COMPARATIVE LAW GLOBAL CONTEXT

This book presents a critical rethinking of the study of comparative law and legal theory in a globalising world and proposes a new model. It highlights the inadequacies of current Western theoretical approaches in comparative law, international law, legal theory and jurisprudence, especially for studying Asian and African laws, arguing that they are too parochial and euro-centric to meet global challenges. Menski argues for combining modern natural law theories with positivist and socio-legal traditions, building an interactive, triangular concept of legal pluralism. Advocated as the fourth major approach to legal theory, this model is applied in analysing the historical and conceptual development of Hindu law, Muslim law, African laws and Chinese law.

WERNER MENSKI is Professor of South Asian Laws at the School of Oriental and African Studies, University of London, where he is also Chair of the Centre for Ethnic Minority Studies. He has published widely in the area of South Asian Law. He has been a Visiting Professor at the Pakistan College of Law, Lahore, the South Asia Institute, University of Heidelberg, the Tokyo University of Foreign Studies, and at ILS Law College, Pune, India.

COMPARATIVE LAW IN A GLOBAL CONTEXT

The Legal Systems of Asia and Africa

Second Edition

WERNER MENSKI

CAMBRIDGE
UNIVERSITY PRESS

CAMBRIDGE UNIVERSITY PRESS
Cambridge, New York, Melbourne, Madrid, Cape Town, Singapore, São Paulo, Delhi

Cambridge University Press
The Edinburgh Building, Cambridge CB2 8RU, UK

Published in the United States of America by Cambridge University Press, New York

www.cambridge.org
Information on this title: www.cambridge.org/9780521675291

First edition published by Platinium Publishing Limited 2000
This edition published by Cambridge University Press 2006
Reprinted 2008

Printed in the United Kingdom at the University Press, Cambridge

A catalogue record for this publication is available from the British Library

Library of Congress Cataloguing in Publication data
Menski, Werner.
Comparative law in a global context : the legal systems of Asia and Africa / Werner Menski.
p.   cm.
Includes bibliographical references and index.
ISBN 0-521-85859-3 (hardback) – ISBN 0-521-67529-4 (pbk.)
1. Comparative law.   2. Law – Philosophy.   I Title.
K559.M46   2006
340′.2 – dc22   2005018618

ISBN 978-0-521-85859-5 hardback
ISBN 978-0-521-67529-1 paperback

Dedicated to Emeritus Professor Masaji Chiba
for his eighty-sixth birthday

17 September 2005

CONTENTS

Preface and acknowledgments   *page* xi
Table of cases   xv
Table of statutes   xvii
List of abbreviations   xx

PART I   **Comparative framework**

Introduction: Globalisation and Asian and African
legal systems   3

1   Comparative law and legal theory from a global
perspective   25
   1.1   The culture-specific nature of law and respect for difference   26
   1.2   Changing global scenario: from colonial transplant to
           ethnic implant   37
           1.2.1   International law and its unifying pressures   38
           1.2.2   Comparative law as a harmonising handmaiden   46
           1.2.3   Assumptions about uniformity: legal transplants and reception
                     of laws   50
           1.2.4   Southern voices: from polite silence to post-colonial
                     reassertion   55
   1.3   New globalisation: reverse colonisation and ethnic implants   58
   1.4   Good practice in studying and teaching comparative law   66
   1.5   World legal history: a deficient model   70
   1.6   A model of pluralist, globality-conscious
           legal education   75

2   Legal pluralism   82
   2.1   Early conceptualisations of legal pluralism   85
   2.2   The historical school of law   88
   2.3   Early legal pluralism: Ehrlich's 'living law'   92
   2.4   Reluctant pluralism: Hart's primary and secondary rules   98
   2.5   Postmodern theories of legal pluralism   103
           2.5.1   Moore's concept of the 'semi-autonomous'
                     social field   104
           2.5.2   Allott's three perspectives on law   108

2.5.3   Griffiths' theory of legal pluralism   113
2.5.4   Chiba's tripartite model of law   119

3   Comparative jurisprudence: images and reflections of law   129
3.1   Traditional natural law theories in outline   131
3.2   Greek legal philosophy   134
3.3   Roman legal philosophy   139
3.4   Early and later medieval developments in Church law   141
3.5   Re-evaluation of natural law during Renaissance and
        Reformation   146
3.6   Legal positivism   150
3.7   Beyond positivism   160
        3.7.1   Socio-legal approaches   161
        3.7.2   New natural law theories   168
3.8   A global working definition of law   173

PART II   **Regional comparisons in a global context**

Introduction   193

4   Hindu law: the search for appropriateness   196
4.1   A historical and conceptual overview   200
4.2   The pre-classical stage: Vedic law (c. 1500 BC to c. 500 BC)   204
4.3   Classical Hindu law (c. 500 BC to c. 200 AD)   209
4.4   Late classical Hindu law (c. 500 BC to c. 1100 AD)   222
4.5   Post-classical Hindu law (after 1100)   234
4.6   Medieval Hindu law under Muslim domination   237
4.7   Anglo-Hindu law   239
4.8   Modern Hindu family law in India   249
4.9   Hindu legal concepts and the Indian Constitution   259
4.10   Searching for composite appropriateness in postmodernity   273

5   Islamic law: God's law or men's law?   279
5.1   Understanding Islamic law from a legal pluralist perspective   281
5.2   The Qur'anic base and its application   289
5.3   The Prophet's roles: leader, judge and guide   294
5.4   Early Islamic law after the Prophet's death   298
5.5   Legal developments in the early Muslim empire:
        the Umayyads   303
5.6   Scholar-jurists and the Abbasids   309
5.7   The central role of jurists   312
        5.7.1   Schools of law and competing doctrines   312
        5.7.2   Shafi'i scheme to unify Muslim jurisprudence   315
        5.7.3   Hadith collections and the 'Schacht controversy'   319
5.8   Continuing diversities after Shafi'i   324
5.9   Judicial administration: *qadis* and *muftis*   330
5.10   Subsidiary sources of law   333

5.11   The purported closing of the 'gates of *ijtihad*'   339
5.12   The shift towards legal reforms   344
5.13   Turkey as a secular Muslim country   354
5.14   Pakistani law and Islamisation   364

6   African laws: the search for law   380
6.1   The denial of African culture and laws   385
6.2   The search for African law and legal theory   390
6.3   The nature of traditional African laws   404
6.3.1   Reflections of early knowledge   404
6.3.2   African worldviews and their conceptual
implications   407
6.3.3   African religions and socio-ritual processes   413
6.3.4   African customary law as a self-controlling system   421
6.3.5   Dispute settlement processes in pre-colonial Africa   435
6.4   African laws under colonial rule   444
6.4.1   The process of colonisation   445
6.4.2   The colonial impact on African customary systems   453
6.4.3   The colonial impact on dispute settlement processes   459
6.5   African laws in the post-colonial period   464
6.5.1   The continuing devaluation of African traditions   466
6.5.2   Debates about custom in modern African laws   470
6.5.3   Dispute settlement and the problems of finding
justice   477
6.5.4   The unification debate as a tool for nation-building   480
6.6   The future   485

7   Chinese law: code and conduct   493
7.1   Scholarly representations of Chinese laws   495
7.2   Traditional Chinese worldviews in their social and
legal context   502
7.2.1   The cosmic dimension: *tao*   503
7.2.2   Self-controlled order, Chinese style: *li*   505
7.2.3   The social context of traditional Chinese legal
regulation   512
7.2.4   The place of customary laws   518
7.3   The classical Chinese legal system: codes and what else?   521
7.3.1   Historical overview of codification in China   521
7.3.2   The conceptual emphasis on penal law   523
7.3.3   The key concept of *fa* and the influence of legalism   525
7.3.4   Confucianisation of the law   531
7.4   The practical application of the law   534
7.4.1   The imperial code system as a formal framework   535
7.4.2   The Emperor as Son of Heaven   538
7.4.3   The imperial legal machinery   541
7.4.4   Avoidance of the law   547
7.4.5   Social and ritual differentiation in the law   555

7.5 Post-imperial Chinese legal systems   560
    7.5.1 Resistance to modernising reforms   561
    7.5.2 Introduction of Western laws in the Republican
        period   564
    7.5.3 The communist foundations of Chinese law   566
7.6 Law in the People's Republic of China   569
    7.6.1 The ambivalent approach to law in Mao's China   570
    7.6.2 The post-Maoist reconstruction of Chinese law   579
    7.6.3 The new legal structures and the future   584

Conclusion: towards global legal realism   594

References   614
Index   659

PREFACE AND ACKNOWLEDGMENTS

While the long-awaited first edition of this book was explicitly directed at a specific student readership, it attracted much attention worldwide as a pioneering model of global legal analysis. This revised second edition ventures further beyond the still somewhat exotic ambit of comparative legal education pursued at the School of Oriental and African Studies (SOAS) in the University of London. It places legal pluralism more confidently into the mainstream study of comparative law, addressing some of the serious deficiencies of comparative law and legal theory in a global context.

Having read much of what appeared since 2000 in this fertile but still largely uncultivated field, I feel empowered to write with more clarity about the challenging experience of applying in practice what some writers, particularly Santos (1995), Twining (2000) and Cotterrell (2003), have been suggesting as viable strategies to promote plurality-sensitive, globality-conscious legal theory. There has been growing recognition of the fact that academic activities in the complex fields of legal theory and comparative law remain underdeveloped and still too eurocentric. As Western academics we seem, by our own histories and training, to be too wedded to ways of perceiving and studying law that do not take sufficient account of the culture-specific social embeddedness of legal phenomena in the world. We continue to ignore principles and models of good practice that have been developed elsewhere, particularly in Asia and Africa. As lawyers, we need to accept that law in its various manifestations all over the world is, and will always remain, culture-specific (Allott, 1980; Twining, 2000). We fail to admit that globalisation does not primarily lead to universal homogenisation, but rather increased legal pluralism in ways that make legal research ever more challenging and complex. Postmodern, globality-focused legal scholarship is a tough enterprise.

Twining (2000: 30) has argued that, unlike the science of geology, which is subject to universal physical laws, law is culturally relative. This basic observation puts a huge obligation on legal theorists and comparative lawyers to educate today's postmodern readership, and our current generation of students, about how to understand law itself and its various manifestations in a truly global context. While none of us can cover everything, some tasks are do-able within a lifetime. There is an urgent need to research particularly how the legal systems of Asia and Africa react today to the demands of globalisation, developing in many cases in ways that we did not expect a few decades ago. We may find it hard to accept this today, because *they* often do not follow *us* and our ideas, but develop their own hybrid methods of dealing with legal issues. In understanding such complex processes of pluralisation, we can count on the active participation of many researchers and teachers from the South. But they, too, often require reminders that globalisation is today not just leading towards a uniform world legal order, given the strong ideological impact of existing eurocentric and uniformising scholarship in the fields of legal theory, comparative law and increasingly international law.

The present study remains geared towards combining inquisitive interrogation of Asian and African legal systems in a comparative global context with a self-critical questioning of dominant Western assumptions about the nature of law itself. The theoretical critique of global jurisprudence of the first edition is retained, and is now interwoven with arguments presenting legal pluralism as an integrated fourth theoretical approach that combines and yet transcends the familiar three dominant major theories in the study of law worldwide, namely natural law, legal positivism and socio-legal approaches. In four separate historically based chapters, the study provides a detailed historical overview of major legal systems of Asia and Africa to critically examine how these legal systems in the countries of the South are developing today in respect of my proposed theoretical approach.

The introduction to this revised edition focuses explicitly on globalisation and its pluralising effects in the legal field, while chapter 1 retains its focus on comparative methodology and emphasises the changing understanding of the nature of law in today's globalising world. The former chapter 2 has been split into two substantive chapters. The new chapter 2 allows for a more specific focus on legal pluralism and a global pluralistic legal theory, while the newly carved-out chapter 3 reassesses the more familiar ground of standard legal theories in their eurocentric, Western-dominated forms. Chapters 4–7 then discuss, in turn, the historical evidence of, and theoretical contributions made by, major legal systems of Asia and Africa, focusing on Hindu, Muslim, African and Chinese laws. The conclusion emphasises the extent to which a globally focused, plurality-conscious jurisprudence accounts for the evidence coming from non-European legal systems about the intrinsically plural nature of all laws in the world, no matter how globalised and commercially interlinked they may have become at a certain formal level. The study proposes that as law continues to be culture-specific all over the world, the key challenge for legal theorists remains to develop a globally valid model of legal analysis rather than more studies on legal eurocentrism. This should permit a deeper investigation of the ways and forms in which hybrid legal phenomena worldwide emerge and are reproduced as a result of interplay between local and global legal inputs and competing elements within the internally plural phenomenon of law. The dynamic interplay and competition of different perspectives in and on law requires constant negotiation in a spirit of tolerance of other viewpoints, rather than myopic assertion of idiosyncratic positions. Plurality-conscious legal construction and debate will remain a constant challenge everywhere.

This book, with departmental plans for its production under discussion since the early 1980s, should have been a co-operative effort involving several regional specialists. However, many factors inhibited co-operation and ultimately prevented a joint project from materialising. The pressures of modern academic life have become such that even speaking to one's colleagues has become a luxury and the e-mail, convenient as it may be, has replaced face-to-face discussion. In addition, modern academic structures do not sufficiently encourage co-operative research efforts across regional boundaries. In the end, this book had to be written, and now rewritten, by one person. This actually helped, looking back at this exciting experience, to achieve greater analytical coherence and depth, and to aid comparability.

Having listened to the lectures of many regional experts over the past twenty-five years, some of them now deceased, while others moved on or retired, I owe an enormous debt of gratitude especially to Professors J. Duncan M. Derrett, Noel J. Coulson (1928–86) and Antony A. Allott (1924–2002), stalwarts of comparative legal studies at the University of London. Each in his own way made sure that the important subjects covered in this book would not be neglected. Many others have contributed to the comparative law programme at SOAS over time, in particular the key course on 'Legal Systems of Asia and Africa'. Their names are too numerous to mention here. They made some input into the present work, duly acknowledged in footnotes and references to published writing, where it exists. Professor Esin Örücü at the University of Glasgow, Professor S. P. Sathe, Honorary Director of the Institute of Advanced Legal Studies in Pune, and Professor Humayoun Ihsan, Principal of the Pakistan College of Law in Lahore, deserve special thanks for engaging discussions about comparative law and global legal issues.

Several helpful research assistants contributed to the first edition, particularly Clare Fazal, Malachi Broome, Eric Bakilana and Samantha Pearce, whose unfailing support helped to make writing this book an enjoyable experience of study and learning in an environment where co-operation and frank exchange of views and perspectives needed to be protected from parochial challenges. The present revised edition has benefited from the critical comments of Professor John Bell of Cambridge University and a number of other reviewers. The partly sceptical feedback given by some colleagues and by many law students at SOAS between 2000 and 2005, especially the classes in 'Legal Systems of Asia and Africa' of 2003–4 and 2004–5, are gratefully acknowledged. All of this enlivened further ongoing thought processes, to which especially Dr Prakash Shah, Dr Ihsan Yilmaz, Dr Lynn Welchman and Nidhi Gupta have contributed. This edition was updated with the assistance of Shahin Baghaei, Biswajit Chanda,

Sameer Bhawsar and Jeremy Brown, who also helped me with the graphics. I also thank Finola O'Sullivan, Jane O'Regan and their colleagues at Cambridge University Press for professional guidance and a smooth production process.

The subject matter covered in this book is of such enormous dimensions that nobody could hope to cover every aspect. Many selections had to be made in view of constraints of time and space. Many difficult technical terms from different languages needed to be used; they are found with explanations in the glossary. Any mistakes and omissions are of necessity mine, and I shall continue to be grateful for constructive criticism from readers, which will in turn it is hoped lead to an updated and revised third edition.

TABLE OF CASES

Abdul Waheed v. Asma Jahangir PLD 1997 Lah 301   306, 373, 568
Abdul Waheed v. Asma Jahangir PLD 2004 SC 219   374
Alhaji Mohamed v. Knott [1969] 1 QB 1; [1968] 2 All ER 563   467
Ali Nawaz Gardezi v. Muhammad Yusuf PLD 1963 SC 51   377
Allah Rakha v. Federation of Pakistan PLD 2000 FSC 1   54, 375, 378, 379
Antony v. Commissioner, Corporation of Cochin 1994(1) KLT 169   271
Attorney-General for Nyasaland v. Jackson [1957] R&NLR 443   463
Baby v. Jayant AIR 1981 Bombay 283   254
Bandhua Mukti Morcha v. Union of India AIR 1984 SC 802   266, 268
Bandhua Mukti Morcha v. Union of India AIR 1992 SC 38   266, 268
Bhaurao Shankar Lokhande v. State of Maharashtra AIR 1965 SC 1564   254, 256
Central Inland Water Transport Corporation Ltd. v. Brojo Nath Ganguly AIR 1986 SC
    1571   270
Collector of Madura v. Moottoo Ramalinga Sathupathy (1868) 12 Moore's Indian
    Appeals 375   248
Danial Latifi v. Union of India (2001) 7 SCC 740   276, 277
Faheemuddin v. Sabeeha Begum PLD 1991 SC 1074   375
Forasol v. Oil & Natural Gas Commission AIR 1984 SC 241   263
Francis Coralie Mullin v. The Administrator, Union Territory of Delhi AIR 1981 SC
    746   271
Jesmin Sultana v. Mohammad Elias (1997) 17 BLD 4   352
Joyita Saha v. Rajesh Kumar Pandey AIR 2000 Cal 109   255
Kunhikannan v. State of Kerala 1968 KLT 19   15, 202, 219
M. C. Mehta and another (1987) 1 SCC 395   263
M. Govindaraju v. K. Munisami Gounder AIR 1997 SC 10   256
Mohd Ahmed Khan v. Shah Bano Begum AIR 1985 SC 945   275, 305, 352
Moottoo Ramalinga case, see Collector of Madura
Nebu John v. Babu 2000(1) KLT 238   271
Noor Khan v. Haq Nawaz PLD 1982 FSC 265   374, 377
P. Mariammal v. Padmanabhan AIR 2001 Madras 350   256
Partap Singh v. Union of India AIR 1985 SC 1695   201
People United for Better Living in Calcutta v. State of West Bengal AIR 1993 Cal 215
    271

Pratheesh Fuels v. Indian Oil Corporation Ltd 2002(1) KLT 296   205
Ramakrishnan v. State of Kerala 1999(2) KLT 725   221, 271
Rani v. The State PLD 1996 Kar 316   371
Rattan Lal v. Vardesh Chander (1976) 2 SCC 103   56
Rudul Sah v. State of Bihar AIR 1983 SC 1086   268
S. v. Makwaneyane 1995 (3) SA 391   489
Safia Bibi v. The State PLD 1985 FSC 120   374
Saima Waheed case, *see* Abdul Waheed v. Asma Jahangir
Shah Bano case, *see* Mohd Ahmed Khan v. Shah Bano Begum
Singh v. Entry Clearance Officer, New Delhi [2004] INLR 515   60, 467
S. P. Gupta v. President of India AIR 1982 SC 149   268
State v. Dosso PLD 1958 SC 533   153, 158
Sumitra Devi v. Bhikhan Choudhary AIR 1985 SC 765   254
Surjit Kaur v. Garja Singh AIR 1994 SC 135   254, 256
T. Damodhar Rao v. The Special Officer, Municipal Corporation of Hyderabad AIR
       1987 AP 171   270
V. Bhagat v. D. Bhagat AIR 1994 SC 710   258

TABLE OF STATUTES

Administration of Justice Regulation, 5 July 1781 [India]   247
Caste Disabilities Removal Act, 1850 [India]   243
Child Marriage Restraint Act, 1929 [India]   243
Civil Code of Egypt, 1949   350
Civil Code on Private and Commercial Law, 1929-31 [China]   565
Code of Civil Procedure, 1932 [China]   565
Code of Commercial Procedure, 1861 [Ottoman Empire]   355
Code of Criminal Procedure (Amendment) Act, 2001 [India]   276, 277
Code of Maritime Commerce, 1863 [Ottoman Empire]   355
Commercial Code, 1850 [Ottoman Empire]   355
Community Courts Act, 2003 [Namibia]   54, 477
Constitution (Forty-Second Amendment) Act, 1976 [India]   265, 269
Constitution of China, 1982   584
      Art. 5   584
Constitution of India, 1950   197, 201, 203, 250, 259, 581
      Art. 12   270
      Arts. 14-16   266
      Art. 21   266, 270, 271
      Art. 32   267
      Art. 39(a)   269
      Art. 44   250, 260, 274
      Art. 48-A   269
      Art. 51-A   250, 269
      Art. 226   267
Constitution of Pakistan, 1973   371
      Art. 2-A   371, 372
Criminal Procedure Code, 1973 [India]
      s. 125   275
Dissolution of Muslim Marriages Act, 1939 [India]   275, 351,
      368
Enforcement of Shari'ah Act, 1991 [Pakistan]   374
Ethiopian Civil Code, 1960   47, 483, 484
Government of India Act, 1935   259

Hindu Adoptions and Maintenance Act, 1956   251
Hindu Marriage Act, 1955 [India]   251, 274
    s. 3   254
    s. 5   54
    s. 7   253
    s. 7(1)   253
    s. 7(2)   253, 255, 256
    s. 8(5)   254
    s. 11   54
    s. 17   54
    s. 29(2)   249
Hindu Marriage (Amendment) Act, 1964 [India]   252
Hindu Minority and Guardianship Act, 1956 [India]   251
Hindu Succession Act, 1956 [India]   250, 251
    s. 14   250
Hindu Widows' Remarriage Act, 1856 [India, Pakistan, Bangladesh]   243
Hindu Widows' Remarriage (Repeal) Act, 1983 [India]   243
Hindu Women's Right to Property Act, 1937 [India]   250
Hudood Ordinances, 1979 [Pakistan]   303
Indian Companies Act, 1866   242
Indian Divorce (Amendment) Act, 2001   201, 274
Indian Evidence Act, 1872 [India, Pakistan]   368
Indian Penal Code, 1860   242, 243, 368, 449, 462
Kerala Joint Hindu Family System (Abolition) Act, 1975 [India]   250
Land Code, 1868 [Ottoman Empire]   355
Land Code, 1930 [China]   565
Marriage Law of the People's Republic of China, 1950 [China]   572
    Art. 1   572
    Art. 2   573
    Art. 6   573
    Art. 8   573
Marriage Laws (Amendment) Act, 1976 [India]   252
Muslim Family Laws Ordinance, 1961 [Pakistan, Bangladesh]   167, 372, 374, 376
    s. 6   54, 375, 376
    s. 7   376, 377, 378
Muslim Personal Law (Shariat Application) Act, 1937 [India, Pakistan, Bangladesh]
    368
Muslim Women (Protection of Rights on Divorce) Act, 1986 [India]   276, 277
Objectives Resolution, 1949 [Pakistan]   369, 370, 371, 372, 378
Offence of Zina (Enforcement of Hudood) Ordinance, 1979 [Pakistan]   374, 377
Ottoman Civil Code, 1877   356
Ottoman Law of Family Rights, 1917   351, 358, 360
Parsi Marriage and Divorce (Amendment) Act, 1988 [India]   201

Penal Code, 1858 [Ottoman Empire]   355
Qanun-e-Shahadat Ordinance, 1984 [Pakistan]   374
Qisas and Diyat Ordinance, 1990 [Pakistan]   374
Revival of the Constitution of 1973 Order, 1985 [Pakistan]   371
Sati Regulation of 1829 [India]   243
Special Marriage Act, 1954 [India]   250, 252
Traditional Courts Act, [Malawi]   477
Tunisian Law of Personal Status, 1956/7   302
Turkish Constitution,   354

ABBREVIATIONS

AD	Anno Domini
ADR	Alternative dispute resolution
AIR	*All India Reporter* (India)
AP	Andhra Pradesh
BC	Before Christ
BJP	Bharatiya Janata Party
BLD	*Bangladesh Legal Decisions*
Cal	Calcutta
CLR	*Pakistan Civil Law Reports*
FB	Full Bench
FSC	Federal Shariat Court (Pakistan)
INLR	*Immigration and Nationality Law Reports* (UK)
J	Judge
Kar	Karachi
KLT	*Kerala Law Times* (India)
Lah	Lahore
LJ	Lord Justice
MFLO	*Muslim Family Laws Ordinance*, 1961 (Pakistan)
NUJS	National University of Juridical Sciences, Kolkata
PLD	*Pakistan Legal Decisions* (Pakistan)
PRC	People's Republic of China
Rs.	Rupees
SC	Supreme Court
SCC	*Supreme Court Cases* (India)
SOAS	School of Oriental and African Studies

PART I

Comparative framework

INTRODUCTION: GLOBALISATION AND ASIAN AND AFRICAN LEGAL SYSTEMS

In the late twentieth century, globalisation seems to have become 'the cliché of our times' (Held *et al.*, 1999: 1). Linked to postmodernism, it has given rise to a large body of writing in many academic subjects.[1] While postmodernism remains heavily contested as a concept and methodology, it seems that globalisation as a widely observable fact is not seriously challenged as a phenomenon. However, scholars argue vigorously about its consequences, and many debates focus on the role of the nation state in newly conceived contexts of global interconnectedness.[2] There is as yet little discussion about how globalisation relates to legal theory and understandings of law. In common parlance, the term creates assumptions about the desirability of increased efficiency in processes of global communication. We immediately think of easier travel, homogenisation of trade laws and harmonisation or integration of all kinds of rules, easing communication processes by recourse to one language, one pattern of doing business, and so on. This is matched by the tempting assumption that there would be less conflict if only all humans thought alike, followed uniform moral standards and respected universal human rights.

However, is this realistic in view of universal plurality? Much universalised thinking about globalisation goes too far in its uncritical acceptance of the advantages of uniformisation. It is rather unreal to expect that the whole world would ever follow one rule system, one language and culture, or one law. George Orwell's famous writings in *Animal Farm* (1945) and in *1984* castigated fake assertions of equality underpinning domination by elites.[3] More recently, Legrand (1997a: 61) has noted that 'globalisation of the world cannot

---

[1] Robertson (1986; 2000; 2003) is a major contributor to the debates. From an Indian sociological perspective, Doshi (2003: 363–6) contains a useful overview on the history of globalisation. A good analysis of the complex political, economic and cultural processes is provided by Held *et al.* (1999). Twining (2000) mainly surveys writing concerned with legal theory, while Harding and Örücü (2002: 305–11) produce a helpful short bibliography of comparative law.

[2] Held *et al.* (1999) distinguish three broad accounts: hyperglobalists (predicting the end of state power), sceptics (arguing that globalisation strengthens state powers) and transformationalists (seeing an uncertain outcome, but a continuing role for the state).

[3] Schott (1995: 39) refers to Orwell's famous phrase that '[a]ll animals are equal, but some animals are more equal than others'.

change the reality of varied historical traditions'. While global uniformity is an idealistic vision, it would not only be boring, taking away all the colourful differences of human existence, but also intrinsically repressive. For, who should ultimately decide the criteria for an envisaged globally uniform system? Whose values, rules and norms should be chosen to dominate the world? To what extent is locally coloured situation-specificity more conducive to justice than following universally fixed models? At the end of the day, what is justice?

The present study explores how globalisation concepts today feed from, and in turn impact on, conflicting conceptualisations of law and justice in a global context. With specific reference to the legal systems of Asia and Africa, it draws attention to a notable conflict of visions and the critical divergence of two basic assumptions among scholars and in the general public. The central question pursued here, through an interrogation of legal theories, is whether the phenomenon of globalisation should and can be premised on a vision of global uniformisation, or whether a vision that emphasises legal pluralism and the pluralising effects of globalisation processes is more realistic, so that globalisation ends up as almost unlimited diversity, indeed as 'glocalization' (Robertson 1995). Given that the current world scenario points towards growing diversity of local solutions despite the ongoing search for global unification,[4] this study argues that insisting on anti-pluralist unification visions may be misguided and quite dangerous for global peace and well-being. In today's world, the most evident conflicting claims arise from competing visions of globalised uniformisation,[5] made by American-led initiatives like the War on Terror and extremist militant versions of Islamic *Jihad*, leading to mutual accusations of terrorism by George Bush and Osama bin Laden as protagonists of two opposing visions of globalisation that seem deficient in liberality. To an extent, this parallels the 'conflict of civilisations' theories proposed by earlier writers. These seem flawed, from a global perspective, because they focused too narrowly on Christian – Muslim contests over global supremacy, ignoring many other globalising claims in the world.[6] The public perception of a bifocal dispute of 'Western' and Muslim visions is too simplistic and dangerous, far too fuzzy and severely limited – what about all the other perspectives?

Whatever the precise nature of the existing conflict between different visions of uniformisation, it seems that peaceful co-existence in a globally interconnected world will not be possible without allowing space for and recognition

---

[4] The newly constituted laws of the Republic of South Africa and of Namibia offer ample material for instructive case studies of culture-specific plural reconstruction, covered here only in passing.

[5] In this context, Werbner (2004: 451) speaks of 'utopian discourses' in relation to millennial Islam.

[6] See in particular Huntington's theory of a 'clash of civilisations' and Fukuyama's (1989) questions about the end of history.

of different visions and thus respecting, as Lyotard (1984: 67) puts it, 'both the
desire for justice and the desire for the unknown'. Instead of asserting the superiority of this or that vision of globalisation, which one then seeks to impose
through various law-making processes, scholars and policy-makers need to
acknowledge the critical role of constant plurality-conscious negotiation of
competing perspectives in a spirit of liberality. Law, the present study argues,
is much more than a body of rules that can simply be imposed on others by
those who dominate the formal processes of law-making. Much current legal
scholarship remains too closely focused on outdated, positivistic approaches,
still proudly claiming their own superiority over all other perspectives. The
onerous task of legal theory in terms of cultivating respect for worldwide plurality rather than pushing for globalising uniformity is therefore enormous.
Recent writing has begun to express this more clearly. While Lyotard (1984: 61)
emphasises dissension and notes that '[c]onsensus is a horizon that is never
reached', Melissaris (2004: 76) concludes:

> The study of the legal must be directed towards the discovery of alternative
> perceptions of the world and justice and of different practices of solving
> practical problems by accommodating competing interests as well as meet-
> ing the prerequisites of substantive justice. The question of law and justice
> then becomes one concerning our whole way of life, how we perceive and
> place ourselves in our surroundings.

Existing theoretical approaches, not only among lawyers, tend to be far too
parochial and eurocentric, failing to take a global, plurality-conscious perspective. Legal scholarship, it seems, lags seriously behind reality, which remains
marked by immensely deep plurality. Global migration patterns, old and new,
and multiple exchanges between different states, economies, societies and legal
systems, on a variety of scales and through different methods, have over time
created transnational, inherently plural, multi-ethnic and multicultural legal
environments, which are becoming ever more prominent in reality today. Far
from creating legal uniformity worldwide, reception of mainstream Western
laws has been leading to an immensely complex further pluralisation of laws all
over the world.[7] Yet, mainstream legal science continues to behave as though
globalisation simply means uniformisation, resisting evidence, from everywhere in the world, that global harmony and understanding will only be
achieved by greater tolerance of diversity, not by enforced uniformity. To some
extent, insistence on liberal approaches remains a viable option, but how liberal
can liberals be when it comes to recognising the views and values of others?
Glenn (2000; 2004), Twining (2000) and others have provided convincing arguments for the recognition of all legal traditions in the world and for a systematic

---

[7] This is acknowledged in recent writing, e.g. Örücü (1999) and even transpires from a careful
   study of Watson (1993).

rethinking of legal theory. The present study develops such encouraging suggestions,[8] applying and extending them specifically to the legal systems of Asia and Africa.

It is evident that globalisation and legal theory are today hugely important subjects (Twining, 2000: 88) and that a plurality-focused international legal science is possible (Zweigert and Kötz, 1998: 45). However, while some traditional assumptions and prevailing orthodoxies are beginning to fade and much rethinking is taking place (Harding and Örücü, 2002: vii), it has proved difficult to reorient traditional legal concepts of theory and analysis.[9] Twining (2000: 232) notes:

> Lawyers and law students encounter normative pluralism every day of their lives, in legal and non-legal contexts. Yet legal pluralism is generally marginalised and viewed with scepticism in legal discourse. Perhaps the main reason for this is that for over 200 years Western legal theory has been dominated by conceptions of law that tend to be monist (one internally coherent legal system), statist (the state has a monopoly of law within its territory), and positivist (what is not created or recognised as law by the state is not law).

Combining comparative law and legal theory, the present study attempts to overcome such narrowly defined traditional legal methods. It emphasises the need for recognition of legal pluralism and therefore of difference, developing methods to account for their effects on legal theory and comparative law. The academic discipline of law, as conceptualised and studied so far, has remained too eurocentric and legocentric (focused on the allegedly central role of state-made law in society and human development) to be able to meet global challenges.[10] Twining (2000: 135) emphasises that '[u]nderstanding law involves taking account of the "realities" of those with power over it and those who are subject to it and many others besides. Understanding law requires multiple lenses.'[11] Zweigert and Kötz (1998: 46) suggest that '[i]f law is seen functionally as a regulator of social facts, the legal problems of all countries are similar' and

---

[8] De Cruz (1999) remains self-consciously limited, still focused on the dominant 'legal families' approach. Conscious of the emerging new world order, the concluding chapter (pp. 475–96) goes well beyond eurocentric visions.

[9] Freeman (2001: 920–1) notes much criticism of legal pluralism and suggests that it makes the drawing of a clear line between state and society problematic. Zweigert and Kötz (1998: 33–4) diagnose legal science as 'sick' and suggest that comparative law approaches can cure it. But, as we shall see, most comparative lawyers have ideological problems with legal pluralism.

[10] As a sociologist of law, Anleu (2000: 10) suggests that 'law' or 'the law' is often taken for granted as a concept and recommends that the numerous dimensions of law must be taken into account in analysing the role of law in social change.

[11] Smart (1989) argues in her feminist analysis that law has failed in this respect by projecting itself as unified, while privileging male perspectives.

call for a universal legal science which clearly implies plurality consciousness. From the perspective of anthropology and law, Sack and Aleck (1992) present a sharp critique of legal scholars' reliance on techniques of self-definition and word plays that constantly shut out plurality and hide the social embeddedness of all law. Such comments by leading scholars in various fields indicate growing awareness that the traditional focus on legal positivism and traditional natural law theories has tended to marginalise the social dimensions of law.[12] The present study presents a methodological approach that integrates the social and ethical elements of law into a necessarily pluralist legal analysis to understand the pervasive role of law in its various social contexts. While a plurality-conscious legal theory cannot afford to overlook or disregard *any one* of the major theoretical approaches to law that have been developed over time, a major challenge for legal theory remains to make sense of how all these elements interact.

Twining (2000) highlights how closely law is everywhere linked with matters of daily life and how the boundaries between what is law and what is not law are not really clear at all. Stating *ex cathedra* that law is pervasive in society (Twining, 2000: 1), his analysis sets the scene for 'a pluralistic vision of legal theory which includes a variety of perspectives and a multiplicity of levels of generality' (p. 13). His brief initial discussion of globalisation reflects the rich social science literature, finding that '[t]hese processes tend to make the world more interdependent, but this does not mean that we are moving inexorably towards a single world government nor does it mean the end of nation-states as the most important actors' (p. 5). Again, this contains a finding of increasing pluralisation rather than global homogenisation. While it is confirmed that the wider literature on globalisation is fairly recent, by the late 1990s, words like 'global', 'globalisation' and 'globalism' were as much in vogue in law as in other disciplines (p. 3).

Portraying globalisation theory as a new academic industry, Twining (2000: 5) refers to the important work of Santos (1995) and his distinction of 'globalized localism' and 'localized globalism'. Law, from this perspective, is seen as interlinked with other aspects of life, and cannot be treated as a closed system. Twining (2000: 7) reports that 'there has been a good deal of self-criticism within disciplines about the extent to which they have over-emphasised the importance of boundaries and have treated societies, states and "tribes" as self-contained, decontextualised units'. While anthropologists and others have learnt some lessons from this, many lawyers still favour perceptions of closed systems and rely particularly on the supremacy of state-made, official law as

---

[12] Leading jurists (Chiba, 1986; 1989; and Hinz, 2003a) argue now that all law needs to be seen as linked to anthropology. However, Sack and Aleck (1992: xx) suggest that anthropologists 'are unlikely to play the prince who will deliver the princess of western legal theory from a hundred years of positivistic coma'.

a regulator of social and other relations.[13] This presents deep methodological problems, sharply identified by Twining (2000: 8):

> The general theme is clear across disciplines: the processes of globalisation are fundamentally changing the significance of national and societal boundaries and generally, but not inevitably, making them less important. This represents a challenge to all 'black box theories' which treat nation states or geographically bounded 'societies' or legal systems as discrete entities that can be studied in isolation either internally or at the international level.

Most writing on globalisation ignores its legal dimensions and, with few exceptions,[14] legal scholarship has yet to tackle the issues that arise. Twining (2000: 2) writes sceptically of the 'loose and possibly rhetorical label of "globalisation"', indicating that lawyers experience problems in understanding the complex implications of globalisation and may have been too quick to welcome them uncritically as an aspect and consequence of modernisation. Twining (2000: 194–244) presents the concept of interlegality, developed by Santos (1995), as a significant new perspective, while Glenn (2000: 328; 2004: 354) prefers the notion of 'interdependence, or of non-separation . . . as the most fundamental idea in the existence of major, complex, legal traditions. It is the fundamental, underlying characteristic of multivalence.'[15]

However modern or post-modern concepts like multivalence, interdependence and global interconnectedness may appear, they are hardly new. One of the leading writers on globalisation, Robertson (2003: 3), cautions that we have no reason to congratulate ourselves today for having invented or created something that people in the past did not realise or could not know:

> [G]lobalization is more than just McWorld or Westernization. It is about human interconnections that have assumed global proportions and transformed themselves. If we focus on globalization simply as a modern strategy for power, we will miss its historical and social depths. Indeed the origins of globalization lie in interconnections that have slowly enveloped humans since the earliest times, as they globalized themselves. In this sense, globalization as a human dynamic has always been with us, even if we have been unaware of its embrace until recently.

---

[13] Cownie (2004) reports that most English lawyers these days have developed a high degree of awareness of the social interrelatedness of law, but are often not feeling comfortable enough on the basis of their own 'black letter' training to attempt socio-legal research themselves.

[14] Apart from Twining (2000) see especially Griffiths (2002) and Flood (2002).

[15] Glenn (2004: 351) explains that multivalence 'asserts that *all* categories are vague and all efforts of separation are arbitrary and artificial'. He contrasts this with bivalent thought, which 'implies clear boundaries between distinct and separate concepts, and prevents mixing and confusion over the boundaries, once they are created. It is very logical, in the way western people have been trained to be logical' (p. 351).

While modern information technology has made huge differences to how we connect with others, modern social scientists have tended to overlook evidence of ancient concepts and early regional, if not global, interaction patterns. Tracing the history of globalisation, Waters (1995) finds that the term 'global' has been used for about 400 years,[16] but that 'globalisation' as a technical term did not exist until about 1960 and was only accepted more widely during the 1980s. A diachronical global interdisciplinary analysis needs to be aware that all major world religions operate on the assumption that their God or gods are more or less 'in charge' of the whole world, and thus make universal and holistic claims, which then of course contradict each other. A sense of being connected worldwide has always united the global Muslim community (*ummah*). Ancient Hindu philosophy, evidence of which is well preserved in Sanskrit texts from at least 1500 BC onwards, perceived the entire cosmos as an interlinked whole and did not limit itself to 'law', politics, environmental pollution or individual salvation. Similar holistically focused global perspectives existed in ancient China, Japan, Africa and elsewhere, but much of such early evidence remains inaccessible, coming from societies and cultures based on oral transmission of knowledge and wisdom. But orality does not mean that brains in those ancient days (or indeed today) were less sophisticated; in fact many people argue precisely the opposite.[17]

   Scholars have drawn close links between postmodernity and global society, so that globalisation is often perceived as a prominent consequence of postmodern, post-industrial socio-economic change. Doshi (2003: 163) captures this in typical optimistic tones which, we should note, stray into questionable legal assumptions:

> Information and knowledge have established linkages between people of the world. Now, the belief that humankind can be turned into a universal community, is getting shape with the processes of globalization and technological knowledge. It appears that the world can develop a cosmopolitan order based upon liberty, justice, and equality for all humanity. Globalization, thus, is a new characteristic of post-industrial society.

In a similar vein, there is much talk of the 'global village',[18] but perhaps, so Twining (2000: 4), '[w]e are now living in a global neighbourhood, which is not yet a global village' and everything in this ongoing process is in flux:

---

[16] This is linked to international sea trade in colonial contexts but it is often forgotten that such exchanges, documented in a large specialist literature, took place much before colonial times.

[17] On the dynamic nature of oral traditions, see Glenn (2000: 7–8) and chapter 6 below on African law.

[18] De Cruz (1999: 29) refers to this as the 'catchphrase of the 1980s and early 1990s'. Doshi (2003: 351) starts his chapter on globalisation stating that '[w]e are now on the road to the formation of a global society', tracing its legacy back to the Enlightenment era and portraying it as the only alternative for the world.

> In the present context the term 'globalisation' refers to those processes which tend to create and consolidate a unified world economy, a single ecological system, and a complex network of communications that covers the whole globe, even if it does not penetrate to every part of it. Anthony Giddens characterises the process as 'the intensification of world-wide social relations which link distant localities in such a way that local happenings are shaped by events occurring many miles away and vice versa'.[19]

Doshi (2003: 351) speaks in this context of 'surface' events, which significantly influence our perceptions of what globalisation may or may not achieve, such as the end of the Cold War and the collapse of communism and the Soviet Union.[20] One must now add to this list the consequences of the 11 September 2001 destruction of the New York Twin Towers as a symbol of globalisation and the 'War on Terror'.

The existing literature recognises that 'globalisation' can mean lots of different things. Glenn (2000: 47; 2004: 51) introduces the subject by saying that '[g]lobalization, or world domination, is usually thought of as a single process', but immediately warns that '[t]he problem with this analysis of the state of the world is that there are a number of globalizations going on . . . There is also, for example, globalization in the form of Islamization.'[21] Especially from a North American perspective, it appears that globalisation can easily be perceived as American domination of the world, a tempting thought for some, but what about all others? From a Southern perspective, Doshi (2003: 352) warns:

> There is no single globalization. There are several globalizations. Its *avatar* is plural, its processes are historical and its outcomes are varying. And, therefore, instead of calling it globalization, we should call it globalizations. Globalization, the world over, does not have a cakewalk. Challenges given to it are by no means ordinary. There is always a fear that the nation-state would lose its identity and importance. And, who knows, the state itself would die. There is yet another fear that the gap between the rich and the poor would increase. It is also argued that globalization is nothing short of a cultural bombardment on the developing countries by the western modernity – capitalism, industrialism and the nation-state system.

This highlights the complexity of processes of globalisation, including both modernisation and postmodernisation. The result is a complex plural phenomenon whose economic elements may be dominant, but encompass all other aspects of life, including law.[22] Modernisation advocated prominently

---

[19] Twining (2000: 4). The reference here is to Giddens (1990: 64).

[20] Riles (2001: 14) emphasises the same point with regard to how comparative lawyers work and think.

[21] Later on, Glenn (2000: 49; 2004: 53) notes that 'as there are multiple globalizations, so there are multiple regionalizations'.

[22] Doshi (2003: 364–6) reports on Robertson's (2000) earlier mapping of globalisation history, which Robertson (2003) now discusses differently as a model of three waves.

an ideology of progressive linear development, spearheaded by the nation-state and its instrumentalist use of law as a tool for reform, leading to the much-revised 'law and development' debates of the past few decades (Trubek and Galanter, 1974; Vyas *et al.*, 1994). Postmodern theories question modernist Enlightenment claims in relation to universality and certainty in reason, truth, knowledge and reality, to the extent that modernity is no longer seen as providing a global solution for human existence and a universal path for understanding the world (Doherty *et al.*, 1992). Challenging the modernist Enlightenment ideal of universal true knowledge, which was thought to be achieved through the exercise of objective human reason, postmodernism suggests that truth, knowledge and even reality are all culturally relative and that human rationality is heterogeneous and diverse. As a result, '[t]he grand narrative has lost its credibility' (Lyotard, 1984: 37). Treating almost everything as subjectively constructed, postmodernism celebrates a plurality of perspectives and emphasises the fallacy of imagining complete, universal knowledge, thus leading (for some observers) to nihilism, pessimistic fatalism, and a 'crisis of representation' in several social science subjects (Marcus and Fisher, 1986).[23] Postmodern legal writers acknowledge that postmodern theory 'protests against the totalising monopolisation of certain types of rationality and against universalist concepts that raise false allegations of absoluteness' (Peters and Schwenke, 2000: 801–2), while most jurists tend to see this as 'nothing less than a rejection of the whole liberal project' (Freeman, 2001: 18).

Postmodernism is methodologically closely linked to postcolonialism,[24] which specifically involved challenging the colonial vestiges of eurocentrism and Western ethnocentricity in dominant discourses about non-Western societies. However, much of the current debate on globalisation seems still inspired by the theme of 'civilising mission', now in the name of universalism and human rights.[25] For, in common parlance today, globalisation seems to mean economic and political domination of a Western-focused, even eurocentric process of development in linear fashion, moving more or less inevitably towards global uniformity.[26]

In debates by social scientists, legal aspects of globalisation are rarely explicitly discussed, but often form an important subtext. Doshi (2003: 374) finds

[23] For example, sociologists are now agonising over the significance of the concept of 'society' which appears to have lost its meaning (Doshi, 2003, citing Bauman, 1992 and others).

[24] Robertson (2003: 11) sees decolonisation as 'a child of globalization and its struggles', but also notes the risks of prospering neocolonialism and its potential to destabilise what he portrays as the third wave of globalisation.

[25] I have discussed elsewhere (Menski, 2003: 11–18) that, while post-colonial theory seeks to reveal the inherent contradictions of the 'civilizing mission' of European colonialism, such falsities have infected even the best of current critical social science scholarship.

[26] Twining (2000: 192) finds it 'disturbing that these alleged universal or general standards are not often subjected to sustained critical analysis'. White (2001: 46) criticises Max Weber's 'relatively anaemic conception of rationality' as excessively myopic.

that '[e]ach scholar has his own logic about the consequences of globalization' and reports much theoretical speculation about how concepts like modernity, postmodernity and globalisation are related. We can therefore not expect a neat pattern of analysis, in which everything becomes clear at the end of the day. On the contrary, as globalisation becomes stronger and more mature, the inherent contradiction between unifying ambitions and plurifying realities becomes more apparent and assumes critical relevance to studying comparative law in a global context. After much debate, the emerging assessment appears to be that globalisation is much more than one single phenomenon and is not actually moving the world in the direction of uniformity. On balance, the constant interaction between the global and the local creates more plurality rather than greater uniformity. The hybridisation inherent in globalisation processes leads to what Robertson (2003) calls 'global localization', which he also referred to as 'glocalization' (Robertson, 1995). Not surprisingly, there is now much controversy over conflicting visions of globality. Doshi (2003: 367–8) captures both sides well:

> The developing countries in Asia and Africa are much scared about the expansion of globalization. They consider it to be a new kind of imperialism, which exercises its hegemony in the fields of economy and culture. The US is the leading champion, which subordinates the nation-state cultures. The nation-state and grass roots culture are always in fear of its extinction. The other side of such a notion is that the proliferation of globalization would in the long run establish a uniform social order. The end of this process is homogenization.

Many writers now point to the large list of negative impacts of globalisation.[27] As the world has shrunk in terms of travel time and ease of communication, global interlinkage has brought new opportunities as well as new worries. The Chernobyl nuclear accident demonstrated that disasters in one part of the globe can have tremendous implications on people living far away. Taking the example of dumping toxic and dangerous wastes in the territories of powerless developing countries, an important study on the future of human rights warns of 'genocidal corporate and international financial institutional regimes of governance' which are, 'to coin a neologism . . . *righticidal* practices of management of *governance*' (Baxi, 2002: 143). Clearly, there are many lurking dangers in the ongoing processes of globalisation. In his exploration of globalisation, Robertson (2003: 3) portrays it as 'everyone's favourite catchphrase today', but his assessment of globalisation is not all positive:

> Indeed, it has become the *bête noir* of analysts angered at the contemporary power and influence of transnational entities, monsters that they believe are

---

[27] Flood (2002: 311) notes that '[a]lthough good things can flow from globalisation, the potential for suffering is omnipresent and rising'.

rapidly homogenizing the world, destroying its diversity, and marginalizing its peoples' hard-won democratic rights.

This leads into an important current debate, in which the image of globalising forces as monsters makes another appearance. One of the leading experts on human rights and traditional governance in Southern Africa (Hinz, 2003a: 114) reports:

> In training programmes of the Human Rights and Documentation Centre at the University of Namibia, we have always paid special attention to the perception of human rights by those who attended our programmes. Some of these perceptions we had to listen to were: human rights are western concepts; human rights interfere with the values of our culture; human rights are there to protect criminals; human rights prevent us from doing the job. Human rights are, so it has been said by a distinguished and well-respected traditional leader, monsters.

This kind of debate reflects lively ongoing worldwide discourses about visions of an ideal society.[28] Not everywhere are global and/or modern Western patterns of thought dominant; indeed, traditional and local concerns often predominate and assert themselves.[29] While liberalism as well as Marxism have their roots in enlightened universalism, which lawyers should recognise as a form of idealised natural law, the new universalism brought about by globalisation is supposed to be inspired and nourished by 'a cosmopolitan world society, a global society in which transnational social bonds and universally held notions of peace, justice, equality and freedom would define the conditions of human existence' (Doshi, 2003: 372). This vision is one in which all of mankind pulls together in building a unified structure, a 'global village' in which everyone can live together happily on the basis of agreed rules. But it should be immediately obvious that such a scenario is simply not realistic. What about normative pluralism and the agency of the individual? What about subaltern perspectives (Guha, 1982)? Do we need to be reminded of multiple legal pluralities by traditional leaders from Namibia to realise that a universally applicable value system for the whole world is little more than a nice illusion,[30] theoretically attractive, but practically impossible?

The concept of 'enlightened universalism', now prominently reflected in lively human rights discourses, has been inspired by a much-noted but imperfectly analysed resurgence of natural law thinking in the twentieth century.[31]

---

[28] For obvious reasons, academic debates are highly activated in post-Apartheid Southern Africa (see Freeman, 2001: 98; Bekker *et al.*, 2002; Bennett, 2004; Hinz, 2003a).

[29] Twining (2000: 249) notes that 'CNN and the Internet may circle the world, but they have not "penetrated" very far in Uganda or India'.

[30] Schott (1995: 38) portrays absolute legal equality as a utopian dream of philosophers ('ein *utopisches Traumziel* der Philosophen') which is an exception in normal human reality.

[31] In his debate about the co-existence of legal traditions, Glenn (2000: 332; 2004: 358) argues that legal diversity is natural and 'looks like it will be with us for a long time. It is sustainable, and perhaps there should even be efforts to sustain it.'

Given that globalisation appears to have created hybrid results rather than uniformity, leading in political science terms to a bifurcated, multi-centric world as a 'hyper-pluralist transnational society' (Rosenau and Tromp, 1989), there is an argument for listening to many voices in the ongoing debates. Enlightened universalism therefore must mean and involve intrinsic respect for plurality and diversity.[32] Hinz (2003a: 117) argues:

> The challenges of the international human rights discourse will only result in responses from which individuals and societies will benefit when local voices are allowed to speak up, when local perceptions are taken seriously, and when local concerns are respected. We must understand that people have a right to call human rights monsters when they are told that there were no human rights in their traditional societies. People have a right to resist human rights concepts imported by religious and secular missionaries who pretend knowledge of everything without having set foot into the areas in which they want to do missionary work.

Hinz (2003a: 117) highlights that there is a need for what he calls the 'soft human rights approach', since traditional societies have the skills to react constructively to new challenges:

> One of the ways to which I would give priority, is to empower traditional communities and groups of stakeholders like traditional leaders consciously to judge the suitability of their own way of doing things in the context of the present enhancement of human rights. This may lead to reconfirming what they have been doing all the time. It may also lead to changes in what they have practised thus far. It may eventually lead to the permanent acceptance of new ways of doing things. One can only hope that it will also lead to the acceptance of a modicum of modesty when people proclaim that they need more time for the adjustments expected of them.

This seems to indicate that, while emphasising ideal notions like the universality of humankind and equality certainly does no harm and has an important symbolic value, in social reality 'on the ground', diversity and plurality continue to be so important to people's well-being that an ultimate ideal of global universality and absolute equality in all respects seems misguided as a blueprint for global development. It appears that post-Apartheid South Africa has explicitly recognised this (Bekker *et al.*, 2002) in order to be able to survive as a rainbow nation. However, this does not mean that respect for pluralism is necessarily and automatically good in itself and can simply be romanticised as an alternative ideal to uniformity.[33] Santos (1995: 114–15) argues that 'there is nothing inherently good, progressive, or emancipatory about legal pluralism. Indeed

---

[32] In this context Twining (2000: 243) claims for himself a perspective of 'innocent realism', leading to agnostic abstinence, recognising the risks of 'sitting on the fence'.

[33] This claim is often made in various contexts. See Freeman (2001: 903ff.) on the romantic reaction to natural law in Germany.

there are instances of legal pluralism that are quite reactionary.' However, does insistence on uniformity magically guarantee the dismissal of reactionary outcomes, or absence or reduction of conflict? Evidently, such debates are closely linked to discourses about equality versus equity and to old debates among lawyers about whether following precedent or working from case to case is preferable.

It appears that plurality-conscious globality-focused legal methodologies will need to emphasise a radical view of equity as a foundation for ultimate equality, and must prefer finding justice from case to case over rigid adherence to precedent. Ancient Hindu texts, among others, strongly advised that this was preferable to avoid injustice.[34] A legal methodology that acknowledges situation-specificity at all times (and thus deep or strong legal pluralism) would seem to be an essential tool in this endeavour. Everywhere on the globe, globalisation remains confronted with massive plurality and diversity and their consequences. In a detailed discussion of the three major challenges to globalisation, Robertson (2003: 13) finds that, in the short term, 'it is the refusal of many societies to accommodate diversity, one of the most important consequences of globalization, that may immediately prove most destabilizing'. Thus, despite ideologically grounded widespread fears and allegations that respect for local diversity and cultural specificity will not lead to a good life for all world citizens, it seems that in social reality plurality and diversity are going to prevail, because that is what people themselves want. This, too, suggests that respect for plurality and equity should be the ultimate aim.[35] Robertson (2003: 13) strongly argues for the enhancement of a global consciousness of plurality, relentless individual and collective empowerment and an inclusive rather than exclusive reading of human history:

> The creation of effective strategies to handle the reality of human diversity is one of humanity's most pressing challenges, as recent wars, ethnic cleansings, genocides, and the restless tides of refugees and displaced persons demonstrate.

In view of such debates, it appears that lawyers will increasingly need to rely on, or must develop for themselves, social science expertise. This means that particular legal methodologies need to be developed, or existing ones reshaped,[36] to analyse law in a global context. In view of southern African socio-legal realities,

---

[34] See *Brihaspatismriti* 2.12, quoted by the Kerala High Court in *Kunhikannan* v. *State of Kerala*, 1968 KLT 19, at 23 (chapter 4, section 4.3 below).

[35] Edge (2000: 6) notes that '[t]he much vaunted "globalisation" process does not have to mean the inevitable march of so-called progress to a sanitised future of dull uniformity'. Glenn (2000: 327–8; 2004: 353–5) warns that simple tolerance, as a Western concept, is not sufficient to cope with pluralism.

[36] Cotterrell (2003; 2004) argues for an empirical legal theory that takes explicit account of individual human autonomy and of 'community'.

Hinz (2003a: 117) emphasises that '[t]he challenges of the international dis-course can best be met by proactive responses to problems emerging from the interface between local perceptions and the international discourse. This is then exactly where jurisprudence and anthropology meet.'

The present study therefore emphasises the need for strengthening socio-legal approaches, which seem to have led a marginal existence within jurispru-dence.[37] But, in itself, this is not enough. A socio-legal focus with pluralist ori-entation must challenge the prevailing 'black box' approaches, as well as 'black letter' law and the predominance of authoritative law-making by rulers and nation states.[38] Taking a self-consciously cautious and conservative approach, Twining (2000: 10) leaves no doubt that 'if legal theory is to engage seriously with globalisation and its consequences a critical re-examination of its agenda, its heritage of ideas, and its conceptual tools is called for'. However, does advo-cating an integrated socio-legal perspective go far enough?

One of the key questions for lawyers today becomes to what extent globalisa-tion will and can mean harmonisation or even uniformisation of laws all over the world. The present study cannot start from an assumption that at some point in the future there will no longer be any Hindu law, Muslim law, Chinese law or African laws in the world. These internally complex legal systems have always changed and will inevitably experience further change, but it is unreal-istic to assume that they will ever give way to some kind of cosmopolitan global law. Abandoning the Western hubris that underpins much of comparative law and most of the current human rights discourse, the present study challenges the claimed superiority of Western models of law as dangerous. Similarly, Glenn (2000: 330; 2004: 356) argues that uniformising visions constitute a form of fundamentalism:

> They elevate one truth, or one tradition, to exclusive status, and seek to impose it. Fundamentalists may thus act in an imperial or aggressive or violent manner. In so doing, they do not reflect the entirety of their own tradition. Nor do they represent a truth which has the potential of becom-ing a major tradition in the world. It is, as interpreted, insufficiently com-plex to attract support across the wide range of human opinion. Complex traditions are therefore by their nature, and in their leading versions, non-universal and non-universalizing. They offer many grounds of accommo-dation with other complex traditions.

While this specific debate focuses on the co-existence of major legal traditions in the world, Europeans may need reminding that the demographic majority in today's world is definitely not in the North and that law everywhere remains a culture-specific and therefore social phenomenon. Asking whether there is a

---

[37] Twining (2000: 26) reports that already during the nineteenth century, the historical school was perceived as a threat and a rival by positivists.

[38] Indeed, pluralist approaches raise important questions about power (Griffiths, 2002: 289).

core in any of the major legal traditions of the world that could supplant all the law of the rest of them, Glenn (2000: 331; 2004: 357) responds: 'The answer would appear to be that there is no such universalizable core. This is good news for the sustainability of the major, complex, legal traditions of the world.'

Globality-conscious legal scholarship therefore needs to become less idealistically committed to certain ideologies, more practicality-conscious and socially and culturally aware of existing pluralities, including more explicit recognition of various Southern perspectives. At the same time, such globality-conscious scholarship needs to allow itself to dream afresh, in remodelled natural law fashion. This needs to be focused not so much (as was hitherto the case) on the supremacy of 'nature' or of 'law', and therefore those (gods or men, normally) who are deemed to have the power to make rules for others. Rather, it should focus on the fact that a good and sustainable global legal order, to cite Robertson (2003: 4) and his vision of the third wave of globalisation, 'suggests the emergence of something greater than the accident of interconnections'.[39] That kind of globalisation cannot hope to live without deep respect for plurality and diversity in the world, based on flourishing and dynamic equity rather than flattening equality. It also has to take account of something as vague as 'public interest' or 'the common good'.[40]

Hence there is a complex prima facie case for studying the legal systems of Asia and Africa in their own right and as integral elements of the global legal order in a spirit of respect for plurality. To what extent the existing methods of dealing with jurisprudence and comparative law are sufficient for this enormous challenge is not the key issue here, since we know that present approaches are not adequate. The main challenge and ambition of this book is therefore to move the existing debates beyond false axioms and simplistic models to a deeper level of legal analysis and understanding.

Following this introduction, which lays out the wider implications of globalisation for the study of law anywhere in the world, the first major chapter of this book reflects in more detail the various methodological difficulties of plurality-conscious global jurisprudence and offers a critical analysis of the ongoing problems faced by comparative law and legal theory as academic disciplines. Discussing and delivering globalised legal education is an ambitious enterprise, but certainly not an impossible goal. The chapter, in several sub-sections, argues

[39] This concept, known as 'super-additivity' in mathematical English and as *Übersumme* in German (Fikentscher, 1995), overcomes the constructed boundaries of 'private' and 'public', which Fikentscher (1993) has traced back to ancient Greek distinctions of *oikos* and *polis*. See also Mahajan and Reifeld (2003). On the idea of India as 'a nation greater than the sum of its parts' see Tharoor (2000: 5).

[40] Much writing exists on this outside anglophone scholarship, particularly the 1970s works of Ernst Fraenkel (Schütt-Wetschky, 1997). Glenn (2000: 320) lists interest analysis ('*Interessenjurisprudenz*') as one of the young traditions or goslings of the legal world and refers to Schoch (1948).

that in a changing world scenario, globalising eurocentric visions appear like another form of postcolonial colonisation, which is now being undermined by the private colonisation of many Northern states through migration from the South, which results in unofficial ethnic implantation of yet more legal hybrids. This chapter also discusses different models for studying law in a global context, based on interdisciplinary consideration of related subjects which should form an integral part of legal education and the study and practice of law today.

Chapter 2 focuses on legal pluralism, arguing that it constitutes much more than plurality of legal rules and should be treated as lying at the very root of all legal studies today, perhaps even as the fourth major methodology of legal theory. Plurality-focused legal analysis requires reconsideration of the concept of 'law' itself and the various ways in which this phenomenon has been studied and used. It is indeed painful, and yet beneficial, for incoming law students to be confronted with the basic fact that there is no universally agreed definition of law. If all existing legal reasoning is ultimately circular (Cotterrell, 2003: 244), students are forced to realise, from the start, that the subject of their study is much more complex than they imagined when they first contemplated a legal career. It excites intellectually alive students to be shown that divergent views about the nature of 'law' are not a result of simple North–South discrepancies or peculiarities of one jurisdiction, but that within any given country there are many different approaches to law which dynamically interact at all times. From the very start of recorded scholarship, the best thinkers of the world did not reach the same conclusions about what law is and means.[41] Learning about plurality within various legal theories around the globe empowers lawyers to think for themselves, rather than to submit unthinkingly to rote learning processes or certain attractive ideologies. If law students can, from the start, develop sensitivity for how different concepts of law have been historically growing within a specific socio-cultural environment, they have also been taught to function as humans, not just to think as lawyers. Studying pluralism of theory and thought in law is not just a matter of recognising some exceptions for strange 'other' systems. It is necessarily an integral part of legal methodology, informing all our systems of thought and behaviour, resulting in an integrated legal education which frees itself from the shackles of 'black box theories' and the virtual coma induced by dominant paradigms of legal positivism.

Chapter 3 covers what would appear to be familiar ground to traditional lawyers, in that it goes in roughly chronological order through the basic ideas, concepts and approaches of the various major schools of legal thought. This necessarily brief and incomplete survey implements a conscious decision for this revised edition to discuss the various theories of law only *after* the reader has been sensitised to the demands for a plurality-conscious globally valid

---

[41] Morrison (1997: 6 n. 9) highlights that even Austin was conscious of legal pluralism and criticises later commentators as presenting his approach as overly simplistic.

methodology of analysing law in chapter 2. It should become obvious, through a fresh reading of established legal theories, that the major debates about the nature of law have remained fragmented and partial, are hardly global and appear now sometimes quite naïve.[42] They represent eurocentric approaches and are frequently just petty debates over little details, full of unnecessary polemics, extended squabbles among experts on particular aspects of European legal systems. Such fragmented debates are deeply unsatisfactory because 'in an era of globalisation, we are under increasing pressure to focus on the whole universe of legal phenomena' (Twining, 2000: 175).

Finally, chapter 3 ventures beyond known territory by suggesting that there is an urgent need to rethink particularly the scope for combination of modern natural law theories with historical and socio-legal approaches. By abandoning the traditional false dichotomy of natural law and legal positivism, significant progress can be made in theorising strong legal pluralism, combining the theoretical approaches of natural law, positivism *and* historical/sociological school traditions in a triangular or concentric model (chapter 3, section 3.8). Since law is itself an internally plural phenomenon, a globally focused legal theory cannot avoid taking a realistic plurality-conscious approach that respects and highlights different perspectives, never totally ignoring consideration of 'the other'. The central field within the triangular model of global legal theory represents the arena of legal pluralism. Within it, the intrinsic pressure and systemic need to develop plurality-conscious justice-sensitive outcomes motivate constant negotiation between potentially conflicting legal inputs.

Four further chapters in Part II of this book apply this plurality-conscious theoretical model, focusing on major Asian and African legal systems and related jurisdictions. Chapter 4 concentrates on Hindu law as a family of laws that falls, like the term 'Hindu' itself, under a conceptual label which hides enormous divergence and internal plurality, and yet seems to make global claims. Proceeding from internal historical perspectives, an understanding of the conceptual foundations of Hindu law produces the realisation that state law is virtually absent within the traditional system, while the key to classical Hindu law seems to lie in appreciating the central role of models of cosmic order, macrocosmic as well as microcosmic, providing an intellectual continuum throughout the history of Hindu societies and legal systems. This set of dynamic natural law presuppositions has, of necessity, important implications for the study of Hindu law as a historical construct, since such indigenous perceptions clashed with the assumptions of outsiders about what 'Hindu law' is and how it manifests itself. The story of how colonial rule influenced the concepts and processes of Hindu law and turned it later into the 'bogus' Anglo-Hindu case law (Derrett, 1977: vii) with bizarre effects (Derrett, 1978: 78), is

---

[42] This seems to go particularly for debates about 'families of law' and the mapping of laws, on which see Twining (2000: 136–73).

followed by a detailed analysis of postcolonial modern Hindu law. This illustrates how, more recently, postmodern Hindu law began to pierce through earlier colonial impositions by the 1970s, rediscovering its roots, a complex process opposing simplistic uniformising globalisation visions, which is now becoming much clearer.

Today, it has become possible to study modern Hindu law as a legal system on its own terms, within a secular official framework, but with richly manifested Hindu conceptual characteristics (Menski, 2003), which are not necessarily 'religious'. Modern India's desire to portray itself as a secular democracy, developing along internationally respected lines, clashes head-on with the complementary desire to construct a legal system that can provide sustainable justice for India's many millions of desperately poor people. Recent legal developments in India show that Hindu law is reasserting itself as a legal system in its own right, borrowing certain so-called Western concepts, but not dependent on them (Menski, 2001; 2003). The diachronic study of Hindu law teaches about the internal diversities of law itself, its contested paradigms and its never-ending multifaceted manifestations within the overarching framework of a plurality-conscious, culture-specific global vision.

Chapter 5 focuses on Muslim law and, while emphasising the unique features of that legal system, problematises the realisation that Muslim law, too, is in reality a family of legal systems with immense internal diversities, rather than one uniform law. All that is common to all branches of this great tree are the basic conceptual roots, evidently of a religious nature, presenting an alternative vision of a natural law system, since Muslim law is not primarily made by the state.

The understanding of traditional concepts of Muslim laws, too, is premised on the realisation that there is a superhuman agency that is believed to have laid down parameters for all forms of life which continue to apply, whether humans accept it or not. This primarily religious tradition with global claims, also locally coloured and historically rooted, may manifest itself in firm religious belief and resulting orthopraxis, itself another heavily contested field. In such basic respects, the only difference between Hindu law and Muslim law is that Muslims clearly acknowledge that this universal Order is under the exclusive jurisdiction of one divine authority, Allah.[43]

Having focused primary attention on one divine authority that is believed to have created the global Order (*huqm*), Muslim law had to develop as a system of rules that would at all times relate back to this central authority. After the death of the Prophet in 632 AD, the urgent need to ensure continuity of

---

[43] Hindus, on the other hand, unable to agree (and never imposing a consensus) on the nature of this superhuman force, settled on explicit recognition of pluralistic tolerance, allowing individuals to believe in whatever superior force they chose, which could, in some highly syncretic cases, include Allah, Christ and others.

thought and of authority led ultimately to various systems of scholarly juristic expertise, which have over time created an impressive body of jurisprudence (*fiqh*), marked by enormous plurality and continuously developed also today, in interaction with many other sources, throughout the Muslim world. The comparative law student needs to understand, as fast as possible, that the Qur'an is not in itself, word by word, God's law (in the sense of positivist law). It is not, in that comparative legal sense, divine legislation,[44] but something much higher and larger: in fact it constitutes a holistic conceptual edifice of natural law. That being so, the Qur'an contains the roots of all good for the world as a whole and all law for all Muslims. The perennial challenge, the continuous task of man, and of every individual believer, is to discover what this law is, hence the crucial importance of juristic effort (*ijtihad*) and of human reasoning (*ra'y*) within Muslim jurisprudence, second only to divine revelation, both inevitably and inextricably linked in a plurality-conscious symbiosis.

The family of Muslim laws contains much evidence of experimenting with different types of reform to modernise, to divest certain religious authorities of their superior standing and to allocate new powers to the state's functionaries. Or the aim was to Islamise, to educate local populations into accepting rules closer to the demands of the Qur'an than traditional local norms. Today, in some cases, the expectations of modern international law are resisted as foreign interventions. Two intriguing case studies are Turkey and its path-breaking modernist legal reforms (chapter 5, section 5.13) and Pakistan (chapter 5, section 5.14), choosing to follow a path of so-called Islamisation, with manifold consequences for law-making in a modern democracy. Analysing those two case studies, and other developments within Muslim laws today, confirms that legal pluralism remains a reality also within the globalised framework of Muslim laws. The purported conceptual uniformity of Islamic law and its pluralistic manifestations are therefore not a contradiction. Such concepts co-exist, as they have always done, and have made the study of Islamic laws challenging for Muslims, experts of Islamic law, as well as for comparative lawyers.

Chapter 6 focuses on African laws, more than any other family of laws a truly extended family, due to the absence of centralising political and religious forces. This inherent plurality has made the study of African laws an immensely fragmented experience. Because it is almost impossible to work on the basis of African universals, many scholars have been frustrated by the masses of small detail required to understand any one legal system, only to see that it has limited application.

Moreover, the colonial agenda and events, and Christian as well as Muslim claims over African souls and people today, have driven the mostly oral indigenous African traditions further into the realm of the unknown. Only a few African thinkers and researchers have dared to stand up to the continued

---

[44] Which, of course, many Muslims take it to be, as a matter of belief.

claims of outside domination, asserting in turn that Africans have always had their own legal traditions. These are African assertions of natural law, which continue to be fiercely resisted. The powerful but of course nonsensical assumption that traditional African societies did not have 'law' still lurks, as evidence of local customary norms is often treated as a sign of backwardness and the prescribed path to a better future involves foreign-dictated outline plans of development that do not, in most cases, take adequate account of local norms and needs. It is no surprise that some Africans are talking about monsters when they refer to globalising pressures. As in the analysis of Hindu law, it is possible today to show how awareness of environment and nature, of complex local representations of global, macrocosmic and microcosmic order, have shaped African legal traditions and continue to influence the way in which African legal systems develop. There is much need for further research on all aspects of African laws, but there are signs of progress in this field, too (Okupa, 1998).

The study of African laws, fragmented as it is, has until recently – at any rate in Britain – mostly concentrated on the impact of colonial rule. The material collected here and the resulting discussions reflect that emphasis. As in post-modern, post-colonial Asia, African legal systems today, including the laws of the newly restructured Union of South Africa, develop within a complex framework of multiple reference and interactions, heavily contested when it comes to issues of dominance. Here, too, at the legal coalface, globalisation results in the creation of new hybrid legal systems such as post-Apartheid South African law, which is clearly not turning out as a carbon copy of Western legal systems. For some time, modern African legal systems have been dismissed as an intractable mess, while we see today that the fault lies more with insufficiencies of research and limitations of our own understanding. It remains enormously difficult to provide the necessary 'internal' African perspectives (Bennett, 2004: 1), given the multiple outside influences on African laws, but it is not possible to deny that African customary laws and indigenous visions of natural law continue to exist today and make their own contributions to today's globalised legal scenario.

Finally, chapter 7 concentrates on Chinese law, also a historically grown and immensely complex amalgam of many different legal systems over time and space with its own ideas about natural law. The formally unified and theoretically focused nature of classical Chinese law created an impression of somewhat rigid uniformity. However, that patina of uniformity disappears as soon as the surface of imperial legal rules is scratched and we discover that the formal rules left much of what we call 'law' today to informal local bodies and to customary laws. State law in classical China, therefore, provided only an extremely thin layer of state regulation and supervision, which neatly parallels the picture emerging from classical Hindu law as well as traditional African and Muslim laws. In other words, the formal superiority but actual remoteness of the respective state's legal system appears to be a remarkably common element of all traditional legal systems in Asia and Africa. In its various manifestations, this phenomenon deserves further comparative analysis.

The material on classical Chinese law is firmly grounded in literary evidence provided by imperial records from the various ancient dynasties of China. While some research continues on traditional aspects of Chinese law, legal attention has focused much more on the unsettled post-imperial era and then particularly on the Maoist period and now on current Chinese legal developments. Earlier Chinese attempts to borrow and adapt legal concepts from the West (and later from Russia) deserve special attention. All of this has more recently been overshadowed by reflections of globalisation, particularly a business-driven hype about the commercial opportunities offered by a modernising, increasingly capitalist China. The focus in studies on modern Chinese law has therefore been on commercial legal developments, as well as matters related to good governance and human rights.

The long-established characterisation of Chinese law as a socialist system with Chinese characteristics reinforces the conceptual paradigm of pluralism and shows that Chinese legal systems, too, must be read as open networks of competing diversities which need to be constantly negotiated. It is not unique to Chinese law that informal methods of dispute settlement have co-existed with official formal types of dispute resolution. While the increasingly well-researched Chinese manifestations of such complex processes continue to excite, comparative lawyers will find many parallel phenomena all over Asia and Africa.

The coverage in this volume could have included other legal systems of Asia and Africa, in particular Japanese law, the various South East Asian laws, and also the laws of the new Central Asian Republics. It seems now unlikely that they will be added into a future edition of this book, unless one contemplates a two-volume study. The exclusion of such legal systems should not signify lack of importance, but does reflect lack of academic coverage.[45] While the present text does not claim to provide a comprehensive overview of all the legal systems of Asia and Africa,[46] the selection chosen aims to introduce key concepts and sources of major Asian legal systems and African laws in their historical and political contexts, from ancient beginnings to the present time. This immense ambit of coverage and range highlights many gaps of knowledge, understanding and academic coverage and often shows how eurocentric approaches, especially in colonial times but still today, have led to crucial misrepresentations. A major aim of this book continues to be, therefore, to attempt a clearer understanding

---

[45] For example, European scholarship on South East Asian laws is now only represented at SOAS in the University of London and at Leiden University, where the historical links with Indonesia have created a special research focus.

[46] For 2006, OUP New York is planning publication of a multi-volume *Encyclopedia of Legal History* (edited by Stanley Katz), which is aiming to be truly global.

of the overarching concepts and structures of Asian and African legal systems within their own contested frameworks of reference and now in the wider context of globalisation. It is hoped that the present volume makes existing knowledge more accessible and will encourage readers to further explore 'other' legal systems. As one cannot emphasise enough, the laws of the South have continued to grow in importance in their own right and will need to be studied by many more lawyers and other professionals if Europe and North America want to remain competitive in a global legal environment.

1

Comparative law and legal theory from a global perspective

The introduction indicated that the current state of jurisprudence and comparative law leaves much to be desired.[1] There are disagreements about how to theorise and apply 'law'. Law's constant demand for clearly defined categories has led to what Cowan *et al.* (2001: 10–11) call 'the *essentialising proclivities of law*'. The discipline as a whole stands accused of misusing social categories and identities, claiming superior universal status for legal rules (p. 6) and 'law' itself has been essentialised in a reductionist manner (Griffiths, 2002: 293). In common parlance, the word 'law' itself immediately sets off all kinds of assumptions: 'The mere word "law" has an honorific ring' (Harris, 1980: 128). But we also know that all legal systems may fail to some extent to provide justice.[2] Historical memories of slavery, Nazism, Apartheid and ongoing genocides evoke mixed feelings about the potential (ab)uses of law and legal systems. For many people 'law' remains associated with misuse of power, and disorder rather than order.[3]

If globalisation means increasing hybridisation in locality-coloured and culture-specific forms worldwide, rather than uniformising homogenisation, lawyers need to be better equipped to understand the manifold pluralities within and between legal systems as complex entities with ragged boundaries. It seems that a plurality-focused understanding of globalisation challenges legocentric Western laws and questions much of what Western culture and modernity claim to stand for. Eurocentric legal theories claim universal validity while representing only a shrinking part of global humanity.[4] Since most thinking about globalisation is still inspired by the 'civilising mission' approach of the colonial period, huge mental barriers appear when people talk and write about this subject, particularly now linked to human rights (Caney and Jones, 2001). Explicit

---

[1] Riles (2001: 1) emphasises that comparison 'is one of the most ubiquitous and yet under-theorized dimensions of modern knowledge'.

[2] On law's ideal as justice, see Cotterrell (2003: 247). Bozeman (1971: xi–xii) notes that, in Asia and Africa, law is generally not perceived as dominant and separate, nor as necessarily good, but closely linked with socio-political elements.

[3] On law as disorder, see Twining (2000: 35).

[4] On the arrogance of this approach, see Dembour (2001: 58) and Caney and Jones (2001: 29). On ethnocentricity, see Renteln (1990: 74–6).

recognition in theory *and* practice that Eastern/Southern values may have an equal claim to universal recognition not only needs to be demanded, but also practised.[5]

In six sub-sections, this chapter analyses the ongoing problems faced by comparative law and legal theory as interrelated disciplines and discusses barriers in providing plurality-focused, globality-conscious legal education. These discussions lay foundations for the detailed study of legal pluralism in chapter 2 and a reassessment of traditional mainstream legal theories in chapter 3. The main concern here is to highlight the need to transfer theoretical jurisprudential awareness that all laws are culture-specific into practical application, for this is where current legal scholarship is seriously deficient. The first three sub-sections situate law as a culture-specific phenomenon within a wider discussion of comparative law and international laws. Largely involuntary and, in some cases, voluntary transplants of metropolitan laws in earlier colonial times are continued in various current receptions of laws today, but what is the impact of such transplants? This issue is analysed in light of current consequences of South–North migration, leading to ethnic implants in the legal systems of the North and posing new theoretical and practical challenges for accommodating plurality within metropolitan laws. Later sub-sections present a critical analysis of models for teaching comparative law, particularly the prevailing American world legal history approach. This discussion aims to demonstrate that such projects require more attention to interdisciplinary studies, which should form an integral part of all legal education to support globality-conscious legal practice. In conclusion, the chapter presents a plurality-focused model which aims to overcome the limitations of current approaches to studying law.

1.1 The culture-specific nature of law and respect for difference

Arguments for recognising the inherent plurality of law are well recognised in the theoretical literature on comparative law. Authors often use different terms and adopt slightly modified forms of reasoning, but there is an emerging consensus that one cannot view law as solely emanating from the state. The present discussion highlights the theoretical challenges faced by comparative lawyers in reconciling their own partially subconscious adherence to positivist axioms with growing recognition of legal plurality as a global reality.[6] Santos (1995, cited in Twining, 2000: 194) argues for recognising the concept of 'interlegality':

---

[5] This does not mean that anything goes. Renteln (2004: 186), one of the main American propagators of partial cultural defence, writes: 'I am not saying that every cultural tradition ought to be tolerated…[T]he consideration of cultural evidence does not necessarily require that courts permit the continuation of all cultural practices.'

[6] Following an overview of recent debates, Woodman (1998: 54) concludes that 'legal pluralism exists everywhere' and advises that comparative research therefore needs to assess degrees of legal pluralism rather than questioning its existence.

We live in a time of porous legality or of legal porosity, multiple networks of legal orders forcing us to constant transitions and trespassings. Our legal life is constituted by the intersection of different legal orders, that is, by interlegality. Interlegality is the phenomenological counterpart of legal pluralism, and a key concept in a postmodern conception of law.

Similarly, discussing the interconnected issues of reconciling legal traditions and respecting diversity in law, Glenn (2004: 349–50) points to an innate pluralistic awareness within all legal traditions:

The complexity of major legal traditions . . . is a fundamental part of their own teaching, of their own understanding of themselves . . . All of these complex, major traditions thus achieve complexity because of their proven ability to hold together mutually inconsistent sub-traditions. They all involve a particular way of thinking, which has become explicit in some of them, though remaining implicit in others. It is a way of thinking which has been described as multivalent, as opposed to bivalent, because sub-traditions are not either right or wrong but may be right in different, multiple (inconsistent) ways. The traditions are hence multivalued . . . all major legal traditions, asian, western and other, appear built on multivalent thought.

Glenn (2004: 351) argues that while the Western world ferociously defends its constructions of bivalent logic, with clear boundaries between distinct and separate concepts, the boundaries within and between all legal traditions are in fact 'fuzzy', reflecting socio-legal reality anywhere in the world. He concludes that diversity in law is a basic fact which is constantly hidden and defined away. Similarly, in her feminist analysis of the power of law, Smart (1989: 1) criticises the tendency of law to make questionable claims about its own uniformity and superiority:

[T]he collectivity to which the label law is applied presents us with the appearance of unity and singularity. Hence law constitutes a plurality of principles, knowledges, and events, yet it claims a unity through the common usage of the term 'law'. I shall argue that it is in fact empowered by its 'singular' image. It is important to acknowledge that the usage of the term 'law' operates as a claim to power in that it embodies a claim to a superior and unified field of knowledge which concedes little to other competing discourses which by comparison fail to promote such a unified appearance.

The tendency to assert the uniformity and superiority of law is often fuelled by those in positions of power, reinforcing positivism. The concept of law itself, and those who engage in the unavoidable word battles over its meaning, possess a significant power to define reality, which can be misused.[7] How do lawyers as theorists and/or practice-focused specialists reconcile rigidified uniformising

---

[7] Cotterrell (2003: 228) notes that law's abstract formality 'can no longer be viewed as embodying objectivity or a neutral approach to the social'. Lyotard (1984) emphasises the

understandings of law with a dynamic postmodern approach, in which almost nothing seems forever certain, and much depends on particular socio-political constellations?[8] It seems that, rather than recognising plurality, lawyers have sought to define what is, and what is not, within the 'law' (Sack and Aleck, 1992: xviii). Such efforts have led to defining away the plurality of law, pulling analysis towards unification and uniformity. Sack and Aleck (1992: xviii–xix) blame 'evolutionism' and its influence over the last 200 years for this tendency:[9]

> The 'natural' laws of history, whose existence is demonstrated by history itself, demand that 'law' becomes increasingly centralized, unified and uniform, because this is progress . . . The actual plurality in the field of 'law' merely shows that we are not as yet living in the best of all possible worlds and that some societies are progressing faster than others – the stragglers (those who try to resist the laws of history instead of letting themselves be carried along by them towards a glorious future) representing the earlier stages of the development through which the leaders have long passed. Hence the latter are not merely entitled but duty-bound to assist the stragglers in the acceleration of their own advancement.

In this way, with the help of anthropology, the history of Western law and of 'progress' became universalised: 'There was only one law with one history, transformed from an (interpretive) art into a science, because this universal history of "law" was assumed to be governed by natural laws which could be studied as if "law" (as well as "society") was a physical phenomenon' (Sack and Aleck, 1992: xix). This dominant approach used evolutionism as 'an essential part of the "positivist" package deal' of modernist rationality, but this is now being challenged by postmodern thought (p. xix):

> This was how things were supposed to turn out. Instead 'evolutionism' itself is disintegrating because people begin to see that the results its implementation produces are neither good nor necessary – and because even the physical universe, as understood by 'post-modern' natural science, is not a strict, predictable rational order but a mixture of certainty, probability and chance, which requires a holistic approach and precludes blinkered and self-assured specialization.

At the same time, disillusionment with social engineering through law is widely reflected in the literature.[10] Postmodern challenges to understanding 'law'

---

manipulation of narrative knowledge. Watson (1993: 118) highlights the place of authority in operationalising legal transplants.

[8] Comparative lawyers now accept that no legal system exists in isolation (Bell, 2002: 238) and stress that all law operates in context. Cotterrell (2002: 52) emphasises comparative law's necessary concern with the social. Freeman (2001: x) acknowledges from the start that legal positivism is not enough for legal analysis.

[9] Criticism of evolutionist thinking also appears in Watson (1993: 13).

[10] See Baxi (1982; 2002). Anleu (2000: vii) notes that '[i]n the wake of reliance on law to further desired social transformations, there is widespread disillusionment regarding the

complicate the picture but also suggest constructively that deeper awareness of interlegality helps to understand how 'law' functions in a pluralistic global context. Law, from this perspective, is no longer neatly packed in toolboxes for easy transportation, application and consumption. Recent scholarship suggests that whole tranches of academic discourse about the relationship of 'law' and 'society' (Cotterrell, 2002), 'rights versus culture' (Cowan *et al.*, 2001) and 'universalism versus relativism' (Renteln, 1990) are built on flawed premises. All of these debates re-examine the extent of legal interaction with socio-cultural plurality, but often fail to examine the nature of law as a plural phenomenon.

It is no surprise that many lawyers do not like such new complications.[11] Is law not supposed to be about certainty, clarity and well-formulated rules? From a conventional perspective, difference becomes an invitation for lawyers to unify, streamline and harmonise. But on what criteria should this be based? Accepting that the plurality of 'law' has no theoretical limits, it 'becomes unproductive to consider the practical limitations of "law" in any given society, let alone in the world. Instead we should be looking at the range of "legal" possibilities human beings have actually realized in the course of their history' (Sack and Aleck, 1992: xxv). This is perceived as a task for anthropologists rather than lawyers, who have focused on unification of laws to combat pluralism. But even the scholar most vigorously cited for supporting legal transplants as a means to global unification envisaged at best a 'virtually unitary system' (Watson, 1993: 101). Having concluded that his study 'can raise questions about the possibility and desirability of a unified system of law, at least for the whole of the Western world', Watson (1993: 100) states that '[o]bviously a complete legal union is neither possible nor desirable'. While greater centralisation or harmonisation of 'laws' may remain a viable aim, it becomes inevitably necessary to recognise deep legal pluralism. Sack and Aleck (1992: xxvi) argue:

> It requires us . . . to learn to live with the fact that 'law' is like a multidimensional net which stretches beyond the horizon in all directions, wherever we stand. We can only lift it at a particular point and inspect its mesh as far as we can see, knowing that it is changing even as we are observing it in response to a multitude of forces of which we ourselves are part – and that even its most permanent configurations are the product of conventionalized and institutionalized human imagination and perception.

However, anthropology 'can only play the role as a midwife in the birth of a "post-positivist" "law" after it has itself been liberated from its own cultural blinkers' (Sack and Aleck, 1992: xxvi). Lawyers, in turn, struggle to understand

persistence of inequalities and the resistance of social institutions and actors to changed legal environments'. Morrison (1997: 13) observes that 'the promises of modernity to construct societies of social justice where people would be happy have proved false'.

[11] Finnis (1980: 279, cited in Freeman, 2001: 179) noted that '[t]he lawyer is likely to become impatient when he hears that social arrangements can be *more or less* legal, that legal systems and the rule of law exist as a matter of degree . . . and so on'.

'society' and 'community' (Cotterrell, 2002) and legal theory must now systematically take account of the notion of 'culture' (Cotterrell, 2004: 1). Riles
(2001: 18) suggests that modern comparative law's 'technocratic devotion to
universalism is something of an embarrassment' today. Such comments show
acute consciousness of plurality and respect for socio-cultural difference in
legal debates. However, few lawyers have penetrated more than the surface of
such recognition.[12] There are many reasons for this. Ignorance may be a factor,
since conventional legal training does not prepare lawyers for such theoretical challenges. Having interviewed many legal academics, Cownie (2004: 58)
observes that:

> [W]hatever they call themselves, the majority of academic lawyers occupy
> the middle ground between the two extremes of pure doctrinal analysis
> and a highly theoretical approach to the study of law. Arguably, law is a
> discipline in transition, with a culture where a small group still clings to a
> purely doctrinal approach, but a very large group (whether they describe
> themselves as socio-legal or not) are mixing traditional methods of analysis
> with analysis drawn from a range of other disciplines among the social
> sciences and humanities.

In this changing climate of legal education, comparative legal work will remain
difficult for anyone,[13] especially for those lacking a pre-disposition towards
accepting difference.[14] Because law is often treated as a segmented, separate
entity by lawyers, and, damagingly, also by other social scientists, critical debates
about development and globalisation are not easily carried into law schools and
socio-cultural specificities of 'the South' are mostly left unexamined. Global
legal debates on human rights and religious law circle uncomfortably around
the often unspoken but systematic denial that anything useful could be learnt
from non-Western socio-legal traditions. Modernism leads itself ad absurdum.
Glenn (2004: 18) claims that '[i]n the west the argument has extended to the
jettisoning even of the notion of tradition itself'. Non-Western laws and their
underlying 'traditional' concepts are, therefore, forever kept on the defensive.[15]

---

[12] Such issues are not discussed in Cownie (2004), while Freeman (2001) recognises the
   need to think further about such matters and introduces a much-noted section on legal
   pluralism. De Cruz (1999: v) focuses mainly on French and German law but acknowledges
   the need for more comprehensive comparative legal study. Cowan et al. (2001) seek to
   push the boundaries of interdisciplinary academic discourse.

[13] Watson (1993: 10) finds comparative law superficial. Legrand (1996: 239) pointedly asks:
   'Who ever claimed that comparative legal studies should be easy? Who ever asserted that
   comparative legal studies should be for everyone?'

[14] It is not clear how one acquires that quality. The biographies of comparative law scholars
   often point to personal histories of migration and plurality-consciousness. See many of
   the contributions in Edge (2000) and Riles (2001) and reference to the insider–outsider
   dichotomy in Riles (2001: 6).

[15] The impact of this on some sections of third world scholarship has been significant. On
   recent arguments for abolishing traditional elements in Indian law see Dhagamwar (2003).

In this context, the inherently individualistic orientation of many non-Western cultural and religious traditions (within cultural traditions that seem to give pre-eminence to the group rather than the individual) has long been purposely underplayed by Western scholarship to hold up the enemy of 'tradition' and 'religion'. Individual agency, like pluralism, fundamentally challenges state-focused notions of law and makes many lawyers uncomfortable.[16] This, among other reasons, may account for the continued dismissal of traditional non-Western legal systems as irrelevant for legal study and contributes to the chorus of denial of the need for plurality-conscious legal studies.[17] Such negative approaches must be understood as self-protection mechanisms on the part of Western secular, state-centred legal establishments.

Individual agency in law is a difficult issue to analyse, given that Western cultural hubris and Eastern political and religious élitism (which both often focus on patriarchal forms of domination, in addition to state centrism and legalism) act hand in hand to deny individual legal agency and the resulting plurality.[18] Accepting every individual's right to determine his or her own set of rules (or at least to have a voice in such processes) challenges the authority of official state law and 'religious' law, Western or Eastern. Arguing for individual discretion as a *legal* element is perceived as subversive, inherently dangerous and non-legal, even anti-legal and, in some contexts, even blasphemous.[19] Whether state law (which might also appear as 'religious' law) would be right in claiming to control all behaviour in all situations is a huge question which cannot be squashed by standard answers to the effect that 'the law' must always prevail, or that a particular religious law or rule is unquestionably supreme.[20] Such positioning displays a lack of plurality-consciousness. While one cannot amend

[16] Holden (2004) shows how Hindu women may arrange their escape from bad marriages into new unions that are socially sanctioned and legally valid, undermining traditional preconceived notions of rigid rules about Hindu marriage and divorce. Twining (2000: 10) stresses the need for re-examination of 'legal personality' and agency.

[17] This is strongly emphasised by Berman (1974) who, from an American perspective, analyses the excessive fragmentation of law and religion and emphasises their factual and intellectual interdependence. Depicting liberal democracy as the first great secular religion (the second is revolutionary socialism), Berman (1974: 74) writes critically of 'the religion of the intellectual'.

[18] On the individual as 'purposeful agent' see Dembour (2001: 59) who asserts that in this respect '[t]he stark divide posited between the West and the rest of the world just does not exist'. The central dispute appears to be over the axiom of equality, when as a matter of fact every individual could be seen as an entity in his/her own right. Radical pluralism of this kind was established in ancient Hindu thought (chapter 4), but is not seen as politically correct today, even in India.

[19] This arises in legal systems where dissent from the dominant view is seen and treated as treason. This used to be possible in English law but is today an issue mainly in Islamic jurisdictions.

[20] Berman (1974: 49) suggests that this approach is dangerous, because law degenerates into legalism and religion turns into private religiosity.

the Qur'an, the Bible or other religio-cultural sources, allowing room for new human interpretations in changing life circumstances becomes an inevitable necessity (chapter 5). Everywhere, the dynamic social (and therefore also religious) embeddedness of law poses huge challenges and existing theoretical approaches do not answer many questions about the extent of legal respect for plurality (O'Dair and Lewis, 2001).

Studying Asian and African legal systems from an internal perspective, attempting to understand 'from inside' how they have developed and function today, it becomes impossible to maintain a eurocentric, statist and purportedly universal set of assumptions about 'the law'. Perhaps that is why many people never even try to go that far. Herein, first of all, lies the central challenge for the comparative law teacher and legal theorist in the field of globalised legal education: the absence of any worldwide agreement, in theory as well as in practice, about the central object of globalised legal studies, namely 'the law' itself. Such definitional and ideological struggles are exacerbated by discrepancies between different religious systems and their competing truth claims.[21] As in religious studies, it seems that, unless we agree to disagree about the basic ingredients of law itself and allow others the space to explain (and live) their culturally conditioned understandings of life and law, no real progress will be made in global legal debate.

In this context, academics often raise the objection of 'essentialising', stereotyping complex entities by emphasising one particular aspect of the whole.[22] Allegedly this happens at the cost of fuller understanding or in disregard of flexibility of boundaries, and has caused enormous frustration in academic discourse (Cowan *et al.*, 2001). However, provided one is aware of the fluidity of boundaries, what is wrong with demonstrating that a certain category or a particular legal system or legal rule is different from others and appears to have certain key characteristics? Academics need such techniques to explain their thoughts. The deeper issue appears to be that the task of the comparatist in cherishing difference involves open-minded appreciation of 'the other', readiness to accept the other system as valid in its own right, thinking in open rather than closed basic categories. Combined with statist legocentric approaches, boxed visions have impoverished legal analysis and made it amazingly easy for positivists to define away the socio-cultural dimensions of law as 'extra-legal'. Mattei (2001: 254) identifies the difficulties of mainstream legal

---

[21] Glenn (2000: 45ff.) considers whether it is feasible to rule the world through truth and, not surprisingly, reaches the tentative conclusion that toleration of pluralism is a demanding task, given a tradition of intolerance and a plurality of claimed truths. Küng and Kuschel (1993: 86) discuss the collapse of eurocentric Christian modernity from a comparative ethics perspective.

[22] On 'essentialism' see Freeman (2001: 40–2). Renteln (2004: 198) notes that some stereotypes 'are true or at least contain a kernel of truth, if by stereotype we mean one group's perception of another group'.

scholarship in adopting more plurality-conscious perspectives and suggests that,

> [L]egal positivism is *the enemy* of understanding in the law. It is a reduc-
> tionist perspective that artificially excludes from the picture the deeper
> structure of the law (things like legal culture, language of legal expression,
> revolutionary moments and so on) as well as (in typical postmodern style)
> the decorative, and symbolic elements of it. Positivism, as a consequence, is
> unmasked as an inherently formalistic approach, in the sense that form pre-
> vails over structure in determining the law's domain. It *outlaws* (considers
> outside the law) deeper structural aspects.

Such shortcomings need to be overcome. Various contested and competing definitions of law need to be combined into a plurality-conscious analytical model, as attempted later (chapter 3, section 3.8). Here it must suffice to note (1) that law appears to be all-pervasive, in all kinds of forms, in our daily lives;[23] and (2) that the dominant assumptions in our minds about the nature of 'law' tend to isolate 'law' and privilege state-made law, so that 'law' becomes primarily a system of state-made rules which is ideally just 'good law'. But that is definitely not the end of the story.[24]

Many important questions arise. How are religion and society linked to law?[25] Do Gods/gods or their human spokespersons make law? Are 'customs' to be treated as law? More specifically, do groups of people in a state have the right to determine their own rule systems if there are formal laws that they should follow? Do we treat such private law-making as evidence of lawlessness, even treason, or do we recognise it as law-making processes by social groups rather than states, and perhaps even by individuals? To what extent is this legitimate and still 'legal'? Does law really govern every moment of our lives, as legocentric approaches would claim? These are complex questions to which no universally agreed answers will ever be found because so much depends on one's perspectives and ideology. Simple eurocentric assumptions about 'law' cannot remain unquestioned in a sophisticated global educational environment. Law students in London or New York probably have quite different thoughts on such issues than budding lawyers in China, India, Namibia or elsewhere in the South.

---

[23] Twining (2000: 1–2; 259) refers to a newspaper exercise, asking students to scan a daily newspaper and to mark all law-related passages. Not only do students quickly realise that law is pervasive in society, they also face difficulties in deciding what is and what is not 'legal'.

[24] In teaching, I often find that Muslim students wish to respond (but tend to remain silent) to statements that the concept of state law is dominant by asserting that God's law, not state law, is superior. As we shall see, this is not unique to Muslims.

[25] A broad range of current issues is covered in O'Dair and Lewis (2001). Emphasising the dialectical interdependence of law and religion, Berman (1974: 137) suggests 'that there are religious dimensions of law and legal dimensions of religion, and that the two cannot survive independently of each other', requiring recognition of their ultimate interaction.

Even if we try to develop a working definition of law in the North/West, from the perspective of a traditional Southern African community leader, the legal world will look very different.[26] Since the word 'law' is used to refer to a variety of concepts, we are offered a bewildering spectrum of definitional propositions from which to make a choice, in the knowledge that both the definitions and the choice are inescapably culture-bound and situation-specific.

Consequently, any attempt to answer the popular essay question whether law is a universal phenomenon is bedevilled from the start by the absence of consensus about methodology and the definition of 'law'. A narrow, state-centred approach would have to conclude that law is not a global phenomenon, as not all human societies (assuming we know what we mean by 'society') have formalised laws laid down by a state. Quite simply and logically, if one does not accept that customs can fall under 'law', then the conclusion inevitably becomes that not all human societies have law. Perhaps this logic is wrong? Do we really have lawless societies, and so-called 'primitive' people have no law?[27] Roberts (1979: 23–5) criticised Hart's (1961) famous model of law, which appears to require centralised legislative and adjudicative bodies to recognise 'law'. A broader, more globally oriented approach should have no problems accepting, for example, that ethnic minorities in Britain could develop their own laws in the shadow of the official English law (chapter 1, section 1.3). Yet such matters are heavily contested, and we are struggling with such issues in Europe and North America at present, agonising for example over whether Muslim women and girls, Sikh men or Jamaican Rastafarians should be permitted to wear 'religious' forms of headgear in certain situations.

A more open approach to the definition of law than currently used in many debates would need to account for different forms of law in all human societies. Thus, in a so-called simple society, where no formal evidence of law exists and where no disputes may arise because everyone knows the basic rules and follows them to the satisfaction of others, there may be no visible evidence of law and of legal processes. A plurality-conscious analysis of law would nevertheless conclude that this society has its own laws, probably internalised to such an extent that nobody needs to write them down and apply them formally. Such a simple society still has a legal system, which perhaps includes the overriding principle that avoidance of disputes at all costs is the guiding principle or the 'golden rule'. So here, the 'rule of law' would be that there should be no recourse to formal law at all.[28]

---

[26] Hinz (2003a). Freeman (2001: 1) emphasises the role of ideological stances, or Holmes' 'inarticulate major premises'.

[27] While Hart (1961) is a major contributor to Western legal theory, what he says about the absence of law among primitive people cries out for revision. Twining (2000: 63) gentlemanly criticises Hart's approach as 'rather simplistic and old-fashioned'.

[28] The same rationale could be applied in a critical analysis of modern contract law (e.g. Collins, 1999), which is far too legocentric.

A globally valid analysis of 'law' needs to be sensitive to such informal and unwritten concepts, aware of many culture-specific and even personal idiosyncrasies. When one travels through Heathrow airport's Terminal 3 these days, one finds on the long walls of the walkways illustrations of common symbols with totally different culture-specific meanings abroad. Such thoughtful mental preparation for international travel indicates that such differences of meaning could become legally relevant when a particular cultural group assigns to some image, concept or human action specific negative or positive values. Legrand (1997a: 61) notes that '[c]ulture remains the most insistent admonition directed at law to recognise its own limits'.

It is impossible for anyone to obtain a full mental map of all citizens of the world in their various life situations. Human life is just too complex; where do we stop? Do we prioritise the views of people in hour-long queues on congested roads in Mumbai's urban jungle over the assumptions carried by people who walk on foot every day through bushland to reach their place of work in the same jurisdiction? Do we make distinctions between rich and poor, rural and urban, dominant and servient, white and black, and so on? Yes, we do, all the time, reflecting the diversities of life. Applying law continuously involves making decisions that take account of different facts and circumstances and must, of necessity, involve consideration of socio-cultural elements. This even goes for commercial law, despite a strong belief that it is culture-neutral.[29]

Legal science has moved through various modernising phases into a position where gradually the formal cosmopolitan law has become the dominant concept, often completely silencing lesser orders, little people and their local concerns.[30] Since postmodern methodology involves a general re-questioning of all human activities, the task for legal scholarship is to build such realisations into a strong plurality-conscious methodology of global validity, focusing on the whole universe of legal phenomena (Twining, 2000: 175). But what are legal phenomena? We are always thrown back to the conundrum of defining 'law'.

In a book on Asian and African legal systems, it becomes impossible to treat law simply according to eurocentric, statist models. However, the comparative legal world, with few exceptions, still ends at the Bosporus or in Gibraltar. However, Western positivist models of law, even in combination with natural law claims to universal validity, run into trouble in the very first session of a comparative law course if a global, plurality-conscious perspective is taken.[31]

---

[29] Foster (2002: 60, 68). Watson (1993: 100 n. 14), while expressing reservations about complete legal union, argued that 'unification of commercial law may be both possible and desirable'.

[30] Sack and Aleck (1992). For references on modernism in legal studies, see the bibliographical note in Riles (2001: 1). Legrand (1997a) vigorously challenges current attempts to reduce diversity through the project of a European Civil Code.

[31] This experience confirms the view of Dennis Lloyd, expressed in 1959, that 'there is nothing inconsistent or incompatible with a positivist outlook, in acknowledging the essential role of values in law and human society' (Freeman, 2001: x).

This indicates that legal science as a whole is sick (Zweigert and Kötz, 1998: 33) and that, '[t]hough the hollowness of the traditional attitudes – unreflecting, self-assured, and doctrinaire – has increasingly been demonstrated, they are astonishingly vital' (p. 33). Lawyers have been slow to globalise their perceptions. The problem may be much deeper, mainly related to a fixation on the project or vision of global uniformisation.[32] Riles (2001: 15) identifies that everything 'is in the service of a goal, in the world, of building a consensus, of *solving*, rather than simply analyzing, the problem of difference'. Jurisprudence, together with other social sciences, has been fixated on, and imprisoned by, a vision of the need to get rid of difference and plurality. One wonders why – clearly there are many hidden agenda.

The present study argues for conscious inclusion of all Asian and African manifestations of legal systems as an integral part of legal theory and education. There is no necessary contradiction between respect for diversity and aiming for greater convergence (Renteln, 1990: 78; in detail Cowan *et al.*, 2001). Increasing globalisation in the form of pluralisation has created an even greater need to have detailed knowledge and better understanding of the complex world and its many types of law.[33] Diversity simply cannot be ignored (Caney and Jones, 2001: 31; Legrand, 1997a; 1997b). This has given rise to new ways of looking at debates about culture and rights, as Cowan *et al.* (2002: 21) conclude:

> But the search for a single theory that would provide definitive guidance in all cases is quixotic, not only because of the existence of irreducible difference and contingency across contexts and situations, but also because it misconstrues what actually happens when universal principles are applied in the real world.

Exposing first-year law students to such ideas, and to the theories of internationally renowned postmodern legal thinkers like Masaji Chiba (1986) and his enormously helpful distinction of 'official law', 'unofficial law' and 'legal postulates' (chapter 2, section 2.5.4) is not too demanding and confusing. Law students tend to be clever people, and they should be keenly interested in problem-solving. I have found most students, including freshers, ready to pick up complex issues and to unpack them, rather than to be given simple paradigms and to be left alone to discover the fuller picture for themselves later. It all depends on what we want to achieve through legal education. As long as much of legal teaching is merely designed, as Legrand (1996: 235) put it, to train 'simple technicians of the national law', neither will there be much progress in comparative law, nor are we going to see many educated, competent

---

[32] Dembour (2001: 73) notes that 'the *prima facie* value of universalism is generally not contested'.

[33] Taking the emotional subject of female circumcision, Dembour (2001: 60ff.) suggests a cautious approach of 'erring uncomfortably in-between' and agrees with Peter Fitzpatrick's view that it is necessary to make constant efforts to find one's way (p. 75).

lawyers with global legal expertise. Studying a few basic rules of international law does not do the trick. Plurality-conscious legal education can do much better than that.

The next section delves deeper into more specific reasons why comparative legal scholarship and legal theory carry epistemological baggage and historical burdens that make it difficult to refocus our lenses, even today, for a plurality-sensitive globally-focused jurisprudential analysis.

1.2 Changing global scenario: from colonial transplant to ethnic implant

Globalisation discourses have awoken the old ghosts of debates about what happens when laws are transplanted from one place to another. Is the current wave of globalisation just a remodelled version of earlier colonial domination, now in the garb of attractive trade deals and development programmes, forcing 'little' local people to comply with metropolitan standards? Colonialism itself was not primarily intent on legal transplantation, it was in the first instance based on conquest. Moreover, many colonial powers were too weak (and far too thinly spread and busy making profit) even to care about what happened to local laws.[34] Often, colonial powers were concerned that too much interference in local affairs might lead to rebellion. De Cruz (1999: 479) suggests that '[o]ne reason why the colonising powers almost always left indigenous customs practically untouched was because of the immense local pride that exists in maintaining well established customs'.

However, it appears that colonial mindsets still influence much thinking about law in the world today. The colonial experience created a strong spirit of Western superiority and a self-conscious claim of a civilising mission. In many colonial territories, and also outside of them (e.g. Japan, Thailand), much European law was transplanted in various processes of reception.[35] Many colonial subjects imbibed such new rules and values and became 'brown sahibs', acculturated copies of their colonial masters. Few protested in words and actions like M. K. Gandhi, India's 'Father of the Nation'.[36] Ideological divisions about how to evaluate such conflicts continue today; much of non-Western scholarship reflects a remarkable 'colonisation of the mind' (Nandy, 1983: xi), and a resulting dearth of adequate socio-legal scholarship is evident.[37]

---

[34] On colonial India, see Menski (2003: 156–85). Galanter (1989: 15) portrays the formation of a unified nationwide modern legal system as one of the major achievements of British rule in India, but how far does a formal legal system interlink with society?

[35] It is rarely mentioned that this was primarily to avoid that the respective local laws applied to the European newcomers, who were initially traders, rather than lawyers and rulers.

[36] Hardiman (2003) examines Gandhi's alternative modernity and the predicaments of the social activist. On African reconstructions of religious thought and political power, see Ellis and Ter Haar (2004).

[37] This has been noted for India by Baxi (1982; 1986) and Menon (1983).

To interrogate such deficiencies in legal methodology, several interrelated themes are explored here to demonstrate that, in today's world, significant socio-legal changes are taking place that demand the attention of an up-to-date plurality-conscious jurisprudence, combined with a refocusing of visions about an ideal world. The major themes are covered in separate sub-sections: (1) the traditional focus on international law and now on human rights as means to create some kind of 'global law' for the world; (2) the role of comparative law as a handmaiden to such aims; (3) related to this, the long history of transplants, reception of laws in colonial and non-colonial contexts, mainly by national legal systems; and lastly (4) the emergence of voices of the South, earlier marked by strategic silences of Asian and African laws and scholars, but now manifested as increasingly self-confident post-colonial assertion of non-Western laws in the countries of the North.

1.2.1 International law and its unifying pressures

A key question for lawyers today is to what extent globalisation means harmonisation,[38] or even global uniformisation of laws, rather than glocalisation or global pluralism. In this debate, the creation of a universal legal order motivates much legal activity, channelling students into public international law courses, often explicitly motivated by concern to safeguard human rights and universal legal standards under the banner of 'rule of law' and 'good governance'. These are exciting agenda. However, it must be questioned whether these are appropriate educational strategies and legal responses to the multiple impacts of globalisation.

Traditional legal studies in Britain have mainly focused on state law and, with some reluctance, on public international law (Twining, 2000: 61). International law as a field of legal study and practice appears to suggest the possibility of constructing a world legal system.[39] Indeed, public international law and its various agencies and bodies today create the impression that a universal legal order has been created. Much of this remains wishful thinking, but while both public and private international law have to compete with jealously guarded state powers and corporate strategies of bypassing all of this, there is so much commitment towards uniformisation that some academics have begun to feel constricted and express concern about pressure to operate only at the global level (Twining, 2000: 248).

The definition of international law depends very much on one's understanding of 'law', but it is essentially a supranational and therefore global system of law (Zweigert and Kötz, 1998: 7) which continues to be concerned about structuring

---

[38] This strategy is emphasised by the Indian Law Institute (1971) through the search for a common core of legal principles, inspired by Schlesinger (see Riles, 2001).

[39] Pathak and Dholakia (1992: 89) see it as an inevitable conclusion that 'its modern evolution is going in the direction of the construction of one united, integrated and coherent system of law', while also recognising the continued claims of state sovereignty.

and regulating international public order (Cass, 1996). International law was famously relegated by Austin in 1832 to the realm of 'law improperly so called' because it did not fit his narrow positivist definition (Freeman, 2001: 270). Public international law emerged in sixteenth-century Europe as 'Law of Nations',[40] essentially for a family of Christian states with a shared European cultural heritage. During colonialism, its reach was gradually extended beyond Europe and today it covers all nations through what looks like global law.[41] There is a long history of employing comparative law techniques to harmonise and unify international law.[42] David and Brierley (1978: 10) argued vigorously for uniformisation of public international law to curtail the continuing plurality of rules, which they depicted as anarchy, and explicitly criticised opponents of legal unification as rooted in nineteenth-century thinking, conveying a sense of urgency (p. 10):

> It is not, after all, a matter of replacing any one national law with a uniform supra-national law enacted by some world-wide legislator; without going so far, some progress towards a gradual improvement of international relations can be made through a variety of other techniques. But some international unification of law is required now and more will be necessary in the future.

Harmonisation as a process of ascertaining the admitted limits of international unification does not necessarily amount to a vision of total uniformity. David and Brierley (1978: 16) concluded, at a time when globalisation was not yet a term of art, that there is 'no true science of law unless it is universal in scope and in spirit'. Linked to their ideas of progress of law, this modernist statement sits uneasily with recognition of legal diversity. David and Brierley (1978: 18) indicated an awareness that a plurality of laws is much more complex than just a diversity of rules:

> It is a superficial and indeed false view to see law as being only composed of the totality of such rules . . . Each law in fact constitutes a *system*: it has a vocabulary used to express concepts, its rules are arranged into categories, it has techniques for expressing rules and interpreting them, it is linked to a view of the social order itself which determines the way in which the law is applied and shapes the very function of the law in that society.

The conclusion suggests that positivist law reform may face significant obstacles. David and Brierley (1978: 18–19) argued:

> The legislators may, indeed, with a stroke of the pen modify the actual legal rules, but these other elements and features nonetheless subsist. They

---

[40] As is widely recognised (Harris, 1991: 17), Indians claim that international law has a much older pedigree as the law governing relations between states in ancient India (Chatterjee, 1958). A recent study even claims that this ancient model is a precursor to the United Nations (Bhattacharjee, 2003).

[41] See Zweigert and Kötz (1998: 24–8); de Cruz (1999: 23–6); Riles (2001: 1–18).

[42] On the need to reduce discrepancies, see Zweigert and Kötz (1998: 24–8) and de Cruz (1999: 23–6).

are not so arbitrarily changed because they are intimately linked to our civilization and ways of thinking. The legislators can have no more effect on them than upon our language or our reasoning processes.

This suggests that law reform would ideally have to consider socio-cultural facts, but this conclusion is significantly not drawn, because the authors are thinking about European civilisation and its global claims to superiority. David and Brierley (1978: 21ff.) proceed from such basic assumptions to their treatment of the concept of legal families,[43] denying in the process that all cultures in the world deserve the same respect. Clearly, their assumptions about 'civilisation' and the need for progressive, modernist law reforms override respect for legal plurality on a global scale.

Historically, this uniformising approach relates back at least to the first International Congress for Comparative Law in Paris in 1900, marked by a strong belief in human rationality and progress.[44] Twenty years after David and Brierley (1978), Zweigert and Kötz (1998: 3) indicate that 'belief in progress, so characteristic of 1900, has died. World wars have weakened, if not destroyed, faith in world law.' They identify a more sceptical way of looking at the world, while the 'belief in the existence of a unitary sense of justice' (p. 3) is still there. Similarly, de Cruz (1999: 496) concludes his discussion of the new world order with a claim for the continued relevance of comparative law 'to remind us that, despite differences in culture, history, law and language, we are all part of the larger community of mankind'.

Zweigert and Kötz (1998: 24–31) show that the focus in such debates has now shifted towards reduction of discrepancies and harmonisation, especially at the European law level, where the aim for many continues to be total unification.[45] This indicates ongoing disagreements over the extent to which different perceptions of law and justice can be tolerated in the world. Such debates often fail to acknowledge that legal plurality does not exist merely between national legal orders and international law but also between different normative

---

[43] De Cruz (1999: 33) seems to accept this method, while Harding and Örücü (2002: viii–ix) indicate that the theory of legal families 'is under attack and is not regarded as useful except as a teaching device'. Riles (2000: 2) suggests that everyone is now a critic of earlier typologies of legal systems. Twining (2000: 152) sees early attempts to use the legal families concept as jurisprudentially naïve.

[44] Zweigert and Kötz (1998: 2–3) outline concisely how the rationale of this movement worked to underpin ambitions of global law-making, 'the development of nothing less than a common law of mankind (*droit commun de l'humanité*). A world law must be created – not today, perhaps not even tomorrow – but created it must be, and comparative law must create it' (p. 3). De Cruz (1999: 23) traces earlier ambitions for global unification to 1851. But in the 1900 International Congress, even English law was hardly represented and no notice was taken of places like South East Asia (Harding, 2002: 263).

[45] De Cruz (1999: 481–94) speaks in this context of European convergence but extends this to the global level.

systems in any one jurisdiction and at different levels, even within state law itself.[46]

Closely linked to such ongoing debates, which are ultimately over values in relation to law, many scholars have noted the revived prominence of natural law approaches in the twentieth century.[47] Human rights jurisprudence has become a 'human rights industry' (Twining, 2000: 192), which relies heavily on unifying assumptions, often assiduously denying the possibility of protecting human rights through reconstructing indigenous norms at local level rather than imposition of globally uniform standards and norm systems.[48] This central issue resurfaces in fierce ongoing discussions over universalism versus relativism (Renteln, 1990; 2004), which have now reached an impasse (Cowan *et al.*, 2001: 5).

Historically, international law rules about protection of human rights against state interference originate largely from the post-1945 period. Before then, individuals were treated as a state's nationals/citizens or as aliens. Protection of minority groups was often regulated by treaties between states, but no general protection was attempted. The evolution of international human rights law has been prominent since 1945, but 'it remains uncertain who in law holds or may enforce the resulting substantive and procedural legal rights' (Harris, 1991: 602). Many states have accepted human rights treaties and are protecting certain rights, but there are a growing number of substantive reservations by states, which cause a lot of irritation on the part of international lawyers (Sagade, 2005) rather than propelling processes of critical self-assessment.

Three generations of human rights are basically (1) civil and political rights deriving from eighteenth-century natural law philosophy, traditionally given priority, such as the right to life; (2) second generation rights, mainly based on twentieth-century socialist philosophies, especially economic, social and cultural rights; (3) third generation rights of the 1970s, mainly supported by developing countries, constituting collective group rights such as the right to self-determination and right to development. Globalisation debates have significantly impacted on the interrelationship of these types of rights. While 'the model of rights is today hegemonic, and imbued with an emancipatory aura' (Cowan *et al.*, 2001: 1), local concerns continue to shape how universal categories of rights are implemented, resisted and transformed.

---

[46] Petersen and Zahle (1995). With reference to Scandinavian concepts of polycentricity of law, see also Woodman (1998: 46).

[47] See chapter 3 below. Nelken (1997: 5), commenting on Hanne Petersen's argument that modern industrial societies undervalue gender and nature, finds that '[t]his means that we need to rethink how law constructs the difference between nature and culture by placing in question even the very notions of law and of science – the subject and methodology of comparing legal cultures'. He therefore calls for a change in legal culture, including the idea of a revival of some new form of 'natural law'.

[48] Cotterrell (2002: 43–5) finds that debates about globalisation and localisation have given fresh impetus to those who seek convergence and harmonisation.

Cotterrell (2002: 44) observes as an impact of globalisation that '[c]ompara-tive law is powerfully driven now, as through much of its history, by the urge to unify or harmonize law. Recognizing difference does not, in these contexts, lead to its celebration, but to devising means of removing it.' However, he also argues that in the area of human rights, 'appreciation of difference alongside a search for uniformity seems widely recognized as a continuing necessity' (p. 45) and explains why there is a continuing struggle:

> [T]he universalization of human rights is a matter of the export, reception or transplanting of fundamental values or beliefs . . . in legal form. These values can be variously interpreted, or confronted by opposing values, in certain settings. Hence the drive for universalism, seeking similarity in human rights jurisdictions, is challenged by so-called cultural relativism that demands the appreciation of difference. Nonetheless, the drive for uniformity is very strong given that the universality of the values to be represented in human rights law is powerfully championed.

Earlier, Renteln (1990) challenged the simplistic bipolarity of discussions about universalism and relativism, suggested that there was room for convergence between the two and queried why 'opponents have been so eager to dismiss outright the notion of overlap' (p. 78). Her conclusion that '[r]elativism is compatible with the existence of cross-cultural universals' (p. 87) introduced the important issue of 'overlapping consensus' into the debate. As a political philosopher, Jones (2001: 34–7) dismisses Renteln's attempt to build a theory of human rights on a global moral consensus as unsatisfactory. In his view, it avoids addressing diversity. Rather, '[w]e want a theory of rights appropriate to human beings who hold different and conflicting beliefs . . . The search for an overlapping consensus is merely the search for an element of uniformity among diverse systems of belief' (pp. 36–7). Jones (2001: 37) suggests that 'a theory of human rights is not to add yet another voice to that cacophony of disagreements' about the standards to follow in life, but rather to 'be concerned with how people ought to relate to one another as people with different beliefs'. This necessitates constructing 'a second-level role in a context of disagreement' (p. 39), which gives a theory of human rights a special status compared to other doctrines. The subsequent debate does not suggest that this refined theory could keep itself totally apart from disagreements, and Jones (2001: 48) finally retracts by saying that 'the search for a single grand theory of human rights may be misplaced'. Cowan *et al.* (2001) also build on Renteln (1990) but seek to move beyond debates on universalism and cultural relativism as opposing poles, exploring the tensions between these two forces as well as between the global and the local. Their discussions are less hostile to the concept of 'overlapping consensus' and take a different route. Noting the increasing deployment of a rhetoric of 'culture', Cowan *et al.* (2001: 3) suggest a new approach, 'shifting attention from a formulation which *opposes* culture and human rights to one in which the pursuit of human rights is approached as itself *a cultural process* which impinges on human subjects and subjectivities in multiple and contradictory ways'.

This debate leads to a sophisticated discourse on 'rights as culture', the right to culture inevitably comes up as an issue,[49] law-as-culture enters the fray and debates about socio-legal interconnectedness move centre-stage again. The advice that 'neither rights nor culture should be essentialized' (Cowan *et al.*, 2001: 28) relies on a number of excellent case studies demonstrating the need for 'a non-essentializing pluralism which, grounded in the reality of people's lives, is neither universalist nor relativist' (p. 29 with reference to Griffiths, 2001). This interactive approach seeks to transcend the global and the local, but remains concerned to protect individual visions of the good life, rather than imposing uniform standards from outside onto communities or individuals. One sees here that the favourite objection to this 'liberal' diversity-friendly approach, namely that one should not romanticise difference and diversity and allow disagreeable rules and forms of behaviour in the process, evaporates as soon as one accepts that there is no need to strive for uniformity. Cotterrell (2002: 49) wisely suggests that the task may sometimes be 'neither to seek similarity nor to appreciate difference, but only to recognize the appropriateness of leaving well alone'. How easily said in an intensely politicised field!

Much recent work on human rights focuses on testing the levels of compliance of particular local or national legal arrangements in countries of the South against supposedly global human rights standards. Such simplistic exercises tend to take a priori negative approaches to Asian and African laws, especially their 'traditional' components and do not reflect the theoretical advances that have been made in recent scholarship.[50] It is evident that the study of Southern local legal norms retains much relevance and prevents exclusive focus on global legal rules (Cowan *et al.*, 2001). For example, in the preface to an annotated bibliography on traditional African laws (Okupa, 1998), Professor Hinz from Namibia argues for the continued relevance of African customary laws:

> The flexibility of customary law stands a chance against Rule of Law campaigners who have never tried to understand the origins of customary law, but also never left the positivistic education behind which taught them a very narrow concept of Rule of Law.

In the complex field of international human rights law, we see no universal agreement about anything. As a result, critical voices about human rights debates are heard everywhere. O'Dair and Lewis (2001: xliii) report that a major conference on 'Law and Religion' found that 'human rights legislation

---

[49] On this see Santos (1995: 262) and his concept of 'right to roots' and 'right to options', which allow the greatest possible scope for personal choice and initiative.

[50] For a recent example, focusing on child marriage in India, see Sagade (2005).

is at best ambiguous in its implications for freedom of religion. At worst, it is dangerous.'[51]

Similar problems of different perspectives and their implications affect the international discussions and practice of private international law, or conflict of laws, a branch of law dealing with cases in which some relevant fact has a connection with another system of law on either territorial or personal grounds.[52] This inevitably raises questions about the application of the appropriate set of rules, exercise of jurisdiction by a domestic or foreign court, and mutual recognition of decisions. Choice of law becomes a critical issue. The need for private international law constantly arises as a direct result of legal pluralism, mainly because different countries have different systems of law, or various rule systems exist within a nation's boundaries, in which case one speaks of internal or 'interpersonal conflict of laws' (Pearl, 1981). In practice, private international law has little to do with public international law. Though it has an international aspect, it is essentially a branch of municipal law, so that every country has its own private international law (Diwan and Diwan, 1993: 37) and there are huge differences between such laws. There are no uniform rules in the world about the circumstances in which municipal courts assume jurisdiction over cases with foreign elements, when foreign law is to be applied or foreign judgments are to be given recognition. Recent attempts at harmonisation are just that, efforts to reduce diversity and conflicts, with no hope of total unification.

By its very nature, private international law is constantly required to use comparative legal analysis and complex methodologies (use of connecting factors like citizenship/nationality, residence or domicile) in attempts to harmonise divergent and often conflicting norm systems. Conflict lawyers should therefore be highly attuned to plurality-consciousness, but that does not mean that they will abandon unifying ideological agenda. More often than not, unifying efforts have been built on assumptions about the innate superiority of one's own legal system and the desirability of global legal uniformisation. Criticising lack of coherence, David and Brierley (1978: 9) wrote:

> This approach would be satisfactory were all countries to adopt uniform rules for finding the answers. But conflicts of laws and conflicts of jurisdiction are, in reality, resolved in any given country without paying heed to any of the rules applying elsewhere. The result is that international relations are, in one country or another, subject to different systems and rules.

In this context, the difficult issue of 'comity of nations' arises. It is seen in the interest of nations 'to accommodate, wherever possible, the laws of other

[51] On plurality-consciousness in global ethics debates, see Küng and Kuschel (1993: 7).

[52] Many writers acknowledge the practical importance of personal religious laws in countries of the South. Older textbooks assumed that such conflicts would rarely arise in Western jurisdictions, but even in the 1970s, there were signs that this would change (Graveson, 1974: 4).

nations. Indirectly this promotes a world order which generates confidence not only for commercial relations but for all manner of intercourse between subjects and governments' (Tan, 1993: 6). Perhaps this does not require uniformity of laws, but more respect for plurality? However, David and Brierley (1978: 9) argued for unification 'to end this anarchy', asserting that a framework for such relations should be put 'on a proper basis' (p. 10), by which they clearly meant uniform rules. There have been constant pressures for the unification of private international law, not primarily to make life easier for lawyers and judges, but to identify what is called 'best practice'. However, whose best practice does one consider?[53] Such battles are now often linked to human rights activism, allegedly protecting non-Western people against their own cultures and traditions. Such attempts to unify or harmonise laws often dictate rules to Southern countries, leading to deliberate non-recognition of their personal laws, hardly in a spirit of comity of nations.[54]

Conversations with well-educated lawyers in practice confirm that the biggest gap in their knowledge often remains sufficient insight into legal systems other than the one in which they are supposed to function as lawyers.[55] The academic subject of 'conflict of laws' is immensely complex and many legal professionals lack expertise in this field. Some aspects of English conflicts law have remained quite unsatisfactory and unable to cope with new challenges posed by ethnic minorities (Pearl and Menski, 1998: 84–117). Bennett (2002: 33) concludes for internal conflicts of law within South Africa that 'it is impossible to eliminate the regulatory orders of semiautonomous social fields. Some form of accommodation is necessary, and thus a perpetuation of the conflict of laws.' However, it is a fact, not just in Britain, that most law schools do not pay sufficient attention to such matters. This needs to change if legal education is to become more globally focused. As the next section shows, even the field of comparative law, which seems ideally suited for tackling plurality-consciousness, continues to suffer from modernist amnesia and eurocentric hubris.

---

[53] The tendency to see one's own system as supreme is a well-known problem. Farrar and Dugdale (1990: 245) critically note 'the erroneous belief that the common law tradition is the most important legal tradition in the world and the . . . related belief that it is in every respect the best system in the world'. They blame the 'narrowness and bigotry of conventional legal education' (p. 245).

[54] For English law, examples are found in Pearl and Menski (1998: 84–117), relating to curtailing polygamy and non-recognition of extra-judicial Muslim divorces. This has particularly pernicious consequences in the context of immigration law (Sachdeva, 1993).

[55] Recent writing notes that huge City law firms, 'operating in a global marketplace in a genuinely multi-disciplinary manner' (Francis, 2004: 327), now 'work across disciplinary boundaries in a way that undermines claims to homogenous legal knowledge for the entire profession. They are working across national borders, working creatively to fill the "black holes" left where international law has not yet been developed' (p. 328). Obviously, this creates new problems for professional regulation and confirms observations that practice has outrun theory (Twining, 2000: 241).

1.2.2 Comparative law as a harmonising handmaiden

The previous section indicated that comparative lawyers have long been fasci-nated by prospects of constructing a world legal system and are often assisting international lawyers in this endeavour.[56] In this context, fierce debates about the balance between the search for similarity and appreciation of difference arise (Cotterrell, 2002).[57] Dupré (2002: 269) puts the historical baggage of comparative law on the table:

> I suggest that in 1900, the approach of comparative law was based on two understandings that were so obvious that they were never really spelled out. The first one was that law, as understood in the West, was a sign of civilization. At that time, only civilized societies were considered to have a legal system. The second understanding was that civilization was mainly European (with an extension to America, due to early European emigration and settlement). To make it simple, at the beginning of the twentieth century, civilization was considered as being mainly Western, white and Christian.

While debates about plurality versus uniformity have arisen ever since compar-ative law came into existence, it seems that comparativists have more recently begun to appreciate plurality more openly.[58] Today they appear to embrace the spirit of postmodern globalisation, not necessarily because their appreciation of diversity has increased, but because they can perhaps see more clearly than other lawyers that uniformising global trends are continuously being defeated by pluralising particularities.[59] Glenn (2004: 359–60) suggests that harmo-nious diversity in law on a global level is viable and should be promoted. But not everyone agrees.

Within a framework of ambivalence about legal pluralism, what is the pur-pose of comparative law? While there seems to be a basic division of regionalists and generalists (Harding, 2002: 250), recent trends indicate 'a renewed emphasis

---

[56] The definition of comparative law remains contested (Watson, 1993: 1ff.; Riles, 2001; Harding and Örücü, 2002). Watson (1993: 6) suggests that it is not the study of one foreign legal system or parts of it, but 'the study of the relationship of one legal system and its rules with another', to enable onself 'to understand the particular factors which shape legal growth and change' (pp. 6–7) and therefore it is 'about the nature of law, and especially about the nature of legal development' (p. 7).

[57] Comparative law is not a value-free scientific instrument. It has been described as 'com-parison *with the purpose of harmonization*' (McDonald, 2002: 194), now put to the test by recent European developments.

[58] Riles (2001) suggests that a re-reading of the earlier masters of comparative law shows many of them attuned to plurality in a way that modernist projects did not wish to accept. Such discoveries link pre-modern and postmodern ways of thinking. A short bibliography of comparative law is provided in Harding and Örücü (2002: 305–11).

[59] Harding and Örücü (2002: vii) indicate a recent combination of forces between supposedly different orientations of comparative law scholarship which extends to a re-questioning of presumed prevailing orthodoxies.

on culture and society as guides to the understanding and analysis of law, and on legality, legal certainty, or the rule of law, as the way forward beyond the crisis' (p. 265). While Harding argues primarily in favour of strengthening comparative public law, Twining (2000: 255) claims that 'in a loose sense, we are all comparatists now'.[60] Decades ago, David and Brierley (1978: 4) suggested three traditional uses of comparative law, including support for international law:

> [I]t is useful in historical and philosophical legal research; it is important in order to understand better, and to improve, one's national law; and it assists us in the promotion of the understanding of foreign peoples, and thereby contributes to the creation of a context favourable to the development of international relations.

These vague words skilfully hide uniformising agenda. David and Brierley (1978: 2) suggested that comparative law first arose 'after the disintegration of the notion of a *ius commune* or law of universal application' as a result of nationalism and the resultant focus on statist positivism. However, positivism quickly created its own claims of universality and 'best practice', especially in post-Napoleonic France, which left no place for comparative law (p. 3). Treating Montesquieu (1689–1755) as one of the fathers of comparative law, Launay (2001: 22–38) demonstrates how his plurality consciousness, which appears like radical relativism, had its own political and rather parochial agenda. Early comparative law first focused on legal history and philosophy and might use 'foreign' material, but did not develop much systematic thinking about plurality, while remaining conscious of diversity.[61]

Secondly, the aim of improving one's national law through comparative legal study led to a unifying focus on 'comparative legislation' during the nineteenth century, the creation of learned societies and 'in a very concrete way, a true concordance of legislative development and not merely a generally similar tendency' (David and Brierley, 1978: 6–7). However, this did not lead to uniformisation, because such reforms were introduced 'with such modifications as may be found necessary because of local conditions or other special considerations which ensure its smooth integration into the legal system' (p. 7). This points to growing emphasis on legal instrumentalism as a tool for social engineering which 'will undoubtedly be increasingly frequent in the years ahead'.[62]

---

[60] Uncomfortable with 'comparative law', Watson (1993: 1) prefers the German '*Rechtsvergleichung*' because it connotes a process of comparison without suggesting a separate branch of law.

[61] For details see David and Brierley (1978: 4–6). The historical approach has been severely criticised (Watson, 1993), also in combination with evolutionism (Sack and Aleck, 1992), for failing to give due recognition to legal plurality in the long run – another critique of uniformising visions.

[62] David and Brierley (1978: 7). The practical use of this approach is evident from the involvement of Professor David in producing the Ethiopian Civil Code of 1960. Hooker (1975: 390–408) discusses the voluntary reception of this Code and hints at some early

Thirdly, comparative law's claim that it can promote understanding of foreign peoples made it particularly attractive for public international lawyers. David and Brierley (1978: 8) noted that different political views might lead to different laws and state structures, elaborating this through examples of how skilful diplomats need to deal with representatives of people from different countries who, 'with their very different intellectual processes, contemplate law and international relations in a manner very different from those in western countries' (p. 9). This conveys the hidden assumption that Western laws are believed to be 'civilised' and superior, while others and their laws are therefore inferior.[63] This suited those who argued in favour of simple transplantation of laws. While lip service was paid to social influence on law, somehow it was taken for granted that progressive initiative should come from the West. It is a fact that legal changes have been forced onto many countries, ultimately denying non-European legal cultures the capacity and the chance to develop on their own terms.[64] This is enforced globalisation, not entirely dissimilar from earlier processes of colonial superimposition of supposedly superior Western laws.[65] Comparative law is strongly implicated as a willing handmaiden in such processes. The basic credo of traditional comparative law, clearly expressed by David and Brierley (1978: 16), that 'there is no true science of law unless it is universal in scope and in spirit', reflects an absence of ultimate respect for global diversity and only tolerates it as an interim measure.

It appears that, in today's global context, the realisation that such shallow comparative approaches lack plurality-consciousness and are marred by accusations of aggressive world domination, has finally hit home.[66] Postmodern comparative legal theory now takes guidance from linguists and aesthetics to understand the nature of comparison as 'both the elucidation of similarities and the elucidation of differences' (Riles, 2001: 17). It is widely acknowledged that the discipline of comparative law (if it is a separate branch of law rather than a methodology) continues to be in bad shape.[67] In this crisis, Riles (2001: 17) sharply observes that 'the loss of grand ambitions for the discipline' separates

---

difficulties. Allott (1980: 207) commented a few years later: 'As an intellectual achievement the Ethiopian Civil Code ranks high. As a practical exercise it was a dismal failure'.

[63] A good analysis of the underlying rationale of such assumptions is found in Bozeman (1971).

[64] Watson (1993: 99) suggests that 'reception is possible and still easy when the receiving society is much less advanced materially and culturally'.

[65] David and Brierley (1978: 11) seem to recognise that comparative law cannot achieve total legal unification as a viable short-term agenda, writing that 'it opens the door to working with those in other countries in establishing uniform conflict or substantive rules or at least their harmonization'.

[66] Bozeman (1971: 175, 178), writing of the reversal of convergence and erosion of respect for the law, seems almost ahead of her time.

[67] Riles (2001: 3) notes 'ubiquitous angst about the disciplinary identity of comparative law today'. This is also brought out by Harding and Örücü (2002: xii–xiii), who note the

the present from the past. In clear text, comparatists have begun to understand that they need to become not just plurality-conscious, but ready to acknowledge that difference per se is not a problem.

Has recent academic scholarship picked up this challenge? Örücü (2002: 1–17) provides a thought-provoking overview and analysis of trends in comparative law. Modern comparative law scholarship in the late nineteenth century focused first on its own methodologies and place within law. It became a historical science with several distinct approaches, but remained eurocentric. Örücü (2002: 5) concedes that research in the field of legal transplanting, in particular, 'has not always been impartial'. Her discussion of legal transplants culminates in endorsing the value of respecting 'differents' within specific legal systems, mentioning for the common law world that 'it is now generally accepted that this unity can be enhanced by diversity' (Örücü, 2002: 8). The contemporary character of reciprocal influence has resulted in a diversified scenario, as 'the influences were not systematic and the solutions did not remain the same upon import' (p. 11).[68] Significantly, Örücü (2002: 12) notes that '[i]t is obvious that how one assesses the process is entirely related to one's stance in these matters. In the plethora of activities and examples one can always choose illustrations to support one's own position.' This seems to indicate that comparatists today are becoming more aware of their own subjectivity and are experiencing postmodernity first-hand. Constantly faced with evidence of legal pluralism, which even the most persistent adherents of unification visions will find difficult to ignore, comparatists are challenged to rethink their own perspectives. Örücü (2002: 14) spots new opportunities for comparative law, but still emphasises the supremacy of Northern legal systems:

> As newly emerging democracies look to the pool of competing models available in Western Europe and America with the purpose of re-designing and modernizing their legal, economic and social systems, a whole new world of research possibilities is opening up for comparatists.

This reflects how reluctant comparativists still are to accept that they are operating in a truly global context. Are there no South–South borrowings in law? Within the global village, the portrayal of future tasks still does not take sufficient account of the existing global fluidity and plurality. Örücü (2002: 16) concludes that 'socio-cultural and legal-cultural differences are the most serious causes of mismatch' and advises that '[i]f communication and conversation are kept moving, then cross-fertilization between the seemingly incompatibles can be facilitated' (p. 16). Örücü (2002: 16–17) predicts that the value of comparative law in the twenty-first century will not diminish, but its utility

growing diversity and popularity of comparative law scholarship, but highlight that 'it is also fraught with internal contradiction, uncertainty, and a sense of mid-life crisis' (p. xii).

[68] For a modernist female Turkish scholar with a strong belief in the power of transplanted law, expressing such sophisticated reservations about modernist claims to uniform regulation indicates critical reflection on recent developments in Turkey (chapter 5.13).

will continue to lie in effectuating uniformisation of law rather than addressing its plurality:

> Globalization is already increasing interest in localization. Both the local and those who study the local feel the need to assert it. The trend to integrate moves the focus to the 'differents' and their value. Thus comparative law will become indispensable in the globalization movement since in the effort to create universalist standards, interest in localised exceptions will flourish. Also, as Twining says: 'processes of globalisation stir up old nationalisms, exacerbate cultural conflict, and encourage post-modern scepticism about the universality of values and ideas'. Comparative law will be needed in the understanding of this diversity to facilitate co-existence and harmony.

While this demonstrates that Twining's theoretical guidance is beginning to have some effect in comparative legal scholarship, the interest in 'differents' is ambiguously phrased – to what extent is it merely a technique to 'know your enemy'? Örücü's (2002: 17) final suggestion that '[c]omparatists will report at the end of the 21st century' wisely leaves the field wide open. It would indeed not be safe to predict that all comparatists are now converted into globality-conscious respecters of difference. Quite apart from limitations of knowledge and expertise in foreign legal systems, the temptations of unifying visions are bound to remain strong.[69] This also transpires from the ongoing debates about legal transplants.

1.2.3 Assumptions about uniformity: legal transplants and reception of laws

Well before colonial times, exchanges of legal, religious and cultural norms took place all over the world as people became interconnected through trade and war.[70] The most noted early legal transplant is the reception of Roman law all over Europe (Watson, 1993). The colonial period brought new exchanges of legal information, normally in the North to South direction.[71] Assumptions

---

[69] Cotterrell (2002: 46) warns that unless comparative law sets its own agenda of finding an appropriate balance between search for similarity and appreciation of difference, 'the residual assumption is likely to be that the aim of all contemporary comparative scholarship must be to facilitate legal uniformity on the widest possible scale'.

[70] Watson (1993: 22) argues that legal transplants 'have been common since the earliest recorded history'. In a pioneering attempt to research the disparities of *dharma*, *li* and *nomos*, May (1985:3) introduces an intercultural process of legal understanding to show that *nomos* as a Western form of legal culture 'is not universally valid or transferable or applicable'. The English preface to Derrett et al. (1979) presents the rationale for a careful selection of topics for intercultural legal comparison, aware of the challenge 'to avoid imposing European concepts upon non-European thinking, admittedly a rather difficult task!'

[71] See in detail Hooker (1975). However, the existence of South–South borrowings should not be overlooked, since also in ancient times most socio-legal systems did not exist in

about the superiority of Western laws meant that legal scholarship has focused mainly on Western inputs.[72] Somehow, the global movement of legal norms and rules has always been assumed to migrate from the West to the East, from the North to the South, and hardly ever in the reverse direction.[73] While this world-wide process of transplant and reception took many different forms (Watson, 1993: 19, 29–30), it has not led to the global uniformisation of laws, creating instead a scenario that defies simple classification and easy models of identifying legal families.[74] Moreover, as simplistic positivist views of legal reception give way to more complex understandings, we realise that received laws have everywhere been adapted to suit local conditions, and transplants everywhere manifest themselves as new hybrids.[75]

Opposition to the idea that a legal rule could just be transplanted from one culture to another is old but still vigorously debated (Nelken, 2002; Nelken and Feest, 2001). Rouland (1994: 20) reports on Montesquieu's views: 'In common with some legal anthropologists today, he believed that the close relationship between law and society militated against the transfer of law from one society to another, unless the societies were themselves similar.' Foster (2002: 58–60) reviews the main positions in this venerable debate between 'culturalists' and 'transferists'. Kahn-Freund (1974) had earlier argued that the success of transplants depended primarily on the respective political system,[76] while particularly Legrand (1997a; 1997b) and Seidman and Seidman (1994),[77] take the view that law as a culturally determined construct cannot be fully transplanted to another culture.

---

isolation. Ancient exchanges between China and India are discussed by Bozeman (1971: 4–6) and Sarkar (1975).

[72] In colonial times, much Anglo-Indian law was transplanted into British African territories, leading to many interesting African contributions to the *Journal of the Indian Law Institute*.

[73] On this subject see Drobnig and van Erp (1999). David and Brierley (1978: 7) emphasised that decisions of English courts have great influence upon judges in Canada, Australia and New Zealand – and vice versa. The authors noted that 'some decisions of the highest courts of the Commonwealth countries are cited in English courts with an authority almost equal . . .' (p. 7), but failed to mention that the global exchange of case law is clearly not multidirectional.

[74] De Cruz (1999: 3) suggests that there are no less than forty-two legal systems in the world, proving that his approach, focusing on families of law, remains deficient in terms of plurality-consciousness.

[75] Örücü (2002: 7) offers a wide range of new terminologies for transplants and reciprocal influence. Legrand (1997b) proposes the impossibility of legal transplants, because all rules have meanings, and these cannot be simply transplanted.

[76] Kahn-Freund (1974: 20) concluded that using the comparative method in law reform 'requires a knowledge not only of the foreign law, but also of its social, and above all its political, context'.

[77] Seidman and Seidman (1974), based on African experience, formulated a law of non-transferability of law. See also Seidman and Seidman (1996) on lessons from recent Chinese legislation.

Against this, 'transferists' argued that legal rules may be successfully borrowed even if the socio-economic, geographical and political circumstances of the recipient are quite different from those of the donor. The theory of legal transplants was famously propounded by Watson (originally 1974, now 1993), under whose banner the 'transferists' congregated, ignoring his warnings against a blind belief in total unification.[78] For, having cautioned that even the possibility and desirability of a uniform system of law for the Western world was questionable, Watson (1993: 100) stated clearly that 'a complete legal union is neither possible nor desirable', so that he cannot simply count as an adherent to unifying global visions.[79] Watson (1993: 82) was fully aware that differences would occur because of many non-legal factors, even a good dose of chance, and warned of exaggerating the extent of transplants (p. 81). Recent debates show that the famous statement by Watson (1993: 7) that 'in the Western world borrowing (with adaptation) has been the usual way of legal development' was overinterpreted, taken out of context and applied globally by eager 'transferists'. They took courage from other statements, such as '[a] successful legal transplant – like that of a human organ – will grow in its new body, and become part of that body just as the rule or institution would have continued to develop in its parent system' (p. 27). But when is a transplant 'successful', and how many different ways are there of growing into a new body? Watson (1993: 82) answers this himself:

> When an institution is completely received it none the less seems almost inevitable that differences will occur even when they are not dictated by social change and progress, and even when the old rule can still be regarded as satisfactory and the new one has no overwhelming claim to succeed.

A re-reading of Watson's transplant theory in light of recent debates is provided in several contributions to Harding and Örücü (2002). It was assumed that Watson's theory considered social factors unimportant, but in his 'Afterword', Watson (1993: 107) emphasises the complex, difficult relationship between law and society. Nelken (2002: 24ff.) finds that subsequent debates between Watson and his critics have been unhelpful and raises important questions about the 'mirror theory of law', according to which law should (but often may not) mirror social norms. At the end, '[b]orrowing other peoples' law is seen as just a method of speeding up the process of finding legal solutions to similar problems – a process being encouraged all the more by the pressures towards convergence brought about by globalization' (Nelken, 2002: 26–7).

---

[78] Watson (1993: 50–1) points out how the reception of Roman law in Scotland 'shows how much legal relationships and transplants may owe to non-legal historico-political factors, to what a plain lawyer might well call sheer chance'.

[79] However, Watson (1993: 100 n. 14) makes a well-known exception for commercial law, and much of the criticism of his approach seems justified; see e.g. Legrand (1997b).

Here the problem of how to assess the impact of globalisation appears again. Cotterrell (2002: 38) notes that '[i]n all modern legal interpretation . . . the search for unity, integrity and consistency of meaning is usually privileged, in certain ways, over the identification of difference'. In this, comparativists are no different from other lawyers (p. 39). Cotterrell (2002: 43–5) finds that the debates about globalisation and localisation have given fresh impetus to those who seek convergence and harmonisation and warns that, unless comparatists identify different regions of the social or of 'community' in relation to law, little progress will be made.[80]

The current transplant debates (Nelken and Feest, 2001) remain inconclusive but show some ways forward. Harding and Örücü (2002: ix) emphasise that transplants continue to be important today and are not always entirely voluntary. The wide scope for showing transplants in an ambiguous light continues (Örücü, 2002: 4–5), as does the significant division of belief among comparatists about convergence or non-convergence.[81] It is now better recognised that Watson (1974; 1993) never claimed that legal transplantation simply led to unification. Having emphasised the importance of official acts of law-making, Watson (1993: 108) writes in his 'Afterword' that '[t]he different sources of law have different impacts on legal change, but at all times and in all places the approach of the lawmakers is affected by their particular culture'. Recent debates rightly note that Watson was not oblivious to interlegality.[82] Örücü (2002: 13) highlights that '[t]he difficulties are not in the transposition of techniques and forms, but of values and contents'. This links well with the debates of anthropologists and other social scientists, but makes the interdisciplinary task of analysing transplants in a spirit of plurality-consciousness more difficult for lawyers. For, how do we deal with knowledge (Lyotard, 1984)? One example of such difficulties must suffice here. Kahn-Freund (1974: 10) prominently uses the abolition of polygamy in Indian Hindu law in 1955 to support his central thesis that Montesquieu's views on the importance of socio-cultural and other non-legal factors are now well out of date:

> Even in relation to the developing world, I would submit, there is a tendency, stronger here, weaker there, and of course of varying velocity, to assimilate the law to that of the developed countries. This is happening even in family law: for me – rightly or wrongly – it is one of the greatest legal events of

---

[80] In another transplant debate, de Cruz (2002: 103) states the obvious when he says that transplantation never occurs in a vacuum, referring to Glendon (1977) and her concept of 'context', which Cotterrell (2002: 46ff.) seems to elaborate through classifying different types of community.

[81] Örücü (2002: 7). Harding and Örücü (2002: ix) still insist that, in comparative constitutional law, 'perhaps there is little room for divergences'.

[82] That differences in rules may irritate especially commercial lawyers was noted by Watson (1993: 97) himself and is not really a new issue, but was developed by Teubner (1998).

our time that the Indian Legislature should have abolished polygamy for
Hindus.

This is factually correct according to the letter of the law,[83] but recent analysis
shows that, in socio-legal reality, Hindu polygamy has remained legally condoned and courts, including the Indian Supreme Court, are now regulating
polygamy in a remarkably postmodern reconstruction (Menski, 2003: 374ff.)
rather than focusing on its illegality and criminalisation. Similarly, on closer
analysis, the purported abolition or at least restraint of Muslim polygamy in
Pakistan through modernising legislation, as envisaged by Kahn-Freund, is just
a pious illusion.[84] While such myths are widely believed, especially by modernists in India who push for reforms to Muslim law in their jurisdiction to serve
various political agenda, current debates about Muslim law reform in South
Africa are beginning to acknowledge that unifying attempts through statutory
reform will remain largely ineffective unless the community itself modifies its
norms.[85] Similar lessons are beginning to be drawn in relation to Muslim law
in Europe (Shah, 2003).

Such examples show that worldwide assimilation of values to dominant
Western legal models and expectations is simply not happening. Using assimilating assumptions as a justification for law reform and transplants constitutes
in itself an abuse of comparative law.[86] Everywhere, unifying global visions
are facing insurmountable challenges of normative pluralism (Twining, 2000:
224–5). Respect for plurality means that possible options need to be scrutinised more carefully as to their suitability for the transplant's recipients. Watson (1993: 113) emphasised the element of chance in transplantation processes,
highlighted the issue of accessibility and observed that certain legal systems use
others as a 'quarry' for mining transplants. This continues to be the case, but
the range of suitable quarries is now much wider, indeed global, including local
customary law rules.[87] It is no longer sufficient to look only for evidence of how
Western laws have been, and can be, transplanted all over the world.

---

[83] Section 5(i) of the Hindu Marriage Act 1955 read together with sections 11 and 17 of the
same Act.

[84] The relevant provision is section 6 of the Muslim Family Laws Ordinance 1961, which
operates in Pakistan and Bangladesh, but has been unable to withstand traditional Islamic-
cum-postmodern interpretations, as shown in an important Federal Shariat Court decision, *Allah Rakha* v. *Federation of Pakistan*, PLD 2000 FSC 1 (see chapter 5, section 5.14
below).

[85] For details see the recent Report of the South African Law Reform Commission (Project
106) on *Islamic Marriages and Related Matters* (July, 2003).

[86] Kahn-Freund (1974: 27), cited by Legrand (1997b: 124) to argue that law is always a
culturally situated phenomenon.

[87] For example, South Africa is now making much use of Indian constitutional law and of its
own customary laws in the ongoing process of post-Apartheid reconstruction. Namibia is
even permitting its local communities to develop their own laws and is including traditional
leaders through the Community Courts Act 2003.

1.2.4 Southern voices: from polite silence to post-colonial reassertion

Given the bad shape of comparative legal studies and the ideological and political domination of eurocentric, globalising pressures around the world, how is it possible to hear the silence of opposition? The claim that the West has supplied all the leading words and concepts (Bozeman, 1971: 35) feeds the impression that, in the field of jurisprudence, the South has nothing to say in response, and nothing to add. How can we understand global law if the necessary evidence is not found in books and on websites, but mainly in the minds of people and in their daily actions, which lawyers find difficult to research? How can one oppose the hegemonistic dangers of legal centralism as the central axis around which all human activity supposedly revolves, when in many parts of the world state law remains peripheral to people's lives and modern states are often the major violators of legal rules? A refreshed, conceptually expanded multidisciplinary approach is required to pick up the sounds and signs of often deliberate silences about law.

While American-led, eurocentric 'melting-pot' ideologies are undergoing serious revision (Alba and Nee, 2003), growing opposition to post-colonial patterns of inequality and exploitation in Asia and Africa has resulted in quiet refusal by many individuals and states to blindly adopt Western-dictated norms. As the demographic balance has irrevocably tipped in favour of Asia, Africa and Latin America, and international migration has created many more transnational global diaspora communities, dominant visions of the global future are becoming more contested (Bozeman, 1971). The erstwhile 'developing world' now speaks with a louder and more confident voice than before.[88] Gradual global power shifts point to substantial redevelopments from which law cannot be excluded. But do we even wish to know? Infected by Western hubris and legocentric orientation, and informed by colonial experience and history, most legal scholars continue to assume that the South should just follow the North and has little or nothing to contribute to thinking about 'development' (Cheru, 2002). Both comparative law and legal theory, as we saw, have been heavily influenced by images of 'the march of common law over the world' and similar empire-building claims (e.g. de Cruz, 1999).

While little is known among lawyers about opposition to law reforms during colonial times,[89] important voices were soon heard from newly independent countries about how to operate inherited colonial legal systems, promoting

---

[88] UN Secretary General Kofi Annan, on the occasion of posthumous conferral of the Sakharov Prize to Sergio Vieira de Mello and other UN personnel killed in Baghdad in 2003 (29 January 2004, reported in *Migration News Sheet*, February 2004: 1–2) criticised the EU's attitudes and policies towards immigrants and refugees, causing 'surprise'.

[89] Certain contested issues, for example restrictions on child marriage and early marital intercourse during the 1890s in India (Menski, 2003: 322ff.), gave rise to public and academic attention.

fresh thinking about European legal influence on post-colonial reconstructions. A powerful example of judicial independence, expressed by the Indian Supreme Court,[90] originates from a landlord–tenant dispute over eviction:

> We have to part company with the precedents of the British-Indian period tying our non-statutory areas of law to vintage English law, christening it 'justice, equity and good conscience'. After all, conscience is the finer texture of norms woven from the ethos and life-style of a community and since British and Indian ways of life vary so much the validity of an Anglophilic bias in Bharat's justice, equity and good conscience is questionable today. The great values that bind law to life spell out the text of justice, equity and good conscience and Cardozo has crystallized the concept thus: 'Life casts the mould of conduct which will some day become fixed as law'. Free India has to find its conscience in our rugged realities – and no more in alien legal thought. In a larger sense, the *insignia* of creativity in law, as in life, is freedom from subtle alien bondage, not a silent spring nor a hothouse flower.

Flowery language apart, this is, at heart, a matter of contract law, based on individualism, closely tied to Western visions of development (Bozeman, 1971: 37–8). The basic unsuitability of a received legal system that individualises transactions and insists on formal, written contracts is a key issue in this case, which prompted Mr Justice Krishna Iyer (as he then was), a major Indian thinker and elder statesman (Singh, 1993; Iyer, 2004) to make such critical comments. Since the late 1970s, similar views have been reflected in many Indian judgments, leading gradually to a reorientation of Indian laws (Menski, 2001; 2003). This post-colonial legal reconstruction opposes uniformising globalisation agenda and is focused on achieving sustainable local solutions. Often carried through in radical fashion, this process clearly distinguishes the new public interest orientation of modern Indian law from the traditional common law focus on private interest, which was seen to be detrimental to national development and, ultimately, to basic justice.

However, there are enormous silences around such issues. Indian legal scholars find it difficult to admit that their country's Constitution means little in reality to many citizens. Who outside India reads about Justice Krishna Iyer's work? Where in the world do law students study Indian public interest litigation? There is silence not only of Southern voices; Western scholars appear complicit in the refusal to debate key issues of justice openly (Twining, 2000: 74). The eurocentric orientation of most legal education has not only created huge ignorance in the West over new legal developments in Asia and Africa, made worse by much misinformation by scholars, it even extends to elite Southern law schools, where students are often not properly taught the law as it exists in

---

[90] *Rattan Lal* v. *Vardesh Chander* (1976) 2 SCC 103, at pp. 114–15, *per* Krishna Iyer J, cited by Derrett (1977: xxi).

their jurisdictions but are indoctrinated in global positivist ideology. There is much complicity by Asian and African lawyers (who are often also leading politicians) with Western agenda of hegemony and colonial-style domination. It often serves the self-interest of local elites to cultivate positivist paradigms. Educating the voting public about comparative analysis and pluralist perspectives would be counterproductive for those concerned to maintain privileges. Legal education, everywhere, easily becomes a willing handmaiden of power politics.

Other interpretations of silence in response to Western hegemonistic onslaughts reflect awareness that any claims on the part of non-Western laws to recognition of their own legal models as globally valid will be dismissed anyway, so what is the point of talking?[91] As a result, the presence of strategic, selective, ideologically motivated breakdowns in globalised legal communication manifests itself legally in what Baxi (1982) saw as 'crisis', a massive disobedience of official laws or disregard, as we so often read, of the 'rule of law' and 'lawlessness'. However, this analysis is too superficial: is a country really lawless if the official law is not strong enough (or not good enough) to assert itself? This image only works from a statist perspective. A legal pluralist would need to ask what other laws apart from state law are actually in operation.

Chapter 2, section 2.5.4 below offers an Asian pluralistic model for interpreting such conflict scenarios, helping us to understand that entire rule systems may be found in silent opposition to the official state law (Chiba, 1986). Unofficial laws may be tolerated for many reasons, but may also be lifted into the hallowed field of 'official law' through formal state recognition. Localised socio-cultural forces, thus, have the potential to effectively oppose globalising legal pressures and may dynamically reshape them so that harmony between 'law' and 'society' (both seen in a very wide sense) may be maintained at the local level, where it is felt that one knows better what is appropriate for the life conditions of local people. Such legal processes of interaction between individual, local, national and global forces have been confirmed, for example, through detailed studies of the Chagga people of East Africa (Moore, 1986). Even in European countries and North America, as we are now beginning to discover, non-Western migrants and their descendants have been reconstructing their legal universe 'on their own terms' (Ballard, 1994), while largely keeping silent, because to claim 'official status', as British Muslims found during the 1970s (and still experience today), results in stubborn silence on the part of the official legal system. While patterns of colonial thinking and its legal nomenclature, such as 'migration of laws' or 'reception of European laws overseas', continue to dominate our minds, it seems that new processes of international migration and private reordering of the legal sphere, leading to ethnic

---

[91] On the refusal to recognise 'Asian values' and the cultivation of 'overlapping consensus', see Peerenboom (2004).

implants as discussed below, are currently observable and require much further thought.

1.3 New globalisation: reverse colonisation and ethnic implants

A major challenge to plurality-deficient theorising in legal academia today arises from the long-term effects of South–North migration on the legal systems of the North/West. Everywhere in the Western world, even in America (Moore, 1999), this issue is now beginning to lead to important new research which demands knowledge of many different legal orders, contradicting earlier assumptions about the American 'melting pot' and the resulting assimilation processes.[92] As awareness of the importance of ethnicity (itself a much-contested concept, related to pluralism) increases all over the world, virtually all countries face questions about how to accommodate diversities within old or new multi-ethnic populations. Desperate attempts by some countries to cleanse themselves of ethnic minorities have ended in failure, as have tough strategies for closing the leaking taps of immigration control.

While political scientists and others have engaged in 'ethnic and racial studies' and currently labour under redefinitions of 'state', 'nation', 'citizenship' and even 'British' (Parekh, 2000), most lawyers are not involved in such social science debates (Schuster and Solomos, 2004). The vigorous development of two related branches of law in Britain, immigration and nationality law (Macdonald and Webber, 2001) and anti-discrimination law (Hepple and Szyszczak, 1992) siphoned off much energy into practice-related activism, while legal analysis suffered. Only recently have lawyers been motivated by the changed social realities of multicultural Britain to develop ethnic minority legal studies (Poulter, 1986; 1998; Jones and Welhengama, 2000; Shah, 1994; 2003).

Tackling such issues, we tend to forget how very skilfully colonial powers ensured that the presence of Western personnel and whole large expatriate communities did *not* result in the application of existing local laws to the colonial rulers and those who came with them, using the principle of extraterritoriality. It seems, therefore, that Asian and African settlers in Europe and North America today hope in vain for official, formal legal recognition of the laws which they brought with them during the post-colonial processes of reverse migration. The new migration patterns today are private migrations, not state-sponsored movements of personnel to secure shares of a colonial cake. As a result, private reliance on extraterritoriality principles is resisted by Northern

---

[92] The classic 'melting pot' image has meanwhile been replaced by the 'salad bowl' model, in which different ingredients retain their previous characteristics but are joined together by some type of sauce or glue. Alba and Nee (2003) produce a detailed assessment of how immigrants to the USA and their descendants continue to combine concern for improvement of social and material circumstances with retention of culture-specific characteristics.

state legal systems. Watson (1993: 29–30) discusses three major categories of voluntary transplants:

> First when a people moves into a different territory where there is no comparable civilisation, and takes its law with it. Secondly, when a people move into a different territory where there is a comparable civilisation, and takes its law with it. Thirdly, when a people voluntarily accepts a large part of the system of another people or peoples.

The current unofficial development of ethnic minority laws within Western jurisdictions has characteristics of all three types identified by Watson. Clearly, it depends on what perspective one takes (Ballard, 1994). How does one oppose the claims of some Muslims, for example, that Islamic law is inherently superior to any Western legal system? Developing a plurality-sensitive legal approach in this new global migration scenario is far easier said than done. The powerful traditional eurocentric presumption among comparative lawyers has clearly been that 'all other systems, no more than survivors from the past, will ultimately disappear with the passing of time and the progress of civilization' (David and Brierley, 1978: 26). If in the modern world, there is no place for traditional Asian and African laws when people from the South enter the domains of Western law, then (so we are made to believe) there is nothing legally relevant to study. Such migrants are simply declared subject to the laws of their new home; all they have brought with them is cultural baggage, customs perhaps, but not law (Poulter, 1986). In a postmodern, globality-conscious environment, lawyers will need to make better sense of such new developments, building on existing legal training, which is actually much more pluralistic than most of us assume.[93] Clearly, we need to sharpen and refocus comparative legal analysis to identify such new scenarios.

Today legal scholars (Poulter, 1998), judges and the wider public appear to be desperately concerned to prevent elements of Asian and African laws gaining a foothold in Europe.[94] It seems that we have responded to South–North migration by insisting on familiar axioms and images of assimilation, like 'when in Rome, do as the Romans do', also in the legal field (Poulter, 1986: v). This is a grave mistake in legal methodology, failing to adopt plurality-conscious

---

[93] Cownie (2004) shows that British lawyers today perceive themselves no longer predominantly as 'black letter' lawyers, but are aware that their training has not equipped them for socio-legal enquiries. Twining (2000: 18) encourages a re-reading of Bentham as an important early scholar who was much more sensitive to plurality than is widely assumed and also shows that Austin was not a pure positivist.

[94] A recent report in *Migration News Sheet* of June 2004 cites (at p. 24) research by Danish professors on the attitudes of Danes towards immigrants, highlighting their fear that Muslims will become a majority in Denmark in the future, even if statistics indicate that 'people and their descendants of non-Western origin will make up about 11% of the total population by 2040'. While one may dismiss such concerns as evidence of xenophobia, legal policies are influenced by such negative apprehensions.

perspectives. For various historically loaded reasons, we may be desperate to ensure that traditional 'personal laws' (mainly different family laws for various groups of people) should not become part of allegedly secular, uniform modern legal systems. Hence the claim that such personal laws should remain at the level of 'custom', 'culture' or 'tradition', outside the formal realm of law. We claim thereby exclusive power to define what the law is, depriving Southern migrants and their descendants of any agency in this respect.

Ignoring such signs of new pluralistic development reflects short-sighted panic about cultural alienation in our midst but cannot entirely solve the various legal problems that appear in daily reality and demand solutions. At present, we are not prepared to tackle such challenges in a spirit of plurality-consciousness and leave ethnic minority laws in a constantly growing sphere of unofficial laws. From a practical perspective, it appears that Northern state laws must eventually take constructive action to regain the initiative and reclaim control over the entire legal field. This control has to some extent been lost, as emerging debates about the activities of Shari'a Councils as alternative dispute settlement fora for Muslims, not only in Britain, demonstrate in full force (Shah-Kazemi, 2001).

To some extent, it is officially recognised that English judges are not fully prepared to handle cases on complex matters of 'ethnic minority custom' and socio-cultural issues.[95] Expert evidence on 'foreign legal systems' or 'foreign customs' is frequently called for. In Britain, the Judicial Studies Board distributed a *Handbook on Ethnic Minority Issues* to every judge in the country.[96] In their daily working life, reflected in many other European jurisdictions and in North America, British judges now have to deal with Asian/African socio-cultural norms to find and protect justice. In different combinations virtually all jurisdictions in Europe and North America are now confronted with such complex issues.[97] The questions that arise do not comfortably stay within the ambit of traditional private international law or conflict of laws.

Thus, a new kind of comparative legal training is required in Europe and elsewhere to respond to such practical challenges. It is too simplistic, dangerous and manifestly unjust, to ignore the fact that millions of otherwise law-abiding citizens operate their own hybrid rule systems, based on Asian and African concepts, which may involve a wide range of combinations: British Hindu law (Menski, 1993), Dutch Hindustani culture (Mungra, 1990) or Dutch

---

[95] However, in some recent cases, there is a notable change of perspective. In *Singh* v. *Entry Clearance Officer, New Delhi* [2004] INLR 515, the Court of Appeal in London recognised an Indian adoption as legally valid (a hugely contested issue in itself) and commented on the increasing pluralisation of Britain and its legal effects (*per* Munby LJ at p. 538).

[96] The first edition of this Handbook, a weighty blue folder, was published in June 1994. The second edition was distributed to all judges in late 1999 and is accessible online at http://www.jsboard.co.uk.

[97] On Muslims and German law, see Rohe (2001).

Muslim legal issues (Rutten, 1988), English and Muslim law as *angrezi shariat* in Britain (Pearl and Menski, 1998), North African Belgian forms of hybridity (Foblets, 1994; 1998) and many more. If German judges may now pronounce *talaq* on behalf of an absent Muslim husband, and unofficial Muslim judges in many European countries have huge officially unchecked powers, of which even Britain's House of Lords is now aware, legal developments have taken place in our own midst which must no longer remain undiscussed (Shah-Kazemi, 2001). Yet the academic analysis of such new mixed systems of social norms and formal laws is still in its infancy (Menski, 2000). It is too simple for lawyers to insist that multi-ethnic hybrids are not legal phenomena and may be ignored. But how far should this pluralisation and its legal recognition go? Starting a discussion implies and begins the process of more formal recognition. Significant compromises have been made in the UK, the USA and other jurisdictions ever since earlier migrant groups like the Jews gained specific legal recognition, which is now being denied to more recent immigrants (Hamilton, 1995).

It is doubtful that the prevalent, stubborn clinging to mono-legal regulation systems is conducive to justice, as Poulter (1986: v–vi) insisted. Can disregard for the legal claims of ethnic minorities really be justified under principles of good governance and human rights protection, as Poulter (1998) argued? Today, the hegemonistic assumptions of Western legal systems vis-à-vis foreign legal orders are increasingly challenged and their proclaimed universality is questioned. Western hubris is faced with an equally defiant assertion of the superiority of non-Western moral and legal orders, now even in Europe and North America itself. There is no doubt that studying Asian and African legal systems can help to equip future lawyers to make better sense of the emerging pluralised globalisation patterns.

The main methodological challenge of ethnic minority legal studies lies in exploration of how official national laws in the receiving states and the unofficial norms of ethnic minority communities may co-exist to produce a new culture-specific socio-legal amalgam. Plurality-conscious jurisprudence demands a lot from lawyers for whom 'law' has remained restricted to state law. Even if they perceive themselves as liberals, they struggle to bridge the mental gap between legal and extra-legal factors. Poulter (1986: v), once a leading British writer on ethnic minority legal studies, applied the popular saying 'when in Rome, do as the Romans do' and established what could be seen as a diversity-blind approach to his subject:

> The issues raised by this well-known saying provide a general framework for much of the legal analysis in this book. Should the ethnic minorities who have come to live here conform to English ways or should they be free to continue to practise their own customs in this country? More specifically, should English law adapt its principles and rules to accommodate foreign customs or should new arrivals bear the burden of any adjustment? Is the political objective to be the 'assimilation' of the minorities into

the wider community or is a pattern of cultural pluralism and diversity something to be officially welcomed and encouraged as valuable in its own right?

By phrasing his arguments in this way, Poulter assumed that modern state law governs all aspects of life, and hence divested common people of any legal agency. According to Poulter (1986: vi), it was the law's task to impose limitations on what newcomers could do in England, 'in the interests of public policy, to protect certain core values in English society and to obviate any genuine and reasonable claim by the majority that ethnic minorities are obtaining preferential treatment or special dispensations which cannot be justified by reference to established legal principles'. This assertion of official law as an idealised uniform legal control mechanism is a typical statist approach to law; there is little genuine liberality here. Though Poulter was trained as a conflicts lawyer, he was unwilling to see ethnic minority customs as 'law'. His approach signified reluctance to go beyond formal paradigms of official law.

A more constructive perspective, using comparative skills to understand how real people order their lives in Britain today – and more or less silently claim the right to do so unofficially – is provided by the anthropologist Roger Ballard (1994: 1–34). He demonstrates how South Asians in Britain have been reconstructing their life in Britain, creating a new culture-specific socio-legal environment for themselves and their descendants. Ballard (1994: 5) shows that anthropologists face similar methodological problems as lawyers when it comes to understanding difference:

> Contrary to the expectations of most of Britain's white natives, settling down has not taken the form of a comprehensive process of assimilation, or even an approximation to it. Thus . . . both the older generation of settlers and their British-born offspring are continuing to find substantial inspiration in the resources of their own particular cultural, religious and linguistic inheritance, which they are actively and creatively reinterpreting in order to rebuild their lives *on their own terms*.

This refusal to submit to assimilationist pressures 'on the ground' constitutes a challenge to statist definitions of law. It questions hegemonic paradigms of interpretation in anthropology as well as comparative law. Ballard (1994: 8) explains the socio-cultural rationale underlying this process and reiterates his finding:

> There is of course a visible difference: several million of Britain's inhabitants have the kind of skin colour which its white natives would like to acquire on expensive tropical holidays, but would be horrified to inherit. But while that difference is literally only skin-deep, the changes precipitated by the new minorities' *ethnicity* – that is their commitment to their own religious, linguistic and cultural traditions – have been far more fundamental. Since their ethnicity is intrinsic to their very being, the resultant loyalties are

a major resource in the construction of survival strategies: hence they are unlikely to be abandoned. If this is so, it follows that short of comprehensive ethnic cleansing – which one hopes is not an option – nothing can alter the fact that the new minorities have become an integral part of the British social order, and they have done so *on their own terms*. Hence the underlying challenge is simple: how – and how soon – can Britain's white natives learn to live with difference, and to respect the right of their fellow-citizens to organise their lives on their own preferred terms, whatever their historical and geographical origins?

Developing an intellectually stimulating concept of immense relevance to lawyers, this analysis draws parallels between bilingualism and multiculturalism, probing the extent of comparative analysis for individuals. Having argued that for Britain's monolingual majority, the absence of cosmopolitan linguistic experience constitutes a barrier, Ballard (1994: 31) continues:

> As with language, so with culture. Just as individuals can be bilingual, so they can be multicultural, with the competence to behave appropriately in a number of different arenas, and to switch codes as appropriate. If this is so, the popular view that young people of South Asian parentage will inevitably suffer from 'culture conflict' as a result of their participation in a number of differently structured worlds can be dismissed. Rather they are much better perceived as *skilled cultural navigators* [emphasis added], with a sophisticated capacity to manoeuvre their way to their own advantage both inside and outside the ethnic colony. While such a perspective radically transforms the conventional understanding of the experience of young British Asians, it would nevertheless be idle to suggest that code-switching is a means by which they can short-circuit all their problems and dilemmas. Far from it. Just because they do not follow a single given set of conventions, all cultural navigators must constantly decide how best to behave in any given context, while also finding some means of switching smoothly from one to the next.

Ballard's concept of the 'skilled cultural navigator', someone capable of switching codes between different culture-specific rule systems, is critically relevant to developing a multidisciplinary approach to global comparative law. At first sight, his discussion appears to relate only to the anthropology of ethnic minority settlement in Britain, but Ballard's findings impact on legal study. But only if comparative lawyers learn to take such findings from other academic disciplines seriously, and stop hiding behind self-erected subject barriers, can real progress in ethnic minority legal studies be made (Menski, 2000). Ballard describes law-in-action, commenting on how South Asians in post-war Britain have opted to retain their own value systems in a reconstructed form rather than to adjust to the white majority systems of norms, values and, ultimately, laws. Many lawyers in the UK and elsewhere, often citing Poulter (1986), continue to rely on statist arguments to suggest that immigrants should adopt and learn the legal system of their new home country as fast as possible. Poulter's last major work (1998) simply denies ethnic minorities the right to develop their own legal norms in Britain and applies human rights arguments to underpin his assimilationist stance.

Undoubtedly, the ethnic minority communities in Britain and elsewhere are experiencing adaptive, assimilative processes and do not simply practise their traditional norm systems unchanged in isolation. British Asians have 'learnt the law', and appear to have done so in stages. The outcome, however, was not simply a one-way assimilation to the dominant English law, but a new hybrid plurality. My research on how British Hindus (Menski, 1987; 1993) and Muslims (Pearl and Menski, 1998: 51–83) have reconstructed their legal environment in Britain during the past few decades and now operate their own unofficial personal law systems closely parallels Ballard's findings. More recent research on Somalis in Britain, who arrived in larger numbers only during the 1980s, confirms that they, too, have been amalgamating Somali norms and British legal elements into something like 'British Somali law'.

Most British law graduates would not be able to recognise such hybrid evidence of legal plurality as a by-product of globalisation, and might simply assume that British Somalis and others, because they live in Britain, are now following English law. The fact that many British Somalis undergo only a customary Muslim marriage in Britain today, and do not register their marriages, would be overlooked or officially dismissed as extra-legal, while such evidence is crucial for understanding and applying today's Somali marriage law in Britain. This demonstrates how crucial it is, as a precondition for progress in global legal studies, to be able to apply different readings of 'law'. It also confirms that interdisciplinary and multilayered comparative legal research can act as an eye-opener for blinkered euro-focused legal scholarship wedded to dominant law-centred paradigms.

However, one still often encounters the increasingly unrealistic assertion that ethnic minorities in Britain have only one legal obligation: to follow English law. This is now interpreted by many immigrants and their descendants as downright unfair, equated to a demand to enter the country and to live as a legal *tabula rasa*, devoid of any cultural and legal baggage. It is like being asked to leave your identity at the door before you enter a new room, full of strangers, and to take on the identity of those strangers. Such perceptions overlook basic facts of human life, such as religious and ethnic allegiances.[98] It should not surprise anyone that many Muslims, in particular, vigorously protest against such assimilationist legal pressures by responding, in similarly myopic fashion, through asserting the supremacy of their religion and culture. If one extremism leads to another, plurality-conscious negotiation risks becoming a casualty. Such exaggerated claims and expectations on both sides lead nowhere

---

[98] They also disregard the defining impact of what Chiba (1989: 180) calls 'identity postulate'.

and are dangerous, damaging relations between communities and world peace (Glenn, 2004).

The hegemonistic claims of official law, underpinned by assimilationist scholarship following Poulter (1986; 1998), are bound to fail in social reality. Among South Asians, it is now rarely the case that new arrivals to Britain come to a place full of strangers; they are likely to join a segment of a transnational global community with more or less shared elements of ethnic identity. The room such a stranger enters reverberates with familiar sounds and operates by rules and in a language normally familiar to the newcomer. We urgently need to know in more depth what implications all of this has for legal developments in the increasingly multi-ethnic states of the North. Are we witnessing the creation of states within states, or ethnic enclaves with their own legal systems? Are we laying foundations for future separatist disasters if we permit too many strangers to enter 'our' space? While these may be uncomfortable questions in terms of policies and politics, what legal sense do we make of them? In a globalised world, what is 'our' space?

Such excursions into fields of study that seem, at first sight, quite unrelated to comparative legal theory confirm that the world around us has changed, and is still changing further. Legal scholarship is evidently finding it hard to catch up with social reality. A few decades ago, comparative legal study was still focused on the colonial experience and English law's influence across the world. Working in London today and thinking about law in a global context is a different experience, not yet sufficiently reflected in comparative legal research (Menski, 2002b). Perhaps out of fear as much as ignorance, most lawyers pretend to have no stake in such issues.

Some progress is being made. Yilmaz (1999; 2005) successfully applied Ballard's concept by exploring different forms of Muslim legal pluralism in Britain, Turkey and Pakistan with particular reference to marriage, polygamy and divorce. This pioneering work demonstrates that Muslims anywhere in the world operate as 'skilled legal navigators', combining the expectations of the respective legal system of their country of residence and of their culture-specific understanding of *shari'a*, the Muslim personal law. This results in various forms of 'living' Muslim law, which manifest themselves as an intricate combination of norms based on religious authorities, local customs and the respective state rule systems. Muslims are not unique in seeking to combine the perceived requirements of their religious and social framework of norms with particular forms of official state law in Europe, Asia or Africa. The resulting combinations of plurality and hybridity are almost limitless. Today we have better knowledge of suitable methodologies to tackle such complex phenomena and there is nothing to stop the development of such multidisciplinary approaches. But do we want to be conscious, at all times, of the need for plurality-focused perspectives? The sections below explore to what extent certain methodologies of legal education may promote plurality-consciousness among lawyers.

1.4 Good practice in studying and teaching comparative law

From the above, it appears that plurality-conscious comparative lawyers can only 'see' and research intricate socio-cultural processes such as international migration and their legal consequences once they are prepared to overcome certain biases, including entrenched assumptions about what is legal and what is not. One should otherwise hesitate to call them comparative lawyers. Plurality-consciousness may not mean that the comparativist has to accept everything that is not legal as legal, as Tamanaha (1993) sarcastically suggested, but this is a difficult issue. Having found that it seems impossible to define law as a clearly distinguishable form of social control, Woodman (1998: 45) notes:

> [I]f there is no empirically discoverable dividing line running across the field of social control, we must simply accept that all social control is part of the subject-matter of legal pluralism. This conclusion is not convenient, but it may be necessary. To invent a dividing line which did not accord with a factual distinction would be irrational and unscientific. For the same reason, Tamanaha's argument, that it is essential to distinguish state laws from other social norms because there is no other means of differentiating law, is also not a valid social scientific argument. The conclusion must be that law covers a continuum which runs from the clearest form of state law through to the vaguest forms of informal social control.

This discussion indicates that drawing one's criteria of what is 'law' too narrowly, confined by statist ideologies rather than open-ended and empirical socio-legal methodologies, impoverishes legal research and understanding. This applies both to research on legal pluralism and to comparative law. In an incisive assessment of the latter, Legrand (1996: 232) notes that we live in an age of comparisons, but these exciting opportunities cannot be utilised because comparative law itself is in such bad shape. To analyse where comparative studies have gone wrong, three main points can be highlighted.

First, comparative law is widely perceived as an exotic, fashionable subject. While comparative law appeals to young, aspiring academics and attracts some of the best minds, this trend has had a negative effect. Comparative law as a field of study is full of 'self-styled "comparatists" who wish to appear savant and relish exoticism' (Legrand, 1996: 234). Comparative law today, perceived as trendy, is taken up by inadequately qualified researchers who lack the necessary skills and erudition to effectively engage in the comparative study of foreign laws. Comparative research and analysis is often undertaken with a myopic view limited to the juxtaposition of the regulations of one legal system with those of another, with little or no critical analysis. Legrand (1996: 234) writes that such comparatists 'do not compare, they contrast'. In the process, they actually fail to ask the most fundamental questions about their subject, and remain unable to appreciate the 'true' nature of the foreign legal systems they study. Such work tends to remain plain and descriptive.

The second, closely related point raised by Legrand concerns the nature of European and North American comparative legal study and the methodological flaws in identifying similarities and relationships between concepts of different legal systems. The almost irresistible tendency of comparative lawyers has been to translate roughly equivalent (or so it appears) concepts from two or more legal systems and then to contrast them, rather than to analyse their respective socio-legal environments. Legrand (1996: 234) advocates that lawyers should not even attempt to translate in this fashion and raises serious general questions about legal translations.[99] One could rely on the wisdom of Rodolfo Sacco, a leading Italian legal philosopher and comparative law scholar, who had forcefully argued that 'the comparatist must learn *not* to translate' (Legrand, 1996: 234). It makes sense to advise that comparative lawyers should abstain from the irresistible desire to draw parallels and to equate concepts between different legal systems simplistically. However, the enterprise of experimenting with conceptual comparison and translation should remain a tool in interpreting foreign legal systems, no matter how problematic those translations may turn out to be. Comparative lawyers are pioneers, they must be allowed to speculate,[100] even to make mistakes; intricate cultural knowledge is rarely served on a silver platter. Of course, cultural and linguistic barriers, in addition to the commitment to theory and interdisciplinarity, make comparative legal work much more challenging than the work of the 'technicians' of the national law.[101]

The third key problem faced by comparative lawyers in Europe and North America in researching Asian and African legal systems is how to accurately understand, interpret and compare the respective normative systems known by the cultures and societies which the comparatist aims to study. This requires extensive, practical research in those countries, not just exotic trips to a leading university library or a brief discussion with some lawyers who may tell researchers what they want to hear. A related issue in this debate involves the negative impact of superficial, ideology-driven comparative legal inquiry. As Legrand (1996: 236) notes, a serious consequence following from the unwillingness or inability to practise thorough comparative inquiry is the *illusion* of understanding other legal systems, which seems to block a desire for deeper inquiry. The result is that we *think* we know, and remain too easily satisfied with our fragmented elements of more or less exotic semi-knowledge.

The result, predictably, could be negative. If other people's laws are only understood in ways that sever them completely from their historically developed contexts, comparative lawyers deny themselves, and us, the chance of gaining

---

[99] On this issue, see also Allott (1980: 5 and 44).

[100] Twining (2000) claims repeatedly that the legal theorist as a paid subversive has a duty to explore the field in innovative ways.

[101] See David and Brierley (1978: 16) with Jhering's reference to 'merely local or provincial jurisprudence'.

important intellectual insights. For example, by ignoring the socio-cultural context of English legal history, a comparative lawyer would fail to realise that English common law is often determined by culture-specific epistemological assumptions, hidden behind judicial decisions or statutes. The purportedly scientific study of law thus remains incomplete, unless one is willing to strive for a deeper understanding of what law is. Legrand (1996: 237–8) comments in detail:

> My point is that the cognitive order within which the common law operates is just as important to an understanding of any solution given to any legal problem in an English court of law as the technical language of the solution itself – if not more so, because it is encrusted in the *longue durée* over which the common law mind has fashioned itself... One simply can not grasp the common law, other than in a superficial and, therefore, meaningless way, unless one understands the common law mind, unless one appreciates the common law *mentalité* – a *mentalité* which is inevitably socially, historically, culturally and epistemologically situated ... Only a keen awareness of this underlying cognitive framework – of the unconscious of law – can guard the comparatist against the misleading conclusions that apparent similarities would otherwise suggest.

Dealing mainly with European legal comparisons, Legrand (1996: 238–42) provides sound methodological advice for plurality-conscious analysis, identifying four major requirements. First, a deep commitment to theory; linked to this, secondly, a commitment to interdisciplinarity. Thirdly, he argues that a comparative lawyer must be ready to acknowledge difference, rather than seeking to operate on the basis of assimilationist undercurrents. Finally, he demands that a true comparative lawyer should remain critical at all times. To analyse in more detail what these four critical elements mean and involve, on the first two points, Legrand (1996: 238) suggests that the socially interlinked nature of law demands an interdisciplinary theory-focused methodology:

> Without doubt, a commitment to theory is paramount if comparative legal studies is to take place in any credible form. Furthermore, this commitment to theory must include a commitment to interdisciplinarity. Law does not exist in a vacuum; it is a social phenomenon, if only because, at the minimum, it operates within a society. For example, the comparatist must realize that she can learn much that is of direct relevance to her work from anthropology ... Similarly, the comparatist must accept that she can learn much from linguistics, specifically from studies devoted to bilingualism.

The third critical element of comparative legal work specifically concerns plurality of perspectives. Legrand (1996: 239) emphasises the need for 'a proclivity on the part of the comparatist towards an acknowledgement of "difference"'. The agenda of the comparative lawyer should be more geared towards identifying differences than seeking to demonstrate similarities. Legrand (1996: 240) advises that 'empathy for alterity thus appears as an indispensable condition of serious comparative work about law', directly opposing scholarly tendencies to look and argue for uniformising trends. Asking for acceptance of any foreign legal system 'on its own terms' (Ballard, 1994) is of course a tall order for lawyers used to statist perspectives. Closely linked to this, according to Legrand (1996: 240–1), the fourth requirement for a serious legal comparatist is almost commonsensical, namely to remain intellectually alert and open to a complex scenario of competing influences.

Legrand's discussion does not make much of the underlying ideological struggles and personal battles which serious comparative legal work may involve. After all, undertaking global legal studies may, like foreign travel in a gap year, alter a person's perception of the world. Is that a valid reason to treat such studies as dangerous, and to suppress them? So much is certain: in the process of learning about different legal systems, mental agony over challenges or collapse of one's pre-conceived notions can only lead to two possible results. If one stalls and retreats to one's own positions for fear of going too far, or out of intellectual laziness, there will be no proper comparative analysis. If one remains curious and goes on probing, the effort tends to become a catalytic force, a positive motivator to learn more and to expand one's horizons ever wider. Is this not precisely what legal education is supposed to achieve?

From the above, it should be evident that, in addition to applying a broad historical grounding in the socio-cultural contexts of the legal systems studied, it is equally important that comparative lawyers must examine their own understanding of law; and pay attention to legal theory. Legrand (1996: 235) advises:

> Most reasonably, comparative legal studies is about law. But who undertakes comparative work equipped with a theory of law? Who has a sense of where the law begins and where it ends? Who has reflected upon what counts as law and what counts as non-law? Where is the boundary to be drawn between the normal and the deviant, the normal and the pathological? For most 'comparatists', the matter is easily resolved. For them, there is no need for theory. Indeed, some of my colleagues . . . are plainly irritated by the mere *suggestion* of the need for theory. In short, the law is to be found in legislative texts and judicial decisions.

This confirms the urgent need for reflection on the nature of 'law' itself.[102] Clearly, a deep enough understanding of law is not found in legislative texts and judicial decisions. Studying 'black letter law' does not automatically create a plurality-conscious understanding of law; rather it impedes it. Legrand (1996: 235) argues that the spirit of a law may emanate from such unexpected sources as a piece of art, and takes the well-chosen example of an 1812 painting, which

---

[102] Along the same lines, Twining (2000) repeatedly stresses the need to combine comparative legal methodology and legal theory and refuses to see them as separate fields.

depicts the Emperor Napoleon in his study drafting the French Civil Code by candlelight. Legrand argues that this image offers deep insight into the French legal mind, focusing on legal codification by the ruler and the resulting restrictions on all other processes of law-making. Legrand skilfully emphasises that our notions about 'law' are always culturally determined and must be carefully considered before one ventures into comparison. Despite this image of Napoleon by candlelight, Legrand (1996: 236) concludes that 'French law is much more than a compendium of rules and propositions' and says that it is therefore quite appropriate to propose that 'French law is, first and foremost, a cultural phenomenon, not unlike singing or weaving'. However, most lawyers will be unwilling, or simply unable, to view the phenomenon of law in this wider, culturally embedded, hybrid way.

There can be no doubt that the range of cultural and other knowledge required is vastly increased when one tries to make sense of Hindu law, Islamic law, African law, Chinese law or Japanese law. But who are 'we' when we are trying to make sense of such laws? Many law students in Britain today are not English (nor even British) and may know very little about English law, which they study as a foreign legal system. Many readers of this book will not be English, either, and are likely to come from quite diverse backgrounds, with widely different educational and life experiences. As the composition of student populations in centres of legal education like London has changed over time, itself a result of globalisation, law teaching should have adjusted accordingly, taking account of new realities. Instead, more or less unthinkingly, most law teachers continue to behave as though students know, first and foremost, quite a lot about English law, and are now to be introduced to a selection of 'foreign' laws. Yet, what seems 'foreign' to the teacher may be intimately familiar to some foreign students. In our new, globalised working environments, law teachers may too easily fail to realise that some students may carry important insights for discussions about comparative law in a London or Harvard seminar. But, assimilationist and supremacist agenda apart, who wants to admit that students may know more about a particular subject than the teacher? Undoubtedly, this is an additional challenge to the comparatist in a global legal environment.

1.5 World legal history: a deficient model

Legrand's discussions about the need for deeper levels of comparative analysis apply even more to attempts to understand how Asian and African legal systems operate and 'tick' as real living systems. Unfortunately, few law courses anywhere in the world concern themselves with detailed comparative studies of such legal systems. The approaches chosen differ and serve purposes often unrelated to understanding law in a global context. The aim may simply be to offer some 'interesting' options that may indulge personal interests (as much of the teacher as of the students) and increase the marketability of degrees. In a largely methodological article explaining why it was perceived necessary to teach American law students something about world legal history, Funk (1987: 723) explained how the matter was then viewed across the Atlantic:

> LEGAL history teachers in American law schools confront one of the educational ironies of the close of the twentieth century: their students need a world perspective in their historical studies more than ever; yet our educational system is less inclined than before to provide it. Law schools cannot make up much for undergraduate deficiencies in world history; but they can provide a world legal history course to future lawyers in the final year of formal education before they go out into the world of affairs.

It is highly unlikely that law students in the final year of their professional legal education (by which time they are postgraduates) would pay much attention to the concepts of any foreign law, unless it was offered to them as part of a professional training programme opening up new markets and fields for lucrative business. Offering legal history by itself does not automatically fulfil the demanding criteria set by Legrand. Other commentators express doubts whether teaching jurisprudence to law students will make them better lawyers,[103] but acknowledge that '[a] "progressive" law teacher would insist that awareness of the social implications of law is of the essence of proper legal training' (Harris, 1980: 2).

Funk (1987: 725) laments that the task of providing a general knowledge of world legal history 'is complicated by continuing cultural diversity', which lays bare the ambivalence with which many American lawyers view attempts to teach legal traditions other than their own, supposedly superior legal order. Not surprisingly, Funk (1987: 726) finds that teaching and writing about world legal history 'requires a certain type of person to write and teach it', and that such teachers cannot expect their course to be popular with students, also since there are no adequate recent materials for teaching world legal history (p. 727). Funk (1987: 728–9) suggests that world legal history should not be limited to the history of Western civilisation with the rest of the world merely 'tacked on', nor should it simply be the history of the West in the world.

Funk (1987: 733–4) also argues that world legal history courses are of great professional importance for American lawyers and benefit national commercial interests, as American international trade and investment are increasing and likely to grow in future. Approximately two-thirds of this trade is with countries outside the Anglo-American legal culture. Tort and other legal problems arising out of foreign travel will increase as more Americans travel abroad, and transnational domestic relations and probate problems will continue to arise in US practice. The obvious conclusion is that the days when American lawyers

---

[103] This is undoubtedly a reflection of earlier assumptions among English practice-focused lawyers that teaching jurisprudence was a waste of time.

can confine their legal knowledge to the common law of the United States, Anglo-American legal systems or those of Western Europe, are long gone. These arguments in favour of world legal history reinforce the commercial orientation of US academic agenda, but tell us little about the need to understand and apply plurality-conscious legal methodologies. It is evident that this kind of comparative law remains a minority occupation in US law schools. Funk (1987: 740) reports how perspective courses that survey a selection of foreign legal systems are generally not popular with students. Within a practice-oriented law school environment, the encouragement for law students to spend intellectual energies on comparative legal studies are restricted to research paper options or one or two seminars. Nothing from the more recent first-hand accounts of Twining (2000) suggests that this is any different today.

How does one read world legal history from a global perspective? In Funk's terminology, the legal systems of the world have been divided into different forms of 'primitive law' (Funk, 1987: 754) and various 'civilized' (p. 759) legal systems.[104] This appears just as insufficient and unsatisfactory as dividing the legal systems of the Western world into major legal families and then lumping all the rest of the world into 'other systems'.[105] Funk's strange terminology and its undercurrents of eurocentrism and US supremacy apart, his model does not leave enough scope for Asian and African legal systems and concentrates too much on the history of American law. In Funk's model, comparative legal study is just a minor adjunct to studying US legal history, rather than an integral component of comparative law teaching. The programme of study also does not question 'law' itself in sufficient detail, so that teaching about 'other' legal systems towards the end of a law student's curriculum appears like running after a fast-moving train of professional brain-washing that will never make a properly scheduled stop for a deeper understanding of Asian and African legal systems. While the need to integrate the teaching of jurisprudence from around the world from the very beginning of a law degree is becoming more apparent as a desirable element of globality-conscious legal education, that will not be a viable option in many US law schools.

There are many ongoing debates about how to teach various types of law, not just in Britain,[106] but worldwide. Attempts to restructure the legal education system of Pakistan a few years ago failed not only because of opposition to US-led interventions, but because of disagreements over basic ingredients of legal education and training. Most Pakistani law students are required to engage in the study of jurisprudence in the first year of their LLB course, having to grapple with Western jurisprudence and Muslim jurisprudence in separate courses in

---

[104] Notably, Lampe (1995) does the same in his approach to legal pluralism studies.

[105] David and Brierley (1978: 26). Twining (2000: 148) suggests that more intellectually ambitious approaches are required.

[106] University College London introduced a new first-year LLB course on World Legal Orders from October 2004, a notable experiment which deserves close monitoring.

the same year. It has always been incomprehensible to me how these two subjects could be kept in their own watertight compartments, in the classroom as well as in the human brain. Is this evidence of lingering colonial influence or simply a sign of intellectual laziness? So far there are no satisfactory answers. While the traditional Indian LLB programmes were similarly unimaginative, offering Hindu jurisprudence as well as Muslim law, the more recent five-year Indian LLB programmes have integrated jurisprudence into the pre-law programme of study where it is now more securely anchored in an interdisciplinary approach. But my observation so far is that during those two years of pre-law study, law students are thoroughly infused with black letter approaches through social science teaching and are, with few exceptions, not guided towards a globally focused legal education.[107]

In Britain, ongoing debates bring out perennial concerns about the dangers of intellectually impoverished legal education, but not enough thinking about globality-consciousness in legal education. Hunt (1986: 292) made a strong case for teaching theory throughout the law curriculum and wrote that 'there is emerging a broad alliance, embracing a range of intellectual positions, which is increasingly outspoken in its criticism of the dominant vocationalism which characterises so much of legal education'. A national survey of jurisprudence teaching in the UK documented a remarkable expansion of the subject. In response to concerns that many law colleges were removing the compulsory status of jurisprudence as a final-year subject, Hunt (1986: 292) commented that the demise of compulsory jurisprudence was not a cause for concern, but advanced a case for more legal theory throughout legal education, insisting that 'legal education must address the "big" questions about the place and function of law'. Hunt (1986: 293) argued for an ideal model of legal education which stands 'for the capacity to take a broad and comprehensive view of one's discipline in its connections with the wider public concerns of the time', throughout the study programme, not just in the final year (p. 294):

> Compulsory jurisprudence suffers from the deficiency which I will call finishing school syndrome. Inserted at the end of the educational process it is both too little and too late. Jurisprudence plays the part of the intellectual icing on the otherwise stodgy cake that is legal education ... Compulsory jurisprudence comes too late because by excluding theoretical/philosophical issues from the preceding years of study it ensures that staff and students alike become imbued with an antitheoretical and empiricist perception of the project of legal education. The result is that jurisprudence is forced to stand in splendid and, all too often, arrogant isolation

---

[107] Attempts to rethink Indian legal education in the context of globalisation challenges have remained sporadic and largely ineffective. See *New vision for legal education in the emerging global scenario*, a publication by the National Law School of India University in Bangalore (2001). Promising models of teaching about customary laws exist in Namibia and some South African universities.

> from the rest of the curriculum . . . Jurisprudence is doomed to failure in
> its role as the finishing school of legal education.

Hunt (1986: 302) therefore suggests that 'theory should be injected at the
beginning of the courses and that we renounce the finishing school role that
has so widely been given to jurisprudence'. Such arguments closely relate to
Legrand's (1996: 241) demands of more reflection on the nature of law itself:

> One particular manifestation of the critical vocation that the comparatist
> must embrace concerns . . . the definition of law itself which must be made,
> in important ways, more open-textured than has habitually been the case.
> This is necessary, even though it may require the comparatist to operate at
> variance with the prevailing views in the legal culture that forms the object
> of her study. If the interpreters of the national law persist in acting as mere
> 'reverberators' of the law, the comparatist must note this fact, integrate it
> into her analysis, and seek to bring to the surface the deeper meaning of the
> 'binding law' to which national positivists confine themselves. She must
> also extend the notion of 'law' beyond that of 'binding law'.

Other recent writing suggests acute awareness of deficiencies in current law
teaching. Banks (1999) considers to what extent law students in Britain receive
a legal education that is meaningful and relevant to them. He highlights that
law teaching today, within the context of higher education and its objectives,
should incorporate contextualised visions of reality rather than purportedly
simple and uniform models of law. This argument is also not explicitly focused
on globalisation and pluralism. Banks (1999: 446) simply suggests that 'legal
education ought to be something more than learning cases and statutes and
applying the law to the facts'. Since legal education does not take place within
a value-neutral environment, all legal education is a highly sophisticated form
of manipulation, even brainwashing, and not just a vocational enterprise. Law
teaching is more closely linked to ideology than most law teachers seem to
realise. It matters therefore what is taught, how it is taught, and students should
be aware of what they are studying and why. Banks (1999: 447) suggests that
law teachers should lay such matters on the table, if only to assist students
in assessing choices about their lives, so that legal education becomes more
than vocational training. Banks (1999: 449) indicates that there are no agreed
answers about desirable subjects of legal study and notes that the demands of
professional bodies often restrict educational initiatives and force students into
'black letter' subjects or 'core courses'. However, there is an expectation that
law must be taught within the context of the society in which it operates. Banks
(1999: 465–6) concludes:

> Not only must differing perspectives and social contexts be integrated into
> the curriculum, they must be integrated *across* the curriculum . . . If only one
> lecturer of 15 places law in a culturally and experientially diverse context, the

message of marginalisation and segregation remains. The more the message is heard . . . the greater the challenge to the assumption of a generalised common interpretation to law.

Significantly, Banks writes as a Canadian law teacher working in a British law school, restricting his examples of the changing world and of exclusion to current concerns of modern Western societies, such as sexual orientation. For a globally focused approach to legal analysis, this kind of activist agenda, meritorious as it may be, is too parochial and unambitious. There are much larger issues of a cross-cultural, multidisciplinary, global nature requiring the attention of comparative lawyers.

1.6 A model of pluralist, globality-conscious legal education

Is there a remedy through the medium of legal studies? This final section presents a model of globalised legal education, practised at the School of Oriental and African Studies (SOAS) in the University of London since 1975, which appears to be well advanced on the road to plurality-conscious global legal education. At SOAS, in the early 1970s, important strategic decisions were made about introducing a system of undergraduate legal education that would tie in with the School's academic focus on Asian and African studies. Law students at SOAS were to be offered courses in English law as well as a variety of courses on Asian and African laws.[108] A new course called 'Introduction to Legal Systems', later renamed 'Legal Systems of Asia and Africa', still the current title, was created as an integral part of the compulsory first-year LLB programme. The ambition was to lay solid conceptual foundations for a broad-based analytical understanding of law as a cross-cultural phenomenon in a global context.

This course threw the cat among the pigeons, as far as comparative legal study and global legal education were concerned. While London as a whole offers a rich field for legal study (Twining, 2000: 55–6), SOAS is not just an exotic flower, but has quietly pioneered explorations of global legal studies.[109] Other colleges tend to teach jurisprudence as the crowning glory of legal studies in the third year, an element of 'finishing school' (Hunt, 1986). SOAS law undergraduates have since 1975 been forced to read and think comparatively and theoretically about the phenomenon of law on a worldwide level from the very first day of study.

---

[108] Some snippets of this are found in Edge (2000) in an account by Professor Allott, then Head of Department, who was instrumental in introducing this unique undergraduate law degree.

[109] Twining (2000: 56) notes that the main cosmopolitan areas of law at postgraduate level 'have not been particularly well-served by legal theory in recent years'. On legal education see also Flood (2002: 322–7).

The new venture at SOAS was much more than a job creation programme for redundant colonial officers, as some cynics might suggest.[110] The leading lights of the Department at the time, Professor Antony Allott, who spearheaded the syllabus developments, Mrs Margaret Rogers, Professor Duncan Derrett and others had first-hand experience of colonial rule. They realised that in the changed post-colonial world of the Commonwealth a new legal education was required, bridging gaps in knowledge between domestic legal science and over-seas jurisdictions and their respective principles and norms. Most of Asia and Africa had gained independence by that time. As colonial legal domination was coming to an end, those who remained closely involved in local developments in the former colonies realised that these new countries would go their own way, politically and legally. It was hazily recognised that it would remain rel-evant for future lawyers to acquire detailed understanding of the conceptual frameworks underpinning traditional Asian and African legal systems and their more recent manifestations. It would be insufficient to study the metropolitan laws' march across the globe. An early inkling of plurality-focused globalisa-tion inspired the innovative SOAS LLB programme of the mid-1970s. Initially though, demonstrating the worldwide movement and continued strength of English common law remained prominent.[111] Whether we look at African law and the later much-maligned Restatement of African Laws project under Allott's direction during the 1960s, or the project of modern Hindu law reforms in India and Derrett's initial advice to modern Indians to restructure their family laws according to English law,[112] for some time colonial patterns of thought and strategy remained prominent. It became a critical requirement that first-year students should learn as fast as possible about the basic concepts of various tra-ditional non-Western legal systems to understand, where relevant, the impact of colonial rule and current tensions within contemporary legal systems of Asia and Africa. How was this going to be achieved? The first textbook for the new SOAS course (Derrett, 1968b) indicated the problem in the Preface (p. xiii):

> One may wonder whether now a man can call himself educated who, having studied, for example, English law for three years goes into the world as a 'lawyer' and has never heard of other systems of law. The present editor once asked a London law graduate what he thought of Indian law, and this was the answer: 'I really don't know anything about it, but I presume they mostly follow English law. I suppose the natives may stick to some bits of their ancient systems where their religions are involved . . . You know, like not eating cows . . . ?' In other words those parts that matter are likely to be

---

[110] Much information about the early history of the SOAS Law Department is found in several contributions to Edge (2000).

[111] See particularly Allott (1968) and other contributions in Derrett (1968b). Old exam papers from the early years of the course strongly reflect this ex-colonial orientation.

[112] Derrett (1957; 1963), but see Derrett (1978), his last major work, where this line is no longer pursued.

as similar to ours as makes little significant difference, and those that are 'religious' are unlike ours, and so fit to be ignored.

Such uninformed responses are still given today. Current students, testing this on co-residents in halls and friends from other colleges and disciplines, often report amazing levels of ignorance about other people's legal systems and the persistence of imperial myths of English law's domination in Asia and Africa. Similarly, it has never been easy for me to explain that I teach Indian or South Asian laws. Many people, Indians and Pakistanis included, instantly respond that I must be an expert in the history of English law or some odd Oriental variation of it. Earlier, Derrett (1968b: xv) noted that even highly educated people, including authors of law books, might not accept that every society had law and would have particular difficulties in recognising African law as legal (Kagan, 1955). The full ambit of Asian and African legal studies was neither popularly understood nor perceived with accuracy by most people, including those who considered themselves well educated, such as practising lawyers and legal scholars.

Faced with such hardboiled eurocentric assumptions, those who devised the new SOAS course had to make important decisions about methodology to counter the prevalent assumption that the importation of European laws had somehow created the Asian and African legal systems we know today, wiping out the legal past and most indigenous concepts. Derrett (1968b: xiv–xv) indicates awareness of methodological ramifications: 'After settling which systems should be explored, and at what level of generalisation, the next question – a more delicate one – was how to explore them.' Here it became difficult. What questions were to be debated, if one did not really know where best to start and how to compare? Derrett (1968b: xv) addresses one of the major methodological issues that has troubled all comparatists, namely how to discuss entirely different concepts and systems in a common language:

> Now no doubt he would prefer to hear about a foreign system of law in the terms used by that system itself. But this involves the hearer in an effort of translation, and that too of much more than words. The nuances of each legal literature, and its presuppositions, are seldom set forth for the foreigner's assistance. No system appears to have a built-in cultural dictionary and guide. Whatever difficulties the qualified man would have, those of the beginner are bound to be daunting.
>
> And yet it is the beginner who needs to know where his own national system of law fits into the patterns created by the ... systems as a consortium. There is little point in exploring the minutiae of one's own system if one has hardly grasped that it is itself only one of a group of intensely developed attempts to effectuate justice amongst human beings.

Derrett (1968b: xv) reassured students that '[t]his book attempts to show the beginner what the specialists would say to him if they spoke his language, knowing his limitations and anticipating his curiosity', but this must have been an enterprise risking many misunderstandings and failed messages. In multicultural classrooms today, establishing a common language and shared understanding of basic concepts becomes an urgent and critical first task in globalised educational processes. Learning and teaching law involves multiple forms of complex communication at various levels. The endeavour to analyse the legal systems of Asia and Africa on their own terms cannot succeed unless one unpacks supposedly universal concepts like 'law' and communicates under-lying pluralities. Simply using familiar eurocentric models puts a straitjacket on any attempt at developing globality-conscious methodology. Allott's impor-tant jurisprudential study (*The limits of law*, 1980) arose from such debates, problematising advanced legal analysis in a post-colonial world, anticipating much of the current globalisation debate. Gradually, a decidedly post-colonial and partly anti-Western perspective began to develop, which would eventu-ally allow the legal systems of Asia and Africa to speak with their own voices (Menski, 2003).

Clearly, such legal studies at SOAS were conceived as a wider educative experience, an international endeavour, involving analysis rather than simple description, elaborate discussion rather than rote learning of fixed rules. The largely unspoken aim was to prepare law students for the global market. Excit-ing legal careers and leading functions in national and international legal fora became possible for those who acquired critical navigation skills that studying Asian and African laws can so uniquely provide. Rather than reducing every-thing to a few basic rules of national law, such legal studies were to involve wide-ranging consideration of multiple particularities on a near-global scale.

There was always a danger that less interested students would remain mere tourists, sampling a few exoticisms and taking no further interest. However, the academic profile of law at SOAS and the tough competition for the few places in this unique programme brought a certain self-selection, which has grad-ually become more pronounced. Yet every year, the initial reaction is mixed and some 'black letter' die-hards from all over the world initially view this compulsory element of their law course as an irritation, an enforced, irrelevant distraction.[113] Today, the contentious issue of how to understand globalisation is immediately on the agenda and most students quickly realise the enormous potential of this kind of global legal study.[114] Some students build up men-tal barriers and struggle with supposedly unpronounceable terms, like *usul al-fiqh* in Islamic law, *smriti* in Hindu law, or the intricate concept of individual conscience (*ātmanastushti*), which contains many lessons about the nature of law (Menski, 2003: 126–7). Some students are nervous about having to study

---

[113] Some opposition to globality-conscious challenges of unification visions is also reported by Dembour (2001: 59).

[114] Some students, however, leave the course and flee to 'safer' programmes of study.

'other' systems which their religious or cultural norms seem to treat as ideological enemies or simply as backward, 'traditional' or 'religious' hocus-pocus; others reach levels of analytical sharpness they never imagined to exist. It has been particularly instructive that not only 'white' students have difficulties in understanding 'the other'. In a globally oriented comparative law class, everyone is in the same boat, having to travel and come to terms with many 'others'.

Sometimes I set students essay questions which ask them to reflect on their experiences of such comparative legal study. Remarkable personal insights have been captured in some incisive comments which were kept on record. Almost all students confirmed that comparative legal study had made them more perceptive and sensitive about terminology, in relation to a subject which they thought they knew, or had not really thought about before. A common starting point for most students, before the exposure to comparative law, was that 'law' was assumed to be state law, represented by officialdom, closely related to retribution. The study of legal systems of Asia and Africa showed such assumptions to be based on ethnocentric, particularly Western premises. Studying the historical evolution of legal systems put such unwitting ethnocentricity in perspective. The importance of customs, local norms, and value systems in legal practice had become more appreciated, and a clearer understanding of the interaction between state law and other rule systems had been achieved. Many students expressed a deeper understanding of criminal law and its role in society. A penal approach was not essential to upholding order in society, which could be achieved in many other ways, including assiduous self-control. Following the law could indeed mean avoiding disputes at all costs, upholding harmony through psychological and social healing processes rather than litigation. Exciting examples of African dispute settlement processes, which appeared at first as healing rituals and would not strike a 'normal' law student as relevant because of the prominence of religious and cultural ritual, turned out to be most instructive examples for studying legal processes in interaction with social life patterns. One student of politics and law, who had apparently come to college in the firm belief that all state law was oppressive and merely designed to uphold the rule by one class over the rest of society, discovered that state law and its application could be negotiated by individuals and social groups in many more ways than he had ever dared to assume. Some students lost all their illusions about the power of law, in which they wanted to partake, and realised how easily such power could be abused in the name of the law. A rather typical, anonymous LLB student wrote:

> My own thoughts were fairly nebulous and confused, with common misunderstandings as to what constitutes a legal system, and a fairly conservative attitude to thinking about different models of law . . . The overlap into the areas of history, ethics, religion and morals has been fascinating when a series of events unfolds to produce the legal systems present today . . . It has become overwhelmingly apparent that there exists a dichotomy between

> what purports to be the official state law and what actually represents the 'living law' of the people . . . In studying different theories of how law evolves and how legal systems develop, the danger of being short-sighted or of having pre-conceived ideas readily shows up flawed theories, which are seen to be prejudiced by trends of a particular time and place, and often the selective use of data, to furnish a constructed model that does not reflect what happens at the level of daily life of a group of people.

One must of course wonder how much can be achieved by introducing one academic course at one British university in the context of one particular law degree. However, this is not the only law course dealing with Asia and Africa at SOAS; there are many regional law options available to students in subsequent years. The fact that top law firms anywhere in the world now recognise that law graduates with a solid grounding in comparative legal theories have that 'extra' quality they expect reassures us that the deeper study of law in a comparative environment is not misguided. It may seem today that the agenda for comparative legal work at SOAS in the mid-1970s were much less ambitious than they are now. There can be no doubt, however, that the SOAS course, explicitly directed towards non-Western jurisprudence as well as the plurality-conscious study of global legal history, has ensured that theory-focused comparative law methods are imported straight into the first year of legal study.[115]

This has had several notable consequences. Students experience a rather more 'exotic' intellectual environment than Legrand (1996) imagines in his comparison of English and French laws. But studying Asian and African legal systems also carries a perceived risk of marginalisation from mainstream British legal education. Adding an intellectually radical rather than merely 'liberal' approach to studying law appears at times to push students into further isolation. Is one really studying 'proper' law when one discusses ancient Hindu visions of cosmic order, the role of the companions of the Prophet in Islam, African concepts of nature, or the concept of *tao* in Chinese philosophy? Does it not disadvantage a law student in Britain today to have studied Indian, Chinese or African laws, or the unofficial *angrezi shariat* of Muslims in Britain? The evidence is to the contrary, as many students report positively of interviewers who wanted to know what had been learnt in such 'new' and unusual subjects. Global law firms (and increasingly high street firms in multi-ethnic Britain) appreciate globality-conscious legal education and now seek to identify not only the brightest trainees, but often prefer those with specialist regionally focused legal knowledge, including language and cultural skills. However, it is

---

[115] The parallel experience of teaching postgraduates who did not go through this kind of undergraduate programme (and undergraduate 'floaters' from other colleges of London University) largely confirms that a plurality-focused globality-conscious legal education from the start creates a higher level of awareness about 'law' and interlegality than is achieved in other study programmes.

still difficult for some students to 'unlearn' in one law class what they have just learnt in another. This may happen not only in the first year, but with even more force in subsequent years, when seemingly conflicting visions of 'law' and 'justice' may cause anguish and confusion in some minds. This creates an extremely productive tension, which permeates virtually the whole of SOAS academia. Perhaps it is precisely this kind of tortuous intellectual experience which creates competent comparative lawyers with an awareness of global legal theory.

It would be foolish to claim that anything more than a certain level of insight into the complexities of global legal education has been achieved by either teacher or student in this enterprise. The globally focused study of Asian and African legal systems at SOAS remains a testing arena and a minority occupation, but it is a model that can easily be replicated elsewhere, particularly in law schools of the South. Contrary to dismissive assumptions, the recipients of such globally oriented, interdisciplinary legal education are recognisable as lawyers at the end of the day. In addition, they have learnt to think as global citizens with a more self-reflective consciousness and a wider range of knowledge and understanding than the standard product of most law schools. It is evident that much more remains to be done, all over the world, to provide firm foundations for plurality-sensitive, globality-conscious legal studies, but a beginning has been made. While colonial assumptions might continue to dominate (Twining, 2000: 150), interlegality, legal pluralism and glocalisation are solid conceptual bases on which to build such education.

2

Legal pluralism

In the postmodern age, lawyers are re-learning that it remains impossible to draw clear boundaries between the legal and the non-legal.[1] Debates about globalisation have precipitated this realisation (Flood, 2002). Several pioneers of legal pluralism studies provided useful starting points for further plurality-conscious analysis.[2] Hooker (1975: 1) highlighted that '[l]egal systems typically combine in themselves ideas, principles, rules, and procedures originating from a variety of sources', adding that '[b]oth in the contemporary world and historically the law manifests itself in a variety of forms and a variety of levels' (p. 1). We know that law is everywhere (Twining, 2000: 1) as a social phenomenon, based on cultural foundations (Chiba, 2002: v), which the dominant positivist approach has unsuccessfully tried to ignore in order to privilege the state and its laws.[3] Studying legal pluralism clearly 'raises important questions about power' (Griffiths, 2002: 289) and thus challenges legal centralist perspectives about state law.

While legal uniformity represents a utopian dream of philosophers, it is therefore an exception in social reality.[4] Questions have arisen about where law begins and where it ends,[5] but perhaps these are misleading questions.[6]

---

[1] Scholars seeking to provide pure legal theory note the 'adulteration' of this purity (Kelsen, 1970: 1). Kelsen's translator (at p. 5) highlights the increasing 'diversity of the contents of positive legal orders'.

[2] For an overview and bibliography see Woodman (1998). Hooker's approach is appreciated by Chiba (1989: 41) as 'an amazing far-reaching understanding of non-Western law', but he is also criticised as 'a captive of Western jurisprudence' (p. 42).

[3] Anleu (2000: 6–7). Griffiths (2002: 293) observes that the pervasive power of the legal centralist or formalist model of law is such that 'all legal studies stand in its shadow'.

[4] Schott (1995: 38) argues that, while legal pluralism is normal in all human societies, legal equality is a rather incompletely realised exception in social and legal orders: '"*Rechtspluralismus*" ist . . . empirisch gesehen, der für alle menschlichen Gesellschaften "*normale*" Zustand, nicht nur in Afrika . . . "*Rechtsgleichheit*" dagegen ist entweder ein *utopisches Traumziel* der Philosophen oder ein in der Realität nur sehr unvollkommen verwirklichter *Ausnahmefall* der gesellschaftlichen und rechtlichen Ordnung.'

[5] Tamanaha's writings (1993; 2001) reflect that lawyers are concerned about ownership of their subject. See also Cotterrell (2002).

[6] Twining (2000: 166) suggests that law may be about groups rather than rules. Accepting that law might be as much about legal rules as social norms, one cannot ignore that values impinge on these rules and norms.

It is a common daily experience that normative pluralism, the coexistence of different bodies of norms within the same social space, is a fact of life.[7] While we may struggle to understand the elusive and dynamic nature of norms, Twining (2000: 246) suggests that pluralism goes much deeper, so that 'to understand law and legal ordering, the study of norms is almost never enough. One also has to take account of values, facts, meanings, processes, structures, power relations, personnel, and technologies. And then there is the matter of multiple standpoints and perspectives.'[8] This suggests that the whole arena of natural law, which according to Lampe (1995: 18) is not primarily legal, cannot be excluded from legal pluralist analysis. Although normative pluralism as a fact is central, Twining (2000: 232) notes that lawyers have problems with handling legal pluralism:

> [L]egal pluralism is generally marginalised and viewed with scepticism in legal discourse. Perhaps the main reason for this is that over 200 years Western legal theory has been dominated by conceptions of law that tend to be monist (one internally coherent legal system), statist (the state has a monopoly of law within its territory), and positivist (what is not created or recognised as law by the state is not law).

This reflects growing realisation that positivistic models of legal study, alone or in combination with idealising natural law approaches, have failed to grapple with global socio-legal realities. If law is a social phenomenon, any legal theory that ignores socio-cultural elements and values in relation to law would yield just a partial vision and remain unrealistic.[9] To take account of interlegality (Santos, 1995), pluralism needs to be conceived as 'a universal phenomenon covering both Western and non-Western societies and, at the same time, appearing in not only the dual structure of state law and minor customary law but also the triple of customary law, national law and international law' (Chiba, 2002: 7–8).

No easy prescriptions for tackling the ensuing tasks are possible.[10] Twining (2000: 2) emphasises that '[e]ach of us has to try to make sense of these bewildering messages in our own way'. Legal theorists and comparative lawyers have to learn how to conduct plurality-focused analyses of law. As we saw, traditional 'black letter' legal study is now recognised as limited (Cownie, 2004). New approaches are needed which reconnect jurisprudence and anthropology

---

[7] Banakas (2002: 182) points out that the great legal anthropologist Bronislaw Malinowski (1884–1942), the founder of functionalism, already described all culture, including legal culture, as 'normative'. On Chiba's (1986) legal postulates and in particular his 'identity postulate' (Chiba, 1989) see section 2.5.4 below.

[8] Örücü (2002: 13) emphasises the importance of values when it comes to legal transplants.

[9] This is one of the criticisms of the pure science approach of Kelsen. For details see Freeman (2001: 255ff.) and Morrison (1997: 323–50).

[10] Twining (2000: 174ff.) emphasises the frustrations of lack of knowledge and understanding. Griffiths (2002: 309–10) suggests a research agenda.

(Hinz, 2003a). Twining (2000: 135) suggests that 'a sound understanding of law as a social phenomenon needs to be rooted in a sound sociology and social theory' (pp. 81–2) and stresses that '[q]uestions of cultural relativism of law are central to contemporary jurisprudence' (p. 156). Since the only closed social system is humanity at large (p. 73),[11] even if we wanted to focus on law itself, 'closure is not an option' (p. 247). Twining (2000: 103) thus sees 'a need for a sophisticated conceptual apparatus which can form both a meta-language for talking about laws in general and a tool-box for expressing laws with precision'. But so far, legal debates about globalisation and pluralism are undeveloped. Twining (2000: 58) indicates:

> Legal theory in London, and in the common law world generally, has diver-sified considerably and shows signs of a confusing, sometimes confused, intellectual ferment. But very little of this seems to be directly related to globalisation, let alone to be a response to it. The two most obvious rele-vant approaches, law and development and legal pluralism have been quite marginal in London and elsewhere in the United Kingdom in recent years. So, too, has historical jurisprudence. Indeed, some of the most fashionable pursuits could be accused of being quite parochial.[12]

Glenn (2000; 2004) demonstrates the multitude of legal traditions in the world. Law is found all over the world and is thus a universal phenomenon in that sim-ple sense. A globally focused study, including the laws of Asia and Africa, cannot avoid taking many culture-specific elements into account. Twining (2000: 101) observes that looking at law from a global perspective 'involves no commitment to naive universalism, rather it puts issues about interdependence, cultural and ethnic relativism, and multiculturalism near the top of the agenda'. This post-modern emphasis on diversity, plurality and socio-cultural elements in their interlinkedness with law inevitably involves a method of legal analysis and theorising that is akin to historical school approaches in jurisprudence (Örücü, 2002: 15–17; Griffiths, 2002). While the modernist phase of legal analysis priv-ileged state positivism and natural law theories,[13] postmodern legal analysis focuses more on the role of social value systems in making law. It therefore draws more attention to socio-legal realities as part of the third triangle of jurisprudence (chapter 3, section 3.8). The question is whether that in itself is sufficient to promote pluralist study.

Adding social dimensions to legal analysis brings nothing much that is new. The dominant positivist and statist assumptions about law never existed in

---

[11] In light of the perceptions of some world religions, such as Hinduism, this assertion can be questioned.

[12] Twining (2000: 3) observes that, by the mid-1990s, the discipline of law as a whole was becoming increasingly cosmopolitan in the UK and the USA, but that the theoretical analysis of law seemed to lag behind.

[13] Typically, Olivecrona (1971: 5) divides theories of law merely into two groups: natural law theory and legal positivism.

isolation from other perspectives and have never been totally unchallenged. The postmodern, pluralist shift of emphasis provides a corrective to the axioms of modernity that made scholars forget or ignore that law everywhere is socially embedded and linked to values.[14] Legal pluralism thus reacts against the monist excesses of modernist legal analysis, but has to be cautious about becoming too diffuse.[15] New pluralist approaches differ from traditional historical methods, however, in that they no longer follow unilinear theories of evolution (Rouland, 1994: 26ff.), which have done so much damage to legal analysis (Sack and Aleck, 1992). Postmodern globality-focused legal analysis is more concerned to capture social plurality in the widest sense from a legal angle than to search for, or even imply, a uniform historical direction. Legal pluralist analysis in this manner is indeed characterised by 'the loss of grand ambitions' (Riles, 2001: 18). As we shall see in chapter 3, section 3, there is more to this, since a deep pluralist analysis also needs to take account of the interaction between the various elements of law.

Providing a plurality-conscious, globality-focused theoretical analysis, the present chapter focuses particularly on those elements of legal theory and comparative jurisprudence that emphasise awareness of the socio-political embeddedness of law. The chapter demonstrates that legal anthropology, comparative law and legal theory as distinct fields of study need each other for deeper explorations of law in its social context. The sections below build on the views of earlier and more recent theorists to develop a legal pluralist approach to studying law. This lays the foundation for critically discussing the traditional eurocentric jurisprudence in chapter 3 and for embarking on a deeper analysis of the nature of legal pluralism in chapter 3, section 3.8.

2.1 Early conceptualisations of legal pluralism

As a theme, legal pluralism is ancient and found especially among people 'who live ecological lives by being chthonic . . . which means that they live in or in close harmony with the earth' (Glenn, 2004: 60). This is an attempt to describe a legal tradition by criteria internal to itself, rather than imposed criteria.[16] It is the oldest form of legal tradition in the world, focused on orality and specific ways of life. Glenn (2004: 61) explains:

> A chthonic legal tradition simply emerged, as experience grew and orality and memory did their work. Since all people of the earth are descended from people who were chthonic, all other traditions have emerged in contrast to chthonic tradition. It is the oldest of traditions; its chain of traditio is as long as the history of humanity.

[14] Even Kelsen (1970: 65) accepted in principle that every law is moral, while he had no time for natural law (Davies and Holdcroft, 1991: 149).
[15] It has been accused of being 'too vague and ill-defined' (Griffiths, 2002: 306).
[16] Glenn (2004: 60) distinguishes this term from the more general 'folk law'.

The term 'legal pluralism' became academically recognised in anglophone scholarship after Barry Hooker's (1975) book on legal pluralism, followed by many important studies and an ongoing lively debate.[17] However, many early thinkers, anthropologists and jurists made contributions which are still relevant today.[18] A brief survey must suffice to indicate that plurality-consciousness is definitely not a new approach. An early pioneer was the French thinker Jean Bodin, who in 1576 directed specific attention to the cultural aspects of law.[19] In rationalist reaction to the natural law of the classical period (see chapter 3), Baron Charles de Secondat Montesquieu (1689–1755) wrote famous works in 1721 (*Lettres persanes*) and 1748 (*De l'esprit des lois*) in which he argued for 'the existence of eternal standards of some kind, antecedent to the positive laws of men, and recognizable to human intelligence' (Kelly, 1992: 259). These were not necessarily natural law elements, but arose from social conventions. Montesquieu drew attention to 'the varying customs of different nations (while giving the usual perfunctory salute . . . to the supremacy of the law of nature) and suggesting that their variety was explained by the variety in their surrounding conditions' (Kelly, 1992: 273). He elaborated on this by creating the famous principle that laws made by the state should be adapted to suit the actual condition of the people concerned.[20] Rouland (1994: 20) writes:

> Montesquieu . . . had the merit of being the only thinker of his period to reject a fixed attitude towards law, and to consider societies which differed from his own. For Montesquieu, law was one of the components of a sociopolitical system and closely involved in its functioning. Thus law was of necessity a changeable entity, varying according to society, time and place.

Rouland (1994: 20) indicates that Montesquieu pioneered what we might call today a holistic perspective and shunned the evolutionary model:

> For him, developments in legal systems are not marked by historical milestones, indicating the march of progress, but depend on much more prosaic

---

[17] On the francophone debates see Woodman (1998). Chiba (1989: 1) confirms that Hooker put legal pluralism on the map. The *Journal of Legal Pluralism and Unofficial Law* offers a wide range of contributions. Twining (2000: 224–33) surveys the literature on legal pluralism. Griffiths (2002: 290) suggests that John Gilissen's (1971) *Le pluralisme juridique* was the first pioneering study and presents a detailed bibliography.

[18] Morrison (1997: vii) expresses shock and bewilderment at discovering Hart's (1961) failure to transmit a complete reading of John Austin's work of 1832. Presented as the pioneer of legal positivism, Austin had been acutely conscious of what we now call legal pluralism (Morrison, 1997: 6).

[19] Chiba (1989: 30). The Société Jean Bodin, established in 1935, has as its aim the encouragement of scholarly studies in the field of comparative history of law and institutions. It publishes the *Recueils de la Société Jean Bodin*.

[20] Seeking to identify what contributes to diversity or convergence in law, Banakas (2002: 184) draws a distinction between Montesquieu's view of law as a product of national and cultural forces and the views of some modern comparatists on the greater importance of the social and political environment. Such debates seem fruitless. In an open system, all these factors may play a role.

agencies, such as the climatic conditions, topography, demography, etc. of a particular society. In his recognition of the variability of law, Montesquieu is the first legal anthropologist of the modern period.

He is therefore also recognised as a protagonist of the legal pluralist approach by various branches of scholarship, including comparative law and the sociology of law (Tamanaha, 2001: 27) and influenced many early thinkers on crime and punishment (Stone, 1965: 112–13). A recent analysis of Montesquieu's radical relativism (Launay, 2001) questions his range of relativity and suggests the impact of fairly narrow political French agenda at the time. It is also critical of Montesquieu's portrayal of Asian despotism, but at least he put Asia and Africa on the map of comparative scholarship about law, society and government.

The leading English jurist Jeremy Bentham (1748–1832) was influenced by Montesquieu's work when formulating his famous concept of utilitarianism, the principle of the greatest happiness for the largest number.[21] Stone (1965: 112) noted that, 'in theory at any rate, Bentham adopted the thesis that law is not to be judged as good or bad in the abstract, but only in relation to the manners, customs and physical environment of the particular people'. Twining (2000: 18) highlights that Bentham not only distinguished 'international jurisprudence' as relations between sovereigns and internal jurisprudence, which comprised national, provincial and local levels, but was willing to recognise a multiplicity of levels of law and acknowledged that local entities could have laws of their own.[22] Twining (2000: 20) also confirms that in considering the influence of time and place on legislation, Bentham was prepared to give some weight to local customs and circumstances and was therefore not a pure positivist. Thus, 'caution needs to be exercised in legislating for a particular country in case expectations based on local customs and circumstances should be disappointed – for the non-disappointment principle is an important principle subordinate to utility' (p. 20). Twining (2000: 66) suggests that Bentham should not be oversold, but characterises him as 'a citizen of the world with an ambitious intellectual agenda' (p. 101) and as 'an optimistic child of the Enlightenment' (p. 107), whose intellectual contribution is still relevant today. Twining (2000: 250) concludes:

> Although he did not develop his ideas very far in this respect, he was more sensitive than most of his successors to the limitations of 'black box' theories of national or municipal legal systems . . . his grand vision of the range of questions that need to be addressed by a general theory concerned with the design of institutions, procedures and laws at all levels from the very local to the global deserves much more attention than it has so far received.

---

[21] On Bentham see Twining (2000: 15–20); Freeman (2001: 200–7).

[22] Today, legal recognition of customs in English law is found in faint remnants, for example the customary right of the fishermen of Walmer to dry their nets on a particular beach (Shears and Stephenson, 1996: 20).

In England, Bentham's theories were soon overshadowed by Austin's theory of positivism,[23] but jurisprudence and legal anthropology all over Europe received important stimuli from a number of other early scholars as proponents of the historical school of jurisprudence.

2.2 The historical school of law

Twining (2000: 26) observes that, for a time in England, the historical school, led by Maine, had threatened to become a serious rival to positivists, but Maine was eventually marginalised by them (p. 33). The historical school of law, which arose side by side with analytical positivism during the nineteenth century in reaction to the earlier dominance of natural law theories, responded to their purported rationalism and individualism, relying on a romantic, 'mystic sense of unity and organic growth in human affairs' (Freeman, 2001: 903). Historical analysis implies a functional study of law in its specific socio-cultural, political and economic context.[24] Among early scholars, Sir Henry Maine (1822–88) is considered significant as the father of comparative law,[25] as well as of legal anthropology (Rouland, 1994: 21), though he is also blamed for producing a much-criticised evolutionist legal scheme that is no longer seen as valid. An early example of a misguided search for the wrong problems comes from Sir Henry Maine's (1861: 3) suggestion that law can be studied like a science:

> If by any means we can determine the early forms of jural conceptions, they will be invaluable to us. These rudimentary ideas are to the jurist what the primary crusts of the earth are to the geologist. They contain, potentially, all the forms in which law has subsequently exhibited itself. The haste or the prejudice which has generally refused them all but the most superficial examination, must bear the blame of the unsatisfactory condition in which we find the science of jurisprudence.

Such historically oriented assumptions about the nature of law have helped to marginalise all traditional legal systems, damaging the worldwide image of all non-Western laws. David and Brierley (1978: 1) may be right in asserting that '[t]he comparison of laws, at least in their geographical diversity, is as old as the science of law itself', but when it comes to intercontinental comparisons, continuing lack of progress must be noted. Few 'indigenous' writers have been

---

[23] For details see chapter 3, section 3.6, but note the reservations by Morrison (1997: vii, 6, see n. 18 above) about viewing Austin merely as a positivist.

[24] Summers (1982: 35) notes that historical jurisprudence was never strong in the USA but claims that 'the work of the American theorists . . . qualifies as America's only indigenous legal theory' (p. 12).

[25] Rouland (1994: 33) sees the Swiss scholar J. J. Bachofen (1815–87) as the founder of comparative law, while Maine achieved prominence teaching the subject at Oxford.

able to take an internal view.[26] Far too often, the starting points for comparative analysis have been colonialist or post-colonialist perceptions and agenda, and they remain strong today.

During the nineteenth century, evolutionary thinking was trendy, Karl Marx (1818–83) was writing *Das Kapital* (1867) and Charles Darwin's (1859) pioneering study on the origin of species gave a biological interpretation to legal evolution and increased the belief in man's capacity for rational action and growth. Maine opposed natural law theories, but did not follow mystical adherence to a folk spirit (*Volksgeist*) as developed by Savigny in Germany (see below). A prominent exponent of evolutionism, Maine knew Greek, Roman, English (and Irish) and some Hindu law. His major work on *Ancient law* (1861) was a typical product of its time, investigating scientifically whether there were certain patterns of legal development which could claim universality. He developed a basic distinction of 'static' and 'progressive' societies,[27] as well as a multi-stage theory of legal development, according to which 'initially, man believed that law was God-given and channelled through earthly rulers . . . ; then law became identified with custom; finally, law acquired a separate identity. In the course of this long evolution law passed from status to contract.'[28] Maine saw it as a characteristic of 'progressive' societies that they went beyond the older methods of law-making and employed three specific methods: fictions, equity, and finally formal legislation. Maine (1861: 1) starts his study with the famous statement that '[t]he most celebrated system of jurisprudence known to the world begins, as it ends, with a Code', a reference to the Twelve Tables (c. 450 BC) and the Code of Justinian (*Corpus Juris Civilis*, 534 AD) in Roman law.[29] While he was aware of the existence of Sanskrit sources for ancient India, which were not accessible at the time, his focus and scheme of analysis are clearly eurocentric and his belief in the superiority of European socio-legal development is evident.[30]

In Germany and Italy, but less so in France, evolutionist theories proved popular, too. In several major German studies, Albert Hermann Post (1839–95) attempted to study all legal institutions in all societies to demonstrate that

---

[26] A famous example appears to be Edward Said's *Orientalism* (1979), while perceptive African writers, in particular, have been ignored by a wider readership.

[27] Rouland (1994: 22) notes that, '[f]or him, far-off societies are stationary and infantile, Europe alone having revealed itself as a dynamic force in the development of legal processes'.

[28] Rouland (1994: 21). Maine's (1861: 182) much-cited statement was that '[t]he movement of progressive societies has hitherto been a movement from status to contract'.

[29] Neither of these really is a code. The XII Tables are 'rather the transcription of a number of customs' (Rouland, 1994: 39), while Justinian's collection comprises many different types of legal text.

[30] While Maine emphasised patriarchal concepts, Johann Jakob Bachofen (1815–87) focused on matriliny and kinship. Lewis H. Morgan (1818–81) developed a theory of social development from savagery and barbarism to civilisation in *Ancient society* (1877), predicting the disappearance of private property (Rouland, 1994: 22–3).

law is a universal phenomenon and therefore a unitary theory is possible,[31] but evolutionism fell rapidly out of favour in the early twentieth century. Charting this decline, Rouland (1994: 31) presents Franz Boas (1858–1942),[32] a German-American anthropologist, as the founder of cultural relativism:

> For him, societies are in essence diverse, because humanity inherits only its genetic make-up, further development depends on specific physical and social environments. In practice, there is little point in looking for large unitary schemes; variety rather than similarity prevails.

This diffusionist school, without rejecting the role of history altogether, condemned the rigidity and uniformity of unilinear evolution, but notably, '[a]s usual, legal writers took some time to react' (Rouland, 1994: 31). Through several early German writers, one can trace how the vision of universal historical laws was rejected at this time, only to see it resurrected later by neo-evolutionists (Rouland, 1994: 31–6). Among the latter, Hoebel (1954) developed the concept of 'trend of law', which does not mean unilinear evolution but, viewed globally, implies a pattern of transition from the simple to the more complex, since simpler societies (he was working on an Inuit community) needed less law. Rouland (1994: 36–7) rightly points out the lurking dangers of such philosophical assumptions about the unilinear direction of human development.[33]

Earlier in Germany, where political fragmentation and a complex variety of local laws had sparked off vigorous calls for comprehensive codification along the French model, the historical school of law had emerged in defence of local peculiarities and in opposition to official state law. Johann Gottfried von Herder (1744–1803) had rejected the universalising philosophical tendencies of natural law, was deeply suspicious of the state and treated its bureaucracy as an oppressive mechanism robbing individuals, as we would say today, of agency. Stressing the unique character of every historical period, civilisation and nation, he argued that different cultures and societies developed their own culture-specific values, so that 'the quality of human life and its scope for self-expression resided precisely in this plurality of values' (Freeman, 2001: 905).

Within this particular socio-political context, debates arose over the relevance of Roman legal traditions. F. Karl von Savigny (1779–1861) was critical of Roman law influence and, like Montesquieu, opposed the classical natural law approach because, to him, law was inevitably part of the culture of a people.

---

[31] Rouland (1994: 29, 65). Post is now a largely forgotten pioneer, soon pronounced guilty of the 'offence' of supporting evolutionism (Hildebrandt, 1989).

[32] Boas was influential in the USA. On his theories and his school, especially Melville Herskovitz and Ruth Benedict, see Merry (2001: 32–3).

[33] Chiba (1989) is dedicated to Hoebel, who has clearly been influential (see also Hooker, 1975: 24–30). Since the 1970s, modern legal anthropology has been dominated by legal pluralism.

He also rejected the Napoleonic Code of 1804 as a suitable model for Germany.[34] Savigny advocated a more realistic investigation into historical facts underlying particular rule systems and argued that all law originates in custom and was only later influenced by juristic activity. He developed the concept of folk spirit (*Volksgeist*), viewed in its particular historical context, which therefore tended to become quite nationalistic. Arguing that any particular system of law was a reflection of this folk spirit, Savigny saw law as 'the manifestation of the common consciousness' (Dias and Hughes, 1957: 392). This approach led him to view customs as the first manifestation of a people's spirit, so that any form of legislated law should always take into account a people's popular consciousness. No official law should be made which would violate local customary norms and the value systems of the subjects of the law. Such views of law and law-making, echoing Montesquieu, inevitably forced lawyers to study non-legal subjects as well, including folklore. In Glenn's (2000; 2004) terminology, it made them take explicit account of the contemporary manifestations of chthonic laws.

Savigny has been accused of overplaying his historical method and of treating it as universal. Such criticisms indicate that emphasis on the social dimensions of law alone is not considered sufficient.[35] Other criticisms relate to the fact that Savigny's model of the *Volksgeist*, applied to a local community, assumes an artificial uniformity but would forever fragment law-making processes by insisting on the superiority of small-scale entities. In the extreme, if any local community were to be allowed to maintain their own system of rules, how could one have viable systems of national law? Savigny dealt with such inherent conflicts by insisting that any legislation must be harmonised with what the people concerned felt was right and wrong. Dias and Hughes (1957: 396) argued that, 'consistently with his theory, Savigny maintained that legislation was subordinate to custom. It must at all times conform to the *Volksgeist*. It would be quite wrong to suppose that he opposed legislation altogether.'[36] Savigny merely warned that careless or rushed legislation would lead to negative consequences, an approach which put him ahead of his time, but also reflects what Montesquieu had said earlier. Freeman (2001: 908) criticises Savigny for underrating the role of legislation in modern society and for overlooking that law may mould customs, rather than just the reverse. A dynamic legal analysis would certainly need to take both types of impact into account.

Influenced by Savigny and Herbert Spencer, Otto Gierke (1841–1921) focused especially on the phenomenon of 'association', seeking to show that the reality of social control was not dominated by the state, but lay in the way in

---

[34] As a result, until 1900, German law largely remained Roman law adapted to local German conditions.

[35] See Freeman (2001: 906–7), where it is also noted that Savigny assumed Roman law to have been adopted into popular German consciousness.

[36] Cotterrell (2002: 41–2) cites Savigny's concept as one of the best known theoretical arguments for uniform law.

which groups in society organised themselves. Gierke (1950: l) stressed the concept of people's law and wrote that '[l]aw, on this view, is essentially *Volksrecht*: it is the product, in each nation, of the national genius'. Such approaches laid foundations for early sociological schools of jurisprudence. Julius Stone (1965: 277) highlighted that the satisfactory application of legal theories required consideration of plurality by what he called 'civilisation areas' and 'civilisation periods'. While the historical school rightly highlighted that law is more than an abstract set of rules imposed on society and is rather an integral part of it, later evolutionist trends in the traditional historical school of jurisprudence, fitting all legal developments into a linear developmental pattern, appear to have contributed to its gradual demise during the late 19th century. Another reason for this decline, which nobody has fully explained, may be that positivist assertions proved more attractive for legal scholars than the more complex, sociologically focused orientation of the historical school. Lawyers prefer certainty, while consideration of social diversity introduces multiple differentiations that are difficult to administer and to analyse. Nevertheless, despite the growing prominence of positivism, some scholars continued to pursue social analyses of law.

2.3 Early legal pluralism: Ehrlich's 'living law'

Operating from within a sociologically oriented approach,[37] later theorists began to develop more specific consciousness of legal plurality. The Austrian jurist Eugen Ehrlich (1862–1922) discussed legal pluralism in detail, without using the term explicitly. He proposed quite radically that 'lawyers' law 'exists side by side with other factors in society which may heavily influence or even in practice override it' (Kelly, 1992: 362). Twining (2000: 226) confirms that:

> [P]ioneers of the sociology of law, most notably Ehrlich, argued that a realistic depiction of the law in action had to take account of 'the living law' of sub-groups, as well as 'the official law' of the state. They saw that these could diverge significantly and that sometimes one, sometime the other would prevail. This was an important step not only in the direction of 'realism', but also away from the idea that the state has a monopoly of law-creation.

Ehrlich saw law as derived from social facts and more dependent on social compulsions than state authority (Freeman, 2001: 670), recognising that the state possessed certain characteristic means of compulsion. Basing his powerful theory of 'living law' on sociological foundations, he said in his brief preface that any attempt to formulate his basic theory in one sentence would be as follows:[38]

---

[37] Ehrlich is discussed by Freeman (2001: 670–2) under sociological jurisprudence as an eminent jurist concerned to explore the social basis of law.

[38] The German original in this and the following quotes is Ehrlich (1913), the English translation is from Ehrlich (1936).

> Der Schwerpunkt der Rechtsentwicklung liege auch in unserer Zeit, wie zu allen Zeiten, weder in der Gesetzgebung noch in der Jurisprudenz oder in der Rechtsprechung, sondern in der Gesellschaft selbst.

> [The centre of gravity of legal development lies, in our time as well as in all times, not in legislation nor in juristic science, nor in judicial decisions, but in society itself.]

For Ehrlich, law can only be properly understood from a sociological perspective. Kelly (1992: 362) emphasises that Ehrlich's theory implies that lawyers' law 'is only one of a series of normative orders which society itself has evolved'. Social institutions such as marriage, succession and business relationships all preceded state regulation and can only be understood within their respective social settings. Hence such factors should in Ehrlich's view be treated as equivalents of law and should be studied by lawyers.[39]

In Ehrlich's view, the norms which govern life within any given society are only imperfectly and partially reflected in traditional formal legal sources, such as statutes and decided cases. Ehrlich's analysis highlights an inevitable gap between the official law and actual practices, so that 'living law' is not simply the law as practised, but an amalgam of the official law and of people's values, perceptions and strategies, constituting a new hybrid entity. Dias and Hughes (1957: 421) suggested that over time courts and legislatures will take notice of people's practices, but 'the formal law can never catch up with the living law. The donkey never reaches the carrot. There must always be the inevitable gap between what the law says about a given topic and the way in which people actually behave . . . Not only does the law lag behind the practice of society, but in some cases it clearly contradicts that practice.' Ehrlich (1913: 11) emphasised that state law was never the only source of law, but that this important fact had been overlooked or, rather, marginalised over time:

> Es hat nie eine Zeit gegeben, wo das vom Staate als Gesetz verkündete Recht das einzige Recht gewesen wäre, auch nicht für die Gerichte und andere Behörden, und es war daher immer eine Unterströmung vorhanden, die dem außerstaatlichen Rechte eine entsprechende Stellung zu verschaffen suchte.

> [There was never a time when law promulgated by the state was the only law, not even for the courts and other authorities, and therefore there was always an undercurrent that tried to establish a corresponding position for non-state law.]

Ehrlich (1913: 15) emphasised that people play many legal roles outside the official legal arena:

---

[39] Cotterrell (2002) argues similarly, encouraging lawyers to venture into different social fields to expand legal scholarship.

Für den aber, der im Rechte vor allem eine Regel des Handelns erblickt...
spielt sich das menschliche Leben nicht vor den Gerichten ab. Schon der
Augenschein lehrt ihn, daß jeder Mensch in unzähligen Rechtsverhältnissen
steht, und daß er mit sehr wenigen Ausnahmen ganz freiwillig das tut, was
ihm in diesen Verhältnissen obliegt; er erfüllt seine Pflichten als Vater und
Sohn, als Gatte oder Gattin, er stört seine Nachbarn nicht im Genusse ihres
Eigentums.

[But for someone who above all perceives regularity of action in the law...
human life does not occur before the courts. It is evident at first sight that
every man is enmeshed in innumerable legal relationships and that, with
very few exceptions, he does entirely voluntarily what he is obligated to do
in such relationships; he fulfills his duties as a father and son, as husband
or wife, he does not disturb his neighbours in the enjoyment of their
property.]

This theoretical approach raises important questions concerning the understanding of law. First, Ehrlich does not say that courts, the legislature, or lawyers
in general, are unaware of the gap between theory and practice. He emphasises
that an understanding of the living law of a community necessitates looking
far beyond formal legal manifestations, concentrating on how people actually
live in society.[40] Secondly, like Duguit and others in France before him, Ehrlich
downplays the significance of the state and its legal institutions as a source of
law. To him, formal legal state norms remain only one factor of social control.
Local, family and group customs, morality, and the norms of specific associations, contribute much more, in Ehrlich's view, to what he called the 'living law'.
Thirdly, Ehrlich therefore emphasises that the key element in norm structures,
whether they be formally propounded as law or informally exist as social rules,
is in every case social pressure.[41] The individual was not an isolated being, but
embedded in a social environment, hence subject to social pressures. Ehrlich
(1913: 29) emphasised that social norms were more important and prominent,
even today, than the officially pronounced rules:

Die innre Ordnung der menschlichen Verbände ist nicht nur die
ursprüngliche, sondern auch bis in die Gegenwart die grundlegende Form
des Rechts. Der Rechtssatz stellt sich nicht nur viel später ein, er wird
auch heute noch größtenteils erst von der innern Ordnung der Verbände
abgeleitet. Um die Anfänge, die Entwicklung und das Wesen des Rechts zu
erklären, muß daher vor allem die Ordnung der Verbände erforscht werden.

---

[40] Noting that Ehrlich minimises the place of legislation, Freeman (2001: 671 n. 81) points
out that he worked in an ethnically and religiously plural part of Europe, the Austro-
Hungarian Empire. Criticism that his general conclusion, reached by observing a culturally
diversified society, may not be applicable in more homogenous societies displays a lack of
plurality-consciousness: Which society is entirely homogenous?

[41] The parallels with Hindu legal debates about this issue are remarkable (Menski, 2003:
25–7). Japanese 'shame culture' (*haji*) relates to this as well (Dean, 2002).

Alle bisherigen Versuche, sich uber das Recht klar zu werden, sind daran
gescheitert, daß nicht von der Ordnung in den Verbänden, sondern von
den Rechtssätzen ausgegangen worden ist.

[The inner order of human society is not only the original but, even in
our time, the basic, form of law. A formal legal rule not only arises much
later, it is still also today largely derived from the inner order of society. To
understand the origins, the development and the nature of law one must
therefore research above all the order of societies. All attempts so far to
understand law have failed because they did not start from the order of
societies but from formal legal rules.]

Ehrlich (1913: 44) similarly insisted that legal institutions did not simply
depend on legal norms:

Es ist nicht richtig, daß die Rechtseinrichtungen ausschließlich auf den
Rechtsnormen beruhen. Sittlichkeit, Religion, Sitte, Anstand, Takt, ja sogar
guter Ton und Mode ordnen nicht bloß die außerrechtlichen Beziehungen,
sie greifen auf Schritt und Tritt auch in das Rechtsgebiet ein. Kein einziger
der rechtlichen Verbände könnte allein durch Rechtsnormen bestehen, sie
bedürfen fortwährend der Unterstützung außerrechtlicher Normen, die
ihre Kraft verdoppeln und ergänzen.

[It is incorrect to assume that the institutions of the law are exclusively based
on legal norms. Ethics, religion, custom, morality, tact, even good style and
fashion do not only order extra-legal relationships, they also intrude with
every step into the legal arena. Not a single legal order could exclusively
exist simply through legal norms, they require at all times the support of
extra-legal norms which would double and supplement their strength.]

From this analysis, Ehrlich (1913: 399) begins to introduce his concept of the
'living law':

Das lebende Recht ist das nicht in Rechtssätzen festgelegte Recht, das aber
doch das Leben beherrscht. Die Quellen seiner Erkenntnis sind vor allem die
moderne Urkunde, aber auch die unmittelbare Beobachtung des Lebens,
des Handels und Wandels, der Gewohnheiten und Gebräuche, dann aber
aller Verbände sowohl der rechtlich anerkannten als auch der von dem
Rechte übersehenen und übergangenen, ja sogar der rechtlich mißbilligten.

[The living law is law which is not fixed in legal statements and yet dominates
life. The sources of its knowledge are above all modern legal documents, but
also the direct observation of life, of trade and other activities, of habits and
customs, and of all organisations, those which are legally acknowledged as
well as those which have been overlooked or marginalised, even the legally
disapproved ones.]

Ehrlich here emphasises how law 'is distilled out of the interplay of social
forces' (Freeman, 2001: 671). Arguing that research on actual contracts between

people would give the clearest picture of socio-legal reality, Ehrlich (1913: 401) continued:

> Lebendes Recht ist vom Urkundeninhalte nicht das, was etwa die Gerichte bei der Entscheidung eines Rechtsstreites als verbindlich anerkennen, sondern nur das, woran sich die Parteien im Leben halten.

> [Living law according to the contents of legal documents is not what the courts recognise as legally binding when they decide a case, but only that which the parties live by.]

This is much more radical than many writers have realised, because there is a tendency to view Ehrlich's 'living law' just as an equivalent of 'the actual law'. What Ehrlich meant, in a deeper sense, is that all law as 'living law' is a complex amalgam of rules laid down as official law *and* social and other norms that affect their operation. 'Living law' is thus never just 'custom' or the law as officially laid down by the state, but the law as lived and applied by people in different life situations as an amalgam. If what people do in such life situations is officially recognised as 'law', then it becomes Chiba's (1986) 'official law', but much of Ehrlich's 'living law' appears to remain under the ambit of Chiba's (1986) 'unofficial law' (section 2.5.4 below).

The effect of Ehrlich's theory was to encourage jurists to emerge 'from the ivory tower of analytical jurisprudence' (Dias and Hughes, 1957: 423) and to test law against real life. By minimising the differences between law and other norms of social control, and placing the state and its attempts at legal regulation on a distinctly lower footing than positivists, Ehrlich developed a socio-legal approach akin to legal pluralism, which continues to make many lawyers feel uncomfortable because it challenges the assumed power of positivist law-making.[42]

Not surprisingly, there have been fierce criticisms of Ehrlich's approach. First, it has been said that his theory 'does not attach sufficient weight to the way in which formal law itself influences and reforms the practices of society' (Dias and Hughes, 1957: 423–4). That criticism could be made against anyone who did not adopt a predominantly positivist approach, but it raises an important analytical point about Ehrlich's failure to evaluate theoretically and empirically the extent to which informal and formal laws interact and in what ways one may supersede the other.

---

[42] This is clearly reflected in the subtle criticism in Freeman (2001: 672) of Ehrlich's failure to appreciate the significant influence of state law. Ehrlich may have 'unduly belittled the primary role of legislation in creating new law (p. 672), but if a reminder of the importance of social norms in relation to law irks lawyers, it shows that they remain sensitive to challenges of the supposed supremacy of law. A reference to the educative function of law is neither here nor there, since society also has educative functions, and the two processes may conflict.

A second criticism questions Ehrlich's approach to custom, alleging that he confused the position of custom as a source of law with custom as a type of law (Friedmann, 1947: 182). Ehrlich's 'living law', however, is clearly not the same as 'custom'. The main argument of such critics is that in modern societies custom is less and less a source of law and that Ehrlich's approach therefore gave it too much importance. Ehrlich would not have agreed, since he clearly saw that custom could also recreate itself in the presence of state law and creates new customs based on (or influenced by) state law. While he did not explain that aspect well enough, the main point of Ehrlich's theoretical approach remains that, even in the presence of state law, people's norms would not automatically become defunct and they would modify the law made by the law-giver into 'living law'. Further issues are raised when in today's globalised world new migrant communities settle in the midst of 'natives' (chapter 1, section 1.3 above). Ehrlich's approach within a global perspective would certainly have been to the effect that hybrid ethnic minority customs, existing in social reality, were equivalent to 'law' and should be studied as a form of 'living law'.[43]

Dias and Hughes (1957: 424) attempted to argue that Ehrlich's approach was outmoded and might in fact be 'much more true of primitive society than it is of society to-day', since the modern state has taken on a more prominent role-making function. However, as Chiba (1986) and others confirm for the late twentieth century, Ehrlich's theoretical approach has lost none of its relevance. Since official law cannot, in social reality, ever exclude the presence of unofficial laws and legal postulates, Ehrlich's 'living law' is present in Chiba's model of legal pluralism and is integral to a globally focused legal analysis.[44] A further criticism of Ehrlich's approach (Dias and Hughes, 1957: 424–5) involves a general challenge to legal pluralism and seeks to defend the typical lawyers' legocentric approach:

> Finally, Ehrlich is guilty of the same confusing tendency as Duguit in that he fails to offer any sharp distinction between the legal norm and other social norms . . . To recognize that the rules of a system of law must be studied in their social context, that they are meaningless outside that context, is of the utmost benefit to jurisprudence; but to allow the legal norms to be

---

[43] The emergence of British Muslim law as *angrezi shariat* (Pearl and Menski, 1998) applies and proves Ehrlich's theory of 'living law'. Glenn (2000: 152) also recognises this, writing that 'while the formal restrictions on the use of foreign sources continue largely to prevail in Europe, notably in France, recent detective work has shown that the comparisons are made anyway, behind the scenes'.

[44] Hooker (1975: 3–4) struggles with this issue and sees one reason for the emergence of legal pluralism in the process of legal transplantation, where 'the original system is by no means displaced in whole or in part by the introduced law' (p. 3), but he maintains the positivist claim that the national legal system 'is politically superior to the extent of being able to abolish the indigenous system(s)' (p. 4). Chiba (1989: 42) correctly notes that Hooker remained a captive of Western model jurisprudence.

submerged and lost in the background of their social context can only be
the death of the separate discipline of jurisprudence.

This anticipates more recent mocking of pluralist methodology that declares
all non-law to be equal to law as an absurd folly,[45] while legal pluralists now
argue that the plural nature of law itself is a fact (Griffiths, 1986; Woodman,
1998) and will not go away. As Griffiths (2002: 307) suggests, '[t]he difficulty
is that legal pluralism rejects a definition of state law which is limited to state
law'. But whose difficulty is this? For a globally focused jurisprudence, such
pluralising elements of legal analysis are important basic building blocks that
cannot be pushed over by narrowly theorising 'law' and insisting on statist
axioms. If lawyers resent that 'their' academic patch is being invaded by other
disciplines, while even state law is shown to be polycentric (Petersen and Zahle,
1995), a constructive reaction should be to educate lawyers better about those
areas of study which potentially encroach on jurisprudence. Clearly, there is a
need to cultivate appropriate interdisciplinary legal approaches similar to those
of Ehrlich (Cotterrell, 2002).

2.4 Reluctant pluralism: Hart's primary and secondary rules

H. L. A. Hart (1907–92), in his major work, *The concept of law* (1961; 1994),
engaged in deep theoretical discussions about law as one of the leading proponents of legal positivism. While he claimed to combine the methods of analytical positivism with social reality, he insisted that law was first and foremost
a matter for lawyers. He described his theory, in response to critics, as 'soft
positivism' (Hart, 1994: 250). He opposed the claims of Austinian positivism
as a sufficiently sophisticated model for conceptualising the complexities of
law and emphasised the multiplicity of law.[46] However, his 'subtle joinder of
formal and informal positivism', according to Glenn (2000: 140), 'has given still
more bite to the idea of positive law', since the power of law seems to derive
from its existence as a fact. To Hart, legal analysis involved an intricate combination of rule-focused enquiry, combined with an understanding of how the
social players in any given group perceive the relevant rule systems and how
they negotiate and apply it. Hart (1961: 55) called this the 'internal aspect'
of rules, which forces the legal analyst inevitably into the position of a social
analyst. According to Hart, law cannot be studied and understood like a natural
science, since it is a human construct, designed to fulfil human needs, which
always involves (and thus also depends upon) human participation. Bix (1996:
42) explains this further:

---

[45] See Tamanaha (1993) and reflections of this approach in Freeman (2001: 672). For a
critique, see Griffiths (2002: 306–7) and Woodman (1998: 44–5).

[46] Bix (1996: 40). Morrison (1997: vii and 6) suggests that Hart's portrayal of Austinian
positivism was merely a convenient caricature of the previous position.

The idea is that one cannot understand a social system unless one understands how the people who created the system or who participate in the system perceive it. This 'hermeneutic' approach – that is, giving priority to trying to understand how other people perceive their situation – is always in tension with those who want social theory to be more scientific.

By saying that all legal norms have social relevance, and must be understood within their social context, Hart came rather close to accepting the position of legal pluralists. However, his concern with conceptualising law, rather than socio-legal theory, made him retreat from this position. Despite the merits of his hermeneutic methodology, Hart's reluctance to abandon the legal positivist emphasis is particularly evident from two aspects of his work. First, his assumptions about primitive societies, which remain in need of critique.[47] Although Hart, in his attack on the inherent flaws of the command theory of law, does not accept conceptualising law simply as formal legal regulations laid down by a sovereign, he subscribes to the misguided assumption that primitive societies are pre-legal because they do not have enough formal legal rules. Hart (1961: 4) explicitly declares that certain types of primitive law differ from Western rule-fixated conceptualisations of law and says that 'it is their deviation in these respects from the standard case which makes their classification appear questionable. There is no mystery about this.' Hart struggles in this debate, like many others, with the ultimate question whether simple or 'primitive' societies have law. His division of rules into different categories reflects this endeavour. In essence, he works on the assumption that certain people did not (and still do not) have law.

Secondly, linked to the above, in attempting a critique of the Austinian command theory, Hart's (1961: 78–9) proposed interaction between primary and secondary rules reinforces eurocentric positivism. He emphasised the critical position of rules in a legal system and distinguished between these two different types:[48]

> Under rules of the one type, which may well be considered the basic or primary type, human beings are required to do or abstain from certain actions, whether they wish to or not. Rules of the other type are in a sense parasitic upon or secondary to the first; for they provide that human beings may by doing or saying certain things introduce new rules of the primary type, extinguish or modify old ones, or in various ways determine their incidence or control their operations. Rules of the first type impose duties; rules of the second type confer powers, public or private. Rules of the first type concern

---

[47] See Twining (2000: 63) on Hart's understanding of 'primitive' societies, which even today does not strike many lawyers as unacceptable.

[48] Anleu (2000: 6) summarises this well: 'Hart (1961) analyses the law in terms of primary rules, which he terms rules of obligation, and secondary rules, which are the rules about rules, such as rules of recognition and adjudication. Thus, he makes a distinction between duty-imposing and power-conferring rules.'

actions involving physical movement or changes; rules of the second type provide for operations which lead not merely to physical movement or change, but to the creation or variation of duties or obligations.

While he discusses customs, Hart (1961: 89) explains that there must be some primary rules in any society, because otherwise there would be total chaos and such a society could not survive. In Hart's scheme of law, however, for proper 'law' to exist, there is a need for more complex legal regulation, 'secondary rules' in his terminology, whose main purpose is to regulate processes of law and to confer legal power. Harris (1980: 106) reinforced this evolutionist approach, claiming that '[t]heir introduction represents a step from the pre-legal to a legal world'. Hart argued that there is a need for secondary rules because simple primary rules, based on ties of kinship, common sentiment and belief in a stable environment, are unable to cope with crises and the increasing complexity of a larger society. He claimed that primary rules suffer from uncertainty, are static in character, and are inefficient in that they fail to punish deviance fast and effectively. Turning to the first weakness, Hart (1961: 90) argued that the uncertain nature of primary rules arises because 'the rules by which the group lives will not form a system, but will simply be a set of separate standards'. More importantly, asserted Hart (1961: 90):

> Hence if doubts arise as to what the rules are or as to the precise role of some given rule, there will be no procedure for settling this doubt, either by reference to an authoritative text or to an official whose declarations on this point are authoritative. For, plainly, such a procedure and the acknowledgement of either authoritative text or persons involve the existence of rules of a type different from the rules of obligation or duty which *ex hypothesi* are all that the group has.

This is totally hypothetical indeed, since Hart here claims that certain groups of 'primitive' people, either in the distant past, or probably in Asia or Africa today, have simply not developed methods of clarifying doubts about any of their rules. Turning to the static character of primary rules as a key defect, Hart (1961: 90) wrote:

> The only mode of change in the rules known to such a society will be the slow process of growth . . . and the converse process of decay . . . There will be no means, in such a society, of deliberately adapting the rules to changing circumstances, either by eliminating old rules or introducing new ones: for, again, the possibility of doing this presupposes the existence of rules of a different type from the primary rules of obligation by which alone the society lives. In an extreme case the rules may be static in a more drastic sense.

Hart here hypothesised that such an assumed 'primitive' society has no means of developing elaborate rules from within.[49] When it comes to the third defect,

---

[49] However, in his posthumous 'Postscript', Hart (1994: 272–6) indicated that even in developed legal systems there may be situations where cases may be unregulated and judges may have to exercise discretion, a position which he vigorously defended.

Hart (1961: 91) was similarly negative about the self-healing powers of the simple society he had in mind:

> The third defect of this simple form of social life is the *inefficiency* of the diffuse social pressure by which the rules are maintained. Disputes as to whether an admitted rule has or has not been violated will always occur and will, in any but the smallest societies, continue interminably, if there is no agency specially empowered to ascertain finally, and authoritatively, the fact of violation. Lack of such final and authoritative determinations is to be distinguished from another weakness associated with it. This is the fact that punishments for violations of the rules, and other forms of social pressure involving physical effort or the use of force, are not administered by a special agency but are left to the individuals affected or to the group at large. It is obvious that the waste of time involved in the group's unorganized efforts to catch and punish offenders, and the smouldering vendettas which may result from self help in the absence of an official monopoly of 'sanctions', may be serious.

Hart (1961: 91) further wrote that '[t]he remedy for each of these three main defects in this simplest form of social structure consists in supplementing the *primary* rules of obligation with *secondary* rules' and he proceeded to discuss those remedies in detail.[50] Hart (1961: 95) concluded that his model, the combination of primary rules and secondary rules, thus truly encapsulates the nature of a legal system. Assuming lack of socio-legal development in 'primitive' environments, he denied that all societies could have law in this sense. Hart therefore failed to offer a globally valid definition of 'law' or 'legal system'. While his concept of the primary and secondary rules and their interaction produces useful categories, his method excludes from the ambit of law certain rule systems that many states and societies in Asia and Africa would recognise as legal. On the other hand, there is much merit in Hart's (1961: 113) emphasis of the inherently social character of law:

> There are therefore two minimum conditions necessary and sufficient for the existence of a legal system. On the one hand those rules of behaviour which are valid according to the system's ultimate criteria of validity must be generally obeyed, and, on the other hand, its rules of recognition specifying the criteria of legal validity and its rules of change and adjudication must be effectively accepted as common public standards of official behaviour by its officials.

It is not clear to what extent Hart envisaged that ordinary citizens, rather than officials, would need to underwrite both types of rules. Hart (1961: 113) notes this duality, but seems to suggest that the approval and activity of officials is the crucial element. But what if, by the inherent rules of 'primitive' societies, *any*

---

[50] Allott (1980: 49–67) discussed the imagined deficiencies raised by Hart.

member can exercise the functions of Hart's imagined official? This possibility is clearly disregarded by Hart's theorising.

Quite how to read Hart's legal philosophy has been debated by innumerable critics.[51] Did he merely say that legal rules were a species of social rule, given that social rules are ubiquitous? Hart indicated that 'rules are members of a legal system if, but only if, they meet the criteria laid down by the rule of recognition' (Harris, 1980: 109). Hart (1994: 261) seems to have accepted that both 'rules' and 'principles' are open categories but his analysis of the nature of law and legal systems remains a theoretical model. Allott (1980: 52) argued that Hart's approach 'would clearly and swiftly lead to an unacceptable paradox: a society which is completely law-abiding, and indeed so law-abiding that there are no occasions for argument as to what is the relevant norm in any particular circumstance, would be deemed to be anarchical and lawless!'[52] Another criticism has been the extent to which Hart's thesis of legal systems relies on anthropological work (Harris, 1980: 111). Did Hart just provide and apply a picture of linear historical development? If so, his model is simply flawed by the assumption that so-called 'primitive' societies do not have secondary rules and therefore lack the key elements of law.

It seems, therefore, that Hart's model is misguided in hypothesising about the nature of law in human society worldwide. Hart's (1961: 244) comment that '[f]ew societies have existed in which legislative and adjudicative organs and centrally organized sanctions were all entirely lacking', should not go uncommented. Hart here posits, in purely speculative form, that certain human societies indeed did not have law. What Hart (1961: 90) called 'unofficial rules', which he clearly saw as 'a simple form of social control', did not qualify as law in his scheme. It appears that this is so because his own positivist assumptions about the nature of law came in the way, so that he expected to see tangible forms of rules and, more specifically, 'secondary rules'. Rather than 'wasting time', as Hart imagined,[53] in the business of self-cleansing of a small community and its legal system, it may be argued that the simple social process of discussing matters, preferably under shady trees than in stuffy courtrooms, may constitute the secondary rules that Hart did not notice in his imagined simple society. Therefore, especially with reference to Asia and Africa, as well as

---

[51] Foremost among them are Lon Fuller and Ronald Dworkin. Bix (1996: 28) suggests that 'the conceptual "debates" in legal theory – debates about how the concepts are best defined – are often best understood as talking past one another'. Twining (2000: 24–5) seems almost dismissive: 'These "debates" can mostly be read as a series of family squabbles with strong Oedipal overtones within English legal positivism.'

[52] Allott (1980: 52) argued against Hart that every society empirically known, however small, seemed to have the elements that Hart imagined to be absent. Allott's conclusion was that '[w]e are playing, then, with definition rather than with substance'.

[53] Hart (1961: 91) speaks critically of 'the *inefficiency* of the diffuse social pressure by which the rules are maintained'.

all chthonic systems, Hart's theory fails to include the conceptually challenging informal legal realities of laws in Asia and Africa. His model of the interaction of primary and secondary rules is, at the end of the day, a model of universal application which appears in endless local, regional and national variations, but it tells us nothing about law itself. Allott (1980: 67) concluded on the subject:

> The case against customary *Laws* and against the existence or efficacy of legal norms in small societies is not made out. The smallness of a society does not limit either the existence or the effectiveness of *Law*, though the smaller and simpler the society, the less *Law* there will have to be.

Twining (2000: 53–4) notes that Hart's efforts to revive the study of jurisprudence during the 1950s succeeded in shifting emphasis towards general jurisprudence, but Hart did not apply his modernist methods fully enough to important sociological concepts. Thus, he perpetuated the failure of mainstream legal theory to address problems of cultural pluralism in relation to law.

2.5 Postmodern theories of legal pluralism

While it is arguable that clear boundaries between 'modern' and 'postmodern' theories cannot always be drawn, the four major writers discussed in this section go much further than Hart (1961; 1994) and share perspectives which clearly identify law as embedded in its respective socio-cultural context, taking many different forms. These writers raise the spectre of lawyers having to work on matters not normally seen as 'legal', a boundary that Hart was not willing to cross. This crossing would appear to be an unavoidable occupational hazard for lawyers engaged in plurality-focused, globality-conscious legal theory when it comes to fully understanding legal pluralism.[54]

We noted earlier that Hooker (1975) was one of the first scholars to tackle legal pluralism but remained far too cautious, too closely wedded to positivist jurisprudence. His basic distinction of 'weak' and 'strong' legal pluralism, which seemed so attractive at the time, was subsequently criticised as a meaningless effort, because both types remain dependent on state sanction and are merely different types of positivist, official law (Griffiths, 1986; Chiba, 1986; Griffiths, 2002). Still, his work remains an immensely useful study, with excellent material on legal transplants and the reception of laws by many countries in Asia and Africa from European, mainly colonial, powers and it shows that the author was well aware of the importance of social factors in relation to law. In the preface, Hooker (1975: vii) portrays legal pluralism as an important form of

---

[54] For excellent discussions of various approaches to legal pluralism and bibliographical details, see Woodman (1998) and Griffiths (2002).

comparative law and indicates his plan to discuss the origins of modern forms of pluralism. He then shows that he was a pluralist at heart, but a positivist by training:

> The fact is that, despite political and economic pressures, pluralism has shown an amazing vitality as a working system. It may well be that it – and not some imposed unity – should be the proper goal of a national legal system. Indeed, even within developed nations themselves, there are signs that a plurality of law is no longer regarded with quite the abhorrence common a decade ago.

Re-reading this almost thirty years later, having closely worked with Hooker during the early 1980s, it is evident that his study focused rather too much on the impact of legal transplants and colonial imposition of laws, in a post-colonial spirit influenced by modernist agenda. While I agree with the fierce, yet sympathetic critique by Chiba (1989: 41–3), who praises his achievements as a scholar of pluralism while portraying him as restricted by his reliance on traditional Western jurisprudence, Hooker was a pioneer in suggesting that there was more to study for lawyers than official state law. The main distinction between him and the four scholars discussed below is that Hooker remained chained to statist concepts of law, whereas postmodern pluralist approaches take more specific account of the polycentric nature of law.[55]

2.5.1 Moore's concept of the 'semi-autonomous' social field

An influential article by this American legal anthropologist on 'Law and anthropology', originally published in 1970 and reprinted in Moore (1978: 214–56), expressed disquiet with legal studies which treated legal rules as though they could be divorced from their respective historical and social environment. Moore (1978: 214–15) laid out her own project:

> Examining different approaches to the classification of legal systems may give us some idea of the magnitude of law as a subject, and of the ways in which anthropologists have perceived the field as a whole. No society is without law; *ergo*, there is no society outside the purview of the 'legal anthropologist.' It is not merely difficult but virtually impossible to control the full range of the available ethnographic information. Every good ethnographic description contains a great deal of legal material, whether or not it is explicitly called 'law' . . . Not only does every society have law, but virtually all significant social institutions also have a legal aspect. This means that to master the whole legal system of one society, procedural and substantive, one must master the whole institutional system of that

---

[55] The precise nature of this process remains debated and contested. For details see succinctly Griffiths (2002) with reference particularly to the work of Merry, von Benda-Beckmann and Woodman.

society – from citizenship and political place to property and economic relations, from birth to death, and from dispute to peaceful transaction.

Moore (1978: 215) shows that she was aware of the potential for taking quite different approaches in the endeavour to understand law in society, distinguishing the methods of the anthropologist from those of the comparative lawyer. The special contribution of the anthropologist's point of view lies in the tendency 'to see the legal system as part of a wider social milieu' (p. 215). She notes that, since different anthropologists use their own criteria for defining society, they also disagree in their approaches to legal systems. Moore (1978: 215–18) outlines that there have been basically three analytical approaches, all of which share the underlying premise that 'there is an intimate relation between law and society, that law is part of social life in general and must be treated analytically as such' (Moore, 1978: 218). The pioneering work of Bronislaw Malinowski (1926) proved influential for the academic study of law, as Moore (1978: 218–19) explains:

> With a few bold strokes Malinowski told the world his idea of what law was, why people obeyed it when they did, and why, sometimes, they did not. Malinowski was indignant about theories of primitive law like Hartland's (1924), which asserted that primitive man automatically obeyed the customs of his tribe because he was absolutely bound by tradition. Malinowski was little concerned with prohibitions and sanctions, but instead was struck by the positive inducements to conformity to be found in reciprocal obligations, complementary rights, and good reputation. He perceived the social and economic stake of the man who wished to remain in good standing among his fellows as the dynamic force behind the performance of obligations. But if the law is so much the stuff of ordinary social life that it is embodied in all binding obligations, then nothing but a full account of social relations in a society will adequately 'explain' the content and working of its law. In a way, this is quite true, and is continuously being rediscovered.

Malinowski's society-focused work was published when endless debates were going on over whether law even existed in primitive societies. Moore (1978: 219) shows how more recent studies on 'primitive law' have treated the subject as though it had no relevance for the present. Such distortions of perspective, due to general assumptions about modernisation and development, have created their own problems for legal studies. Moore (1978: 219–20) criticises that many recent studies on jurisprudence:

> [T]reat the law of technologically simple societies as the historical or typological precursor of modern law – as an early stage subsequently replaced by that supposed apogee of excellence, the Western European tradition, or perhaps still better, the Anglo-American tradition. The law of pre-industrial society is not examined to see whether it operates on sociological principles

that apply equally well to some aspects of social control in industrial society. On the contrary, it is treated as a phenomenon that has been superseded, rendered obsolete by later improvements.

The assumption that earlier laws will simply be replaced over time and will disappear was even criticised by David and Brierley (1978: 26), who saw such views as evidence of 'a rather naïve sense of superiority' which 'does not acknowledge an observable reality in the modern world'. Moore (1978: 220) notes that Malinowski's work 'was received only to be placed in a very narrow niche reserved essentially for exotica and historical background, rather than being understood as something that might have theoretical relevance to the present'. Moore (1978: 2) emphasised the limits of legal regulation in a social context, criticising legal centralism, in a manner close to Ehrlich:

> Ordinary experience indicates that law and legal institutions can only effect a degree of intentional control of society, greater at some times and less at others, or more with regard to some matters than others. That limited degree of control and predictability is daily inflated in the folk models of lawyers and politicians all over the world.

As a result, we can at best talk of partial legal control, with the law being subject, in terms of effectiveness, to many non-legal factors. Moore (1978: 3) wrote that we are therefore at best 'dealing with *partial* order and *partial* control of social life by rules', and that an approach to legal studies that focuses on compliance with rules 'reduces the colorful hurlyburly of social life and the dynamic logic it has for the actors' (p. 3) to such an extent that we overlook the social rules that operate within a particular society. Evidently, realisation of such analytical limits has important consequences for law-making, too. Moore (1978: 4) points out:

> A central concern of any rule-maker should be the identification of those social processes which operate outside the rules, or which cause people to use rules, or abandon them, bend them, reinterpret them, sidestep them, or replace them. To recognize that such processes are inescapable aspects of the use of rule-systems and to try to understand as much as possible about the conditions of their operation would probably be far more effective than taking the view that such activities might be fully controlled simply by tighter drafting of 'loophole-less' legislation. Social transactions usually take place in the service of objectives to which legal rules are merely ancillary shapers, enablers, or impediments. Conformity to the rules is seldom in itself the central objective.

Legislation is here depicted as piecemeal legal intervention, not as a simple means to create order and to dominate a society top-down. Moore (1978: 9) explicitly commented on this:

> The piecemeal quality of intentional legal intervention, whether legislative, executive or judicial, is due to its construction as a response to particular

circumstances at particular moments. The accretion of many such responses over time makes for a composite, unplanned total result. Even though, at various times and places, there have been attempts to codify everything once and for all, in the long term all legal 'systems' are built by accretion, not by total systematic planning.

Legislation is, then, only one part of legal regulation.[56] Moore (1978: 29) wrote that 'the law of the central state is but one kind of reglementation emanating from one kind of organization', and concluded therefore that, over time, control through legal regulation remains necessarily incomplete. Since the consequences of legal regulation are never fully predictable, any legal analyst would at best study how partial ordering systems and partial controls operate in specific social contexts. Moore's work as a legal pluralist, ready to see that law and legal regulation manifest themselves in many different ways and that the official law is never the only legal force in any given social field, has been seminal, particularly her concept of the 'semi-autonomous social field'. Arguing that there is a certain fallacy in assuming that law alone controls society, and stipulating the possibility that 'it is society that controls law and not the reverse' (Moore, 1978: 55), she emphasises that '[l]aw and the social context in which it operates must be inspected together' (p. 55). Focus on the semi-autonomous social field is therefore an appropriate methodological tool to understand the operation of law in society (pp. 55–6):

> The semi-autonomous social field has rule-making capacities, and the means to induce or coerce compliance; but it is simultaneously set in a larger social matrix which can, and does, affect and invade it, sometimes at the invitation of persons inside it, sometimes at its own instance. The analytic problem of fields of autonomy exists in tribal society, but it is an even more central analytic issue in the social anthropology of complex societies. All the nation-states of the world, new and old, are complex societies in that sense. The analytic problem is ubiquitous.

This definition is further elaborated when Moore (1978: 57–8) emphasises that the semi-autonomous social field and its boundaries are not only identified through organisational structures but also by processual characteristics, in particular the fact that such social fields can generate their own rules and will then expect more or less strict compliance with them. Since complex societies are made up of many semi-autonomous social fields, the anthropologist needs to study also the interactions between such fields, a methodology further developed by Chiba's (1986) concept of constant interaction between official and unofficial laws and legal postulates (section 2.5.4 below).

---

[56] Customary laws, as more recent writing from South Africa explicitly acknowledges, remain part of the present, they are 'at one and the same time, both young and old' (Bennett, 2004: 2).

For comparative legal analysis, this image of interconnecting social fields means that what lawyers normally define as 'law' is far too imprecise. Moore's seminal work shows that, in any given legal system, a variety of sub-systems exercise limited autonomy in the construction and application of socio-legal norms. An understanding of law that is narrowly focused on state law and on national legal systems is therefore too rigid, insufficient particularly for understanding how Asian and African legal systems operate. Lawyers do not have to study anthropology to make sense of what Moore is arguing, but legal scholarship needs to take account of social facts and factors more explicitly than has so far been done (Cotterrell, 2002). Indeed, many scholars have taken account of Moore's work.

2.5.2 Allott's three perspectives on law

Approaching the study of law from a wide comparative perspective with an African flavour, Allott (1980: 1–44) considered in detail the limits of law and introduced three different typographical forms of the word 'law' to pinpoint important aspects of the concept which are not normally thought about. This strategy may be seen as 'relatively unambitious' (Bix, 1996: 29), since it only makes claims about the way we use language (Bix, 1996: 10), but Allott extended this debate to consider legal pluralism. Allott (1980: 1) argued that we need to be aware that law can be understood in at least three different ways. First, there is its metaphysical understanding as an abstraction; secondly, the social understanding of law in terms of its function as a legal system; and, thirdly, the linguistic understanding of law. To reduce the linguistic confusions about the English term 'law', Allott (1980: 2) proposed three different forms of typography:

LAW = the general idea or concept of legal institutions abstracted from any particular occurrence of them

Law = a coherent, total, particular legal system prevailing in a given community or country

law = a particular normative provision of a *Law*; a rule or norm of a given legal system.

Stating that *Law* and law are certainly more easily understood than LAW, which seems to have been debated much more than the others, Allott (1980: 2–5) first considered in detail what is meant by LAW and emphasised the idiosyncratic nature of the three concepts:

> LAW by definition is an *abstraction* from reality, from particular *Laws* or laws . . . There is no way in which one can dissect the abstraction and expose the essence at its core . . .
>
> Abstractions therefore are idiosyncratic. But, since their use is not only in analysis but in communication with others, I must so use the abstraction as to convey some meaning to my hearers. It may not be the same meaning,

as I may well discover on further investigation of what they have received, and what *they* perceive (p. 2).

Thus, continued Allott (1980: 2), what those three types of law mean to us is clearly a matter of individual choice, 'but if our usage diverges too far from what other people do and is thereby unintelligible or unacceptable to others, our communication fails'. Allott (1980: 3) therefore explained that we should not immediately look for a general or universally valid definition of LAW:

> Because LAW is an abstraction from particular *Laws*, it is useless to attempt to define it or elucidate its abstract and general meaning before looking at the particular on which it rests. We must therefore start with the particular = the actual legal systems or *Laws*. There is an analogy here with LANGUAGE, which is an abstraction from natural or actual *Languages*. Linguistic studies must start with, and be anchored in, the actual *Languages* used.

Allott argued in effect that taking a universalist natural law perspective would be less productive than a socio-legal approach to legal theory. Debating assumptions about the universality of law, Allott (1980: 18) identified a popular tendency to be misled, so that 'LAW is thought of as of universal application, because the laws of nature or physical laws are by definition without exception'. Given that all scientific laws are universal, a confusion of categories occurred when the images of physical laws and their regularity were transposed to legal images. Allott (1980: 19) concluded that '[t]here was thus an illegitimate corruption of (juristic) *Laws* and laws as terms to be used in the analysis of legal systems'.

Analysing the concept of *Law*, Allott (1980: 3) had already said, while discussing LAW, that '*[l]aws* or actual legal systems are a social reality. A given society will continue to think about it. *Law* . . . has abstract qualities as well as a concrete substrate. Its perception as a system, and the extent of the phenomena covered by that system, depend on a process of abstraction by an observer.' Searching specifically for a definition of *Law*, Allott (1980: 5) wrote that '[a] *Law* or "legal system" is a *system of communication*. That is, it is a member of the same super-genus as a Language. The features of a *Law* are thus the same as those of any communication system.' Allott (1980: 9–12) explored this in a technical sense, showing that one can understand and treat law as a complex system of communication, with an emitter and recipients, a code and a message – and the possibility of massive, multiple failures of communication. Regarding this complex process of communication, Allott (1980: 9) emphasised:

> The ordinary subject of a *Law* in a society perceives and receives, not *Law*, but laws, i.e. norms which purport to guide his behaviour. Who emits these laws or norms? Western jurists of the positivist school, Austin and after, would answer: the determinate sovereign in that society. Verbal contortions

> have to be performed to identify such a sovereign in a federal state, in a diarchy, or in a society ruled by customary *Law*. The effort is not worthwhile; the 'sovereign' is a lay figure manipulated by the analyst, a construct.
>
> If we start at the opposite end, and consider an act of legal communication in a real society, preferably one devoid of lawyers and jurists, the recipient of the normative statement perceives that it is transmitted to him by the fellow-members of his society generally . . . whether or not they are in authority over him; by those who are recognised as official spokesmen or enunciators of the norms, such as judges or other members of courts, arbiters, diviners, oracles, priests. Most of the normative statements are *transmitted*, not *originated*, by the emitter/enunciator. In other words, the emitter of the norm does not claim to be its originator; the people say that they are quite literally transmitting or handing on the customs of the ancestors . . . In fewer cases the emitter will himself (or themselves collectively) be and claim to be the originator of the norm.

This totally opposes legal positivism and its assumption that someone 'in authority' may just make laws for others, which then have to be obeyed. Allott (1980: 10) pointed out that norms do not have to be precisely articulated to affect behaviour. While the act of articulation is important to the recipient, 'what matters is whether he thinks he has received a normative message. If he conforms his conduct to it, and sufficient of his fellows do likewise, then when a context arises in which a norm might be articulated to cover the case, there is a likelihood that the articulated norm will reflect the inarticulate assumption' (p. 10). While in earlier societies, there may be little material evidence of such transmission of norms, as a society develops, 'specialist transmitters and workers-over of norms' appear (p. 10). Still, their involvement does not simply mean that the emitters of norms are automatically effective law-makers. Allott (1980: 10) argued that '[m]ost societies empirically known include persons who are or hold themselves out to be, or are recognised by the society as being, special authorities in the handling of normative statements'. For example, in African customary laws, spokespersons or enunciators of norms and skilled judicial experts were recognised and had important functions.

Allott (1980: 10–11) showed that law-making, even in the modern world, does not ultimately depend on the involvement of legal professionals – not a popular message for lawyers. His view that the all-important people in legal communication are the recipients of the messages, not the senders, indicates Allott's endorsement of Ehrlich's 'living law'. Although lawyers tend to consider themselves important, since they 'make' the law, while common people 'receive' the law, apply it and follow it, *Law* as a set of communication only achieves its purpose if it affects human behaviour. Allott (1980: 11) showed that the nature of communication itself is such that nobody can receive a message fully and precisely as transmitted, so that multiple deficiencies of communication are bound to occur. Since *Law* can be defined as a system of communication and the function of all kinds of institutions, Allott (1980. 8) depicted legal systems as manifestations of human relationships, since there are real people behind the institutions that make up the *Law*:

> A policeman is tangible. But when we say that the police are one institution of the *Law*, we mean that the *Law* has created or recognised them as an institution. The body of men who are police are only an institution of the *Law* to the extent that they carry out the function or role attributed to them by the *Law* . . .
>
> Similarly with relationships functioning as institutions of the *Law*. The *Law* can take an existing relationship, e.g. the family group, and recognise or define it as a legal institution. Or the *Law* can invent an institution, which, though it has some physical connexions or implications (without these it could not operate in the real world), is an abstraction: a limited liability company springs to mind. All relationships defined as legal institutions are thus abstract with real connections.

Next, Allott (1980: 8–9) discussed the normative character of legal systems, touching on the important distinction between 'is' and 'ought'. He concluded that *Law* both is, and is not, a fact. It is not the case in all human societies that norms have to be articulated to be obeyed. In other words, there may be a *Law* in existence which is totally invisible but operates as an unwritten norm system in a given society. Based on his deep exposure to African legal systems, often simple societies which many scholars have declared to be 'without law', Allott (1980: 9) found that while 'a *Law* or legal system is a *fact*, in the sense that the existence of legal systems is open to experimental observation and confirmation', at the same time it 'is *not a fact*, in that its laws/rules/norms do not describe what has happened, but prescribe what is to happen, and which in fact need not happen' (p. 9). To Allott, therefore, a *Law* is neither a sociological statement of fact nor purely theoretical, nor is it a complete system of control, because the examination of *Laws* in simpler societies would easily show that 'legal norms are not necessarily obeyed because they have physical force lurking behind them' (p. 9).

The final element of Allott's tripartite model refers to law as a single rule or norm. Allott (1980: 16) demonstrated that norms may include rules, principles and policies, as well as legal institutions and processes. Allott (1980: 16–17) distinguished a binding norm from an empirically observed form of behaviour by demonstrating that the daily streams of commuters in central London may well show a habitual, customary pattern of behaviour, but it would be wrong to see this as a binding norm, because such patterns are not based on a command. Normative statements expressed in the imperative are more than simple commands. Allott (1980: 17) found that '[n]orms are not necessarily legal. Any norm of behaviour may be analysed as a hypothetical-conditional. Legal norms are distinguished by the identification of the emitter of the norm, and the nature of the consequences specified by it.'

This seems to suggest that a norm is a legal norm only when it has been expressed or stipulated by a legal agent. This does not clarify the nature of 'law' itself because it depends on a circular definition of law. Allott (1980: 17) tried to look for the defining characteristics of a legal norm, another way of posing the basic question about what law is. It transpires that there is no clear answer. It all depends on what one is looking for, and from what perspective the enquirer comes. Allott (1980: 18) provided several examples, including the command theory of Austin, to show that legal norms may set prescribed patterns of behaviour for a particular community or for sections of it. As Allott (1980: 18) showed, skilful legal interpretation has over time enlarged the sphere of law, since '[l]ater juristic opinion has managed to include such individual pseudo-norms within the definition of legal norm by the simple device of prescriptive definition: it is so because I say it is so.' This is entirely circular, a classic illustration that 'the rationality of modern law is a piecemeal rationality' (Cotterrell, 1989: 6).

As Allott (1980: 18) noted in his debate about universality, 'the word "law" (and its cognates at different levels) induces in the hearer/user a notion of *regularity* or even of universality. This is a fact of linguistic behaviour, borne out by the etymological connection between "rule" and "regular".' This neatly demonstrates how popular assumptions about LAW as an abstract, related to physical laws of nature, have made us believe that legal norms must also be universal and 'regular'. In this context Allott (1980: 19) spoke of the 'illegitimate corruption of (juristic) *Laws* and laws as terms to be used in the analysis of legal systems'. This helps to explain why most law students come to law school assuming that law can be studied like a natural science.

In Allott's view, several examples of law-making challenge the claim to universality. For example, some legal rules may only apply to certain categories of people (such as rules about naturalisation of foreigners, or immigration laws) or to certain specific situations. Allott (1980: 19–23) considered whether various facilities, institutions, processes and principles in a legal system are norms, finding that norms can be of different types. Allott (1980: 23) explained:

> The reason is that a *Law* is a system; it is a system with feedback; each element in the system pre-supposes and depends on many other elements. It is unreal, and analytically absurd, to attempt to abstract one norm in isolation from those others which relate to it and give it meaning or control its operation. A simple norm apparently directed to the behaviour of individual subjects of the *Law* implies many norms, of which the most general is:
>
>   'Let there be a legal system!'
>
> A simple norm without implementing norms is and must be ineffective. Implementing norms will often consist of instructions to and about the

institutions and processes of the law; what we would otherwise call meta-norms. The circle is a closed one.

Thus, Allott again concluded with a totally circular argument: Law is law because it is law! It is law because certain people declare it to be law and it is perceived as a necessary condition of human existence. Highlighting the importance of a legal system in itself, Allott stipulated a natural, instinctive, human *grundnorm* to the universal effect that there must be law, similar to familiar calls for application of the 'rule of law'.[57] If it is indeed a basic behavioural imperative in all human societies that there should be law, then the debate about whether law is a global phenomenon or not becomes nonsensical, unless we were to go so far as to deny human status to certain societies in earlier times or in Asia and Africa today. Such a position is clearly untenable.

Allott's debate, therefore, does not tell us much about the nature of law other than that it is extremely diverse and has limits. But his exercise concerned not only the linguistic use of 'law'. Leading us around in circles, this debate was also designed to illustrate that law is an immensely complex, plural, globally present, internally diverse and culturally relative phenomenon. The global presence of law as a concept and a reality does not imply automatic uniformity, nor indeed universality of rules, but brings with it enormous diversities on local, regional and national scales. Later sections of Allott's important book show to what intricate extent law is interlinked with other norm systems in different parts of the world, confirming Allott's overriding argument that the presence of non-legal norm systems makes law itself, in many situations, an ineffective and even defunct regulatory mechanism. Law, so his central thesis, has crucial limits and will not be effective unless one considers and understands its interconnectedness.

2.5.3 Griffiths' theory of legal pluralism

While Sally Falk Moore combined her theoretical discussions mainly with field-work on African societies, other theorists of legal pluralism have been content to remain within the realm of theoretical analysis. A much-cited work of this kind is John Griffiths' (1986) article on legal pluralism. The author's note (Griffiths, 1986: 1) emphasises that the article was originally written when legal pluralism as a concept among lawyers was still in its infancy, in fact a 'combative infancy' (Woodman, 1998: 22). Griffiths (1986: 1) indicates his conceptual indebtedness to Moore (1978), employing her phrase about legal pluralism as 'the presence in a social field of more than one legal order'. Griffiths (1986: 1–2) begins with a sharp critique of 'legal centralism', whose dominance

---

[57] Using different language, Fikentscher (1995) refers to the concept of 'super-additivity' (*Übersumme* in the German original) as a form of higher public interest that connects communities of people to a particular legal system.

as an ideological construct reflects the ambitions of the modern nation state of total legal control, obfuscating the understanding of legal pluralism, and deeply opposed to it (Woodman, 1998: 22). Griffiths challenges in particular the popular understanding of Hooker's (1975) colonially induced form of legal pluralism, which in his view is not real pluralism, but just a sub-category of state-dominated legal centralism. Griffiths examines the work of several legal scholars who provided explicit definitions of legal pluralism, Hooker, John Gilissen and Jacques Vanderlinden, showing that they all relied ultimately on legal centralist assumptions. However, various other theories that consider the place of law within social structures were found useful to develop a theory of legal pluralism. Griffiths (1986: 2) explicitly mentions Pospišil's (1971) theory of 'legal levels', Smith's (1974) theory of 'corporations', Ehrlich's (1936) theory of 'living law' and Moore's (1978) concept of the 'semi-autonomous social field'. Griffiths shows all of these approaches to be inadequate in some way, but helpful in his own construction of a descriptive conception of legal pluralism.

Noting that social fields vary in their extent of plurality, but that all fields (with very few exceptions) are plural, Griffiths (1986: 2) aims to provide a basic working definition of legal pluralism as 'that state of affairs, for any social field, in which behavior pursuant to more than one legal order occurs'. In his first major section, 'The intellectual context of a descriptive conception of legal pluralism', Griffiths (1986: 2–8) locates his debate of legal pluralism within existing writing and thinking. Griffiths (1986: 3) defines the concept or ideology of 'legal centralism', according to which 'law is and should be the law of the state, uniform for all persons, exclusive of all other law, and administered by a single set of state institutions. To the extent that other, lesser normative orderings, such as the church, the family . . . exist, they ought to be and in fact are hierarchically subordinate to the law and institutions of the state.' Griffiths (1986: 3) explains that, from this perspective of legal centralism, law as an exclusive and uniform system of hierarchical ordering has been understood either in legal positivist fashion as a top-down phenomenon, or as a bottom-up system of control deriving its validity ultimately from some moral norms in a natural law context. In either case, this supreme legal authority, whether embodied in a sovereign or found in something like Kelsen's *grundnorm* or *lex natura*, has simply been accepted by dominant legal scholarship as a fact. Griffiths (1986: 3) argues that the assertion of factual legal state power, combined with the moral authority of norm systems, has created the impression that binding laws exist, but criticises this approach as a damaging ideology for understanding pluralism. In fact, legal centralism as an ideology relies on the same circular argument identified above in Allott's (1980) attempts to define law. This critical discussion of legal centralism evidently benefited from Moore's (1978) analysis of partial state legal control. Griffiths (1986: 4) strongly criticises the inability and unwillingness of legal scholars to perceive social reality without blinkers:

> The ideology of legal centralism . . . has made it all too easy to fall into the prevalent assumption that legal reality, at least in 'modern' legal systems, more or less approximates to the claim made on behalf of the state. Lawyers, but also social scientists, have suffered from a chronic inability to see that the legal reality of the modern state is not at all that of the tidy, consistent, organized ideal . . . but that legal reality is rather an unsystematic collage of inconsistent and overlapping parts, lending itself to no easy legal interpretation, morally and aesthetically offensive to the eye of the liberal idealist, and almost incomprehensible in its complexity to the would-be empirical student.

Griffiths (1986: 4) argues that 'the theory of law in "primitive" society has also suffered indirectly, by way of "false comparisons" with the idealized picture of law in "modern" society'. Legal theory as well as social research on law are found in deep crisis and the ideology of legal centralism and observable reality clearly do not match. Griffiths (1986: 4) cites Galanter (1981: 20) to support his claim that the dominant ideology of legal centralism has effectively prevented official recognition of the power of legal pluralism because that would undermine the hegemonistic claims of the modern nation state and dominant positivist legal ideology, which work hand in hand. Griffiths (1986: 4–5) then powerfully asserts his own position:

> Legal pluralism is the fact. Legal centralism is a myth, an ideal, a claim, an illusion. Nevertheless, the ideology of legal centralism has had such a powerful hold on the imagination of lawyers and social scientists that its picture of the legal world has been able successfully to masquerade as fact and has formed the foundation stone of social and legal theory. A central objective of a descriptive conception of legal pluralism is therefore destructive: to break the stranglehold of the idea that . . . law . . . is a single, unified and exclusive hierarchical normative ordering depending from the power of the state, and of the illusion that the legal world actually looks the way such a conception requires it to look. In short, part of the purpose of this article is a simple debunking, as a necessary prolegomenon to any clear empirical thought about law and its place in social life.

Griffiths (1986: 5) deepens his analysis by introducing the distinction between 'strong' and 'weak' legal pluralism. To him, legal pluralism in its 'strong' sense is 'a situation in which not all law is state law nor administered by a single set of state legal institutions, and in which law is therefore neither systematic nor uniform' (p. 5). It is, hence, an observable state of affairs that within any given social group there may be co-existing legal orders which do not belong to the same system (Griffiths, 1986: 8). This shows that Griffiths recognises the potential legal impact of certain social norms which may not be officially recognised because it is morally and ontologically excluded by legal centralist ideology (Griffiths, 1986: 5). From a positivist perspective, therefore, 'strong' legal pluralism is a conceptual impossibility and is simply denied. 'Weak' legal pluralism, on the other hand, operates within the ideology of legal centralism and could therefore be treated as a particular sub-type of law, rather than merely a social phenomenon. Griffiths (1986: 5) explains that in this 'weak' sense:

> a legal system is 'pluralistic' when the sovereign (implicitly) commands (or the *grundnorm* validates, and so on) different bodies of law for different groups in the population. In general the groups concerned are defined in terms of features such as ethnicity, religion, nationality or geography, and legal pluralism is justified as a technique of governance on pragmatic grounds . . . Within such a pluralistic legal system, parallel legal regimes, dependent from the overarching and controlling state legal system, result from 'recognition' by the state of the supposedly pre-existing 'customary law' of the groups concerned. While such pluralism is not limited to the colonial and post-colonial situation, that is certainly where it is best known.

This definition is not fundamentally inconsistent with the ideology of legal centralism (Griffiths, 1986: 8). Confusingly, 'weak' legal pluralism has a nominal resemblance to legal pluralism, because separate laws exist. However, such 'weak' pluralism is no more than a plural arrangement in a diversified legal system whose basic ideology remains centralist. The legally recognised elements of 'weak' legal pluralism are only law because state law accepts them as such. One major reason why even 'weak' legal pluralism, especially as manifested in personal law systems, is disliked so intensely by most lawyers, is that such 'weak' legal pluralism often exists because the respective state has actually been forced to accept socio-cultural and religious norms as part of the official law.[58]

However, Griffiths (1986: 6) is on shaky ground when it comes to researching when 'weak' legal pluralism began. He suggests that '[t]he modern history of legal pluralism in this weak sense begins at least as early as 1772', when Warren Hastings famously introduced a regulation for the new judicial system established in the Indian territories administered by the East India Company, providing for separate legal regulation of Muslim and Hindu law in British India mainly in respect of family law and related issues. Relying on Hooker (1975: 61), Griffiths assumes that legal pluralism in this weak sense was a consequence of the colonial experience, carried over into the post-colonial legal systems of Asia and Africa. While this is not totally wrong, in that colonialism introduced new types of legal pluralism, Griffiths overlooks the fact that other forms of legal pluralism, probably strong and weak, had been in existence well before the intervention of the British in India and elsewhere. Hence weak legal pluralism as a phenomenon is neither just a colonial invention nor an element of legal modernity. Nor is pluralism something introduced by earlier Muslim rulers of the subcontinent. Rather, it is an ancient integral feature of legal regulation

---

[58] This argument is elaborated and illustrated by Chiba's (1986) distinction of two types of 'official law' (section 2.5.4 below).

characteristic of plurality-conscious chthonic laws everywhere in the world.[59] While Griffiths is not a legal historian, he could easily have supplemented his claim that legal pluralism is a fact by asserting that it is an ancient, well-recognised fact, probably in all human societies. For a globally focused analysis of legal concepts, such an important aspect should not be overlooked. It will resurface in all subsequent chapters of this book.

What Griffiths has to say on the mechanisms of operating weak legal pluralism with particular reference to Indian laws is too detailed for the present discussion. However, he makes valuable comments about the tensions between maintaining 'weak' legal pluralism in the shape of 'personal law systems' in the post-colonial world and the centralist agenda of unification of laws. Maintaining 'weak' legal pluralism is widely seen as evidence of a deficiency in modern development. Griffiths (1986: 7) writes:

> Formal acquiescence by the state in a situation of legal pluralism in this weak sense adds a formidable layer of doctrinal complexity on top of the complexity normally incident to a supposedly uniform state legal system. The resulting state of affairs is regarded by almost everyone concerned as profoundly defective. It is the messy compromise which the ideology of legal centralism feels itself obliged to make with recalcitrant social reality: until the heterogeneous and primitive populations of ex-colonial states have, in the process of 'nation-building', been smelted into a homogeneous population of the sort which 'modern' states are believed to enjoy, allowances must be made.

However, as Griffiths (1986: 7–8) continues immediately, the proponents of legal centralism are unhappy and quite impatient with a pluralist scenario,[60] even where this is largely on terms set by the state itself:

> But unification remains the eventual goal, to be enacted as soon as circumstances permit. While law ought not to and cannot depart from local expectations so quickly and radically that it ceases to 'function', upsets expectations, and unsettles the social order, it should nevertheless exercise a constant pressure in the desired direction. Uniform law is not only dependent upon, but also a condition of progress toward modern nationhood (as well as of economic and social 'development'). In one form or another, the literature of and about legal pluralism, in the weak sense primarily associated with colonial and post-colonial societies, is almost all written under the sign of unification: unification is inevitable, necessary, normal, modern and good.

Hence, within the framework of legal centralism as an ideology, 'weak' legal pluralism belongs to the ambit of law, and yet it is rejected because of visions

---

[59] Glenn (2004: 350) highlights in this context the multivalence of all traditional legal systems.
[60] An instructive example is found in Dhagamwar (2003), complaining vigorously that Indian family law and religion still encroach today on the formal system of criminal law.

of legal uniformity that have remained mere illusions.[61] Griffiths (1986: 8) clarifies this ambivalent complex process:

> 'Legal pluralism' is thus but one of the forms in which the ideology of legal centralism can manifest itself. It is to be sure, by the terms of that ideology an inferior form of law, a necessary accommodation to a social situation perceived as problematic. But it is nevertheless only intelligible as an expression of that ideology. It is the fact that 'legal pluralism' is defined as an imperfect form of law by the very ideology which gives it meaning as a concept, that accounts for the low opinion of 'legal pluralism' held by so many of those who write within and about it, and it is thus not surprising that even lawyers and scholars who live in states whose legal systems are formally pluralistic take a dim view of that state of affairs.

Here we find another explanation for the meaningful silence of writers from non-Western jurisdictions when it comes to defending Asian and African legal systems and their internal arrangements against Western criticisms. Real, i.e. strong, legal pluralism is a phenomenon which academic writing prior to 1986 had hardly touched upon. Griffiths (1986: 9) complains that '[t]here are practically no explicit definitions of legal pluralism, in the descriptive sense with which we are concerned, to be found in the literature. What there does exist is not generally of great use.' Griffiths (1986: 9) finds that Hooker's (1975) concept of legal pluralism was not moving away far enough from legal centralist ideology.[62] Real legal pluralism, in the sense used by Griffiths, would imply that the law explicitly recognises that there are other bodies of rules which also regulate and influence human behaviour, and which are therefore legally relevant.[63]

Griffiths' purely theoretical discussion makes no attempt to test his model through empirical study. Moore (1978; 1986) and Chiba (1986; 1989) researched the realities of strong legal pluralism. Chiba's model of the interaction of official law, unofficial law and legal postulates focuses precisely on the theoretical concerns identified by Griffiths. Both writers published their work in 1986 and initially were not aware of each other.[64] In today's pluralising global environment there is increasing evidence to support Moore's assertions of partial legal control. The final dictum of Griffiths (1986) remains only too correct: legal pluralism is simply a fact. Woodman (1998: 54) strongly endorses this, seeing legal pluralism as 'a non-taxonomic conception, a continuous variable,

---

[61] Allott (1980: 216) wisely portrayed India's attempts to envisage a Uniform Civil Code for all citizens as 'no more than a distant dream'.

[62] Woodman (1998: 26) notes that it was not Hooker's aim to develop the concept of legal pluralism.

[63] On his own concepts of 'deep legal pluralism' and 'state law pluralism', see Woodman (1988).

[64] The same goes for Poulter (1986), who represents what he perceived as liberal legal centralism.

just as ... "law" is'. The challenge then, indeed, becomes to examine this phenomenon 'in terms of the degrees of legal pluralism present' (p. 54).

2.5.4 Chiba's tripartite model of law

Masaji Chiba's work, built on the assumption that legal pluralism is a universal phenomenon, is mainly found in two major studies (Chiba, 1986; 1989). Taking an Asian, and to some extent Japanese perspective, Chiba (1989: 1–2) asserts that legal pluralism as a phenomenon is increasingly well recognised, writing that '[t]he conception of legal pluralism emerged when other systems of law were found working in reality together with the "law", whether in harmony or in conflict, typically in non-Western society and in Western society as well'. Various labels have been used to describe the different forms of non-state law (Baxi, 1986) and the coexistence of state law with various types of non-state law was noted in earlier studies (Galanter, 1981). However, in such contexts, the concept of 'legal pluralism' has remained generally based on the assumption that official law will ultimately prove to be superior to any other form of legal regulation.

Chiba (1989: 2) portrays the concept of legal pluralism as 'an effective attack on the common sense of orthodox jurisprudence, because it means to reject the believed-in oneness of state law as law or universality of Western law among all the people in the world'. While the relativisation of 'law' is not reversible, in Chiba's view, it should not be taken as far as to negate the universality of Western law altogether. Hence, Chiba (1989: 2) writes, '[t]he true problem must be to distinguish between universality and relativity inherent in Western law, both of which coexist with non-state law or customary law in legal pluralism'. In a number of publications, especially the introduction to a collection of essays on the interaction of Asian indigenous laws and received laws, Chiba (1986) developed a complex concept of legal pluralism of immense relevance for globality-focused legal study. His holistic theory of law and legal pluralism takes explicit account of social realities and values and refuses to distinguish the strictly 'legal' from the 'non-legal' or 'extra-legal'.[65] Applying Chiba's methodology, one also overcomes the private/public divide in law, another one of the 'completely suspect' (Tamanaha, 2001: 67) axioms of centralist legal theory that prevent creative thinking about legal pluralism. In Chiba's tripartite model of a legal system, 'official law' is always seen as interacting with 'unofficial laws' and 'legal postulates'. None of these elements ever exists in isolation; they continuously interact in dynamic fashion. Law, thus, is always plural.[66] The key

---

[65] Rudolf von Jhering spoke of 'extra-legal' conditions for social life only when these were 'realized without any intervention of law, e.g., climate, the fact that the earth is fertile, that there is air to breathe' (Dias and Hughes, 1957: 412).

[66] The basic underlying concept, that law is but one factor in a social field, was earlier explained by Moore (1978), on whose field-based theoretical work Chiba relies.

passages of this model are found in Chiba (1986: 1–9), but some important points are already made in the preface. Chiba (1986: v) starts immediately with a strong criticism of Western presuppositions about the nature of non-Western laws and their dependency on Western legal models:

> Western law is normally regarded as universal when considered from the fact that it has been received and utilized by non-Western countries as the basis of their own state legal systems. It is accordingly natural that jurisprudence, among both Western and non-Western scholars as well, tends to observe the development of a non-Western legal system as a history of received Western law. In fact, because of their different underlying cultural histories, there have been countless incongruities and conflicts between received Western law and indigenous non-Western law. However, these points have rarely been taken seriously by orthodox jurisprudence – a situation which may seem reasonable from the Western point of view, but is certainly not from the non-Western.

From a non-Western perspective, reception of foreign laws did not just involve simple replacement of one set of rules with another, but a complex process of cultural interaction with many facets.[67] Chiba (1986: v) emphasises that people in non-Western societies have 'cherished their indigenous law as an integral part of their cultural heritage'. He demonstrates that the reception of foreign laws, whether voluntary or not, has at times involved peaceful assimilation, while often there have been conflicts between indigenous and received law, as a result of which, in some cases, indigenous law may not have survived. In other cases, the indigenous law may have rejected received elements outright, or it may have adapted itself to preserve its cultural identity. Chiba (1986: v) argues that the contemporary laws of Asian countries are found in 'an ongoing process of self-developing indigenous law whether successfully or not'.[68]

The problem identified by Chiba's analysis, in a nutshell, is that the non-Western patterns of legal pluralism, historically developed in interaction between Asian indigenous laws and various received laws, have not been researched and explained sufficiently well from an Asian perspective. The main problem for legal analysis, according to Chiba (1986: 1), is that law has been studied unsatisfactorily in isolation from its social environment:

> There has been a long-established belief among both specialists and laymen that law is a special mechanism for social control isolated from other social mechanisms and, for this reason, that the scientific study of law should be confined to the special capacity of traditional, model jurisprudence. But since the beginning of the twentieth century this common belief has

---

[67] This is clearly a Japanese perspective. For details see Igarashi (1990), Oda (1992) and especially Dean (2002).

[68] Ethnic self-development also appears as a prominent element in the reconstruction of Asian concepts in the West today (Ballard, 1994; chapter 1, section 1.3 above).

been challenged by new ideas concerning both the objectives and methods of the study of law. As a result it has become more evident that law is so inseparably rooted in society as to be approachable by sociological methods. Furthermore, it has also become accepted that law must be recognized as an aspect of the total culture of a people, characterized by the psychological and ideational features as well as the structure and functional features of each fostering people, and may therefore be approached by anthropological methods.

This positioning immediately indicates that Chiba views law not as an isolated phenomenon, but as a complex social element which may have its own, legal characteristics, but is 'inseparably rooted in society' and thus not fully accessible through mono-focused legal analysis. Chiba (1986: 1–2) challenges in particular the universalist claims of Western model jurisprudence:

> The popular negligence of the cultural factor of law may have been partly caused by the alleged universal nature of traditional jurisprudence, prevailing as in *the* model science of law in the world. Contemporary model jurisprudence is indeed established on a universal basis. Its overwhelming prevalence in the world seems to leave little room either for serious consideration of its cultural specificity or for doubt as to its applicability to the different cultural specificities of other countries. But the Western conception of law, created and supported by model jurisprudence, has been bereft of its cultural specificity when comparatively analysed with the conceptions of law in other cultures . . . Truly, contemporary model jurisprudence is a product of long Western history and is coloured by a Western culture based on the Hellenistic and Christian view of man and society. While we acknowledge the universalistic achievements of Western jurisprudence as the most advanced science of law ever accomplished by man, we cannot disregard its cultural specificity. That specificity may have been in some cases diffused by or assimilated into different specificities of different cultures, but in other cases it has conflicted with or been rejected by them. In all cases, model jurisprudence, convinced of its universality, will not pay due attention to the cultural problems which accompany such diffusion or conflict between Western specificity and non-Western specificities.

Chiba's critical analysis of Western 'model jurisprudence' rests on two main arguments. First, legal analysis has tended to overlook socio-cultural factors in their interaction with the law and has therefore become too legocentric (Legrand, 1996: 242). Secondly, by assuming its own universality, Western 'model jurisprudence' has rendered invisible the specific experiences of non-Western cultures and legal systems. By not explicitly admitting the contribution of culture-specific elements in the development and operation of Western laws, Western model jurisprudence has therefore made claims to universality which are not maintainable. Chiba argues in legal terms similar to Ballard's (1994) anthropological analysis. Debating the nature of law, rather than simply blaming Western scholars for misrepresentations of universality, Chiba (1986: 2) politely explains the problem as a result of deficient cross-cultural communication:

> [T]he peoples and scholars of non-Western countries who have cherished their own jurisprudence with specificities quite different from the Western, have not succeeded nor even attempted to present the achievements of their jurisprudence before the world circle of legal science forcibly enough to cause the proponents of Western jurisprudence to doubt their conviction of its universality. Without presenting the achievements of their own jurisprudence before world bodies specifically aimed at self-reflection of model jurisprudence, they would be disqualified from criticizing the ethnocentricity of the latter, as recently pointed out by some Western scholars...and insisting upon the *raison d'être* of their own jurisprudence. Such a negative or passive attitude may be another reason why model jurisprudence has in general disregarded the jurisprudence of different cultures... Vital to the proper understanding of law in non-Western culture is, firstly, for native scholars to present their own data and views positively in order not to negate the significance of model jurisprudence, but to maintain a sound understanding of its nature when utilized in different cultures.

The 'negative or passive attitude' on the part of 'native scholars' which Chiba identifies here can be related to the purposeful silence among Asian and African scholars (chapter 1, section 1.2.4) in reacting to Western assertions of superiority. It is not that 'native scholars' have nothing to say to Western scholars, but they may well take the view that there is no point explaining their views on law and their own cultural perceptions, since these will be haughtily dismissed offhand, as continues to happen only too often, now prominently in the context of international human rights debates and in relation to 'Asian values' (Peerenboom, 2004). Chiba politely suggests some historical explanations as to why non-Western jurists have not managed to raise their own voice and have instead given more emphasis to the interaction between their own indigenous laws and received laws. In this respect, Chiba (1986: 3) asserts that various Asian philosophies and religions should be seen as comparable to those of the West and that the Asian legal systems found today are an amalgam of all kinds of cultural influences on legal processes and institutions. Chiba (1986: 3) calls for a new methodology in studying this complexity, writing that 'we wish to take a step forward in establishing how such struggles developed, or are developing, whether harmoniously or with conflict, and also to determine whether the results should be judged as successful or unsuccessful'.

Chiba (1986: 4) then refers to a number of earlier thinkers who have brought out the cultural nature of law, mentioning among others Savigny, Maine, Post, Kohler, Ehrlich and his 'living law', Weber and Malinowski. Thus situating his own work firmly within the wider context of social science approaches to law, Chiba (1986: 4) introduces his highly instructive model of the three-level structure of law, which demolishes legal centralism:

> The point is that the whole structure of law of a people is not limited to the monistic system of state law as maintained by model jurisprudence in accordance with its methodological postulates. The whole structure of law as an aspect of culture should include all regulations, however apparently different from state law, which the people concerned observe as law in their cultural tradition, including value systems; the very cultural identity of a people demands that we include all of them in a whole structure. Thus, the whole structure of law is plural, consisting of different systems of law interacting with one another harmoniously or conflictingly. Our first methodological requirement then is to frame a new conceptual scheme sufficient to allow us to observe the relevant facts accurately and to analyse them into theoretical formulations. Thus we arrive at our first working hypothesis: the three-level structure of law.

Chiba explains that the cultural origins of law and its continuing interlinkedness with state law may be viewed as another form of 'reception of law'. For him, this reception is not only a matter of unequal interaction between Western and non-Western legal rules, as most writers suggest, but a complex process of competition and mutual accommodation between different socio-cultural forces within any given non-Western legal system. Chiba (1986: 4–5) criticises the fact that Western research has mainly focused on assessing to what extent Western legal influences have been unidirectionally received, rather than taking a more sophisticated plurality-focused perspective:

> Reception of law is one of the topics frequently discussed by the proponents and students of model jurisprudence. But their point of view is, generally speaking, limited to confirming how Western law has been adopted or permeated into the official legal systems of non-Western countries, with only occasional recognition of its conflict with or rejection by indigenous systems. In this view, main concern is given to the destiny of the received Western law rather than to the receiving indigenous systems. For the receiving peoples, in contrast, main concern must be given to the whole structure of their indigenous systems, with focus upon assimilation of the received law while firmly maintaining their cultural identities. Unfortunately, the point of view clearly centring on that concern has been neither established nor systematically attempted. This, then, would be [the] second methodological requirement necessary for our purpose: Interaction between received law and indigenous law.

Having emphasised the dialectic process of interaction between received and indigenous law in various contexts, Chiba (1986) provides a theoretical model which he then aims to apply to a number of national scenarios (Egypt, Iran, Sri Lanka, India, Thailand and Japan) and proceeds to develop a set of working hypotheses for his three-level structure of law and for the interaction processes between received law and indigenous law. The major elements of the three-level structure of law, comprising of official law, unofficial law and legal postulates, are neatly outlined by Chiba (1986: 5–6):

> *Official law* is the legal system sanctioned by the legitimate authority of a country. *State law* is ordinarily understood as a typical official law or even the only official law. Truly, it is directly sanctioned by the legitimate authority of the government of a state to have overall jurisdiction over the country. But as a matter of nature it is only one among many official laws of a country, however dominant it may appear over the others. For instance, as in most contemporary countries with established religions, religious law may be partially included in or accommodated by state law, but partially functioning out of the jurisdiction of the latter, thus forming its own system different from state law. Canon law, Islamic law, Hindu law, Buddhist law, and Judaic law are among typical examples. Other examples may be found in the laws of marriage and family, land and farming, local organizations, professional guilds, castes and stratifications, ethnic minorities, and so on, insofar as officially sanctioned by state law in one form or another. Each of these official laws of a country is sanctioned first by an authority of its own. But all of them are required to keep consonance with one another. To fulfil this requirement, each of them must, finally, be sanctioned by the state authority.

At first sight, this concept of 'official law' coincides with state law. However, showing that state-sponsored legal rules form only one of the possible components of an official law, Chiba introduces religious law and people's customary norms as actual or potential elements of official law. This pluralising perspective on the composition of state law challenges and actually destroys the assumption that all official laws are made by the state. Chiba indicates instead that a state may have to accept (and in that sense receive) bodies or elements of rules from other, non-state sources, which may then be formally incorporated into the official law, but were not made or created by it. Indicating that such rules also interact with each other, and are likely to conflict, Chiba prepares his later discussion about interaction patterns between competing legal elements. This most important finding brings out the internally plural nature even of 'official law'.

Similarly, Chiba's concept of 'unofficial law' signifies an internally diverse and diffuse phenomenon, more so than the official law. 'Unofficial law' is not just custom, since many aspects of custom may already have become part of the official law, as explained above. Apart from circumscribing the phenomenon of 'unofficial laws', Chiba (1986: 6) again emphasises complex interaction processes:

> *Unofficial law* is the legal system not officially sanctioned by any legitimate authority, but sanctioned in practice by the general consensus of a certain circle of people, whether within or beyond the bounds of a country. That

general consensus may be either consciously recognized and expressed in formal rules, or unconsciously observed in particular patterns of behaviour. However, not all such unofficial practices supported by general consensus are to be included in unofficial law. Unofficial law is here limited to those unofficial practices which have a distinct influence upon the effectiveness of official law; in other words those which distinctively supplement, oppose, modify, or undermine any of the official laws, including state law. The effectiveness of the total system of official law is thus dependent upon the *status quo* of the unofficial law of the country concerned. One of the most important problems of unofficial law is therefore its positive or negative influence upon official law as well as its cultural background. While model jurisprudence has tended to disregard it, unofficial law has been treated in various rubrics in sociological and anthropological trends. For example, such rubrics are frequently found as customary law, living law, law in action, primitive law, tribal law, native law, and folk law, although their specific connotations should be carefully distinguished from one another.

Chiba then moves towards the third, critical element of his three-level structure, namely 'legal postulates', or value systems of various types. He views these less as bodies of rules, but rather as norms or values, which are created neither by the state nor by a social group. They simply exist in their own right as elements of a specific cultural context, intimately connected to official law and unofficial law. Chiba (1986: 6–7) defines a legal postulate as:

[A] value principle or value system specifically connected with a particular official or unofficial law, which acts to found, justify and orient the latter. It may consist of established legal ideas such as natural law, justice, equity, and so on in model jurisprudence; sacred truths and precepts emanating from various gods in religious law; social and cultural postulates affording the structural and functional basis for a society as embodied in clan unity, exogamy, bilineal descent, seniority, individual freedom, national philosophy, and so on; political ideologies, often closely connected with economic policies, as in capitalism or socialism; and so on. The legal postulates of a country, whether official or unofficial, are as a whole required to keep a certain degree of consonance with one another. But complete consonance cannot be expected. First, because as each legal postulate is in support of a particular system of official or unofficial law, the potential of conflict with other systems, as pointed out above, is high. Second, because the legal postulate may tend to upset the *status quo* of its supported official or unofficial law in order to improve or even replace the latter.

Interaction between received law and indigenous law forms a further key element of Chiba's theory of legal pluralism. Focusing first on the element of received law, Chiba (1986: 7) emphasises that '[t]he whole structure of law of a non-Western country is, seen from a cultural point of view, formed in the interaction between received law and indigenous law'. Chiba (1986: 7) then continues:

Received law is, in a broad sense, that law which is received by a country from one or more foreign countries. Reception may take place in a variety of forms or processes; for instance, partially or wholly, systematically or unsystematically, formally or substantially, rapidly or gradually, voluntarily or involuntarily, in one or more of the three levels, exclusively between Western or non-Western countries, or, finally, between Western *and* non-Western countries. Most crucial for our purposes, however, is the reception of Western state law by non-Western countries in modern times, which we might consider as the narrower sense of 'reception of law'. It is crucial because it is the one in which the cultural conflict between received law and indigenous law is most conspicuous, and because the reception process, in the truest meaning, has not yet been completed. The modern reception has taken place rather formally and systematically in the level of official state law, whether imposed by Western countries or voluntarily accepted by non-Western countries, and some might see the reception as completed by the formal enforcement of received law. But in the actual process of the history of receiving countries, it is only the beginning of their struggles to assimilate the foreign systems of law of different cultures with their own indigenous law. Notable is the fact that in this struggle process the foreign law originally received can be more or less assimilated with existing indigenous law so that it may assume a character of indigenous law, while it may still be discriminated as a different system of law.

The complex category of 'indigenous law' is explained broadly by Chiba (1986: 8) as 'law originated in the native culture of a people'. But he also suggests that it is virtually impossible to find purely indigenous law: 'It may thus be defined as law existing indigenously in the native culture of a people prior to the reception of Western state law in modern times, although it may include some assimilated law which was originally received in earlier times' (p. 8). In Chiba's view, it is instructive to analyse how indigenous laws have developed in interaction with received laws. The process of reception, seen by many scholars as imposition, remains incompletely understood. Chiba (1986: 8) argues:

> The actual interaction between received law and indigenous law differs widely from country to country. Generally speaking . . . state law is framed after Western models in its formal structure, adopting into its substantial contents various rights, duties, and legal institutions and procedures originated in Western law . . . But interaction is not limited to such a static structure. It takes place rather in a dynamic process of mutual influences between both types of law, whether through institutional revisions at a long range, or through individual authoritative judgements and peoples' behaviour at a short range. It is a process of accommodation or conflict, with legal postulates for both types of law playing an important role as they ideationally encourage the peoples concerned to protect or reformulate the law they support against rivalling law. Official law other than state law may originate in indigenous law or in received law as in the case of established

religious law, though generally assimilated as if indigenous. Unofficial law is mostly occupied with indigenous law, except in cases where new reformative ideas of rights, such as environmental or consumers' rights, or legal institutions such as socialist ones in capitalistic countries, come to have certain effective influence as unofficial law. And finally, legal postulates constantly accompany all forms and cases of official and unofficial law, both received and indigenous.

The tripartite model was applied in further studies by the author himself and by others.[69] In the conclusion to his 1986 study (Chiba, 1986: 378–94), satisfaction is expressed that his theory could be successfully applied to six Asian country studies, while much further research needs to be undertaken to elucidate the processes of continuous interaction. Chiba (1986: 388) writes:

> Truly, as seen by the proponents of model jurisprudence, official law may have the capacity to reject unofficial law at its command, but that rejection never results in the annihilation of the unofficial law in reality. The reality is nothing more nor less than a continuous struggle between the two, with coexistence as the best, and the undermining of the official law as the worst possible cases.

Law, therefore, even where an official law *appears* to be dominant, is always a plural phenomenon and remains always part of a dynamic interaction process between different legal sources, akin to what Fitzpatrick (1984) characterised as 'integral plurality'. However, Chiba's 1986 model is premised on the existence of an official law, which can then be distinguished from 'unofficial law'. Despite being anti-positivist, this model relies deeply on positivist assumptions, which causes problems if one seeks to apply it to traditional legal systems in which state law is not dominant. Aware of the need to analyse with more clarity the role of cultural values in relation to law, Chiba (1989) examines more closely how 'legal postulates' are placed within the interactive patterns of different types of law. Chiba (1989: 1–9) offers a rethinking of legal pluralism focused on the significance of culture in relation to legal pluralism. Chiba (1989: 3) throws a challenge to all legal theorists:

> As a matter of fact, there is no legal pluralist whose argument of culture or legal culture is substantial enough to invite the interest and discussion of cultural anthropologists, specialists in the science of culture. Such legal pluralists might be viewed by the specialists to be frogs in the well, essentially not different from the lawyers who are satisfied by working in the isolated domain of orthodox jurisprudence. A true legal pluralist may be required to observe and analyze culture in law on the basis common to that of the specialist of culture.

[69] Yilmaz (1999; 2005) applied Chiba's model successfully to the study of Muslim legal pluralism in the UK, Turkey and Pakistan.

Arguing that the 'voices of non-Western peoples represented by native scholars are indispensable to correctly present needed data' (Chiba, 1989: 4), the analysis then proceeds to develop a revised model of 'three dichotomies of law', building on the earlier 'three-level structure of law' (Chiba, 1986). The three dichotomies are easily explained in terms of the 1986 model:

1. Official law v. unofficial law
2. Legal rules v. legal postulates
3. Indigenous law v. transplanted law

The first dichotomy (Chiba, 1989: 177–8) reiterates the crucial distinction of different types of official law, basically state-made and state-acknowledged, interacting with different unofficial laws. It is evident that Chiba still does not say enough about the fact that state law is itself a social fact. The second dichotomy (Chiba, 1989: 178) focuses on the contrast and interaction between positive rules and postulative values, indicating that 'legal postulates are by and large difficult to isolate' but 'have the potential of reactivating outdated legal rules or even creating new legal rules to embody themselves'. The third dichotomy (pp. 178–9) emphasises the complex interaction of these two major elements, which are themselves hybrid amalgams of different indigenous and transplanted elements.

Chiba (1989: 180) then introduces the overarching concept of '*identity postulate of a legal culture*', which 'guides a people in choosing how to reformulate the whole structure of their law . . . in order to maintain their accommodation to changing circumstances'. The reference to 'a people' reflects Chiba's focus on Japanese legal culture, but this will need to be researched much further in terms of internal pluralities *within* any one legal culture. Chiba's advanced theoretical model suggests that law is everywhere a culture-specific plural phenomenon. Chiba's work demonstrates the possibility, in practice and not just in theory, to develop plurality-conscious methodologies to study law as a universal, global phenomenon. His findings confirm that law can be seen as a multidimensional net (Sack and Aleck, 1992: xxvi), that different sources of law have different impacts in all places (Watson, 1993: 108) and above all that values (Örücü, 2002: 13) as part of various legal structures are of critical relevance in a plurality-conscious legal analysis.

In view of such theoretical findings of global relevance, we are now better prepared to reassess the eurocentric nature of mainstream legal theory. The next chapter critiques traditional jurisprudential approaches, highlighting their inherent limitations in adopting an isolated focus on one particular aspect of law or any one particular methodology.

3

Comparative jurisprudence: images and reflections of law

The previous chapters confirmed that legal academics are still struggling to free themselves from the shackles of 'black letter' traditions (Cownie, 2004) and 'black box' approaches (Twining, 2000). Given that 'one of the main jobs of jurisprudence is the critical exploration and evaluation of prevailing assumptions underlying legal discourse – both law talk and talk about law' (Twining, 2000: 12), a radical reappraisal of old-established Western concepts and assumptions of legal theory in the light of globality-consciousness and sensitivity to legal pluralism is needed. Indeed, 'it is clear that if legal theory is to engage seriously with globalisation and its consequences a critical re-examination of its agenda, its heritage of ideas, and its conceptual tools is called for' (Twining, 2000: 10).

Such critical re-examination of global validity must demonstrate that general jurisprudence is more than a Western phenomenon. All around the world, different legal cultures have developed their own ways of 'law talk and talk about law', which a plurality-conscious global jurisprudence must account for. Observing that globalisation has already stimulated major rethinking in many fields, Twining (2000: 50) argues that 'jurisprudence has so far responded only patchily to these challenges, but that the prospects for a sustained response are better than might appear on the surface'. Sharing Twining's optimism, I hope to have shown through the previous chapters that significant progress has already been made in conceptualising legal pluralism and globality-consciousness in law. But there is much more to do, and legal pluralism as a term and methodology remains unacceptable to many legal scholars. The axioms of Western legal theory, Chiba's (1986) Western 'model jurisprudence', remain firmly imprisoned by statist and positivist assumptions about the nature of law. Together with idealistic, but equally prescriptive and conceptually rigid natural law speculations about universal values, they persistently prevent lawyers from developing plurality-conscious thinking about law. Lawyers remain uncomfortable about facing the boundaries between social (in the widest sense) and legal fields. While a fully integrated theoretical approach is asked for in principle, in practice legal theorists balk at the challenge and constantly divert their attention to a maze of marginally 'new' theories that 'critically' question the issue of global interconnectedness, but do not really tackle it.

The sub-sections below comprise a historically grounded analysis of legal theories within their Western contexts in roughly chronological order, adopting a pluralist perspective as developed in the previous chapters. Focusing on the emergence of Western thoughts about law, with initial emphasis on chthonic natural law, its later Christianisation and a subsequent gradual shift towards rationality and 'secular' approaches, this brief historical analysis demasks general legal theory as 'Western' rather than universal.[1] The aim is to re-examine what to many readers will be familiar perspectives on traditional jurisprudence in the light of globality-focused approaches, testing to what extent they are still useful in an interactive, global context.[2] The task is to point out where and how eurocentric assumptions have made significant impacts and where (to be expanded in later chapters) the legal systems of Asia and Africa have made similar or identical contributions to legal theory which have been overlooked. This analysis prepares the ground for the final sub-section, a detailed discussion of a triangular model of global jurisprudence which takes more explicit account of law's socio-cultural embeddedness and plurality-conscious analysis in a global context. So far, virtually all major jurists have not taken sufficient account of non-state law and have focused too much on positivist methodologies.[3] Twining (2000: 76) provides a revealing example of what he calls 'the disastrous influence of Austinian analytical jurisprudence' and complains that '[f]or almost a century an impoverished version of conceptual analysis, under the name of analytical jurisprudence, dominated legal theory in Britain' (p. 97). There is a strong view that much of the recent debate about positivism and its adversaries has been 'repetitious, trivial and almost entirely pointless' (p. 119). Positivism, however, is itself a reaction to natural law (Olivecrona, 1971), which must come first in any chronological survey of legal history and conceptual analysis.

Further, in contrast to the historical experience of many Asian and African legal systems, it appears that in European conceptualisations of law, religion was from at least medieval times gradually divested of its dominant position. Law became eventually conceived in the modern liberal West as a product of human rationality and effort rather than arising from divine power or will.[4] This does not mean that religion became irrelevant in European legal thought, but Western legal theory has clearly privileged law, as a human creation, over the competing claims of religion, in a way that most evidently Islamic jurisprudence is not willing to contemplate to that extent.[5] Other reactions to inflated

---

[1] Many jurists (e.g. Olivecrona, 1971; Kelly, 1992) have explicitly stated that they are only dealing with modern Western society.

[2] For a more detailed survey, see especially Freeman (2001) and Morrison (1997).

[3] Twining (2000: 61) indicates that Llewellyn and Finnis may be an exception.

[4] This leads to the liberal Rule of Law model, discussed in detail by Unger (1976, ch. 3)

[5] This is not unique to Islam or some forms of orthodox Judaism. Militant forms of *hindutva* (Hindu-ness), coupled with belief in divine revelation of ancient legal texts, employ similar

claims of Western conceptual domination and globalising pressures may be less articulate, but no less powerful.

3.1 Traditional natural law theories in outline

Starting with natural law makes sense for historical reasons and provides an effective entry point to legal philosophy's maze. It also demonstrates that Western legal theory has never been entirely removed from the spiritual and the 'religious', and is therefore of necessity culture-specific in its own way, with a Christian bias. The origins of natural law theories are rooted in the distant past,[6] arising from moral and more or less 'religious' sets of assumptions about reality, to the effect that there is a force larger than man, against which all human actions must be measured.[7] If the earliest legal systems were all chthonic (Glenn, 2004: 61), the first forms of natural law everywhere must be chthonic, too. Historically, it is not the prerogative of the West to have thought about legal theories, the origins of law, its morality, and its potential for abuse since ancient times. These universal questions have arisen everywhere in human societies, from earliest times, but within quite specific cultural contexts, giving rise to different, culturally conditioned answers.[8] It seems that eurocentric assumptions about the primitivity of non-Western 'others' have hindered acknowledgment of such early contributions to legal theory.[9]

In jurisprudence, there have always been huge debates about ethics and morals as part of law (Freeman, 2001: 47–51). Attempts by some positivists (in particular Kelsen) to banish value judgments from juristic study have been unconvincing.[10] Thus 'it will be found impossible to disregard the role of value judgments in legal activity, and we cannot exorcise this functional role by stigmatising such judgments as merely subjective or unscientific' (p. 51). A typical definition of natural law which overstressed the universality of the concept was provided by Olivecrona (1971: 8):

    arguments. Muslims might simply assert the superiority of Islam and oppose eurocentric 'rule of law' concepts by their own legocentric claims to the effect that the Qur'an is binding divine legislation.

[6] Cotterrell (2003: 115) summarises the natural law position 'that law cannot be properly understood except in moral terms, that it is fundamentally a moral phenomenon', and notes that '[i]ts history extends through at least 2,500 years of Western philosophy'.

[7] As we shall see, another challenging question may be whether this force is actually larger than any particular God.

[8] Chapters 4–7 below are going to show in detail that Hindu law, Islamic law, African law and Chinese law each have their own culture-specific forms of natural law.

[9] Weber (1972: 143) expressly denied any type of natural law in the traditional Hindu system. Due to their ancient status and prevailing orality, evidence may of course not be recoverable, a problem particularly for, but not unique to, African legal philosophy.

[10] Twining (2000: 62) treats Kelsen as relevant, 'if only as a worthy opponent' and goes on to say that he represents an 'illuminatingly misguided position'.

> In contradistinction to positive law, 'natural law' generally means a law that has not been posited. Even if it is ascribed to the will of God, it is supposed to have always existed. Its validity is not thought to be limited to a certain people or a certain time. The law of nature is timeless and universal.

Early Western natural law theories are immensely diverse,[11] trace their origin in Greek civilisation (Morrison, 1997) and were much debated until the nineteenth century, when natural law largely fell out of favour in Europe. Many of the earlier assumptions are now rejected as false and 'it must not be supposed that the phrase "natural law" has had a constant meaning: it has meant different and often contradictory things in the course of its long history.'[12] The common feature of natural law theories is that they 'all turn away from the reality of an actual legal system and purport to discover principles of universal validity in some external source' (Dias and Hughes, 1957: 372). Natural law implied throughout a search for ideals higher than positive law: 'The history of natural law is a tale of the search of mankind for absolute justice and of its failure' (Friedmann, 1967: 95) and its main attraction as a legal philosophy 'has been as often the justification of existing authority as a revolt against it' (p. 95). At different times, natural law 'has been used to support almost any ideology; but the most important and lasting theories of natural law have undoubtedly been inspired by the two ideas, of a universal order governing all men, and of the inalienable rights of the individual' (Friedmann, 1947: 19).

Twining (2000: 61) depicts classical natural law as 'a tradition which has claimed universality for its principles and which significantly antedates the rise of the nation-state'.[13] While natural law theory has fulfilled many functions, with changing socio-political and socio-cultural conditions, its notions have constantly changed also in Europe. Ideas about nature, justice and the appropriateness of certain rules are everywhere in the world culturally conditioned and culture-specific, notwithstanding claims to universality.[14] Here lie some of the roots of current problems with debates on globalisation and the superiority claims of Western normative systems. From a European perspective, by the eighteenth century, natural law had become explicitly Christianised and was unashamed about claiming global validity. Kelly (1992: 259) cites what Sir William Blackstone (1723–80) wrote in 1765. To him, natural law,

> being coeval with mankind and dictated by God himself, is of course superior in obligation to any other. It is binding over all the globe in all countries,

---

[11] For details see Freeman (2001: 90–102).

[12] Dias and Hughes (1957: 350). New natural law theories during the second half of the twentieth century are discussed in section 3.7.2 below.

[13] Part II of this study demonstrates that the latter observation also applies to all major legal systems of Asia and Africa.

[14] In discussing the concepts of natural law as applied by the Dutchman Hugo Grotius (1583–1645) and the German jurist-historian Samuel Pufendorf (1632–94), who separated natural law from theology, Olivecrona (1971: 8–25) explicitly acknowledges the influence of their own times and location on their thinking.

and at all times: no human laws are of any validity, if contrary to this; and such of them as are valid derive all their force, and all their authority, mediately or immediately, from this original.

Many jurisprudential studies do not recognise that non-European cultures may have something to say on natural law theories.[15] Leading early scholars denied that non-Western cultures had developed natural law concepts, which implied deficiency in civilisation and inability to contribute anything useful to global reflections on natural law, condemning them to silence.[16] Typically, the taxonomies of legal families in the world also disregard natural law criteria. Western hegemonistic claims receive endorsement when David and Brierley (1978: 28) deny the presence of natural law concepts in Far Eastern civilisations such as China, since 'there is no question of studying an ideal distinct from rules laid down by legislators or simply followed in practice'. This is quite inconsistent with their own recognition that in Africa, like in Far Eastern cultures, 'the principal objective is the maintenance or restoration of harmony rather than respect for law' (p. 29). How would members of such cultures perceive this higher harmony, if not through perceptions of a higher entity than positivist law, very much akin to European natural law theories? It is one thing for comparatists to assert, as David and Brierley (1978: 26) do, that non-Western countries 'remain very largely faithful to philosophies in which the place and function of law are very different from what they are in the West', and quite another to spot similarities in culture-specific assumptions about natural law and justice.

The failure of most natural law theorists to even contemplate that there may be different cultural forms of natural law is highly significant for the present study. This may have come about because most early Western natural law scholars were engaged in debates between positivist and natural law concepts, and largely ignored social variations. A notable exception is the neo-Kantian, anti-Marxist German scholar Rudolf Stammler (1856–1938), who cultivated a theory of 'natural law with a changing content', which holds that 'while the ideal of justice is absolute, its application must vary with time, place and circumstance'.[17] Among these variations, moral attitudes are prominent. Freeman (2001: 93–4) gives a telling example: 'The Greeks did not think slavery was wrong: we do. In which case to concede that the content of natural law may vary with social differences is to give up any attempt to construct objective norms and values.' Stone (1965: 167–81) brings out that even in the early twentieth century this was a matter of concern for pioneering thinkers from the German tradition of historical jurisprudence. Discussing Stammler's difficult

---

[15] Freeman (2001: 103 n. 11) acknowledges traces of natural law among almost all peoples, but necessarily directs attention to the Greek roots because they are better researched.

[16] See for example Weber (1972: 143) on India. As noted in chapter 1, section 1.2.4, awareness of such biased views seems to have silenced non-Western voices.

[17] Freeman (2001: 93). Hart's marginal contribution to this debate is dismissed as rather weak (p. 94).

'pure' theories about the 'right law' and assessing his contribution, Stone (1965: 172) shows that,

> his design was to seek, not universal *rules* of just law (which he thought quite unattainable), but merely a universal *method* of ascertaining just law in empirically conditioned situations. In theory this *method* should be absolute and universal, though even as to this, Stammler was sufficiently a twentieth century child to admit that 'a systematic and universal view of law may also undergo change and progress'.

Stammler's promising approach anticipates that emerging debates about globalisation, in the sense of global plurification and their legal recognition, will pose a significant challenge to the universality claims of Western natural law. On the other hand, since the key issue for natural law theories of any description is 'not whether law can be morally evaluated but whether its *essential character* must be explained in moral terms' (Cotterrell, 2003: 119), many writers have taken the view that natural law ideas lack any convincing theoretical justification.[18] However, such secular approaches and challenges to natural law are mainly of more recent provenance. Historically speaking, also in Europe, the dominant early views of natural law theories are linked to various kinds of religious belief and are culture-specific while making global claims.

3.2 Greek legal philosophy

All European textbook authors agree that the roots of European thought on philosophy, politics, society and law can be traced to ancient Greece. Friedmann (1947: 3) stated that 'Greek thought has developed all the principal problems and put the questions which have occupied Western legal thought ever since' and 'all the main issues of legal theory were formulated by Greek thinkers, from Homer to the Stoics' (Friedmann, 1967: 5). Legal theorists have studied not so much Greek law as it existed in reality, but the emerging philosophies of law produced by ancient Greek thinkers, based upon teleological views of human nature (Morrison, 1997: 41). The Greeks themselves were 'comparatively uninterested in the technical development of law' (Freeman, 2001: 103), but speculation about the relation of higher justice to positive law was propelled by practical problems. Friedmann (1967: 5) notes that 'a unique gift of speculative insight and intellectual perception, a sense of tragedy and human conflict which is apparent in Greek philosophy and poetry, made possible the Greek contribution to legal philosophy'. In the classical era, there was frequent turmoil and no unified Greek state or legal system. Within this diffuse political framework, 'the idea of law, in a sense which the word conveys immediately to the modern mind . . . is fluid and elusive . . . [W]e are seeing Europe in a

---

[18] Cotterrell (2003: 119) cites Habermas (1974) to this effect.

pre-legal condition' (Kelly, 1992: 7).[19] Greek legal philosophy, disgusted with abuses of the law, focused on higher things than human arbitrariness. Jones (1956: 98) characterised the early genesis of Greek natural law theories as linked with natural sciences:

> The notion of a law of Nature is one expression of the belief that there are certain legal principles and institutions so firmly in the general scheme of things that they represent something inherent in all ordered social existence. The concept was originally bound up with that of physical laws. In the philosophy of the Pythagoreans and Stoics, the whole Universe was conceived as a Cosmos or ordered whole, governed by a creative force called by them Nature or God or the Universal Law; and particular things were believed to be an emanation from the Universal through the operation of this Law. Since individual human beings are a part of Nature their only chance of achieving Man's highest purpose and attaining true happiness seemed to lie in ordering their lives according to this law of Nature. To the Stoics, life in accordance with Nature was what was meant by Virtue, for Man's individual reason should also be a reflexion of the Universal Reason which they held to be the divine element in the Universe and the final standard of conduct. Human laws and institutions thus came to be regarded as a realization, however imperfect and partial, of the law of Nature, which stands behind them and provides rules by which men should regulate their actions.

Much of this basic framework of natural law thought remains debated today (Freeman, 2001: 103ff.). Man-made rules in this perceived system of macro-cosmic order, which, not by coincidence, resembles the oldest known Hindu assumptions about the nature of the Universe and man's place in it,[20] were tested against moral criteria which could be seen as universal values. Kelly (1992: 7) emphasises the religious basis of ancient Greek understandings of law:

> There is no 'legislature'. The king does not 'make' laws, in the sense of rules which the people must obey. There is no apparent consciousness of custom as something normative. Instead, there is a *themis*: a word whose force is difficult to grasp, but which is applied to an area at the centre of which is perhaps the idea of a god-inspired decision or directive or finding. This finding is not arbitrary, but reflects a shared sense of what is proper. It is the word used to convey rulings of the gods as well as of kings.

---

[19] Legal fluidity appears to be seen here as 'primitive' rather than a sign of pluralist sophistication. Unger (1976: 76–7) suggests that this local cherishing of difference was a shattering discovery which sparked off the search for higher universal principles.

[20] See chapter 4 below. Philological 'Orientalist' research suggests that the ancient Greeks and Indians (Aryans) were close cousins who, in search of greener pastures, settled in different parts of the world. Some nationalistic Indian research claims that the Aryans originated in the subcontinent, refuting the idea that Indian culture may have European roots. This approach also challenges the globalising claims of Western culture and defensively asserts a particular 'indigenous' element in the admittedly hybrid socio-cultural developments in India.

This early religious basis of understanding human life as linked with various gods is not expressed in cosmic terms, but there are remarkable parallels with early Hindu thought.[21] Friedmann (1967: 6) notes with reference to Homer's work that '[l]aw is embodied in the Themistes which the kings receive from Zeus as the divine source of all earthly justice and which are based on custom and tradition'. Kelly (1992: 7–9) argues that, in this early pre-legal age, Greek philosophy developed no clear concept of state law but concentrated on nature and justice. Friedmann (1967: 98) explained:

> First among its forerunners is Heraclitus. Trying to find the essence of being, Heraclitus finds it in the rhythm of events. This he called destiny (ειμαρ-μενη), order (δικη), and reason (λογος) of the world. Here, for the first time, nature is not just substance, but a relation, an order of things. This provided the basis for the Greek school of enlightenment (Sophists). The movement developed in the fifth century BC when the high state of political, social and spiritual development of the Greek city states and resulting problems of political and social life forced upon thinking people a reflection on law and order. Laws changed frequently in the democratic republic, and the human and changing element behind the laws became visible. Philosophers began to think about the reason for and validity of laws. At such a point the conception of nature, as an order of things, could be utilised. With a generation sceptical of itself, weary of the arbitrariness of human government, conscious of oppression and injustice, nature came to be opposed to the tyranny of men . . . From this arise demands for justice which anticipate the principal demands for social justice, raised and disregarded again and again in modern history.

Out of this contrast of supposedly perfect universalist order and imperfect human ordering arose powerful social criticisms,[22] in which law, already at that early stage, received a bad press. Law in its various manifestations was seen as inherently plural. Dias and Hughes (1957: 351) indicate that the Sophists explicitly recognised the relativity and subjectivity of human ideas and perceptions. Observing the unsatisfactory legal realities around them, they argued that both the makers and the subjects of law just acted in self-interest, so that law was little else than expediency. They argued therefore that law was not founded on universal principles, such as justice, but was subject to multiple manipulations by rulers and subjects.

An opposing and eventually dominant conceptualisation of natural law among early Greek thinkers was more guided by uniform principles (Dias and Hughes, 1957: 351). The Greek philosopher Socrates (c. 470–399 BC) and his pupil Plato (429–348 BC) emphasised the existence and immutable nature of

[21] For details on the old Hindu concept of *rita* (macrocosmic Order) see chapter 4, section 4.2.

[22] Freeman (2001: 89) notes that in modern times natural law 'has formed an important weapon in political and legal ideology'.

basic moral principles, laying foundations for the later dominant uniformising strand of European natural law. Their theories were elaborated by Plato's star pupil Aristotle (384–322 BC), who still accepted, however, that 'among men, even natural justice was not unchanging' (Freeman, 2001: 103). Friedmann (1967: 10) showed that Aristotle exerted a major influence on the development of Western philosophy through his doctrine of the dual character of man as part and master of nature. Through his *Logic*, Aristotle suggested that the world could be seen as a universal totality comprising the whole of Nature. Friedmann (1947: 22) noted:

> Man is part of nature in a twofold sense; on the one hand he is part of matter, part of the creatures of God; as such he partakes of experience; but man is also endowed with active reason which distinguishes him from all other parts of nature. As such he is capable of forming his will in accordance with the insight of his reason.

Thus, man as part of the universe and subject to its universal laws, has at the same time the potential to dominate nature, since he is able to distinguish between good and evil, and can exercise his own free will. This increasingly anthropocentric development of Greek philosophy is also reflected in traditional Hindu conceptualisations of the universe and the role of man, in which the latter remains at all times subject to the laws of the universe, but individuals in their social embeddedness assume central agency.[23] Aristotle's recognition of human reason as part of nature later provided the basis for an elaborated Stoic conception of the Law of Nature. The Aristotelian philosophy of law treats state law as inferior in status compared to the higher, 'natural' law. Kelly (1992: 13–19) shows that the ancient Greeks, observing socio-political reality, were well aware of the potential for unjust laws and abuse of legal processes. Philosophers could clearly see the self-serving class interest of law-making at the time (p. 22). The earlier thoughts of Aristotle were then adapted by the Stoics,[24] who focused on human reason. By arguing that reason governs the entire universe, of which humans are a part, they identified natural law as living according to reason. The Law of Nature thus became identified with a moral duty.[25] Gierke

---

[23] This parallels the shift from macrocosmic *rita* to microcosmic *dharma* in traditional Hindu law (chapter 4, sections 4.2 and 4.3). Similar tensions in Islamic jurisprudence between Allah's supreme Order and the need for man-made rules to implement it are discussed in chapter 5.

[24] Stoicism is a school of philosophy, founded by Zeno of Citium (350–260 BC) in about 300 BC. He was influenced by Socrates, Aristotle and Plato. The Stoics held that all reality is material and is shaped by a universal working force that pervades everything and could be seen as God. The Stoics argued that by performing one's duty with the right disposition, one can live consistently with Nature and thus achieve true 'freedom'. There are many parallels with ancient Hindu thought (see chapter 4).

[25] Olivecrona (1971: 13) discusses the reflections of such thoughts in seventeenth-century Germany: 'Pufendorf propounds a general principle of natural law: that everybody ought

(1950: xxxv–xxxvi) explained how this gave rise to an early vision of global uniformity from a Greek perspective:

> Nature was synonymous with Reason, and Reason was synonymous with God. They believed that the true city or polity of mankind was a single 'city of God', or cosmopolis . . . which was also a city of Reason and of Nature. They believed that true law was the law of the city – the law of Reason; the law of Nature. According to the teaching of Zeno, the founder of Stoicism, men should not live in different cities, divided by separate rules of justice; they should consider all men fellow-citizens, and there should be one life and order, as of a flock on a common pasture feeding together under a common law.

Significantly, the Greek word for 'law' as reason (Friedmann, 1967: 6), *nomos*, is the same as that for pasture, except for a difference of accent. However, this rural, idyllic image of law as a shared resource, available to all members of a social group, does not necessarily mean that all such members would be equal. Gierke (1950: xxxvi) pointed out that '[i]t was an ideal law which could only become actual if men were purely rational. Its principles were ideal principles. Among these ideal principles was that of equality. By nature, and as reasonable creatures, all human beings were equal. By nature the woman was equal to the man, and the slave to the master. This was the teaching of Zeno.' Friedmann (1967: 100) explains that the Stoics used the postulates of reason as a universal force to develop the first great cosmopolitan philosophy of Western thought: 'Men are endowed with reason, irrespective of nationality and race. The difference of city states, of Greek and barbarian, is rejected, and a universal world-state postulated in which men live as equals.' Freeman (2001: 104) traces the emergence of this understanding of natural law as a universal system:

> Until the Stoics 'nature' had meant 'the order of things': with them it came to be identified with man's reason. When man lived according to 'reason' he was living 'naturally'. To the Stoics precepts of reason had universal force. They stressed the ideas of individual worth, moral duty and universal brotherhood, and though in the early days theirs was a philosophy of withdrawal enjoining conformity to the universal law upon the select few of wise men alone, in its later development . . . in the second century BC, stress was placed on its universal aspects . . . for all men.

However, while in an earlier golden age of absolute natural law there were no distinctions in terms of family, slavery, property or government, all these institutions were later perceived as necessary by the Stoics because of the moral

---

to contribute to the maintenance of a peaceful community with all others, in accordance with the disposition and purpose of humanity. From this principle all special maxims of natural law are to be deduced.' A similar sense of 'duty to do the right thing at the right time' is reflected as the core meaning of Hindu *dharma*, Chinese *li*, Japanese *giri* and the Islamic *shariah*.

deterioration of mankind (Friedmann, 1967: 101). Faced with this dilemma, it was believed that 'relative' natural law would lead to legislation guided by reason, which should conform as closely as possible to absolute natural law. Current visions of uniformising globalisation and endeavours to create a global legal order marked by observance of human rights and 'rule of law' clearly relate back to, and feed on, early ancient idealised understandings of universal principles and the equality of man. Ancient Greek philosophy, in particular Aristotle's work, as Friedmann (1967: 13) notes, 'thus anticipates all the major themes and conflicts of modern Western legal thought'.

3.3 Roman legal philosophy

The Romans laid the foundations for modern analytical jurisprudence but made only minor contributions to legal philosophy (Friedmann, 1967: 5). Once they became familiar with different Greek philosophers, the Romans took particular interest in the Stoics, finding it attractive to use their conception of nature based on reason 'to transform a rigid system into a cosmopolitan one fit to rule the world' (Friedmann, 1967: 101). Kelly (1992: 47–8) summarises the essence of Stoic philosophy as received by the Romans:

> [I]ts central message was that everything in nature is to be explained by reason; and every act must be justified by reason. The wise man, therefore, must live in accordance with the reason which is identical with nature; his conduct in accordance with that principle will enable him to rise superior to the application of any force or temptation. It is this element of sovereignty, of serenity, available to everyone who practises such wisdom, that provides the link with the modern usage of the word 'stoic', meaning calm steadfastness in adversity . . . [H]ere was a training in individual character that would reward its practitioner with a vital inner independence.

Although the practical impact of Greek legal models on Roman law 'was nil, or virtually nil' (Kelly, 1992: 48), Stoic elements of Greek legal philosophy found a fertile soil in Rome. Emphasis on austerity and indifference to good or ill fortune were deeply admired qualities and almost all the Roman jurists followed Stoic teaching. Marcus Tullius Cicero (106–43 BC) became its most prominent and productive representative through his concept of natural or true law as 'right reason in agreement with nature' (Freeman, 2001: 104). Jones (1956: 99) noted:

> Cicero often uses the word *Natura* – either alone or in such phrases as *ius natura, ius naturae, lex naturae* – to mean primarily some sort of objective and universal order, emanating from divine reason, yet at the same time holding sway over gods as well as men; but he also has in his mind a *ius naturale* comprising those half-legal, half-ethical rules which express the principles of human justice, because they have a special bearing upon the relations of men living in society upon their duties to one another and to the gods.

Freeman (2001: 104) highlights that Cicero was the first natural lawyer advocating the striking down of positive laws which contravened natural law, comparing corrupt legislatures to a band of robbers.[26] Roman developments at this stage involve a secularisation of approaches taken to natural law. In Rome and later in many parts of the empire, lawyers 'had to administer the law to hundreds of non-Roman peoples and tribes living under different customs' (Friedmann, 1967: 101). Less concerned with pantheistic speculations on the nature of the Universe than with practical legal administration, the Roman jurists preferred a pragmatic approach (Freeman, 2001: 104) and developed a practical science rather than a theoretical body of knowledge. According to Kelly (1992: 49–50):

> The formulation of great first principles and grand generalities was quite foreign to them. They were strictly practical, concentrating on the concrete individual cases in regard to which they had been consulted as to the law (hence their name *iuris consulti*, 'persons consulted about the law'), and giving their view tersely, without rhetorical or philosophical flourish, mostly also without any full statement of reasons (though often citing in support the congruent opinions of other or earlier jurists).

By the time of Cicero, three different Roman conceptions of law became prominent. Apart from *ius natura*, we find *ius civile*, the particular law applicable only to Roman citizens, and *ius gentium*, which applied to all members of the Roman Empire and did not distinguish between citizens and non-citizens. *Ius naturale* was not commonly distinguished by Roman lawyers from *ius gentium* (Jones, 1956: 101–2), following Stoic teaching, and became identified with *ius natura*. In practice, *ius gentium* was developed by Roman magistrates as a body of general legal principles, derived from foreign laws and customs which appeared capable of general application, mainly through maritime trade in the Mediterranean (Friedmann, 1967: 101). These general principles of justice and reason were developed from case to case, leading to the *ius gentium* 'as the embodiment of the law and usages observed among different peoples, and representing general good sense' (p. 101).[27] In practice, this widening concept encompassed mainly a body of commercial laws concerned with contracts, defined as universal,[28] while *ius naturale* remained a general legal ideal. These two notions of

---

[26] St Augustine (354–430 AD) referred to Cicero's scepticism about positive law, asking rhetorically: 'What are states without justice but robber-bands enlarged?' (Harris, 1980: 8). Kelly (1992: 57–63) discusses many different approaches in Roman theories of natural law after the early views of Cicero.

[27] Freeman (2001: 105) suggests that this development demonstrates a confusion of 'is' and 'ought', and therefore an early example of the 'naturalistic fallacy', the convenient definition of moral norms in terms of suitably agreeable facts. It may also be seen as a jurisprudence of common sense, with an acute awareness of legal pluralism.

[28] This indicates one reason why commercial law and contract law are perceived as more global than other types of law.

universal law co-existed, *ius natura* of more religious nature and *ius gentium* of more secular orientation, together forming a 'universal' common law.[29] Friedmann (1967: 102) notes that '[n]atural law, apart from transforming the old *jus civile*, now created the basis on which Roman and foreign people could live together under a common rule of law'.

Later Roman law was much influenced by Christian thinking. Early Christians in the Roman period laid the foundations for arguments that nature, including mankind, had become corrupted and that, as the exponent of divine law, the Church could interfere with the state and override its laws (Dias and Hughes, 1957: 355). Therefore the late Roman period, influenced by Christianity, ended with a reassertion of the superior status of religious natural law. Watson (1993: 116) shows that the Emperor Justinian (482/3–565 AD) 'defined natural law as that which nature has taught all animals, whereas *ius gentium*, the law of nations, is that used by all peoples'. While Watson may be right to assume that this distinction was made to deny significance to natural law and to privilege positive law, this was also a particular form of religious positivism. Later reinterpretations of this distinction of natural law in a primary and secondary sense (Watson, 1993: 116–17) confirm that Justinian may have laid foundations for eurocentric hubris, reinforcing assumptions that uncivilised people had no proper law.

3.4 Early and later medieval developments in Church law

For many centuries, as Friedmann (1967: 104) notes, 'the Fathers of the Church, of whom Ambrose, Augustine and Gregory are the most notable, preserved the continuity of the idea of natural law and, at the same time, began to give it a different meaning and foundation'.[30] The Stoic distinction of an ideal absolute natural law and a 'second best' relative natural law was linked more definitely with original sin (p. 104). The revival of Roman legal scholarship in Europe, starting from Bologna in the eleventh century, meant that Roman law became a widely studied subject from the twelfth century onwards and '[t]hroughout the Middle Ages, the theology of the Catholic Church set the tone and pattern of all speculative thought' (Freeman, 2001: 105).[31] Earlier Roman patterns of thought were now heavily overlaid with Christian philosophy, leading to the Christianisation of European natural law (Dias and Hughes, 1957: 355).[32] Gierke (1950: xl) noted that law became 'the expression of human reason in a great body of scripture . . . the heavenly Scripture committed to the Church'.

[29] Unger (1976: 77) notes that the precise nature of *ius gentium* remains disputed.
[30] Friedmann (1967: 104–7) neatly summarises five major trends running through this period.
[31] This is a typical eurocentric statement, ignoring the non-European world.
[32] A detailed analysis of Christian legal philosophies with reference to different Christian orientations is found in Kelly (1992).

The Catholic Church made a traditional distinction between the absolute Law of Nature and the relative Natural Law. The first is to the effect that by nature, i.e. God's law, 'men are free from the State, they own all things in common, and they are equal to one another' (Gierke, 1950: xxxvii).[33] The relative Natural Law, now justified in Christian terminology by the imperfect condition of man after the 'Fall from Grace', and therefore rooted in and tainted by sin (Freeman, 2001: 105), allowed for human law-making, which could potentially violate all the ideal principles of the absolute Law of Nature. Gierke (1950: xxxvii) explained:

> The State, and property, and even slavery, can all find their place in the scheme of this law; but they must all have something of an ideal character . . . The relative Law of Nature is a sort of half-way house between an absolute ideal, vanished beyond recall, and the mere actuality of positive law. It was not easy to occupy a half-way house without being exposed to attacks from either side.

St Thomas Aquinas (1226–74) became a key figure in the development of a universal divine law, synthesising the philosophy of Aristotle with Catholic faith (Freeman, 2001: 105).[34] As a philosopher, he drew a distinction between reason and belief. While his theories assert that God's law is always superior to that of man,[35] by abandoning the idea that all human law-making was inherently tainted, he granted a rightful place to positivism, setting in train reinvigorated thinking about how to harmonise legislative power with natural law axioms and opening avenues for the later domination of legal positivism. In fact, Aquinas was an unacknowledged early legal pluralist. His theories are based on the understanding that different types of law co-exist and interact with each other harmoniously and conflictingly. Harris (1980: 8) explained:

> His legal theory encompasses four types of law. 'Eternal law' comprises God-given rules governing all creation.[36] 'Natural law' is that segment of eternal law which is discoverable through the special process of reasoning mapped out by the pagan authors – intuitions of the natural and deductions

---

[33] Similar claims, it should be noted, are made for Islamic law.

[34] For details on Canon Law see Brundage (1969) and Helmholz (1996).

[35] Again, one notes parallels with Islamic thought. According to Aquinas, '[d]ivine law is supreme. But the whole of divine law is not accessible to men' (Friedmann, 1967: 108).

[36] Freeman (2001: 106) sees this *lex aeterna* as 'divine reason, known only to God and "the blessed who see God in his essence". It is God's plan for the universe, a deliberate act of God and everything, not only man, is subject to it.' From a comparative perspective, we note that this concept is also reflected in other legal traditions, particularly in the Islamic concepts of Allah's omniscience, the privileged position of the Prophet Mohammad as the only human in close contact with God, and the competing claims of later jurists (chapter 5).

drawn therefrom.[37] 'Divine law' has been revealed in Scripture.[38] 'Human law' consists of rules, supportable by reason, but articulated by human authorities for the common good.[39] As to the interrelation between these different types of law, two crucial propositions stand out in Thomist philosophy. First, human laws derive their legal quality, their power to bind in conscience, from natural law . . . In some instances, the content of law is deducible from first principles of natural law; for the rest, the legislator has the freedom of an architect. Secondly, any purported law which is in conflict with natural or divine law is a mere corruption of law and so not binding by virtue of its own legal quality; nevertheless, even if an enactment is contrary to natural law and so 'unjust', obedience may still be proper to avoid bad example or civil disturbance.

This approach underwrites legal positivism as long as it remains subservient to religion. Friedmann (1967: 109) noted that '[h]uman law is part and parcel of divine government; there is no schism between faith and reason; on the contrary, reason is a partial manifestation of faith.' This shows that later European legal philosophy could leave the fields of 'eternal law' and 'divine law', which focused on the afterlife, largely to religious studies,[40] while focusing on the two more secular elements of Thomist thought, which focused on this life. Dias and Hughes (1957: 356) confirmed that '[t]he identification

---

[37] This is *lex naturalis* or *lex natura*, which 'consists of participation of the eternal law in rational creatures . . . in so far as this is intuitively and innately known and knowable' (Freeman, 2001: 106). This natural law is the same for all men, since all people are rational. However, Aquinas himself conceded that 'the will to do right and awareness of what is right may be distorted by habit, custom or temperament' (p. 106), which further confirms that Aquinas was an early legal pluralist.

[38] Putting this type in second place, which indicates its closeness to the concept of *lex aeterna*, Freeman (2003: 106) simply notes that '*lex divina* is the law of God revealed in the Scriptures'. Friedmann (1967: 109) uses this concept to explain the late medieval Church argument that '[a]ll law enacted by human authority, that is positive law, must keep within these limits. In a hierarchy of legal values, *lex divina* is perhaps the least necessary of the categories. But it served to cement the position of the Church as the authoritative interpreter of divine law laid down in the Scripture.' In comparative perspective, this concept is found when some Hindus believe (which they need not do) in the divinely revealed nature of their most ancient texts, the four Vedas ('knowledge'), and when Muslim scholarship makes a fine (often overlooked and undervalued) distinction between Allah's supervening authority and His revelation in the Qur'an.

[39] Friedmann (1947: 28) noted that 'Natural Law is a part of Divine Law, that part which reveals itself in natural reason. Man, as a reasonable being, applies this part of Divine Law to human affairs, and he can thus distinguish between good and evil. It is from the principles of eternal law, as revealed in natural law, that all human law derives.' Freeman (2001: 107) sees *lex humana* as positive law and demonstrates the huge difference between practice and theory in the medieval period.

[40] This appears to be an important distinction from Islamic jurisprudence, in which concern with God's law in both senses of Thomist thinking has remained linked and thus 'religion' remains theoretically dominant for those who wish to assert this.

of natural law with reason helped the separation, which came about much later, of natural law from theology'. This indicates that the secularisation of law appeared on the philosophical horizon much earlier than in political action.

Moreover, human laws 'are recognised to be variable according to time and circumstances' (Friedmann, 1967: 109) and thus seen as culture-specific, anticipating utilitarianism. While some assumed basic principles of natural law, such as 'do harm to no man', are commonly treated as universal and immutable,[41] it became now possible, through deductions from first principles, or through additions from natural law, to modify laws as the ruler pleased. Olivecrona (1971: 23) examined this linkage between natural law and positive law:

> Since positive law is based on the law of nature, its contents must be in harmony with this law. But the lawgiver has got the right to supplement the law of nature in many ways according to the needs of the particular society. The right of property, for instance, has been introduced by positive law. This is also the case with punishments. The precepts of the law of nature are not devoid of sanctions: their sanctions are the pangs of conscience. But human punishments are a human invention, though the justification of punishment rests on the law of nature.
>
> The law of nature, therefore, gives wide scope to the activity of the sovereign as lawgiver. But he cannot do anything contrary to the law of nature. If he did so, his precepts would lack binding force; they might create fear, but they could not impose obligations.

In Part II of this study, the culture-specific early concepts of governance in Hindu, Islamic and Chinese legal traditions are examined in further detail. It appears that this linkage of natural law concepts and positivist empowerment is familiar to Asian and also African legal systems,[42] but in all cases, as suggested here by Olivecrona's analysis, positivism is put under the shadow of the higher category of natural law.[43] A ruler, unlike in later European secular thinking which sought to divorce law and religion, would not be able to claim absolute authority. Since recourse to natural law theory now gave a presumptive moral status to all legislation, even where positive law manifestly conflicted with natural law, obedience to the law-maker would still be morally required.

Late medieval developments in legal philosophy thus tolerated that human law could be manifestly unjust,[44] to such an extent that the Church exposed

[41] It may be doubted whether such a supposedly 'first principle' would necessarily be acceptable in Hindu, Chinese, Muslim and also African laws, where the requirement of adherence to a specific higher Order may override the evidently good expectation not to do harm to others (see later chapters).

[42] This throws a shadow of doubt over European assertions of 'Oriental despotism'.

[43] The Islamic concept of *siyasa shar'iyya* (governance in accordance with Allah's law, see chapter 5) has conceptual parallels in Thomist thought (see Friedmann, 1967: 109–10).

[44] This was hardly new, in view of what the ancient Greeks had to say on the subject.

itself increasingly to criticism for lack of vigilance about justice or, as we would say today, lack of respect for human rights, especially in relation to slavery (Kelly, 1992: 105–6). In these early debates, the term 'positive law' is frequently used for rule systems imposed by rulers of various descriptions with the sanction of the Church. Aquinas still took a somewhat idealistic and defensive perspective of the legitimacy of such law-making, as Harris (1980: 10) indicated:

> Aquinas showed how the bindingness of positive law actually derived from natural law, so long as flexible notions like the rationally-conceived common good were not overstepped; and he thus threw over positive law a halo of moral sanctity. Later writers, using the same process of reasoning from nature, evolved the conception of natural rights, infringement of which entitled citizens to revolt.

The examples of the American uprising against British rule in 1776 and the French Revolution in 1789 illustrate the eventual political use made of such concepts in order to justify political protest. What is 'just' in particular circumstances may not be universally agreed, even among Europeans. The optimistic presumption that natural law theories can provide universally valid guidance on moral and legal standards was increasingly questioned at this time; natural law theory as interpreted by the Church came under enormous challenge. At an early stage, the Catholic Church asserted its claim to moral superiority, based on the assumption that man's sinful condition had to be supervised by spiritual authority.[45] Friedmann (1947: 25) noted the perceived task of the Church to require the utmost approximation of human laws to eternal Christian principles:

> For this purpose, the Church is given absolute supremacy over the State which is bad, but which can justify its existence by protecting the peace and the church and striving to fulfil the demands of eternal law. The otherworldliness of a pessimistic doctrine is thus ingeniously coupled with a philosophical justification of the claim of the church for sovereign political authority.

Because Christianity eventually became the dominant religion of Europe, intimate links between temporal and spiritual power structures worked in favour of the Church (Friedmann, 1947: 26). Since spiritual and worldly order (unlike in early Christianity) both professed the same religion, a theory of law based on Christian values could claim superior status in emerging Christian states without much opposition. It became easy to create laws for medieval European societies which legitimised certain hierarchical structures and abuse of

---

[45] This issue is familiar, among others, from the Islamic belief that after death a person faces divine judgment, from Hindu notions of *karma* and from Buddhist ideas about karmic accounting.

political power in the name of the Church.[46] The Thomist system protected both the *status quo* of spiritual superiority *and* of political power, leaving no scope for the rights of individuals (Friedmann, 1947: 29). Despite endowment with intelligence, they were merely objects of the legal order. Given that one of the most ancient motors of legal philosophy appears to have been concern for justice, a constantly recurrent theme,[47] this *status quo*-ist position led ultimately to radical refocusing of legal thought in Europe as well as political revolt.

Throughout the above account of legal philosophy, its eurocentric orientation, almost totally unconcerned about the rest of the world,[48] should have become apparent. Muslims or Hindus, for example, might well find it agreeable to go along with a general view of a universal and immutable 'law of nature'. However, their perceptions would not be independent of culture-specific parameters, such as a particular divine authority in the case of Muslims, giving rise to Muslim concepts of natural law. This would have been similar for other legal traditions in the world. The culture-specific nature of European natural law debates thus becomes deeply problematic when they claim universal validity. Assuming that people in other cultures could not possibly take a different view, or simply had no thoughts about this, seems a little naïve. Alternatively, one might argue that European claims to universality were made in deliberate opposition to other views of the world, as far as they were known at that time. For, by the time of Aquinas, Islam was well established and its conflicting universalising claims were increasingly known. While mainstream Western legal scholarship, even today, largely fails to discuss this competing global diversity, a globality-conscious jurisprudential approach cannot close its eyes to this. Clearly, there have always been alternative forms of natural law in existence on the globe. These are discussed in Part II of this study.

3.5 Re-evaluation of natural law during Renaissance and Reformation

The Renaissance, the Reformation and the rise of the nation state in Europe, roughly between 1350 and 1600, engendered important reassessments of older theories. The Renaissance involved a reconstruction of classical thought patterns, destroying the medieval order in which the individual had been perceived only as a minute part of a universal organism, liberating the critical, sceptical individual as an entity in its own right. It 'led to an emphasis on the individual

---

[46] Much the same appears to happen today when a Muslim-dominated state declares its intention to 'islamise' the laws. For the Pakistani example see chapter 5, section 5.14.

[47] For later periods see Friedmann (1947: 59 and 62).

[48] Freeman (2001: 110) presents an interesting discussion about the status of native Indians in America, showing that some earlier thinkers were not willing to submit unquestioningly to eurocentric hubris.

and free will and human liberty and a rejection of the universal collective soci
ety of medieval Europe in favour of independent nation states' (Freeman, 2001:
107–8). This movement was supported by the Reformation, a deep-running
critique of Catholic Church domination, which resulted in various forms of
Protestantism, separate national Churches, and generally strengthened individual freedom of conscience (Friedmann, 1967: 114). Both movements led
to a secularisation of political concepts, exemplified by Machiavelli's famous
political philosophy (Freeman, 2001: 108). New competing expectations arose.
Dias and Hughes (1957: 356–7) highlighted the desire of the rising commercial
classes to pursue their trading activities free from wanton interference, which
placed trust in national sovereigns as guarantors of rights. Great advances in
knowledge about the physical operations of the material world affected the
intellectual sphere, leading to adaptation rather than disintegration or complete
rejection of the Thomist worldview (Dias and Hughes, 1957: 357). Protestant
denial that the Church had any authority to expound the law of God meant
that the individual received more prominence, though such arguments were
hotly contested (Freeman, 2001: 108).

Accredited with the secularisation of natural law, and with being the father of
modern international law,[49] the Protestant Dutch philosopher Grotius (1583–
1645) claimed that '[e]ven if God did not exist . . . natural law would have the
same content; and just as God cannot cause that two times two shall not be
four, so he cannot cause the intrinsically evil to be not evil'.[50] The intellectual
authority of reason attempted to substitute the spiritual authority of divine natural law, claiming no lesser authority. In this period, according to Friedmann
(1967: 115), '[n]atural law is not yet the rather vague guide to the right path,
which it has become in modern times. It is the superior law.' Friedmann (1967:
115) also noted that for Grotius, the idea of natural law 'assumed once more
a constructive and practical function, comparable to that which it had exercised at the time of the growth of Roman law towards a cosmopolitan system'.
This new practical approach did not deny the existence of God, but asserted
that there was a higher standard of goodness to which man, through reason,
could appeal.[51] Later natural law thinkers, particularly Samuel von Pufendorf

---

[49] For details see Freeman (2001: 109, 110–11).

[50] Harris (1980: 11). Freeman (2001: 110–11) indicates that more recent research sees this
more as a shift of emphasis and that Grotius did not expel God from his natural law
doctrine. Olivecrona (1971: 15) claims that 'he actually has a better theory – a theory
explaining the origin of the law of nature as a set of prescriptions or commands', suggesting perhaps that there is another higher power behind God. This kind of thinking is
familiar from Hinduism and other non-monotheistic religions which are not based on the
commands of a monotheistic God.

[51] It could be argued that this theory shares striking similarities with the Hindu conceptualisation of *rita*, macrocosmic Order, as a higher, superhuman standard which binds all
individuals, rulers, as well as all divine beings (chapter 4).

(1632–94), developed from such thoughts principles focusing on the duty of individual self-perfection as the principal command of natural law.[52]

The new mental chemistry of this time is closely linked to the emergence of social contract theory, an analytical construct used to present conflicting political ideals (Freeman, 2001: 111). Such theories mark the stronger emergence of individualism, with basic features going back to Plato,[53] representing a gradual shift of attention to human agency rather than divine or superhuman will. Friedmann (1967: 118) explains:

> From a state of nature, in which they have no law, no order, no government – this state of affairs appears to some writers as a paradise, to others as chaos – men have at some time passed to a state of society, by means of contract in which they undertake to respect each other and live in peace (*pactum unionis*). To this contract is added simultaneously or subsequently a second pact by which the people thus united undertake to obey a government which they themselves have chosen (*pactum subjectionis*).

Individual rights to life, liberty and property had existed before there was any society; now they began to be seen as inalienable human rights which needed to be defended. New idealistic natural law thinking perceived the state as originating in a contract, through which individuals surrender their innate sovereignty to the ruler and pledge obedience in return for protection. This was designed to overcome the earlier state of nature, marked by 'a war of every Man against every Man' (Freeman, 2001: 111).

Thomas Hobbes (1588–1679), together with Locke and Rousseau, further developed the social contract theory from Thomist thought. The concept of individual consent began to be discussed (Olivecrona, 1971: 12; Freeman, 2001: 109, 114). As a scientific materialist, Hobbes vigorously denied the authority of the Church as the authoritative interpreter of God's law and allocated power, in his scheme, to a utilitarian secular sovereign, which 'marked the final break up of the Catholic international order of things' (Dias and Hughes, 1957: 359). However, this created a new problem, not unfamiliar since Greek antiquity. The strengthening of the political sovereign's power through social contract raised questions about how to control rulers' appetite for absolutist rule. Since the social contract theory was used by Grotius and Hobbes to justify authoritarian government (Freeman, 2001: 112), the only guarantee against abuse of power by the ruler was now that he, too, was bound by natural law (Dias and Hughes, 1957: 358). The paramount need now became to safeguard the individual against the abuse of sovereign power (p. 359).

John Locke (1632–1704), different from Hobbes, became the theoretician of the rising middle class (Friedmann, 1967: 123). He perceived the state of

---

[52] Friedmann (1967: 115–16). This approach finds striking parallels in the central Hindu concept of *dharma* as the individual's duty to do the right thing at any one time (chapter 4, section 4.3).

[53] Friedmann (1947: 35). On the Greek roots of this concept see Kelly (1992: 14).

nature prior to the social contract as an idyllic near-paradise, in which property was not secure, so that '[t]he purpose of government was the protection of human entitlement' (Freeman, 2001: 112). Later, Locke argued that unlimited sovereignty and its abuse were a violation of natural law.[54] Rulers who violated their obligations betrayed the trust of their subjects and rendered the social contract invalid, thus justifying revolution or disobedience.[55] Revolution, for Locke, was not an act of revenge, but a restoration or recreation of a violated political order.[56]

During the seventeenth and eighteenth centuries, new perceptions of 'secular' natural law arose. Gierke (1950: xlii) observed that this new natural law became more academic: 'The theorists of the new Natural Law might often pass into the service of the State, and hold judicial or administrative or diplomatic posts; but in itself Natural Law was a speculation of theorists and professors. It had . . . an academic quality. Its immediate life was the life of lectures and text-books.' As the theorists of Natural Law came into closer contact with leading philosophers, both disciplines were mutually enriched. Among the many writers, Montesquieu (1689–1755) is credited with propounding the theory of the separation of powers, and presents an argument seeking to guard the individual from state lawlessness. Rousseau (1712–88) also sought to protect individual interests against the sovereign but has been seen as 'a Janus-like figure in the history of the School of Natural Law'.[57] Dias and Hughes (1957: 361) emphasised that Rousseau's teachings, glorifying popular sovereignty, underpin the philosophy of the French Revolution. Rousseau's philosophy also provided a notable link between the natural law school and early German historical jurisprudence.[58] Gierke (1950: xlv) explained:

> The final sovereign of Rousseau is not an individual or a body of individuals . . . The sovereign of which he speaks is a 'moral person'; and the final norm is the 'general will' of that person . . . Rousseau was a romantic before Romanticism; and he prepared the way for the new style of German thought which was to divinise the Folk-person, and to historicise law as the expression in time of the general will or consciousness of right which proceeds from that person. Hegelianism and the Historical School of Law can find their nutriment in him.

---

[54] This argument is also found in the Hindu concept of *artha*, 'worldly power', which is subordinate to the overriding requirements of *dharma*, the duty to do the right thing. Hence, the Hindu ruler remained at all times a servant of *dharma*, with implications for good governance and accountability of all those who rule (see chapter 4, section 4.9 below on public interest litigation in India).

[55] Freeman (2001: 114). Again, this is familiar from different legal traditions.

[56] Freeman (2001: 115). This debate is followed (pp. 115–17) by an interesting discussion on concepts of property and the views of Locke on entitlement to welfare rights.

[57] Gierke (1950: xliv); Freeman (2001: 117). Friedmann (1967: 125) notes that his work abounds in contradictions.

[58] Freeman (2001: 120) discusses how in this age of Enlightenment, Montesquieu perceived mankind as influenced by a variety of factors.

During the eighteenth century as an age of reason,[59] a group of Scottish intellectuals attempted to study society scientifically (Freeman, 2001: 120). The philosopher David Hume (1711–76) interrogated the theoretical basis of natural law by arguing that natural law ideas had confused the meaning of reason in three different ways (Friedmann, 1967: 129–31). First, they had wrongly assumed that inevitable and necessary truths (of which there are very few, save certain mathematical principles) could exist in the subjective realm of human behaviour. Secondly, they had assumed that cause-and-effect relationships between facts are a matter of experience and observation, whereas in fact this is not logical, as such relationships have only been based on subjective and selective empirical correlation. Thirdly, natural law theories misleadingly assumed that there was such a thing as reasonable human conduct, which, based on rational principles, had universal validity. Hume's incisive analysis destroyed the conceptual underpinnings of traditional natural law theories and leads over to a modern theory of natural law (Freeman, 2001: 121). He laid foundations for distinguishing between natural and social sciences, an issue later taken up by neo-Kantianism. This analysis heralded a new anti-metaphysical, scientifically minded and utilitarian era (Friedmann, 1967: 130).

Thus, as natural law concepts were subjected to severe scrutiny, many were rejected as unscientific and simply false. Gradually, natural law went out of fashion and on the whole the nineteenth century was hostile to natural law theories: 'The rival movements of historical romanticism, utilitarianism, scientific positivism and economic materialism were united in their opposition to natural law' (Friedmann, 1967: 132). Such strongly adverse reaction led to the emergence of, and focus on, analytical and historical approaches to law in Europe.[60] However, during the twentieth century, there has been a significant revival of natural law thinking, discussed in section 3.7.2 below.

3.6 Legal positivism

Olivecrona (1971: 141) noted that, when nineteenth-century positivists 'wanted to make a clean break with natural law doctrine, they ceased to cite the old authorities. But as a matter of course they took over their fundamental concepts.' He therefore argued that one cannot understand modern discussions about legal positivism without going back to traditional teachers of natural law. From within a eurocentric civilisational model, David and Brierley (1978: 2)

---

[59] Griffiths (2002: 291) notes that '[o]ut of Englightenment came an interest in tracing the evolution of human development in which law played a key role because it was viewed as representing rationality over other forms of order, created, for example, out of self-interest or force. Thus law became the index of a "civilized" society, marking a transition for humanity and society from an irrational to a rational state of being.'

[60] Friedmann (1967: 132–51) traces further developments of natural law ideas in English law and in American jurisprudence.

commented on the shift from a theoretical natural law focus towards the more practical concerns of legal positivism:

> For many previous centuries, the science of law was devoted to discovering the principles of just law, that is to say law conforming to the will of God, to nature and to reason, and there was little concern for positive law or the law as it applied in fact. Local or customary law was of importance to practitioners and the legislative measures of ruling sovereigns were of interest to governments of other countries, but neither was of any real significance to those who meditated upon and wrote about law. Positive law in either form was neglected in the universities. There the principal study, once thought more noble and more suitable to true legal training, was the search for just rules that would be applicable in all countries. This search, which was to reveal the true science of law, was best carried out in the study not of the various national or local laws but rather in Roman law and Canon law, the only laws common to the whole of the civilized (i.e. Christian) world.

Much earlier, Aquinas had introduced among his four types of law two categories which can be seen as 'positive law', namely 'divine law' as revealed in scripture, and 'human law' as articulated by human authorities (section 3.4). The concept of positive law at this early stage comprised both religious and temporal authority.[61] This legitimation of religious-cum-temporal authority reflects an early European theory of positive law in which the ultimately superior authority lies not yet with a temporal law-giver, but with a religious or spiritual authority, ultimately, in Catholic theology, with God Almighty.[62] This is evidently quite different from later, secular theories of positive law, but the principle of making law for all subjects, ultimately the whole of humanity, was clearly established. Through secular methods of enquiry, it became possible to develop legal positivism, 'based on the simple assertion that the proper description of law is a worthy objective, and a task that need be kept separate from moral judgments' (Bix, 1996: 35). This methodology was articulated more fully, not without criticism, by Friedmann (1947: 135):

> Positivism mistrusts *a priori* assumptions and ideas, it places its faith in observations. The scientific method is extended to 'practical reason,' including law. Accordingly the number and variety of positivist legal theories is as great as that of the sciences, each claiming certainty and accuracy in its own field. Therefore, positivism in jurisprudence comprises legal movements, poles apart in every respect, except for their common aversion against metaphysical theories and natural law in particular. As often

---

[61] Much of Islamic legal scholarship also treats religious law as 'positive law' and goes as far as portraying the Qur'an as divine legislation. For details see chapter 5 below.

[62] Evidently, in this respect, early Muslim concepts of positivism simply put Allah in the same place as the Christian God.

as not, however, positivist theories substitute for the articulate idealism of the theories which they fight an inarticulate idealism of their own, which is presented as a scientific fact based on observations.

Friedmann (1967: 256–7) summarises five basic elements of positivism according to Hart. These are (1) the assumption that laws are commands of human beings rather than gods; (2) the contention that there is no necessary link between law and morality, and thus between law as it is and ought to be; (3) the conviction that analysing the meaning of legal concepts is worth pursuing and differs from historical and sociological enquiries; (4) the assumption that legal systems are closed logical systems which can be objectively analysed; and (5) the contention that moral judgments cannot be established by rational argument. Friedmann (1967: 257) portrays the separation of law and morality, of 'is' and 'ought', as the most fundamental philosophical assumption of legal positivism. Freeman (2001: 199) links the origin of positivist legal thinking to the rise of the nation state and 'a departure from the medieval idea of law as being fundamentally custom, and legislation merely a form of declaring the existence of new customs'. This engendered the idea of unfettered human legislative capacity, virtually unthinkable earlier under natural law. The new secular positivist approach paid mere lip-service to natural law. Now, '*positive* law, in the sense of the law of the state, is something ascertainable and valid without regard to subjective considerations' (Freeman, 2001: 200).

Olivecrona (1971: 7) noted that, while the term 'positive law' was not employed in antiquity, *ius positivum* is documented from about 1140 onwards, though it may have been known earlier; certainly by the thirteenth century it was in popular use. The general sense of 'positive law' is that it has its origin in human activity (not necessarily legislation) and that it has been 'posited' or laid down (p. 8). While legal positivism has several meanings, most of its followers would accept two basic propositions. First, the definition of 'law' should not depend on questions of moral validity. Secondly, law should only be identified in terms of tangible formal provisions, such as legislation, case law and customary traditions. As a result, positivists refuse to incorporate any moral assessment in their definition of law. While most adherents of this method do not deny that justice remains an important consideration, discussing justice is often seen as irrelevant and confusing.[63] Others have argued that '[s]ince positive law is based on the law of nature, its contents must be in harmony with this law' (Olivecrona, 1971: 23).

---

[63] According to Dias and Hughes (1957: 372), English judges and jurists have remained dominated by this way of thinking, which may explain why certain legal problems in English law today, especially relating to ethnic minorities, seem so difficult to tackle (Jones and Welhengama, 2000). Friedmann (1967: 257) argues that the theoretical elimination of values in positivism 'does not imply any contempt for the importance of values in law'.

A value-neutral approach can be criticised as myopic, disregarding the incontrovertible fact that national legal systems are always underpinned by certain values,[64] which may cause specific cultural and legal problems for newcomers, minorities and dissenters of various descriptions. If law is simply law because it is said by someone in authority to be law (Morrison, 1997: 1), we face a dangerous circularity problem. Presuming that law can be a stand-alone factor must be seen as 'the great positivist fallacy', which has made 'pure' positivism unrealistic, as Hans Kelsen, its most famous proponent, found to his dismay.[65] A purely analytical interpretation of law, if it means a value-free and entirely objective assessment, is therefore inherently impossible, as Hume had realised and taught earlier in a different context, referring to 'utility' (Freeman, 2001: 200). Since the major aim of analytical jurisprudence remains, even today, to analyse 'law' in the abstract, it appears that the earlier intellectual superiority claims of natural lawyers are now being countered by positivists, asserting that their method is the highest form of legal theory. One wonders how productive such positioning can be. Olivecrona (1971: 77–8) argued that positive law simply did not exist:

> No rules of law at all are the expression of the will of an authority existing prior to the law itself. What we have before us is a body of rules that has been slowly changing and growing during the centuries. It would be no use to call this body of rules positive law. The adjective 'positive' is entirely superfluous; it might be misleading because it is connected with the idea that the law is 'posited' in the sense of being the expression of the will of a lawgiver.
>
> The term 'positive' law may therefore conveniently be dropped as a term for an objectively existing phenomenon . . . When speaking of the law itself, it is much better simply to say 'the law' without the adjective 'positive'.

Most lawyers will not be willing to listen to such critical remarks, and legal positivism has remained the dominant Western legal ideology.[66] Legal positivism was clearly not invented in England,[67] even if the first great positivist was Jeremy Bentham (Olivecrona, 1971: 27) as the founder of 'naturalistic positivism' (p. 67). It has been argued that 'all law is positive in the sense of being an

---

[64] Chiba (1986) speaks in this context of 'legal postulates' (chapter 2, section 2.5.4).

[65] Kelsen's 'pure theory' of law was famously interpreted by Pakistani judges to legitimise military rule. See *State* v. *Dosso*, PLD 1958 SC 533. Freeman (2001: 221) refers to debates about whether Nazi abuses of law were caused by the application of positivist thought.

[66] However, Chiba (1986) has importantly pointed out that 'official law' consists of two types, directly posited law and pre-existing law accepted by the state, which is what Olivecrona had in mind.

[67] The ancient Greek philosophers saw it in action and did not like it. So, evidently, did Bentham. The ancient Hindus and the Chinese apparently abhorred it (see Lloyd, 1991: 15), realising the potential for abuse of power, appealing instead to self-control order mechanisms (see chapters 4 and 7).

expression of the will of a supreme authority'.[68] But who or what is a supreme authority?[69] English legal scholarship has primarily focused on English thinking within its specific historical context, but there is (almost) a worldwide debate.[70] Sir William Blackstone (1723–80) had still insisted that human law derives its validity from natural law, and that any man-made law that violated natural law was a nullity. This approach was vigorously refuted by Jeremy Bentham (1748–1832), the founder of English legal positivism.[71] Twining (2000: 93–4) suggests that Bentham should be seen mainly as a jurist, though he is better known as a philosopher, political theorist and social reformer. He wanted to be to jurisprudence what Luther was to Christianity or Newton to science (p. 94). Bentham (and later Austin) adapted the older concepts of Jean Bodin (1513–96) and Thomas Hobbes (1588–1679), who had still related authority within natural law concepts to divine power, but had attempted to secularise these concepts, so that 'the sovereign was not he who by divine or natural right could tell us what we ought to do. The sovereign was identified by the fact that he was obeyed, and his commands were those facts which people call "laws"' (Harris, 1980: 25). Bentham as a philosopher and reformer started from the principle of utility, the ideal that the greatest happiness of the greatest number should be promoted. He applied this as a practical method to evaluate law-making and was deeply shocked when he attended lectures by Sir William Blackstone and heard that the common law of the time could be defended by reason and through reference to natural law.[72] Blackstone's definition of law was mocked by Bentham 'as pure tautology – "a rule of conduct for those who are to observe it, prescribed by those who prescribe it, commanding what it commands, and forbidding what it forbids"' (Jones, 1956: 91). Blackstone had asserted the legislative supremacy of Parliament which, as a concept, is not different in principle from Bentham's and especially Austin's later circular definitions of law as 'the will or command of the legislator'.[73]

Bentham advocated social reform through law and mainly sought to develop scientific principles to guide legislators; he subscribed otherwise to a *laissez-*

---

[68] Freeman (2001: 207 n. 46) with reference to Olivecrona's (1971: 61) reliance on German *Rechtspositivismus*. Potentially this is a pluralist interpretation which ultimately, as Freeman (2001: 860) indicates, throws out the baby of positivism with the bath water.

[69] The critical question whether this may include any individual was raised in chapter 2 above.

[70] Twining (2000: 97) notes that '[p]ositivism versus anti-positivism is still treated by many Anglo-American jurists as the main battleground of jurisprudence'.

[71] Recent discoveries from his enormous opus allow much more differentiated assessments. For details see Twining (2000: 91ff.); Freeman (2001: 202).

[72] Freeman (2001: 200) refers to Blackstone's approach as 'complacent and uncritical' and highlights Bentham's famous statement that to speak of natural rights was 'nonsense upon stilts' (p. 201, n. 10).

[73] It is no surprise that Bentham came close to conceptualising a doctrine of judicial review (Freeman, 2001: 204).

faire approach (Freeman, 2001: 201). He saw jurisprudence as 'an experimental science founded upon the careful observation of legal realities' (Jones, 1956: 92) which, to him, were thoughts and acts of men. While he had his own reservations about law-making as a necessary evil, his prime concern was to make laws better. Hence, Bentham was far less of a positivist than his pupil Austin.[74] Bentham clearly saw the distinction between social desirability and logical necessity (Freeman, 2001: 203). His distrust of the state, shown by his reactions to Blackstone's arguments, was coupled with a focus on sanctions and punishments as a motivator for human action, and thus law-making. Interestingly, this links to a consideration of duties as an element of legal analysis.[75] Harris (1980: 24–5) explained:

> Where an act was commanded or prohibited, it was the subject of a legal duty. 'Duty' was the lowest common denominator of all laws. All other legal concepts, such as right, power and property, were to be translatable into their relationships to duties. Having decided, on the basis of utility, what acts ought to be made the subject of duties, and what incentive to compliance (whether punishment or reward) was desirable, scientific codes could be worked out.

However, Bentham's ideas were not fully publicised until quite recently.[76] Twining (2000: 97) presents him as a soft positivist: 'Bentham's theory arguably has affinities with pragmatism, the sociology of knowledge, and even some of the milder kinds of post-modernism'. But rather than Bentham, John Austin (1790–1859) has become prominently linked to the command theory of law.[77] Every aspect of Austin's work has been subjected to much criticism,[78] but the basic concept of law as 'command of the sovereign' or law as 'state law', has become dominant, at least in the West. It was reinforced by those who discussed Austin's model, so that after Austin, positivism developed its own momentum. Austin's exposition of this theory in 1832 laid foundations for the 'analytical school of jurisprudence', which is not Austin's term (Twining, 2000: 23). Harris (1988: 4) notes:

> Austin treats rules, including legal rules, as though they were amenable to analysis 'in a vacuum' . . . in a manner divorced from social contexts or settings. For Austin, the hallmark of a legal rule (which he terms 'positive',

---

[74] Morrison (1997: vii and 6) points out that Austin himself was evidently not a pure positivist.

[75] Freeman (2001: 204). This is interesting because Asian and African legal thinking is focused on duties rather than rights.

[76] Twining (2000: 93) reports that over 20 million words of Bentham's writings still survive, only a fraction was published during his lifetime, and some very significant material is still available only in manuscript form today, awaiting to be included in a projected sixty-eight-volume edition of Bentham's *Collected Works*.

[77] Freeman (2001: 207ff.) indicates much criticism of Austin's approach.

[78] For details see Hart (1961; 1994) and helpfully Freeman (2001: 207–21).

or man-made, law) lies in the manner of its creation. He defined law as the *command of the sovereign body* in a society (which may be a person, such as a king or queen, or a body of elected officials such as our own law-making body which we refer to formally as 'the Queen in Parliament'), and these commands are backed up by threats of sanctions, to be applied in the event of disobedience.

Austin insisted on a determinate person or body as the source of a command (Freeman, 2001: 208). Much debate has softened this narrow positivist stance, so that 'it is often replaced nowadays by colourless designations like "imperatives" or "directives"' (p. 209). Notably, Austin avoided the word 'state' and focused on theoretical deliberations about 'sovereignty', much criticised in the light of more recent legal developments.[79] Relying on earlier thinkers, Austin's theorising about sovereignty appears muddled and superficial today, lacking a sense of practical application. His failure to distinguish *de jure* sovereignty, the authority to make law, from *de facto* sovereignty, the power to enforce obedience, avoids many critical questions that arise in a global legal context.[80] Since Austin notably recognised that 'law cannot itself be based on law but must be based on something outside law' (Freeman, 2001: 212), he grounded it upon fact, manifested in habitual obedience of most subjects of the law, which is equally meaningless (p. 213).

The most important academic element of English positivism as represented by Austin remains the rigid separation of law and morality.[81] This approach does not recommend itself as a useful tool for understanding law and 'remains essentially an idealist search for absolute truth in the realm of values' (Freeman, 2001: 215). In terms of the present globality-focused analysis, it is evident that Austin's model and methods (as perceived in jurisprudential scholarship) are simply not sufficient to explain law as a global phenomenon.

More recently, Chiba's (1986) tripartite model suggests that law is never just positive law in isolation (chapter 2, section 2.5.4). Clearly, Austin's theory and method were complex, but far from universally applicable. His use of the word 'proper', in particular, drew much polemic criticism, for what is a 'proper' law? He excluded not only customary law (unless it had been adopted by a state organ as a rule) but also rules of international law, constitutional conventions, divine commands and rules made by private people. His intricate distinctions between commands which were not laws and those which were, relying on his understanding of the central role of sanctions, remain severely disputed (Freeman, 2001: 215–19).

---

[79] For details see Freeman (2001: 209–14).

[80] Freeman (2001: 210) shows through the example of South African courts and their refusal to be bound by rigid concepts of sovereignty that Austin's theory is limited in practice. Similarly, sovereignty problems of UK law in relation to European law (pp. 211–12) suggest the 'unreality of repeating the formula of irreversible parliamentary sovereignty' (p. 212).

[81] Twining (2000: 111). Cotterrell (1989: 120) confirms this.

Twining (2000: 21) emphasises that both Bentham and Austin are subject to multiple interpretations and suggests that Austin's originality and influence have often been greatly exaggerated (p. 25). He was never accepted uncritically even within English positivism (p. 24). The Austinian basis of analytical legal theory has now largely been discarded (Harris, 1980: 25) and the rejection of Austin's simple sovereignty model is not controversial (p. 34). Twining (2000: 48) notes, however, that despite such challenges, analytical positivism 'remains the dominant force in our academic culture'.

An explicitly rational approach to understanding law was promoted by Hans Kelsen (1881–1973), whose pure science of law has been treated as the highest development of analytical positivism, but is now seen in a different light.[82] In his Kantian quest for 'pure theory',[83] Kelsen searched for formal elements as concepts of the human mind to understand the structure of legal systems and, ultimately, of law. His approach rejects both legal positivism, because it confuses law with fact, and natural law theory, because it confuses law with morality (Freeman, 2001: 256), totally isolating law from ethics, politics, sociology, history and religion for the purposes of his 'pure' theory.[84] Kelsen's approach focused on jurisprudence as a science of 'norms' or normative propositions with their own hierarchy.[85] Freeman (2001: 256) explains:

> For Kelsen, the law consists of norms: a norm cannot be derived from facts, but only from other norms. The relationship between norms is one of 'imputation', not causality . . . [N]ormative science, such as law or ethics, is concerned with conduct as it ought to take place, determined by norms.[86]

Kelsen saw norms as expressing expectations, not facts. A norm in his scheme is therefore not an 'is', but an 'ought'. Law then becomes a normative order

---

[82] For a detailed discussion of Kelsen and the pure theory of law, see Morrison (1997: 323–50) and Freeman (2001: 255–330). The earlier view of Kelsen as a 'positivist of positivists' (p. 256, n. 6) has been revised, since Kelsen distinguished 'is' and 'ought', but largely ignored the 'ought' for his 'pure' analysis.

[83] Kant's approach to the theory of knowledge sounds postmodern, in that he taught that 'the objective world is transmuted by certain formal categories applied to it by the mind of the onlooker' (Freeman, 2001: 255). In other words, all perceptions are subjective and 'constructed'. See Kant (1965).

[84] Freeman (2001: 257) notes that 'Kelsen is not disinterested in justice or sociology or psychology' but he evidently had no ambition to solve real legal problems through his theory.

[85] He also emphasises their dynamic character (Freeman, 2001: 263), but by wishing to restrict his theory to the 'legal', sets himself up for criticism: 'A legal system is not an abstract collection of bloodless categories but a living organism in a constant state of movement' (p. 264). To Kelsen, then, a legal system is much more than 'law' in his narrow sense.

[86] The concept of 'imputation' (German *Zurechnung*) signifies responsibility, more specifically accountability, of the individual.

regulating human conduct in a particular way. Kelsen argued that norms exist within systems of norms and derive their validity from being part of a system. Arguing that norms derive their validity from other norms, Kelsen developed the famous concept of 'basic norm' (*Grundnorm*), asserting that in every legal system a hierarchy of norms is traceable to the most basic of norms. Kelsen accepted that such a norm could take different forms, and even acknowledged that there could be more than one *Grundnorm*, though he argued that a legal system could not be founded on two conflicting basic norms. This may suggest that his understanding of 'legal system' lacked sufficient attention to the internal plurality of legal traditions and their multivalence (Glenn, 2004: 347ff.). In Kelsen's model, the basic norm ultimately must be extra-legal because by definition it does not depend on another legal norm.[87] Thus law is shown to be dependent on socio-cultural factors, but Kelsen remained silent about this aspect. Freeman (2001: 265) comments that legal science has 'reached the stage where it is pointless to look for further *legal* justification. And this is what Kelsen recognises'. Such comments are based on strict theoretical discussions of what is 'legal', with no attempt to reflect socio-political reality.

Kelsen's theory of law was used in Commonwealth countries, prominently Pakistan, Uganda and Southern Rhodesia, where the legality of revolutionary movements was at issue or newly empowered usurpers sought to legitimise their rule through Kelsen's theory of law.[88] Kelsen himself was appalled that his 'pure' theory was applied for such political purposes in ways which he had not foreseen.[89] He insisted that his theory of law was merely a theory, but obviously had no control over how his attractive model would be used by judges in courts of law under political pressure. Kelsen has intellectually excited many commentators. Freeman (2001: 276) remains impressed with Kelsen's learning, but partly unclear about what he was trying to say through his 'pure' science of law. Morrison (1997: 350) respects Kelsen's project and his 'desire to protect the language game of the jurisprudent from being sucked into ideology'.

Much of the continuing focus on analytical jurisprudence has to do with H.L.A. Hart (chapter 2, section 2.4 above) who replaced Austin's model by constructing his own positivist theory of law (Twining, 2000: 24). Hart insisted that Austin's model of law based on coercive sanctions was too narrowly focused on criminal law and failed to take sufficient account of modern legal systems which confer public and private legal powers. He introduced his dual model of 'primary rules' and 'secondary rules', which reflects an implied, though reluctant

---

[87] Freeman (2001: 259). This is 'a very troublesome feature of Kelsen's system' (Freeman, 2001: 264).

[88] For Pakistan, see *State* v. *Dosso*, PLD 1958 SC 533. Further references are provided in Freeman (2001: 268 n. 80). A useful explanation of the political use of Kelsen's theory is found in Harris (1980: 71–3).

[89] Freeman (2001: 259) suggests that Kelsen avoided writing about the state, since he wanted his theory to be relevant to all scenarios, even primitive contexts.

recognition of legal plurality and led to a much more realistic methodological approach to understanding law's social interlinkedness.

Academic debates of Hart's work and his critics continue to inspire many legal scholars.[90] Twining (2000: 24–5) seems critical of these debates with their Oedipal overtones within English legal positivism.[91] He strongly suggests the need to develop 'a sophisticated conceptual apparatus' for developing a legal theory that can respond adequately to the challenges of globalisation (p. 36). But how? In an excellent essay on the Hart/Dworkin debates (Twining, 2000: 15–49), various intricate differences between the approaches of Hart (supposedly, general jurisprudence) and Dworkin (broadly, particular jurisprudence) are brought out. Both scholars seem to be involved in the respective other field, too, and have different but overlapping agendas (p. 40). Freeman (2001: 332) suggests that '[t]he search for what it is that separates law from other normative phenomena remains a positivist project', even among those who have started to write about 'inclusive legal positivism' (Waluchow, 1994 and 2000; Coleman, 2001). However, such writers studiously avoid the tainted term 'legal pluralism' and concentrate on the contested interactions between analytical positivism and natural law paradigms. This search may have taken jurists into new terrain (Freeman, 2001: 333), so that positivism is no longer as easy to pigeon-hole as it once was (p. 334). Positivist activities today can be identified by two central tenets (Freeman, 2001: 334): 'the so-called "social thesis" (what counts as law in a given society is a matter of social fact); and the "separability thesis" (there is no necessary connection between law and morality)'.

The wide gulf between 'inclusive legal positivism', to which one must count Hart and his 'soft positivism' (chapter 2, section 2.4 above), and 'exclusive legal positivism' seems unbridgeable. It appears that legal positivism as a method remains insufficiently concerned about socio-cultural legal facts to become deeply incorporated as a separate entity into a plurality-conscious, globality-focused analysis. The problem appears to be that a positivist scholar who becomes involved in socio-cultural dimensions of law ends up dropping out of the safe box of positivist pigeon-holes into the more turbulent sphere of legal pluralism and risks being tainted.[92] Sometimes intellectual snobbery, rather than deep concern for understanding law in a global context, seems to prevent focus on legal pluralism. Clearly, there are many reasons why positivists are reluctant to cross the boundaries between what is properly (in their limited understanding) 'law', and what a deep plurality-conscious global jurisprudence would need to take into account to understand law as an interlinked

---

[90] See the detailed chapter on 'Modern trends in analytical jurisprudence' in Freeman (2001: 331–522).

[91] On the famous Hart/Dworkin debate see Twining (2000: 33–47). Twining recounts his own experience as a law student during the 1950s, involving exposure to particular legal jurisprudence (p. 34) and its intellectual challenges.

[92] On the problematic nature of legal pluralism, see Freeman (2001: 919–21).

phenomenon. Positivist approaches to legal theory and 'general jurisprudence' on their own can only offer limited contributions to the development of a globally valid jurisprudence. Morrison (1997: 4) notes that positivism has lost its dominance in recent years because its projects of conceptual analysis failed to take account of 'the entirety of the legal enterprise and they lacked social awareness as to the law's social effectivity'. Indeed, as Legrand (1997a: 59) argues, '[l]egal positivism and the closed system of codes which the fetishism of rules commands must be regarded as obsolete'.

3.7 Beyond positivism

The inherent circularity of legal positivism and the potential for its abuse led to much distrust and deep rethinking of its premises, especially after 1945. However, the recognition that the state, in whatever form, is needed to maintain stability and order in society has remained strong, and positivist ideology has developed new dynamics and mechanisms of self-interested defence.[93] A renewal of the social contract through restructuring of the welfare state became a prominent strategy in the countries of the North to argue that the state and its laws remained central.[94] Different ideologies were pursued, prominent among them communism and the resulting emergence of socialist legal systems of various descriptions.[95]

While common sense suggests a focus on interlegality or interlinkedness, we saw that pluralist approaches are not yet accepted as mainstream legal methodology. As a result, it seems, general jurisprudence has languished and a confusing array of not-so-new 'schools' has arisen during the twentieth century, often seeking to combine certain methodological elements of the three major theoretical approaches in a new way, but never really all three together. While discussions of positivist ideologies in relation to morality are an 'old hat', the combination of positivism and socio-legal approaches was famously argued by Hart and his 'soft positivism' (chapter 2, section 2.4) and is now prominently pursued by Tamanaha (2001). Few writers have sought to explore how the legal factors within morality/ethics and society may be combined, because the prominence of legal centralism continues to treat non-positivist laws as 'extra-legal'.[96] The trend among authors to create their own theory leads to an even more confusing picture of growing multiplicity.[97] Particular difficulties arise in

---

[93] In fact, one positivist reaction to the atrocities of the pre-1945 period has been fear of what is unknown, and thus of difference and 'the other' (Legrand, 1997a: 52–3).

[94] On the welfare state in Britain and new approaches see Fraser (1984), Cochrane and Clarke (1993), Giddens (2000).

[95] See Butler (2003) and earlier editions on Russian law.

[96] Notably, the later work of Lon Fuller moved in that direction. For details see section 3.7.2 below.

[97] For a fairly detailed overview of major new writing on sociological jurisprudence and the sociology of law, see Freeman (2001: 659ff.).

comparative law methodology (chapter 1, section 1.2.2), over the inclusion of non-Western legal systems, and in relation to law and religion. An unfriendly commentator might characterise the current picture as extremely fragmented and marked by cluelessness about the 'bigger picture'.

Since comprehensive coverage is impossible, the present sub-section only discusses two major developments in jurisprudence during the twentieth century. The increasing attention to socio-legal approaches in a variety of schools is examined first. Secondly, the resurgence of natural law has led to significant new growth in jurisprudence, mainly focused on human rights, but has also experienced the old problems of constructing a general jurisprudence from a eurocentric bias. As modern human rights jurisprudence has, with increasing vigour and self-confidence, claimed moral superiority over everything else, old disputes over the religious/rational divide in natural law theories have broken out afresh, exemplified by the current burgeoning interest in studies on law and different religions.

Overall, coupled with uniformising idealistic visions, the forceful modernist and secular assertion of rational superiority has revived the risk of global clashes of cultures (Huntington, 1998) and is being perceived in some quarters as a new form of dictatorship of an intellectual elite, linked to neo-colonialism. While the social embeddedness and culture-specific nature of law are generally more openly acknowledged than before, it appears that the combination of eurocentric focus and Christian civilised hubris has strengthened positivist claims by the state as well as the moral apostles of global universalism. Despite much global rhetoric,[98] this seems to have led to further marginalisation of the rest of the world, denying Southern legal concepts and systems a place at the high table of legal theory.

3.7.1 Socio-legal approaches

At roughly the same time as positivism emerged in reaction to natural law theories, the historical school of jurisprudence also developed all over Europe. Details of its early developments were traced in chapter 2, sections 2.2 and 2.3. Preceding sections of the present chapter demonstrated that much of natural law philosophy, and particularly the subsequent shift of focus to positivism, tended to marginalise the study of law as a historical and sociological phenomenon.[99]

Have recent sociological approaches to understanding law, widely seen as a characteristic of our age (Dias and Hughes, 1957: 408; Freeman, 2001: 659), made any significant contributions towards global jurisprudence? Socio-legal approaches consider law in its social context and give explicit recognition to

---

[98] The hidden agenda of uniformisation were examined in the Introduction to this book.
[99] Twining (2000) comments repeatedly on the virtual disappearance of the historical school. Summers (1982: 35) notes that the historical school was never strong in the USA.

the social dimensions of law. However, like positivists and natural lawyers, socio-legal experts appear to have become mired in endless debates about the complex nature of the social.[100] How wide can the socio-legal net be cast? Do lawyers have to become sociologists? To what extent can we expect lawyers to become cultural experts, not just in one culture, but in several? Freeman (2001: 659) notes that '[l]egal thought has tended to reflect the trends to be found in sociology', so that lawyers have over time changed their perspectives and it becomes difficult now to identify any central proposition of sociological jurisprudence (p. 659). Growing belief in the non-uniqueness of law, a vision that law is but one method of social control, coupled with increased recognition of relativism (p. 659) can be identified. Rather than just focusing on the analysis of rules, sociological jurists prefer studying law in action, and often focus on social justice. This offers some hope that the methodological requirements of a plurality-conscious globality-focused jurisprudence can be met through such approaches. Freeman (2001: 660) provides a helpful overview of earlier scholarship that underpins sociological jurisprudence:

> It depends upon how one defines sociological jurisprudence as to how far back it goes. Hume, who provides one of the intellectual foundations of positivism, wrote of law as a developing social institution which owed its origin not to man's nature but to social convention. Vico too rejected the fixed concept of human nature which had characterised social thought since Aristotle . . . Montesquieu argued that law was a product of numerous factors, for example local manners, custom, physical environment: a good law, he maintained, conformed to the spirit of society. The historical school of jurisprudence emphasised the dynamics of legal development and showed how law was closely related to its social context. All of these have contributed to the growth of sociological jurisprudence.

Since the nineteenth century, the new science of sociology and an emerging sociology of law have promoted critical thinking about legal institutions.[101] The important contributions of Auguste Comte (1798–1857), who invented the term 'sociology', Herbert Spencer (1820–1903), Rudolf von Jhering (1818–92), Max Weber (1864–1920) and Emile Durkheim (1858–1917) constructed mainly evolutionist models of historical human development that tended to disregard people and societies outside the European cultural context.[102] The new science of sociology, and with it an emerging sociology of law, promoted critical thinking about legal institutions. The emphasis on empirical study meant that fresh questions were now being asked about the purpose of law. An important thinker in this field was Rudolf von Jhering (1818–1892), widely seen as the pioneer of sociological jurisprudence, whose interpretation of law

---

[100] Cotterrell (2004) seeks to assist by clarifying this aspect.

[101] For an impressive documentation of the sociology of law worldwide see Ferrari (1990).

[102] For details see Freeman (2001: 659ff.).

as a part of human conduct proved influential. Dias and Hughes (1957: 411) discussed this approach in some detail:

> Law is only an instrument for serving the needs of society; its purpose is its essential mark and this purpose is to further and protect the interests of society. But the social impulses and interests of man are clearly not always in accord with his individual or selfish interests. The grave problem of society is to reconcile selfish purposes with social purposes, or to suppress selfish purposes when they clash dangerously with social purposes. The state must therefore employ devices to encourage the social purposes which are inherent in every individual; and one of the chief methods is to identify his own selfish interest with some larger social interest. This is done by the two principles of Reward and Coercion.

The most important point emerging from Jhering's analysis was that he treated law as only one means of social control, one factor among many, and thus refuted legal centralist assumptions to the effect that law, as state law, could actually dominate people's lives to the exclusion of all other factors. Jhering's studies emphasised that law operated in a social context, that many factors interacted in the development of legal rules, and that law therefore needed to be studied and understood mainly as a social phenomenon. In taking this approach, Jhering also admitted that the problems of law-making could not be easily solved and that the reconciliation of conflicting interests would be a constant challenge in any society.

Seeking to measure law by social criteria, the French scholar Duguit (1859–1928) sought to develop a new theory of justice, but the problem continues to be that what is 'just' remains subject to social interpretation. The sociological approach alone, useful as it is, also does not answer the 'won't-go-away questions' about law in terms of morality and justice. Max Weber, whose work remains influential for sociologists and lawyers, wanted to understand the development of Western society and of capitalism through much-discussed comparative studies on the world's major civilisations.[103] Focusing on law as a rational element and reacting, eventually, against simple evolutionism, Weber developed a pattern of 'ideal types' of legal institutions, claiming famously that formal rationality was unique to modern Western civilisation.[104] He rejected Marxist economic determinism,[105] but emphasised the role of bureaucracy and legal personnel in establishing the foundations of rational legal

---

[103] There is a huge literature on Weber. For some details, see Freeman (2001: 662–6) and Kantowsky (1986).

[104] The famous statement about Qadi justice in Islamic law goes back to him (Freeman, 2001: 663).

[105] In its purest form, according to Karl Marx (1818–83) and Friedrich Engels (1820–95), economic determinism is used to the same effect as legocentric ideology by lawyers. The key argument is that economic facts and factors determine human behaviour more than anything else (see Freeman, 2001: 953ff.).

systems.[106] Durkheim's sociology focused on criminal law and contract, viewing law as the measuring rod of any society.[107] Durkheim saw law as closely linked to and derived from a society's morality, but tended to underestimate conflict and overestimate groupness (Freeman, 2001: 669). Building partly on such classical models, different types of socio-legal studies emerged, emphasising the importance of placing law in its social context, using social-scientific research methods and recognising that many traditional jurisprudential questions are empirical in nature (Freeman, 2001: 684).

Reacting to the dominant *laissez-faire* approach of early twentieth-century America and the positivist formalism of common law, legal realism became a prominent new movement, particularly in the USA.[108] Legal realism focused on the gaps between legal rules and actually lived social norms, but was soon widely accused of remaining too descriptive, lacking analytical depth, and working on the basis of unquestioned positivist premises.[109] Law continued to be perceived as occupying a central hegemonic position in relation to society. The pioneer stage of the sociology of law, identified with Roscoe Pound (1870–1964), a leading American jurist influenced by Jhering,[110] perceived lawyers as social engineers and focused on exploring how to harmonise different interests in law and society within a Western democratic context. Freeman (2001: 672) explains how the character of early twentieth-century American society favoured an interdisciplinary approach to law that sought to understand how law as a form of social control could be used effectively to solve old and new problems over justice and distribution. Pound viewed law as a technology, a scientific method applied to solving social problems. This new functional approach was practice-centred and less interested in theory, with much focus on the judiciary, another typical American aspect in the modern sociology of law. Pound's distinction between social and individual interests has remained of major concern to jurists, but 'reads rather like a political manifesto in favour of a liberal and capitalist society, as well as suffering from excessive vagueness' (Freeman, 2001: 675). Seeking to develop a theory of law and justice, Pound was thinking about the values which law should underwrite in a well-organised, well-functioning society. However, Pound's vision of 'good law', of social order as a harmonious

---

[106] Harris (1988: 8–9) neatly summarises Weber's writings about different types of authority in social groups, charismatic, traditional and rational-legal.

[107] For details see Freeman (2001: 666–70).

[108] Freeman (2001: 665). See also Summers (1968; 1971; 1982). Olivecrona (1971: 171) noted that the American realists used similar arguments as Bentham and shared his empiricist basis. The roots of realism can be traced back to Plato (Harris, 1980: 93). The term itself seems disputed (see Dias and Hughes, 1957: 467–78). For a more recent discussion, see Freeman (2001:799–820). It is a hallmark of different schools of modern legal realism that they combine analytical and sociological approaches, pushing natural law to the periphery.

[109] For details of these critiques, see Freeman (2001: 684f.).

[110] On Jhering's influence, see Summers (2000: 21–42).

whole, so that law comes to represent the consciousness of a whole society, does not reflect social reality anywhere and thus fails to make practical sense. Freeman (2001: 676) notes:

> Pound is describing a society which is homogenous, static and coherent, one with shared values and traditions and a common cognition of reality. Whatever society Pound thought he was describing, it certainly was not the United States, nor, it may be added, can British society be recognised in this model.

The approach underlying Pound's jurisprudence of interests seems built on the idealistic American dream of a cohesive society and is, like this rosy vision,[111] deficient in plurality consciousness. Not surprisingly, his idealistic consensus model has been criticised and replaced by a conflict paradigm focused on exploring class interests in relation to the law.[112] Twining (2000: 54) notes that sociology of law has become ethnocentric under American influence, too particularistic and parochial.

Oliver Wendell Holmes (1841–1935), a judge of the Supreme Court, provided much intellectual inspiration, introducing a strong court-centred bias focused on the role of judges in applying and making law. Holmes saw law in terms of predictions about what courts would decide and advised that practical social sciences could be of assistance in catering to the legal needs of a highly developed society. His ideas were taken up by Karl Llewellyn (1893–1962) and Jerome Frank (1889–1957). Respectively an academic and a judge, Llewellyn and Frank shared a desire for better justice. Focusing on the judiciary and judicial processes,[113] rather than the whole field of law, Llewellyn cautioned that blindly applying legal rules, and treating them as binding law, did not match reality. Warning against such 'book law', Llewellyn as a weak positivist (Twining, 2000: 79) saw law as an organised activity centred on certain 'law-jobs',[114] and was concerned to research how such law-jobs are carried out in various social settings. Llewellyn saw his theory as universal but has been criticised for overlooking power differences in various social settings, using a simple appeal to common sense, while the realist school faced criticism for being conservative and intellectually insignificant (Freeman, 2001: 806–12). Frank

---

[111] Exemplified in the traditional 'melting pot' image, which has now been replaced by the 'salad bowl' approach, which accounts more accurately for plural realities (Alba and Nee, 2003).

[112] Freeman (2001: 676) suggests that the consensus model is reflected in Ehrlich's approach. However, Ehrlich was certainly aware of the potential for conflict and resolved this by observing that social forces would override or manipulate legal inputs, a message that lawyers do not like and that Ehrlich himself probably played down.

[113] The typical focus of American legal thinking on judges and their roles is highlighted by Llewellyn and Hoebel (1941: 310) and contrasted to German methods of scholarly analysis.

[114] See Freeman (2001: 805–6) and Twining (2000: 79–82).

criticised Llewellyn as a mere 'rule-sceptic',[115] proposing that realist legal analysis needed to involve scepticism of rules and facts.[116] Taking law as a means to settle disputes, the various realist approaches merely question whether formal legal rules are all that matters or whether legal certainty can be achieved by making rules and rigidly applying them. A later stage of realist argument focused more on theory,[117] in which the complex relationship between different sociological approaches and claims to legal centrality have remained key issues (Freeman, 2001: 678–703). More or less guarded criticism of the lack of theorising has continued.[118]

While the explicit focus on judicial activities makes the ambit of most American realists rather narrow, the so-called Scandinavian realists took a wider, more philosophical approach.[119] These authors share a positivist outlook (Freeman, 2001: 858), emphasising that 'law' only corresponds to a psychological reality, so that the mere label 'law' or 'rule' has no inherent authority and law needs to be studied as a matter of fact. The most influential author in this field, the philosopher Axel Hägerström (1868–1939), focused on criticism of the will-theory and laid the foundations for a non-voluntaristic theory of law (Olivecrona, 1971: 84).[120] He wanted to free legal thinking from lawyers' myths to establish a realistic legal science to improve society and combat exploitation of people through law. Hägerström denied the existence of objective values, dismissing all conceptual thinking as metaphysical or ideological, thus (however unconvincingly) refuting natural law methodologies. Dias and Hughes (1957: 482) explained his approach:

> This leads Hägerström to deny the possibility of any science of the Ought. All questions of justice, aims, purposes and the reality of law are matters of personal evaluation and not susceptible to any scientific processes of examination. In this way many of the traditional problems of legal philosophy

[115] This relates to legal uncertainty about what the law means, while 'fact sceptics' are concerned about the unpredictability of court decisions as a result of the assessment of facts. Freeman (2001: 803 n. 25) identifies a third category, 'opinion-scepticism', which relates to judicial subjectivity and discretion, which is also difficult to predict.

[116] Frank thought mainly of lower courts and observed that their assessment of facts was fraught with many imponderables. Legal rules, to him, 'are little more than pretty playthings' (Harris, 1980: 95).

[117] Twining (2000: 75–6) highlights Llewellyn's contribution to methodology and the teaching of professional legal skills.

[118] Summers (1982: 273–4) discusses possible reasons for the failure to produce a coherent American realistic legal theory.

[119] Freeman (2001: 855–901) presents the Scandinavian realists as emerging from relative insularity, marked by a penchant for social welfare, a rejection of metaphysics and a down-to-earth approach to crime. For details see also Olivecrona (1971: 174–82).

[120] Such a theory would appear to emphasise that law is not just based on the will of a sovereign or a myth of its own inherent authority, but needs to be studied as a socio-legal fact.

become illusory, and must be replaced by an examination of the actual use of legal terms and concepts and a psychological analysis of the mental attitudes that are involved.

His friend Vilhelm Lundstedt similarly 'insisted that rights and duties are chimeras' (Olivecrona, 1971: 176) and suggested that 'all talk of rights and duties should be banished from jurisprudence' (p. 176), though he himself kept using the terms. Lundstedt asserted that legal rules are mere labels, resembling recommended procedures for achieving a particular purpose, hence potentially meaningless scraps of paper, because the rules might be ignored altogether.[121] Further, Lundstedt 'emphasized that what we call the law is a vast and complicated working machinery in a society' (Olivecrona, 1971: 84). Such radical suggestions did not meet with much approval, but inspired further debates about the concept of rights.

The writings of Karl Olivecrona (1897–1980) and Alf Ross (1899–1979), now partly available in English, also created much interest. For Olivecrona (1971), rules of law are 'independent imperatives', not just statements of fact, but propositions in imperative form, used as bargaining chips in a dynamic interactive socio-legal environment. He rejected the idea of a generally binding force of law, since it was observable that not all laws were treated as binding. Like Allott (1980), this discourse enters into limits of law debates, and radically challenges fundamental assumptions of legal positivism. Olivecrona (1971: 80) commented on the misguiding nature of the dominant natural law/positivism debates:

> The voluntaristic assumption, which seemed so natural, has been like a signpost through which generations of philosophers and jurists have been induced to take the wrong road. This was a road that led to an impasse. In most cases, it was not even noticed that there was another road which took off from the main thoroughfare of legal theory at an earlier age. This road was far less conspicuous and it was seldom taken.

The alternative road, described from this perspective as non-voluntarist theories, implies historical and socio-legal approaches. Olivecrona (1971: 80) pointed out that in the beginning these theories 'were put forward in a tentative way and were lacking in clarity'. This is in line with the findings of the present study about the peripheral nature of socio-legal approaches in legal theory as a whole, while the third triangle of society and its norms (section 3.8) maintains a constant presence. Closely related to this, Alf Ross preferred to see law as 'directives' or 'quasi-commands' but made a distinction between rules in statutes and legal statements in textbooks. To him, the study of law was an

---

[121] An example of such rules may be found in Pakistan's Muslim Family Laws Ordinance of 1961, which manifestly do not mean what positivist lawyers have read into them (chapter 5, section 5.14).

engagement in constructing assertions, and lawyers appreciated his respect for statute law as 'valid law' (Freeman, 2001: 861). However, he later modified his perspective to see legal norms as directives to judges rather than the public at large, a position that was not maintainable.[122]

Through highlighting the subjectivities of law and its constructed nature, the realists 'did much of the initial spade-work' (Freeman, 2001: 813) for later schools of legal thought, especially the Critical Legal Studies movement, feminist jurisprudence and postmodernism.[123] Freeman (2001: 685) suggests that, while contemporary scholars try to focus on understanding the place of legal systems in relation to wider social structures, fears of mutual colonisation between lawyers and sociologists seem prominent. Law as a field, and much legal scholarship concerned with it, continues to close itself off as superior in relation to social sciences and maintains a legocentric stance. There are few exciting studies with a global perspective. Taking a social theory approach, Unger (1976) appears to look beyond the confines of modern law and predicts something akin to postmodern legal development (Freeman, 2001: 691–2). Recent socio-legal scholarship remains too abstruse and parochial, or too focused on specific narrow agenda (Cotterrell, 2004) to make deep contributions to a globality-focused jurisprudence.

3.7.2 New natural law theories

Despite the disillusionment with positivism,[124] and its continued potential for abuses, the twentieth century did not disown legal positivism. It has continued to remain a central focus of legal theory and many new theories strengthened positivist methodology, often subjecting state law to vigorous tests of moral evaluation.[125] This process went hand in hand with a remarkable and widely noted resurgence of natural law theory (Olivecrona, 1971: 6), which began around 1900,[126] grew slowly until after the Second World War (p. 43), and led to a huge literature on natural law theory between 1945 and 1960.[127] While positivism could not provide answers, according to Cotterrell (2003: 115–16),

---

[122] For details of this intricate discussion see Freeman (2001: 862–3). For new thinking about law and language see Freeman (2001: 863–5).

[123] For details on all of these see Cownie (2004: 50–4) and the new chapter 8 in Cotterrell (2003: 209–36). In America, legal realism has also led to the interrelated movements of jurimetrics and judicial behaviouralism, discussed by Freeman (2001: 813–17).

[124] Olivecrona (1971: 47) refers to the widespread view that the positivist doctrine of the legal omnipotence of the law-giver was the Fall or *Sündenfall* of legal positivism.

[125] Olivecrona (1971: 42–3) noted that it is impossible to make clear-cut distinctions between positivists and natural lawyers.

[126] Cotterrell (2003: 122–3) explains this resurgence as a reaction to the claimed victories of analytical jurisprudence towards the end of the nineteenth century, which still could not explain how and why legal outcomes should change, and as a reaction to Nazi atrocities.

[127] See Olivecrona (1971: 48 n. 84) and Freeman (2000: 123ff.).

natural law theory has postulated the existence of moral principles having a
validity and authority independent of human enactment, and which can be
thought of as a 'higher' or more fundamental law against which the worth
or authority of human law can be judged . . . Natural law thus requires no
human legislator. Yet it stands in judgment on the law created by human
legislators.

The debates between natural law and legal positivism are ongoing. Freeman
(2000: 123) suggests that rediscovery of the concept of practical reason, especially in the work of Finnis (1980) and Raz (1979), bridged the gulf between
positivism and natural law. George (1999) discusses the Grisez–Finnis theory
of the 1980s and suggests in defence of natural law theory that it need not rely,
and has not depended on, what Finnis called the 'illicit inference from facts
to norms' (George, 1999: 3), meaning that this new natural law theory claims
renewed superiority over everything else. Cotterrell (2003: 120) observes that
discussions about the nature of law almost inevitably turn into political debates,
so that '[n]atural law theory, when taken seriously, becomes a force in political
struggle – usually in defence of existing legal and political systems (by demonstrating their legitimacy grounded in "reason" or "nature") but occasionally as
a weapon of rebellion or revolution'. Thus, the main difference between positivism and natural law 'is not a polar opposition but a difference as to how
far inquiries about law's ultimate authority should be taken' (Cotterrell, 2003:
120). Since most positivists accept moral evaluation and natural lawyers tend
to recognise the law-making powers of the state, the scope for taking different political perspectives became ever wider.[128] In this context, Finnis (1980:
364–5) pointed to the lingering problem that unjust laws may still be seen and
treated as valid laws and that the perception of what is 'just' remains subjective.
Cotterrell (2003: 121) notes:

> So the conflict between natural law and positivism tends to become a dis-
> pute as to whether the authority of a legal system as a whole can only be
> understood and judged in relation to some specific moral *purpose* (such as
> promoting the common good) for which all legal systems exist. In general,
> the answer of natural lawyers is yes, and of positivists, no.

Modern theories of natural law can still be divided into religious and secular
categories. Olivecrona (1971: 48) firmly opposed the former and concluded
that '[t]he religious foundation of the law of nature appears to be illusory from
religion's own point of view'. Modern secular theories of natural law deny any
form of divine will as a source of natural law, making it possible to reject the
term 'law of nature' itself,[129] and to replace it with discussions about rights

---

[128] Cotterrell (2003: 123) rightly notes the new focus on Rule of Law as a 'defence against
uncontrolled terror and arbitrary violence'.

[129] Cotterrell (2003: 117–9) discusses whether natural law is dead and concludes, relying on
Habermas (1974: 113) that in the view of many writers, natural law ideas are 'devoid of
any and every convincing theoretical justification'.

and duties. However, this refocusing just revives old problems over defining what is 'just' and 'good'. Olivecrona (1971: 50) highlights that modern natural law theories simply seem to take legal positivism for granted and focus on the judgment of values, widely recognised as variable:

> The principles that are supposed to follow from the fundamental values are not said to be eternal and unchangeable. They must be adapted to circumstances of time and place. If a 'law of nature' is spoken of at all, it is therefore held to be variable. Many authors prefer to use Rudolf Stammler's expression 'right law' (*richtiges Recht*).

This suggests a need to rethink the combination of modern natural law theories with historical and sociological approaches to the study of law. Like 'pure' positivism, theorising law in secular, rational, natural law fashion is clearly not sufficient to understand the global phenomenon of law. The traditional false dichotomy of natural law and legal positivism, which failed to give a voice to the socio-cultural aspects of law, did not explain why particular values should be 'good', but traditional natural law terminology continues to be used by many recent thinkers. The key challenge continues to be that idealising statements about 'law' need to be matched with evidence that in real life justice is being respected. Combining such theoretical approaches with reality-conscious sociological methods might be more fruitful for a globally focused jurisprudential analysis. It appears that, for a globally valid definition of law, positive law must be measured against morality, which remains subjective and culture-specific, so will need to be tested against social realities to ascertain what is perceived as appropriate at any given point of time. Since we are dealing with perceptions rather than physical truths, debates about law will forever remain a hotbed of subjective contest.

It is evident that none of the major theoretical approaches to the study of law on its own has been able to provide globally valid and agreed answers even about the nature of law itself. The search for agreeable universals has virtually been abandoned and declared useless by important scholars like Unger (1976: 265). It is clearly too simple to portray certain values as universally good and globally binding, since those who assert such positions come from particular backgrounds and tend to overlook the fact that there are many people in the world who may not share such perceptions for sound cultural or other reasons, rather than alleged disregard for universal human values, which is often used as an argument to silence opponents today.[130] It has also been overlooked rather too fast that badness is another universal phenomenon with which legal analysis has to grapple.[131]

---

[130] This technique of discourse carries striking similarities with the Islamic technique to declare the opponent 'un-Islamic', a *kafir* (non-believer) or simply *haram*.

[131] Freeman (2001: 683) notes that greed is also a universal value.

Since scientific analysis cannot solve the problem of how one measures 'justice' without taking account of culture-specific values, and a purely objective and scientific analysis of values is a contradiction in terms,[132] significant progress may be made in theorising the central role of legal pluralism for understanding global plurality. However, no amount of shifting of categories and understandings can overcome the basic and universal problem that abuses of political and legal power continue to be a reality, so that vigilance, in practice as well as in theory, remains crucially important.

Seeking to explain the recent 'rebirth' of natural law, Cotterrell (2003: 121–2) suggests that debates about the nature of legal authority tend to resurface when political and legal authority are under challenge. In times of stability, positivist approaches seem good enough to explain 'law', but when political authority faces challenges, moral considerations are brought in and '[q]uestions as to what rules are valid as law become elements of ideological struggle; a matter of winning hearts and minds for or against established regimes' (p. 122). To assess what may be seen as good or bad, one is then always thrown back to the level of society, thus drawing the third triangle of socio-legal approaches back into the discourse. While this approach appears to be familiar from Stammler's theory of natural law with its changing content and his subjective concept of 'good law', few legal theorists have gone down that route, fearing presumably that the resulting legal insecurity would be too cumbersome. Finnis (1980: 279) warned that most lawyers would be impatient with legal uncertainty, but he did not say that 'good' law should not take account of such factors and actually stated quite clearly that '[i]t is a philosophical mistake to declare . . . that a social order or set of concepts must either be law or not be law, be legal or not legal' (p. 280). So what is 'good' depends ultimately to a large extent on social construction and considerations of situation-specificity and it may not matter whether we agree on whether this is 'legal' or not.

This more sophisticated kind of socio-legal understanding is reflected in recent literature on social and legal theory, but scholars still seem afraid to grasp the nettle,[133] and we lack a systematic exposition of how it is possible to combine the triangle of the three major theoretical approaches to law, rather than just focusing on two aspects. Cotterrell (2003: 132–6) discusses Fuller's (1969) important critique of positivism in relation to the common law tradition. In the process, he makes several significant comments that require further analysis and a fresh reading of Fuller's important later work in a global

---

[132] Freeman (2000: 93–4) comments on Stammler's suggestion that differences in moral attitude are a normal part of human life, and that this means giving up any attempt to construct objective norms and values. This would indeed rescue natural law theory from uniformising visions.

[133] For example, Freeman (2000: 692) discusses Unger (1976) as 'one of the most stimulating essays of legal and social theory to have appeared for many years', but does not take up the challenges posed by Unger's analysis.

context.[134] In particular, Fuller's emphasis on the processual nature of law, his suggestion that human interaction gives purpose to law and that, ideally, law everywhere should manifest itself as 'the collaborative working out of a reasoned view of human affairs' (Cotterrell, 2003: 134), point to a focus on dynamic socio-legal processes. Finding striking parallels with traditional common law thought, Cotterrell (2003: 135–6) highlights the re-emergence of customary law as a central element in Fuller's later writings:

> Customary law, for Fuller, consists of the established patterns of social interaction that provide the stable structure of expectations within which people can co-operate, negotiate, plan and act. Social science shows how important these stable structures are – often much more important than those provided by enacted law.

This line of thought, focusing on expectations, must be pursued further. Freeman (2001: 139) emphasises the need to study law in the context of other disciplines, but remains unclear as to how this is to be done. Cotterrell (2004) has more recently renewed efforts to explore 'community' in relation to law. Unger (1976: 251ff.) explicitly focuses on custom; in fact he advocates a return to a customary law or tribalist society and the reassertion of communitarian concerns, emphasising 'the logic of the situation' as an explanatory model (p. 255). This is not unlike the 'situation-specificity' advocated by the present study. A plurality-focused approach would need to remain open to such socio-legal perspectives and would always need to build scope for different perspectives and disagreement over basic values into any theoretical model. Here again, the claims of universalising idealism and realistic particularism clash head on and allow no simple compromise.

Even citizens of the supposedly most advanced legal system in the world, that of modern Western liberal society, find it both necessary to struggle for the rule of law and impossible to achieve it, given the common experience of 'the sense of being surrounded by injustice without knowing where justice lies' (Unger, 1976: 175).[135] In view of Unger's (1976: 174) observation about the 'nonexistence of an order men can accept', I suggest that all such critiques are symptomatic of a persistent failure to take account of the dynamic systemic, and therefore flexible and open, interaction of all three major law-making elements. Unger (1976: 249) emphasises that '[n]o conduct has meaning independent of its social context' and compares this to language as a 'collective patrimony' (p. 249). Unger (1976: 262–3) concludes with two possible suggestions for understanding social cohesion:

---

[134] For a detailed discussion of Fuller's contribution see Freeman (2001: 124–9). Morrison (1997: 391) criticises Fuller as too optimistic.

[135] The recent legal ban on fox-hunting in England offers an example of violent disagreement over what is 'right'.

One can look for a general conception of the social bond that somehow synthesizes the doctrines of legitimacy and instrumentalism such as to avoid the defects of each. Or one can abandon the search for a comprehensive thesis as futile and try to ascertain the circumstances to which each account of social order most suitably applies.

Unger (1976: 262) also suggests a middle path, but ultimately questions 'our ability to universalize the experience of community' (p. 265) and finds 'no assurance of ever answering completely the theoretical question of social order' (p. 265). It appears that the moment we rid ourselves of the pressures to think in 'black boxes' and binary pairs and accept methods of thought such as 'overlapping consensus' (Twining, 2000: 69, 71), many of the problems of uniformising global legal theory cease to be problems – legal uniformity simply does not exist as a fact, so its pursuit in theory is futile. Twining (2000: 74) suggests that concern for the position of the least advantaged (the disadvantaged 'other') is most important, and thus endorses the concept of a higher common good as opposed to self-centred autonomous individualism based on arbitrary assumptions of equality. This is clearly another aspect of socio-legal natural law realism that a theory with claims to global validity cannot ignore.

3.8 A global working definition of law

Searching for the authority of law, Raz (1979: v) warns against unrealistic expectations and suggests that 'all legal systems contain gaps calling for the exercise of discretion and for reliance on extra-legal considerations by courts in certain cases' (p. vii). We have seen in abundance that, instead of making hasty claims of universality, law talk needs to guard its language while referring to 'Western' law. Using the term 'law' itself immediately raises enormous conceptual complexities. The challenge at this point is to explore in more depth, from a plurality-focused perspective, what may be meant by 'law'. This concluding section culminates in presenting an intricate triangular model of legal pluralism and interlegality.

The usefulness of trying to define 'law' has been questioned by many writers, and the concept itself has created hostility in many parts of the world (Lloyd, 1991: 11). Positivist analysis has been criticised for being too narrowly focused on rules,[136] natural law theories are viewed with suspicion for ending up as 'religious positivism',[137] and socio-legal approaches face fears about fuzziness.[138] Earlier, Olivecrona (1971: 272) found that '[a] definition of the

---

[136] See e.g. the famous 1958 Hart/Dworkin debate.

[137] Finnis (1980: 388–9) argues that 'God' is a term with many meanings and circumscribes D, 'of which all that has been affirmed is that it is a state of affairs which exists simply by being what it is, and which is required for the existing of any other state of affairs'.

[138] Cotterrell (2004: 1) notes that legal theory must now systematically take account of culture and suggests that '[l]egal theory requires a sociologically-informed concept of community'.

supposed concept of law cannot be given'. The simple model of law as a system of rules is perhaps nothing more than a tool of description (Twining, 2000: 37). It is superficial and false to treat law as only composed of the totality of rules: 'Each law in fact constitutes a *system*' (David and Brierley, 1978: 18; Allott, 1980). Such a system may be changed by law-makers, yet there is something, supposedly universal, beyond these rules which one can also study as 'law'.

A postmodern approach would question attempts to universalise one particular concept of law and emphasise instead its inherent plurality.[139] Twining (2000: 231) suggests that a general definition of law within the conceptual context of legal pluralism may be misleading, because 'the indicia of "the legal" are more like a continuum or more complex mix of attributes, which it is not necessary to set off artificially from closely related phenomena except for pragmatic reasons in quite specific contexts'. Bell (2002: 236) notes that 'generic statements of the functions of law are of limited value. A comparatist has to examine not only rules and functions, but also the context in which legal problems arise. Only by understanding this context or institutional setting can we make effective comparison.' This leads to the argument that looking for law as an ordered system is itself highly problematic. Sampford (1989) argued that it is fundamentally misleading to think of law anywhere as self-contained and systematic. Twining (2000: 35–6) comments that '[h]is picture of law as being part of a "social mêlée" at both national and international levels is very much in tune with the thrust of those aspects of globalisation theory, and of legal pluralism, which challenge all "black box" conceptions of law'.

Faced with such widely divergent perspectives, is it possible to come to any general understanding of the meaning of 'law'? Simon Roberts (1979) refuted the usefulness of the word 'law' itself, arguing that the analysis of aspects of order and the maintenance of such order through dispute processing, would take better account of the realities of everyday life for people whose ideas of legal rules differed significantly from our own. It would be unrealistic to assume that we could search for any neat, agreed definition of law.[140] Bix (1996: 8) suggests that it all depends on what categories one chooses, as '[t]he question is one of inclusion and exclusion'. Any realistic jurisprudential approach is therefore forced to take account of plurality at various levels and of the dynamic interaction between different elements of law. But jurisprudence is described as a 'wasteland of false polemics' (Twining, 2000: 39) and asking about the nature of jurisprudence itself opens up ideological battles. Freeman (2001: 1) warns that:

---

[139] Twining (2000: 138) notes that globalisation makes more salient the multiplicity of legal orderings and proceeds to discuss different levels of law and the mapping of law. From a social theory perspective, see Unger (1976).

[140] Lloyd (1991: 326–7) finds it 'hardly surprising that no universally acceptable pattern of the idea of law emerges from a study of human society at all its varying stages of development'. Nader (1992: 5) notes that direct attempts to define law 'have not borne much fruit'.

not only does every jurist have his own notion of the subject-matter and proper limits of jurisprudence, but his approach is governed by his allegiances, or those of his society, by what is commonly referred to nowadays as, his 'ideology'. No doubt such ideological factors are frequently implicit rather than openly avowed.

While the impact of their training and professional environment seems to unite lawyers, 'the close relation of law to the social structure inevitably brings into prominence the ideological context of legal theory' (Freeman, 2001: 2) and therefore leads to different approaches and petty politics. Harris (1980: 3) points out that jurisprudence 'is a scavenger, as well as a ragbag; having no perimeter to its field of enquiry', identifying the definition of law as the central problematic in jurisprudential enquiry (p. 5):

> Whether labels matter when it comes to the word 'law' itself – a question which is highly controversial in the areas of 'primitive law' and 'living law' . . . – it is surely the case that labels do not matter in assigning the proper fields for 'jurisprudence', 'legal theory' and 'legal philosophy'. It is the won't-go-away questions which count.

Freeman (2001: 3) provides some help in defining jurisprudence, indicating what may be included and excluded from a working definition of law:

> Jurisprudence involves the study of general theoretical questions about the nature of laws and legal systems, about the relationship of law to justice and morality and about the social nature of law. A proper discussion of questions such as these involves understanding and use of philosophical and sociological theories and findings in their application to law. A study of jurisprudence should encourage the student to question assumptions and to develop a wider understanding of the nature and working of law. Questions of theory constantly spring up in legal practice, though they may not be given very sophisticated answers.

This statement clearly takes a holistic perspective of law, but does not explicitly include consideration of law outside the eurocentric realm. Later, Freeman (2001: 10) perceptively notes that '[i]t is difficult to characterise jurisprudence; there are many rooms in its mansion.' We enter this vast mansion, aware of the risks of rule-centredness, with the familiar assumption that law is a collection of rules made and enforced by the state through various official organs and institutions. The practical application of rules in social reality creates dynamic interaction processes, which are not only influenced by the state, requiring the analyst to look beyond positivism. While positivism is not enough to understand 'law',[141] it remains the dominant approach, but statist rule-fixation does

---

[141] Dennis Lloyd, writing in 1959, in his Preface to the first edition of what is now Freeman (2001: x).

not match with how most people in the world experience law and handle disputes in their day-to-day lives. Moreover, it is a fact, insufficiently reflected upon by lawyers, that most disputes never formally go to 'the law'.

The normative character of law is self-evident.[142] Laws are, generally speaking, 'rules or norms, which prescribe a course of conduct, and indicate what should happen in default' (Freeman, 2001: 11). This is still quite a positivist, even Austinian take on the definition of law. Farrar and Dugdale (1990: 246) take a more relativist approach, recognising that 'law is more an expression of the culture of the lawmaking élite rather than that of society at large, and that the variety of interests and attitudes possessed by such elites may thwart attempts to generalise'. Emphasising the purposive nature of law, Harris (1980: 130) noted that '[a]ll legal systems seek to govern conduct', while immediately admitting that 'all legal systems fail by some of the criteria to some extent' (p. 131). Law manifestly fails to govern conduct when, for example, some people drink and drive in clear violation of legal rules and hope not to be caught. To what extent law can deter people from wrongdoings or can guide actions are ancient problems of a global nature.

The prevailing focus on fixed legal rules and institutions,[143] combined with the realisation that life and law may not match, raises further complexities about how 'law' may be defined. It is evident that people may use norms and whole rule systems that are not defined as legal, but appear to have the same effect as legal commands or regulations.[144] If definitions of law are more or less arbitrary and culture-specific, does it matter whether a particular norm or rule system can be defined as 'legal' or not? Where do we draw the boundaries? Dominant Western theories of analytical positivism treat law as separate from social institutions and ethical norms – but this is only *one* way of looking at law. Is it not that ideologies, politics, economics, socio-cultural factors and religions have played a critical role in shaping legal systems anywhere in the world? If that is so, then how do we understand law and isolate it as a separate phenomenon in a coherent, globally valid theory?

Most writers actually accept the plurality and interlinkedness of law. We saw that even Austin was conscious of legal pluralism (Morrison, 1997: vii, 6). Charting future research agenda, Lloyd (1991: 334, originally published in 1964) suggested that 'it seems not improbable that the idea of law which will prevail among lawyers in the near future will be one which emphasizes not so much the

---

[142] Twining (2000) notes repeatedly that we are surrounded by normative plurality in our daily lives.

[143] Bix (1996: 7) treats law as 'an English term which refers to a certain collection of institutions and practices'.

[144] In this context Moore (1978) introduced her important concept of 'semi-autonomous social fields' (Chapter 2, section 2.5.1). Freeman (2001: 8) notes in hermeneutical debates that '[s]ocial life has an internal logic which must be understood by the social scientist'. But what about the lawyer's understanding?

self-contained character of law, but rather its function as an instrument of social cohesion and social progress'. Even Kelsen (1971: 64) noted the 'extraordinary heterogeneity . . . of what men in fact have considered as good or evil, just or unjust, at different times and in different places', so that 'no element common to the contents of the various moral orders is detectable' (p. 64).

There have been so many different attempts to understand law that nobody could hope to represent them all today in a readable study. It seems that two approaches to conceptualising law, focused either on justice and morality (broadly, natural law), or on rules and regulations (broadly, legal positivism) have been most prominent.[145] Putting these two together, as we saw, has led to needless polemics.[146] But there is also potentially a more integrated third way of analysing law, focusing on socio-legal approaches, as indicated by Freeman (2001: 3, cited above) and elaborated earlier by Summers (1982), who treats the historical school as the third major legal theory.[147] The present study argues that there has in fact been a fourth approach, centred on legal pluralism, which most lawyers seek to ignore as it is messy and requires crossing boundaries into the so-called 'extra-legal' domain. Reacting to this plurality of approaches, most scholars have taken sides rather than considering the whole picture and have construed an avalanche of 'realistic' and 'critical' theories which are all segmentary and fragmented. Part of the resurgence of natural law in the twentieth century (section 3.7.2) has been the concern with substantive questions of justice, rather than legal structures, and the claim that this concerns everyone. In this context, Harris (1980: 2–3) wrote:

> The won't-go-away questions are not and should not be the lawyer's preserve. Everyone has a right to ask whether the ideal of the rule of law has value; whether there is any moral duty to obey the law . . . ; whether the law ought to diminish our liberty for our own physical or moral good . . . ; what it is, if anything, that justifies the institution of punishment . . . 'Out of office hours', we all stand on the same (usually shakey) ground when we debate the merits of proposed legislation in terms of the public good . . . or of justice.

These are important indications that discussions about the moral claims *of* the law, on law *as it ought to be*, and of moral claims on the law *as it is*, remain

---

[145] Olivecrona (1971). Lloyd in Freeman (2001: viii) emphasises the central controversy between positivists and natural lawyers. Twining (2000: 61) argues that most major theorists 'tended to assume that a theory of law is only concerned with two types of law, viz. municipal state law and public international law', and thus tend to overlook non-state law and natural law concepts.

[146] Podgorecki and Whelan (1981: 10) note that, while especially analytical jurisprudence 'has achieved a good deal by way of semantic clarification, it has never really *explained* law'.

[147] Notably, Summers (1982) presents as a fourth approach American pragmatic instrumentalism, which does not appear to have been accepted in recent scholarship.

a central matter of jurisprudential debate and public interest (Freeman, 2001: 11–13). But in eurocentric legal debates it is often forgotten (or more or less purposely overlooked) that the world extends far beyond the realm of the office of 'white men' and Judaeo-Christian concepts. How universal are some of the supposedly universal elements of complex Western jurisprudential debates? This question will definitely not go away for students of non-European laws and globally focused jurisprudence.

To answer the question what legal systems consist of, Allott (1980: 6–7) tried to explain that '[t]he short answer conventionally given is that *Law* is a system of rules; and that, in the juristic world in which we now move, those rules are restricted to rules about behaviour; and that, to avoid over-extension of the term *Law*, the behaviour meant is the behaviour of persons in a political society; and that, to avoid legitimating the illegitimate, only rules made by a competent and legitimate authority within that society may be called rules of *Law*'. However, Allott (1980: 7) immediately pointed out:

> All of these elements are challenged. Dworkin, among others, argues that a *Law* includes principles, policies and standards (as defined by him) as well as rules. The legal sociologists tell us that *Law* includes institutions and relationships as well as rules (or that rules themselves are merely one type of such institutions). Pospišil would argue that *Law* cannot be restricted to a political society, and that any subgroup of a society can have its law. On this view *Law* would extend to rules imposed by the Mafia or the IRA on their members.

This was getting close to arguing, daring for an English law professor, that law could include all kinds of elements despite doubts over legality and legitimacy. Allott (1980: 7) therefore proceeded to state his own views categorically, providing a wide-ranging definitional framework:

> A *Law* or legal system comprises norms, institutions and processes. The norms include rules of law, as well as principles (in Dworkin's sense). The rules include both *primary rules*, which directly prescribe behaviour, and *secondary rules*, which govern the application of the primary rules and the functioning of the institutions and processes of the system, including the process for adding to or varying rules.
>
> The institutions of the *Law* comprise both the *facilities* (e.g. judges) for the operation of the processes and the application of the norms, the *statuses* and the *relationships* identified and controlled by the norms, i.e. the relationships on which the norms operate.
>
> The processes of the *Law* describe the norms and institutions in action. Adjudication is one process of the law; making a contract is another.

Allott (1980: 7–8) further discussed this definitional cluster, relying on Moore (1978) and returning to his earlier concern over the possible illegality of law:

> A *Law* or legal system is a function of an autonomous and distinct society or community, that is, an organised body of persons. To say that the society

is autonomous is not to say that it is independent in a formal sense, but that it has its own system of regulation. Thus a tribal group having its own customary *Law* within a modern state is autonomous to the extent that it generates and applies its own system of norms. Although it is theoretically possible to include in such a society one which is illegal or unrecognised by a superior order in the larger society of which it is part, it appears convenient to introduce some notion of *legitimacy* into our definition of a society which, though autonomous, is politically part of a larger whole. Our amended version would then read, 'an autonomous and *legitimate* society or community'.

Chapter 2, section 2.5.2 showed that Allott's (1980) discussion of law and its limits ended in a circular argument, to the effect that law is law because someone says it is law.[148] Such definitions remain meaningless (and dangerous) unless we accept, from the outset, that there are many possible agents for asserting what is law. In the absence of a globally agreed definition of law, an effort is made below to develop a plurality-focused definition by laying dominant preconceived assumptions on the table for further analysis.[149] But let us not be deluded: If it is pointless to search for a uniform scientific definition, because 'law' manifests itself in so many different ways and is everywhere culture-specific, this exercise will only result in a collection of open-ended thoughts, not because we cannot handle the challenge, but due to the nature of the subject. That is the dilemma of plurality-conscious legal theory: it has to remain at all times so plurality-conscious that no one prominent legal theory must be allowed to dominate.[150] This is why we need a theoretical model which can incorporate and interlink all major approaches.[151]

Reflection on law in a global context leads us into an intellectual labyrinth (Morrison, 1997: 3), since law can take a variety of forms, can be 'made' in a number of ways, and may originate from quite different and potentially competing sources. Law is always something particular, not just a generalised phenomenon, and it is culture-specific because its manifestations depend on socio-cultural settings that differ from place to place and through time. Assuming generally that law is 'a body of rules made and applied by a particular group of people' (rather than restricting this immediately in legocentric fashion to

---

[148] Olivecrona (1971: 1) immediately shows concern about how to avoid this circularity. The same problem is faced by the analysis of Tamanaha (2001) and is pointed out by Cotterrell (2003: 244).

[149] Freeman (2001: 1) refers in this context to 'inarticulate major premises'. Unger (1976: 11) notes that rationalism, too, cannot operate without the 'perplexing but inevitable introduction of empirical assumptions'.

[150] Putting it this way adopts the advice of Legrand (1996) and is inspired by Chiba (1986; 1989).

[151] Summers (1971: 103 n. 4) argued that talk of definition of law and of morality should be abandoned because 'it only invites confusion'. However, Summers (2000: 82) acknowledges that 'general theory profoundly influences the law, something of which those in the law should be more conscious'.

state law, or just saying that law is a body of good rules), we see that this wide definition already contains three basic elements.[152] The first element may be expressed in a variety of ways, using English words with slightly different nuances. Thus, for the simple 'a body of rules' we might substitute:

- a collection of rules
- a system of norms
- a set of rules, norms or conventions.

Whatever form of words we use, this first definitional element comprises not a single unit, but immediately a combination of elements that may or may not be coherent, a plurality. This potentially wide definition tells us nothing about the nature of interaction between those rules, unless we want to read a significant difference into 'body of rules' and 'system of rules'. If we are tempted to imply that the body of rules must have been made by someone or a group of people authorised to do so, then we are back in the legocentric cul-de-sac, where law is only law because it is asserted or recognised as law. In a wider, globally conscious definition, law as a body of rules remains an inherently diverse and plural phenomenon that could take many forms. All the time, much depends on our unspoken assumptions about law-making (Unger, 1976: 11).

If we want to give this definition a narrower ambit and de-pluralise it, reducing the diversity within the body of rules does not help. Whether we speak of 'a body of rules' or 'a small body of rules' makes no difference in principle; a small body or set of rules is still inherently plural. So would it be different if we perceived 'law' as a single rule? The definition would then simply read that law is a rule. Like the previous wider definition, this does not explain what kind of rule we mean. But can one define law in the singular, or is law always more than one rule, and always a plurality, so that the little category of 'law' as 'a particular normative provision of a *Law*' (Allott, 1980: 2) exists, but never in isolation? Asking whether a single rule is law, we find that this may be so, but not all single rules are law, nor are all laws single rules. Searching for universality necessitates a wider definition of law which requires an interactive plurality rather than a single entity. Our probing yields the result that we are probably more impressed with a definition of 'law' that retains the image of a *system* of rules rather than a single rule. Going further in this analysis, one may next tackle the second element of the basic definition given above and ask how law as a body of rules came about or what effect it has. This yields two possible types of verbal constructs:

- a body or system of rules made by . . .

---

[152] This particular approach seems to run against 'the more progressive view that law simply cannot be captured by a set of rules . . . and that there is, indeed, much "law" to be found beyond the rules' (Legrand, 1997a: 58), but the discussion below will it is hoped free itself from the 'fetishism of rules' (p. 59).

or:

• a body or system of rules applying to . . .

In the first phrase, the additional words indicate the origin or sources of the law, while the second phrase specifies its application. Many new questions arise: Does law *have* to be made in some form or can it just exist in its own right? The definition would then read: 'A body of rules that exists.' That does not help, since there is no real difference between 'a body of rules' and 'a body of rules that exists', unless we want to engage in complex arguments about meta-language.

It is perhaps more productive to ask whether 'made by' in the definitional construction can be replaced by other words. What if the body of rules was imposed by someone, or an institution, and had been developed in a particular way? We have a wide choice of English words to circumscribe how a particular body of rules was created, but different words will set off various assumptions: while 'made by' remains general, 'chosen by', 'developed by' or 'imposed by' all connote particular processes of rule-making. How wide or specific can a definition of law be? Do we envisage law only as a body of rules imposed by someone (Austin's sovereign) or a group of people, or can law just develop or grow, more or less haphazardly, perhaps in a totally unplanned manner, resulting in a quite unsystematic collage, but a system nevertheless? Legal presumptions tend towards viewing 'law' as an ordered system, but several scholars have shown that law can be messy, incoherent and self-contradictory. Having clarified the nature of *Law* as a deficient system of communication (chapter 2, section 2.5.2), Allott (1980: 6) questioned our assumptions about *Law* as a legal system:

> Is a legal system natural or contrived, pre-existent or imposed? Like many of the essentialist questions one has to pose in this study, the answer, unsatisfactorily, is 'both'. A legal system is composed of many elements or items, some of which appear in the real world, like policemen, judges, prisons, lawyers, law-books; while some appear to exist only in the meta-world, a mental world floating in the air over the real world: such abstractions as rules, principles, standards, institutions, norms. *Law* has abstract elements as well as tangible elements. As a complete system it continues to function (as already remarked) even if no one is thinking about it, even if no one sets out consciously to design and operate it as a system. In this sense it is natural.

We clearly have several options to avoid definitional blind alleys. Understanding 'law' as a systematic, planned, well-developed body of rules made for a particular purpose seems sensible, but does not match reality. We may agree that it would be good if law was a straightforward, 'easy-to-comprehend' and 'simple-to-apply' system of rules, but is that always so? Do people not come to study law (or approach dispute resolution mechanisms) precisely because the law is often not clear? If law was always certain, lawyers would have much less work. If one agrees that we need highly trained specialists to think about legal problems and to solve conflicts, then one can hardly proceed on the basis of a definition of law which assumes that definitions of law and its application are simple, uncontroversial and uncontested.

We must assume that 'law' may be made in a variety of ways which need to be examined further. In every case, questions arise because it makes a difference whether we accept that a haphazardly developed 'people's law' can be 'law' just as much as legislation imposed by a state. This is where Hart's (1961) general model seems flawed by an overly narrow approach. We are beginning to ask here whether law as a body of rules can also be made by a non-human agency, or can just develop organically from human consciousness. In the extreme, would sets of rules that individuals may make for themselves also fall within the definition of law? How far are we prepared to deviate from standard assumptions about law as 'made by the state'? Can we devise an English wording like 'established by' that conveys a message covering all these possibilities? We return to this issue further below.

The second combination of words used above to provide better particulars involves law as 'a body of rules applying to . . .'. This incomplete definition immediately raises further questions: applying to whom or what? The obvious answer would be something like 'a group of people'. If law is a body of rules applying to a particular group of people, are we saying that law cannot just apply to a specified individual? Does law always have to be a group phenomenon? Does it make a difference whether that group is small or large, and how it is composed? Can we have a law that applies to all people in the world, assuming a universal, global nature? All possibilities seem possible if we take a globally focused perspective. Further, we may replace the above phrase by other words, such as 'a body of rules imposed on . . .' or 'governing . . .', which introduces important qualifications. It may make a crucial difference whether a body of rules is formally imposed on a group of people or has organically grown and now applies to a particular group of people. The critical question remains at all times whether such rules can fall under the definition of 'law'. A tentative conclusion might be that they do, but then we are using a rather wide and diverse definition. To what extent is that acceptable to lawyers? Should one not go for a tighter definition? To explore this issue further, we need to test our perceptions about who makes laws and to whom they apply. We do this all the time, simply by adding more specific words, for example we say that 'law' is:

- a body of rules   made by   a state

or

- a set of rules   applying in   a particular country.

Both of these phrases, for which many other words could be used to similar effect, have in common that they relate to the state as a law-making agent. Such definitions will be uncontroversial for positivists and match dominant Western ideas about law. However, the second phrase above may not necessarily be read in a positivist sense, since the set of rules applying in a particular country might be religious or cultural norms rather than state-made law,[153] raising the familiar problem that positivism is only one possible approach to conceptualising law. Since the phenomenon of law must definitely extend beyond state law when we take a globality-focused approach, we require more detail and different words to describe rule systems *not* made by the state. For example, we could think of:

- a body of rules   developed by   a certain group of people
- a set of norms   applying to   a particular social group

or

- a body of rules   laid down by   God
- a set of norms   applying to   a religious community.

All these definitional phrases have in common that they signify rules not made by the state, but by other sources, applying to people as members of a social group or a religious community. Readers will have to decide for themselves whether they can accept that such bodies of rules may fall under the definition of 'law'; a plurality-conscious approach must necessarily be inclusive. Judgment on these matters concerns morality, religion and community as much as law, and it will be necessary to respect a diverse range of opinions. Bix (1996: 57–8) provides the useful example of a religious person denouncing the act of adultery as a doctrinal matter of God's law and the futility of debating this. Because not all religions and cultures may share such doctrinal views, the discussion shows that a single global understanding of law cannot be achieved, and can be neither formulated nor taught. Ultimately, it depends on an individual's capacity and will to accept a variety of views. This is also why a moralistic definition of law which simply stipulates that law is 'a body of rules that is good' will not be conducive on its own to the development of legal theory anywhere, as citizens of the world will forever argue and disagree over what is 'good'.[154] It makes no sense to argue that there should be no such argument. Who are we to say whose views should prevail globally?

While the dominant model of law appears to be that 'law' is first and foremost what the state, in whatever form, has laid down as a body of rules applying to its citizens (and, in many cases, to everyone within the jurisdiction of that state), a wider definition of law would also need to take account of the presence of bodies of rules made by groups of people for themselves, and of religious

---

[153] This could be akin to Chiba's (1986) second type of 'official law', or it might be unofficial law, but is still a system of rules.

[154] Summers (1982: 41) rightly suggests that 'any general theory of law which fails to address issues of value is fundamentally incomplete' and highlights 'change-mindedness' (p. 57), which appears to be a form of plurality consciousness or situation-specificity.

or ethical/moral laws and concepts. Where a particular community, perhaps within a state, or perhaps in the absence of a state (though that is rare, nowadays) makes bodies of rules for itself, we may speak of customs, social norms or different types of Moore's (1978) semi-autonomous legal field. The critical question, again, remains whether we are prepared to accept that such customs and norms are a form of law. Following Chiba (1986), we may assume without difficulty that certain customs may be co-opted by a state as law, in which case they might no longer be seen as customs, but as 'official law', while other customs will be treated merely as local norms without binding legal value. But does this make them less effective in social reality? And, what if the effect of legislation is the emergence of new customs, a new 'living law'? These are complex issues to which no easy answers are found unless we open our eyes to plurality-consciousness and recognise that not accepting plurality creates barriers to holistic legal analysis.

Similarly, by considering religion as a source of law, we may find that certain state laws have silently incorporated religious norms and rules into their official legal system. The more critical question is what happens if a state refuses to do so, as is today the case in Northern states with large Southern ethnic minority and migrant populations (chapter 1, section 1.3). Again, such arguments are dependent on worldviews and personal opinions, and are therefore intractable. From the perspective of certain religions, God's law may be treated as superior to any form of state law. But controversies will start with the basic question whether there is God, of whatever name or description (Finnis, 1980). At the end, a plurality-conscious, global definition of law that includes every possible stakeholder turns out so general that it seems meaningless. Law then becomes, in a form of English that remains open to all possible kinds of interpretation, simply:

- a body of rules established by an entity.

A legal system, in the same vein, would then be something like a body of rules applied by an entity, which may be a collection of entities, in specific contexts. The notion of 'system' increases the perception of dynamism, but law itself is internally dynamic from the very start. This discussion was not designed to show the absurdity of efforts to define law, but to illustrate that a universal definition of law is only feasible if it accounts for the immensely plural phenomenon of law itself. As a working hypothesis for a globally conscious understanding of law, the following propositions and consequences arise from the above discussion:

- law is a phenomenon that is universal but manifests itself in many different ways;
- law constantly needs to be worked out or negotiated in a culture-specific social context, and is thus inherently dynamic and flexible;
- law not only takes different forms but also has different sources;

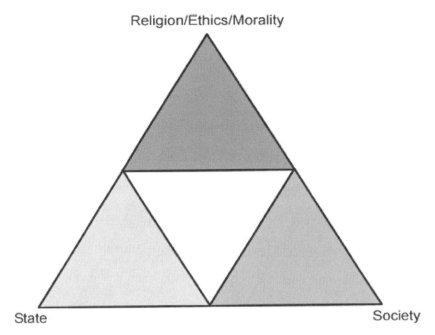

Figure 1

- these sources, in essence different manifestations of the state, society and religion/ethics, compete and interact in various ways;
- any given body of such rules will also contain components of the other two elements, which adds another (generally invisible) layer of plurality;
- this can be illustrated in a fairly simply triangle as shown in Figure 1;
- lawyers as professionals and theorists have tended to emphasise the centrality of state law and have thereby underplayed the role of non-state sources of the law including ethics, and particularly society and the element of culture, seriously underestimating the potential for the co-existence of various rule systems;
- whether something is legal or not may well ultimately be determined by lawyers, but they have used the alleged centrality of law to promote a world-view in which 'law' is dominant. One might call this 'legal determinism', a form of positivism, which turns out as legal centralism;
- this may not be a view consistent with people's experiences anywhere in the world;
- such legal centralism therefore needs to be challenged and a wider, global perspective on law needs to be taken.

Within a global framework for the comparative study of law and legal systems, it is evident that a narrow approach to law as state law leads neither to appropri-

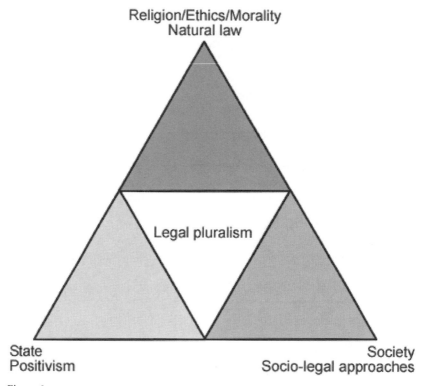

Figure 2

ate understanding of non-European societies and cultures nor to satisfactory analysis of the phenomenon of law even in its European manifestations. If we do not want to be mere technicians of a particular national law (Legrand, 1996) or end up in eurocentric dark alleys or circular parts of the legal maze, arguing that law is simply law because someone said so (Tamanaha, 2001), taking a pluralist legal perspective is an inevitable requirement. To state this is easy; to perform the necessary tasks is an enormous challenge.

Based on the above discussions, the present study proposes a plurality-focused model of understanding law that takes implicit account of all three major elements of the triangle as shown in Figure 1 above, their intrinsically plural nature, and their constant dynamic interaction. This model introduces legal pluralism as a major fourth methodological approach of legal theory. Of necessity, this methodology places legal pluralism at the centre of the triangle. The triangular model would then look as shown in Figure 2.

Legal pluralism fills the central space in this triangle because it signifies all those scenarios and conflict situations in which neither of the three major law-making sources rules the roost absolutely. The centre of this triangle would

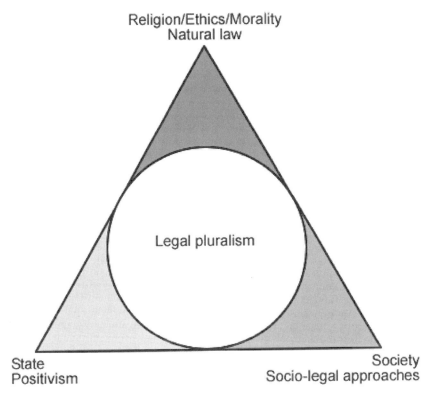

Figure 3

appear to indicate 'perfect' justice as the result of an equilibrium between the various competing forces. It is in the nature of an equilibrium to be unstable, however, so there will be a continuous need for renegotiation of this central ideal. This is the dilemma of all law. However, Figure 2 shows that exclusive and 'pure' reliance on either positivism, natural law or socio-legal concerns may be the exception rather than the rule, as clearly represented by the three thinning edges of the triangle.[155] Since the ambit of legal pluralism within this model should be shown as large as possible, it makes sense to represent the centre of the triangle as large as possible, and therefore as a circle rather than an inner triangle. The model would then look as shown in Figure 3.

I suggest provisionally that this methodological approach can at all times take proper account of the inherent plurality of law and illustrates the necessarily interlinked nature of all law. However, testing this model on real legal systems

---

[155] This may mean that much of social control is not exclusively within the social field. Woodman (1998: 45) argues that 'all social control is part of the subject-matter of legal pluralism'.

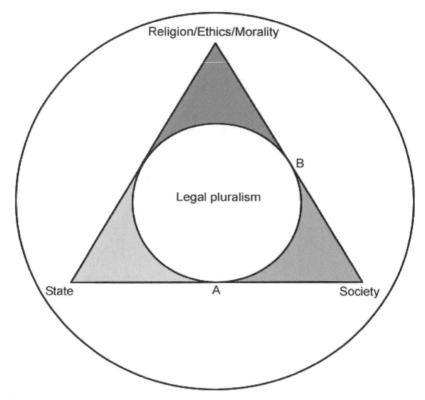

Figure 4

showed very soon that there is much more law than could be encompassed in any single triangle. The laws of the world comprise an enormous plurality of triangles in both time and space, and it is impossible to represent this visually. Law is indeed so plural that it can hardly be grasped in its theoretical totality, let alone be configured in simple models. The first amendment to the above model, in the light of foreign legal transplants in many countries (chapter 1, section 1.2.3) and ethnic implants into the various legal systems of the North (chapter 1, section 1.3), implies that a large circle will need to be drawn around the entire triangle, representing the whole of humanity, better still, the whole cosmos. This is because legal elements like 'ethnic implants' and 'extraterrito- riality' are not located within the space of the triangle, but more or less closely attached to it from the outside, strategically implanted at a particular point of the periphery. Point A then represents foreign transplants, and point B ethnic implants into any particular legal system.

This new global image of law, which still hides more intricate pluralities than the ones directly identified here, confirms that it was not sufficient for

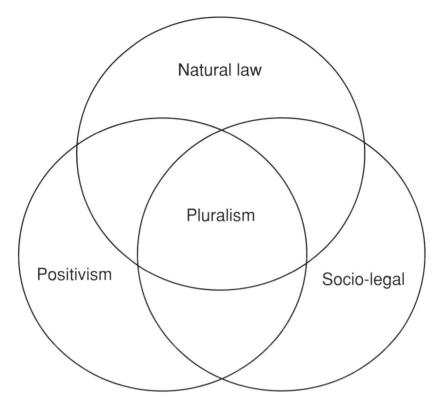

Figure 5

ameliorating earlier theories, even Chiba's (1986) with its partly state-centred focus on 'official law', to simply add more explicit concern for social elements to legal analysis. Earlier I went along with Cotterrell (2004: 1) who suggests that 'legal theory, must, it seems, now systematically take account of the notion of culture' and 'requires a sociologically-informed concept of community' (p. 1), a point argued by an increasing number of theorists.[156] I suggest now that, while leaving out culture-specificity definitely does not make sense, the model as a whole still needs to be more dynamic than it is widely perceived. Chiba (1989: 180) emphasised these interactional elements through his revised model of the 'three dichotomies' and especially his suggestion of an 'identity postulate' that marks all legal systems as distinct and therefore 'ethnic' entities. If that is correct, then we have another problem of legal plurality, because whenever we deal with

---

[156] 'Culture' would in the above models be found within the triangles of religion/ethics and morality as well as society, and to some extent even within the triangle of the state. I am grateful to Sanjay Gandhi for drawing my attention to this difficult issue.

ethnicity, we are always confronted with the possibility that self-assessment and being assessed by others might diverge.

A graphic alternative to the triangular models would be to illustrate the interlinked elements of law through circles rather than triangles, with the same result as above, but an emerging awareness that there may be different kinds of natural law, positivism and socio-legal norms as a result of influence by the other law-making factors. This is shown in Figure 5.

Concentrating only on one particular triangular or circular element, questioning for example whether social norms are legal rules, or whether certain values can constitute law, which has engaged much jurisprudential effort so far, has clearly been too shallow. To achieve a deeper globality-conscious, plurality-focused understanding and approach, we have to look at all times at the internally complex structures of law as a whole and the mindboggling, constantly changing plurality of interactions of its various plural elements across time and space, working from situation to situation. At the same time, it seems possible to conceive of a global definition of law in this way, which will now need to be tested with reference to the legal systems of Asia and Africa.

PART II

Regional comparisons in a global context

INTRODUCTION

Part I demonstrated from a variety of angles that cross-cultural legal comparison continues to face major global challenges. The overview of Western legal theory in chapter 3 confirmed that we have only just begun to appreciate the limits of theoretical endeavour in capturing the complex reality of legal pluralism as a global phenomenon. We are now able to see that no single major legal theoretical approach on its own, whether positivism, natural law or socio-legal methods, can encompass the internally plural phenomenon of law. Their pluralist methodological combination, in ways yet to be analysed and explored, promises a deeper understanding of the complex nature of law, but theory will never be able to capture the practically limitless real plurality of law. Problems over the acceptance of radical legal realism are clearly exacerbated by insistence on visions of globalising uniformity that fly in the face of plural socio-legal reality and end up in prescriptive normative tyranny. Part II provides many examples of such clashes of values and their implications. But the legal systems of Asia and Africa will not disappear, nor will they ever merge fully into some 'global' legal framework.

A major critique of existing efforts to make sense of other people's legal cultures still needs to be written and is not possible within the present study. The globally focused analysis of Asian and African legal systems raises complex but surprisingly familiar conceptual questions. The three major sources of law and the resulting theoretical approaches identified in Part I reappear, but not necessarily in the same manner. Statist positivism is not absent in Asian and African cultures but is not immediately perceived as central. An equivalent for 'law' (as 'state law') may even be absent in ancient languages that express instead some form of holistic 'order', as much social as legal. Legal centralism could not thrive in such an environment. In holistic Asian and African socio-cultural traditions, legal, social and religious authorities were not treated as distinct elements, but formed part of the various culture-specific visions of a larger whole which tend to be inherently global. Thus, Hindu macrocosmic conceptualisations, African and Chinese assumptions about the nature of the universe and the world, and Islamic belief in Allah's universal order, co-exist and compete with each other and with Western ideas about the nature of law in a globalised world.

It may surprise positivists and secular natural lawyers that all traditional non-Western legal systems appear to give little or even no importance to state law, emphasising instead culture-specific concepts of universal order as a matter of religion and culture. But religion, like law, is itself a cultural construct, a culture-specific interlinked element within context-specific scenarios and cannot simply be treated as superior to everything else. Religious centralism, like legal centralism, is also an unrealistic analytical tool. It is not possible, therefore, to view non-Western laws simply as religious systems, since religion is manifestly an element of legal ontology in the 'West', too, and non-Western 'religious' laws contain many elements that are not primarily religious. Even Muslims, most vociferous proponents today of the view that everything legal is religious, have had to accept a long time ago that this perspective is not unchallenged within their own tradition (chapter 5). Religion is simply not the same as law, and law, anywhere in the world, is not just based on religion, ethics and morality.

Evidence of the widespread refusal to give a central place to law in Asian and African cultures may be stronger in some legal traditions than others. David and Brierley (1978: 26) distinguished two basic groups:

> In non-western societies the governing social principles to which reference is made are of two types. On the one hand law is fully recognized as being of eminent value but the law itself is a different concept than it is in the West; on the other, the very notion of law is rejected, and social relations are governed by other extra-legal means. The first view is that of Muslim and Hindu societies, while the latter is that adopted in countries of the Far East and large parts of Africa and Malagasy.

Consequently, David and Brierley (1978: 27) make a distinction between a scenario where law is seen as 'a model of ideal behaviour, one not to be confused with the actual rules', while they note that in the Far East, especially China, 'the very value of law itself is put into question' (p. 28), while in Africa, where 'the principal objective is the maintenance or restoration of harmony rather than respect for law' (p. 29), one must doubt the existence of law altogether. Other authors (for a survey, see Zweigert and Kötz, 1998) have used different criteria, but there is certainly no global agreement on the taxonomy of various families of law.

Apart from evident eurocentric biases in much of the existing writing, a difficult challenge for Part II is that appreciation of cultural specificities continues to be a major stumbling block for fruitful intellectual exchange. Few conceptually sound analytical writings exist on some legal systems, while much was written on others but often in difficult languages. While Islamic law, Chinese law and to some extent also Hindu law are well served, writing on African law continues to suffer from the tenacious assumption that most African laws are too primitive to be classed as 'law'.

The won't-go-away question whether socio-religious concepts or the world-view of a particular traditional society should be seen as 'law' and recognised as encompassing and dominating legal regulation, will constantly arise throughout Part II. Can we still speak of law when we deal with religion and myriads of oral customs? To what extent are we impressed by claims of religious supremacy and of social norms that continue to deny a central place to the model laws of the modern state? We constantly return to questions about our theoretical understanding of 'law' as a global phenomenon and must seek to maintain a holistic, dynamic, plurality-focused analysis. This goes not only for the respective traditional legal systems, but also their modern and now postmodern manifestations, whereas uncritical assumptions about reception of Western laws would easily lead to unjustified assumptions about the eradication of non-Western laws. If the dominant presupposition among Western lawyers remains that all legal systems in the world should ultimately follow Western models, i.e. if we accept globalisation visions that are directed towards uniformisation or convergence rather than just assimilation and harmonisation, there needs to be much future change in Asian and African legal systems. But what if globalisation has in fact pluralising and glocalising effects, so that the present picture of global diversity remains and is further embellished? Since the latter scenario seems much more realistic than eurocentric speculations about a uniformised world legal order, we clearly need to know much more about the development of Asian and African legal systems, past, present and future. The chapters that follow seek to provide material for further study and argue that plurality-conscious traditional adherence to situation-specificity in Asian and African laws, a key element of their holistic past, will remain a core feature of these legal systems. The discussions within these chapters also help us to return eventually to a final analysis and exposition of what a globally valid general jurisprudence might look like.

4

Hindu law: the search for appropriateness

A conceptual overview of Hindu law must of necessity proceed chronologically. One cannot understand Hindu law and the present Indian legal system while ignoring the rich tapestry of older concepts. To demystify this confusing diversity, the present chapter starts with a brief historical overview, and then examines in detail ancient pre-classical, classical and late classical, post-classical and medieval Hindu concepts of law, before moving on briefly to Anglo-Indian laws and modern Hindu laws. This analysis aims to present the totality of 'traditional' Hindu law as an interlinked sequence of sub-systems, emphasising the inherent dialectics and dynamisms within traditional Hindu law and its enormous scope for flexibility and internal reform.

The study of Hindu law has long been neglected due to at least four major factors. In combination, and over time, these have led to worryingly low levels of knowledge, prompting even the Indian government to reinvigorate classical learning in this field (Narang, 1988; Sivaramayya, 1988; Jois, 1990). The first major factor responsible for insufficient depth in Hindu law research is declining knowledge in its classical, Sanskrit-based foundations, which has led to a vicious circle of suffocating scholarship. Today there are simply not enough Sanskritists interested in legal study, while 'lawyers with Sanskrit' have long been extremely rare. Recent efforts in this field reflect the urgent need for better understanding,[1] or one simply reprints older work (Nanda and Sinha, 1996).

Secondly, lack of professional interest has taken away a major motivation for studying Hindu law. The combined effects of Anglo-Hindu interference and modern Indian legal developments made traditional Hindu law appear irrelevant to most practising lawyers. Some recent legal writing (Singh, 1990; Purohit, 1994) reflects a realisation, shared by some scholar-practitioners (Dhavan, 1992; see also Larson, 2001) that Hindu law does remain relevant, but there is too little depth in such efforts.

Thirdly, the largely codified Hindu law of modern India, the major jurisdiction which applies Hindu law as a personal law to now well over 800 million

---

[1] The *Indian Journal of Juridical Studies*, Vol. 1 (2003) is the most recent attempt to bring together relevant scholarship on ancient Indian legal thought.

people, appears to relate mainly to family law issues. Modern pressures of political correctness, partly a side-effect of globalising tendencies, meant that modernist scholarship, also in India itself, has further marginalised Hindu law, treating it as a reactionary, misogynist remnant of a deficient past (Dhagamwar, 2003; Sathe and Narayan, 2003). Teaching and studying Hindu law has come to be seen as a dubious scholarly activity, and there are few academic positions dedicated specifically to Hindu law in the world today. However, the view that Hindu law is increasingly irrelevant has turned out to be a huge misconception. Major areas of Indian public law, whether access to justice and fundamental rights (Ahuja, 1997), environmental law (Jaswal and Jaswal, 1999) and consumer protection (Singh, 1996) have recently been restructured through the almost invisible use of Hindu concepts. The much-amended Indian Constitution of 1950, outwardly secular but South Asian in spirit, now reads in parts like a Hindu manifesto. Recent developments in Indian family law (Menski, 2001) also point to a half-hidden conceptual reconstruction of modern laws along chthonic lines with a Hindu flavour (Menski, 2003).

Fourthly, Indian legal scholars appear unable to discuss their own legal systems within a global framework of reference. The leading law schools focus on issues of globalisation in an international legal context, pursuing agenda of uniformising visions that denigrate traditional Indian laws and overlook the growing gap between law as taught in law schools and Indian law 'on the ground'.[2] Recent attempts to make the study of Hindu law easier (Agarwala, 2003) fail to portray Hindu law in a plurality-conscious global framework of reference.[3]

At the same time, various politicised attempts have been made to glorify and idolise traditional Hindu law. Hindu law has long been under threat from various quarters and has had to prove its worth to hostile foreign lawyers and observers. Respect for Hindu law, which had earlier been given (albeit with reluctance) by Muslim rulers, became an increasingly crucial issue under British influence (from 1600) and British rule (1858–1947) in India. While the old *pandits* of the British time asserted that the Hindus had 'law', the stage was set for colonial reconstruction of Hindu law as a strange amalgam of ancient textual authority, case law and legislation. Huge misconceptions resulted; we labour with some of them until now. Towards the end of the colonial period, the seven monumental, scholarly volumes of Kane's *History of Dharmaśāstra*

---

[2] See 'New vision for legal education in the emerging global scenario' (2001), www.abc-india.com/lawcoll/bangalore/vision.htm.

[3] For example, Agarwala (2003: 4) rightly states that Hindu law is different from the Austinian concept and 'cannot strictly be said to have been promulgated by any Sovereign within the meaning of Austin's definition of law' (p. 6). However, this is taken back (p. 8) when it is suggested that acceptance by the Sovereign of the rules of Hindu law somewhat brings it within Austin's definition. This is a feeble attempt to make Chiba's (1986) distinction between rules made by the state and accepted by the state.

(1968) constituted a final massive effort to prove to the British colonial power that Hinduism and Hindu law are not inferior. In the process, Kane purposely overstated his case for the recognition of Hindu law as a legal system in its own right, and portrayed his subject to some extent in terms recognisable to Western lawyers, infusing positivist concepts into his portrayal of Hindu law which continue to confuse today's lawyers.

While efforts to rewrite Hindu scriptures are doomed to dismal failure, as rewriting the past will never undo it, there has been much writing about ancient Hindu models of good governance and good behaviour, and about *dharma* as a global ethic (Jois, 1990; 1997). However, if some orange-clad 'holy men' might in our day feel tempted to resurrect what they think is an ancient tradition of laying down the law for all Hindus, they are simply playing mischief and overstepping their limits. Hindu law has always been a people's law, not a body of rules made by powerful old men to be obeyed by all others. Despite the alleged recent shift towards Hindu-ness (*hindutva*), widely portrayed as Hindu 'fundamentalism', this basic message remains alive, but is not cultivated.

The nature of Hindu law itself has remained open to searching questions. Massive ignorance must be diagnosed, even in India itself. If the Sanskrit language does not even have a neatly translatable term for 'law', does it mean the ancient Hindus did not have law? It is a fact that the pioneering nineteenth-century European translations of ancient Indian texts are often misleading, even outrightly wrong, when it comes to understanding legal issues. The great pioneers of indological scholarship saw their task as making ancient Sanskrit texts accessible to Europeans, providing translations into English or often German.[4] But translation, often drowned by wealth of detail, did not manage to convey that these texts were cultural documents, not legal codes. While the old translators were excellent philologists, they did not always test their translations and interpretations against socio-legal reality. A new generation of translations mainly by US-based scholars has begun to emerge (Larivière, 1989; Olivelle, 2000), but some old problems of presenting Hindu law to a global readership remain.

Most relevant for the present study is the cardinal mistake of translating the key term of Hindu law, *dharma*, the all-encompassing duty to do the right thing at the right time, at any point of one's life, simply as 'law'. That is inadequate and misleading; other mistakes have inevitably followed.[5] Such misconceptions

---

[4] For example, the *Manusmriti* was first translated in 1794.

[5] The title of Bühler (1975), *The laws of Manu*, continues to impress scholars who should and do know better. Olivelle (2000: vii) speaks in his Preface simply of 'the law book of Manu', notes the special challenge of translating *dharma* (p. xvi), and then explains (p. 1): 'The term *dharma* may be translated as "Law" if we do not limit ourselves to its narrow modern definition as civil and criminal statutes but take it to include all the rules of behavior, including moral and religious behavior, that a community recognizes as binding on its members.'

resurface today when Glenn (2000: 255; 2004: 276), partly through no fault of his own, assumes that Manu was the great law-giver of the Hindus, an equivalent of Moses or Mohammad. That is simply not the correct interpretation, although many Hindus appear to subscribe to the idea of ancient law-making by sages.[6] In view of such fundamental misunderstandings, attempts to capture the key concepts of Hindu law and to gauge their relevance today remain regrettably limited. Such misconceptions about the processes of law-making in Hindu law have enormous implications for current debates about law reform and the application of state law (Menski, 2003).

The alleged *sadhu*-friendliness of the so-called Hindu communalist Bharatiya Janata Party (BJP) cannot hide the truth that 'holy men', despite the tempting old image of Manu as the law-giver, have never been in a position to 'lay down the law' for all Hindus.[7] Hindu legal concepts are inherently inimical to strictly monotheistic revelation-based legal regulation or Austinian positivism. Current fears that a resurgence of Hinduness would lead to dramatic legal changes are therefore quite baseless, even frivolous.[8] Some academics seem to have become masters at playing with such confusions for the sake of academic profiling, without checking their understanding of Hindu law (Rajan, 2003).

Such dramatic positioning on many stages shows that Hindu law is still being challenged, and is on the defensive today, over specific issues and as a legal system in its own right. To many Hindus, however, their concepts of truth seem so universal that they are unchallengeable. All others are happily invited to state their own positions within this universalising Hindu ambit, one aspect of the well-known Hindu 'tolerance' towards other traditions. Thus, as long as Christians and Muslims are prepared to accept that their respective Gods are but one of many, and respect the Hindu method of postponing final judgment on Truth into limitless eternity, co-existence and toleration can be practised. But if non-Hindus seek to ridicule Hinduism and its underlying values, insisting that they alone are right, then defence mechanisms can be triggered off and there may be violence (Engineer, 1989; Das, 1990). This is not seeking to explain or condone 'ethnic' or 'communal' violence: the point is that anything 'Hindu' continues to be widely portrayed as primitive, traditional, weird and simply bad in our day and age, and Hindus have become angry about this.

In such a competitive, lively forum of intercultural and interreligious competition, there are many meaningful silences which the non-specialist legal

---

[6] Glenn (2004) relied mainly on Diwan (1993), who excelled in perpetuating myths about the genesis of Hindu law. On the two extreme views (divine origin and customs), see Agarwala (2003: 7).

[7] The BJP was in government until early 2004; politicised discourses around a resurgence of Hindu nationalism have somewhat died down since then.

[8] Hindus in diaspora have much to do with such confusions, adding their own subjectivities and agenda in the process. See the Special Issue, Vol. 23 No. 3 (May 2000) of *Ethnic and Racial Studies.*

observer will easily overlook in the cacophony of competing claims. Most of this vigorous struggle has escaped outside observers, because Indian legal authors on whom an educated Western readership tends to rely often fail to capture recent developments adequately. Writing many years ago, they were often not up-to-date on current socio-legal developments and theoretical legal scholarship. There is more to such deficiencies than meets the eye.

While earlier comparative scholars (David and Brierley, 1978: 447–76) managed to portray the concepts of Hindu law quite well, it is disappointing to see recent writing on the subject so uncertain about how to view Hindu law. Glenn (2000: 86, 251ff.) treats Hindu law as a kind of leftover at the bottom of his 'bran-tub', the huge container in which the indefatigable legal comparatist may find all legal traditions of the world.[9] Nobody ever claimed that Hindu law was an easy field of study, but knowledge of this legal system remains today insufficient and not easily accessible. Much of the blame falls on Indian legal scholarship, which has been in deep crisis for many years (Baxi, 1982; 1986), suffering either from positivist amnesia or illusions of spiritual superiority, unable to find a realistic middle path that makes sense in a global context and speaks in clear text to comparative lawyers and legal theorists.

4.1 A historical and conceptual overview

It is crucial for a solid conceptual understanding of the Hindu system to distinguish at least four interlinked stages of conceptual development within 'traditional' Hindu law itself, from the macrocosmic universal Order (*rita*) of the Vedic system to the microcosmic self-controlled order (*dharma*) of classical Hindu law proper, and the deterrence-based stage of punishment (*danda*) and more or less formal dispute processing (*vyavahāra*) in the late classical and post-classical system (Menski, 2003: 81). Thereafter, Hindu law did not whither away under Muslim and British domination. Rather, the official Anglo-Hindu law changed into a complex, artificially constructed and hence largely 'bogus' system of Hindu case-law (Derrett, 1977: vii). More recently, as the dominant personal law in modern India, Hindu law has been reformed and secularised by statute, but the spirit of the old Hindu law and its continuing concern for the relativities of justice are found not to be controllable by modern state law. Thus, the recent re-emergence of Hindu principles in the reconfiguration of postmodern Indian laws (Menski, 2003) should not come as a surprise.

Hindu law is certainly not the same as Indian law. A huge country by all standards, India has never been the exclusive home of Hindus, apparently themselves early immigrants to India. India respects the personal laws of Muslims, Christians, Parsis and the few remaining Jews. Many of these laws

---

[9] Huntington (1998: 14) admits that he did not consider Hindu civilisation for his study.

were until recently arcane and outdated.[10] Even today, local and tribal customary laws continue to play a much larger role in Indian law than lawyers
readily admit.[11] Modern Hindu law in India also governs the Sikhs, Jainas
and Buddhists, despite Sikh objections,[12] and this artificial unity of Hindu
law appears designed to promote nation-building and a composite, pluralistic,
national spirit. The Constitution of 1950 has, through its secular *grundnorm*
(secularism in India means equidistance from all religions) sought to protect
and nurture a multi-ethnic, multi-religious concept of Indian citizenship, albeit
with a definite Hindu flavour.[13]

Over time, in Hindu law itself, two major elements of continuity and pluralisation have been visible, both socio-cultural factors rather than legal elements.
First, the production of many Hindu cultural texts since c. 1500 BC has tempted
lawyers to imagine ancient codes, when in fact such texts are neither law-focused
nor produced by and for lawyers (on the debates, see Larivière, 1976). Secondly,
the complex socio-political and cultural sphere, with its dominant influence of
innumerable Hindu customary laws spread over a huge territory, has militated
against legal uniformity, as well as legal domination of the social sphere, thus
giving pride of place to custom rather than law (Derrett, 1962; Menski, 1992b).
The key to understanding Hindu law as a holistic system lies in concepts of
Hindu culture, such as *dharma*, which are so diffuse that most analysts appear
to have given up interpreting them, while they are so firmly internalised by
Hindus themselves that they do not appear to warrant detailed explanation.
We thus find enormous silences and gaps of communication about the inherent nature of Hindu law and misunderstandings in the transmission of legal
messages.

Hindu law is, not as much as African law but similar to Islamic law, a family
of laws rather than a single unit. The label 'Hindu law' covers a large variety of different legal systems and thus reflects the endless internal diversity
of Hinduism, a term that means little in the singular (Sontheimer and Kulke,
1989). When the term 'Hindu' was first used, by the Greeks, who called them
indoi in their language, 'the people living near the river Sindhu', now the Indus

---

[10] Parsi law is now quite modern. The Parsi Marriage and Divorce (Amendment) Act 1988
was partly a political move to reassert the separate existence of Parsi personal law, not
just a modernising reform. Indian Christian law came under vigorous attack for being
discriminatory against women (Champappilly, 1988). The Indian Divorce (Amendment)
Act 2001 has rectified the situation.

[11] The prominence of such laws, particularly in north-east India, is well documented. See
Kusum and Bakshi (1982); Dev and Lahiri (1983). On Panjab customs, see Diwan (1984).

[12] A much underrated aspect of Khalistan debates, Sikh resistance to Hindu domination has
focused on politics and economics rather than law. Male Sikh resistance to modern Hindu
law reforms which give property rights to women appears in *Partap Singh* v. *Union of India*,
AIR 1985 SC 1695.

[13] This reflects and confirms Chiba's (1989: 180) concept of the 'identity postulate' as a
composite cultural entity.

in Pakistan, it appeared to have neither a religious nor a legal meaning, but geographical and ethnic connotations. Since both Hindu law and religion have always been extremely complex constructs, it has been quite appropriate to speak of 'unity in diversity' (Derrett, 1966; 1979). While this diversity is held together by an underlying conceptual core, which is in itself a complex plural system, Hindu law has always been a living socio-legal system marked by much dialectic dynamism, forever evading codification and, thus, the control of powerful men who might have wanted to dictate legal rules to all others. Had Austin been able to work with Sanskrit sources, and to acquire an internal perspective of Hindu law, he would undoubtedly have had to give up the theory that made him famous.

The earliest layers of Vedic texts, seen as divinely inspired (*śruti*), tempt us to view them as the basis for a formal, codified Hindu rule system. However, there was never a Napoleonic code of Hindu law. The most striking element of Hindu law throughout has been its unlimited diversity and flexibility, which observers find confusing, have far too often reduced to a few basic items, and have taken out of context. Here we see lack of plurality-consciousness in operation. Hindu law strongly emphasises the rhetoric and practice of plurality and of relative justice, displaying tolerance almost to the point of selfless extinction. Legal diversity forms such an essential part of Hindu legal philosophy that uniformity of legal rules is often portrayed as a manifestation of injustice.[14] Thus, in many ways, the modern Indian legal system with its continued respect for legal diversity may be better equipped than purportedly uniform legal systems in promoting and achieving situation-specific justice and equity. Indeed, the project of an Indian uniform civil code has become subtly redefined over time to take account of plurality-consciousness (Menski, 2004).

Hindu law today remains manifestly culture-specific wherever it applies in the world.[15] It has resisted all unifying tendencies, while at the same time retaining a global orientation. It is virtually impossible to speak about Indian legal systems, or Hindu law, without reference to a particular time, locality or situation. The mere size of India and its multi-ethnic and plural composition have always worked against certainty and uniformity of legal rules. Not surprisingly, legal uniformity has remained a 'distant mirage' (Allott, 1980: 216) in modern India. Aiming for legal uniformity has meant following a false blueprint for legal development (Menski, 1990; 2001), which is currently being revised, not

---

[14] This was noted by the Kerala High Court in *Kunhikannan* v. *State of Kerala*, 1968 KLT 19, at 23. See also Agarwala (2003: 20–1).

[15] Twining (2000: 182) is wrong to assume that Hindu law is nowhere a state legal system. Nepal is a Hindu kingdom, while the colonial Anglo-Hindu law remains an outdated and ignored minority law in Pakistan and Bangladesh (for the latter see Menski and Rahman, 1988). On Hindu law in Britain, see Menski (1987; 1993a). There is also much Hindu law in other parts of the world (Trinidad, Guyana, Fiji, Mauritius, parts of Africa and South-East Asia).

because India has turned fundamentalist, but because the Indians have realised over the past two decades that transplanted and partly indigenised Western legal models on their own are not suitable tools for creating a sustainable legal system for over a billion people (Menski, 2003). Yet the Indian Constitution would appear at first sight totally Westernised. Glenn (2004: 296) is thus absolutely right when he notes that modern Indian law 'looks a lot like US law, yet there remain profound differences'. India is often mistakenly portrayed as a common-law country (de Cruz, 1999: 125–6), hardly an adequate description of Indian law, because this ignores the complex mixture of various legal systems that constitutes Indian law. This is, first of all, a political message, to the effect that India was, and continues to be, under British influence, rather than the French colonial model. Further, it flatters the élite perceptions of the colonial past as well as those sections of the present Indian élite who have imbibed the message that anything South Asian is intrinsically inferior.

These are important lessons for comparative lawyers. Indian law, through the conceptual elements of Hindu law, teaches us to look out for the larger issues raised by governing unimaginable multitudes of people, whether in ancient times or in a modern nation state. This does not just concern India, but also China, Indonesia, Brazil, South Africa and many other large nations. Hindu law never took the stance that human conduct can be totally regulated by external force or state-made laws. There has been from the start an anti-legal attitude inherent in the system, similar to the Chinese aversion to *fa* as 'state law' (chapter 7). Thus the ideal of human self-controlled order within a higher, cosmic superstructure is placed in the centre of Hindu law as an early global vision. Modern India, it is now being realised, has neither the legocentric power nor the economic resources to provide more than the most basic framework of legal protection, but was earlier lured into following modernist Western models of positivist legal regulation. Today, rethinking this process leads beyond the familiar diagnoses of dysfunction and lawlessness (Baxi, 1982) towards postmodern legal analysis (Menski, 2003). The realisation that ancient Hindu legal models are not only available as a blueprint for a sustainable legal future but have already been unofficially practised, is gradually becoming more concrete (Menski, 2004). While such lessons may strike observers who know ancient Hindu law, it should be possible for comparative lawyers to appreciate how the operation of a legal system without much official legal input might achieve new prominence in an Asia-focused global analysis. Self-controlled ordering is not only cheaper, it is a democratically sustainable system of legal regulation, provided some safeguards exist to allow redressal of injustices if self-controlled ordering fails. It appears that traditional Hindu law practised legal pluralism, and that the systemic benefits of doing so explain to a large extent why today's postmodern Hindu law is not just a Western-inspired reconstruction but a plurality-focused construct that takes account of all elements within our conceptual triangle (chapter 3, section 3.8).

4.2 The pre-classical stage: Vedic law (c. 1500 BC to c. 500 BC)

The rich literary heritage of ancient India, with the Vedic literature (from about 1500 BC) in prominent place,[16] provides much valuable detail about this distant period,[17] though we know little about the actual legal systems at this time. The Sanskrit literature reflects not what actually happened, like an anthropological report, but often takes the form of mythological account and fiction. Importantly, the Vedas are primarily ritual manuals, designed to bring about beneficial effects through ritual performance inspired by an intricate vision of cosmic interlinkedness as a kind of Kelsenian *Grundnorm*.

Through the Vedic hymns, we learn of the worldview of the Vedic Hindus (Miller, 1985). Macrocosmic 'Order' (*rita*) is the earliest core concept of Hinduism, and thus of Hindu law. Its relevance in legal terms is almost a matter of commonsense: life is seen as a complex experience, in which everybody and everything is interconnected and has a role to play. These roles are, of necessity, specific to different people and situations, and they depend on factors like gender, age or status in society. There is nothing essentialising or essentially 'Hindu' about this, the key notion is symbiotic interaction and intrinsic diversity of all manifestations of life. The ideal is an ordered universe, in macrocosmic and microcosmic dimensions, a kind of ecologically sound symbiosis in which every component part plays its proper role. This represents the dominant Indic, South Asian or Hindu conceptualisation of natural law, at once religious and secular.[18] In the Vedic system, the emphasis is still more on the macrocosmic superhuman whole,[19] rather than on the duties of the individual, which only become central in the classical period with a shift of emphasis towards *dharma*. The ideal of *rita* is holistic, focused on a pre-existing natural order and concerned to protect that order. The Vedas are first and foremost a collection of ritual verses and material, designed to be used in huge public Vedic sacrifices, whose main purpose was to safeguard the continuation of the universe, over which man had only limited control. The Vedic rituals, connecting the human sphere with the supernatural world, reflect a chthonic worldview with a literary tradition of its own which remained oral for a long time.

---

[16] The term *Veda* comes from the Sanskrit root *vid*, 'to know', 'to understand' or 'to discover', and thus relates first of all to a pre-existing form of knowledge. There are four hymn collections of Vedas, the Rigveda, Samaveda, Yajurveda and Atharvaveda.

[17] The standard work on the history of Indian literature is still Winternitz (1968). A series of separate volumes on specific aspects or periods of Indian literature, edited by Jan Gonda, has appeared since 1975 as *A history of Indian literature*.

[18] The terminologies are hotly contested, but these squabbles are irrelevant for comparative legal analysis. Vedic law seems to contain all four types of Aquinas' natural law (chapter 3, section 3.4). Eternal religious law is *rita*; the secular observable natural law is *satya* (also 'truth'); *śruti*, primarily the Vedic texts, equates to the divine law; and *smriti* (revealed knowledge) or *dharma* ('duty') represent human law. Research relying on Max Weber's approach (see Kantowsky, 1986) tends to overlook Hindu natural law.

[19] Agarwala (2003: 7) speaks rightly of non-human law (*apaurusheya*).

As predominantly ritual manuals, the Vedas did not by any means 'lay down the law', as some scholars have been tempted to argue.[20] They contain primarily sacrificial hymns, invocations to the pantheon of Vedic gods, and give little indication of any legal rules other than by coincidence. While real human life is of little direct concern to the Vedas, the hymns are quite realistically self-protective and often ask for strength, wealth, many sons and long life. Beyond that practical sphere, early Hindu life involves being conscious of *rita* (later *dharma*), envisaging increasingly a continuous process of harmonising individual expectations with concern for the common good, at least by the classical period,[21] ascertaining the appropriate balance between good and bad, right and wrong, the permissible and the prohibited. Hindu law is therefore from the start based on a continuous, complex dialectic process, centred on a natural law approach. Much of this search for absolute 'truth', another translation offered for *rita*, is internalised, as is later brought out in dramatic illustrations of the great Hindu epics, which sought to teach about 'order' and the role of law.

The key concept of *rita*, cosmic Order or 'truth' (Day, 1982; Lüders, 1959), is a complex system of unknown origins, with underlying rules that are not known to man, while the parallel Sanskrit term *satya*, also rendered as 'truth', signifies secular dimensions of the natural order. Vedic Hindus respected the limits of human knowledge and, probably observing the regularities (and occasional irregularities) of nature, like sunrise, sunset and different seasons, as well as the sudden force of the monsoon, floods and other disasters, came up with an understanding of invisible mechanisms for the maintenance of this order that involved gods and men alike. There was no agreement as to who or what was in charge of this Order, that was not the most pressing issue. To that extent, too, the Vedic worldview was practical and commonsensical. There was no doubt that this higher Order existed, so that humans would do well to mark the invisible cosmic links not just through consciousness (as in the later philosophical literature) but primarily through ritual action.

We find here an elaborate record of early chthonic Hindu thought. Man's major duty, or perhaps temptation, at this early stage appears to have been to invoke the benign influence of various gods, who were themselves seen as subject to this higher Order, through elaborate and solemn sacrifices. The combination of seeking protection for oneself through these rituals, as well as fulfilling a cosmic obligation to strengthen the universe through appropriate ritual action, illustrates the assumed early interlinkedness of man with the cosmic whole. Here lies the key to understanding later Hinduism as well as Hindu law (Menski, 1993b; 2002). Any individual is, thus, not alone in this

---

[20] It appears that much of this is inspired by inferiority complexes in view of Muslim and Christian claims of revealed Truth.

[21] Modern Indian constitutional law now incorporates this concept within 'public interest' with its significant emphasis on duties rather than rights (section 4.9). For the argument that principles of natural justice are subservient to public interest see *Pratheesh Fuels* v. *Indian Oil Corporation Ltd*, 2002(1) KLT 296.

world, but is interlinked in many ways, to family, clan, village, society as a whole, ultimately the universe. The Vedic ritual system focuses on the macro-dimension through ritual specialists and does not yet involve every individual. Monotheistic Hindu dogma did not develop because this Order was not related to one creator-God, but to an unknown force, about whose nature there was endless speculation, but no agreement. Thus the ancient Hindus agreed to differ and left this issue open, with the result that a Hindu is not defined by allegiance to a particular God or gods, but to the conceptual system as a whole and, later, to a way of life relating to such concepts. Law is perceived as an integrated whole, certainly not simply a matter for the state. Law here becomes conceptualised as a culture-specific way of life.

Vedic man assumed that it was necessary to ritually enact human inter-linkedness with the universe, as much for his own protection as for the sake of universal Order. Thus perfect sacrificial action forms the core of Vedic con-cerns. We see Vedic man seeking to sustain and influence the course of the world, as well as events in his own life, through sacrifices to those gods that are seen as upholders as well as servants of *rita*. Prayers for strong sons and great riches, combined with invoking the many Vedic gods with specific functions in maintaining *rita*, are constantly reinforced through ritual performances. At this stage not every Hindu took a direct, active part in the ritualised process of cosmic maintenance. The major religious activities appear restricted to a small élite class of literate ritual functionaries, Brahmin priests, who acted as repre-sentatives of a particular section of society, families, clans, a village, a region or a whole kingdom. The involvement of more or less powerful rulers in such ritu-als (as sponsors rather than ritual experts) also legitimised the ruler's position, while it remained quite clear that even the most powerful ruler would remain a servant of this higher Order, not its master (Agarwala, 2003: 7). The continued political fragmentation of ancient India, in contrast to China, prevented the institution of Indian kingship from becoming an important determinator of religious ritual and of legal rules.[22]

Classed as 'revelation',[23] the Vedas give little indication of any legal rules. While it was an obligation for ritual specialists to be extremely punctilious,

---

[22] Even in China (chapter 7), rulers did not control 'Heaven' but merely held its mandate.

[23] The technical term is *śruti*, from the Sanskrit root for 'to hear'. While other religious traditions rely on divine revelation from one God to one chosen person, Vedic Hinduism remains purposely vague; there are many myths about which god created the universe and how revelation took place. Since this is not a linear process of transmission from one God to one man, the concept of revealed authority in Hindu law is comparatively weak. Indeed, it is not a core element of Hindu belief, as a Hindu is defined by a variety of criteria. Attempts to argue that Hinduism is based on divine revelation reflect sectarian views and indicate that many Hindus today feel it is 'proper' for a religion to follow this pattern – one needs to remember that Christians and Muslims have shared the same living space with Hindus for well over 1,000 years.

it could only be claimed that obedience to the Veda was a legal duty in the sense that there was a human obligation to assist in maintaining cosmic Order. Agarwala (2003: 7) makes an interesting distinction of two extreme views on the origins of Hindu law by orthodox Hindus and European jurists: 'According to one view it is of "divine origin" while the other view is that it is based upon immemorial customs and usages.' This Indian student textbook typically portrays Hindu law as a combination of divine natural law in one place,[24] and a more secular type of sociological construct in another.[25] No clear distinctions are made, though all of this fits comfortably into what Aquinas as a legal pluralist said in his time about four different types of natural law.[26]

We know a lot about the Vedic rituals and also about early socio-political organisation of the Vedic people (Kosambi, 1992). But when it comes to positive law, rules imposed by rulers, there is little evidence; indeed Agarwala (2003: 4) confirms that 'the law according to Hindu philosophers and sages is not the king-made law'. We know that ancient Indian society was mainly, as today, organised on patriarchal principles, but matriarchal elements (as today) are also strongly evident (Subba Rao, 2003). Whether one should speak of 'primitive communism' or early despotism of the Roman *pater familias* type remains unclear. Early Hindu law developed informally in society and was applied locally. Early Hindu conceptualisations of law feed on all aspects of the triangle of global legal theory (chapter 3, section 3.8), though giving little importance to state-made law. We have no hope of ever tracing recorded socio-political and legal evidence from early antiquity; all we have are the Vedic texts themselves, and they are certainly not legal texts, and many scholars would not even see them as Hindu texts.

It is not surprising, therefore, that the category 'Hindu' has remained contentious and impossible to define (Derrett, 1966; 1979; Sontheimer and Kulke, 1989). Since Hinduism does not require its adherents to accept the supremacy of a particular God and to submit to His Order, the conceptual basis of Hinduism and Hindu law is not personalised in theistic fashion, although this has become a strong element in modern sectarian Hinduism. Instead, Vedic and more explicitly classical Hindu religion and law are focused on man's inevitable involvement in an invisibly ordered universe, in which gods and men, animals

[24] Agarwala (2003: 4) asserts: 'Hindu law is considered to be of divine origin. It is revealed by the Almighty God to our great sages, philosophers and jurists who had attained spiritual hights . . . Hindu law, according to our *Dharmashastras*, is sacrosanct, inviolable and immutable.'

[25] Agarwala (2003: 1) claims that Hindu law 'was given by Hindu seers and sages who after their long penance and meditation discovered certain rules of conduct which, according to them, are necessary for peaceful co-existence of society. The principles of law discovered by these ancient seers, who were sociologists in the true sense, have great relevance even today.'

[26] See chapter 3, section 3.4 above and note 18 in this chapter.

and all other beings have their place, and to which everyone and everything must relate. From a Hindu perspective, there may be no choice in this matter, a view which establishes the universalistic and cosmic claims of Hindu concepts, so easily exploited today in communalistic *hindutva* fashion.

This Vedic understanding of ordering clearly gives less importance to the individual as an ordering force than to elements beyond human control. The Vedic texts, as sacrificial manuals, depict in confusing abundance all kinds of gods and other superhuman beings in positions of influence over the ordering processes. The idea that appropriate sacrifices will yield appropriate results was taken to intricate heights, as the sacrifice itself was viewed as an ordered microcosm. It was believed that, to be efficacious, rituals had to be executed with utmost precision. Vedic hymns and verses (*mantras*) had to be spoken and sung with strict attention to the minutest detail; any incorrect syllable would ruin the attempted ritual reconstruction and re-creation of cosmic order. Thus, complex ritual sciences developed and the emphasis on correct pronunciation of every syllable of the Vedic texts explains why the Vedas were so faithfully transmitted over a long time.

Later portions of the Vedic literature, especially the texts on marriage and other social aspects in Rigveda 10, prepare the ground for classical Hindu law's key concept of *dharma* as every individual's duty. Vedic knowledge was passed on and preserved by descendants and pupils of earlier sages. According to Vedic *Mīmāmsā* philosophy, the Veda is eternal, self-existent and of absolute authority (Kane, 1968, V, 2: 1269), a statement reflecting concerns to uphold the supremacy of the Vedas as a source of law. This has remained a minority view (Derrett, 1968b). While that school of thought is now virtually defunct, it continues to fascinate scholars because of its intellectual sharpness and perhaps because of its hidden positivistic messages about law-making by gods and men.

Thus, while LAW in Allott's (1980) sense was for Hindus to a large extent determined beyond man's control, actual legal systems (Allott's *Law*) and individual rules were at this stage largely, if not exclusively, left to custom, although Maine's (1861) notion of 'caprice' of the powerful and strong male would have played a certain role in mainly patriarchal contexts. The existing Vedic literature does not discuss legal questions, nor the nature of human law. It is thus not legal literature (Lingat, 1973: xii), but because it focuses on aspects of cosmic law, it is crucially relevant for understanding the deeper meanings of Hindu legal systems as natural law.

As in other early societies, various forms of social organisation, from small family groupings and acephalous societies to centrally structured large kingdoms, must have maintained order, as well as trying to support macrocosmic Order at the local level. Due to the interaction of the various forms and spheres of the visible and the invisible worlds, customary rules were closely linked with magic and religion. To what extent such rules were 'Hindu' in nature will be impossible to ascertain; the nature of this ancient subject is such that we will

never find 'proper' evidence. One must assume a gradual process of Hinduisation, shown for example in the late Vedic models for marriage solemnisation
in Rigveda 10.85 and Atharvaveda 14 (Menski, 1984). Such models reflect how
the Vedic worldview became more prominent among local Hindu chthonic
populations, but a picture of customary diversity prevailed and is later explicitly referred to in all *dharma* texts (Olivelle, 2000: 18). Vedic Hindu law clearly
had both religious and secular natural law characteristics, and both of these
developed further in classical Hindu law.

4.3 Classical Hindu law (c. 500 BC to c. 200 AD)

Vedic concern about utmost ritual precision and its effects on Nature also
explains the ultimate demise of this ancient sacrificial system, which fell into
virtual oblivion around the end of the Vedic period which overlaps with the
onset of the classical or formative period.[27] Vedic man learnt, probably quite
fast, that relying on sacrifice alone for the maintenance of Order was not good
enough. While images of hungry Vedic gods in some of the texts confirm the
collapse of the old order, the key concept of *karma*, often translated as 'action',
more precisely 'action and its inevitable result',[28] was now reconfigured to adapt
to the emerging classical Hindu worldview based on *dharma*, correct or 'good'
action of all individuals, at any moment in their life.[29] Hinduism now became
a plurifocal way of life, and Hindu law experienced socio-legal reconfiguration
as every individual was now held to account, giving rise to a shift towards
socio-legal approaches rather than reliance on Nature.[30]

It appears that early Vedic belief in the more or less direct effects of ritual
action soon metamorphosed into a more realistic secular belief system which
envisages effects from all kinds of human action, not just ritual performance.
Classical Hindu law, built on macrocosmic Vedic conceptual foundations, now
developed a number of interrelated ideas about man and the world into a
coherent system of obligations centred around the more secular aspects of
karma and *dharma*, leading to a system of self-controlled order, a perception
of an ideal state of humankind or a Hindu vision of the Golden Age. This ideal
of self-controlled order would not be maintainable in real life, as 'the big fish',

---

[27] Using this periodisation, I am not suggesting any fixed dates, but approximations over
which much scholarly debate can be held. Rocher (2002: 3) puts the period of the
dharmasūtras at 600–300 BC, followed by the *dharmaśāstras*.

[28] For details see Tull (1990), Mohanty (1992) and Glucklich (1988).

[29] Rocher (2002: 3) notes that there is no Western equivalent for the Sanskrit term, which
'encompasses any kind of injunctions, legal or other, that govern the life of a Hindu'.

[30] Agarwala (2003: 4) notes that early Hindu jurisprudence made no distinction between
legal, moral and religious rules, typically overlooking the social element, and portrays
śāstric law as dynamic (p. 7) without exploring the theoretical implications. Mani (1989:
4) defines *dharma* as 'the totality of rules governing the social order'.

as many *śāstric* texts elaborate, would simply take advantage of their might.[31] In reality, thus, the conceptually sound ideal 'Golden Age' of Hindu law, where all people simply did their best to follow *dharma*, cannot have lasted for long.[32]

The strictly classical configuration of Hindu law is thus based on approximation to an ideal that is unworkable in social and legal reality.[33] Still, it makes sense to distinguish this idealistic classical Hindu law from late classical Hindu law (section 4.4), though both will have overlapped in time during this formative period of Hindu law. The *śāstric* literature, originally oral and immensely diverse, presents material for both concepts in the same texts and it is not possible to neatly divide several historical periods in the way they are presented here for the sake of analysis.[34] Certainly, there is no simple evolutionist progression from *dharma* to *danda*, to *vyavahāra*, rather a gradual sophistication of Hindu approaches to conceptualising the internally plural phenomenon of law. An increasing awareness of the plural nature of 'law' is not explicitly discussed, but is reflected in the texts and seems to be taken for granted.

It is instructive to draw conceptual distinctions between classical and late classical Hindu law. The former is manifestly based on the idealistic assumption that *rita* and *dharma* are maintained by individual self-control through constant, conscious subordination of personal desires to higher concerns. The latter is premised on the probably more realistic observation that individuals are selfish by nature and need reminders of obligations, so that some form of systemic support (the threat of punishment, *danda*, and negotiation over obligations, *vyavahāra*) are needed to strengthen individual and social self-control. I therefore speak of assisted self-control in which Hindu law takes on an even more plural conceptualisation and now falls squarely within the centre of our conceptual triangle (chapter 3, section 3.8). While all these concepts remain premised on the supremacy of self-controlled action, which is the hallmark of the entire Hindu law system, there is a significant shift of emphasis within the classical paradigm.

Since classical Hindu law is distinguished from Vedic law primarily by putting more emphasis on individual action and accountability, it manifests itself as a never-ending chain of role conflicts, processes to ascertain duty and find one's

---

[31] This sounds familiar as a characteristic of power imbalances within any human society (Dahrendorf, 1969) and reverberates with Unger's (1976) findings on the impossibility of achieving ideals in real life. The Hindu chaos theory of 'shark rule' is found in the concept of *mātsyanyāya* ('rule of the fish').

[32] The 'Golden Age' is linked to the complex Hindu theory of four eras (*yuga*), from the most ideal to the corrupt present stage of the *kaliyuga*, in which *dharma* is perceived to be in danger (Derrett, 1968b: 88).

[33] Following Unger (1976), this makes it akin to modern 'rule of law' ideals in which there is an idealised balance between competing legal interests.

[34] Compare traditional Chinese law and the competing visions of Confucianists and Legalists, which led to 'confucianisation of the law' (chapter 7) at roughly the same time.

path, later viewed in more individualistic tones. Sacrifice, still very important, is carried into every Hindu home, so that every Hindu is now expected to engage in sacrificial rituals as part of *dharma*, while it is quite evident that ritual action alone would not suffice to maintain cosmic order. *Dharma*, the originally élitist Vedic expectation of correct ritual action, now becomes enlarged and popularised to include all human actions. It is at first redefined as expectation of right ritual action for every Hindu, then expanded into the secular realm to include any appropriate action at any time, the idealised microcosmic conceptual core of classical Hindu law. Concurrently, Vedic Hinduism (some scholars call it Brahmanism) evolved into classical Hinduism, which even changed its gods and its forms of sacrifice, but not the theoretical basis of the centrality of Order/order and the inescapable interrelatedness of man and universe. The concept of *dharma* is clearly central to the whole of Indian civilisation (Olivelle, 2000: 14) and is inherently pluralistic. Kane (1968, I, 1: 3) explained that *dharma* passed through several transitions of meaning, so that ultimately its most prominent significance came to be 'the privileges, duties and obligations of a man, his standard of conduct as a member of the Aryan community, as a member of one of the castes, as a person in a particular stage of life'. Olivelle (2000: 14) traces the development of *dharma* in close interaction with *karma*, while *rita* gradually fell into oblivion as a technical term:[35]

> As *karma* is primarily ritual action, so *dharmas* are the rules of correct ritual procedure. As the semantics of *karma* widened to include moral/immoral actions, so *dharma* came to include norms of correct behavior within both the ritual and the moral/social spheres. These two spheres of activity appear to be poles apart to the modern mind; it was not so to the traditional Indian mind. The ritual, the moral and the social constituted a continuum. In the Dharmasūtras we see the one overlapping the other and the authors passing from the one to the other imperceptibly.

This comes very close to a finding of plurality-consciousness that includes the legal sphere, but Olivelle's analysis does not extend to legal theory. Kane's seminal definition (quoted above) was adopted by European scholars. Lingat (1973: 4) wrote:

> In internal terms, *dharma* signifies the obligation, binding upon every man who desires that his action should bear fruit, to submit himself to the laws which govern the universe and to direct his life in consequence. That obligation constitutes his duty: and that is a further sense of the word.

Thus, *dharma* now covers the eternal order of the universe (the primary Vedic preserve of *rita*) as well as order in any particular life situation. It is both religious and secular. It concerns all levels of existence, macrocosmic and microcosmic.

---

[35] While Hindus today are aware of the term, it has become so internalised that it is hardly ever discussed, which creates barriers for outsiders in understanding Hindu law.

By placing every Hindu individual into this network of cosmic interrelation-
ships, any human activity, including inaction, becomes perceived to have potentially wide-reaching consequences. The parallel conceptualisation of *karma*
into 'retribution as a result of action' has the effect that *dharma* and *karma*
together established a complex system of moral demands, retributional threats
and promises, all aiming to elicit and promote ideal 'appropriate' behaviour,
whatever that may be in a given situation. This is pristine Hindu law, in its
truly classical conceptual form, still not dependent on state law. It is centred
on the individual as a cosmically linked social being and a legal agent with the
potential for internal self-control. For the present analysis, the most relevant
aspect is the conceptual shift within the meaning of *dharma* from ritual action
to 'good action'.

The resultant need to define what is 'good' or 'bad' in *dharmic* terms provided significant impulses to develop entirely new classes of Hindu literature
and led to creative thinking, akin to the search for justice in Western legal theory.[36] Built on Vedic foundations, and often intricately intertwined with it, new
material was created by many learned men, probably with no clear agenda, but
searching for equity and 'goodness'. For the resulting texts, neither fixed dates
nor identified authors are known; we find a floating mass of originally oral
literature which only later manifests itself in identifiable texts.[37] Even today, it
remains correct to say, with Derrett (1968a: 81), that '[t]he fundamental rules
of law and their spiritual supports are available in texts which are usually dated
between 500 BC and AD 200. Exact chronology is defied by these traditional
materials which had so long a working life.'[38]

In this literature, divine inspiration and authority is not altogether absent,
but is hidden behind, and eventually totally overshadowed by, the huge body
of human knowledge now being elaborated by a small, literate élite and subsumed under *smriti*.[39] These texts are clearly not just law books; they remain
premised on holistic visions and the importance of individual self-controlled
action within the context of communities and show no direct concern for
state law. This is legal pluralist literature as cultural text, so massive in scope
that specialisation became more and more necessary. The *dharmasūtras* and
dharmaśāstras emerge as major guidelines on *dharma*, while important earlier
texts on domestic rituals (*grihyasūtras*) provide specific guidance for the Hindu
householder, developing elaborate ritual models for the celebration of various

---

[36] Olivelle (2000: 15) rightly emphasises the epistemological concerns of the ancient authors.

[37] For details see Olivelle (2000: 1–18); Rocher (2002: 3–5).

[38] Recent painstaking research efforts among American indologists have tried to provide
more precise chronologies, which are not so important for the present conceptual study.

[39] The concept of *smriti* as opposed to the Vedic *śruti* comes from the Sanskrit root for 'to
remember' and relates to a vast category of Hindu cultural texts composed or collected
over time. While this may be originally revealed knowledge, it has been transmitted by
human effort. On the changing concept of *smriti* see Klaus (1992) and Wezler (1999).

rites de passage (Menski, 1984; Pandey, 1969). Following the Vedic tradition of 'schools', based on the various sacrificial specialisations, numerous school traditions developed in this period. None can claim exclusive authority over the others. Only much later did medieval writers on dispute settlement (*vyavahāra*) seek to establish practical guidelines on relative authority, not unlike a comparable process in Roman law.[40] One should partly read this as evidence of scholarly (or saintly) politicking: the classical Hindu texts abundantly acknowledge a variety of views, plurality of rules and relativity of justice. It is unthinkable, from internal criteria alone, to assume that any one of these texts could unilaterally and uniformly determine Hindu law. These are innumerable private efforts to provide some form of guidance. A finding of legal pluralism in action would be in order, but is not made even by leading experts because they are not thinking as comparative lawyers. Olivelle (2000: 18) concludes:

> The expert tradition of Dharma during the centuries immediately preceding the common era appears to have been vibrant and dynamic as shown by the numerous contradictory opinions of experts recorded in the extant Dharmasūtras. Such diversity of opinion belies the common assumption that ancient Indian society was uniform and stifling under an orthodoxy imposed by Brahmins. If even the experts recorded in these normative texts disagree so vehemently, the reality on the ground must have been even more chaotic and exhilarating.

While there was undoubtedly much socio-cultural plurality, this body of humanly transmitted knowledge could claim considerable religious authority, though much less stringently defined than in Islamic law (chapter 5). The scholarly authors of *smritis* were clearly not just jurists, no matter how tempting a thought for lawyers that may be. The emerging central concept of classical Hindu law, *dharma*, 'what is conducive to ordering', 'appropriateness', now turns into the system's keyword as 'duty', the obligation of every Hindu individual, in fact of every living being, to act appropriately. But what is appropriate? *Dharma*, in its idealistic conceptual focus, is radically plurality-conscious and universalistic; it could not develop an absolute, measurable notion of 'good', while *adharma* could not simply be interpreted as the equivalent of 'bad'.[41] In certain situations, as illustrated by the famous scene in the epic poem *Bhagavadgītā*, when Lord Krishna explains to the warrior-hero Arjuna that he must, however reluctantly, kill his relatives in battle to fulfil his *dharma*, we are shown that Hindu law refuses to lay down generally applicable rules such as 'Thou shalt

---

[40] Here the mythical law-maker figure of Manu appears and the text ascribed to him, the *Manusmriti*, is declared (first by the text itself and later by the British) to be more authoritative than any other. There are several reasons for this misguided approach, including a desire to emulate Roman 'codification' and a copying of Maine's evolutionist model.

[41] On *āpaddharma*, the colourful rules on what may be permitted in emergency situations or distress, see Derrett (1968b: 95).

not kill'. Clearly, following *dharma* may demand killing in certain situations. It appears, therefore, that one-sided overemphasis on certain notions, like non-violence (*ahimsa*), has created the misguided image of Hindus as soft pacifists who have no will to fight. Arjuna's dramatic battle of conscience, as well as communal violence in modern India, forcefully disprove such notions. At the same time, violence without justification is clearly not condoned by *dharma*. To take an example from India's rich fable literature, it is the lion's *dharma* to kill in order to survive, but senseless murder violates even the predator's code of conduct.

Quite soon, the science of *dharmaśāstra* developed further, defining the main Hindu aims of life, *dharma* (spiritual merit), worldly possessions (*artha*), sensual gratification (*kāma*) and ultimately salvation (*moksha*).[42] In this integrated society, where the spheres of law, morality and religion overlap (Allott, 1980: 25), one may perceive *dharma* and its implications as religious, but it evidently operates together with other forces and is neither simply law, nor just religion. While the current study suggests a pluralistic perspective taking account of all elements of the conceptual triangle (chapter 3, section 3.8), Indological scholars have maintained artificial boundaries between legal and extra-legal elements. As a French civil lawyer, Lingat (1973: 4) wrote that *dharma* 'is essentially social in the sense that, in a social order visualised as one with the natural order, the individual who obeys its precepts performs a duty which is as much social as religious'. This strong force of *dharma* was further emphasised by Lingat (1973: 5):

> It follows, as a matter of course that, for authors committed to the religious significance of action, society's essential end is realisation of *dharma*, when each individual can put his duties into effect. So their structure of law has *dharma* as its axis.

Rather than turning into an absolute standard, *dharma* had to remain an essentially relative criterion, since its precise definition depends on particular situational contexts. Illustrating this, the *smriti* texts themselves explain that they are not uniformising law books, though this impression persists well into our time.[43] Such misconceptions are constantly reinforced by carelessly equating *dharma* with law. Similarly, statements like 'Hindu law has always been a book law' (Derrett, 1968a: 83) mislead readers who share a presumption that law is only found in written form: what the author really meant here was that the *śāstric* Hindu law, as opposed to Hindu customary law, relies on texts.

---

[42] Agarwala (2003: 2–3) discusses these concepts as elements of Hindu social structure and links them to the Hindu stages of life (*varnāśramadharma*).

[43] The standard translation of the *Manusmriti* used to be Bühler (1975), whose title, *The laws of Manu*, continues to perpetuate misguided notions about legal texts in Hindu law. It does not help that other scholars (Doniger, 1991, using the same title) simply insist that they *mean* the right thing when they refer to Hindu law books, for this continues to confuse students, lawyers and scholars alike. See also note 5 above.

If we read such comments in context, we find a familiar phenomenon: law and legal scholarship seem inherently focused on tangible sources, primarily texts, while the less tangible conceptual and anthropological aspects of legal study and their evidence in real life among Hindus received comparatively less attention. Evidently, it has been far easier for lawyers to study texts than to conduct fieldwork or enter into philosophical or philological debates about basic, but extremely complex, concepts of rights and duties. This has had immense consequences for the study of Hindu law. As fieldwork on classical Hindu law is out of the question, since evidence of litigation only takes us back to courtrooms in the seventeenth century (Smith and Derrett, 1975; Davis, 1999; 2005), we are largely limited to reading classical texts. But the numerous *smriti* texts do not tell us about the 'living law' of their time. They might at best propose ideal models which may or may not have been followed in social reality. Several texts indicate that what was commonly known need not be stated, so one should always ask why certain statements were made and recorded. Olivelle (2000: 11) suggests that the implied audience of the texts is composed of Brahmins, and 'when no class is explicitly mentioned or when the subject is referred to simply by a pronoun, then a rule refers to the Brahmin'. The function of Indian cultural texts is therefore clearly not that of law books (Hoadley and Hooker, 1981: 1–9; Derrett, 1968b: 148ff.). These texts are first of all cultural documents of a private nature, written by men of a certain class in society. They offer guidance about what was considered appropriate in certain situations (Larivière, 1993).

The guidance given may be quite specific, but could never be binding legal prescriptions for all Hindus and for all circumstances, because that would clash with the situation-specific expectations of *dharma*. That the precise nature of duty depends on social context is evident from the complex concept of *varnāśramadharma*, the duty of an individual according to caste and stage of life, which becomes an idealised model at this stage. In seeking to circumscribe *dharma* for individual cases, important questions must have arisen about the relationship of various local and family customs and the *smriti* rules, especially the relationship between custom and *dharma* and, at a deeper level, of individual discretion and divine Order.[44] The earlier *smriti* texts do not provide much discussion on this, list a hierarchy of only three major sources of *dharma* and leave out *ātmanastushti*, the explicit reference to individual conscience.[45] In *Manusmriti* 2.6 and 2.12, however, and in a few other places,[46] we find reference

[44] Instructive parallels are found in intriguing observations by Rosen (1995) on the customary nature of Moroccan Islamic law. See similarly Falaturi *et al.* (1986).

[45] Islamic jurisprudence appears to go further in its negation of individual discretion by not indicating any role for the individual among the sources of *sharia*. After the Qur'an and the Prophet's *sunna*, the other two sources, *ijma* (consensus) and *qiyas* (analogy), are based on juristic reasoning and élite rule-makers.

[46] Further details are found in Agarwala (2003: 6 and 14).

to four sources, which allows us a glimpse of the 'living Hindu law':

> 2.6: The whole Veda is the first source of *dharma*, next *smriti* and the
> virtuous conduct of those who know (the scriptures well), also the example
> of good people, and finally the individual conscience.
> 2.12: The Veda, *smriti*, the customs of good people, and one's own satisfac-
> tion they declare to be visibly the fourfold means of defining *dharma*.[47]

These statements establish an obvious hierarchy of sources, down from the
divinely inspired, 'revealed' Veda to individual, intuitive discretion of the 'reasonable Hindu'. However, this hierarchy of sources does not make sense in
real daily practice. Hindus would not ascertain their *dharma* first by looking
up rules in Vedic texts, they would certainly start the other way round and
examine their conscience first.[48] It is necessary here to explain this more fully
to test our understanding of basic concepts of Hindu law and their practical
operation. In practice, Hindus have never looked to *śruti* first and to *smriti* next
for ascertaining *dharma*. In social reality, the sequence of sources of *dharma* is
completely reversed. To find the actual sources of classical Hindu law, we must
read this hierarchy in reverse order. Thus, individual satisfaction about 'doing
the right thing in the right way at the right time', collectively and individually experienced, is chronologically and factually the first source of *dharma*. It
may well settle close to 100 per cent of all legal issues or situations of insecurity, so that Hindus who found the answer to a problem by examining their
own conscience need not go further. However, this does not make recourse to
individual conscience the most authoritative source of *dharma* in social reality, since this would imply, ultimately, that all Hindus could just follow their
whims. Recourse to individual conscience does not envisage an autonomous
Hindu individual. Individual discretion is seen within a community context,
influenced and circumscribed by situation-specific social contexts, as well as
the wider cosmic context. Absolute relativism and Maine's 'caprice' as a free-
for-all is theoretically precluded by the social and cosmic interlinkedness of all
Hindus, which does not mean that wide discretion is not possible.

Scholarly reactions to the question of how to ascertain *dharma* have been
remarkably confused. From a positivist perspective, an interpretation of the
hierarchical textual model marginalises the Hindu individual's rights to participate in the rule-ascertaining process, typical of lawyers' reluctance to recognise socio-legal factors, let alone the individual's role. Lingat (1973: 6) argued
expressly that it did not seem proper to give a voice to the common Hindu in

---

[47] My own translation, modified from Bühler (1975: 30–1).
[48] The same must be true for Islamic law, where individual believers must have the freedom
to ask themselves whether they have strayed, or should stray, from the path of *sharia*.
Self-examination as an internalised process, and not just direct recourse to the Qur'an,
will inevitably be a feature of the Islamic way of life, too.

law-making:

> But if 'inner contentment' – we should prefer to say the approval of one's conscience – really is a source of *dharma*, it does not strike us as quite properly placed here, following upon sources which possess an authority exterior to man.

This refusal to accept a law-making role for the Hindu individual strongly reflects Lingat's training as a civil lawyer, but this interpretation does not match the conceptual framework of classical Hindu law and also does not fit Lingat's express recognition (cited above) of the social dimension of *dharma*. Leaving the decision first of all to the individual gives primary importance to individual perceptions of right and wrong. Classical *dharma*, thus, relies on the individual's self-controlled ability to discern appropriate action, almost by intuition. This internalised process does not lead to visible action in terms of dispute settlement and is therefore impossible to quantify, but that does not mean it can be ignored and defined away by lawyers. Here is a classic case of declaring a manifestly legal process in a particular culture as 'extra-legal'.

The discrepancy between Lingat's interpretation and the present plurality-conscious analysis becomes more obvious if we consider briefly the meaning of *sadācāra*, 'model behaviour', the third source of *dharma* in the verses cited above. Indian authors and Western scholars have been happy to allocate authority to learned men (and thus indirectly to *dharma* texts) rather than to common people, but this reflects élitist patriarchy and must be questioned. For, what is *sadācāra*, if a basic translation must be 'behaviour of the good'?[49] Are only learned men 'good' for the purposes of this concept, or can Hindus, in social reality, legitimately try to ascertain what the people around them consider right and proper? Can one's peer group (of whatever caste or gender), parents, or a wise grandmother's guidance, replace the advice of a learned man who (ideally, it seems) relies on scriptural authority? All these forms of guidance fall under *sadācāra* and can be envisaged in constructing 'living law', but standard translations and scholarly interpretations have underrated this pluralist perspective, overstating the roles of scripturally posited authority and learned men as its representatives. This indicates that scholars love and perpetuate scholarly authority, and will see it even where it may not exist. It also confirms how easily scholars, perhaps unwittingly, can perpetuate and reinforce patriarchal notions.

When one Hindu individual consults another or others for guidance, and we find the element of *sadācāra* in operation, this again need not be a visible process, since one may simply observe others, or listen silently to guidance, not giving away (not even being aware, perhaps) that one is in fact ascertaining *dharma*. Further, these may be split-second decisions. Of course, this process may be formalised, but unless it involves recourse to a source of guidance based

---

[49] Notably, Bühler (1975: 30) assumes 'the customs of holy men' for *Manusmriti* 2.6 and 'the customs of virtuous men' for 2.12 (p. 31).

on scriptural authority or knowledge, texts do not appear as a source of legal authority. This means indeed that we should look upon *sadācāra* as the major source of *dharma* and of Hindu law (Derrett, 1968b: 156–7). I suggest therefore that, in real Hindu life, recourse to scriptural guidance was then (as it is now) of secondary importance, a matter of last resort. There is no disagreement that *sadācāra* can refer in various ways to custom, better perhaps 'good' custom. *Manusmriti* 8.46 explicitly recognises this when it advises the ideal Hindu ruler:

> What may have been practised by the virtuous, by such twice-born peo-
> ple who are devoted to *dharma*, that he shall establish as the rule, unless
> it is opposed to the customs of countries, families and castes. (Author's
> translation.)

Since *sadācāra* is primarily based on social norms, the texts would have to remain a residual source where evidence of custom was available.[50] The idealised self-controlled order of Hindu law was thus primarily achieved by two types of internal self-regulation, either through an invisible mental process (asking one's conscience) or through consultation within the immediate social environment. Both might never strike us (and did not appear in Hart's concept of 'secondary rules') as a legal process so long as we remain fixated on formal legal methods.

Phrasing this discussion in terms of dispute resolution, we see that the state and any other formal sources of law play at best a peripheral role in classi- cal Hindu law, which remains premised on the supremacy of self-controlled ordering processes and informal mediation and thus relies heavily on cus- tomary laws.[51] This is excellently illustrated in the edicts of Emperor Aśoka (c. 274–232 BC), a Buddhist ruler with many Hindu subjects who explicitly appealed to the conscience and social norms of his citizens by issuing edicts on his famous stone pillars that were moral guidelines rather than legislation as we know it.[52] Nikam and McKeon (1962: 42–3) translated Rock Edict XI, in which Aśoka says:

> There is no gift that can equal the gift of Dharma, the establishment of
> human relations on Dharma, the distribution of wealth through Dharma,
> or kinship in Dharma.
> That gift consists in proper treatment of slaves and servants, obedience to
> mother and father, liberality to friends, acquaintances, relatives, priests and
> ascetics, and abstention from the slaughter of animals.
> Father, son, brother, master, friend, acquaintance, or even neighbour ought
> to say, 'This has merit. This ought to be done'.

---

[50] This is akin to the finding in Part I that where non-state sources of law exist, the state will be put under pressure to accept those as official law.

[51] For an overview of the segmentary state see Kulke (1995: 134ff., 348).

[52] On Aśoka and his wheel of law, see Jacobsohn (2003: 5–8), presenting *dharma* as perpetually moving and thus inherently dynamic.

If one acts in this way, one achieves the gift of Dharma happiness in this world and infinite merit in the world to come.

Glenn (2004: 155) shows how recent writing in the civil law tradition now accepts and almost invents the notion 'that legislation and its interpretation are simply means of continuing the discussion, and not in any way means of bringing it to an end or limiting its breadth'. It appears that the Emperor Ašoka was familiar with such ideas. Based on his internalised understanding of Hindu *dharma*, he could never claim the authority to posit legislated norms to control his people's daily actions. All he did was to appeal to people's sense of self-controlled order.

This kind of legal evidence from ancient India raises the wider, important issue of the relationship between Hindu customs and texts as a source of guidance on *dharma* and law. The co-existence of local practice and textual model is regularly referred to in the *śāstric* texts, not only in the context of marriage rituals (Derrett, 1968b: 159), with local practice fully acknowledged as a supreme force overall, even by the texts themselves. For example, *Āšvalāyanagrihyasūtra* 1.7.1–2 (Sharma, 1976) starts its treatment of marriage rituals with an important reservation about textual authority:

> Immensely diverse, indeed, are the customary practices of different countries and villages; one should follow these in marriages. What, however, is common to all or most shall be declared here. (Author's translation.)

Other texts indicate that old women, rather than learned men, are an authority on customs (Derrett, 1968b: 159), and this can still be observed today (Menski, 1987: 197). The supremacy of local practice over textual rules, of concern for social reality rather than general principle, comes up in the context of equity (Agarwala, 2003: 20–1) and was explicitly recognised in *Brihaspatismriti* 2.12,[53] to the effect that '[n]o sentence should be passed merely according to the letter of the law. If a decision is arrived at without considering the circumstances of the case, violation of justice will be the result.' This shows that justice (*nyāya* or *yukti*) is sought from the situational context, not in abstract rules. Classical Hindu law evidently has terms for 'justice', but no precise equivalent for 'law' as state law. That, itself, confirms inherent plurality-consciousness.

The relationship of the various customary laws and the *smriti* texts suggests that customs, even in derogation of textual rules, would be valid.[54] Potentially, this puts custom and *smriti* into open conflict; there must have been many occasions for this. Older studies often misunderstood the relationship of text and custom, and some authors (Winternitz, 1968, I: 233) wrongly claimed that the old texts actually record the customary law in tremendous detail. Since

[53] This text was quoted as late as 1968 by the High Court of Kerala in the case of *Kunhikannan* v. *State of Kerala*, 1968 KLT 19 at 23, to save an innocent victim of police overzealousness.
[54] See in detail Menski (1992b; 2003: 121–30).

the texts themselves do not claim to say the last word on any matter, we find processes of negotiation, interaction and mutual influence. While textual rules must have contributed to Hinduisation and Sanskritisation (Srinivas, 1973) of local and caste customs, so that customs have changed through incorporation of *śāstric* ideals, much of the *śāstric* material is itself based on observations of custom, but is certainly not what lawyers might call 'codified custom'. Derrett (1968b: 206) suggested that customary law 'moved towards the *śāstra*' in various ways. A gradual process of Hinduisation must be assumed, since many people lived at that time on the fringes of Hindu civilisation.

The gradual acceptance of child marriage is perhaps one of the best-documented examples for social change. The Vedic ideal appears to have been that only a fully mature girl, ready to give birth, was to be given in marriage, because the most important expectation of a woman's contribution in terms of *rita* and *dharma* focused on her potential for strengthening the husband's family. In various *dharmaśāstra* texts, marriage is advocated within a speci-fied period after puberty (puberty plus three years) at first, later about three months after puberty, then marriage on puberty, and finally pre-puberty mar-riage (Menski, 1984: 751ff.). The main consideration here changes over time, apparently from earlier concerns that fertile periods should be utilised, to later concerns of controlling illicit sexual relations. Here we see two competing *grundnorms* in operation, the older one being that members of society have an obligation to ensure the survival and growth of the next generation, so that con-jugal sex becomes a matter of cosmic obligation for both partners, while later Hindu traditions focus especially on concerns over female chastity. One may analyse this in terms of a *grundnorm* shift: eventually, it was considered more important for *dharma* that a woman's chastity be protected, which had impor-tant implications for widow remarriage, and even the killing of wives, leading to dramatic *dharma* dilemmas (Datta, 1979) as such basic norm patterns and their change were vigorously contested.

There are strong voices from within Hindu tradition, reflected in virtually all Indian legal textbooks, which claim that the ancient texts are based on Vedic revelation, directly in the case of *śruti* and indirectly in *smriti* texts, and thus possess a superior form of authority, which individuals disregard at their peril.[55] The Mīmāmsā schools of Hindu philosophy, in particular, attempted to develop a theory that the Vedic texts, as divine revelation, were binding law, a form of religious positivism. Did they learn anything from early Christians or Jews about the power of religious law? Not surprisingly, this school of thought with its arcane techniques, though intellectually stimulating and influential, never gained the upper hand over continuing awareness of real life (Derrett *et al.*, 1979: 32–7). As we saw, the Vedas would certainly be difficult to use for ascertaining the actual law. The complexities of the later *śāstric* literature made

---

[55] Agarwala (2003: 4) suggests that their violation is deemed as a sin (*pāp*).

attempts at finding the law in this sea of texts deceptively easy, for anything could be 'proved' from this ocean of material. But would any particular text possess any authority? Indications from more recent Hindu practices suggest that collective reference to 'the Vedas' as a convenient label for an authoritative corpus of texts remains a popular strategy to back up the opinion of individuals who claim traditional learning. Lipservice to the Vedas is used to legitimise what is in reality much more recent authority and, one suspects, often a variant of *sadācāra*.

A brief comparison with the similarly structured system of Islamic law may help to elucidate why Hindu law has developed its particular characteristics of textual fluidity and the overriding force of custom. In Islamic law, only one man, the Prophet Mohammed, is held to be the direct recipient of divine revelation, which could then as the Qur'an become the primary textual basis of Muslim law. Hindu law is neither premised on the authority of one personalised God nor on the records of revelation from a specified, central divinely appointed source. The divinely inspired knowledge of the Vedas (*śruti*) was not received as revelation by one historically verifiable man, but by an indeterminate number of ancient sages, who admittedly (the *smriti* concept itself suggests this) created new forms of knowledge through the process of transmission. Hence we find that scriptural authority in Hindu law was from the start extremely dissipated, difficult to ascertain and impossible to use as the basis for a tightly formulated central creed. The Hindu evidence of Vedic revelation was simply not conducive to building up a uniformised legal system based on holy scripture, as has been claimed with more persuasive success in Islamic law.[56]

The consequences of relying on the individual Hindu's conscience within its social context as a major ingredient for the development of classical Hindu law are thus apparent. In an ideal world, all individuals would follow their specific group *dharma* and a constant balance of symbiotic co-existence would be sustained, rather like a stable ecosystem or a healthy immune system.[57] As Vedic concepts of ordering moved from macrocosmic *rita* to microcosmic, idealistic self-controlled ordering through *dharma*, different kinds of specialised *dharma* came to be recognised, such as every individual's obligation (*svadharma*), women's duty (*strīdharma*), the ruler's set of duties (*rājadharma*), all within the all-encompassing *varṇāśramadharma* ideology, so that everyone's caste status

---

[56] Muslims, too, do not, as a matter of practice, refer first to the Qur'an when they require guidance on what is right and wrong. They, too, tend to seek solutions first from within themselves, whether as individuals or as members of a specific social group. These are simply facts of life, not a matter of religious doctrine, and they are not necessarily in contradiction with maintaining the superiority of the Qur'an as God's word (chapter 5).

[57] Glenn (2000: 79–80) also notes the implications of such attitudes for environmental protection issues. They are felt strongly in modern Indian environmental laws and manifest themselves for example in banning of smoking in public places in Kerala, as in *Ramakrishnan* v. *State of Kerala*, 1999(2) KLT 725.

and stage of life have a bearing on *dharma*. In its unlimited generality, which at the same time provides for equally unlimited specificity, this looks like plain commonsense in terms of socio-economic and political division of labour. Later texts and especially secondary interpretations often provide a rigidity of views and concepts which are more ideological than real. Here again, scholarly reconstruction introduces fixities into an inherently dynamic framework of reference and thus denies and buries traditional plurality-consciousness, often in the name of modernity and progress. ·

The internalised dialectics of cosmic order as a never-ending process rather than an idyllic vision of a final state of development imply that the ideal of balance is always necessarily accompanied by imbalance, requiring constant vigilance and re-balancing. Human greed and other inadequacies, as many Hindu textual statements indicate in the late classical period, necessitate that self-controlled order should be assisted, since self-control cannot be relied on. The idealised pattern of self-regulation in an imagined Hindu Golden Age, the truly classical period of Hindu law, is soon replaced, in reality as well as in principle, by a methodology of supervision. Its underlying aim appears to be, as in Chinese legal culture (chapter 7), to strengthen and support individual and local self-regulatory processes. While early rulers like Aśoka, as we saw, issued edicts as moral guidelines, later Hindu rulers may have felt authorised to stipulate harsh penalties for their subjects to improve self-control processes. In this process, the temptation to lay down fixed rules for everybody, to create 'real law' in a positivist sense, will have increased. But to the classical Hindu ruler, 'real law' could never mean state-made law outside the Hindu conceptual context. Everything and everyone, including the ruler as judge and eventual appellate authority, would have to respect the invisible norms of self-controlled order. Classical Hindu law was inherently plurality-conscious and certainly not legocentric.

4.4 Late classical Hindu law (c. 500 BC to c. 1100 AD)

As indicated, the borderlines between this and the previous period are fluid and the periods partly overlap. Most writers treat 'classical' or 'traditional' Hindu laws as one category, and thus lump together the four periods of Hindu law distinguished here. At the fluid end of the classical period, which probably overlaps with the early beginnings of the late classical period, the stage is set for more active involvement by forces outside the individual and the immediate social group, supporting self-healing mechanisms where self-controlled order breaks down or is inefficient. The individualistic classical Hindu method of strengthening universal order through individual self-control appears to give way to an assumption that simple self-control is not effective enough in safeguarding *dharma*. Unlike Aristotle, whose idealistic views of human nature fit well into the classical period of Hindu law, the ancient Indians argued now that man's conscience needed a little help to maintain good order. The centre of activity in maintaining cosmic order, earlier shifted from heaven to earth, now moves from individuals and social groups towards specific processes and institutions that support *dharma* in various ways. Maintenance of cosmic order now begins to involve what we might call public agents rather than simply individual self-consciousness and local social self-control.

Late classical Hindu law takes certain characteristics which require separate treatment. Above all, the shift to supervised self-control through the threat of punishment (*danda*) – deterrence rather than cruel punishment itself – throws the spotlight on the functions of the Hindu ruler (*rājā*).[58] There is a great degree of scriptural continuity (Lingat, 1973: 107) or, put differently, the *śāstric* texts appear to oscillate between the two conceptual models of self-controlled order and assisted self-control. It is impossible to draw dividing lines because the texts themselves were not composed in one piece and were probably the product of a collection of authors rather than one person.[59] Several important later texts, such as the *Nāradasmriti*, *Brihaspatismriti* and *Kātyāyanasmriti*, develop earlier concepts and build on the foundations of the classical age.[60] An increasing variety of textual sources was created, including new independent works, and eventually commentaries on older ones (Lingat, 1973: 107ff.; Kane, 1968, I, 2), famous dramas and great epic tales. From the seventh century onwards, a fair number of traveller's reports and a variety of historical records were available to the researcher.

If order was maintained primarily at local levels and by recourse to custom rather than texts, this meant that justice was relative, and law had to remain relative and the equity of the situation remained of paramount concern. The absence of a strong political centre for most of Indian history further strengthened the trend towards diversity rather than unification of laws. The shift towards assisted self-control is most clearly evidenced by the emergence of the concept of the threat of the punishing rod, *danda*. The *Manusmriti* contains a string of verses on this subject; verse 7.18 is a good example. In my translation, *danda* is rendered as 'punishment', but it really signifies 'threat of punishment', emphasising the deterrent effect:

> Punishment alone governs all creatures, punishment alone protects them, punishment watches over them while they sleep; the wise declare punishment to be identical with dharma.

The concept of self-controlled ordering appears defunct here and requires support through deterrence. Similarly, *Manusmriti* 7.22 (Bühler, 1975: 219)

---

[58] *Danda* has a deterrent as well as coercive and punitive aspect, like *hadd* in Islamic law (chapter 5), and the similarly dreaded *fa/hsing* in classical Chinese law (chapter 7).

[59] Glucklich (1988) correctly writes throughout of 'the authors of Manu' rather than envisioning a single law-making Napoleonic figure.

[60] For details see Jolly (1977); Rocher (2002: 4). On the third text see in detail Derrett (1968b: 148ff.).

suggests that '[t]he whole world is kept in order by punishment, for a guilt-less man is hard to find; through fear of punishment the whole world yields the enjoyments (which it owes)'. The Hindu ruler, as stated in innumerable texts, should employ the punishing rod, a conceptual device as much as a real stick,[61] to inflict appropriate punishment after due consideration. The idea that the threatened punishment should fit the crime, an important concept also in Chinese law, reinforces the cosmic context within which punishment processes (whatever form they may take) should take place. If the underlying aim is to strengthen an invisible balance, any disregard for balance, also in pun-ishment, would create further imbalances rather than contributing to *rita* and *dharma*. The texts therefore allow us to measure such balancing acts, provided we understand that the cruel punishments often stipulated constitute expres-sions of (mostly Brahmin) disgust and dismay over certain practices, rather than offering legitimation for cruel punishments by self-appointed guardians of morality and 'proper' standards.[62]

The Hindu ruler's major new function, maybe first through exhortation and later explicitly through deterrence, which may extend to stipulations of most cruel deterrent punishments, and only in the extreme their execution, was premised on ensuring that this equilibrium of relativities was not unduly tilted in any direction.[63] Hindu law does not cultivate the same elaborate taxonomies of penalties to 'match the crime' as Chinese law (chapter 7, section 7.3.2). Apart from treason, specific attention needed to be given to abuses of power on the part of the most powerful individuals and groups in society, visualised in the 'rule of the fish' (*mātsyanyāya*), where the big fish devour all the small ones, which is ultimately not to the benefit even of the big fish. An image of ordered chaos emerges, a system which constantly strives towards synergetic symbiosis, to be somehow kept in check by a ruler wielding a stick. This, in outline, is the Hindu model of assisted self-control. The system as a whole still relies heavily on the self-controlled agency of every Hindu individual through conscious or intuitive mental processes, whether as a matter of free will or under some form of social or circumstantial coercion.

While the individual Hindu still carries major responsibility for the main-tenance of *dharma*, the Hindu ruler as a figurehead now gains prominence as *dharma*'s guardian, reflected by stressing the supervisory function of rulers. Ideally, like in ancient China,[64] the ruler need not be called into action, as

---

[61] The Chinese bamboo stick seems more designed to be actually used (chapter 7), though in Chinese law, too, the element of deterrent threat is important.

[62] The fact that some texts were taken verbatim later does not prove that these injunctions were binding 'law'; the power to punish could always be abused.

[63] This may denote efforts to keep legal processes as closely to the centre of the triangle of law as possible.

[64] For an instructive comparison of *dharma, li* and *nomos*, see May (1985), with numerous references to Chinese law and its allegedly cruel approach to crime, which also takes

self-control is still supposed to work effectively. Yet where it breaks down, the ruler is to step in through deterrence in the form of harsh and often quite grue-some punishments (Day, 1982; Menski, 1992a). These are often elaborated in later texts and clearly belong to the late classical period. Such punishments are reinforced by penalties of a more religious nature, since transgressions of *dharma* are also seen as sins, which require penances and/or attract con-sequences in the unseen world, either immediately or after a person's death. Clearly, a variety of views existed on that subject, and *karma* was and is no simple exercise of adding up points for an imaginary bank balance.

Comparative lawyers might see more here than early glimpses of criminal law. However, it is still not the state which determines the rules of human co-existence in traditional Hindu law; the primary rules are still a cosmic given with local flavours. The late classical reorientation of *dharma* turns violations of ideal behaviour potentially into what lawyers would call a matter of public concern and thus public law, attracting a threat of punishment by the ruler and other representatives of the state. But does the Hindu ruler represent the state in this sense, or is it still his primary function to protect the cosmos? The conceptual development of *rājadharma* as a specialised branch in the science of duties offers further explanations. From a political perspective, it is not unreasonable that a ruler figure should have some kind of concern for, and control over, what 'his people' should not do.

The texts emphasise that the ideal Hindu ruler now takes the functional char-acteristics of Varuna, the divine Vedic guardian of *rita* (e.g. *Manusmriti* 9.245). The subject of *rājadharma* becomes an important topic in its own right. Soon the rulers, and increasingly their judicial functionaries, are depicted in situa-tions akin to litigation and dispute settlement. The epic and dramatic literature in Sanskrit and various old local languages (different forms of Prakrit) provides much evidence of this development, too. While rulers and their representatives appear to be given guidance in such texts about how best to secure *dharma*, *all* Hindus are taught about *dharma* in this way, which in that sense also protects the public against rulers who are tempted to overstep their limits. However, the Hindu ruler is still not the creator of primary legal rules in Hartian terms. Fulfilling his special obligation to act conducive to cosmic order, in late classical Hindu legal theory, he still *makes* no law. Rather, he *administers* what his people perceive to be their law, seeking to ensure thereby that society does not disregard morality and that the individual perceptions of rights and duties remain within the overriding ambit of *dharma* in its macrocosmic and microcosmic dimen-sions. Without making law himself, he cultivates a control function that seeks to keep all law within the centre of our pluralistic triangle (chapter 3, section 3.8).

account of cosmic balances. The deterrent approach of Islamic *hadd* punishments serves a similar function in terms of preserving God's order, though the individual Muslim seems to play a minimal role in this (see Falaturi *et al.*, 1986).

The texts provide rich evidence of this new function, making it apparent that local customary notions of appropriateness remain the major source of law in social reality. The ruler has to respect such customs and must give them effect, thereby following his own *dharma*. A few examples may illustrate this here. Kautilya's *Arthaśāstra* 3.7.40 (Kangle, 1972) advises a dutiful ruler that '[w]hatever be the customary law of a region, a caste, a corporation or a village, in accordance with that alone shall he administer the law of inheritance'. *Manusmriti* 8.41–2 (my own translation) provides:

> A ruler who knows his duties according to *dharma* must inquire into the customary laws of castes, districts, guilds, and families, and thus settle the law peculiar to each. For men who follow their respective occupations and who abide by their respective duties become dear to people, even though they may live at a distance.

Even when a new territory has been conquered, there should be no simple super-imposition of the new ruler's law but respect for people's customs. *Manusmriti* 7.203 (my own translation) clearly indicates that this is a matter of political expediency as well as *dharmic* duty of the ruler towards his new subjects:

> Let him make authoritative the customary laws of the inhabitants of that territory, just as they are stated to be, and let him honour (his representative) and his chief servants with precious gifts.

The late classical Hindu ruler's main role is therefore still not to posit and enforce his own law, but to enable his subjects to follow their own respective *dharma* as far as possible. There is no simple operative concept of positive law in ancient India, rather a more intricate, plurality-conscious conceptualisation of supervision of communities. Austinian legal positivism is conceptually blocked by the all-pervasive pre-existing norm system of cosmic, universal order, to which all forms of existence are linked, whether they like it or not. The Hindu ruler, therefore, who earlier was more evidently a protector of his people against outside aggression (hence the importance of *kshatra*, the legitimising power to protect), now acts more and more as a guardian of *dharma*, indeed as its servant, and hence the classical Hindu ruler provides a critical service to his people, rather than ruling over them.[65] Even late classical Hindu law remains hostile to positivist conceptualisations of law and upholds a plurality-conscious methodology of legal realism.

In addition, one further Hindu legal concept marks the shift of emphasis from processes of idealised self-control to situations where official agencies of 'the law' appear to provide more input. Faced with many competing claims, the

---

[65] The concept of public interest litigation in India, with spectacular growth since the late 1970s, is partly based on classical concepts of 'accountability'. Those in positions of power are seen as accountable, visibly to their constituents or clientele, but also, one suspects, invisibly to the higher order of which everyone is aware.

Hindu ruler as a model figure gradually acquired another key function beyond punishing or threatening to punish. Textual statements about the functions of the Hindu ruler in late classical literature introduce the concept of *vyavahāra* as a device to settle disputes and to uphold cosmic order. This again puts the spotlight on the Hindu ruler, placing more emphasis on formal litigation processes, it seems. However, it would be wrong to assume that the primary traditional reliance on individualistic, situational self-control was abandoned.

The ruler figure now becomes more of a justice facilitator, the key person involved in the gradually emerging concept of dispute settlement, *vyavahāra*.[66] This is often blandly translated as 'litigation' (Kane, 1968, III: 242ff.), which addresses a Western audience and lawyers, but does not properly convey the full ambit of this concept in classical Hindu law. At first sight, it seems that references to dispute settlement reflect an increased perception of the need for state law and judicial intervention. This necessity for 'lawsuits' seems to be suggested at the very beginning of the later *smritis*.[67] Thus *Nāradasmriti* 1.1 to 1.2 (Jolly, 1977: 5) reads:

> 1. When mortals were bent on doing their duty alone and habitually vera-cious, there existed neither lawsuits, nor hatred, nor selfishness.
> 2. The practice of duty having died out among mankind, lawsuits have been introduced; and the king has been appointed to decide lawsuits, because he has authority to punish.

The more recent translation by Larivière (1989, II: 3) sees *vyavahāra*, like Rocher (2002: 4) as 'legal procedure' rather than litigation or lawsuits:

> 1.–2. When men had dharma as their sole purpose and were speakers of the truth, then there was no legal procedure, no enmity, and no selfishness. Legal procedure came into being at the time when dharma was lost among men. The overseer of legal procedures is the king; he has been made the rod-bearer.

Similarly, *Brihaspatismriti* 1.1 (Jolly, 1977: 277) provides:

> In former ages men were strictly virtuous and devoid of mischievous propensities. Now that avarice and malice have taken possession of them, judicial proceedings have been established.

Such textual statements and their translations confirm perceptions of declin-ing Hindu self-controlled ordering and a strengthening of the ruler's posi-tion as justice administrator. Other texts indicate that experts in the *śāstra*, now moving into positions as legal advisers, assessors and even judges, should

---

[66] Rocher (2002: 4) suggests that '[w]hat is understood as "law" in the West is expressed in Sanskrit by the terms *vivāda* and *vyavahāra*, the former corresponding to substantive law, the latter to legal procedure'.

[67] I suggest below that we should rather think of dispute settlement processes generally, not lawsuits.

become increasingly involved in the administration of legal rules. All this seems to increase the importance of state law, of texts and textual knowledge as a source of Hindu law.[68] But all of this together still does not mean that earlier cosmic concerns became marginalised or were superseded and that the centre of gravity now shifts to rule-making by the state. Law here does not replace *dharma*, the concept of *vyavahāra* simply strengthens the input of 'the state' in the widest sense but maintains the interlinkedness with the other two elements of our conceptual triangle.

The above positivist assumptions about a movement from *dharma* to law collapse as soon as we remember that *vyavahāra* can mean anything from a mental process of sorting out a doubt to a full-fledged formal court hearing before the king as final arbiter.[69] Often circumscribed as 'removal of doubts', *vyavahāra* is envisioned as the extraction of a thorn or a dart (*Nāradasmriti* 1.3.16–17; *Manusmriti* 8.12). It is the thorn of actual or potential injustice that needs to be removed through processes of ascertaining *dharma*. However, the general meaning of this term is more like 'action, conduct, behaviour', even 'custom' (Monier-Williams, 1976: 1034),[70] and it is only with reference to the *Manusmriti* and other *śāstric* texts that 'legal procedure, contest at law, litigation, lawsuit, legal process' are indicated in the dictionary.

Based on my own translation and interpretation of these texts, I suggest that a plurality-conscious rather than a positivist reading is preferable. Clearly, the process of formal or informal dispute settlement is focused on removing doubt about *dharma* and is designed as a search for truth. *Nāradasmriti* 1.3.18 (Jolly, 1977: 40) concludes:

> That is not a judicial assembly where there are no elders. They are not elders who do not pass a just sentence. That is not a just sentence in which there is no truth. That is not truth which is vitiated by error.

Larivière (1989, II: 22) translates this as follows:

> A court is not a court if there are not elders. Elders are not elders unless they pronounce dharma. Dharma is not dharma unless there is truth. Truth is not truth if it is mixed with sophistry.

The emphasis here is evidently on 'truth' (*satya*), not on cosmic Order (*rita*), which confirms that late classical Hindu law focuses more explicitly

---

[68] There has been some discussion on whether a legal profession existed in ancient India and the answer appears to be in the negative (Kane, 1968, III: 288ff.). Even if certain experts assisted litigants with their case, their primary duty remained to explain the *śāstra* and to monitor compatibility with *dharma*, not to represent a client. Such experts served the system as a whole, not an individual seeking to establish a claim or to evade retribution.

[69] See section 4.3 above on how individuals ascertain *dharma* through mental processes.

[70] This is also the popular meaning of the term in languages like Hindi today: 'behaviour . . . transaction, practice, usage . . . application' (Chaturvedi and Tiwari, 1975: 728).

on ascertaining what is appropriate and correct among humans in the context of *dharma*. The process of ascertaining this truth is, however, not restricted to formal court proceedings, it remained in my submission an integral element of daily Hindu life, simply part of the process of living a good life. While the relevant texts make the loss of illusions about the Golden Age quite evident, the human task and challenge of making sense of a complex socio-legal reality is emphasised. Rather than imagining that all this removing of doubt about *dharma* and truth has to take place in formal legal settings, indologists should realise and emphasise the importance of informal dispute settlement as part of Hindu law. I accept that the texts appear to suggest formal settings with 'kings' and 'courts', but all those terms can mean a wide range of things, so that 'ruler' could be the head of a family, a local village headman or a clan elder, and 'court' can be a shady space on the village common. Indological constructions of necessarily formal dispute settlement at this historical stage, based on the textual statements that we have, are not sufficiently plurality-conscious to allow us to gauge what really went on among Hindus at that distant time. The absence of a developed literature and deep thinking on informal dispute settlement among Hindus, the trendy alternative dispute resolution (ADR), seems directly related to the exaggeratedly positivist reconstructions of Western indologists about key concepts like *vyavahāra*. With such reservations in mind, a brief fresh look at the verses from *Nāradasmriti* 1.1 to 1.2 (my own translation) can be undertaken:

> 1. So long as people were intent on following their respective duties and were habitually veracious, there existed neither the need to resort to formal dispute settlement, nor hatred, nor selfishness. The practice of *dharma* having ceased among the people, formal dispute settlement has been introduced, and the ruler has been appointed to decide such matters, because he has been made the bearer of *danda*.

Similarly, *Brihaspatismriti* 1.1 (my own translation) simply conveys: 'In former times people were strictly virtuous and devoid of mischievous inclinations. Now that avarice and malice have taken possession of them, dispute processing has become necessary.' This does not mean that informal dispute settlement no longer occurs among Hindus. The scholarly tendency to assume the predominance of formal processes has been strengthened by the fact that some texts now elaborate in much detail how such processes are to be executed. Investigation and critical evaluation of textual evidence becomes a new focus of interest for the *smriti* authors. These are clearly 'rules about rules', Hartian secondary rules that give power to officials. Remarkably parallel to early Islamic law, an impressive body of procedural rules emerges in the texts from this period. Doubts whether these texts reflect actual practice resurface, since they often overindulge in classifications and hairsplitting distinctions, leading to a virtual science of dispute processing. They are clearly not a realistic reflection of actual legal practice

According to these *śāstric* texts, rulers were called upon to settle disputes, as well as to punish criminals. The former was the case in disagreements between individuals or social groups based on conflicting claims, the latter presumably when grave violations of *dharma* had occurred and local control mechanisms had failed. However, the severity of a transgression alone could not determine whether a matter was dealt with by a ruler. Non-metropolitan local fora in India, to this day, claim and exercise the right to devise appropriate punishments, including the death penalty, which is not so much evidence of corruption or lawlessness, as modernist observers insist (Dhagamwar, 2003), but a systemic pattern of informal dispute settlement or local justice, internally perceived as self-controlled cleansing. Such dualisms of practice and perceptions about 'truth' and 'justice' highlight of course the legitimation crisis of modern Indian state law (Baxi, 1982), which seems undermined by continued application of the 'old order'.

In the late classical period, the overriding concern in practice must have continued to be *dharma* and the equity of the situation rather than intricate arguments about procedural niceties.[71] If order was still primarily and informally maintained at the local level, the Hindu ruler would exercise at best a supervisory function. He would not even come to know of most disputes, unless they affected his rule or occurred in the capital, where access to the ruler's court was less difficult. Rulers themselves would not want to be involved in petty matters, unless they were corrupt and saw judicial administration as a means of exploitation or a chance to increase revenues. While this cannot be excluded as a possibility, many texts show that vexatious litigation and litigiousness were not favoured and were actually punished.

Other verses elaborate the four basic stages of *vyavahāra*, plaint, answer, examination of evidence and judgment, though there is little harmony between individual texts on points of detail (see e.g. *Brihaspatismriti* 3.1ff.). The late classical texts became increasingly arranged subjectwise and the eighteen 'titles of law', the 'substantive law' (*vivāda*) that Rocher (2002: 4–5) highlights, receive prominence. All major texts contain such a list.[72] While *Manusmriti* 8.4–7 merely listed them (see also Rocher, 2002: 4–5), the *Nāradasmriti* treats them in considerable detail: (1) debt; (2) deposits; (3) partnership; (4) resumption of gifts; (5) breach of a contract of service; (6) non-payment of wages; (7) sales affected by another person than the rightful owner; (8) non-delivery of a sold chattel; (9) rescission of purchase; (10) transgression of a compact; (11) boundary disputes; (12) mutual duties of husband and wife; (13) law of inheritance; (14) heinous offences; (15) and (16) abuse and assault; (17) games;

---

[71] Indeed, the warning of sophistry in the *Nāradasmriti* (Larivière, 1989, II: 22) reverberates here.

[72] Rocher (2002: 4–5) suggests that, from the *Manusmriti* onwards (which he sees as the earliest text in this category), there are always eighteen titles, though with variations.

(18) miscellaneous (Jolly, 1977: vii–viii). The *Brihaspatismriti* produces these topics in a slightly different order, but does not otherwise vary much from the *Nāradasmriti* (Jolly, 1977: ix).

Rather than evidence of substantive law-making, this offers a detailed classification of the categories under which substantive rules might be brought, which makes a crucial difference for evaluation. The texts appear to reflect an academic exercise, not a process of laying down rules for people to apply. Moreover, *vivāda* does not simply mean 'law' in Sanskrit. Monier-Williams (1976: 986) lists 'dispute, quarrel, contest between . . . or with . . . or about . . . , legal dispute, litigation, lawsuit', so that the term equates largely with *vyavahāra*, and *vivādapada* is significantly given as 'subject of a dispute or lawsuit' (p. 986), so it may be quite informal and placed in the social sphere. There is clearly no case here for seeing any form of substantive positive law in late classical Hindu law. Procedural niceties abound, but there are certainly no Hartian primary rules made by the Hindu ruler.

Increasing formalisation of legal rules and of administration of justice at the highest level is reflected in verses that *appear* to give the Hindu ruler the last word in deciding disputes. These verses establish another hierarchy of sources of law (or rather of *dharma*?) markedly different from *Manusmriti* 2.6 and 2.12 (section 4.3 above). This indicates probably an advanced discussion about the sources of *dharma*, an issue which is still virtually unexplored (Derrett, 1968b: 148). Lingat, as Derrett (1968b: 154–5) tells us, saw these verses as statements about methods of dispute settlement or means of proof. This seems only one part of the complex message which such texts convey. As a starting point, one may take *Nāradasmriti* 1.10 (my own translation):

> Virtue (*dharma*), a judicial proceeding (*vyavahāra*), evidence of custom (*caritra*) and a verdict from the king (*rājaśāsana*) are the four feet of a lawsuit. Each following one is superior to the one previously named.

Jolly (1977: 7–8) tried to explain the meaning of this verse, based on the rather rudimentary efforts of *Nāradasmriti* 1.11, whose terse language does not give many clues. Derrett (1968b: 148ff.) indicated in detail how this hierarchy of sources of law should be read. Taking the text of the *Kātyāyanasmriti* as a basis, he argued, firstly, that where both parties to a dispute act truthfully and the wrongdoer admits his misdeed, the outcome is achieved through *dharma* (Derrett, 1968b: 149), thus still by self-controlled ordering. Derrett's interpretation and the original text leave it open whether such cases would have to come to a formal court, or whether *dharma* here includes reference to internal processes of self-control as in classical Hindu law, perhaps a public admission on the part of a wrongdoer, once challenged, that a particular action was contrary to *dharma*. This could be a form of settlement before trial, informal self-settlement, maybe again just a mental process. If that is correct, the term *dharma* here definitely refers to continuing relevance of informal self-control mechanisms. In this particular sense, *dharma* itself continues to be a source of *dharma*, and is therefore properly placed in a prominent position in the present hierarchy of four sources, which appears to start in realistic chronological order, beginning with the least authoritative and most informal source.

Continuing this dual imaging of sources of *dharma* and methods of settling disputes, the second element in this hierarchy, *vyavahāra*, signifies any form of contested ascertainment of *dharma*, not necessarily recourse to formal processes of dispute settlement. The boundaries may be drawn somewhere between *dharma* as virtually invisible 'self-settlement' and *vyavahāra* as visibly 'assisted' settlement of a dispute. This makes sense, particularly if we remember that the conceptualisation of late classical Hindu law is based on the image of a corrupted ideal: in the bad *kaliyuga*, the worst age, where self-control has largely broken down, more elaborate mechanisms for dispute settlement need to be pursued. Derrett (1968b: 149) reports Kātyāyana's view that *vyavahāra* involves the settling of disputes by recourse to *smriti* rules, i.e. the formal application of textual guidance. However, this conclusion does not necessarily follow from verses like the one cited above from the *Nāradasmriti*. In fact, *Nāradasmriti* 1.11 explains that 'a judicial proceeding (rests) on the statements of witnesses'. Thus, I would argue, formal methods of dispute settlement do not by necessity demand recourse to *śāstric* texts, unless we restrict witnesses to learned men. As Derrett (1968b: 149) indicates, the *smriti* authors may here be conducting 'a self-conscious and tendentious debate' among themselves. They might be less concerned to explain how *dharma* is determined, and more keen to highlight their own importance, particularly since in Hindu social reality textual authority remained just a subsidiary source of *dharma*. In an age of prevailing self-interest (*kaliyuga*), it is hardly surprising that these authors should suggest an increased role for their texts and expertise. Another explanation could be that recourse to texts here means reliance on new rules about evidence rather than older *śāstric* sources. This would lead to the same conclusion: the *vyavahāra* experts are effectively advertising themselves and their products and services. Are these Hindu 'lawyers' in fact attempting to establish a Hindu legal profession or a version of legal centralism? They would not have come very far, but they might have tried.

The third element in this scheme is *caritra*, a colourful term which can mean many different things, just as *ācāra* or *sadācāra* in the classical scheme, since all three terms involve different types of human behaviour. Derrett (1968b: 149) translates from the *Kātyāyanasmriti* that 'whatever a person practises, whether it be in accord with *dharma* or not, is declared to be *caritra* because it is the invariable usage of the country'. At first sight, this means that appropriate behaviour serves as a source of *dharma* and requires no intervention from anywhere, in which case one must wonder why it is listed here separately. If we view *caritra* as a method of dispute settlement, however, it could refer to documentary evidence of what is right and proper (Jolly, 1977: 7). Again, this does not need to imply recourse to *smriti* texts, but could be a written or orally documented confirmation of particular local or caste practices, a form of expert evidence with evidentiary value. The precise meaning of this term needs to be investigated further. It would be wrong, in my submission, to think immediately of highly technical, notarised affidavit procedures.

Lastly, the ruler's edict or verdict (*rājaśāsana*) must also be seen in this dual fashion. It is not just, in legocentric manner, the authoritative final verdict of a supreme judge, who is also the ruler. Contextually a source of *dharma*, it could fall under the classical category of *sadācāra*, being based on what the leader figure, as a person of authority and eminent standing, considered appropriate.[73] But how did a ruler reach his decision? It could be the result of patriarchal despotism and brazen force, but this is probably not what the Hindu texts had in mind. While Jolly (1977: 8) thought lawyer-like of 'the pleasure of the king' (which is dangerously close to Maine's 'caprice' or Austin's command of the sovereign), he omits to explain *how* a Hindu ruler would come to a decision and to what extent this should be binding. The *Kātyāyanasmriti* indicates generally that texts do play an important role in ascertaining 'relative appropriateness' (Derrett, 1968b: 150). The suggestion that a circumspect ruler would consult experts in the *śāstric* literature makes sense, but does not answer the critical question about the standing of the ruler's verdict or decision. This could again be read as evidence of self-advertisement in the late classical age, this time by rulers seeking to legitimise their involvement in dispute settlement processes in conjunction with experts of the *śāstra*. A commonsense interpretation would be that a good ruler would give a decision after due consultation with wise advisors. Most importantly, in acting as a 'judge', the ruler would be a justice facilitator, an assessor of competing perspectives, rather than a direct source of law in common law fashion. Moreover, his decision had no standing as a precedent, a notion that violates the situation-specificity of Hindu law.

While it seems premature to draw final conclusions from this particular set of texts about the sources of law and of *dharma*, it is apparent that custom con-tinued to play a large role in practice in combination with locally conditioned reference to textual sources.[74] Whatever we call it, the supremacy of this local customary law is further underlined by frequent statements to the effect that a valid custom need not be in accordance with *smriti* rules. Even custom in derogation of *smriti* continues to be perfectly valid in Hindu law and has to be given effect in dispute settlement scenarios, an important lesson that the British were to learn during the nineteenth century.

---

[73] Not, however, the model behaviour of the ruler, because he had his own particular *rājadharma*.

[74] Davis (1999: 191ff.) discusses the concept of *deśamāryāda* (local law) in Kerala, insisting that this should be called 'law' rather than 'custom' because it did not arise only from local norms but represents the outcome of a combination of textual and other sources. Here, too, we see struggles over defining 'law'.

All this shows clearly that late classical Hindu law, too, did not simply allow the ruler to 'make law', but tied him firmly into a local framework of relativities and, within our conceptual framework, pulled him towards the pluralist centre of the triangle (chapter 3, section 3.8). The fact that the ruler increasingly delegated his judicial functions to experts (Derrett, 1968b: 183; Derrett *et al.*, 1979: 65ff.), some of whom we might now call judges and/or jurists, had some influence on the consideration of these relativities, but case-law and statute did not become formal sources of Hindu law until British intervention many centuries later. Increasing awareness of procedural intricacies is not sufficient proof that late classical Hindu law had become 'law' in the dominant Western sense of state-made rules.

4.5 Post-classical Hindu law (after 1100)

Post-classical Hindu law probably represents a shift in emphasis from internalised processes of ascertaining *dharma* to more visible attempts at finding the right balance in tangible and more public processes of conflict resolution. This still does not mean, however, that we now find a separate sphere of 'law' within the Hindu cultural context. Increasing importance was given to 'secular' concerns and there is much evidence of a more explicitly 'legal science' within *dharmaśāstra*, but all of this visible (*drishta*) activity is still perceived as being connected to the invisible (*adrishta*) sphere of the holistic *rita/dharma* complex.

Within the context of *dharma* and *vyavahāra*, later *smriti* texts assume various important functions. Where they comment on older rules, their aim is often to update such rules and to make them more applicable to contemporary situations (Lingat, 1973: 109ff.; Dasgupta, 1973, I: 6). The interesting, clever device of declaring older and now unacceptable practices as *kalivarjya*, not allowed in the *kaliyuga*, the current immoral and utterly bad era of human existence, appears here (Derrett, 1968b: 88–9). For example, it was difficult to accept later that ancient sages apparently enjoyed eating beef, or that great women, like Draupadī in the epic *Mahābharata*, could be married to five brothers at the same time (Datta, 1979). Various devices to explain such unpalatable evidence away show concern for use of the older texts as guiding models in a new social setting. As today, rewriting the ancient texts was not a realistic aim, so later generations of Hindu textual specialists engaged in creative reinterpretation through a complex and rich commentary literature (Menski 2003: 146–52; Rocher, 2002). This remains virtually unexplored, but seems to be full of ingenious arguments regarding almost every problem under the sun. Some of these texts read like legal commentary and have been interpreted as such, with the word 'jurist' in frequent use, but one must advise caution: the cosmic framework of traditional Hindu law, also in this period, still puts powerful brakes on all human law-making and requires pluralist circumspection. Hence, the commentators should not simply be perceived as jurists in the sense in which we normally use that word, they were specialists in the science of *dharmaśāstra* and might have a special interest in grammar or philosophy, rather than law. They remained plurality-conscious in a culture-specific Hindu manner and did not aim to develop a separate science of law.

In this context, the *Mīmāṃsā* school traditions for harmonising texts and social reality acquired new prominence.[75] An important device in their method-ologies became the distinction between rules of greater and lesser authority, *vidhi* and *arthavda*, binding injunction and descriptive account of how a prob-lem may be solved (Derrett, 1968b: 87f.). Debates about these concepts circum-scribe efforts to apply textual statements to factual situations. In addition, this device allowed the authors and collectors of new *smriti* material to develop rules in accordance with new preferences and to update the *śāstra*, often according to their own taste, while not entirely disregarding the older textual models. Attempts to maintain textual and conceptual continuity, in a complex society which was by no means static, led to much personal opinion masquerading as authoritative rule. Perhaps that had always been so under the mantle of *smriti*.[76] While some authors made genuine attempts to clarify contested positions and to offer solutions, the potential for vain casuistry, poetic licence and simple abuse of the system was enormous. Like we complain about lack of quality control on the internet today, we should assume that post-classical Indian highways of information were full of spam.

Many speculative post-classical efforts indicate recognition of gaps between theory and practice and there are many attempts to reduce such gaps (Derrett, 1968b: 192 and 196). Statements in texts are later more closely related to actual problems, even to legal cases in which appropriate solutions are sought by reference to texts (Derrett, 1962: 17). Later literature, now ascribed to individual authors, often high-ranking officials with expert status in the administration of justice (Lingat, 1973: 110), offers fuller accounts of the author's thoughts. Such texts often look more like rough drafts than finished products, incomparable to the polished earlier *śāstric* aphorisms that were designed to be remembered.

From the post-classical period come two important texts, the *Dāyabhāga* of Jīmūtavāhana, an independent work (Rocher, 2002), and the *Mitākṣarā* of Vijñāneśvara, seen as a commentary on the *Yājñavalkyasmriti*, but in real-ity more like an independent work on matters of property and succession (Sontheimer, 1977). Both texts appear to have been composed around 1120–5 (Rocher, 2002: 24). Focusing on technical legal questions and dealing in

---

[75] This is originally a Vedic system of epistemological and hermeneutical investigation and efforts to understand the Vedic textual sources as authoritative rules of law in relation to *dharma* (Jha, 1942). Inevitably, it clashed with customary concepts in Hindu law (Derrett, 1968b: 86, 148–70).

[76] Similar observations can be made about the concept of *sunna* in Islamic law (chapter 5).

depth with matters of property, these texts were in use when the British first made attempts to understand Hindu law during the seventeenth and eighteenth centuries and continued to be used after the British took over legal administration.[77] The abundance of later textual material, very little of which is accessible in European languages, clearly reflects increasing concern with formal processes of administration of justice. The ground was being prepared for a cross-cultural (but unsuccessful, as we shall see) attempt at a meeting of minds, as colonial administrators would be looking for formal evidence of Hindu law, while the *śāstric* experts were seeking to enlarge their role in terms of legal administration while continuing to think about strengthening *dharma* through appropriate textual guidance.

In real life, the majority of conflict situations within the various Hindu communities continued to be dealt with locally and customary laws remained the most important yardstick. Textual sources remained of peripheral influence to how local Hindu laws developed; to what extent text influenced custom (and vice versa) remains the subject of much debate. Most of Hindu law at this stage remained informal, unrecorded and inaccessible to formal legal analysis. The post-classical Hindu legal system as a whole remained rooted in self-controlled order and cosmos-conscious action. State law could not, and did not, take over the entire field.

Looking at the Hindu ruler as a justice facilitator in view of the textual evidence, the post-classical system produced rich evidence of creating a still more formalised system of secondary procedural rules. These are found, for example, in immense detail in the *Nāradasmriti*, which Larivière (1989, II: x) refers to as 'the juridical text *par excellence*' and sees as 'the only original collection of legal maxims (*mūlasmriti*) which is purely juridical in character' (p. ix).[78] I have reservations about this assessment, to the effect that this text, and later ones like it, may well *appear* familiar to lawyers, but these are still *dharma* texts that operate within a very different socio-cultural, and hence legal, context than any Western system of law. Thus they have to be read within their culture-specific conceptual framework. The same mistake of interpretation was made with regard to the *Arthaśāstra*, ancient India's handbook on politics and international law, a guidebook for Hindu rulers who wish to survive multiple challenges (Kangle, 1972). While the material on *artha* (acquisition of worldly goods and power) may look entirely secular to outsiders, it has an invisible *dharmic* dimension and should be interpreted within the wider conceptual context of the *rita/dharma* complex. The fact that the author of the *Arthaśāstra* did not spell out the critical continuing importance of *dharma*, let alone of *rita*, is not evidence of gradual secularisation of Hindu law, but confirms that the conceptual presence of *dharma* in its various shades of meaning was taken

[77] Today they are a matter of legal history (Rocher, 2002: vii).
[78] Rocher (2002: 4) supports this view.

for granted. Such texts were not written for foreign scholars and comparative lawyers and contain meaningful silences, of which outside observers and interpreters must remain aware.

Thus, despite much evidence of formal Hindu law rules, it should be understood that these remain largely procedural, secondary rules in the Hartian sense, while the primary rules of ancient Hindu society and its historical successors remain firmly in place. The cultural factors that Chiba (1986) referred to as 'legal postulates' or 'identity postulates' (Chiba, 1989: 180) continue to dominate the practical application of such formal rules. In a sense, there is still no official Hindu law, if by that we mean legal rules made by the state. There is only a different type of literature on *dharma*. Classical cultural understanding of the interlinkedness of higher cosmic order and Hindu socio-legal realities is now matched and harmonised with increasing recourse to more formalised processes of dispute resolution, while the Hindu cultural core remained invisible and internalised. To keep it that way became to some extent a strategy of survival, as Hindu law was about to lose its position as a politically dominant element.

4.6 Medieval Hindu law under Muslim domination

The political fragmentation of medieval India made it laborious and yet fairly easy for any strong force to take over substantial parts of the subcontinent and to establish a central government. Eventually, a politically unified central state was firmly established in Delhi from c. 1100 onwards, leading to Muslim rule over huge Hindu populations (Wink, 1990). The consequences for Hindu law have not been as negative as is often claimed. Certainly, Hindu law did not cease to exist and was applied at various levels. Now it simply became a personal law within the emerging Moghul Empires rather than the official law of a Hindu state. If we apply the criteria of 'weak' and 'strong' pluralism, Griffiths (1986) would have been pleased with the result: far from being forced to exist on terms dictated by the now dominant Muslim law, Hindu law became itself part of the official law, but largely on its own terms, so the result was an emerging pattern of strong legal pluralism.

Although there was now a Muslim ruler at the political centre, little may have changed for the average Hindu, since the central ruler would have remained a remote force unless one lived in or close to the capital. Being a small minority in demographic terms, Muslim rulers learnt fast that it would be impossible to impose Islamic law on all subjects, the vast majority of whom (a figure of 95 per cent is quoted) remained rural Hindus (Jain, 1970; Ojha, 1978: 119–26). As the desire to sustain a viable central rule prevailed over ambitions to regulate the daily lives of all citizens,[79] Muslim rulers sought to uphold the authority of Islamic law for themselves and fellow Muslims, while developing a more

---

[79] If such ambitions ever existed, given the nature of Islamic law (chapter 5).

detached, secular approach towards their subjects of different faiths, letting them carry on their own affairs within their own communities.

In this way, Hindu law remained a personal law, but now in politically subservient status (Hooker, 1975). On the ground, the existing pattern of an 'essentially isolationist society' (Ingalls, 1954: 37) remained almost totally undisturbed, and Hindu law continued to be applied at all levels of society. Allowing many Hindu sub-rulers to remain in their place, provided they paid the appropriate tribute (Ojha, 1978: 119), most Muslim rulers did not interfere with the administration of local justice. As the effects of Muslim rule remained largely restricted to the cities (Shrivastava, 1981: 112–28) and the Muslim rulers were mainly concerned with the collection of taxes and the administration of criminal law (Banerjee, 1962: 33f.), the duty of common Hindus towards the state was fulfilled by discharging tax burdens. Many Hindus would, then as now, have felt little impact from centralised political rule. Indeed, there is a popular saying in India to the effect that 'Delhi is far away' (*dilli bahut dūr hai*). This image, diametrically opposite in significance to the French painting of Napoleon making law by candlelight (Legrand, 1996: 235), tells us more about the *mentalité* of Hindu and Indian laws than the study of textbooks and judicial decisions.

The preservation of Hindu self-ordering processes and customary laws in this period was probably promoted by the traditional reluctance among South Asians to carry one's disputes beyond the family or the clan.[80] There is evidence that some Hindu law cases did reach higher urban fora of dispute settlement.[81] These were often interesting civil disputes with useful information about procedural details (Derrett et al., 1979: 76ff.). Such disputes might also be brought before Muslim rulers, some of whom applied Hindu law not only in cases among Hindus, but also in Muslim–Hindu disputes.[82] Perceived or real risks of non-Hindu interference would have reinforced resort to local dispute resolution mechanisms, which could still be seen as socio-cultural self-healing processes.

While there can be no doubt that Hindu customary law continued to operate during this period, the development of *smriti* texts did not come to a halt either. Huge collections of *smriti* material were produced, which some scholars view as a defence mechanism against Muslim aggression. Such collections took the form of digests or *nibandhas*, like the *Krityakalpataru* of Bhatta Lakshmīdhara,

---

[80] Basu (2001) discusses how this avoidance of formal litigation hinders Hindu women today who may wish to claim their rightful entitlements to shares in family property. On women's property rights see Agarwal (1994).

[81] For a well-documented example from the Maratha period see Smith and Derrett (1975). On Kerala and the intriguing concept of intermediate realms of law, see now Davis (2005).

[82] Derrett et al. (1979: 84) provided an instructive example. There was a notable vacillation in the approach to Hindu law between leniency (the extreme is perhaps Akbar, who sought to fuse Hinduism and Islam) and early forms of Islamic 'fundamentalism', whose representatives would refuse to take official account of Hindu law.

probably of the twelfth century, and many later ones.[83] Often following the pattern of 'titles of law', such digests comprise and collect all kinds of relevant statements from earlier *smriti* texts, subjectwise and frequently without comment. These enormous collections were never practically useful in ascertaining 'the law', and this was probably not their purpose. Perhaps such collections also served as a memory bank or training manual for the few remaining experts on the *śāstra*. A well-trained *pandit* would be in a position to cite numerous verses on particular topics, or only those that made a particular point useful to a specific scenario, or, indeed, he might express his own opinion on the matter. The textual experts exercised a virtually uncontrollable monopoly of knowledge and thus achieved a position of considerable power, which could be abused and exploited, as the British eventually discovered to their cost.

A phenomenon about which we appear to know far too little is the use of the village Brahmins or 'neighbourhood *pandits*' as self-professed experts or advisers on *dharma* and their role in local dispute settlement processes.[84] Fitting the pattern of *sadācāra*, this meant that *śāstric* concepts could continue to percolate to the local level. For a variety of reasons, the complex processes of interaction between local customary laws and Hindu scriptural authorities and their interpreters never ceased during this period, the vast field of Hindu law remained alive, and the substance of Hindu law did not change as a result of Muslim domination.

4.7 Anglo-Hindu law

The impact of colonial rule on the structures and concepts of traditional Hindu law led to the introduction of an originally non-indigenous legal framework in India which later developed its own momentum. The British first came to India to trade, officially from 1600 onwards, but soon ended up (as elsewhere) as colonial administrators and local rulers. This created a need for knowledge of Hindu law, since disregarding Hindu (and Muslim) law altogether was simply not a politically viable option. The British had enormous reservations about taking account of Hindu law, but since it was a legal system governing, even then, huge masses of people, political expediency dictated caution. How could the British administer a virtually unknown legal system, respecting it in some form, while not totally giving up control over it?

It did not take long to develop a system of judicial administration, since there were practical pressures.[85] From 1600 onwards, various Royal Charters

---

[83] Kane (1968, i, 2) contains some material, but far too little is as yet known about these texts.

[84] Similarly, the ordinary Muslim might ask for a *fatwa*, a form of legal opinion, from the local religious leader, the *maulvi*.

[85] As elsewhere in the Empire, adjudication of legal matters among mercantile and later colonial staff, who would not have wanted to be subject to Muslim law (the official law

gave the British East India Company first the right to trade and then the power to establish courts in their territory. Such Charters did not specify which law was to be applied, leading to considerable insecurity.[86] Under a new Charter of 1668, the East India Company was required to work towards creating a new legal system, in effect 'to enact laws "consonant to reason and not repugnant or contrary to" and "as near as may be agreeable to English law"' (Pearl, 1979: 23). In this way, notice was given that the British would eventually reform substantive parts of the law applying to the people of the subcontinent. In a Charter of 1726, Mayor's Courts were established in the Presidency towns of Madras, Bombay and Calcutta (Banerjee, 1984: 11), thus a beginning was made in creating a colonial judicial system. It was still not expressly stated in such Charters which law should be applied, and it is evident that strategic planning about formal structures preceded substantive involvement with local Hindu or Muslim laws. While hardly anything was known about those laws at the time, technical 'choice of law' questions began to arise in more and more disputes between British and Indian litigants. Something had to be done, and without much delay.

Practical experience quickly showed that the application of English law and judicial procedure would be quite unsuitable to the local population.[87] As a result, Hindu customary laws were increasingly, albeit reluctantly, recognised (Banerjee, 1984: 9), leading to 'the beginnings of the co-existence of English law with Indian laws prevailing in the region concerned' (p. 9). This process of hesitant local coordination, first in Bengal, follows earlier South Asian patterns of co-existence of a 'soft' official and general law and concurrent personal laws of different communities. While such legal pluralism was familiar, the meeting of a European legal system and Western legal concepts with the various Indian laws was a dramatically new experience.

The East India Company obtained *Diwani* rights over parts of Bengal, Bihar and Orissa in 1765, which meant in effect that it became a local authority under the sovereignty of the Moghul ruler in Delhi, while also operating under the sovereignty of the British Crown (hence the problems of diarchy, which

until 1858) or Hindu law became a concern. Swift action had to be taken to introduce English law for such specific purposes; the next question then became to what extent Indians should and could also be governed by English law.

[86] For details see Banerjee (1984: 1–27). In Bombay, for example, English law was applied under a Charter of 1661 (Pearl, 1979: 22).

[87] Glucklich (1988: 1) with reference to Derrett's writings. Many earlier authors argued that the Charter of 1726 simply implied the application of English law. The myth that India just applies English common law originates from such assumptions. Even a more recent specialist study supports the 'general view' that the Charter of 1726 introduced the laws of England, as they stood at that date, into the Presidency towns (Banerjee, 1984: 11). However, Banerjee (1984: 21) admits the increasingly obvious absurdity of enforcing a selection of substantive rules of English law on the Indians. As more calls for restrictions on applying English law in India were heard, something had to happen about involving Hindu law.

also needed to be resolved). Now the pressure to develop a suitable method of judicial administration for local populations became stronger. In 1772, Warren Hastings, then Governor of Bengal, issued his famous Regulation, which included provisions to the effect that, 'in all suits regarding inheritance, marriage, caste and other religious usages and its institutions, the laws of the Koran with respect to the Mahomedans, and those of the Shasters with respect to the Gentoos, shall be invariably adhered to'.[88]

This important Regulation had several effects. First of all, it indicates British recognition of Hindu law, assuming that these laws were found, more or less codified, in the *śāstras*. Secondly, this Regulation effectively confirmed that the British would not introduce English law in all respects and subjects. By preserving the so-called 'listed subjects' (see the Regulation above) to which succession was added in 1781, as the domain of the personal laws, notice was given that Hindu law was to be applied to Hindus even before much was known about their law. Thirdly, the Regulation gave notice that the British intended to exercise more direct control over public law, with criminal law as a priority. Again, this follows earlier South Asian patterns of legal development: the Muslim rulers had retained the personal laws of the various religious communities, concentrating on tax laws and criminal law. The interaction of the new 'secular' laws with the religion-based personal laws now became a matter of growing interest.[89]

At first the British tried to ascertain Hindu law from texts, but this strategy was soon abandoned, as it proved cumbersome and impractical (Menski, 2003: 165–74). Prior to 1793, when the so-called Cornwallis Code was introduced, there had been no general Code of Laws and Regulations in British India.[90] Influenced by British legal theory at the time, prominently Bentham,[91] codification began to be considered essential for good administration (Banerjee, 1984: 167). James Stewart Mill viewed the *śāstras* as compilations of Hindu law by the *pandits*, but took a rather disparaging view of the texts and the legal standing of their authors, while recognising that Hindu customary law was powerful. Such observations laid the ground for a strategy of codification, extending eventually to all those areas of Hindu law not covered by the 'listed subjects' of the Hastings Declaration. Provisions were made for an Indian Law Commission,

---

[88] For details see Banerjee (1984: 30), Derrett (1968b: 231ff.). Interestingly, the Muslim rulers at the time were quite unhappy that Hindu law was put on an equal footing with Islamic law.

[89] The topic is well covered in a number of studies and Anglo-Hindu law continues to interest some British (and Japanese) historians today. For details on early developments see Banerjee (1984), Fawcett (1979) and Jain (1981).

[90] Banerjee (1984: 166). The new Code brought many innovations (for details see Jain, 1981: 137ff.).

[91] Bentham noted the importance of Hindu customary law and observed that practical application of this law was marked by mysterious procedures. For him, the case for codification of Indian laws was absolutely clear, as introducing a proper written law would amount to bringing civilisation.

the first of which started work in 1835 (Jain, 1981: 411ff.). Its first task was to prepare, under the lead of Macaulay, a draft Penal Code, submitted in 1837.[92]

A major aim of this codification process was uniformity and certainty (Banerjee, 1984: 171). Since the usefulness of 'native laws' was not accepted by Macaulay and others at the time, the new Codes were mainly based on principles taken from the laws of England. The new criminal law was drafted so that certain technicalities and local peculiarities of English law were removed, while some modifications to suit the circumstances of British India were introduced (Banerjee, 1984: 173 and 177). Thus a new law was created, tailor-made for the subcontinent, not just a transplant from England. Macaulay, who was Scottish, purposely introduced civil law elements, and acknowledged his debt to the French Code and the Code of Louisiana, while on closer examination one finds many Indian elements, too (Banerjee, 1962: 129ff.). The result of Macaulay's labours was a systematically arranged, fairly precise and intelligible Penal Code, which is to this day hailed as a model of successful codification.[93]

There appears to have been little Indian opposition to the Indian Penal Code of 1860, but it remains doubtful whether it was as widely known as has been claimed (Banerjee, 1984: 179; Dhagamwar, 1992: 9–10). Silent non-acceptance of the Code seems a likely reaction of the vast Hindu population, while the fact that the Code offered new remedies and some tough punishments (Fisch, 1983) made it popular with those who could afford to harass their enemies, including of course the colonial regime. The Penal Code did not govern all aspects of criminal law in all parts of India (Banerjee, 1984: 179). Above all, much of India never came under direct British rule. Thus, in practice such codification was less comprehensive and less successful than appears at first sight.

After British sovereignty had been firmly secured in 1858, the British codified many other areas of the law, leading to charges of 'over-legislation' (Banerjee, 1984: 180–90). During the particularly active period after 1860, the Third and Fourth Law Commissions operated under instructions to use the law of England as a basis, while making some concessions to local conditions, native habits, and modes of thought (Banerjee, 1984: 182; Jain, 1981: 430ff.). Banerjee's simplistic view (1984: 182) that 'thus it was decided that India was to be governed under English law' is therefore misguided. Codification meant the creation of a new legal system, in which English law had an important influence, but the law of England did not directly apply. Acts like the Indian Companies Act 1866 might not look very different from their English model, but they were also adjusted, at least to some extent, to subcontinental conditions.

---

[92] At this time, the British argued keenly that Muslim criminal law, then the official law of India, was totally inadequate and needed to be replaced (Malik, 1994).

[93] The Draft Code evoked considerable opposition among the British in India, and was reworked several times to become law in 1862, as the Indian Penal Code of 1860. For details see Jain (1981: 441). With further modifications, it was later introduced into many other parts of the British Empire, especially Africa (chapter 6, section 6.4).

While all major areas of general law, except tort law, were codified in this way, the codification process was not restricted to the 'unlisted subjects'. In derogation of the Hastings Regulation of 1772, the British also began to interfere in Hindu law, particularly when they found certain Hindu practices cruel and inhuman.[94] Often they did this cautiously, aware of hostile public opinion. Through the Sati Regulation of 1829, the British aimed to protect Hindu widows from being burnt on the husband's funeral pyre. The Caste Disabilities Removal Act 1850 provided that Hindus who were excommunicated from their caste would not thereby also lose their interest in property. The Hindu Widows' Remarriage Act 1856 removed, by the stroke of a foreigner's pen, all legal disabilities against the remarriage of a Hindu widow.[95] In addition, despite much criticism about the speed and amount of Indian legislation (Banerjee, 1984: 187), the general law was constantly expanded at the expense of the 'listed subjects'; no neat borderline could be drawn between the 'general law' and Hindu personal law. Ultimately, vigorous Indian opposition to some amendments of the Indian Penal Code at the end of the nineteenth century, relating to the age of consent, slowed down the British legislative zeal (Heimsath, 1962; Anagol-McGinn, 1992). Thereafter, only few selected reform measures, like the Child Marriage Restraint Act of 1929, were introduced. In this case, it became obvious that Western-educated Indian opinion-makers were arguing for such legislation just as much as the British, who continued to look down on Hindu society and sought to introduce civilising social reforms through law.

Towards the end of the nineteenth century, most important areas of law had been taken out of the ambit of Hindu law altogether and were administered according to colonial codes and procedures. The official law had pushed Hindu law into an enclave, a kind of ethnic niche, the realm of the 'Hindu personal law'. Because Hindu law continued to be seen as an inferior system of law lacking official authority, many British administrators refused to pay much attention to Hindu law, even though the practical demands for settling disputes under Hindu law made themselves increasingly felt.

Professor Derrett has, in many articles, depicted the complex story of the administration of Hindu law by the British in India (Derrett, 1968b: 225–30). His work distinguishes two major aspects: (i) the role of the *śāstra*, i.e. the changing role of texts as a source of law under British rule, and (ii) the process of administering Hindu law through a subtle combination of English and Hindu principles of adjudication, involving the use of precedents and the introduction and creative use of the important formula of Justice, Equity and Good Conscience (Derrett, 1978a; Pearl, 1979: 27ff.). Regarding the role of

[94] The concept of repugnancy was known but became prominent only later, particularly in the colonial administration of African laws (chapter 6, section 6.4).
[95] This Act was quietly taken off the shelf in India by the Hindu Widows' Remarriage (Repeal) Act 1983. It was never an effective Act in the first place (Derrett, 1968a: 99).

texts as a source of Hindu law, the British appeared for some time genuinely concerned to discover what the law was, but proceeded on the false assumption that the Hindu law was found in books. Of course, this was not totally wrong. Derrett (1968b: 229) confirmed this from a legal perspective:

> But it is certain that amongst Hindus the *dharmaśāstra* held very high pres-
> tige, served as the only indigenous system of jurisprudence, and supplied
> actual rules of law in a wide variety of contexts, especially (in Northern and
> Eastern India) in matters of inheritance. The native professors of the *śāstra*
> were therefore consulted on such matters.

Significantly, Derrett does not speak of 'jurists' here, referring instead to Hindu 'legal' experts in a more neutral way. Obviously, in the eighteenth and early nineteenth century, it was too much of a challenge for outsiders to appreciate fine points in the conceptual foundations of classical Hindu culture, nor did the British obtain a full picture of Hindu socio-legal reality. While they observed that *pandits* might be consulted in legal matters as experts on the *śāstra*, they also noticed that neither the *śāstra* nor *pandits* might be consulted (Derrett, 1968b: 230).

It was more or less inevitable that the help of Hindus should be sought, since the British required some inside knowledge to administer Hindu law without causing too much offence. Thus, indigenous legal experts, as the British saw those *pandits* who offered their assistance, were employed at all levels of the official court hierarchy soon after 1772. These native experts on Hindu and Islamic law acted as some form of expert witness,[96] with the title of 'assessor', guiding the British court personnel on matters of Hindu and Muslim laws. This system was maintained until 1864, when it was believed that enough precedents had been accumulated.[97] The *pandits* and *maulvis* who were so appointed treated their new employers almost like a Hindu or Muslim ruler (Derrett, 1968b: 268) and their methods in the use of textual authority were adjusted to the new expectations.

Actually, this particular scenario led to a crucial intercultural breakdown of communication over the meaning of 'law'. The court system demanded specific solutions to often complex issues. Unaware of the basic principle of situation-specificity in Hindu law, and lacking in plurality-consciousness, the colonial administrators asked the *pandits* questions about 'law', while the *pandits* responded in terms of *dharma*. While the British wanted to know about a general rule of law, the indigenous experts provided situation-specific assess-ments of the case in question. Unsurprisingly, the British soon discovered with

[96] I find myself today acting in a similar capacity when English judges and legal professionals require expert assistance.
[97] There were other reasons for 'sacking' the native experts, prominently lack of trust. The British had not realised that those who offered themselves for appointment might not be the most qualified persons. A purity-conscious high-caste Hindu expert of the *śāstra* might never want to be involved with the British.

dismay that different answers were given by various experts, even by the same person, based on different texts or simply representing a considered personal opinion. It took the colonial officials a while to realise this, but the damage was done. By the time this particular system of ascertaining Hindu law was abandoned in 1864, Anglo-Hindu case law had become a conglomerate of precedents built on shaky textual authority, now developing its own momentum. Evidently, this law was neither Hindu law nor English law, but a deeply problematic construct.

The 1772 Hastings Regulation shows that the British had understood *śāstra* as a collective term for written codes of Hindu law, unaware of the complexities of this literature as cultural text. It also transpired only gradually that what was presented to courts as *śāstra* was rarely the oldest layers of literature, ancient *sūtras* or the *Manusmriti* and similar texts,[98] but later commentaries and extracts from digests (Desai, 1982: 48). This updated *śāstric* material was, in the extreme, influenced by the *pandit*'s own opinion on the matter, which could – and did – create considerable confusion and was often seen as evidence of outright mischief when private opinion was clothed in the mantle of a nebulous *śāstric* text.

To restrict the freedom of indigenous experts to expound 'the law' as they pleased, the British hoped initially that codification of Hindu law would lead to greater certainty. Since codification of law was the 'flavour of the day' among lawyers, it was a tempting thought to improve on the abstruse Hindu texts by producing some new, authoritative *śāstras*. Early on, the British engaged learned *pandits* for compilations of new digests on Hindu law, sometimes in conjunction with early indologists. The first work so commissioned, the *Vivādārnava-setu* or *Vivādārnava-bhañjana*, was compiled by 1775 (Derrett, 1968b: 239). Such compilations of *śāstric* rules under English legal headings were initially assumed to be authoritative statements of Hindu law, and the British anticipated that these texts would eventually be followed by all court *pandits* (Derrett, 1968b: 239). However, that was clearly a misguided assumption and this codification process 'failed to deflect *pandits* from their normal sources of information, and merely added another to their many reference works' (Derrett, 1968b: 241).

The first digest was at best 'a somewhat qualified success' (Derrett, 1968b: 242) and the wide ocean of the *śāstra* continued to provide rich fishing grounds for *pandits* looking for an appropriate textual authority. Other attempts at codification followed, the most successful being Jagannātha's *Vivāda-bhangārnava* ('Ocean of Resolutions of Disputes'), which was even translated into English and quite often applied for some time (Banerjee, 1984: 43f.; Derrett, 1968b: 245ff.). In this code the learned author 'recorded the state the *śāstra* had reached' (Derrett, 1968b: 249) by compiling a collection of earlier textual authorities. This scholarly product was not usable in practice, even in English translation,

---

[98] The *Arthaśāstra*, which was only rediscovered in the early years of the twentieth century (Kangle, 1972).

because a British judge could now see for himself that, on any one question under Hindu law, there were many possible textual authorities which disagreed widely on points of detail and sometimes even on basic principles.

This obvious dilemma had several important consequences. First, British efforts to restate traditional Hindu law in codified form were swiftly abandoned. There was manifestly no point in pursuing this flawed strategy, which would have involved much Sanskrit expertise. Construction of case law as a familiar common law technique offered a more productive method of legal development. For some time, though, the court personnel, guided by the *pandits*, waded through this shallow lake of material, making numerous decisions along the way that began to lay down a new precedent-based form of Hindu law, Anglo-Hindu case law. Thus, the British created what Derrett (1977: vii) has called the 'bogusness' of Anglo-Hindu law, a 'hybrid monstrosity' without parallel in the world (Derrett, 1968b: 298). This happened because the indigenous scholar-jurist perhaps did not quite understand the British lawyer's concept of 'law', and vice versa, while both attempted to make the best of the situation – a classic case of failed intercultural communication. The resulting case-law system of binding precedent radically violated the most basic principles of Hindu self-regulated order and of situation-specificity. However, this Anglo-Hindu case-law was officially treated as persuasive and some authors, especially among the emerging Bengali intelligentsia, welcomed judicial precedent as the most important source of Anglo-Hindu law, superseding the unwieldy digests (*nibandhas*) and the numerous commentaries (Sarkar, 1940: 37). The switch to English as the language of Hindu law further reinforced the growing impression, in learned circles and among the wider population, that the official Hindu law was now administered on the lines of a Western law. Insufficient attention was given to the fact that there was much more to Hindu law than this new colonial construct. This strengthened later moves towards codification and further legal intervention by the British-controlled state.

The use of Hindu texts within the British court system also meant that parts of certain texts (prominently the early medieval *Mitākṣarā* and the *Dāyabhāga*) now gained a supra-local authority which they would never have acquired in the indigenous system. Since later texts and commentaries were often more conservative than the early *śāstric* texts, many elements of 'traditional' Hindu law built by the British into the new patchwork system reinforced the growing impression that Hindu law was outdated and in urgent need of reform. Fragments of such texts were built into the system of precedent; only in later years were obvious mistakes discovered (Derrett, 1968b: 301). While some defects were remedied later (Derrett, 1968b: 310 and n. 3), the Indian Supreme Court may still find itself asked to correct an earlier position taken by Anglo-Hindu law (Venkataramiah, 1982).

Ignorance about Hindu law persisted once the indigenous experts were relieved of their duties in 1864. This must have got worse over time. The British judges, often faced with assumed lacunae, had to fill these gaps themselves. While they could still seek help from 'native' experts, an easier method needed to be found, freeing the process of reconstructing Anglo-Hindu law from the shackles and vagaries of Hindu jurisprudence and its fickle representatives. The problem itself was not new, and an early, potent solution had been found: the Administration of Justice Regulation of 5 July 1781 had already introduced Justice, Equity and Good Conscience as a residual source of law. This now became the most important device in the development of Anglo-Hindu law after 1864 (Derrett, 1968b: 289, 311; Derrett, 1978a). Since a judge could under this principle make reference to any legal rule known to him, reference to Justice, Equity and Good Conscience implied, in many cases, the application of rules of English law (Derrett, 1968b: 311). As the judicial personnel began to give up looking for Hindu law sources and turned to guidance from other legal systems, Anglo-Hindu law became still more indebted to English law, but also to Roman law and other legal systems. Even if it had been recognised earlier that local Hindu customs were of major importance (recognised even by Lingat, 1973: 137), it was too late after 1864 to redirect the course of legal history. Inevitably, Anglo-Hindu law had become a court-centred law relying on foreign legal concepts. Derrett (1968b: 311) suggests that this was not a conscious process of planned legal development but evidence of globalising visions:

> This happened frequently even without conscious reference to Justice, Equity and Good Conscience, the residual source of law, since . . . the Judges were not aware that in applying English common law or Equity they were doing anything else but expounding the Hindu law on the point. So many rules of English law seemed to be merely rules of universal law.

The haphazard introduction of fragments of imported law from various sources led to an extremely hybrid system of court-law, an official legal system known only to specialists, while the 'living law' of the Hindus remained quite different. This partly explains the astonishing popularity of Anglo-Hindu law with some Indian litigants: It offered new remedies and alternative strategies to harass one's adversaries and, though the stakes were high, the gamble was often considered worthwhile. As a flood of litigation developed, litigiousness was attributed to Indians by many authors (Derrett, 1968b: 232, 279, 286). Historians of South India have shown that litigation with armies of lawyers now replaced traditional warfare among ruling clans (Dirks, 1987; Price, 1979).

The increasing divergence between customary practice and official law led to an important change: custom was now in competition with case-law and legislation rather than *śāstric* texts as before. Naturally, those in charge of the official legal system preferred to follow the 'letter of the law' rather than vague, unwritten rules based on extremely diverse socio-religious native traditions. Anglo-Hindu law became an élite phenomenon, focused on the written word, an official law in every sense. Thus, the gap between official Hindu law and

Indian society became wider than it could ever have become in traditional contexts. The British administration of justice in India, unaware of the role of every Hindu individual within the *rita/dharma* complex, and only partly knowledgeable about the Hindu ruler's function in maintaining *dharma*, more or less completely stepped out of the Hindu conceptual framework and acted within the conceptual realms of positive and common law, with a sprinkling of natural law ideas. Sensitivity to the indigenous pluralistic harmony of principles governing the interaction of dominant and subordinate legal systems was lacking. Anglo-Hindu law went its own way in searching for justice and moved outside the centre of our conceptual pluralist triangle (chapter 3, section 3.8), veering towards positivism.

The chthonic, culture-specific elements of Hindu law were not entirely disregarded, however, since the importance of custom was recognised and administratively regulated in some places (Lingat, 1973: 137). Importantly, it was judicially fortified in the early case of *Moottoo Ramalinga*,[99] holding that proof of custom would override the written text of Hindu law. After this precedent, Hindu litigants could try to prove that they were not governed by the Anglo-Hindu law in a particular matter, but by custom (Derrett, 1957: 7). Custom, once proved, would totally displace the official Hindu law (p. 27), but there was a strong presumption in favour of the official Hindu law (p. 78). Anglo-Hindu law laid down such stringent conditions for proof of custom that very few managed to become judicially recognised (Desai, 1982: 67f.). Full-scale recognition of custom was not considered a viable option for the official law. Since the British were merely paying lip-service to the principle of upholding custom, and were not really concerned to find out what 'the people' considered to be their law, protests arose. An English judge based in Madras by the name of Nelson, an early warning voice, observed that 'his' local people were following customs that diverged significantly from the emerging official law (Lingat, 1973: 138 and Derrett, 1961). He was silenced.

Subsequent judicial administration purposely ignored the many statements in the ancient texts asking rulers to put the customary laws of their subjects into effect and thus did not act in accordance with the *rita/dharma* expectations surrounding *rājadharma*. It was unrealistic in the circumstances to expect the British to develop a Hindu law based on local custom (Derrett, 1968b: 317), because they would have had to deal with hundreds of different customary legal systems, a problem that also resurfaced in Africa. The reaction, significantly, was further breakdown in legal communication, another meaningful silence, as common Indians had only one way to show their disapproval, namely to avoid recourse to this new law altogether. As Derrett (1986b: 316–17) put it, '[p]ublic opinion had no organ of expression'.

[99] The full citation is *Collector of Madura* v. *Moottoo Ramalinga Sathupathy* (1868) 12 Moore's Indian Appeals 375. On details see Desai (1982: 64–7).

There has been some discussion whether these developments of Hindu law have been beneficial. On the negative side, the spontaneous growth of Hindu law was to some extent stopped by the emergence of the official Anglo-Hindu law (Desai, 1982: 72; Derrett, 1968b: 318). From a lawyer's perspective, '[t]he law became, for all its many anomalies, more certain and much more uniform' (Derrett, 1968b: 316). But such views only take account of the official law. Obviously, 'the great chasm between custom and law remained' (Derrett, 1968b: 305), as Anglo-Hindu law and the actual social realities of Hindu law continued to diverge. While Derrett (1957: 78) emphasised that the British period 'saw the elimination of a great many customs diverging from the Anglo-Hindu law', judicially unrecognised Hindu customs would not thereby cease to exist in social reality. Hindu customary law had become an enormously important and flourishing unofficial law. As the scope for the application of the traditional texts became smaller and smaller, many unresolved questions related to the role of the innumerable customary laws and their relationship with the official law arose. Tackling this challenging task was left to the post-independence government of India.

4.8 Modern Hindu family law in India

On independence (15 August 1947), India inherited an extremely complex legal system characterised by remarkable plurality of laws. While Anglo-Hindu law was earlier turned into an official legal system based mainly on case-law, postcolonial Hindu law is best characterised by the prominence of legislation as a source of official law.[100] But that does not mean modern Indians or the Indian legal system have now wholeheartedly embraced legal positivism. The post-colonial Indian law-makers, so much is evident, did not just copy all kinds of Western laws, as is often assumed, to construct a new state-made family law. The law-makers still knew the old law fairly well and, most importantly, they were aware that it would continue to apply even after the Hindu law had been codified and secularised.[101]

[100] For useful surveys of Indian legal systems see Galanter (1989) and Baxi (1982; 1986). On selected aspects of family law, see Dhagamwar (1989), Diwan (1993), Parashar (1992), Menski (2001; 2003).

[101] An instructive example is the Hindu law on divorce. The wrong but widely supported perception has been that traditional Hindu law did not know divorce, hence modern Hindu law copied this remedy from England. In reality, Hindu law has always been familiar with divorce, but gave it different names (Larivière, 1991) and treated it as an infringement of the *śāstric* ideal of sacramental marriage, something that low-caste people might do. In reality, customary laws on divorce existed in all communities. When modern Hindu law made divorce available to all Hindus, the impression was created that every Hindu divorce now had to go through the courts. However, customary divorces were expressly saved by section 29(2) of the Hindu Marriage Act 1955. The picture 'on the ground' is therefore extremely pluralistic (Holden, 2004).

The restructured plurality included the system of traditional personal laws, with Hindu law as the majority personal law, but also Muslim, Christian, Parsi and Jewish laws as well as an optional secular family law.[102] Buddhists, Jainas and Sikhs are now governed by the codified modern Hindu law, officially to reduce diversities. Sikh protest against this went as far as demanding their own state (Khalistan), while the Jainas seem to have quietly withdrawn from official legal processes and cultivate self-regulation and little is known about how Buddhists reacted. Independent India is treading a difficult but historically familiar path between formal legal uniformity and informal diversity. This helps to explain why Article 44 of the Constitution, requiring the State 'to endeavour to secure' a Uniform Civil Code for the whole of India, has remained a pious declaration, despite continuous rhetoric about the supposed advantages of legal uniformity. The diverse Hindu foundations of modern Indian law, as well as the considerable conceptual input from Muslim law, preclude an easy path of formal uniform legal development in accordance with Western models. Modern Indian law is, and will remain, an Asian legal system in its own right, not an imperfect copy of some Western model. As suggested earlier (Menski, 2001, ch. 6), legal plurality in Indian law will never disappear because it makes sense to retain it in a vast country conscious of its composite legal culture.[103] In this case, pluralism is definitely an asset rather than a liability.

However, modernism privileges legal uniformity and statist centrism. The trend of modernising and unifying Hindu family law had first been promoted by the British during the nineteenth century and was adopted by some sections of the Indian élite, who were instrumental in securing further legislative reforms, particularly the Hindu Women's Right to Property Act of 1937, which gave Hindu widows a 'limited estate' in the share of the deceased husband to ensure their maintenance. Modern India went much further in seeking to modernise and secularise Hindu law.[104] Heated debates about Hindu law reforms took

---

[102] The main provisions of this are now found in the Special Marriage Act 1954.

[103] This was subtly written into the Constitution of India, 1950 through important amendments in 1976. Article 51-A(f) makes it a duty of every citizen of India 'to value and preserve the rich heritage of our composite culture'. The Uniform Civil Code debate continues to excite many commentators: see Khodie (1975), Dhagamwar (1989), Deolekar (1995), Deshta (1995), Khan (1996), Raina (1996), Ratnaparkhi (1997).

[104] However, modernist reformers did not dare abolish the traditional joint Hindu family altogether (Sontheimer, 1977). This only happened in Kerala through the Kerala Joint Hindu Family System (Abolition) Act of 1975. The Hindu Succession Act of 1956 goes much beyond the 1937 Act and secures, on paper at least, greater rights for Hindu females as absolute owners of property that used to be joint family property earlier. Section 14 of the 1956 Act made widows absolute owners of any share they previously held as a 'limited estate', leading to thousands of cases filed by enraged males, including many Sikhs. The transition from joint family ownership to individual property rights was never complete, and postmodern Indian law (section 4.10) has begun to rediscover the role and value of the joint family as the most basic element of social welfare.

place prior to independence and during the 1950s; they are well documented (Derrett, 1957; 1970). Closely linked to this are vigorous discussions about the position and future of India's various personal laws (Mahmood, 1986; Agnes, 2000; Parashar, 1992). It is a hallmark of modern legal reform in South Asia that the majority personal law is tackled first, so in India Hindu law was subjected to reform, while in Pakistan legal reforms were introduced for Muslim family laws (chapter 5, section 5.14).

Immediately after independence, vigorous debates about the future of Hindu law resulted in the preparation of what is often misleadingly called the 'Hindu Code' (Derrett, 1957). However, this ambitious project of comprehensive codification (which also involved much Westernisation) was defeated and instead India created four separate Acts of Parliament which regulate most aspects of modern Hindu family law.[105] These Acts are not a comprehensive code, and do not even purport to abolish the entire old Hindu law. They represent an uneasy compromise between tradition and modernity, abolishing polygamy for example, but retaining the traditional law on Hindu marriages. Apart from legal uniformisation, the agenda of secularism indicate that law was assumed to be a magic tool to create a nation.[106] In family law, while awaiting the implementation of a Uniform Civil Code, the modernist expectation included the gradual creation of secularised, modernised Hindu law.[107] This reformist approach, initially pursued in a spirit of post-colonial euphoria, has led to enormous tension between uniformity and diversity, official legal regulation emanating from various power centres and the spontaneity of India's many communities, and between official law and unofficial law, state law and people's law. To understand this legal labyrinth from a globality-focused perspective, one has to look well beyond official law reports and statutes. While the real differences

---

[105] These are the Hindu Marriage Act 1955, the Hindu Succession Act 1956, the Hindu Adoptions and Maintenance Act 1956 and the Hindu Minority and Guardianship Act 1956.

[106] This concept, in modern Indian law, does not mean the same as in Western countries (i.e. legal rules are not to be determined by religion, but by the state). The Indian concept of secularism arose from historical awareness of plurality of religions and their co-existence in the socio-political field. Hence, the new leaders of India (initially of Pakistan as well) used this concept to promise religious minorities that they would not be treated as second-class citizens. In India, 'secularism' therefore means first of all equidistance, equal respect by the state for all religions, as a *grundnorm* of the modern Indian state and a basic value that the Indian Constitution protects. This has been so more explicitly since 1976, despite multiple political disturbances. The experience and memory of massive ethnic cleansing on the basis of religion following independence on 14–15 August 1947 still haunts many people. Since the multi-ethnic, multi-religious nature of the Indian polity needs constant vigilant protection, religion cannot be denied a role as a legal force, but it needs to be kept under control.

[107] In this specific context, 'secular' has its usual Western meaning, indicating that Indian discourses are partly confused about the relevant terminology. On secularism see Madan (1987; 1994), Baird (1989; 1993), Shourie (1993a, 1993b).

between personal laws are now small,[108] politicised sloganeering has constantly overplayed them, working with simplistic models to fool everyone. The secular framework of the Constitution, which does not easily permit a religiously coloured legal discourse, creates massive silences (Sathe and Narayan, 2003).

It is now obvious that the extensive reforms to modern Hindu law in India during the 1950s were partly designed along an outrightly reformist path. The initial aim, of some reformers,[109] was to secularise modern Hindu law to such an extent that it might eventually become acceptable to all Indians. This hidden uniformising agenda was later reinforced by the Hindu Marriage (Amendment) Act 1964 and the Marriage Laws (Amendment) Act of 1976, in particular. Both Acts created further harmony with the provisions of the secular general law of the Special Marriage Act of 1954. However, this strategy of artificial uniformisation has not worked in practice, as it turned out to be intrinsically hostile to women and children and assuming gender equality in a patriarchal setting created new legal problems (Derrett, 1978b). Further, the modernist ideology of legal uniformisation collapsed as soon as the Hindu nationalist BJP rose to prominence in the 1990s and many people realised that insisting on a Uniform Civil Code could now turn into demands for imposing Hindu law on all Indians. Since then, the Indian debates over unification of family laws have partially subsided and there are significant new developments (section 4.10).

This particular uniformisation strategy was bound to fail for many other reasons, one of which is central to the present conceptual analysis. The modern statutory system of Hindu law still contains structural elements that negate the possibility of total legal uniformity in Hindu law. In a sense, the past as legal tradition (Glenn, 2004) slipped back into the framework of modern legal provisions, which themselves accepted that the past had a useful role to play. Recent recourse to many old Hindu concepts is therefore not a mistake or an oversight, but perhaps even a calculated element of modernist legal reform, suggesting that the law-makers themselves were aware that the modern statute law could not completely replace the old order. The instrumentalist use of legal positivism to reform Hindu law points to a modified strategy and strain of legal positivism, not its 'pure' Western-style variety. This is crucial evidence to demonstrate that complex family law systems like modern Hindu law cannot simply be reformed along Western lines of supposedly global standards.

---

[108] The most prominent examples cited are always that Muslims in India may have up to four wives and can pronounce an instant *talaq*. But Hindu polygamists benefit from lenient implementation of the relevant law, which should put polygamists in jail for up to seven years, but has ended up administering the consequences of Hindu polygamy (Menski, 2001). Hindu men have also found it much easier over the years to engineer divorces (Derrett, 1978b), so there are no real legal differences left and the Hindu/Muslim legal contrast is just politically exploited.

[109] Dr Ambedkar and those who followed him wanted to radically de-hinduise Hindu law and give it a secular shape.

To do so, and to rid themselves of 'custom' through ignoring the socio-legal part of the conceptual triangle (chapter 3, section 3.8) means depriving one's own people of finely balanced pluralist legal mechanisms, including methods of socio-economic survival through family solidarity and principles of visible and invisible interlinkedness. It appears that the Indian law-makers wisely realised the perils of individualised atomisation for the masses and combined legal positivist strategies with explicit recognition of local socio-cultural norms. Therefore, Indian legal positivism explicitly accounts for social norms as well as local values within the legislative provisions. The positivist corner of the triangle of Indian law is not only composed of positivist law, but contains elements of natural law and of socio-legal concerns. It constitutes a deliberate plurality-conscious construct that is impossible to understand through superficial positivist analysis.

At first sight, the picture seems modern, reform-focused and uniform: on paper, polygamy was banned for Hindus,[110] divorce on many fault grounds and later by mutual consent was introduced for Hindus,[111] and reformist euphoria ruled for some time.[112] But reality is much more complex. There is only space for one example here. Solid evidence of recycling old substantive rules, found in the modern garb of statutory regulation, comes from the analysis of how the modern Hindu law on marriage solemnisation and registration was dealt with. At first sight, it looks modern and Westernised in its codified form, but it actually preserves the diversity-conscious, situation-specific methods of the old Hindu law *in toto*. Section 7 of the Hindu Marriage Act 1955 regulates the solemnisation of Hindu marriages and provides:

7. Ceremonies for a Hindu marriage

(1) A Hindu marriage may be solemnized in accordance with the customary rites and ceremonies of either party thereto.

(2) Where such rites and ceremonies include the *saptapadi* (that is, taking of seven steps by the bridegroom and the bride jointly before the sacred fire), the marriage becomes complete and binding when the seventh step is taken.

The first sub-section shows that the legal validity of a Hindu marriage in modern India is not determined by recourse to procedures introduced by the state, but the relevant criteria are still found within the old Hindu system of marriage solemnisation with all its inherent pluralities. Thus, customary Hindu tradition still rules the roost, and the modern state has merely fitted the old *śāstric* law into statutory form, but has not changed its substance nor challenged its universal validity. It has thus become important for Hindu litigants, in case of

---

[110] For details see Menski (2001, ch. 3; 2003, ch. 10).
[111] For details see Menski (2001, ch. 2; 2003, ch. 11).
[112] Doubts began to surface during the late 1970s: see especially Derrett (1978b).

doubt, to be able to prove that they followed the respective customary norms of marriage solemnisation. The role of custom as a source of law has thereby been explicitly respected by modern statutory Hindu law, and custom was built into the modern statute. This, too, was achieved in an articulate, plurality-conscious fashion which recycles tradition in a surprisingly liberal manner. Section 3 of the Hindu Marriage Act of 1955 provides:

> 3. Definitions
> In this Act unless the context otherwise requires—
>
> (a) the expressions 'custom' and 'usage' signify any rule which, having been continuously and uniformly observed for a long time, has obtained the force of law among Hindus in any local area, tribe, community, group or family:
> Provided that the rule is certain and not unreasonable or opposed to public policy and provided further that in the case of a rule applicable only to a family it has not been discontinued by the family . . .

The major issue here is that a legally valid custom under the newly codified Hindu law need no longer be, as under the strict and hostile Anglo-Hindu law (section 4.7), a custom observed 'since time immemorial' but only, as seen above, 'for a long time'. How long, then, is 'long'? This has been the subject of many extremely instructive cases.[113] This debate is highly relevant to a globally focused analysis of legal regulation in modern Hindu law. Modern Hindu law on marriage solemnisation, given that marriage is a key element of society, continues to measure the legal validity of a Hindu marriage not by modern criteria provided by state law, such as registration of marriage,[114] but by recourse to traditional socio-cultural norms. This does not mean that religion is treated as superior to law, but it is evident that legal positivism, in its manifestation as modern Hindu law, takes account of socio-cultural factors and thus is explicitly concerned to include the socio-legal angle of our conceptual triangle to achieve

---

[113] Detailed research (Menski, 2001; 2003) uncovered two lines of judicial decisions, one of which reflects patriarchal interference with basic gender justice through positivist impositions, while the other approach accounts for customary plurality and sensitivity to socio-cultural factors. The opposing poles are represented by the misguided precedent of *Bhaurao Shankar Lokhande* v. *State of Maharashtra*, AIR 1965 SC 1564 and by *Sumitra Devi* v. *Bhikhan Choudhary*, AIR 1985 SC 765. Legal insecurity continues, even among overseas Hindus, because of more recent inadequate decisions, in particular *Surjit Kaur* v. *Garja Singh*, AIR 1994 SC 135. Clearly, local practice proved to exist over a few decades qualifies for official legal recognition, especially if many people are involved, as in the neo-Buddhist case of *Baby* v. *Jayant*, AIR 1981 Bombay 283. New customs can thus be built into the modern statutory law, which explicitly allows for such dynamism.

[114] Section 8(5) of the Hindu Marriage Act of 1955 provides that '[n]otwithstanding anything contained in this section, the validity of any Hindu marriage shall in no way be affected by the omission to make the entry'. This means that the modern Indian state (like many states in Asia and Africa) accepts that the ultimate legal criterion of legal validity of a marriage remains a matter for society.

situation-specific justice. Modern Hindu law thus silently admitted that there are limits to statist positivism and did not fuss about preserving religious tradition. One could interpret this as recognition of tradition or as the consequence of resource limitations, but probably both factors have played a role. Surely, this is not an oversight or a slippage. How could the modern Indian state even begin to monitor comprehensively and reliably how several hundred million people marry in their homes? Any bureaucratic solution would be out of the question.[115] The ancient model of self-regulated order was accepted by India's postcolonial positivists as a useful ingredient for reconstructing modern Hindu law.

This conclusion is well supported by many other elements of modern Hindu family law (Menski, 2001). A brief look at sub-section 7(2) of the Hindu Marriage Act, as cited above, helps to bring out another dimension of the complex interaction between ancient legal order and modern legal system. The assumption of the modern statute clearly is that the Hindu ritual of *saptapadi*, which may be executed in many different ways, or not at all, depending on custom, shall be the precise point at which a Hindu marriage becomes legally valid and binding. This would mean that the legal validity of the contract of Hindu marriage,[116] at least in cases where the seven step ritual is performed, can be pinpointed to a specific time. It is remarkable that this rule was copied directly from *Manusmriti* 8.227, where it had the obvious function, in the context of contract law, to suggest precisely when a Hindu marriage should become binding.[117] The sacramental Hindu contract of marriage, according to the *Manusmriti* as well as section 7(2) of the Hindu Marriage Act, is completed on the seventh step of this particular ritual. Manifestly, the new legal order has just recycled the old law, even if such use of tradition may carry particular risks.

Attempted abuse first arose when some Hindu husbands started to argue that, because they had not performed the ritual of *saptapadi*, they were not

---

[115] It remains an option for the élite or those who require official documentation (to go abroad, for example) to register their marriages, but registered Hindu marriages by themselves are not treated as legally valid in India, a fact which has recently caused some surprise in several European embassies. See *Joyita Saha* v. *Rajesh Kumar Pandey*, AIR 2000 Cal 109 and Mody (2002).

[116] Contrary to almost every textbook on the subject, emphasising only the sacramental nature of Hindu marriage, a Hindu marriage is clearly both a solemn contract and a sacrament.

[117] The verse stipulates that the performance of some rituals, and the use of *mantras*, are an indication that Hindu marriage rituals are being performed, but the decisive ritual in terms of legal validity shall be the seventh step of the *saptapadi*. One can envisage many situations where it would be crucial to know when precisely a marriage was legally valid. What if the prolonged marriage rituals were disrupted by raiders and the groom was killed? Was the bride now a widow, or was she capable of undergoing a fully ritualised idealised virgin marriage to another man? Not only common sense, but concern for the *rita/dharma* complex demanded a clear answer. Notably, the dominant criterion was not virginity, but ritual status.

validly married, and thus had no legal obligations towards a woman or her heirs who made claims (mostly related to property or maintenance) based on such marriage.[118] Such legal mischief was aided and abetted by some judges, mainly high-caste tradition-fixated male black-letter lawyers lacking plurality-consciousness, even in the Supreme Court, who read into section 7(2) that it required every Hindu couple to have undergone a *saptapadī*.[119] That was neither the rule of ancient Hindu law, which left the matter to local custom, nor correct statutory interpretation, given the unambiguous wording of section 7(2). The battle over this issue continues in India today, since patriarchy and crafty lawyers are not easily silenced, and some litigants will misuse the law if they see a chance of success. Significantly, modern Hindu law applies (as did the old law) a strong presumption of marriage, as authoritatively stated in one of the leading hand-books for practitioners, Mulla's *Principles of Hindu law* (Desai, 2004: 770–1):

> Where it is proved that a marriage was performed in fact, the court will presume that it is valid in law, and that the necessary ceremonies have been performed . . . There is an extremely strong presumption in favour of the validity of a marriage and the legitimacy of its offspring, if from the time of the alleged marriage, the parties are recognised by all persons concerned as man and wife and are so described in important documents and on important occasions. The like presumption applies to the question whether the formal requisites of a valid marriage ceremony were satisfied.

This reinforces another key argument in the present analysis of modern Hindu law as a reconstructed version of ancient Hindu law in modern garb. Modern Hindu law, like the old system, has to rely ultimately on judicial alertness, the skill of judges in 'extracting the thorn' (*vyavahāra*) in relation to dispute-processing. The primary function of the modern judge continues to involve removing social hurts or injustices, to secure justice above all, and not simply to apply the modern statute blindly by enforcing positivist law without considering the facts and circumstances of the case. The ancient Hindu method of working on a situation-specific, case-by-case basis, application of the *dharmic grundnorm*, remains pertinent in Hindu law today. A reading

---

[118] Indian law successfully counters such obfuscation by liberal application of presumptions of marriage.

[119] The leading case, now thoroughly discredited, but still cited as an authority by mischievous lawyers, is *Bhaurao Shankar Lokhande* v. *State of Maharashtra*, AIR 1965 SC 1564, asserting that every Hindu marriage must involve a *saptapadī* and invocation of the fire to be legally recognised. This is not what section 7(2) of the 1955 Act says, and has led to blatant injustice, as *Surjit Kaur* v. *Garja Singh*, AIR 1994 SC 135, demonstrates. Here, male chauvinist contempt for a remarried Sikh woman, slandering her in order to grab property, did not strike the two Hindu judges as blatant abuse of the modern law by what ancient Hindu law perceptively called 'sharks'. For excellent examples of judicial alertness, see *M. Govindaraju* v. *K. Munisami Gounder*, AIR 1997 SC 10 and *P. Mariammal* v. *Padmanabhan*, AIR 2001 Madras 350.

of modern Hindu family law through the lenses of the old law thus contains many lessons for comparative lawyers and for global legal theory. Regrettably most modernist observers cannot perceive Hindu law in this way, as it requires respect for traditional Hindu concepts, which are unfortunately branded as politically incorrect. In the context of a globally focused legal analysis, however, away from the Indian politics of religion, culture and community, it remains imperative to keep an open mind.

A positivist summary of the main sources of official modern Hindu law would find that these are now legislation and precedent, and only to a very limited extent custom and the traditional textual provisions. But a deeper, plurality-conscious analysis of modern Indian law suggests a different hierarchy of norms in working out the 'living law' (Ehrlich, 1936). Hindu natural law is still in evidence through the values and ethics permeating society. Since the conceptual realm of the *rita/dharma* complex was not superseded by the new positivist Hindu law, who or what actually decides, at the end of the day, whether something is right or wrong, and what should be the solution to particular problems arising at any specific time? Evidently, such matters are still decided and worked out within the social realm. We are merely asking the same questions today as the ancient Hindus thousands of years ago, long before legal positivism became a domineering influence. The answer given in the ancient tradition was clearly that there is a method of ascertaining *dharma* and finding justice which has several elements and strategies within itself (section 4.3). The question to ask in the context of a globally focused jurisprudential analysis must be whether the old answers given by Hindu tradition still have validity today.

To test this proposition, we are thrown back to the ancient techniques of ascertaining one's *dharma*. The individual examination of one's conscience (*ātmanastushti*) and the search for guidance or a good model within one's peer group, family or local environment (*sadācāra*) are clearly timeless universals. In India today, these informal self-ordering processes remain prominent, much as before, at the individual and local level, whether with explicit reference to *sadācāra*, or simply by relying on what is today considered just and proper. We may safely conclude that these two techniques of ancient Hindu law have remained valuable tools for today's legal processes, and will continue to do so.

Yet, difficulties arise over the other processes of ascertaining *dharma* today. In the old system, ultimate recourse was supposed to be taken to *smriti* texts and guidance by those who knew them, and then finally to *śruti*, Vedic revelation. Section 4.3 above demonstrated that these two sources were probably always of less practical relevance. This cannot be really different today. While the formal effect of British and modern Indian interventions in Hindu law has been to replace recourse to *smriti* and *śruti* with the application of modern codified Hindu law, including case law, the old law and its processes have not gone away. In a typical reflection of legal centralism and positivist ideology, the official assumption may now well be that modern Hindus are first of all bound by modern statutory laws. If they have a legal problem, they should turn to modern state laws, and not traditional sources. However, such legal centralist claims do not match with social reality: as before, most Hindus do not turn straight to lawyers or courts, they first negotiate within their respective socio-cultural spheres. Even if they eventually turn to the Indian state and its modernised Hindu laws, the official law itself refers Hindus back to their own customs and local processes for dispute settlement and ascertainment of what is appropriate, as shown above. The same happens to a very large extent in Hindu divorce law,[120] though sometimes the courts have had to intervene to separate the warring parties.[121]

The complex, conceptually mature nature of modern Hindu family law is beginning to become more apparent as we understand better today how the modern Indian state manages to regulate modern Hindu family law in a uniquely hybrid manner, constructing a social welfare system in the process (Menski, 2001). The strategically wise and financially prudent reliance of the modern Hindu law on self-control mechanisms from within society confirms that modern Hindu family law is definitely not built on a primary assumption that total legal control of society can be exercised by state-made law. We could speak of 'soft legal centralism' or 'soft positivism' here. The critical element for present analytical purposes is that modern Hindu family law has continued to delegate much legal authority to society. Crucially, it seems to trust society to evolve solutions that will avoid recourse to formal dispute settlement and yet produce just results, thus keeping social harmony and securing basic rights for all citizens. The 'soft positivism' of modern India is able to trust the social sphere, it seems, because both have been sharing the same social space and awareness of ancient legal tradition and are sensitised to each other. We see here how deeply a 'semi-autonomous social field' (Moore, 1978) can influence the development of formal modern law. The mutually beneficial collaboration between the old order and the new dispensation is clearly a plurality-conscious reconstruction within Indian Hindu law. The inevitable result of this strategic alliance must be that the modern state law has thereby delegated a considerable amount of legal authority to the social sphere. Where does this leave the Indian Constitution and 'rule of law' if India's modern judges, at the end of the day, are rather like the ancient *śāstric* expert or adviser, who only enters the arena when social relations have seriously broken down, and when expert help is required?

[120] This is a huge and complex area (for details see Menski, 2001; 2003). A recent study on Hindu customary divorce and women's agency in remarriage proves that official law and socio-legal reality are often wide apart (Holden, 2004).

[121] The disgust of modern Indian judges with a Hindu couple who would not stop washing their dirty linen in court is elaborately expressed in *V. Bhagat* v. *D. Bhagat*, AIR 1994 SC 710, which changed the judicial approach to irretrievable breakdown of a Hindu marriage as a ground for divorce, allowing it in exceptional circumstances without opening the floodgates. Significantly, the husband in this case was a senior lawyer.

4.9 Hindu legal concepts and the Indian Constitution

One might have expected the analysis of modern Hindu law in India to end with the examination of modern Hindu family law and its eventual secularisation and de-Hinduisation. To modernists, it seemed, there was nothing more to say about the secular Indian Constitution and the general Indian legal system in relation to Hindu law. However, a plurality-conscious analysis of Hindu law must dig deeper to uncover some of the complex legal realities which challenge the globalising and uniformising claims of strong legal positivism in Indian laws. The present section explores to what extent Hindu law has also remained a much more important ingredient of modern Indian constitutional law than the modern state and modernist writers would readily want to concede. Clearly, the realities of 'soft legal positivism' in Indian family law impact on the whole legal system and offer a blueprint for sophisticated legal development, even if this partially undermines positivist and uniformising claims and endangers various fictions of secularism.

This section demonstrates that Indian constitutional law, too, is deeply influenced by traditional Indian and often explicitly Hindu concepts of governance. This may not have been intended when the current system was first put into place, since the roots extend to the colonial period.[122] However, especially since the late 1970s, Indian constitutional law has experienced what may be called a plurality-conscious re-indigenisation. My first argument here is that the modern secular Indian law is secular only in terms of the constitutionally prescribed legal non-discrimination against non-Hindus which is a *grundnorm* of the modern Indian state that certainly requires vigorous protection. It is the vision of a nation in which all citizens, irrespective of religion, should be able to live together under one rule of law.[123] However, the legal stipulation of Indian secularism, suggesting that all kinds of Indian citizens should be equal before the law, really means that Hindus as an overwhelming majority of the population are not superior to anyone else – the Hindu majority is legally required to respect the equal rights of non-Hindus. Many Hindus have begun to notice this anti-majoritarian rule and some have reacted, defensively and even violently, in what may be called *hindutva* fashion. That apart, if this is indeed the real underlying message of Indian secularism, there is simply no contradiction between India's unique policy of secularism and new legal developments that recognise an important place for traditional Indian socio-cultural and legal concepts, even more specifically Hindu legal concepts, in the interpretative reconstruction of India's secular Constitution.

There can be no doubt that Indian constitutional law has always been deeply infused with Indian values and concepts, while the formal body of the modern

---

[122] In particular, the Government of India Act 1935 which forms a strong base of the Indian Constitution of 1950.

[123] On theory and practice of the rule of law in India, see Baxi (2004).

Constitution is a complex hybrid of provisions adapted from all over the world.[124] There can also be no doubt that India's composite culture is to a large extent influenced by Hindu concepts. The previous section showed that the Indian Constitution allows for the continuation of personal laws and merely gives notice, through Article 44, of the modernist agenda of eventual uniformisation. Since according to modernists the co-existence of general and personal laws perpetuates legal inequality, about fifty years after the introduction of the Constitution, the now seriously strained argument continues to be that there should be a secular Uniform Civil Code (Dhagamwar, 1989; 2003) and that the modernist constitutional promise should be kept and implemented (Kumar, 2003). Section 4.10 below demonstrates that significant recent legal developments in Indian family laws have been ignored by such commentators, who should know better, but are blinded by legocentric perspectives.

The second and central argument here is that, over the past few decades, the indigenous nature of modern India's Constitution has gradually become more obvious and has visibly and invisibly been reinforced. This happened because modernist, positivist models and strategies failed to produce the desired socio-legal results that the new legal order of independent India had been promising to all citizens. Equality has not been achieved, poverty has not been abolished, justice is still not safely guaranteed, the state itself (in its various manifestations) continues to be the biggest violator of law (Ahuja, 1997). After initial euphoric assessments, a hard look at reality during the 1970s showed that the entire legal system faced a fundamental crisis. This culminated in Indira Gandhi's Emergency from 1975 to 1977, a momentous and cathartic phase of Indian national development, during which Indian constitutional law was dramatically restructured, occasionally by explicit reference to Hindu concepts, which one can interpret as injections of Hindu-inspired self-cleansing mechanisms.[125] The evidence, discussed further below, supports a further major argumentative strand in the present globally focused analysis. Not only are the so-called religious and personal laws of Asian and African countries showing a resilience that opposes all major positivist assumptions about legal modernity, progress and the superiority of the 'rule of law'. The evidence now indicates, at least from the perspective of modern Indian constitutional law, that these 'traditional' laws and their socio-cultural norms are clawing back territory that seemed lost earlier and have also infiltrated and hence (from a legocentrist perspective) undermined and subverted modern state laws in Asia and Africa.

[124] On the Indian Constitution see Austin (1966); on questions of secularism see Larson (2001).
[125] Modernist analysts tend to overlook this dimension: see Iyer (2000). It is also not considered to what extent Indian developments at this time were influenced by the Chinese Cultural Revolution (chapter 7, section 7.6.1) and its related agenda of restraining a new emerging elite.

Arising from such observations, the crucial question for a globally focused jurisprudential analysis must be whether these new developments are conducive to justice, or are maldevelopments that need to be controlled through more intensive modernist legal intervention.[126] We know what the answer to this question from a legal positivist and modernist position would be, there is no silence here, rather a lot of noise and pompous claims about the power of law: in the global, intercultural battlefield of competing legal concepts and assumptions, 'tradition' is denigrated by modernist posturing and positivist assertions (Mattei, 2001). However, we have now gone well beyond earlier battles over tradition and modernity (Menski, 2003) and the limits of law are a reality that needs to be built into plurality-conscious global analysis.

More difficult to handle is the assertion that the main concern for global jurisprudence must remain justice itself, in all its variant socio-cultural and legal manifestations, for what is justice? Putting this concern at the centre would privilege natural law approaches, but these are dangerously contaminated either by excessive reliance on religious authority or by excessive secular idealism and always need to be tested in social environments. In India, positivism has clearly lost credibility and has limited moral authority: insistence on simple 'rule of law' arguments and/or globally uniform standards of human rights sounds somewhat absurd for the Indian legal system, which fails to take care of hundreds of millions of people living below the poverty line.[127] How does one protect the rights of those who have no means to assert them? Many debates have been conducted, and they will continue. In a futuristic study, Baxi (2002: vi) notes that human rights 'are not the *gifts of the West to the Rest*', and argues that '[t]he local, not the global . . . remains the crucial site for the enunciation, implementation, enjoyment, and exercise of human rights' (p. 89). Similarly, religio-centric natural law approaches would inevitably lead to global clashes and communal disasters in the subcontinent, sponsoring either saffron-clad Hindu dictatorship in India, or barely concealed religious fundamentalism as in neighbouring Pakistan and now in Bangladesh. These are definitely not viable options for countries with a proud tradition (albeit constantly smirched) of respect for composite co-existence of different communities and cultures.

That leaves us to consider the third element of the global legal triangle, socio-legal approaches. Left to dominate, this would induce the collapse and destruction of an intricately constructed nation state that is as much the result of historical accidents as a legal and economic reality today, a huge internal market and an increasingly powerful global economic player. An India composed of Mahatma Gandhi's envisioned village republics is not a realistic option either,

---

[126] Anxieties over this issue underlie many worthy academic studies, too numerous to list here. However, much of this 'activist' writing lacks plurality-consciousness and is outrightly partisan.

[127] Jaswal (1996: vii) poignantly notes that 'excellence comes only after existence'.

as such an India would not be able to compete in a global economic context. All of this leads to the conclusion that modern India needs a sensible state, a soft and yet strong central state that can play its rightful role in the global international arena and can assert itself also vis-à-vis its component parts. But to what extent is this possible without empowering the state too far so that it abuses its powers and exploits positivism? What is the concept of the Indian state? Clearly, this must be the subject of another book, and much debate about this central issue is needed; this is a seriously neglected area.

Here, we can only scratch the surface and raise some pertinent issues in the context of a plurality-focused global legal analysis. As indicated, something happened in India between 1975 and 1977 that demonstrated to Indian leaders, and the judges of the Supreme Court, that strong legal positivism and modernist instrumentalism by itself was also not a sustainable tool for mature modern Indian legal development. It was evident that the initial modernist approach favoured the rich and powerful, underwriting huge abuses of law by the elite and by the state itself. This abuse of positivist modernism needed to be curtailed. The process through which this self-cleansing was achieved turned out to be the dreadful, much-misunderstood event of the Emergency imposed by Mrs Indira Gandhi, then Prime Minister of India, the major crisis point of Indian governance to date. A legal interpretation of Mrs Gandhi's role, from the perspective of traditional Hindu law, is that she acted as the archetypal classical Hindu ruler by wielding the threatening *danda*, telling everyone to get their house in order, above all questioning the efficiency of the modern legal system in delivering justice to all Indians. It is of course self-contradictory that this had to be done through imposing an Emergency, which also undoubtedly had other agenda (Tarlo, 2002). The damning self-critique of Indian postcolonial development, straight from the top of the positivist pyramid, especially of massive misuse of law by lawyers and politicians, shocked the nation, but also led to significant ameliorative action. By showing everyone that the entire legal and political system could just be dismantled through an Emergency, and that positivism could indeed be its own worst enemy, this modern 'Mother India' taught everyone ancient Hindu law: power, too, is relative and interlinked, and it needs to be controlled. Those in power cannot just do what they want, they are supposed to be accountable to the nation and its collective good. This was giving the nation, without saying it in so many words,[128] a practical lesson in *rājadharma*, illustrating abuse of power through her own action, as much as by punishing others who had forgotten the ancient lessons of interlinked responsibility and accountability. Of course, many lawyers and commentators

---

[128] Silence about the input of something like 'Asian values' (Peerenboom, 2004) and specifically of Hindu norms must be explained as strategic. Mrs Gandhi was certainly concerned to protect her credentials as a modernist reformer and knew that she could not avoid being caricatured as a Hindu despot. Speaking openly about Hindu cultural elements in relation to law would simply have been unwise. Actions speak louder than words.

saw only abuse of the rule of law as Mrs Gandhi bullied India into examining and changing its culture-specific path of legal development by more explicitly introducing Hindu concepts, in terms of both substance and procedure. The significantly reconfigured post-Emergency Indian constitutional legal system combines multiple recourse to Hindu concepts with showing how modern globalised law can indeed be culturally restructured and localised to face the challenges of the future. This is what I see as postmodern Indian law, an intricate combination of old and new, no longer blind belief in the modernist axioms of instrumentalism, linear progress and the unique power of legal positivism (see further section 4.10 below).

Earlier developments had seemed to put India on the road to following the West. Anglophilic Indians, often Bengalis (who claim longer exposure to British influences than other Indians) have proudly boasted that 'almost the entire legal system of India is today based on English law' (Banerjee, 1984: 288). However, what does 'based on English law' really mean? While the Indian Constitution is written in English, the UK does not even have a written constitution that could have provided a model for India – the image itself is faulty and the Indians manifestly chose *not* to copy English law and English blueprints like the famed Westminster model. It is certainly also no longer as true as a few decades ago that the Indian courts 'often appeal to English precedents' (Banerjee, 1984: 288) in interpreting constitutional and other legal provisions.[129] English constitutional law is now only relevant to modern Indian law as a matter of comparative interest, despite learned assertions to the contrary (Sathe, 2002). While the links in commercial law have remained strong, post-Emergency Indian constitutional developments continue to irritate foreign commercial interests. In many respects, however, Indian public law is today well ahead of Western counterparts in its explicit thinking about relative and absolute justice, because it has to deal with a very different socio-legal and demographic set-up than Western countries and has to protect the nation against foreign neo-colonial subjugation. Rather than copying Western models, a reverse process of learning should occur, therefore, and becomes possible when judges and scholars from different jurisdictions meet.[130]

[129] Much evidence of post-colonial reconstruction could be adduced. For example, the Indian courts have explicitly rejected English precedents in tort law with specific reference to liability for pollution. See *M. C. Mehta and another* (1987) 1 SCC 395. For comments on the value of foreign decisions for Indian courts see *Forasol* v. *Oil & Natural Gas Commission*, AIR 1984 SC 241, at 259.

[130] Some recent reforms in English law appear to have borrowed Indian concepts, but this will hardly be admitted officially, since the flow of models of 'good practice' is supposed to be the other way (chapter 1, section 1.2.3). Drobnig and van Erp (1999: ix) indicate that judges are beginning to recognise the usefulness of comparative law, but their study also emphasises the many barriers of communication. Larson (2001) points to promising initiatives of US–Indian exchanges. Jacobsohn (2003) compares India, Israel and the USA.

The tremendous initial reformist euphoria for restructuring the Indian legal system along Western lines has never been unopposed or unquestioned. As a result, modern Indian law has always been a hybrid conglomerate of many models. However, after the cathartic experience of Mrs Gandhi's Emergency, there has been a significant increase in recourse to traditional Indian legal concepts. One might be tempted to say that these are not traditions, rather re-inventions, but the models were actually 'in the air' as a floating tradition, they just needed to be used, and Mrs Gandhi knew this only too well.

It was indicated earlier that the re-traditionalisation of modern Indian law went hand in hand with a conscious and vocal rejection of Western models and legal rules. This trend was wisely foreseen by Professor Derrett in the 1970s. He noted that prominent Supreme Court judges like V. R. Krishna Iyer were turning their back on the 'Anglophilic bias in Bharat's justice, equity and good conscience', arguing that 'free India has to find its conscience in our rugged realities and no more in alien legal thought' (cited in Derrett, 1977: xxi). Much stronger judicial statements have been made in the past few years and whole new areas of law have been developed in India, outwardly built on secular rhetoric and human rights principles, but more firmly founded on indigenous concepts of justice.[131] Such new developments focus on duties rather than rights, on accountability in terms of 'public interest', which one can read as a modern translation of reference to a higher order in the classical Hindu sense, rather than the private interest of an individualistic and rights-based modern jurisprudence.

To analyse modern Indian constitutional law, therefore, has become a task for indologists or specialists in religious studies as much as for lawyers; neither can quite succeed without the assistance of the other, and interdisciplinarity is necessary. But regrettably such interdisciplinary co-operation has remained undeveloped. Only few studies (O'Flaherty and Derrett, 1978; to some extent Dhagamwar, 1992; Larson, 2001) attempt to combine the two approaches, while most legal writing follows the black letter tradition and legal centralism, which is easier on the author and on readers than complex critical analysis.[132] In earlier decades, when the possibility of a 'return' to Indian idioms had begun to raise its head, Professor Gledhill poignantly warned in his Inaugural Lecture at SOAS in

---

[131] Mr Justice V.R. Krishna Iyer, one of the major judicial pioneers of this movement, said in a lecture in London during the early 1980s that he would have been ridiculed if he had cited Hindu law principles while introducing public interest litigation into Indian law. Referring to American cases, he earned praise and international recognition, but in his mind he connected the American concepts and their Hindu equivalents and found the Indian principles more solid and endurable. This confirms that even the finest thinkers about Asian values are forced to remain silent before a wider public.

[132] Earlier criticism of insufficient analysis is found in Baxi (1982; 1986). Recent writing from India, however interesting, does not show much improvement. See e.g. Verma and Kusum (2000), Kirpal et al. (2000), Noorani (2000), Anand (2002).

1955 that strengthening Hindi as a national language in India at the expense of English would cause multiple damage, not only to British interests. Remarkably, Gledhill (1956: 19) also sympathised with Indian lawyers, who would have to bear the brunt, since '[t]he change will bear hardly on the present generation of judges and lawyers, who think about law in English'.

Indira Gandhi, however, must have thought about law in Hindi. Despite all her selfishness and personal interest that numerous critics have identified, she never forgot that she was Prime Minister of a country relying on ancient Indian cultural norms. She saw her duties to the nation, and to the system as a whole, not just its élites. Compared to outside observers like Gledhill, she felt the pulse of her nation more directly. Certainly, there can be no doubt that she understood the power of the ballot box and sought to manipulate it. Perhaps this, too, explains why she had learnt to think about all Indians, not just propertied men, lawyers and judges – even the most recent elections demonstrated the massive power of 'backward' rural voters as equal citizens when it comes to elections. Her most famous electoral slogan, *garībī hatāo* ('banish poverty!'), was probably more than just a political slogan. It was also evidence of concern for the most disadvantaged,[133] as well as a manifesto of better development that could not be implemented unless the ancient concept of inevitable interlinkedness and responsibility for 'the other' was practised. The desperately poor, everyone knew, would not be able to help themselves out of their wretched situation without far-reaching socio-economic as well as legal restructuring. This was to include abolition of the fundamental right to property in 1978, a radical and much-resented step.

How did Mrs Gandhi go about recycling ancient Hindu concepts? India turned more openly towards certain indigenous concepts to restructure its own model of 'good governance' along ancient Indian principles when, in 1976, the Preamble to the Indian Constitution was reworded, to the effect that India now became a 'sovereign socialist secular democratic republic'. The new explicit emphasis on 'socialist' and 'secular', as well as a number of important other amendments, were introduced by the Constitution (Forty-Second Amendment) Act 1976. Several more dissertations need to be written on what these terms may mean. Quite to what extent do they have ancient Hindu connotations?

On paper, at least, the Constitution governs the lives of all Indians irrespective of religion, race, caste, sex or place of birth. It would appear at first sight, and is a fact according to positivist dogma, that the Constitution has superseded the traditional Indian systems of differential statuses, but for most rural Indians the Constitution and its rules have remained remote (Dhagamwar, 1992: 9–10). Realising that the social norms of India's multi-ethnic, hybrid society and

---

[133] Twining (2000: 74) writes in the context of a global debate about justice that 'the position of the least advantaged is one important measure of just institutions'.

the new constitutional norms are quite different categories of law, we need no longer be surprised that modern positivism did not succeed in creating social facts and only produced 'paper law' and 'paper rights'. Indian law destroys the legocentric fallacy by showing that positivism as a specific type of law just cannot control and override (as it continues to claim) religious/ethical and socio-legal norms. Positivism is a competing norm system, not automatically superior to everything else, and it has to negotiate its claims with the other two claimants to the label of 'law', natural law concepts and social norms. In practice, thus, Indian social inequality and inequality before the law were not wiped out and state law remains little more than a thin layer of official law, as everyone concerned knows and judges have lamented *ad nauseam*.[134] But does this mean that the modern law will therefore look on impassively as the sharks devour the small fish? Mrs Gandhi evidently faced the chaos of 'shark rule' and jumpstarted a democratic rejuvenation through her Emergency.

Well before Mrs Gandhi's drastic interference, the Indian Constitution contained many elements that reflected and incorporated traditional Indian norms and concepts. With the explicit purpose of redressing historical imbalances, the Indian Constitution allows and in fact demands various forms of differential treatment or 'protective discrimination'. The equality provisions in Articles 14–16 were from the start qualified to take care of traditional inequalities, which the modern state was supposed to remedy. The special provisions for certain groups of chthonic people, Scheduled Castes and Scheduled Tribes, and (more controversially) other backward classes, especially as far as access to higher education and government employment are concerned, have had considerable effects, albeit, as Galanter (1984) claimed, at a huge cost. These policies continue to be challenged and have bred much resentment, especially as the former 'underdogs' gain better positions and challenge the privileges of higher caste Hindus (Jaffrelot, 2003). As in North America, such policies have been vigorously debated (Menski, 1992c), but India remains faithful to the basic principle that such historical imbalances need to be redressed in some form, while politicised disputes have focused on the extent of such reservations. However, such policies are only creating new patterns of inequality, perhaps best characterised as a more equitable system of inequality, not ultimately a society based on total equality. Given the socio-historical conditions that legitimised the reservation policies in the first place, these remain (with important modifications, which have partly been worked out) justifiable in terms of strengthening equality and safeguarding basic fundamental rights for all Indians. Significantly, Mrs Gandhi did not tinker with these policies.

While it has been fashionable to see this difficult legal problem as proof of dysfunction in modern Indian law, careful reading of jurisprudential work

---

[134] For example, when it comes to bonded labour, a modern form of slavery, see *Bandhua Mukti Morcha* v. *Union of India*, AIR 1984 SC 802 and AIR 1992 SC 38.

(Dahrendorf, 1969; Unger, 1976; Kelly, 1992) indicates that no legal system in the world actually achieves equality. It is an ancient Indian truth, well documented, that the question of equality or inequality is a jurisprudential won't-go-away question. Hindu tradition has been acutely aware of such problems. The principle of cosmic interlinkedness contains an element of ultimate equality, linking all unequal social elements of creation equally into one central, unknowable force of natural law. While social inequality is evidently a fact of life, every person can therefore in principle still be seen as equal. It is thus misleading and unfair to treat Hindu law as the epitome of legalised inequality and Indians as fixated on differential statuses – there has always been overlapping consensus in this area, too. Only in modernist ideologies is absolute equality even envisaged as an ideal in real life, which remains forever unattainable. Unger's (1976) analysis suggests that no social system or legal culture in the world can claim to have found the holy grail of perfect justice.

Looking more carefully at the Indian Constitution, one finds that it is much more Indian and also much more plurality-conscious than its founding fathers wanted to admit to an international public and perhaps even to themselves. I select here two aspects to highlight the recycling of ancient Indian and often explicitly Hindu concepts within the positivistic edifice of modern Indian constitutional law: the emergence of Indian public interest litigation, and the current creation of an intricate new jurisprudence on fundamental rights protection. Both processes appear to break some fundamental principles of formal positivist law-making. Both movements are fed by supervening concern for substantive justice rather than adherence to form. Both developments share an idealistic tint which makes them more akin to idealised ancient reasoning about duties than modernist assertive insistence on rights.

In cases of direct violations of fundamental rights, direct access to the Supreme Court and High Courts, India's legal watchdogs, was explicitly provided through powerful judicial review mechanisms, found in Articles 32 and 226 of the Constitution. Somehow, the specific words used were not interpreted in the same way earlier, but these skilful protective provisions were implanted in 1950. They would not strike modern lawyers as functional equivalents of ancient Indian ideas about direct access to the ruler's court, but that is what they have turned out to be. After the Emergency,[135] Indian judges developed a radical reinterpretation of Article 32, which guarantees the fundamental right of access to the Supreme Court 'by appropriate proceedings'. Under the inherited Anglo-Indian procedural model, this necessitated formal filing of a petition through a lawyer. Much expenditure and courage were required before the constitutional protection mechanisms could be activated. During the late 1970s and early 1980s, the Indian Supreme Court created a virtual revolution in *locus standi* jurisprudence and developed what came to be known as public interest

---

[135] During which, to their collective shame, Indian judges did not raise their voices.

litigation, ameliorating access to justice in the process (Ahuja, 1997; Bakshi, 1999). Some activist judges, realising that the formal operation of the law had been disadvantaging the downtrodden still further, made radical changes to improve fundamental rights protection in India.

Following a landmark case in which the self-interest of the legal professions is evident,[136] it became possible to use the new 'epistolary jurisdiction' and to send a fax, telegram, or a postcard from jail, directly to the Supreme Court. This would then be converted into a writ petition by the Court, whose judges might also act *suo motu*. Any Indian could now approach the Supreme Court directly in case of violation of a fundamental right, provided the claim was *bona fide*. This powerful innovation (which can of course easily be abused) claimed to seek to ensure social justice and above all better access to justice for those many millions for whom official law is remote and inaccessible, so that even in the most atrocious circumstances justice remains an empty shell. Public interest litigation is evidently based on the ancient Hindu strategy of opening the door of the court to anyone who has a grievance.[137] It was an important aspect of *rājadharma* that the ruler should listen to complainants to protect 'little fish' from the 'sharks'. This technique has radically changed modern Indian law, as the courts have to some extent moved away from the adversarial model of the colonial system (Bakshi, 1999: 118) which intrinsically favoured the privileged. Public interest litigation has had enormous success in many courtrooms and continues to develop. Cruel injustices have come to light in such petitions, often perpetrated by the state and its agents,[138] and appropriate remedies are not always readily available. While the Indian courts recognise such limits, this does not mean that the search for feasible remedies has been given up.

Indian public interest litigation is therefore not a modernist borrowing or an offshoot of American law, but needs to be understood as an intricate blend of modern human rights concerns and traditional Indian concepts of relative justice and balance in society. It is also not correct to assume that only a few maverick judges of the Indian Supreme Court have promoted this movement. It is now a broad-based phenomenon through which much progress has been made in alerting the Indian public to the need for greater accountability of those in positions of power. Today, South Asia and particularly India appear

---

[136] In *S. P. Gupta* v. *President of India*, AIR 1982 SC 149, the independence of the judiciary was at stake and was taken as a matter of public interest. Baxi (1985: 61) calls this 'a superb example of judicial statespersonship'.

[137] Most writing suggests an American heritage for this movement, but this confirms the inability of analysts to access knowledge of classical Hindu law.

[138] *Rudul Sah* v. *State of Bihar*, AIR 1983 SC 1086, brought to light the illegal detention of a man who had been acquitted many years before. *Bandhua Mukti Morcha* v. *Union of India*, AIR 1984 SC 802, involved bonded labourers living and working in atrocious conditions. The same case, taken up under a 'rolling review' and reported in AIR 1992 SC 38, showed that the conditions of about 2,000 people had still not improved.

to lead the world in thinking about judicial activism and the related concerns for public accountability (Menski, Alam and Raza, 2000). Rising awareness of public accountability in India, by no means on a steady curve of progress, is a reliable indicator that concern for justice, which is neither Hindu nor Muslim, but a universal natural law element, can be linked to ancient concepts about ordered spheres, in which state law is but one small aspect.

This duty-focus is also obvious from an analysis of important recent Indian developments in the reconstruction of a sustainable and effective regime for fundamental rights protection. The traditional position after 1950 was that only the Fundamental Rights of the Constitution (Part III) were justiciable, while the numerous Directive Principles of State Policy (Part IV), focusing on socio-economic rights, were not directly accessible to litigants and were not justiciable. These Principles were a kind of blueprint for government, pro- grammatic ideals which might be put off indefinitely. One of the most obvious examples from this category would be Article 39(a), according to which '[t]he state shall, in particular, direct its policy towards securing (a) that the citizens, men and women equally, have the right to an adequate means of livelihood . . .'. The wonderful objective of a welfare society has, however, never been imple- mentable, so these must sound like hollow words for most Indians.

A number of other constitutional provisions in this category of Directive Principles of State Policy were introduced through the 42nd Amendment of the Constitution in 1976. Much of this concerns environmental protection, a new growth area. Thus, Article 48-A, headed 'Protection and Improvement of Environment and Safeguarding of Forests and Wild Life', provided that '[t]he State shall endeavour to protect and improve the environment and to safeguard the forests and wild life of the country'. Even more explicitly, Article 51-A, on 'Fundamental Duties', introduced as part of the constitutional restructuring by Mrs Gandhi in 1976, reads almost like the edicts of the Emperor Aśoka, admonishing, even requiring, all Indian citizens not only to abide by the laws of the country, and to protect its institutions, but to cultivate self-improvement. Such provisions appeal directly to the conscience of the individual, the critical agent in Hindu law for assessing appropriateness. Subsections (e) to (j) of Article 51-A illustrate the culture-sensitive tenor of these duties:

(e) to promote harmony and the spirit of common brotherhood amongst all the people of India transcending religious, linguistic and regional or sectional diversities; to renounce practices derogatory to the dignity of women;

(f) to value and preserve the rich heritage of our composite culture;

(g) to protect and improve the natural environment including forests, lakes, rivers and wild life, and to have compassion for living creatures;

(h) to develop the scientific temper, humanism and the spirit of enquiry and reform;

(i) to safeguard public property and to abjure violence;
(j) to strive towards excellence in all spheres of individual and collective activ-
    ity so that the nation constantly rises to higher levels of endeavour and
    achievement.

One could read almost all of this as statements on Hindu *dharma*, which shows
that recent developments in Indian constitutional law have begun to combine,
more explicitly than ever before, new elements of the modern Constitution
and ancient holistic concepts, allowing for different ways of reading this kind
of rich text. Some alert Indian judges have constructively used such provisions
to generate a duty-based jurisprudence that ties every individual into the public
interest web, so that the standard phrase that the Constitution is the new conscience of the nation can easily be understood from a Hindu perspective, too. At
a formal legal level, the Indian judiciary developed an intricate jurisprudence to
combine Fundamental Rights and Directive Principles, arguing that the guarantees of the former do not make sense if the latter are not implemented as well
(Jaswal, 1996). Almost imperceptibly interlinked is a different level of analysis
according to which some of the most basic fundamental rights, such as the right
to life in Article 21 of the Indian Constitution, are now being linked with some
of the Directive Principles, including elements of the Fundamental Duties, to
construct a new jurisprudence that requires, at the end of the day, that the
division between public interest and private interest should be minimised.[139]
This new constitutional *dharma* is to the effect that every citizen should act
in such a way that the common good is not unduly damaged, a reflection of
ancient cosmic and social linkages as much as modern positivist state law. This
is plurality-consciousness in action, right in the heart of modern-sounding
constitutional jurisprudence.

Using such borrowing from the legal past in the garb of modern constitutional rhetoric, it has become possible for modern Indian constitutional law,
within a framework of outward secularism, to develop a new culture-specific
style of plurality-focused legal positivism influenced by Hindu principles. Relying on ancient holistic concepts of duty, Indian public law can actually make
larger claims on citizens than Western-style law, so that fundamental rights
might become enforceable even against individuals, not just the state and its
agents. Enormous technical legal consequences can flow from this, which we
can only begin to indicate here.[140] In *T. Damodhar Rao* v. *The Special Officer,
Municipal Corporation of Hyderabad*, AIR 1987 AP 171, it was held that building

---

[139] Intellectual foundations for this were laid by K. K. Mathew's work, discussed in Baxi
(1978).
[140] The concept of the 'state' under Article 12 of the Indian Constitution has been expanded
to an extent that would cause enormous problems of accountability in some Western
states. See *Central Inland Water Transport Corporation Ltd* v. *Brojo Nath Ganguly*, AIR
1986 SC 1571.

residential houses on land reserved under local development plans for recreational purposes undoubtedly amounted to a violation of the constitutionally guaranteed right to life. It was held, at p. 181:

> [I]t is clear that protection of the environment is not only the duty of the citizen but it is also the obligation of the State and all other State organs including Courts. In that extent, environmental law has succeeded in unshackling man's right to life and personal liberty from the clutches of common law theory of individual ownership. Examining the matter from the above constitutional point of view, it would be reasonable to hold that the enjoyment of life and its attainment and fulfilment guaranteed by Art. 21 of the Constitution embraces the protection and preservation of nature's gifts without [which] life cannot be enjoyed. There can be no reason why practice of violent extinguishment of life alone should be regarded as violative of Art. 21 of the Constitution. The slow poisoning by the polluted atmosphere caused by environmental pollution and spoliation should also be regarded as amounting to violation of Art. 21.

Similarly, in *Antony* v. *Commissioner, Corporation of Cochin*, 1994(1) KLT 169, it was held that life 'no longer means animal existence . . . but includes the finer grades of human civilisation'. These are not stray cases decided by maverick Hindu judges, there are many others with the same message, including from the Supreme Court of India.[141] More recently, evidence of further judicial activism in the field is found in *Ramakrishnan* v. *State of Kerala*, 1999(2) KLT 725, in which K. Narayana Kurup J, speaking for the Bench, banned smoking in public places all over the state of Kerala, *inter alia* on the ground that, under Article 21 of the Constitution, a person is entitled to protection of law from being exposed to the hazards of passive smoking.[142] This may sound like a copy-cat reaction to much-publicised, multi-billion dollar law suits in the USA, but there is more to this than meets the eye. While the learned Indian judges in Kerala are aware of foreign jurisprudence, their concerns are focused on alleviating specific problems in their local arena, seeking ways to make their own people's (and their own) living environment better, not only with regard to smoking.[143]

One must wonder to what extent positivist legal thinking and Hindu legal norms are in such cases coagulating into the reported outcomes. Having

---

[141] On the right to life see earlier *Francis Coralie Mullin* v. *The Administrator, Union Territory of Delhi*, AIR 1981 SC 746. The balance between environment and development is discussed in depth in *People United for Better Living in Calcutta* v. *State of West Bengal*, AIR 1993 Cal 215. Similar jurisprudential developments have occurred in Pakistan, where the right to life has also emerged as an important issue linked to environmental law (chapter 5, section 5.14).

[142] This has since been followed up in other parts of India.

[143] In *Nebu John* v. *Babu*, 2000(1) KLT 238, the same learned judges enforced the ban on smoking through contempt of court proceedings and punished a chain-smoking bus driver, making a public example of him because he was a public servant and therefore had a definite duty to obey the law.

discussed this issue with several of the judges involved in such cases, I am fortified in my analysis that they formally act as judges under the Constitution of India, but see no conflict in making their decisions as highly educated thinking individuals influenced by traditional cultural norms of appropriateness and duty.[144] They may also be influenced by very personal histories, as the biography of V. R. Krishna Iyer (2004; Singh, 1993) and much other evidence discloses.

It appears that the politician-law-makers of modern India, as well as many judges, are now appealing more openly to the duty-consciousness of modern Indians at several levels at once. They are asking for greater moral integrity, *dharma*-sensitivity as well as obedience to the rules of modern state law. The new hybrid Indian legal system, like the old model, is manifestly still to some extent built on idealised cultural elements of legal relevance, rather than just positivist legal rules. However, this new amalgam, which matches our triangular analytical concept even if different labels are used for the various elements, still requires a number of support mechanisms, in the same way as the sophisticated late classical Hindu law taught: While self-controlled order is expected, punishments threaten those that overstep their limits, and formal processes of dispute settlement are available if needed. All these techniques are of course not foolproof, since a lot depends, as before, on idealist renunciation of selfishness. What is evident, though, is that the most important institution in this complex legal scenario is still the judiciary on behalf of the state, offering an open ear to hear complaints as well as providing incentives (if necessary through punishment) for everyone to do the best they can to work for the common good. The amazingly activist developments in recent Indian human rights jurisprudence have gone a long way to alleviating some of the worst abuses that used to go unremedied, but of course much more remains to be done.

Detailed research could chart massive evidence of the reappraisal of traditional values and concepts in Indian law, initially during the 1980s, but extending to the present. This would probably confirm the present argument that the modern law of India has been moving along the road to further indigenisation in two major ways: First, through increased awareness of the continued relevance of traditional socio-cultural and hence legal concepts; secondly, through stronger realisation that the application of foreign-style laws and particularly of some Western legal concepts and strategies, like emphasis on individualism, and privileged treatment of contract law and private property, do not suit Indian socio-economic and legal conditions and have to be either discarded, restructured or more explicitly re-indigenised.

The modern Indian legal system remains on constant alert to the need for relative justice, operating a complex ordering process of disparate units, rather

---

[144] Some indications of how an activist South Asian judge thinks and decides cases are found in the Foreword by Mr Justice A. S. Salam to Menski, Alam and Raza (2000: x). See also Baxi (1985) on 'social action litigation'.

than simply a uniformly and formally egalitarian approach as preferred by Western legal systems. That seems a prudent and realistic approach to the existing challenges. Legal uniformity by itself is no longer seen as desirable. Indian culture has always contained the message that formalistic equality cannot work in reality, because it would further disadvantage the disadvantaged. The lessons learnt by post-colonial India in this respect point to serious dissatisfaction with the positivistic Western model of state law and the realisation that making a Constitution does create legal facts, but not social facts. This was one of the major messages of Mrs Gandhi's call to the nation thirty years ago. Ever since, much fresh thinking about 'law' and 'justice' has been taking place in modern India. There is nothing religious or fundamentalist about this, as most Indians (but not many academics) seem to appreciate. The search for appropriateness and justice is not a doctrinal matter of religious belief or social doctrine. From a Hindu perspective, it is a clamour for the cosmic good, another variant of an idealistic approach in which religion and ethics, society and state, and really all aspects of life, are intimately interconnected.

4.10 Searching for composite appropriateness in postmodernity

In the previous section, postmodern Indian law was portrayed as an intricate combination of old and new, questioning and abandoning blind belief in modernist legal axioms and linear progress. Tharoor (2000: 76) emphasises that Indian identity celebrates diversity and 'India . . . is a *thali*, a selection of sumptuous dishes in different bowls', so that 'the singular thing about India is that you can only speak of it in the plural' (p. 6). It remains to be discussed here briefly to what extent it is appropriate to speak of plurality-conscious Indian law, including Hindu law, as a postmodern legal system. What implications does such plurality carry in relation to searching for approximation to the centre of our conceptual triangle (chapter 3, section 3.8)?

The composite pluralist nature of Indian legal systems has been discussed in detail. Legal uniformity per se is no longer seen as desirable in India (if indeed it ever was, across the board) and seems an unattainable goal in view of the realities of life and past experience. Indian legal realism, theoretically still at embryo stage, has managed to cultivate the customary plurality of Hindu family law, but by listening to 'tradition' it has not given up on reformist agenda. Its agenda are more focused on socio-economic aims than on intellectual dogmatisms. Indian law, as a matter of self-preservation in terms of retaining legitimacy, is desperately searching for practical justice and appropriateness, not for an ideal ideology.[145] In the field of Indian family laws as a whole, this has become a little clearer in the past few years. As I see it at present, the reformist strategy

---

[145] From that perspective, one may appreciate that Indians simply have no time for legal theory, but must take the time to take the right action. The observation that 'practice has outrun theory' (Twining, 2000: 241) clearly applies not only with regard to comparative

of postmodern Indian law, restructuring the entire system by more explicit reference to traditional concepts of self-controlled ordering, is much more than a cost-saving exercise or an avoidance tactic to negate the need for legal aid for millions of poor people. There is a much broader social welfare agenda now, with enormous implications which nobody (least of all any government in power) dares to spell out, because there would be murderous criticism from many quarters. Most academics have anyway been too busy with their own often idiosyncratic politics to even notice what is happening under our very eyes.

In brief, there are several, interrelated major recent developments that make it possible to speak of postmodern Hindu law within the wider context of the plurality-conscious restructuring of the entire Indian legal system today. First is the skilled maintenance of the personal law system itself, superficially in disobedience of constitutional guidance from Article 44 about the need to 'endeavour to secure' a uniform civil code for the citizens. What actually does this mean? Who said that this had to be a totally new code (Kumar, 2003)? Why did we assume this for so long? Positivist phantasising misguided two generations of scholars. Indian family law has today reached a sophisticated stage of equitable harmonisation across the board, while retaining the personal law system itself. More precisely, all personal laws have gradually been brought more closely together, so that today it makes hardly any difference whether the people wishing to marry, make polygamous arrangements, divorce or deal with affairs relating to their children or maintenance are Hindu, Muslim, or anything else. While the last bastion always appears to be Islamic law, I do not agree at all with the common assessment, informed by communalist politicking and deliberate silences rather than detailed legal analysis, that Indian Muslim law remains out of line. True, it is not formally codified, but its provisions are remarkably similar to all the other personal laws today. In fact, Islamic law has exerted a huge influence on how postmodern Indian family laws have developed, but nobody in Hindu-dominated India wants to take credit for that.

An important date in the Indian legislative calendar, hardly noticed (Menski, 2004), was 24 September 2001. On that day, two small Acts of Parliament were passed, one after much debate and strenuous lobbying, the other after a lot of behind-the-scenes shadow-boxing which needs to be explained further below. The easier task is to analyse what happened when India's Christian divorce law was totally reformed and updated by the Indian Divorce (Amendment) Act of 2001 (Act No. 51 of 2001). Clearly, the modernists won a huge battle, since the seriously outdated colonial and religio-centric Christian divorce law (which refused most spouses the right to divorce) was finally brought in line with the secular divorce law of India and the provisions of the Hindu Marriage

law in general. Indian practical legal realism, as the examples below demonstrate, is far ahead of theoretical analysis.

Act 1955 as amended to date.[146] Now modernist reformers are preparing to tackle afresh what they perceive to be the only remaining major hurdle to a Uniform Civil Code in this area, namely Islamic divorce law. But Islamic divorce law is so liberal (arguably for both men *and* women) when it comes to the right to divorce that there is little need for the state to become involved to liberate spouses from marital chains. The need is rather to protect Muslim women against being simply thrown on the street. The real problems therefore lie elsewhere, in the socio-economic arena and the law relating to post-divorce maintenance entitlements.

Since 2001, it should have been evident that Indian laws on divorce constitute a largely uniform law across the board, permitting divorce on a large number of grounds, with encouragements to process divorces speedily, *while retaining the personal law system.* It seems nobody noticed. This realisation has not struck many Indians because the state itself is keeping quiet over such matters. One reason for this is the desire, for reasons explained throughout this chapter, to promote self-controlled ordering. In all personal law systems, most definitely including Islamic law, informal dispute settlement is preferred to going through formal legal proceedings. Postmodern Indian family law operates now a plurality-conscious, situation-sensitive system of divorce laws which is uniform in its diversity, hardly a new feature, but a new constellation after the quiet legislative activity of September 2001. One waits to hear what comments this new scenario will elicit.

The second major scenario of postmodern legal development searching for appropriateness is still more intricate and extends over various areas of law which must be seen – and can only be understood fully – as interlinked aspects. To unravel this, it makes sense to start with the fact that, in 1973, Indian law quietly changed the definition of 'wife' under section 125 of the secular Criminal Procedure Code of 1973 to include 'divorced wife', so that such a wife remained entitled to maintenance from the former husband also after divorce.[147] Obviously, this was not unwelcome as a social welfare measure, especially for near-destitute people,[148] but Indian Muslims began to claim that they should be exempted from this law, since their religious law stipulated that a divorcing husband was only required to maintain an ex-wife for the *iddat* period, no more than three menstrual cycles.

Then came the 'big bang' of the much-discussed Shah Bano affair.[149] An old Muslim woman, who had been divorced by her husband, a senior Muslim

---

[146] The Parsi law had already been brought into line in 1988 (see note 10 above). Muslim law permits rather too easy divorce to the husband. Indian Muslim women, like their sisters in Pakistan, could claim rights under the Dissolution of Muslim Marriages Act 1939.

[147] This means that an Indian husband can more easily get rid of responsibility for his wife if she is killed, an awful thought, but a possibility.

[148] Which is clearly why it was introduced, with an upper limit of Rs. 500 per month, now just over £6.

[149] *Mohd. Ahmed Khan* v. *Shah Bano Begum*, AIR 1985 SC 945.

lawyer, was granted the right to maintenance till death or remarriage by a bench of the Indian Supreme Court, composed of five Hindu judges, who held that India's secular law on post-divorce maintenance and Islamic law as found in the Qur'an did not conflict, and at any rate the secular law prevailed over the personal law. The ensuing riots pressed the government of the day, led by Rajeev Gandhi, in record time, to pass the Muslim Women (Protection of Rights on Divorce) Act of 1986, which was commonly believed to have taken away the right of divorced Muslim wives to extended post-divorce maintenance and thus nullified the Shah Bano position. However, since at least 1988, several Indian High Courts have held in a growing number of cases that the 1986 Act in fact gave Muslim women this contested right to maintenance and, more notably, there was no financial limit to what such a woman could claim (Menski, 2001). Nobody wanted to know; all major scholars (and many others, including the press to this day) insisted that Rajeev Gandhi had let down Muslim women. The uniform civil code lobby was up in arms and filed numerous constitutional petitions challenging the constitutionality of the 1986 Act. Remarkably, these were not decided by the Supreme Court until 2001 – hardly a coincidence. In *Danial Latifi* v. *Union of India*, (2001)7 SCC 740, it was held that the 1986 Act indeed gave Muslim women appropriate rights to post-divorce maintenance till death or remarriage and was perfectly constitutional. This caused no riots, and seems to have emboldened the Indian government to make the next move on the chessboard of far wider social welfare agenda.

To understand this, we have to turn again to what happened in Parliament a few days later, on 24 September 2001. The second Act on family law passed that very day has been surrounded by ominous silence and even official ignorance (Menski, 2004). The Code of Criminal Procedure (Amendment) Act 2001 (Act No. 50 of 2001) removed the uniform Rs. 500 ceiling and thus now permits all Indian wives (and ex-wives, by definition) to claim whatever is appropriate as post-divorce maintenance. This amounts to a silent, highly explosive revolution of gender relations in India, a time bomb which nobody wants to detonate. Some further explanations are needed to appreciate the implications.

Protracted debate over the uniform civil code has been an attractive political football, but such games have distracted from the really important issue for governments of all hues, perhaps remembering the lessons of the Emergency. For, the issue of how to avoid depriving millions of women and children of legal rights against men who simply flout their moral and legal obligations for selfish reasons has not gone away. 'Shark rule' persists within Indian patriarchal structures and these are not likely to be overthrown. So the new chessboard strategy of a destitution-conscious government is to hold those in charge of resources responsible for the socio-economic welfare of others. This, again, is a quiet duty-focused approach rather than the loud rights-based claims of the various human rights lobbies. Since modern Indian law faces huge problems of gender balancing linked to social welfare in such enormous dimensions, the state has had to devise a sustainable form of welfare provision to avoid or at least minimise social disasters and massive claims against the state. From this perspective, the Indian government seems to have remembered the institution of the family (savaged by modernists as the source of all suppression of individuality) and appears to have fallen back on joint family concepts and issues of corporate responsibility for the benefit of needy individuals. This will, no doubt, have important repercussions on how debates about women's property rights are going to develop in future. For the moment, there is embarrassed silence.

Taking a holistic approach to the development of Indian personal laws, one can therefore see that the postmodern Indian state values substantive reforms more than rhetoric uniformity, especially when financial implications are involved (Menski, 2001). The new Act No. 50 of 2001 means, in practice, that within the continuing patriarchal system of India, men will have to pay for their privileged entitlements and access to material resources by being put under a legal duty, not just a moral obligation, to maintain those family members that may require assistance, or simply want to claim a more equitable share of the cake. Since this was already the legal position under the 1986 Act for Muslims, Indian law has in one stroke also ingeniously managed to reinstate legal uniformity across the board. The Muslim experiment of the 1986 Act and the abstruse *Danial Latifi* decision created no new riots, and I am not aware that Indian men went on the streets to protest against the new law on 24 September 2001. In an equally sophisticated manner, the Indian state has thereby managed to reassert its formal control over the entire legal field, while at the same time allowing huge scope for self-controlled ordering. For, the intelligent expectation must be that this new official law, as 'symbolic legislation', will lead to a significant informal reassessment (by working on individual consciences) of what is considered appropriate by the various communities in all the crucial areas of law that this development touches.

I predict that this exceptionally sophisticated legal rearrangement, outwardly engineered by swift positivist law-making but inspired by deeply considered socio-legal and ethical concerns, will in due course be understood as a key example of postmodern legal reconstruction. It not only demonstrates a spirit of plurality-consciousness in terms of the plurality of personal laws in India, but also helps to understand the plurality of law as a global phenomenon. Hindu law, so much is sure, is not a legal system that can be legislated away overnight, least of all in India. Its principles and concepts have shown a resilience on the ground which is entirely in line with the jurisprudential axiom, propounded by this study, that all legal systems are culture-specific.

The universalistic foundations of India's composite cultural traditions, dominated to a large extent but not exclusively by Hindu models (which are themselves internally hybrid), thus provide one culture-specific global model for sustainable legal development in the future. A further globally relevant lesson to draw from the Indian Hindu law case is that Western legal models are now merely a distant quarry for transplants (Watson, 1993). Traditional transplant techniques may now not even be used, since the conceptual spring of Hindu legal traditions in one's own backyard, and the trickle of inspiration that it provides even now, remain a useful source of inspiration towards achieving a higher form of plurality-consciousness and appropriateness of legal outcomes in line with the composite identity postulates of India as it is today and will develop in future.

5

Islamic law: God's law or men's law?

The present chapter aims to provide a detailed historical overview of Islamic law in comparative perspective. It seeks to demonstrate that Islamic law, too, is built on a notion of plurality-consciousness and can be examined within the triangular model of global legal theory explored in the present study. In comparison with Hindu law, scholarship on Islamic law seems to be much more securely anchored around the world. This does not mean that knowledge about Islamic law is better developed or that its place within a plurality-focused global analysis is easier to define. Scholarship on Islamic law is spread widely, available in many different languages apart from Arabic and English, and so diffuse in terms of approaches, sectarian and school traditions that a full overview is impossible.[1] The present analysis concentrates on those aspects that further understanding of how Islamic law, as a religion-based legal system, manages to reconcile the doctrinal centrality of religious belief with its inherent plurality of socio-cultural manifestations. It is a case study mainly in how natural law and socio-legal approaches interact, while concepts of state positivism are not absent. This chapter highlights how Islamic law has achieved and largely maintained a sophisticated degree of plurality-consciousness, albeit often obfuscated by theological polemics and political rhetoric.

The chapter explores in depth the tensions within Islamic law concerning its claims to uniformity and global validity and the pluralities created by human social and political life. Focusing first on the Qur'an and the Prophet, his companions, the early Muslim rulers and judges, and then the emerging class of Muslim jurists, Islamic state law is found to develop gradually in interaction with primarily religious structures and social norm systems, never able to dominate the entire field. This illustrates how the conceptual global legal triangle (chapter 3, section 3.8) operates culture-specifically in theory and practice among Muslims worldwide. The analysis includes two contrasting examples of Islamic law in the modern world. Turkey officially abolished Muslim law during the 1920s and constructed a secular legal system following Western models. In contrast, post-colonial Pakistan has sought to Islamise its legal system,

[1] The four volumes of the *Oxford Encyclopedia of the Modern Islamic World* (Esposito, 1995) are a rich reference source.

particularly since the late 1970s. Both strategies raise complex jurisprudential issues of particular relevance for discussions of modern Islamic state law
(Ahmed, 1987).

Some old leading studies (in particular Schacht, 1979; 1984) are challenged by new critical research, which has opened up the entire field to re-
examination.[2] Prominent among the contested issues is whether the supposed
'closing of the door of endeavour' (Glenn 2004: 191) or gates of *ijtihad*, and
thus the intellectual stifling of medieval Islamic scholarship that some Orientalist scholarship saw, ever happened in practice.[3] There is no doubt that it
was debated in theoretical terms, but in a field of enormous research efforts,
subjectivity and personal opinions (*ra'y*) continue to remain deeply contested
(Hallaq, 1992). The phrase '*sunna* of the Orientalists', linked to allegations that
Western scholars distorted Islamic traditions, signifies resentment over some
of the representations of Islamic law by non-Muslims.[4]

Despite a central religious ideology of binding divine revelation, universal
agreement among Muslims beyond certain basic tenets has proved problematic.
All Muslims, irrespective of sect or tradition, must constantly affirm belief in
Allah as their God and the Qur'an as His word, but fundamental differences
arise even over the position of the Prophet Mohammad.[5] Some communities
who view themselves as Muslims have therefore been declared non-Muslims.[6]
The internal pluralism of Islam continues to be as big a challenge to Muslim
scholarship and communities as making sense of global legal pluralism. Links
are now beginning to be drawn (Dupret *et al.*, 1999; Loimeier, 2000).

Islamic law as a global legal system struggles with the concept of pluralism,
but has ingeniously succeeded to some extent in handling the inherent plurality
of the global Muslim presence. The explosive tensions within Muslim jurisprudence require a basic spirit of human tolerance,[7] evidently not always present.
Islamisation, as a process of seeking to make an existing Islamic system more
faithfully Islamic, has been a constant challenge for Muslims. Islam has had
to protect itself from within as well, reflected in constant intense conflicts and
tensions about correct methodology (Coulson, 1969).

---

[2] See especially Hallaq (1997; 2001); Melchert (1997; 2004); Motzki (2002).

[3] *Islamic Law and Society*, Vol. 3, No. 2 (June 1996) carries excellent articles on *ijtihad* and
taqlid.

[4] Significantly, this links to debates over borrowings from other Middle Eastern traditions
(Hallaq, 1992).

[5] On the early struggles between the majority Sunni Muslims and the Shi'a minority see
section 5.4 below.

[6] The Ahmadis or Qadianis, a Hanafi Sunni group of Muslims who follow their own leader,
are seen to challenge the dogma of the finality of the Prophet Mohammad. In Pakistan,
this group has been outlawed and declared non-Islamic, so that many Ahmadis have had
to seek refuge abroad. In several other countries, they face persecution, too.

[7] This is remarkably akin to Legrand's (1996: 239) emphasis on 'proclivity on the part of the
comparatist towards an acknowledgement of "difference"'.

5.1 Understanding Islamic law from a legal pluralist perspective

The difficulties in understanding Islamic law are exacerbated because it is, similar to Hindu and African laws, a complex family of laws rather than one single legal system. The terminology 'Islamic' or 'Muslim' law itself gives rise to debate.[8] Protracted politics over terms like 'Muhammadan law', which is specific to Indo-Muslim law and the historically grown 'Anglo-Muhammadan law', continue to excite some authors.[9] Muslims themselves tend to emphasise the unity of the worldwide community of believers (*ummah*) and resent being divided, more so after 9/11. As Islam is a way of life manifested in widely disparate local traditions which might cause some raised eyebrows,[10] the immense plurality of locally coloured customary and religious practices leads some scholars to speak of 'Islams' rather than 'Islam'.[11]

While nobody seriously doubts that Islamic law is law, in contrast to perceptions of African laws (chapter 6), many questions arise about the nature, structure and development of Muslim law. The central problematic in Islamic law is the tension between its doctrinal and religious claims to global validity and its practical application in diverse and complex socio-cultural contexts. As a divine system of Truth for Muslims, Islam demands explicit allegiance and claims innate supremacy over other belief systems, since the time of its emergence soon after 600 AD. Offering an alternative model to European Christian natural law, Islamic claims to global validity raise the critical issue of how one treats 'others', particularly non-believers. Early Muslims were a minority, aware of the existence of many other communities. This is not different today when Muslims have become a worldwide community of over a billion people: Muslims are still bound to accept that the world holds many more non-Muslims. A good Muslim, as stated in the Qur'an itself, cannot insist that all people in the world should follow Islam, or a particular kind of Islam.[12] A good Muslim is therefore, of necessity, a pluralist.

---

[8] I use mainly 'Islamic law' and 'Muslim law' as interchangeable terms with no significant difference in meaning. Fyzee (1999: 2) finds 'Muhammadan law' deeply unsatisfactory and calls it 'an ugly term'. While he defends its use for the Indian subcontinent, he argues that '[t]he correct term in English would be "Islamic law"' (p. 13).

[9] Mahmood (1986: 49–94) elaborately critiques the grave distortions of Islamic law in the Indian subcontinent. He blames authors and judges alike (pp. 52–5), as well as the *maulvis*, the film industry, and all intellectuals, claiming to be able to discover its 'true' spirit.

[10] For example, observance of Hindu customs by some Indian Muslims (Husain, 1976; Miller, 1992). See also Rosen (1989) on understanding law as a cultural phenomenon in the Maghreb and Berber law in Morocco.

[11] Glenn (2004: 194); Bistolfi and Zabbal (1995). On Muslims in Europe, see Nielsen (1995).

[12] In this context, Afghanistan's President, Hamid Karzai, responding to a question whether Islamic fundamentalism is a threat to human beings and peace (*India Today*, 28 February 2005, p. 38), stated: 'I am a fundamentalist Muslim. I believe in the fundamentals of Islam. It is extremism that is wrong. We must not allow extremism in religion. In our case extremism came from abroad. Afghans are not extremists.'

As a historical latecomer, Islam displays an in-built awareness of other rule systems and religions that also claim universal validity.[13] Glenn (2004: 170) emphasises that '[b]y the time Muhammad . . . began to hear the voice of God, or Allah, there were many kinds of law around him'. Early Islam tackled this issue of diversity by claiming superiority to everything before it. While some would argue that Islamic law remains a religiously based tradition unamenable to modernity and globalisation, Glenn (2004: 51) highlights that Islam has now become part of globalising processes, so that 'there are a number of globalizations going on. It is not just the spread of western technology, open markets and human rights. There is also, for example, globalization in the form of islamization.'

Islamisation here means the spread of Islam across the world and the growth in numbers. Glenn (2004: 51) observes that '[w]hile globalization has been going on above, islam has been expanding on the ground'. This image might suggest that Western-driven globalisation takes place above ground, at an official level, while Islamisation is an underground, even subversive process in the unofficial realm.[14] It has been easy to play mischief with such images in a scenario of competing discourses.[15]

From a conservative Islamic perspective, comparative legal work may be looked upon with considerable reservation.[16] If the sole aim of comparison were to demonstrate the superiority of one's own system, there is really no point in comparative study. Conversely, if Muslim scholars simply treat all others as inherently inferior, advertising their own law as divine legislation and the sole 'real law', they are bound to be criticised and risk outright dismissal.[17]

Islamic law asserts itself, through numerous spokespersons (not all male) and various approaches, as first and foremost a religious law based on divine revelation.[18] But it is also a scholars' or jurists' law, which raises at once the clash of revelation and reason as a core problem in Muslim jurisprudence. If

---

[13] From a polytheistic Hindu perspective, Allah is one of many gods, making it fairly easy for South Asians to accept Islam (especially in its Sufi forms) but more difficult to internalise its exclusive claims. Unsurprisingly, South Asian Islams represent many hybrid beliefs, also reflected in the laws of the region (Husain, 1976).

[14] This may not be what Glenn means, but it could be seen as inherently subversive from a modernism-focused perspective that opposes tradition and religion.

[15] For writing on Islamophobia and related issues see Stone (2004). On British Muslim identity, see Ansari (2004). Mamdani (2004) focuses on US approaches.

[16] Despite such difficulties, there is an immensely rich scholarship in the field of interreligious dialogue. For a recent survey, see Cohn-Sherbok (1997); Morgan and Lawton (1996) is a much-used student handbook on ethical issues in six religious traditions. A major specialist journal is *Islam and Christian–Muslim Relations*.

[17] For an example of such a debate, over justifying polygamy, see Khan (1989) and Menski (2001).

[18] We saw in chapter 4 that the internal perspective of Hindu legal scholarship was to similar effect.

God made all law, what is the scope for human law-making? The two opposing fiercely debated positions are clearly outlined in Coulson (1969) as binding oneself totally to revelation (*ahl al-hadith*), or engaging in private speculation as to what God may have meant (*ahl ar-ra'y*). One should never expect total agreement. From the start, the divine message of unity and equality before God co-exists with observable facts of diversity, differential statuses and the need to construct a living Muslim tradition.

In terms of religion, the internal perspective on divine superiority is clearly a matter for believers (on the Qur'an, see Cook, 2000). In terms of comparative legal analysis, this issue is not so simple. Familiar debates about the supremacy of religious natural law promote the perspective of religious centralism or religious positivism, which culminates in assertions that God's law is supreme and that, for Muslims, the Qur'an is simply 'the law'. Many Muslims rashly assert this, especially in political contexts.[19] In turn, legocentric secularist outsiders might dismiss Islamic claims as evidence of religious extremism. For believers in other religious traditions, Muslims become enemies. If all these people had their way in their respective subjective assessments, debates about law and religion would simply become a clash of civilisations (Huntington, 1998) and talk about legal pluralism becomes blasphemy. This is where discussion stops and mutual accusations of terrorism arise.

But there has always been an overlapping consensus, often hidden by strategic silences and internal and external politics: accepting that Islamic law is more than God's law and has man-made elements as well, requires pluralist perspectives. Many Muslims are uncomfortable with this because it appears to challenge the supremacy of divine revelation. Yet Muslims also know that the Qur'an does not answer all legal questions directly but offers a broadly guiding ethical framework. To live ideally as good Muslims, they have to find daily guidance for themselves. Islam as a way of life and a lived experience is thus intricately linked to Muslim law as a matter of belief *and* socio-cultural acceptance and interpretation.[20] While many early jurists, as private citizens without power-centred agenda, were intensely concerned to get as close as possible to the divine truth through the process of interpretation (*ijtihad*), later

---

[19] Muslims in Western countries have long been calling for better recognition of Islamic personal law by portraying themselves as a religious minority (Modood, 1993). See also Ansari (2004).

[20] The duty of the Muslim individual is to seek guidance primarily from God's law, rather than from within. Muslim jurisprudence is reticent on the individual's role, and also on custom as a source of law, because they are seen as human sources. Since even the holiest and best religious expert remains fallible (the *ikhtilaf* principle of tolerated diversity), and one does not know whether an individual could plead mercy on judgment day by reference to bad advice, commonsense suggests circumspection and the Muslim individual must have the freedom to decide for himself or herself. Seeking advice locally becomes a matter of commonsense but remains risky.

generations of jurists, probably encouraged by their potential roles in relation to state law, might be tempted to exploit their specialist knowledge.[21]

At its base, the religious Muslim law is clearly a matter of natural law philosophy; it is not a form of legal positivism originating from the state. Conceptual analysis of early Islamic law is confronted with the virtual absence of the state, which is of course not unique to Islamic law. At first sight, this creates analytical problems in applying the conceptual triangle (chapter 3, section 3.8) because religion is treated as entirely dominant and the triangular interlinkage seems to be denied. However, since the focus on religious authority serves to promote the experience of a good life in Islamic terms, and Muslims are normally also members of communities, which exercise their own authority as a human and thus secondary source of guidance,[22] the result is not just another clash of positivism and natural law but a triangular dynamism. Muslim individuals and communities are expected to orient themselves first of all towards God, not a state. But the state is not entirely absent: the Prophet was the first ruler, judge and leader of the emerging faith community, and others followed him. Legal positivism seemed an attractive concept to ancient Arabs,[23] but as a human construct it remains inferior to the divine revelation of Islam, while social embeddedness is taken for granted.

Examining the time of the Prophet in seventh-century Arabia allows a better understanding of why and how Muslims may perceive state authority and customary laws as subordinate. In the pluralistic socio-cultural environment of the Prophet's time, with Islam as a new minority religion, Islam had to assert itself in a hostile environment by creating a new identity for its adherents. This confirms the critical importance of Chiba's (1989: 180) '*identity postulate of a legal culture*', giving it 'ethnic' characteristics. The new belief system of Islam offered an attractive, innovative and holistic system for believers, a powerful message that subjected everything to a new ethical assessment. Hence, the Qur'an is much more than a Napoleonic code of law, it is received as a comprehensive guidance for Muslim life, a code of ethics that leaves nothing uncovered. However, as it needed to be applied in practice, the Prophet and later his Companions and Muslim scholar jurists were needed as human agents to interpret this divine revelation and make it applicable to Muslim daily life. Herein lies the core dilemma of Islamic jurisprudence. As a matter of religious doctrine, it asserts superior divine authority, but when it comes to real life, human interpretation and application are central to establishing the rule systems we now know as Islamic law.

---

[21] The almost illiterate village *maulvi* in South Asian Muslim communities who advises his 'flock' in accordance with *izzat* (his own assumptions about honour), but declares this Islamic, is a common feature of contemporary Islam (Mahmood, 1986: 55–7).

[22] On the role of custom, especially in Hanafi law, see Mahmood (1965) and Libson (1997).

[23] Mayer (1990: 179–80) reports that a high government official, Ibn al-Muqaffa', who died c. 759 AD, proposed unsuccessfully that the Caliph should codify the law to remove the confusions arising from excessive scholarly diversity. See also Coulson (1964: 52).

The Prophet as the recipient of the divine messages and the first leader of the Muslim community had a central role in this process of harmonising divine revelation and social reality. This immediately combines all three elements of the triangular model of law (chapter 3, section 3.8). He acted as ruler, human recipient and guardian of the divine message, and as head of the emerging Muslim community. Even during the time of the revelation, a long process (610–32 AD), this rendered Islamic law of necessity immediately plurality-conscious, despite the monotheistic focus on God, His message and its transmission through the Prophet.

Since this divine Order needed to be applied by Muslims in daily reality, guidance about God's will was required. That guidance came originally from the Prophet as the recipient of the divine messages, who had to be extremely careful not to turn into an Austinian law-maker. It is evident that he succeeded in maintaining the distinction between being God's messenger and being an emerging ruler by subjecting himself to divine authority. Acting primarily as a mouthpiece of God and only secondarily as a leader of the emerging community, the Prophet's positing of new rules was designed to explain the greatness and goodness of God's Order, not to assert his own personal rule. Here lies the origin of the claim that all political (and hence positivist legal) as well as social authority in Islamic law must be seen as subject to the divine will. More strictly circumscribed than in Hindu law, therefore, the Islamic ruler is from the very start a servant of this divine Order and can claim only a limited role in making law.

Islam also teaches that the Prophet was a very special man and nobody after him can claim to fully understand God's will.[24] Consequently no Islamic jurist could ever claim to have found 'the Truth' through his own effort of interpretation (*ijtihad*). Thus, striving for Truth at the highest level of Islamic understanding becomes an ultimately unachievable ideal. Muslim jurists as learned individuals can view themselves only as faithful interpreters of the divine will, never as autonomous law-makers, since they themselves remain a fallible tool, a socially conditioned element of human interpretation of the divine will. The principle of limitation of human knowledge and the resulting axiom of 'tolerated diversity' or 'margin of error' (*ikhtilaf*) suggest that pluralism is structurally inherent in post-revelation Islamic law.

Hence it is inadequate and confusing to speak simply of Qur'anic 'legislation' (but see Hallaq, 1997). While the Qur'an must be seen as *lex divina* in Thomist terminology (chapter 3, section 3.4), Islamic law comprises other categories of

---

[24] His remarkable privilege according to Muslim tradition was that he could still ask direct questions from God. No human after him could do so; the closest we get in the Muslim system to divine inspiration is the Shi'a concept of the *imam*, who is deemed to be a direct descendant of the Prophet's family and thereby possesses innate legitimising legal authority.

Thomist natural law as well.[25] The Prophet was by all accounts a simple man, but he had common sense and he lived in an environment where plurality was a daily experience (Glenn, 2004: 170–1). The divine revelation that he applied left no theoretical loopholes, and in this sense it is deeply plurality-conscious. However, claiming that this divine revelation is simply 'the law' masks the fact that divine law-making by itself could never become a legal system in its own right. A God who makes rules needs people to apply them. Allah needed the Prophet as a tool, as other Gods before him required a messenger (Glenn, 2004: 171). It seems to be accepted therefore by all major Muslim scholars that the Qur'an contains the essence of God's law, but is not the law itself. Weiss (1978: 200) explains:

> Strictly speaking, it is not the Law as such which is interpreted, but rather the sources of law. The Law as a topically-organized finished product consisting of precisely-worded rules is the *result* of juristic interpretation; it stands at the end, not at the beginning, of the interpretive process. Yet it would not be acceptable to speak of those who interpret the sources as in any sense creating law. It is much more appropriate to refer to the interpreter as one who *discovers* the law. The theory of *ijtihad* presupposes that the process of producing rules is a process of elucidating that which is *present* but yet is not self-evident. In principle, the Muslim jurist never invents rules; he formulates, or attempts to formulate, rules which God had already decreed and which are concealed in the sources. These rules, which constitute the ideal Law of God, exist objectively above and beyond all juristic endeavour.

The core predicament of Islamic law-making therefore lies in the 'margin of error' (*ikhtilaf*), to which all human interpretation of the divinely revealed word remains forever subject. Nobody, according to strict religious interpretations of Islam, can ever totally grasp God's message, no human could ever claim to possess perfect knowledge of the divine truth. Weiss (1978: 204) explains:

> The notion of opinion suggests the possibility of error, and error is contemplated by *Sunni* theorists as an inevitable fact of legal life. Opinion is frankly admitted to be fallible: liable (although not necessarily prone) to error. The factuality of error is implicit in the *ikhtilaf*, the disagreements among the great jurists. Unwilling to succumb to an ethical-legal relativism, Islamic jurisprudence insists that the truth of God is one and that there is only one correct rule with reference to every human act. Accordingly, when jurists disagree on a particular rule, they cannot all be right. Because the positions taken by jurists regarding a particular legal question are all opinions, one cannot know which opinion happens to be correct. If one could know an opinion was correct, erroneous opinions would necessarily be eliminated.

---

[25] The comprehensive divine Order of Islamic natural law is found in *huqm*, the Qur'an equates to *lex divina*, while the later concept of *siyasa shar'iyya* (government in accordance with God's law) represents secular strands within Islamic natural law.

> In such case, knowledge would be existent and would prevail over opinion
> because opinion is only binding where knowledge is lacking.

A globally focused jurisprudential analysis of Muslim law must be aware of
this core element of Islamic epistemology from the start. Muslims, therefore,
have to continue to argue over how to understand their uniform revelation.
This explains why translating *shari'a* simply as 'law' is just as inadequate as
doing the same to *dharma*.[26] Muslims as believers, when they treat God's word
as 'the law', appear to think as religious natural lawyers and accord secondary
importance to any human laws. Aquinas would have had no problems with
that; his system indicated different categories of divine law but also recognised
what we now call secular dimensions of law, perceived as subject to divine rules.
The facile assertion that law and religion are co-terminous, and that Islamic
law is a codified system of God-made rules ready for human consumption,
simply conflates the various categories of natural law identified by Aquinas.
However, the meaning of Allah's message in the Qur'an has to be ascertained
through human effort to turn it into 'living law'. While the Prophet faithfully
fulfilled that function in the early days of Islam, after him that task became
much more difficult to execute as many later Islamic leaders could not resist
positivist ambitions.

The globally-focused comparatist, recognising that law manifests itself in
several different ways, cannot be impressed by extremist Islamic religious doctrine. Various competing approaches to understanding Islamic law and its rule
systems become visible if one applies the conceptual triangle of global law
as developed in chapter 3.8. Indeed, in Islamic legal history, transmission of
the Prophet's advice (*sunna*) becomes the second most authoritative source of
Islamic law after the Qur'an (Burton, 1994: ix). It inevitably contains some
human intervention, since the Prophet had to match situation-specific justice
with adherence to divinely revealed rules. Since the Qur'an always remains
the starting point of Islamic law, neither religious positivism nor the secular
ideology of legal positivism, which appears at first sight culturally alien to Muslims,[27] make sense on their own. Submission to the divine will as the first rule
of Islamic law (Coulson, 1968: 54, cited below) precludes questioning of the
goodness of God.[28] This is a difficult issue for Muslim scholars and individuals

---

[26] See chapter 4. Glenn (2004: 173) notes that *shari'a* means basically the way or path to
follow.

[27] It raises questions, which also arise among Hindus and Buddhists over *karma* and *kamma*,
whether God really sees everything and whether retribution (in whatever form) really
exists. Such speculations assume that we know what the results of our actions will be.
Since we do not possess such knowledge, following any form of guidance becomes a
matter of calculated risk for individuals. A 'secular Muslim' might be treated as an odd
description for somebody who hopes that God might not notice everything.

[28] It is considered presumptuous to assume that Allah needs human help in running the universe. He simply sits in judgment of individual action. The individual Muslim, therefore,

faced with manifestly bad realities. How does one explain misfortune striking Muslims? Familiar questions from natural law debates raise their head.

Later developments of Muslim jurisprudence allow for secular manifestations, for which separate terms have been used, *qanun* for state-made law, the secular *mazalim* courts, which dealt with mundane matters (Amedroz, 1911) and *siyasa shar'iyya*, 'government in accordance with *shar'ia*' (section 5.9). A succinct insightful summary of traditional Islamic law was provided by Coulson (1968: 54):

> Islamic law (known in some parts of the world as 'Muhammadan law') is a body of rules which gives practical expression to the religious faith and aspiration of the Muslim. Total and unqualified submission to the will of Allah is the fundamental tenet of Islam, and the law which is associated with the religion defines the will of Allah in terms of a comprehensive code of behaviour covering all aspects of life. *All* aspects of life: for ritual practices, such as prayer, fasting, alms, and pilgrimage, the subjects of permissible foods and styles of dress, and social etiquette generally are as vital and integral a part of the system as those topics which are strictly legal in the western sense of the term. Known as the 'Shari'a', a derivative of an Arabic root word meaning 'track' or 'road', this law constitutes a divinely ordained path of conduct which guides the Muslim towards fulfilment of his religious conviction in this life and reward from his Creator in the world to come.

Allott (1980: 141) emphasised a relationship of fusion and intimate connection of Islamic law and religion: '[t]he sacred law, the Shari'a, is more than a law in the western sense . . . it contains an infallible guide to ethics. It is fundamentally a DOCTRINE OF DUTIES, a code of obligations.' Complex interlinkage of law and religion, ultimately law and life, meant that religion could assert its claims to superiority over law. However, Derrett (1968b: ix) protested that religion was not really, if one studied the subject carefully, a source of law:

> The notion that in oriental societies relatively immune from western influence law is derived from religion is deeply engrained. It is difficult to shake off the mistaken notions of our former teachers on this subject . . . The improbability of this we have already stated: it is rather the case that religion suits society than that society has to suit the religion.

However, even if religion was not a direct source of law, this did not mean that it was not an important subject of study for lawyers. Derrett (1968b: xviii–xix) concluded:

> Meanwhile, so long as determinations of 'our rights' continue to expose our individual weakness and moral poverty, judges there must be. But

bound through declaration of faith, does well to consider whether certain actions will be meritorious or not and thus needs to know about God's will, much more so than the pious Hindu or the good Buddhist.

we respond to a primeval superstition, one which externalises an inborn intuition, when we believe that there is a judge above all judges. Law, for all its majesty, is a temporary expedient . . . Man, however, senses that above laws there is a standard, which is *just*.

Thus, as we have seen, religion is not a true source of law, but, at most, part of the conceptual framework within which a legal system and legal propositions take their places; likewise beside the ultimate requirements of morality all such law is dwarfed, and in this conclusion it seems that Christians, Muslims, Hindus and Jews are agreed. A superstition in which all the great civilisations are at one speaks for a constant factor of the human make-up which can only be ignored at one's peril.

This is still sound advice to secular scholarship today which seeks to shut out that various religious beliefs are an important element of human existence for many people. Global legal theory cannot ignore the presence and impact of concepts of religious natural law. However, religious positivism goes one step too far: if Islamic law had operated on a different *grundnorm*, there would have been Muslim leaders claiming with due authority that they knew exactly what God's will was. No doubt, such men would have been tempted to lay down entire legal systems on that basis for all Muslims to follow globally. Fortunately for Muslims as well as non-Muslims, and particularly women, this was not God's will. It would have opened the door to patriarchal tyranny in the name of Islam. Viewed from this perspective, it could be argued that the lessons from plurality-conscious Islamic jurisprudence help to protect the world from the potential excesses of unbridled positivism.

5.2 The Qur'anic base and its application

The revelation of the Qur'an to the Prophet Mohammad (c. 570–632), an Arab from Mecca, which was then a holy place for Jews, occurred over a period of some twenty-two years between 610 and 632 AD, until the Prophet died and the revelation was completed.[29] The term *qur'an*, 'that which is revealed', is often translated as 'reading' or 'recital' and over 6,000 verses were revealed in this way. During this process, Mohammad migrated from Mecca to Medina, where he established the first Muslim community in 622 AD.[30]

It is known that the oral revelations, which did not appear in any particular order, were written down on various materials and kept safe (Glenn, 2004: 172). They were not systematically sifted, it appears, until after the death of the Prophet. The process of organising this collection took some time, but within twenty years of the Prophet's death a formal text of the Qur'an existed. The

---

[29] On the eternal and universal nature of Islam see Fyzee (1999: 13). The Prophet received these revelations through the Angel Gabriel, who appeared to him in various forms.

[30] A detailed historical account is provided in Hosain (1995). The Islamic calendar starts from the year 622 AD.

production of six copies of this text was safeguarded during the rule of the third Caliph, Uthman (644–56 AD). The Qur'an was collected into 114 *suras* or chapters, varying in length from three to 286 verses, in no particular subject order but according to length.

The legal discussions about the nature of this revelation suffer from many conceptual imprecisions as writers, both Western and non-Western, have not reflected about using the word 'law'; it is left to the reader to gauge the appropriate nuances of meaning in a particular statement. From a religious perspective, for the Muslim believer, God's revelation is of supreme authority and is 'law'. For the modern period, too, the continuing supremacy of Islamic revelation is unambiguously expressed when El Alami and Hinchcliffe (1996: 3) begin their study with the following statement:

> For Muslims, the Shari'ah is the law of God. God alone is the giver of law; the function of man is to comprehend the law and to obey its divine provisions. The Shari'ah covers all aspects of life and every field of law – constitutional, international, criminal, civil and commercial – but at its very heart lies the law of the family.

More than a statement of faith, this reflects how a Muslim variant of legal centralism only speaks of God's law, while the comparative analyst knows that God's law does not cover the entire field as understood by Western legal theories. Since the Qur'anic law goes much beyond the ambit of any positivist law-making and encompasses every aspect of life, including the hereafter, that field is much wider than conventional legal studies would wish to reach. This is subtly expressed in the juxtaposition of 'all aspects of life' and 'every field of law'. Studying the whole of Muslim law, therefore, requires first of all analysis of its religious foundations. Coulson (1969: 1) correctly emphasised:

> The fundamental question of the nature of law is answered for Muslim jurisprudence, in terms that admit of no compromise, by the religious faith itself. Law is the divinely ordained system of God's commands. To deny this principle would be, in effect, to renounce the religious faith of Islam.

Coulson saw the contrast of this Islamic axiom with theories of Western jurisprudence of positivism or various natural law approaches and opened a window for the reader to show multiple interactions between different types of law. In the literature generally, however, including important textbooks (Hallaq, 1997), the Qur'anic revelation is misleadingly portrayed as legislation, often without further explanation. Even Coulson (1964: 11–20), taking a historical approach to Islamic law, seemed at times to think too much like a lawyer and comes across as too legocentric. Coulson (1964: 20) speaks of an 'objective assessment of the Qur'an itself as a legislative document', whereas earlier he had expressly pointed to the limits of law-making through the Qur'an: 'For those who were pledged to conduct their lives in accordance with the will of

God the Qur'an itself did not provide a simple and straightforward code of law. As a legislative document, the Qur'an raises many problems' (p. 17).

The somewhat misleading references to 'legislation' are clarified elsewhere when Coulson (1964: 12) states that 'the primary purpose of the Qur'an is to regulate not the relationship of man with his fellows but his relationship with his Creator'. This important conceptual distinction appears to have been overlooked by others. The writing of some Muslim lawyers, reflecting Western legocentric training, shows that they see, as Muslims, every reason to declare God's law as 'the law'.[31] Sometimes, the term 'legislation' is even applied to the role of the Prophet. Rahim (1994: 16), in a brief overview of the history of Islamic law and jurisprudence in four periods, writes:

> The first period . . . has been rightly called the 'legislative period' of Islam when laws were enacted by the divine legislator and promulgated in the words of the Qur'an, or by the precepts of Muhammad. These are the texts upon which as their foundation the superstructure of the four Sunni schools has been constructed.

This is conceptually imprecise and misleading for non-specialist readers, conflating the Qur'an and the Prophet's *sunna*, creating an impression that both can be treated as the same type of law.[32] It is understandable that Muslim scholars refer to divine revelation as 'legislation', but the sayings and decisions of the Prophet are certainly not appropriately termed 'legislation'.[33] Unreflected mixing of different legal categories occurs; global legal application of the Qur'an is entangled with Western legal concepts and must be questioned.

The Qur'an was not revealed into a dialectic vacuum, but entered the crowded socio-cultural space of the Middle East at the beginning of the seventh century AD. It created a new ethical system of evaluation of all human actions, on a scale ranging from 'obligatory' and 'recommended' to the neutral 'permissible', as well as 'disliked', and finally 'illegal' or 'prohibited' (*haram*). The pre-Islamic period, referred to as *jahiliyah*, was characterised by the co-existence of Arab communities, which lived by chthonic, cosmos-loyal ethics (Glenn, 2000: 157), with communities of Jews, Parsis, Christians and others. Pre-Islamic Arabian society was dominated by tribal law, polytheism and adherence to patriarchal norms, in an environment of much social and political instability. Some Muslim authors have been tempted to depict this period as primitive, but that created delicate dilemmas, since the revelation of the Qur'an

---

[31] Doi (1984: 2) begins his chapter on the *shari'a* with the declaration that 'Allah is the Law Giver', again a statement of Muslim faith rather than a legal comment.

[32] It seems that Hallaq (1997: 3ff.), portraying the Qur'an as a legal document, goes too far in speaking of 'legislation'.

[33] Rahim (1994: 18) discusses the powers of the later Caliphs, clearly distinguishing the absence of any legislative power of such human functionaries, while 'God alone is the legislator in Islam'.

did not totally wipe out the existing social and legal patterns. To depict Muslim cultural history as based on backwardness carried certain risks.[34] There was no doubt that it would be possible to improve on the existing conditions.

An important aspect of pre-Islamic Arabian society concerns the position of women (Esposito and Delong-Bas, 2002). There is wide agreement that the Qur'an specifically addressed some of the legal problems of women and lifted them out of a disadvantaged social status (Fyzee, 1999: 5–6). Coulson (1964: 14) emphasised that '[w]ithout doubt it is the general subject of the position of women, married women in particular, which occupies pride of place in the Qur'anic laws'. Islam not only encouraged women to become Muslim, it significantly enhanced their socio-legal position and life chances.[35] Coulson (1968: 56) summarised this process:

> The legal status of women was greatly improved in a variety of respects, *inter alia* by the rule that the dower, or payment made by the husband in consideration of marriage, belonged to the wife herself and not, as was common previously, to her father or other guardian who had given her in marriage. And yet most of these rules have the appearance of *ad hoc* solutions for particular problems. There is no real attempt in the *Qur'an* to deal with any one legal topic or relationship comprehensively. Its regulations set out to modify the existing customary law in certain particulars rather than to supplant that law with an entirely new system.

The new set of rules introduced by the Qur'an was achieving two important things at once. It provided a new faith, which all people could opt into, and it stipulated important socio-cultural reforms. Hence, apart from its religious objectives, the revelation would also have significant legal effects and consequences. However, the category of law now being introduced through the Qur'anic provisions is not the same kind of law as the pre-existing category, best classified as local Arab customary laws. Aware of competing conceptualisations of law, given that the Qur'an is an all-comprehensive divine law, we have to analyse carefully what legal impact the comprehensive new revelation was about to have. It is interesting to see how Fyzee (1999: 6) viewed the matter, writing that '[i]n pre-Islamic times law proper, as we understand it today, was unknown. Tribes and chieftains acted in accordance with tradition and convention.' While he saw no state law, he was not willing to treat the pre-Islamic law as

---

[34] Indeed, Fyzee (1999: 6) suggests that *jahiliya* does not mean the period of 'ignorance', but rather of 'wildness' or 'intrepidity'. See also Muslehuddin (1980: 61–4); Endress (1988: 116ff.); with a South Asian slant see Purohit (1998: 3–7).

[35] Prominent examples include that marriage was more of a sale of the woman than a contract, that men could marry as many women as they liked, and that they could divorce them as they pleased. The dower (*mahr*) given to a woman in marriage was earlier handed over to the male guardian, rather than the woman herself, and the property rights of women generally were strengthened through new rules on succession. For details see Doi (1984) and Coulson (1964: 14–17; 1971).

a form of law. However, Fyzee (1999: 7) explicitly recognised the existence of two types of customary law, inter-tribal customs and 'customs which regulated the relation of the individual to his own tribe'. Fyzee (1999: 7–10) provides a number of examples to illustrate the far-reaching and humane nature of the reforms brought by the new revelation, but the legal categories used lack precision.

By its very definition and position the Qur'an was of course not customary law. But it had the effect of criticising and challenging many rules within the various customary legal systems, particularly relating to women and the relationship of clan and nuclear family. Coulson (1964: 15) noted that the Qur'anic regulations 'modify in certain particulars rather than supplant entirely the existing customary law'. This could not have been any different, first because Qur'anic 'law' could not just replace custom, and secondly because many people of course did not become Muslim. The new rules did not constitute territorial law, applying only to people who chose to submit to them. For persons who did not convert to Islam, the new rules might remain largely irrelevant, but how did Qur'anic law affect the growing number of converts to the new faith? The inevitable outcome was that the new Qur'anic rules and existing social rule systems at the time would need to be harmonised. Within the socio-cultural space of Arabia, it would take time to evolve a 'living Muslim law' which followed the letter and spirit of the Qur'anic law. Individuals might accept the new faith, but their daily activities would still have to be restructured to fit the new norm system. Application of the new ethics of Islam implied a new way of life. The daily challenge would lie in making the new law practically applicable to society, and it was not even relevant to consider what role the state could play in this context. Coulson (1968: 54) noted this challenge, but immediately focused on the position of jurists, characteristically overstating the role of juristic doctrine,[36] while underplaying the role of the common Muslim:

> From the advent of Islam in early seventh-century Arabia the task assumed by Muslim jurisprudence was the discovery of the terms of Allah's law for Muslim society. Legal scholarship gradually built up a corpus of doctrine, and by the end of the tenth century Shari'a had achieved a definitive formulation in legal manuals composed by individual jurists.

This fast-forward focus on doctrine, and the swift move towards the jurists, who are not an institutional feature of Islamic law from its very start, obscures the key role of individual activities, and to some extent of the Prophet, as catalysts in the process of creating an early living Muslim law.[37] In later Islamic

---

[36] More recent research on Islamic law has begun to challenge the dominant focus in older studies on doctrine, and argues that developments in the history of Islamic law should be analysed more specifically within their socio-cultural context. For a recent example see Hurvitz (2000).

[37] Hallaq (1997) shows that an early stage of development, personal discretion (*ra'y*), played a critical role, which was only later restricted.

doctrine, the terms of Allah's law were to be discovered from the text of the Qur'an. Since the Qur'an is not a Napoleonic code, finding guidance on 'the law' inevitably involved human agents. In that sense, the Prophet was also the first Islamic jurist, just as he was the first leader and judge, but the proper category of the 'jurist' appears much later and has specific functions (section 5.6). The question whether any particular manifestation of Islamic law in the world was God's law or men's law did not concern the Qur'an, but became critical later. Submitting to God's will may be simple, the real challenge for believers presented itself in ascertaining the right thing to do at any one moment of their life, a universal challenge.[38] As shown in abundance below, God's revelation needed to be protected by Muslims not only from the challenges of outsiders, but from internal subversions of various kinds.

It would be too simplistic for legal analysts to argue that the main problem lies in the nature of the Qur'an because it is not a comprehensive code of law. No law code is ever going to cover everything; all law-making must remain a piecemeal human endeavour (Moore, 1978: 9). The precise number of explicitly legal verses in the Qur'an has been assessed as not more than 80 to a maximum of 600 out of a total of about 6,000 verses, mostly in books two and four. Coulson (1964: 12) wrote that '[n]o more than approximately eighty verses deal with legal topics in the strict sense of the term'.[39] While God did not legislate on everything through the Qur'an, it is quite clear that this revelation introduced a comprehensive all-encompassing new ethic, a new natural law. It therefore created solid foundations for what Chiba (1986) called 'legal postulates', but not an official legal system by which a state would henceforth govern its subjects. Given the nature of this revelation and the socio-cultural conditions at the time, many important questions were bound to arise, particularly in relation to the role of the Prophet.

5.3 The Prophet's roles: leader, judge and guide

The Prophet of Islam undoubtedly played a crucial role in the early development of Islamic law because he alone knew directly about the new system of ethics during the long period of revelation. As leader of the first Muslim community, he was closely involved in advising fellow Muslims about legal issues, acting as community leader and administrator of justice. He was the leader, judge and spiritual guide of the emerging community. While the message of the new rules was spread by the Prophet to a wider public, several people close to the Prophet

---

[38] Islam, too, is focused on the concerns of the individual, and hence brings about, in its own way, what the Hindu concept of *dharma* and the Chinese understanding of *li* sought to achieve (May, 1985). The individual Muslim has an obligation to follow *shari'a*, the 'path to the watering hole'.

[39] Hallaq (1997: 3) notes that 'Muslim jurists and modern scholars are in agreement that the Quran contains some 500 verses with legal content'.

gained deeper insight. They became known as the Companions of the Prophet (*sahabah*) and were bound to play a crucial role especially after the Prophet's death.

Coulson (1968: 56) reported that '[d]uring his lifetime Muhammad was accepted as the supreme arbitrator of the community and solved legal problems, as and when they arose, by interpreting the relevant Qur'anic revelations'. Coulson (1964: 21) emphasised that the function of Mohammad as a legal arbiter was legitimated by the Qur'an itself, denouncing the customary pattern of recourse to a soothsayer or pagan arbitrator (*kahin*).[40] This strengthened the inner cohesion of the Muslim community and allowed the Prophet to apply the stipulations of the Qur'an in difficult situations. Thus, Coulson (1964: 22) wrote, 'Muhammad had been elevated to the position of judge supreme, with the function of interpreting and explaining the general provisions of the divine revelation', but he also emphasised that 'Muhammad made no attempt to elaborate anything like a code of law on this basis' (p. 22) and 'was content to proffer *ad hoc* solutions as problems arose'. Obviously, the Prophet could not have done anything else to fulfil his divinely ordained task of applying God's law. In particular, he could not claim to make law without challenging the revelation. Schacht (1984: 10) writes a little confusingly that 'as the Prophet he became the ruler-lawgiver of a new society on a religious basis', reiterating this by reference to 'the legislation of the Prophet' (p. 11), though his overall analysis does not suggest that the Prophet was engaged in positivist law-making. The multiplicity of the Prophet's functions shows that he was primarily engaged in applying God's law, inevitably involving human discretion. Later law-makers might ignore the requirement of relating every human action back to Qur'anic authority and run the risk of being accused of introducing their own personal opinion (*ra'y*). Indeed, while the Prophet was trusted to apply God-given rules and remain faithful to Qur'anic revelation, his death and the activities of later interpreters precipitated allegations of abuse (see below). The Prophet's involvement as a judge must have created many personal dilemmas. He was at the same time a member of society, and the chosen Messenger of God's word. His special position in rule formation highlights critically important conflicts in early Muslim society, resulting from divergence between pre-existing laws and some explicit provisions of the Qur'an. Seeking to strengthen the legal position of women and the nuclear family against the patriarchal clan, the Qur'an introduced new rules on succession. In conflict situations, God's new law needed to be applied to bring about the first process of Islamisation in the local community at that time, Islamising local normative orders. The Prophet was uniquely placed to propel this process.

---

[40] The socially central role of wise men (or women), acting as arbitrators in ritualised forms of dispute settlement, was traditionally important everywhere in Asia and Africa. Since these people had a lot of influence on local normative orders, seeking to curtail their impact makes sense.

In the famous case of Sa'd, succession law issues came to a head and the Prophet's guidance was invoked. The widow of Sa'd, a soldier killed in battle, had complained to the Prophet that her husband's brother, as the nearest male agnate relative, in accordance with local customary norms, had claimed the entire estate and totally excluded her and her two daughters.[41] The Prophet, with reference to explicit Qur'anic provisions about apportioning of shares, decided that the Qur'anic heirs should have first claim on the property of a deceased, not the agnates as in the old system, thereby placing the Qur'anic rules above local traditions. He ordered that, in accordance with the Qur'an, the widow should receive one-eighth of the estate, the daughters two-thirds, and only the residue of five twenty-fourths should go to the male agnate, who was not totally excluded, but took only after the Qur'anic heirs. Coulson (1968: 57) called this 'the golden rule of the Islamic law of inheritance'. The effect of such amalgamation of old law and new Qur'anic rules was to lay foundations for the immensely complex system of Muslim succession law.[42]

The Prophet's advisory and judicial activities until his death in 632 AD created a large body of rulings, regulations, decisions and statements. These were not systematically collected but were remembered by the people closest to him, prominently the Companions. Neither a rudimentary body of case law nor legislation, it was a haphazard collection, recording solutions offered for socio-legal problems arising at the time. It could not have been any different, since none of the components in this complex cauldron of legal norm-making would be able to claim superior status to the exclusion of all other potential sources. While the Qur'an was applied by the Prophet as the most authoritative yardstick for all cases, neither could custom be totally ignored, nor could some measure of personal discretion be entirely excluded. Coulson (1968: 57) highlighted this complex scenario: 'The fundamental problem facing the Prophet and his successors in their judicial capacity was the precise determination of the relationship between the new Qur'anic provisions and the traditional standards of the customary law.' Noting that the Prophet had to balance the conflicting expectations of the new Qur'anic provisions and the rules of society around him regarding succession law, Coulson (1968: 58) concluded that this led at times to a restrictive interpretation of the Qur'anic provisions and that 'the perpetuation of the traditional standards of the customary law was by no means confined to inheritance, but was a central feature of general legal development in the

---

[41] Such problems are known to exist in many African communities, too, where a brother or close male relative of the deceased will inherit not only the property, but also the widow herself. Such chthonic rules are also documented from ancient Indian society, which knew levirate marriages. On marriage as a dynastic matter see Derrett (1968b: 355).

[42] This has been the subject of many detailed studies. See e.g. Coulson (1971) and Khan (1999), mainly on Sunni law. The Shi'a system of inheritance later went even further and, saying that the Qur'an constitutes the new law, gave nothing to the agnates ('dust in the jaws of the *asaba*').

Medinan period'. So the reformist provisions of the Qur'an, in particular their pro-women slant, were beginning to be applied with a less reformist effect than a reading of the Qur'an would suggest. At that time, however, nobody read the Qur'an as we do now. This is not to suggest that the Prophet and those around him ignored certain Qur'anic provisions, but there was much scope for human interpretation, influenced by the 'legal postulates' of a clan-focused, honour-driven patriarchal Arab society.

In this context, the concept of *sunna* becomes extremely important; it has at least two distinct meanings, which must not be confused. Their co-existence illustrates the early conflicts and tensions faced by the Prophet, who had the religious obligation to apply the Qur'anic law, but could not avoid taking account of customary norms. The concept of *sunna* at first referred to 'good local practice'.[43] Schacht (1984: 17) confirms this, while his legocentric use of the word 'precedent' is misleading:

> At an early period the ancient idea of *sunna*, precedent or normative custom, reasserted itself in Islam. The Arabs were, and are, bound by tradition and precedent. Whatever was customary was right and proper; whatever the forefathers had done deserved to be imitated. This was the golden rule of the Arabs whose existence on a narrow margin in an unpropitious environment did not leave them much room for experiments and innovations which might upset the precarious balance of their lives. In this idea of precedent or *sunna* the whole conservatism of the Arabs found expression . . . The idea of *sunna* presented a formidable obstacle to every innovation . . . Islam, the greatest innovation that Arabia saw, had to overcome this obstacle, and a hard fight it was. But once Islam had prevailed, even among one single group of Arabs, the old conservatism reasserted itself; what had shortly before been an innovation now became the thing to do, a thing hallowed by precedent and tradition, a *sunna*. This ancient Arab concept of *sunna* was to become one of the central concepts of Islamic law.

This early process of Islamisation of the central customary concept in Arab society was subsequently continued when everything the Prophet declared to be correct practice also became known as *sunna*, and was thereby turned into the second primary source of *shari'a*, Islamised good custom as tested and approved by the Prophet (Pearl and Menski, 1998: 5). Because it was the Prophet who approved of such customs, in the emerging scheme of Islamic law this *sunna* was to have a superior place. Schacht elaborates on this transition in the meaning of *sunna* while discussing the role of Shafi'i, the first major juristic theoretician of the Islamic legal system (section 5.7.2). Shafi'i laid down a formal system of four sources of *shari'a* in which the role of the Prophet's *sunna* is clearly identified as second in line immediately after the Qur'an. However, the term

---

[43] This shares similarities with the Hindu concepts of *smriti* and *sadācāra* as 'tradition' and 'good custom'.

sunna existed much earlier and referred to a quite different category of law.[44] Schacht (1979: 2) wrote that Shafi'i was the first lawyer (an inappropriate use of the word) 'to define *sunna* as the model behaviour of the Prophet, in contrast with his predecessors, for whom it was not necessarily connected with the Prophet, but represented . . . their "living tradition" on an equal footing with customary or generally agreed practice'. Through creating the new *sunna*, the Prophet produced authoritative statements on the newly Islamised 'living law' of his people, a process reminiscent of common law techniques of judicial restatement.

The recollections of what the Prophet said and did were unsystematically recorded, mainly by the Companions, and became later subject to standardisation and selection (Doi, 1984: 48). The collections of these sayings were later called *hadith*, constituting the records of the Prophet's *sunna* (Burton, 1994). The process of their formal collation and editing took some two hundred years (section 5.7.3).

5.4 Early Islamic law after the Prophet's death

Mohammad's death in 632 AD created a dilemma, as from that point onwards revelation ceased and there could have been a break in the emerging Muslim legal traditions. However, in political and legal terms, there was continuity. Coulson (1968: 56–7) wrote that 'the mantle of the judicial authority was assumed by the Caliphs, who succeeded to political leadership, and their decisions, together with those of the Prophet, marked the beginning of the growth of a body of law which supplemented and expanded the general precepts of the Qur'an'. Marking a new phase in the development of Muslim law (Rahim, 1994: 17), the task of spiritual and worldly leadership of the community now devolved on the Companions, the next most reliable source of guidance when new questions and conflict situations arose. Rahim (1994: 17–18) discusses their methodology of decision-making in this early formative period of Islamic law:

> If a text of the Qur'an or pronouncement of the Prophet covered a point, or if the Prophet had decided a similar case, there could be no difficulty. But fresh facts and new circumstances often arose for which no provision had been made, specially as the affairs of the community became more complex with the growth of empire. In the absence of authority, the Companions had to guide themselves by the light of their reason, having in regard those usages of the community which had not been condemned by the Prophet. Those who were associated with the Prophet as his companions, and often shared his counsels, must have known, as if by instinct, the policy of Islamic law, and whether a particular rule or decision was in harmony with its principles. It is presumed, therefore, that an agreement among the companions in a

---

[44] See in detail Schacht (1979: 58–81).

particular view vouched for its absolute soundness, and even their isolated opinions are regarded as of high authority.

The concept of 'agreement' or 'consensus', *ijma*, was later to become a critically important source of Islamic jurisprudence (Hasan, 1984). In its early beginning, *ijma* refers to the involvement of the Companions as a new source of legal authority, which the Companions collectively shared on account of their previous physical proximity to the Prophet, whose pronouncements they had witnessed or heard of, and whose views they had known. The first *ijma* in the history of Islamic law is therefore the agreement of the Companions of the Prophet over something heard from him or observed through his actions. This is a different kind of *ijma* than the later 'juristic consensus', based on study rather than participant observation. Further, the concept of *ijma* as 'consensus of a community', based on custom rather than recourse to text,[45] may refer to a locally agreed norm system that was not necessarily tested in Islamic terms. Based on human discretion, it does not figure among the later approved sources of Muslim law, which are focused on juristic techniques (section 5.7.2).

Studying the first century of Islam, Schacht (1984: 15ff.) emphasised that this early formative period was crucial, but there are severe limits to knowledge about law-making processes at that time.[46] Schacht (1984: 15) reports that '[w]hat little authentic evidence is available shows that the ancient Arab system of arbitration, and Arab customary law in general, as modified and completed by the Koran, continued under the first successors of the Prophet, the caliphs of Medina (AD 632–61)'. The four so-called Rashidun ('rightly guided') Caliphs, as political successors of the Prophet, could not totally fill the unique position of the Prophet and turned their attention to other legal matters, less focused on the Qur'an. Some form of what one could call 'secular' Islamic law-making began here.[47] The emphasis of law-making shifted gradually from consideration of the God–man relationship to the continuing process of Islamising interhuman relationships and more attention was given towards administration, developing secondary rules in a Hartian sense. Concentrating on such secondary rules, these early rulers made numerous administrative decisions and regulations. Schacht (1984: 15) wrote:

> In their functions as the supreme rulers and administrators, though of course devoid of the religious authority of the Prophet, the caliphs acted

---

[45] Like *sadācāra* in Hindu law, which also occupies the ragged boundary between custom and textual authority.

[46] A specialist journal, *Islamic Law and Society*, contains evidence of recent lively debates about this period. See Schneider (1999) and Motzki (2002).

[47] However, from an internal Muslim perspective, all secular law-making is still perceived as subject to God's Order. In that conceptual sense, truly secular law-making in Islamic law is impossible, but there is much scope for the practical regulation of life in accordance with Islamic principles.

to a great extent as the lawgivers of the community; during the whole of this first century the administrative and legislative activities of the Islamic government cannot be separated. This administrative legislation, however, was hardly, if at all, concerned with modifying the existing customary law; its object was to organize the newly conquered territories for the benefit of the Arabs.

Such law-making could not remain in a water-tight compartment and inevitably also influenced, as examples cited by Schacht show, the continuing process of applying the Qur'anic norm system. A relevant example concerns the introduction of stoning to death as a punishment for unlawful intercourse (*zina*), not mentioned in the Qur'an but taken from Jewish law.[48] This shows, like other examples, that the borderlines between 'religious' law-making and secular legal regulations could not be neatly maintained by these more practice-oriented early rulers. Man-made Islamic law began to grow. Inevitably, internal conflict among the Companions arose not only over questions of succession to the political authority of the Prophet (Coulson, 1964: 23) but over the legal standing of the administrative acts of the first two Caliphs. Positivist ambitions of these early leaders must have been resisted and resented since there should in principle be no human law-making. It is evident that sticking to that position rigidly would have either prevented, and certainly slowed down, further formal legal development.

Little seems to be known about Abu Bakr, the first Caliph (632–4), who was elected, according to Sunni Muslim accounts,[49] as the successor or who may have been recommended by the Prophet himself. He faced a revolt against Islam, which was put down by him (Muslehuddin, 1980: 68–9). Doi (1984: 66) emphasises that Abu Bakr attempted to base his rule on the principle of *ijma* of the Companions, but frequent disagreements arose. The Caliph Umar (634–44) introduced certain rules on tax and land law (Coulson, 1964: 23), but also faced much opposition and was subsequently assassinated. The dilemma of continuous arguments over law-making is most clearly illustrated by the actions of the third Caliph, Uthman (644–56), who finally made sure that an authoritative collection of the Qur'an was prepared.[50] Uthman himself eventually lost control of the growing Muslim empire and was also killed.

Coulson (1964: 23) wrote that the Caliphs and their advisors had the duty of implementing the Qur'anic provisions 'in the same spirit as their former leader', and emphasised that the first two Caliphs were quite ready to take

---

[48] Schacht (1984: 15). This debate resurfaced in modern Pakistan a few decades ago (section 5.14).

[49] On the Shi'a opposition and claims, based on the position of Ali as the Prophet's son-in-law, see further below. For a history of the Ismailis, a major Shi'a group, see Daftary (1998).

[50] Details of this process are discussed by Muslehuddin (1980: 71), who reports that the task took several years, and the results were verified by a committee.

advice from pious and respected persons (p. 25). Coulson (1964: 23ff.) depicted this prolonged process as a complex conflict between old and new orders and provided several examples of interesting succession cases decided at this time. In addition to their judicial functions, the later Caliphs were becoming more involved in 'positive legislation' (Coulson, 1964: 26), justified by reference to the Qur'an, but 'the precise nature and scope of this legislative activity remains clouded in obscurity' (p. 26). Overall, Islamic law asserted itself and '[i]n a spirit of compromise . . . a population deeply attached to its traditional values had come to terms with the dictates of its new religious faith' (p. 26). However, with the fourth Caliph, Ali (656–61), one particularly critical and important matter came to a head. It had long been simmering below the surface, and now led to the Sunni/Shi'a split in Islam. While the term 'Sunni' is linked to the due observance of customary practice, *sunna*, the name 'Shi'a' derives from the term for supporters or followers of Ali, the *Shi'at Ali*. Both terms developed later (Bharatiya, 1996: 17) and their history reflects the deepening doctrinal and legal differences between the two groups.

This complex subject has many political aspects, but goes far deeper than politics.[51] At its core was a dispute over whether, in succession to the Prophet, family relationship or esteem in the community should prevail, and so whether family ties or nomination should be the main legitimising element of Islamic leadership.[52] Ali, an early convert to Islam, had married Mohammad's daughter Fatima and had claimed succession to Mohammad, who had no son. His argument was based on the closeness of family ties as well as his alleged designation as successor by the Prophet himself, which Sunni doctrine does not accept. The principle of family or blood relations, as against standing in the Muslim community, in this case measured in terms of moral probity and closeness to the Prophet,[53] surfaced here for the first time.[54] Since Ali's claims were not accepted on a number of grounds,[55] others were nominated before it was

[51] Esposito (1995) contains several relevant entries with further details of the resulting conflict.

[52] Early indications of this simmering problem under the early Caliphs are discussed in Schacht (1984: 15), who refers to social criticism by a poet, a popular means of political commentary.

[53] At this early time, of course, jurists did not yet exist. Only later did classical learning become a major criterion for merit.

[54] It continues to be a qualifying element for Shi'a jurists to be able to trace descent to the Prophet, whereas for Sunni jurists the qualifying criterion is classical learning. In terms of law-making, too, Shi'a *imams* claim the power to legislate with divine authority (a modern example is the Aga Khan of the Ismailis), while the development of Shi'a law mainly took place under the Safavids in Persia. On the terminology regarding *imam* see Hidayatullah and Hidayatullah (1990: xiv). On Shi'a law generally, see Schacht (1979: 262–8).

[55] It appears that one of these was the apprehension that Ali might claim to continue the Prophethood, which would have challenged the position of Mohammad as the 'seal of

eventually Ali's turn. After Umar's death, the Caliphate had been offered to Ali, on condition that he would uphold the laws established by the two previous Caliphs, but he had declined, 'declaring that in all cases respecting which he found no positive law or decision of the Prophet, he would rely upon his own judgment' (Bharatiya, 1996: 15). The Caliphate was therefore offered to Uthman, who soon lost control of governance and was assassinated in 656, which opened the way for Ali to become Caliph.[56] Endress (1988: 36ff.) provides a detailed account of the various battles and manoeuvres leading to the eventual assassination of Ali, who also could not control the growing political turmoil. Ali had two sons, who were also killed in this struggle.[57]

The period of the Caliphate thus ended in turmoil. Political agenda threatened to overshadow and marginalise the core religious issues. It began to dawn on many Muslims at this time that the provisions of the Qur'an would now need to be studied, since leading members of the community could no longer be trusted to uphold God's divine order. Divine revelation was constantly watered down by human discretion, and blatant exercise of political power without reference to the Qur'an interfered in all walks of life. The conceptual origins of Muslim jurists as a class are found here, removed from and in opposition to political office and power, in a piously motivated desire to ensure that God's word would continue to be applied and Islam would be spread.

Most standard textbooks and studies of Islamic law treat the jurists as very important, but forget to reflect on why they were needed in the first place. Rather than assuming that somehow they appeared on the scene, it is important to realise that the Muslim jurists as individuals and as a 'profession' did not just materialise from nowhere. Clearly, they had their own agenda, which also require analysis. At this critical juncture of Muslim legal history, the earlier process of Islamisation needed to be revived and reactivated, because the death of the Prophet and eventually of all those who had known him in person and had seen him perform his functions, had created new problems for the community and for the future of Islam. While some copies of the Qur'an existed, all the important people in society seemed to be too busy fighting over power and riches, while the existence of the revelation itself was relegated to the realm of a receding collective memory.

Prophets', the last one to whom divine revelation could be made. Evidently the Companions closed ranks to prevent this. The ultimate split could not be avoided, however, because both sides continued to insist on their respective claims. An excellent brief account is given by Esposito (1995, II: 247–54).

[56] For details of the history and the political battles see Bharatiya (1996: 15–17) and Endress (1988: 35–9). The Shi'a position is highlighted by Ahmad (1985: 4), to the effect that Shi'as regard the first three Caliphs as usurpers.

[57] The younger son, Husain, was killed in the famous battle of Karbala (in today's Iraq) in 680. For details and implications for Shi'a practices today, see Esposito (1995, 2: 150–1 and 153–5).

5.5 Legal developments in the early Muslim empire: the Umayyads

The growing threat to the continuation of the Qur'anic tradition did not seem to be of much concern to the new rulers following the Caliphs, the ortho- dox Sunni dynasty of Umayyads or Omayyads, who ruled from 661 to 750, based in Damascus, and were followed by the Abbasids (750–1258), who ruled from Baghdad. While the earliest developments concerning juristic scholarship remain inadequately researched (Motzki, 1999; 2002), much of the existing writing about this period focuses on the political activities of these new rulers, arising from local ruling clans, who were no longer elected on the basis of cri- teria that linked them to the Prophet and understanding of the Qur'an. Now political and military power counted foremost and the Umayyads saw their role mainly as continuing the Islamic military conquest. They were, by all accounts, practical-minded rulers who built up administrative structures for the rapidly growing empire.[58] As these Empire builders wielded their political power in the name of Islam (Coulson, 1964: 27), the risk became that, rather than being servants of their religion, they might turn into its masters.[59] This is proba- bly especially true for the early period of Umayyad rule, focused on creating new legal and administrative structures that looked and operated like secular institutions. Such legal creativity led to charges of abandoning Islam,[60] which in turn produced a reorientation of Umayyad rule towards Islamic norms in their later period of rule. Schacht (1984: 23) seems justified in defending the Umayyads against accusations by Arab historians, whose writings seem to have relied heavily on arguments of the competing Abbasid dynasty, who eventually took power from the Umayyads in 750.

Under the early Umayyads, the process of legal restructuring involved fre- quent borrowing of legal models from other legal systems in the region. There is much evidence of such legal transplants in all directions in the early Middle East. Probably the most well-known example is that of the market inspector, the *muhtasib*, an institution copied from Byzantine law (Coulson, 1964: 28). This official possessed limited jurisdiction over such things as weights and measures; in modern terms he was engaged in consumer protection. However, he was also given the duty to safeguard proper standards of *hisba*, religious

---

[58] This included more systematic tax laws and new rules for non-Muslim minorities, the *dhimmis*, whose legal status was modelled on Roman law concepts, and for whom specific legal regulations needed to be developed.

[59] Faruki (1987: 24) speaks of the 'secular Umayyads'. Rahim (1994: 21) sarcastically noted that 'they were not generally speaking noted for their knowledge of the sacred laws'. Hallaq (1997: 8) suggests that 'it is fairly clear that the early caliphs, including the Umayyads, considered themselves as deputies of God on earth and looked to the Quran as a source from which they could draw their legal decisions'.

[60] Motzki (2002) disagrees with Schacht and suggests that caliphal influence was small.

morality (Coulson, 1964: 28), while his main function was clearly administrative. While the Byzantine model was Islamised, it still looked like a secular office.[61]

The Umayyads also created the formal office of the *qadi*, whom Coulson (1964: 28) called 'a judge of a special kind'.[62] The first Muslim *qadi* had been appointed by the Caliph Umar (Rahim, 1994: 20). This was a specialised legal office, reflecting some practical division of labour and focused on administrative efficiency rather than religious elements that were originally taken care of by the Companions. The formal appointment of *qadis* by the early Umayyads as an attempt to create an administrative judicial bureaucracy also represented a further step in restricting the activities of the old *ad hoc* arbitrators, who were still available as informal sources of guidance and dispute settlement in society.[63] Most writers explain the appointment of *qadis* as a matter of administration, but there is also an element of Islamisation, beyond the superficial aim of increasing bureaucratic efficiency and strengthening the claims of the state to control dispute settlement. Schacht (1984: 26) captured this when he wrote that 'care for elementary administrative efficiency and the tendency to Islamicize went hand in hand'. Coulson (1964: 29) found that the early *qadis* took charge of all administrative matters and became exclusively concerned with judicial business only towards the end of Umayyad rule. This reflects an important change in the institution of the *qadi*, since focus on dispute settlement rather than administration reinforced religious elements in the judicial function of the Muslim judge. This created its own problems in a political environment where the rulers' Islamic credentials were constantly questioned and where ruler and judge might disagree. Many accusations against the Umayyads boil down to criticism of a growing state legal system that asserted positivist law-making over Islamic religious foundations. Widespread criticism was expressed not only in political rebellion and dissent, but in the private activities of many pious Muslims who endeavoured to find out for themselves what the Qur'an had stated. This provided added impetus and an even more fertile ground for the emergence of Islamic jurists as a whole class.

The growth of the Muslim empire, and the realisation that administrative efficiency was essential, led to the appointment of many *qadis*. The activities of these judges inevitably 'produced a growing diversity in Islamic legal practice' (Coulson, 1968: 58). Coulson (1964: 30) emphasised the virtually unrestricted

---

[61] See also Schacht (1984: 52). Anyone reading about Islamic law might commit the same methodological error as pointed out for Hindu law (chapter 4), where institutions like the ruler may appear secular to us, and may be so portrayed, without indicating their 'invisible' religious aspects.

[62] On negative American assumptions about '*qadi* justice' see Makdisi (1985).

[63] This may be read as an attempt to control 'extra-legal' mediation. We saw in section 5.3 that the Qur'an opposed recourse to such local non-Islamic guidance and the Prophet claimed the right to decide disputes in the community.

power of these judges to decide cases and the lack of governmental supervision. Since there was no hierarchy of appeal courts, and no case law system, there was no unifying force. Coulson (1964: 30–1) wrote:

> Apart from their limited scope, whether or not the Qur'anic norms were applied at all depended simply upon the degree of knowledge and piety possessed by the individual judge. But even for the pious *qadis* the interpretation of the Qur'anic provisions was largely a matter of personal discretion, so that, apart from the simple and basic rules, their application often added to rather than subtracted from the prevailing diversity in legal practice.

In actual practice, the Qur'anic law was now only one of several sources of law. It seemed no longer necessary to test every decision explicitly against religiously dominant ethical standards. Not only were decisions beginning to look more and more administrative and secular, they were often reached by recourse to secular techniques of law-finding, rather than by Islamic methodologies. Coulson (1968: 58–9) identified two major sources of conflict in the context of growing diversity of judicial practice. First, the extent of reliance on the Qur'an and *sunna* depended on the knowledge and piety of the individual *qadi*. The result of intensive efforts to apply Qur'an and *sunna* inevitably led to numerous divergencies and outright conflicts of interpretation. The Qur'an as a holistic code of ethics, rather than a code of law, was open to human interpretation that inevitably produced different results.

Coulson (1968: 58–9) discussed the example of the Muslim husband's obligation, after divorce, to make a fair provision (which came to be known as *mut'a*) for the former wife, still a heavily contested issue among Muslims today.[64] The relevant Qur'anic provisions (2.236 and 2.241) urge husbands to be fair to the women they divorce, but are only phrased in general terms and do not specify for how long the former husband should maintain the wife, or how much he should pay her. The interpretation by early *qadis*, within the context of their local social norms, first considered this rule obligatory and fixed three *dinars* as appropriate. Some thirty years later, another *qadi* decided that this obligation was only directed at the individual's conscience, an obligation only on pious Muslims and not a general legally enforceable requirement.[65] While Coulson (1968: 59) suggests that further debates took place, we know from later developments in juristic reasoning that the husband's obligation was defined away by most jurists through reference to individual conscience, and such liability was later even outrightly denied. This shows that despite the presence of a

---

[64] See also Coulson (1964: 31–2). This continues to be an important issue and led in Indian Muslim law to the famous case of *Shah Bano* in 1985 (see section 4.10 above).

[65] Indeed, Coulson (1964: 32) also reported that a husband who had refused to treat his former wife with fairness might not be accepted as a proper Muslim witness of high moral probity. Like early Hindu law, Muslim law at this stage also attempted to rely idealistically on the individual conscience.

women-friendly general Qur'anic rule, men's later interpretations took away
such protective mechanisms.

The second major reason put forward by Coulson (1968: 59) for explaining
the growing diversity of judicial decisions under the wide mantle of Islamic law
concerns the role of the *qadis* as 'the spokesmen of the local customary law,
which varied considerably'. A prominent example for this concerns the right of
a Muslim woman to give herself in marriage without a guardian, again an issue
with which modern Muslim societies today, as well as judges and jurists, continue to grapple.[66] Contrasting the Medinan traditional social norms with the
more cosmopolitan views and practices of Kufa at the time, Coulson illustrates
the powerful influence of local customs on decisions made by *qadis*, adding to
this diversity borrowed elements from other legal systems.[67] Coulson (1968:
59) concluded that '[a]s a result of these diverse influences and local standards,
Islamic legal practice under the Umayyads lost the unity and cohesion it had
enjoyed during the Medinan period'. Indeed, a lot of opposition to the legal
effects of Umayyad rule came from Mecca and Medina, relating to the Maliki
school (see further below). From a comparative legal perspective, pluralisation
of laws as an inevitable consequence of the growth of empire troubled many
pious Muslims, seeing that God's universal message to man could now be interpreted in hugely diversified ways through human effort. Was this still God's law,
or was it now becoming men's law? This won't-go-away question in Islamic law
continued to agitate many minds. Coulson (1964: 33) showed through several examples of Islamic equity jurisdiction that the *qadis* gradually acquired
a more prestigious role, moving up from subordinate roles of legal secretary
to the higher echelons of public service. By the end of the Umayyad period,
the *qadis* had become 'an integral and important part of the administrative
machinery, no longer controlled by, but themselves controlling, the customary
law and by their decisions adapting it to meet the changing circumstances of
society' (p. 33).

Coulson (1964: 34) further commented on the haphazard process of legal
growth in which a lot depended on the discretion of the individual judge, so that
the specifically religious or Qur'anic element 'had become largely submerged'
(p. 34). The Umayyads had succeeded in establishing a practical system of legal
administration, not a science of jurisprudence (Coulson, 1964: 35). For the
later period of Umayyad rule (about 715–20), Schacht (1984: 26) emphasised
that *qadis* were becoming increasingly specialised, not as legal technicians in a
positivist sense, but as pious private individuals concerned about the nature of
the Islamic norm system:

> The main concern of these specialists, in the intellectual climate of the
> late Umayyad period, was naturally to know whether the customary law

---

[66] The important *Saima Waheed* case in Pakistan is discussed in section 5.14 below.
[67] See also Pearl and Menski (1998: 8–9); Schacht (1984: 26–7).

conformed to the Koranic and generally Islamic norms; in other words, the specialists from whom the *kadis* came increasingly to be recruited were found among those pious persons whose interest in religion caused them to elaborate, by individual reasoning, an Islamic way of life.

The inevitable conflicts between state-sponsored legal administration and the emerging class of private jurists led to new activities by the *qadis*, whose primary concern now became to safeguard the Qur'anic foundations of Islamic law. This was more a private activity of pious individuals who were concerned to ascertain God's will. Their tendency to rely on Qur'an and *sunna*, rather than unbridled personal opinion, would put them in inevitable opposition to the latent positivist ambitions of Umayyad rulers. By eventually becoming *qadis* themselves, mainly under the Abbasids, early jurists did not resolve these problems, rather they were increased. Once Qur'an-oriented scholars rather than efficient administrators offered themselves for appointment as *qadis*, the ruler of the day might attempt to influence the *qadi* rather than submit to his views, which were supposed to be legally superior because of reliance on Qur'anic guidance and *sunna*. Again, religiously founded authority and positivist political power had ample opportunity to clash.

The multi-layered opposition to excessive human law-making in this period is crystallised to some extent in the concept of *ra'y*, 'personal opinion'. It has a variety of connotations, depending on the context, and can sometimes dismissively mean 'outright speculation'. In the extreme, it is merely classed as 'conjecture' (*zann*).[68] Views based on *ra'y* may be entirely sound, but they are considered arbitrary (Faruki, 1987: 25) if reached without due reference to God's law. The term *ra'y* therefore encapsulates any form of human law-making, but later lost ground to *ijtihad* (Hallaq, 1997: 19). It was bound to be criticised for excessive reliance on human subjectivity. Coulson (1969: 4–5) explained the discretion of the individual with reference to the early beginnings of Islamic law and highlighted the inevitability of some element of human interpretation:

> The first 150 years of Islam were characterized by an almost untrammelled freedom of juristic reasoning in the solution of problems not specifically regulated by divine revelation. Such rules of law as the Qur'an and the *sunna* established were regarded simply as ad hoc modifications of the existing customary law. This existing law remained the accepted standard of conduct unless it was expressly superseded in some particular by the dictates of divine revelation. And when new circumstances posed new problems, these were answered on the basis simply of what seemed the most proper solution to the individual judge or jurist concerned. In the expression of his personal opinion, known as *ra'y*, the individual was free to take into account any factors he deemed relevant. In short, in these early days law

---

[68] Hallaq (1997: 15) demonstrates that early *ra'y* was not so strictly censured, but later it was virtually ousted.

had a distinctly dual basis. It was a compound of the two separate spheres of the divine ordinance and the human decision.

Coulson (1969: 5) concluded this discussion of *ra'y* by saying that 'this pragmatic attitude soon fell victim to the increasing sophistication of theological and philosophical enquiry'. Perhaps this moves a little too fast into the doctrinal realm of the jurists, since the use of *ra'y* was always an inevitable element of practical Islamic law-making and remained a term that jurists have been using to criticise each other. As a technique, it was an inevitable part of the process of Muslim law-making. Coulson (1969: 4) highlighted this need for human involvement:

> But the Qur'an and the *sunna* taken together in no sense constitute a comprehensive code of law. The legal material they contain is a collection of piecemeal rulings on particular issues scattered over a wide variety of different topics; far from representing a substantial corpus juris, it hardly comprises the bare skeleton of a legal system.

The task of human interpretation arises from the piecemeal nature of substantive legal provisions in Qur'an and *sunna*. Constructing a Muslim way of life in accordance with the supreme guidance of Qur'an and *sunna* inevitably required human discretion. Coulson (1969: 1–2) wrote succinctly:

> But while law in Islam may be God-given, it is man who must apply the law. God proposes: man disposes. And between the original divine proposition and the eventual human disposition is interposed an extensive field of intellectual activity and decision.

Starting with the Prophet, Muslim law-making had always required human activity. While the Prophet's sagacious use of discretion would be accorded the highest *bona fide* standing among Muslims, the Companions clearly found it difficult to maintain consensus. As methodological criticisms became more sophisticated, the rapidly escalating debates about *ra'y* demonstrate the wide scope for Muslim scholars to distinguish mere 'speculation' from proper methodology and *bona fide* 'personal opinion', guided by a person's own understanding of God's law. This is the 'margin of error' (*ikhtilaf*) that Muslim jurisprudence has had to grapple with ever since, protected by the unspoken agreement that no individual scholar could ever fully understand God's will.

Under Umayyad rule, increasing allegation (and evidence) of wanton exercise of human discretion led to apprehensions about positivist law-making and strengthened calls for re-Islamisation. Rising awareness among Muslims at the time that recourse to God's law was slipping away because the classical knowledge base had become so tenuous led to efforts to make the divine law and the *sunna* more widely available in writing. While some copies of the Qur'an existed, it appears that expert knowledge of Qur'anic provisions was not well developed initially, and certainly the *sunna* of the Prophet was increasingly difficult to ascertain. It became increasingly easy to allege *ra'y* rather than proper reliance on Qur'an and *sunna*. Since every Muslim was required to make personal decisions all the time, the nature of knowledge itself became an issue in the construction of subjective and objective 'truths' (Sarup, 1993).

The observable excesses of secularisation and positive law-making under the Umayyads suggested that something should happen to put Islamic law back on a rightly guided path. Two remedies were possible at this stage. First, renewed efforts in faithful preservation and painstaking study of God's word. Secondly, the systematic collection of the Prophet's *sunna*, which was then still widely scattered, became an urgent task. Criticism of Umayyad rule and its effects thus gave an enormous boost to the emerging groups of scholars who had been watching the development of Islamic law with growing concern.

5.6 Scholar-jurists and the Abbasids

Muslim jurists now formed a liaison with the political opposition, the rival clan of the Abbasids, who favoured more explicit recourse to Qur'an and *sunna* over political and administrative expediency. Political and ideological opposition to the Umayyads came from various quarters. Not only were the Shi'as, now sidelined, in opposition to the ruling dynasty, there was also the rival clan of the Abbasids, and many non-Arab Muslim groups had remained wary of Arab domination (Esposito, 1988: 47–57). As we saw, the Umayyad rulers with their pragmatic approach to law-making had alarmed many pious Muslims who took the view that God alone made law, and man should merely apply it.

Among these pious Muslims, the Kharijites warrant special mention, since they represented an early example of radical dissent and fundamentalism (Esposito, 1988: 47). Having witnessed the violent struggles over the Caliphate between Ali and his opponents, they had taken the unequivocal stance that only God can decide the crucial matters that were being contested (Esposito, 1988: 48). As pious believers in divine authority, they took the ethical norms of the Qur'an as absolutes and rigorously claimed that all human acts were 'either good or bad, permitted or forbidden' (p. 48). Consequently, they treated all actions contrary to the religious law as sins and went as far as justifying the killing of sinners on various grounds. Having established their own secluded communities, they ended up fighting other Muslims in Arabia in an ultimately unsuccessful attempt to assert their own views of how Islamic life should be lived (Schacht, 1979: 260–1).

Rahim (1994: 21) emphasises that, during Umayyad rule, legal knowledge 'grew and developed only in the lecture rooms of the professors, who did not come into contact with the practical concerns of the administration of justice'. Coulson (1964: 37), discussing the embryonic stage of Islamic jurisprudence, suggested that early jurists might more properly be called experts of religion rather than of law:

Islamic jurisprudence thus began not as the scientific analysis of the existing practice of courts whose authority was accepted, but as the formulation of a scheme of law in opposition to that practice. The first scholar-jurists were men of religion rather than men of law, concerned, almost exclusively, with the elaboration of the system of ritual practices. Their interest in the field of legal relationships strictly so called was a subsequent development, deriving its major impetus from the political ideals of the Abbasids, and their approach to law, therefore, was initially that of religious idealists. Such an activity of academic speculation contrasted sharply with the pragmatism of Umayyad legal tradition and marked a new point of departure.

Little is reported about the early beginnings of the emerging mainstream Sunni schools of jurists.[69] Coulson (1968: 59) wrote:

> Pious scholars, concluding that the practices of the Umayyad courts had failed properly to implement the spirit of the Qur'anic precepts, began to give voice to their ideas of standards of conduct which would represent the systematic fulfilment of the true Islamic religious ethic. Grouped together for this purpose in loose studious fraternities, they formed what may be called the early schools of law. These schools marked the true beginning of Islamic jurisprudence, and their development derived a major impetus from the accession to power of the Abbasids in 750; for the legal scholars were publicly recognised as the architects of an Islamic scheme of state and society which the Abbasids had pledged themselves to build.

Rahim (1994: 22) highlights the supportive role of the Abbasids, who 'loved to patronize learning and extended special encouragement to the jurists, partly it may be from political motives'. Based in Baghdad, the Abbasids ruled from 750 to 1258, when the Moghuls sacked their capital. Coulson (1964: 37–8) reported that, under the early Abbasids, learned scholar-jurists were appointed to positions as *qadi* and their legal advice was valued. Schacht (1984: 49) emphasised that they 'continued and reinforced the Islamicizing trend which had become more and more noticeable under the later Umayyads'. Proclaiming their policy to establish the rule of God on earth, they 'recognized the religious law, as it was being taught by the pious specialists, as the only legitimate norm in Islam' (p. 49). Initially it appeared the Abbasids would be serious about translating their ideal theory into practice, and they won the respect and support of scholar-jurists. Later, however, positivist ambitions again won the upper hand over religious idealism. Schacht (1984: 49) commented that '[i]t soon appeared that the rule of God on earth as preached by the early Abbasids was but a polite formula to cover their own absolute despotism'. Under the early Abbasids, a *qadi* had to be a scholarly specialist rather than a skilled arbitrator or administrator (Schacht, 1984: 50). However, growing confidence of the scholar-jurists as *qadis*

---

[69] For recent research in this area, see Dutton (1999), Gleave and Kermeli (1997), Melchert (1997); Hurvitz (2000) writes on the Hanbali school.

programmed conflict into the ruler–judge relationship and often put them in opposition to the ruler of the day. Schacht (1984: 50) noted that with increasing despotism the Abbasids became more and more unwilling to tolerate any independent institution, so that 'the *kadis* were not only subject to dismissal at the whim of the central government, but had to depend on the political authorities for the execution of their judgements'. Again, positivist ambitions and Islamic methods of law-making clashed. The result was considerable interference in judicial administration and the eventual creation of the more or less secular, separate jurisdiction of the *mazalim* courts (Schacht, 1984: 50ff.). Complaints might also be directed against the *qadis*, so this became a competing jurisdiction which the rulers might use to keep efforts at religious law-making in check (Schacht, 1984: 51).

A related subject of much interest concerns the Muslim state's power to legislate. The Umayyads, in their efforts to build an efficient administrative system, ended up creating much new law without reference to religious norms. During Abbasid rule, much of this was challenged by the increasingly confident jurists, but the rulers began to argue that their administrative law-making was in the nature of Hartian secondary rules, while the realm of primary rules was left to supervision by religious authority. In this way, as Schacht (1984: 54–5) outlines, religious law-making and secular law-making could co-exist and the result was a dual system:

> [A] double administration of justice, one religious and exercised by the *kadi* on the basis of the *shari'a*, the other secular and exercised by the political authorities on the basis of custom, of equity and fairness, sometimes of arbitrariness, of governmental regulation, and in modern times of enacted codes, has prevailed in practically the whole of the Islamic world.

The zenith of Islamic aspirations in terms of secular law-making is documented from an early stage when a highly placed government official by the name of Ibn al-Mukaffa suggested to his ruler that the state should have total control over law-making, and thus over religion, too.[70] His proposals, to the effect that uniform laws for all subjects could be promulgated by the ruler, who should have the authority to determine and codify *sunna* as he saw fit, represent an explicit assertion of positivist law-making over adherence to religious rules. Probably, this was too early in the history of Islamic jurisprudence to be considered acceptable. Referring to this episode, Coulson (1964: 52) concluded that the policy of the Abbasids 'had endorsed the idea that the Caliph was the servant of the law, not its master; legal authority was vested in the scholar-jurists and not in the political ruler'.[71] This shows that God's law remained central and explains

---

[70] However, he was put to death in 756 (Schacht, 1984: 55).
[71] The idea of the ruler as servant of a higher order is also familiar from Hindu law (chapter 4), various African laws (chapter 6) and Imperial Chinese law (chapter 7) and its 'Mandate of Heaven'.

why the Islamic scholar-jurists became a central agency from the Abbasids onwards (Coulson, 1968: 59).

5.7 The central role of jurists

In this section, the analysis focuses first on the emergence of distinct early Muslim schools of law and their use of different sources of law in developing a jurisprudential corpus. This complex process led inevitably to many conflicts and tensions (Coulson, 1969). In the constant attempts of Muslim jurisprudence to retain religious control of a sprawling system, and seeking to unify it, the jurist Shafi'i occupies a central role. Finally, attempts of Muslim scholars to collect the sayings and traditions of the Prophet into a body of authoritative rules prompted Schacht (1979, originally written in 1950) to challenge the authenticity of much of that material.[72]

5.7.1 Schools of law and competing doctrines

Traditional Islamic law or *shari'a* had long made the distinction between the Muslim individual's obligations to God (*ibadat*), and the obligations to individuals *(muamalat)*. Both require individual effort on the part of every believer to ascertain God's will.[73] The emerging scholar-jurists, on the basis of classical learning and pious endeavour (*ijtihad*), acquired a central role in developing the classical knowledge base about what constituted right and appropriate conduct for Muslims. The prominent classification of Muslim law as a 'jurist's law' has its roots here, but early jurists were first of all private scholars, probably concerned as much for their own salvation as for the guidance of fellow Muslims. Their approach was often explicitly critical of actions and decisions by early *qadis* and government officials. To an extent the early scholar-jurists represented a social protest movement and self-controlled ordering mechanisms within Muslim society. Describing these scholars as 'juristic theologians' puts more emphasis on the religious aspect and is certainly appropriate. Such scholars often established a *madrasa*, or school, to spread and discuss their views. Out of such institutions grew many identifiable schools of law, of which four major ones survive among the Sunnis to date.

The major geographical centres of early learning were Medina and Mecca and slightly later Kufa and Basra and the major aims of these schools were

---

[72] Schacht's research is now being challenged by several more recent scholars, in particular Motzki (2002). For a brief overview, see Hallaq (1997: 2–3).

[73] Apprehensions about *ra'y* on the part of individuals rather than scholars question individual agency. Academic focus on juristic concerns provides little juristic recognition of individual conscience as the first *locus* of ascertaining *sharia*. This approach has been challenged by women writers (Mernissi, 1975) and there is now a huge literature on women and Islamic law (e.g. Esposito and Delong-Bas, 2002).

identical and idealistically motivated (Coulson, 1968: 60). Before the emergence of formal schools, certain methodological approaches had been developed by some early jurists, and there was still immense scope for *ra'y* (Hallaq, 1997: 15). The individual's effort to apply reasoning in the process of ascertaining God's will now became redefined as *ijtihad*,[74] a 'total expenditure of effort' (Weiss, 1978: 200) and increasingly focused on the role of scholars (*mujtahid*) and textual sources (Hallaq, 1997: 18–19). Through their human efforts to formulate 'the ideal scheme of Islamic law' (Coulson, 1968: 60), scholars had ample opportunity to criticise each other's conclusions on the basis of excessive use of *ra'y* or 'private opinion'.

In the early schools of Medina and Kufa, the Maliki and Hanafi schools respectively, various techniques were developed to harmonise local practices and the requirements of the ethical code of Islam. While *ra'y* played a large role in this, the gradual consolidation of the early schools into what Glenn (2004: 175) appropriately calls 'pools of consensus' gave more importance to agreement between a group of scholars. Thus, *ijma*, which had been in existence as a concept since the time of the Companions (section 5.4) now metamorphosed from local agreement into more formal consensus of a group of scholars and the community (Hallaq, 1997: 20). The term *sunna* then acquired another nuance of meaning (Coulson, 1964: 39):

> With the gradual growth of agreement between the scholars of a particular locality the doctrine was expressed as the consensus of opinion in the school. Then, as the consensus remained firmly established over the course of the years, the concept of the *sunna* of the school appeared. *Sunna*, literally 'beaten path', had originally meant the actual customary practice, whether of pre-Islamic tribes or of seventh-century Muslims; but in the jurisprudence of the eighth century it had come to bear a different connotation. In the language of the scholars, *sunna* was now the ideal doctrine established in the school and established by its current representatives. From its very nature it did obviously not coincide with the *sunna* of Umayyad courts.

Coulson (1964: 40–1) emphasised that this growing notion of *sunna* as 'established doctrine of a school' led to it being legitimated by reference back to earlier generations of Muslims. The inevitable outcome of this technique was that 'the process ended in claiming the authority of the Prophet himself for the doctrine' (p. 41; Hallaq, 1997: 17). To minimise *ra'y*, some scholars argued more strictly that only analogical reasoning (*qiyas*) should be used.[75] Coulson (1968: 60) explained:

[74] Bharatiya (1996: 27). Faruki (1987: 25–6) defines this term as 'systematic reasoning' and 'disciplined striving'.

[75] Glenn (2004: 175) is correct to emphasise the restrictive agenda of *qiyas*. Elevating this concept or technique to a major source of law sought to block recourse not just to *ra'y*, but to custom and other potential human sources.

The originally accepted freedom of speculation (*ra'y*) in the absence of any
explicit text of divine revelation began to be questioned, and many argued
that reasoning should be more disciplined and by way of deduction (*qiyas*)
by means of analogy from established rules.

The growing intensity of methodological debates led to the emergence of *usul
al-fiqh*, classical Muslim jurisprudence, the result of *ijtihad*. Fyzee (1999: 17)
explains that *fiqh* literally means 'intelligence' and a *faqih* is a 'jurist', a person
skilled in the law, which here is evidently not positivist law, but the *shari'a*.[76]
Within this context, later classically formulated by the jurist Shafi'i, several
concurrent debates were conducted, but the basic problems are always centred
around two major conflicts and tensions: divine revelation versus human reason, and uniformity versus diversity. While the earlier schools of the Malikis and
Hanafis 'took the Koranic norms seriously for the first time' (Schacht, 1984:
29), they still exercised considerable flexibility in attempting to make sense
of God's law, which elicited criticism about *ra'y*. A radical revelation-based
approach was adopted by the Kharijites, discussed above. Other proponents of
ahl al-hadith, the 'supporters of *hadith*' (Coulson, 1969), argued that use of
juristic reasoning itself was questionable and dangerous. Coulson (1968: 61)
explained the growing trend to ascertain the Prophet's *hadith*, which was not
yet systematically compiled:

> This group of scholars, representing opposition to the current legal method
> of both the Hanafi and the Maliki schools, maintained that the use of juristic
> reasoning in any form was both illegitimate and unnecessary. Outside the
> Qur'an, they argued, the only true source of law lay in the practice of the
> Prophet Muhammad, the one person who was qualified to interpret and
> explain the divine will. His practice or *sunna*, was to be found in Traditions,
> or *hadith*, which described what the Prophet had said or done on particular
> occasions. And since the Qur'an had declared that 'man was not left without
> guidance,' the *sunna* of the Prophet was without doubt comprehensive.
> It was simply the task of the jurists to discover this *sunna*, through the
> *hadith*, rather than to indulge in speculative reasoning as to what Allah's law
> might be.

Reliance on divine revelation became central to many scholars in whose philosophy of law the legal sovereignty of God was all-embracing. Diluting it by
human interpretation amounted to impermissible pollution. Coulson (1969:
5) commented:

> To allow human reason to formulate a legal rule – whether by continued
> recognition of a customary law or by juristic speculation on a new problem –

---

[76] Fyzee (1999: 17–18) highlights the distinction between any form of knowledge or learning
(*ilm*), from which the term *ulema* or *ulama* derives, and those forms of knowledge (*fiqh*)
which require both intelligence and independent critical judgment. Schacht (1984: 28)
distinguishes *ulama* as 'scholars' and *fukaha* as 'lawyers'.

was tantamount to heresy. In the language of Islamic theology it was 'to set up a competitor with Allah' and to contradict the fundamental doctrine of the omniscience and omnipotence of the Creator.

The conflict between the two approaches 'hardened in the eighth century into the first fundamental conflict of principle in nascent Islamic jurisprudence and epitomized the tension between the divine and the human element in law' (Coulson, 1969: 5). During 770–800, 'the reasoning of individual scholars, local consensus and the reported precedents of Muhammad lay in uneasy juxtaposition' (Coulson, 1964: 43). During this period, legal compendia of major scholars appeared and added to the growing diversity of juristic opinion. The first written text of this kind is the *Muwatta* of Malik Ibn-Anas, an early leading scholar from Medina (Dutton, 1999). He died in 796 and the Maliki school was later named after him.[77]

5.7.2 Shafi'i scheme to unify Muslim jurisprudence

It fell to the prominent jurist Shafi'i to attempt to reconcile the various conflicting positions. Muhammad Ibn Idris Al-Shafi'i (c. 767–820) was born into the clan of the Prophet. He studied first in Medina with the founder of the Maliki school, but disagreed with his teachers and later interacted in Kufa and Basra with the Hanafi school, before settling in Egypt. Dissatisfied with almost everything he saw and heard, he developed his own theory, 'the principle that certain knowledge of Allah's law could be attained only through divine revelation' (Coulson, 1968: 61), and that, outside the Qur'an, 'the only other legitimate material source of law lay in the decisions and precedents of the Prophet Muhammad' (p. 61). Coulson (1964: 53ff.) referred to him as the 'master architect'. Hallaq (1997: 18) notes that he 'insisted, consistently and systematically, that the Quran and the Sunna of the Prophet are the sole material sources of the law', but 'his theory was by no means universally accepted at the time' (p. 18).

Shafi'i was above all concerned to check the growth of speculation (*ra'y*) in the existing school traditions. He was engaged in the never-ending process of Islamisation, concerned that there should be only one Islamic law, while regional variations among the Maliki and Hanafi schools alone were already so wide that Shafi'i must have realised the tough task of unifying Islamic jurisprudence in theory, quite apart from application in practice. As a theoretician, he is rightly praised for his significant jurisprudential contribution. Coulson (1964: 55) described him as 'the colossus of Islamic legal history'. His *Risala*, composed in Cairo during his last five years, created a new systematic scheme

---

[77] For details see Coulson (1964: 43–7) and Doi (1984: 101–3). Guraya (1985) is a specialist study of this text by a Pakistani author.

of jurisprudence with much impact on ongoing discussions.[78] But, despite the brilliance of his theoretical construct, Shafi'i did not manage to unify the diversity of opinions. In fact, another school in his name arose, and the creation of schools did not stop thereafter.[79] Esposito (1988: 78) describes his central role in classical Muslim jurisprudence:

> Al-Shafii was primarily responsible for the formulation that, after great resistance and debate, became the classical doctrine of Islamic jurisprudence, establishing a fixed, common methodology for all law schools. According to al-Shafii, there are four sources of law (*usul al-fiqh*, roots of law): the Quran, the example (*Sunna*) of the Prophet, consensus (*ijma*) of the community, and analogical reasoning or deduction (*qiyas*).

This hierarchy of sources is obviously in descending order of importance, with the Qur'an in first place.[80] Next, therefore, the *sunna* of the Prophet was taken by this theory as the second most important source.[81] Shafi'i in fact 'taught that there were only two material sources of law: the Quran and the Sunna of the Prophet, as preserved in the *hadith*' (Esposito, 1988: 79). He relied for this theory on repeated commands in the Qur'an itself to the effect that God and the Prophet should be obeyed (Coulson, 1964: 55). The consequence of this strict theory is clearly that only God's law, either in its directly revealed form, or in the shape of the inspired example of the Prophet, is to be accepted as a source of *shari'a*. So far, this is just the old position of those who relied on revelation as a source of legal rules, constituting a refutation of all legal positivist claims in their legislative, administrative or judicial shape, as well as rejecting various chthonic forms of customary and other traditions as sources of law. Neither custom nor the state, in this scheme, would be a legitimate source of law – the triangular model of the present study would not have appealed to Shafi'i.

However, because he also included two other sources of *shari'a* in his scheme, namely *ijma* and *qiyas*, he also explicitly recognised that there was inevitably a role for human law-making and for human reasoning, but at all times subject to the overarching ambit of God's law. This is the plurality-conscious compromise position that Shafi'i is famous for. It may be religio-centric, but it recognises a limited plurality of law-making sources while claiming pride of place for the religious natural law of Islam. This compromise position did not go as far as accepting human law-making in principle, however. Coulson (1968: 62)

[78] A major critical study on Shafi'i's theories is Schacht's pioneering work, originally published in 1950 (Schacht, 1979), which also contains the much–discussed debates about the authenticity of the Prophet's *hadith*.

[79] The fourth major Sunni school of law that survives today, the Hanbali school, arose after Shafi'i and was founded by a man who attended the lectures of Shafi'i and adopted an even more rigid approach. For details see Rahim (1994: 28–9) and Hurvitz (2000).

[80] On the Qur'an as a source in Shafi'i's scheme see Esposito (1988: 79–80).

[81] On the *sunna* of the Prophet under this theory, see in detail Schacht (1979: 58–81) and Esposito (1988: 80–2).

noted that '[t]he function of jurisprudence was not to make law but simply to discover it from the substance of divine revelation and, where necessary, apply the principles enshrined therein to new problems by analogical reasoning'. Proper law in this scheme could not be rules made by man without reference to divine legitimation.

Coulson (1968: 62) rightly emphasised that Shafi'i's main aim was 'to instil into Muslim jurisprudence a uniformity which was conspicuously lacking at this time', but he underestimated the sophisticated pluralistic message of this ingenious scheme, which gave a pre-eminent position to the Prophet's *sunna* (Hallaq, 1997: 29). Insistence that the Prophet's legal decisions were divinely inspired (Coulson, 1964: 56) was hardly a new argument, but it had not been strictly followed. He therefore redefined and restricted the term *sunna* to the 'model behaviour of the Prophet' (Fyzee, 1999: 26),[82] and 'it came to be identified solely with the divinely inspired practice of Muhammad and no longer with tribal custom or the consensus of law schools' (Esposito, 1988: 79). The most significant result of his method was, therefore, to elevate the *hadith* of the Prophet 'as a source of the divine will complementary to the Qur'an' (Coulson, 1964: 56), an argument which proved irrefutable. Coulson (1964: 57) added that Shafi'i aspired to eradicate a root cause of diversity between the several schools and instil uniformity into juristic doctrine by arguing that there should be only one genuine Islamic 'tradition'. This elevation of the *hadith* to the practically most important source of guidance obviously boosted the incentives to collect the Prophet's Traditions (section 5.7.3). In terms of practical application of his theory, Shafi'i propounded a complex theory of abrogation (*nashk*) to deal with the inevitable diversities and conflicts between different *hadiths* of the Prophet (Hallag, 1997).

Regarding the additional source of *ijma* as 'consensus', Esposito (1988: 79) suggests that it became 'the third infallible source of law'.[83] The *mujtahids*, 'authorized by divine revelation, are thus capable of transforming a ruling reached through human legal reasoning into a textual source by the very fact of their agreement on its validity'.[84] But *ijma* as a juristic technique, like *qiyas* (reasoning by analogy), is not a textual source, and thus implies human lawmaking. Shafi'i argued that the human element in those two techniques should be as minimal as possible, but could not totally exclude it. Coulson (1964: 59) remarked that with regard to *ijma*, too, Shafi'i 'takes up an existing notion and gives it a new connotation designed to achieve uniformity in the law'. He explained that, while Shafi'i denied the scholars of any particular locality the authority to establish binding consensus, thus challenging the various emerging

---

[82] Esposito (1988: 80) speaks of the 'normative model behavior of Muhammad'.

[83] For detail, see Schacht (1979: 82–97); Esposito (1988: 84–6).

[84] Hallaq (1997: 1). Esposito (1988: 84) comments that 'consensus served as a brake on the vast array of individual interpretations of legal scholars and contributed to the creation of a relatively fixed body of laws'.

'pools of consensus', he argued that there could be only one valid form of *ijma*, that of the entire Muslim community, including all members irrespective of learning.[85] Esposito (1988: 84) points out that the position of *ijma* as the third source of law is normally derived from a saying of the Prophet, to the effect that his community would never agree on an error. He therefore sees the consensus of the early community in Islam 'as a check on individual opinions' (p. 84), which allows the conclusion that Shafi'i himself appeared to trust the community as a whole to self-control in accordance with divine commands, an idealistic approach which later jurists did not share:

> [T]wo kinds of consensus came to be recognized. The consensus of the entire community was applied to those religious duties, such as the pilgrimage to Mecca, practiced by all Muslims. But despite al-Shafii's attempt to define the fourth source of law as this general consensus, classical Islamic jurisprudence defined the community in a more restricted sense as the community of religious scholars or religious authorities who act on behalf of and guide the entire Muslim community.

Coulson (1964: 59) wrote that Shafi'i admitted the theoretical assumption, to the effect that the Muslim community as a whole would never agree on anything contrary to the Qur'an or the *sunna*, but 'he also realised that the formation or ascertainment of such an agreement had ceased to be practical once Islam had spread outside the boundaries of Medina'. With respect to *ijma*, then, as in the case of *sunna* which could mean so many things, *ijma* is now under pressure to be restricted to some kind of universal agreement about a few basic rules, such as the pilgrimage to Mecca or the performance of daily prayers. Coulson (1964: 59) subtly indicated that this doctrine of *ijma* 'is therefore essentially negative, designed to the end of rejecting the authority of a local or limited consensus and thus eliminating the diversity of law which resulted therefrom'. Within a comparative legal analysis, this looks like a focused attack on the role of local and community custom as a source of legal rules in different societies. However, Shafi'i addressed scholars, not local people, and he may have overlooked and underestimated the pluralist implications of his own theory with regard to local practice. As we know, not the least from Coulson's work, many differences between the Maliki and Hanafi schools are due to customary local norms which impressed the scholar-jurists as agreeable with the spirit of the divine will.

There is evidence that this aspect of Shafi'i's brilliant theory was later modified by the jurists themselves as pious but reality-conscious members of local communities. This is subtly indicated by the quote from Esposito (1988: 84) above. If that is correct, it contains a significant lesson for Muslim jurisprudence as well as global legal analysis, namely that exclusive domination of religion over

---

[85] The inclusive nature of this concept would probably later prove attractive to Muslim converts in South India and especially in South East Asia, the current stronghold of the Shafi'i school.

the other two law-making and law-founding elements, in other words religious centralism, is as unrealistic as legal centralism (Griffiths, 1986).

Finally, the fourth source in Shafi'i's scheme is *qiyas*, analogical reasoning,[86] a particular method of *ijtihad* (Coulson, 1964: 60). Shafi'i's theory further restricts the discretion of learned jurists, who are not to be guided in their reasoning by reference to local practices, administrative preferences and the like, but by a mental process of comparison on strictly circumscribed terms. Coulson (1964: 60) wrote that 'the role of juristic reasoning is thus completely subordinate to the dictates of divine revelation'. Esposito (1988: 79) explains:

> Finally, the role of personal reasoning in the formulation of law was restricted. Where no explicit revealed text or community consensus existed, jurists were no longer free to rely on their own judgment to solve new problems. Instead, they were to resort to deductive reasoning (*qiyas*) to seek a similar or analogous situation in the revealed sources (Quran and Sunna), from which they were to derive a new regulation. Reasoning by analogy would eliminate what al-Shafii regarded as the arbitrary nature of legal reasoning prevalent in the more inductive approach of those who relied on their own judgment.

Esposito (1988: 83) elaborates further that the general term for human reasoning, *ijtihad*, comprises all kinds of reasoning and that *qiyas* is 'a more restricted, systematic form of *ijtihad*'. The aim of Shafi'i's theory, to focus at all times on the divinely inspired roots of Islamic law, was thus to be achieved not only by direct reference to the Qur'an and *sunna*, but also through applying revelation-focused methodologies of harmonising this religious law with the facts of life, a continuous challenge demanding plurality-consciousness. Schacht (1984: 46) commented sceptically that the strict practical application of Shafi'i's theory over time 'could only lead to inflexibility' and 'could hardly be productive of progressive solutions' (p. 47). At the time, the new emphasis on the *sunna* of the Prophet demanded as much certainty as possible about the Prophet's *sunna*, but certainly could not totally control human effort and subjectivity.

5.7.3 Hadith collections and the 'Schacht controversy'

Shafi'i's theory about the sources of *shari'a* recognised a central position for the *sunna* of the Prophet, the only divinely inspired person, whose acts had model character. Coulson (1964: 42) showed that the earlier expansion and misuse of the concept of *sunna*, declaring numerous practices and concepts as ultimately relating back to the Prophet without proper evidence, led to agreement about the importance of the Prophet's role in principle, but also created evidence problems. While Shafi'i criticised the methods employed to ascertain *hadith*,

---

[86] See in detail Schacht (1979: 98–132) and briefly Esposito (1988: 83).

his principled position was that the Prophet's true *sunna* alone was the second source of *fiqh* and thus of *shari'a*.

How could one properly ascertain, in a largely oral society, what the Prophet had really done or not done, or said and left unsaid? Since his lifetime, many reports had begun to circulate, not all genuine, which was painfully clear to Shafi'i. Schacht (1979: 140–62) showed that many of the emerging traditions of the Prophet were the subject of intense polemics. Those arguing a particular position were not always scrupulous in providing proper evidence. Also, not everything that the Prophet ever said and did was dutifully accepted by society around him – after all he was a reformer who spearheaded a religio-ethical revolution in his society. Schacht (1984: 35) confirmed that, for a long time, '[t]raditions from the Prophet had to overcome strong opposition' and were subject to much polemical discussion, evidently since their effect was often to challenge what local communities considered appropriate. Coulson (1964: 43) indicated more generally that the genuine core of the Prophet's sayings gradually 'became overlaid by a mass of fictitious material'.[87] Oral transmission of the Prophet's sayings originated from the people closest to him, the Companions and his own family, and gradually extended to more people as the community grew. After the Prophet's death, his Companions took the initiative to collect his sayings, but also recounted orally what the Prophet had said. The preservation of the Prophet's sayings and the memory of his actions as model behaviour were considered important because of his special authority, which no human after him could claim.[88]

While the Qur'an had been collected under state supervision, particularly the Caliph Uthman, the post-Caliphate Muslim state did not seem to be concerned about recording the Prophet's sayings. Hallaq (1997: 8) argues that 'it is fairly clear that the early caliphs, including the Umayyads, considered themselves the deputies of God on earth, and thus looked to the Quran as a source from which they could draw their legal decisions'. This fits the picture of the Umayyads as practice-focused administrators, rather than religiously inspired leaders. Collection of *hadith* was a private activity, not the business of the Muslim state. Bharatiya (1996: 25) confirms that 'collection was left to the piety and private enterprise' of Muslims. This process of unsystematic and patchy collections and recordings spanned two centuries. The constant demand for authoritative statements kept this system active and gave prestige and power to individuals engaged in collecting and ascertaining the Prophet's *sunna*. Later, Shafi'i's theory provided critical impetus for renewed efforts to collect all sayings and records relating to the Prophet during the ninth century.

---

[87] Hallaq (1997: 13–14) refers to the important role of storytellers.

[88] The unsuccessful claims of Ali to succeed the Prophet were there for all to see, and must have left their impact on the appreciation of the special position of the Prophet as the 'seal of Prophets'.

But that theory itself did not supersede all other views, and the stricter definition of *sunna* in Shafi'i theory was not adopted by later writers. For example, Doi (1984: 52) writes that the *hadith* of the Prophet 'enshrines the Sunnah or the "Way of life" the custom and practice of the early Muslim Community'. This is not what Shafi'i meant by *sunna*. It may explain to some extent why the *hadith* collections were challenged. What was being recorded was not only the actions of the Prophet, but practices in his time that were presumed to be part of *sunna*, the generally agreed 'good custom'. Not only were the processes of collection subject to contamination, therefore, but the basic definitions of the object of scholarly attention remained imprecise. One can understand therefore why some Western scholars found it impossible 'to share the confidence of the Muhammadan scholars in what they consider first-class *isnads*'.[89] What was being collected was not just the sayings of the Prophet. Ideally only direct statements of the Prophet should have been recorded. But who, in the seventh century, thought of the worldwide spread of Islam and the conflicts and tensions this would give rise to? Even soon after the death of the Prophet, few Muslims would have realised how crucial it would eventually become to ascertain what the Prophet had said or done. As we saw, the *sunna* of the Prophet was not originally a separate concept; it floated within the more general social definition of *sunna*. Some pious Muslims apparently became engaged in the emerging science of *hadith*,[90] long before the methodological requirement of legitimation by recourse to Qur'an and *sunna* of the Prophet was fully formulated. Soon after the death of the Prophet, alarm bells started ringing in some minds and Muslims, according to Doi (1984: 52), 'began to compile everything that he had said and done; what he had refrained from doing; what he had given quasi-approval to by silence. Above all, a record was being gathered of all the cases he had judged and of his decisions; of all the answers which he gave to formal questions on the religious life and faith.'

In this process, a lot of material was collected whose authenticity was later questioned. From this kind of literature, as in the Hindu commentary literature of roughly the same time, almost anything might be shown to be good or bad by reference to a particular chain of tradition. But was that chain authoritative and authentic? Was it a reliable source of religious legitimation? Such questions propelled Shafi'i into formulating his strict methodological approach and inspired Schacht's (1979: 37, 165) critical questioning of reliance on *hadith*.

Over time, these collection efforts were intensified, resulting in six massive Sunni collections of *hadith*, with several thousand traditions each, eventually

---

[89] Schacht (1979: 163). An *isnad* is a chain of submission, crucial for testing the veracity of a *hadith*.

[90] In contrast, the early Hindu *śruti* sources (chapter 4, section 4.2) did not concern verification of religious fundamentals and were focused on religious ritual designed to support macrocosmic Order. Allah needed no such help – it would be preposterous for traditional Sunni Muslims to claim that rituals could achieve cosmic changes.

produced and published between 850 and 900.[91] They are almost universally accepted by all Sunni Muslims, and the most authoritative ones are considered to be the collections called *Sahih* by al-Bukhari (died 870) and by Muslim ibn al-Hajjaj (died 875).[92] Doi (1984: 54) reports that elaborate critical techniques were used to sift out and select the truly authentic material. For example, Bukhari is said to have examined 600,000 traditions, but accepted only 7,397.

A *hadith* consists of two parts, the report itself, and the list of its authoritative transmitters, or chain (*isnad*), which may be quite short, but would in later *hadiths* be long and complex. This is the element that Schacht (1979: 163) found the most arbitrary part, observing that transmission was often attributed in a rather haphazard manner. Doi (1984: 55) appreciates the methodological stringency that Shafi'i (and later Schacht) wanted to see applied, but also envisages the purpose of producing these vast collections for guidance of the community, rather than ascertaining the divinely revealed will from the reported actions of the Prophet only for scholars. This probably reflects the motivation of the original compilers, prior to Shafi'i's strict concepts, who were seeking to promote *sunna* as the consensus of the community. Doi (1984: 54) writes:

> Their purpose was to assemble a body of traditions which would serve as a rule of life for practising Muslims, so their primary interest was in selecting such Traditions as would give clear guidance concerning what Muslim [*sic*] belief and practice should be, what things were permissible and approved, and what were not permissible and disapproved.

Doi (1984: 55) argues that all the important early jurists gave tremendous importance to the traditions of the Prophet and thus relied on more or less remote participant observation of the Prophet's actions rather than the strictly limited *qiyas* demanded later by Shafi'i.[93] Doi (1984: 56) affirms that '[t]he Companions of the Prophet followed the footsteps of their master scrupulously', a typically idealistic statement. Shafi'i himself emphasised this element of self-control in the *Risala*, writing in detail about the qualifications of the transmitters of *hadith* (Doi, 1984: 56). The tests of authenticity developed by Muslim scholars concentrated on the chain of transmission (*isnad*) and thus established a classification from 'excellent' to 'weak' (Doi, 1984: 54), giving rise to a new science. The tradition of *hadith* scholarship continues until today.[94]

---

[91] For details see Doi (1984: 51–63) and Burton (1994).

[92] This title means 'true' or 'authentic'. The Shi'a Muslims prepared their own collections, since they questioned the authority of some of the Companions. Four authoritative Shi'a collections are recognised, prepared slightly later than the Sunni collections, at around 1100 AD (Esposito, 1995, II: 83–7).

[93] See also Motzki (2002). Hallaq (1997) takes a different view.

[94] For a good overview see Doi (1984: 55ff.) and Esposito (1995, 2: 83–7).

Esposito (1988: 82–3) reports on the controversy over the authenticity of *hadith*, prominently linked to Schacht's critical analysis, with which most Muslim scholars have disagreed, despite their own reservations about questions of authenticity (see Hallaq, 1997: 2–3). Schacht (1979: 163–75) had argued, building on the work of Goldziher, that the bulk of the *hadith* attributed to the Prophet was the result of 'an artificial growth' (Schacht, 1979: 169) of *isnads*, and that many of the most reliable *hadith* had been written much later. Schacht argued that, since it only became important to attribute authority to the Prophet after Shafi'i's theory, and as the term '*sunna* of the Prophet' had only developed then, it was unlikely that there were authentic earlier traditions that could be attributed more or less directly to the Prophet. He claimed that he had found no evidence of legal traditions before 722, almost 100 years after the death of the Prophet, and went as far as speaking of 'large-scale circulation of spurious traditions' (Schacht, 1979: 170). Esposito (1988: 82) summarises Schacht's main argument:

> Thus, he concluded that the Sunna of the Prophet is not the words and deeds of the Prophet, but apocryphal material originating from customary practice that was projected back to the eighth century to more authoritative sources – first the Successors, then the Companions, and finally the Prophet himself.

It is no surprise that Muslim scholars should be appalled by such arguments of an Orientalist scholar, since it created 'an unwarranted vacuum in Islamic history' (Esposito, 1988: 82). Schacht's approach also dismissed offhand the reliability of an old chthonic tradition of orality, a speculative academic enterprise, no matter how one feels about the transmitters of the *hadith*. He relied upon his own assumptions, highlighting a problem that Muslims themselves were certainly not unaware of (Schacht, 1979: 172), but did not raise. It is evident that Schacht's thesis has not been totally refuted (Melchert, 2004: 407), but the strength of his challenge to the authenticity of the Prophet's *sunna* did not give a good press to the 'Orientalists' (Said, 1978).

We are told that Shafi'i's thesis, that human reasoning should at all times be subordinate to divine law, 'was never after him seriously challenged' (Coulson, 1964: 61). This makes sense as a fundamental religious issue, since the supremacy of God's law over any form of human law could not be denied or questioned by pious Muslims. However, from a plurality-conscious legal perspective, the perennial problem for Muslim law, also today, remains how to make practical and sustainable legal arrangements on the part of states, communities and individuals without appearing to override what is supposed to be God's law.[95] Within the pluralistic model of the conceptual triangle of law

---

[95] So far, Turkey is the only Muslim majority country in the world to have created a fully secular system of law (section 5.13).

(chapter 3, section 3.8), challenging the supremacy of Islamic natural law could be seen as blasphemy. But accepting the supremacy of religious law does not make the other types of law non-existent as law.

Precisely this was an acute problem faced immediately after the demise of the Prophet, and it was earlier experienced by the Prophet himself who carried the burden of balancing those competing legal inputs.[96] In principle, taking it as a *grundnorm* of Islamic law that divine law is always superior to human law, there had been nothing new in the theory of Shafi'i. Muslim jurists have always argued about the dynamic interaction of various methods of law-making. Shafi'i reminded everyone of the critical relationship between human and divine law, raising similar issues as the later natural law debates by St Thomas Aquinas in Europe (chapter 3, section 3.4). The theoretical distinction of religious and secular elements confirms awareness that neither of the two was ever totally absent, another form of overlapping consensus. Islamic jurists would have been as reluctant as medieval Christian natural law theorists like Aquinas to admit the presence of secular laws. Aquinas wrote in detail about this, the Prophet was clearly sensitive to this distinction, and the later Umayyad administration system enlarged the scope for administrative law-making and legislation (Hallaq, 1997: 10), probably under the banner of good Islamic governance. Shafi'i tried to insist that God's law was always superior, but, as we saw, he did not deny that there were other types of law.

5.8 Continuing diversities after Shafi'i

The period of Islamic law after 820 is characterised by increasing diversity of theory and practice, as Shafi'i's unifying and Islamising theoretical efforts confronted living realities and ever greater diversity of local Muslim traditions. The growing geographical spread of Islam constantly demanded negotiations of what Yilmaz (2005b) calls dynamic legal pluralisms among Muslims. Conflicts and tensions over revelation and reason remained lively. Coulson (1968: 62) summed up Shafi'i's limited practical impact, noting that 'his dream of a basically uniform and common law for Islam was not to be realised. In fact, as a result of his work, two more schools of law were formed in addition to those which already existed.'[97] Schacht (1984: 59) also noted the failure of Shafi'i's efforts to supersede the growing plurality of law by a new unifying doctrine.

---

[96] Coulson (1969: 60–1) commented that, in Islam, 'there is a particularly significant tension between the legal ideal and the social reality'. One could rephrase this to speak of a tension between religious ideal and socio–legal reality.

[97] Coulson (1964: 70) mentioned three further schools, including the Zahiris, who did not sustain a following. They were publicly reviled, and their books burnt in Spain, for denouncing the use of all analogical reasoning as 'a perversion and a heresy' (p. 71). Because of rigid adherence to their original principles, the Zahiris became extinct in the Middle Ages (p. 73).

Shafi'i's attempt 'to erect the traditions from the Prophet, instead of the living tradition and the consensus, into the highest authority in law was short-lived in its effect' (Schacht, 1984: 59–60).

Coulson (1969: 22) emphasised that the Shafi'i and the Hanbali school 'were both born out of the jurisprudential controversy which arose during the ninth century on the subject of the sources of the religious law'. The earlier Maliki and Hanafi traditions adopted some elements of Shafi'i's thought, but continued to use various other juristic techniques which were now contemptuously treated by their new opponents as *ra'y*.[98] Coulson (1964: 71) noted that, within these established schools, 'the interests of past local tradition necessitated a cautious approach' to Shafi'i's thesis.[99] Regarding the Hanafis, Bharatiya (1996: 28) writes that '[a] high degree of reasoning, often somewhat ruthless and unbalanced, with little regard for practice, is typical of Abu Hanifa's legal thought as a whole ... and was rejected by his disciples'. Still, his pupils carried on under the banner of their teacher, and the Hanafi school remained a major Sunni school of law under this name.

Several of Shafi'i's students founded their own schools, but only two of those became prominent and survive today. These two new schools did not occupy a particular territory and were free from the primary need to link in with a local population, but were distinguished by methodological criteria. Both emphasised in different ways that the Prophet's *sunna* was of paramount authority. Some pupils of Shafi'i' formed the Shafi'i (sometimes spelt Shafei) school soon after his death in 820. The Hanbali school was founded in about 850 under the leadership of Ahmad bin Hanbal (780–855), another student of Shafi'i.[100] He took a much more traditionalist approach and sought to minimise recourse to human interpretation and law-making. Hanbal himself challenged the ruler of the day, was promptly victimised for his views and became a martyr figure, though he was not killed (Doi, 1984: 110). Rahim (1994: 28) emphasises that this school allowed only 'a very narrow margin to the doctrines of agreement

---

[98] Their respective founders, Malik Ibn Anas (713–95) and Abu Hanifa (699–767), each had a large following of scholars. Modern research emphasises that it is misleading to focus just on the views of the eponymous leader. Within all schools, all shades of opinions were represented, as the differences of opinion between Abu Hanifa and his two major pupils illustrate.

[99] See Coulson (1968: 63). An example given by Coulson (1964: 72) of how the Hanafis managed to get around the theoretical superiority of *sunna* while maintaining their own interpretation of it, relates to the right of an adult Hanafi Muslim woman to give herself in marriage. There was a traditional *sunna* to the effect that, if a woman marries herself without a guardian, her marriage will be null and void. The Hanafi jurists, 'in order to preserve their rule that an adult woman had the capacity to conclude her own marriage, had to interpret the Tradition ... as referring to minor females only' (p. 72). On a relevant recent case in Pakistan see section 5.14 below.

[100] For details see Doi (1984: 108–11). Hurvitz (2000) focuses on the Hanbali school and questions the prominent notion of regional schools.

and analogy'. Hanbal's large following of scholars ensured that his school tradition would survive and, since 1930, his school has represented the official law
of Saudi Arabia and also applies in Qatar.

After Shafi'i, the various groupings of jurists needed to harmonise their
methodologies to some extent with his now dominant theory. The Hanafis,
through juristic reinterpretation, maintained a system of rules that they preferred locally, in contradistinction to traditional *sunna*. Coulson (1968: 63)
wrote that 'once this process of adjustment was complete, the Hanafis and
Malikis formally acknowledged the principle of the supreme authority of
hadiths', but gave much importance in real life to local traditions. At the other
end of the spectrum, the Hanbalis came to accept *qiyas* as a necessary instrument
in the elaboration of law. So did the Muslim jurists after Shafi'i meet somewhere
in the middle and did the earlier conflicts and tensions abate? Coulson (1969:
24) suggested that the fiction of uniformity 'created an impression that the
schools spoke with one voice on all fundamentals and only differed on minor
issues'. In social reality as well as jurisprudential practice, however, immense
plurality remained prominent.

After Shafi'i, Islamic law became even more of a plural jurist's law under
the umbrella of *usul al-fiqh* (Hallaq, 1997: vii), in a similar sense that Hindu
law became a complex 'book law' (Derrett, 1968a: 83). Coulson (1969: 60)
observed that Muslim jurisprudence became an introspective science as scholars now defined themselves more clearly as jurists,[101] and the requirements of
proper scholarly qualification attracted growing attention. To exercise authoritative *ijtihad*, a scholar now needed to be a fully trained and qualified expert,
a *mujtahid*. Coulson (1968: 63) explained that such a scholar exercising proper
ijtihad 'must first seek the solution of legal problems in the Qur'an and the
sunna, and failing any specific regulation therein must then use the method of
analogical deduction or *qiyas*'.

The dogma of superiority of God's law firmly established and agreed, post-
Shafi'i concerns could shift towards administrative legal processes and took
some focus away from juristic methodology. As the unity of the old Islamic state
collapsed, and several Muslim states emerged, the old ruler–jurist dichotomy
with its attendant clashes about who can claim higher legitimacy took on different, more localised Islamic forms. Positivist ambitions still needed to be harmonised with the principle of superiority of religious law. Secular Austinian
legal positivism could not develop in this climate and, where it did, it was
widely perceived as abuse. Depending on the politics of the situation, critical

---

[101] The other possible job description appears to be 'traditionalist', which is the label given
to the eponymous leader of the Hanbali school by many scholars, who saw him more as a
religious activist than a man who wrote learned treatises (Fyzee, 1999: 35). To call them
'lawyers' reflects Western thought patterns rather than Muslim practice. Hallaq (1997)
uses 'legists' and suggests rather wide scope for human 'legislation'.

questions would always need to be asked about how the customs of various Muslim communities, guidance on spiritual and legal values by jurists and the powers of state-made laws interacted.

In this dynamic triangular field, jurists once again invoked the concept of *ijma*. It now became redefined, as Coulson (1968: 63) explained, as 'the agreement of the qualified legal scholars in a given generation, and such consensus of opinion is deemed infallible'. The jurists thus strengthened their own position and invented a new weapon for themselves in the never-ending debates about God's law. Again, any dissident opinion would be termed *ra'y*, 'private opinion', but a new term appears, 'conjecture' (*zann*), to the effect that no opinion voiced by a single jurist could now be accepted as more than a 'tentative or probable conclusion' (Coulson, 1968: 63). This links in with the important concept of 'margin of error' (*ikhtilaf*), discussed further below. Assuming that only *ijma* as consensus of jurists had validity served to control *ra'y*, customs and the claims of individual jurists. Coulson (1969: 23) noted:

> But the conclusion that an individual jurist might reach, in terms of a substantive doctrine derived from the recognized sources, was in the nature of a conjecture. Whether he was deciding upon the precise meaning of a Qur'anic text or resolving a novel problem, his conclusion could only amount to a tentative, or probable, statement of the divine law.

This could be read to mean that no individual jurist could henceforth claim to have reached a conclusion entirely by his own effort of *ijtihad*. While that strict approach protects the profession against 'cowboys', which may have been one of its purposes, another implication is equally important: no single Muslim scholar could ever claim that he alone knew and understood God's law perfectly. In this way, Islam as a religion protected itself from claims by new Prophet-like figures who might simply claim to be God's representative on earth.[102] In Islam, no human interpreter could know God's law totally. Coulson (1969: 24) commented:

> Where the Muslim jurists could not agree, they agreed to differ. It is a candidly pluralistic philosophy of law, which recognizes that no individual can claim, as against other variants, a unique authority . . . Discussion of a controversial problem and an assessment of the various possibilities often ends with the words: 'but Allah alone really knows.'

This shows that, apart from being brilliant theoreticians, the Muslim jurists were also reality-conscious people with common sense. Without this, the whole field might have developed very differently. However, while opposing the trend towards strict *taqlid*, mere copying or 'imitation', the creative and empowering use of *ijma* also operated as a legitimator of plurality for Muslim jurists and even

---

[102] The Catholic institution of the Pope in Rome was of course known at this time.

individual believers. In theory, conclusions reached by the general agreement of all scholars had been declared as binding and infallible *ijma*. But this was difficult to maintain in practice for a growing, diverse community of scholars, and led inevitably to greater diversity. The example of the Hanafi woman who can give herself in marriage, while any Muslim woman from another school tradition cannot do so, confirms a picture of internal diversity within the scholarly consensus of *ijma*, a plurality of opinions hidden under the mantle of a uniformising redefinition. As the Tunisians were to confirm in the 1950s, the interpretations of the Qur'anic verses about the permissibility of polygamy never yielded total consensus from the start, leaving a trail throughout Muslim jurisprudence of 'minority' and 'majority' interpretations which has become a useful tool for more recent law reforms. Coulson (1968: 64) indicated tentatively that 'variant opinions are recognised as equally valid attempts' to define the divine will, elaborating this to show that *ijma* became the legitimising force of internal difference as well:

> In the first place *ijma* operated as a permissive principle to tolerate variations in substantive legal doctrine between the different schools and individual jurists. The acceptance by Muslim jurisprudence of the phenomenon of variant versions of Shari'a law is reflected in the alleged words of the Prophet Muhammad: 'Difference of opinion within my community is a sign of the bounty of Allah.' With a philosophy of candid pluralism, the four schools of law . . . are blended together as inseparable manifestations of the same single essence under the blanket authority of the principle of *ijma*.

An overall picture of uniformity, stipulated by *ijma* as the concept of juristic agreement, thus hid an immense diversity which required explicit juristic recognition.[103] Coulson (1968: 64) concluded that the various schools 'represent essentially distinct systems whose individual characteristics were fashioned largely by their circumstances of origin and growth', a subtle reference to the important role of custom in Islamic societies and law. Coulson (1968: 64–5) emphasised the practical implications of this diversity in that the 'philosophy of the mutual orthodoxy of the schools should not obscure the fact that geography and history created a four-fold division in the legal practice of Sunni Islam'.[104] Schacht (1984: 67) confirmed that acceptance of difference in Islamic jurisprudence was not a new phenomenon:

> In their relationship to one another, the orthodox schools of law have . . . generally practised mutual toleration. This attitude goes back to the time of the ancient schools of law which had accepted geographical differences of

---

[103] Since *ijma* might also mean consensus of a particular local population, this diversity is potentially much larger. For the same process, compare debates over the ambit of *sadācāra* in chapter 4, section 4.3.

[104] On Shi'a jurisprudence, see Coulson (1968: 65–6).

doctrine as natural. The maxim that disagreement (*ikhtilaf*) in the community of Muslims was a sign of divine indulgence had already been formulated in the second century of the hijra, though it was put into the mouth of the Prophet only much later. This mutual recognition was not incompatible, and did indeed go together with vigorous polemics and the insistence on uniformity of doctrine within each geographical school.

The geographical focus in Schacht's arguments is questioned in recent studies which suggest 'circles of masters and their disciples' (Hurvitz, 2000: 37). Esposito (1988: 85) saw a danger in overemphasising the unity and fixed nature of Islamic law:

> [W]hile an overall unity or common consensus existed among the law schools . . . the divergent character of the law schools was preserved by differences in such areas as the grounds for divorce, the levying of taxes, and inheritance rights. Acknowledgment of this diversity within the unity of law was embodied in the doctrine of *ikhtilaf*, divergence of legal opinions.

The important concept of *ikhtilaf*, 'difference of opinion', is ancient and still underpins the mutual orthodoxy of the various schools of Islamic law today. Faruki (1987: 166) translates *ikhtilaf* as 'disagreement' and justifies it on socioreligious grounds, emphasising that the extremely limited recognition of *ikhtilaf* in classical legal theory contrasts with the fact that there are *hadiths* relating to it. Rather, '*ikhtilaf* is not recognised, as some have alleged, in a reluctant fashion in order to conform theory to reality, but is regarded with approval as possessing a positive, definite, intrinsic value' (Faruki, 1987: 167). Through examining the difference between *ikhtilaf* as 'disagreement' and *niza* as 'dissension', this Pakistani author's analysis confirms how simple it has continued to be for Muslims to declare any form of disagreement as dissent, which is then taken to endanger the community and can lead to a charge of heresy. Here, as elsewhere, it is evident that freedom of thought and speech are contested concepts, in discussions of Muslims with non-Muslims, as well as among Muslims.[105]

The inevitable consequence of such plurality-conscious thought processes had to be even more plurality and diversity. A prominent argument is that *ijma* was used by jurists as a block on *ijtihad* of the individual scholar and therefore a device to restrict independent reasoning and to curtail individual speculation. Thus, the jurist's task eventually came to be seen as imitation (*taqlid*) rather than innovation (*bida*), a term with negative connotations. The expectation was that the student should absorb what had already been absorbed, tread along trodden paths, critically examining but following those earlier thought processes, which increased the strength of *ijma*, rather than developing new views. This technique was probably also motivated by a desire to dissuade students from searching for their own path. This precluded the development

---

[105] Faruki (1987: 166–241) contains a long discussion and develops a complex theory.

of new schools, but also possibly softened the differences between the various schools. All of this serves as intellectual justification for *taqlid*, which was to become the key word linked to the purported 'closing of the gates of *ijtihad*', discussed further in section 5.11 below.

5.9 Judicial administration: *qadis* and *muftis*

While jurists might devise ways to exclude eccentric or unorthodox opinions among themselves by policing *ijtihad* and enforcing a move towards *taqlid*, it would be much more difficult for them to exercise control over state-dominated adjudication and the normative patterns of local Muslim societies. A brief examination of this issue conveys an acute sense of awareness about the living reality of diverse opinions, encapsulated in the term *ikhtilaf* ('tolerated diversity of opinion'),[106] a form of 'Muslim legal pluralism' (Yilmaz, 2005b), which remained a central feature of early medieval Islamic law and society. How did Muslim judicial administration cope with this plurality?

Earlier jurists, focused on pious endeavour to ascertain God's will, might not have been interested in judicial office. Coulson (1969: 58–9) reported that the '[l]egal literature abounds with such expressions of distaste, on the part of medieval jurists, for the office of judge'. Under the late Umayyads (section 5.5) the *qadi* became more of a legal specialist than an administrative officer, and juristic knowledge became an essential qualification for a judge. However, conflicts arose if pious jurists as *qadi* then made decisions that did not please the ruler. Coulson (1968: 67) noted:

> As delegates of the political ruler, in whom was vested supreme executive and judicial power, the *qadis* never formed an independent judiciary. The jurisdiction of the Shari'a courts was always subject to such limits as the political sovereign saw fit to define, and when a clash occurred between the terms of the Shari'a and the interests of government it was perhaps inevitable that the political sovereign should curtail the powers of his Shari'a courts and recognise alternative organs of jurisdiction.

Claims about the superiority of God's law notwithstanding, rulers would be tempted to assert positivist claims. As long as rulers did not violate the basic principles of Islam and adherence to the faith itself, they might not be vigorously challenged, but many conflicts over self-control must have arisen.[107] Since the *qadi* should resolve legal problems by reference to Qur'an and *sunna*,[108] he

---

[106] Surprisingly, this term does not appear in the index of Dupret *et al.* (1999) and Yilmaz (2005b).

[107] In distinction to Hindu law, Chinese law and also African laws, a bad Islamic ruler could not be deposed on religious grounds. It appears that his due punishment would arise only after death.

[108] For some details see Glenn (2000: 163–6; 2004: 176–9). An excellent German study on the *qadi* and dispute settlement is found in Falaturi *et al.* (1986).

would have to be learned. Less learned *qadis* might be preferable for rulers, particularly if they were also willing to engage in administrative legal tasks. Coulson (1968: 68) suggested that the rigid adherence to civil and criminal procedure, based on idealised assumptions about the probity of the good Muslim witness, yielded the result that 'the Shari'a courts proved an unsatisfactory organ for the administration of certain spheres of the law'. Those areas of law which involved largely (but of course not exclusively) administrative issues rather than questions of religious law, were put under the jurisdiction of the *mazalim* courts since the earlier Umayyad period (Amedroz, 1911). Coulson (1968: 68) reported that this jurisdiction developed in competition with the *shari'a* courts and created a clear dichotomy:

> All functions in the Islamic state were theoretically religious in nature. But the distinction between the *Mazalim* and *Shari'a* jurisdictions came very close to the notion of a division between secular and religious courts, the *qadi* being regarded as the representative of God's law, and the *Sahib al-Mazalim* as the mouthpiece of the ruler's law.

While *mazalim* courts might also function as courts of appeal and developed their own hierarchies, officials and procedures, the familiar division in legal systems of Asia and Africa between general law and personal laws now became more visible.[109] Coulson (1968: 68) observed that mainly because of the importance of local customary laws in many Muslim communities, 'even in the sphere of the family law, which is regarded as an essential and integral part of the religious faith, Shari'a doctrine has been by no means universally applied throughout the Muslim world'.

Within the limits of their jurisdiction, the courts of the *qadis* 'also deviated in certain limited respects from the strict doctrine of the Shari'a texts on the ground of social or economic necessity' (Coulson, 1968: 69). Examples include the complex subjects of unjust enrichment through interest (*riba*) and uncertainty (*gharar*). In the classical system, based on idealised notions of good Muslim status, unrealistic and impractical ideal standards had been laid down. These ideals could often not be upheld through judicial decisions without infringing on commercial interests and local customary norms. In many cases, the *qadis* gave in, officially recognising customary institutions (Libson, 1997; Arabi, 2001). Through judicial sanctioning of such practices, on the grounds of economic necessity, 'un-Islamic' practices might become part of the body of rules recognised by *shari'a* courts. Such debates, for example over excessive interest (*riba*), continue in many jurisdictions today. Related to this, an important feature of Islamic dispute settlement and jurisprudence is the use of certain devices or strategies, known collectively as *hiyal*, which might be used to circumvent strict *shari'a* rules not acceptable in society. Coulson (1968: 69–70) reported:

---

[109] This was earlier known from Roman law and the *ius gentium* (chapter 3, section 3.3).

Hanafi and Shafi'i courts generally accepted the validity of such *hiyal.* But the Malikis and Hanbalis, displaying a greater concern for the real intention behind overt acts, roundly condemned this manipulation of the letter of the law to achieve a purpose fundamentally contrary to its spirit.

Such examples confirm an overall picture of much diversity in theory and practice, despite the overarching authority of the religious norm system. Esposito (1988: 85) concludes that '[t]his diversity continued in practice as judges applied the laws of the various law schools in their courts'. As noted, the ruler's control over the judiciary might be achieved more effectively by having less qualified *qadis.* This leads to the institution of the *mufti.* Like the jurist, he was a private scholar, sometimes a support mechanism for a *qadi* who was not learned enough to decide matters of religious law, or he might be acting as adviser for a litigant. The scholar as *mufti* thus performs a function as a jurisconsult, an expert on religious law capable of giving authoritative opinions.[110] Among the first specialists, whom he does not yet call 'jurists', Schacht (1984: 27) found the very first *muftis* in Islam. Under the Umayyads, qualified *qadis* were still acting as *muftis* themselves. However, whenever a *qadi* lacked qualifications of juristic expertise, he required the help of a *mufti.* Questions put to the *mufti* were answered in the form of authoritative opinions on a particular matter (*fatwa*), and though they never had the value of precedents as in common law, they were considered authoritative opinions and were collected in large important works.[111] Coulson (1968: 70) argued that the *muftis* were largely responsible for using various devices and thus 'accommodating the classical doctrine to the needs of Muslim society'. In relation to social norms, too, the religious doctrine of the superiority of the religious law did not mean in practice that custom could not be accepted as valid law in derogation of a religious principle. While Esposito (1988: 86) argues that 'limited legal development and change did occur' through the involvement of *muftis,* Coulson (1968: 70) suggested that 'such concessions to practical necessity were always made reluctantly and by way of exception to the general rule that the courts were rigidly bound to the doctrine of the classical manuals'. However, the *muftis* might well be paying lip service to the religious system by acting contrary to its spirit. Coulson (1968: 70) concluded that divergence from the path shown by the classical texts 'constituted a deviation from the ideal standard', but that does not explain why such departures were so frequent and significant that everybody knows of them.

Evidently, the religiously inspired ideal that God alone should be the lawmaker was constantly infringed by *qadis* and *muftis* through their professional

---

[110] On his position see in detail Glenn (2004: 178).

[111] See in detail Hallaq (1994) and the bibliographical notes in Glenn (2004: 178). Modern means of communication have introduced some changes and media *muftis* are becoming popular (Yilmaz, 2005a).

activities. Exploring the nature of Islamic legal 'tradition', Glenn (2004: 179) suggests that the *qadi* and the *mufti* lacked institutional support and that Islamic law is simply sustained by Islamic communities, so that 'legal authority is in a very real sense vested in the private, or religious, community and not in any political ruler'. That amounts to the familiar finding that all law has critical social dimensions (Griffiths, 1999), falling in line with Ehrlich's theoretical model and the assertions by scholars (e.g. Unger, 1976; Cotterrell, 2003) that the realities of law are constantly being worked out in society. If Islamic law 'is simply sustained by the islamic community' (Glenn, 2004: 179), this is perhaps adequate for explaining the nature of Glenn's concept of 'legal tradition' with regard to Islam, but it does not tell us enough about how the complex edifice of various Islamic laws has been worked out over time (Hallaq, 1992), seeking to maintain sustainable balances between the dogma of religious superiority, the reality of social embeddedness, and the claims of various political entities in the Muslim world. The following sections explore in more detail how the continuing process of negotiation within the triangular model of plurality-consciousness led to significant changes within Islamic jurisprudence, building on earlier experience but facing new challenges as well.

5.10 Subsidiary sources of law

Many potential sources of law were considered unsuitable for inclusion in Shafi'i's scheme of the roots of Muslim jurisprudence and the reassertion of the religious basis as dominant (Coulson, 1964: 91) because they constitute various kinds of human law-making. Weiss (1978: 202) wrote that '[t]hese appear to have originally represented independent human judgment of expediency or public utility'. Though *ijma* and *qiyas* are also techniques that necessarily involve human activity in ascertaining rules, they were not supposed to contain more than an absolute minimum of human endeavour, thus making them acceptable and usable within Shafi'i's scheme.

Various elements, referred to as 'additional sources' (Weiss, 1978: 202) and generally linked to *ra'y*, served as interactive components in law-making processes. These supposedly minor, informal sources have continued to play an important role in the construction and reproduction of 'living Muslim laws'. The role of these minor sources has often been underplayed, relegating them to the unofficial realm outside the four 'official' sources. Shafi'i rejected them because they all involved human reasoning and facilitated *ra'y* to an extent which he did not find acceptable. Hence, they figure more prominently in Maliki and Hanafi legal theory than in the later Shafi'i and Hanbali schools. Coulson (1964: 60) emphasised that through his repudiation of these 'undisciplined forms of reasoning', insisting on strictly regulated analogical reasoning, Shafi'i was attempting to reduce differences of opinion to a minimum. Listing some of these sources, Fyzee (1999: 22) argued that they mainly reflect 'the difference of opinion among jurists in matters where discretion can be exercised and lead to refinements and distinctions which have become questions of controversy among the adherents of various schools'. This is precisely the kind of situation that Shafi'i wanted to avoid. Weiss (1978: 202) argued that 'these so-called sources were eventually assimilated into the textual sources and were thereby deprived of their independent status'.

Analysing this is difficult because different jurists and scholars have given different names to similar concepts. Fyzee (1999: 22) wrote of 'material sources of law' and argued that these cannot be neglected. He listed pre-Islamic customs, some elements of Roman law, the local customs of different people, as well as later English law influences through 'Justice, Equity and Good Conscience'. This incomplete collection appears to lack coherence, but the emphasis on custom is relevant. The main concepts to consider here first are *istihsan*, 'personal preference', and *istislah*, 'public interest', both methods of interpretation rather than substantive sources of law. Coulson (1964: 91) explained that flexibility of legal reasoning was the keynote of the Hanafi principle of *istihsan*, 'juristic preference', and to some extent also of the Maliki principle of *istislah*, 'consideration of the public interest'. Shafi'i vigorously opposed them since they contradicted his *grundnorm* that Qur'an and *sunna* were absolutely dominant and that human reasoning should not be allowed to prevail on any ground (Hallaq, 1997). Coulson (1964: 92) highlighted the difference between legal theory and reality:

> Although legal literature, from classical times onwards, naturally tended to minimise the importance of these supplementary principles, they in fact represent the real sources of the bulk of Hanafi and Maliki law; their survival, under the umbrella of *ijma*, shows how successfully the early schools had absorbed the shock of ash-Shāfi'i's attack, and why they were able to preserve the distinctive characteristics which stemmed from their circumstances of origin.

Similarly, Esposito (1988: 84) suggests that the subsidiary sources were invisibly integrated into the formal system:

> While all came to accept the four sources of law, Islamic jurisprudence recognized other influences, designating them subsidiary principles of law. Among these were custom (*urf*), public interest (*istislah*) and juristic preference or equity (*istihsan*). In this way, some remnant of the inductive human input that had characterized the actual methods of the law schools in their attempt to realize the Sharia's primary concern with human welfare, justice and equity were acknowledged.

As Weiss (1978: 202) explains, *istihsan* could be seen as a form of analogy, which also involves a process of selecting one interpretation in preference to another:

[s]ome jurists claimed that *istihsan*, far from being an expression of personal preference, was nothing more than the repudiation of one rule based on analogy in favor of the adoption of another based on a more subtle – but ultimately more plausible – analogy.

If this selection involved purely methodological criteria rather than social concerns, *istihsan* would even be acceptable within Shafi'i's scheme. Similarly, the concept of *istislah* as 'public interest' could be used to justify various interpretations. The most acceptable for Shafi'i would have been the interest of the Muslim community as a faith group, i.e. the protection of Islam itself. The most prominent term for this appears to be *maslaha*, also translated as 'public interest', a notion which can be brought under Shafi'i's scheme, whereas *istihsan* and *istislah* are normally excluded.[112] Weiss (1978: 202) writes that *maslaha* was eventually classified by Sunni theorists as a category of purposes of the divine law, 'to be discovered, not through a free exercise of reason or intuition, but as a result of an inductive exegesis . . . of the texts'. Hence, it could become acceptable. Doi (1984: 81–2) provides a useful discussion:

> Public interest is also regarded in Shari'ah as a basis of law. The jurists of different schools have used different Arabic terms to describe it. The Hanafis call it *istihsan* meaning equitable preference to find a just solution. Imam Malik calls it *Al-Masalih al-Mursalah* that is the public benefit or public welfare . . . Imam Ahmad bin Hanbal calls it *istislah* seeking the best solution for the general interest. The Hanbali scholar Ibn Qudamah as well as the Maliki jurist Ibn Rushd have occasionally used the term *istihsan*. The only school which does not recognise *ihtisan* as a source is the Shafi'i school. According to Imam Shafi'i, if it is allowed, it can open the door to the unrestricted use of fallible human opinions since the public interest will vary from place to place and time to time.

Doi (1984: 82) further highlights that concepts of public welfare and general interest can be seen as an equitable consideration that was not even denied by the Shafi'i school, which used *istidlal*, 'argumentation', to achieve similar results by avoiding strict application of *qiyas* that might result in injustice or a socially unacceptable theoretical conclusion.[113] The Shafi'i school also recognises the concept of *istishab*, 'presumption of continuity'. This is different from the other categories discussed above since it is a technique or rule of evidence (Doi, 1984: 83). It concerns a legal presumption to the effect that a state of affairs known to have existed in the past continues to exist until the contrary is shown. This would become relevant in situations where a missing person may either be presumed dead from the date of disappearance, after some specified time, or

---

[112] See Coulson (1964: 144), Hallaq (1997) and in detail Esposito (1995, III: 63–5).

[113] Doi (1984: 82–3) provides useful examples. The modern use of 'public interest', accepted now as Islamic in Pakistan (Menski *et al.* 2000), clearly has deeper Islamic dimensions (section 5.14).

that person may be presumed alive until the contrary is known. This might affect succession questions and the position of married spouses.[114]

Continuous debates arose over the role of custom and legislation, neither of which are recognised as classical formal sources of Islamic law. Official statements that 'custom' is not a source of Islamic law, so often found, can be read to mean, therefore, that custom should not influence the human mind in interpreting God's law. But because Muslims have always had to ascertain God's law (Weiss, 1978: 200), since the time of the Prophet customary influences have inevitably played a large role in shaping authoritative Muslim interpretations of Qur'an and *sunna*. Statements about the irrelevance of custom for Islamic law become even more unreal in view of the enormous diversity among Muslims. Schacht (1984: 62) highlighted that 'custom and customary law have co-existed with the ideal theory of Islamic law, while remaining outside its system, in the whole of the Islamic world. As a point of historical fact, custom contributed a great deal to the formation of Islamic law.' The classical theory, concerned with the systematic foundation of the law, led to a consensus of scholars that denied recognition to custom. In principle, this is the same process that makes the negation of moral values and social input by legal positivism so unreal. Theoretical Islamic scholarship deliberately denied itself plurality-consciousness to maintain the assertion that God's law was supreme at all times. But does assertion of divine supremacy require a denial of the role of custom and legislation? Doi (1984: 84) explains that traditional Muslim jurists were plurality-conscious, but sought at the same time to maintain the superiority of God's law:

> *Urf*, the known practices and *Adat* or Customs are recognised as a subsidiary source by all schools of Jurisprudence. The Maliki school attaches more importance to custom than other schools. But customary rules are valid as long as there is no provision on the matter in the Qur'an and the Sunnah. If any of the customs contradict any other rule of Shari'ah, they will be considered outside the pale of Islamic Law.

Being placed outside the strict ambit of Islamic law does not erase custom from Muslim social reality and the legal framework of certain states. Should we then speak of unofficial customs, or un-Islamic customs? Coulson (1969: 54–5) emphasised that this conceptual tension has accompanied Islam throughout its history since the time of revelation:

> Inevitably perhaps, in Islam as in other philosophies of life, there has always existed some degree of conflict between theory and reality and of tension between the religious idealism of the doctrine and the demands of political, social, and economic expediency. On grounds of practical necessity Muslim states and societies have recognised and applied laws whose terms are

---

[114] For details see Coulson (1964: 92–3) in the context of unity and diversity in *shari'a* law. This became relevant in Turkey (section 5.13).

contrary to the religious doctrine expounded in the medieval legal manuals. Within the vast geographical spread of Islam and the many different peoples who make up its four hundred million adherents, customary law has always controlled many aspects of life.

Observing how learned past scholars scrutinised different school approaches, Coulson (1969: 34) claimed that 'Islamic law takes on the appearance of a built-in comparative legal system'. Such internal comparisons not only provided substance for polemic battles but also engendered a spirit of valuing difference among Muslims, akin to what Legrand (1996) demands of all comparative legal scholarship.

The same goes for state-made laws, prominently legislation, since case law has not been a feature of traditional Muslim law, given that every case was judged in its own right, and the idea of precedent, while not absent, was perceived to endanger justice.[115] The official view has always been that no ruler or government can change the *shari'a*,[116] but positivist law-making was never totally absent. Most likely, it was treated as an aspect of efficient administration, implying the production of secondary rules in Hartian terms, but it is asserted by Hallaq (1997) that early Muslim law knew and used legislation. A Muslim ruler could certainly introduce administrative regulations without direct reference to religious law, which does not mean that this becomes 'secular' law, since it still applies the values and spirit of God's law. We find confirmation here of explicit conceptual (and plurality-conscious) recognition that Muslim positive law contains religious values and consideration of social normative orders, so Muslim legislated law would be internally plural and not just posited law in a strictly secular Austinian sense. Conceived as internally plural, respecting the superiority of God's law, this precludes the emergence of Islamic absolutism. Starting from the Prophet, and more so in the time of the early jurists, Islamic governments appear to have been conscious of the need to remain at all times under the religious umbrella while pursuing positivist law-making. As fierce criticisms of the early Umayyads (section 5.5) showed, pursuing legal positivism without explicit reference to religious norms would be branded as misguided. However, from earliest times it was possible to legitimise this through juristic reasoning, which then deflected criticism to the jurists and their methodologies. This probably allowed Islamic rulers to get away with much positivist law-making in the name of Islam.

Mayer (1990: 179) argued that Islamic law, rather than becoming a 'jurist's law', might just as well have turned into a codified system. Her assumptions do

---

[115] Hallaq (1997) seems to suggest a role for decisions as a help in solving other problems.

[116] There is a rich literature on concepts of the Muslim state. See Rosental (1958; 1965), Asad (1961), Faruki (1971), Enayat (1982). With particular reference to the modern world, see Khadduri (1970), Hassan (1984), Halliday and Alavi (1988) and Ferdinand and Mozaffari (1988). Tibi (1997) focuses on Arab nationalism.

not stand up to scrutiny from a globally focused comparative perspective and require some comment here. They explain why many Western legal writers may not have been able to grasp the nature of Islamic legal arrangements. Mayer (1990: 179) starts from wrong assumptions about legal codification:[117]

> The tradition of codification was well established in the ancient world as well as in ancient Middle Eastern culture, and the choice could have been made at the outset of Islamic legal history to devise Islamic codes that would have been promulgated by the ruler. That is, it would have been perfectly possible for the Shari'ah to have been introduced in a codified formulation.

Mayer certainly has a point that codification would have been possible. Section 5.3 explored why it could not have been done by the Prophet without drastically changing the nature of Islamic law. The roots of Islamic law had to remain within the conceptual triangle of natural law and ethics to achieve the purpose of the new divine message and could not be transplanted to the triangle of the state. Simply replacing an unsatisfactory positivist order by a new positivist order was not a viable option. Even later, despite many positivist ambitions of early Islamic leaders, this basic liaison of a new value system and legal rules could not be modified without challenging the entire edifice of Islam. Mayer's modernist interpretation seems to ignore the central role of religion as an aspect of natural law, which then infuses any positive law. From a plurality-conscious perspective, the task of humanity appears to be to harmonise human ways of life with the perceived requirements of those unseen higher forces that are perceived to control the universe in some form and gave rise to the various beliefs that we know, including the religion of agnosticism. Ignoring, in this case, Allah's natural law and its globalised claims to superiority, Mayer's approach completely excludes the overriding religious claims of Muslim law and is too positivist in tone.

It is not surprising that debates over the relationship between state-made law and religious law have not led to any conclusion. This neatly mirrors the never-ending dominant discourse in Western legal theory between positivists and natural lawyers, with the crucial difference that Islamic discourses tend not to question the religious nature of natural law and would provide a different interpretation of 'secular' law-making and theorising. After the ninth/tenth century AD, the focus in the Islamic world remained on expansion and administration of ever-growing empires, while the jurists were carrying on intensive debates in their learned circles as before but linked, from time to time, into those political developments. At first sight, little attention was paid to socio-legal issues. This, too, reflects the European experience, where the historical school

---

[117] I assert this in light of the analysis of Emperor Ašoka's 'legislation', which turned out to be an appeal to self-controlled order rather than statist law-making (chapter 4, section 4.3), the colonial misconstruction of ancient Hindu texts as legal codes (chapter 4, section 4.7) and in view of lingering concerns that the interpretation of old Middle Eastern codes has been heavily influenced by Maine's (1861) evolutionist thinking and may be too positivist.

of jurisprudence was yet to emerge. People's law was still a social matter for people, not so much for 'legal' scholars, who were more concerned about their own universe than local concerns. Plurality-consciousness, it seems, remained somewhat deficient, as indicated by the following section.

5.11 The purported closing of the 'gates of *ijtihad*'

This much-debated episode confirms that Islamic legal history, too, follows a cyclic pattern of dialectical ups and downs rather than a linear progression of development. The concept of the so-called 'closing of the gates of *ijtihad*' is an important issue for late traditional Muslim jurisprudence. As the growing diversification in Muslim jurisprudence around 950 reached more complexity and confusing multiplicity, calls for the unification, streamlining and continued Islamisation of Muslim law were again becoming louder. The result was assumed to have been the closing of the famous 'gates of *ijtihad*', a term used by some Western scholars to claim that Islamic jurists stopped thinking for themselves during medieval times.

However, such a fresh uniformising endeavour in Islamic jurisprudence could not be completely successful. What gradually emerged was a new system of 'living Muslim law', in which formal rules and social reality were realigned to adjust to new conditions. Like Shafi'i's theory, the 'closing of the gates' was an excellent theoretical argument (Hallaq, 1986: 141), but it had to fail in practice, as even Coulson (1969: 44) began to realise, and more recent scholarship (Hallaq, 1984; 1986; 1997) confirms. No law can completely shut out the freedom of the intellect, nourished in this case by Muslim jurists' thirst for knowledge of God's law. Just as a customary tradition cannot be frozen forever by turning it into statutory law, a living scholarly tradition cannot be arrested at a certain point. It would not be healthy for the continuing harmonisation of Islamic religious doctrine with legal and social developments to refuse a place for interactive dynamism. The doors of *ijtihad* thus never really closed, as scholarship today recognises. Inherent plurality-consciousness among Muslims all over the world made sure the doors stayed ajar. Just as religion cannot be abolished for ever, the 'gates of *ijtihad*' could not be closed for good.

The period between 1000 and 1300 was productive for the four major schools, as many handbooks of *fiqh* were compiled and became classical works, above all used by scholars and *qadis*, supplemented where necessary by the *fatwas* of *muftis*, who would themselves consult such works. After centuries of enormous conflicts and tensions, it appeared that a certain consolidation had taken place. Esposito (1988: 85) captures an atmosphere of settlement by the tenth century, based on consensus among jurists that Islamic law as a jurisprudential system had been sufficiently clarified and documented in juristic literature:

> This attitude led many to conclude that individual, independent interpretation (*ijtihad*) of the law was no longer necessary or desirable. Instead,

Muslims were to simply follow or imitate (*taqlid*) the past, God's law as elaborated by the early jurists. Jurists were no longer to seek new solutions or produce new regulations and law books but instead study the established legal manuals and write their commentaries. Islamic law, the product of an essentially dynamic and creative process, now tended to become fixed and institutionalized. While individual scholars like Ibn Taymiyya (d. 1328) and al-Suyuti (d. 1505) demurred, the majority position resulted in traditional belief prohibiting substantive legal development. This is commonly referred to as the closing of the gate or door of *ijtihad*. Belief that the work of the law schools had definitely resulted in the transformation of the Sharia into a legal blueprint for society reinforced the sacrosanct nature of tradition; change or innovation came to be viewed as an unwarranted deviation (*bida*) from established sacred norms. To be accused of innovation – deviation from the law and practice of the community – was equivalent to the charge of heresy in Christianity.

Coulson (1964: 73) left little space between developments after Shafi'i and the later supposed 'closing of the gates':

> With the spread of the area of law covered by divine revelation came an increasing rigidity of doctrine; the scope for independent activity was progressively restricted as the particular terms of the law, through the Traditions, were identified with the command of God. The spring of juristic speculation, which had supplied the rapidly moving stream of Islamic jurisprudence in its early stages, gradually ceased to flow; the current slowed, until eventually and inevitably, it reached the point of stagnation.

This is certainly no longer maintainable today. There may have been conceptual stagnation in jurisprudence, for what else could have been said after it had been established and agreed that God's law was supreme? There was maybe a slowing down of Islamising activism after Shafi'i convincingly asserted the supremacy of God's law, but no overall stagnation or a closing of minds, as new research richly documents (see below). During the 1960s, scholarship was still impressed with the image that the gates of *ijtihad* were closed. Coulson (1968: 64) relied on the internal duality of *ijma* methodology to argue that Islamic jurisprudence had gone into decline:

> [T]he consensus of opinion . . . endorsed the variant doctrines of the four schools as equally legitimate. But *ijma* also operated as a prohibitive and exclusive principle. For once *ijma* had cast the umbrella of its infallible authority not only over those points which were the subject of a consensus, but also over the existing variant opinions, the contemporary situation was irrevocably ratified inasmuch as to propound any further variant opinion was to contradict the *ijma*, the infallible expression of God's will, and so to be guilty of heresy! Hence the right of independent effort, or *ijtihad*, to ascertain Allah's law disappeared. *Ijma* had set the final seal upon the doctrine which, as it existed in the early tenth century, was represented as the culmination of the quest to express the law in terms of the will of God;

and Muslim jurisprudence recognised that its creative force was now spent
by declaring that 'the door of *ijtihad* was closed'.

Schacht (1984: 70–1) imagined how a consensus gradually grew among the
jurists that *taqlid* rather than *ijtihad* in the sense of independent assessment
should be used and wrote (p. 71):

> This 'closing of the door of *ijtihad*', as it was called, amounted to the demand
> for *taklid*, a term which had originally denoted the kind of reference to
> Companions of the Prophet that had been customary in the ancient schools
> of law, and which now came to mean the unquestioning acceptance of the
> doctrines of established schools and authorities. A person entitled to *ijtihad*
> is called *mujtahid*, and a person bound to practice *taklid, mukallid*.

But how far would the scholars, as vigilant guardians of God's law and its interpretation, actually go in this respect? Could human reasoning ever be totally
excluded? Schacht's view that there was now mere 'unquestioning acceptance'
has been challenged by more recent scholarship, especially Hallaq (1984) and
Gerber (1998), discussed below. Schacht (1984: 71) was correct to emphasise
that the transition from *ijtihad* to *taqlid* was a gradual process, so that the
doors were perhaps gradually closing, rather than being shut tight. But were
they ever completely closed? Rather than answering this particular question,
Fyzee (1999: 36–7) offered a different view, which makes much sense in terms
of juristic politics:

> The earlier jurists had greater powers; the later ones could not cross the
> barrier and were classified as of lower and lower rank. The classification
> of lawyers in this period is very elaborate; seven different grades are rec-
> ognized, beginning from the Imams as founders down to the ordinary
> jurisconsult or *mufti*. Practically, in every case the later lawyers were con-
> sidered lower in grade; until, after a time, the exercise of independent
> judgment was not permitted at all. This is known as 'The Closure of the
> Gate of Interpretation' during the fourth/tenth century.

This gradual watering down of juristic status was also observed by other scholars. Schacht (1984: 71–2) recognised that '[e]ven during the period of *taklid*,
Islamic law was not lacking in manifestations of original thought in which
the several schools competed with and influenced one another'. While Schacht
assumed that such original thought could only be expressed in abstract terms,
he had an inkling that the 'closing of the gates' was perhaps not total. Schacht
(1984: 72) in fact provided several examples of articulate scholarly opposition
to the total closing of the gates. These include arguments that it would be 'dangerous to follow blindly the authority of any man, excepting only the Prophet,
in matters of religion and religious law' (p. 72).

While there was still a need for *ijtihad*, the focus shifted to critical reception
based on study rather than idiosyncratic 'speculation', *ra'y*. The freedom of
the pioneering scholar was restricted by masses of existing *fiqh*, but *taqlid* did

not simply mean uncritical mindless reception or copying, but a prohibition on flying off into private speculations. In this sense, *taqlid* is a methodological requirement of circumspection and caution for all Sunni jurists, expecting them to search for the correct opinion in the plethora of sources, rather than claiming too rapidly to have found the right answer themselves. This methodology again asserts revelation over human reasoning, but does not imply the abolition of critical legal scholarship. This was recognised by Rahim (1994: 33):

> I may observe here that a notion exists that henceforward there has been no further exposition of Islamic law, the ancient doctors having anticipated every question and laid down a rule for its solutions. Such a notion is prima facie untenable, nor is it founded in fact. It would be more accurate to say, as held by jurists of authority, that the principles that have been hitherto established would, if properly applied, furnish an answer in most cases.

Could this approach, which certainly involved curtailment of 'speculation', really end up in total censorship and stagnation? Scope for restriction is strongly reflected in the older literature and many traditional textbooks were content to simply state that the gates had closed. Bharatiya (1996: 28), in one sentence, reinforces an image of stagnation and juristic introspection, claiming that '[a]fter the establishment of the four Sunni Schools, there has been no independent exposition of Muslim law, and jurists have been busy, within the limits of each School, in developing the work of its founders'. A leading Indian textbook on Muslim law (Hidayatullah and Hidayatullah, 1990: xxv) discusses the need for Muslim law reforms in modern India, imagining that no help can come from Muslim jurists, since the doors of *ijtihad* have been firmly shut forever and the only suitable remedy, a classic positivist prescription, is legislation:

> This reform cannot obviously be left to scholars. The scholars today cannot reopen the closed doors of *ijtihad*, even if it were possible. Moreover, where are the scholars who can be said to possess the necessary qualifications? The only alternative is legislation and to a certain extent, liberal judicial interpretation of the root principles where possible.

Thus, a misleading impression has been created that there could be no further legitimate development within Islamic law through juristic innovation. Many Western observers welcomed the resulting conclusion that Muslims had restricted themselves to medieval states of knowledge and development. The modernists rejoiced: Islam was not able to handle the modern world, it would not be part of a global future. However, this has been challenged recently: global Islam has become a lively and much larger family of Islams, whose internal diversities have increased rather than being suppressed. It appears now that traditional legal scholars fell into a trap of their own making, out of which Islamic scholarship has only recently emerged.[118] Given that the input

---

[118] See in particular the special issue of *Islamic Law and Society*, Vol. 3, No. 2 (June 1996).

of human law-making had to be accepted all along in Islamic jurisprudence, imagining a final seal, encouraged by Coulson's (1968: 64, cited above) image of the final seal of *ijma*, in analogy to Mohammad as the 'seal of the Prophets', reveals wishful positivist thinking in Western scholars and Muslim jurists. An immensely intelligent theoretical construct, the clever image of the shut door reflects a deficiency in plurality-consciousness. In practice, this door must have remained almost as widely open as before, but now had a veil put before it that filtered visions and imaginations. The effects of this veiling created a public image of Islam worldwide as a stagnant religion, as Muslims were to discover to their own cost. Since such a thick blot in legal history cannot just be wiped away by a revision of theories, the damage was done.

The first major challenge to the image of the closed gates of *ijtihad* came when Hallaq (1984: 4) argued that the prevailing views about the closing of the gates 'are entirely baseless and inaccurate' and that the gate was closed neither in theory nor in practice. Hallaq (1984: 5) described *ijtihad* as a religious duty and argued that the Muslim community as a whole could not survive without *ijtihad*. Hallaq (1984: 22–3) reasoned along with some Hanbali jurists:

> Therefore, should this activity be abandoned, the Muslim community would inevitably be in error, something which cannot possibly happen. Moreover, the community would fall into anarchy and the edifice of Shari'a would be demolished should ijtihad cease to exist, because ijtihad is the only means by which the believers can pursue the true path of God whenever a new case comes up.

In his concluding analysis, Hallaq (1984: 33) therefore argued that 'in Islamic legal theory ijtihad was reckoned indispensable in legal matters because it was the only means by which Muslims could determine to what degree their acts were acceptable to God'. He even challenged the existence of a consensus about the closing of the gates, and concluded on the basis of his research that the gates were never closed. Hallaq relied for his study on Hanbali arguments, to which Schacht (1984: 72–3) had earlier drawn attention. This critique did not challenge the interpretation of *taqlid* itself as pure imitation. Weiss (1978: 200) had taken this to be 'a term which refers to the acceptance of a rule, not on the basis of evidence drawn directly from the sources, but on the authority of other jurists'. In this sense, the jurist who employed *taqlid* was still using his skills and was not just a mindless imitator. A more recent author, who examined the *fatwa* collection of a seventeenth-century Palestinian *mufti*, argued that, contrary to Western assumptions about the increasingly obsolete and rigid nature of Islamic law in the post-classical period, it 'contained an important element of openness and flexibility' (Gerber, 1998: 167). The law in this period was not frozen and petrified, the *mufti* whose work he analysed was very much aware of *ijtihad* and, above all, 'the law contained many unsettled issues that constituted an intellectual space in which *qadis* and *muftis* were allowed to – indeed had to – use their personal discretion' (Gerber, 1998: 194). Gerber (1998: 173 n. 31) also challenges the understanding of *taqlid*, saying that '[t]he translation of *taqlid* as imitation is not only pejorative, but factually wrong. *Taqlid* is mainly used in the context of accepting the intellectual authority of someone', thus confirming that the jurist still needed to exert effort. In the process, Gerber also has much to say about the role of custom as an important source of law and an element of continuous flexibility. The widespread assumption and popular image of the closed door of *ijtihad* is therefore now shown as a useful image for a shift in emphasis, not as an illustration of the confinement and suffocation of Muslim legal scholarship through more or less total prohibition on creative juristic thinking and flexible application.

5.12 The shift towards legal reforms

Scholarly activities continued during medieval times but appeared less prominent than before, contributing to the image of the closing gates. Attention shifted away from Islamic scholar-jurists and towards human law-making by states. Scholars could now concentrate on writing commentaries on older works, and advising in the capacity of *muftis*, without the spotlight on them that had earlier scrutinised every methodological technique and its implications. Human law-making remained necessary to make sense of God's word in a new age and in different socio-political circumstances. Doi (1984: 51) notes that the Qur'an 'is still insufficient by itself without the assistance of Fatawa (a religious decision) and Tradition'. This expresses the need, also highlighted by Hallaq (1984; 1994) and Gerber (1998), for Muslim societies to continue searching for further guidance regarding the right path. It reflects constant plurality-conscious efforts to ensure that the pluralistic circle at the centre of our conceptual triangle (chapter 3, section 3.8) reflects 'goodness' and 'justice' among Muslims, seeking to discover *shari'a* as the ideal path or road to follow.

Because of the assumption that Islamic scholarship had been suffocated, most textbooks do not tell us much about this period.[119] Bharatiya (1996: 29) merely warns that, unless reforms are made to the law, the *shari'a* will remain fossilised, indicating further that '[r]ecent trends and developments in Muslim law effected by different Islamic countries are indicative of a new trend'. As the drive for reforms became a major theme, the focus shifted to critiques of the legal arrangements in various Muslim states, stirring up legal and religious politics. Efforts to introduce reforms through simply enforcing religious law – always a tempting thought for religious positivists – and bypassing existing state-made laws, were doomed to failure (Hallaq, 1984). Schacht (1984: 86) argued that reforms would have to be directed at state legal systems.

---

[119] Hallaq (1994; 1997) is an exception; see also Dupret *et al.* (1999) and Arabi (2001).

In this context, the division between 'private law' and 'public law' becomes important. While Western positivist theory insists on this distinction, non-Western legal systems find it difficult. For them, divisions of private and public may well exist at the visible level, but, at the invisible level of the higher Order, everything is subject to one overarching higher legal authority. While secular positivist lawyers refuse to treat this higher Order as law, Islamic law does not have this option: God's law is supreme at all times. Anderson (1960: 187) emphasised that it is 'impossible even today really to understand the Muslim mind, Muslim society, Muslim ideals, politics, and reactions, without some knowledge of that law which, in theory at least, still molds and pervades them all'. Gerber (1998: 169) argues that it is a serious fallacy to claim that 'Islamic law suffered from a deficiency qua law because it was also religious law'. From a Muslim perspective, nothing a human being does would be able to escape divine notice. The division of private and public, as in Hindu, African and Chinese laws, creates no barriers for the supervening authority beyond man, whatever culture-specific names it is given. Hence, nothing that a Muslim ruler does can evade divine judgment and for Muslims, all positive law and all legal actions remain subject to the supervening religious authority (Anderson, 1960: 187).

Beyond that, the realisation that Muslim rulers could make law in accordance with God's will, provided they affirmed their allegiance to Allah, opened the door for positivist law-making under the principle of *siyasa shar'iyya*, 'government in accordance with *shari'a*', which explicitly allows Muslim rulers to legislate. Coulson's useful discussions of the binary axis of *ahl al-hadith* and *ahl-al-ra'y* can now be brought within the pluralist legal triangle of our present model (chapter 3, section 3.8). Islamic law-making by the state is now tested in terms of its acceptability to religious values (natural law) *and* social norms, opening the door for social reforms through legal instrumentalism.[120]

The older legal literature, focused on Western positivist agenda and on Islamic scholar-jurists as key players in jurisprudence did not capture this triangular relationship, but Johansen (1997; 1999) portrays a complex socio-legal picture in which normative pluralism and inherent flexibility are key elements. Among earlier writers, Anderson (1959) focuses explicitly on socio-legal contexts. Both Anderson and Coulson wrote much about legal reforms to Muslim law, with rich evidence of political struggles and religious politics. Traditional defensiveness became apparent in book titles like *Modernization menaces Muslims* (Siddiqi, 1981), which signify a siege mentality in which calm discussion and necessary constructive interaction become difficult (Pearl and Menski, 1998: 83).

---

[120] Fresh questions over custom as a source of Muslim law arise. Hallaq (1984: 5) shows that familiarity with customs was treated as a qualification required for *ijtihad*, since it is essential 'to determine God's law in the light of the exigencies of human life'. Mahmood (1965: 102) confirms that 'consideration has always been shown to the force of general usage, insofar as it did not contravene the basic tenets of Islam'.

Coulson (1964: 128–9) pointed out that the concurrent jurisdictions of the *qadi* courts and the *mazalim* courts 'came very close to the notion of a division between secular and religious courts', public and private law. Traditional Islamic law had long made the distinction between the Muslim individual's obligations to God (*ibadat*), and the obligations to individuals (*muamalat*). The Muslim ruler was now taken to task for both sets of obligations. Coulson (1964: 129) confirmed that '[l]egal scholarship from the eleventh century onwards evolved a doctrine of public law which rationalised the place which the Shari'a had in fact come to occupy in the organisation of the Islamic state'. Under this scheme, the two key conditions for a Caliph were being a pious Muslim and the ability to exercise *ijtihad*. This device 'recognised that a ruler so qualified had the power to take such steps as he saw fit to implement and supplement the principles established by the religious law. This system of government was known as "government in accordance with the revealed law" (*siyasa shar'iyya*)' (Coulson 1964: 129). It implied that the Muslim ruler 'was bound to give effect to the general purposes of God for Islamic society' (p. 129). The ruler's duty as a Muslim individual was now enlarged to that of protecting the *shari'a* of his realm and his people.[121] The ruler was now made explicitly subservient to the *shari'a*, a step which had significant consequences, as political sovereignty was Islamically legitimated. Coulson (1964: 129–30) noted that 'the wider and supreme duty of the sovereign was the protection of the public interest; and in pursuance of it he was afforded an overriding personal discretion to determine, according to time and circumstances, how the purposes of God for the Islamic community might best be effected'.

This is not simply legal positivism in Western secular form, but the Islamic version of positivism, allowing a ruler to administer, legislate and operate judicial activities while remaining conscious of the higher Order of God's law. Doi (1984: 467) writes that '[i]t is a technique through which certain so called reforms were introduced in Shari'ah as an escape from the application from strict Shari'ah principles' but expresses much criticism about Islamic rulers. It was certainly an idealistic system of political arrangement that relied on the individual ruler's conscience. As Coulson (1964: 133–4) showed, abuse of this idealistic system was widespread, because not enough attention had been paid to political theory and to the risks of unfettered legal positivism:

> Doctrine had granted the ruler such wide discretionary powers on the assumption that he would be ideally qualified for office. But it is precisely here that the idealistic nature of the doctrine is at its most apparent; for there existed no constitutional machinery, and in particular no independent judiciary, to guarantee that the ruler would be so qualified and that those powers would not be abused. Although the doctrine expressed to

---

[121] The Hindu ruler had much earlier been enjoined to protect the *rita/dharma* complex, so that the obligation to protect *dharma* made him a servant of this higher Order (chapter 4).

perfection the concept of a state founded upon the rule of God's law, it never seriously challenged the ruler's autocratic power to control the practical implementation of that law; and it finally reached the point of abject surrender and recognition of its total impotence by acknowledging the principle that obedience was due to the political power whatever its nature, and that even the most impious and tyrannical regime was preferable to civil strife. The order of allegiance expressed in the Qur'anic verse: 'Obey God, his Apostle and those at the head of affairs' had been reversed, and the only limits upon the *de facto* power of the ruler were those that he found in his own conscience.

Hassan (1984: 52) confirms that the problem of the unrighteous ruler 'was never really faced by the main body of Islamic opinion, either Sunni or Shia'. Coulson 1964: 134) argued that the concept of *siyasa shar'iyya* implied that *shari'a* law forms only part of an Islamic legal system:

> The doctrine of *siyasa shar'iyya*, based on a realistic assessment of the nature of Shari'a law and the historical process by which it had been absorbed into the structure of the state, admitted the necessity for and the validity of, extra-Shari'a jurisdictions, which cannot therefore be regarded, in themselves, as deviations from any ideal standard. Islamic government has never meant, in theory or in practice, the exclusive jurisdiction of Shari'a tribunals.

Coulson (1964: 130–1) demonstrated how the jurisdiction of the *mazalim* courts was used by rulers to develop Islamic law, almost parallel to how equity jurisdiction in English law had allowed legal growth. The most prominent area of the ruler's discretion under *siyasa shar'iyya* was the criminal law, both in terms of procedure and substance (Coulson 1964: 132). This is confirmed for Nigeria, where, apart from his duty of punishing in terms of *ta'zir*, the Muslim ruler also acted in the wider public interest under *siyasa*, which concerns 'the ultimate right and duty of the Ruler to safeguard the moral and material welfare of the community' (Anderson, 1978: 195). Apart from *hadd* offences, the grave crimes (as well as sins) specified by the Qur'an itself, namely drinking, extra-marital sex (*zina*), robbery with violence, theft, and false accusation of unchastity, the ruler could now determine *ta'zir* punishments, whose main purpose was deterrence (Coulson 1964: 133).[122]

Thus, the Islamic ruler, legitimised in Islamic terms and not effectively enough controlled by idealism, could now proceed to make law and to abuse power. Doi (1984: 467–9) complains that Muslim rulers were given too much discretionary power and often neglected their religious obligations and obligations to their subjects. Hassan (1984) claims that this problem has not been properly addressed by Islamic jurisprudence. The bad Muslim ruler's punishment, it seems, is reserved for the time after death.

---

[122] The concepts of *danda* in Hindu law (chapter 4) and *hsing* and *fa* in Chinese law (chapter 7) show remarkable parallels.

Interactions between Muslim rulers and their subjects have not been of much interest to writers on Islamic jurisprudence. Coulson (1964: 135) observed that converts to Islam would be expected to abandon and modify their pre-existing social norms, thus becoming Muslims in terms of religion as well as practice. While this would be less difficult for people in Arabia, he found that, for other people, 'the reception of Shari'a law posed serious problems, for its basic concepts were often wholly alien to the traditional structure of their societies' (p. 135). His examples from the Berbers in Morocco, Indonesian Muslims and the Yoruba in Western Nigeria show that many communities accepted Islam, but not fully Islamic ways of life, thus becoming only superficially Islamised.[123]

During the Middle Ages, following the fall of the Abbasid Caliphate in 1258, the political structure of Muslim states remained basically static (Coulson 1964: 149). In this atmosphere of relative stability, *shari'a* law was often able to accommodate successfully to new circumstances. The increasingly complex political scenario of the time allows only some broad contours of the new picture. Instead of one large Muslim empire, there were eventually several sultanates, prominently the Ottomans of Turkey, whose empire covered not only Turkey, but most of the Middle East and Eastern Europe (section 5.13). Under the protection of the Safavids in Persia (1501–1722), Shi'a jurisprudence developed into several separate legal schools. Further East, the Sultanate of Delhi, established in 1192, metamorphosed into the Moghul Empire during the fourteenth/fifteenth centuries and lasted until 1858, when Queen Victoria became Empress of India.

Coming to more recent reform concerns, Coulson (1964: 150) argued that Muslim criminal law and the rules on civil and commercial transactions were perceived to be deficient, speaking even of the 'total inadequacy to cater for modern systems of trade and economic development'. There seemed 'initially at any rate, no alternative but to abandon the Shari'a and replace it with laws of Western inspirations in those spheres where Islam felt a particular urgency to adapt itself to modern conditions' (Coulson 1964: 149–50). Particular points of criticism were the perceived harshness of some criminal sanctions, a reflection of colonial discourse (Fisch, 1983), the continued application of homicide as a tort, involving 'blood money' or compensation (*diya*), and the wide arbitrary powers vested in the Muslim ruler under *ta'zir*.[124] Coulson (1964: 150–1) showed how the presence of non-Muslim communities and observations of their extraterritorial legal systems taught Muslims that maybe other systems of law could be usefully imitated. Action soon followed and took various forms. Coulson (1968: 70) wrote:

---

[123] On Nigerian Islamic law, see Coulson (1964: 157–9, 162) and Ajijola (1989). In India, evidence of Muslims applying Hindu law gave rise to interesting case law (Mahmood 1977: 21–33; Diwan and Diwan, 1991: 36).

[124] Coulson (1968: 70–6) provides relevant examples.

> During the nineteenth century the impact of Western civilisation upon
> Muslim society brought about radical changes in the fields of civil and
> commercial transactions and criminal law. In these matters the Shari'a
> courts were now wholly out of touch with the needs of the time, both in
> their procedure and in the doctrine which they were bound to apply.

The idea of borrowing from non-Muslim legal systems developed in two ways,
first in terms of copying certain legal elements or aspects piecemeal. Only later
was the wholesale transplant of Western laws contemplated. Since the value systems underlying such laws were outside the Islamic legal system, many scholars
objected to the importation of secular laws.[125] Coulson (1964: 160–1) claimed
that this 'was never strong enough to constitute a formidable obstacle. In general, the attitude was taken that it was better to let the Shari'a pass peacefully
away from the field of legal practice', rather than attempting radical surgery of its
principles to suit modern conditions. From this perspective, the introduction
of modern, even Western laws could be justified as long as they were brought
under the umbrella of the religious law. Since Islamic legal tradition had long
recognised the ruler's right to introduce 'secular' administrative regulations as
'secondary rules' in Hartian terms, the same process could now be followed
to incorporate Western-style laws into Muslim law, either in piecemeal fashion
or as whole codes. There was no agreed methodology, no trodden path in this
respect that promised the right rewards.

Various methods were tried; it is not possible to provide much detail here.
Section 5.13 below discusses Turkish legal developments, which are unusual
because Turkey radically went outside the Islamic legal system during the 1920s
after earlier attempts to bring about internal reforms, and is 'positively un-
Islamic' (Coulson 1964: 223). Rather than copying European laws wholesale and
abandoning the Islamic legal framework, all other Islamic states have attempted
to work on piecemeal reforms, both in terms of substantive and procedural
law.[126] Modernising states such as Egypt, from 1875 onwards, adopted French
law in the form of codes both for civil and criminal law. Coulson (1964: 152)
reported:

> As a result of these initial steps taken during the Ottoman period, laws of
> European origin today form a vital and integral part of the legal systems
> of most Middle Eastern countries. Criminal law and procedure are almost
> completely Westernised, though the last few years have witnessed a move-
> ment away from the French Codes towards other sources . . . As for the law
> of civil transactions and obligations, this has become increasingly Western-
> ised, throughout the Middle East generally, during the present century.

---

[125] Having stated their conviction that the gates of *ijtihad* were firmly closed, Hidayatullah and
Hidayatullah (1990: xxv) noted in the Indian context that 'there is, however, considerable
opposition to the Legislatures and Courts playing the role of *mujtahids*'.

[126] For some details see Pearl and Menski (1998). On Egypt see Dupret *et al.* (1999).

The early prominent trend of almost indiscriminate borrowing of European laws was soon replaced by more intricate methods of adaptation, moulding the Western laws to fit them into the specific conditions of the receiving societies,[127] a process of Islamisation of foreign elements (Coulson 1964: 153). Another prominent method of avoiding conflict and cultivating plurality-conscious adaptation was to ensure that, in cases where there were perceived gaps in the law, local norms rather than foreign legal principles should apply. Coulson (1964: 153) provided the example of the Civil Code of Egypt from 1949, which provided that the courts should follow 'customary law, the principles of Islamic law, or the principles of natural justice'. Such provisions gave explicit authority and important incentives to judicial creativity, particularly in jurisdictions under common law influence. British Indian courts had a pole position in this field, but operated in a secular framework of reference, staffed by secular judges, who might be educated Muslims, but not traditional scholar-jurists.[128]

In many jurisdictions, Islamic law became a personal law for Muslims, which were then subjected to some state-sponsored legal reform, often in piecemeal amendments to any particular school tradition. National personal laws were dominated by a particular Sunni or Shi'a school tradition (*madhab*), as determined by the ruler, who might follow a different *madhab*. Coulson (1964: 183) affirmed the right of a Muslim to be governed by the law of his school in matters of personal status. The freedom of a Muslim individual to change his or her school became a matter for debate, but has been upheld in principle, protecting pluralist flexibility. Since the Sunni schools were recognised as mutually orthodox, in the Hanafi law of British India, rules from another school tradition were introduced by the ruler or through cases. Application of the principle of mutual orthodoxy, according to which all major Sunni schools were united under the broad canvas of *ijma*, was helpful to allow Muslim law to develop by recourse to Muslim concepts rather than foreign legal elements. Coulson (1964: 185) characterised this form of transplant as an important aspect of *siyasa shar'iyya*:

> *Takhayyur* is the general Arabic term for the process of selection; and if we omit the case of a restricted choice from among Hanafi variants only, such as had taken place in the Ottoman *Majalla*, it will be seen that the exercise of *takhayyur* falls under three distinct heads which may generally be regarded as chronological stages in the development of the principle.

Coulson (1964: 185–201) discussed this in detail, providing many examples from various fields of family law to show that, despite the dominant ideology

---

[127] Similar processes of learning to adapt foreign laws, rather than simply copying them wholesale, can be observed in Chinese law after 1911 (chapter 7) and are evident in Japanese law, too.

[128] Earlier the *maulvis*, Indian *muftis* employed by the British as 'assessors' between 1772 and 1864, were sacked when it was felt that modernity required more recourse to Western-type laws and legal methods (chapter 4, section 4.7).

of *taqlid*, intricate processes of legal choice were taking place all the time. Such evidence further undermines assumptions that *taqlid* was completely restrictive and supports the research of Gerber (1998). The juristic techniques of *takhayyur* are certainly not mindless imitation, blind copying of some legal rule; they are the very opposite and demand precisely, as Gerber (1998) showed, an intensive search for the right solution. Hence this is another form of *ijtihad*.

Three stages of *takhayyur* can be identified. The first technique would be to consider the doctrines of any other Sunni school and to adopt one of its elements. A prominent example is a Muslim wife's right to divorce, which was severely restricted by traditional Hanafi jurisprudence, but was more widely available in Maliki law. This method was first used for the Ottoman Law of Family Rights of 1917 and was later applied to the reform of Muslim divorce law in British India, under the Dissolution of Muslim Marriages Act of 1939. One of the express purposes of this Act was to allow Muslim wives to escape from an unhappy marriage without having to abandon Islam, which had become necessary for desperate wives, given the strictness of traditional Hanafi law.

The second stage of *takhayyur* was purposeful reliance on 'the authority of individual jurists whose opinions had preceded or were in conflict with the dominant doctrines of the four Sunnite schools as a whole' (Coulson 1964: 193–4). The example here is child marriage, for which permission by a court might now be demanded, based on the opinions of 'marginal' jurists. The selection technique of *takhayyur* is seen here searching in the vast bran-tub (Glenn, 2004) of Islamic legal norms propounded by earlier jurists, no matter how remote and arcane. The purpose is to find an Islamic rule that suits the social purpose, and to give it authority on that basis.

The third stage of *takhayyur* has its own technical term, 'patching' (*talfiq*), which made Coulson (1964: 197) note that 'the claim of *taqlid* by the legislators becomes little more than an illusory formality'. Coulson explained (p. 197):

> Legal rules are ostensibly constructed by the combination and fusion of juristic opinions, and of elements therefrom, of diverse nature and provenance; and to this activity is given the description *talfiq* (literally 'to make up a patchwork, to piece together').

This convenient technique, under the official mantle of the juristically acceptable *taqlid*, allowed a reformist ruler or judge to incorporate any useful element from anywhere, reconstructing a new rule system that was still Muslim law, while no longer owing its standing to the efforts of a particular jurist or school of jurists. Coulson (1964: 197) spoke of the production of a 'composite legal system' and provided several examples. Coulson (1964: 201) concluded this discussion with some important points about the plurality-conscious nature of modern Islamic law reforms, highlighting the expectations of society:

> When the traditional authorities had to be manipulated in this fashion to yield the required rule, any claim that this process constituted *taqlid* had

become nothing more than a thin veil of pretence, a purely formal and superficial adherence to the established principles of jurisprudence, which masked the reality of an attempt to fashion the terms of the law to meet the needs of society as objectively determined. This new attitude of modern Islamic jurisprudence, which is, of course, the antithesis of the classical view that the only legitimate standards for society are set by the law, was inherent in the process of reform from the outset; for in fact, *takhayyur* was essentially the selection of views on the basis of their suitability for modern conditions. And as time went on, an increasing emphasis was placed upon practical and social considerations.

This recognised that, behind the supposedly closed doors of *ijtihad*, protected by the convenient myth of *taqlid* as 'imitation', modern Islamic law gradually changed its nature in a process lasting several centuries. One of the most recent developments in this context is what Coulson (1964: 202–17) discussed as *neo-ijtihad*, based on the argument that 'the exercise of *ijtihad* or independent judgment was not only the right, but also the duty, of present generations if Islam was to adapt itself successfully to the modern world' (Coulson 1964: 202). Several examples of modern Muslim family law reforms are most clearly based on *neo-ijtihad*, such as the abolition of polygamy by the Tunisian Law of Personal Status of 1956/7.[129] This was legitimised by revisiting the relevant decidedly pro-women Qur'anic verses on polygamy, restricting the Muslim husband's prerogative of polygamy to four wives on condition of equal treatment. According to modern Tunisian interpretation, based on a re-reading of the Qur'an and taking the minority view, this meant that no man after the Prophet could be allowed to be polygamous, since it was humanly impossible to treat two women completely on equal terms. In this way, it appears that older pro-women layers of juristic interpretation, which were often overlaid by later, patriarchally influenced juristic views, may be uncovered and used for modern legal reforms through statutes or case law, with the socially desirable effect that Muslim women should not be disadvantaged in patriarchal societies.[130]

During his time, Coulson (1964: 217) merely commented in upbeat fashion that '[t]he era of *taqlid* now appears as a protracted moratorium in Islamic legal history. Stagnation has given way to a new vitality and potential for growth.' But there has been real change only in method, not in principle, since it appears that traditional *shari'a* law cannot be simply replaced by modern statute law (section 5.14). State-made laws have existed ever since the first Islamic Caliphs began to regulate the affairs of their people, but God's law is still superior to men's law.

---

[129] For details see An-Na'im (2002: 182–5); earlier Coulson (1964: 193).

[130] This was illustrated by the Shah Bano controversy in India, which involved virtual neo-ijtihad by five Hindu judges. See *Mohd Ahmed Khan* v. *Shah Bano*, AIR 1985 SC 945. For details see chapter 4, section 4.10 above and Pearl and Menski (1998: 209ff.). See also the attempt to follow Tunisian law in Bangladesh in *Jesmin Sultana* v. *Mohammad Elias* (1997) 17 BLD 4.

To that extent, there is no real difference between Muslim tradition and Muslim modernity. However, at the level of visible legal reality, men's laws have become much more self-assured in their use of Islamic legal pluralism. The study of Islamic laws seems to teach a globally focused jurisprudential analysis about the need to recognise that men's laws could never really override God's law unless one denied the existence of God, which is not really an option for Muslims. However, since God's law is a different category of law than positivist state law or the social norms applied by communities, there is no either/or scenario. The plurality-conscious legal analysis cultivated by the present study yields the important finding that such different categories of law co-exist and need to be harmonised. Thus, it depends on the situation-specific context which of the three elements prevails. The present plurality-conscious analysis of Islamic law confirms the presence of three interacting kinds of legal rules, whose precise relational dynamics are subject to an unlimited diversity of imponderables. According to Muslim legal doctrine, *shar'ia* law is always superior, but there have been many assertions that modern legal reforms constitute 'the law'.[131] This axiom has continued to assert itself, even if more in principle than in practice. It even seems to have re-incorporated Turkey into the Islamic fold to some extent, causing much anguish in current negotiations over Turkey's accession to the European Union. This shows that no matter how modern Islamic laws may appear, even if one secularises them, as Turkey claimed to do, and no matter how 'patched together' such laws may be, they are still Islamic laws if the people who live this law are Muslims.

As both the Turkish and the Pakistani examples below show, legal modernisation in Muslim countries is a complex process of pluralist reconstruction, which inevitably involves difficult conflicts and tensions. Manipulating the interaction of the three major legal components that the present study has identified, Muslim communities everywhere in the world will inevitably negotiate and create different types of Islamic law. These may be official or unofficial, in an Islamic state or outside it, and they are always culture-specific, irrespective of Western or Islamic theories of law, because they are lived systems, managed and manipulated by real people. These people may make mistakes in the tortuous process of negotiating their legal systems, but nobody can deny them the right to live their laws as they think right. As Muslims, for whom submission to Allah is the first of all duties, they are united in adherence to a global vision. Beyond this, as the Pakistani example in section 5.14 below shows in detail, the perennial questions over what Muslim and 'Islamic' means have not been resolved in

---

[131] Apprehensions about the direction of changes are widely reflected in books written by Muslim authors. Doi (1984: 469) expresses doubts about the moral integrity of some of the modern laws. Hassan (1974: 50) asks whether the Islamic system has the capacity to provide a successful combination of Islam and modernity and proclaims that '[t]he answer is assertively in the affirmative', which he then seeks to prove, throughout his book, by showing the Islamic system as superior to Western modernity.

any way. Clearly, the Muslim world has its own culture-specific problems with defining plurality-consciousness in a global context.

5.13 Turkey as a secular Muslim country

Modern Turkey is a secular republic in which the overwhelming majority of citizens are Muslims, a unique phenomenon in the world's legal history. Turkey appears to have placed the Islamic system of religious law at a lower hierarchical level than state positivism, and has visibly put men's law above God's law. This bold legal innovation is explicitly protected by Article 174 of the Turkish Constitution, and it is unlikely that the old position will be restored.[132] The development of Turkey's modern legal system cannot be properly understood without first providing a brief historical backdrop. One needs to examine first why and how the Ottoman Empire struggled with internal reforms and then combined concepts of Western laws with notions of Islamic law before considering how the conceptual entity of a secular Muslim state was created, leading to the culture-specific Turkish vision of a secular state full of Muslims.

The traditional Islamic Ottoman Empire, with the Sultan as a typical Islamic ruler, recognised until 1839 the superiority of religious norms, while hesitatingly introducing new legal provisions for administration and governance under *siyasa shar'iyya*. Initially, 'reform was far less the result of any popular demand than imposed on the people from above, in the interests . . . of administrative efficiency and national progress and in the desire . . . to satisfy foreign opinion' (Anderson and Coulson, 1967: 36). Several Ottoman Sultans during the sixteenth century had made determined efforts to build efficient systems of administration based on *shari'a* (Schacht, 1984: 89–90). Preservation of Islam was at the heart of the developments in this period (Starr, 1992: 3). Ably supported by some *muftis*, in particular the newly created Grand Mufti of Istanbul, attempts were made to harmonise reformist administrative laws with religious norms. During this process, the limits of traditional *shari'a* principles as tools for legal reform became apparent, leading to new internal reform efforts. Schacht (1984: 90) referred to a number of directives by the Grand Mufti to the *qadis*, instructing them 'to follow one of several opinions admitted by the Hanafi authorities', laying down that *takhayyur* should be applied. The courts were more explicitly supervised by officers of the state, and great Ottoman Sultans like Suleyman I (he ruled 1520–66) became famous for introducing many state laws (*qanun*). The overall picture of an efficient, effective legal framework under the umbrella of God's law prevailed.

Some writers claim that the need for reform was beginning to be recognised in the seventeenth century when the Ottoman state began to lose strength,

---

[132] One of those factors remains Turkey's ambition to join the European Union. Since 1963, it has had associate status, with full membership denied so far because Turkey is still not trusted.

realising that the other Muslim states would go their own way and the scope for a unified Muslim Empire was forever gone.[133] The focus was still on internal reforms and attempts to strengthen central government authority. Gradually, some Ottoman intellectuals and statesmen, probably inspired by growing knowledge of Western laws, and later pressures of extraterritoriality, began to consider the viability of Westernisation, but this was a long process. As Starr (1992: 7) shows, Ottomans firmly believed in their own superiority until well into the nineteenth century and even 'saw no reason to learn anything about European culture', remaining proud of the 'Ottoman way'.

Early reformist initiatives were driven by the bureaucratic and military élite. During the nineteenth century, the basic concern of Ottoman reformers was primarily to Westernise the military and to introduce secular educational structures in addition to traditional systems. Starr (1992: 8–9) shows how political reasons created an initial bias in favour of French language and institutions. As a new educated élite emerged, more people came to believe that the state's future could be safeguarded through acceptance of Western technology and institutions, including legal codes. Could foreign implants be adapted to an Islamic society without accepting Western civilisation itself? Doubts about this led eventually to a dual legal system and dual institutions, rather than wholesale importation of foreign codes. Instead of destroying the traditional institutions, the reforms of the nineteenth century created new constructs designed to co-exist with a modified traditional but still dominant Islamic system which was only changed in the 1920s.

The introduction of Western-style systems of law into the Ottoman system begins with the *Tanzimat* ('regulation') reforms from 1839 onwards, lasting until about 1876 and aiming to prevent disintegration of the vast Empire by bringing about modest reforms.[134] Some constitutional reforms began in 1839, extending to private law through promulgation of a series of Codes based mainly on French models. The early enactments comprised the Commercial Code of 1850, a Penal Code of 1858, a Code of Commercial Procedure of 1861 and a Code of Maritime Commerce in 1863. These new secular transplants were perceived as laws in addition to, and not replacements of, the relevant provisions in the *shari'a* law. Hooker (1975: 363) showed that the Land Code of 1868 still retained all the traditional *shari'a* classifications of different types of land. The law-makers of the time were well aware that an altogether new category of law was being introduced, but would not and could not just erase existing legal arrangements overnight. Plurality-consciousness manifested itself when the reformers took a few bricks from *shari'a*, but made the whole building

---

[133] Iqbal (1989: 125). Others are less clear about this. Siddiqi (1981: 41) notes that '[t]he rot in Islamic society was brought into focus by a sudden decline in Muslim fortunes' and reports on Turkish discussions about restructuring the state (pp. 55–60).

[134] For a detailed, plurality-conscious discussion, see now Yilmaz (2005b: 83–123).

look like a new edifice. The Ottomans also created a new secular court system, the *Nizamiyya* or *Nizami* courts, to apply the new law. None of this was as revolutionary as may seem at first sight to an external observer; the new laws were virtually optional codes, co-existing with the old legal order. There are no indications that the new system created a flurry of litigation or was welcomed by a wider public. While the Ottoman Empire was now getting used to human law-making, it was also evident that 'the Shari'a had never in fact been exclusively or comprehensively applied, but that customary law, and the orders or caprice of the executive, had frequently prevailed' (Anderson and Coulson, 1967: 38). That did not seem to change as a result of partial legal transplantation.

While some secularisation occurred since 1839, the ambit of classical Muslim law was gradually restricted by the new codes. Total legal reform was not on the agenda. Anderson and Coulson (1967: 37) emphasised that the Ottoman reformers at this stage resolutely refused to abandon even such controversial provisions in the sacred law as the death penalty for apostasy from Islam or the ineligibility of non-Muslim witnesses in a law suit between Muslims. Especially concerning contract and tort, the bureaucrats, now known as 'Young Ottomans' (Starr, 1992: 10), began to face opposition against more use of European laws. Against reformist agenda, it was argued that codification based on Islamic laws should be attempted to safeguard the link between tradition and modernity. Initially, this view prevailed. The result was a unique enactment, the *Majalla* or *Mejelle*, an Islamic civil code based on modified Hanafi law which took many years to produce (1869–76). Schacht (1984: 92) commented:

> Ottoman Turkey is the only Islamic country to have tried to codify and to have enacted as a law of the state parts of the religious law of Islam. This is the *Mejelle* . . . which covers the law of contracts and obligations and of civil procedure in the form of articles, and was promulgated as the Ottoman Civil Code in 1877. According to the explanatory memorandum, its purpose was to provide the recently created (secular) tribunals with an authoritative statement of the doctrine of Islamic law and to obviate (without forbidding it) recourse to the works of Islamic jurisprudence which had proved difficult and impracticable.

This is the conceptual starting point in the Muslim world of *shari'a* law as positive law. Schacht (1984: 92) noted that '[s]trict Islamic law is by its nature not suitable for codification because it possesses authoritative character only in so far as it is taught in the traditional way by one of the recognized schools'. A codified body of Islamic law, as men's law, might not be taken seriously. The dilemma was that 'the experiment of the *Mejelle* was undertaken under the influence of European ideas, and it is, strictly speaking, not an Islamic but a secular code' (Schacht, 1984: 92). Whatever one calls this new legal construct, it led a strange existence, since it was not applied by the *qadi* courts, and its rules were different from those that people were used to. For example, witnesses in litigation no longer needed to be Muslim. Through the process of constructing the *Majalla*, Muslim jurists were seeking to increase the internal flexibility of Islamic laws, using *takhayyur* techniques, but they were still restricted in their options to variant Hanafi views (Coulson 1964: 185). The *Majalla* remained in force as official law of the Ottoman Empire and has influenced the laws of many successor states. It was abandoned in Turkey in 1926 when the Swiss Civil Code was introduced.

The *Majalla* did not cover Muslim family law. As one of the last bastions of traditional jurists' law, family law was most resistant to bureaucratisation and secularisation, mainly because it depended on popular acceptance. The jurisdiction of the *shari'a* courts, which continued to apply the old law, encompassed marriage, divorce, paternity suits and guardianship, succession, *waqfs* and some other subjects. There was no doubt for most people, including intellectuals and bureaucrats, that 'Islam, as "a mental moral map" and as practice, was still an integral part of the Ottoman state and Ottoman consciousness at the start of the twentieth century' (Starr, 1992: 12).

Since the early reforms had created an optional dualist legal structure, they were an addition to the classical Islamic system (Hooker, 1975: 362), rather than a replacement. The interaction of this new official law with the traditional legal system still needed to be worked out. This task fell to the new dual court system. Anderson and Coulson (1967: 37) emphasised that '[t]his clear-cut dichotomy between "secular courts" and "religious" courts was a startling and radical development'. It was made more radical since the secular courts were given more general and residuary jurisdiction, so that the *shari'a* courts were increasingly restricted in their competence. The plurality of courts was increased by special 'mixed' courts for cases involving non-Muslim subjects, and the various personal law systems (*millets*) among non-Muslims retained their own tribunals and internal hierarchies. Overall, the new reforms brought a significant structural change to the Ottoman legal system. The scope of Islamic law was now severely and openly restricted, 'its place taken by legislative enactments which found their inspiration largely in the West' (Anderson and Coulson, 1967: 38).

While the area of Islamic religious jurisdiction was gradually reduced, causing *de facto* secularisation of principal state institutions, a further period of substantive reform and rethinking is found in the modernisation of Turkey under the 'Young Turks' after 1889.[135] They followed on from the 'Young Ottomans', and were especially active between 1908 and 1918. Now the idea of reforming Islamic laws from within began to be abandoned. Coulson (1964: 184) indicated that the Ottoman legislation of 1915 built on earlier reforms that had allowed *shari'a* courts more discretion in applying *takhayyur*. Anderson and Coulson (1967: 39) commented that Muslim laws of marriage, divorce and inheritance

---

[135] Starr (1992: 10) reports that the idea of a distinct Turkish loyalty, as opposed to an Islamic or Ottoman identity, was first mooted by expatriate Turks in France around 1870.

had always been most meticulously applied and it was not considered a viable option to import foreign models into family law. Schacht (1964: 184) reported that internal reforms were built on *takhayyur* or 'selection':

> Family law, or substantial parts of it, was codified on the juristic basis that the sovereign, as part of his acknowledged *siyasa* powers, had the right to define the jurisdiction of the courts, in the sense that he might order them to apply one among several existing variant options. These codifications also contained regulations . . . which set procedural limits upon the competence of the courts; but the vast bulk of their substance consisted of those rules which had been selected from the whole corpus of traditional Shari'a doctrine as most suitable for application in modern times.

Further reforms were introduced in 1917, but 'the opinion prevailed that the family law must remain essentially the province of the Shari'a' (Anderson and Coulson (1967: 39). Coulson (1964: 186) referred to the Ottoman Law of Family Rights of 1917 as 'the first great monument of reform in the traditional family law'. Enacted on 25 October 1917, this eclectic legislation reflected and amalgamated the views of different juristic schools, going beyond the traditional four Sunni schools by incorporating views of some minor jurists, using *talfiq* techniques. This was modestly modernist legal intervention (Schacht, 1984: 103). Reforms were introduced to provide more grounds for judicial dissolution of marriages for women whose husbands were either seriously ill or had deserted them without their whereabouts being known (Anderson and Coulson, 1967: 39). The new law tried to give marriage a more formal legal character by providing that the unilateral *talaq* in the presence of two witnesses would no longer suffice to terminate a marriage and that the presence of a judge or a deputy was required by the law (Starr, 1992: 39). Every marriage and divorce was now expected to be legally conducted according to state procedures, a serious imposition of state law on an area so far totally outside positive law. The new law also allowed women, at the time of betrothal, to write certain conditions into the marriage contract, for example if the husband should take another wife, the marriage would be null and void. Such attempts to change family law rules, achieved largely through *takhayyur* and *talfiq*, must count as pioneering experiments in social engineering through law by the modernising élite in a Muslim society. While the reformers were probably aware that the new law would not be widely followed, it offered members of the élite new avenues for legal redress. To an extent, this was law-making by an élite for themselves, but it served a wider purpose by demonstrating that Muslim family law could be reformed from within. This legislation was repealed in Turkey in 1919, under foreign pressure and concerns about extraterritoriality, because it also attempted to uniformise all *millets* and thus touched 'foreign interests'. But this Act remained valid in other countries arising from the Ottoman Empire (Schacht, 1984: 103; Anderson, 1959) and has been quite influential. It remains an important early legal document of internal reforms in Muslim family law, perceived as necessary because of the central role of the family in transmitting socio-cultural values.

These reformist agenda were taken up by the emerging Turkish nationalists, the Kemalists, named after the founder of the Republic, Mustafa Kemal (1881–1938). Later known as Kemal Atatürk, he introduced a cultural transformation of society through legal means. Following the defeat of the Ottoman Empire in 1918, the Ottoman state rapidly collapsed. After the Treaty of Lausanne in 1923, and the founding of the Turkish Republic on 29 October 1923, the duality of modified Islamic laws and Western legal codifications was finally resolved in favour of wholesale official acceptance of Western civilisation and laws. The Kemalist élite, no longer interested in integrating Islamic institutions and laws with Western concepts and structures, decided to abandon Islamic laws. An official state policy of secularism (laicism) was implemented through a series of legal steps to oust traditional Islamic law from its dominant role in the state. leading to disestablishment of Islamic law (Yilmaz, 2005b: 83, 96). Religion was now treated as a private matter of individual conscience, while the public sphere was entirely subject to positivist law-making.

Eventually, Islam ceased to be the official religion of the state. It was abolished in 1928 (Hooker, 1975: 364), and modern Turkey became a truly secular republic in the traditional sense of the word in 1937.[136] During the 1920s, a reconstruction of Turkish identity took place (Starr, 1992: 13–14), involving changes to the language, its alphabet and dictionary, the dress code, the calendar and much else. The educational system was significantly remodelled and Islamic education was denied state support. The dress rules had particularly strong symbolic value, as Starr (1992: 14) explains:

> Symbolic aspects of Ottoman culture were disparaged in dress. Western-style hats with brims were substituted for the red Moroccan fez, the distinctive mark of the nineteenth-century Ottoman man. This particular change was significant: Muslim men do not remove headgear when praying; a hat with a brim prevents a forehead from touching the ground, an essential act in the Islamic ritual of prayer . . . In some places Islamic women covered their faces with veils or long head scarves, which was now strongly discouraged.

In positivist culture-blind fashion, all Turkish men and women became equal citizens of one central state; everybody was amalgamated into the national mainstream, constructing a new nation.[137] The various personal laws of the traditional *millet* system, including the Islamic personal law, were abolished;

---

[136] This is very different from the Indian model of secularism (chapter 4, section 4.9) with its guarantee of non-discrimination against minorities, which has remained a major weak spot of Turkey's legal system.

[137] Significant exchanges of population took place at that time, especially with Greece; ethnic cleansing was a prominent feature in this period following the First World War.

all Turks were now governed by the same state-controlled laws. All religious courts were replaced by secular ones. The new secular law, a means of social engineering, was just as alien for Turkish Muslims as for non-Muslims. Based on a vision of what the élite wanted everyone to be, it was a programme for the future, built on men's law, leaving God out of the picture. This entirely new official legal system, constitutionally protected as the vision of the new Turkey, focused on the ideological message of Kemalism in six areas: nationalism, secularism, republicanism, populism, statism and reformism. This looks at first sight like pure positivist law-making in Western style, but deeper analysis demonstrates a high level of plurality-consciousness. There was no expectation that every aspect of this new law would be meticulously observed by all Turks. Most obviously in family law, the rulers did not expect immediate compliance (Yilmaz, 2005b: 104ff.).

Family law reforms gained a prominent place in this cauldron of social engineering through law. The *Mejelle* and later the new Ottoman Law of Family Rights of 1917 had brought certain improvements in the legal position of women, but neither had superseded the conceptual framework of traditional Hanafi family law. After proclamation of the Republic in 1923, special committees were appointed through the Ministry of Justice to prepare the framework for a new set of secular codes. Their advisory reports showed that traditional Muslim principles still figured prominently in the mind of the reformers. Therefore, the internal reform project was dropped and the government decided to adopt foreign models, particularly the Swiss Civil Code, the Italian Criminal Code and the German Commercial Code. Copying European models was now seen as essential to achieve modernisation and uniformisation. According to the then Minister of Justice, trained in law at Lausanne, and cited by Starr (1992: 16):

> We are badly in want of a good scientific Code. Why waste our time trying to produce something new when quite good Codes are to be found ready made? Moreover, what is the use of a Code without good commentaries to guide in the application of it? Are we in a position to write such commentaries for a new Code? We dispose neither of the necessary time nor of the necessary precedents in practice. The only thing to do is to take a good ready-made Code to which good commentaries exist, and to translate them wholesale. The Swiss Code is a good Code; I am going to have it adopted, and I shall ask the Assembly to proceed to a vote *en bloc*, as Napoleon had his Code voted. If it had to be discussed article by article, we should never get through.

This style of pure positivism, pushing through an entire system of codes without concern for social acceptance, shows that the reformers were primarily focused on the vision itself, introducing a new ethic as well as a new official law – the people would have to get used to this. The Codes were duly adopted in 1926 as wished by the Minister. The speaker of the Justice Commission argued that the Swiss Civil Code would be compatible to the Turkish character, since it was based on principles of justice and human rights and that the proposed abolition of polygamy and better divorce rights for women would be required for a civilised nation. These radical reforms to Turkish family law were introduced when most people lived in villages and the government was a remote institution. While the Islamic law of personal status, abolished in 1924, was officially superseded by this new civil code, taken more or less verbatim from Swiss models, what happened in terms of practical application?[138]

Many writers have focused on formal structures rather than social processes of legal adaptation.[139] A new law school was opened in Ankara in 1925 to train judges and lawyers in the new secular law (Starr, 1992: 16). At the opening ceremony, Kemal Atatürk, the first dean of this law school, announced the government's intention 'to create completely new laws and thus to tear up the very foundations of the old legal system' (quoted in Starr, 1992: 16). By 1926 a more or less entirely secular legal system had been put in place, in 1928 the clause that had made Islam the state religion was abandoned, and in 1937 Turkey was formally declared a secular state. This shows that secularisation was perceived as a gradual process, not a sudden revolutionary cut-off. Initially quite militant and inspired by the French experience, the secularisation movement in modern Turkey later settled into laicism, intellectually linked to the French Third Republic. This meant that religions should stay in the conscience and places of worship and not be mixed with public life. In Turkey, Islam as a religion is firmly under the control of the state and a unique Turkish form of secularism has been developed (Yilmaz, 2005b: 100).

However, it is now increasingly recognised that the influence of Islam in Turkish public life has not diminished as much as reformist ambitions expected.[140] The triangle of Islamic religious and ethical values, secular state laws and local customary norms continues to determine the socio-legal realities of the complex 'living law' of modern Turkish people. While state law is officially in control, the other elements are by no means absent in the legal field and local Islam and local practices continue to have much influence. While it used to be assumed that modern Westernised urban élites and the rural masses would be found at opposite ends of a spectrum, new research indicates that modern urban Turks are not immune to the influences of religious and social norms which conflict with dominant modernist assumptions. A distinctive Turkish culture of hybrid modernity has been created through plurality-conscious interaction of dynamic legal pluralisms in Turkey. Muslim Turks 'have reconstructed their Muslim laws to meet the demands of both official and unofficial laws' (Yilmaz, 2005b: 104).

Especially in rural areas, Turks still regard official law as 'government law' and may not follow it, without being directly affected. Earlier research on this showed that the new law might have only limited effect on villagers (Hooker,

---

[138] Yilmaz (2005b: 84) reports that, on 27 November 2001, the Turkish Parliament enacted a totally new Civil Code after a long drafting period.

[139] On the latter, see now in detail Yilmaz (2005b: 104–17).

[140] For a detailed analysis, see Yilmaz (2005b: 104–23).

1975: 365). The fervent expectation that local people would learn and follow only the official *lex loci* by abandoning the *shari'a* and their local norms has turned out to be unrealistic and raised huge questions about the limits of law (Allott, 1980: vi). Starr (1992: 17) reports from her earlier field research that the reformist aims 'were mostly achieved in western Anatolia by the mid-1960s'. Hooker (1975: 365), relying on Turkish research from the 1950s, demonstrated that '[i]t is freely admitted that informal marriages and the concomitant problem of illegitimacy represent a failure of fusion of religious and code provisions'. Thus, according to Hooker (1975: 365):

> In peasant society the religious ceremony is all and it alone is regarded as valid: a civil marriage alone is not regarded as valid by the peasant community. The Turkish position, wherein civil and religious forms are separate and only the former has legal validity, immediately suggests the dominant–servient dichotomy, despite the sociological fact that the question of which is dominant and which servient is answered differently according to whether one is a judge or a peasant farmer. A suggested solution to the problem is to use the religious official (in the majority of cases the *Imam*) to conduct a marriage ceremony in which religious and civil elements are combined.

Such dichotomies have continued to exist in Turkey, where more recent statistics indicate that 85 per cent of all marrying couples may be undergoing both a civil and a religious marriage, while close to 10 per cent have only a civil marriage, and almost 5 per cent undergo only religious ceremonies and consider themselves legally married.[141]

If we take the example of polygamy, another legal issue of outright contrast between the old *shari'a* law and the modern Turkish state law, which banned and criminalised it, the literature shows us a different kind of legal assimilation. Hooker (1975: 366) suggested that,

> although the Civil Code prohibits polygamy, this injunction has remained in a significant majority of cases a dead letter: it is part of 'government' law and so has little effect on the life of the village. The only success the Code has had in this respect is to create, in some measure, a social sense that polygamy is no longer acceptable, but this is a change in social psychology, a field in which legislation is at best of dubious value.

Statistics indicate that in traditional Ottoman society only about 2 per cent of marriages were polygamous, as in Turkey today, with polygamy now often occurring in modern metropolitan contexts (Yilmaz, 2005b: 114). The effectiveness of modern laws remains doubtful, since legal penalties may be avoided by performing only an informal or consensual religious marriage, the *'imam*

---

[141] Updated statistics are found in Yilmaz (2005b: 105–17). Research in Britain shows similar patterns among modern, urban South Asian settlers, often British citizens who follow hybrid norm systems on their own terms (Ballard, 1994; Yilmaz 2005b: 49–81). Pearl and Menski (1998: 74–7) explain the concept of *angrezi shariat*.

nikahi' (Yilmaz, 2005b: 106). Other areas of legal concern have been child marriages and divorce. The Muslim *talaq* is deemed to have been subjected to the formal requirements of secular Turkish law, but husbands may not observe this, and wives may find themselves in 'limping marriages' (p. 117). Since total disregard for the hybrid reconstructions made by Turkish people would damage the interests of women and children, as in modern India (chapter 4, section 4.10) the modern Turkish state had to react. It has done so in an instructive manner, as Hooker (1975: 368) noted:

> Since the majority of marriages contracted in the villages are illegal according to the code, the result has been a great increase in illegitimacy as defined in law. The response to this has been the passing of a series of enactments to make legitimization an extremely simple matter. Such a position is highly undesirable in any legal system and smacks strongly of 'juridical double think'.

Chapter 2 showed that Hooker was criticised by Chiba (1986), Griffiths (1986) and others for failing to be a real legal pluralist. His unsympathetic comment on the amnesties in Turkish marriage and child law, the last in 1991 to make sure that law and life remain in step,[142] indicates a serious deficiency in plurality-consciousness. Turkish legal remedies like these official amnesties can be seen as instructive examples of how postmodern state laws in Asia and Africa today may retain formal control despite massive social subversion.[143] Hooker merely suggested the positivist remedy of better administrative practice, and did not seem to realise that this is what the Turkish amnesties are. Today, the Turkish evidence of hybrid marriage laws is an excellent, culture-specific illustration of Ehrlich's (1936) 'living law' and of Chiba's (1986) theory of the continuous interaction of official and unofficial laws. It is a model example of plurality-conscious legal pluralism in action, placed in the centre of the circle of our conceptual triangle (chapter 3, section 3.8). What irked the lawyer in Hooker, and baffles positivists, is that the state should give in to its people. From a plurality-conscious perspective, the Turkish evidence shows how modern states in Asia and Africa may use legislation as a means for discussion (Glenn, 2004: 155), a bargaining tool, rather than purely a positivist instrument of asserting power. Noting the continued effectiveness of Islamic law 'or what passes for such, in the villages' (Hooker, 1975: 371), questions arise whether Islamic law can be deemed to be abolished as a marker of personal status among Turkish people. While Hooker (1975: 371) saw the success of legal modernisation as 'at best only partial', recent research confirms that the intended secularisation of Turkey has resulted in Turkish assimilation to secular law in culture-specific terms, which remain contested and debated (Yilmaz, 2005b: 84, 95).

---

[142] Yilmaz (2005b: 119) indicates that a new amnesty law is currently being prepared.

[143] On Indian examples of tolerating polygamy see Menski (2001). Egyptian evidence is discussed in Dupret *et al.* (1999: 194–6).

The present study observes such developments as a backlash against excessive globalising pressures and evidence of glocalisation. Earlier, Starr (1992: 19) affirmed the need to strengthen the universalist message of modern Turkish legal reformers, arguing that 'Turkey's secular court system asserts universal legal norms of individuality and equality and, like other civil law countries, uses established norms of proof and systematic legal procedures, required by the rule of law'. Unilateral assertion by modern state law of its own superiority and assertion of supposedly global values cannot mask the problem of having to work out a plurality-conscious compromise that suits Turkey as a whole. Leaving aside the question of Islam and its contested superiority as a religion, Turkish people as an integral element of the conceptual triangle of law have clearly reasserted their perspectives in a plurality-sensitive legal scenario. Turkish people basically had three alternatives: avoidance of state law, following state law, or developing a hybrid combination of traditional and modern laws (Yilmaz, 2005b: 104). Turks chose the third option, developing a new Muslim law, a hybrid norm system in which the religious expectations and ambitions of *shari'a* and modern secular state law, of God's law and of men's law, are being combined (p. 104).

Such a finding contains useful lessons for intercultural and comparative legal studies. Where a modern state is willing to leave scope for citizens to construct their own form of 'living law', harmonious co-existence between the various competing legal forces remains possible, and a plurality-conscious legal system under state control can be maintained. However, this does not mean that all the rules of the 'living law' were made by the state. The official law contains many elements of law arising from ethical values and social norms and the emerging legal system is a sophisticated culture-specific socio-legal construct. For most Europeans, as eurocentric closet Christians, the Turks have not gone far enough in assimilating to an allegedly global vision: they are still Muslims. Legal positivists will find much to criticise in a state that is seen to 'give in' to influences from 'religion' and 'culture'. Conversely, for many Muslim observers, the Turks have gone too far by placing men's law visibly above God's law. Nobody seems satisfied with the plurality-conscious Turkish solution to the conundrum of making law, and these issues remain contested and debated (Yilmaz, 2005b: 95). Nothing else can be expected from a perspective of plurality-conscious awareness that all legal systems in the world have to find their own 'identity postulates' (Chiba, 1989: 180), and that law everywhere in the world remains embroiled in triangular dynamism.

5.14 Pakistani law and Islamisation

Allama Muhammad Iqbal's famous study on *Reconstruction of religious thought in Islam* (1989: 121) asserted his belief that 'we too one day, like the Turks, will have to re-evaluate our intellectual inheritance'. But modern Pakistan pursued a very different route from Turkey, going to the other extreme by seeking to Islamise its legal system. On independence (14 August 1947), it was clear that its historically grown legal structures, contaminated by colonial interventions and local customs, were confused about whether God's law or men's law was supreme and raised critical questions about Islamisation.

We saw that Islamisation occurred throughout Muslim legal history, constantly demanding recognition of the supremacy of God's law, seeking to ensure that Muslims stay on the path of permissible behaviour and that new converts accept Islam not only as a faith but also as a way of life. Conceptually embedded in Middle Eastern thought, Pakistani Islamisation politics also display the crucial relevance of local factors. The desire to show themselves, and the world, that they are proper Muslims, capable of running an Islamic legal system, became an aspect of postcolonial reconstruction. Dreams of historical recreation of past Moghul structures offered little more than temporary distraction from an unsatisfactory present. Attempts to cleanse the inherited Anglo-Indian legal system of unacceptable elements, including any Hindu heritage, mask shameless political use made of Islamisation as a concept and strategy. In Pakistan, it became a positivist, state-driven phenomenon, a culture-specific method of social engineering through law, while the sceptical outside observer may question whether there is any such policy. Is it just a trend, a pull in a particular direction, with difficulties discovered only once the bandwagon had started rolling, crushing women, minorities and anybody who seemed to represent un-Islamic views? Nobody can tell us, it seems, what Islamisation in Pakistan actually means and how its legal implications fit into a plurality-conscious global framework of analysis.[144]

Within a historical framework, we first see early Arab traders coming to the subcontinent around the eighth century AD, settling along the Western coast even before Islam appeared. Arab occupation of Sind occurred in 711 and was followed by the intrusion of a small conquering foreign élite from the North-West. Sunni Hanafi Muslims became the dominant group. As the Muslim population continued to grow, mainly through conversions, Islamic law soon became the second most important personal law of the subcontinent. By about 1100, when Muslim central rule was firmly established at Delhi, Hanafi law became the official law of a new Muslim empire. Most Muslim rulers were content to restructure local tax laws and criminal laws, leaving most legal administration to local agents and to local people, mainly Hindus, whose rulers were often allowed to stay in power under Muslim supremacy. Apart from becoming a personal law, Islamic law was a 'soft' fragmented official state law, concerned mainly with some aspects of public law rather than comprehensive governance by *shari'a*, an inevitable result of political expedi-

---

[144] Mehdi (1994: 1) portrays Pakistani law as 'an inconsistent and unstable legal system in a peripheral capitalist state'.

ency. Like the early Muslim rulers of Arabia, the Moghuls vacillated in their policy approach to non-Muslims between tolerant leniency, official blindness to 'the other' and attempts at imposing Islam more rigidly.

Before British supremacy, the penal law prevailing in India was the so-called 'Muhammedan law' (Banerjee, 1962: 33) and little was known about early Muslim law in India.[145] The Muslim rulers of India could not have enforced 'pure' shari'a law, given the distance from the Muslim heartland, the absence of religious scholars, at least initially, and the importance of local customs.[146] Hai (1977: 77) realistically depicts shari'a and local exigencies as the main sources of rules. Local, pre-Islamic customary laws were widely recognised, making deeper Islamisation desirable. In particular various Shi'a communities, the Khojas, the Cutchi Memons and the Mapillas in Kerala (Miller, 1992), applied various forms of local Hindu succession and property laws. Further north, in what later became Pakistan, Pathans, Baluchis and Panjabi Muslims followed local customs and codes of honour apart from Islamic legal principles.

The rules of the official legal system were not well known, it seems. Banerjee (1962: 62) pointed out that '[i]n practice, what was the exact law on a particular crime or what was the punishment for it, would never be known before the pronouncement of sentence by the Quadi or Magistrate'. Islamic law took time to develop into an official law, a process not helped by traditional reluctance to approach official courts and deterrent hadd punishments.[147] Eventually, two officially recognised authoritative medieval juristic texts, the Hidaya or Hedaya (Hamilton, 1891) and the Fatawa-i-Alamgiri, commissioned by the Moghul Emperor Aurangzeb as a digest of fatwas mainly on Hanafi law, became local written sources (Baillie, 1865; Banerjee, 1984: 55; Mahmood, 1982: 16). Both collections remain of great interest to researchers, but were of uncertain legal authority (Pearl, 1979: 22). By 1858, when Moghul political power collapsed and a British colonial administration took control, South Asian Muslim laws were quite different from Middle Eastern Muslim laws.

Islamic law stood to lose much from the new bureaucratic arrangements, and the creation of Pakistan in 1947 can be seen as a Muslim attempt to regain control of their own state. Derrett (1968b: 318) went too far in claiming that Islamic law died under the British, but it suffered loss of status and massive interference (Mahmood, 1986: 49–94). Similarly with Hindu law, the official starting point for Islamic law under British domination was the Warren Hastings Scheme of 1772 (chapter 4, section 4.7), officially recognising the 'Laws of the Koran' as Muslim law for the 'listed' subjects, mainly family law matters.

[145] Banerjee (1962: 32–67) contains useful material on the pre-British Islamic law. Other studies (Pearl, 1979) give attention mainly to the British influence.

[146] Pearl (1979: 21) highlights the particularly Indian flavour of the subcontinental Islamic laws, which Mahmood (1986: 49–94) discusses in detail.

[147] According to several sources, human life became rather cheap just before the British interfered in the administration of justice (Fisch, 1983).

The wording was amended in 1793 to 'Mohammedan law', reflecting ambiguity over Islam but also growing British knowledge of the complexity of Islamic law. Growing recognition of diversity within South Asian Islamic law followed the realisation of the importance of jurists and various schools of law.

Juristic scholarship in Indian Islamic law seems to have fared better under the British than its Hindu counterpart. Distrusted like the Hindu *pandits*, the Muslim *maulvis* who acted as law officers between 1772 and 1864 apparently claimed a high degree of authority vis-à-vis the British judges.[148] Banerjee (1984: 31) notes that, because only a *kazi* as a qualified jurist could reject a *mufti's* opinion, British judicial officers, unqualified infidels from a Muslim perspective, were bound by opinions of the *muftis* or *maulvis*. While not unquestioned, the *maulvis* argued that their texts supplied ascertainable rules for most situations (Derrett, 1968b: 318), reducing the scope for residual sources of law, so that the application of 'Justice, Equity and Good Conscience' would be less pervasive than in Hindu law.

Authoritative Anglo-Mohammedan case-law gradually built up, largely a judicial restatement of Islamic law principles as considered applicable in South Asia (Mahmood, 1982: 14ff.). According to common law principles, the courts would then look to those precedents. English and Muslim law principles worked together to block the path to a re-evaluation of the sources of Islamic law. The notion of the 'closed gates of *ijtihad*' perfectly suited the agenda of the British juristic élite as well as the *maulvis*, later impressing Schacht, Coulson and others, who overlooked that most Muslim jurists in the subcontinent were not of high calibre.[149] Courts in India would have found it difficult to exercise *ijtihad*, even if allowed to do so, and *taqlid* became firmly accepted in South Asian Muslim law (Wilson, 1921: 44). Another remarkable feature in South Asian Islamic law is that academic authors of reference books became an important source of law as jurists. Mahmood (1982: 16–17) lists the most authoritative authors, including a number of judges, whose pronouncements on Anglo-Mohammedan law might turn into exhaustive monographs on difficult points of law (Wilson, 1921: 45). Such textbook jurists (also in Pakistan later) almost seemed to codify the law, but Mahmood (1982: 17) rightly expresses reservations about treating such books as codes. Such works aimed to clarify the law, not to fix it forever, although Western and Islamic notions of law-making seemed to mix in the minds of the authors.

Not surprisingly, a fiercely contested element of South Asian Muslim laws has been customary law, providing additional arguments for Islamisation well before Pakistan came into existence. The requirement that custom should be considered, and took precedence, in most parts of India (Wilson, 1921: 33–4;

---

[148] For details on this period see Anderson and Coulson (1967: 41–4).
[149] The British judicial system was not able to handle some difficult situations and outright mistakes were made (Anderson and Coulson, 1967: 44).

Pearl, 1979: 36; Mahmood, 1977: 19) was initially observed without much difficulty in Hindu and Muslim law. Unlike the Hindu model of four sources of *dharma* (chapter 4, section 4.4), Shafi'i's theory of the four sources of *shari'a* ignores custom (Mahmood, 1965). However, in social reality, individual Muslims would also first examine their conscience when a legal insecurity arose, and thus almost inevitably turn to custom. The divergence of practical application and Islamic legal theory was not addressed and gave rise to tensions 'on the ground'.

Mahmood (1977: 19–20) argued that the British misunderstood the position of custom and usage in Islamic jurisprudence. In 1874, the Supreme Court of Bombay had to decide two cases of Muslim women who claimed a share in their father's estate, denied to them by male relatives relying on Hindu customary laws that excluded daughters from inheritance. The decision that these customs had been proved and prevailed over Islamic law caused severe criticism and led to re-evaluation of customary practices in such communities.[150] The end result was the Muslim Personal Law (Shariat Application) Act of 1937, still part of the law of Pakistan today. The Act did not totally abrogate all un-Islamic customary laws of South Asian Muslims (Pearl, 1979: 37), since its rules did not originally apply to agricultural land.[151] This Act is an early example of attempted Islamisation under colonial administration. Wilson (1921: 38) indicated that whole communities drew up petitions about wanting to be governed by Muslim law. Pearl (1979: 37) noted 'a desire by the religious Muslim community to reduce the role of custom', creating the impression of a community effort. In fact, the *ulema*, alert Islamic guardians of religion, pressed for this Islamisation (Mahmood, 1977: 21) to protect their own powers.[152] Ambiguous reforms of Indian Muslim law occurred also through the Dissolution of Muslim Marriages Act of 1939, designed to improve the position of Muslim women, giving them the right to ask a court for divorce under nine specified grounds. This short Act, still in force in India, Pakistan and Bangladesh today, was also a result of Islamisation, since one of its purposes was to prevent Hanafi Muslim wives from abandoning Islam to bring about a divorce.[153]

Much earlier, Islamic criminal law had been abrogated by the Indian Penal Code of 1860, promulgated from 1862.[154] The Islamic law of evidence was superseded by the Indian Evidence Act of 1872. The recent Islamisation of laws in Pakistan has reintroduced certain provisions of Islamic criminal law which were abolished during the nineteenth century by these early British Acts. While

[150] See Wilson (1921: 34–9); Pearl (1979: 35); Hidayatullah (1982: 22ff.); Fyzee (1999: 48–54).
[151] This was changed in Pakistan in 1948, evidence of Islamisation before it became a controversial issue (Pearl and Menski, 1998: 42–3).
[152] Details are found in Mahmood (1977: 22ff.; 1982: 24ff.) and Hidayatullah (1982: 22ff.).
[153] The Act offered Hanafi Muslim wives more divorce grounds through the use of *takhayyur*.
[154] For details see Banerjee (1962: 68–180) and important recent work (Fisch, 1983; Malik, 1994).

Anglo-Mohammedan law became a modified South Asian version of *shari'a* law, Muslim law codification was not favoured by anyone, and it was doubted whether codified law would be accepted as authoritative (Mahmood, 1977: 18). Only in the early days of Anglo-Mohammedan law were some areas of law regulated by statute (Mahmood, 1982: 16 lists such enactments), later the British left Muslim law alone. In 1947, Anglo-Mohammedan law was a hybrid law, heavily influenced by English principles of law, with rules borrowed from a number of foreign legal systems.

The rationale for Pakistan as a homeland for South Asian Muslims included the aim to cleanse Muslim law of the impurities of colonial domination and pervasive Hindu cultural influence, important aspects of Pakistani Islamisation which many observers overlook.[155] Islamisation also involves anti-Western and anti-secular messages, proud assertions of Islamic values in explicit anti-globalisation opposition to Western value systems, as Glenn (2000: 47; 2004: 51) highlights. The internal dynamics of the Islamisation agenda in Pakistan are extremely complicated and to some extent historically predetermined. Soon after independence, Pakistan celebrated the newly found freedom to reconstruct its legal system, free from colonial rule and Hindu domination, along Islamic lines by passing the much-quoted Objectives Resolution of 1949, which was by 1985 made an integral part of the Pakistani Constitution (see below). The process of putting Islamisation on the national agenda has been extremely complex. Far above mundane political squabbles, the poet Iqbal (1989: 122–3) provided a philosophical model for Islamisation which harmonises the conceptual conflict between the superiority of God's law and the need for human law-making. He argued that the divine revelation, *tauhid*,

> as a working idea, is equality, solidarity and freedom. The state, from the Islamic standpoint, is an endeavour to transform these principles into space–time forces, an aspiration to realize them in a definite human organization. It is in this sense alone that the state in Islam is a theocracy, not in the sense that it is headed by a representative of God on earth who can always screen his despotic will behind his supposed infallibility. The critics of Islam have lost sight of this important consideration. The Ultimate Reality, according to the Qur'an, is spiritual, and its life consists in its temporal activity. The spirit finds its opportunities in the natural, the material, the secular. All that is secular is, therefore, sacred in the root of its being. The greatest service that modern thought has rendered to Islam, and as a matter

---

[155] Chaudhary (1999: 22) emphasises legal pluralism as 'the reality of multiple choice' and cites Hoebel (the reference to 1967 is not identifiable) who noted that '[t]he legal system of Pakistan does not constitute a neatly integrated whole; it is made up of an unlimited multiplicity of subsystems . . . Most obvious among these systems is the Formal National law which arches as an ethereal dome above all the lesser systems . . . a vast array of local folk systems of law . . . Ideologically, it incorporates Islamic law, but the folk ignorance of Islam is in fact profound' (Chaudhary, 1999: 23).

of fact to all religion, consists in its criticism of what we call material or natural – a criticism which discloses that the merely material has no substance until we discover it rooted in the spiritual. There is no such thing as a profane world. All this immensity of matter constitutes a scope for the self-realization of spirit. All is holy ground. As the Prophet so beautifully put it: 'The whole of this earth is a mosque.' The state, according to Islam, is only an effort to realize the spiritual in a human organization.

This is a powerful assertion of religious natural law as well as an elaborate justification for an Islamic state, following *siyasa shar'iyya*. Watching the Turkish example, and initially tempted to follow the route of positivist law-making, early Pakistani leaders realised that they could not secularise their legal system in the same way without being grossly misunderstood by their own people. Following the Indian model of secularism of guaranteeing equal treatment for all members of the new state (chapter 4, section 4.9) was also not particularly attractive. Pakistan wanted to be a Muslim state mainly for Muslims. Following the Turkish path was simply out of the question for a new Muslim nation. The early Pakistani leaders were therefore unable to secularise as the Turks had done, and could not modernise as the Indians were about to do; they had to find their own way. This particularly Pakistani way centred on the Islamic identity of the country and most of its people.

Landmarks of the Pakistani process of Islamisation include the Objectives Resolution of 1949, according to which the nation's business should be conducted such that collective and individual Muslim identity and existence would be strengthened. The key sections of this text illustrate the wide ambit of the new Muslim state's programme and contain an immediate affirmation of the global ambit of Islam and its supremacy in the new state:

> Whereas Sovereignty over the entire Universe belongs to Almighty Allah alone, and the authority to be exercised by the people of Pakistan within the limits prescribed by Him is a sacred trust;
> And whereas it is the will of the people of Pakistan to establish an order-
> . . . .
> Wherein the principles of democracy, freedom, equality, tolerance and social justice, as enunciated by Islam, shall be fully observed;
> Wherein the Muslims shall be enabled to order their lives in the individual and collective spheres in accordance with the teachings and requirements of Islam as set out in the Holy Quran and Sunnah;
> Wherein adequate provision shall be made for the minorities freely to profess and practise their religions and develop their cultures;
> . . .
> Wherein shall be guaranteed fundamental rights, including equality of status, of opportunity and before law, social, economic and political justice, and freedom of thought, expression, belief, faith, worship and association, subject to law and public morality;

Wherein adequate provision shall be made to safeguard the legitimate interests of minorities and backward and depressed classes;
Wherein the independence of the judiciary shall be fully secured . . .

This Objectives Resolution then became the Preamble to all Pakistani Constitutions, first in 1956, then in 1962, and finally in 1973. During the process of explicit Islamisation under General Zia-ul Haq, starting from 1977,
many legislative measures were taken and a new structure of Shariat Courts
was introduced, comprising today the Federal Shariat Court and the Shariat
Appellate Bench of the Pakistani Supreme Court. The potential impact of this
restructuring has been huge (Lau, 1996: 378) and it represents and has led to
'a significant increase of judicial power' (p. 379). The function of these courts
is to test whether any laws of the country are violative of the 'Injunctions of
Islam', which primarily means Qur'an and *sunna*. As hybrid legal creatures,
Pakistani judges quickly learnt that justice is a globally understood legal value,
and have not hesitated, as Muslims, to emphasise that Islam stands for justice,
thus seeking to legitimise their own position.[156] An important Amendment to
the 1973 Constitution, which was brought into force in 1985, was the inclusion
of Article 2-A, inserted by the Revival of the Constitution of 1973 Order, 1985
(President's Order 1985), which runs as follows:

2-A. The Objectives Resolution to form part of substantive provisions
The principles and provisions set out in the Objectives Resolution . . . are
hereby made a substantive part of the Constitution and shall have effect
accordingly.

The Objectives Resolution, as the Preamble to the Constitutions of Pakistan, had
until then been unenforceable in the courts. Its inspirational guidelines about
how the Constitution and all laws of the country should be interpreted could
now be used more directly in providing important guidance for government
policy and legislation. The assimilation of these provisions into the substantive
provision of Article 2-A has had a deep effect on the interpretation of the Pakistani Constitution.[157] It is relevant to examine here how these provisions relate
to visions of an Islamic society and legal system. At first sight, the conceptual
tension between the secular fundamental rights of the Constitution and the

---

[156] Such assertions are repeated from time to time, but not without risks. In *Rani v. The State*,
PLD 1996 Kar 316, a staunchly Muslim judge criticised excesses of so-called Islamisation
and acquitted a woman who had been convicted of *zina* while the men who had molested
her had been let off. Sadly, such forthright, intelligent judges in Pakistan may find that
the political climate will not tolerate their presence in office – the services of this learned
High Court judge were soon terminated. Judicial activism has become important in public
interest litigation. For details see Lau (1996) and Menski *et al.* (2000).

[157] The rich Pakistani constitutional law literature strongly reflects Western positivist
predilections. See e.g. Mahmood (1973) and Khan (1990). For an overview from the
external perspective of a political scientist, see Newberg (1995).

possibly more restrictive Islamic laws is striking. As in India, the concurrent operation of a diversifying personal law system with a uniformising constitutional regime creates many inconsistencies (Mehdi, 1994: 4–14). We know today that the inclusion of the Objectives Resolution as a substantive provision of the 1973 Constitution enabled the Pakistani judiciary to use Islam, especially the Islamic right to justice, as a powerful tool and new inspiration to constitutional interpretation. This is particularly evident in the newly emerged field of public interest litigation. In this context, Article 2-A became a powerful tool to chip away at established, restrictive, Anglo-inspired precedents, and to open the courts to an Islamic version of justice-focused public interest litigation.[158]

Apart from the critical field of constitutional law, in which endless debates and politicking prevented even the establishment of the first Constitution for many years, Pakistani legal developments focused initially on family law. In uneasy tension with the programmatic commitment to Islam, initial reformist efforts involved modernist legislation on Muslim family law through the Muslim Family Laws Ordinance of 1961. This Ordinance,[159] the watered-down outcome of modernist proposals emanating from a Commission set up in 1955, caused huge controversies because the suggestions for reform had included curtailing the rights of Muslim men to polygamy, abolition of the simple 'triple *talaq*', and compulsory registration of all marriages and divorces, in addition to changing the scheme of succession for orphaned grandchildren. Coulson (1964: 214) observed that the methods of *ijtihad* used here were not very 'Islamic':

> [I]t is evident from the deliberations of the 1955 Commission and from the terms of the Ordinance that the *ijtihad* on which the reforms are allegedly based is of a very different nature from the conscientious reinterpretation of the original sources as practised by the Middle Eastern reformers. Eminently 'Islamic' though the system of Arbitration Councils may be, this does not appear to be a deliberate attempt to implement the Qur'anic provisions, while the rules concerning polygamy are conditioned by straightforward criteria of social desirability rather than by the Qur'anic injunctions of financial capability and impartial treatment. As has always been the case since the first legislative interference in the domain of Shari'a law in the Indian sub-continent, the problems of the juristic basis of reform have not commanded the same attention as they have in the Middle East. In short, therefore, the Ordinance continues the particular tradition of Anglo-Muhammadan law in a manner which is certainly practical and probably best suited to the present mood and aspirations of Pakistan.

This somewhat dismissive approach to South Asian Muslim law as an inferior cousin of the 'proper' Islamic system should not distract from the fact that

---

[158] See in detail Khan (1993); Menski *et al.* (2000). In Pakistan, public interest litigation developed similar characteristics to its Indian counterpart, but has been explicitly Islamised and stamped with a Pakistani Muslim identity.

[159] It is not an Act, because it was put into effect by a military dictator.

Coulson identified a major problem with human law-making in Pakistan. His observation that the legal reformer was not even properly paying attention to accepted methods of *ijtihad* to create a new Islamic norm system is correct; the agenda were directed at social reform and the amelioration of the position of women. Coulson could have said more clearly that all Muslim law reforms in Pakistan, particularly Islamisation processes, have been influenced by political considerations in ways that earlier Islamic rulers did not need to bother about: they were not dependent on an electorate that wanted to see the government act in the best interests of the nation. In Pakistan, the politicised temptation to invoke Islamisation whenever it seems useful for ambitious politicians is still abundantly evident today. Mehdi (1994: 18ff.) stresses the need for ideology in post-colonial Pakistan, but deplores the lack of consistency and coherence. Much earlier, Coulson (1964: 220–1) made further negative comments about Pakistani attempts at Islamisation which are useful for a comparative analysis:

> If the outright recognition of the needs of society which jurisprudence has thus endorsed in many respects is to be regarded as modern *ijtihad*, it is obviously a very different concept of *ijtihad* from that we have seen operating, for example, in relation to polygamy and repudiation, where reforms are based on particular interpretations of specific Qur'anic injunctions. In sum, it appears that modern jurisprudence has not yet evolved any systematic approach to the problem of adapting the traditional law to the circumstances of contemporary society. Lacking any consistency of principle or methodology, it has tackled the process of reform as a whole in a spirit of juristic opportunism.

Subsequent events in Pakistan were to show that this process was more than just 'juristic opportunism',[160] namely planned, politically motivated use of Islam as a slogan to bring about a more favourable public opinion towards the law-maker (whether elected or not) by relying on traditionalist social rather than religious norms. In this complex politically driven process of Islamisation, there have been many confusions and disagreements over what it means to construct an 'Islamic' society. Moralising *mullahs* have joined hands with self-appointed guardians of Islamic values to criminalise women and minorities, leading to massive abuses of law and legal procedures which continue to some extent today.[161] Such abuses relate especially to the introduction,

---

[160] In an early article which asked whether Pakistan was an Islamic state, Anderson (1967: 136) concluded his assessment by comparing the people of Pakistan with a boy flying a kite on a misty day: 'They cannot see it; they cannot tell where it is going; but they certainly feel the pull.'

[161] This explains partly why a case concerning the right of a Hanafi Muslim woman to choose her marriage partner made such headlines. Here was a runaway couple in a 'love marriage', following 'Western' patterns of behaviour and thus endangering Islamic values. The court in *Abdul Waheed* v. *Asma Jahangir*, PLD 1997 Lah 301, eventually agreed that the woman had the right, under Hanafi law, to select her spouse. The decision was confirmed by the

under a military regime, of the Offence of Zina (Enforcement of Hudood) Ordinance in 1979, as well as several other Ordinances.[162] There is a considerable amount of legal literature focusing on women in Pakistan.[163] Some of those studies bring out how the slogan of 'Islamisation' was used as a new weapon in petty, personal vendettas.[164] It is apparent that Islamisation could be abused to control women, even to blame them for moral lapses in society. Pakistani judges took some time to control these kinds of abuses and blatant excesses,[165] and the risks for individuals are by no means over, as many applications for political asylum continue to document. Beyond the headlines, there is immense apprehension about victimisation of individuals in the name of Islamisation, sustaining a pervasive element of fear, not so much fear of God as a resigned awareness that abuses of men's laws in the name of religion are not effectively controlled in countries like Pakistan. On the other hand, strict punitive measures are portrayed as a necessary tool for creating a better Islamic society. A prominent former Chief Justice of Pakistan (Shah, 1999: 66) writes:

> The Hadd punishments have been provided to ensure preservation of values that Islam upholds for the dignity of human society. Furthermore, Islamic punishments are also designed for the spiritual and moral purification of the human beings in this world and for their expiation in the world hereafter, which concept is absent in any other legal system.

Apart from the *hudood* laws, recent developments in Pakistani family law place debates about Islamisation into a wider framework. The Muslim Family Laws Ordinance of 1961 (MFLO),[166] asserting the right of the modern state to legislate and to make rules different from traditional Muslim law, has been questioned as un-Islamic and hence unconstitutional. It has never been properly clarified what the relationship of state-made Muslim law would be with the traditional *shari'a* law. Could men in Pakistan make law in derogation of God's law? Two

Pakistani Supreme Court in *Abdul Waheed* v. *Asma Jahangir*, PLD 2004 SC 219. Since the traditional Islamic law in question here was more liberal and pro-women than the local customary norms, the case is not a good example for those who argue that Islamisation is necessarily bad for women. For details see Lau (1997). On secularism and Islam see Jan (1998).

[162] These are the various Hudood Ordinances of 1979 and 1980 as well as the Qanun-e-Shahadat Ordinance of 1984, which concerns evidence law, the Qisas and Diyat Ordinance of 1990 (for the full text see Mehdi, 1994: 298–323), and the Enforcement of Shari'ah Act of 1991, which aims to make the country a 'truly Islamic state' according to the Statement of Objects and Reasons.

[163] See Balchin (1994), Mehdi and Shaheed (1997) and Shaheed *et al.* (1998).

[164] See further below the case of *Noor Khan* v. *Haq Nawaz*, PLD 1982 FSC 265.

[165] A prominent example is the case of *Safia Bibi*, a partially blind young victim of rape, who had to be rescued by the Federal Shariat Court from a prosecution for *zina* after the lower courts abysmally failed to do justice. The case is reported at PLD 1985 FSC 120.

[166] On all aspects of this Ordinance, see in detail Pearl and Menski (1998).

brief examples, relating to polygamy and *talaq* divorces, illustrate the resulting confusions and current uneasy compromise. On polygamy, section 6(1) of the MFLO provides:

> No man, during the subsistence of an existing marriage, shall except with the previous permission in writing of the Arbitration Council, contract another marriage, nor shall any such marriage contracted without such permission be registered under this Ordinance.

It was long known that if a Pakistani Muslim husband ignored this state law and contracted a polygamous marriage in derogation of this section, the resulting polygamous Muslim marriage would be legally valid under Pakistani law,[167] while the criminal penalties stipulated in other parts of section 6 would remain ineffective if nobody complained. More recently, Pakistani courts have begun to make some negative comments about polygamy, significantly from a justice-focused perspective, for example criticising men who fail to tell a second wife that they are already married.[168]

In a landmark decision of the Federal Shariat Court,[169] now pending on appeal to the Shariat Bench of the Supreme Court, several provisions of the MFLO were challenged as violative of the 'Injunctions of Islam', a standard phrase in Pakistan with reference to Qur'an and *sunna*. The traditionalists' constitutional challenge to the provisions of section 6 of the MFLO had been that, since the Qur'an permitted Muslim men to be polygamous, it should be struck down because it restricted the Muslim male's freedom to marry polygamously. In response, it was confirmed by the Federal Shariat Court that the state-made Islamic law of the Ordinance did not clash with, nor override, the traditional *shari'a* law. What was not said is that section 6 of the MFLO could not become effective in practice because it is a different type of law from the one it was purporting to replace or amend. This extremely elaborate and learned decision, citing relevant Qur'anic provisions and much *sunna* material, without saying so explicitly, engages in a plurality-conscious reconstruction of how the two types of Islamic law in Pakistani law interact. By treating *shari'a* law as a form of natural law which is God-given, it implies that the state could not possibly have intended to replace the traditional permission for the Muslim husband to have up to four wives with a restriction on polygamy. All the modern positive law did, in effect, was to introduce an optional new procedure, according to which a husband should seek permission from his existing wife or wives. This means that 'shall' in the above section of the MFLO – and throughout that Ordinance – means something akin to 'should', and probably rather *Inshallah*,

---

[167] Numerous court decisions confirmed this. For details see Pearl and Menski (1998: 256–67).

[168] See *Faheemuddin* v. *Sabeeha Begum*, PLD 1991 SC 1074. This criticism was reiterated in *Allah Rakha* v. *Federation of Pakistan*, PLD 2000 FSC 1.

[169] *Allah Rakha* v. *Federation of Pakistan*, PLD 2000 FSC 1.

'If God pleases'.[170] This confirms that Pakistani state law never achieved a reform of Muslim polygamy.[171] Rather, the traditional *shariat* continues to provide the primary rules on this matter, while the MFLO is merely a set of secondary rules.

The panel of learned judges considered such matters with grave concern. Launching into an historical analysis of Muslim polygamy, they emphasised the Qur'anic toleration of polygamy with some safeguards. While section 6 of the MFLO did not prohibit polygamy and polygamy remained 'a permissible act' in Islam (p. 57), this section appeared designed to ensure that a polygamist treats his wives equally and was thus 'reformative only' (p. 57). The Court's reasoning that 'only a procedure has been prescribed' (p. 56) implies that Pakistani Muslim women today, as in earlier times, need some protection from abuse of the husband's right to polygamy. Therefore, protective mechanisms for women who wished to complain needed to be strengthened. It was held (p. 57):

> [W]e are of the view and accordingly recommend that the Arbitration Council should figure in when a complaint is made by the existing wife or her parents/guardians. The intention is to protect the rights of the existing wife/wives and interest of her/their children. The wife is, therefore, the best judge of her cause who or her parents may initiate the proceedings if her husband intends to contract another marriage.

This benign social reform in the name of Islamisation is also observed regarding *talaq* divorces. In modern Pakistani society, a major problem has been that Muslim husbands can use the disreputable but convenient 'triple *talaq*' or *talaq al-bidah* to divorce a wife virtually instantly, simply pronouncing *talaq* three times, to the effect that the wife is instantly and irrevocably divorced. There is no set form of words, a mischievous husband might not even tell the wife and he might just abandon her without even pronouncing the *talaq* in front of witnesses, let alone writing anything down. The woman is socially and religiously considered a divorcee because of the claim that there has been a triple *talaq*. Since this caused socio-economic hardship to many Muslim women, the 1955 Commission had recommended that all divorces should be registered by the state and should only become effective after the *iddat* period, and not instantly, as in the dreaded *talaq al-bidah*. The 1961 Ordinance introduced a watered-down compromise favouring (through silence about the implications on the validity of such a divorce) Muslim husbands who simply ignored the state law and relied on the pre-existing *shari'a*. Section 7(1) on *talaq* provides:

---

[170] Still, this does not make the MFLO a meaningless scrap of paper, as Scandinavian realists (chapter 3, section 3.7.1) might have suggested.

[171] However, as noted in chapter 4, modernist Indian authors in particular have been claiming that the Pakistanis abolished polygamy. That is obviously an activist myth.

> Any man who wishes to divorce his wife shall, as soon as may be after the pronouncement of *talaq* in any form whatsoever, give the Chairman notice in writing of his having done so, and shall supply a copy thereof to the wife.

Accepting the pre-existing Muslim law, according to which there needs to be a *talaq* in some form, section 7 of the MFLO expects the husband to give notice only after the *talaq*. If he pronounced a triple *talaq*, which in traditional *shari'a* law becomes instantly effective and legally valid, any form of notice is clearly pointless. The provisions of section 7 of the MFLO aimed to establish a fiction, found in section 7(3), that the divorce would only be effective ninety days *after* the husband had given notice, turning an instant *talaq al-bidah* into the more acceptable *talaq al-hasan*, which would still give the wife three menstrual cycles of 'security'. However, where a husband does not give notice, the instant divorce would have become valid under *shari'a*, while it would be deemed ineffective under the fictive provisions of the MFLO.

The established position after an early precedent in 1963, almost universally accepted,[172] became that formal notice of divorce was essential for its legal validity. But this created a strange situation, for a Muslim husband might now abandon his wife, refuse to give her a *talaq* and keep her in legal limbo. She might not be aware of this, given the effects of patriarchy and the state of education in Pakistan. Under the official MFLO, such a marriage was treated as subsisting and legally valid, while socially and religiously the marriage was doubtlessly over, though not properly terminated. The medieval *Hedaya* (Hamilton, 1891), it was discovered recently, knew a term for this, namely 'implied divorce' (*talaq al-qinayat*), which is what Muslim wives in Pakistan have been subjected to for centuries.

This systematic abuse came to light as a direct result of Islamisation in Pakistan during the late 1970s, when devious men brought prosecutions for *zina* under the notorious Offence of Zina (Enforcement of Hudood) Ordinance of 1979 against women who had been sent away by their husbands but not formally divorced. Most instructive on this is *Noor Khan* v. *Haq Nawaz*, PLD 1982 FSC 265. Here an illiterate mother of many children was thrown out by her husband without an explicit *talaq*, considered herself divorced and arranged a marriage with another man, from whom she had another set of children. Several years later, a relative of the first husband, an army officer, brought a vindictive *zina* prosecution, manifestly *mala fide*, against the woman and her second husband. The Federal Shariat Court vigilantly spotted that such abuse was facilitated by the newly Islamised law and set the woman and her husband free. This shows that the judges, rather than legislators (in Pakistan often military dictators) are

---

[172] *Ali Nawaz Gardezi* v. *Muhammad Yusuf*, PLD 1963 SC 51. For details see Pearl and Menski (1998: 334–73).

the real guardians of justice, which is of course precisely their constitutional function.

In the context of constitutional challenges to section 7 of the MFLO in *Allah Rakha v. Federation of Pakistan*, PLD 2000 FSC 1, such evidence of plurality-consciousness and sensitivity to Islamic justice was again manifest. The constitutional validity of section 7 of the MFLO had been challenged by traditionalists *inter alia* because the supposedly mandatory requirement to give notice of divorce, and the provisions about punishment for failure to give notice, contradicted the Qur'an, which knew of no such notice requirements (p. 58). While criticising the 'over exuberance of legislation in a new field' (p. 60), the FSC refused to hold (as Islamists had hoped) that the notice requirement was un-Islamic. Finding instead that 'the purport of section 7 of the Ordinance is regulatory only' (p. 60), the Court played the same word games observed above with regard to polygamy. The legislator in his exuberance might have overlooked a few fine points, but the notice requirement itself was merely an optional procedure and 'no valid objection can be raised to the spirit of section 7 of the Ordinance' (p. 61). To hold anything else would have meant that the FSC treated the notice requirement as mandatory, so that without official notice a *talaq* could not become legally valid. Thus, again, modernist interpretations as well as 'fundamentalist' arguments stand defeated.

Performing such elaborate plurality-conscious balancing exercises, Pakistan's FSC protected virtually the entire MFLO from long-standing conservative onslaughts and clarified that the current Islamic law of Pakistan contains two co-existing and potentially conflicting Muslim law elements, MFLO law and *shariat*, setting God's law against man-made Islamic law. Modern Pakistani Islamisation policies seem to combine a commitment to Islam and strict punitive responses to violations of sexual morality with reformist, pro-women agenda in family law. Both are policies designed to bring about a better Muslim society in contemporary Pakistan, but they inevitably clash. The ongoing challenge to the MFLO demonstrates that the country remains uncomfortable with this dualistic presence of Islamic law as well as the continued presence of non-Muslim minorities, including the Ahmadis, who consider themselves Muslims. Pakistani policies of Islamisation have undoubtedly led to massive human rights violations. Their Islamic credentials remain dubious, because Islamisation policies are based on man-made reconstructions of certain laws, and fierce lobbying for certain values, rather than direct reliance on Qur'an and *sunna*.

Unlike the Turks, therefore, it seems that the Pakistani law-makers did not have a clearly defined programme and vision of the future of their country and its people. While the Turkish law-makers, implanting a foreign set of legal rules, made that vision a massive legal reality at the official level, and then waited to let the system settle down, evidently expecting a new 'living law' to emerge, the Pakistanis were not able to plan more than general programmatic statements like the Objectives Resolution of 1949. Following this and half-hearted experiments with legal modernisation of family laws in 1961, the formal legal process of Islamisation from the end of the 1970s could not assert itself as a coherent legal policy and caused, predictably, some massive failures of justice. It appears that early observers like Coulson (1964) were correct to find that the Pakistanis were not really engaged in a 'proper' process of Islamisation. There is a lot of jurisprudential confusion and dishonesty here, exploited by all concerned. After *Allah Rakha*, as it stands at present, it is evident that Pakistan is not a theocracy, and that what it means to be or become an Islamic country is still not openly discussed. Clearly, the arena for conflicts and tensions remains firmly within the realm of human law-making. Given the 'margin of error' in all of Muslim jurisprudence, no other result could have been expected.

Just as the Turkish state has found that it needs to negotiate the modalities of legal modernisation with the people concerned, the Pakistanis have discovered that real Islamisation rather than sloganeering involves effort on all sides, a process of *ijtihad* that is not limited to juristic endeavour. Despite the messy observable 'reality of multiple choice' (Chaudhary, 1999: 22), this deeper message is not forgotten by many Pakistanis, who remain concerned that a sustainable plurality-conscious method of dealing with conflicting expectations within a Muslim society with South Asian characteristics needs to be found. Pakistani Muslim law, too, confirms the culture-specific nature of all law and the global predicament and constant challenge of finding a system of justice that can take care of all kinds of scenarios.

For a globally focused legal analysis, the overall conclusion on Islamic laws remains that the various national manifestations of Islamic law today exhibit the multiple plurality-conscious interactions between the spheres of state law, religious and moral values and social norms among Muslims within the global *ummah*. Apart from the *grundnorm* that binds all Muslims into this universal community, namely that God's law is superior to men's law, the culture-specific modalities of human law-making remain as contested, locally and nationally, as in the various Western manifestations and theories of law. The Muslim *grundnorm* in all of this, preventing Islamic law as a complex natural law system from easily admitting secular elements, shows that even a deliberately modernist Muslim country like Turkey cannot avoid some kind of official recognition of Islamic claims and theories about the dominant concept of Islamic law as religious natural law. In a global context, this does not set up a binary polarity of East and West, nor a clash of civilisations involving Judaeo-Christianity versus Islam,[173] but indicates rather a global plurality-focused scenario that is much more complex and definitely multipolar. As demonstrated here for Islamic legal systems, this multipolarity, emphasising the culture-specific nature of all law, can indeed be understood through application of the conceptual triangle of law developed by this study.

---

[173] See to the same effect Yilmaz (2005b: 123).

6

African laws: the search for law

The sub-title of this chapter indicates deep problems in the discourse on African laws. For many reasons, African laws and African jurisprudence have always faced a barely hidden undercurrent of denial of African laws and their potential contributions to jurisprudence. Previous chapters demonstrated a serious deficiency of plurality-consciousness in understanding non-Western laws, mainly implicating positivist presuppositions, which have also heavily impacted on how African laws are perceived. While Islamic and even Hindu religious law dogma tends to overemphasise the place of divine legislation, thereby conflating positivism and natural law, scholarship about African laws remains heavily influenced by a brand of deficiency in plurality-consciousness which denies the existence of law in social contexts. Positivist bias is strongly reflected, leading to claims that there was no proper law in traditional Africa. Comparative law scholarship, too, has struggled with accepting that Africans have 'proper' law. More recently, the voices of Africa have been in danger of being drowned out by assertions of global human rights, to the effect that there is nothing of value in traditional African laws to contribute towards a better future for the world as a whole and the understanding of law as a global phenomenon.

A plurality-conscious perspective on the laws of Africa cannot ignore the people of Africa and their many cultures and languages. But can one even speak of 'African law', given this immense diversity? The short answer is that 'African law' is merely a kind of ethnic label and the collective term 'African laws' comprises evidently many different types of legal systems. But there is much more at stake here than taxonomy, legal theory or the evaluation of customary laws. The presence of African laws as a separate family of laws continues to be denied and defined away.[1] This is presumably a consequence of historical marginalisation of the 'dark continent'. The present chapter must therefore first address the huge problem of concerted efforts to deny a place to African laws at the global table. Arguments that Africans are somehow primitive, do

---

[1] Woodman and Obilade (1995: xxvi) argue that, rather than contributing to construction of new theories on African law, theoretical scholarship on African laws may play a significant role in developing a global jurisprudence. Glenn (2004) treats African law under chthonic legal tradition, with the (probably unintended) result that African law becomes invisible in this taxonomy.

not have proper laws and should modernise out of their depressed conditions as fast as possible through reception of Western laws have been powerful and pervasive. Since Africans were widely assumed to lack the capacity for sophisticated rational thought and modern administrative arrangements, culture-blind European legal observers ignored massive evidence of mainly oral African laws and brushed it aside as 'culture'. In the context of plurality-sensitive efforts to devise a globally valid legal theory, such myopic views are seriously outdated. African laws are as legal as other laws, but they may well have specific characteristics unique to them, defining their 'identity postulates' (Chiba, 1989: 180).

There is much earlier evidence of systematic denial of African laws. Today's scholarship only *seems* more open-minded about Africans and their laws. Africans anywhere in the world still face vigorous denial of the validity of their culture-specific legal norms and postulates, now often on universalising human rights grounds. While many allowances are made for African Muslims in the name of religion, African people are almost everywhere treated in a colour-blind, culture-neutral fashion that denies their value systems adequate legal recognition. In addition, young black males everywhere seem to be systematically criminalised and punished for being 'different'.[2]

A globally focused analytical perspective must account for the fact that one can easily identify culture-specific African concepts of a pre-existing, superhuman Order. African natural laws feature strongly (Ayittey, 1991), emphasising humankind's link with Nature, Earth and various gods, thereby also challenging assumptions that Africans do not have 'proper' religions. Ultimately, African people, too, have to constantly balance different conceptualisations of law in their daily lives so that here, too, the analytical triangle (chapter 3, section 3.8) applies and works well. In Africa, too, positivism and state laws, natural law concepts and values, and socio-legal normative orders (mostly as customs) have been interacting dynamically at all times as powerful claimants for the attention of individuals, communities, whole states and academics. Individuals could choose to ignore the inherent tensions between different types of law, but the ideologies of secularism and of man's mastery over the world have not become a prominent feature of African thought. Chthonic people do not put themselves above nature, they live with it (Glenn, 2004, ch. 3). Traditional Africans perceive themselves as tied in with everything around them, applying culture-specific holistic, chthonic perspectives as a fertile conceptual base for the production of innumerable legal systems. To what extent African conceptual clusters and culture-specific values facilitate adjustment to new circumstances remains to be seen. The simplistic view that traditional African laws are just

---

[2] For uncomfortable British evidence of the criminalisation of African people, see Hood (1992). For communication problems between minorities in America and courts, see Moore (1999). Glenn (2000: 80) notes that 'chthonic people, in many instances, are the principal occupants of prisons'.

'customary law' reflects, first of all, an outsider perspective (Mensah-Brown, 1976: 7) and seems to arise from the myopic positivist argument that traditional African law is not really law.

African legal history may be divided into three major periods: pre-colonial, colonial and postcolonial African law (Allott, 1965). Traditional African laws, as floating oral masses of non-state laws, were not easily recognisable as law and attracted anthropological rather than legal research. Moreover, continuing biases against anything related to Africa and to Black people as primitive, dangerous and somehow not quite as human as others must be noted.[3] Few studies managed to understand Africa as 'an ancient, remarkably resilient culture world, capable of coping with foreign intrusions, however determined the thrust, without easy loss of authenticity' (Bozeman, 1971: 86). Most authors simply assume that colonial legal systems intervened in traditional legal arrangements and destroyed them. It is much closer to reality to note that much of traditional African law became invisible unofficial law as a result of colonisation. In postcolonial Africa, fierce debates are continuing over the status of traditional African laws and the value of retaining African legal traditions. Much scholarship continues to portray African laws as impediments to globalisation, 'development' and gender justice.

Because of the absence of written evidence from earlier times, it does not make sense to divide traditional African laws into chronological sub-segments.[4] The present chapter analyses first the traditional legal systems of Africa, their internal structures and holistic manifestations, directing the spotlight in turn towards conceptual underpinnings, the role of custom, morality and religion, and dispute settlement. Next, various impacts of colonial rule are examined, leading to a multitude of plural legal systems in different combinations, complex legal arrangements about recognition of custom and tradition, the restructuring of dispute settlement processes and debates about legal reforms. Analysis of the post-independence period concentrates on the place of customary laws in today's modern African legal systems and considers evidence of strategies to deal with legal plurality, modifying dispute settlement processes, and the scope for legal reforms, including unification of laws.

The great variety of African legal systems precludes sweeping generalisations. In addition to African laws, Islamic law applies to many African people in all Northern African countries, in the Sudan, Somalia and many other countries,

---

[3] On ethnic minorities in English law and perceptions of black people see Jones and Welhengama (2000: 5ff.). A much-used teachers' handbook is Mothe (1993). On education and racism see Sarup (1991). Notably, the English language even has a particular word for blackening or defaming, 'denigration', use of which is now seen as politically incorrect. This was not the case in the 1960s (Kuper and Kuper, 1965: 17).

[4] Attempts to make such distinctions are frustrated by the orality of African legal traditions and the fact that such 'traditions' continue to be accepted today, 'always on the understanding that the old is new' (Bennett, 2004: 2).

including Mozambique.[5] Islam travelled with traders along the ancient trade routes across the Sahara to West Africa, and along the East African coast.[6] In Southern Africa, apart from various local laws, and Muslim and Hindu laws, Roman-Dutch law applies.[7] Post-apartheid South Africa, engaged in post-modern legal reconstruction, as various Law Commission Reports document, finds that local legal norms remain extremely relevant. In addition, Africans as a global transnational community have taken their traditions and laws with them all over the world, especially to the Caribbean and America,[8] Brazil,[9] and into almost all countries of the developed world, where African refugees have become prominent new groups.[10] We concentrate here on sub-Saharan Africa and the large extended family of African laws. Not surprisingly, questions have arisen whether in view of such diversities a label like 'African law' is useful and appropriate.[11] While there is no such thing as one African law, and despite enormous diversity on the ground, it is possible to treat African laws as forming a coherent unit for comparative study. Allott (1968: 131) argued:

> Not the least of these reasons is that the literature on African law ranges widely over the African continent and its peoples; the writings of one scholar supplement those of another in building up a comprehensive view of Africa and its laws. But, more fundamentally, African laws reveal sufficient similarity in procedure, principles, institutions, and techniques for a common account to be given of them. The variations, some minimal, some major, which may be detected between different African systems do not obscure, but rather illuminate, the reasons for and the advantages of each system in its own environment.

The elements of similarity of African laws listed here are all ingredients of every legal system in the world; all legal systems have procedures, principles, institutions and techniques. Therefore, are we asking for 'ethnic' African

---

[5] On Mozambique, see Sachs and Welch (1990); more generally see Young (1994).

[6] On Islamic laws in sub-Saharan Africa see Mensah-Brown (1976: 47–53). On Nigerian Islamic law see Ajijola (1989) and Ebo (1995: 34). On Morocco and the anthropology of justice see Rosen (1989). On North African Muslim laws, see An-Na'im (2002b).

[7] For a good overview see Bekker *et al.* (2002) and Rautenbach and Goolam (2002). On customary law see Bennett (1991; 2004).

[8] For an overview, see Franklin (1947), also published in German (Franklin, 1983). A rich collection of material specifically written for British schools is found in Addai-Sebo and Wong (1988).

[9] For an overview, see Levine and Crocitti (1999). On African religions in Brazil see Bastide (1978). Davis (1999) argues for better legal recognition for Afro-Brazilians, countering the modern nation state's uniformising pressure and highlighting racial discrimination against black Brazilians. See also Reichmann (1999).

[10] See Kibreab (1985) and CIMADE *et al.* (1986). Kibreab (1987) provides insight on displaced people in Africa. On the disorientation of Somalis, and the reconstruction of their lives abroad, see Farah (2000).

[11] For details see Allott (1960: 55–71). Mudimbe (1988) adopts an Afro-centric approach.

characteristics, or are we relying simply on geography, so that African laws are the laws of Africa? Faced with the enormous internal diversity of African customary laws, David and Brierley (1978: 506) asked: 'Does this mean, then, that there is no *legal* unity among these various communities, that there is no "African" law properly speaking?' While opinions have differed on this issue, there is now 'general agreement that certain characteristics common to all African laws do set them off from the laws of Europe' (p. 506), presumably some conceptual elements of African social order. Allott (1965: 217–18) had earlier discussed the changing definitions of African law in different periods. He noted 'a certain ambiguity in the term, giving rise to doubts as to the existence of an externally isolable and internally coherent body of laws describable as African law' (p. 217). The frequently used term of native law 'would have had a faintly derogatory implication, as if the law of the natives was not real law' (p. 218). In the post-colonial era, the existence of African laws was institutionally recognised by the creation of academic posts and courses in African law, which reflected the perception of African law as a family of legal systems. Allott (1965: 218) commented:

> The acceptance of this position did not imply the existence of any fundamental uniformity in African legal systems, still less of a single type of African law with local variations; but it did imply that the geographical contiguity and the comparable histories and backgrounds of the people subject to these laws, and the character of the laws themselves, were such that it had become meaningful to study them in this way.

The end of the colonial era in Africa brought further changes of perspective and the earlier distinction between African laws and received English or other laws ceased to be relevant. Allott (1965: 219) argued therefore that the definition of African laws had been significantly enlarged:

> All laws in independent Africa are now 'African' and African law no longer means simply the indigenous customary laws deriving from antiquity, but the modern statutory laws as well; in other words, African law is the totality of African legal systems. At this point one might well ask: Does the mere fact that legal systems are to be found in the same continent give them anything in common? Is not 'African law' now an empty term, like 'European law'?

One notes an important shift here towards the inclusion of modern Western-style laws as African laws and concomitant neglect of traditional African laws and cultures. Debates have persisted about the subject itself,[12] but modern scholars of African law may now have very little knowledge of traditional African legal systems. Since the redefined field includes numerous Western-style positivist laws and legal processes, questions about the relevance of traditional African laws and procedures may seem almost irrelevant: there is so much new official African law to study. However, the living realities of African laws suggest

---

[12] Mensah-Brown (1976: 7) indicates some elements of these debates.

that traditional law lives on today (Bennett, 2004) and that by merely study-ing modern African laws as copies of Western laws one misses critical cultural dimensions.[13] Academic debates about the reconstructed nature of modern African laws (Chanock, 1978; 1985) deny to some extent that understanding traditional African laws remains crucial today. As for Hindu and Islamic law, the conceptual input of indigenous African legal values and traditions into modern legal systems seems much larger than most legal scholars are able or willing to see. In the context of a plurality-conscious global jurispruden-tial analysis, a conceptual understanding of traditional African laws in their diachronical manifestations remains a critical tool. First, however, the unpleas-ant reality of powerful assertions that traditional Africans had no law must be faced.

6.1 The denial of African culture and laws

The modernist prescription for all aspects of African existence involves an outright deracination and derogation of anything African, so much so that the literature is full of statements of Afro-pessimism focused on the 'broken' traditions or 'broken heritage' of the African continent and its many different peoples.[14] Almost as soon as European 'civilised people' arrived in the 'dark continent', Africans were declared to be uncivilised, unlettered, devoid of proper political and legal structures, waiting to be subjugated and enlightened.[15] Such undercurrents of racist thought have severely affected much of the international scholarship on African laws.[16]

Negative views about Africa and Africans can be traced back well before European colonialism, which is popularly blamed for all African ills. The process of denying value to anything African started at least with the ancient Greeks and

---

[13] The same observation was made in chapter 4 for Hindu law and modern India.

[14] Okupa (1998: xi) writes that '[t]he disintegration of pre-colonial African empires, states and their legal institutions could have been brought about by a combination of many lethal situations: disintegration of families during the slave trade, the spread of Islamic conquest, Christian missionaries against heathenism and the white man's aggression. In the nineteenth century, Africans were traumatised.' Serequeberhan (1991: 23) writes of the need for 'the revitalization of the broken and suppressed indigenous African heritage'.

[15] Mensah-Brown (1976: 19) calls this 'ethnocentric thought control' and illustrates the simple binary pair of Christian = civilised = possessed law and African = pagan = uncivilised = possessed no law. Okupa (1998: 1) indicates that at an early stage of European interaction, just prior to colonisation, the picture may have been a little more harmonious: 'In pre-colonial Africa, the missionaries, adventurers and traders had found systems of family law, family property, succession, inheritance, criminal law and compensatory jus-tice, but it was not the positivist law that they knew. Nevertheless, the early Europeans had co-existed peacefully with the natives.'

[16] Maathai (1995: 6) emphasises that 'this must not be an excuse of the African people for the perpetual litany of woes about colonialism, slavery, and other injustices against them. Indeed, this is part of their heritage. These gross violations of the rights of the African peoples should be living examples of the many battles they have fought and won.'

later the Romans, who were, in the view of African writers, not forthcoming enough about whence they gained some of their knowledge. Most Europeans do not realise that St Augustine and other early prominent Europeans were Africans. St Augustine (354–430), originating from what is now Algeria, is the famous early thinker to whom the saying that '[w]ithout justice states are nothing but organised robber bands' is attributed (Allott, 1980: 151). It is possible that this statement, a classic natural law argument, was inspired by his African 'roots' and has a deeper meaning than obvious critique of excessive positivism. Famous Greek thinkers like Plato and Aristotle, it appears, took much inspiration from Egypt, which African writers quite properly count as their territory.[17] Writing about African philosophy, which is not even supposed to exist because Africans were assumed to be too primitive to think in an abstract way, Onyewuenyi (1991: 31) speaks therefore of 'a concerted effort on the part of Western scholars to deny Africa any contribution in the field of philosophy'. Thus, notes Serequeberhan (1991: 4):

> African historical existence was suppressed and Africa was forced to become the negative underbelly of European history. What is paradoxical in all of this is the fact that Europe undertook the domination of Africa and the world not in the explicit and cynical recognition of its imperial interests but in the delusion that it was spreading civilization.

Citing Rudyard Kipling and the famous verses on the white man's burden, this leads almost directly to Gramsci's critique of the orientation of modern European thought as a 'singular globalized cultural totality' (Serequeberhan, 1991: 5). Such assumptions are manifest in the views of leading European thinkers, who are said to represent the best of rational traditions, but appear racist and irrational. Serequeberhan (1991: 5–6) notes:

> Hume and Kant held the view that Africans, in virtue of their blackness, are precluded from the realm of reason and civilization. As Hume puts it, 'I am apt to suspect the negroes, and in general all the other species of men (for there are four or five different kinds) to be naturally inferior to whites. There never was a civilized nation of any complexion than white.' Kant, in agreement with Hume, asserts that '[s]o fundamental is the difference between the two races of men, and it appears to be as great in regard to mental capacities as in color.'

Such authoritative, influential statements from spokespersons of the 'enlightened nations' made it child's play to assert that Africans were child-like,[18] and

---

[17] Such material is collected by Onyewuenyi (1991: 35–7), who argues that accounts of African philosophers were purposely withheld from history (p. 35). A comparative perspective needs to note that the ancient Greeks were probably also influenced by Indian concepts (May, 1985). Middle Eastern scholars and individuals, however, will claim Egypt and much of North Africa as 'their' territory.

[18] Mamdani (1996: 4). The same point was made for colonialism generally and its impact on the Indian psyche by Nandy (1983: 11–12).

simply had no philosophy, a view that did not take long to become common knowledge. It was only a little step from there to assert that Africans did not have any laws either. The same chain of reasoning was applied to African religions, despite a lot of early knowledge.[19] Some early European observers understood that Africans saw the entire world as interlinked,[20] but did not take this as evidence of a sophisticated, holistic understanding of man's existence. Rather, for some observers, this indicated a deficiency in African thought processes. Non-recognition of division of the metaphysical sphere from the physical served as proof that Africans had no speculative inclinations, and hence no proper religion (Ayittey, 1991: 11).[21] This is the age-old issue of separating religion and law. Missionaries were largely responsible for the dissemination of irrational information about indigenous laws. Okupa (1998: xiii) emphasises that they wanted polygamists killed and their idols burnt. Ayittey (1991: 14) notes that 'rather strangely, Christianity is called a religion. So too is Islam. But that of the natives is called paganism.'[22]

Legal scholars could not remain insulated from such negative approaches to everything African, especially since early European legal scholarship arose out of philosophy (chapter 3, section 3.2). Lawyers came to the study of African laws fairly late, which further reflects the approach that there was nothing 'legal' for them to study. Earlier comparative law scholars (e.g. Kagan, 1955) were not interested in African law and might not recognise it as a legal system (Derrett, 1968a: xv). Such negative assumptions still underpin assertions that post-colonial Africans really have no proper religious, cultural and legal traditions to fall back on and the only viable method of development is to modernise Africa and Africans along Western lines. While this eventually became 'politically incorrect' during the post-colonial era, a lot of damage had already been done, and some developments have become irreversible. The prevailing negative assumptions about African laws are strongly reflected in legal scholarship and old negative views have significantly influenced the study of African legal systems. Okupa (1998: 177) notes critically:

[19] On African religions, a good overview is found in Shorter (1991). On the role of religion in African politics today, see Ellis and Ter Haar (2004).

[20] Much like the Hindu vision of *rita* as a macrocosmic Order to which man was subject (chapter 4, section 4.2). Such parallels with Hindu law as another chthonic tradition are strong. Ayittey (1991: 11–12) explains the parallel African concepts.

[21] Comparative lawyers have committed similar methodological blunders, taking their own confusions as justifications to deny Africans the power to think, and to make distinctions of their own. For an example, see David and Brierley (1978: 507).

[22] Scholarship on African Christianity and Islam in Africa seems to be much more prominent than studies on indigenous African religions. For details see Dickson (1974); Shorter (1975); Young (1986); Parratt (1987). On African Islamic laws, see Anderson (1978); Ajijola (1989); An-Na'im (2002b). On the influences of Christianity and Islam on traditional African laws see David and Brierley (1978: 509–11), concluding that 'Christianity and Islam deprived custom of its magical and supernatural basis, and thus began the process of its decay' (p. 511).

Legal anthropologists have analysed and interpreted African indigenous laws but with very little reference to the philosophical input of the people who formulated the principles of the customary law. For example, the indigenous child law and succession law that govern the matrilineal *Himba* and the patrilineal *Tiv* may be similar but the underlying jurisprudence may vary enormously. What has emerged when one trawled through the literature on legal anthropology was that most writers did not take cognisance of négritude, Bantu philosophy or the ferocious debate in ethno-philosophy. Hardly any jurisprudential or anthropological notice was taken of the philosophy of the indigenous law.

Okupa (1998: 177) therefore takes the view that 'legal anthropology is languishing because it cannot be studied independently of indigenous philosophy, in spite of its new names'. Earlier, Onyewuenyi (1991: 35) supported such arguments, speaking from personal experience when he reports a familiar phenomenon for scholars who work on supposedly arcane topics, which are not even supposed to exist:[23]

> Philosophy has come to be identified with Descartes, Spinoza, Leibnitz... Since there are no such names associated with Africa, philosophy is denied Africa. (In conversation with professors and students in America who knew I was teaching African philosophy, the question always put to me was: Are there African philosophers and what have they written? I have not heard or read of any.) In other words, if there are no known academic philosophers in Africa, then there is no African philosophy.

Okupa (1998: 1) indicates that early visitors to Africa found all kinds of legal systems in operation and recognised familiar features, but their views were probably dismissed as romantic infatuation. Later, for legal scholars infused with Western positivism, African law was not law because it was just a vast jumble of local customary laws. Due to the prevalent orality of African cultures, lack of dependence on written documentation, and reliance on unacceptable 'primitive' value systems, it was considered impossible to find proper law.[24] While such difficulties may exist for foreign observers, Africans knew that they had laws, and their ancestors had laws, too, and they experienced their respective 'living law'. Such manifold breakdowns in communication when it comes to understanding culture-specific concepts of law are again marked by meaningful silences and gaps of communication.

The popular view that Africans would do best to copy either the Western (Christian) or Muslim systems of law to develop into civilised members of the modern world is rightly perceived as hurtful by many Africans. There

---

[23] I have similar experiences regarding Hindu law, which is either assumed to have been abolished or anglicised beyond recognition.

[24] Even Llewellyn and Hoebel (1941: 313) note that, in descriptions of African laws, there is no evidence of intricate developments akin to what they found among the Cheyenne.

is much evidence of protest. Okupa (1998: x) strongly refutes comments by earlier writers that 'Africa never invented anything, but has always received from others', an assumption which does not make sense if the claim that humankind started in Africa is correct.[25] Exasperation of the mature scholar who has to debunk hardened myths about the predominant reception of European laws is expressed by Okupa (1998: x):

> Even a simple human intellectual activity such as the formulation of laws is purported to have been received by Africans. This is one of those assumptions about Africa that has perpetuated the myth that Africa has no laws. Today, archaeologists, ethno-archaeologists and oral historians are beginning to piece the evidence together that there were multi-ethnic city states, as well as stateless societies in pre-colonial Africa since the beginning of the first millennium. There were public infrastructures of roads, city walls and market spaces, as well as exchange standards in gold dust, gold ingots, brass ingots, cowrie shells and barter.
>
> There was justice; anarchy did not reign. According to the records of Arab geographers and historians, African kings were renowned for their sense of justice. The communities formulated their own laws setting out some basic legal principles to meet their needs.

Defining his basic concepts of LAW, *Law* and law, Allott (1980: 4) sought to explain how Western people reached the premature conclusion that traditional Africans had no law. Allott debated what would happen if an imaginary person, who had never thought about LAW in the abstract, a kind of 'noble savage' (Allott, 1980: 3), were to look for *Law* comparable to his own among the files of the United States Supreme Court.[26] Allott (1980: 4) argued that '[h]e may find the imaginative effort too much, and deny that they are really *Laws* or laws'. In Africa, according to Allott (1980: 4):

> Exactly the reverse happened in the history of western jurists and their encounter with African customary legal systems. Equipped with their knowledge of western *Laws* at different points of time, they had constructed an abstract LAW, which to them expressed the essence of LAW. They came across customary legal systems, found they did not match with western *Laws* in various ways, and concluded that they therefore were not LAW, or that these societies did not have or recognise LAW.

As a legal anthropologist and an African area specialist with a theoretical interest in law, Moore (1978: 214) countered such legocentric preconceived notions by emphasising the inevitable interlinkages between law and society:

[25] Onyewuenyi (1991: 30) provides evidence of how cleverly European scholarship has been trying to ensure that African contributions to humankind do not become known, since this would challenge eurocentric hegemonistic claims.

[26] Allott (1984: 128–9) asked the reader to imagine the absence of writing in a Western-type legal system and speculated about the consequences.

> No society is without law; *ergo*, there is no society outside the purview of the 'legal anthropologist.' It is not merely difficult but virtually impossible to control the full range of the anthropological information. Every good ethnographic description contains a great deal of legal material, whether or not it is explicitly called 'law'. . . . Not only does every society have law, but virtually all significant social institutions also have a legal aspect. This means that to master the whole legal system of one society, procedural and substantive, one must master the whole institutional system of that society.

Moore's excellent review of legal anthropology research highlights that early legal authors behaved like legal technicians or administrators, not disclosing their underlying assumptions as postmodern methodology demands.[27] While early anthropologists like Malinowski (1926) tried to show how socio-legal relations between people worked in practice, among lawyers at the same time, 'dullish debates were going on over whether there was such a thing as law at all in primitive societies' (Moore, 1978: 219), much of this with an eye to African societies. Because early African law scholarship was produced by anthropologists rather than lawyers, various social inputs were emphasised and portrayed as social factors rather than legal structures. Radcliffe-Brown and Forde (1956: 1) emphasised typically that '[f]or the understanding of any aspect of the social life of an African people – economic, political or religious – it is essential to have a thorough knowledge of their system of kinship and marriage'. It is significant that this statement did not refer to law at all. Remarkably, historians have contributed little to African legal studies, though some important anthropological works have a historical slant.[28] Okupa (1998: 178) traces the progress of legal anthropological studies through various stages, emphasising the role of the 'tribal law school' and the 'functional tribal school', until modern lawyers, such as Elias (1956) and Allott (1960), took up a more legally focused study of African laws and thus showed that Africans did indeed have law.[29]

6.2 The search for African law and legal theory

Academic voices in defence of 'indigenous' African traditions and laws have grown louder over time. An international bibliography of African customary

---

[27] Moore (1978: 223) refers to Schapera (1938), a pioneering study of legal rules in an African society, which 'set an unprecedented standard for the detailed reporting of rules, but it did so without the slightest nod in the direction of theoretical questions, simply proceeding in a businesslike manner to describe as succinctly as possible such rules of law as were enforced by the Tswana'. For further references on this kind of study see Okupa (1998: 178ff.).

[28] See in particular Kuper and Kuper (1965). Chanock (1978: 80–1) notes that historians have mainly concentrated on the repugnancy clause and 'indirect rule', focusing on British legal elements.

[29] Allott (1984: 125) indicates that not all scholars agreed with his positive views of African laws, mentioning 'the challenge now not infrequently offered by those who deny that there are laws or legal systems (in a universal or comparative sense) in traditional African societies'. A detailed research survey is found in Woodman and Obilade (1995: xii–xxiv).

law (Okupa, 1998) vigorously advocates a continued search for the widely scattered principles and material relating to the study of traditional African laws.[30]
Manfred Hinz, Professor of Law at the University of Namibia, welcomed this
new bibliography in his preface, noting that it places the reading of African laws
and the painstaking dryness of bibliographical collections into a real African
context:

> After generations of missionaries, anthropologists and lawyers, whose first
> interest was to force African customary law into the Procrustean bed of
> either the bible, civilisation or a western paradigm of Rule of Law, African
> Customary Law begins to breathe again: to breathe the air of Africa. The
> flexibility of customary law stands a chance against Rule of Law campaigners
> who have never tried to understand the origins of customary law, but also
> never left the positivistic education behind which taught them a very narrow
> concept of Rule of Law.

Emphasising that '[t]he vision of this bibliography is of the dignity of Africa and
its mission to rediscover the principles of African Customary law', Hinz points
out that a recent major work on African laws (Woodman and Obilade, 1995)
denied an imminent prospect for the emergence of an African legal theory, but
not its relevance. Whether there is an African legal theory or not, evidence for
the past and present existence of African laws and their underlying theoretical
edifice exists in abundance and is undeniable. In her introduction, Okupa
(1998: ix) asks why African customary law has not fallen into abeyance, despite
the onslaught of authoritative modernity in the form of state laws, military
decrees and, one should add, repeated scholarly assertions about the futility
of using African customary laws as tools for sustainable future development.
The answer she gives is that people in Africa simply need their local laws, as
before, to survive. That appears to be a sensible message of enormous relevance
to a globally focused legal analysis: laws are not just there for lawyers; laws are
about life and real people. Allott (1984: 124) asserted that '[t]he legal system is
not a self-justifying system. Law is merely instrumental to certain ends, notably
the good order of society and the apportionment of claims and responsibilities
within it; and thus the question relates rather to the effective ordering of society.'
Legocentric hubris, and a certain blindness when it comes to African laws, can
be identified in David and Brierley's (1978: 507) observation that traditional
African law does not make a clear-cut distinction between juridical and moral
obligations, which led to some strange conclusions:

> While this distinction can be drawn in respect of African customs them-
> selves by European jurists, it is, for the Africans, difficult to understand in
> a country where there is neither any legal science nor jurists. In the same
> way, the distinctions between public and private law, civil and criminal law,
> law and equity, *a fortiori*, unknown; the law of property, contract and

---

[30] Woodman and Obilade (1995) highlight the earlier efforts of Jacques Vanderlinden in
producing a series of *African law bibliographies* with entries in many languages.

tort, linked to the notion of status, depend upon, or form part of, the law of persons. In the face of this apparently considerable confusion, European authors have asked themselves whether it is artificial to attempt to seek out our western ideas of law and whether the customary laws of Africa and Malagasy ought not, more properly, to form the subject of anthropological rather than legal research.

Awareness of interlinkedness and of what Santos (1995) calls 'interlegality' is here portrayed as confusion of the mind, much in the same way that legal pluralism has been portrayed as messy. These authors appear to suggest, firstly, that Africans do not understand their law because they do not have lawyers to explain it to them. This confirms that they did not grasp the internal structure of African laws and their integral interaction with societies. The confusion is clearly that of the observer, not the observed. The second point made above, that the private/public divide is not drawn in the same way as in European laws, reinforces evidence of the lack of plurality-consciousness: traditional legal systems know such distinctions, but draw lines differently than modern Western scholarship. The final suggestion, that it may be better to treat traditional African laws as a matter of anthropology, reflects adherence to old negative views about African laws as non-laws. Against such barriers to the pursuit of knowledge, Allott (1968: 132) took an expressly historical approach to studying legal phenomena, laying open the assumptions of evolutionist scholarship:[31]

> The picture commonly built up of the universal pattern of legal develop-ment is from one where the society was small, based on kinship, techno-logically backward, and dominated by the hopes and fears of the other world just as much as by the rigours of the present, to one which is large, complex, equipped with an advanced technology, and controlled by secular or materialistic preoccupations. The laws have, on this view, correspond-ingly developed: unwritten customary laws based on religious belief and sanctioned by religious practices give way, it is said, to legislated laws admin-istered and studied by professional lawyers, where the sanctions now rest on the enhanced power of the state machinery rather than on fear of the supernatural or the strong arm of the complainant.

Allott (1968: 133) further highlighted how such speculations, in particular the assumption that law in its developed form needs to be manifested in codi-fied form, automatically marginalised the study and understanding of African laws:

> Speculative thought has dominated historical jurisprudence. From a few ambiguous clues provided by classical Roman law, eked out by reference to Hindu and Scandinavian sources, Maine was willing to infer a general

---

[31] Allott (1984: 127) held Sir Henry Maine responsible for creating eurocentric and legocen-tric images about the nature of law. See also Allott (1980: 169).

historical law of the disintegration of the family and the movement of 'progressive societies from status to contract.' The evidence from African laws is much fuller. It enables us to say whether such laws hold for these simpler societies in the nineteenth and twentieth centuries. Relatively hard facts (though the interpretation of some of them is hotly contested) thus take the place of inference and speculation.

Before Allott (1980) produced his challenging study on the limits of law with numerous examples from African jurisdictions, vigorously illustrating the lively existence of 'indigenous' African laws, Moore (1978) had published fieldwork-based work demonstrating the realities of legal pluralism in colonial and post-colonial Africa and the strength of local elements in interaction with new centralising forces (see also Moore, 1986). Everybody concerned realised the enormity of the task, but the general paradigm was established: law, even as modern state law, could not be properly studied in isolation if one wanted to understand how a particular legal system in Africa worked in social reality. To restrict oneself to studying formal state laws would allow only a severely limited vision of the fullness of legal reality.[32] African legal scholarship needed to be necessarily multi-layered, interdisciplinary, and aware of many hidden aspects of the law that might not interest the practising lawyer, but were relevant for deep socio-legal analysis. Allott (1968: 133–4) had earlier warned that different manifestations of law would be encountered by students of African laws and had emphasised that unwritten African laws were laws:

> To say that there were no law books is not to say that there were no well-recognised principles or rules of law, or no specialists in legal theory and procedure. The African evidence thus contradicts Maine's speculation (p. 7) that 'Law scarcely reached the footing of custom: it is rather a habit.' In some respects African law could be highly formal (especially with the routines for the creation of a marriage, the transfer of property, or the disposal of an estate). Every adult member of the community might be expected to know the generally accepted principles of law which obtained there, but legal specialists were also recognised in many societies, persons who by reason either of their training (which was often hereditary) or of their frequent involvement in legal disputes were esteemed to know more of the law and its implications than the ordinary citizen.

Allott (1968: 132) placed African laws as customary laws into the wider context of 'ethno-jurisprudence', which would include customary laws of the ancient Greeks, Germans and Anglo-Saxons, as well as American Indian, Indonesian and Polynesian laws, and many others. He argued that significant resemblances between such kinds of customary law outweigh the differences, and that the

---

[32] The criticisms elaborated in Chiba's theory of the three-level structure of laws and their interaction were therefore applied by Africa-related socio-legal scholarship well before Chiba (1986) was published.

study of African law had much to offer for a better understanding of customary laws worldwide. This debate has resurfaced now in discussions of 'chthonic laws', seen as a kind of 'folk law'.[33] Within the historical school of jurisprudence as represented by von Savigny and others (chapter 2, section 2.2) such legal traditions cannot be understood through positivist methodology. As Glenn (2004: 60) notes, '[f]olk law is also perilously close to folk lore', indicating a risk that such laws will not be recognised as law.[34] Glenn (2004: 60) attempts a legal definition of chthonic laws, which relates to 'people who live ecological lives by being chthonic, that is, by living in or in close harmony with the earth'. On that count, all Asian and African legal systems would more or less qualify as chthonic laws. Glenn (2004: 61) makes an attempt 'to describe a tradition by criteria internal to itself, as opposed to imposed criteria. It is an attempt to see the tradition from within, in spite of all the problems of language and perception.' This methodological approach, taking an internal perspective, should be a methodological requirement for all comparative legal work. Regarding a more specific description of what a chthonic legal system involves, Glenn (2004: 61) writes:

> There was no point of origin of a chthonic legal tradition. There was no recorded revelation; no dramatic rupture from other traditions; no single, literally unforgettable achievement. A chthonic legal tradition simply emerged, as experience grew and orality and memory did their work. Since all people of the earth are descended from people who were chthonic, all other traditions have emerged in contrast to chthonic tradition. It is the oldest of traditions; its chain of traditio is as long as the history of humanity.

In his treatment of such legal systems, Glenn subsumes African laws, thus veiling the culture-specific, uniquely indigenous elements of traditional African laws and their internal diversity. He portrays chthonic systems well, highlighting the key elements of orality and informality, from which numerous consequences flow for the practical application and operation of such laws. Of course, this methodology contradicts the inherent reservations of many people about the existence of traditional African laws. One can immediately see how conservative, essentially racist, anti-African assumptions and modernist views about the inherent superiority of international legal norms and regulations go hand in hand with positivist assertions that only certain people in the world have valid laws.

Apart from questioning the existence of law in Africa, the use of African law terminology has been much contested. Allott (1965: 217–19) portrayed

---

[33] That term is also used by Woodman (1988) in an interesting article on the creation of customary laws in Ghana and Nigeria, apart from lawyers' customary law and sociologists' customary law. For details on chthonic laws, see Glenn (2000: 56–85; 2004: 59–91).

[34] Glenn avoids the term 'native law', which is probably seen as tainted. In a North American context, it has of course specific meanings.

the gradual changes in the nomenclature and perceptions of African laws and identified subtle, 'faintly derogatory implications' (p. 218) in the use of certain terms.[35] More recently, Okupa (1998: ix) justified her choice of terminology:

> It is necessary for me to explain the use of the term 'indigenous law'...
> [V]arious terms have been used by scholars to designate the systems of laws, norms and customs found in Africa. Sometimes, it is referred to as 'native law', 'native laws and customs', 'native customary law', 'primitive law', 'folk law', 'informal law', 'living law', 'positive morality', 'non-state law', 'non-government law', 'autogenous regulation', 'native justice', 'indigenous law', 'customary law', 'people's law', 'vernacular law'. There is an ongoing debate among international Africanists as to the conceptual question of nomenclature, and the nature of African law. The terminology argument either illuminates or conceals the scholar's preference of the meaning of 'law' as it applies to the African phenomena.
>
> My preference is for the use of 'indigenous law' when it is applied to a particular community, 'tribe' or ethnic group . . . because the ethical basis of the principles of their law is indigenous to that particular community.

This term is similarly preferred by Mensah-Brown (1976: 18), who also uses 'autochthonous law'. Okupa (1998: ix–x) further defines indigenous African laws as 'a related family of laws composed of principles of moral philosophy and prescriptions of behaviours recognised by the dominant patrilineal or matrilineal groups within each specific society'. Following colonial interference, various forms of African state law remained only one possible form or manifestation of African laws, and the indigenous laws of the various communities, 'tribes' or 'ethnic groups' within a state could be termed the 'customary law' as distinct from the state law. Okupa (1998: xiii) emphasises that the various explanations for the continuing importance of indigenous or customary African laws should leave no doubt that African people would remain serious about observing and preserving their laws and reports that, '[f]rom the empirical evidence, it is apparent that most people take their indigenous law very seriously' (p. xiii). While she emphasises socio-economic reasons for the continuation of traditional legal systems, a different conceptual perspective is presented by Glenn (2004: 71–2). There is simply no escape route from the global ambit of chthonic laws:

> Chthonic laws will therefore protect you, but you have few means of protecting yourself against it . . . If no one can create the tradition, no one can escape its teaching and the roles it defines, except by departure (and there may be no place to go). This represents a classic problem that no one, anywhere, has solved.

[35] Mensah-Brown (1976: 31) reports that, during the 1970s, Ghana proscribed the use of the word 'tribe' and its derivatives. In the 1960s, Kenya replaced the word 'native' wherever it occurred in legislation with 'African law and custom'.

African laws, whether one calls them 'chthonic', 'native' or 'indigenous', or classifies them into different types of culture-specific local African laws, do exist as lived and living realities of human existence. The major challenge for all legal scholars and practitioners seeking to make sense of them has been to unravel their culture-specific conceptual and practical complexities and to find their 'identity postulates' (Chiba, 1989: 180). African laws may be oral, but they are definitely not simple. They may be informal and plurality-conscious, but that does not mean that anything goes. They may be flexible, but there are limits to such flexibility. Since legal positivist methodologies of research and analysis on their own are insufficient, locating indigenous African laws requires a plurality-conscious, multidisciplinary approach which must be at liberty to cross academic boundaries as and when required to follow the traces of oral traditions and local practices.[36] As indicated earlier, there have been interesting recent debates about the scope for African legal theory (Woodman and Obilade, 1995: xi–xxix). This debate is not recent, as Kuper and Kuper (1965: 17) explicitly claimed a place for African theories of law within the context of debates about the continent's adaptation and development processes:

> The adaptation of African systems of law will be affected not only by the theories of law of the colonial powers or of Islam, but also by African theories of law, whether explicitly formulated or implicit in legal institutions. Probably there are many different theories of law in African societies, varying perhaps in their relative emphasis on imperium, tradition, and divine revelation. They have not been much studied in the past. Now emancipation from colonial rule is stimulating this study. Denigration of African society and law naturally provokes the demonstration that traditional African societies were regulated by just and efficient systems of law . . . Racial counterassertation may emphasize a more democratic participation in the work of the courts, or deeper concern in African law for the human quality of a person, or stronger group consciousness and a more sensitive awareness of the social context, encouraging the reconciliation of persons rather than the apportionment of blame, regardless of disruptive social consequences.

More important than various observations about the counterassertiveness of African arguments is the suggestion that variant theories of law might vacillate between the triangle of state, society and religion or, in the terminology of the Kupers, quoted above, 'imperium, tradition and divine revelation'. This approximates the conceptual triangular model developed by the present study (chapter 3, section 3.8). As anthropologists, the Kupers were less interested in legal theory than in the political dimensions of the creation of an African theory of law, which they portray as an aspect of the complex process of reasserting

---

[36] Kuper and Kuper (1965: 5) disagreed with Hart's formalist distinction of 'primary and secondary rules' as a useful measure for the existence of law, stressing that '[a] flexible and eclectic approach, rather than a firm semantic commitment, seems necessary'.

African values and concepts against the eurocentric domination of legal and political science. This is evident when Kuper and Kuper (1965: 17) emphasise that '[m]any pressures, political, economic, and social, impel the quest for appropriate theories of African law'. They listed the need for stability and unity in newly independent states; the internal struggles for power, in which theories of law may be used as political tools; economic pressures and the search for effective modernisation strategies; debates about socialism versus capitalism, as well as Pan-Africanism. In their conclusion, Kuper and Kuper (1965: 17–18) warn that modern legal thinking about African legal theories will be dominated by positivist assumptions:

> It is in such milieus of thought and action that theories of African law may emerge as by-products of political and economic processes. The changed situation from colonial subjugation to national independence, with the realization of sovereignty and the compulsions to modernize, seems likely to encourage an emphasis on imperium as the source of law. The influence of purely legal considerations, such as a tradition of civil or common or sacred law, may not be decisive. In many respects, it may convey more understanding to analyze the new theories of law in the period of their emergence as ideologies. Once established, they no doubt exert an independent influence on other aspects of the society.

The above discussion clearly indicates that legal positivism by itself may not be central and decisive, but that political considerations would dominate. While the close links between politics and state-made laws are highlighted in this debate, the competing centrality of social aspects does not receive enough recognition as a potential ingredient for an emerging postcolonial African theory of law. The present plurality-focused legal analysis offers a fuller picture of African legal thought and practice as a complex expression of the aspirations of all African people within their specific socio-cultural, legal and political environments, recognising that African legal systems are as complex, internally diverse and dynamic as other legal systems. Considering recent developments of African legal theory, Woodman and Obilade (1995: xxiv) first establish an ideal definition of legal theory, stipulating that, as a construct built within this field, it should be 'a comprehensive, coherent analysis of the principal features of law or legal systems'. Woodman and Obilade (1995: xxv) use this definition to suggest that 'there is no imminent prospect of the emergence of an African legal theory in this sense'. But what is a comprehensive, coherent analysis of the principal features of law or legal systems? Given the fundamental disagreements in the scholarly world over the nature of law, and over the status of African customary laws as law, how can we assume that there could be agreement over what is comprehensive and, even more so, over what is coherent? Woodman and Obilade collected significant evidence of theoretical writing on African laws which provides clear pointers to future work. Why do we refuse to recognise that this writing amounts to a theory? The final suggestion by Woodman and Obilade (1995: xxvi) that there is no value in African legal theory as such, and that it should be incorporated into global legal theory and jurisprudence, seems to deny African legal theory a voice of its own. It is instructive to examine this issue in more detail.

Their discussion begins with the statement that the title of their book 'implies the possibility of a literature devoted to distinctively African legal theory' (Woodman and Obilade, 1995: xi), while 'it is not immediately obvious how this field may be delimited' (p. xi). African legal theory can mean neither a body of thought first formulated in Africa, nor something formulated by Africans, it must be something else. The authors suggest 'that African legal theory, if it exists, must be distinguished by a predominant concern with characteristic features of African laws' (p. xi). They continue:

> That proposal pushes the enquiry back to the question: what are the characteristic features of African laws? The subject-matter which requires investigation is initially identified by social geography. African laws are the laws of societies indigenous to Africa. This category has blurred edges but a firm core, and consideration of doubtful cases need not detain us.

Since it might be wrong to assume that African societies have common characteristic features, the authors insist that we must continue to speak of 'African laws' rather than 'African law'. African law is thus in good company as an internally plural conglomerate and conforms to the characteristics of other major legal systems of the world. Next, Woodman and Obilade (1995: xi) identify three major factors which make African laws distinctive. These are the experience of colonisation and the large-scale reception of law, the aspiration to use law as a tool for legal development, and the continuing importance of indigenous customary laws. While these three features are not unique to law in Africa (p. xii), it is suggested that their particular combination may well be a key feature of African laws. Considering the available written material, the authors assert that '[i]t cannot be claimed that there is yet even one developed African legal theory with a distinct content' (p. xiii). Relying on an African writer, they neither find an intellectual tradition in Africa, nor do they hold out hope, in view of the absence of such a tradition and resource problems, for the development of African jurisprudential endeavours. They note that 'there is a great deal of theoretical reflection in Africa – both popular and specialist – about legal matters' (p. xiii), that 'there is clearly concern with and interest in the development of theory. Why, then, is there not yet an African legal theory?' (p. xiii).

This negative conclusion can be challenged. For a start, the African author cited as claiming that there is no intellectual tradition in Africa did not really say this; rather he made a different theoretical point.[37] Ojwang (1995: 351)

---

[37] Actually, this is also noted by Woodman and Obilade (1995: xxiii and xxv).

considered the possibility of a jurisprudence of development and the focus on rights, finding that writers on African legal issues, whether Africans or African-ists, 'take for granted an operational linkage with Euro-American legal tradition and juristic thinking, hardly at all subjecting this to the test of original analysis' (p. 351). This, according to Ojwang (1995: 351–2), is quite unsatisfactory:

> A scholar involved in the sphere of African legal development ought to address certain basic questions: Is there a legal theory that would explain the particular characteristics of the law and the legal process in the form in which they operate in Africa? Do Africans, taken as a general category, manifest any peculiar approach to legal thought? Or is Africa merely an appendage of the Euro-American world, in terms of perception on law and the legal process?

Ojwang (1995: 352) does not answer these questions and merely indicates his hypothesis that 'the dominant notions of legal rights and of justiciability, are rather skewed and mainly reflect the experience of the industrialised countries of the West'. Ojwang (1995: 378) argues that a 'jurisprudence of development' offers the most appropriate agenda for African scholars of legal theory. Various angles of this debates continue to occupy many minds, now also in relation to human rights (An-Na'im, 2002a) and globalisation (Cheru, 2002). Setting out a development-conscious approach to legal theory, Ojwang (1995: 378) suggests a domestication of governmental machineries in Africa so as 'to serve the social purposes of Africa in an authentic fashion'; the modern state and its laws should be reconstructed to suit the needs of society. Ojwang (1995: 379) emphasises that '[t]he most important concern and reality is the current low level of social, economic and political development. This undermines the material basis to support schemes for the enhancement of legal rights.' However, he does not ask whether the state and the official legal system are actually more a hindrance than a help to development. His approach is not radical enough and remains too closely wedded to the foreign positivist models that he criticises as unsuitable.[38] Here is a theoretically oriented African author, attempting more than simply calling for placative Africanisation or grappling with the visible problems of 'underdevelopment' in Africa, but not critical enough about the state. This is also not a people-centred theory, nor is it a holistic approach, simply a materialism-oriented theory of development, too influenced by Western models, and simply not African enough in content or approach.[39] Like Hooker (1975), it appears that Ojwang (1995) remains enchained in positivist thought.

[38] Woodman and Obilade (1995: xxv) also note that Ojwang seems to follow the very route he wishes to escape and point to Chiba (1984) for a more thorough critique of Western legal theories.

[39] For an elaborate African critique of Western models of development see Maathai (1995), now holder of the Nobel Peace Prize, 2004.

Woodman and Obilade (1995: xiii) indicate that authors who might want to develop an African legal theory 'may also find it more attractive to contribute to the jurisprudential debates of the west'. Indeed, if one wants to develop a field that is not supposed to exist, one faces many more obstacles than one's own limitations of skills and knowledge. Seeking to contribute to a larger debate, the academic jurist as 'a licensed dilettante as well as a hired subversive' (Twining, 2000: 90) is forced to speculate beyond known boundaries. Ojwang (1995) apparently played safe and chose a well-trodden path. But, by following models of Western scholarship, he ended up in a vicious circle, depriving scholarship on African laws of crucial new energies. Thinking about avenues for developing legal theory, Woodman and Obilade (1995: xiv) stress that an emphasis on customary law might well be a crucial element of African legal theory:

> Customary laws structure most social life in Africa. In this continent any general theory of law must give attention to customary laws, if only to argue (contrary to linguistic usage) that they do not belong to the subject-matter of legal theory. There has indeed been a tendency to equate African law with African customary law in discussion of the theory, concepts, classification and content of African law.

Surely, equating African customary law with African law makes sense, provided it is not taken to mean that other forms of law do not exist in Africa? A methodological approach that emphasises the predominance and factually dominant position of African customary laws, as opposed to legal approaches that take a positivist stance or a religion-centred approach, seems viable. However, merely emphasising the importance of social norms as legal norms does not pay sufficient attention to the dynamic interaction which Chiba (1986, 1989) and the triangular model of the current study emphasise. A plurality-conscious interactive approach would lead towards the conclusion that traditional African laws appear to value the balanced interaction of all three elements of the triangle and seek to privilege none. This commonsensical pluralist message is one that comparative legal scholarship does not convey. It reflects an unwillingness to recognise plurality as normal, and seeks always to assert the dominance of one factor over others. Traditional African law turns out to be intrinsically sensitive to plurality and dynamic interaction, and thus is truly holistic, perhaps more so than other legal systems. Most legal scholars instinctively look for certainty and dominance of one element rather than interactive fusion with fuzzy boundaries. But, if theory and reality do not match, more questions should be asked about the theory, rather than denying the validity of reality. Scholarship on African law, as the above examples show, continues to suffer from legocentric myopia and has not been ready to embrace the proclivity for difference that Legrand (1996) advised.

Woodman and Obilade (1995: xviii) indicate that, by questioning the assumption that African customary law may not be law, 'African legal theory might assist in the development of legal theory generally'. The authors suggest that this work has not been done and seem to expect proof of a theory. But what more is there to prove? What sense do we make of the numerous statements by African lawyers, refuting the claims of Western 'analysts' about the alleged absence of African laws? When Western scholarship asserts that something is a fact, it becomes a fact, it might even become a theory, which then becomes hard to debunk.[40] When African or Asian authors do the same, it tends to be disregarded and treated as unscientific. Is global scholarship therefore applying different criteria for the definition of 'theory', depending on who writes? Or is there something inherently wrong, for legal scholarship, in seeking to develop an African legal theory? While Woodman and Obilade do not question the need for an African legal theory as such, they want to see it subsumed in a global jurisprudence. Can the two not co-exist? Is African legal theory not something that could also be valid in its own right? The final argument in Woodman and Obilade (1995: xxv–xxvi) leaves doubts over the proper balance between globalising trends and paying attention to regional and local particularities:

> [I]t is submitted that a programme to construct an entirely new African legal theory or set of theories would be intellectually wasteful and probably in the end futile. A great deal in the existing, western literature of legal theory enhances our understanding. While no doubt it needs modification in order to provide equal understanding of law in Africa, it would seem likely, since societies in both the west and Africa are human societies, that the necessary modifications are less than total abandonment and replacement. The construction of new theories would be like reinventing the wheel in order to use a different type of road.
>
> The programme which is suggested would aim to use African legal experience to contribute to general legal theory. Current legal theory is deficient in so far as it advances general propositions about law which are true of western but not of African experience. It can clearly be improved by reference to such experience. This should not be seen as a contribution from Africa to western theory. To view the process thus is to concede ownership of legal theory to the west, and that is effectively a surrender to the claims of western ethnocentrism. The proponents of African legal theory are not required to choose between being camp followers of the western intellectual world or setting up their own, unique theoretical system. They may instead play a significant part in the development of a global jurisprudence.

These are important, constructive comments for promoting a global theory of law, advising against the reinvention of wheels and opposing ethnocentric claims to European ownership of global jurisprudence. But as previous chapters showed, there is no agreement over the nature of law, let alone its global ownership, even among Western scholars. One needs to think, therefore, about

---

[40] See in this context Griffiths (1986) and his counter-assertion that legal pluralism is a fact (chapter 2, section 2.5.3).

the scope for readjusting the deficient general propositions that different types of Western jurisprudence make about law rather than discarding them altogether. We need to build on existing knowledge, rather than assuming we could start afresh.[41] Instead of reinventing wheels, one might look at a reconstruction process, a careful testing of existing knowledge, leading to a new bricolage made up of existing known components. If the aim is to offer the theoreticians of African law a place in international debates about the nature of law, we may find that all the places at the table have already been taken and nothing really new can be said. The main contribution of African legal theories would then be to bring to this global table a myriad of culture-specific combinations of various types of laws. That in itself would be a never-ending task, but one suspects that there may be more to say. Earlier lessons from history, for example when St Augustine became Christian and was appropriated by Europe, seem instructive.[42] Who and what will guarantee that the contributions of African scholarship will be valued appropriately as African contributions? That remains a major problem.

I agree with Woodman and Obilade, as cited above, that attention to customary laws and their continued relevance in modern Africa today must be a key ingredient for an Africa-centred approach to legal theory. But this does not mean that customary law in Africa ever ruled the roost to the exclusion of all other potential sources of law. In particular, various African assumptions about pre-existing superhuman forces will exert their own culture-specific influences (Section 6.3.3), and various forms of African state structures will be relevant, too. Thus, as for Hindu and Islamic law, an analytical starting point could be that the primary power centre of all African legal activity lies outside the realm of human law-making and somewhere in the area of 'religion' or values. There is a shared assumption in all African legal systems concerning the existence of a superhuman order of some kind, undefinable but ever-present, to which everyone and everything is somehow subject. Everything will be evaluated and in some form judged against that culture-specific backdrop, which is why some writers have proposed that African laws are in essence religious laws (e.g. Allott, 1968: 131). Perhaps that suggestion relates to a simple general principle, a potentially universal pattern which applies all over the world, except in systems where Western liberalism seeks to suggest that God in any form is not involved in law-making (Unger, 1976). Against this untypical modernist development, at least throughout Asia and Africa, the basic chthonic principle of a 'religious' natural law appears to bind African laws as much

---

[41] Such arguments also appear in Islamic debates about the closing of the gates of *ijtihad* (chapter 5).

[42] Chiba (1984) discusses this in detail and doubts the willingness of scholars to accept the unjustified ethnocentrism of Western legal theory.

as Hindu and Islamic laws and many other legal systems in the world. The culture-specific content of the various African laws produces different names and terms for concepts of superhuman order and their different manifestations (Section 6.3.2). Any human form of rule-making, any socio-legal organisation of any kind – and that includes custom – can therefore be seen as secondary and will need to be measured against, and harmonised with, the perceived expectations of that superhuman order – which is, however, itself a cultural construct. This is what many legal theorists appear to have forgotten in the frantic clamour to assert rationality over religion, or the reactionary defence of religion against such claims. Hindus assume they are expected to behave in certain appropriate ways which cannot be fully defined in advance and experience mindboggling confusions about *karma* and *dharma*. Muslims are brought up to believe that God will judge them after death. Many Buddhists of various descriptions may constantly calculate their cosmic bank balances and seek to achieve their culture-specific vision of salvation and the afterlife. Africans, as this chapter shows in detail, have their own ideas about such matters, as have the Chinese (chapter 7). To research such cultural constructs of 'religion' and its various dimensions requires more than legal skills and knowledge, but to deny their legal relevance is intellectually dishonest and has been damaging to comparative legal scholarship and especially to the project of constructing a global legal theory.

Coupled with the undeniable presence of positivism in its many forms, globality-conscious legal analysis means that emphasising a central role for customary laws in African legal systems cannot by itself make the African experience unique. The present comparative analysis has earlier demonstrated the importance of customary laws and cultural norms for South Asian societies and laws (chapter 4) and for Islamic legal systems (chapter 5), but they were never ruling the entire legal field to the exclusion of other sources of law. Why should we expect anything different for African laws? Selective blindness in theory grounds inadequate scholarship, as Kuper and Kuper (1965: 5) stressed a long time ago:

> The social scientist must, however, attempt both to interpret single, historically unique societies and to relate and classify them in more general categories. To refuse to speak of law, politics or religion because nothing quite like them is to be found in other societies would be to refuse recognition of the study of 'society' as something common to all forms of human existence.

The present chapter provides evidence that the suggested focus on 'society' or 'community' as the primary locus of human law-making and dispute settlement among Africans may well be the individual human brain. Legal analysts will tend to be myopic in this regard, arguing that mental dispute settlement is not a legal activity. But the crucial role of individual agency in any form of human application of laws can hardly be denied.[43] African laws may sound idealistic about negotiated dispute settlement, emphasising harmony and the need to work together. They still tend to rely ultimately on individual self-controlled order mechanisms, expecting every individual to do the right thing at the right time within specific social contexts. As demonstrated for Hindu law (chapter 4, section 4.3), invisible mechanisms of mental dispute settlement are a central but largely unexpressed cultural expectation. Self-controlled order is perceived not only as inherently good, it is systemically required. This remains most obvious in chthonic contexts, where the inherent requirement is, at all times, to remain in balance with nature and the environment. The interlinkages of the legal and the religious, the overlap of crime and sin, ultimately the need to restore any imbalance through human action, which may or may not include explicitly ritual action, was evident in Hindu and to some extent also in Muslim law and appear in African laws, too. These highly sophisticated methods of socio-legal organisation are designed to produce harmony not just among the living, but for the larger world (Maathai, 1995). It appears that Africans have known this all along. While the journey through African law may be arduous, I believe with Woodman and Obilade (1995: xxvi) that the detailed study of African laws can make a valuable contribution to the development of a globally focused jurisprudence, even if at the end it only reinforces a commonsensical, pluralistic and culture-specific message that may have been forgotten in the frantic search for 'modernity'.

6.3 The nature of traditional African laws

In this section, the development of traditional African laws is portrayed as a journey through history. The complex webs of traditional African legal systems are analysed by emphasising, in turn, the various interconnected elements of traditional African worldviews and assumptions about the world as a whole, African customs and their development, morality and religion, and finally processes of dispute settlement. Initially, early evidence from Africa, on which there is not much to say, sets the scene for the external and often negative evaluations of early African laws.

6.3.1 Reflections of early knowledge

Allott (1968: 133) emphasises that '[o]ur knowledge of the customary laws of antiquity is meagre, despite the clues which may be gleaned from Tacitus and Homer'. Fisch (1998: 85) reports in the context of a comparative global study

---

[43] On the neglected role of the individual see Takirambudde (1982).

on death rituals, especially the processes of following others in death,[44] that there is much more documentary evidence from Africa on this topic than from anywhere else in the world. While many early reports were based on hearsay rather than direct observation, Fisch (1998: 86–7) notes that many European observers were keen to portray Africans as cruel barbarians and purposely exaggerated their accounts to justify colonialism and the slave trade. From a comparative legal perspective, David and Brierley (1978: 505) indicate that there were many different ancestral customs in the vast African territory and paint a broad, general picture:

> The parts of Africa south of the Sahara . . . were ruled for centuries by their own ancestral customary laws. Obedience to custom was generally spontaneous since it was thought that one was obliged to live as one's ancestors had; the fear of supernatural powers and of group opinion were most often sufficient to assure a respect for the traditional ways of life. The fairly complex social system had means for the resolution of disputes or the creation of new rules of conduct when new circumstances created fresh problems for the community in question.

A general picture of complexity in local, unwritten, informal, non-technical legal systems is evident from the literature. Laws were deeply integrated in society, flexible and dynamic. While this could be seen as desirable attributes of a legal system, many early observers and latecomers who gazed at the past from a vast distance produced inadequate, even hostile interpretations. Mensah-Brown (1976: 22) remarked critically:

> Very often indigenous African law is indiscriminately defined in terms of a law derived from custom. As a result it has for some time been (and still is) projected as a phenomenon with origins in usages established in a nebulous, immemorial past by the ancestral founding fathers of a given African community, and sacredly handed on to succeeding generations and solemnly observed by the community. First of all, indigenous African law . . . is not synonymous with customary law. Secondly, the view assumes that indigenous law is a static phenomenon. This position does not correspond with living realities. It has been (and is still being) debunked by the interaction of the juridical behaviour of the communities with the imperatives of political, socio-economic and related variables prevailing at various given points in time.

Many African writers have reacted defensively to observations about the primitive nature of Africans and their laws. Ebo (1995: 33) protests that '[i]n their

---

[44] Fisch (1998: 89–128) shows in detail that such ritual killings had an institutionalised character and were closely linked to assumptions about religious core elements as well as African political philosophy. Such practices were designed to provide ritual support to political structures of a community, but they could be abused for the ritual aggrandisement of powerful individuals.

pristine state of society, Nigerian people were not lawless men living in a state of permanent anarchy. They observed elaborate rules of law, which were seldom apparent to a casual observer because they were not codified but formed a part and parcel of the fabric of local tradition.' Okupa (1998: 63) portrays the image of brutality in African societies and life as a convenient colonial invention to justify the imposition of foreign laws and the subjugation of the 'natives':

> It is a myth that pre-colonial African societies were anarchical and brutal; a society where tribesmen were nearly always at the ready to throw poisoned spear heads at each other. Violence and cruelty in human society have nothing to do with men's ethnic origin, as illustrated by twentieth century wars . . . As such, African societies did not have a monopoly of violence, some indigenous communities were as beastly and cruel as the societies of the colonial powers. The myth of violence and brutality were perpetuated to justify the application of colonial penal laws, public hangings and incarceration.

Other authors indicate that early misconceptions led later to the 'propagation of mutilated and confused exposition which required rectification and clarification with the tools of informed African jurisprudence' (Mensah-Brown, 1976: 22). Allott (1968: 135) emphasised against such earlier reflections of deliberate distortions that traditional African law 'is not an arcane mystery but a matter of public concern'. He also stressed that rather than learned debates about technical legal details or procedural niceties, justice in line with the facts and circumstances of each particular case, rather than fixed principles, was considered most important. As a result, according to Allott (1968: 133), '[a] broader, more ambitious and humane approach dominated the law, namely to render essential justice in the particular case in conformity with the general principles and the appropriate patterns of behaviour recognised by custom for each relationship or transaction'. Allott (1968: 131) therefore emphasised that legal research in Africa offered unique methodological insights:

> The legal scientist thus finds in Africa the possibility (so often denied to him elsewhere) of investigating the consequences of a variation in legal structure where other elements in the social situation remain constant. Society A recognises exclusively matrilineal succession, for instance; its neighbour, society B, comparable in all respects except this, recognises patrilineal succession; the effect of this difference on parental authority, the structure of the corporate family, or the rights of an inheritor can be readily compared. Such a situation, for example, prevails among some of the peoples of southern Ghana, and among different Ibo-speaking peoples of south-eastern Nigeria.

A useful comparative perspective was provided by Allott (1968: 131), who introduced a major article on African law in a positive spirit. Rather than questioning the existence of African laws, he tried to compare it with other legal systems:

> AFRICAN LAW has many points of contact with the other legal systems
> . . . Like Jewish, Islamic and Hindu law, for instance, it is, though not a
> religious law in a strict sense, yet a system predicated upon a particular
> set of supernatural beliefs and ritual practices. Like Chinese law, its main
> source of law has been ancestral custom. But equally there are profound
> differences which strike the observer: of these the most notable are that this
> is the law of preliterate societies, and that it is not (perhaps in consequence
> of this) a jurist's law. Most important of all, it is not (and here it differs
> radically from all the other systems represented here) a single system, even
> one with variant schools, but rather a family of systems which share no
> traceable common parent.

The intimate linkage of law with the socio-cultural environment, skilfully indicated in this statement, suggests that socio-legal approaches are essential for
researching African laws. But there is no deliberation about whether on its own
this would be sufficient. Like traditional Hindu law and Chinese law, African
law is ultimately people-centred, not state-focused. For African laws generally,
Okupa (1998: x) emphasised that '[i]t is a person's relationship to his or her
community and the character of that person that make up the indigenous law
and count as virtues and justice. Indigenous law is the acceptable norms that
most people in the community comply with.'

The old question whether traditional Africans had rules, or just norms, has
led to protracted debates. These continue,[45] but seem pointless: the evidence is
clearly that early Africans lived by law-like rules and norms, and that they used
a variety of processes to apply and develop such normative plurality. Much of
this would have been invisible because norms and processes in a self-controlled
order system remain intangible. Debate may not be necessary when everyone
in society seems to know how to maintain harmony. In that idealistic sense
– for it could not be a permanent state of affairs given human nature – even
the simplest African societies would have had functional equivalents, however
invisible and undeveloped, of primary and secondary rules, which Hart saw as
a precondition for the existence of law. Early African societies, so much is clear,
certainly had laws, but they did not manifest themselves as formal laws. In fact
they might be heard rather than seen, even today, since so much depends on
the spoken word in the orality-focused context of traditional African societies.

6.3.2 African worldviews and their conceptual implications

The generally integrated, holistic nature of African laws is noted by many writers, but with quite different consequences, since not all scholars writing on
African laws have been able to make sense of such concepts.[46] Sanders (1987: 39)

---

[45] For a brief overview of the various positions see Woodman and Obilade (1995: xvii).
[46] Early collective efforts to understand the quintessence of the traditional African way of
life are reported in Fortes and Dieterlen (1965).

emphasised that '[t]ogetherness is what law is about', and relied on Allott's (1980: 96–7) discussion of Somali *heer*, 'custom', 'contract' and 'law', which originally meant the rope used to bind or fasten the roof of the nomadic Somalis' huts. David and Brierley (1978: 5–6) started off well:

> In the African mind, ancestral custom is linked to a mythical order of the universe. To obey custom is to pay respect to one's ancestors whose remains are fused with the soil and whose spirits watch over the living. Violations of custom will release unknown but certainly unfavourable consequences in a world where forces natural and supernatural, man's behaviour and the movements of nature are all linked.

However, observing that African customs are based upon notions entirely different from those in modern Western thinking, David and Brierley (1978: 506–7) drew seriously questionable conclusions:

> The African conception of the world is essentially static; it rejects the idea of progress and, therefore, frowns upon any act (such as the sale of land) or institution (such as prescription or usucapion) which has the effect of changing a previously established situation. The principal concern is for those social groupings (tribes, castes, villages, blood lines) which endure throughout time, rather than, as in the West, those which are more transient (individuals, couples, households). Land belongs to one's ancestors and to future generations as much if not more than to those living. Marriage is an alliance between two families rather than a union between two people. The individual is not ignored, and his personality is recognized, but the group is the visible basic unit.

None of this leads necessarily to the authors' conclusion that traditional African laws were static. Realities of life and the preservation of community and group concerns required constant dynamism, which simply escaped the authors' attention. African laws do not reject the idea of progress, but have a different vision of the world than Western unilineal 'progressive' thinking. The African world is a never-ending continuum of past, present and future; Africans find themselves on a slowly moving conveyor belt through history, a low-speed train that never stops at all, perhaps better envisaged as an endless chain stretching from past to future (Ebo, 1995: 38). Concern for the preservation of established situations, a certain innate conservatism, is hardly the same as being 'essentially static'. Such interpretations simply failed to balance two sides of the same coin.[47] Next, David and Brierley (1978: 507) tackle the issue of the individual's position, finding that:

> Such a view of the world leaves little place for the notion of individual rights deriving from the personality of individuals. Much greater emphasis

---

[47] Ayittey (1991: 11) indicates that such misrepresentations 'stemmed from ignorance of the true nature of African philosophical thinking. African expressions appeared complicated or chaotic, but they had simple internal logic.'

is placed upon the *obligations* of each person, given his social condition; and obligations properly juridical in character are not clearly distinguished from those which may be classed as simply moral.

This suggests that societies which treat morality and law as fully complementary or totally overlapping are somehow deficient in their legal understanding, a classic case of legocentric blindness on the part of positivists. While David and Brierley (1978: 509) are able to identify a key principle for Malagasy society, they do not realise, despite their privileged position as comparative lawyers, that they are looking at the African equivalent of 'duty' or 'appropriateness'.[48] Hence David and Brierley (1978: 509) do not quite see the wood for the trees, waiting for Africans to explain in writing what they, in their oral societies, seem to imbibe with the mother's milk, namely the sense of doing the right thing at the right time:

> No indigenous writings exist to simplify an investigation of these customs or an analysis of their major principles. In Africa, a purely oral customary tradition has been preserved. Malagasy codes and legislation do not constitute a true exception; they do no more than supply a number of special provisions or introduce a type of administrative regulation. The social order was, in general, and in its detail, ruled by the *fomba* or custom, comparable to Chinese ritual practices or the *giri* of Japanese law.

The reference to Chinese law and Japanese law here is correct, since *giri* is the conceptual equivalent of Hindu *dharma*. The authors should at least have noted explicitly that China's *li* is also a conceptual parallel. Their reference to 'ritual practices' obscures this, since *li* is not just a matter of religion or ritual but constitutes the key concept of Confucian self-controlled order (chapter 7). Despite their recognition of the importance of social harmony and self-controlled order for Africans, it does not occur to the authors that Africans must know a parallel concept. One must wonder why: perhaps this happens when researchers narrowly study every jurisdiction as a separate entity or 'black box' (Twining, 2000). This example confirms that a socio-legal framework relying on idealistically self-controlled order appears to be a shared feature of all traditional Asian and African societies, manifesting itself under different names. There is no reason why African law should be any different from other legal systems in this regard. What makes it African, then, are simply the respective culture-specific elements.

Some African authors have provided detailed descriptions and analysis of the typical African worldview.[49] Significantly, most law books do not discuss such issues, since religion or philosophy are not seen as a matter of law. From the perspective of religious studies, Shorter (1991: 426) indicates awareness of cross-disciplinary interlinkedness, noting that '[r]eligion permeated every

---

[48] See Hindu *dharma*, which David and Brierley (1978: 448–9) discussed very well.
[49] Ayittey (1991: 10–14) is excellent on this, but see also Yelpaala (1983) and Ebo (1995).

aspect of life in traditional African societies and its history is inseparable from that of their social and political institutions'. Apart from his strange use of the term 'non-ethnic',[50] Ayittey (1991: 10) is helpful in introducing the most basic African philosophical tenets:

> Africans have always believed that their universe was composed of three elements: the sky, the earth and the world. The sky and the earth made up the world, which was the place where all people, ethnic and non-ethnic, lived. Each component, however, could not exist independently of the others, but the sky was recognized in many ethnic societies as supreme.
>
> The sky was the domain of the spirits of the living and the unborn as well as thunder, lightning, rain, drought and other natural phenomena. The earth was the burial place of dead ancestors and other tribesmen as well as being the dwelling place of the people and their activities . . . The world was the domain of all people, both ethnic and non-ethnic, and as such embraced inter-ethnic relationships.

Ayittey suggests the existence of a more or less common African macrocosmic view of the world, a typical chthonic vision, in which the spheres of the dead and the ancestors, the living and those as yet unborn are all interlinked in an endless chain. We are also beginning to see elaborations of such beliefs in terms of the environment, a key element of chthonic cultures, so that philosophy, religion, social arrangements and the wider environment are all seen as interlinked.[51] Ayittey (1991: 11) explains this further and brings out the many assumed correspondences between different levels of this global vision of an ordered universe, which are remarkably similar to Hindu law (chapter 4, section 4.2):

> Most traditional African societies believed the universe, composed of the three elements (the sky, the earth and the world) was ordered like one giant equation. Each being had a specific place in this universe. Human animation corresponded to the animation of nature and each gesture correlates with some aspect of the universe. African art, dance, music and other human activities were a reflection of the rhythms of the universe. Hence, the metaphysical sphere was not abstractly divorced from concrete experience, especially since the physical and the metaphysical were aspects of reality and the transition from one to the other was natural.

Ayittey (1991: 11) quotes several other African authors to emphasise the internal logic of the African worldview. He stresses that belief systems had

---

[50] The critical point is that everybody is 'ethnic' in some form. Ayittey's problem appears to be that he wanted to avoid the word 'tribal' when making distinctions between those who belong to the main group, and 'the others'. It cannot be a racial category, since we are dealing here with a social scenario in which probably all participants are indigenous Africans. On ethnicity in Africa, see Gorgendiere *et al.* (1997) and Hameso (1997).

[51] See on this Maathai (1995: 7) with an elaborate defence of indigenous African methods of earth-centredness against the unscrupulous greed of modern positivism. On the role of traditional leaders in relation to the environment, see Hinz (2003).

enormous implications for the internal organisation of traditional African societies, including their legal structures. It constituted, indeed, a pre-existing all-comprehensive system of order in which individual humans were little else than temporary participants with limited powers and situation-specific obligations. Because the supernatural forces involved in the cosmic correspondences had manifest powers, which could be beneficial as well as lethal for man, human relationships had to be kept in harmony with the higher norms of supernatural elements. Ebo (1995: 38–9) elaborates on the religious dimension of African laws:

> The most potent source of authority behind indigenous law is instantly available from the religious beliefs and rituals of the community. An aspect of the traditional belief-system which deserves special mention holds that the group or community is a continuing, endless succession of generations, a self-perpetuating corporation embracing both the living and the dead. The law of the community, therefore, is conceived and accepted as the possession and heritage of an endless chain of generations. It enjoys the moral support and is the object of jealous vigilance, not only of living contemporaries, but also of departed ancestors. The stake of the latter in seeing that the authority of the law is upheld at all times . . . is an absolutely essential part of the integrative myth to which all adult members are exposed during the socialisation process.

This central role of the ancestors, which is also a feature of traditional Chinese law (chapter 7), has important implications for the individual conscience and thus contributes to a familiar internalised model of self-control. Ebo (1995: 39) brings out the element of individual conscience:

> This faith that the spirit of the ancestors is incarnate in the law is a precious and powerful factor from which derives an 'inner concern' felt by an individual member and which influences his behaviour toward the mores and folkways of his community. This spiritualization of law and its sanctional sources, and indeed of life in general, operates to surround law and its procedures with an aura of sanctity and to endow it with the instantaneous ability to evoke voluntary compliance with its dictates as an exalted religious obligation. This is also the principal explanation for the fact that sacred rituals and ceremonies form such an inseparable part of the legal process.

Manifold conceptual parallels to the Hindu transition from macrocosmic *rita* to microcosmic *dharma* (chapter 4, section 4.2) can be drawn. Such traditional African conceptualisations were given different names in different communities.[52] Ayittey (1991: 11–12) showed how such belief systems interlinked closely with human relationships:

---

[52] Among the Ovahimba in Namibia, the key term *oveta*, the duty to do the right thing, involves above all a fine balancing between matrilineal and patriarchal principles (Okupa, 1996). Ayittey (1991: 11) reports that the Nandi of Kenya called this *kiet*. The Tswana employ a variety of terms to signify rules of conduct, speaking of *maitseô* (manners, etiquette, polite usage) and *tshwanno* for 'duty' or obligation (Schapera, 1955: 35).

[M]etaphysically, the cosmos ran in a strictly orderly manner. It was essential for the components to be in perfect harmony and order . . . If an element was out of balance, there would be chaos, disease and death. For example, if the sky was out of equilibrium, thunder or floods would result. Similarly, if the earth was 'angry', there would be disease, poor harvests, famine and barren women.

An individual was not a mere spectator in this potentially turbulent cosmos . . . An individual's personality was the outcome of the interplay of natural forces. A 'good' child resulted from the concurrence of agreeable forces whereas a 'bad' child signified the wrath of some 'displeased' force. Sickness and death were similarly interpreted. . . .

All these supernatural forces were believed to have emotional intelligence and certain rules of prohibited human behaviour. Compliance with these rules was blessed in the form of longevity, freedom from sickness and individual prosperity. Violations elicited punishment which often came in the form of sudden death, affliction by a terrible disease, or financial ruin on an individual basis and collectively by poor harvests and barren women.

All of these belief systems, therefore, had manifold correspondences with the socio-legal normative orders and were reflected in arrangements that African people made among themselves to live within their specific environment. The inherent environmental consciousness of Africans is beginning to be discussed in more depth (Maathai, 1995; Hinz, 2003). Ayittey (1991: 14) emphasises that '[i]n traditional African societies, as in other, non-African cultures, there is acute awareness of the effects of the environment on people'. Glenn (2000: 79) writes from a comparative perspective:[53]

> The influence of chthonic thought on the environmental debate in the west has already been noted. The response has been at many levels: philosophical, economic and legal. No winner has yet been declared. What chthonic thought represents is a radical alternative, intellectually coherent and with thousands of years of experience and application. All other shades of green become tested against it, in terms of feasibility and results. The externalities of western thought can therefore no longer be ignored.

The belief systems of Africans also carry enormous implications for patterns of dispute settlement. The interlinked roles of medical and social healing are frequently ritualised in public performances which serve multiple reconstructive purposes. The natural world serves as a background to all of life and law, and the supernatural world is clearly not separated from the physical world. Any form of human law-making would not be able to ignore such deep-rooted cultural assumptions about order, illustrating the axiom that law is everywhere mixed up with culture. Ancestor worship was always an

---

[53] Interestingly, Glenn (2004: 84) takes notice of African perspectives, prefacing this quote with the comment that '[i]t is said in Africa that western culture has "a big mouth and small ears"'.

important ritualised element in African cultures, linking the spheres of the living and the dead, and many different types of ordeals would become part of the legal processes among Africans. In all of this, the spheres of human law-making and the pre-existing order needed to be harmonised in a spirit of intrinsic plurality-consciousness. Far from being primitive pagans, traditional Africans were highly sophisticated operators of their train through history.

6.3.3 African religions and socio-ritual processes

Outside the Muslim and Christian realm in Africa, the absence of codified religious writing made for complex relationships between religion and law. Within the overarching framework of a locally centred but ultimately global cosmic vision, most indigenous African societies recognised a hierarchical ordering of supernatural and cosmic forces at different levels.[54] These could range from a high God to local deities and spirits to certain forms of medicines and holy objects.[55] Given the holistic nature of African worldviews, religion (like law) was not seen as a separate concept and many African languages do not have a technical term for 'religion'.[56] African indigenous religions are more than just a collection of particular symbols, beliefs, myths and rites; they are holistically focused, complex constructs developed and manipulated by humans all the time to link themselves to the wider order of Nature. African religions give more importance to religious practice, good behaviour and ritual action than to dogmatic, fixed forms of belief. Certain beliefs may be shared by all in a particular community, but they need not be precisely circumscribed.[57] It is evident that African religions are not closed systems with fixed boundaries.

Given the openness of these various African belief systems, human constructs built upon the observable reality of a pre-existing natural order, nobody could

---

[54] See also Ayittey (1991: 12). Many Africans, probably most of them, relate to this today. Shorter (1991: 436) discusses modern developments in African religions and reports that '[i]t has been estimated that between 30 and 40 per cent of the population of contemporary Africa still practise traditional African religion'. He adds that, if the additional recourse of Christians and Muslims to traditional practices is included, 'then the percentage might reach 70 per cent'.

[55] For example, the Subia in Northern Namibia believe that the universe is composed of the heavens (*iwulu*), the sky (*mbimbiyulu*) and the earth (*lifasi*). The Subia also believe in the existence of a supreme being (*Shandandulo*) or creator (*Ireeza*). The Owambo share such cosmological ideas and believe in a supreme being called *Kalunga* who, as father of all gods, is endowed with highest authority (Malan, 1995: 28). The Tswana people of Botswana refer to *Modimo* as the Great God or Great Spirit. The Shona in Zimbabwe know *Mwari* as the great God, who can only be approached through ancestral spirits.

[56] This, again, is a parallel to Hindu law, where *dharma* meant neither 'law' nor 'religion', although it is often wrongly translated as such.

[57] Again, we see parallels with Hindu approaches to similar questions. It matters less which particular god one chooses to address. What counts is situation-specific appropriate behaviour, not a dogmatic form of theism, and certainly not monotheism.

claim to have the 'right truth' and then attempt to monopolise religion. In Africa, too, this temptation must have been there, but was probably defeated by the prevailing orality and local differentiation. Academic writing on African religions does not point to efforts to preserve and protect the superiority of religious authority, a central feature of Islamic religio-legal debates (chapter 5). If fluidity and plurality were taken for granted among Africans and the religious sphere did not make any specific demands on human law-making, it was not necessary, in fact it was impossible, to insist on the formal superiority of religious norms, quite in contrast to Islamic law. Since everybody and everything constantly needed to be linked to the pre-existing order, the performance of ritualised actions, in many different social contexts, became critically important, as in the *dharma* system of the Hindus. This confirms that right action, not right belief, orthopraxis rather than orthodoxy, constitutes the key element of African religions. African traditional rituals are, then, legally relevant methods of linking the human sphere with the superhuman cosmic level. Participation by all concerned may be not only expected but required, and there may not have been many barriers to participation, especially where different ethnic groups lived in close proximity, knowing of each other's belief systems.[58] Some of the literature suggests that, rather than piety in view of a central deity, awareness of culture-specific cosmic interlinkages and their re-creation is the main focus of African ritualised action.[59]

Much could be said about concepts of ritual (Grimes, 1982). Relevant here is that rituals constitute a fresh performance every time, rather than following a fixed, ritualised, pre-set pattern which needs to be endlessly repeated. Every ritual performance becomes an entity in its own right, since the train of time never stops, and the participants, even if they are the same as before, are no longer truly the same. Such dynamic perceptions also impact on conceptualisations of custom, which similarly suffer from rigidity complexes in the minds of foreign observers, but not among Africans. Traditional African custom, like ritual, is much more inherently flexible and dynamic than lawyers are willing to accept.

African rituals have not only recreative functions, they also dramatise latent ambiguities about whether something is good or bad, so one could use the potential ambivalence of rituals for many purposes, and a positive or negative cause may be the reason for ritual action in the first place. This reflects the African experience of nature as 'either life-fulfilling or life-diminishing'

[58] On different types of strangers in African societies, see Shack and Skinner (1979). One could imagine the possibility of ritual action to persuade one's rivals' gods or spirits to be kind, a clever politically motivated ploy expressed through ritual action, also known from Hindu rituals. In Africa, too, this could involve Muslim sorcerers such as the *mallams* of Ghana (Lowy, 1978: 119).

[59] Shorter (1991: 434) proposes that seeking out forces of evil for the sake of self-protection takes precedence over worship.

(Shorter, 1991: 428). A celebratory thanksgiving will involve rituals quite different from those that seek to protect the participants from bad influences. Such considerations become centrally relevant for dispute settlement processes in African societies, which appear as traditionally ritualised processes (section 6.3.5 below). No matter how secular they look to us, they have an invisible cosmic dimension that may not be expressed, but is nevertheless present. Ritual activity is different from ordinary life; sacred spaces will be important, and the ritual time may also be different from ordinary time. New ritual identities may be assumed by the participants, and such rituals serve many purposes. Ayittey (1991: 12) explains:

> There was the need to communicate with these gods and spirits, to placate them in order not to incur their displeasure or wrath and to make atonements in cases of wrongdoing to prevent vengeful acts. Above all, however, it was essential to maintain order and a state of harmony between the sky, the earth and the world. To agricultural societies, the harmony between the sky and the earth was particularly important. The set of beliefs associated with this harmony is known as the earth cult. An aspect of this cult was the attribution to the earth of the power to bring good or bad fortune to the people in such matters as fertility of the land in crops and fertility of wives.

Ritual activity would therefore seek to promote fruitfulness, strength, wealth in children and cattle, and renewal in life in every possible respect. It would be more concerned with immediate effects in everyday life, concerning health, wealth and children, rather than a distant cosmos, although that is also a dimension which ritual performances account for. Depending on a society's belief system, ritual performances can also be seen as entertainment of deities or spirits. Such performances also bring people closer together and may be designed to strengthen social harmony, in addition to being educative and entertaining.

Turner (1965; 1968) developed the concept of social drama through his studies on African ritual performances, showing how breaches of social relations could develop into a crisis, so that redressive action in the form of dramatic rituals might be required to restore imbalances and strained networks. His work emphasised the distinction between, and co-existence of, instrumental and expressive aspects of human behaviour. Lawyers are more interested in the instrumental aspects; an observable function of many rituals is to bring about a healing of damaged or endangered social, and thus legal, relationships. This shows that religious ritual also serves as a means to heal rifts in society and becomes a form of dispute settlement, leading to the reintegration of an offender, for example, or the execution of serious offenders through poison ordeals. Other rituals may constitute a public effort to assist, and if possible rescue, a member of society suffering from some unexplained misfortune. Since a religious ritual may constitute a healing ritual as well as a dispute settlement process, it becomes difficult to distinguish the various strands. Ritualisation of human actions and behaviour can be designed to confront individuals, groups and whole societies with the immediate conditions of their existence and may impress on individuals or whole groups that certain redressive action is required in order to protect the threatened order of society and of the wider world. This ritualised correction of imbalances at various levels is not unique to Africa, it plays a prominent role in all traditional contexts.

All of this is premised on assumptions about the effects of human action or non-action, which means that Africans, too, have culture-specific equivalents to the *karmic* assumptions of Hindus and other people in the world. In the African case, this may be more centred on instant effects than distant moral accounting, so a person's illness may be perceived as the almost instant result of a failure to perform proper rituals, or to act in a particular way. Rather than blaming themselves, however, members of traditional African societies also display the universal human pattern of blaming others for their misfortunes.

In this context, witchcraft becomes a prominent issue.[60] Shorter (1991: 428–9) explains that '[t]he ultimate source of evil and disorder in the world is rarely personalized as a spirit, but more commonly traced to the witch, a human being who possesses preternatural powers to harm others secretly and malevolently'. Belief in witchcraft is also a technique or method to explain misfortune, illness or death. A witch is seen as evil, selfish and secretive, working against the social welfare of the group. A witch may or may not be aware of such processes, and it is easy to understand how such concepts could be misused by manipulators to suspect and even terminate socially marginalised individuals who fall outside the norm system, or to exploit this for power politics or financial gain. Accusations of false magic are frequent.[61] Evans-Pritchard, working on the Azande during the 1930s, found that more or less every death was attributed to witchcraft. Shorter (1991: 434) writes that '[a]t the popular level the African believer is often more engrossed in the identification of human sources of evil, and in counteracting them, than in the acknowledgement and worship of superior forces of good'. Some reports suggest that witchcraft was on the increase during the twentieth century, mainly because of the destabilisation of society.[62] But quite where witchcraft begins, and where it ends, has never been easy to decide. This topic provided much food for thought to the colonial authorities in Africa.

[60] On witchcraft, see Ellis and Ter Haar (2004: 149ff.). For traditional judicial processes, see Elias (1956: 225–6).

[61] This is also a feature of South Asian and Islamic societies, where concepts like the 'evil eye' and various magic spells are prominent.

[62] Maathai (1995) reports on recent Kenyan efforts to control witchcraft and devil worship, but argues that there are more important things to do for modern African governments than to go witch-hunting. Further, '[t]o many African devotees of Christianity and Islam, seeking African spiritual heritage is devil worship' (p. 10). Ayittey (1991: 14) also suggests that prejudices against African traditional religions are widespread among Muslims and Christians.

African religions know a variety of deities and spirits in different combinations; there is simply no uniform pattern.[63] In some traditions, the concept of a high God is used,[64] a creator figure, who can be a woman and may be the first ancestor of a particular group. Beneath that, a range of deities may be found, mainly nature gods, as well as spirits of the land, the water, trees and mountains. Other 'objects with power', sometimes referred to as 'medicines', such as certain plant and herbs, or a shrine, might play an important role in local cults.[65] The conceptualisation of medicines is highly developed, and specialist knowledge about such matters would naturally be linked to higher powers. Ancestors occupy a most important role in this context, and are placed at various levels in the overall hierarchy by different African traditions. They also play a very important role in the shaping of customary norms, discussed further below.[66] Shorter (1991: 429) explains:

> Although there are some well-documented instances of totemic spirits who are invoked as the guardians of clans and lineages, the patrons of society are usually the spirits of the dead, the ancestors. The spiritual world of the ancestors is patterned after life on earth. The recently dead and the unremembered collectivity of the remotely deceased, are invoked by, and on behalf of, the family community. The territorial spirits who are the ancestors of chiefs or who are eminent personalities of the past are invoked on behalf of larger social groupings. Ancestors are thought to be mediators in one sense or another . . . More often they are plenipotentiaries of the supreme being, mediating his providence and receiving worship in his name. Occasionally they are seen as mankind's companions in the approach to the supreme being, guarantors of authentic worship. Much of traditional morality is concerned with pleasing the ancestors and living in harmony with them, since they are the most important members of the total community.

The widespread belief that the ancestors watch over everything and need to be obeyed would have much influence on processes of norm-construction. It also had many ritual implications. Shorter (1991: 433) notes that '[a]ncestors are credited with exceptional knowledge and power, and sacrifice to them is an acknowledgement of their powerful role in human society. Misfortunes are very frequently attributed to a failure to offer sacrifice in due form or due time.'

Ayittey (1991: 12) points out that the function of linking people and the three dimensions of the universe around them, and of maintaining harmony and

---

[63] For some details and examples, see Shorter (1991: 428); Ayittey (1991: 12).

[64] In some cases, the development of a High God may have to do with Christian and Islamic influences.

[65] Among the Xhosa in South Africa, the herbalist (*ixhwele*) dispenses medicines and communitates with the ancestors. In the Hambukushu and Bayeyi communities of Namibia, Shamans and herbalists (*nganga*) are seen as connected to the supernatural world. See Siyabona Africa (2005), at http://namibia.safari.co.za/africa_bushmen.html.

[66] Ayittey (1991: 21–2) explains concepts about the presence of ancestors and the need to follow their trodden paths.

order, fell to certain ritual leaders or priests. The ability to conduct or supervise such rituals meant gaining access to powers, which might be good, bad or ambivalent. Ritual experts might be heads of families, or they might be formally recognised individuals and ritual functionaries and experts, ambiguous figures whose position depended on formal initiation into a cult. Such individuals might be able to exercise considerable power and would then become functional equivalents to the Hindu *pandits* or Muslim jurists or *maulvis* if they began to be seen as living authoritative representatives of a particular religio-cultural tradition. But how far could they go in trying to control religious beliefs and practices, and, in that sense, putting religious law above custom? There are no simple answers to this question. The use of oaths and ordeals by some religious functionaries clearly gave them powers over life and death. In some chiefly societies, chiefship was determined through rituals, so here the 'priest' might have a competitive relationship with the ruler.[67] Both might play a role in social control mechanisms, sometimes through use or control of witchcraft, but no clear picture emerges about the relationship between religious authority and socio-political authorities. Ayittey (1991: 13) emphasises the power of human intermediaries:

> Accordingly, there was also a hierarchical ordering of intercessors. At the lowest levels were such posts as . . . diviners, witches, sorcerers, witch doctors, priests, medicine men, who together with shrines, fetishes or other objects embodying supernatural powers were the agents that were believed to be capable of communicating with the supernatural world and able to influence the impact of supernatural power on human affairs or to influence its aid in attaining desired goals. Such goals included the averting of misfortune or inflicting injury on adversaries.

The socio-political structures of a particular society largely influenced what kinds of religious functionaries developed. Shorter (1991: 430) indicates that '[l]eadership in traditional Africa was basically ritual leadership, whether of divine kings, or of prophet-arbitrators or spirit-mediums'. This fails to distinguish between the leadership ambitions of religious figures and more explicitly political rulers, whose position was legitimised by links to important ancestors or, in some cases, a creator god.[68] The prevailing image of interlinkedness between religion, law and morality suggests ample room for conflicts, and there must have been many tensions. Allott (1968: 135–6) noted that many questions which modern jurists or law reformers pose become almost meaningless when directed at traditional African law, where law, religion and morality overlap:

---

[67] The relationship of ruler and priest is well documented in Indian writing as a relationship of mutual dependence, as they both need the other but control each other, too (Altekar, 1958: 53–4, 168).

[68] For details see Shorter (1991: 431).

> The attempt, for example, to separate legal norms from those which are merely of moral obligation presupposes . . . a state of society in which there can be a serious lack of correspondence between what ordinary members of the community feel to be a proper way of behaving towards each other and what the official organs of the society say should happen. African traditional law was not like this. The law expressed the common moral code of the people; if the code changed, the law would automatically change as well. Similarly with religious beliefs and practices. There was no conflict or opposition between the religion of the community (a religion which was the shared system of belief of all those in the community – a state religion, if one likes) and its legal institutions. The religious beliefs permeated the whole of the secular world: the family structure was often organised around the cult of the ancestors, with whom the living head of the family acted as the official channel of communication; and this substratum was brought out . . . in the ideology of the family property system, in which the ancestors might be viewed (as in many of the peoples of West Africa) as in a sense co-proprietors with the living members of the family. What was punished as crime was often what society treated as sins or breaches of taboo.

This integrated African model indicates that none of the three competitors in the triangular relationship of state, society and religion/ethics could be set up as supreme, as all three spheres had to work hand in hand. While the possibility of conflict cannot be ruled out and avoidance of conflict remains a constant challenge, Allott (1968: 136) cautioned against overemphasising the role of traditional religions and portrayed law as a central component in an integrated culture:

> [T]he law could not punish many breaches of morality or compel everyone to act morally; much of the law was completely secular in tone. But the general point remains: African society enjoyed an integrated culture, or set of institutions and beliefs, in which the law occupied a central position.

It seems that Allott overstated the centrality of law. Later, Allott (1968: 142) emphasised that 'custom and tradition are by no means the only sources of law', adding to his matrix some forms of legislation, precedent, equity and legal fictions.[69] Finally, Allott (1968: 145) mentioned the main legal areas where religious belief was significant, highlighting oaths, the law of crimes, family law and land law. Religious considerations must have played a role throughout the fully integrated traditional African societies, but as part of a larger whole.

Exploring the limits of law, Allott (1980: 25) highlighted that '[t]he area of law is entirely located within the sphere of societal morality'. Thinking of the

---

[69] On equity, Allott (1968: 144) points out that it is not a separate source of law in traditional African customary practice, since the system itself had an in-built awareness of the need for justice and equity.

problems of modern African states, Allott wanted to show that traditional laws might be more effective than modern state laws because their normative foundations were embedded in traditional society and not imported from outside. The observation that '[c]oncentricity and concurrence of spheres of morality, convention and *Law* mean *reinforcement* of the legal message' (Allott, 1980: 25) could be understood as a typical legocentric conclusion. However, it could also be read to imply that traditional African laws maintained a healthy balance between the competing elements of law-making. Allott did not comment further on that issue but seemed to suggest that something that the traditional system knew about had been lost in postcolonial law-making.

Regarding traditional, pre-colonial African systems of law, then, the question to ask is to what extent one of the three competing law-founding elements might have sought to set itself up as superior. Researching this is a virtually impossible endeavour, since truly traditional African customary laws developed in the distant past, of which records are not preserved. Although there is a wide range of early literature on African laws (Woodman and Obilade, 1995), evidence only takes us back into the twentieth century and at best the late nineteenth century. But absence of evidence should not prevent discussion about the conceptual implications of what we know must have been there.

Some of the earlier evidence would confirm that traditional African societies, prior to colonial interference, managed to maintain a symbiotic equilibrium between the three competing law-founding elements, developing this into an oral African theory, but a theory nevertheless, of symbiotic balance: none of the three elements should ever be allowed to claim superiority to the exclusion of the others. Such a central theory will naturally be challenged by those who assume that Africans were incapable of sophisticated thought, but they must be wrong, and this can be proved. The key words to watch out for are balance, harmony and co-operation. That almost innate sense of symbiotic balance, reflecting an inherent plurality-consciousness and an affinity with strong pluralism, appears to have been disrupted and often ultimately ruined by colonial interference, particularly in the areas of Africa subjected to civil law. British colonial 'indirect rule' remained mostly a form of 'soft' positivism (section 6.4.1 below). Importing a foreign model which privileged legal positivism and unbalanced the traditional symbiotic plurality-consciousness impacted on and probably ruined the idealistic, self-controlling system of traditional African laws. Many modern African leaders would later come to advocate legal centralism (section 6.5 below), because it seemed to legitimate the new ruling élites of Africa, who often studied metropolitan law, empowering them to manipulate the old triangular balance of traditional societies in their favour. It is not surprising that some of these new rulers should be afraid of belief in the power of their ancestors.

This particular line of argument throws light on many discussions about traditional African laws. We know that traditional African laws practised and cherished the integration of the visible and invisible worlds, and that political rule was in the main seen as a matter of trust from the people.[70] In fact, the living were using the earth and all its resources during their lifetime as a matter of trust. Owning nothing absolutely, they lived on this train through history, enjoying their time if they could, knowing that their active time was limited, and that they had obligations to ancestors as well as to future generations. Within any of the three areas of potential law-making, the principle of collegiality was treated as supreme, so that reaching joint decisions was treated as a value in itself. Seen in this light, long debates about how to decide a particular matter are not a waste of time, but reflect a consensus-sensitive strategy to maintain balance and harmony, the key elements of traditional African societies. As in other traditional societies, the individual is recognised in traditional African societies as a separate entity, but is at all times subordinated to the collective and, of course, the cosmic order.[71] There is a role for the individual, and it is an obligation on the individual to be active, which exists even for young children, as vividly illustrated through fieldwork in Namibia (Okupa, 1996). Traditional African law was also quite clear about the fact that nobody is on a lone journey through the world. Therefore, not by coincidence, one of the severest punishments is to be found in the form of exile: the offender is just pushed off the slowly moving train. It would be up to him or her to join another moving train, to build up a new train with some pieces from the past, or to perish. The image of a journey through history helps to explain certain key features of traditional African systems and can serve as a useful illustration for understanding how law and legal rules in Africa, and perhaps everywhere, are conceptualised.

6.3.4 African customary law as a self-controlling system

The above hypothesis about self-controlled balancing as the central integrative element of traditional African legal systems requires further search for evidence to assess whether traditional customs were able to rule independently, or whether and how they were controlled and kept in check in various forms. Could powerful individuals just do as they pleased, imposing their laws on society? An affirmative answer is predictable, since perfect balance is always an ideal, and there were many traditional political arrangements among Africans, ranging from large kingdoms to acephalous or polycephalous societies. The endless diversity of traditional African customary laws is beyond description,

---

[70] This is illustrated by the Tswana maxim that 'a chief is a chief by the people' (Bennett, 2004: 4).

[71] Ebo (1995: 40) writes that, in the process of a trial, discovering the applicable rule of law is not the aim, since 'that is a settled and foregone conclusion'. The pre-existing legal order is thus taken account of, and the focus of the proceedings is on rectifying the breach of that pre-existing order. That is familiar from Islamic and Hindu law.

and largely beyond reach for legal researchers. Any attempt to be comprehensive seems foolish and unrealistic. Bennett (2004: 1) notes critical methodological issues:

> Customary law derives from social practices that the community con-
> cerned accepts as obligatory. Normative systems of this nature are never
> directly accessible to the outsider. They must be discovered by questioning
> informants and on-the-spot observation, which are methods typical of the
> social sciences, or by consulting authoritative texts, which is the traditional
> legal method. In either case, the resulting data present a construction of
> reality that is coloured by the preconceptions of the informants and the
> researchers.

The culture-specific local or communal nature of customary laws and their situation-specificity are universal phenomena. As elsewhere, traditional African customary laws relate to a specific area or group of people, and are not a nationally agreed body of rules. Traditional customary laws, as people's laws, grew and developed out of practice. Allott (1980: v) indicated that his doubts about the limits of law 'started off with a concern with African customary laws, legal systems in which the community makes law, and changes it by its changing practice without help from the legislator'. The customary rules in many societies were constantly stated and restated for debate, and remained subject to reconfirmation or modification. It was certainly not a static system, as Maine (1861) and others imagined from an armchair perspective. The constant internal dialectic processes of testing and trying point to simmering conflicts and tensions within the social sphere. This partly explains the lack of interest in such research among lawyers, even about dispute settlement, as earlier anthropological studies indicate (e.g. Gluckman, 1955).

Traditional social systems in Africa typically included wide-ranging family relationships and joint family arrangements, but the nuclear family is in many communities the primary unit. Traditional African economic systems include extremely diverse forms of settled agriculture, nomadic pastoralists (Masai, Barabaig, Turkana), hunter-gatherers (San Bushmen, Hadza, Ituri) and many coastal and river fishing communities. Individual rights and duties flowed from people's roles in society, their kinship networks, occupational groupings, local alliances and, not necessarily co-extensive with those, religious groupings. Allott (1968: 131–2) commented that major influences on customary laws were the environment, the social system and orality:

> Many of the similarities of customary laws in tropical Africa are due not
> so much to any genetic relationship between the inhabitants or of cultural
> influence between one society and the next as to uniformity of response to
> the challenge of a shared environment. There are also similarities implicit
> in the social system. Of these the most obvious is the absence of writing,
> and hence the absence of all written legislation, law reports, and juristic

analyses. A purely oral legislated law is possible; but in practice, unwritten law tends to consist mainly of customary law. The African legal systems share, then, the common characteristic that they are all unwritten and mainly customary in origin.

Since similar social systems and climate zones also exist elsewhere in the world, none of this is new or peculiar to Africa in any sense, and the only uniquely African feature is the factor of orality and its various consequences. Allott (1968: 133) elaborated:

> African customary laws were not book-law. There were no legal texts or manuscripts, no statements of claim formulated on pieces of paper, no summons or writ of execution, no conveyances in writing, no learned commentaries by doctors of law. These facts inescapably determine the style of the law, the relationship of the law both to those who administered it and those who were subject to it, and the processes of legal development.

Allott (1984: 128) suggested further that '[i]t is sometimes difficult to make the imaginative leap to see into and understand the profound effect that the absence of writing will have on the quality, character and operation of a legal system'. Asking the reader to imagine what the impacts would be if a Western-type legal system were to have no writing, Allott (1984: 128–9) suggested several practical consequences:

> We should immediately have to alter radically the style and function of our legal institutions, of our legal academies. The lawyer could not 'look up' a point; he could only consult his memory or that of those around him. The student would not be told to read a book in the library – there would be no library and no book in it. Instead, he would have to have recourse to those older and wiser than he, who might, out of their accumulated knowledge, say what the law has been and aims to be. Our courts would change as dramatically: their writ . . . would run only as far as the spoken word might carry and the strong arm prevail; they would tend inexorably towards the local settlement of local problems. Nor would their judgments remain in the same form – no one would collect and perpetuate them. They would have to be published by word of mouth, by public speech.

Allott identified that orality would decentralise legal processes and the production of law. Orality meant that the law came closer to the people to whom it applies, increasing the scope for legal diversity in different parts of a territory or state. This must be a worrying thought for positivists, although even the United States has not managed to create a nationally uniform legal system. If the Americans can live with locally anchored legal plurality, why not Africans?

Many writers on custom are not as helpful as one would hope. Mensah-Brown (1976: 23) remains too engaged with defending African laws, and gets entangled in rhetorical debates to prove that African customary laws make distinctions familiar to English law (pp. 19–20). We learn surprisingly little about the nature of traditional African customary laws from legal writers.[72] As a general rule, a traditional African elder would explain his system by saying that 'it traces back to the immemorial customs of the tribe. It is "the law of the ancestors," "the law of long ago"' (Allott, 1968: 140). Many outside observers, judges, anthropologists and administrators, have taken custom for granted, seeing customary law as 'inflexible in its structure and incapable of deviating from the routines and principles handed down from the dead and now given a quasi-religious status' (Allott, 1968: 140). This almost conflates custom and religion, but Allott (1968: 140–1) refutes the idea that traditional African customary laws were inflexible in all respects, arguing that the opposite is true:

> [T]he impression one derives is not that of unthinking adherence to immutable principle but precisely the reverse. The style of African adjudication is flexible; the principles are there, but so general are many of them in content that it is a moot point how to apply them to a given circumstance. Often the principles themselves form no more than a starting-point for the negotiation between the contending parties as to the most suitable settlement of their quarrel, or a court may allow a deviation from the rule in the interests of a lasting harmony between the disputants.
>
> The history of African law argues the same way. Enormous changes have taken place in customary law, both before and after the advent of colonial rule. Many of these changes have emerged from the heart of the traditional system in response to changing needs . . . or a changed assessment of a role or status.

This confirms that customs are norms and rules handed down since ancient times, and yet they may change over time, a notion that does not match traditional English lawyers' understanding of custom. Bennett (2004: 2) notes that 'customary law is always up to date, because, ancient though it may seem, no custom is ever older than the memory of the oldest living person'. Section 6.4.2 below elaborates on how rigid official understanding of custom affected British colonial administration in Africa. The British largely had a different understanding of custom from that of local people.[73]

---

[72] Some earlier writers, anthropologists rather than lawyers, fiercely debated methodological and substantive issues about traditional African customary laws. On the Bohannan–Gluckman debate, see Woodman and Obilade (1995: xvi). Most writing focuses on African customary laws in the colonial and post-colonial periods and takes ambivalent views of the nature and place of customary laws.

[73] Compare the famous Nelson controversy in India (chapter 4, section 4.6). For Africa, Mamdani (1996: 109ff.) discusses how indirect rule impacted on customary law, arguing that, over time, there was a shift 'from a civilizing mission to a law-and-order administration' (p. 109).

In terms of social organisation, it is evident that individualistic, positivistic law-making was not a feature of traditional African laws and the key word is 'cooperation'.[74] Ayittey (1991: 15) highlights that such cooperation was necessary for the survival of the group. Individuals were first of all seen as members of families and kinship circles.[75] Ayittey (1991: 2) explains that '[e]ach person was attached to several latent groups of solidarity which provided mutual support for its members'. The clan was the main source of an individual's identity, reputation and pride. This also implied social control and basic law-making by the clan, as this 'often served as a form of behavioural control as a person would desist from acts likely to bring shame to the clan as a whole' (p. 2). This conceptual parallel to the Hindu concept of 'model behaviour' (*sadācāra*) seems to fulfil the same function of guiding the individual's conscience in the case of doubt. Since the individual is closely tied into socio-economic and socio-cultural networks, grave rule violations by errant individuals would be rare, and disputes over existing rules might not be frequent. We see here glimpses of familiar visions of a Golden Age, an idealised self-controlled order expected to function for a higher purpose. Ayittey (1991: 6–7) points to the Asante, among whom it was the task of the family head (according to an English author who wrote in fairly formal language in 1911):

> to instruct his wards in the ways of loyalty and obedience. He was held responsible for the freaks of recalcitrant members of his family, and he was expected as well to keep them within bounds, to insist upon conforming to the customs, laws and traditional observances of the community.

This sounds like positivism and rigid law enforcement, and it would certainly have been strict, but not necessarily oppressive.[76] This practice was followed in a spirit of submission not just to the dictates of a family elder, but to the perceived needs of the three worlds, which can never be left out of this picture because they were an ever-present, albeit invisible, feature – another level of meaningful silence about a traditional worldview which is simply present and does not need to be discussed.[77] Ebo (1995: 36) discusses this in the context of crime and compensation:

---

[74] With an eye to Marxist excesses in Africa, Ayittey (1991: 20) makes a neat distinction between 'cooperation' and 'collectivity': 'Collectivism precludes individualism or independence whereas cooperation permits some degree of independence and volition. To characterize the traditional African society as "collectivist" would be inaccurate.' Collectivism is, then, another form of positivist interference in traditional African self-controlled balancing systems.

[75] On individual versus society see in depth Ayittey (1991: 14–22), with many interesting examples.

[76] One could compare this to the law-making by the Emperor Ašoka in India (chapter 4, section 4.3), which only appeared like positivism at first sight.

[77] The same was found for Indian cultures (chapter 4). An excellent analysis of these issues is found in Ebo (1995: 36ff.).

Hence the African idea of justice demanded that the loser's group regain what had been taken from them plus such additional transfer of goods as would ensure that aggression of any sort always meant punishment; and not punishment merely of a symbolic sort, such as we mistakenly suppose imprisonment to be, but of a kind that impoverished not merely the wrong doer but also his group.

Whoever dares to upset the prevailing state of social balance by injuring the generally recognised rights of another must in all cases emerge from the dispute 'not richer or more favoured, but poorer and less favoured than before'.

This kind of thinking, also evident from ancient China (chapter 7), has important implications for strengthening individual self-control. Ayittey (1992: 2) reports about the role of the lineage or clan as the next largest unit in society, emphasising its socio-economic insurance functions, again matched with legal responsibilities, like in a 'corporate body'. Membership meant agreement to the internal rules of a larger group of people, a kind of social contract. The fact that land use, rather than land ownership, often depended on the clan or lineage explains traditional African concepts of property law. Not even kings owned the land (Ayittey, 1991: 5). Traditional African worldviews implied that the living generation merely held the right to usufruct of any property in their area, passed on from those who were there before them; this right would in turn pass to the next generation. The unstoppable train of African traditional history makes such concepts and arrangements appear sensible and practical; it certainly worked well as long as there was enough land for everybody.[78]

Ayittey (1991: 3) emphasises that tensions within the family group or village would inevitably arise and that someone who was unhappy could always leave.[79] If there was any fundamental disagreement between family members, one could agree to disagree and everyone would carry on as they thought fit, providing growth points for traditional customs. In Africa, as elsewhere, 'local language groups, tribes and kingdoms have always stratified into the inevitable patterns of

---

[78] Ayittey (1991: 19) shows that concepts of individual property co-existed (as they did in India) with ideas about the communality of property. The individual was free to enjoy individual property rights, 'so long as the pursuit of wealth or prosperity did not conflict with the greater interests of society'. These are important starting points for developing African principles of public interest in the context of modern nation states. See further Ayittey (1991: 23–30) on African concepts of wealth. On the sharing of wealth and resources, Yomo Kenyatta is cited by Ayittey (1991: 30–1) and property claims are discussed more specifically (p. 56ff.).

[79] The exit from joint family property through formal partition was always a legal possibility also in India. Ebo (1995) introduces the distinction of 'private law' and 'public law' in this context. This is not convincing because all violations of order are perceived to have a public dimension. However, Ebo (1995: 36) rightly argues that the gravest offences in public law provide a reason to exile a person and treats ridicule and ostracism as the African equivalent of 'sending a malefactor to Coventry' (p. 39).

superordination and subordination' (Reisman, 1982: 9). As against fission and dispersal, African traditions would emphasise the strategy of winning friends and allies, holding the system together, with the effect that 'indigenous African social and political cultures are characterized by remarkable entrepreneurship in acquiring followers and making alliances' (Ayittey, 1991: 4), leading to a perennial 'intense competition for people' (p. 4). Linked to such strategies, flexibility in negotiation and norm-construction on a roughly democratic basis is seen as preferable to positivist law-making. Negotiated arrangements rather than dictatorships will have been common, because a dictator who failed to maintain alliances and to consider his people's interests might simply be abandoned.[80] Ayittey (1991: 15) indicates the limits of individual action:

> Normally, an individual's power was not considered adequate to overcome or to mediate between the society and the natural environment. Auxiliary power was required, which could come from several sources: from his own intelligence, capabilities, ingenuity; from the ancestors; or from magic or even witchcraft.

In every case, as Ayittey (1991: 15) demonstrates through examples, promoting cooperation and group effort were seen as vital. Containing and controlling conflicts, preventing them from becoming larger battles, was seen as a matter of survival for traditional societies. Ayittey (1991: 9) notes that 'heavy emphasis was laid on restoring harmonious social relationships rather than the pursuit of abstract notions of justice'. Here again, finding justice from case to case was considered more important than sticking to fixed rules. The relationship of individual and society, and the position of individuals, became a controversial but undeveloped topic among specialists on African studies (Takirambudde, 1982). Ayittey (1991: 16) reports:

> At any rate, the African emphasis on cooperation did not rule out the existence of an individual as a person capable of making an effort on his own initiative. This issue of the individual versus the community has been the source of much confusion. In the West, individuals would say, 'I am because I am and I want what I want when I want it.' In Africa, the peasant would say, 'I am because we are.' . . . The *we* or *us* connotes kinship. The community plays a crucial role in the individual's acquisition of full personhood.

This is supplemented by comments to the effect that '[s]urvival is the primary objective of the leader of every African tribe' (Ayittey, 1991: 16) and that 'primary duty is owed to the community' (p. 16). The notion of individual self-sufficiency, which underlies positivist, absolutist ambitions, was treated as absurd, as Ayittey (1991: 17) explicitly highlights with reference to the Kuranko

---

[80] Ayittey (1991: 75) indicates that '[a] despotic headman soon found himself abandoned by some of his people'.

of Sierra Leone and the Fanti, whose system of ethics is said to be anti-egoist.[81] With regard to the scope for individual discretion, Ayittey (1991: 18) has interesting things to say:

> The boundaries within which the individual could exercise 'unlimited freedom' were prescribed by the cultural norms and practices of the community. These norms were in turn influenced by the need to maintain harmony among the cosmic forces and to comply with behavioural rules required by ancestors as well as the supernatural forces. In other words, the philosophical beliefs, social mores, obligations and value systems merely set the parameters within which the individual could operate freely.
>
> The limits were in general not imposed by the chief or king – an important distinction. The imposition of rigid boundaries is the hallmark of dictatorship whereas the prescription of limits by the community, or the people themselves, is not. Thus, reluctance on the part of an African to do something does not necessarily signify an obedience of an order from a chief.
>
> The limits set by the community, of course, varied from one tribe to another. Further, the degree of individuality or independence also varied from tribe to tribe. But the preeminence of the societal interests prevailed in all systems. Accordingly, it would be more useful to consider the ontological schema as a continuum along which various African ethnic societies may be placed, depending upon the degree to which the 'I' or the 'we' is emphasized.

Several examples are given to illustrate this model, providing for a large variety of balances between individual ambition and group expectation, emphasis towards individualism and independence, or greater disposition towards cooperation. Ayittey (1991: 18) shows that '[n]o able-bodied African native could expect to receive hand-outs from the group to which he was attached . . . [S]upport was mutual, not unilateral and a great deal of emphasis was placed on reciprocity.' Ayittey (1991: 20–1) then identifies precisely the issue that the present globally focused legal analysis has identified as a key element for understanding traditional African legal systems:

> Imprecise definitions and poor understanding have given rise to much confusion about African philosophy and spurned various bastard ideologies that bear little relation to indigenous African value systems.
>
> Much of the difficulty originated, as we have seen, from lack of understanding of indigenous African philosophy and therefore African personality. In the West, the individual is answerable to himself and God, if he is religious. In the communist countries, the individual owes primary allegiance to the state. In Muslim countries, he is answerable only to Allah. The

---

[81] Ayittey (1991: 17) demonstrates how easy it has been for modern African leaders to abuse this balance and to emphasise and superimpose their individual will. For details see section 6.5 below.

average African, on the other hand, is subject to four levels of authority or sources of control. In ascending order, Yelpaala (1983: 375) states:

> First, there is the authority of the living exercised by such personalities as the king, the chief, and the lineage heads. Second, there is the authority of the ancestral spirits over the living. The authority of the living, particularly that of the lineage heads, is monitored and subordinate to that of the ancestors. Third, there is the authority of other supernatural forces whose cosmic norms and authority take precedence over those of the ancestors and the living. Finally, there is the authority of the supreme omnipotent being, who rewards or punishes the dead according to the quality of their lives on earth.

The average African must consult four standards before initiating any action on his own and resolve any resultant conflicts and contradictions. Obviously, it is far more complex and taxing than answering to one or two lines of authority. This is not to suggest that the average African is far more intelligent than other species.[82] The main point is that, foreigners who consult only themselves or Allah may not understand the African who consults, not only himself but also four other authority reference points as well.

Similar issues were discussed with reference to Hindu law (chapter 4) and Muslim law (chapter 5). The cosmic responsibility of the Hindu individual indicated an individual-centred but not egocentric informal, invisible interlinkage of individual and cosmos, paralleled in Islam through the accountability of the individual believer to Allah. In the Hindu, Muslim and African scenarios, individuals are at all times accountable to various levels of authority outside themselves, arising from their specific socio-cultural environment. The socio-legal triangle in such cases is always plurality-conscious and takes account of ethical values and positive laws, where they exist. The pluralistic African model presented above appears to undervalue the social input into the triangular negotiation process, emphasising the political dimension and particularly religious forms of authority. The Hindu system explicitly recognised that the individual conscience (*ātmanastushti*) was to be consulted first. Significantly, this is left out of Ayittey's and Yelpaala's schemes, though they both recognise the individual as an active participant and not just a mental space. One might therefore suggest a fifth level of authority in African culture, the self-controlled order mechanism within individual consciousness. Only if that level has been passed and the question is still unanswered, will the process of consulting other levels of authority continue and become, probably but not necessarily, more visible.

Yelpaala's scheme emphasises the authority of the living, represented by personalities with authority or power. This is perhaps too male-centred and certainly too positivist and rule-centred, particularly for Western readers, who would imagine too fast that authority-bearing males would apply legal rules

---

[82] This wording seems to assume that Africans or black people are a different species, an assertion which may need to be examined, but not here.

or norms as some kind of advisory jurisdiction. In reality (compare section 4.3), processes of ascertaining guidance would still remain primarily mental processes through silent observation or participation in social activities. There is no need for debate and formal verdicts; all this can be handled by individuals in total silence. The African conceptual equivalent to Hindu *sadācāra*, Muslim *shariat* and Chinese *li* relates to the socio-political level as well as religious authority, and thus comprises all three elements of the conceptual triangle of law-making. In the African scheme, Yelpaala (1983: 375, as cited above) next lists the ancestors, as much a separate category as they are directly linked to the king, chief or lineage head, which Yelpaala recognises. They are, thus, a separate source of authority, as in China, and yet they are not. They deserve to be listed separately as a source of guidance because they are at the same time a human source of authority and no longer a purely human source. In the Hindu system, where they also play a certain role, they were not listed in the ancient texts as a source of legal rules.

The other two levels identified by Yelpaala and Ayittey are explicitly religious authorities, the familiar lower deities and the high god of whatever description. Yelpaala does not indicate whether the four levels of authority should be understood as a hierarchical structure. Indeed it seems that all these sources of authority in the African system may be consulted simultaneously. None excludes the other, as was assumed for the Hindu system with its hierarchical structures (chapter 4, section 4.3). The African model thus emphasises the all-pervading authority of socio-religious authorities, but does not give them a hierarchically superior position. This confirms the hypothesis that in traditional African processes of law-finding, several potentially conflicting sources of authority were always ideally harmonised into one system of interacting equals rather than allowing any one element superiority over the others.

It now becomes more obvious how conceptually different the Islamic perspective on the same legal predicament is and how explicitly religion-focused Muslim theoretical discussions have been (chapter 5). Muslims anywhere in the world would need to seek guidance from several sources of authority, too, but the official religious message is that God's law and guidance are supreme, claiming superiority for religion over society and the state. This contrasts with African systems of thought and methods of law-finding. It may explain why many Africans have not rushed to become Muslims, or have become Muslims but maintain their lines of communication to African traditional authorities, replacing visions of an African supreme omnipotent being with belief in Allah while retaining the traditional plurality-consciousness of African cultures.

The above discussion confirms that there was no conceptual ingredient in traditional African laws which was allowed absolute pre-eminence. For the three competing sources of law, the central requirement was that of balancing and harmonisation. This central element, described in different terminology and in a different context, also appears when Ebo (1995: 34) emphasises the concept of 'equilibrium':

> The primary purpose of indigenous justice is to maintain equilibrium between interests and forces whose dynamic interplay form the substance of human societies. Justice makes a common demand on all, namely, that nothing be done to destroy equilibrium between groups. It accords the chief place among unjust and harmful acts to what can be called belittlement, or the denial of equilibrium conditions.

For this reason, 'the end of justice is not served by the prescription of a set of penalties' (Ebo, 1995: 34). Every infringement needs to be looked at in the light of its particular circumstances, justice is not served by uniform standards. More important than punishment is recognition that any infringement of equilibrium requires healing of the interpersonal relationship that would have been damaged by a wrongful action. Repairing breaches of social equilibrium therefore requires more than just punishment, as Western criminal law assumes. Here again, the social and religious spheres come together. Ebo (1995: 39) argues:

> A legal offence is not merely a simple matter of a transgression of a rule of custom or good behaviour. It is also a breach of some spiritual observance. To make amends for violating a rule of law by paying due compensation that restores the condition of the status quo ante is not the end of the matter. There is a spiritual dimension to attend to before the matter is finally set to rest.

Ebo (1995: 39) emphasises that this gives traditional African law added strength. His approach, typical of a legal writer, does not relate the topic to the individual, looking instead to authority outside the human brain, in this case religious authority. Ebo (1995: 39) argues:

> Because of this pervasive religious nexus, indigenous law is usually possessed of enough inner virility and power to be almost self-acting and self-contained as regards its in-built capacity to enforce its verdicts once they are pronounced by competent sources.

Ebo is unclear about the role of individual conscience as a controlling mechanism, but admits that, in view of strong internal mechanisms of self-control, it may not be necessary to police the norms of society. This leads Ebo (1995: 40) to conclude that, in the absence of a police force, 'every bona fide member of the community is supposed to be an honorary police of law and order'. Making it a presumed civic duty to report any acts of violation that come to one's notice, this captures a vision of public vigilance and public interest with modern activist characteristics.[83] Ebo (1995: 40) discusses the notion that an infringement may be seen as 'an offence against public interest', but his public/private distinction is

[83] This is precisely the underlying philosophy of South Asian forms of public interest litigation (chapter 4, section 4.10 and chapter 5, section 5.14), where any *bona fide* petitioner can bring any matter of public interest or, in Pakistan, any issue of 'public importance', to the attention of the superior courts (Menski *et al.*, 2000).

not maintainable and obfuscates the main issue. The critical element is that 'the soul of justice lies in the determination of equitable equilibrium compensation' (Ebo, 1995: 41).

This discussion of how traditional Nigerian societies maintained protective mechanisms for societal equilibrium takes into account only two dimensions. Ebo (1995: 41) writes that 'especially the apparently harmonious coexistence and co-action of two quite different levels of legal system in the behavioural equipment of the individual mind' provides salient lessons about processes of modernisation. Significantly, his analysis misses the third element of the interactive pattern that Chiba (1986) identified through his tripartite model and that the present study cultivates through the triangular model (chapter 3, section 3.8). Ebo shows only that religion and society interact to produce balancing mechanisms, overlooking the state, in whatever form, as the third party in the triangular dynamic. It would not be fair to say that Ebo did not notice this third element. However, despite recognising it, he does not draw it into his analytical framework. This confirms that law tends to be seen as a separate force in a 'black box' also by African authors.

Other legal authors have not even noticed this intrinsic balancing within traditional African laws and have been characteristically legocentric. A mild example of selective myopia in Western legal scholarship is found in Allott (1984). Thinking about why knowledge of customary laws in Africa mattered, Allott (1984: 124) started with general reflections about law, underplaying critical distinctions between customary laws and positive law and conflating the two, as well as overlooking the role of the individual as a potential law-finder. Later, turning to the customary nature of African indigenous laws, Allott (1984: 129) shows clearly that he was alert to the social relevance of customary law-making processes, but he did not go far enough in emphasising considerations of balance and coordination:

> If one bases a law . . . on popular practice, then it is at least probable that the laws will also be popular in a quite different sense. In this latter sense, the laws tend to be knowable, expressed in a form capable of knowledge, because they spring from the same people who will then be subjected to them. Such laws may well be mediated through courts, tribunals and authorities at some stage; but these courts and authorities themselves tended in African customary practice to incorporate the ordinary people or a representative sample of them, whether as participants and parties, or as spectators allowed to venture opinions. Once laws are processed through such channels, they naturally emerge in a form and with a content which ordinary people comprehend and accept.

This awareness of processes does not extend to primary patterns of rule-construction in the human brain. However, careful reading of this article brings out awareness of the principle of internal balancing of the various conflicting law-making forces, but only with reference to particular individuals, such as priests. Allott (1984: 130) indicates that 'the law or legal system as a whole was not seen as the private possession of such priests and religious functionaries; and though their practices might be arcane, they purported to administer laws which all could understand and accept'. Hence, law-making is more than just a legal process. But did such priests in fact 'administer' laws, as Allott suggests here, or were they above all engaged as dramatic characters in the continuous balancing and reproduction of legal norms and principles, playing their own interactive role in this? This question is left open. Similarly, Allott (1984: 130) briefly examines the suggestion that a dominant political elite in ethnically stratified societies might exploit the 'aristocratic privilege' of imposing laws as they pleased, and without public control. Allott (1984: 130) seems to accept this to some extent, especially when he asserts that laws 'might be out of the control of the ordinary people; but they were in no real sense generally foreign to them'. Similarly, the absence of a professional lawyer caste, which Allott portrays as 'somewhat surprising' (p. 130), is not further explored.[84] Were there inherent barriers to the emergence of such a class which go beyond orality, publicity of laws and the desire to keep everything local and public? Could it be that traditional Africans sensed that allowing lawyers to dominate law-finding processes might be bad for balance and justice? These are speculative thoughts which require further investigation. Allott (1984: 131) confirmed that the inherent publicity of traditional African laws was important:

> Many commentators have remarked how African judicial or arbitral pro-
> ceedings did more than settle cases; they settled law too. Furthermore, they
> had an educational function in reminding participants and spectators of
> the basic norms of the society and its legal system, and spelt out the social
> obligations which flowed from these norms. A legal proceeding could thus
> perform a most important, secondary, integrative role, binding the mem-
> bers of society more closely together by reminding them of their obligations,
> and the practical meanings of them in relation to the various roles which
> they might occupy.

Allott continues that we should not assume that legal knowledge was equally and uniformly dispersed throughout society, but asserted that general levels of public knowledge about the laws, and of comprehension, were high. He explained this not as a safety mechanism to ensure equitable balancing between competing inputs but as the result of orality and hence the absence of a special code of legal language. Thus, '[i]n the absence of writing and the often generalised character of legal norms and principles, there could be no vast accumulation of laws which the ordinary person could not master' (p. 131). Allott (1984: 132) went further, emphasising the close links between legal norms and the lives of African people:

---

[84] Chapter 7 demonstrates clearly expressed ancient Chinese reservations about lawyers as 'litigation tricksters'; it was almost a crime in ancient China to hold oneself out as a lawyer.

Everyone lived within the society and in accordance with the life which the law sought to regulate. So any individual could readily attach the norms and principles he was expected to assimilate to the institutions which they regulated. The norms he dealt with referred to the acquisition and tilling of land, the making of marriage, the infliction of simple harms, such as wounding. . . .

There were substantial benefits from this common knowledge and acceptance of laws. The laws became more effective, and the requirements of a good political society were more easily met. One must not exaggerate: not all was sweetness and light. There were conflicts, misunderstandings, attempts to bypass or stretch the law; but the law which was so stretched was a known and generally accepted law. If it was not known and generally accepted, then it would tend to become non-law, to lose its legal force.

Allott's focus on knowledge brings out several important points to test the hypothesis of the plurality-conscious, ideally balanced nature of traditional African laws. Other legal writing emphasises that, depending on the political organisation of an African community, some form of legislation might appear in the form of oral decrees by a chief (in council) or by elders. Such laws were not derived from formal legislation, but were rather drawn principally from how people thought one ought to behave. Precedents of previous cases were remembered and could be used as a subsidiary source of law if the facts and circumstances matched, but precedent was not really a source of African law (Ayittey, 1991: 62).[85] There are many indications that custom needed to remain flexible to serve its social purpose and to fulfil the perceived obligations of people towards the pre-existing higher order, including the ancestors. Lack of adaptation in customary law would force it to become out of touch with society, which is difficult to imagine. As Allott explained in the citation above, this would inevitably lead to its demise.

Allott's approach confirms the idealistic assumption that everybody knew more or less implicitly what the law is. Public debates about disputes, ritualisation of conflicts, publicity of proceedings and a high level of general public participation in law-finding made it a rather democratic mechanism for harmonious living. There were experts, to a limited extent, but they never managed to hijack the law, as modern lawyers have done, appropriating it for their own benefit, while professing to act in the public interest and public service. There was little room for positivist manipulation in traditional Africa, and there was clearly no legal profession. Being a lawyer-like specialist was a matter of a person's life experience, knowledge and skill in balancing the constantly competing claims of religion, governance and society. As in Hindu, Islamic and Chinese laws, such experts would acquire high status in society, provided they used

---

[85] Allott (1968: 143), however, suggests that precedent is a major source of law and gives examples. Although these seem to indicate that remembrance of earlier cases was important, they did not necessarily act as precedent in the sense of a binding model.

their skills for the public good. Such persons were not above the law, which was found outside the human sphere. Being a lawyer of whatever description, in the lego-philosophical context of Africa, was not a crime. There were no prominent bad sayings in Africa about 'litigation-tricksters', as in China, but instead many proverbs about selfish individuals. Those who were experts in legal matters were supposed to act in the context, and for the benefit, of the wider community. Apparently, some African communities saw the onus of office rather than its attractions and expressed themselves in many ways against having leaders, or joining a team of leaders (Ayittey, 1991: 79). The principle that '[a]utocracy was always a theoretical possibility in government' (p. 79) worried many African societies. Such issues are further tested below in relation to dispute settlement processes.

6.3.5 Dispute settlement processes in pre-colonial Africa

Traditional African dispute settlement, though at first sight centred on conflict, probably also operated on the idealistic basis of recognition that it was better to balance and harmonise conflicting claims in society than to engage in constant warfare and fighting. Plurality-consciousness then becomes a means to maintain harmony. Much of the legal literature concentrates on ways of maintaining social order and settling disputes in pre-colonial African societies. Questions arose over whether one can have laws without a legislator, law enforcement without a police force, and proper settlement of disputes without courts. It is evident that such questions all start from positivist assumptions. The structures of traditional political systems in Africa showed great variety and it seems that all forms of political organisation have appeared on the continent in one form or another. The range extended from large kingdoms and chiefly societies with urban centres down to polycephalous and acephalous communities and small groups of hunter-gatherers.[86] New states and communities evolved through migration, conquest and settlement; empires and kingdoms rose, flourished and decayed. Small-scale societies might thrive in self-governing family or village units. Generally speaking, political authority never went much beyond the village level, which was often dominated by the rule of elders, a kind of gerontocracy, but often depended on age-sets, where the strongest and most active males as a group were collective leaders. The internally stratified system of traditional African societies is explained by Ayittey (1991: 8–9), who identifies four groups. First, the 'founder group' of members, descended from the original forefather, believed to be the founder of a particular society, and hence often the clan(s) from which any leader figures might be drawn. Secondly, the 'commoners' who were not necessarily related to the governing class and normally formed the majority. Thirdly, 'strangers' who had been given permission

---

[86] On acephalous societies and African segmentary systems, see Middleton and Tait (1958).

to reside in the area occupied by a group,[87] and finally 'servants' or a servile class which might often include slaves.

An influential classification found in Fortes and Evans-Pritchard (1940) distinguished often highly structured, 'centralised' communities from headless or 'acephalous' societies. Centralised ('Group A') societies had organs of government with centralised authority, administrative machinery and judicial institutions. The ruler(s) often commanded an organised force, and cleavages of wealth, privilege and status among the people in such societies corresponded to the distribution of power and authority within a defined territory. Hart (1961) would have had few problems in recognising the existence of law in such societies. Examples include the Zulu, Tswana, Basotho, Bemba, the various kingdoms of East Africa, such as Buganda, Bunyoro, Ankole and Ruanda, the Yoruba, Benin and Ashanti in West Africa. Constitutions of such states tended to balance power with responsibility,[88] and saw the duties of rulers and subjects as complementary, implying a model of 'rule by consent'.[89] In terms of dispute settlement machinery, many of these societies had formal courts with some specialised legal personnel.[90]

Acephalous ('Group B') societies were stateless or republican groupings which lacked central authorities and sharp divisions of rank.[91] Their lineage or descent system and age grades, in particular, regulated political and social relationships. In such societies, community mattered more than territory. Examples include the Igbo, Ga, Kikuyu, Nandi and Nuer. Simpler segmentary societies might still have local legal specialists, such as the *muthamaki* among the Kikuyu in Kenya (Allott, 1968: 134). A third type of traditional African society was recognised, comprising very small societies within which the largest political unit was just a family group. The major examples in this category are the San Bushmen, Hadza and Ituri.[92]

African lawyers, as well as Western experts and commentators, have written much on African dispute settlement processes.[93] Holleman (1974: 16) indicates that 'the merits of the tribal system have been seriously doubted, especially by those who have never attended a tribal process'. Okupa (1998: 115) refutes the

---

[87] For details on various kinds of strangers in African societies see Shack and Skinner (1979). Ayittey (1991: 8) provides a politically instructive Bantu example.

[88] Compare for Hindu law *rājadharma*, the specific set of duties for the ruler (chapter 4, section 4.4) and for Islamic law *siyasa shar'iyya*, government according to *shari'a* (chapter 5).

[89] For example, there is a Sesotho saying that '[a] chief is a chief by the people' (*morena ke morena ka batho*) (Bennett, 2004: 4) and there would be many phrases like this. For a detailed bibliography on various types of chieftaincy see Okupa (1998: 25ff.).

[90] For details see Allott (1968: 134).

[91] 'Polycephalous' might be a more realistic image; there was no legal void, as 'acephalous' might suggest.

[92] On the !Kung Bushmen, see Ayittey (1991: 84–91).

[93] For bibliographical details see Okupa (1998: 115–33).

assumption that traditional African processes of dispute settlement resulted in injustice, claiming that '[i]t is a myth that anarchy reigned in pre-colonial Africa. Many people in rural societies did not dissipate their energy and man-power in war, as they had to battle every day with their often harsh physical environment.' Thus, certain legal institutions were formed 'to make peace-ful co-existence and survival easy for everybody, men, women and children' (p. 115). Allott (1968: 136) emphasised that African communities were gener-ally small, from only about fifty persons in Bushman bands to half a million or more people in larger kingdoms, e.g. the Ashanti. However, the typical African system of government meant that even in the largest empires most govern-mental functions were carried out in a restricted local community, usually by functionaries who lived in and came from that community. Allott (1968: 136–7) commented:

> The fact that government and the processes of law and dispute-settlement were mostly confined within a community of limited area and popula-tion lent a distinctive character to African law. Face-to-face contacts, both between potential disputants and between a disputant and one who might later judge his case, were frequent. Neighbours knew each other, for better or ill. Relationships between parties in dispute often extended far beyond the issue which had brought them to quarrel before a court.

Allott (1968: 137) emphasised how this might confuse Western observers, since many of their cherished principles and assumptions found no place in Africa:

> The judge was not a remote member of an official order, but the man in the next hut. The English fiction of judicial ignorance would have been severely strained in African customary processes. Not only did the local judge or arbitrator often know most, if not all, of the facts of a dispute before ever it came officially to his notice, but he would also probably be aware of the previous history of the relationship between the contestants; he would know that X was always quarrelling, that Y beat his wife, that Z was a stranger who only came to the community a few years ago; and so on.
>   Equally it would be much more difficult for the litigant to pull the wool over the eyes of a court consisting of his neighbours who knew him well. The gap between legal truth and actual fact was thus diminished. Rules of evidence were less formalistic and restrictive than those of English law or those of Islamic law.

Allott (1968: 145) noted that '[a]t the heart of African adjudication lies the notion of reconciliation or the restoration of harmony' and offers some realistic insights how injustice might be minimised in informal traditional societies where all dispute settlement was subjected to public scrutiny. Allott (1968: 145–6) explains why decisions were respected by all concerned:

> At the heart of African adjudication lies the notion of reconciliation or the restoration of harmony. The job of a court or an arbitrator is less to

find the facts, state the rules of law, and apply them to the facts than to set right a wrong in such a way as to restore harmony within the disturbed community. Harmony will not be restored unless the parties are satisfied that justice has been done. The complainant will accordingly want to see that the legal rules, including those which specify the appropriate recompense for a given wrong, are applied by the court. But the party at fault must be brought to see how his behaviour has fallen short of the standard set for his particular role as involved in the dispute, and he must come to accept that the decision of the court is a fair one. On his side he wants an assurance that once he has admitted his error and made recompense for it he will be re-integrated into the community.

These are the objectives which a customary court will set itself. Only in this way will the judgment receive the endorsement of the community as a whole. Mutual acceptance of a judgment and subsequent reconciliation are the only guarantee, in view of defective enforcement procedures, that a judgment will be duly executed.

Holleman (1974: 18) argues that traditional African dispute settlement must be viewed in its particular socio-cultural setting, which creates a very different style of law and legal processes. The community must and does take a vital interest and a decision of a lawsuit strictly according to formal rules of law is unrealistic and inadequate, unless it 'has the effect of *removing the cause of the conflict and of reconciling* the litigating parties'. Formal rules of law only serve as a basis for discussion rather than as binding rules, so that 'indigenous administration of justice aims at *solving* the conflict between the parties rather than *deciding* its legal aspects in terms of law. Justice . . . becomes a process of persuasion with the accent on the reasonable behaviour of all concerned in a spirit of give and take . . . The successful end of a tribal process is a judgment which both parties formally agree to accept and observe' (Holleman, 1974: 18). Such comments show the author's deep insight into the psychology of traditional African systems. David and Brierley (1978: 508), on safer ground while writing about procedures, also found that traditional Africans put justice above procedure:

Law and justice in the context of the small, pre-colonial societies of Africa and Malagasy are inevitably different from what they are in the vast communities of the European states. Native justice is an institution for peace rather than a means for the strict enforcement of law; its purpose is to reconcile the parties and to restore harmonious relations within the community. Searching for an agreement is all the more necessary in view of the lack of procedures for the enforcement of judgments which, in any event, because they are based only on some principle of authority, might well be of no effect whatsoever. Moreover, it is not rare, we are told, for the successful party, acting in that generous spirit characteristic of African society, to forego the enforcement of his judgment.

These authors begin to indicate the implications of the supervening African desire for amicable settlement of disputes, but doubt whether the mechanisms of authority in African societies would be sufficient to ensure compliance. From the holistic perspective of African laws, where legal action is concurrently a social process, a political gameplay and a matter of religion and social healing through ritual, compliance is certainly less problematic than a mono-focused legocentric approach assumes. Allott (1968: 134–5) focused on the informal oral nature of these proceedings, showing that informal law-making was practised in various ways:

> The fact that the law and procedure were oral naturally led to simplicity and directness in its formulation. Rules and principles were expressed in everyday language which the ordinary citizen could understand. Technical legal terms were known and employed; but these formed no barrier between the legal expert and the litigant. The very process of adjudication and the promulgation of new statutes contributed to this popularisation of the law. Thus among the Tswana new laws were deliberated and enacted at a *pitso*, or general assembly of all the adult males of the tribe. In theory, every man could attend and take part in its deliberations; and there was a similar right to attend and participate in a case before the court of a local chief. Not every African law went as far as that of the Tswana in permitting popular participation in law-making and adjudication; but the general drift is clear. The law is not an arcane mystery but a matter of public concern.

Maine's (1861) assumptions about the exclusivity of legal knowledge and its monopolistic position among the aristocracy, or a juristic oligarchy as universal depositories and administrators of law, are thus proved wrong. Allott (1968: 135) argued that such ingenious speculation 'is completely contrary to most African judicial practice: African customary law was not and is not known only to a privileged minority.' Allott (1968: 135) emphasised that, because legal processes were generally localised rather than remote and customary law was expressed in simple language, virtually all citizens could take part in its making and administration:

> Wherever there was a community, be it a village or extended family unit, there was machinery of greater or less formality for the public settling of disputes. Every man thus had a court of some kind on his doorstep (perhaps one should say the threshold of his hut!). To adjudicate or arbitrate in disputes is in traditional African society an essential appurtenance of office, so that not only the chief or village headman but the lineage elders and the father of a restricted family would be expected to settle cases which arose between those subject to their authority.

This indicates a sense of obligation to participate in dispute settlement for the good of society, a notion still widely present today and often leads to large

crowds and a market atmosphere (Achebe, 1958: 64). Ayittey (1991: 43) emphasises that settlement processes, especially in acephalous societies, such as those
of the Arusha in Tanzania, achieved and constituted a number of things at
once:

> The settlement process was partly an informal consensus in that discussion
> took place until an agreement was reached. It was partly a bargaining process
> in that offers and counter-offers were made until agreed terms were reached.
> It was also a negotiating process partly because persuasion, artifice, and
> stratagem were employed to reach an agreement. At the same time, however,
> it constituted an adversary process as each disputant was represented by
> spokesmen or counsellors.

In more formalised states with more official-looking procedures (Ayittey, 1991:
44ff.), there might be a hierarchy of courts, depending on the nature of the
dispute and its potential implications. The potential abuse of powers by such
institutions and office holders was of concern to traditional African societies.
For chiefly societies, Ayittey (1991: 94) paints the image of a leader surrounded
by an inner council with regular meetings who 'was not bound to follow their
advice and might ignore it if he wished. But he would not deliberately do so
and risk the withdrawal of their support. This inner council, thus, constituted
the first line of defense against despotism.'

Ayittey (1991: 95) relies on earlier researchers to show that the council had
two functions. Apart from advising and assisting the chief in administrative
matters, it had the duty 'to act as a brake on the chief, preventing abuse of
power, voicing dissatisfactions, criticising and generally to keep the Chief under
the necessary control' (p. 95). The same is reported from the Akan in Ghana,
among whom the chief was forbidden to act without the knowledge, approval
and concurrence of the council. Other research reports that, on accession to
power, a chief would have to swear that he would act only in consonance with
his council. Traditional African political structures therefore militated against
dictatorship and Maine's (1861) imagined power of *caprice*. Further down the
line, too, the system of checks and balances was continued, as reported by
Ayittey (1991: 95ff.) for the Asante and many other groups. Among various
communities in Ghana, complaints about the ruler or chief could be made
to one or more members of the council, and the ruler might be admonished
or, if this did not help, could be deposed or de-stooled. Thus, as in the Chinese ruler's Mandate of Heaven, the leader's authority was subject to public
approval and satisfaction. Absolutist rule by an Austinian law-maker was possible, but is conceptually incompatible with the idealised African legal and political traditions about maintaining an equilibrium between all three law-founding
elements.

Disputes between people would inevitably arise (Ayittey, 1991: 3). Since a
small personal quarrel could quickly lead to a wider dispute, engulfing many

more people and thus costlier on every count (Ayittey, 1991: 9), the need to avoid conflict was paramount. While disputes would often arise over property, Ayittey (1991: 39) emphasised the crucial importance of social harmony:

> [W]ithin the traditional African *modus operandi*, there was an additional unique dimension. Individual attachment to lineages and latent groups of solidarity always carried the potential risk of transforming personal disputes into broader group conflicts as was often the case among the Nuer and the Ganda. Consequently, great emphasis was placed on peaceful resolution of disputes and the promotion of social harmony while upholding the principles of fairness, custom and tradition.

Ayittey (1991: 40) emphasises the cosmic dimension, so that the requirement to achieve harmony remains not just a matter for human society at the time, but extends much beyond the present moment. The living have obligations towards the ancestors as well as those yet to be born:

> Cosmological factors provided additional reason for the general emphasis on peaceful resolution of conflicts. It may be recalled that Africans stressed the maintenance of order and harmony in the universe which consisted of the sky, the earth and the world. Order and harmony in the universe required the maintenance of corresponding conditions within the various kinship groups in the ethnic society as well. Gikuyu elders considered as their primary duty the prevention of strife between members of a lineage or between lineages and the prevention of both from resorting to supernatural powers and open hostilities.

Recourse to supernatural powers as a means of dispute settlement (section 6.3.3 above) can be matched by preventing access to such forces in their negative, destructive shape. Supernatural forces could be invoked in various legal processes, for example in installing or anointing a king or chief by oaths, to initiate litigation as oracles, oaths or ordeals to make difficult decisions, as 'masquerades' to coerce stubborn litigants, or in witchcraft as a means of causing or attributing harm, or deterring or detecting harm caused. Ayittey (1991: 65–6) quotes evidence from other authors to support his points:

> In law procedures, the influence of the supernatural is most dramatic and visible. The importance of the supernatural can be seen in dispute settlement. Because they are omniscient and all powerful, cosmic forces are called upon to judge the probity of a witness if the veracity of a testimony is in doubt. Among the northern tribes of Ghana, the most powerful supernatural force that can be called upon in trials is lightning (*saa* among the Dagaaba). Disputants and witnesses are often required to swear under oath to be struck by lightning if they perjure themselves. So immediate and dramatic is this punishment that litigants are not prone to lying under oath. If someone nevertheless perjured himself, 'he must act swiftly to pacify this highly temperamental supernatural power by telling the truth and

providing some sacrificial offerings to the custodian of that power (*saasob* or *saadaana*) for pacification' (Yelpaala, 1983: 375).

Ayittey's research demonstrates that the religious sphere is firmly integrated into the legal processes of traditional African dispute settlement and society monitors that supernatural powers are not exploited by humans.[94] Secular lawyers would be unable to understand such processes 'from within'. Ayittey (1991: 40) shows that traditional African dispute settlement processes had several layers and dimensions, focused all the time on one central ideal aim, equilibrium at all levels, here expressed in social harmony and the best possible form of cooperation:

> The maintenance of peace within most African communities followed four principles. The first was settlement of disputes by deliberation and discussion, rather than by force. The second was the correction of wrongdoing by compensation except in serious offenses such as murder. The third was adjudication and assessment by elders who were considered to be impartial. The fourth was fairness. These principles were upheld by the use of courts, their constitution and the right to appeal.

Ayittey (1991: 63) further analysed the legal and philosophical dimensions of such dispute settlement processes, bringing out the situation-specific nature of traditional African dispute settlement:

> A kind of 'situation' ethic was applied with the aim to resolve conflicts in accordance with general social values rather than predetermined codes of law. Certain acts were recognised as crimes: theft, rape, extortion, murder, assault, etc. and were punished accordingly. But punishment alone, which of course varied from one society to another, was not enough to heal the social wounds.
>
> Most native Africans believed wrong-doing strained social relationships and displeased the ever-present spirits of the ancestors. Thus, while the concept of justice was clearly known, it was pursued within certain parameters or with additional objectives: repairing frayed social relationships and pacifying the ancestral spirits.
>
> Thus unlike the Western legal system, the indigenous African arbitration process laid a great deal of emphasis on reconciling the disputing parties *to promote social harmony* rather [than] on the punishment or the settlement. Justice was pursued with broader societal and spiritual objectives ... In this way, the peasants were able to adjust legal arbitration decisions to changing values, standards and circumstances of the community.

Ayittey's analysis confirms the internally balanced nature of traditional African societies and their laws as an inherent concept. The related conceptualisation

---

[94] Poison rituals and ordeals are covered by Okupa (1998: 63–79). Lowy (1978), working on a more recent period in Ghana, illustrates the frequency of recourse to various supernatural powers.

of a duty to do the right thing at the right time is brought out when Ayittey (1991: 65) writes:

> It may be recalled that African peasant's maxim was: 'I am because we are.' The teleological emphasis on the community overshadowed the interests of the individual. Consequently, in African law, the fundamental principle was embedded in a contractual liability to maintain what Davidson (1970) called the 'ideal equilibrium.'
>
> This equilibrium or principle, expressed in every aspect of the social fabric, upheld that any action intending to harm others was a threat to the whole society, and must be purged by appropriate counteraction. Right behaviour was accordingly seen in terms of debt: of a negative liability on the individual not to do what was wrong, but also a positive liability to do what was right. Purging and punishment were frequently a matter of compensation.

Ayittey (1991: 67–8) therefore concludes overall that the indigenous court system stressed reconciliation and promotion of social harmony to resolve disputes and conflicts while pursuing a fair degree of justice:

> Court hearings were open and the administration of justice was flexible. Indigenous courts were not conducted according to a rigid and abstract code of law. This flexibility was necessary to permit the court system to achieve its twin objectives of justice and social harmony. Perhaps, this was the prime reason why the proceedings were open to the public or any interested person. Those present could 'speak their minds' freely and contribute to the administration of social justice. Thus, a fair trial could be ensured and, moreover, court decisions could be appealed.

Holleman (1974: 3), having witnessed such dispute settlement processes, reports on extended discussions, occasional disintegration into a free-for-all, and the sometimes quietly listening chief, who might appear to have lost control. However, such first impressions are deceptive:

> It may strike us as a sign of weakness and lack of authority on the part of the chief and his court. But is it? Isn't this rather the very nature of indigenous jurisdiction, a direct consequence of a predominantly communally-adjusted frame of mind? A case in which every personal matter brought before a public forum is of public interest, that is, not merely as a matter of curiosity regarding the affairs of one's neighbours, but in a very real sense a conflict that belongs to the community itself and which has to be thrashed out and settled, not only in public, but by the public, that is, by the *community itself?* The answer seems to be in the affirmative, because whenever there is a question of public reconciliation of parties by means of meat killed and eaten, or snuff taken, *all present* partake in the act of reconciliation: chief, parties and public alike.

'Public interest' appears here again as a powerful social balancing mechanism in which the rough edges of injustice and disputes are smoothened, and everybody is encouraged to give and take a little for the wider common good. Ayittey (1991: 72) claims that Africans may have developed an alternative form of 'rule of law', which should be taken seriously. This debate confirms that traditional African systems of law operated on the basis of a skilful combination of various kinds of law within an overarching philosophical framework that sought to serve the interests of individuals as well as of the universe. The incoming colonial powers, not aware of such legal postulates and underlying conceptualisations, looking upon law from a positivist angle, were thus destined to interfere dramatically in the traditional systems, impacting on the traditional ideal of equilibrium in a distorting manner.

6.4 African laws under colonial rule

Lawyers are the first to proclaim that the imposition of colonial rule on the various African territories had a profound effect on existing legal orders in Africa. However, the slow-moving train of African legal history did not even stop to take on colonial baggage. Like a band of marauders, colonialists imposed their concepts onto existing structures, claiming overall control, but the train kept moving and did not change its basic characteristics as much as the literature has claimed.

It is amazing how self-contradictory the legal arguments over colonial rule in Africa are. While many authors realise that pre-colonial Africa had its own, well-established legal systems and was not a *tabula rasa*, those same authors often apply culture-blind legocentric assumptions, behaving as though modern Western laws simply brought salvation to Africa. In light of the previous sections, it is doubtful whether enforced introduction of Western laws into Africa could be positive. Elevating the colonial state and its formal legal machineries into a privileged law-maker position, using what Kuper and Kuper (1965: 17) called 'imperium', would automatically unbalance the intricate network of traditional African legal systems. This would tilt the balance of power dangerously towards those who could claim to control the official law, leading to a potential increase in perceived injustice through marginalisation of the indigenous equilibrium ideal.

The present section examines briefly how colonial changes affected the pre-existing concepts and structures of African laws. It is not the case that everything changed in Africa overnight; first of all, the incoming colonial laws merely formed a new layer of official law. Colonisation became an extended series of superimpositions, not a sudden legal transformation. Indirect rule gradually changed, 'from a civilizing mission to a law-and-order administration' (Mamdani, 1996: 109). The new official laws remained largely distant and inoperative for most Africans,[95] an observation which holds true even today. The focus in

---

[95] Achebe (1958) portrays a different picture, but suggests that there were ways to evade or avoid the new regime.

the literature on structural changes introduced by colonialism wrongly suggests that the traditional systems were either destroyed or totally abolished. They were modified and restructured, but, within the largely invisible unofficial realm, there was also much continuity – the result was a new hybrid, not a replacement of the old order. In colonial Africa, too, state positivism could not just abolish people's religions and worldviews and their traditional socio-legal systems of community-based regulation by the stroke of a pen. The incoming colonial positivist laws naturally claimed superiority, denying equal status to the other two claimants for law-making authority, religion and society. Such an imbalanced approach, represented through the ideal model of 'rule of law' as a great achievement of Western civilisation and Western legal theory, was bound to upset the subtle traditional balances that African laws had been so concerned to preserve throughout the pre-colonial period.

Within the triangular interactive model of jurisprudence cultivated and tested in the present study (chapter 3, section 3.8), introducing and superimposing state law as the dominant element would mainly create new official laws, while the pre-existing legal systems would become either partially integrated into this new official law or would continue in existence, but now as unofficial laws. No legal author on colonialism appears to have considered Chiba's (1986) 'legal postulates' in relation to Africa, while Ayittey (1991), without using the term as such, accounts for this concept and has used it for his analysis. It is evident that eventually the British model of 'indirect rule' managed to create a sustainable, plurality-conscious balance. The present section explores this complex process, first discussing the general process of colonisation and then examining in detail its impact on customary laws and processes of dispute settlement.

6.4.1 The process of colonisation

Like almost all South Asians and many Muslims, most African people have experienced that the colonial state law introduces a new language and a conceptually different framework of reference. Traditional multilingual African legal orality was drawn into increasing competition with received European languages and colonial legal concepts. As a result, African laws are now found not only in various local idioms, but above all in one of the languages of the colonial powers, mainly English, French and Portuguese (Read, 1997). This new linguistic plurality impedes communication and has contributed to various discrepancies between official and unofficial laws in Africa.

The process of colonisation in Africa started comparatively late. While the British started trading in India as early as 1600 (chapter 4, section 4.7), were involved in local law-making from 1765, and were firmly established as the supreme power in the subcontinent by 1858, most of Africa was for a long time still more of a dangerous coastline for European sailors trying to get to India and the Far East than a continent that could be colonised. The Roman

Empire had for some time extended into northern Africa; Muslim invaders and travellers had reached North Africa by the seventh century, invading Spain in 711. The famous Muslim traveller Ibn Battuta sailed from Aden in 1330 along the eastern coast of Africa and met many Arab traders on the way.[96] In 1351 he went overland from Morocco to Mali, crossing the Sahara, spent several years in the area and left detailed records of his travels. Such early evidence reflects the Muslim domination of much of North and East Africa from an early stage.

Most European powers did not get a secure foot on the ground for a long time. During the fifteenth century, Portuguese seamen explored the Atlantic coast of Africa and eventually sailed into the Indian Ocean, seeking to find a way eastwards that would allow them to avoid contact with Muslims, who were expanding further into Europe (and East Africa) at that time. The Portuguese established trading posts all along the coast, and started building up a slave trade, but did not find interior Africa attractive. Between 1500 and 1800, as Portuguese power gradually declined, Dutch, English and French sailors took over, and trade with Africans began to grow.[97] Apart from a few missionaries, Europeans did not develop detailed social contacts with Africans. Many of the earlier Portuguese trading posts were abandoned. In 1652, the Dutch made a decision to establish a port in the Cape region of South Africa, only to find that their home country was absorbed by France in 1796. This meant that the Dutch settlers in South Africa were suddenly unprotected and eventually came under English control.[98]

The early slave trade was dominated by Arabs; when the Europeans tried to join in, friction was created. Needless to say, the Africans were not pleased, did not like the Europeans, and retreated inland. All these factors together impeded European attempts to penetrate Africa.[99] Only after the Muslim domination of the Mediterranean had been broken and the Suez Canal inaugurated in 1869, did Europeans become emboldened to 'open up' Africa. Between 1880 and 1900 the greater part of Africa was divided, like a juicy melon, among originally six European powers. The motivation for this was largely economic, as the potential for extracting raw materials and agricultural produce from Africa was realised in connection with the industrial revolution. Okupa (1998:

---

[96] The Europeans were to discover later that the eastern coast of Africa was heavily dominated by Arab traders and thus stayed mainly in western Africa.

[97] Names such as Ivory Coast and Gold Coast date from this time.

[98] By 1800, some 26,000 Europeans were settled in South Africa. Details of fights between Dutch Boers and the British in 1880–1 and 1899–1902 do not concern us here. South Africa became a self-governing Dominion in 1910, with a legal system dominated by Roman-Dutch law (Bekker *et al.*, 2002).

[99] Liberia is an unusual case. From 1820 onwards, it was set up for former slaves repatriated to Africa from the United States and became independent in 1822. Earlier, Britain had also resettled some slaves in Sierra Leone, hence the name Freetown, given in 1792. Sierra Leone became a British Protectorate in 1896. Some commentators speak of deportation of subjects of the Crown rather than a humane act of resettlement (Shah, 2000).

xi) writes of the 'historical accident of colonialism', even though it also looks like a planned venture. An international European conference was held in 1884 in Berlin, agreeing that claims to any territory in Africa must be upheld by effective occupation. Inevitably, this gave rise to a rush towards inner parts of Africa, starting from various trading posts, since most interior parts of Africa were then still white patches on maps. Numerous treaties were eventually made with, and mainly imposed on, local African rulers to extend the sphere of influence of a particular European power. By 1914 the melon called Africa had been carved up, and most of the present political boundaries had been drawn. This often happened in an arbitrary fashion and took little account of geography, ethnicity, and the customs and ideas of local people, leading to ongoing concerns (Mamdani, 1996).

The consolidation of European occupation involved the creation of colonial legal structures and important legal changes. The various powers took quite different approaches. The French, Spanish and Portuguese followed a state-centric policy of assimilation, claiming that all men were of equal worth, but that European civilisation was superior to that of Africa, thus inviting individual Africans to join the colonial establishment to demonstrate their advanced stage of development.[100] The French had occupied parts of North Africa since 1830 and claimed colonial possession of Algeria in 1834, though they had to fight for many years to consolidate their position. Tunisia became a Protectorate in 1881 and Morocco was gradually subjugated between 1904 and 1912. The French also established a consolidated colonial territory in West Africa, which completely surrounded the four British territories of Gambia, Sierra Leone, Ghana and Nigeria. Madagascar became a French colony in 1896.

Between 1884 and 1900, the Germans claimed Togo (1884), Cameroon (1884), Tanganyika, and South-West Africa (now Namibia). Okupa (1998: 2) indicates that the early plans for codification of African customary laws by the Germans were a result of the view, based on the historical school of jurisprudence, that codification of laws should rely on existing indigenous customs. Based on questionnaires sent out to Africa, the Germans initiated a codification process which was never completed. After the First World War, the German colonial territories of Togo and Cameroon were divided between France and Britain, while German East Africa was split into Ruanda-Burundi under Belgian authority and Tanganyika under British mandate. From 1920 South West Africa was administered by the Union of South Africa.

After 1885, the Congo was claimed by the Belgians, who speculated on its enormous economic potential, and it became a colony in 1907, after much opposition by the Portuguese, who had claimed prior rights. The Belgians also

---

[100] The French even had African members of Parliament and ministers. The 1946 French Constitution still provided that the native populations would retain their *statut personnel*, thus continuing to offer Africans a choice of law.

used French-style assimilation policies but were less hostile to local customs than the French. Respect for native custom was officially declared and later reaffirmed by a colonial Charter of 1908.

The Portuguese, after their early pioneering ventures and the establishment of trading posts, took little interest in their possessions in Africa until the other European powers began to divide up the continent. They ended up with a fairly small share, comprising a few small Atlantic islands, the territory of Portuguese Guinea (1879), and Angola and Mozambique. Closely linked with the Portuguese colonies in India (especially Goa), Mozambique was consolidated as a Portuguese territory only between 1886 and 1919 (Sachs and Welch, 1990). The Portuguese, like other Latin colonial powers, were fairly hostile to local custom. Spanish interests in Africa have always been limited, while the Italians were not given much territory after 1884 and could only claim, apart from Libya (1911), the Protectorate of Eritrea (1889) and Eastern Somalia. They tried to occupy Ethiopia, but were unsuccessful,[101] except for a brief spell during the 1930s.

Virtually all of Africa came under colonial rule in this way.[102] David and Brierley (1978: 515) emphasised that the new laws obviously reflected the legal ideas of the respective colonising nation. The differences between French and English policies, in particular, came out quite clearly in public law. Generally speaking, direct control of the mother country was the civil law principle, while English common law developed patterns of administration along the lines of a simple protectorate and particularly the system of 'indirect rule', which seems more plurality-conscious than the French expectation of assimilation. The British acquisitions were spread all over Africa. In West Africa, Gambia, Sierra Leone (Protectorate in 1896), the Gold Coast, later called Ghana, and Nigeria were in British hands. In East Africa, Kenya and Uganda became Protectorates in 1894/5, and British involvement in Southern and Central Africa was extensive, too. David and Brierley (1978: 516) reported:

> In territories under British control, British subjects and those to whom British protection was extended – as distinct from the native population – were subject to the regime established by way of order in council and local legislative measures. In West Africa, Northern Rhodesia (Zambia), Nyasaland (Malawi) and British Somaliland, English law . . . was in force as it stood at a specified date (1874 for the Gold Coast; 1880 for Sierra Leone; 1888 for Gambia; 1900 for Somaliland; 1902 for Nyasaland; 1911 for Northern Rhodesia, etc.). In East Africa reference was made to the law of British India as it stood in 1897 for Kenya, in 1902 for Uganda and in 1920 for Tanganyika, English law, as such, having only a subsidiary status.[103]

[101] In 1896 Ethiopia defeated Italian invaders in the battle of Adowa, preserving their independence.
[102] For extensive detail, see the four volumes of Middleton (1997).
[103] For further details see Allott (1970: 28–69).

This meant that there was no uniform way of dealing with law-making in the various British African territories and growing legal pluralism was in evidence, as it is today. First of all, there was certainly a need for Europeans living in Africa to make sure that the local indigenous laws would *not* govern them (Mensah-Brown, 1976: 36). But the colonial administrators did not necessarily apply the corresponding English law at the time, reserving some discretion in constructing rule systems for themselves. London was far away, and local discretionary patterns were appreciated by early traders. David and Brierley (1978: 514) indicate that for dealing with disputes between Africans and Europeans, or between Africans belonging to different groups or those who had left their own communities, a new conflict of laws or *ius gentium* had to be created. The introduction of English law in some territories from a certain date, especially in West Africa, was combined especially in East Africa with the introduction of much Anglo-Indian law, which possessed the advantage of being more extensively codified than English law at the time. In this way, important statutes like the Indian Penal Code of 1860 became part of the laws of Africa. Allott (1968: 137) succinctly but rather vaguely characterised the colonial law-making process:

> During the latter part of the nineteenth and first part of the twentieth centuries there were superimposed, swiftly and overwhelmingly, upon the traditional customary laws of Africa, highly organised legal systems developed in an utterly different environment, motivated by different objectives, following procedures far removed from those of African law, and backed up by the administrative systems and military and police forces of the colonising powers.

Allott (1968: 137–8) suggests subtly that the Africans at the time were illiterate and worlds apart from the colonisers. The enormous gap between conquerors and conquered led to communication problems which unsurprisingly affected law-making processes. The integrated traditional African systems of sociocultural and legal organisation were 'grossly disrupted' (Allott, 1968: 136) by the intervention of European colonial powers, modern commercial activities and foreign religions. However, the colonial law-making process did not lead to complete codification, which was still foreign to common lawyers. David and Brierley (1978: 516) emphasised that the reception of European law was neither final nor total, since local legislative authority could modify received laws, and the courts had powers to exclude application of any rule considered inappropriate to local conditions.

While much writing is totally legocentric, Allott (1984: 132–3) raises the pertinent point that the alien laws thus imposed remained largely inaccessible in practice for virtually the whole indigenous population and for many years to come. They remained out of reach for most Africans, in an alien language, did not match with their ways of doing things, and required foreign interpreters. As a comparative lawyer in the emerging 'law laboratory' of postcolonialism, Allott (1968: 140) even suggests the exciting possibility that legal systems in other parts of the world can learn something about processes of legal development from the African experience. However, the reluctance to learn anything from Africa would probably be just as great as the aversion to learning anything from Hindu or Muslim laws.

British colonial administration in Africa was undoubtedly informed by earlier Indian experiences. Finding it impossible to conquer the entire subcontinent and to impose English rule and laws directly, the British had entered into numerous treaties with local rulers and princes, ensuring British political sovereignty, while leaving local legal regulation largely to existing rulers. This created a system of indirect rule which later served as a model for Africa through the notion that some respect for existing indigenous institutions and laws was an appropriate policy. The use of different terminologies in India and Africa does not mean that the model itself is not quite similar. David and Brierley (1978: 512) noted that, in contrast to the French and other Latin powers, the English adopted a policy of 'indirect rule' and did not make much effort to instal their own ideas in their territories. This meant that they allowed the Africans some self-rule according to their customs, but under British supervision. Okupa (1998: xii) comments wryly that '[t]he natives were governed by "indirect rule" as long as they were submissive, paid their head or hut tax, and let themselves be flogged or imprisoned for criminal offences'. Allott (1968: 138) explained the background to the system of 'indirect rule':

> In British colonial thinking this approach was systematised in the writings of Lord Lugard and Sir Donald Cameron, and the policy of 'Indirect Rule' which they both advocated and applied in such territories as Nigeria and Tanganyika. Indirect rule meant in particular the preservation of local government by traditional chiefs and elders following their own customs and procedures. The native courts of such rulers were officially recognised by the British colonial administrations and became the lowest grade in the judicial system. Often the supervision of these native courts was kept away from the professional judges and magistrates (who, it was feared, might subvert the traditional laws and try to force them into conformity with the technicalities of English law) and entrusted instead to administrative officers who could take a friendlier and less formal view of customary law.

Sir Frederick (later Lord) Lugard published his famous study on *The dual mandate in British tropical Africa* in 1922. Allott (1980: 182) confirms that Lord Lugard did not originate this policy, whose doctrine implies using the traditional chief, his council and his court as instruments of colonial rule. Recognition of such Africans structures did not involve appreciation of the intrinsic interlinkedness of chiefs and other institutions into the traditionally subtle balancing act between various law-making agents. Applying this doctrine, the

British assumed that they were relying on rudimentary African positivist legal structures, even in acephalous and polycephalous societies.

British indirect rule created dual or plural systems of laws with three major elements. First, the recognition of indigenous customary laws, unless they were seen as repugnant to natural justice, equity and good conscience, or were inconsistent with legislation, allowed the colonial administration to be seen to be concerned and even 'liberal'. In reality (see section 6.4.2 below), local customs could be extensively manipulated and turned into official customary laws, while many other customs remained in the unofficial realm. Secondly, the recognition of traditional African authorities and the strategy of investing them with considerable judicial, executive and legislative powers at local level, served the same purpose and also allowed for extensive interference in the operation of such bodies. Thirdly, the establishment of English-style courts, Magistrates' courts, High Courts, various Courts of Appeal and ultimately access to the Privy Council in London provided legal supervision for the entire British African colonial legal system and ensured that it would acquire some official cohesiveness that might not have been achieved otherwise (Elias, 1965). The resulting formal dual model was really a more explicitly plural structure, given that various European laws, Islamic law and in some territories Hindu and Parsi law would also operate within any given system. Allott (1968: 138) noted some criticism:

> This policy, which one might have thought would have earned commendation as showing a proper respect by the alien rulers for the traditions of their subjects, has recently been criticised as being equivalent to setting up 'anthropological zoos': just as the wild-life was preserved in game-reserves, so the traditional institutions were artificially preserved in the 'native reserves'.[104]

Allott (1968: 139) argues that this policy shows that 'not every conqueror has automatically assumed his institutions to be superior and fit for immediate and total application in his conquered territories', which helps to explain why African indigenous institutions have survived to the present day. It is almost like arguing that colonial rule preserved African customary traditions. Certainly, traditional African customary concepts and laws were not left in isolation. Allott (1968: 139) explained that the parallelism between indigenous customary laws and received European laws provoked a dialogue, but more often competition and conflict:

> As time has gone on, each law has penetrated more deeply into the other: European legal ideas have infiltrated into customary law by legislative act, by judicial decisions, and by imitation; while customary laws have been applied by the western-type courts and have modified or displaced some of the rules and principles of the western laws.

---

[104] On this issue see David and Brierley (1978: 523 n. 4).

Allott entered here into an interesting discussion about customary laws (continued in section 6.4.2 below). Other authors provide contradictory messages about the process of colonial law-making in Africa and much of such legocentric writing is internally inconsistent. It has to admit that traditional Africans had their own laws, while arguing that these existing laws were too undeveloped to be of use for colonial rule. Such arguments hide that colonial law-making, despite the 'indirect rule' image, could be seen as unscrupulous, culture-blind legal positivism, with almost total disregard of religion and society, using the Napoleonic or Austinian principle as a legitimising tool. David and Brierley (1978: 513) justified colonial legal interference by observing that modern laws were required because African customs could not cope with the expectations of civilisation and modernity:

> There was first of all a reception of a modern legal system needed to regulate the many questions arising because of the transition to a new civilization and for which native customs were unable to provide any practically useful solutions. Secondly, a transformation of customary law took place in those areas where it already provided a complete system of rules and concepts either because the colonial power in question may not have considered it sufficiently civilized or because the law itself may have been forced to adapt to the changes taking place in other fields.

It is amazing with what ease the 'native customs', whose prior existence as a complete system of rules and concepts is explicitly admitted, are just brushed aside here as irrelevant elements for colonial reconstruction or as 'uncivilised'. In the next section of their book, explaining the need for new law, David and Brierley (1978: 513–14) concede that traditional African laws constituted comprehensive systems of legal regulation that might have been developed further without massive outside intervention and the superimposition of European laws. However, the Europeans were in a hurry to modernise:

> Custom was originally sufficient for the regulation of all aspects of social life in Africa and Malagasy. It settled all social, political and economic problems as well as family matters, commodity exchange and criminal law and procedures . . . It was clearly not suited, however, to bring about, with all the speed that was desirable, an adaptation to the entirely new social order . . .
>
> Enactment of new law was necessary in a number of fields, especially in modern commercial law where there was no indigenous basis at all. Customary law anticipated only a limited number of contracts, those known to rural life. The whole of the law of business and commercial associations, bills of exchange, maritime law, and even the totality of contract law itself, had to be imported from the West.

This quote indicates that the Europeans were rushing, but also did not really care to ascertain traditional African laws before employing their own legislative and administrative tools. Having learnt tough lessons earlier in India, where they had tried to ascertain the 'native' laws but eventually given up (chapter 4, section 4.7), the British would have been aware of the difficulties in ascertaining traditional African laws, given their oral nature, their extremely diffuse distribution and language barriers. A mixture of civilisational hubris and civilising mission, pragmatism as well as lack of effort, led to the result that positivist ideology anyway suggested as ideal. In this way, the carefully cultivated existing balances and symbiotic co-existences within traditional African legal systems were significantly affected. However, the old system could not be totally abolished, a critical point which most authors have simply overlooked. African customary laws were of such a nature as laws that colonial legislation could never, in its totality, have superseded the traditional system – it was a different type and category of law, as illustrated by the conceptual triangle (chapter 3, section 3.8). But we should not expect legal scholars of colonialism to admit this – they are blinded by familiar positivist myopia. In socio-legal reality, the British colonial system thus only superimposed a new official law on top of existing customary structures and declared the new system 'dominant', in the sense that Hooker (1975) used this term to explain colonial law and 'weak pluralism'. The traditional African legal systems, now 'servient' (Hooker, 1975) to the colonial order, co-existed with the new official system and became largely what Chiba (1986) called 'unofficial law'. As shown in chapter 4, section 4.7 for colonial India, the official new colonial law in the various British African territories could never have achieved total abolition of the pre-existing African customary laws and the value systems underpinning them. It is therefore necessary to investigate further to what extent colonial intervention has impacted on the wide field of customary laws and on dispute settlement patterns. In other words, how did colonial impact negotiate its own conditions? We shall see below that the new official law remained under enormous pressure to give official legal recognition to various aspects of African customary legal traditions.

6.4.2 The colonial impact on African customary systems

Allott (1984: 136) wrote of 'a twisted story' in dealing with African customary laws, the stuff of people's daily life. Section 6.3 above demonstrated that traditional African customary laws were not fixed entities and are more than just 'traditions'. As chthonic traditions (Glenn, 2004), they are never static; they are 'at one and the same time, both young and old' (Bennett, 2004: 2). Allott (1968: 140) noted that '[e]normous changes have taken place in customary law, both before and after the advent of colonial rule. Many of these changes have emerged from the heart of the traditional system in response to changing needs.' The gradual shift in African land laws towards more individualised concepts of property ownership (Allott, 1968: 141–2) illustrated this. David and Brierley (1978: 517) emphasised changes of traditional customs

through the influence of Christianity and Islam, especially with family structures moving from matrilineal to patrilineal patterns after conversion. Colonial
influence accelerated this evolutionary process and created a 'hot-house' atmosphere. Noting that '[m]ost Africans may well have continued to live as their
ancestors had, but a growing number put into question their ancestral customary practices and institutions', David and Brierley (1978: 518) acknowledged
change as well as continuation of tradition. Doubts whether legal positivist
claims existed perhaps only in the law-makers' imagination were expressed
(p. 528):

> There must be no misconceptions. Much of the new legislation, especially
> that which purports to reform the whole fabric of the family structure,
> affects the general population very little and has not yet changed the tradi-
> tional African way of life. Behind the façade which this legislation really is,
> the peasants, in particular, continue to live the life of their ancestors, wholly
> unaware of the law of the cities and the new institutions set up. According to
> well informed observers, 80 or 90 per cent of the population still lives by the
> old ways quite oblivious to the whole movement towards modernization.
> Ancient custom is in fact still followed and the state courts are by-passed in
> favour of arbitration or, even more frequently, conciliations according to
> traditional procedures. The new law will only be fully applied when society
> as a whole sees true justice in it and much remains to be done before such
> a state of affairs will exist.

The emerging pluralistic framework is not analysed, but David and Brierley (1978: 530) blamed colonial administrators for simply copying laws from
Europe which turned out to be ineffective. Earlier, though, a legocentric picture had been painted, claiming that the entire system had been changed. David
and Brierley (1978: 518) claimed that no meaningful action had been taken to
protect traditional African customs:

> If there had been any real desire to preserve the traditional system, it was
> not sufficient merely to proclaim the principle that native custom was
> to be protected. Such an affirmation was altogether meaningless so long
> as no steps were taken to enable it to survive. Positive measures such as
> clarification, reform and systematizing of the custom would have ensured its
> place next to European law. Little effort was made, however, along such lines.
> The colonial powers did declare, as a matter of principle, their intention to
> respect customary law, but the actual measures implemented with a view
> to guaranteeing its application resulted in its complete deformation.

For various reasons, the colonial rulers were neither able nor interested to work
within the parameters of traditional African legal systems, about whose internal
working far too little was known.[105] The British system of indirect rule meant

---

[105] Bennett (2004: 2) notes that 'it is impossible to imagine a Western court working with
unwritten laws'.

that there was no longer a pressing need to consider the codification of African customs. The British were content to prohibit 'repugnant' customs that were considered opposed to justice, equity and good conscience. Allott (1984: 134–5) showed that the British made some attempts to understand African laws to improve colonial administration:

> If we turn to the agents of colonial power, some of them – the district officers – made a commendable effort to learn about indigenous institutions, gaining anthropological or legal qualifications and producing a flood of useful books, reports and articles on customary law topics. But, especially in the superior courts, there was practically no knowledge of customary laws – how could there be? – so that judges had to resort to other means . . . Methods of judicial ascertainment of customary law in the British territories included, first and most important, by means of witnesses, usually 'expert' (a challenging notion in itself). Customary law, in other words, was a matter of evidence and proof. As the courts became familiar with customary law, they were entitled to take 'judicial notice' of it, an English legal term which translates as 'judicial knowledge' . . . Resort to judicial knowledge of customary law was, however, meagre in the colonial period. Assessors drawn from the relevant indigenous group could, under many colonial laws, sit with the presiding judge and advise him as to the pertinent rules of customary law. Provision was made in some instances for the receipt of reports by way of an official reference to a native court or a customary local authority, who were asked to advise in the abstract on what was the customary law in a particular case.

It is evident that the British also experimented in Africa with earlier strategies used in India until 1864, appointing local 'experts' to assist the judicial personnel in the law-finding process. However, once custom became a matter of evidence and proof, easily restricted by formalising criteria, the marginalisation of custom, previously observed in Anglo-Indian laws (chapter 4, section 4.7) also occurred in Africa. Allott (1984: 135) commented:

> [I]t resulted in establishing an apparently inferior status for customary law as compared with the law of the land; and it also led to the emergence of what I call 'judicial customary law', especially in Nigeria and Gold Coast (later Ghana). By the operation of the doctrine of precedent, judicial statements of customary law came to prevail over what the people did in practice; so that there was a disconnexion between practised law and judicial law. 'Knowledge' of customary law thus took on a different meaning, in which knowledge of what people actually did (practice) or what those traditionally acting as repositories of law thought the law was (opinion) became of less importance.

For the French domain, David and Brierley (1978: 515) explained that colonial legal regulation limited customary law to private rights and duties in areas such as family law and land law, the classical private law subjects of the French *droit civil.* They also argued that, even where custom had been retained, it might still be replaced if people themselves chose to accept European law by opting into it through some form of registration. For example, land rights might be registered with the colonial authorities and then took a different form, or a traditional marriage between two Africans might be registered under a colonial ordinance, which would then render it monogamous, with all kinds of formal legal consequences for the couple, not the least monogamy.[106] David and Brierley (1978: 525) noted that, in territories under British rule, 'custom was declared and applied by the native courts and was considered to be no more than a fact when invoked before the African "English Law" courts'. In criminal law, while the French claimed total control of this area, the Belgian Congo and the British territories gave considerable importance to customary norms also in criminal law. David and Brierley (1978: 519–20) concluded that apart from discarding traditional dispute settlement processes, the greatest change in customary law under colonial rule was brought about by the new formalistic view of social order – a hidden reference to social segregation and apartheid. Imposition of this exclusionary system elicited in most Africans a response of silent withdrawal and avoidance of contact with officials. It is significant that legal writers observed this, but did not comment further. Allott (1968: 138) noted another strategic silence, since traditional African customary laws were not wiped out by colonial interference:

> Naturally one would have expected the indigenous laws to crumble and wither away under such an impact, just as the previously viable indigenous technology, art, education, religion, and economic systems gave way or were displaced by the products of European civilisation. But this did not happen: customary laws largely held their ground.

Allott (1968: 138) discussed several reasons for this resilience of African customary laws from the perspective of the law-enforcer. First, the colonial institutions were initially more concerned with establishment of peace and order, consolidation of their own power, rather than intervention in African institutions. Grave social abuses would be suppressed, but 'the rest of the law (and of the customs which underlay it) was allowed to continue'. This legocentric wording suggests that, with better manpower and resources, the British might control or even override African customs. It is not clear whether during the late 1960s Allott still accepted legal positivism to such an extent. Allott (1968: 138) indicates the official view that it was preferable to respect the existing indigenous institutions, perhaps a colonial policy of preservation of power rather than

---

[106] Africans themselves may not have seen the matter like that and used registration of marriage, in particular, as a measure of social standing. But choosing English-style law did not mean in practice that African law became irrelevant: two types of legal marriage now co-existed and the positivist fallacy did not work. Such legal issues now concern courts in the UK as a result of ethnic implants (chapter 1, section 1.3).

reflection of respect for African traditional laws. Certainly Allott (1980), in a spirit of self-doubt, demonstrates that legocentric optimism had gradually evaporated.

Since the overwhelming majority of Africans continued to follow traditional customary laws, colonial Africa now had several types of customary law. The indigenous customary traditions, of course not entirely unaffected by the colonial presence, now co-existed in dynamic interaction with what Allott called 'judicial customary law'. This eventually gave rise to lively debates among scholars about its constructed nature (section 6.5.2 below). The inherent flexibility of the indigenous system, custom itself being so supple, since 'the rules of an oral regime are porous and malleable' (Bennett, 2004: 2) cultivated situation-specific adaptability as the highest value and maintained traditional concerns about equilibrium. The colonial model of custom, based on rigidifying inflexible English notions, looking for certainty and fixed patterns of behaviour rather than fluid situational adjustments, gave rise to some interesting litigation and observations of native litigiousness, reminiscent of colonial India (chapter 4, section 4.7).

Growing realisation that traditional African customary laws would eventually claim their place also in post-colonial Africa underlies the well-known Restatement of African Law Project, which began under the direction of Professor Allott at SOAS in London in 1959. A reformist project (Cotran, 1963), it turned out to be too ambitious, but produced some extremely interesting studies. David and Brierley (1978: 522) characterised this project as '[a]n ambitious plan for a systematic exposition of African customary law' and provide details of some efforts to improve knowledge of customs in various countries. Twining (1963: 221) saw this project as 'a venture of major significance', outlined the project's aims and pointed out that it relied on earlier colonial models of restatement such as Rattigan's *Digest of customary law* in the Panjab in India. Twining (1963: 221) was mildly critical of the project at that stage, arguing that the 'desire to please both scholars and practical men may lead to some awkward dilemmas, which could be difficult, if not impossible, to resolve'. Allott (1984: 136) explained that the project 'was intended to fill the gap which had developed between the superior courts and the customary laws they were to apply'. The restatements of African customary laws were not intended to be codes, but manuals of guidance, containing systematic presentations of information about such laws, group by group, with specific reference to family law, succession and land laws. The project focused on the recording of oral traditions, which created its own methodological and jurisprudential problems and sought to produce agreed positions on customary traditions as a tool for eventual legal unification, which became a matter of 'a running battle' (Moore, 1978: 249) in many African countries. The main aim was to ascertain details of local African customary laws in Kenya, Malawi, Zambia and Botswana as a preparatory stage to customary law reforms. Many questions arose over the appropriateness of such a project and its implications.[107] The project was eventually abandoned, reflecting a shift in attitudes to the study of African customary laws and to codification of laws. Allott (1980: 184) points specifically to the 'obstinate resistance of the people', reflecting a reorientation in the understanding of law reforms in modern Africa. Allott (1984: 136) still mounts an elaborate defence of the original aims of the project, linked to pragmatism and in particular the needs of judges, rejecting academic criticisms about the inappropriateness of the project:

> There has been some criticism – informed or otherwise – about this type of project, which has been imitated in some of the African countries, and which currently forms the thinking of a number of them. This criticism is directed at the alleged rule-based character of the restatements produced, it being argued that these mean a divorce of the rules from the processes and the societies in which the rules are to operate. Indeed, the anti-rule squad has attacked them on the familiar ground . . . that law is not solely, principally, or perhaps even at all, about rules. All these criticisms . . . can be accepted in part, but only in part. Clearly, law does not consist solely of rules. Rules can give too fixed and firm an appearance to what may be fluid and flexible. These are perils which one does well to recall and guard against from time to time. But, like it or not, judges proceed and decide by rule; they will continue to do so whether academic commentators think it right for them to do so or not; when they decide customary law cases they need to know what principles they are to apply. Supplying this deficiency of knowledge is surely better than leaving them to flounder or misdirect themselves in ignorance.

Here, Allott not only defends 'his' project, but also refers to ongoing debates and unresolved questions about the nature of law. Discussions about the Restatement project do not bring out clearly that the attempt by lawyers to wade into the muddy field of customary norms and to reconstruct agreed statements of principles and customary rules were not successful. They created an artificial body of rules, useful as guidance for judges and administrators in particular cases, but they might not serve justice in other cases, because the stated law and the actually practised customary rules were significantly different. Even minor differences would be significant, a point which Cotran (1963) in the exposition of his techniques and approach underrates. It appears that the project of restatement and unification of customary laws was fundamentally flawed at source because it undervalued the situation-specific nature and requirements

---

[107] For details see Cotran (1966: 86–9), responding to some of the criticisms. Cotran emphasises the practical utility of the project, but its abandonment points to a variety of problems which go beyond the definition of customary law. On the thinking behind the project, Cotran (1963) is most useful. Some of these issues are discussed in ongoing debates about adaptation of African traditions to new conditions (Gluckman, 1969; Cheru, 2002) and reforms of African customary laws in human rights contexts (Shivji, 1989; An-Na'im 2002a).

of African societies and appeared to be lacking in plurality-consciousness about the constant intricate balancing of African norms and values on a case-by-case basis.

The African Restatement project exemplifies that any attempt to restate, record and codify customary laws would always only result in yet another competing set of rules about customary laws, but never a definitive collection of rules. The proponents of the Restatement project may have known this, but they were also imprisoned by their own positivist thinking and the purported practical usefulness of their project to realise what problems they were creating. Later, Allott (1980: 196–202) excellently explained the various resistances to transformation and confirmed that many lessons were learnt from this project about how *not* to deal with customary laws.

6.4.3 *The colonial impact on dispute settlement processes*

Another arena of debate about African customary laws has been the closely related wide field of dispute settlement. Once the colonial powers had decided to introduce their own legal regime, it was necessary to adjudicate over disputes. David and Brierley (1978: 514) provided a typical colonial justification for the construction of dispute settlement mechanisms under colonial control:

> The application of this law newly imported from the West could not be entrusted to the court system or the procedures already established by custom. In all the countries . . . courts of the European type, therefore, distinct from the native tribunals, were set up to deal with these cases – where custom could not apply, where disputes involving non-Africans occurred, and where new questions arose as the result of the many new matters for which the customs provided no rules.

The perceived needs of modern administration totally dominated the agenda. Consequently, throughout the various colonial territories, different administrative and judicial systems were set up, marking a break with customary institutions. Depending on the policy of the respective colonial rulers, either local mechanisms and fora of dispute settlement were totally excluded and suppressed, or attempts were made, especially within British indirect rule, to reorganise and activate them for colonial purposes. In some cases, new local assemblies were constituted. In every case, even where there was an underlying intention to preserve the traditional system, lack of knowledge and understanding about the indigenous system and its functioning meant that colonial intervention became an invasive procedure.

Traditional African judges and dispute processors knew that after a case they would have to live with the litigants, often the proverbial 'man in the next hut'. Traditional judges were also concerned that the litigants themselves would have to live together in future, so that their minds were focused on reconciliation and integration rather than on adversarial processes. The social and ritual processes of indigenous systems were discussed earlier (section 6.3.5). Under the colonial system, an enduring perception built up that Africans were 'naturally and typically litigious, ready to resort to law at the slightest opportunity, and to pursue their case, whether well-founded or no, through every channel of appeal' (Allott, 1968: 147). Such readiness to resort to litigation was explained by reference to traditional patterns of African dispute settlement, which encouraged participation and discussion about appropriate solutions to problems. Assuming the disappearance of the traditional courts, Allott (1984: 133) argued that the open opportunity for ordinary people to participate in dispute settlement through the 'previously existing continual seminar in customary law which traditional proceedings provided', was now missing. While this meant that '[y]ou cannot learn your law in court and through court any more' (pp. 133–4), traditional dispute settlement also had an entertainment value and other functions, which were emphasised by Allott (1968: 147):

> [I]f we seek for an explanation of this litigiousness it is partially to be found in the traditional availability of courts of law. The judicial arena was not something strange and forbidding; it was rather like a football pitch, to which everyone might resort for entertainment and excitement and to challenge.

With respect, such arguments trivialise the matter and do not tell us that a major reason for the avid use of the new courts by some Africans might have been to seek an alternative forum for dispute settlement in which their claims might be heard and dealt with in a different way than in the traditional systems. The traditional courts did of course not disappear, but continued to operate within the unofficial realm – but most legal writing does not make that clear. Using the official colonial 'native' courts could therefore become a convenient method for some litigants to assert their claims before a colonial tribunal, knowing that under the traditional system they would receive a different response.[108] Using the new avenues for litigation, some individuals who were, unlike rural women, in a position to exploit the new legal intervention to their own lasting benefit, learnt important new lessons. Watching colonial administrators in action, some Africans began to learn that the new official system could be easily manipulated in favour of their own egoistic ambitions. The new processes of dispute settlement offered a small agile élite of Africans the chance to learn about modern, Western-style adjudication. This became a training ground for future politicians and lawyers, an emerging élite who were to benefit most from colonialism in the long run, because they would eventually be the new rulers of Africa.

---

[108] Such observations are, for example, made by Chanock (1978), who shows how women used the new courts in Malawi to assert rights to divorce, upsetting the men. See also Wanitzek (1990–1) for Tanzania, and Griffiths (2001) for Botswana.

Notably, the legal literature, politely or innocently, does not highlight this sufficiently, while Chanock's (1985) important observations focus on the tensions which the new forms of dispute settlement created within African societies.

Under the British system of indirect rule, the selective use of some locals and 'invented' local chiefs for the advancement of colonial rule and policies further distorted traditional balances of power and law.[109] Ayittey (1991: 78–9) notes with reference to acephalous societies that Westerners might see the absence of the state as a recipe for chaos. Thus, as Ayittey (1991: 82) explains:

> The colonialists had the most difficulty in dealing with stateless societies. The colonial authorities sought responsible office holders with 'power' in such societies. Finding no such power figures, the colonialists then 'created' them. But these 'leaders' lacked authority since they were not part of the kinship group and were treated as external representatives of an alien government. Within the tribe they had little authority and what little they had was considered tyrannous by the people under them.

Such arbitrary processes of allocating authority to individuals without traditional authority and standing constituted enormous interference in indigenous processes of balancing different sources of law. Suddenly a new legal authority, backed by positivist theory and the might of a colonial government, had the chance to intervene in customary processes. The results are quite predictable if one remembers how traditional Africans would react to a situation where an autocratic person tried to grab power in despotic fashion. Avoidance reaction or violence would be the result. Violence against those who sided with the new colonial authorities would be fatal.[110] The earlier traditional pattern of mass flight of families, seeking to avoid the imbalanced rule of an autocrat, was now replicated in massive avoidance of formal dispute settlement processes by entire communities, clearly an act of defensive self-preservation rather than evidence of uncultured backwardness. That so many Africans continue having recourse to indigenous patterns of informal dispute settlement, bypassing the formal courts, indicates that they clearly did not trust the new system to provide the customarily flexible and finely balanced justice they had been used to (Ebo, 1995: 33–4).

In Nigeria, the British policy of indirect rule involved acute consciousness of indigenous micro-politics and 'encouraged the establishment of what are known as "native courts" where cases arising from customary rules and regulations are settled according to home-grown principles and procedures' (Ebo, 1995: 33). In such cases knowledge about such rules posed challenges for judges without knowledge of indigenous rules and adjudication processes. Apart from absence of relevant knowledge, deliberate abuse for selfish reasons was probably

---

[109] Mensah-Brown (1976: 37) emphasises that the colonial government gradually increased the extent of its control over the indigenous courts.

[110] Achebe (1958, ch. 20) illustrates this very clearly.

an equally important factor in the tortured history of colonial African dispute settlement. In many British areas, under the policy of indirect rule, personnel chosen by the British administration would include many persons who used this position to serve their own agenda.[111] The British, innocent of intricacies of local politics and law, as David and Brierley (1978: 518) indicated, 'often supported chiefs who had lost their recognized place or relied upon native institutions that were discredited'. This allowed further abuse of the traditional balancing systems by exploitative and manipulative individuals and shows that those who sat in judgment and some litigants might now collude in intricate gameplays to bypass the traditional balancing mechanisms of indigenous legal systems. David and Brierley (1978: 518) noted vaguely that such appointment processes led to the eventual distortion of African customary laws. Colonial intervention, often more innocently than deliberately, opened the doors widely for some Africans to abuse their own systems of law and their own people. The foundations for post-colonial tyrannies and the present refugee disasters with millions of internally displaced people in Africa (Hampton, 1998; Cheru, 2002) were partly laid here.

In other areas, especially in East Africa, penal codes based allegedly on nineteenth-century English law were used, tailor-made Anglo-Indian codes produced for the Indian subcontinent, not really English law, as many writers insinuate or assume. The Indian Penal Code of 1860 in locally modified forms became the official law of many African territories; the same happened to many other Indian laws.[112] For the French territories, David and Brierley (1978: 518) explained how the administration of justice was entrusted to civil servants, assisted by native 'assessors', the functional equivalent of the Indian *pandits* and *maulvis* (1772–1864). In areas where penal codes had been introduced, customary criminal laws had officially only a minor role, but social reality might be very different. Since the newly received codes were based on different notions of crime, responsibility and punishment, this caused considerable problems. David and Brierley (1978: 518–19) indicated:

> In both French and British Africa, the important point is that customary law, and its application, became distorted because of the view which held that it could be treated as though it were a western law. In the desire to rid African society of arbitrary action and establish a new security in legal relations, the very role and working conditions of the native courts were altered. By attempting to make them the guarantors of the rights of individuals, the

[111] For Ghana see Quaison-Sackey (1963: 7), cited further below. The same happened earlier in colonial India, certainly when it came to the appointment of *pandits* and *maulvis*.

[112] An interesting side-effect of this has been the attractiveness of study at Indian law colleges for African law students, who can in this way avoid the exorbitant fees of the UK or the USA and still obtain a relevant legal education. Strong links between African and Indian lawyers are evident from the *Journal of the Indian Law Institute*, which regularly carries articles by African legal scholars.

courts lost their traditional function, which was to compose conflicts and bring about reconciliations. They thus became mere statutory creations having little or no connection with traditional custom.

More specifically, Ebo (1995: 33) demonstrates how interference in indigenous systems of adjudication led to significant changes in the criminal law system and its administration. Some traditional practices, now deemed repugnant to the idea of natural justice and morality in the eyes of the colonial power, were modified or no longer permissible. New institutions were introduced, particularly the use of imprisonment for certain crimes and misdemeanours and the creation of channels of appeal from the native courts to higher levels of courts. Repugnancy is discussed in detail by Hooker (1975: 130–5). It is 'a term used to indicate that customary law will not be admitted "if repugnant to justice, morality or good conscience" or some such similar phrase' (p. 130). Woodman (1988: 194–7) provides fifteen examples of situations in which this clause has been used. The issue can be illustrated by the introduction of Witchcraft Ordinances and the reluctance of the superior colonial courts to recognise any form of belief in witchcraft as a defence. In a case reported from Nyasaland in 1957, a man by the name of Jackson, who felt that a spell had been cast on him by a witch, had killed her and was now charged with murder. In the lower court, he was acquitted on the basis of self-defence, which means that the lower court applied African norms. Typically, the Attorney-General appealed and the appeal was allowed, on the basis that Jackson was guilty of murder because his belief, which was not an English belief, was repugnant and thus could not serve as a valid defence.[113]

Not surprisingly, many Africans would seek to retreat from contact with a superimposed law that did not respect indigenous norms. David and Brierley (1978: 520) indicated awareness that things went wrong:

> The results are today severely criticized. By wishing to install prematurely the rule of law, such as it is understood in the West, we have upset the old order in societies which were not ready to receive western legal ideas. African civilization was founded on certain values: a sense of community, respect for the aged, the absence of class antagonisms; it has been too readily accepted that these values could be destroyed without assuring that new ones will take their place. Unconsciously, perhaps, we have thus contributed to the breaking up of the ties of family and clan, and we have been incapable of replacing them with a sense of solidarity extending to African society as a whole.

We are not told here what the real implications for the traditional customary legal systems were; the assumption that everything changed and broke to pieces overlooks the internalised strength and resilience of traditional African

---

[113] *Attorney-General for Nyasaland* v. *Jackson* [1957] R&NLR 443.

customary laws. Eventually, widespread dissatisfaction about how colonial legal systems operated does not figure as a major reason for African countries to demand independence. Even after formal independence, countries such as Kenya continued their legal administration almost as before, using foreign judicial personnel for many years, partly operating on the basis of the formal colonial legal systems, although some significant changes were made.[114] Many questions arise, therefore, over what the impact of political independence for African states has actually meant for the position of African laws today. They are undoubtedly African laws, but to what extent are they still indigenous? And what does 'indigenous' mean, given the fairly long period of colonial rule and the formal strength with which colonial legal structures have been implanted on African soil?

6.5 African laws in the post-colonial period

Until the early 1950s, only Liberia (1822), Ethiopia (1853), Egypt (1922) and the Union of South Africa (1931) were independent African countries. The independence of Ghana in 1957 produced a signal effect, encouraging other African states to claim independence.[115] Allott (1968: 132) noted that the characteristics of contemporary African life were basically set in the colonial period and compared the process to handing over a baton in a relay race. Albeit a little too legocentric, the image of handing over something official to a new official source of power fits well. However, one must ask how much effect less than a century of colonial domination could have had on the many peoples of Africa, rather than the systems that ruled them officially. Cotran (1966: 77) emphasised that '[i]t would indeed be surprising if an alien rule lasting over half a century did not materially affect both the application and content of customary law'. But what customary law are we speaking of?

We return to this particular question in section 6.5.2 below. It is evident that the continued importance of unofficial laws and of African legal postulates is not taken into account by most commentators on modern African law. This typical positivist perspective still overlooks most legal realities of Africa today

---

[114] For some details see Cotran (1966: 78).

[115] The events leading to the end of the British empire in Africa are discussed in Lapping (1989). Listed according to year of independence, the independent countries are first of all Libya 1952; Morocco, Tunisia and Sudan 1956; then Ghana in 1957. The radical reorganisation of French colonial possessions after the Constitution of the Fifth Republic in 1958 led to the independence, in 1960, of the Ivory Coast, Dahomey, Upper Volta (Burkina Faso), Niger, Chad, Central Africa, Congo (Brazzaville), Gabon, Mali, Senegal, Mauritania and Madagascar. Cameroon, Togo, Nigeria, Somalia and the former Belgian Congo (Zaire) also became independent in 1960. Sierra Leone followed (1961), Algeria, Uganda, Ruanda and Burundi (1962), Kenya (1963), Tanzania and Malawi (1964), Gambia (1965), Botswana (1966), Swaziland (1968), Angola and Mozambique (1975) and Zimbabwe (1980). Namibia finally separated itself from South African rule in 1990.

and also mars discussions about the future of African legal systems (section 6.6 below). For a globally focused interdisciplinary legal analysis, it is insufficient to consider only the sphere of official laws. Okupa (1998: xi) pertinently notes:

> As a result of the historical accident of colonialism, most African states now have several models of law: their many indigenous laws; the legal extensions imposed by the colonial powers; Common law, Civil law, Roman-Dutch law, and by Islamic conquest of some communities by Sharia law, and finally Hindu law. Some African political elite [sic] also flirted with Socialist law.

A significant feature of modern Africa is that the new national boundaries were often hastily drawn in the early colonial period without recognition of ethnic, historical and geographical facts. This has been causing huge problems to many African countries, giving rise to violent clashes, perpetuating an image of Africa and Africans as cruel, lawless and totally underdeveloped.[116] Some legal writers emphasised the stabilising effect of legal continuity beyond independence. David and Brierley (1978: 520) wrote that, on the whole, Africans have considered the evolution in their countries since colonialism as inevitable. Briefly noting that the democratic ideas and agenda of the new governments for nation-building are often diametrically opposed to traditional structures, David and Brierley (1978: 520–1) observed efforts to complete the European civilising mission:

> The law of western inspiration established by the colonial powers has been confirmed in all the new states; as yet no voice has been raised in favour of its abrogation, even in those states which have declared themselves to be socialist. No important legislation has been repealed with a view to returning to the past. Various steps taken in different parts of the continent clearly indicate the intention to retain, and to perfect, the 'modern law' put into operation during colonial times.

Few steps have been taken to reduce the influence of European legal domination over African laws.[117] The prevailing impression continues to be that modern African laws have become clones of European models; there are many non-legal reasons for wishing to keep matters that way, but these are not explained in standard legal textbooks. Ayittey (1991: 69) severely criticises modern African governments and their representatives for arbitrary seizures of other people's property and for running robber band states that are in danger of descending into anarchy. One of the examples of police lawlessness cited by Ayittey in this context is from Somalia, where matters became so bad during the 1990s that

---

[116] On the international law dimensions of such issues see Zartman (1985), Elias (1988) and Keller and Rothchild (1996). Linked to globalisation, see Cheru (2002).

[117] For details on some reforms in Ghana and Zaire, and the abolition of appeals to the Privy Council in London by most former British colonies, see David and Brierley (1978: 521). East African developments are summarised by Cotran (1966).

Somalis themselves are perturbed as to how this could have happened and now, as asylum seekers spread all over the world, find that they have no country to return to (Farah, 2000: 7).

The present section, divided into four parts, briefly presents some indications of the continued devaluation of everything African before revisiting the debates about African customs and their constructed nature. Linked to such issues, it is then examined to what extent modern policies of unification and codification of customary laws are feasible and useful for the development of sustainable legal systems in African states. A further sub-section discusses significant evidence that the plurality of dispute settlement mechanisms in Africa is continuing, creating fierce debates about how best to protect the rights of African individuals, particularly women and children, and whether an emphasis on individual rights is an appropriate approach, given the split realities of modern Africa.

6.5.1 The continuing devaluation of African traditions

The risk of complete marginalisation of everything African continues, and the world cannot ignore 'centuries of cultural adulteration of the African people through religious and mental indoctrination against their heritage' (Maathai, 1995: 4). In the context of a reassessment of the human rights discourse on and in Africa, Shivji (1989: vii) emphasised the intellectually backward nature of that discourse, 'even by the standards of the African social science' and pointed out that this is not intellectually innocent. His study provides good insight into the ideology of domination which is being continued through the modern human rights discourse. Shivji (1989: 3) emphasised explicitly that 'human rights ideology is part of an imperialist ideology', but relies too heavily on his own modernist agenda. Without reaching sufficient depth in the analysis of indigenous African values, this valuable study remains too tightly fixed on the notion of rights. Shivji (1989: 21–2) merely notes that the African conceptualisations emphasise obligations rather than rights. More recent debates, influenced by the realisation that 'human rights are the right to be the same and the right to be different' (An-Na'im, 2002a: 1), are attempting a more sophisticated approach.

Despite widespread realisation that most Africans have continued to adhere to their own perceptions and practices of 'indigenous' African traditions, the assumption that this is evidence of continuing cultural backwardness and lack of 'development', rather than a skilful survival-centred method of exploring sustainable legal arrangements has continued to be strong. It does not help that lawyers in the academies of the North remain puzzled by how to handle evidence of traditional African laws and their continuation today. From a South African insider perspective, Bennett (2004) does not perceive such continuation as a problem, but many lawyers and anthropologists continue to have difficulties recognising customs as law. Freeman (2001: 910) notes that '[e]ven in the twentieth century anthropologists using a folk rather than an analytical concept of law have been inclined to deny that simpler societies had law'. He confirms that such views were influenced by legal positivism and were only partly revised later. Today, 'definitional questions are sidestepped' (Freeman, 2001: 912), the focus has shifted to examining methods of dispute settlement and handling legal processes, but '[j]urists and anthropologists are not agreed on the relationship between custom and law' (Freeman, 2001: 914). As a result, scholars continue to agonise over definitions of law, and remain diffident about legal pluralism, and dismissive of African 'culture'.

Such ambivalent messages from academia have exerted enormous influence on global public opinion as well as on Africans themselves.[118] The colonial impact went well beyond law reform and the construction of new official laws. It also affected the psyche of many Africans, who were made to feel inferior by white-dominated discourses about globalisation, eurocentric policies of legal regulation and social reform, and the latent general contempt of black people, their cultures and their achievements. African people, despite legal attempts to root out discrimination,[119] are often made to feel that they cannot achieve those purportedly global standards, because these are predicated on 'white' models and ideals.[120] Equally negative is the realisation that African people themselves, and their cultures, achievements and laws, are not being accepted as equal or equivalent to others.[121] Despite statements to the contrary, Africans and their laws are simply not fully respected in their own right.[122] At the international

---

[118] Two specialist journalists based in East Africa noted that European newspapers are more interested in reporting about elephants than the 500 million people of Africa (Hoering and Wichterich, 1991: 9). On the ambivalent attitudes of Indians towards Africans see Gupta (1991).

[119] Allott (1980: 226–36) discussed in detail the difficulties for anti-discrimination legislation 'as programmatic law in its acutest form' (p. 234), especially if destruction of privileges of their former bearers are fiercely resented.

[120] This is probably less true of people of African descent who have lived outside Africa and may be more deeply influenced by 'Western' ideas about equality, human rights and the values of uniformising globalisation. No agreement on such ultimately very personal issues is to be expected. Insistence by people of African descent that they are equal to others cannot nullify the views of those who do not agree. This is the major dilemma of ethnicity, always dependent on the potentially conflicting perspectives of how an individual or group perceives itself, and how others perceive that individual or group. Self-righteous, aggressive self-definition can pinpoint outright racism, but is not sufficient to persuade others out of their views, however untenable.

[121] The Court of Appeal for Eastern Africa in 1963 still refused to accept an African marriage as equivalent to a proper marriage (Cotran, 1966: 90–1). This also happens with regard to South Asian jurisdictions, with some recent evidence of changing judicial approaches in *Singh* v. *Entry Clearance Officer, New Delhi* [2004] INLR 515. Evidence of judicial attitudes in the UK is collected in Jones and Welhengama (2000: 59–89).

[122] This also goes for Asians in Africa: current South African law continues to discriminate against Muslim and Hindu marriages. Sometimes recognition is achieved after a long battle, but these are much-debated exceptions; see *Alhaji Mohamed* v. *Knott* [1969] 1 QB 1; [1968] 2 All ER 563.

level, too, pious talk about inclusion of all humans is often not put into practice
when it comes to drawing up instruments of international law and regulating
their application. In the minds of many, Africans have remained backward
people who need to be taught about modernity and who are simply not 'up
to speed' on progress and development. Such earlier views and perceptions,
however obnoxious, have remained tenacious.[123]

While most Africans remain silent about such matters, some articulate scholars and writers oppose such oppressive modes of thinking and action (see
Maathai, 1995; and Okupa, 1998). Such voices assert that there are inherent
values in African cultures and traditions, including the traditional laws, which
are not only useful, but almost essential for the construction of a sustainable
legal order in the future.[124] Some Africans proudly claim that they and their
cultures, values and laws can make a contribution to global legal progress.[125]
What they are really saying is that there is an African natural law that needs to be
taken seriously and which demands respect in a global context. An impressive
voice in this respect is Professor Wangari Maathai, a Kenyan woman and now
a Nobel Peace Prize winner (2004). In the Schumacher Lecture of 1995 for a
distinguished audience of environmentalists, she made an elaborate case for
the relevance of African cultural, and therefore by definition legal, traditions
in today's world. Maathai (1995: 10) explained in detail why the world seemed
to derecognise everything related to traditional Africa, thus creating barriers
and bottlenecks for development for Africans, who had been taught to despise
themselves:

> Spiritually, Africa looks for inspiration from the Christian and Islamic
> worlds. None of the spiritual experiences of Africa has been given atten-
> tion because none of them is coded in scriptural writings associated with
> prophets and holy men. The indigenous spiritual heritage of many Africans
> has largely been relegated to primitive expressions more akin to the unholy
> dark world of the evil spirits and the devil. To many African devotees of
> Christianity and Islam, seeking African spiritual heritage is devil worship.
> To many other peoples, seeking African roots, once condemned and over-
> whelmed by foreign cultures, is a fulfilling experience.

---

[123] Quaison-Sackey (1963: 9) recounts being confronted on the street in Oxford, during his
student days in 1949–52, by questions like, 'Which of our possessions do you come from?',
and reports racial violence against African students in London at the time. Evidence of
black people being lost to unexplained custodial deaths in many jurisdictions and day-
to-day street experience of people of African descent speak their own language also today.

[124] Chanock (1978: 80–1) opposes and ridicules this as counter-myths to the colonial myths,
speaking disparagingly of the 'Garden of Eden view of African law' (p. 84). These are
familiar accusations also levelled against 'Asian values' (Peerenboom, 2004).

[125] In the late 1950s euphoria of independence in Ghana, Kwame Nkrumah coined the
term 'African personality' as an indicator of new-found pride and status. For details see
Quaison-Sackey (1963).

Therefore, much of the African traditional wisdom and cultural heritage has been destroyed. Indeed, Africans have been encouraged to be ashamed of their heritage and to ape foreign cultures and values, much to their detriment.

People who are robbed of their heritage during occupation, enslavement and political and religious colonization become disorientated and disempowered. They lose self-respect and self-confidence as well as the capacity for self-guidance, leadership and independent decision-making. Kenyans are today worried about devil worship. Yet the constitution guarantees the freedom of worship. At the same time, a group of individuals who have tried to re-introduce the form of worship of their forefathers has been declared an illegal assembly. The freedom of worship is therefore only guaranteed to people who accept foreign faith. It is easy to appreciate why the colonial government would have prevented indigenous forms of worship so that the natives could be more easily converted to the religion of the master, but it is astonishing that African leaders should deny freedom of worship to indigenous people.

All human beings have their traditional culture, knowledge, wisdom and values. These have been accumulated for thousands of years . . . They have been passed from one generation to another. This accumulated heritage directs communities in times of peace, insecurities, and in times of birth, life and death. It is their antennae into the unknown future and their reference point into their past. While some peoples have invented the art of reading and writing and have been able to record their accumulated knowledge and wisdom, others pass it through oral instructions, stories, ceremonies and customs.

When this rich heritage is used to disempower the African people, it becomes a bottleneck of development when it should have been the source of empowerment.

This deep analysis claims respect for African natural law traditions without saying so explicitly. Maybe this should be made clearer. Maathai links the African image of the never-stopping train of history to the needs of the modern world, claiming that Africa has a valid contribution to make to future policies for the survival of mankind. This is not a lone voice, as the discussions below illustrate. It is also not an idealising fantasy, as Chanock (1978) and others have tried to suggest, nor a 'counter-myth' fabricated by Africans against the colonial myth that Africans were cruel, barbarous and unable to govern themselves.[126] There is much substantial evidence that the idealistic balancing systems of traditional African cultures continue to exist in social reality. Africans face difficulties in making themselves heard because, '[w]ithout an indigenous art of literacy and lacking in technological advances to put the record straight, the Africans are unable to correct the distortions paraded as truths so often and for so long that even the victims have begun to accept them as truths' (Maathai, 1995: 6).

---

[126] In this context, Mamdani (1996: 3) speaks of 'a paralysis of perspective'.

It remains an enormous challenge to make European writers on African laws 'see' and understand the African worldview in the constructive way that for example Hinz (2003) and Bennett (2004) have achieved. There is a huge task for African legal scholars in this field, but they, too, often seem more interested in black-letter law than in the exploration of African contributions to global legal theory.

6.5.2 Debates about custom in modern African laws

These ongoing debates raise doubts over whether black-letter lawyers, even if they appear to be anthropologically inclined, have actually understood the difference between customary laws that were modified by the state under colonial rule and later, and those that were not so modified, but still changed as a result of being 'living law'.[127] The argument that African customs are no longer really 'traditional' and hence superseded by modern law is impressively challenged by Bennett (2004), Bekker *et al.* (2002) and other writers particularly from Southern Africa. There is massive evidence of enormous distances and gaps of communication between modern African states and their peoples' customary, normative orders. Realisation of the limits of official law-making, particularly in Africa, was earlier reflected in Allott's discussion of resistances to transformation. Allott (1980: 197) emphasised that law-makers seem unable to slip into the shoes of those for whom they make new laws:

> These resistances have been consistently under-estimated by legislators in developing countries, who, with their centralist and 'capitalist' . . . values, cannot make the imaginative effort to project themselves into the minds of those at the periphery who will be affected by these changes. The attitudes of those at the periphery are demonstrated by their behaviour rather than their assertions – they carry on as if the new laws had not been passed. Examples of this general passive resistance are too numerous to mention.

This candid assessment offers a glimpse of meaningful silence, when 'little' people just continue to do what they consider appropriate and seem to ignore the modern state's laws. Few other writers have gone that far in questioning legocentric delusions and false axioms. Modern 'rule of law' models claim constitutional supremacy for the state and its agents. However, modern legal systems have been making highly selective and often immensely technical decisions about what counts as legal and what does not.[128] Such distinctions are

---

[127] This is clearly identified by Bennett (2004). An instructive parallel with these confused debates may be the debates in Muslim law over the various definitions of *sunna* as different types of good practice, which included the '*sunna* of the Orientalists' (chapter 5).

[128] This has not been properly researched for Africans in Britain. On Asians and the concept of *angrezi shariat* as British Muslim customary law in the UK today, see Pearl and Menski (1998: 65–117).

convenient tools of governance, as much during the colonial period as today. It remains unclear how the various definitions of African customary laws fit into this matrix of official and unofficial laws, supplemented and infused by underlying values, which Chiba (1986) identified as 'legal postulates'. Most lawyers simply assume, it appears, that the introduction of modern state laws into Africa turned all customs automatically into some form of state-made customary law, which was then judicially assessed and filtered, and is therefore no longer truly indigenous customary law. But what is custom? Cotran (1966: 72) emphasised that even two days of debates among specialists during the 1960s did not produce an agreed definition. Debating this in the context of East Africa, Cotran (1966: 74) highlighted the confusion without clearing it up himself:

> What was often forgotten, and I am afraid is still forgotten by many people, is that customary law governs the personal everyday relations of probably 90 per cent of the population of East Africa . . . In these circumstances it is in my view rather ludicrous to speak of customary law as being a special law and the received English law as being the general law.

The point is well taken, but quite what is 'customary law'? If 90 per cent of the East African population continued to live by customary laws, but the Ugandans had at that time already declared that they wanted custom to whither away and did not care less,[129] while the Tanzanians abolished customary criminal laws altogether and no longer took account of it,[130] and the Kenyans were not happy with operating a customary system either, where does that leave the customary normative orders that people continue to apply and develop among themselves, away from direct state control? Do we not have another type of African customary laws here, a type which lawyers neither like, nor understand, nor write about? What do we call this modern unofficial customary law which is not supposed to exist? It clearly dominates a lot of people's lives all over Africa today and is the 'living law' for most people, even in urban centres. This is a challenge which European legal scholarship on African laws has studiously avoided, it seems, by talking about the 'constructed' nature of African customary laws (Chanock, 1978; 1985). Far away from the world of scholars and administrators, hiding their own ignorance about 'traditional' systems, the overwhelming majority of Africans in the former colonies continue to adhere to what they understand as their own indigenous customary laws.[131] Generally speaking, non-customary laws are still a recent phenomenon in Africa, and

---

[129] Cotran (1966: 89) states that 'the expectation or hope of the Uganda Government that customary law will whither away and that everybody will soon accept statutory civil law is simply wishful thinking'.

[130] See Cotran (1966: 80) and in detail Moore (1986).

[131] This debate is familiar from South Asia, where the virtual collapse of Indian socio-legal scholarship is contrasted by growth of the 'black letter law' tradition (Galanter, 1989: xvii–xviii).

the traditional customary laws continue to be extremely important.[132] David and Brierley (1978: 522) suggested that African leaders, themselves members of 'traditional' African communities, valued such customary laws to a certain extent:

> Independence ushered in a new attitude towards traditional law. The leaders of the new African states were raised in milieux where custom was observed; because of this background they intend to affirm and maintain certain of its moral values which they hold in high esteem. They profess the belief that when purged of certain abusive elements custom may be able to form the basis of African private law. All the traditional social values are not to be rejected.

This confirms what Maathai (1995), quoted in the previous section, said about modern African leaders. They profess to be real African leaders, but reject certain elements of African culture and will now use the force of law at their disposal to get rid of such elements. The agenda of the new leaders will dominate legal policies, not primarily the concerns of their people, raising the spectre of dictatorships. The word 'certain' in the above quote indicates a certain readiness to grant a place to custom within private law, but not in the sphere of public law.[133] It does not seem to strike David and Brierley, as quoted above, that taking out certain elements from a people's tradition might disturb the subtle traditional balancing exercise that indigenous law was constantly focused on. To take the Kenyan example used by Maathai above, outlawing ancestor worship would certainly remove a critical element in the bricolage of the traditional worldview. Therefore, the debate needs to be about much more than the removal of certain abusive elements or supposedly cruel rules in a traditional, customary legal system. We need to reassess the criteria for what is 'repugnant' and are therefore still arguing over competing values. Why do lawyers not discuss this in terms of natural law debates? Whose interests would be harmed by respecting the ancestors of a traditional African? A loud and clear message is found in the existing literature, but is hidden from lawbooks. Glimpses are found in David and Brierley (1978: 522):

> De-colonization was frequently accompanied by declarations that justice should be rendered according to customary law. If the new leaders are to be believed, their intention is to rehabilitate the traditional legal systems. On

[132] Mensah-Brown (1976: 35–6) contains an interesting calculation table, suggested by Professor James Read, about the sources of colonial African law. While 25 per cent is allocated to colonial administration and law, 20 per cent is given to 'traditional' African legal principles. Again, it appears that the calculator has left out the 80–90 per cent of Africans who do not link in with the official state system, and whose 'indigenous' laws form a different category.
[133] Freeman (2001: 921) perceptively notes that a failure to draw a clear line between state and society, between the private and the public, remains problematic for lawyers.

this point there has been a reaction to the condescending and sometimes disdainful attitude which, it is thought, the Europeans held in its regard.

While the authors themselves appear to express doubts whether the new leaders can be trusted, the language used here is significant. Declarations of intent do not need to be followed by legal action. David and Brierley (1978: 523) recount how the new leaders, 'drawn from the evolved segments of African society which have modelled themselves on western patterns, have certainly exalted negritude and affirmed their africanism in their public speeches'. Yet, as they report a little later, 'all of them have, however, in the end, acted in a manner detrimental to the survival of custom' (p. 523). More specifically, in the context of debates about unification of laws, their argument against the use of customary laws is that it would allow too much loyalty to tribal units rather than to the modern nation state (David and Brierley, 1978: 523–4). For political reasons, therefore, the new African rulers had no interest in restoring customary laws (p. 524):

> If there had been a real desire to respect and perpetuate African legal tra-
> dition, it would have been necessary to . . . restore the supple methods by
> which it was applied and developed. In other words, a pluralist concept
> of society would have had to be admitted: the groups that had developed
> a custom should have been entrusted with its continued administration,
> because without this there can be no real customary law. Once, however, the
> state assumes the place of the original group in the function of articulating
> and applying custom, its destruction is certain.

Significantly, this debate discusses social pluralism, but not legal pluralism. David and Brierley (1978: 524) concluded that, 'while the new law may well have been based in some measure upon custom, this new state law is not customary law, even though it has been thought desirable to retain the term in official terminology'. Thus, this debate about African customary laws again just turns into the familiar question whether a state-sponsored customary law can still be called custom, an issue that has occupied virtually all recent scholars on African laws. David and Brierley (1978: 524) argued that, because traditional African customary laws were based on the ideas of harmony and reconciliation, modern state involvement had fundamentally changed its nature:

> [T]he attempt to introduce the rule of law, understood as being the guar-
> antor of individual rights through legislation and judicial decisions, and
> the view that the latter contained rules to be followed strictly rather than
> a point of departure for the amicable settlement of disputes, has led to the
> repudiation of the very essence of custom.

David and Brierley (1978: 525) argued further that '[b]y placing custom under the control of jurists and, even more so, by leaving it to their direct administration, traditional law has been hastened to its complete decadence'. It is evident that in this discussion the authors rushed to declare African customs dead and focused only on the new 'official' customary law, ignoring the fact that probably more than 80 per cent of all Africans, as they themselves report (p. 528), might continue to use updated versions of traditional norms and processes in their daily lives. In their line of argument, therefore, the officially stated desire to save customary law may well contribute to its further decline. Thus, David and Brierley (1978: 525) stated:

> The truth is that while custom has become law it has lost its soul. There must be no illusions on this point: the custom which is now fully law has very little in common with traditional custom. De-colonization has not contributed to the rehabilitation of custom, it has sounded its death knell.

These authors have thus managed to declare traditional African laws almost dead. Riddled with unacceptable injustices, traditional law is so deformed by modern state interference that it is no longer worth being called custom. To contend this legocentric perspective, one needs to accept that custom has remained practically important because the constantly changing indigenous customary traditions which African people have continued to apply in their daily lives are still around us (Bennett, 2004). Thus, custom remains 'law', and the current plurality-conscious analysis demonstrates that it is a different kind of law than state law. Again we see that 'black letter' lawyers are simply not equipped to understand this, but there are outstanding studies of legal pluralism in Africa.[134] It is certain, though, that simply reconstructing the past state of indigenous African customary laws through studying their present manifestations is not a methodologically sound enterprise. Allott (1968: 133) advised:

> African customary laws, existing in our present age and accessible to profound study by anthropologists and others, appear to be available to fill the gap. This is perfectly true: the study of contemporary African laws can supplement, on the role of customary laws in the evolution of law, the deficiencies or challenge the presumptions of Maine, Vinogradoff and Diamond (none of whom wrote with any personal or reliable secondary knowledge of the legal institutions of Africa). But there is a real risk in this procedure. Modern Bushmen, and *a fortiori* modern or recent Baganda, Ashanti, or Barotse, are not ancient Britons, Germans or Greeks; still less are they representative of palaeolithic or neolithic man in prehistoric times. So to argue backwards from African laws of the last two centuries to what law was like before the Indo-Europeans colonised Europe is a suspect undertaking.

Much recent writing among African law specialists discusses the constructed nature of 'customary' African laws in modern states.[135] Allott (1984: 135–6) reported that in the period following independence, the trend for customary

---

[134] Moore (1986) focuses on Chagga law around Mount Kilimanjaro. Less versatile lawyers venturing to undertake such complex research would face linguistic problems and methodological biases, which might exclude religion and other non-legal factors.

[135] On this see especially Woodman (1988; 1995), Chanock (1995), Bennett (2004).

laws to be more vigorously applied in the court system of several countries has accentuated a change in the status of custom. Whereas 'real' indigenous customary law was earlier generated and accepted by the people subject to it, judicial customary law has become officially more dominant in independent African countries. This kind of African customary law is often reconstructed and conflated from rules prevailing in different social groups into a generalised, somewhat uniformised law, no longer strictly affiliated to any particular group, nor recognisable as such.[136] Allott (1984: 136) argued that this ongoing process threatens to move African customary law in the same unifying direction as English common law, a prospect positively welcomed by the rulers and courts of some states. Custom as people's law is perceived by many lawyers as totally drawn under the influence of the modern state; it has ceased to exercise its traditional role as 'people's law' and now becomes a form of official law that is declared and applied, from time to time, by the judges. This is a fine example of how custom can gradually become an important element of the official law (Chiba, 1986), while other forms of customary law, not brought under the direct influence of the modern state and its law-making agents, continue to exist as unofficial laws.[137]

Rather than focusing on the interaction between such new forms of official law and unofficial customary laws in modern African states, legal scholars have, as we saw, conducted a polemical debate about the constructed nature of African customary laws. Allott (1984: 133) acknowledged this debate but distanced himself from it to some extent:

> [T]here are critics who wish to assert that so-called 'customary law' is no more than the creation of the colonial system; it follows that comparison of knowledge of it now with knowledge of it in the pre-colonial era would be pointless. However, though there is a grain of truth behind the labelling of contemporary customary law, that is all that there is. The grain of truth is a recognition of the fact that the agencies which used to create customary law are no longer active, or no longer active in the same way.

Indeed, as Allott (1984: 133) observed, modern African customary law now had a different validator and was thus no longer the same as 'indigenous' African customary law:

> Practice does not necessarily define valid customary law today. Valid customary law is defined by the (western-type) courts, administering their own tests, recognising their own precedents. Nor do the traditional customary courts and tribunals, which were also generators and declarers of customary

---

[136] As later Islamic juristic techniques (chapter 5, section 5.12), choosing and picking suitable rule elements from different school traditions were referred to as 'selection' (*takhayyur*) and 'patching' (*talfiq*).

[137] For the colonial and early postcolonial period, Cotran (1966: 74ff.) provides a useful discussion of governmental lack of interest in customary laws.

law, any longer function in this way. Their place has been usurped by local statutory courts, which may be called 'customary courts' but which in truth are far from customary, either in personnel or method. Statutory local customary courts have no special acquaintance with customary law or special talent in finding what it is. Often such courts are now presided over by the products of law schools and training institutes. Finally, the indigenous political authorities, chiefs, councillors or elders, have generally lost all their power over customary law, except perhaps that which relates exclusively to their own traditional position; so the other great source of customary law has also been capped.

Allott (1984: 134) was more concerned about the impact of this new law on the people whom it was supposed to govern. He spotted another 'limits of law' issue, since ordinary people now knew much less than they did before about their own law. Allott concluded that '[t]his disconnexion between people and law has grave consequences for the authority of the law' (p. 134). Even here, legocentric concerns dominate the agenda. Allott, too, did not consider those Africans who maintain a cautious distance from modern state laws and practise what they perceive to be their indigenous customary laws within their own socio-cultural environment. Immediately after this, Allott (1984: 134) turned to the public use of customary laws, but still thought of state-controlled custom:

> It is surprising that, despite all this, customary laws, though attenuated and changed in many ways, receive the definitive endorsement of being voluntarily followed by large numbers of the population. Proposals to change or abolish parts of this law can excite bitter controversy. At the same time, there are ever-wider calls for major change.

It is not quite clear what type of customary laws Allott was thinking about here, but the ambivalence of the discourse is brought out well. African people wish to continue applying 'their' customary laws, while positivism-biased legal scholarship and power-hungry politicians as Austinian law-makers collude in denying a rightful place to custom. The picture 'on the ground' in every independent African country may be diffuse but one thing is certain: massive avoidance tactics among African villagers (and even urban settlers) when it comes to using state courts and their constructed 'customary' laws confirm a significant divergence between socio-legal reality and official views and their reflections in legal scholarship. However, almost the entire current legal discourse on African customary laws continues to disregard socio-legal realities and the currency and internally updated and self-constructed indigenous nature of customary laws in Africa. Most of the current legal discourse, as before, disregards and disempowers traditional African normative orders, behaving as though the state-controlled customary norm systems now extend over the entire social field. Coupled with disregard for African natural law, this means that legal analysis of modern African customary laws has suffered the same negative consequences as other legal discourses suffocated by the predominance claims of legal positivism. It remains to be seen, in relation to processes of dispute settlement, whether reality-consciousness will prevail to reimport some respect for plurality-consciousness.

6.5.3 Dispute settlement and the problems of finding justice

Official disregard for indigenous customary structures and values is also strongly reflected in the field of dispute settlement. A central problem facing African post-colonial governments relates to the place of customary law and customary courts in the modern legal system. If customary law was to be retained, questions arose whether there was a case for codifying it or for integrating it with the general law (Cotran, 1963). Different countries chose one option or the other, or a mixed form. Kenya went furthest in the reformist direction, deciding that customary courts should be abolished altogether. Malawi extended their jurisdiction under the Traditional Courts Act, and most recently Namibia has passed the Community Courts Act of 2003 (Act No. 10 of 2003) to give extended powers to traditional authorities. There is no one trend that would characterise African development, though a streamlining of various court systems and a policy of national uniformisation can be observed in the transition from 'native administration' to the creation of national judicial systems with their own specific hierarchies. Allott (1980: 183) emphasised that 'integration' of courts and laws was the watchword of the 1980s. This does not tell us anything about how the interplay of official and unofficial customary courts would develop in practice.

In view of the discussion in the previous section, and the present interdisciplinary conceptual framework, doubts about the role of custom in African dispute settlement processes remain puzzling. While it remains possible to delineate to what extent customs may be incorporated into official dispute settlement mechanisms, the massive presence of the unofficial realm cannot be discounted. That raises the burning question whether it really was an option for modern African states not to retain legal recognition of custom in any form. Were the Kenyans, Ugandans and others right to disregard customary law, expecting it to whither away? Different grades of myopia exist among African leaders about the extent to which their people have continued to follow traditional legal systems outside state-centred court structures. One could ask interesting questions about the relationships of ruler and ruled, and the implications of the modern constitutional right to culture (Bennett, 2004, ch. 3). Allott (1984: 134) still concentrated on the difficulties of the courts in dealing with 'customary' law:

> Those with positions of power in the customary society are now increasingly divorced from administering 'their' customary law; those who administer the customary law may lack the traditional authority and position for doing so. The result is a grave diminution in the knowledge of customary laws

in the lower, first-instance courts. The position is not totally black, nor is the process complete. There are many customary and local courts whose members still have special knowledge of customary law; but their role is inevitably in decline.

Earlier, David and Brierley (1978: 527) indicated that large numbers of new codes were produced, especially in the former French colonies, and often judicial organisation was reformed as well. Ayittey (1991: 68) is particularly critical of the failure of modern African leaders to develop dispute settlement mechanisms to avoid continued severe bloodshed among rival groups of Africans:

> [I]t is African governments and elites, if anything, who should have drawn pointers from and built upon the indigenous African system of law. Tragically, they failed to strengthen the indigenous institutions for resolving inter-tribal disputes and conflicts during the post-colonial period. This explains the proliferation of ethnic rivalries and hostilities.

While Cotran (1966: 78–86) deals in a balanced manner with post-independence legal changes in East Africa, which he experienced first-hand, Quaison-Sackey (1963: 7) recounts from experience in Ghana that the effects of indirect rule under the British had been extremely beneficial for a small élite, virtually teaching them to abuse the system and their own people to fulfil their selfish agenda:

> [S]uch a system tended to enhance the prestige and power of the chiefs without taking into consideration the wishes of the governed and the traditions of the land. In Ghana, for example, a chief had never been permitted to speak in public, for tradition decreed that no one should bandy words with him; his thoughts and wishes were expressed through an intermediary, often a linguist, who had been trained for the purpose and who, in fact, served as a repository for the history and traditions of a particular state. And yet, under British colonialism, our chiefs spoke freely in public, carried out the bidding of British governors instead of the wishes of the people, and . . .
>
> Under the colonial system, therefore, the power of the chief in Ghana increased out of all proportion to his traditional role. As a result, some chiefs . . . became more and more divorced from the traditional sources of their power . . . Such was the abuse of traditional custom, under the colonial regime, that even when the people exercised their ancient prerogative of 'destooling' (dethroning) a chief they no longer wished to have rule them, the Governor could, through his provincial and district commissioners, refuse to recognize the destoolment and so maintain the unpopular chief in office. And reverse situations also occurred.

In this way, indigenous rulers learnt to fight among themselves over positions of power and influence, forgetting their obligations to their people.[138]

---

[138] Okupa (1998: 28–9) has interesting things to say about inheritance battles, which parallel Indian evidence about succession struggles, conducted during British times with armies of lawyers rather than soldiers.

Despotism had never been absent as a possibility in traditional African contexts, but a new type of ruler, administrative functionary and judge, began to emerge now. Those men learnt to bypass the traditional methods of safeguarding the subtle balances between the three competing law-founding elements in traditional societies. They could do this under the protective mantle of the indirect rule system, protected by the positivist bias of colonialism which continued after independence. Ayittey (1991: 69) criticises such abuses and comments on the resulting failure to ensure protection of justice in modern African states:

> The native system of justice was not perfect. However, regardless of its imperfections and defects, the 'primitive' legal system was far superior to the kangaroo courts and tribunals that are ubiquitous in modern Africa. In most tribal systems, there was no such thing as a 'kangaroo court.' At least, the peasants understood and safeguarded rights unlike many modern African governments which arbitrarily seize property without due process of law.[139]

Ayittey (1991: 17), citing examples from the Ivory Coast and Liberia, shows how conceptually un-African many modern leaders became in emphasising their own position, boasting of their uncontrolled absolute power. These were model pupils of Western notions of legal centralism and positivism. The presence of such leaders in many countries and the widespread public disgust with their exploitative regimes explains further the massive withdrawal of Africans from the official legal system. Ebo (1995: 33–4) candidly reports for Nigeria:

> [I]t remains an open secret that many cases involving violations of some aspects of local custom are still decided at the village level by clandestine or ad hoc tribunals, in spite of the existence of native courts and other modern British-oriented judicial institutions. On such occasions, in which the underlying spirit of indigenous justice bursts through the façade of the imported system to reveal its residual vigour as a living force in the mind of society, the law-enforcement agencies carried over from British rule invariably talk about people 'taking the law into their own hands'.

Given such breakdown of relations between rulers and ruled, and such innate violations of old culture-specific African codes about the maintenance of equilibrium, it is no surprise that the debates about nation building in Africa are bitterly politicised, while debates about legal theory remain undeveloped. Shivji (1989: 5) emphasises that '[t]he battle-cry of the day is for a second independence, not just independence'. However, we hear about dispute settlement processes in modern African jurisdictions only when something has gone drastically wrong, or a particular lobby sees some mileage in raising issues of concern. One element of particular prominence in this respect has been the treatment of

---

[139] Ayittey (1991: 69) provides a number of examples of government lawlessness, relating to Somalia and Kenya.

women in African courts,[140] and the related issue of legal literacy (Tsanga, 1997). The emerging human rights literature on Africa cannot be covered here.[141]

6.5.4 The unification debate as a tool for nation-building

Allott (1980: 182) emphasised that it would be wrong to see the trend towards unification of laws and social reforms through law as a product of the attainment of independence, since '[t]he policy long antedates independence, both in the civil law and the common law areas of Africa'.[142] The extremely politicised agenda of nation-building in modern Africa are discussed by many authors, most of whom are not concerned with specific legal issues.[143] Maathai (1995: 4) indicates that three major objectives occupied the minds of the new rulers. First, to oversee the decolonisation of the entire continent, secondly to promote African unity, and thirdly to bring about economic development. None of these aims is explicitly legal or particularly focused on the benefit for common people in Africa. Kwame Nkrumah, the first leader of Ghana, had optimistically declared after his country's independence in 1957 that, following political freedom, all else would happen more or less automatically. Such optimism is not shared by many observers and was clearly not realistic. Maathai (1995: 4) critically notes that 'decolonizing territories is only the first step. African unity and economic development have completely eluded the subsequent generation of African leaders who largely became dictatorial chieftains of their now impoverished and collapsing states'. Maathai (1995: 6) went much further in her criticism:

> Leadership in Africa has been more concerned with the opportunity to control the State and all its resources. Such leadership seeks the power, prestige and comfortable lifestyles that the national resources can support. It is the sort of leadership that has built armies and security networks to protect itself against its own citizens. With the new wave of people's urge for democratic governance and for more freedom, ethnic nationalism is being encouraged by such leaders in desperate move to hold onto power. With this type of leadership in place it is difficult to help Africa.

---

[140] For the earlier period see Chanock (1978). Hay and Wright (1982) constitute an important collection of material; Wanitzek (1990–1) discusses the problems created for legally unrepresented women in Tanzania.

[141] See Shivji (1989), Cheru (2002), An-Na'im (2002a). The *Journal of African Law* remains an excellent starting point for researching current issues in African laws.

[142] Allott (1980: 182–3) also points out that the French unexpectedly moved more slowly in terms of codification than the British, who gradually modified their assumptions about 'indirect rule' and began a more explicitly interventionist policy of uniformising lawmaking.

[143] See Häckel (1974). Cotran (1963) is an important early contribution to the debate, still defending the agenda and particular methods of unification. Allott (1980: 182–6) provides an overview and concludes that there is no uniform policy of unification in Africa.

Maathai (1995: 7) argues further that the various instruments and control mechanisms in traditional African societies, which were originally intended to provide checks and balances and to prevent dictatorial tendencies, have been bypassed by post-colonial African rulers to ensure that they themselves stay in power and enjoy the privileges which the various instruments of the modern state control. This is a serious indictment of legal positivism and institutions controlled by autocratic state bureaucracies. Institutions like the police, the judiciary and the press are often heavily manipulated, misused and censored by heads of states, so that, '[s]o poised, many of the current African leaders enjoy immense power and control and indeed run states as if they were their own personal property' (Maathai, 1995: 7). Okupa (1998: ix) highlights that the concerns of the ruling élite, the *Wa Benzi* or *Ova Benzi*, the 'people of the Mercedes', dominate over the public interest, while common people's adherence to custom continues to be defined and perceived as a threat. Such individuals are still African, no matter how 'evolved',[144] but they do not act like the ideal, duty-conscious African who has first of all obligations to others and to the common good.

The processes of post-colonial reconstruction and nation-building often concerned issues of territories and divided ethnies, an important matter for which we have no space here.[145] Many politicians paid lip service to customary laws and some countries, like Tanzania, tried to codify and unify some aspects of their customary laws, an arduous and ultimately ineffective procedure, since the modern official customary law would always co-exist with the continuing unofficial customary laws. Most states have tried to ignore these important legal issues, concentrating instead on other projects. Okupa (1998: 1) notes:

> Since colonialism, drastic measures have been applied to African indige-
> nous laws to clone or to transform them into western law with an African
> backdrop. After the attempted codification, there followed a period of the
> recording, the restatement, and the unification of African customary law.
> Today, it has become development and harmonisation of customary law for
> social engineering. The indigenous laws are still with us, albeit a modified
> version of their former selves for the survival of the majority subject to
> them. What is responsible for the resilience and longevity of indigenous
> law? . . . [W]e shall see that the majority of the rural people have had only
> very limited direct involvement with the changing political and statutory
> legal power structures in their new states.

In terms of the political restructuring of modern African states, Maathai (1995: 6) emphasises that 'people conveniently forget that, prior to the "discovery" of Africa, many African "states" were governing themselves through unwritten

---

[144] This term was repeatedly used by David and Brierley (1978). Its use here does not imply that it is considered appropriate or a fair description of the persons concerned.

[145] See Ihonvbere (1994) for a good discussion and further references.

constitutions which ensured peace, liberty, prosperity, resulting in a feeling of happiness and self-fulfilment'. This indicates the persistence of a major lie about traditional Africa, to the effect that it did not know the principle of good governance and had no good forms of government. Maathai (1995: 6) comments that such purposeful deception serves to uphold Western ideas of superiority. Since democracy is treated as a Western value now being exported to Africa, this offers a chance to some 'nationalist' African leaders to refuse such models as unsuitable for their countries, while they themselves know that traditional Africa practised well-balanced models of government, especially in acephalous societies. In this regard, Maathai states categorically that, in her own Kikuyu community, a pre-colonial democratic governance existed, 'which was better than any in the world today' (Maathai, 1995: 6). This is much more than a statement of ethnic pride: it is the outcome of a painful analysis and realisation that modern African governments do not deliver justice to their people. Maathai (1995: 7) writes:

> Africans, like all other human beings, want justice, equity, transparency, responsibility, and accountability. They want respect and human dignity . . . They want to create a strong civil society which can hold its leaders account-able and responsible, as well as sustain mechanisms of governance which ensure the security of the people rather than the security of heads of states and the small group of supporters and political opportunists who surround them.

She also demonstrates the linkages between non-accountable and non-transparent governance and environmental mismanagement, claiming that '[i]t is, therefore, impossible to protect the environment unless there is a government which is accountable to its people' (p. 7).[146] While David and Brierley (1978: 530) blamed colonial administrators for simply copying laws from Europe, entirely missing the point of the necessary debates, African writers have been vocally critical of their post-colonial leaders, who are seen to abuse old African notions of good governance and the balanced equilibrium of state, religion and society for their own benefit. Ayittey (1991: 17) shows how un-African many modern leaders have become, emphasising their own position and ignoring the collective needs of their people (Ayittey, 1991, 22–3). African policies of nation-building and unification have had to grapple with the lack of credibility of many leaders, and with massive resistance against centralisation and unifica-tion by centrifugal forces. Häckel (1974: 119) suggests federalism as a possible administrative and legal solution to maintaining the viability of African states. Important law reform movements took place in various African countries with

---

[146] Hinz (2003) discusses the role of chiefs in the context of nature conservation. This links with the right to life debate and an emerging jurisprudence under that heading in South Asia (chapter 4, section 4.10 and chapter 5, section 5.14).

a view to promoting the unification of law at the national level and stimulating general development. Probably the most extreme example was Ethiopia, which tried total codification of its laws, guided by advice from none other than Professor René David. Allott (1980: 185) commented:

> Of all the codifying legislation in the independence era in Africa, the Ethiopian Civil Code was the most frankly programmatic: its purposes, as was officially emphasized on its introduction, were to build national unity and to procure the modernisation of Ethiopian institutions. It thus combined three aims – unifying, modernising and secularising. So ambitious a law could not possibly hope to be made effective overnight; but its draftsman declared himself content if it was eventually adopted within a century or two.
>
> A law like this is not like laws enacted by the British Parliament, which make an instant demand for compliance; the Civil Code was a goal or target, at which it was hoped that the people would eventually aim.

Evidently, such positivist law-making, typical of Asian and African laws, left many question marks over the nature and application of law. Allott (1980: 187) noted that the provisions of the Ethiopian Civil Code 'would not be out of place in a modern European country' and commented on the 'stark reversal of the previous position, when religion had been one of the most important factors both as a source and as a control of *Law*' (p. 187).[147] Allott (1980: 207) described the Ethiopian Civil Code as 'the comparatist's joy':

> As an intellectual achievement the Ethiopian Civil Code ranks high. As a practical exercise it was a dismal failure. The law was programmatic in the most distant sense, in that it set a programme to which the nation and its disparate parts might eventually work and which might eventually succeed. It seems unfair, given this perspective of centuries, to measure its success in a couple of decades; but that we must do.

Allott (1980: 208–9) summarised the Civil Code's assessment by Professor Jacques Vanderlinden, to the effect that '[t]he judges of the courts which should be applying the Code have not resorted to it. Worst of all, the population at large has been unaffected by the Code.' Extremely high illiteracy rates, problems of language, and especially the fact that the Civil Code constituted entirely new law, were listed as reasons for programming failure. Not surprisingly, this Civil Code did not survive for long and probably contributed to the general feeling of dissatisfaction with the government. Ethiopia's new revolutionary rulers

---

[147] Hooker (1975: 399) notes that the drafting of the Code, originally in French before its translation into Amharic, was 'in terms cognizable only in a West European code system'. Hooker discusses the Ethiopian law in detail and compares it with Thai and Turkish law. Allott (1968: 156) portrays the Code as '[o]ne of the most extreme examples of the modern transmogrification of African customary law'.

abolished it after coming into power in 1974. Remarkable legocentric myopia is evident when David and Brierley (1978: 511) claimed that '[n]o voices were raised in protest' at the introduction of the Civil Code. They probably assumed that the Civil Code had only been abandoned because of the socialist revolution in Ethiopia. This would be far too simple as an explanation, since the Civil Code represents a classic case of extreme legal positivism. It could never have succeeded in becoming the operative law of Ethiopia, and its demise is probably a blessing rather than a disaster. The hubris of the law-makers and their highly qualified European advisers received a severe knock in this case, but it does not appear that enough lessons have been learnt in the discourse on transplants (chapter 1, section 1.2.3).

Codification in various African countries was discussed by Allott (1980: 185–6). Tanzania constitutes an interesting example for the study of unification policies and their limits. Strong belief among lawyers in the desirability of unification of laws and related reformist policies was evident. Allott (1965: 217) had outlined earlier how the Tanzanian government went about consulting local authorities, but not traditional customary authorities, to seek local consensus on customary normative orders that might then be introduced in codified form. Allott (1968: 156) predicted:

> Unification and codification of the laws will be the end-product of this reformist movement; but there is a possibility that the new African legal systems will retain some of the better and more suitable features of the old laws, although the old institutions will emerge in a completely transformed state, both as regards form and content.

At that time, Allott still saw the Ethiopian Civil Code as a blueprint for a bright future, an optimism that was to be shattered. Allott (1980: 186) summarised African unification policies:

> [P]ractically every African country has now adopted the unification of laws policy. The way in which they go about it, and the speed at which they move, may vary; but the effects are the same. The eventual shape of the resultant uniform legal system can vary widely, according as the governments adopt a liberalising, secularising or mobilising policy concomitant with the initial purpose of unification.

Such vague assessment disguises emerging self-doubt (Allott, 1980: vii) and a lost sense of direction. Outright positivist legal codification was clearly not a useful strategy, while simplistic arguments about returning to traditional African values and structures are just as illusory. A new middle 'third way' will have to be found. There is no agreement on what that way should be. The challenge for postcolonial and now postmodern African states remains to search for the Holy Grail of a sustainable balance between the competing elements of state law, different value systems and local normative orders.

6.6 The future

What are to be the goals for Africa's legal development, and to what extent is there a place for African legal traditions in the future of the continent? Attempting to answer such questions, the task is to investigate what claims Africans can make to a culture-specific contribution in the context of a global legal theory. Much earlier, Kuper and Kuper (1965: 17) perceptively emphasised the continuing need for recognising the ever-present dynamic 'relative emphasis on imperium, tradition, and divine revelation' in African laws. By now it should have become clear that Africans have largely forgotten such ancient lessons, or have been brainwashed into accepting Western legocentric models that would not contribute towards maintaining the desire for the ideal equilibrium.

There is, however, increasing recognition that Africans and their laws cannot simply assimilate into a global North-dominated agenda of legal uniformisation. Recent developments in Southern Africa, in particular, point to intriguing evidence of plurality-conscious reconstruction processes with much signal effect for other African jurisdictions. Dogged adherence to positivist circularity did not secure a sustainable future for the earlier South African Apartheid regime. If even the tower of centralising, legocentric white domination on the African continent now opens its doors quite widely for recognition of African customary laws within the newly constructed rainbow nation of the Republic of South Africa (Bekker *et al.*, 2002; Bennett, 2004), academic debates, even on a global level, cannot remain what they were. Widespread evidence of state dysfunction, legally induced disasters and massive failures of justice in many African states today are no longer due to colonialism, but to abuses of law by current rulers who have learnt to copy the bad and dangerous elements of positivist circularity.

How can global legal theory assist Africa in producing better laws? To what extent can Africa contribute to that theory? Those questions are as controversial as ever. New 'little' countries like Namibia are working hard to develop sustainable policies (Hinz *et al.*, 2000) at the coalface of legal innovation, experimenting with plurality-consciousness. It is evident that neither a return to a mythological, over-idealised past nor a simple copying of Western statist models is appropriate. Placative advocacy of a return to 'custom' and 'tradition' is too simple as a remedy. But complete denial of a place for custom and tradition within the dynamism of legal reconstruction in African laws is also far too simplistic, since the input of social norms and common people's values into law-making remains a universal phenomenon. This demonstrates that the comparative analytical framework of the present study is also valid for African legal developments of the future: to achieve justice-conscious laws for Africa, there need be fresh efforts towards promoting an intricate balancing of all three law-making elements identified in the present study (chapter 3, section 3.8) while taking account of local African specificities, past, present and future. This is a constant challenge wherever one looks. A plurality-conscious legal analysis of current Southern African legal developments may indeed offer some pointers for reconstructing a more people-centred and justice-focused approach to African laws, but only if the voices of African people are allowed to be heard and if their minds are allowed to make crucial inputs into the resulting legal systems.

Maathai (1995: 8) claims that the ills of modern Africa appear to be tolerated by the world only because they happen in Africa, and that this would never happen in Europe.[148] Particularly corruption, a worldwide crime, 'reaches devastating proportions in Africa because it is coupled with undemocratic and, therefore, unaccountable and non-transparent leadership which cannot be held responsible by its people' (Maathai, 1995: 8). Lack of accountability to the public interest and the larger public good is clearly a major problem which, many people claim, was first implanted into African legal systems by colonialism and is now skilfully exploited by reliance on statist doctrine, if not outright 'shark rule'.[149]

Many modern African leaders have skilfully learnt, above all through colonial rule, how to manipulate the state and its laws to their own benefit. Hence, it is politically beneficial for them to use placative recourse to Africanisation, employing it as a rallying cry for national construction and reconstruction, regrettably without implementing in most cases what they preach. African traditions manifestly did not stand for exploitation of all resources to the best of one's abilities and powers. Traditional rulers were subject to a higher vision of Order, and could be overthrown if they overstepped their limits and became autocratic despots. Perhaps the last thing today's African rulers would want to happen is to find themselves accountable to their various peoples to the same extent as they would have been under the traditional system, which was infinitely more democratic, in its ideal form, than the European-based systems copied into Africa. If modern rulers in Africa had been concerned to be duly accountable to their people, the modern ideal of African democracy should have created a better reality. Western liberal democracy is idealistically based on an understanding that 'the other' also has a voice and a right to live, that there is a right to opposition and an inherent claim to demand the balancing of competing interests and agenda. However, in Africa, as anywhere else, too

---

[148] The largely unsuccessful and certainly incomplete interventions of European NATO powers in Kosovo and other parts of the world appear to contradict such observations. Europe, too, does not have a ready recipe for remedying blatant exploitation of power and struggles with maintaining balanced equilibrium models. It is precisely in the nature of such basic models, which often stress the geostrategic proximity of problem areas to Europe and North America, that the core element of latent violence presents a constant challenge to stability, peace and justice in Africa.

[149] This concept was identified as the biggest threat to order in traditional India (chapter 4, section 4.3).

many allowances seem to be made for the tyranny of a ruling class through the self-legitimising mechanisms of majoritarian legal positivism. Many African rulers appear to have become star pupils in the art of legal exploitation of their own people, ripping to shreds the old balancing mechanism that they know still exist in the villages in which most of their subjects live.

So we find a new form of inadequate dualism in modern African laws, which has not been sufficiently studied by experts on African law, who do not even touch the dirty subject of legal abuse of positivism in Africa and have instead continued to blame African traditions for the multiple ills of Africa. The 'modern' debates about the constructed nature of African customs distract from the real socio-legal issues at the heart of modern Africa's woes. Modernist discourses, assuming and asserting the all-pervasive presence, supervening authority and bureaucratic officialdom of modern Western-style positivist laws all over Africa, ignoring the socio-legal realities of 'living law' and of culture-specific natural laws, blur our visions and prevent exploration of the scope for retrieving useful elements of traditional African concepts about good governance at every level of life. The legocentric nature of scholarship on African law itself, therefore, prevents a constructive reassessment of the potentially highly instructive role of 'indigenous' traditions in the rebuilding of future legal structures in Africa.

It is instructive to compare this negative assessment briefly to debates in Pakistan (chapter 5, section 5.14) and India (chapter 4, section 4.10) today, where Western-inspired modernisation and colonialism also left indelible marks and led to a notable colonisation of the mind (Nandy 1983: 11–12), with similar effects as in Africa. Pakistan, still confused about the real meaning of its Islamic path, permits people to kill each other over disagreements on Islamisation strategies. The realisation that one Pakistani government after the other has taken the name of either Islam or modernisation, or both, and has then devised still more intricate means to avoid accountability to the public, has led to a remarkably widespread and deep public distrust of all politicians, who more often than not are lawyers steeped in positivist extremism. The current power vacuum, confusingly filled again by a 'concerned' army general, contains a message to the nation which politicians find hard to express in clear language, but which judges (some of whom may then face dismissal, as we saw) seem to understand better. Muslim concepts of balancing different types of conflicting legal rule and value systems need to be strengthened in an Islamic republic to protect and offer better justice. Pakistan has begun to learn that lesson and finds it less difficult than African countries to attempt to implement this realisation, perhaps because it is linked to religion. The explicitly Islamic redefinition of public litigation in Pakistan today (Menski *et al.*, 2000) clearly reflects the postmodern search for an idealised local version of balanced Islamic justice.

In India, where the almost schizophrenic use of an ambiguous secular label virtually outlaws official recourse to traditional Hindu concepts, we find a scenario surprisingly akin to modern Africa. The local chthonic traditions have been declared unacceptable, and avenues for law improvement by recourse to tradition have appeared as blocked as in Africa. Modernist reformers obstinately decry evidence of massive recourse to local customary laws (Dhagamwar, 2003) as a relapse into pre-colonial anarchy, in a way that would be unthinkable today in Southern Africa. But the Indians, though many commentators still find this unbelievable, have actually managed to lift themselves out of the conceptual jail of blind adherence to axioms of modernity and state positivism. India was led along a plurality-conscious road first by Mahatma Gandhi and his principles of self-controlled local order which India did not want to adopt officially, but tolerated and recently reinstated to some extent through strengthening local authorities (*panchayats*). By the 1970s, Indira Gandhi's key role as a Hindu queen with a secular crown, severely misunderstood by modernist commentators, nudged India back to the recognition that 'shark rule' was not a sustainable blueprint for the future. We still do not fully understand why and how some Supreme Court judges managed to wrench Indian constitutional law into developing concepts for holding the modern state accountable in ways that continue to upset and frighten many Western lawyers. The lessons that India learnt from this, and is still learning, despite widespread denials, are being kept under wraps for as long as possible. These are strong lessons about accountability of the state and its agents to the people which please neither Westminster nor New Delhi. Being held accountable to the nation makes governance a duty, not a democratically legitimated right or privilege. The implicit messages and practical consequences of holding everyone in positions of responsibility accountable to the public good and the public interest are lessons about plurality-conscious balancing of competing claims to legal authority that global legal theory has yet to learn, but Indian governments are beginning to fear. The almost fanatical earlier denial of the relevance of Indian, Hindu-inspired traditions for the reconstruction of modern Indian private and public laws has now been demasked as a clever tactical ploy (Menski, 2003). India has begun to break out of this vicious circle because at least some of her rulers and judges have found the strength to admit that law-making for the benefit of the public is indeed an immensely complex balancing exercise and not just a matter of a few elegant pen strokes.

The new focus on indigenous reinterpretation of public interest litigation in modern India offers a valuable model to modern African states. Indeed, some of them have begun to explore such plurality-conscious avenues. Studying and testing such comparable models appears to be vital for improving justice in modern African states. Blatant abuses of power are being tolerated with a growing sense of frustration and powerlessness, while the continuing blacklisting of indigenous African thoughts on law and justice prevents meaningful discussions and justice-focused reforms in Africa. Labels like 'grass-roots justice', 'bottom-up approaches', decentralisation and federalisation grope in vain around the principle of equilibrium and ever-lasting balancing exercises between the competing law-founding elements of religion, society and the state. Discussions of *ubuntu*, the new magic word in South Africa,[150] do not yet convey sufficiently clearly the need for a holistic and plurality-conscious reconstruction of the entire system, not just the importation of some African 'culture', community consciousness, or respect for local traditions.

Manifest misappropriations of the necessarily plurality-conscious balance, hidden by clever lies and assertions to the effect that Africa had no indigenous concepts of good governance and democracy, of human rights and of justice, is a reality. It was possible to get this far into the morass because of unwitting collusion by scholars on African affairs and the beguiling assertion by most of modern Africa's élite rulers that there is only one way forward, namely either through more copying of Western models and government-directed reforms, or a return to 'African values'. It is beginning to be realised that neither route by itself is a safe one. The crisis point in modern Indian legal history, exploding in the Emergency declared by Indira Gandhi in 1975, has been reached in many African countries, too. But African rulers do not seem to have the nerve to subject themselves to traditional systems of accountability and advance all kinds of arguments for why they must be allowed to 'protect' their nations when they really wish to protect themselves against scrutiny by their own people. The present analysis should not be misread as a political tirade against African rulers. It is the outcome of a globally focused comparative legal analysis that is concerned to explain the legal mismanagement of much of Africa through lack of plurality-consciousness, and is designed to propel discussions on creating a better future. Post-cathartic India did not turn into a Hindu republic, but progressed quite remarkably in justice-consciousness. African countries can certainly achieve similar advances, but there are neither easy roads, nor is success (as we know from India) guaranteed – many problems of justice are so intractable that we should have no illusions about easy prescriptions.

Returning from such flights of comparative analysis to the dry reality of post-colonial writing on African laws leaves a feeling of severe disappointment. Older commentators pursue petty points of their own agenda, but have no overall vision of a future for African laws. This is bleak and depressing, a stark contrast to Allott's enthusiasm during the early 1960s, when legal research on African laws began to prosper for some time.[151] As Allott's comments indicate, and his later work (Allott, 1980) confirms, studies on African laws were

---

[150] This is a term for 'an ethical framework that contains a range of indigenous rights' (Bennett, 2004: 82). It look like a natural law concept, though a South African case, *S. v. Makwaneyane*, 1995 (3) SA 391, describes it more as a concept concerned with communality, social interlinkedness and interdependence of the members of a community.

[151] Allott (1968: 155) noted the paradox that 'the study of African laws has never been so advanced as at present, when the laws themselves, and the societies which produced them, are undergoing profound and irreversible changes'. Allott (1984: 136) observed

evidently not grounded in a sufficiently deep interdisciplinary environment, and often remained technical legal manuals. Much reform-centred research pushed along some strangely misguided paths, mainly because of blind belief in the advantages of modernisation and unification of laws. A small selection of comments on such issues must suffice here to illustrate this dissatisfaction. While even Mensah-Brown (1976: 16) seemed to indicate that globalisation would eventually swallow African laws up altogether, Allott (1965: 238) had earlier thought that African customary law would vanish, just as it had done in England. However, Allott (1968: 156) concluded:

> [I]t is likely that African customary laws will leave their impress on the African codes of tomorrow; but if this is to happen, then more intensive legal study of the customary laws, and their analysis in the light of comparative legal insights, is urgently required so as to facilitate that harmonisation of western and African legal ideas which is the declared aim of contemporary African law-givers.

These are interesting and relevant insights, but not enough intensive study has been undertaken on these matters by scholars of African law, and African rulers have been unwilling to implement what they publicly declare to be their aims. We know why only the most public-spirited of modern African rulers would wish to restore critical legal and moral aspects of the past, in particular community control and family co-operation, because this would manifestly limit their own room for manoeuvre, nipping their absolutist ambitions in the bud. Significantly, David and Brierley (1978: 529) noticed such abuse of political power, but their prescriptions for remedies involved asking for more law rather than less:

> In the absence of professional organizations and legal practitioners the law runs the very serious risk of becoming a dead letter or used only to the profit of the more evolved elements of society whose already privileged position will thereby be reinforced and not, as desired, reduced.

The entirely Western-focused thrust of recommendations for legal improvements in Africa confirms selective culture-blindness as a feature also in comparative legal studies.[152] David and Brierley (1978: 528) asked whether there was perhaps too much close modelling on European blueprints and suggested a re-thought programme of legal reform for Africa focused on development as the principal objective. But such reshuffling of parameters does not tackle

---

that customary law appeared to be considered more worthy of study as its use declined, which was 'the final irony in a twisted story'.

[152] To their credit, David and Brierley (1978: 530) suggested that looking at other less highly developed countries, especially Mexico, might be useful. However, this reinforces the impression that only Western-inspired models are treated as useful quarries for legal transplants (Watson, 1993).

the roots of the dilemma: they proceed to recommend further modernising, formalising reforms, such as extended legal education, publication of legislative texts, judicial decisions and legal writing (p. 529) in total disregard of African cultural traditions and skills of orality. Criticising the fragmentation of Africa, they recommended larger collectivities to aid development, pointing to the model of the European Union (p. 531). Other issues are thrown in for good measure, such as restructuring the relationship between public and private law, property laws, and even legal controls on 'unproductive expenses such as marriage and funeral ceremonies' (p. 529), which shows that these European legal scholars had only limited understanding of how non-Western societies function. Finally, the magisterial advice is given that African states should be 'constant in the quest for the realization of justice' (p. 532). But what is this justice? In view of our findings about how traditional African legal systems sought to achieve sustainable balances through constant negotiation, one-sided positivist prescriptions seem quite inadequate and inappropriate as guidance for modern African states. The disastrous advice given to Ethiopia, fortunately abandoned in due course, was there for all to see: modernise as fast as you can, get rid of anything African as fast as possible, and join us, the West, on the global train through history, which alone leads to development.

Against such modernist illusions, Ebo (1995: 41) argues that the image of 'stronger' and 'weaker' cultures is not only entirely misguided, but leads to the planned extinction of the 'weaker' culture, since '[t]his view implies that traditional, and, therefore, vulnerable cultures subjected to important modern stimuli are embarked on a journey from one state of affairs to another pre-destined end'. The present analysis has shown that indigenous African customary laws, in their various forms, will continue to be crucial for the future of Africa. Their presence in a scenario marked by legal pluralism cannot be denied; no amount of legal obfuscation or scholarly reconstruction can make it non-existent.

Ideas about reforms of African customary laws and their role within plurality-conscious reconstructions will clearly continue to pull in different directions. Problems in relation to intestate succession and bridewealth lead to continuing arguments that old patriarchal norms need to be reformed, while in the case of polygamy, one strong African view appears to be that outright prohibitions on monogamy should be relaxed, reflecting local cultural norms and, not the least, the wishes of women who participate in such arrangements.[153] In this way, the struggle between two apparently contradictory tendencies, modernisation and Africanisation, which is also a battle between uniformising and glocalising visions of globalisation, continues unabated. Arguing against the capacity of Africans to re-create their traditions on their own terms not only

---

[153] It is no coincidence that Indian (Menski, 2001) and Pakistani laws (chapter 5, section 5.14) have recently come to the same conclusion.

denies Africa the indigenous capacity to be modern or postmodern, it deprives African people of the right to their own culture and, hence, to their own culture-specific forms of law. If we want to take the voices of the South seriously, how can such loud messages be ignored?

The continued relevance of African customary laws within the triangular framework is a matter of observing social facts as well as legal realities. African customary laws remain relevant today, not only because governments consider whether or not to use customary laws in their schemes to perpetuate their rule, but mainly because people themselves are taking recourse to such rules while state institutions are not able to lend them much support in sorting out problems in their daily lives. As in India, and indeed in most countries of Asia and South America, people in Africa are thrown back to customary laws (in the widest sense of the word) not only by the inefficiency of modern state legal systems, but by inherent cultural concepts which remain a viable support strategy for the future, no matter what governments or modernist scholars say. Okupa (1998: ix) emphasises that '[t]oday, African customary law is still the law that regulates the lives of most people in rural Africa, especially children, who because of their minority, do not have a choice of law. An understanding of customary law is crucial for the protection and survival of the poor and powerless.' This plea for taking African customary law seriously is opposed to the claims of the *Wa Benzi* or *Ova Benzi*, the African ruling class, who copy Western models and habits without sparing a thought about the realities of life of their own people, whose votes they might need, but whose concerns do not really interest them. Okupa (1998: ix) argues forcefully:

> The law of non-imposition of law only goes to show that for the majority of the citizens of the new states, the laws cloned from the colonial countries have been irrelevant to what the people do and the factors that determine their life style. The consequence of this non-imposition of law is that only the bureaucratic elite make the choice of relying on the imposed law and customary law when it suits them.

Similarly, Maathai (1995: 6) demands recognition of the need for a human-centred, participatory, bottom-up approach in African laws, based on trial and error, not on prescribed blueprints imported from abroad. These last two messages come from African women, which indicates that there may be some truth in the argument that women anywhere in the world seem more sensitive to the task of balancing conflicting expectations and tensions than men. The presence and viability, in theory and in practice, of 'indigenous' culture-specific African laws, whether in their ancient forms or in their current supposedly con-taminated manifestations, cannot be denied. Whether there is an independent African legal theory or not, the search for African law as an integral element of a plurality-conscious global future is certainly not a vain enterprise.

7

Chinese law: code and conduct

Compared to Hindu and African law, the study of Chinese law faces a much less hostile research environment. While China's size, volatility and importance remain a challenge,[1] the codification of imperial Chinese laws impressed most Western observers and left little room for doubt that the ancient Chinese had law. This also provided sufficient reason for comparative lawyers to include Chinese law among the legal families, though its precise place in global taxonomies remains debated.[2] Since the existence of law in China has never been challenged,[3] the present chapter only briefly considers different scholarly representations. It focuses on key aspects of Chinese laws,[4] highlighting the plurality of legal systems under the collective term 'Chinese law'. The core element is visibly the imperial Chinese system of statutory laws, a manifestation of legal positivism which extended, with numerous modifications, from 221 BC until 1911.[5] Equally important in social reality, however, are various uncodified systems of Chinese cultural norms and values, often subsumed (and thus not clearly enough distinguished as natural law and custom) under the label of morality or 'Confucian ethics'. These Chinese postulates (Chiba, 1989:

[1] Glenn (2000: 279; 2004: 301) rightly emphasises the size and importance of what he calls 'An Asian legal tradition', but muddles many different legal systems instead of focusing properly on Chinese law. Huntington (1998: 13) noted the rise of Chinese power.
[2] David and Brierley (1978: 28–9) list Chinese law under 'other systems' and 'Far East'. De Cruz (1999: 203–11) briefly discusses traditional and modern Chinese law under 'Other types of law'. Zweigert and Kötz (1998: 286–302) cover Chinese and Japanese law under 'Law in the Far East' and distinguish it from the religious legal systems of Islamic law and Hindu law. For a recent analysis of scholarship on Chinese law, see Peerenboom (2003).
[3] Bodde and Morris (1967) defend the Chinese throughout against Western allegations of cruelty. Indications of aversion to the Chinese, mixed with admiration, are reflected by McAleavy (1968a: 105), reporting that China and other traditional societies are referred to as 'primitive' (p. 107). The perceived cruelty of punishments is highlighted in the comment that '[d]uring the last hundred years there has grown up in the west a sort of "black legend" about the Chinese penal system which lingers in people's minds even today' (pp. 122–3).
[4] Literature surveys are found in a number of recent studies, for example Chen (1998), Wang and Zhang (1997), Lubman (1996), Zheng (1988) and Glenn (2004: 339–42). The early German writing on Chinese law is discussed in Gniffke (1969); for more recent times see Münzel (1982).
[5] Some commentators give this date as 1912.

493

180) are of immense relevance for understanding the social reality of ancient and modern Chinese law. They point to inherent plurality-consciousness also within Chinese law.

At first sight, the discourse on Chinese law appears to give far less importance to 'custom' than to the Codes or the philosophies of Confucian ethics, suggesting that this legal system is incomparably unique in its reliance on philosophy and state-made codes. Closer analysis brings out the familiar dynamic interplay of state law, social norms and value systems throughout Chinese legal history. More recent types of Chinese law are the borrowed Western codified rule systems brought into China during the early twentieth century, initially through Japan, which made modern Chinese law a positivistic civil law system facing much difficulty to assert itself. Partly in reaction to this, the later development of Chinese law after 1949 as a socialist legal system with Chinese characteristics,[6] and finally the modern laws of the People's Republic of China, are also subsumed under 'Chinese law'.[7]

A globally focused comparative analytical matrix demands consideration of culture-specific Chinese characteristics of law to assess the nature of the interplay between the law-founding elements of religion/ethics, society and state, which have unquestionably all been present throughout in China in their culture-specific variants. As elsewhere, exclusive focus on the state's law-making processes, here the official imperial system of laws, would not permit deep analysis of the culture-specific interaction processes observable throughout Chinese legal history. In many respects, Chinese law is no different from other legal systems in that it is a culture-specific manifestation of how different types of legal rules interact. The subtitle of this chapter is designed to highlight this fact: there is much more to Chinese law and its large and undoubtedly important Imperial Codes than meets the eye at first sight. As elsewhere, the balance between the competing law-making realms of religion, society and state needs to be investigated for Chinese law in light of the working hypothesis of the present study (chapter 3, Section 3.8), focusing on the triangular pattern of competing legal elements. It appears that the formal structures of Chinese state law have continuously acted as catalysts (and have themselves been transformed) in the ongoing process of searching for subtle balancing between the spheres of religion, society and state at all times. Whenever this balance was not considered

---

[6] De Cruz (1999: 2) suggests that, following significant changes, the socialist legal system 'no longer warrants equal coverage as a major legal system in the late 1990s'.

[7] In addition, the laws of Taiwan form a separate legal system. Many overseas Chinese people in large diasporas all over the world today, especially in South East Asia, apply customary Chinese laws among themselves (see Ho, 2000 with further references). Chinese legal influence extends today to Korea, Japan, Vietnam, other parts of South East Asia and now the USA, Canada and the UK. On Chinese law in the USA, see Doo (1973) and Moore (1999). Far too little is known about Chinese Islamic law, prevailing among people in the north-western provinces and also in south-west China (Dicks, 1990; Dillon, 2001; 2004). See also briefly van der Sprenkel (1977: 8) and Sarkar (1975: xxiii).

important, or was simply not achieved, it appears that the formal legal system faced turmoil and transited from one dynasty to another, until it collapsed in the early twentieth century after unsuccessful attempts at internal reform and transplantation of foreign laws. Later, Chinese law went through many more muddled convulsions during the early twentieth century and again in the Cultural Revolution of the late 1960s, from which postmodern Chinese law is now beginning to emerge.

This chapter begins with a brief discussion of some scholarly representations of Chinese law, followed by an exploration of major elements in the Chinese worldview. Attention then turns to the classical imperial legal system, which lasted until 1912 (McAleavy, 1968a: 114). The post-1912 period, marked by the attempted reception of Western laws, is treated in close interaction with the early communist period of Chinese legal development. Finally, modern China and its increasingly formalised socialist legal system are presented as a modern Asian legal system with its own, culture-specific characteristics, now under pressure to globalise. The tendency to view Chinese law as a matter of codes is constantly sought to be balanced by analytical emphasis on human conduct and the resultant ever-present risk of sliding into imbalance and turmoil.

7.1 Scholarly representations of Chinese laws

A brief exploration of some scholarly assumptions about the nature of Chinese laws, especially in terms of religious content and impact, is necessary to understand why there are such different analyses of Chinese law. A particular kind of selective myopia is manifested in the writing on Chinese law. Morris (1967: v) emphasised that '[t]he scholarly literature in Western languages on the traditional law of China is relatively meagre. The materials, however, are voluminous.' Van der Sprenkel (1977: 1) pointed immediately to problems for scholars in ascertaining what is properly 'legal':

> Anyone who sets out to study Chinese law – even supposing that he has a working knowledge of the language – is faced at the outset with a number of problems. He is confronted with a great deal of material of different kinds, all of which appears to have something to do with what is called law in other societies, yet it is difficult to see exactly what in China corresponded to the different branches of law as we know it – a problem familiar to students of pre-[modern]-industrial societies.

Scholars realised that traditional Chinese laws, together with other Eastern legal conceptions, 'traditionally perceive law as playing a minor role in the sense that it is simply another vehicle for maintaining peace and social order' (de Cruz, 1999: 203). Lloyd (1991: 15) noted that the ancient Chinese perceived law negatively and as a tool of social control:

> In ancient China of the third century BC we find . . . the important school of so-called 'Legists', who argued that man's nature was initially evil and that

the good ways in which men often acted were due to the influence of the social environment, particularly the teaching of rituals and the restraints of penal laws. 'A single law, enforced by severe penalties, is worth more for the maintenance of order than all the words of all the sages,' was one of their governing maxims.

Apart from different perceptions of law, many legal scholars argue over whether ancient China had religion or philosophy. Within a plurality-conscious global analysis, this distinction does not really make a difference. It seems absurd for lawyers and others to argue that the Chinese had great philosophies but no religion; it is not clear how such distinctions are to be drawn. As there is no universally agreed definition of law, the same goes for defining 'religion'. Hence, certain scholarly presuppositions impact significantly on interdisciplinary legal analyses. Lawyers have either paid insufficient attention to this issue or have sought to deny that religion influenced ancient Chinese law. Most lawyers are on shaky ground, however, when they deny religious input in Chinese culture, or attempt to declare Chinese law secular, or simply ignore the sphere of religion and ethics as much as possible. Such academic pigeon-holing and stereotyping is bound to run into difficulties since traditional Chinese law, through the ancient device of confucianisation of the law (section 7.3.4), constructed plurality-conscious methods of keeping socio-legal control that extend beyond the black boxes of standard academic disciplines.[8] One recent example of muddled thinking must suffice as an illustration. Compared to Hindu and Islamic law, Chinese law appears to many researchers as a secular legal system, focused on philosophy rather than religion, and thus much closer to European patterns of thought.[9] The reason for this is apparently that the various Chinese religious traditions do not focus on divine revelation. Glenn (2004: 302) questionably suggests:

> Religion and revelation have little place in Asian legal tradition. In this, Asian law is perhaps closer to western law than it is to explicitly religious

---

[8] Despite the supervening conceptualisations of Confucianism, organised religion never dominated China and could not claim predominance within the triangular framework of law-founding sources as Islam and its 'jurists' could do. Van der Sprenkel (1977: 25–6) confirms that '[g]enerally speaking, priests did not rank high on the social scale, they were not influential as a class, and some had to earn part of their living by other work. Religions other than the official Confucian cult, which was somewhat remote from people's personal lives, were not centrally organized.' McAleavy (1968a: 123–4) emphasises that oaths or ordeals played no role in the Chinese courts. This could be taken as evidence of secular orientation or of an unspoken assumption that perjurers would shoot themselves in the foot, since nothing could escape the pre-existing order system. From that perspective, even torture could be justified as a device to avoid perjury and cosmic imbalance.

[9] See the taxonomy in Zweigert and Kötz (1998). McAleavy (1968a: 119) speaks favourably of early Chinese achievements in law-making. On religion, the alleged contrast between India and China is brought out well in Sarkar (1975: 1), a specialist early study from 1916, seeking to demonstrate that the trends of religious evolution in ancient China and India have been more or less along the same lines.

legal traditions, though you can perhaps find religion everywhere if you look hard enough. In both Asia and the west, however, there is no explicit reliance on religion or revelation as an immediate source of law.

This unhistorical comment must be challenged not only for China, but also for the West in light of the Christianisation of early medieval European laws (chapter 3, section 3.4). Much more needs to be said about such matters (section 7.2). Bodde and Morris (1967: 3) wrote earlier that Western scholars on China had, with few exceptions, shown little interest in the study of Chinese law,[10] but indicated that Maoist China had, more recently, motivated fresh efforts to study Chinese legal systems. They explain the paucity of earlier legal scholarship on Chinese law primarily by lack of legal training or interest among sinologists, the traditional specialists on classical China.[11] Secondly, they cite the difficulties of style and vocabulary in the complex Chinese legal literature, as well as the assumption among Chinese scholars that this legal literature was only of a practical nature and had no aesthetic value.[12] Bodde and Morris (1967: 6) speculate further that 'the real reason for Western neglect of Chinese formal law is that this law is not inherently deserving of much attention'. They see this as unfortunate and wrong, arguing first that 'law is an important touchstone for measuring any civilization' (p. 6), a typical legocentric argument which makes some sense for China. Secondly, they argue that the different role of law in China compared to Western countries 'points to basic societal differences between the two civilizations which deserve detailed analysis' (p. 6). This comment indicates a rather too placative use of 'Western', as though there was one standardised Western method of dealing with law. What is meant here, probably, is that the Chinese did not like law and associated it with evil (Lloyd, 1991: 15). In addition, Bodde and Morris (1967) highlight that the extra-legal sphere (as they call it), because of the informal mode of operation and the absence of written records, would be most difficult to study. It can indeed be a powerful disincentive for legal research if such work is not primarily perceived as legal. Notably, the legal literature on formal Chinese law, in particular the imperial codes, reflects a much higher level of scholarly attention from lawyers than other aspects of Chinese legal study.[13] While a fairly recent study

[10] See also Bodde and Morris (1967: 49). A detailed bibliography is found in May (1985), and Glenn (2000: 314–17; 2004: 339–42) has useful entries. More recently, bright market prospects have attracted much more interest in Chinese law, but not in the context of legal theory.

[11] This is similar to scholarship about ancient India, where the phrase about 'Sanskritists without law, and lawyers without Sanskrit' exemplifies the same lack of interdisciplinary mobility.

[12] McAleavy (1968a: 124) argues that traditional China did not possess a developed science of jurisprudence and cites the classicists' aversion to law as a technical vocation as an additional factor (p. 125).

[13] Van der Sprenkel (1977) effectively combines the two approaches.

of Chinese religions (Ching, 1993) provides a well-balanced and informative analysis,[14] David and Brierley (1978: 478) illustrated the problems that lawyers often experience with other people's religions and traditions:

> The traditional Chinese concept of the social order, which had developed apart from any foreign influence until the nineteenth century, is completely different from that of the West. The fundamental idea (distinct from any religious dogma) is that there is a cosmic order of things involving a recipro-cal interaction between heaven, earth and men. Heaven and earth observe invariable rules in their movement, but men are masters of their own acts; and, according to the way in which men behave, there will be order or disorder in the world.

Such muddled thinking is reflected in more recent summaries of the Chinese conception of law which feed on the above statement (de Cruz, 1999: 204). Have we not read similar descriptions of African and Hindu law? Should we only think of post-Enlightenment claims that man rules the world? The above statement appears misleading in at least three respects. First, it overemphasises the contrast with Western worldviews and posits that there is just one uniform Western approach. What about natural law concepts? Do they not shine through the above descriptions? And how would they match with the claims of man's domination of the world? Still more unsatisfactory is the assumption that Chinese concepts should have developed in total isolation from other socio-cultural and religious systems in Asia. This appears to be a scholarly device to cut corners: How is it possible that a huge empire of the size and importance of China should not have been influenced by 'foreign' elements of thought and practice, especially in the early, formative periods? What about early trade links and information about other people's belief systems, cultures and habits, especially from other parts of Asia? We know, for example, that monks of different religions were constantly on the move all over Asia and engaged in discussions,[15] and what about early trade and its many implications? Most significantly, apart from denying the presence of religious normative assumptions, it does not appear to strike these comparative scholars that their description of Chinese ideas about the world is rather similar to that of other Asian cultures and African traditions. The foundations of Chinese culture, as expressed through their earth-centredness, are clearly another culture-specific form of chthonic legal tradition (Glenn, 2004: 319) and natural law. There is

---

[14] On Chinese religions see also Saso (1991), emphasising that 'Chinese religion is . . . a cultural rather than a theological entity' (p. 344) with major influences of Confucianism, Taoism and Buddhism.

[15] McAleavy (1968a: 105) begins his discussion of Chinese law with the assumption that we must concede to China 'a remarkable degree of cultural self-sufficiency'. Van der Sprenkel (1977: 8) emphasises a sense of stability in that, until the nineteenth century, the effect of foreign contacts 'was usually to enrich, sometimes to disturb, but never to disrupt, the existing society'.

no case at all for treating Chinese law in total isolation as a unique example of a legal tradition that is more or less incomparable. Like all laws, it is simply a culture-specific manifestation of a universal phenomenon.

But scholarly efforts to treat Chinese law as unique are frequently found.[16] Foreign influence is refused acknowledgment when Morris (1967: v) indicates that '[t]his vast system was indigenous; only in the nineteenth and twentieth centuries has the legal thought of other countries influenced Chinese law.'[17] The contrast with assertions about the denial of indigenous customs in Africa is remarkable. Bodde and Morris (1967: 49) emphasise that 'Chinese legal development is in many ways sharply different from that experienced in other civilizations'. Van der Sprenkel (1977: 8) also takes an isolationist, but far more balanced position:

> The civilization which flourished for thousands of years in relative isolation from the rest of the world, against the background of physical and cultural variety referred to above, had three broadly unifying features which were themselves interrelated: dependence on irrigated agriculture; a centralized, bureaucratic administration; and a literary tradition, the most important elements in which were ethical philosophy and history. A centralized hierarchical bureaucracy, which identified itself with an ethical and political orthodoxy, was able to impose on the governed a picture of society in which the unity of the whole was exaggerated, its own role was overstressed and the value of Confucian thought was overweighted in relation to that of other schools.

This ethical emphasis is often juxtaposed to the penal orientation of the Chinese Codes. Bodde and Morris (1967: 3) highlighted that 'the written law of premodern China was overwhelmingly penal in emphasis, that it was limited in scope to being primarily a legal codification of the ethical norms long dominant in Chinese society, and that it was nevertheless rarely invoked to uphold these norms except when other less punitive measures had failed'. Bodde and Morris (1967: 3–4) emphasised therefore that 'Chinese traditional society . . . was by no means a legally oriented society despite the fact that it produced a large and intellectually impressive body of codified law'. This indicates close interaction of law and morality, a significant feature of all traditional legal systems in Asia and Africa. The overriding aim in both systems, the ethical and the legal, was to protect society from disturbances and to prevent total disorder and breakdown. Chinese legends of a lost Golden Age (McAleavy, 1968a: 106) mirror evidence from Hindu law and its image of eras (*yugas*), reflecting perceptions of human regression. At the same time, the lawyer's temptation to perceive legal regulation

---

[16] See also, though perhaps unintentionally, de Cruz (1999: 204).
[17] If the author thought (which is rather likely) only about the formal imperial system, that may well be the case, but it would not be an appropriate assumption for the whole of Chinese culture, as Sarkar (1975) and Ching (1993) clearly show.

as exclusively secular seems difficult to control. Despite what they said earlier, Bodde and Morris (1967: 49) asserted that 'law in China was from the beginning viewed in purely secular terms'. McAleavy (1968a: 106) emphasised that the prolonged period of turmoil in ancient China led to concentrated, practice-oriented thinking about theories of government.[18] He then noted (p. 107):

> In the process of digesting this material into a coherent philosophy, Confucius performed one operation in particular which profoundly modified the quality of Chinese intellectual life. He eliminated theology altogether, declining utterly to express any views on such matters as the immortality of the soul, or the existence of a personal god.

Eliminating theology, however, is not the same as arguing that religion plays no role in the development of traditional Chinese law. Largely for ideological reasons, one must suspect, much scholarship on traditional Chinese law has refused to acknowledge the presence of religion, speaking instead of morality or philosophy. Sarkar (1975: xvii) noted that Chinese people themselves might describe Confucianism as a set of morals rather than a religion,[19] but responded that '[i]t is sometimes alleged that Confucius was an atheist or a materialist; this accusation is not just considering that he believed in the existence of a Supreme God. In the "Classics" there are many passages which prove this' (p. xviii). Arguing that his silence on this point should not be taken to mean that he was an atheist or materialist, Sarkar (1975: xviii) confirms meaningful silences in ancient literary texts, asserting that it was unnecessary for Confucius to speak in detail of religious belief, which was taken for granted. Sarkar (1975: 61) goes further:

> [I]t seems absurd to ask the question: 'Is Confucianism a religion or simply a system of morals?' The proper question rather is: 'Should the Chinese religion of the classical age or of the age of Confucius be called Confucianism? What is the contribution of Confucius to the making of this religion?' It would have been clear that Confucianism as a title applied to Chinese religion down to the 6th century BC is a misnomer.

Sarkar (1975: 61–2) argues that both ancient Indian and Chinese religions have many conceptual elements in common; both are focused on some kind of eternal order or permanent cosmic system linked to nature (de Cruz, 1999: 204). Bodde and Morris (1967: 8–9) emphasise the close links of law with religion in many early civilisations, which then gave rise to speculation on the divine

[18] Comparable Indian evidence comes from the *Arthaśāstra* of Kautilya, an early handbook on statecraft, which was also too narrowly seen as a secular manifestation of ancient Indian thinking.

[19] This sounds familiar in light of modern Japanese assertions about the absence of religion. On the separation of law and religion in Japan, see Oda (1992: 123–4).

origin of law. However, they asserted that Chinese legal culture had developed in stark contrast to other traditions since 'in China no one at any time has ever hinted that any kind of written law – even the best written law – could have had a divine origin' (p. 10). This point may be valid for the written law, but quite what definition of law is being applied here, and what concepts were applied for the comparison with other legal cultures? Bodde and Morris did not deny that the Chinese envisaged a higher cosmic order to which humankind was subject, but, because they did not accept that order as a legal element, they did not include it into their legal considerations. One wonders why it did not strike them more clearly that Chinese natural law was making its presence felt here.[20] Confusion of basic categories is the result of arguments designed to portray Chinese law as a unique legal experience. Significantly, Bodde and Morris (1967: 9) had declared Indian law predominantly based on religion, although they also noted traces of secular approaches. For China, in contrast, they emphasised the secular approach and the nature of law as a political tool. Hence Bodde and Morris (1967: 12–13) wrote:

> A notable feature of Chinese historical and philosophical thinking, apparent already in early times, is its strongly secular tone. In general, it prefers to explain human events in terms of the rational (or what seems to it to be rational) than in terms of the supernatural. . . .
>
> When we turn to the legal sphere, therefore, it should not surprise us that here too the atmosphere is secular. What is really arresting, however, especially when we remember the honored status of law in other civilizations, is the overt hostility with which its appearance is initially greeted in China – seemingly not only as a violation of human morality, but perhaps even of the total cosmic order.

Van der Sprenkel (1977: 1) writes much more cautiously that '[i]t appears that much of Chinese social organization had a legal aspect, but it is not clear what relation law had to other institutions, nor what value legal studies have for a knowledge of Chinese society'. Bodde and Morris (1967: 10–11) even refuse the idea that economics could have provided an important stimulus to legal development in China, stressing that 'in China the initial stimulus for law was no more economic than it was religious'. All this leads to the argument that law in ancient China was predominantly a political phenomenon, as Bodde and Morris (1967: 11) explain:

[20] Bodde and Morris (1967: 29) suggest *li* as an embodiment of natural law. In their conclusion (pp. 48–9), they avoid a full discussion but provide useful further references, particularly to Needham (1956). Shapiro (1981: 158) notes that '[w]hether or not the Chinese had a concept of natural law similar to that in the West is unclear'. Unger (1976: 100) assumes the absence of natural law in China because there was no God: 'It became impossible to develop the view that nature and society are governed by universal laws of divine making'. All of this seems deeply unsatisfactory and requires further research in a plurality-conscious context.

Economic growth, to be sure, no doubt played a role in transforming the society of feudal China to the point where it could no longer get along without a written law. When this law appeared, however, it was used neither to uphold traditional religious values nor to protect private property. Rather, its primary purpose was political: that of imposing tighter political controls upon a society which was then losing its old cultural values and being drawn by inexorable new forces along the road leading eventually to universal empire.

Did this political focus really operate to the exclusion of all other elements? Why should it have to be an either/or scenario? It is particularly surprising that these authors should deny that the old law was used to uphold traditional religious values. Surely, the importance of cultural key concepts like *li* and *fa*, and their various shades of meaning, cannot be fully understood without linking them to the formal structures of the Chinese legal system and its underlying aims? The perspective adopted by Bodde and Morris seems partially too legalistic, and therefore, too impressed with the early evidence of positivist law-making in ancient China. Scholarly attempts to divide the field into legal and other segments are unhelpful for a comprehensive analysis of ancient Chinese modes of legal regulation.[21] State law, in whatever form it may appear, together with society and religion, interacted in traditional China in complex, culture-specific ways as everywhere.

7.2 Traditional Chinese worldviews in their social and legal context

The earliest beginnings of Chinese cultures remain hidden through orality, lack of records, and mere efflux of time. The study of Chinese worldviews may not primarily appeal as a legal topic. Moreover, the presence of large imperial codes suggests that there is enough tangible evidence about the official legal system to keep lawyers busy. However, for an interdisciplinary, plurality-conscious legal analysis, detailed examination of the intricate legal consequences of traditional Chinese systems of ethics and morality is indispensable. The present section focuses first on ancient concepts of superhuman order and naturalism, in particular *tao*, and then proceeds to a detailed analysis of *li* as the key concept of Chinese legal thought, representing an ideal model of self-controlled ordering which foreshadows communist theories of law. As David and Brierley (1978: 479) put it, '[t]he ideal is that laws never be applied and that the courts never render decisions'. A further sub-section discusses in more detail how these societal, moral and ethical values worked within the social context and prepares the ground for their legal application.

---

[21] Bodde and Morris (1967: 5) clearly depict clans and guilds as 'extra-legal bodies', again disclosing a lack of plurality-consciousness.

7.2.1 The cosmic dimension: tao

Some scholars make no clear distinctions between earlier and later stages of Chinese conceptualisations of the universe and their implications for law, but are aware of numerous philosophical ideas. De Cruz (1999: 204) summarises:

> A predominant principle of the traditional Chinese conception of law has been the belief in a cosmic order of the universe, involving an interactive relationship between heaven, earth and men. The universe is seen as the basis of law. China's 3000 year old history produced numerous philosophical ideas, with three main philosophical traditions influencing the development of the legal system in China: the Confucian, Legalist and the Buddhist. Chinese sources of law, thus, derive from these traditions.

Like in Hindu law (chapter 4), it is possible to distinguish certain phases of development which are then interwoven into key concepts.[22] The early philosophy of Taoism is linked to the teaching of Lao-tzu, an older contemporary of Confucius, whose major work, *Tao-te ching*, dates from the late fourth or early third century BC.[23] It is not one single strand of a theory but a complex of interlinking concepts and ideas, often rendered in English as 'The Way' (Ching, 1993: 85).[24] It appears to have started off as a secretive body of knowledge for ascetics and recluses, with an emphasis on embracing nature itself. Ching (1993: 91) explains philosophical Taoism, which has been compared to Greek Stoicism. Ling (1988: 105–6) argues that its quietism led to its decline and made it unpopular in China. But there is much more to this philosophy than equanimity and stoic tolerance of adversity. It also has ancient religious aspects and knows many forms of divine beings. Ching (1993: 113) explains that 'Taoists believe in the supernatural, not only as *powers*, but also as *beings* ... a hierarchy of gods – including mythical figures, and many divinised human beings, under the supremacy of the highest deity'. This is further supplemented by the evolution of a whole 'pantheon of innumerable spiritual beings, gods or celestials and immortals, as well as deified heroes and forces of nature' (p. 114). Glenn (2004: 315) explains Taoism as part of a larger Asian tradition that refuses to take positive laws seriously:

[22] Apparently, there were hundreds of philosophical schools in ancient China (Feng, 1952–3).

[23] Bodde and Morris (1967: 22 n. 38). Ching (1993: 85) explains that only fragments of this and another early text by another author have survived. She discusses Taoism in chapters 5 and 6. See also Saso (1991) and succinctly Ling (1988: 104–6). The transliterations of Chinese names and technical terms can be confusing, since different scholarly conventions have been followed over time. No attempt is made here to use one style and the conventions used by the authors whose work is cited are followed.

[24] The idea of the way or the right path is not unique to Chinese thinking. It appeared in Islamic law (*shari'a*) and in Hindu law (*mārga*), and is also evident from African legal traditions.

Taoism, the other great religion of China, has historically been linked with buddhism in its disdain for worldly concerns. It propounds the philosophy of doing nothing (wu-wei), inevitably attractive for many, and gives profound and succinct reasons for doing so. Tao teaching says that 'the more laws are promulgated, the greater the number of thieves'.

The focus on nature and self-controlled ordering, in particular, has had important ramifications for how people in China see themselves linked with the natural world.[25] Since early Chinese philosophy had evolved the concept that heaven and earth were governed by one principle, *tao*, a form of natural order or natural law, the next logical step was that human activity became linked to this, and *karmic* correspondences were established, akin to Hindu law.[26] The assumption that any disturbances in human society, or acts contrary to this natural order, resulted in disruption of the harmony between heaven and earth, led to a belief that disasters such as floods, droughts and internal disorders had underlying causes at the human level. These techniques to explain natural disasters and misfortune on a large scale led to political consequences which related to the choice of rulers and the assumption that there was a Mandate of Heaven for the righteous ruler. It is quite difficult to establish where Taoism has made an input and where Confucianism is the main conceptual force.[27]

Regarding religion, van der Sprenkel (1977: 25) writes that most Chinese people were eclectic in matters of religion, so that rituals practised in their homes, villages and guilds were combined with attendance at Taoist and Buddhist temples on certain occasions.[28] Van der Sprenkel (1977: 130) explains that Buddhism and Taoism displaced Confucianism in popularity as an organised religion. While Confucianism was mainly limited to the educated class, its ethical framework continued to infuse the whole of society and Confucian ethics had a pervasive influence on practical affairs, provided the norms for socio-economic life and underpinned the legal system. Bodde and Morris (1967: 43) emphasised that violations of the social order, 'in Chinese eyes, really amounted to violations of the total cosmic order because the spheres of man and nature were thought of as forming a single continuum'. The legal implications of such concepts were to some extent inherent in Chinese culture, as Bodde and Morris (1967: 43–4) explain:

[25] On Chinese concepts of the environment see in detail several essays in Callicott and Ames (1991).

[26] The Hindu concept of *rita* (chapter 4, section 4.2) parallels this conceptualisation. It is unproductive to argue over whether any of these two cultures borrowed from the other. There is no patent on Nature's law.

[27] On Confucianism see in detail Ching (1993). Ling (1988: 101-4) provides a succinct overview, as does Saso (1991).

[28] Like most Hindus, Africans and even many Muslims, the Chinese are playing safe by addressing various levels of superhuman force.

This concept of harmony or one-ness, expressed with varying degrees of explicitness, underlies a great deal of Chinese thinking. It is very prominent, of course, in Taoist philosophy. As developed into an elaborate political theory, however, it is particularly the work of the 'cosmologists' or 'naturalists' – men who tried to explain all phenomena, both natural and human, in terms of the eternal interplay of the positive and the negative cosmic principles (the *yang* and the *yin*) and of the five Chinese elements (soil, wood, metal, fire, and water).

The basic theory of these thinkers was that the human and natural worlds are so closely interlinked through numerous correlations that any disturbance in the one will introduce a corresponding disturbance in the other. If the ruler, for example, shows an overfondness for women, this will lead to an excess of the *yin* principle in the human world (since the *yin* is feminine), which in turn will cause a corresponding excess of *yin* in the world of nature. Inasmuch as one of the many correlates of the *yin* is water, the concrete result may well be disastrous floods. In order to avoid this kind of situation, therefore, it becomes the ruler's prime duty to cultivate himself morally, to see that his institutions accord with the natural order, and to maintain cosmic harmony by the correct performance of ritualistic observances in which sympathetic magic plays an important part.

This theory reached a high point during the Han dynasty (206 BC to 220 AD), with significant legal implications of this naturalisation. Bodde and Morris (1967: 45) explain this with reference to the 'belief that serious legal proceedings, and especially death sentences, should be carried out only during the autumn and winter months, inasmuch as these are seasons of decay and death, and should be totally avoided during spring and summer, these being seasons of rebirth and growth'. Such ritualistic, nature-focused concepts led to accepted patterns of practices, which were maintained over centuries. Influences of other religions are recorded, too, as Bodde and Morris (1967: 46) report:

> Jumping forward to the T'ang Code of 653 (the earliest surviving code), we find in it a great proliferation of the periods tabooed to executions. Many of the new taboos are inspired by the then extremely powerful influence of Buddhism, with its opposition to the taking of life.

Until the Ch'ing Code of 1740, these taboos were retained in a virtually unchanged manner. Bodde and Morris (1967: 48) see in this later change a 'weakening belief by Ch'ing times in the doctrine of the oneness of man and nature', but such underlying beliefs have been maintained, more or less invisibly, throughout history as an integral element of Chinese culture.

7.2.2 Self-controlled order, Chinese style: li

May (1985: 143) emphasises that the Chinese key concept of *li* as the idealised form of 'appropriate behaviour' in human conduct is immensely complex; it has a long history of changing and often more specialist meanings. It defies all efforts to capture it in one term, so that, 'in a strict sense *li* is untranslatable'. Glenn (2000: 282–3) highlights that *li* 'means many things but most of all means denial of the lasting and effective normativity of formal law and formal sanctions'. May (1985: 140) emphasises:

> [*L*]*i* was not codified and remained unwritten during most of the Chou dynasty, being orally preserved and transmitted by means of example and education. Thus, *li* was modelled from within and not imposed from above, devoid of any individual author, whether human or divine. *Li* owes its invention to man's endeavour to fit into the natural harmony of things; to give active support to it, appropriate conduct is sought.

Here again,[29] there is a movement from the sacrificial sphere to the general human level, as May (1985: 140) clearly shows:

> While the early phase saw little disposition to the supernatural sphere, disclosing *li* as an attentive and appropriate expression in form of sacrificial ceremonies, the following phase exhibited a movement of *li* into the natural human spheres of life, where *li* was regarded as a suitable action or reaction in correspondence with the visible and invisible natural forces. *Li* behaviour became an essential part in human relations with almost no propensity to the supernatural; it was socially legitimated and under constant survey by the whole community in its *wu lun* organization with an accent on hierarchical modifications.[30]

Bodde and Morris (1967: 19) describe the basic elements of this Chinese key concept well, but ignore the close equivalent of the ancient Indian concepts of *rita* and *dharma*.[31] They also undervalue the fact that *li* encompasses all aspects of human life, not just those of 'polite' society,[32] as they put it:

---

[29] In classical Hindu law (chapter 4, section 4.2), we saw a parallel movement from *rita* to *dharma* in various stages that follow a remarkably similar pattern.

[30] On the *wu lun* or 'five relationships', see the next section below.

[31] In chapter 4, section 4.3, the conceptual movement from *dharma* as 'right ritual action' to *dharma* as 'the duty to act appropriately at any moment in life' was depicted; a similar thought process appears here. The ancient Indians and Chinese had multiple cultural contacts, despite the geographical barriers represented by the mountain chain of the Himalayas. May (1985: 119) emphasises that the earliest conceptual beginnings of *li* stretch back to at least 1122 BC. Nobody knows to what extent ancient people at that early time were in contact with each other. May (1985: 199) in his comparative concluding discussion indicates his observation of 'a sound parallelism instead of more or less vague correspondences'.

[32] The applicability of *li* to everyone in society is not only exemplified by the system of the *wu lun*, but by the fact that individuals from higher status groups should receive higher penalties for disturbances of order than a person of lower rank. The same pattern is known from classical Indian sources, where a Brahmin thief, for example, would be punished more severely than a person of lower status.

As against the Legalists' *fa* or law, the key Confucian term is *li*. This word has an extraordinarily wide range of meanings. In its narrowest (and probably original) sense, it denotes the correct performance of all kinds of religious ritual: sacrificing to the ancestors at the right time and place and with the proper deportment and attitude is *li*; so is the proper performance of divination. In this sense *li* is often translated as ritual or rites. In a broader sense, however, *li* covers the entire gamut of ceremonial or polite behaviour, secular as well as religious. There are numerous rules of *li* for all customary situations involving social relationships, such as receiving a guest, acquiring a wife, going into battle, and the many other varied duties and activities of polite society. In this sense, *li* is often translated as ceremonial, politeness, etiquette, or rules of proper conduct. Finally, *li* in its broadest sense is a designation for all the institutions and relationships, both political and social, which make for harmonious living in a Confucian society. The *li*, in short, constitute both the concrete institutions and the accepted modes of behavior in a civilized state.

The reluctance of the authors to portray *li* as a truly holistic principle, with comparable equivalents in other human cultures, is remarkable. Van der Sprenkel (1977: 31) reports a wider perspective from her research:

> Dr Needham defines *li* as the customs of the society based on ethics and on ancient tabus, including in addition all kinds of ceremonial and sacrificial observances. For another modern Chinese writer, the essential element in *li* is the exercise of reason and judgment. He analyses *li* into three aspects: first, an ordering of society such that each individual knows his rights and duties, so that obedience to the natural order will naturally ensue; second, a code of morality which, being based on human nature, operates not by external control but through individual conscience; third, *li* provides an ideal of social harmony emphasizing the individual's obligation to society. The common element in all these theories seems to be that *li* implies the performance of right actions because, through habituation, they are felt to be right, and without external compulsion.

These interpretations begin to bring out the critical role of individual conscience, which is also a feature in Chinese legal culture. While it is not discussed in depth by the main legal textbooks, the role of individual consciousness and conscience is explicitly noted by May (1985: 141):

> As to the operation of *li*, we may assume that the practice of it was internally enforced, working upon man's consciousness in form of an inner-constraint or compulsion to comply with its rules and models, so as to demonstrate one's personal ability to support universal harmony as well as to contribute to the cultivation of society and oneself. Everybody had to have, and to do, his duty, namely conforming to the way of conduct in accordance with *li*, or he was likely to bring about disorder in his relationships and personal misfortune.

This interpretation, which closely matches the equally idealistic binding assumptions about *dharma* and *shari'a* (and various African concepts) within their own specific cultural contexts, is not specifically elaborated in the literature on Chinese law. It appears that the debate in China about the scope for individual responsibility for good or bad acts has manifested itself only within debates about the balance between *li* as the Confucian self-controlled order and *fa* as the legalist control mechanism that would exert pressure on the individual conscience, overlooking comparative contexts. Van der Sprenkel (1977: 31) reports that Mencius,[33] who went further than Confucius in advocating state intervention to stimulate prosperity, regulate agriculture and promote education, favoured only a minimum of interference when it came to enabling people to follow their own nature and did not accept that the state should dictate to people how they should make moral decisions. The careful and detailed analysis by May (1985: 119–55) supports this and shows that the concept of *li* underwent a long period of extension of meaning in ancient China, and then experienced an even longer period of consolidation. At the end of the day, the idealised expectation of this key concept is that no support mechanisms should be needed to ensure that everyone does what should be done. May (1985: 155) argues:

> Granted, the topos of *li* from the Confucian point of view is the proper means of government and education, capable of ensuring the good of man, namely social harmony, *fa* is, plainly speaking, superfluous. And supposing that *li* works properly, especially within the *wu lun*, and the ruler himself is a model (father and mother) to his people governing his state by observing the *li*, little or nothing is left to require him to govern by *fa*.

Van der Sprenkel (1977: 32) notes that punishment did have a place in the scheme of Confucian ethics, but it was to be used sparingly, and merely to support moral discipline. As threat of punishment, *fa* (in this sense similar to *danda* in Hindu law) should be strategically employed to buttress self-controlled ordering, but should not be punishment for the sake of punishment, which would from this perspective amount to pure tyranny. Van der Sprenkel (1977: 32) elaborates:

> Hsün-tzu, who was the Confucian philosopher closest to the Realists, did not believe that human nature was naturally good, but held that it could be made good by cultivation and that this was the function of the *li*. According to Hsün-tzu, it was part of human nature to have desires which, if unchecked, would lead to strife and disorder. 'The cure for strife and disorder is to lay down rules concerning the position and status of individuals and classes in society. This would define what everyone is entitled to and the

---

[33] This is an important older scholar whose dates are not securely established. Bodde and Morris (1967: 20) assume 371-289 BC but leave question marks over these dates. Mencius believed in the goodness of humankind.

precedence of the different claimants. This is Shyuntzyy's [Hsün-tzu] conception of morality, which is to enable people to reap the benefit of living in society while avoiding the accompanying evils.' It is clear from the Chinese that the 'rules' referred to are those of morality (*li* and *i*), not laws (*fa*).

May (1985: 129) emphasises correctly that the Chinese system of conceptualisations of human duties 'did not give way to the "superstructure" of an all-powerful personal lawgiver'. Against this, the legocentric assumption that *li* had to be created by men,[34] rather than being a pre-existing idealised vision of human conduct, is reflected when Bodde and Morris (1967: 19) write:

> The Confucians believed that the *li* had been created by the ancient sages, and that the disorder of their own age resulted from men's failure to understand or live according to these *li*. A prime Confucian duty, therefore, was to study and interpret the *li* as handed down from antiquity so as to make them meaningful for the present day. This idea led the Confucians to prepare several written compilations of *li* which, however, did not assume final form until near the end of the feudal age and during the early part of the empire.[35] During most of the Chou dynasty, consequently, the *li* were transmitted in unwritten form only. At the same time, their large number, complexity and refinement meant that they were largely an upper-class monopoly.[36] Indeed, what most readily distinguished the Confucian ideal gentleman (the *chün-tzu* or Superior Man) from ordinary men was his mastery of the *li*.

Again, this is an élite representation of *li* which roughly parallels that of Hindu *dharma* in terms of knowledge and ability of specialists to handle the rules of the *śāstric* texts. However, to what extent were such idealistic rules and norms among the Chinese to become embedded in daily life, rather than retaining an elegant, refined pre-occupation with style for members of the élite? May (1985: 162) is quite clear in his final summary that *li* concerned everybody, not just an upper layer of persons:

> [T]he topos of *li* emerged from the ancient forms of ancestor worship in combination with sacrificial actions and ceremonial usages and, gradually moving into all spheres of life, created, socially accepted, a vast body of concrete and distinctive rules of behaviour.

Bodde and Morris (1967: 19–20) provide no further guidance on this issue and turn instead to another matter, seeking to compare Chinese law with Western legal concepts:

---

[34] In chapter 4 above, the myth of the Hindu 'law giver' Manu made an appearance with inflated claims. It appears that the ancient Chinese were similarly tempted to imagine the actions of some great men of antiquity behind their normative orders.

[35] These appear to be functional equivalents to the Hindu *dharmasūtras* and *dharmaśāstras*, which served a similar purpose but were, as emphasised in chapter 4, not law books.

[36] All of this goes with equal strength for the Hindu equivalents.

[T]he Confucians believed that underlying the minutiae of the specific rules of *li* are to be found certain broad moral principles which gave the *li* their validity because they are rooted in innate human feeling; in other words, they represent what men in general instinctively feel to be right. It is this interpretation of *li* which has caused some modern scholars to suggest that a comparison may be made between Confucian *li* and the Western concept of natural law in apposition to a comparison between Legalist *fa* and Western positive law.

The point made here about natural law reinforces the finding of the present globally focused comparative analysis that all human societies appear to have their own natural law assumptions about what is good. There is nothing Western as such about natural law; analysts have tended to overlook this because of their eurocentric orientation, background and training.

Bodde and Morris (1967: 20–1) list a total of seven points that a Confucian would put forward to explain that ideally self-controlled order, rather than government-sponsored top-down guidance, is the best possible way to safeguard order and harmony in society. This amounts to the Chinese credo of the idealised balance that human society should be able to achieve but never manages to maintain. The major points in the debate between *li* and *fa* can be summarised as follows:

1. The underlying assumption is that man is by nature good, or at least capable of learning to be good. Therefore a society based on *li*, idealised self-controlled order, will have the capacity to shape individuals into socially acceptable human beings that do the right things at the right time. This means that through its own internal power of goodness, *li* is seen as capable of guiding individuals away from evil. On the other hand, *fa* would only come into action once an evil act has been committed. However, this theoretical perspective does not take account of the (probably only later, Confucianised) conceptualisation of *fa* as a deterrent, so that individuals would fall back on *li* despite the presence of *fa*, realising that they are better off following the path of right conduct. We see further below that this is the main reasoning underlying the policy of 'confucianisation of the law'.

2. A political arrangement based on the principle of self-controlled order or virtue is said to 'win the hearts of men' (Bodde and Morris, 1967: 20), while the use of *fa* principles would only result in outward submission to the legal rules, but not necessarily mental processes that underwrite virtue in its own right. This is a subtle argument which accounts for the crucial element of individual conscience, which the present comparative legal analysis has identified as central to every Asian and African legal system. This chain of arguments also emphasises that a government which itself relies on self-controlled order rather than the punitive elements of *fa* is driven by a very different legal philosophy than the positivist law-making approach. Here is a conceptual parallel with arguments inherent in traditional African societies

that positivist law-making, on its own terms, would facilitate abuse of power and lead to imbalance (chapter 6).

3. The universal validity of *li* is portrayed as a result of its creation by 'intelligent sages of antiquity in conformity with human nature and with the cosmic order' (Bodde and Morris, 1967: 20–1). It is not clear why this is portrayed as such, for the next sentence potentially contradicts this argument, stipulating that '[l]aw has no moral validity because it is merely the ad hoc creation of modern men who wish by means of it to generate political power' (p. 21). One fails to see a necessary difference between the creation of *li* by ancient sages and the creation of *fa* by modern men, since positivist law-making is not always abused, and the ancient sages might have had their own positivist agenda. It seems to be overlooked here that *li* as a more or less natural cultural code of appropriate behaviour need not have been promulgated by wise men in antiquity; it might have just developed organically out of the experience of that specific society in its own time and environment.

4. This argument is reinforced by the statement that the differential status relationships in Chinese society are in themselves 'instinctive to man and essential for a stable social order' (Bodde and Morris, 1967: 21), so that *li* only strengthens what is already inherent in society, it does not impose new rules. While this makes sense also in a cross-cultural analytical context, the assumption that *fa* would of necessity change this seems wrong. The statement that 'law obliterates the relationships by imposing a forced uniformity' (p. 21) has slipped in here, it seems, with an eye to Western law-making, while even the pure *fa* theory of Chinese law would perhaps not be able to have such a fundamentally revolutionary and equalising effect.

5. An additional small point is to the effect that *li* is the real 'stuff of life', while law, 'on the contrary, is mechanistic and devoid of emotional content' (Bodde and Morris, 1967: 21). This seems to suggest that the lived reality of *li* and its constant recreation and reconstruction is much more dynamic than the rigid rule of law model.

6. An important argument in favour of *li* is that a government based on the self-control principle 'functions harmoniously because the *li*, being unwritten, can be flexibly interpreted to meet the exigencies of any particular situation' (Bodde and Morris, 1967: 21). On the other hand, the argument is that state law, by stipulating fixed rules, encourages people to circumvent these norms without paying attention to the underlying moral dimensions. Thus, the argument is that governmental law will foment litigation rather than help to avoid it.

7. Linked to the above, the final argument is that '[l]aws are no better than the men who create and execute them. The moral training of the ruler and his officials counts for more than the devising of clever legal machinery' (Bodde and Morris, 1967: 21). This contains a warning, pertinent in all legal systems, that any form of law-making can be abused.

The gist of these arguments, from a Confucianist perspective, is that self-controlled order is inherently better than a system of state-made legal rules superimposed on people. The Confucian worldview preferred rule-application in the socio-religious sphere, ideally internal to man, to external imposition of rules. Confucianism therefore strongly argues that self-control through individual conscience is the ideal *locus* of normative creativity. This supports the argument that in Chinese law, too, the individual mind or conscience is the primary testing ground for appropriateness, determining whether a particular matter or dispute will be carried to a wider forum or not.

The argument against state-made laws is not only grounded in suspicion about abuses of legal and political power, but reflects mainly a concern that the self-controlling and self-healing faculties within traditional society, and thus within the individual's conscience, might be weakened if individuals as citizens of a state were to get used to following external standards automatically, without subscribing to them in their hearts.[37] Worse, the allegation that such state-made laws might simply entice people to become devious is a serious indictment of the lack of moral underpinning that such official legal rules might have. Similar to ancient Greek thinkers, probably, early Chinese philosophers as participant observers in an essentially unstable and immensely competitive environment were disgusted with political abuses of power. Bodde and Morris (1967: 21–3) provide several interesting quotes from different sources to indicate that opinions about good governance in ancient China diverged widely, but that Confucian idealistic assumptions were underwritten by a strong belief in the power of internal balancing. While this kind of discourse on traditional Chinese law is not explicitly conducted with reference to the competing roles of religion, society and the state, the long-running debate between Confucians and Legalists is very clearly concerned with the triangular pattern of conflicting sources of normative orders that lies at the heart of the present comparative legal analysis.

7.2.3 The social context of traditional Chinese legal regulation

The focus on the individual conscience and the requirement to ascertain for oneself what is right or wrong directs attention to the social arena within which individuals act and interact, emphasising the social dimensions of traditional Chinese societies.[38] Glenn (2004: 319) sees this as a general Asian pattern:

> Guanxi or relations are thus the key intermediaries between the individual and larger harmonious groupings, and remain so throughout Asia today. Grounded in natural human affections, the entire society is meant to have a

---

[37] Allott (1980) raised this as a central issue for law-makers in his discussion on the limits of law.

[38] In Hindu law (chapter 4, section 4.3), the notion of 'model behaviour' (*sadācāra*) constituted the parallel phenomenon.

dynamic of its own, requiring little external intervention or threat of force to make it coherent.

McAleavy (1968a: 106) portrayed traditional Chinese cultural concepts and beliefs very much like secular and commonsense criteria, highlighting the need to have sons and to cultivate the land according to the seasonal rhythm. Beyond that, there was necessarily much speculation, as behind the phenomena of nature a Chinese person 'detected the presence of divine beings whose good-will he sought to gain by prayers and offerings. He pondered on the mystery of death and thought that perhaps the spirits of his ancestors were among the denizens of this kingdom of shadows, and could be sustained and made happy by ritual sacrifices' (p. 106). McAleavy (1968a: 107) argued that this was prob-ably not unique to the Chinese, but overemphasised the peculiarity of Chinese assumptions about the links between humankind and nature:

> They regarded mankind as being so organically a part of the system of the universe that not only did human society depend in the final resort on natural forces but that these forces in their turn were themselves affected by human conduct. Any action by man which was not consonant with the natural order tended to disrupt the cosmic rhythm, and if serious or widespread enough could result in calamities of the gravest sort.

Interestingly, David and Brierley (1978: 478–9) made a clear distinction between two major aspects of the overarching requirement for harmony on which the world's balance and man's happiness depend:[39]

> It is first of all a harmony between men and nature. Human behaviour must be co-ordinated with the order of nature. To avoid epidemics, poor crops, floods, earthquakes and other natural disasters, one must take into account the cycle of the seasons, the position of the stars and various events of nature when proceeding to various acts of public and private life. Persons in authority must set the example of lives conforming to the order of nature; that indeed is their essential role. Virtue and morality are more important in administrators than any technical expertise.
>
> The second harmonious relationship that must exist is that between men.[40] The ideas of conciliation and consensus must be primary in social relations. All condemnations, sanctions, majority decisions must be avoided. Contestations and disputes must be *dissolved* rather than *resolved* or decided; the solution proposed must be freely accepted by each because he considers it to be just; no one, therefore, should come away with the feeling that he has lost face. Education and persuasion, not authority or force, must prevail.

---

[39] All of this could be said about African laws, and is also familiar from Islamic law with its primary distinction of human relationship to God and relationships between humans.

[40] This parallels the Islamic law concepts of obligations to God (*ibadat*) and to other people (*muamalat*).

Van der Sprenkel (1977: 26) perceptively advises that we should look for connections between religious concepts and law within the social arena, 'in the
microcosm of the small group' in which members knew one another personally.
McAleavy (1968a: 107) emphasises this social dimension as a secular element
of Chinese culture:

> Filial piety and its extension to the veneration of the dead ancestors were the
> corner-stones of his social system, but it was left to every man's private judg-
> ment whether or not to believe that the forebears to whom he was so scrupu-
> lous in paying his respects and at whose shrines he reported the important
> transactions of his career really survived as conscious personalities. In other
> words, the phrase 'ancestor-worship' commonly employed in the west to
> designate Confucian practice, is highly inappropriate and misleading.

Based on his assumption that 'Confucius ignored the next world', McAleavy
(1968a: 107) emphasised that Confucian teaching, in secular fashion, attached
the most serious importance to man's duties in this world, and hence also
underwrites the primacy of filial piety. Bodde and Morris (1967: 20) are quite
clear about the social interlinkages between key concepts like *li* and the social
structures in traditional Chinese societies but emphasise the social distinctions:

> [T]he early *li* were the product of a society in which hierarchical difference
> was emphasized. That is to say, the *li* prescribed sharply differing patterns of
> behavior according to a person's age and rank both within his family and in
> society at large (one pattern when acting towards a superior, another toward
> an inferior, still a third toward an equal). This idea of hierarchical difference,
> with resulting differences in behavior and privilege, has remained alive in
> Confucianism throughout imperial times, despite the disappearance of the
> pre-imperial feudal society that first gave it birth.

This basic division of society into those who labour with their minds, and those
who labour with their hands is also brought out by van der Sprenkel (1977: 9),
who emphasises that '[o]rdinary people, who performed the drudgery of life,
were thought to be incapable of being cultured', and then quoted Mencius (p. 9):

> [T]here is a saying, 'Some labour with their minds and some labour with
> their strength. Those who labour with their minds govern others; those who
> labour with their strength are governed by others. Those who are governed
> by others support them; those who govern others are supported by them.
> This is a principle universally recognized.'

This clearly justifies political rule by an upper class, but the dual systematisation
should not lead to the conclusion that the lower classes of society were exempt
from observance of *li*.[41] Van der Sprenkel (1977: 8–9) reports in a more
balanced and broad manner:

---

[41] Indeed, van der Sprenkel (1977: 9) clarifies that while few people could read, so that their
knowledge of the ethical teachings was only second-hand, 'they did share in some of the
beliefs which inspired it (as, for example, in the necessity of rites for departed ancestors)
and they did therefore more modestly try to imitate the ritual practices of their "betters"'.

From the orthodox point of view society consisted of two broad divisions, people of culture and common people. The former were those who devoted themselves to classical learning, educating others and assisting the ruler in governing the mass, while in their leisure they pursued scholarly recreations like poetry and painting. They were supposed in their lives to set a good example to others by putting into practice the ethical teaching – as re-stated by Confucius, Mencius, etc. from the earlier *ching* or classics and developed by their successors and commentators. The core of this was that good was to be promoted by the cultivation of personal virtue, which consisted in defining and conducting personal relationships with propriety, laying particular stress on relationships within the family. One owed respect, obedience and support to family superiors during their lifetime and veneration with prescribed ritual and within prescribed degrees after death. From these obligations there arose other derived obligations: to value one's body as a gift from one's forebears, to add lustre to the family name, to continue the line of descent and to acquire the means to provide fittingly for the departed.

The key elements of ancestor worship, filial piety and consequent duties to the social environment are emphasised by all major writers. Bodde and Morris (1967: 39–43) offer particularly detailed observations, placing filial piety (*hsiao*) within the context of the family into a central position, while also emphasising the principle of *chung*, loyalty to a superior. In case of conflict between the two, '*hsiao* is to hold priority; in other words, father and family are to take precedence over ruler and state' (p. 39). This is important for understanding the practical operation of Chinese laws, since the story used to illustrate this kind of conflict shows that a son would have a supervening obligation to protect a father from the 'arm of the law', should he have committed a crime, such as the theft of a sheep (p. 40). The consequences were significant, as 'we find that already in Han times close relatives were permitted to conceal the crime of one of their members without legal penalty and were not compelled to testify in court against him' (p. 40). Still more significant and extreme than this general right of concealment were various provisions that made it a crime in itself to bring a case to court against a more senior family member.[42] Bodde and Morris (1967: 40) report:

> [A] son who brings an accusation of parental wrongdoing before the authorities is thereby unfilial and hence subject to heavy punishment. Under the Ch'ing Code, for example, such an accusation, if false, was punished by strangulation, but even if true, it brought three years of penal servitude plus 100 blows of the heavy bamboo. The same punishments applied to a wife accusing either her husband or her parents-in-law, and lesser punishments applied to less close relatives. Probably China is the world's only

---

Bodde and Morris (1967: 39) provide examples of a code of *noblesse oblige*, amounting to stricter rules for officials than for the common Chinese person.

[42] Significantly, in cases of treason or rebellion, this rule did not apply (Bodde and Morris, 1967: 41).

country where the true reporting of a crime to the authorities could entail legal punishment for the reporter.

May (1985: 133) highlights that the ordering of society in *wu lun* (the five relationships) made a distinctive contribution to Chinese organisation of life. The *wu lun* are outlined by May (1985: 135) as:

> the distinguished relationships between father and son, ruler and subject, husband and wife, elder and younger (brother), and between friends. Taken together, they shape the whole society in a natural and characteristic manner so as to secure a plain and reliable order under the proposition that they are interlocking with their circle of duties and their corresponding performances which demand due attention to *li* expressing an expected correct and proper behaviour. In fulfilling one's duty *li* is the manner of how to do it, and so 'the outward expression of inward feeling' or, perhaps more likely, the inner constraint to act or react expectedly, in accordance with usage.

Numbering in fives is a distinct element of Chinese culture.[43] May (1985: 135) adds that '[t]he observance and performance of *li* becomes the fruit of the respective five (moral) lessons, the *wu chiao* or the five instructions of how to behave', which in turn created numerous particular kinds of *li*, polite and decent ways of conduct and usages in a situation-specific context. All of the above taken together meant that self-controlled ordering mechanisms were expected to take place within the conceptual framework established by Confucian teaching.[44] Rather than relying on the state or other external agents to maintain social control, internal control mechanisms within the realm of society and religion were preferred, which is why we are told in so many different ways that the ancient Chinese did not like law.

For the present cross-cultural comparative analysis, it is evident that the ancient Chinese were not opposed to law and legal processes as such, but were extremely wary of, and conceptually opposed to, the idea that human ordering processes should be imposed on people from above, by other people. This indicates a deep suspicion of positivism and its potential abuses. The conceptual requirement from within traditional Chinese cultures was that appropriate balances should be achieved through dialectic processes within the socio-cultural realm, for the benefit of the cosmic order as well as all members of society. This confirms that traditional Chinese laws are really no different from African laws and from Hindu law, all of which rely on the primacy of internal self-controlled ordering mechanisms. The consequence of this conceptual basis for traditional

---

[43] This is also noted and further explained by Bodde and Morris (1967: 76–7).

[44] Confucius (551–479 BC) evidently owed his prominent status not so much to his originality as to his ability to rephrase the guiding principles of traditional Chinese culture in a coherent fashion. McAleavy (1968a: 106) emphasised that 'he himself very truthfully declared that he was a transmitter, not a creator, of ideas'.

Chinese societies and legal arrangements over disputes point towards social patterns of dispute resolution rather than state-sponsored official fora. This again
is not different in principle from African and Hindu legal contexts. Focussing
on China, van der Sprenkel (1977: 26) indicated:

> [T]he internal jurisdiction of groups based on kin, neighbourhood and
> craft constituted an important extension of the official legal machinery, and
> I would suggest that the power of such groups to control their members
> was considerably enhanced by their religious beliefs and practices. Without
> entering into the detail of these, I think it is clear that participation in ritual
> observances made individuals conscious of the ties by which they were
> bound to fellow-members ... and the mutual dependence and responsibility
> these implied. Moreover, the solemnity of ritual occasions and the dignity
> acquired by those who took a leading part in them was easily transferred to
> other occasions. To take an example of the sort of thing that happened in
> all the groups, *mutatis mutandis*: those present in the ancestral hall when
> the head of the *tsu* made offerings to the *tsu* ancestors, in an atmosphere
> of extreme reverence and awe, must have received an intense impression,
> as the result of which the leading figure and the setting would alike be
> associated in their minds afterwards with thoughts of ancestors, solemnity
> and power. This both facilitated acceptance of the *tsu-chang's* authority
> in other matters and inspired respect for rules recited or displayed in the
> ancestral hall.

The shared obligations to common ancestors, in particular, created an internalised pattern of solidarity which encompassed all aspects of life.[45] Van der
Sprenkel (1977: 81) emphasises how the processes of socialisation in traditional China involved the deliberate inculcation of personal virtues linked to
filial piety, such as deferring to one's seniors, supporting parents in old age, and
yielding to others for the sake of avoiding disputes and to save face. Lapses in any
of these areas would be first criticised and, if necessary, punished by the heads of
families and clan elders, which shows that Chinese societies relied on a range of
internal, informal dispute settlement processes, which have prominently been
described as 'extra-legal', while plurality-conscious analysis indicates that these
processes are very much of a legal nature. Van der Sprenkel (1977: 85) demonstrates that these processes would be powerful mechanisms for exercising social
supervisory control:

> To be summoned to appear before the whole *tsu* or its leaders was a humil-
> iation in itself, even if the offender were let off with a caution. The action
> taken by them would vary according to the particular rules of the *tsu* and

---

[45] Van der Sprenkel (1977: 80) shows how this affected land-holding patterns, with the
existence of clan lands, income from which could be used for the upkeep of the ancestral
hall, looking after graves and the performance of rites, as well as serving as a social security
mechanism for members of the *tsu*.

the seriousness of the offence. Physical punishments were administered with bamboo or wooden boards; fines could be exacted; his name might be marked in the genealogy to record his offence; he might be deprived for a time of his share in the *tsu* income, and in some cases near relatives had also to be punished. To be omitted from the genealogy altogether was a serious matter, but according to Hu the most severe and effective punishment of all was that of expulsion from the *tsu*, involving loss of all privileges attaching to membership. Anyone who had been expelled could not take part in rituals, or enjoy material benefits during his lifetime, and after death his name would not be included in the *tsu* genealogy nor his tablet in the ancestral hall, and no one would perform rites for him. This was to be 'shut out from the community of the living and of the dead members of the *tsu*'.

Chapter 6 showed that Africans reserved for themselves the right to push an offender off the slowly moving train through history if the norms of the group had been severely violated. Various forms of exile are known from Hindu law, while Islamic law seems to suggest the death penalty in cases of grave *hadd* offences (chapter 5). Van der Sprenkel (1977: 85–6) stresses that being disowned by one's own community was the ultimate sanction and '[f]or a Chinese this would represent failure in the most important things in life'. In all of this, the absence of the state and its formal legal institutions is significant. Van der Sprenkel (1977: 127) suggests for traditional China that the ultimate source of law would be traceable to the common belief, never openly challenged, in an overriding obligation to preserve the harmony of the universe and to avoid evil consequences as a result of disturbing the natural order. She argues that '[i]t was this belief and this fear that led Emperor, officials and people to accept theoretically the necessity for the enforcement of morality, administrative requirements and legal custom' (p. 127). The so-called 'extra-legal' nature of the traditional Chinese legal system is therefore just a deficient scholarly construct and a significant misnomer in the context of a plurality-conscious global legal analysis. The ancient Chinese had and used a lot of law, discussing their various normative systems all the time. Typically, all of this took place, as much as possible, without the involvement of the state and of formal law and legal processes.

7.2.4 The place of customary laws

Not surprisingly, in view of the conceptual requirements of self-regulatory order, customary normative orders must have been of pre-eminent importance in traditional Chinese law. However, this important social fact is not adequately reflected in the legal literature. Lawyers and legal scholars tend and prefer to concentrate on codes and official state-made laws rather than the diffuse field of customary norms, which are perceived as the province of anthropology and sociology. Despite the central legal relevance of Chinese customary laws, such views appear to predominate among legal scholars, so that one finds relatively few comments on Chinese customary law and little specialist literature.[46] Bodde and Morris (1967: 5–6) emphasised the centrality of customary laws in view of the all-pervasive effects of the ethical norms of Confucianism:

> Here it should be stressed that in China, perhaps even more than in most other civilizations, the ordinary man's awareness and acceptance of such norms was shaped far more by the pervasive influence of custom and the usages of propriety than by any formally enacted system of law. The clan into which he was born, the guild of which he might become a member, the group of gentry elders holding informal sway in his rural community – these and other extra-legal bodies helped to smooth the inevitable frictions in Chinese society by inculcating moral precepts upon their members, mediating disputes, or, if need arose, imposing disciplinary sanctions and penalties.

While one must wonder why customs should be more important in traditional China than elsewhere in the world, the frequent designation of customary laws as 'extra-legal' is clearly too legocentric from a global analytical perspective. The term 'extra-legal' appears frequently in writing on Chinese law.[47] This is misleading and entirely arbitrary, reflecting lack of reflection about the various interacting concepts of law identified in the present study. Despite their lack of plurality-consciousness, Bodde and Morris (1967: 6) emphasised the links between formal and informal methods of dealing with disputes:

> The workings of such unofficial agencies were complemented by procedures on the part of the government, procedures which, despite their official inspiration, functioned quite separately from the formal legal system. These extra-legal organs and procedures, then, were what the Chinese everyman normally looked to for guidance and sanction, rather than to the formal judicial system per se.

Admittedly, the important sphere of the so-called extra-legal world is difficult to access for lawyers. Bodde and Morris (1967: 6) emphasised that the various extra-legal bodies for social control, despite their obvious importance and the many references to them, are 'very difficult to study with precision because of their scattered and informal mode of operation, and the fact that what they did and said was often either not written down at all or, if written, not readily

---

[46] An instructive collection of essays is found in a specialist volume on customary law produced by the Société Jean Bodin, in which see Benecke (1992), Shiga (1992) and Tsien (1992). Benecke (1992: 427) distinguishes at least four different types of custom. In Hong Kong and South East Asia, in particular, various forms of Chinese customary laws became important elements of the respective legal system, and proof of custom would then be required. For some material on this see Ho (2000).

[47] David and Brierley (1978: 481) note that everything in China systematically discouraged people from using the courts and 'encourages the use of extra-judicial techniques for the settling of disputes'.

available in published form'. Orality, therefore, also presented huge problems for plurality-conscious Chinese legal analysis. McAleavy (1968a: 110–11) tried to help by suggesting that, despite the enormous size of China, there was not actually a huge variety of customary norms:

> The great size of China would lead one to believe that there must be a pro-found divergence of custom between one part of the country and another, and indeed the Chinese themselves have from the earliest times constantly remarked upon the variations of their local habits. Yet in this as in other respects foreigners would be well advised to be on their guard against overemphasis. It is the unity rather than the diversity of Chinese culture which should engage the attention. The stories we are so often told of a babel-like confusion of dialects, to mention only one subject of misunder-standing, are a grotesque distortion of the truth.

McAleavy proceeds to argue that the centralised imperial form of government in traditional China, maintained almost without interruption for nearly 2,000 years, created uniformising trends which had their own effects on the mutual comprehension of different local languages, the standardisation of education and the harmonisation of some assumed national standards of social norms. However, this did not result in unification of customary laws.[48] It is remark-able how McAleavy (1968a: 114–15) eventually concludes this discussion by emphasising that custom actually overrides the written letter of the law, as was also seen for ancient India:

> It has seemed necessary to discuss this topic at length in order to clarify one most important proposition, which is too often lost sight of by western observers, namely, that to ascertain the effective rules of traditional Chinese law in what we should term private or civil matters, one must exclude statute in favour of custom.

In order 'to study what in the West would be called Chinese private law, one must thus look to Chinese custom' (David and Brierley, 1978: 482). The reali-sation that customary Chinese laws have remained of great practical relevance is also reflected when van der Sprenkel (1977: 103) notes that, during the early years of the post-imperial Republic, in 1925, a compilation of legal customs prevalent in different parts of China was made for the purposes of drawing up a civil code. This included provisions for a wide range of matters, as detailed examples demonstrate. Van der Sprenkel (1977: 111) concludes this discussion by emphasising that, in disputes arising out of customary and contractual agree-ments, 'custom – which I have suggested is here to be equated with local law – must be upheld and customary contracts must be honoured, if the life of the community was to go on'. This signifies a strong interest in seeing the content of

---

[48] This discussion parallels arguments over the unification of customary laws in East Africa (chapter 6, section 6.5.2).

individual and local agreements fulfilled, as well as concern about preventing friction between the parties. This confirms that, at the local level, customary norms in all their potential diversity would override other concerns, provided upholding custom would strengthen harmony and order. This has also been an important feature in more recent periods of Chinese legal history. For example, McAleavy (1968a: 128) emphasised that 'the Nationalist codes were a façade, behind which 95 per cent of the people continued to regulate their lives by the customs of their forefathers'.[49]

As in the study of other Asian and African legal systems, therefore, we see that the practical importance of customary laws is recognised, albeit with some reluctance, by legal scholars who prefer to work with 'real' law. A recent analysis by Lubman (1995: 2) rightly recognises that a theme of fundamental importance, also in the study of modern Chinese laws, remains 'the pervasive influence of a number of strands in Chinese legal culture'. The positivist inclinations of legal scholarship on Chinese law therefore do not allow a finding to the effect that, when it comes to custom in China, everything is different from other legal systems. As in Africa and elsewhere, most of the evidence of customary legal activity in China remains of course inaccessible, but its existence cannot be denied. However, the most impressive early codification of criminal and other public laws, to which the present comparative analysis now turns, does distinguish China from other jurisdictions.

7.3 The classical Chinese legal system: codes and what else?

In this section, the main aim is to examine the impressive, tangible body of Chinese imperial codes and to analyse their underlying, often intangible conceptual roots. It is necessary to explore in some depth the practical implications of having codified laws of this type within a society that manifestly disagreed, in principle, that laws made by the state were conducive to establishing better human relations and to maintaining cosmic order and harmony. Following a brief historical overview of codification in China, major subsections focus first of all on criminal law, then on the core concepts of *hsing* and *fa*, and finally on the confucianisation of laws in traditional China.

7.3.1 Historical overview of codification in China

Bodde and Morris (1967: 15) introduce the earliest Chinese code, which comes from the early Chou dynasty (c. 1027 to 221 BC), a feudalist environment. They paint a picture of a supreme ruling house, the Chou kings, 'who exercised nominal sovereignty over the entire Chinese cultural world' (p. 15), while vassal

---

[49] The same point is reiterated by David and Brierley (1978: 478), noting that in China 'social relations continue to be ruled in large part by the traditional models'.

lords ruled over certain segments of the realm and those areas, in turn, were under the authority of local lords and officials, who ruled the peasants. However, gradually the Chou overlordship collapsed and the vassal kings became independent rulers, creating a plethora of small states around the sixth century BC. The turmoil caused by such inherently unstable political constellations is depicted by Bodde and Morris (1967: 16):

> The final centuries of the Chou dynasty, appropriately known as the Period of the Warring States (403–221 BC), saw increasingly bitter warfare between the few large states still surviving, till one of them, the state of Ch'in, succeeded in swallowing up its rivals one by one, and in 221 BC finally created the first centralized empire in Chinese history.

Prior to this period of the warring states, the creation of the first Chinese codes of written law had taken place in the late sixth century BC. Bodde and Morris (1967: 16) report that 'the earliest reliably known to us is the "books of punishment" (*hsing shu*) which Tzu-chu'an, prime minister of the state of Cheng, ordered to be inscribed in 536 BC on a set of bronze tripod vessels'.[50] Similar efforts to promulgate and record laws were made in several states in 513 BC, 501 BC and later, but all the texts of these 'codes' have been lost. The first imperial code of China, in the third century BC, could therefore draw on various fragments from more ancient Chinese laws. Bodde and Morris (1967: 7–8) wrote about the early phases:

> For previous dynasties there also exists a sequence of earlier codes going back to the T'ang Code of 653, in 501 articles. Before this date, no codes survive save for scattered quotations in other works. However, a study still in progress has already yielded a wealth of information on the code and judicial procedure of the first lengthy imperial dynasty, that of Han (206 BC–AD 220).
>
> Prior to the Han and its short-lived predecessor, the Ch'in dynasty (221–207 BC), no centralized empire yet existed in China. At that time there were only a number of independent and mutually warring principalities. This pre-imperial age, often called the age of Chinese feudalism because of its institutional similarities to medieval Europe, is also the age that saw the formative beginnings of Chinese written law.

There was significant opposition to such promulgations of law, basically grounded in Confucian arguments that self-controlled order is better than state-sponsored rule by law. Bodde and Morris (1967: 17) emphasise that the most significant argument in this context is 'insistence upon the moral and political dangers involved in the public promulgation of legal norms', a view

---

[50] To the same effect, Bodde and Morris (1967: 8) report that '[e]xcluding unreliable myth and legend, the earliest datable evidence of such written law is the promulgation in 536 BC of certain "books of punishment" in one of these principalities'.

of law which 'seems to have no real parallel in any other civilization' (p. 17). There is much more to say about this particular conflict of opinions about how best to maintain social order, internal peace and justice. Evidently, the earlier reliance on principles of self-controlled order was now being challenged by an understanding that stating rules of punishment would deter people from committing bad deeds. Bodde and Morris (1967: 16–17) report on an acerbic exchange of correspondence between high dignitaries from the sixth century BC, arguing over the good and bad points of promulgating a code of law. While the early Ch'in code was based on strict legalist principles, from the Han code onwards, law in imperial China 'became the embodiment of the ethical norms of Confucianism' (Bodde and Morris, 1967: 5), as subsequent sections show in more detail.

The general picture clearly shows that, from 221 BC until the end of the Chinese empire in 1911 or 1912, each successive Chinese imperial dynasty pro-mulgated a new, revised and elaborated code, sometimes a radical modification of the laws of their predecessors. The Ch'ing Code, the last major codification of imperial China, assumed definite form in 1740 during the rule of the Ch'ing or Manchu dynasty (1644–1911).[51]

7.3.2 The conceptual emphasis on penal law

The logical consequence of accepting self-controlled order as the supreme prin-ciple would be that ideally no state-made criminal law should be required within the Confucian framework of reference. If the ruler himself was follow-ing *li*, there should be no need for law (May, 1985: 132–3) and there ought to be total harmony. However, this manifestly idealistic and idealised approach did not preclude the emergence of the so-called 'legalist' school of thought in ancient China. May (1985: 149–50) reiterates the ideal of harmony in accor-dance with Confucian and other traditional philosophies and religious beliefs in traditional China. In view of what we know about the practical importance of the so-called 'extra-legal' sphere, it is conceivable that the state would not necessarily be involved in disputes between individuals, even in cases of mur-der.[52] Van der Sprenkel (1977: 29) doubted whether Chinese peasants were interested in the theoretical justifications of political rule, but emphasised that they would have 'a practical interest both in order being maintained, so that they could labour undisturbed and enjoy the products of their labour, and in

---

[51] Imperial legal documents were not restricted to codes. Case reports existed in large collec-tions, the largest and best dating from 1736 to 1885, with more than 7,600 cases, and there are also some treatises on legal history. For details see Bodde and Morris (1967: 7–9).

[52] Bodde and Morris (1967: 4) confirm that governmental law only impinged on people at the *hsien* or district level, so what kind of law was being applied below that level? The writ of state law did not automatically reach every conscience, as a legocentric approach would like to claim.

the maintenance of public works necessary to the irrigation system'. Thus, the need for government was accepted so long as it was efficient and its demands were kept within recognised limits. The image of governance as cooking a small fish, which appears frequently (Glenn, 2004: 316), expresses well that good governance is an extremely delicate task. Van der Sprenkel (1977: 29) explained that the explicitly ethical character of Chinese society and the intermingling of ethics and administration would have a peculiar impact on how the state would make laws:

> To govern, in the Confucian view, was to set a good example and promote good behaviour among people, that is, to create conditions in which people could live without disturbing the natural harmony. Any such disturbance was in itself a sign of the failure of government, and this was an inducement to conceal or play down lesser disturbances and to pretend that all was well. If in practice this was impossible, action had to be taken to fix responsibility somewhere, and due amends had to be made for the disruption in order to prove that government was in capable hands. The belief that disastrous natural phenomena – floods, droughts, tempests, insect pests – were the consequence of human disorder provided further theoretical justification for punishment of wrongdoers: they were a double menace to society.

The state might therefore intervene to ensure that disorder was avoided. May (1985: 136–7) explains the resulting emphasis on penal law:

> Offences in disregard of one's duty called for appropriate treatment in order to restore the lost equilibrium of nature, the harmonious interaction between the human and the non-human spheres. The *wu hsing* (the five punishments) are regarded as such treatment; they are to be considered in correspondence to the *wu chiao* (the five educational lessons of conduct (duty)) within the five relationships and their implicit order to conform to the respective rules of *li*.

The severe and formidable five punishments, and to a lesser degree the five forms of banishment, were primarily intended to prevent offences that caused the dreaded disturbances of natural harmony. Belief in what the present study subsumes under natural law meant that the whole legal field could never be totally dominated by the state. From the start, therefore, legalist approaches in ancient China did not assume that state law could ever cover the entire social field. Bodde and Morris (1967: 4) explained that the penal emphasis of the law meant that matters of a civil nature (such as contracts) were either completely ignored or were given only limited treatment in relation to property rights, inheritance and marriage. Also, the law was only secondarily interested in defending the rights, especially the economic rights, of individuals or groups against other individuals or groups, and not at all concerned about defending such rights against the state. Thus, what really concerned the formal law were all those acts of moral or ritual impropriety or criminal violence which were perceived as violations or disruptions of the total social order. State law served as a method of assisted self-control, as found for Hindu law (chapter 4, section 4.4). Bodde and Morris explained:

> The existence of the norms of propriety was intended to deter the commission of such acts, but once they occurred, the restoration of social harmony required that punishment be inflicted to exact retribution from their doer. In the final analysis, a disturbance of the social order really meant, in Chinese thinking, a violation of the total cosmic order because, according to the Chinese world-view, the spheres of man and nature were inextricably interwoven to form an unbroken continuum.

Thus the imperial laws of China acquired a penal orientation which remained its basic characteristic until well into the twentieth century. Remarkably, despite what they said above about the law as a tool for the maintenance of cosmic order, Bodde and Morris (1967: 49) emphasised the secular orientation of such primarily penal laws and linked this to hostility towards such law:

> Unlike many other major civilizations, where written law was held in honor and often attributed to a divine origin, law in China was from the beginning viewed in purely secular terms. Its initial appearance, indeed, was greeted with positive hostility by many as indicative of a serious moral decline.

The bitter controversy between Confucians and Legalists from 536 BC onwards reflects different evaluations among the ancient Chinese about the role of state-made laws. For some time, it appeared as though the legalists would become dominant; but Chinese law soon developed an intricate compromise between Confucianism and Legalism. Before we can analyse that compromise and its consequences, it is necessary to consider in some detail how legalist concepts operated in ancient Chinese law and what effects they had on law-making.

7.3.3 The key concept of fa and the influence of legalism

As we saw, from the perspective of the idealistic self-control model of Confucianism, *fa* should be entirely superfluous (May, 1985: 154–5). The concept of *fa*, 'law' or 'legal regulation', has at least two meanings.[53] It is first the idea of law as a tool to control society. Secondly, *fa* refers also to the resulting regulatory law itself.[54] Legalism was one of the four main philosophical schools at the end of the Chou dynasty in the period of the Warring States, prior to 221 BC. Legalists believed that a good ruler should govern his subjects by three means: (1) The law (*fa*) in the form of a code should be clearly written and made public. All people under the ruler were equal before the law. The law itself is higher than the ruler, clearly an early Chinese model of 'rule of law'. (2) The

---

[53] See http://en.wikipedia.org/wiki/legalism_(philosophy).
[54] On *fa* and its various meanings see Unger (1976: 102–5).

concept of *shu* (the 'art of kingship') concerned elaborate methods of control through secretive techniques to encourage the ruler to make sure that nobody else could take control of the state. This identifies the Chinese ruler as a circumspect servant of the higher Order.[55] (3) The concept of *shi* refers to legitimacy, power and charisma and indicates that the position of the ruler, rather than the ruler himself, is the central axis of control. Rulers are, thus, replaceable if they fail to fulfil their role. All of this indicates that legalists, aware of a higher order encapsulated in *tao*, took a pragmatic view of the instrumentality of law, constructing a positivist approach to human law-making with agenda beyond the ruler's command, but in conceptual tension to Confucian trends of reliance on self-controlled order (*li*). Bodde and Morris (1967: 18) clearly emphasise the practical nature of legalist thought, but do not disregard higher concerns:

> Opposed to the Confucians were men who, because of their ardent advocacy of law, eventually came to be known as the Legalists or School of Law (*fa chia*). Most of them were less theoretical thinkers than tough-minded men of affairs who, as administrators, diplomats, and political economists, sought employment from whatever state would use their services. Their aim was direct and simple: to create a political and military apparatus powerful enough to suppress feudal privilege at home, expand the state's territory abroad, and eventually weld all the rival kingdoms into a single empire. . . Their insistence on law, therefore, was motivated by no concern for 'human rights,' but simply by the realization that law was essential for effectively controlling the growing populations under their jurisdiction. In thinking and techniques they were genuine totalitarians, concerned with men in the mass, in contrast to the Confucians, for whom individual, family, or local community were of paramount importance. Yet it would be unfair to regard them merely as unscrupulous power-hungry politicians, for they sincerely believed that only through total methods could eventual peace and unity be brought to their wartorn world.

Pragmatic legalist approaches signal some disillusionment with the idealistic assumptions of Taoist and Confucian self-control. These objectives were voiced with particular vigour by Han Fei Tzu, an outstanding spokesman of the legalist school, who died in 233 BC. May (1985: 158) summarises his main arguments, to the effect that man's nature is evil, moral education through *li* is considered ineffective, and reliance on self-control creates social disorder. Thus, *fa* as 'strict prescription laid down in writing, made publicly known, and applicable to everybody concerned without regard for any distinction whatsoever' (p. 159) is seen as an appropriate remedy for upholding social and legal order. Bodde and Morris (1967: 11) emphasise that the word *fa* was already in common use before its appearance as the most important word in the Chinese legal

---

[55] Again, this parallels Hindu concepts and the reference to secretive techniques mirrors the *Arthaśāstra*, India's Machiavellian guidebook for rulers.

vocabulary: 'Its root meaning is that of a model, pattern, or standard; hence of a method or procedure to be followed. From this root meaning comes the notion, basic in Chinese legal thinking, that *fa* is a model or standard imposed by superior authority, to which the people must conform.' This indicates that *fa* covers both Allott's (1980: 2) concept of LAW as a global abstraction and 'law' as legal rules. In its latter meaning, it becomes an archetypal term for legal positivist intervention. But could a state regulate, to the last dot, what its people should be doing? Bodde and Morris (1967: 11–12) remain silent on this; instead they are concerned to emphasise the importance of another old key term:

> [P]erhaps even more common than *fa* in early legal references, is *hsing*, sig-
> nifying 'punishment' (or 'punishments'),[56] but more specifically 'corporal
> punishment.' That the latter is its primary meaning is indicated, among
> other things, by the inclusion in the written character for *hsing* of the graph
> meaning 'knife.' There is every reason to believe that such punishments as
> nose-cutting, leg-cutting, castration, and the like were current in China well
> before the enactment of any systems of written law (*fa*). Once written law
> came into existence, however, the meaning of *hsing* was extended to include
> not only the punishments per se, but also the written prohibitions whose
> violation would result in these punishments. In this important secondary
> usage, therefore, *hsing* may be fairly understood in the sense of 'penal law'
> (or 'laws'). The frequency of its occurrence in the early legal passages –
> both alone and as an alternative for *fa* – is indicative of the antiquity of
> the Chinese view which sees written law, *fa*, as signifying primarily penal
> law, *hsing*. Until as recently as the administrative reforms of 1906, this idea
> was perpetuated in the name of the highest governmental legal organ, the
> Hsing Pu or Board or Ministry of Punishments.

May (1985: 137) confirms that the concept of *hsing*, 'punishment', especially as *wu hsing*, 'the five punishments', was in use long before the concept of *fa* acquired its specific meaning, indicating also that both were said to have foreign origins.[57] This is elaborated by Bodde and Morris (1967: 13), who recount an ancient story, which attributes the invention of *fa* to a barbarian group of non-Chinese people, the Miao, and dates it back supposedly to the twenty-third century BC and a legendary sage called Shun.[58] This myth was to the effect that the Miao people 'made no use of spiritual cultivation, but controlled by means of punishments (*hsing*), creating the five oppressive punishments which they

---

[56] This is because, in Chinese languages, there is no marker for singular or plural (Bodde and Morris, 1967: 63).

[57] Glenn (2004: 305–7) summarises this subject well. For the legalist position see David and Brierley (1978: 481–2).

[58] Indian myths about Manu as the first law-maker are quite different in type, but also emphasise (chapter 4, section 4.4) the importance of threatening punishment with a punishing rod (*danda*). The use of myth to explain how formal law-making comes about is a remarkable feature of ancient chthonic traditions.

called law (*fa*)' (p. 13). Reports of this myth confirm that the Miao people used punishments such as castration and amputation of body parts. The cruelty and resulting injustice of this system is a key element of the story and this important myth takes on another important message, which Bodde and Morris (1967: 14) bring out:

> Shang Ti or the 'Lord on High' (the supreme god of the ancient Chinese), seeing the resulting disorder among the people, felt pity for the innocent and hence exterminated the Miao, so that they had no descendants.

This story illustrates an early example of excesses in positivist law-making and government lawlessness. The message for ancient Chinese law-makers was therefore ambivalent: law could be used as a tool of governance, but needed at all times to be prevented from creating injustice and cosmic imbalance. Too much law would be bad, disturbing subtle balances. We must note that legal centralism received a resounding early disapproval here. Traditional Chinese codes of law were not to be used as autonomously produced and applied human tools for governance, but were to serve a higher purpose. In this sense, too, Chinese law is also somewhat religious. However, this is not the interpretation of Bodde and Morris (1967: 14):

> The abhorrence of law expressed in this story no doubt reflects a period in legal development (sixth or fifth century BC) when written law was still a novelty and hence viewed with suspicion. In later centuries, when law became more prevalent and the need for its existence became increasingly recognized, various non-mythological and soberly 'sociological' explanations of its origin appeared. Although their attitude was no longer hostile, they all agreed with the unknown author of the Miao legend in explaining the origin of law in strictly secular terms.

In this myth, law as a human secular means of social control fails to perform. Hence the mythological Miao people had to die out or be dispersed to remote corners of the world, from where they could not return to China. Bodde and Morris (1967: 14) show through other literary examples that the ancient Chinese had a vision of even earlier human society as being badly organised and governed. Bodde and Morris (1967: 14) cite a myth to the effect that earlier people were wicked and depraved, and that wise men among them established laws (*fa*), legal controls of all kinds of abuses, including consumer protection measures, reminiscent of Indian *danda*. Bodde and Morris (1967: 14–15) report from another sample of myth:

> Law (*fa*) has its origin in social rightness (*yi*). Social rightness has its origin in what is fitting for the many. What is fitting for the many is what accords with the mind of men. Herein is the essence of good government. . . Law is not something sent down by Heaven, nor is it something engendered by Earth. It springs from the midst of men themselves, and by being brought back [to men] it corrects itself.

> The sages, being enlightened and wise by nature, inevitably penetrated the mind of Heaven and Earth. They shaped the rules of proper behavior (*li*), created teachings, established laws (*fa*), and instituted punishments (*hsing*), always acting in accordance with the feelings of the people and patterning and modeling themselves on Heaven and Earth.

The conclusion need not be, as seems manifest for Bodde and Morris (1967: 15), that positivist law-making should therefore be employed and would in itself be sufficient. The message of the early sages is clearly that laws established by men would need to be balanced and measured against higher standards. Here, too, is a familiar message about seeking to maintain an equilibrium, which legocentric interpretations of Chinese law have failed to bring out as fully as possible.[59]

The main arguments in favour of the Legalist position are discussed by Bodde and Morris (1967: 23–7), supplemented by a number of quotes. The major arguments are, first, that humans are inherently selfish and act out of self-interest,[60] hence 'stern punishments are necessary' (p. 23). Secondly, law-making by the state should destroy factionalism and privilege, and the laws should be applied impartially to all. Thirdly, the fluidity and inherent flexibility of *li* is rejected as a basis for a stable government, which should in the legalist view be based on known and fixed rules which are the same for all. This sounds modern and appears like a 'pure' form of legal positivism. Fourthly, group responsibility is suggested as an inherent element of administration at the lowest level, holding individual members of such groups responsible for the wrongdoings of other members, thus seeking to achieve a higher degree of compliance with state laws. Again, this is a positivist device to achieve state control down to the lowest level of society, which sounds like a useful principle, but will be difficult to implement in practice, as modern Chinese experience confirms.[61] Fifthly, there is a modernisation argument to the effect that self-controlled order was perhaps good enough for small-scale societies with few worries about basic resources. In a more sophisticated and crowded environment, laws become a necessary tool of governance and organisation. Sixthly, and dangerously, the argument is in favour of total uniformisation, so that '[a] state that is strong is one that maintains a single standard of morality and thought for its people. All private standards must be suppressed if they no longer agree with the public standard as prescribed by law' (Bodde and Morris, 1967: 24). This modernist argument can be easily twisted as a government sees fit.[62] Seventhly, the legalist philosophy suggests a system of rewards for those individuals, especially officials, who fulfil the targets of the state-made laws, but matches this with punishments for

---

[59] These messages are also relevant to interpretations of post-Maoist law-making in modern China, which exhibit definite traits of legalist philosophy (section 7.6).

[60] Exactly the same argument was used in ancient India to keep people's selfishness in check.

[61] It appears that later communist techniques of law-making and modern Chinese law have relied on such philosophical underpinnings to achieve a higher degree of state control.

[62] This, again, is an argument that later Chinese governments have abused to cruel extremes, and all of these points can be read as elements of socialist legality.

falling short of required standards. Eighthly, it is suggested that even a mediocre ruler could, under the legalist system, maintain order when there is an efficient legal machinery. Finally, Bodde and Morris (1967: 24) stipulate:

> 9. Laws that are sufficiently stringent will no longer have to be applied because their mere existence will be enough to deter wrongdoing. Thus harsh laws, though painful in their immediate effects, lead in the long run to an actual reduction of government and to a society free from conflict and oppression.

In this way, a different type of self-controlled order is envisaged, in which the same idealistic principles apply as in the Confucian model – and later in Chinese socialist models. The only difference appears to be that in the legalist model the determination of what is good and bad depends on criteria set by the state, rather than local norms. In this sense, Legalism may also be interpreted as an attempt to squash the local dominance of custom and the pervasive influence of different religious and philosophical norms. Legalism is therefore a multi-faceted, sophisticated method of positivist law-making, potentially legocentric and thus endangering the triangular polarity of religion, society and the state in favour of one-sided state control of the entire field. It is not a surprise, therefore, that this model, in its pure form, was not what traditional China chose to be governed by. In its purely legalistic form, it lacked plurality-consciousness and concern for situation-specific justice. The dialectic outcome of the intensive and lengthy continuing debates between legalist and Confucian ideas had to be a sustainable compromise, which is admirably found in the 'confucianisation of the law' (section 7.3.4 below).

In ancient China, while these debates between the Confucians and Legal-ists were going on, the Ch'in dynasty enforced the legalist approach through codification and achieved a dramatic but unsurprisingly short-lived success. Bodde and Morris (1967: 27) report that the legalist techniques of governance enabled the Ch'in dynasty, in 221 BC, to triumph over all its rivals and to estab-lish the first universal Chinese empire,[63] based on a centralised bureaucracy, whose cadres were non-hereditary, salaried appointees of the state, a system which stayed in place until 1912. Interestingly, the Ch'in rulers tried to erase an unsatisfactory past by burning the books of *li*, a futile exercise of course, but significant nevertheless, as well as killing scholars who spoke in favour of Confucian ideals. David and Brierley (1978: 482) emphasise that the legal-ists 'attempted to replace government by men with *government by laws*', and continued:

> The legalists' theories, as expounded in the works of Han-Fei-tzü (d. 233 BC) stated the need for permanent laws which would be known by the servants of the state and to which individuals would, without exception,

---

[63] The term 'universal' is of course misplaced in the context of a globally focused study.

be subject. On the whole, these theories express a concept of legislation (*loi*) and law (*droit*) very close to the western idea. J. Escarra observed that the theories of Han-Fei-tzü seem to express ideas so natural with us that they appear to be somewhat 'naive.' These theories have remained however completely foreign to the Chinese mentality in general. They were too radical a departure from accepted thinking, and the legalists had only a passing success. They did not gain any general acceptance for the notion of permanent rules and the concept of sovereign law in China.

While the outright legalist process of law-making proved unacceptable in ancient China, the impact of Legalism as a concept has been lasting, as noted by Bodde and Morris (1967: 28–9) with various examples:

> Its influence probably explains, for example, the continuing penal emphasis found in all the imperial codes, and the resulting fact that their treatment even of administrative and other noncriminal matters usually follows a standard formula: 'Anyone who does x is to receive punishment y.' Or again, the background of Legalism probably explains certain important features of imperial judicial procedure: the non-existence of private lawyers; the assumption (nowhere explicitly stated but everywhere implied in the treatment of defendants) that a suspect must be guilty unless and until he is proven innocent; or the legal use of torture (within certain specified limits) for extracting confession from suspects who stubbornly refuse to admit guilt despite seemingly convincing evidence against them. Still another idea which probably owes much to Legalism is that of group responsibility (especially conspicuous in treason cases and the like).

While Legalism as an official Chinese ideology was terminated as early as 206 BC, influential strands of legalist thought have reappeared in China's legal history also during the troubled twentieth century, when the temptation to use law as a means of all-powerful government raised its head again and again in different forms. These scenarios are analysed in more detail further below. At this point, it is necessary to consider to what extent classical Chinese law developed a hybrid form of legal regulation that sought to combine internalised Confucian idealism and external legalist force.

7.3.4 Confucianisation of the law

The final stage of the conceptual development of *li* in classical China is represented by its incorporation into the administrative and legal structures of imperial China. May (1985: 161) expresses this well when he explains that the formal incorporation of the Li Chi (the Book of *li*) into the classical canon by the Han dynasty constitutes the concluding phase for the consolidation of *li* as a most important element in traditional Chinese socio-cultural life. The early Chinese debates about the advantages and disadvantages of stating rules of punishment in a code (Bodde and Morris, 1967: 16–17) brought out the debate between Confucians or Confucianists and Legalists. The argument that self-controlled order should be allowed to take its course, and codes were not only unnecessary but actually detrimental to such self-controlled ordering processes, led to the important later compromise embodied in the phrase 'confucianisation of the law'. Bodde and Morris (1967: 18) report:

> Confucians were staunch upholders of the traditional 'feudal' scale of values. Hence it is natural that they should be bitterly hostile to the new law, especially in its early stages. Later, however, as it became increasingly apparent that law had come to stay, the Confucians softened their attitude to the point where they accepted law – although grudgingly – as a necessary evil. Even then, however, they remained Confucian in their insistence that the public enacting of law is not necessary in the ideal state, and that even in the inferior administration of their own times, government by law should always be kept secondary to government by moral precept and example.

It is unsurprising for an interdisciplinary comparative legal analysis that the supposedly triumphant legalist march into power under the Ch'in empire in 221 BC was short-lived. There is nothing amazing about this, as Bodde and Morris (1967: 27) seem to suggest. The death of a ruler in 210 BC and the subsequent rebellion and disorder merely show that the legalist ideology had been an imposed value system that was not shared by rival contenders for power, nor by the people at large. The Han empire (206 BC to 220 AD) adopted all major elements from the bureaucratic structures of the Ch'in model of governance, but did not follow strict legalism as a state ideology. Bodde and Morris (1967: 27) comment that 'in one of the amazing reversals of history, Confucianism replaced Legalism as the dominant ideology. Already by 100 BC Confucianism was beginning to gain recognition as the orthodoxy of the state.' May (1985: 165) shows that the process of confucianisation of the law was a long process:

> As known from researches concerning the completely preserved T'ang Code (653 AD) and its fragmentary precursors a gradual process of Confucianization of *fa*, or, conversely, the slow infiltration of *fa* into the realm and relations of *li*, had taken place from the beginning of the Han dynasty continuing through the centuries of the imperial history.

As shown earlier, one should not assume that Legalism disappeared totally, but it clearly was no longer the dominant philosophy of governance. Bodde and Morris (1967: 50) characterise this system of law in imperial China as a hybrid of Legalism and Confucianism, which retained the penal orientation of the legalists and some elements of the harshness of the law, but adopted from Confucianism the hierarchical structuring of society and the idealist approach that harmonious functioning of all components at their respective different levels should be encouraged to form an ordered whole. Thus, the formal legal system was redesigned to discourage its own use, since recourse to formal litigation was seen as negative in itself. Bodde and Morris (1967: 27–8) explain that the new system represented a symbiosis of the two approaches, because 'the Confucianism which triumphed in Han times was a highly eclectic thought system – one that borrowed extensively from its philosophical rivals'. Since one of those rivals was legalism, the formal eclipse and abandonment of legalism did not mean the complete disappearance of legalist ideas and practices. Formally, severe penalties were decreed against those who infringed the imperial statutes (McAleavy, 1968a: 109), but what would happen in reality? The resulting symbiosis of different concepts is explained by Bodde and Morris (1967: 29):

> [T]he really spectacular phenomenon of imperial times is what has been aptly termed the Confucianization of law – in other words, the incorporation of the spirit and sometimes of the actual provisions of the Confucian *li* into the legal codes. This process got under way during Han times only gradually and thereafter continued over several centuries. By the enactment of the T'ang Code in 653, however, it had effectively closed the one-time breach between *li* and *fa*. Customary morality (*li*) achieved official status in the form of positive law (*fa*), or, to reverse the equation . . . positive law (*fa*) achieved moral status as the embodiment of natural law (*li*).

May (1985: 167) emphasises in conclusion that the supervening influence of Confucianism meant that avoidance of recourse to the law was built into the formal system:

> Continuous endeavours at giving no rise to litigation through moral education reveals once more that there is in fact an alternative in a self-regulating procedure of *li*, the substantial consolidation of which is capable of maintaining social harmony on a broad scale, and thus making the old 'legalistic' use of *fa* and the handling of *sung* (litigation) completely undesirable and in practice possibly superfluous.

The desire to avoid litigation remained a superior norm in practice, so that the Chinese codes could not be read like Western legal statutes. It is here, too, that the most confucianised interpretation of *fa* as 'deterrent punishment' would make an appearance, designed to prevent wrongdoing by reminding the individual's conscience that infringement of the formal law might have drastic consequences, while not necessarily assuming that the law would come into action. Bodde and Morris (1967: 29–31) explain how the combination of the two inherently conflicting principles led to a hybrid system of formal governance, which not only left much room for particularisms but also continued to rely on self-controlled order. Further, the basic Confucian principle that the punishment should fit the crime needed to be applied on the basis of several differentiating considerations, in particular regarding motivation for the crime, the respective status of perpetrator and victim, and an assessment of the situation-specific nature of the occurrence. Bodde and Morris (1967: 31–2) outline the need for maintaining flexibility in order to fulfil this Confucian *grundnorm*:

> The principle of differentiation was no doubt introduced into the codes with the aim of maximizing justice by enabling the law to fit as closely as possible every foreseeable circumstance. In actual fact, however . . . the principle often made justice more difficult because it compelled the judge, faced by a case involving circumstances not exactly covered by any existing statute, to choose as best he could between the several statutes most nearly applicable.
>
> The usual device for handling this situation was the judgment by analogy.

The practical application of this confucianised system of official law therefore posed two grave risks. Either it might lead to more or less total ineffectiveness by applying the principle of avoidance of litigation too widely, allowing the official laws to be bypassed altogether. In the other extreme, the formal laws might be abused by those in positions of power to criminalise certain types of actions and to victimise certain individuals, apparently legitimised by the provisions of the imperial codes. McAleavy (1968a: 109) was quite right when he emphasised that '[t]he legal history of China is therefore to a large extent made up of the interaction of these two divergent tendencies'. As the next section demonstrates, while blatant abuses of legal power were widespread, Confucian perceptions of balance and harmony would be able to intervene and might protect citizens from the worst excesses of abuse. Equally interesting for a comparative legal analysis, however, is the phenomenon of avoidance of the formal system of laws by recourse to various informal methods of dispute settlement within society. The phenomenon is certainly not unique to China and is a hallmark of all Asian and African legal systems. However, the particular culture-specific legitimations for the prominent use of so-called 'extra-legal' or alternative dispute resolution (ADR) procedures in traditional China certainly deserve specific attention.

7.4 The practical application of the law

The co-existence of formal imperial codes, focused on criminal laws and deterrence, and the officially informal, but in their own way formalised, local methods of handling litigation and disputes of any kind established a pattern of intensive interaction that is perhaps unique to traditional China (McAleavy, 1968a: 109). This co-existence over an extremely long period was facilitated by political factors, above all the political unification of the Chinese empire, in marked contrast to the Indian pattern of multiple fragmentations, the African mass of communities that each followed their own patterns of self-regulation and the volatility and fragmentation of Muslim empires over time. Chinese law, in comparison, appears to exhibit a greater degree of uniformity.[64] On the other hand, not only the formal legal system but also in particular the informal sector have always been characterised by fluidity and internal flexibility, conceptually

---

[64] Indeed, several authors try to emphasise this, for example McAleavy (1968a: 110–14).

required in view of the overarching situation-specific Confucian assumptions about harmony and balance. Thus, over time it was necessary to adjust local customary norms, while the provisions of the great imperial codes could also be modified. An overall impression of consolidated stability and uniformity in Chinese law thus masks a reality of multiple pluralisms and constant dynamic interaction, systemically required to fulfil the social tasks of the formal as well as the informal legal systems within Chinese law. From a comparative perspective, there is nothing unusual about this, but the culture-specific Chinese manifestations offer intriguing evidence of plurality-conscious constructions over time.

The present section first provides a historical overview of the system of Chinese imperial codes. The analytical focus then shifts to the Chinese Emperor as the figurehead of the legal system and its various legal functionaries. Two further sub-sections elucidate how the imperial law worked in practice, either through avoidance of formal litigation in the first place, or by a variety of techniques designed to achieve situation-specific justice rather than a uniformised pattern dictated from above.

7.4.1 The imperial code system as a formal framework

Bodde and Morris (1967: 7) contrast the patchy academic coverage of Chinese customary law with that of the formal legal material:[65]

> The literature on formal Chinese law, by contrast, is large in quantity, fairly readily available and covers a longer time span than that of any other present-day political entity. It includes . . . above all the voluminous codes of successive dynasties. The codes, in particular, have a continuity and authoritativeness which make them unrivaled instruments for measuring precisely, dynasty by dynasty, the shifting configurations of Chinese social and political values as officially defined.

The major focus of legal research on the Chinese imperial codes has put the various codes of the Ch'ing dynasty (1644–1911) at the centre of attention.[66] Bodde and Morris (1967: 7) explain that this formal edifice was compiled in definitive form in 1740 and consists of 436 sections that contain a greater number of statutes and approximately 1,800 sub-statutes. The statute law, portrayed in typical Austinian fashion, 'derived its formal validity from its promulgation as the will of the Emperor' (McAleavy, 1968a: 119), although the institution of the codes themselves had a lengthy pedigree, going back to the seventh century AD.

---

[65] In contrast, McAleavy (1968a: 110) notes the slight esteem felt by Confucian scholars for legal texts. Bodde and Morris (1967: 52–5) provide an overview of the major materials and the extent of indigenous and foreign scholarship.

[66] Useful chronological overviews are found in Bodde and Morris (1967: 56–7) and Ching (1993: xiii–xv).

McAleavy (1968a: 109–10) emphasised their Confucian nature, since they remained criminal codes throughout, and 'there is nothing bearing the faintest resemblance to a civil code'.[67] While the codes concentrated on matters of criminal and administrative law, certain customary rules of private law were incorporated and penalties were stipulated against those who infringed such rules. This shows that in Chinese law, too, the boundaries between the private and the public sphere, between family law and criminal law, and therefore also between primary and secondary rules (Hart, 1961), could not be drawn with utmost precision. Subjects like contract and topics of commercial law were conspicuously absent from the imperial codes,[68] reflecting legalist focus on governance rather than on the regulation of socio-economic relations between people, and a focus on Hartian secondary rules. The general pattern of these codes followed a dual structure, with the body of statutes (*lü*) at the centre, and sub-statutes (*li*) to supplement the more general rules. Bodde and Morris (1967: 63) explain that, beginning in imperial times, '*lü* replaced *fa* as the regular technical designation for the individual "statutes" collectively comprising a code', and highlight the importance of the term *lü* and its double meaning:

> [L]*ü*, though very important in the law codes of imperial times (221 BC onward), appears only rarely in a legal sense in earlier texts. As used in these codes, it is the technical designation for the major articles into which the codes are divided, and as such may be translated as 'statute'. It can also, however, refer to the entire body of such statutes as a collective entity, in which case it may conveniently, though a little loosely, be rendered as 'code'.[69]

McAleavy (1968a: 119) explained the structure of the early T'ang code (653 AD). It was composed of two sections, a body of statutes called *lü*, a criminal code which stipulated penalties for the commission of certain acts, and a collection of positive ordinances called *ling*, essentially an administrative code. Bodde and Morris (1967: 63) emphasise that '[a] study of the individual statutes found in successive dynastic codes shows that many of them have survived unchanged from one code to another', so that perhaps 30–40 per cent of the *lü* in the Ch'ing Code of 1740 can be traced back unchanged to the T'ang Code of 653. This means, of course, that 'the other 60 to 70 per cent *did* change' (Bodde

---

[67] Despite this, McAleavy (1968a: 119) still wrote of a *corpus iuris*.

[68] McAleavy (1968a: 110) argued that it scarcely mattered for cosmic order what rules were created in such fields, an unconvincing argument, since every aspect of human life mattered in terms of cosmic relations.

[69] Bodde and Morris (1967: 12). They further list a third meaning of *lü* as a collective designation for several statutes (p. 63), so that it could mean (1) an individual statute, (2) a collection of several such statutes, and (3) the whole body of statutes, thus almost 'code', as in the quote above. Thus, as McAleavy (1968a: 120–1) explains, 'from the 18th century the official title of the criminal code was Ta Ch'ing Lü Li, or the Lü and the Li of the Great Ch'ing (Dynasty)'.

and Morris, 1967: 63) and that ancient China was not a monolithic entity (p. 64).[70] McAleavy (1968a: 119) confirms that 'their unchangeability was merely relative' and explains that a *lü* might be in need of modernisation (p. 120):

> It happened occasionally that the *lü*, for all the deference paid to their immutability, were felt to have outlived their usefulness. Now and then this situation was remedied by dropping the *lü* in question from subsequent editions of the code. . . More often, however, the difficult *lü* was permitted to remain in the book, but was qualified by the addition of a supplementary statute called a *li*, which was not considered to be so sacrosanct as the *lü*, and to have a temporary nature. By the nineteenth century these supplementary statutes had become about four times as numerous as the *lü* they were designed to qualify, and amounted to some 1800 items.

The importance of the sub-statutes, which could be translated as 'principle, pattern, norm, or example', even 'precedent' (Bodde and Morris, 1967: 64), is highlighted in the context of maintaining flexibility within the adjudication system. Bodde and Morris (1967: 32) noted:

> Still another device providing for greater latitude in what would otherwise have been a relatively static body of law was what in this book is called the *li* or sub-statute (a word different from *li*, 'rites'). In contrast to the statutes (*lü*), which constituted the primary framework of the dynastic codes and often passed from one code to another with little or no change, the sub-statutes (*li*) could be promulgated by imperial edict at any moment to meet a given situation. Although the term *li* or substatute did not itself come into common use until the Ming dynasty (1368–1643), clear prototypes of it are to be found in earlier dynasties. These *li* or sub-statutes . . . were often more particularistic than the statutes to which they were appended. Thus, their proliferation during the Ming and especially the Ch'ing dynasties by no means obviated the continued need for judgment by analogy.

As a device to adjust the statutory law to new situations, this technique of introducing new 'sub-statutes' was certainly widely used, and some of the *li* might in due course become enshrined by a later dynasty as a *lü* in their own right.[71] The internal flexibility of this statutory system was not only required by Confucian ethics but kept law and society in harmony. Bodde and Morris (1967: 67) explain that 'it was a regular principle in Ch'ing law that whenever a statute and a sub-statute were both applicable to a given case, the decision was to be based on the sub-statute rather than the statute, even though this might sometimes result in serious modification or even virtual nullification of the intent of the

---

[70] This can be contrasted with the perspective taken by David and Brierley (1978: 481) who envisage an 'essentially static concept of society' and overemphasise this throughout their analysis.

[71] Bodde and Morris (1967: 65–7) explain how various separate collections of *li* were also produced.

statute'. The internal diversity of the codes created its own difficulties, but also allowed this formal statutory system the flexibility to develop and to adjust to new situations.[72]

7.4.2 The Emperor as Son of Heaven

The Confucian system of ethics required that the Emperor, as the figurehead of the entire system, should ideally be a model of utmost integrity. Van der Sprenkel (1977: 28) explains:

> In an extension of this theory the Emperor, with the title 'Son of Heaven', was seen as poised between heaven and earth and as endowed by heaven with a mandate to rule the earth so long as he was capable of maintaining the harmony undisturbed. This harmonious order it should be noted, was not man-made, but existed naturally throughout the universe and had merely to be preserved. If the Emperor proved incapable of doing this, he would be responsible to heaven for the disturbance of the natural harmony and the mandate would be transferred to another. This doctrine implied a right of revolution, and if the revolution succeeded in establishing an effective new government, it established at the same time its legitimacy.

Similarly, McAleavy (1968a: 109) wrote that the Mandate of Heaven 'was ordinarily taken to denote impersonal Nature, which had conferred on the monarch a Mandate to rule, simply by permitting the founder of the dynasty to triumph over his rivals in the struggle for the throne'. This authority could then be passed on from father to son, provided the new ruler was able to fulfil the tasks (p. 109):

> For an unworthy holder, or at least a series of unworthy holders, would inevitably cause the loss of the Mandate, which would pass through rebellion and chaos into the hands of someone better fitted to exercise such a function, and thus a new ruling house would come to power. While on the throne, the Emperor was surrounded by every mark of the most profound respect, yet his commands deserved obedience only in so far as they were declaratory of the natural order. When, as might occur under a bad ruler, an imperial decree was issued in flagrant violation of the principle it was a subject's highest duty to remonstrate, not to obey.

These comments confirm that the Chinese Emperor was not an absolute ruler, rather he served a higher order, to which he himself was subservient as well, like the Hindu ruler, Muslim kings and African rulers. McAleavy (1968a: 119) further explained that, if the Emperor's will conflicted with the order of nature, 'disobedience was justified, but the justification would be acknowledged only by posterity, or after the overthrow of the tyrannical regime, and pending such a revolution the imperial command was binding on the officers of state'. In reality, then, might was to some extent right, and Kelsen's (1970) 'pure' theory

---

[72] On commentaries of the codes, see Bodde and Morris (1967: 68–75).

of legal positivism might apply. However, the ruler's Mandate of Heaven was clearly under question whenever there were disasters and disturbances. Thus, this theory not only legitimises political power, it also permits the overthrow of inefficient political rulers and thus constitutes a powerful element of ancient Chinese political culture. Van der Sprenkel (1977: 34) emphasises the important ritual aspects of the ruler's functions:

> The first duty of a ruler was to maintain harmony with the other elements in the universe. Though this had the widest implications, it was symbolized by the carrying out of certain propitiatory rites. At the appropriate season, for example, the Emperor went out to the temples of earth and heaven and sacrificed at them, and then ceremonially ploughed the first furrow – to win heaven's favour for agricultural operations throughout the Empire for the year.[73] Such ceremonials gave further emphasis to the agriculturalists' need for an exactly calculated calendar. The belief that heaven's pleasure or otherwise with the Emperor's performance of his duties could be judged from the occurrence of certain phenomena of nature, such as eclipses and sun-spots, led the Emperor to take an interest in them and appoint officials whose duties included the careful observation of such portents.

The role of the Emperor as a model for others, despite his unique position, is emphasised by van der Sprenkel (1977: 34) in the context of ancestral rites:

> Next a ruler was expected to encourage virtue, industry and learning among all his subjects both by example and precept. The practice of filial piety demonstrated in the ceremonial of venerating the Imperial ancestors and observance of mourning may be seen as setting his subjects an example in these most important matters. From time to time exhortations to virtue were also published with instructions that they should be publicly read at *yamens* throughout the Empire.[74]

Van der Sprenkel (1977: 35) emphasises that the Emperor's duty of watching over his subjects might require punishments for those who failed to act in consonance with the assumed requirements of harmonious order. Such supervisory function had to be delegated in a large empire; numerous classes of local officials were given important duties in identifying and punishing wrong doers of all kinds. Chinese imperial rule is much more complex than a simple absolutist system of governance in which a strongman lays down the law for all. The higher pre-existing law, as in other Asian and in African legal systems, was found in an imagined, more or less universal normative framework to

---

[73] On the critical importance of this ritual see Murphey (1967: 314).

[74] This looks like the Buddhist Emperor Aśoka's 'law-making' by publicising the obligation of all citizens to do the right thing at the right time. Similar techniques have been used by communist rulers in China to reinforce policy statements representative of the will of the ruler (especially Chairman Mao) rather than a restatement of ancient codes of obligation. One could see this as new forms of Chinese ethics, replacing earlier Confucian models.

which all human activity needed to be constantly adjusted. In such a wider conceptual context, one-man rule was an impossibility and delegated chains of duties, as highlighted by van der Sprenkel (1977: 28–9), were important:

> Authority in China was always accompanied by responsibility for ensuring that the natural harmony was preserved within the area of activity over which that authority was exercised. The Emperor owed responsibility to heaven, under pain of withdrawal of the heavenly mandate if he failed in the duty entrusted to him; lesser people owed responsibility to their immediate superiors – through a chain of delegated authority which reached down to the head of the household.
>
> It was in virtue of this pervasive responsibility that those in authority could lay down precepts to be followed by those in their charge, and require obedience to standards of conduct covering all aspects of life, and take action, both positive and negative, to promote and restore the harmony which it was their responsibility to preserve. The authority of law and government derived directly from the doctrine of responsibility which, as it infiltrated every department of public and private life, provided theoretical justification for law and government to be all-embracing too.

Van der Sprenkel (1977: 126) shows that the ruler was at the top of this hierarchy, and yet he was not above the law:

> All law . . . was enforced by command of the Emperor, if only by much delegated authority. The position of Emperor was thought of as being mediate between mankind and heaven, and on this account one might suppose him to be above the law. But this view is not tenable, since the reigning Emperor could himself be criticized and the mandate to govern could be withdrawn from him if his administration did not maintain harmony in the human part of the universe.

In this context the long-lasting, vigorous debates between Confucianists and Legalists assume specific relevance. Van der Sprenkel (1977: 30) captures this well:

> While Confucian thinkers asserted that the end of all governments was to promote wellbeing and preserve social harmony, the Realists (*Fa Chia*, sometimes called School of Law, or Legists) subordinated everything to building up the strength of the state.
>
> The Confucians taught that if a ruler, basing himself on the sage rulers of antiquity, set his people an example of benevolence and encouraged them to observe the proprieties in personal relationships, the good of the community would automatically follow. The Realists believed that this doctrine, though it may have suited a small community in the past, was inadequate to serve as the basis for a state strong enough to subdue its neighbours . . . People had to be made to contribute to the strength of the state – even against their natural inclination – by clearly defined and impersonal commands and penalties.

Thus, even concerning the ruler himself, the Legalists came to quite different conclusions than the Confucians, who remained therefore all the more distrustful of legalist legality.[75] Van der Sprenkel (1977: 33) explains:

> A ruler, according to the Realists, did not need to bother with setting a virtuous example; his weapons were: *fa*, defined as 'that which is recorded in the registers, set up in the government offices, and promulgated among the people', and *shu*, 'the true arts of kingship', which consisted chiefly in establishing objective criteria for judging men and policies so as to make the rules independent of flattery and corruption, arbitrariness and personal foibles. Rewards and punishments were the two 'handles of the ruler'.

Van der Sprenkel (1977: 37) reports that the ancient Chinese machinery of government remained recognisably similar throughout the imperial period. Heading this complex system, '[t]he Emperor himself was no mere figurehead but was daily consulted and daily gave decisions on cases sent up from all parts of the Empire' (p. 37). In particular, the Emperor himself handled capital cases, but only after revision by the Supreme Court (pp. 67–8), and he had a definite, naturalistic role in making final determinations over who would be killed when he ceremonially endorsed the list of candidates for execution with a vermilion brush, to the effect that '[p]risoners whose names he had marked were then executed; a lucky few were pardoned; the rest waited for the same procedure next year' (p. 68). Despite such observations and some evidence of direct legal involvement of the Emperor, the realities of legal development in traditional Chinese law could not be ascertained from a study of the recorded decisions and activities of the various emperors. As in any legal system in the world, most legal business was conducted at lower levels.

7.4.3 The imperial legal machinery

Highest after the Emperor in terms of legal authority were the Six Boards or Departments of State in Peking, also called Ministries, concerned with Civil Office, Revenue and Population, Rites and Ceremonies, War, Punishment, and Works.[76] While these Boards covered a wide ambit, '[i]n view of the heavy penal emphasis of Chinese law, it is not surprising to find most statutes in the Ming Code falling under the division corresponding to the Board of Punishments' (Bodde and Morris, 1967: 59). The Board of Punishments (*hsing pu*) exercised final jurisdiction over all cases involving homicide, 'except cases punishable by death, which went further upward through a body known collectively as the Three High Courts, and from it to the emperor himself for final ratification'

---

[75] Van der Sprenkel (1977: 33) emphasises specifically the need to recognise the eclectic blend of hitherto conflicting schools.

[76] For some details see McAleavy (1968a: 119–20) and Bodde and Morris (1967: 59–60 and 113ff.).

(p. 116).[77] At lower levels, while a magistrate could in more serious cases 'do no more than pronounce a provisional sentence and await confirmation from above before carrying it out' (p. 115), judicial commissioners as full-time legal experts acted at provincial level to review decisions made by magistrates.

Despite this hierarchical ordering and other formal remnants of legalism in the codes, it is important for the present analysis to note that the entire administration system was thoroughly infused with Confucian ideology, which underpinned the legal administration of imperial China for almost 2,000 years down to 1912. Shapiro (1981: 160) confirms that '[t]he Legalists as a distinct political group vying for control of imperial policymaking were resoundingly defeated by their Confucian rivals'. Legal administration was therefore not a separate, secular government activity but an integral part of the administrative machinery in an integrated system. Bodde and Morris (1967: 113) outline the wider conditions under which the Chinese appellate system functioned, emphasising

> the fact that the judicial system of imperial China, like the governmental system as a whole, was a centralized monolith with no division of powers; that there was no private legal profession; that on the lowest level of the *hsien* (district) or *chou* (department), where all cases originated (save those in the capital or in frontier regions), the magistrate rarely possessed any specialized legal training and handled the cases that came before him simply as one of many administrative duties; that, however, he often personally employed a non-civil service private legal secretary who did possess specialized knowledge of the law; and that all but minor cases automatically went upward from the *hsien* or *chou* to higher levels for final ratification, some as high as the emperor himself.

Bodde and Morris (1967: 5) noted that to avoid miscarriage of justice on the lowest administrative level, a carefully defined system of appeals existed. It automatically took all major cases to higher levels for final judgment, with capital crimes ultimately decided by the Emperor himself.[78] Van der Sprenkel (1977: 36) emphasises that executing the various government functions throughout the vast Empire required the services of capable men who, in ancient China, were identified through a system of competitive examinations in the Confucian classics.[79] McAleavy (1968a: 109) emphasised the critical role of classical ethical education and the potential openness of the system:

> [T]he sovereign in his task of administration was assisted by the wisest heads in the country. Civil servants – 'mandarins' as westerners called them – were recruited by public examinations open to all males irrespective

---

[77] Further details on this Board are found in Bodde and Morris (1967: 122–31).

[78] Shapiro (1981) rightly notes that researchers' focus on such 'higher' criminal cases has reinforced impressions of the harsh nature of Chinese law as well as leading to neglect of civil law cases (see Buxbaum, 1971).

[79] Bodde and Morris (1967: 113–14) and van der Sprenkel (1977: 50–5) provide details of the administrative hierarchies.

of their wealth and social position . . . and although since education was private the sons of the rich had a decided advantage in the competition, yet enough poor men rose to the top to justify the claim that careers were open to talent.

Van der Sprenkel (1977: 10) confirms this, noting that because of the prestige conferred by learning, which might open the door to power and influence, many peasants were ready to make considerable sacrifices to educate their sons in the classical system.[80] McAleavy (1968a: 111) wrote that the state examinations system was throughout at the heart of the traditional system of education, 'success in which gave entry to a privileged class of literati and with luck to a career in government employment, the great goal of every ambitious man'.[81] The structure of the administration system and its personnel are described by van der Sprenkel (1977: 37–55).[82] She emphasises that '[t]he counter over which "the government" did business with "the people" was the magistrate's *yamen*' (p. 40). McAleavy (1968a: 122) reported that the basic administrative units in the nineteenth century were the approximately 1,500 districts, with an average population of about 200,000, governed by a magistrate.[83] Van der Sprenkel (1977: 40) elaborates:

> The *fu, chou* and *hsien* magistrates were the general administrative body of the provincial civil service. Their tasks included the collection of revenue, the maintenance of order and the primary dispensation of justice, as well as the conduct of literary examinations and of the government postal service – in short, all the immediate functions of public administration. 'They are commonly spoken of as *Fu Mu Kuan*, or officials . . . who are the "father and mother" of the people.'

Bodde and Morris (1967: 4–5) report that on the lowest level, the *hsien* (district or county), where the official law impinged most directly upon the people, legal administration was conducted by the *hsien* magistrate as merely one of several administrative functions and, '[a]lthough he usually lacked any formal legal training, he was obliged to act as detective, prosecutor, judge, and jury

---

[80] Van der Sprenkel (1977: 13) emphasises the importance of connections with someone in authority, which might bring positive implications not just for the individual, but for the entire village or town.

[81] Van der Sprenkel (1977: 50) depicts the homogeneity and formidable solidarity in the community of scholar-officials who formed 'a body apart, formally distinguished from "the people", strongly conscious of its own separate character, and imbued with a marked *esprit de corps*'. Such people were attracted to an official career as a way to gain prestige and wealth, while '[s]ervice to the wider public did not usually enter into their thoughts' (p. 54). All officials 'would try to satisfy their superiors by fulfilling tax and grain quotas expected of them in any given district and to give an impression of order and well-being in the area under their charge to superiors or itinerant inspectors' (p. 54).

[82] See also Shapiro (1981: 171ff.).

[83] For an earlier period, Bodde and Morris (1967: 114) report approximately 1,300 districts. Hsiao (1960) indicates about 250,000 people per magistrate in the nineteenth century.

rolled into one'. Van der Sprenkel (1977: 44) explains that the magistrate's *yamen* was both his official residence and the office for the transaction of all kinds of public business:

> The size of the building and the staff employed naturally depended on the size and importance of the place. The offices in every *yamen*, however, reflected in some way the functional division of public affairs observed in the government departments at the capital. In the larger *yamens* (and in all *fu yamens*) there were actually six offices, each with its staff, to correspond to the Six Departments at Peking. Where the volume of work did not warrant organization on this scale a smaller staff divided the duties between them. Besides the clerks there were various messengers and attendants, runners and gaolers.

Thus, like the Emperor, the magistrate had his own network of delegated authorities, providing employment for many people, who might use their office to enrich themselves rather than observing the ground rules of Confucian ethics. But making money out of delegated legal authority and observance of *li* might not be as contradictory as appears at first sight (see next section below). Indeed, since Confucianism discouraged recourse to formal laws, the magistrate's *yamen* became a symbol for cruelty and was definitely a place which a good Confucian would avoid at all cost. Demanding bribes became a way to teach people to avoid the courts, treating them with cruelty in the course of a hearing taught everyone lessons for life about the value of self-controlled order. Van der Sprenkel (1977: 44) indicates, in addition, that a magistrate might not be able to detect abuses of power among his staff:

> Theoretically the magistrate was free to choose his own staff and to dismiss them, but in practice the breadth of his duties and the fact that he was appointed to a province other than his native one made him very much dependent on his staff and gave them a corresponding measure of independence. A new incumbent would come as a stranger to take up his appointment, ignorant of local custom and precedent, and it would be most natural to re-employ those who had had experience under his predecessors and who wished to serve under him.

Similarly, McAleavy (1968a: 111) showed that '[t]hose fortunate enough to be chosen as instruments of the imperial rule were invariably sent to posts outside their native province, to forestall the emergence of local autonomous regimes', which left a newly appointed magistrate somewhat at the mercy of his local staff. He was dependent on specialist help, since the public education system did not prepare candidates for judicial administration. Van der Sprenkel (1977: 46) comments that the magistrate appointed certain specialist advisers who acted as his personal assistants within the sphere of their competence. Bodde and Morris (1967: 5) also emphasise the need for specialist legal support:

Fortunately for the operation of the system . . . the magistrate was commonly assisted in his judicial work by a legal secretary who *did* possess specialized knowledge of the law, and who, on behalf of the magistrate, could prepare cases for trial, suggest appropriate sentences, or write the legal reports which went to higher governmental levels. Yet it is indicative of the Chinese attitude toward law that this secretary did not himself belong to the formal administrative system. He was merely a personal employee of the magistrate, who paid his salary out of his own private purse. Hence the secretary was not permitted to try cases himself or otherwise to take an active part in the trials.

These legal advisers, described as the 'friend behind the curtain' (*muyou*) or 'guest behind the curtain' (*mubin*), assisted the magistrate in making appropriate decisions and avoiding mistakes that might tarnish his professional reputation. Van der Sprenkel (1977: 69) elaborates this with reference to legal expertise in ancient China:

[M]agistrates customarily employed two expert advisors, one of whom specialized in legal matters. This man, whose knowledge of the code and experience of precedents was at the disposal of the magistrate, was the only person openly concerned in the action whose job it was to know the law. The emergence of a legal profession to serve the interest of litigants, either for pleading or offering opinions on points of law, was officially discouraged by articles in the *Ta Ch'ing Lü Li* which penalized those who incited others to undertake litigation or made a profit out of managing a lawsuit. This restriction of professional activity to official advisors or clandestine lawyers was clearly a barrier to the technical development of law in China.

In this context we read about the bad reputation of any form of legal profession in ancient China. Bodde and Morris (1967: 4) report that '[n]o private legal profession existed to help individuals plead their cases, and, even in the government itself, because law was only the last of several corrective agencies, officials exclusively concerned with the law operated only on the higher administrative levels'. McAleavy (1968a: 125) explained that the classically trained Confucian gentlemen did not want to get involved in legal administration:

[T]he drudgery of becoming familiar with the letter of the law was relegated to a subordinate race of clerks. These men, who handed down their craft from father to son, hailed for the most part from the city of Shaohsing, about two hundred miles south of Shanghai. . . The 'Shaohsing clerks' formed a numerous but compact trade union. They were paid by the magistrates who employed them and often became indispensable to their masters, who carried them along in their own ascent on the ladder of promotion. Even so, there was a sharp social distinction between these lawyers and the mandarinate proper.

The low status of any form of legal profession must be seen in relation to Confucian ethics, according to which disharmony and litigation were negative forces and being involved with them was in itself negative, all the more so if one helped a guilty person plead innocence. McAleavy (1968a: 125) highlighted that 'the giving of legal advice to the public was regarded as an encouragement of litigation, and was a crime'. Thus, traditional China knew neither a real science of law nor a legal profession. If being an active lawyer was itself a crime, this field of learning and knowledge could only prosper in relation to official judicial administration through magistrates, not as an independent profession. Van der Sprenkel (1977: 70) summarises various implications for the legal field as a whole:

> The real weakness of the Chinese system sprang from the fact that the application of the law was entrusted to the administrative officers of the Empire. The court of law was, like the militia, part of the machinery for maintaining order and good behaviour throughout the district. It provided no check on the executive power, and this the system as a whole provided only very indirectly through the power possessed by administrative officials to punish other administrative officials. When government was efficient, legal machinery functioned efficiently; when it was not, legal machinery offered no correction and was itself corrupt. In a trial of what would be a civil suit in English law, the magistrate would have little interest in doing justice as between the parties, except in so far as it was more likely that a just decision would lead to peace and harmony in the neighbourhood. The legal system subserved administrative ends.

Clearly, the formal legal system primarily served the conceptual needs of the dominant Confucian worldview in which litigation was perceived to risk potential disturbance of cosmic harmony. However, private disputes were of course not non-existent. Even though avoidance of disputes was the underlying conceptual objective, the above quote subtly indicates the presence of civil litigation also in magistrates' courts.[84] The following sub-section explores some structural reasons for the massive avoidance of formal law in China. This is not the same as avoidance of law altogether, however, since the practical effect of the operation of the classical imperial Chinese legal system was to redirect as many disputes as possible to the social sphere, away from the state-sponsored legal machinery.[85] Since both the state system and the private mechanisms of dispute settlement were supposed to operate on the basis of Confucian ethics, avoidance of official disputes does not completely fulfil the idealistic expectations of Confucian self-controlled order. While the imperial state legal system might have taught people not to use it, further questions

---

[84] More recent American scholarship explodes the long-held myth that the ordinary Chinese were averse to litigation, uncovering from the archives of district courts of the eighteenth, and nineteenth centuries strong evidence of the emergence of a new kind of traditional law, seen as 'civil law'. For details see Shapiro (1981: 168–9) and especially Buxbaum (1971).

[85] Shapiro (1981: 192) speaks in this context of 'the desire to carefully husband and ration the scarce judicial resources available', seeing this as a worldwide phenomenon.

must be asked about how and to what extent the so-called 'extra-legal' sphere (Bodde and Morris, 1967: 5) actually discouraged litigation. It seems that there are some old-established myths in this area which need to be examined.

7.4.4 Avoidance of the law

The comparative analysis of Chinese legal concepts has so far demonstrated that legal writing on China developed its own conventions about the term 'law', thus to some extent impeding cross-cultural comparisons. In the Chinese context, avoidance of the law means first avoidance of any form of litigious activity as an indication of selfishness and as a threat to universal cosmic harmony. That more explicitly Confucian sense is not, however, the one which most legal writing employs. Avoiding the law is envisaged merely as avoidance of the imperial formal law and its complex structures and its potentially painful consequences. Chinese law is therefore not totally premised on avoidance of law altogether, but on achieving an idealised balance between competing rule-making forces for the universal good. In this sense, despite different rhetoric, Chinese law is not different in principle from African laws and from Hindu law in that it seeks to rely on internalised, self-controlled order in the first place and, only if that fails, tries to keep the violation of harmony and order at the lowest possible level, given that fomenting litigation is a negative act in itself (Shapiro, 1981: 157–8). Individual and local instincts of self-preservation together with imperial bureaucratic ideology strengthened a tendency to avoid formal dispute processing. The culture-specific characteristic of imperial Chinese law arises from the presence of the imperial legal regulations with their deterrent criminal law focus and the Confucian expectation that this particular legal field should be avoided.

Without an awareness of such underlying conceptual tensions, readers are easily confused about what specialists on Chinese law are trying to convey. Thus, when McAleavy (1968a: 129) claimed that 'the Chinese are a supremely unlitigious people, and it may be confidently predicted that for many years they will manage their family affairs in their own way without benefit of courts or lawyers', does this mean that Chinese husbands and wives would necessarily put up with each other, come what may? Similarly, if van der Sprenkel (1977: 79) claims that 'to adopt the course of going to law was exceptional in China', or asserts that 'the provisions of the penal code were not always invoked' (p. 27), we should not imagine a lawless society, but a culture-specific conceptualisation of law which operates in the minds of Chinese people as well as legal specialists studying that system. The idealised nature of Chinese law is brought out well when van der Sprenkel (1977: 79) writes that '[t]he law remained synonymous with a morally desirable standard: the Chinese never developed it as the concept of an enforceable minimum. As 100 per cent performance was not to be expected, evasion was natural.' Similar comments could of course be made about African laws and Hindu law. Muslim jurists, in their own way, have also always had definite problems with this issue of perfect performance, since the 'margin of error' (chapter 5) never allowed absolute certainty over what exactly the expected standard was. David and Brierley (1978: 480) discussed such issues at some length for Chinese law and considered the implications for legal processes:

> The Chinese . . . normally live outside or apart from the law. They don't seek out whatever rules the law contains or claim their day in court, but settle their disputes and regulate their dealings with others according to their own idea of what is proper, without assertion of their rights and with conciliation and harmony as goals in mind. The re-establishment of harmony is made easier because of the fact that the education of all concerned naturally prompts them to seek the origin of conflict in their own deficiencies, carelessness or blunders rather than to attribute them to the bad faith or fault of an adversary. . . In such an atmosphere, where each is ready to recognize his faults, it is easy to lead people into making concessions and to accept the intervention of a mediator. This acceptance may, however, be more forced than voluntary, given the fear of public opinion.

The alleged Chinese aversion for law is also said to be increased by poor judicial administration. David and Brierley (1978: 480) observed:

> The official called upon to judge a dispute is removed from the litigants: not legally trained, recruited in principle from another province, he is not familiar with either the dialect or the custom of the region in which he acts. The clerks with which the pleader has to deal are corrupt and purposely prolong the litigation from which they draw fees; the litigant is subjected to countless humiliations and the outcome of the trial is, in all events, very doubtful. According to popular maxims, 'of ten reasons by which a magistrate may decide a case, nine are unknown to the public' and 'a case won is money lost.'

Such quotes indicate a preference for avoidance of formal litigation, influenced by various mechanisms within the social sphere of the customary Chinese legal system. The intricate cooperation of both levels, bound together in principle by the same conceptual element, confucianised legalism, discloses a picture in which there is plenty of evidence of legal activity, but as little recourse to the formal imperial system as possible. McAleavy (1968a: 115) showed that the imperial legal system was not making positivist claims that it should control the entire legal field:

> The Confucian state was well content that its subjects should settle their private disputes between themselves without recourse to its laws. In most cases the mere fact of appealing to a magistrate, even where the appeal had right on its side, stamped a man as a trouble-maker. In the seventeenth century, one of the greatest of Chinese rulers, the Emperor K'ang Hsi,

went so far as to declare that 'lawsuits would tend to increase to a frightful amount, if people were not afraid of the tribunals, and if they felt confident of always finding in them ready and perfect justice. . . I desire therefore that those who have recourse to the tribunals should be treated without any pity, and in such a manner that they shall be disgusted with law, and tremble to appear before a magistrate.' In fact, because of the lack of civil procedure, a litigant could invoke the help of the state only by accusing the other party of a crime, as for instance of fraud in the non-payment of a debt, and even if his resentment was so strong that he was willing to incur the odium of taking so drastic a step, he had to bear in mind that if he failed to establish his case he himself would be punished for wrongful accusation.[86]

So unwelcoming were the courts towards litigants, that they often gave the appearance of being reluctant to interfere, even where the wrong complained of contained a criminal element.

Bodde and Morris (1967: 6) wrote similarly that '[i]nvolvement in the formal system was popularly regarded as a road to disaster and therefore to be avoided at all cost. "Win your lawsuit and lose your money," runs a Chinese proverb.' In principle, anyone had the right to ask the district magistrate to investigate a case and to punish offenders, and all had the duty to report crimes within the area of their responsibility.[87] However, if a magistrate investigated a matter and then decided that the accused was innocent, he had to prosecute the accuser for bringing a false or malicious accusation (van der Sprenkel, 1977: 67), which reflects Confucian approaches to preventing *mala fide* legal actions. The magistrate himself would probably conduct the examination of the defendant, 'questioning and cross-questioning to get at the true facts' (van der Sprenkel, 1977: 68) comparable to Max Gluckman's research on African procedures among the Lozi, where a similar form of aggressive trial 'makes it *appear* that the defendant is assumed guilty unless he can prove his innocence, instead of the contrary' (van der Sprenkel, 1977: 68).

Thus, the 'unavoidable consequence of a legal case once started was punishment for at least one person. It could end in punishment for the accused, if judged guilty; if he were not, punishment would be assigned to the unjustified accuser' (van der Sprenkel, 1977: 69). Even witnesses were likely to incur punishment during the course of the proceedings,[88] and the general rule and experience was that embarking on a legal case 'involved the certainty of fees to various officials through whose hands it passed' and many more related

---

[86] This point is also made by David and Brierley (1978: 482–3).

[87] Van der Sprenkel (1977: 66). See to the same effect McAleavy (1968a: 123): 'Although the courts were purposely unwelcoming to would-be litigants, everyone had a right to petition the magistrate for justice, and there was a general obligation to report crimes. The magistrate was bound to conduct an enquiry.'

[88] Van der Sprenkel (1977: 77) indicates the problem of torture to 'assist' those required to give testimony.

expenses (p. 70). Once the ball had started rolling, it was difficult to get a case withdrawn, even though it might lead to financial ruin for both parties. Litigants therefore 'had little confidence of obtaining justice in return for their money' (p. 71) and would keep their distance from the *yamen* and its officials. McAleavy (1968a: 123) found that 'it must be admitted that the conduct of criminal trials by the courts themselves was a disgrace to Chinese justice', and commented that the magistrates and their staff could not be accused of laxity in their Confucian duty to make the *yamen* a most unpleasant place.

Acting in line with the highest dictates about making recourse to the law a punishment in itself, magistrates also had to consider their own reputation when it came to dealing with cases. The best possible magistrate in the imperial system was clearly someone who had no disputes to report from his district. The non-specialist local magistrate was continually exposed to the risk of reprimand or degradation for making a procedural mistake in his application of the code (van der Sprenkel, 1977: 69). He was also dependent on his *yamen* staff for the version of the evidence he received, because he did not necessarily understand the local language (p. 75). Thus, the magistrate himself had multiple interests in ignoring cases, quite apart from the question of bribes. Van der Sprenkel (1977: 72–3) brings this out well:

> The report of a legal case, especially a serious one, drew attention to his area as being one where all was not well; if harmony was disturbed, this implied that he was incompetent and blemished his record, and a mistake in dealing with the case might bring unwelcome consequences for himself. It was therefore in his interest to suppress cases altogether, or in his submission to alter details of fact to make them appear less serious than the true facts would have been, or even to make the case under consideration appear similar to one previously dealt with without hazard.

Because the emergence of a legal case itself was treated as an indication of disturbance, cases were frequently repressed, even though, according to various articles in the imperial codes, the elders of a locality were required to report crimes involving death or magical practices. From various angles, therefore, there was a higher purpose in hushing up litigation and avoiding recourse to the magistrate's court and the unsatisfactory character of Chinese courts was to some extent deliberate. Van der Sprenkel (1977: 78) concluded therefore that the self-control mechanisms of society were supposed to take care of most disputes:

> There was a general predisposition on grounds of expense, uncertainty, risk and harshness not to set the official legal machinery in motion, nor to get involved as witnesses, if it could be avoided, but rather to leave other units of social organization to deal with all matters they were capable of handling, and only to bring the official system into action when they had failed or when some blatantly violent occurrence could not be officially ignored.

Van der Sprenkel (1977: 33) explained this two-faced approach as linked to the system of 'confucianisation of the law', which she portrays as 'refurbished Confucianism', with a higher purpose, 'the notion underlying the whole edifice being that those who observed the *li* should be treated with benevolence and rewarded, while harsh punishments and executions should be applied to those who were too uncouth or too obtuse to do so' (p. 33).[89] Hence, '[l]aw, equated with a system of punishments, was in its nature harsh and to be avoided by reasonable men' (p. 33). The public image of the imperial control system headed by an Emperor masked, in effect, the predominance of the local customary norm systems and local methods of informal dispute settlement. Van der Sprenkel (1977: 127) explains:

> It might appear from this that law derived from the combination of Emperor's command and people's consent. The words 'resignation' and 'acceptance' might better describe the attitude of the ordinary Chinese towards officialdom, but even so, much of their lives was governed by custom, which, when it was publicly enforcible, we are justified, I think, in calling customary law, though it was never officially promulgated.

David and Brierley (1978: 483) confirmed this, observing that '[t]he Chinese codes and laws were traditionally only applied to the extent that they corresponded to the popular ideas of equity and propriety. When they conflicted with tradition, they were in fact ignored.' McAleavy (1968a: 111) emphasised that the essential features of social organisation, as provided by the Confucian canons of appropriateness and established basically throughout the country, had created over centuries 'a solid substratum of beliefs upon which a superstructure of social institutions could be firmly erected'. Chinese people turned to these informal, assumedly extra-legal structures when they required assistance in litigation. Van der Sprenkel (1977: 114) emphasises:

> Chinese philosophical predispositions ... favoured the resolving of disputes by mediation and compromise. Positively, the idea of harmony or agreement (*ho*) ranked high in the scale of values; negatively, conflict was feared because it was fraught with risks for all and undermined group strength. In philosophical and religious thought Chinese as individuals were eclectic and tolerant; rather than admit the exclusive claims of any one system of ideas, they preferred a blend of what was valuable in each. Parallel with this, conduct likely to minimize friction or reconcile conflicting interests received general approbation.

While the wrong people were not always discouraged (p. 122) and some cases entered the *yamen*, it was considered infinitely more meritorious to give way

---

[89] Similarly van der Sprenkel (1977: 125): 'The juxtaposition of morality and harsh punishments in the official code has puzzled many observers ... admitting the need for punishments to deal with the uncultured people who could not be controlled by *li*.'

and to avoid loss of face. Van der Sprenkel (1977: 114) highlights this inherent desire for harmonisation:

> It was thought better to yield ground (*jang*) and meet an opponent half-way than to stand on principle: then if both parties behaved in this way compromise would be possible without either of them losing face and thus group cohesion would be maintained. If, of two parties to a dispute, one were willing to give way, while the other insisted rigidly on what was due to him, public opinion would always side with the more accommodating party. The idea found general favour that if losses had to be borne, they should not all fall on one party.

There were various local levels to turn to, depending on the nature of the issue at stake. For the present globally focused comparative legal analysis, we can assume that Chinese individuals facing difficulties over ascertaining their *li* would first seek guidance in themselves and in the immediate social environment. In cases of conflict, such issues would then first become a matter for the closer family. Van der Sprenkel (1977: 14–15) explains:

> The head of the family, *chia chang*, managed the business affairs of the household, exercised authority over its members and was its representative to the outside world. The *chia chang* was usually the eldest male member, most frequently the father of the family, but the eldest brother might act as family head on his father's death or retirement, or, exceptionally, the role might be filled by a widow of strong character.

From this perspective, only if it was absolutely necessary would larger fora be involved. However, Buxbaum (1971) and Shapiro (1981) argue that the local magistrate was often involved when a litigant wanted to avoid the politics of the local patriarchal setting and sought a fairly quick civil law decision. Van der Sprenkel (1977: 100) writes in detail on dispute settlement in villages as an important task of village leaders and the local gentry. She reports that '[p]rivate mediation was often effective in settling such arguments, particularly the sudden quarrel or the cases where breaking-point was reached, but when they were not easily settled or when the contestants required public satisfaction, the village leaders were called in to arbitrate' (p. 101). To maintain harmony, such conflict needed to be brought to an end, and, for upholding village values and future peace, a solution which allowed both parties to save face and which both would therefore accept needed to be found. Sometimes, leaders from a neighbouring village were involved in arbitration, and only in disputes between two villages would a higher authority need to be involved (pp. 18–19).

While the government had no official representative of its own in the innu-merable villages, leaving villagers to manage their own affairs as long as they paid their taxes and fulfilled other obligations without major disturbances, the magistrate normally recognized one person in each village as his local agent. Usually known as the *ti pao* or *pao chang*, he had the duty of passing on to his fellow residents the demands of the *yamen*, and was held responsible for producing offenders or witnesses for legal hearings, if necessary (van der Sprenkel, 1977: 46–7). Otherwise, local communities managed their own affairs under the leadership of family and lineage heads, village leaders, guild officials or organisers of ad hoc associations, who owed their position to seniority, prestige or competence. This system of rural self-government was in the main effective and economical, and it certainly saved the magistrate the expense of establishing local sub-offices in every village.[90] It also protected him from having to report all kinds of legal matters, which meant, of course, that even many local cases of murder never reached the *yamen*. In this sense, the official imperial system was formally superimposed onto the local level, but it seemed in nobody's interest, and against the underlying philosophy of the Confucian legal system itself, to ensure that every 'legal' matter came to the notice of the official legal system.

Van der Sprenkel (1977: 95) confirms that the same applied to the commercial affairs of guilds (*hong*),[91] local trade associations of craftsmen and merchants, whose internal tribunals 'operated with the knowledge and approval of magistrates and saved them a great deal of trouble', so much so that '[g]uild regulations were quoted and regarded as authoritative in official courts and magistrates would refer questions to guilds for their opinion or even send cases which had bypassed the guild to them for decision' (p. 95). Van der Sprenkel (1977: 91) further explains:

> The chief functions of the craft guilds were mutual protection (by controlling the conditions of trade, nominally in the interests of all) and resistance to official demands in excess of what custom allowed . . . In order to control the craft or trade, they had to control their own members, and in order to maintain solidarity in their ranks in the face of officialdom, they had an interest in minimizing friction between their members. The guild therefore acted as an agency for enforcing control and a tribunal for settling disputes. Guilds sometimes also undertook relief among their needy members and other charitable projects.

Van der Sprenkel (1977: 94) also reports that guilds had a number of sanctions at their disposal to enforce obedience, including the frequently imposed fine of paying the cost for a feast or a theatrical performance for entertaining members after the cathartic resolution of a dispute. This is familiar, especially from Africa,

---

[90] Van der Sprenkel (1977: 48) reports that, for administrative purposes, town and cities were divided into wards. Shapiro (1981: 192) highlights the need to ration official conflict resolution services.

[91] Van der Sprenkel (1977: 89) notes that 'Western observers have frequently expressed surprise that the Chinese, who have such a reputation as traders, should have been so reticent on the subjects of commerce and industry in their legal codes'. While in the Ch'ing code only a few articles deal with these matters, the conclusion cannot be that the Chinese had no commercial law. Rather, detailed regulation was purposely left to the associations of craftsmen and merchants concerned (p. 90).

where the interlinked social and ritual functions of dispute settlement are often elaborately expressed as social healing mechanisms designed to restore social harmony and to enhance natural and cosmic order. In the Chinese context, the element of 'face' has been highlighted, because this kind of penalty for the guilty party allows the defeated litigant to regain dignity by playing the part of host. Here, as elsewhere, the guild's power to expel a recalcitrant member also existed as an ultimate sanction. In principle, the traditional Confucian state was quite happy to allow a large extent of self-controlled order. Zweigert and Kötz (1998: 291) identified this as a key element of traditional Chinese legal regulation:

> Thus one can see that only a very small proportion of 'private law' disputes ever came before the state courts in imperial China. This was perfectly acceptable to the Chinese emperors and their governments, for it meant that most of these disputes were 'self-regulating' within the local communities on the basis of the traditional rules of behaviour which were dependent on status, that individuals stayed rooted in their narrow social context, and that the state administration was largely relieved of the duties of judicature and legislation in the field of Civil Law. Not until the end of the nineteenth century was there a gradual change.

Attempting to link the official legal and the so-called extra-legal sphere, van der Sprenkel (1977: 96) suggested that we may treat the family and guild tribunals as extensions of the official system:

> The *tsu* and guild tribunals may perhaps be thought of as subsidiaries of the official courts, exercising delegated powers, the one as a community, the other as an association, in connection with matters which came within their range of operation. On this view, they were part of the hierarchy of courts, from which the magistrate's court constituted the first court of appeal. The defects of the system lay in the inefficiency and corruption of the official court rather than in the exercise of delegated authority.

Against this, it appears just as sensible to treat the entire so-called 'extra-legal' sphere as a matter of customary law or, in line with Chiba's (1986) model, as 'unofficial law'. However, scholars of Chinese law do not seem too keen on this, since the image of Chinese law as a legal system with impressive codes would be dented if Chinese law were to be located prominently within the realm of customary legal systems. These are matters of scholarly politics, similar to the insistence of Hindu law scholars that 'their' legal system contains codes (which are in reality cultural texts) rather than a lot of customary law (chapter 4). A plurality-conscious comparative legal analysis finds little difference between African laws, Hindu law and Chinese law in terms of the predominance of local customary dispute settlement processes, which all have the same basic aim, namely to avoid disturbance of the culture-specific cosmic sphere and super-structure, as well as to block or prevent access to formal dispute settlement processes operated by the state. A major benefit of this strategy would be protection of fiscal resources from wastage by a lot of 'small' legal business. Traditional Chinese law, like other Asian and African legal systems, exhibits a desire to tolerate the sphere of societal self-regulation and norm-making and is prepared to support society as a law-making force against the positivist claims of the state. In China, in the absence of organised religion as a powerful claimant to law-making authority, the major axis of conflicts and tensions within the traditional legal system as a whole lies therefore between society and state as competing law-making forces.

McAleavy (1968a: 118–19) opposed as unwarranted the idea that 'the legislative and judicial functions of the traditional Chinese state were in a relatively undeveloped condition'. While there were extensive areas of social behaviour into which the Emperor and his officials did not seek to intrude, Confucian ethics provided solid conceptual underpinnings for official non-interference. In addition, immense local resistance would have resulted if the state had sought to extend its grasp beyond a supervisory criminal law framework. The ancient codes as state-made law and the Confucianised self-regulatory order of Chinese society co-existed in a constantly tested equilibrium, which may well have contributed to the long duration of the unified Chinese imperial system as a stabilising factor. It appears that post-Imperial attempts at state-sponsored law-making in China attempted to reproduce that scenario, but not without much disturbance (section 7.5 below).

7.4.5 Social and ritual differentiation in the law

Evidence of differential statuses is very strong in China and permeates the informal and the formal Chinese legal systems. Given the internal diversities within the imperial and customary traditional Chinese legal systems, two major areas of analysis arise, First, evidence of socio-legal differentiation arises as a result of the traditional status hierarchies within Chinese societies. This is of limited interest to the present legal analysis and only a few illustrative examples can be given.[92] Secondly, evidence of differential legal treatment by the imperial legal system on the basis of social and ritual considerations helps to throw some light on how traditional legal systems were concerned to find the right balance between the intrinsic concerns of the spheres of religion, society and the state. The hypothesis is that traditional Chinese law has been constantly engaged in negotiating the subtle balances between religiously inspired norms, society's normative orders and state laws with a view to achieving legal outcomes that are acceptable and imposing punishments that 'fit the crime'.

The dominant values of the 'five relationships' (*wu lun*) and the principle of filial piety (*hsiao*) meant that parental authority would inevitably have an

---

[92] For details on Chinese family and kinship see for example Baker (1979).

important place within the Chinese legal system, even at the local level. Here again, the place of individual discretion becomes relevant and the most immediate social control functions operate within the nuclear or extended family. McAleavy (1968a: 116–17) explained:

> As regards the junior members of a family, an extensive jurisdiction was conceded to the parental authority. Only in the gravest matters, such as treason, could a son or daughter denounce a parent to the magistrate. Any attempt by a child to invoke the protection of the state against parental ill-treatment was itself a most enormous crime, striking as it did at filial piety, that corner-stone of the social structure, and was punishable by death. In theory, parents did not have the right themselves to put a child to death: this, as well as lesser penalties, would be inflicted by the state at the parents' request. But the death of a child as a result of parental chastisement incurred no blame, and a cursory reading of Chinese newspapers of the last years of the Empire reveals numerous instances where unfilial sons or daughters were even drowned or buried alive with apparent impunity by their indignant families.

While this may set off alarm bells for protection of individual rights, the duty-focused orientation of *li* should not be forgotten. Rather than judging China by our present standards, the analytical task is to understand how Chinese legal systems operated in traditional contexts. McAleavy (1968a: 117) confirms that parental rights were matched by the rights of children, so that parental authority was not unlimited and absolute. In particular, there were recognised limits to the rights of parents over their children when basic parental duties had not been observed. Although the state would do nothing to restrain a parent at the request of a child, since for a child to make that request was itself considered an unfilial act, a magistrate or a local body might intervene to uphold the rights and legitimate expectations of a child. For example, a father as head of the family was the manager, but not the owner, of the family property. A careful buyer of any property would also seek the explicit agreement of the sons, which shows that a father could not just frustrate a son's expectation to inherit by disposing of the family property as he pleased. Again, these were not primarily matters for the magistrate's *yamen* but for the local fora of dispute settlement and supervision, so that, 'in practice, where an improvident father was squandering the estate, senior members of the clan would often intervene in the interests of the children' (p. 117). This confirms that the clan was the most important source of private law, 'indeed, the clan would assume many of the functions of local government' (p. 117).

McAleavy (1968a: 118) confirms that decisions concerning clan affairs were made by the clan council of senior men. This body, by no means an assembly of equals, with all its members in graduated relationships towards one another corresponding to their generation and age, might cause severe problems for certain individuals. Local mediation by village elders or gentry might be partial and some individuals might prefer to approach a magistrate (Shapiro, 1981: 191). Generally speaking, though, the self-controlled order system of traditional Chinese law was perceived as a core element for the basic requirement to achieve situation-specific justice. Bodde and Morris (1967: 35) emphasise that family matters constitute 'the very heart of the Confucian system' and highlight the patterns of ritual mourning, as found in the 'five degrees of mourning' (*wu fu*), which corresponded to the closeness of kinship with the deceased (p. 36). They assert that such an intricate system of ritual distinctions and their consequences in family law 'almost surely has no parallel elsewhere' (p. 37).[93] Polygamy and the changing rules about the legal position of concubines in Chinese family law interested McAleavy (1968a: 112–14), who showed that the need for sons remained a major motivating factor for concubinage. Closely related to this, the Chinese laws on adoption are of much importance, since 'the Chinese attached enormous consequence to the provision of ritual successors to keep alive the memory of parents after their death. Where there was no natural son, the room was filled by adoption' (McAleavy, 1968a: 112).

In terms of dispute settlement generally, even within the customary informal sector it was considered important to keep the dispute at the lowest possible level. If a family could not settle contentious matters within the four walls of the home, for example in matrimonial disputes, involvement through mediation by the two families might be required. Still, balancing and harmonisation were considered more important than determining who was right and who was wrong. McAleavy (1968a: 118) emphasised:

> It was a cardinal principle in this sort of arbitration that neither party should be granted an outright victory. Considerations of 'face' as well as the desire of appeasement invariably recommended a compromise, no matter how slight the grounds for such an arrangement might be by any western standard.

The underlying conceptual requirement, at all levels and in all areas, to find the right balance between conflicting or competing positions, and the need to redress balances where disturbances of harmony and order had been caused, had to have significant impact on the imperial system of criminal laws. Punishments might be stipulated in the codes, but they would differ from case to case, depending on the relative rank of the people involved.[94] Differentiation by social status in relation to punishments under the imperial system is discussed in detail by Bodde and Morris (1967: 33–8 and 76–112). The examples given show that punishments varied in accordance with the social status of the victim and the perpetrator of the offence. Thus, if a person hits someone

---

[93] Mourning patterns in various African and other Asian societies may correspond to such structures and would also have religious and legal consequences.

[94] In this situation, analogy becomes an important legal technique (Chen, 1970).

of a higher status, the punishment is increased to some extent. For example, '[d]ecapitation is the penalty for a slave who strikes his master (irrespective of whether injury results), whereas no penalty attaches to a master who injures a slave, unless the injury leads to death' (p. 33). Privileged social groups were given special treatment, to the effect that 'members of officialdom (and their immediate relatives) could not be arrested, investigated, or tortured without permission of the emperor' (p. 34) and other special considerations, such as the facility to pay fines instead of being hit with the bamboo, or worse punishments, were in operation. On the other hand, there was the expectation that members of the elite would behave better than normal mortals (p. 35):

> Confucian morality expected members of the official class to set a moral example to those beneath them, and hence to live according to a code of *noblesse oblige* which for certain offenses exposed them to heavier punishments than were prescribed for the ordinary man. . . An official who debauched a woman living within his jurisdiction would receive a punishment two degrees greater than the normal punishment for this offense.

Regarding differential punishments within the family, Bodde and Morris (1967: 37) discuss the example of a son who strikes or beats a parent. As a result, the son

> suffers decapitation, irrespective of whether or not injury results. However, no penalty applies to a parent who beats his son . . . unless the son dies, in which case the punishment for the parent is 100 blows of the heavy bamboo if the beating was provoked by the son's disobedience, and one year of penal servitude plus sixty blows of the heavy bamboo if the beating was done wantonly. Likewise a wife who strikes her husband . . . receives 100 blows of the heavy bamboo, whereas a husband who strikes his wife . . . is punished only if he inflicts a significant injury (the breaking of a tooth, a limb, or the like), and if the wife personally lodges a complaint with the authorities; in that case the husband is subject to a punishment two degrees less than the norm (he receives eighty blows of the heavy bamboo).

Various methods of punishment, imprisonment and fines, beating with light and heavy bamboo sticks, penal servitude and various forms of exile, are discussed in detail by Bodde and Morris (1967: 78–91).[95] The central concept of filial piety (*hsiao*) had important implications when it came to ascertaining punishments.[96] Thus, an only son sentenced to death or long-term servitude 'might have his sentence commuted in various ways . . . in order that he might remain at home to care for the parents' (Bodde and Morris, 1967: 41,

---

[95] McAleavy (1968a: 123) merely summarises that '[m]ethods of punishment were, essentially, flogging, transportation, death by strangulation or beheading'.

[96] A detailed table of punishments is found in Bodde and Morris (1967: 77–8, with further details at pp. 102–4). Minor punishments are the wearing of a wooden collar (*cangue*), tattooing and marking crimes on people's bodies, as well as torture (pp. 95–8).

139).[97] Much emphasis was given to fitting in with nature when executing death penalties.[98] McAleavy (1968a: 124) indicated that the Confucian doctrine of the connection between human conduct and the rhythm of nature 'was observed in the general rule that executions should not take place in spring and summer, when the life-force was in the ascendant, but in autumn when the year itself was declining'. According to Bodde and Morris (1967: 42):

> Many death sentences included the standard formula, 'after the assizes,' which meant that they could not be executed until reviewed at the Autumn Assizes annually held in the capital, at which time they were often, though not invariably, reduced to a lower sentence. Amnesties, either general or for specified groups or individuals, also occurred fairly frequently.

The standard death penalties under the imperial system had been strangulation and decapitation, while death by 'slow slicing', the most severe form of death penalty, was only added later (p. 77).[99] Van der Sprenkel (1977: 62) comments:

> The forms of the death sentence themselves represented an ascending scale of intensity. Strangulation was considered preferable to beheading as it did not involve mutilation of the body, while the most ignominious was the dreaded *ling ch'ih* – slow and painful execution, inflicted on those convicted of parricide or high treason. This involved the offender's being tied to a cross while, by a series of painful but not themselves mortal cuts his body was sliced beyond recognition, after which the head was exposed for a period. As the intention was to prevent the continued existence of the criminal's spirit in recognizable form, the slicing would still be carried out even if he had committed suicide.

Bodde and Morris (1967: 92) explain the links of such punishments with Confucian concepts of filial piety:

> [O]ne's body is not one's own property, but a bequest from his parents. To mutilate one's body, therefore, or allow it to be mutilated, is to be unfilial. Strangulation, from this point of view, is superior to decapitation since it leaves the body intact. Furthermore, by the same token, strangulation is superior because it leaves the spirit of the executed man an intact body which it can continue to inhabit.

[97] Bodde and Morris (1967: 41) add that '[i]n 1769 this principle was broadened to include criminals who were the sole male heirs of *deceased* parents; these too were permitted to remain at home so that they could continue the family sacrifices to the ancestors'. The authors argue that 'in some respects, the law of imperial China was more humane and intelligent than its Western counterpart' (p. 41). It certainly appears to have taken notice of social welfare considerations, rather than blindly punishing offenders, as is also evident from ancient and modern Indian laws.

[98] Bodde and Morris (1967: 131) note the 'insistence in Chinese law on careful scrutiny of every capital case at the highest level, including imperial ratification, before life may be taken'.

[99] For details see Bodde and Morris (1967: 93–5).

It is obvious that an offender who was cut to pieces would not be able to join the ancestors, so this gory death penalty is also a device, more definite than exiling a criminal, to exterminate the person from the universe, with the most de-humanising methods and effects possible. All writers suggest, however, that outside observers should not forget that Western styles of punishment were and are not exactly lacking in cruelty either.[100]

As we reach the end of the imperial system in China, it appears that prominent and systematic inequalities in the Chinese penal codes, insisting upon the sanctity of rank, privilege, and seniority, constituted one major element of severe criticism, mainly by outsiders, as a barrier to justice. However, from an internal Chinese perspective, relative justice, situation-specificity and a consideration of the facts and circumstances of every case, rather than uniformised law-making, appeared to be preferable. In this regard, too, traditional Chinese law is not really different from other Asian and African laws. Traditional efforts in finding human methods of law-making that could be harmonised with the assumed pre-existing natural system of order clearly involved much less law-making by the state than the presence of the imperial codes suggests to the outsider at first sight. This typical non-Western approach, which the present globally focused comparative analysis has identified as a key ingredient of all Asian and African legal systems, is therefore also a strong and integral element of traditional Chinese law.

As in other traditional legal systems, the attempted transition to Western models of legal regulation and administration in China, mainly during the twentieth century, had to cause enormous upheavals. As we shall see, despite formal declarations to the contrary, and significant silences in the legal literature, the traditional legal postulates of Chinese culture have continued to form an important ingredient of all post-imperial Chinese laws. For the present globally focused analysis this will mean that China, too, must continue to search for its own, culture-specific path to legal modernity and will not be able to simply copy transplants from foreign models.

7.5 Post-imperial Chinese legal systems

Like Africa (chapter 6, section 6.4.1), towards the end of the nineteenth century China was treated as an area of the world on which European powers had their own designs. It appears that China narrowly escaped full colonial domination.[101] Some processes of Chinese legal reform, initiated under the last few imperial rulers, therefore need to be seen as responses to threats and challenges from European powers, especially Britain and Germany. In this regard, China

---

[100] For details see McAleavy (1968a: 123) and Bodde and Morris (1967: 41–2).
[101] On Hong Kong and its eventual transfer to the People's Republic of China see Cottrell (1993) and Menski (1995).

at this time, Japan earlier and Ottoman Turkey later (chapter 5, section 5.13) have quite a lot in common.

Initial Chinese resistance towards modern reforms, resulting to a large extent from perceptions that China was the centre of the world and far superior to anything coming from outside, led at first to a defensive strategy of attempting internal reforms. However, these were not successful and a major phase of legal and conceptual development followed in which China sought to transplant Western laws, initially through Japan. As this also failed, and the Empire collapsed, the post-1911 Republican period again witnessed various attempts by the Chinese to copy Western laws into their legal system. Quite predictably, such a bold endeavour could not succeed and ended in confusion and official lawlessness. An overlapping subsequent phase, in reaction to the assertion of positivist law-making through transplants and new codifications, witnessed the gradually emerging communist rule of parts of China, marked by attempts to restructure local legal systems and later the whole of Chinese law in line with communist principles, another process of borrowing Western ideas and concepts. That period reached a critical point in 1949 with the formal establishment of the People's Republic of China (section 7.6 below).

7.5.1 Resistance to modernising reforms

Van der Sprenkel (1977: 78) notes that the traditional reluctance of the Chinese to go to law itself acted as a barrier to developing a more flexible legal system, alleging that '[t]hough Chinese merchants were not slow to appreciate the protection of Western law when they were brought into contact with it, no influential element in Chinese society had a clear interest in the creation or emergence of an efficient system'. Clearly, there were several important reasons why late imperial China resisted change and foreign influence. Chen (1998: 20) follows some historians in dividing the early developments into three stages: 'the period 1861–1894 initiated by the Self-Strengthening Movement of the 1860s; the period 1895–1919 initiated by China's defeat in the Sino-Japanese War of 1894–1895; and the modern period beginning with the May Fourth Movement of 1919'.[102] He writes that in the first period only superficial attempts of modernisation were made, but gradually the Chinese began to realise that their system might not be as superior as they had thought. McAleavy (1968a: 127) provided a brief overview of the starting phase of legal reforms in China, which partly resembles Ottoman perceptions and experience:

> The Opium War with Britain ended in 1842 with the Treaty of Nanking, the
> first of the so-called Unequal Treaties which in the course of the nineteenth

---

[102] Detailed coverage of this period is provided in Volume 11, Part 2, of the *Cambridge History of China*, see Fairbank and Liu (1980). A detailed review of this publication with much relevant legal commentary is found in Rodzinski (1983).

century turned China into what Mao Tse-tung terms with justice a 'semi-colony.' Yet it took an amazingly long time for even the most intelligent Chinese to grasp the immediacy of the danger which threatened their country. By the 1860s the government recognised that western military techniques were worth imitating, but not for another forty years was it seen that China had anything to learn in the sphere of law and government. Meanwhile the traditional civil service was for the ambitious still the supreme avenue to success, and only occasional students tried to advance their career by acquiring foreign knowledge at military schools or abroad. It was not until the early years of the twentieth century that the abolition of the old civil service examination opened the gate to modern education. In 1912 a wave of national revolution swept away the imperial system.

The Opium War arose in essence because Western traders were unwilling to submit to Chinese jurisdiction and insisted on the principle of extraterritoriality, according to which their legal affairs, even in China, would be governed by their respective European domestic laws. The Chinese were offended and not ready to give way because of their sinocentric perceptions and feelings of superiority.[103] Rodzinski (1983: 76) highlighted that the traditional Chinese, and especially the gentry, 'clung stubbornly to their cherished beliefs in the superiority of Chinese culture and to their view of the West as barbarian'. More recently, Chen (1998: 20) notes that '[t]raditional China regarded herself as the centre of the world and her civilisation and culture as superior to all others'. A combination of cultural conservatism and concern over the loss of traditional privileges prevented the Chinese bureaucratic élite from taking decisive action towards legal modernisation. Unlike the Ottoman rulers at roughly the same time, therefore, the Chinese imperial leaders did not actively engage in the process of promoting knowledge of 'the enemy' and took their time, until it was too late, to introduce some limited reforms. Unprepared to counter challenges on an intellectual level, and subjected to intense foreign political and military pressures, the Chinese developed much resentment, rather than studying and copying the aggressive methods of foreigners in China. While the Turks responded by sending students to Europe, especially France, at government expense, the Chinese only took some tentative initiatives.[104] From

---

[103] Relevant material is found in several recent articles. He (1995) is an excellent detailed study of Chinese perceptions of identity which highlights the strength of sinocentric perceptions but argues that '[n]evertheless, throughout the course of Chinese history, this Sino-centric perception of the world, had not been unchallenged' (He, 1995: 131). Significantly, an early challenge came from Buddhism, which 'had been imported from India in the middle of the 1st century' (p. 131) and led some Confucians to call for the defence of indigenous Chinese culture. In this context, the pioneering research of Frank Dikötter on racial perceptions in China are of much interest (e.g. Dikötter, 1990).

[104] Lee (1987: 166) reports that, in 1905 and 1907, the Chinese sent study commissions to Europe, Japan and America. This article by Lee, as well as Fan (1997) on the reception of German criminal law in China, represents an interesting sub-category of the literature on Chinese law.

1903 onwards, a number of Chinese students went to Japan, which was to have tremendous impact on the Chinese political arena, since many of these students later became leaders of the early Republican movement, including their principal leader, Sun Yat-sen (Rodzinski, 1983: 78–9).

Chapter 5, section 5.13 showed for Ottoman Turkey that special legal conditions for foreign residents as well as the presence of non-Muslim minorities in their personal law system (*millet*) forced the Ottoman Muslims to recognise that there were other forms of legal regulation that might in fact be useful for all citizens. There is no such comparable evidence of Chinese readiness to learn from 'the other' and to adjust, although there was some evidence of legal pluralism in China itself at that time, particularly regarding Muslims (Dillon, 2004). Since the European powers regarded Chinese law as primitive and saw the criminal law as uncivilised (Chen, 1998: 21), it appears that the outcome had to be a violent clash. It is suggested by He (1995: 133) that '[t]he intrusion of the Western powers into China in the mid-19th century shattered the Sino-centric perception'. McAleavy (1968a: 127) highlights the critical role of extraterritoriality of laws for the newly resident foreigners living on Chinese soil while claiming allegiance not to the Emperor but to a foreign sovereign:

> One consequence of the Unequal Treaties had been the granting to foreign residents of the privilege of extraterritoriality. Indeed, from what has been said about the conditions of legal administration, it will be easily understood why westerners should have been reluctant to entrust themselves to it and insisted on being amenable only to the law of their own countries. It will also be obvious that extraterritoriality was looked upon by patriotic Chinese as a particularly odious stigma, which must be erased as soon as possible. To this end it was necessary to equip the country with a modern system of law. The first tentative steps in this direction were being taken in the last years of the Empire, but the coming of the Republic was followed almost at once by the chaos of the warlord period.

The principle that foreign residents wanted to be governed by their own laws is familiar from other legal systems of Asia and Africa. But was the desire to get round extraterritoriality of foreigners in China really so strong that it motivated the Chinese to reform their own system in line with the laws of those foreigners? If that had been the case, surely not enough preparatory work had been undertaken to consider the implications of wide-ranging legal and administrative reforms.

During the period up to 1911/12, the Chinese had to begin thinking about international law, as growing foreign pressure propelled the movement towards change. While the Emperor decided to implement reforms in 1898, after the manifest failure of the Self-Strengthening Movement with its reliance on Confucian norms, the various foreign powers introduced more of their own laws and procedures into the limited areas that they controlled. The pressure on the

Chinese was intense, and it did not help at all that the Japanese, perceived as inferior cousins, were intent on occupying parts of China and actually defeated the Chinese in 1894/5. Chen (1998: 21) suggests that the Japanese experience of copying Western codes and their success in relinquishing Western control motivated the Chinese to follow suit. However, the measures taken were simply too little too late. Chen (1998: 21) summarises the developments between 1904 and 1911, which included some attempts to reform certain legal elements like cruel punishments and the sale of persons. The imperial Board of Punishments was abolished in 1907 and replaced by a Ministry of Justice and a Supreme Court. Finally, the remnants of the imperial system were unceremoniously overthrown in 1911.

7.5.2 Introduction of Western laws in the Republican period

David and Brierley (1978: 483) observed that '[t]he ideal of a society without law appeared to be put into question following the Revolution of 1911. The desire to be freed of western domination led the Chinese to adopt a series of codes manifestly based on western models.' The provisional Republican government established by Sun Yat-sen in Nanking immediately began a law reform programme, but was overthrown within three months. China then entered, for fifteen years, into another period of competing warlords, some of whom attempted some legal reforms, but there was no consistence and no stability. McAleavy (1968a: 127–8) reported on the next phase:

> [I]t was not until the Nationalist Revolution of 1926–1928 had established a new government at Nanking that the task of legislation could begin. Between 1928 and 1935 a complete system of modern law was promulgated, patterned for the most part on the codes of Switzerland, Germany and France, though in the civil code the sections dealing with the family and succession retained a good deal of the traditional institutions adapted to modern conditions.
>
> It is however, only fair to say that this formidable achievement was almost entirely a dead letter, owing to the administrative impotence of the Nanking government.

Chen (1998: 22) shows how the Kuomintang, the Nationalist Party, promulgated a series of comprehensive codes of law which were really an amalgam of different legal systems and norms. They were partly based on European continental laws, especially from Germany, Japan and Switzerland, with some elements of Anglo-American laws, to some extent still relying on the legal traditions of the late Ch'ing and warlord periods. These new laws were collectively known as the Six Codes or the 'Collection of the Six Laws'. Because the Kuomintang never managed to establish control over the whole of China, having to fight the Chinese communists and the Japanese at the same time, these legal reforms remained largely ineffective and basically existed only on paper.[105] Bodde and Morris (1967: 50) noted that '[o]nly in the present century was serious challenge made of the Confucian doctrine of the natural superiority of the high over the low, of the old over the young, of man over woman', but these were only formal legal challenges that may not have had any real impact. Such legocentric assumptions disguise the fact that the Six Laws were certainly not effective laws. The sociological analysis by van der Sprenkel (1977: 103) captures socio-legal reality more fully. In a situation of legal insecurity, customary rules and general principles offered a fall-back position:

> The important place formerly occupied by custom in matters of what we should call civil law was underlined when the modernization of the legal system was attempted in the early years of this century. One of the reformers' objectives appeared to be attained when the power of the judiciary was separated from that of the executive. The newly independent courts found, however, that in civil matters there was little formal law for them to apply. The Supreme Court ruled that cases should be decided according to the express provisions of law, if any existed; in the absence of express provisions, then according to custom; and in the absence of custom, then according to juristic principles.

But whose general principles would one apply? David and Brierley (1978: 483) noted that the desire to be freed of Western domination had led the Chinese to adopt a series of codes based on Western models, a Civil Code on private and commercial law in 1929–31, a Code of Civil Procedure in 1932, and a Land Code in 1930. Their comment is interesting because they claim China for the civil law world: 'In appearances, therefore, Chinese law has been Europeanized and can be ranked within the family of laws deriving from the Romanist tradition.' Yet it was also noted (p. 483) that the new laws were not able to make an impact:

> Behind this façade, however, traditional concepts have persisted and, several exceptions apart, have continued to dominate the realities of Chinese life. The work of a few men wishing to westernize their country could not possibly have resulted in the sudden transformation of Chinese mentality or accustom the people and jurists of China, in only a few years, to the Romanist concept of law . . . In the early period, no resort was had to the courts, either because the law was unfamiliar or because there was a wish to avoid the resulting disapproval of society. Social relationships continued to be governed in this way, as they were in the past. If, in exceptional cases, one did go before the courts, the Chinese judges still decided by the standards set by Confucius rather than by an application of the rules of written law.

David and Brierley (1978: 477) raised a general point about Far Eastern laws when they emphasise that '[m]ost far eastern countries adopted codes and it

---

[105] Finally, this legal system migrated with the Kuomintang to Taiwan, where it forms the basis of the present legal system. For details see Chen (1998: 22) and Cohen *et al.* (1980).

appeared that they had thereby rejected their traditions in favour of Romano-Germanic law as the basis for social relations. At later moments, some of these countries, moreover, indicated a desire to transform society through Communism.' However, they continued (pp. 477–8):

> The effect of these changes has been considerable. But those accomplished, as well as those now underway, are far from having wiped out all traces of special traditions. The western structures and institutions in many instances are no more than a façade, behind which social relations continue to be ruled in large part by the traditional models. And apart from that, it is very clear that mental attitudes anchored in traditional ways of thinking must be taken into account by present day ruling forces. Thus China, for example, has embarked upon a very different route than that of the Soviets, in the construction of Communism.

Thus, there is no evidence to indicate that China's reluctant move during the 1920s and 1930s to introduce Western-style laws was a success story. Glenn (2000: 305; 2004: 329) merely comments that '[t]he Six Codes remained essentially paper law'. Because of the political uncertainties during the 1930s and 1940s, and the growing influence of the Communists, attention now shifted towards their ideas about law-making and their approaches to law itself.

7.5.3   The communist foundations of Chinese law

The Communist Party of China had been founded in 1921 and had initially cooperated with the Kuomintang during the period 1923–7. However, once the Kuomintang started persecuting them in 1927, the Communists tried to develop their own system of local government in the rural areas under their control (Leng, 1967: 93). In 1931, the Communists proclaimed a Chinese Soviet Republic and gave themselves a legal structure modelled on Russian laws, including a system of people's courts. During this period of the 'New Democratic Revolution' (1931–49), a large number of laws were promulgated. Chen (1998: 23) explains their reformist orientation:

> The laws introduced... in the revolutionary bases were described in Chinese texts as 'anti-imperialist' and 'anti-feudal' in nature. Many were directed towards the overthrow of the 'feudal landlord class' in the rural areas. Different approaches were adopted in accordance with changing circumstances. At some stages the law provided for the reduction of land rent and interest so as to protect the peasants. At other stages, landlords' land was confiscated and given to the peasants.

Chen (1998: 23) provides an overview of the various laws introduced in this early period, and argues that many features of legal processes developed at this time also became elements of the post-1949 communist system. Leng (1967: 93) confirms this, writing that '[m]any features of "socialist legality" in Communist

China today have their roots back in the early years of the revolution' and distinguishes '(1) the Soviet period, 1927–34, (2) the Yenan period, 1935–45, and (3) the post-war period 1945–49' (p. 93). He shows that 'people's justice' began to make an appearance as early as 1926–7 in Hunan Province. The demands for wide-ranging reforms crucial to a rural population became especially prominent. Leng (1967: 93) reports:

> The peasant associations of Hunan adopted during these years a series of measures to enforce land reform, reduce interest rates, abolish exorbitant levies, advance women's rights, prohibit gambling and opium-smoking and eradicate corrupt officials and landlords. In a resolution on the judicial problem passed in late 1926, the First Peasant Congress of Hunan Province called for the elimination of illegal and oppressive acts of judicial personnel and the complete revision of civil and criminal laws.

It is evident that these organisations acted as a new local government and attempted to remove exploitative aspects of the traditional system rather than seeking a total abolition of the past. However, in this revolutionary climate, excesses were predictably unavoidable and Confucian ethics did not protect individuals accused of being enemies of the revolution. The main victim group of these early revolutionist endeavours were members of the upper classes, landlords and gentry, treated as 'local bullies' and 'counterrevolutionary elements'. They were dragged before tribunals, had normally no right of appeal, and were victimised, in the name of the revolution, which in the view of Mao Tse-tung had a necessary element of cruelty.[106] Thus, more or less encouraged from the top, a violent rural restructuring swept through the areas under communist control between 1926 and 1931. Chen (1998: 23) notes that many features of law from this period reappeared later in the post-1949 period:

> Examples are differential treatment according to a person's 'class background', the use of violence and terror and the arousing of 'class hatred' in dealing with 'enemies', 'reactionaries' or 'counter-revolutionaries', the practice of 'mass trials' (*gongshen*), the systems of people's assessors, procurators, and adjudicative committees within courts, and the use of conciliation and mediation to settle disputes.

The formal establishment of the Chinese Soviet Republic, with a Constitution adopted on 7 November 1931, created a democratic dictatorship of the proletariat and the peasantry, designed to cover the whole of China and free the country from foreign domination. Major policy aims were the destruction of all remnants of feudalism and an improvement of the living conditions of workers and peasants. A number of laws were enacted in 1931, relating to land law,

---

[106] Leng (1967: 94) reports that 'some 1822 landlords were executed within a few months' and 'even women were aroused to kill the condemned landlords with spears before the applauding masses'. On the position of Mao Tse-tung, see Kampen (1986).

labour law and marriage regulations.[107] Further laws on marriage and regulations for punishing counter-revolutionaries were introduced in 1934 (Leng,
1967: 95). Complex court structures were set up for criminal, civil and special cases. In effect a new bureaucracy was created and '[t]he primary task of
the soviet judiciary was to protect the "socialist" order against class enemies
and counter-revolutionaries' (Leng, 1967: 97), while '[o]ne serious problem
in judicial work was the shortage of qualified personnel in the soviet areas'
(p. 97). Because of widespread abuses, torture and corporal punishments had
to be explicitly prohibited and Mao Tse-tung criticised them as feudalistic and
barbarous remnants unsuitable for the Soviet style of people's justice.

The effect of applying Soviet-style class justice was to turn the traditional
hierarchy upside down, so that people from privileged backgrounds were now
treated without any leniency, while a common person could expect better treatment. Leng (1967: 99) writes that '[p]ersons of the "exploiting classes" therefore
received severe punishment, as did the principals and those who persisted in
falsification without repentance'. Mass trials were used as an instrument of
public education as well as indoctrination, and they often ended in immediate
execution of the 'enemy'.[108] The toughness led to a lower level of crime, and
Leng (1967: 100) reports that even the Kuomintang had to admit that 'respect
for the law and relative freedom from corruption were among the strong points'
of the Soviet judicial system.

The Yenan or Yunan period of 1935–45 is described in detail by Leng (1967:
101–8). Most significant during this phase was the growing control of the
Communist Party over the judicial system, a shift from the realm of society to
that of the state, with the risk of creating new imbalances. A second new element
was the slightly less aggressive approach to members of the upper classes, which
went hand in hand with some attempts to democratise justice. Still, as Leng
(1967: 105) shows, the most prominent feature during this period was the
'mass line' trial system, which was again used for public education and social
engineering through law. A major case reported from that period concerned
the validity of a marriage in the absence of consent by the girl's father. The
marriage was held to be valid on the basis that free choice of partners was a
good principle.[109] During this period, Leng (1967: 107) found 'marked progress
in developing judicial organs and procedures', but also identified continuing
problems, including the lack of trained personnel. Interestingly, the suggestion
that local people should not be ignored in legal processes and that 'three old
peasants are equal to a local judge' (p. 108) appears here, too.

---

[107] For late imperial China, with particular reference to the New Territories of Hong Kong
and property law, see Palmer (1987c). On the period between 1931 and 1934 see in detail
Butler (1983). On land laws during this period see Elvin (1970a; 1970b).

[108] Leng (1967: 99–100) provides some examples.

[109] This issue in patriarchal Asian societies was also highlighted for Muslim law, particularly
the case of Saima Waheed in Pakistan (chapter 5, section 5.14).

The post-war period of 1945–9 saw the final power struggle between the Kuomintang and the Communists. Leng (1967: 109) reports that during this period the focus on land reform again ended up victimising land owners and even middle farmers, leading to excesses which even the Communist Party did not underwrite and which were publicly admitted by Mao Tse-tung (p. 110). The two main features of the system developed prior to 1949, according to Leng (1967: 114), were the use of legal instruments primarily for enforcing state policies rather than protecting individual rights and the special role given to extrajudicial organs and procedures for imposing sanctions and settling disputes.

Looking back at the traditional Imperial system, it appears that the changes in the post-Imperial period are not really of a dramatic structural nature. All that has changed is that the policies of the new government have replaced those of the old order, so there is a change of political control, and a formal change of positive official law. Much of the pre-existing social system (except in the Communist areas) remained in place, and traditional values and ethics also retained significant importance. As found for all legal systems analysed in the present study, during the period of contact with Western laws and Western legal ideas, the incoming modern legal systems represent an altogether different category of law and simply do not have the capacity (despite positivist claims) to wipe out everything of legal relevance that pre-existed the importation of the new legal models. The enormous importance given to extra-judicial organs and procedures is clearly not a new feature of Chinese law at this historical stage. Evidently, in the pre-1949 period, the old order had merely been overlaid with two thin new veneers, one in the form of the Republican Six Laws, the other through creating new normative orders of a socialist nature. While the former was to be formally abolished by the Communists in 1949, the latter would need to be expanded into a full-fledged legal system for the new China in the socialist vision of its post-imperial leaders.

7.6 Law in the People's Republic of China

Chen (1998: 24) indicates that academic views of this period are quite mixed, since 'a commonly expressed assessment by mainland Chinese scholars today is that while significant achievements have been made, painful mistakes have also been committed at some stages; the journey has not been an easy and straightforward one'. The journey towards establishing a fully functional modern and now probably postmodern legal system for over a billion people is still an ongoing process and remains an enormous challenge.[110] The risk for scholarly commentators who lack historical knowledge of Chinese law and plurality-consciousness is that new legal developments in China are simplistically taken and portrayed as a unique experience. At one level, this it undoubtedly the case,

---

[110] On various challenges relating to Chinese society, see Stockman (2000).

since the identity postulates (Chiba, 1989: 180) of China will not be shared by other jurisdictions. However, there are also many comparative elements and familiar patterns in the context of a globally focused interdisciplinary analysis. Some useful starting points for such analytical expeditions are found in the earlier literature. For example, Bodde (1954: 54–5) noted fifty years ago:

> There is a partial similarity at this point between Confucianism and the ideology of the men who today control the destinies of China. For these men, too, like the Confucianists, proclaim the people's welfare to be their highest aim, yet at the same time insist, again like the Confucianists, that the achievement of this aim depends on the leadership of an élite controlling group – in their case the Chinese Communist Party. This is but one of several significant parallels to be found between these two seemingly sharply antithetical ideologies.

The old ideal of the doctrine of the golden mean (Feng, 1952–3), a balancing act in which also doing nothing was counted as an activity,[111] first in conceptualisations of *tao*, then in the ideal of *li* as good governance, was picked up by the Communist leadership and turned into a public interest concept germane to China as a socialist system with Chinese characteristics. In the present section, the momentous events of the formal establishment of the People's Republic of China (PRC) in October 1949 are briefly analysed in light of the present globally focused comparative legal analysis. The material falls into two major sections, covering first the beginnings of the establishment of the PRC and the various phases of consolidation and unrest, including the Cultural Revolution of 1966 and its aftermath, which show an extremely ambivalent approach to the role of law. Secondly, the post-Mao developments in modern Chinese law are examined in two parts and assessed in the light of interdisciplinary, cross-cultural attempts to understand the nature of modern Asian laws and the scope for their future development in the era of postmodernity.

7.6.1 The ambivalent approach to law in Mao's China

Leng (1967: 111) reports that, on 14 January 1949, Mao Tse-tung included the abolition of the Nationalist Constitution and the old legal system as two of the eight conditions for peace. However, the warring parties fought on and no compromise could be found. In February 1949, the Central Committee of the Communist Party of China issued instructions which officially abolished all existing laws of the Kuomintang, confirmed in September 1949.[112] On

---

[111] This appears like a Stoic concept, but is also familiar from the Hindu/Buddhist notion of *karma*.

[112] McAleavy (1968a: 128) was slightly imprecise when he wrote that '[i]n September 1949, on the eve of the establishment of the People's Government, the Communists proclaimed the abrogation of all Nationalist laws', since they merely reissued the earlier proclamation.

1 October 1949, China became a People's Republic as a result of the Communist Party victory under Mao Tse-tung and gave itself a provisional constitution.[113] Bonavia (1982: 157) notes that '[i]n theory, it should have been feasible to replace rule by the emperor and his officials with rule by the Chairman and the Party cadres', adding that '[m]any of the attributes ascribed to Mao in the Cultural Revolution were semi-divine in nature' (p. 157). However, the theory that a new political rule can just replace an old order of a different kind is evidently flawed. Despite all the personality cult around Mao, he and his new system could not entirely replace the old system, which was a more holistic legal order than the communists wanted to know. Traditional values and social norms were not simply going to be wiped out by a revolution in the sphere of positivist law-making. One must assume that Mao knew this quite well, but pressed on with reforms nevertheless, driven by a vision of a strong New China.

Most legal scholarship, focusing on legal processes, pays minimal attention to such conceptual stumbling blocks for legal reforms. Chen (1998: 24) correctly points out that the new government was most concerned to abolish the old laws and that '[t]he first step in the construction of the new legal system was the abolition of the existing one which was considered to have supported "semi-feudal and semi-colonial rule"'. This is correct as a statement, since Chen does not claim that the communists tried to totally abolish the imperial order. But were the pre-existing, Confucian elements still in existence in 1949, or were they deemed to have been abolished earlier by the paper reforms of the Republican period? No precise answer is given by legal commentators. From the perspective of a cross-cultural comparative legal analysis, it is highly significant that legal writers have tended to discuss this subject as though the pre-Communist legal system now only comprised of the Western-inspired laws of the Kuomintang. No conceptually focused discussion about the place of the pre-existing Confucian worldview and its socio-legal normative implications in China during the period of communist revolution appears, apart from a few stray comments or some specialist articles by non-lawyers.[114] Even Glenn's (2004: 330ff.) recent study on the relevance of tradition for today's legal reconstructions remains too general on this central issue. Discussing the position of socialist law in Asia, Glenn (2004: 330) flippantly suggests that socialism means little else than a hyper-inflated public law sector, but recognises (p. 331):

> Socialist law in Asia is different, necessarily a kinder, gentler form of communism, though of course equally savage when necessary. Asian communism is different because Asia is different, and there is less place for formal law in it, whether of socialist or capitalist tendency.

[113] For details see Chen (1998: 24) and in particular Zheng (1988: 1).
[114] Murphey (1967: 313) notes that, two decades after the communist revolution, a wider perspective was beginning to be taken, recognising continuities with the pre-Communist past as well as discontinuities. The study by He (1995) provides an insightful analysis of different perceptions of tradition and of law.

The realisation that cultural influences might mean giving increased importance to traditional Chinese teaching and values emerges only gradually in this extended discussion. Noting correctly that 'Confucianism, if not explicitly resurrected, has become an ally in the effort to generate loyalty and preserve structures', Glenn (2004; 332) does not appear to realise that Confucian values in today's manifestations have been re-employed by the Chinese state and the all-dominating Party as a critical tool for the plurality-conscious reconstruction of today's immensely hybrid Chinese legal system. All that we are told in this thoughtful but flat excursion is that '[t]here's lots to think about in socialist Asia' (Glenn, 2004: 336). One possible explanation for such meaningful silences must be that legal writers still do not consider the sphere of the Confucian worldviews and their current manifestations as sufficiently legal to warrant explicit recognition of such values as legal inputs.

Several decades ago, David and Brierley (1978: 484) noted in typical legocentric fashion that 'the "common programme" of 1949 abolished in one stroke all existing laws, decrees and courts. It was thus urgent to rebuild the framework of society with all speed.' Because it was thought that the quickest and most effective means for totally transforming society in preparation for the advent of communism was official legal reform, 'a series of fundamental laws were adopted from 1949 onwards, in line with the Soviet model, for this social reorganization' (p. 485). The authors at least noted that the operation of the new legal institutions caused many problems and that 'the principle of legality was established only with difficulty' (p. 485), but do not link their comments elsewhere about the continuation of traditional norms with this theme. Similarly, Zweigert and Kötz (1998: 292) only commented that '[o]ne of the first acts of the new government was to abrogate all the legislation of the Kuomintang period as "reactionary" and "Western in spirit", and for many years nothing was put in its place, apart from a law of marriage in 1950'. This sounds as though there were huge legal voids in China, which cannot be correct. In reality, there have been deadly struggles over what the law was, but there was definitely not a legal vacuum.

The new communist marriage law, promulgated on 1 May 1950 as the Marriage Law of the People's Republic of China, illustrates perfectly the ease with which Maoist law-making assumed a single-minded positivist stance and behaved as though no other law existed on the same subjects. Even if it did, the new law-maker's positivist hubris claimed to just wipe it out by the stroke of a pen. Article 1 of this law provided as follows:

> The feudal marriage system based on arbitrary and compulsory arrangements and the supremacy of man over woman, and in disregard of the interests of children, is abolished.
> The New-Democratic marriage system, which is based on the free choice of partners, on monogamy, on equal rights for both sexes, and on the protection of the lawful interests of women and children, is put into effect.

Similarly, in Article 2, it was simply provided that '[b]igamy, concubinage, child betrothal, interference in the re-marriage of widows, and the exaction of money or gifts in connection with marriages, are prohibited'.[115] Article 6 of this law required both spouses in person to register the marriage 'with the people's government of the district or township in which they reside' and thus suggests that all marriages would henceforth need to be officially registered.[116] The desired impact of the new marriage law on every adult member of society is probably most evident from the wording of Article 8:

> Husband and wife are in duty bound to love, respect, assist and look after each other, to live in harmony, to engage in productive work, to care for their children and to strive jointly for the welfare of the family and for the building up of the new society.

These examples must suffice to demonstrate the ease and revolutionary optimism with which the new law-makers of China assumed their role. The period 1949–53 counts as a phase of transition to socialism. Zheng (1988: 1–2) comments that '[t]he stated major political task of this period was to eliminate the remnants of the old regime', which seems to relate more to structures than ideology. Therefore, this period was dominated by several mass movements initiated by the Party and directed from the top. Chen (1998: 24) argues that '[t]hey were considered necessary to enhance the "political awakening" of the masses, to break down the old social order and to establish in its place a new revolutionary order'. As before, this was achieved through public trials, which often got out of control. Chen (1998: 25) reports:

> In these trials, the accused were subjected to verbal and physical attacks and cruel and inhuman treatment; they had no right to defend themselves. Feelings of hatred on the part of the assembled crowds were stirred up; they often called for the death penalty and for no mercy for the accused. The number of 'class enemies' executed in this way ranged from 800,000 by Mao Zedong's own admission in 1957 to several million as estimated by scholars. Many more were sentenced to long terms of 'reform through labour'. The practice of mass campaigns and mass accusation and struggle meetings was to become a common feature of Chinese political life until the death of Mao in 1976.

Various mass campaigns like the Land Reform Movement of 1949–51 and the Movement Against the Three Evils of 1952 (corruption, waste and

---

[115] McAleavy (1968b: 76) explained that the communists hated polygamy because 'it was peculiarly redolent of class exploitation', especially because landlords had abused it to take the prettiest daughters of their tenants as concubines.

[116] McAleavy (1968b) reported on the ineffectiveness of these measures, comparable with evidence from Turkey (chapter 5, section 5.13), noting that there needed to be 'a government able and ready to assert for itself a monopoly of force' (p. 81). In view of the pre-existing pattern of societal self-regulation, widespread non-compliance with new state laws should have been no surprise.

bureaucratism in the party, in government and in state enterprises) and the Movement Against the Five Evils of 1952 (bribery, tax evasion, theft of state property, cheating on government contracts and stealing state economic information) all concerned economic issues and economic crimes. Chen (1998: 25) suggests that these campaigns targeted particularly the 'national bourgeoisie' and also shows that, through the Judicial Reform Movement of 1952–3, 80 per cent of judges inherited from the Kuomintang regime were removed. These revolutionary movements were clearly designed to dislodge and even exterminate most members of earlier élites in economic and legal fields. Many of the policies produced during this time were codified as laws before 1954, mainly concerning land reform, punishment for counter-revolutionaries and corrupt people, trade union law and marriage law.

Chen (1998: 25) reports that the second stage of transition towards socialism is 1953–6, 'a period of planned development and rapid growth', even a 'golden age' (p. 26). Following the Russian legal model as well as the Russian economic blueprint with expert help from Soviet legal advisers, the Chinese introduced the concept of 'socialist legality'. This amounted to the deliberate acceptance of law as a means of governance, an embodiment of naked power-conscious legal positivism in socialist dress. Chen (1998: 26) explains:

> According to the new orthodoxy, although law represented decay in capitalist societies, law and 'revolutionary legality' in the socialist state was the most highly developed form of law and represented the will of the people. Law was therefore a creative force and had a positive role to play in the construction of a socialist society.

In this context, the first Constitution of the PRC of 1954 was promulgated, an eclectic document which relied to a large extent, but not exclusively, on Russian models. Together with this Constitution, five basic laws relating to the structure of the state were passed, so that a full-fledged legal and constitutional framework had been established. The next step in the socialist transformation of China related to agriculture, handicrafts and the entire commercial sector, which was put under regulatory control.[117] In this way, the state began to encroach on an area traditionally dominated by guilds and trade associations and left to supposedly 'extra-legal' regulation. Together with the First Five Year Plan (1953–7), all aspects of economic life in the PRC now became more closely regulated. Chen (1998: 27) shows in detail that during this period the demand for well-trained legal administrators and hence also the need for lawyers was beginning to be recognised. Legal education was encouraged, law schools were set up, and lawyers began to practise, although still at the edge of legality.

---

[117] For details see Zheng (1988: 2–3), incorporating the 'Great Leap Forward' of 1958 and the observation that the economic reforms were accompanied 'by a shift in ideology from a moderate realistic view to an extreme idealistic approach' (p. 3), which signals further encroachment on the social and ideational sphere.

This economy-focused policy was confirmed at the National Party Congress in 1956, which turned its attention particularly to issues of future economic development. This meant, as numerous public declarations proclaimed, that the old conflict between the common people and the capitalist élite had lost its relevance and importance. The new issue now was that the existing economic and cultural conditions did not permit the fullest possible extent of economic development for all people and for the nation. Chen (1998: 28) stipulates that '[t]he main task ahead was therefore the development of the productive forces of society'. For this purpose, further legal codification was envisaged and a better understanding of the 'rule of law' and of legality was promoted.

However, the Chinese remained evidently aware that they could not just copy the Soviet model, and debates over priorities and policies continued within the party leadership.[118] David and Brierley (1978: 484) noted the initial adherence in communist China to Marxist-Leninist teaching, but cautioned that China's situation was very different from that of the Soviet Union, not the least because of its enormous population. In their view, China's situation was also different because the country had historically taken a different approach to state law and because of recent experience, 'the principle of law is detracted; it represents for the Chinese nothing more than a brief period of their history, an episode of the western imperialism of which they are now free' (p. 484). Thus, the Chinese were aiming for a culture-specific form of state capitalism (p. 486). While the economic dimensions of development and the property law aspects were certainly very important, '[i]n China, priority is to be given to social transformation rather than economic growth; a new relationship between men must be established in order to end any possibility or trace of exploitation' (p. 486). This, as subsequent events showed, appears to have been at the heart of Mao's attempts to reform the Chinese system. However, the above analysis leaves out of the equation that the Confucian worldview of the common Chinese people had not just been blown away with the storm clouds of the revolution. It is evident that Mao Tse-tung was well aware of this, and it appears that he attempted to tackle this issue through a strategy of constantly reviewing the spirit of the revolution as an ongoing process with an enormously wide agenda, rather than a one-off political *fait accompli*.

Indeed, while in 1956 the party had encouraged critical voices to come forward for the benefit of the nation through the slogan 'Let a hundred flowers bloom and a hundred schools contend', by 1957 the resulting flood of criticism of party excesses and violations of legality had become so strong that another clampdown, the Anti-Rightist Campaign, was used by the party to purge the critics and to concentrate again on ideology rather than economic development.

---

[118] However, Glenn (2004: 331) points to research which shows that the Chinese soon realised that they could not make Soviet institutions function in Chinese society. De Bary (1991) discussed unsuccessful attempts by Mao to turn Confucianism into a museum piece.

Again, the party violated basic principles of legality and hundreds of thousands of people were designated as 'rightists' and sent to 'rehabilitation' farms for 're-education through labour' without recourse to any formal court procedure. Many lawyers, jurists and judges became victims of this Anti-Rightist Campaign as well and the small beginnings of legal growth and respect for the law were cut back, as Chen (1998: 29) reports:

> After 1957, the prestige of legal institutions such as the courts and the procuratores fell sharply. Lawyers ceased to practise, the publication of legal materials declined, the law schools switched to teach politics rather than law . . . In 1959, the Ministry of Justice and the organs of judicial administration under it were abolished. All the following principles or practices were denounced as bourgeois and reactionary: judicial independence, procuratorial independence and the role of the procuratores in legal supervision, equality before the law, the emphasis on procedural regularity, the system of defence lawyers in criminal trials, the principles of 'no criminal punishment without a violation of a specific law (*nulla poena sine lege*), correspondence or proportionality between a crime and the punishment for it, socialist humanism in penal policy, the heritability of bourgeois legal ideas, the presumption of innocence on the part of the accused, and the idea of human rights. The system of public trial virtually came to an end.

Chen (1998: 29) reports that, in the early 1960s, Mao Tse-tung again accepted that lawyers were needed, and that civil and criminal codes should be produced. However, by the time of the Cultural Revolution of 1966,[119] everything fell again into limbo, this time for an extended period which lasted beyond Mao's death in 1976. Zheng (1988: 4) argues that the developments during the early 1960s 'significantly undermined the role of the legal system in Chinese society' and that the law commanded less and less respect, officially because of the argument that in a truly communist society no law should exist. However, there was more to come, as Maoist China struggled with its own split attitudes to law, lawyers and the place of authority and order.

As Chen (1998: 30) demonstrates, 'appealing to the anti-bureaucratic instinct of the masses', Mao was able to mobilise millions of Red Guards to pursue a policy of total social transformation through a comprehensive anti-authority campaign. This led to many years of civil anarchy and terror, as these mainly young people branded anyone in positions of authority as 'reactionary' and inflicted their own reign of terror on the country without regard for any kind of law or legal system. Murphey (1967: 325), writing at the time of the Cultural Revolution, shows clearly that the Red Guards were specifically charged by Mao 'with continuing the struggle against the "four olds": the old ideas, culture,

---

[119] On this complex subject see in some detail Chen (1998: 29–30). Ladany (1992) focuses particularly on the concept of legality.

customs, and habits of the degenerate past'. It is evident that this violent rejection of anything linked to the past and its authoritative internal structures would have to end in disaster, as exterminating the past meant questioning an integral part of every Chinese person and thus, ultimately, eliminating each other. Unsurprisingly, China was thrown into total chaos, mass trials took place again, as well as 'struggle meetings', in which the accused would be treated without respect for dignity and human rights. In retrospect, this phase is widely seen as 'a catastrophic period for justice in China' (Bonavia, 1982: 154).

It appears that, as a by-product of this violent rejection of Confucian values, explicitly legalist thinking and methods resurfaced in modern China in a modified form. During the period of the 'Great Proletarian Cultural Revolution' there was certainly no recognition of a balance between different normative orders and consequently no restraint on the conduct of those who claimed they were right to protect socialism in the way they did. Re-reading the descriptions of Bodde and Morris (1967) and others on legalism (section 7.3.3 above) one is struck by many parallels in argumentation between the ancient Legalists and the Red Guards, who relentlessly pursued anyone accused of an offence. The evident imbalance between the normative orders of Chinese society and the shifting norm catalogue of the revolutionary cadres during the Cultural Revolution appears to underlie the 'twisted logic' that Chen (1998: 31) identifies:

> Thus cruelty towards class enemies . . . was glorified as 'revolutionary action' and praised as a moral virtue. Indeed, according to this twisted logic, the more inhuman and cruel the manner in which one behaved towards 'class enemies', the more one showed the firmness of one's 'proletarian class standpoint'. Human rights and dignity were therefore deliberately trampled upon; the theory and practice of class struggle eroded the traditional values of benevolence, compassion, sympathy and trust and brought into being a society filled with suspicion, hostility and the revolutionary 'virtue' of 'class hatred'. The legitimacy of a sphere of private life for each individual was also denied; every single act done or word uttered could be examined and used to incriminate the actor or speaker as a counter-revolutionary.[120]

Class hatred is here equated with contempt of the legalist enforcer for the accused under the ancient legalist code. The legalist assumption that offenders are basically incorrigible adds to the ferocity of conviction that extermination is the only cure, for the overriding benefit of the new social order. While Chen did not further analyse such issues in terms of conceptual tensions, He (1995: 141) perceptively explains that Mao 'felt that his revolutionary goals had been sabotaged by the moderate faction in the leadership and that the monopoly of culture by the remnants of the old society had not been broken'. This seems to

---

[120] Chen (1998: 31) provides a number of examples of these excesses of revolutionary 'legalism'.

indicate an attempt to rid the country of its old traditional imperialist, now redesignated 'feudal', legal postulates, an endeavour that had to end in failure and led to backlashes. These were reinforced when anti-government demonstrators of 1976 demanded again more emphasis on material development and in effect told the government and the Party to scale down the desperate attempts to remodel the spheres of culture and societal norms through ideological rectification. From a legal angle, Chen (1998: 32) focuses on the impact on the legal system as a whole:

> The demise of the legal system in the Cultural Revolution period was not merely an incidental side-effect of the fanatic and violent political campaigns, mass movements and social upheavals associated with the intensive struggles of those eventful days. The legal system was one of the targets of deliberate attack by the radicals. The very idea of law was discredited and held in contempt... In 1967 the *People's Daily*, the Party's leading newspaper, published an article entitled 'In Praise of Lawlessness', denouncing law as a bourgeois form of restraint on the revolutionary masses.... The Chinese people were urged to be guided by Chairman Mao's thought instead of by law. Under slogans such as 'smash the Public Security, the Procuratores and the Courts', or 'the more chaos, the better', legal institutions were attacked and paralysed or dismantled. Law schools were closed down. Members of the legal community were persecuted or forced to shift to other kinds of work. In short, law neither existed as an academic discipline nor as a rational mechanism of social control. It was struggled against and purged.

The radical control of all legal affairs by the Party continued after 1969 and it was not until 1972 that the court system was gradually re-established. Until Mao's death in September 1976, and the downfall of the 'Gang of Four', legal and political turmoil continued, and also immediately afterwards confusions over China's future direction prevailed. Zheng (1988: 5) writes that '[o]ne of the painful lessons that the country has learned from the Cultural Revolution is the importance of an authoritative legal framework to the overall political and economic stability of the country'. This sounds simply like a plea for strong positivism. None of the legal authors who comments on this crucial period appears to bring the critical and centrally contested legal element of the pre-existing and continuing, resilient Confucian order into the analytical equation. Here and there, lip service is paid by legal writers to the critical role of Chinese society,[121] but nobody seems to recognise the central importance of what Chiba (1986) called 'legal postulates' in this revolutionary cauldron.

---

[121] Lubman (1995: 16) writes in the context of an assessment for the future that legal developments 'must be considered together with other forces that are likely to influence the trajectory of Chinese legal development, emanating from Chinese society rather than the Chinese state'. Such argumentative chains must assume that these social forces were ever-present, albeit not unchanged and inflexible.

7.6.2 The post-Maoist reconstruction of Chinese law

Government policy after Mao emphasised 'democracy and the rule of law' (Zheng, 1988: 5), and, 'following the purge of Mao's radical supporters in 1976, highly significant reform policies have been instituted in various areas of social life' (Palmer, 1986–7: 41). The post-Maoist leadership under Deng Xiaoping has been characterised as pragmatic rather than ideologically activist, but a policy of pragmatism will have its own underlying ideological foundation. It is certain that the shock waves of the Cultural Revolution had significant cathartic effects on the superior Chinese leadership, in that it was now explicitly acknowledged that a stable law was essential for creating an orderly socialist future for China. But what kind of law was needed? Given the ambivalent approach of modern China to the various kinds of laws it has operated during its long history, what would be the most appropriate sources of law for reconstructing a feasible socialist legal system? Having rejected virtually every single element of the indigenous legal armoury, China had forced itself onto a path of legal modernisation that seemed to necessitate use of foreign models and yet, at the same time, a recognition that those foreign models and ideas might not be entirely suitable. In a spirit of remarkable realism, not to say cynicism, therefore, post-Mao China has not embarked, like Turkey much earlier, on full-scale copying of foreign legal models, but has chosen to be selective and extremely eclectic. By the late 1970s, there were other legal models in the world that the Chinese could look to. Instead of just Western laws, whether capitalist or communist, there were other attempts to reconstruct socialist legal systems in the world that may well have influenced the way in which the Chinese leadership went about reconstructing the post-Maoist legal system.

Outwardly and most significantly for lawyers, positivist techniques of law-making received most attention. Soon after the end of the Maoist period, decisive steps were taken to rebuild the legal system through a programme of extensive legal codification.[122] Most of the Chinese laws and regulations that are currently in force come from the period after 1979, including the 1982 Constitution (Zheng, 1988: 5). Chen (1998: 33–4) helpfully recounts the main events that display the new thinking about the need to strengthen the socialist legal system as a means to safeguard people's democracy, quoting Deng Xiaoping (p. 33):

> In order to safeguard people's democracy, the legal system must be strengthened. Democracy needs to be institutionalised and legalised so that such a system and such laws would not change merely because of a change of leadership or a change in the leader's views and attention. The present problem is that the laws are incomplete; many laws have not yet been enacted.

---

[122] Detailed overviews and analyses of the modern legal system are found in Chen (1998), Zheng (1988) and Münzel (1982). On family laws see especially Palmer (1986–7; 1987a; 1988; 1992a; 1996; 1997).

Leaders' words are often taken as 'law', and if one disagrees with what the leaders say, it is called 'unlawful'. And if the leaders change their words, the 'law' changes accordingly.

This series of statements is extremely significant,[123] since it shows that Deng, at any rate, had realised the dangers of making the law of the nation dependent on the ruler's view. Austinian law-making did not recommend itself in Chinese circumstances. Law needed to be something above the person in charge of the political realm, in the same way that in the old Confucian order the pre-existing *tao* had been an ever-present reality above the Emperor. Of course Deng, soon after the disaster of the Cultural Revolution, could not simply refer back to the old Confucian order. This shows that, as in postcolonial India, the political leadership cannot be entirely frank about its ideological agenda when it comes to law-making. What Deng stated in public is highly significant, however, since it amounts indeed to an explicit rejection of the Austinian perspective on law-making. Law could not be what the ruler said it should be, so much could be said without raising political heckles. As the new ruler, Deng therefore publicly renounced any claim to personify the law, which had under Mao brought so much misery to the country. The new aim for the reconstruction of Chinese socialist laws would henceforth be to develop a system of rules operative above the political level and, thus, more stable and less subject to fluctuations of the kind experienced in Maoist China between 1949 and 1976.[124] Lawyers will primarily see that law as the new Constitution of China, introduced in 1982. But merely by promulgating a new Constitution, China solved none of the problems that underlie its ongoing doubts about legality and 'rule of law'.

During the late 1970s and early 1980s, there were only a few indications of debates about the role of the indigenous value system in the reconstruction of modern Chinese laws. Most attention appears to have focused on the instrumentalist view that laws are needed to promote socio-economic development. The Fifth National People's Congress in February 1978 enacted the new Constitution, and Deng reiterated the message that economic development instead of class struggle should be at the centre of everybody's concerns. In view of such deliberate policies to write socialist democracy into the law, Chen (1998: 34) comments that '[j]ust as the sabotage of the legal machinery was deliberately engineered by the radicals in the Cultural Revolution days, the return to the idea of the socialist legal system (and the related idea of socialist democracy) was the result of a conscious policy choice by the post-Mao leadership'. Chen (1998: 34) identifies two major reasons:

> First, the weakness of legal system and, in particular, the lack of acceptance of authority of law and the concept of fidelity to law, has been identified

---

[123] It is also reminiscent of many critical assessments of postcolonial African law-making and governance.

[124] On the role of modernisation through law and the place of elections in China see Cheng (1986).

as a partial cause of, and a condition precedent for, the radicals' successful usurpation of political power and their large-scale persecution of alleged 'rightists' and 'counter-revolutionaries' during the Cultural Revolution. Law and legal system must therefore be emphasised to prevent the recurrence of the errors and tragedies of that period.

The most important lesson, a global issue rather than just a matter for Chinese politics or legal reconstruction, was that the uncontrolled authority of the party activists had been able to throw the nation out of balance. The absence of a binding, recognised, supervening code of conduct for all citizens, of agreement about the law itself, actually of something higher than the sum of the whole (Fikentscher, 1995), had allowed mayhem to prevail for too long. It was realised that there needed to be a set of norms above the realm of politics, independent of the will of a particular group of people who represented the state. The trend in public speeches at the time was to blame the insufficiency of the existing laws, and thus to legitimise fresh law-making. However, in the minds of those who spoke there must have been more or less hidden deeper issues, which the present globally focused analysis needs to uncover in more detail.

It appears that, similar to post-Emergency India in the late 1970s (chapter 4, section 4.9), and therefore more or less exactly at the same time, it was not considered politically correct to speak in public of recourse to ancient traditions and to understandings of law that were independent of the state. Yet both Indian and Chinese leaders at the time of crisis seem to have remembered that there were in existence, deep within the realm of society and in the minds of people, certain value systems, albeit carrying dangers of their own, which might perhaps be at least partially useful and might be re-used for national reconstruction. While India restructured the Constitution of 1950 through important amendments in 1976 and 1978, incorporating ancient Hindu values dressed up in modern language (chapter 4, section 4.9), it appears that China attempted something similar, but for obvious reasons also did not admit this publicly. Thus, in both cases, meaningful silences about the process of socialist reconstruction can be noted. The Chinese realisation that something needed to be done to safeguard the country's future is expressed well in a quote from the *People's Daily*, reported by Chen (1998: 35):

> The ten years of chaos have given us a lesson about law, one that is unforgettable for life: once the proletariat has grasped hold of political power, it must construct and consolidate a legal system and use it to protect the interests of the proletariat and all the people. Not to emphasise the legal system, not following the law and acting as if there were no law above oneself – this only benefits bad elements and does not benefit the people. This painful lesson is one which we must always remember.

Obviously, the reference to 'law above oneself' contains a subtle hint that the old Confucian order as a Chinese form of natural law might after all still be a useful legal element for post-Maoist legal reconstruction. There is only a faint indication here of what legal authors might mean when they point to tensions between government policy and the social sphere.[125] It would not have been wise to express any thoughts about this matter openly at the time, and it is probably still a tricky issue, given the history of Chinese law. However, from the perspective of a comparative legal analysis, what does 'a law above oneself' mean in the Chinese cultural context? Deng Xiaoping himself had declared, as cited above, that the state could not necessarily be trusted to create a law that would be above those who ruled. It appears that here are important flashpoints and incentives for fresh thinking about socialist legality which require further debate. Chen (1998: 35) rightly indicates that there was a second factor which made the post-Maoist leadership realise that more law was needed:

> A second factor, which is closely related to the first, was the feeling that law and legality can contribute to political stability and social order, and afford protection to the basic rights of the citizen. All these were believed to be what China deeply and urgently needed to have after the Cultural Revolution era.

The public, it appears, felt that the legal void created by the formal abolition of the old order had not been filled by a reliable replacement that could fulfil the task of balancing the competing pulls of social norms and the state's legal apparatus. The experience of the Cultural Revolution had shown that the state machinery had been abused as an instrument of terror, quite like the old legalist order 2,000 years ago. In a sense, therefore, modern China was now engaged in fresh efforts to combine legalist toughness and overall supervision by the state with explicit concern for the welfare and best interests of the people, a new form of Confucianisation of the law – yet ideally minus the Confucian element. Since the legal postulates of Confucianism were ideologically tainted, they could of course not be used openly for the reform of post-Maoist China, in the same way that post-Emergency India could not admit publicly to recycling elements of the ancient Indic or Hindu value system.

The publicly conducted discourse in modern China, as reflected in the legal literature, has therefore been, as in India, about law in relation to socialism, with only occasional comments about the place of the more than one billion people to whom any legal reconstruction would need to apply. In the Chinese legal discourses, one major point of emphasis in the debates has been the reconstruction of socialist legality.[126] But quite what does that mean? A Party

---

[125] For example, Palmer (1986–7: 43) reports that governmental attempts to influence social norms 'inevitably have encountered resistance', and writes that, '[a]s a result, the authorities in the PRC hold an inherently ambivalent attitude toward the family and operate a variety of policy measures and ideological devices designed to affect the structure and quality of relationships within the family'.

[126] The other key point, mentioned by a number of authors, is the need to construct a legal system that allows foreigners to feel comfortable about doing business with China.

resolution from 1981, quoted by Chen (1998: 36), offers a typical, ideologically correct and to that extent meaningful answer:

> We must turn the socialist legal system into a powerful instrument for protecting the rights of the people, ensuring order in production, work and other activities, punishing criminals and cracking down on the disruptive activities of class enemies.

This kind of programmatic statement reflects awareness that law as a whole has a number of basic functions in terms of protecting the public interest, the state as a whole, and all the people. We must note that the items and concerns listed above correspond more or less exactly to the functions that the traditional division of labour between the Confucianised imperial law and the similarly Confucianised realm of so-called 'extra-legal' social control had fulfilled in long-tested historical conjunction. In addition, the newly phrased element of 'cracking down on class enemies' is not really new in principle, since the old imperial order certainly knew how to handle treason and subversion, and had its own ideas of who constituted a class enemy. Thus, the coded legal message that modern China gave itself after the lawlessness of the Cultural Revolution was that it wanted again an internally balanced system of legal controls that could act as a supreme, general supervisory mechanism for the public good. Post-Maoist China was searching for a plurality-conscious reconstruction to suit the new conditions, reinventing the triangle, so to say.

This, indeed, is quite different from Western understandings of a 'rule of law' model, since the Chinese do not appear to assume that the state should control every activity and that state law could be the only law in the field (Peerenboom, 2004). China remains typically Asian in that even its most modern legal philosophy and theory recognises through silent acknowledgment that the state is not the only law-making agent. Modern Chinese legal philosophy has therefore tried to develop nothing else but a culture-specific balance between the expectations of the modern Chinese state and its positivist ambitions and the manifest needs of the masses of Chinese people, for whom an overbureaucratised legal machinery would probably mean unnecessary and duplicitous intrusion as well as unwarranted expense.

Since it remains difficult to suggest in public that the realm of Confucian legal postulates (albeit in modified form) has continued to operate at the core of the entire system, and since the Chinese leadership was intent on pursuing the path of socialist reconstruction, the public message that was spread everywhere had to be, quite clearly, that modern socialist law was the critical tool in the national

---

Chen (1998: 36) highlights the 'growing demand for a respectable and trustworthy legal system which can ensure that the rights and interests of foreign parties will be fully and effectively recognised, protected and enforced'. Lubman (1995: 1) emphasises that '[t]he surge of foreign direct investment . . . makes necessary further development of the legal framework for foreign trade and investment'.

rebuilding process and that this tool should be used to remodel the realm of social normative ordering. Such programmatic statements could be made, so much is certain, without saying in detail what 'socialist law' actually meant. It certainly did not mean something specifically 'religious', but it undoubtedly refers to a culture-specific value system that the present study has identified throughout Asia and Africa as a form of natural law.

Legal authors have overlooked this. They have, typically, focused on positivist aspects of legal reconstruction and have emphasised the progress made by modern China in using particular aspects of law-making as a tool for development. Thus, Chen (1998: 36) argues that 'the main task of political-legal work in the new era was to contribute to economic development and socialist modernisation', which 'is of course natural since economic development has now been officially designated as the major and central task' (p. 36). In the same way as Mrs Gandhi in India, a few years earlier, had coined her slogans about banishing poverty through socialist reconstruction, the Chinese leadership promised the people a better future through legal reconstruction, thus legitimating law-making along the lines found appropriate by the leadership at the time. Chen (1998: 36) emphasises the impact of the new economic policies in terms of bureaucratic planning and administrative directions, thus indicating again that the modern state increasingly involved itself in the socio-economic spheres traditionally controlled by informal legal mechanisms rather than the state itself.

7.6.3 The new legal structures and the future

Looked at from a technical legal perspective, modern Chinese legal reconstruction is therefore a process of creating ever more law, although some perceptive observers are beginning to doubt that this is what we see,[127] emphasising 'how far away China is from establishing a notion of the supremacy of law' (Lubman, 1995: 2). It is evident that, since 1979, enormous progress has been made in China in terms of constructing a formal, official legal system. In the period 1979–89, approximately 3,000 laws and regulations have been enacted, including more than 100 major codes and laws (p. 2).[128]

Significantly, the Constitution of 1982, the fourth one of the PRC, affirms the idea of legality and related concepts and principles, providing expressly in Article 5 that all state organs, hence also the Party itself, must operate within the scope of the Constitution. Chen (1998: 36–7) reports that much progress

---

[127] Lubman (1995: 2) uses the familiar image of a filling glass, arguing that '[t]o some foreign eyes, the glass into which they peer may seem to be filling, especially when they count up laws and regulations. There is, however, much evidence to suggest how empty the glass remains.'

[128] For details on many of these enactments see Zheng (1988). Earlier, authors often reported difficulties in obtaining information on Chinese laws, e.g. Münzel (1982: 1).

has been made in building legal institutions, and that legal education and legal writing have been revived. A significant element are the concerted efforts to educate the public about the new laws, so that '[l]egal education has become an integral part of the day-to-day output of the official propaganda machinery, encouraging people to obey the law and to understand their legal rights' (p. 37). But how far can this go, given that the whole system is entirely idealistic? Bonavia (1982: 159) perceptively noted that 'the good intentions of the Chinese lawmakers of the 1980s are clear', but we have had many years since to see that the balance between state control and people's justice is perhaps doubly deficient, in that the party manifestly intervenes too much in legal processes and within the social realm there remain massive concerns about violations of basic justice.

Looking back at Chinese legal history, perhaps even the legal history of humankind, it is necessary to recognise that the constant requirement of balancing different law-making sources into a sustainable equilibrium is a task that must of necessity concern all legal systems anywhere in the world. Law everywhere is a social phenomenon that must perforce interact with the respective social field. This was realised and practised under the old Confucian idealistic division of legal labour between informal social justice and formal imperial code. This was supposed to bring about appropriate conduct through self-controlled ordering mechanisms, if necessary with a little help, and if not achievable, then maybe by the harsh hand of the executioner, which would be needed to help restore a disturbed balance. This was the beauty of the old model of 'confucianisation of the law'.

Following the collapse of the formal Imperial legal order, but not the main vestiges of Chinese natural law, post-Maoist China has been facing the same conceptual conflicts and tensions that China has forever faced. The ideology of the revolution appears to have deprived the modern Chinese legal system of the facility to fall back on the Confucianised value systems of Chinese culture and has thus, officially, eliminated a key element in the triangular interaction pattern that is, in social reality, still a key fact. There is a crucial mismatch, then, between the official legal rhetoric and the lived social reality of Chinese people today. Hence, law and society need to explore afresh how to find a new strategy of harmonious balancing of different and yet interlocking normative orders within the desired framework of the new socialist order.

The situation-specific need for modern China is therefore to define what socialism actually means in China, and to relate this to concepts of socialist legality and of public interest that may well have been developed elsewhere, for example in South Asian jurisdictions, but which can be applied to Chinese conditions. Given that those public interest concepts are most concerned about accountability of those in power, and thus about the duty of those who govern, rather than their rights and privileges, it appears that this approach might achieve what modern China has desperately wanted to pursue. The fact that those who operate the state's law always tend to form a new ruling class that might not be controllable in the long run has been a major problem that China has sought to eliminate through various campaigns from time to time, but probably cannot ever solve. Maybe this is simply a problem that can never be solved, because how do you grasp an ideal balance forever? But one can try to create conditions that support sustainable balances, as traditional Asian and African legal systems have done for millennia. At present, China seems to be pursuing this goal by focusing on economic growth and development.

The second, equally tricky issue is to what extent traditional, even 'religious' morality and ethics, rather than modern socialist value systems, can be the foundation for a socialist order. The critically relevant question for the reconstruction of a modern socialist Chinese society and legal system with culture-specific characteristics is therefore how to remodel the value systems operating among Chinese people today so as to harmonise them with the desired norms of socialism. This means, however, that state-made law has to give up its claim to be able to dictate to society. Both need to learn to interact, and to listen to each other in order to find a *modus vivendi* that contains enough supervisory mechanisms for both to control each other. This is the critical socio-legal challenge for modern communist China, a lesson from ancient China that was somehow lost in the turmoils of the Republican era, the later Communist revolutions and certainly the Cultural Revolution. This is, in principle, no different from the challenge for modern India, for innumerable African countries and, despite the outwardly different discourse because of the rhetoric of religion, for the Islamic countries of the world. It is, indeed, a universal legal challenge, with many different culture-specific variants, for it is a myth that Western laws govern the social field to the exclusion of all other law-founding elements.

The study of Chinese legal history demonstrates therefore that the apparent conflict between Confucian tradition and modern socialism is not necessarily based on a conceptual contradiction, and is not difficult to resolve, provided one recognises and accepts that tradition can be modern and that law can take different forms and makes different inputs into a pluralistic whole. There is plenty of evidence from China to the effect that selfish behaviour which would have been criticised under Confucian ethics is now similarly objected to as anti-social and 'bourgeois' (Palmer, 1986–7: 43, cited further below). Lubman (1995: 18) clearly demonstrates that the complaint that there is no law in China refers to government lawlessness and abuses of the law by conceited party officials, not the absence of law itself. As other commentators have highlighted,[129] abuses of the law by the Party and by corrupt pompous officials, exactly those people whom Mao found it appropriate to purge from time to time, continue to pose a risk to justice, since the modern Chinese system, so far, 'gives no democratic safeguards against the subversion of the system through political

---

[129] See especially Bonavia (1982: 152–72) with insightful comments, Lubman (1995) and Palmer (1992b: 72).

coercion or simple unfairness' (Bonavia, 1982: 172). The problem is not the lack of democracy, which superimposes a Western discourse and agenda; the basic threat is the lack of plurality-conscious balance between the three constituent elements of law within modern China. If modern Chinese leaders talk about socialism but practise private enrichment, while telling their people to adhere to the party's value system and to renounce private ambitions in favour of socialist goals, they are doing exactly the same as African leaders who preach African values to their people but abuse their version of the modern law (chapter 6, section 6.6). This is a truly universal human predicament.

When it comes to modern China's struggles over such questions, some of the literature seems helpful to understand the predicament of lacking plurality-consciousness. Several older commentators emphasised that rebuilding modern socialist China is an enormous task which cannot be achieved overnight, and cannot be expected to yield perfect results. Much earlier, Bodde (1954: 54) discussed the long-term impact of confucianisation on China's methods of governance:

> The Confucian theory that has since prevailed has been democratic in the sense that it has consistently emphasized the ideal of government *for* the people, has tried to counter absolutism by the weight of a morally-educated non-hereditary bureaucracy, and has sanctioned occasional political change as an escape from tyranny. It has been undemocratic, however, in the sense that it has never recognized the need of government *by* the people as a whole, has always regarded such government as the particular preserve of a small ruling élite, and has sanctioned political change only in terms of shifting personalities, not of basic change in the social and political order.

This combination of seeking a more or less codified system of official rule, while leaving most matters of conduct to the individual within specific social contexts was only to some extent disrupted by the communist revolution, as more commentators now realise. Bodde and Morris (1967: 28) wisely noted that it would be strange 'if legalism did not leave a lasting mark on law', but did not take this matter beyond the imperial system. Interestingly, McAleavy (1968a: 128) stated that it was impossible to ascertain to what extent old customary traditions survived in communist China, but customary traditions had prepared the country well for the road it had chosen to follow. McAleavy (1968a: 128–9) explained:

> The cardinal principle of the Confucian system was that society is built upon the notion not of rights but of duties, and although prior to 1949 this doctrine was impugned by 'progressives' of every hue, it accords admirably with Maoism in action, and indeed with the ideology of the Cultural Revolution. The Confucian aversion to litigation found an echo, before 1949, in the Communist courts' refusal to hear civil cases until arbitration had been attempted, and although this is no longer the rule, there is the strongest

pressure to submit to arbitration first, and in China now law is studied only as a subsidiary branch of administration. Legal knowledge is no more essential for judicial office than it was in Ch'ing times. Lawyers in private practice have almost disappeared. Defence 'counsel' are usually laymen.

Such observations, made during the Cultural Revolution, are much more than speculation from a safe distance, they subtly reflect the traditional Chinese approach of distrust of positivist law-making and internalised reliance on a system of duties. The conceptual input of the social sphere in traditional China is not, however, discussed in sufficient depth by most legal authors, showing the limitations of legocentric methodologies, which do not produce a comprehensive enough picture of legal reality 'on the ground'. Chen (1998: 37) comments, from a legal perspective which takes account of other factors, on the scope for legal development in China:

> [I]t must constantly be borne in mind that it is a grand and laborious project of which only the early beginnings have been seen. A legal system, and, in particular, those elements of legal culture and infrastructure which constitute the necessary conditions for the effective operation of laws, are not something which can be established and perfected in a decade, or even in a generation's time. So a long uphill journey still lies ahead. At present, the PRC legal system suffers from a number of major problems and limitations, such as the shortage of trained legal personnel, the short history of legal system building and hence lack of experience and tradition, the past habit on the part of law-enforcement official of not paying attention to the law, the dominance of the Party apparatus over the state, and the Party's unwillingness to subject itself to the supremacy and autonomy of the law.

Such thoughtful comments indicate that old problems as well as new interferences in the smooth operation of a balanced coordination between the spheres of religion and worldview, society, and the state are making themselves felt. Chen (1998: 37–8) emphasises practicalities such as the permanent shortage of trained legal personnel and thus highlights elements of practical legal concern, as most lawyers have tended to do. However, in his final analysis, Chen (1998: 38) turns to important conceptual issues:

> Cultural and ideological obstacles to the strengthening of the legal system are also not easy to overcome. The traditional Chinese approach to law has already been mentioned. . . Marxist-Leninist ideology converges with Confucianism in a sense: they share a common distrust of or lack of respect for the rule of law. Many legal textbooks in China today still portray, and many officials still regard, law as an instrument for class rule, and law in the socialist society – before social evolution into the classless communist society of the distant future – as a tool for the dictatorship of the proletariat and for suppression of the enemies of socialism. Within such a framework of thought, the idea of law as a vehicle for enshrining the individual's rights and human dignity will take time to mature.

This vision of a classless society is remarkably similar to the 'Western' idealised society of the future in which everybody is supposed to be equal in terms of human rights. Thus, at one level of debate, the issue of differential statuses continues to occupy analysts and will in all likelihood remain a major issue in the global arena of legal debates, where Western-dominated agenda and concerns continue to attract most of the attention. The same will go for the international commercial issues, whose needs in a globalised environment cannot be denied. While political economists have long been worried about the identity and integrity of China as an economic superpower (Goodman and Segal, 1994), more recent studies (e.g. Chao and Dickson, 2001) still skirt vaguely around the issues that the present study seeks to address and do not discuss legal policies in depth.

In view of the pressing needs of day-to-day co-existence between hundreds of millions of citizens and the central state, massive economic development and the resulting hypes, as well as emerging problems over environmental pollution and other 'big issues', we are distracted and our views are clouded about deeper analysis of current Chinese legal developments. The need for balancing the three competing law-making forces that the present globally focused comparative analysis has identified as critical remains a major challenge for China's safe future. We have seen that, within the framework of an interdisciplinary plurality-conscious legal model, it is not possible to simply throw out religion or questions of worldview as irrelevant or immaterial. In the current process of restructuring laws in China, it needs to be realised that socialism is also a worldview and a form of natural law. The supposedly obvious conceptual incompatibility of socialism and whatever traditional 'religion' the analyst may imagine cannot wipe away the reality of intense intellectual tension and debates.[130]

Some of these are brought out by He (1995: 145) who emphasises that '[a] controversial issue in the re-invention of national identity was how to assess Confucian tradition, previously conceived by many as the core marker of Chinese identity'. While one would not expect any agreement over such critical issues, there is much evidence from various quarters to the effect that post-1979 ideological restructuring in China does not involve a total refusal of Confucian principles and values, but their redefinition and re-evaluation within the overarching framework of China's socialism, which has outwardly become the dominant legal norm. This is one reason why China proudly acknowledged that it operated a form of socialism with Chinese characteristics, rather than copying

---

[130] An interesting discussion about how Confucian teaching was perceived during the 1970s is found in von Senger (1983). Evers (1989) reports that in March that year a leading paper in Beijing declared in headlines that religion and socialism were irreconcilable. The fact that the matter was debated publicly at all is seen by Evers (1989: 50) as an indication that the modern state recognises that there are some elements of traditional culture which are useful for the reconstruction of the modern socialist system.

the Russians or a Western model. Along the same lines, post-Maoist China has probably begun to rediscover the usefulness of indigenous cultural traditions for the legal reconstruction process.[131] However, instead of proclaiming a new confucianisation of law, which would be politically and ideologically unacceptable, like talking of 'Asian values' only to be derided (Peerenboom, 2004: x), we find that post-Maoist China has embarked on a silent socialisation of Confucianism or, put the other way round, a quiet re-confucianisation of Chinese socialism in the shadow of multiple revolutions. This largely invisible indigenisation of the outwardly modern legal structures that China has been producing, more for its own internal consumption than to show the world, might be seen as a postmodern plurality-conscious reconstruction akin to what is happening in India (chapter 4, sections 4.9 and 4.10).

While such a conceptual analysis cannot expect to receive universal agreement or approval, given the contentious nature of the subject and the many ideological issues involved, there is much evidence to support such a finding. For example, it is quite significant that the negative impact of the Cultural Revolution, during which any disagreeable form of action or behaviour could be branded as 'counter-revolutionary', giving rise to punishments of extreme proportions, has not led to a different strategy of dealing with disagreeable behaviour in the post-1979 period. Palmer (1986–7: 43) reports that 'a family member who places undue emphasis on her or his legal rights *vis-à-vis* other members is considered to be acting in a manner typical of the "bourgeoisie"', and is hence likely to be forced, for example in a situation of breakdown of marriage, to take a course of action that accords with the new socialist value system. But that purportedly new value system, the new 'general models of correct conduct' (p. 42), cannot be said to be new; it is merely an ideologically redefined variant of the old social order. In this context, the requirement of mediation achieves utmost relevance. Zweigert and Kötz (1998: 293) noted:

> Mediation and compromise, the traditional method of resolving disputes, are still used by the state itself: countless people's arbitral committees and other similar bodies have been set up and the courts have been told that in all suitable cases they should either seek compromise themselves or remit the matter for this purpose to one of the bodies mentioned.

Research on social control and criminal law in China shows that, in the predominantly rural environment of China, informal social control mechanisms retain a most important position (Rausch, 1987: 40). Preservation of honour and 'face' count heavily within the social environment (p. 43) and the walls of silence are high when it comes to letting lapses reach wider publicity. All of this points to the continuing critical importance of individually and locally

---

[131] This matches India's rediscovery of the usefulness of the family as a social welfare institution (Menski, 2001), which is also confirmed by Chinese evidence.

self-controlled ordering mechanisms. The same image appears from important research during the past two decades on extra-judicial mediation in China,[132] linked to questions about family law,[133] women and reproduction,[134] and criminal law (Ainsley, 1986), all of which confirm in several ways that the co-existing continuities and discontinuities which Murphey (1967: 313) identified long ago have remained a core element of modern Chinese law.[135] This ambivalent scenario reflects an internal contradiction of concepts, principles and practice which, in socio-legal reality, needs to be, and can be, harmonised. A powerful indication of plurality-conscious harmonisation is that family law in modern China has been used 'to reshape the family in order to make it more consistent with the new economic and social orders being created in the era of reform' (Palmer, 1995: 110). However, this is patently more difficult than positivist law-making would like and 'it is clear that in several significant respects the new legislation on the family has been very ineffective and failed to produce desired changes in social practice. As a result, the rapidly evolving system of family law sometimes gives the appearance of being out of control.'[136]

To a large extent, therefore, modern socialist China has not escaped the universal predicament that law-making is not an activity that can be exercised by one single actor to the exclusion of all others. The people may need the state to provide a legal framework for human co-existence, but the state also needs the active support of all members of society to make life easier for everyone and to provide a postmodern framework of social welfare that does not burden the state's coffers.[137] It is an ancient Chinese lesson of Legalism (as it is of 'pure'

---

[132] See Palmer (1987b; 1989b; 1991) on extra-judicial mediation as the preferred form of handling civil actions.

[133] Palmer (1986: 2) analyses China's adoption law and indicates efforts by the state to re-order certain aspects of family and household life so that the domestic unit might play an even more important role in welfare matters. On child law, see Palmer (1992a). Palmer (1996: 155) confirms that '[i]n the post-Mao years the family has re-emerged as the basic unit in China's development policy, and the authorities have sought both to use and to control the family'.

[134] Palmer (1995) analyses recent extensions of legal protection for the health of mothers and children. On the one-child policy see Bianco and Chang-ming (1988).

[135] On Chinese constitutional law, see Barrett (1983), Weng (1982; 1984) and some articles in Chao and Dickson (2001). For a brief overview in relation to commercial laws, see Zheng (1988).

[136] Palmer (1995: 110). As an example, Palmer (1995: 118) notes that '[t]he failure to register marriage remains a problem today' and shows to what extent up to 80 per cent of people in some areas might go to avoid the modern state regulation. In light of such evidence, the Turkish figures for non-registration of marriages (chapter 5, section 5.13) appear almost insignificant.

[137] In the context of adoption law, Palmer (1989a: 373) notes that law-making in modern China has been concerned with 'the direct insertion of extrinsic political norms and values into the law' and demonstrates how the promotion of 'civil adoption' by the state is designed to achieve a dual social welfare objective as 'the state is concerned not only to

positivism) that simple, positivist law-making from above does not function well and is too easily open to abuse. Exploring the basic characteristics of the modern socialist Chinese legal system, Palmer (1992b: 72) highlights that 'the principal "socialist" characteristics of contemporary China's socialist law is party domination of the legal system, and the subordination of law to policy. In the last resort the party is above the law.' These comments were made soon after the Tiananmen Square events of June 1989, and it is no secret that party interference, and abuses of power as a result, have become a grave matter of concern. Palmer (1992b: 72) reports that '[a]mong young and even middle-aged people in legal circles there is widespread cynicism about socialist law', a comment which can be read in various ways.

It remains a fact that modern Chinese law, too, needs at all times to remain conscious of the constant need to maintain a viable balance between freedom of thought and direction from above, between local self-controlled order and bla-tant abuses of such legal plurality, between state intervention and self-healing within social circles. Given the unrealistic resource implications of establishing a fully functional formal legal system that covers all aspects of life for such a huge population, postmodern China is clearly pushed towards experimenting with a compromise between old and new, between local tradition and cen-trally determined ideology, between the higher legal orders inherent in the traditional legal postulates of the population and the claims to superior status of the modern socialist value system. Zweigert and Kötz (1998: 294) argued quite perceptively that China realises that 'its economic development needs a solid legal infrastructure', but added at once that '[i]t is quite another question whether the regulations are affecting people's conduct and are being applied by administrative and judicial authorities in quite the manner which the Western observer takes for granted'.

This leads to the conclusion that any attempts by the state in China to deter-mine people's conduct through imposing codes from above, whether through legislation, the courts or party policy, will always only remain one of several influences on the consciences of individual Chinese people. At the end of the day, whatever lawyers say and write, it is people in their specific socio-cultural environment that determine, in the first place, what kind of conduct they wish to pursue. Drafting new legislation, partly with foreign assistance, is a diffi-cult enterprise (Seidman and Seidman, 1996). There are whole new areas of law in China which we cannot discuss here.[138] The cathartic lessons of the Cultural Revolution in China clearly put a dampener on positivist ambitions of comprehensive law-making along newly configured legalist lines. Given the

pass on to the family the costs of furnishing care for needy children but also to impose on adopted children who have matured into adults the obligation to support their ageing adoptant parents' (pp. 375–6). For India's comparable technique of creating a sustainable social welfare system see Menski (2001).

[138] On environmental law, see Palmer (1999).

continuing, strong foundations of Confucianist and other indigenous perceptions about what is right and wrong, any form of state law in modern China will
continue to face significant limits when it comes to the implementation and
effectiveness of rules that Chinese natural law in all its diverse manifestations
does not accept. The Asian and African legal message to the world, that constant
balancing and equilibrium are always required, is as valid as ever. China may be
perceived as a threat, given the rise of Chinese power (Huntington, 1998: 13),
but it seems well advanced today in finding its own, culture-specific security in a
plurality-conscious process of balancing inherently conflicting and competing
law-making sources.

CONCLUSION: TOWARDS GLOBAL LEGAL REALISM

Building on earlier pluralist models, this study began life in its first edition as an elaborate argument for greater recognition of socio-cultural factors in relation to law and global legal analysis. In its revised incarnation, this argument has been enlarged and modified to include more explicit emphasis on the need to perceive all law as constantly changing and inherently dynamic processes rather than merely a more or less static collection of rules. While law is about rules, it is also about their immensely diverse application in human societies. Consequently, the present study developed in Part I an interactive triangular model of law (chapter 3, section 3.8) centred on legal pluralism as a complex, constantly contested amalgam of state law, values/ethics/religion and socio-cultural norms. Analysis of the legal systems of Asia and Africa strongly confirmed the global presence of such simmering conflicts and tensions in various culture-specific manifestations.

One major dilemma exposed through such pluralist perspectives is that law can probably never fully satisfy all expectations.[1] Law everywhere is constantly involved in negotiation, over time and space,[2] so that it becomes virtually impossible to envisage such interactions in graphs on paper, which tend to give static impressions and do not bring out the inherent dynamism and volatility of legal processes. Nevertheless, towards the end of this chapter, a further graphic model is introduced to illustrate the complexity and fluidity of law as a global phenomenon.

Further analytical depth became possible after it was found and acknowledged that the three elements of this triangle broadly match with the familiar major theoretical schools of legal positivism, natural law and historical/socio-legal approaches. Adding a fourth, pluralism-centred dimension to this model of global legal theory, the present study then proceeded to map and analyse different non-Western legal systems in Part II, in particular Hindu law, Muslim law, African laws and Chinese law. It was found that the plurality-conscious model of legal analysis can indeed be applied in myriad scenarios all over the world and thus appears to have global relevance as a useful approach to legal

---

[1] Glenn (2000: 323; 2004: 348) speaks in this context of the indecision of relativism.
[2] The image of legal rules used as bargaining chips (Olivecrona, 1971) proved useful.

realism.[3] The present study argues and demonstrates, therefore, that law is probably everywhere a complex internally plural field involving constant negotiation between its own different, potentially conflicting manifestations *and* other elements from outside the field of law.

But where are the boundaries of law? Determining and defining the wide boundaries of law was not a major aim of this study.[4] The present study confirms that there is simply no universally agreed definition of law and that legal theory, like Wittgenstein's trapped fly in the flybottle, has so far attempted in vain to find an exit route to salvation. Instead, determined efforts were made to understand better how several vastly different approaches to the study of law from all over the world have contributed to conceptualising 'law' itself. Observing that positivists, natural lawyers and socio-legal scholars of various descriptions took remarkably different perspectives of what law meant to them, and, aware that there is no globally agreed definition of law, the working assumption for the present study clearly had to be that law itself is a plural phenomenon.[5] Consequently, law would clearly be more than just a collection of legal rules; to that extent the 'rule-sceptics' around Dworkin (1986) certainly have a point.

The present comparative analysis found that the criticisms of the undeveloped nature and methodology of legal comparisons are fully justified. There is neither a developed methodology for meaningful cross-cultural legal comparison, nor a blueprint for the universal application of such studies. All we have are different theories of law, in many different shades with their own, potentially extremist assumptions about the nature of law and the ways in which it should be applied and studied. None of the existing three major approaches to the study of law by itself will ever be able to explain fully how the plural phenomenon of law works out in reality. Pluralist methodology appears to offer a remedy.

Enlightenment and modernity have clearly played havoc with realistic assessments of what law is all about, permitted the most atrocious aberrations in the name of law, and strangled plurality-conscious legal theory. More recently, newly invigorated, exaggerated claims of modern 'secular' natural law as a guarantor of justice and human rights seem to have committed the same methodological error of proudly asserting their own supremacy, instead of recognising the need for constant dynamic legal interaction of competing elements of law.[6]

---

[3] This provides a clear answer to Twining's (2000: 90) question whether we can ignore Islamic legal theory.

[4] Finding the available terminology too limiting, Allott (1980: viii) distinguished LAW, *Law* and law, a method which evaded deeper exploration of law's internally plural nature, but prepared the ground.

[5] Woodman (1998: 54) endorsed the view that legal pluralism is a fact and is 'a non-taxonomic conception, a continuous variable, just as . . . "law" is', so that the challenge becomes to examine legal pluralism 'in terms of the degrees of legal pluralism present' (p. 54).

[6] Chapter 5 showed that Islamic jurisprudence continues to be troubled by the same predicament, viewing itself as a natural law system that privileges religious authority over all human

Simply asserting that certain values are globally valid and must be followed by all just ends up in various forms of fundamentalism, as Glenn (2000; 2004) rightly warned. This is not an appropriate method to conduct a global legal debate.

From a postmodern legal perspective, while harmonisation of laws remains a practically desirable undertaking, all uniformising approaches that seek to totally wipe out 'the other' appear therefore unrealistic, because they fail to account for the inherent plurality of all law. The present study demonstrates that claims to globalising uniformisation are little more than questionable attempts to privilege one type of law-making, or of law, over all others. Positivist law-making at the international level ultimately seeks to supersede nation states, which themselves have unsuccessfully sought to override and legislate away various local forms of law-making. In reality, local and global elements of law are always involved in visible and invisible dynamic interaction, leading to pluralistic glocalisation rather than uniformising globalisation. New secular natural law ideologies, seeking to place themselves above all other forms of law, even the laws of Gods, merely insist in familiar legocentric (and hence myopic and unrealistic) fashion on the superiority of their own values, which evidently the whole world does not share. Here again, Western hubris and so-called rational superiority attempt to dictate to all 'others' how they should develop their laws, with predictable reactions of opposition or simple silence, which remains a powerful strategy to avoid plurality-conscious negotiation with a participant unwilling to take account of the basic facts of legal pluralism worldwide. Mainstream legal theory, it appears, has yet to learn to negotiate plurality rather than to search for and then dictate idealistic visions. The critical question, at all times, is whether all factors within a particular legal field or scenario have been realistically accounted for in working out a plurality-conscious balance that satisfies the expectations of the people involved in these negotiations *and* basic criteria of justice and equity.[7]

Inventing and using different terms for the various aspects of law has evidently been necessary over time because 'law' itself has always been so plural that lawyers and other people thinking about law were constantly pushed beyond the boundaries of any one discipline to achieve a deeper legal analysis. In that sense, legal theory is of necessity an interdisciplinary enterprise. The voices from Asia and Africa, which this book has sought to make more audible, not only speak vastly different languages, they often react in self-protective and more or less self-contained silence against the relentless pressure to globalise

---

law-making and thus contrasting (or rather, competing) with Western, allegedly secular models.

[7] This needs to be emphasised because history has repeatedly shown that a people may develop (or fail to oppose) a system of rules that is clearly not 'good' for them or for others. But what is good or bad still remains subject to multiple subjectivities.

and to join McWorld.[8] One of the most obvious stumbling blocks for comparative legal studies has been that regional specialists have developed their own conventions about use of language, definitions and the nature of their subject, impacting of necessity on their approaches to 'law' and creating further barriers to cross-cultural comparative communication. Hence the specialists on African laws and on Chinese law, for example, appear to have found virtually no common ground, whereas the respective people in those parts of the world face quite similar legal predicaments. Good governance everywhere is a delicate task that demands vigilance and balance. Whether we express this in images of a blind goddess holding the scales of justice, the old ideal of the doctrine of the golden mean (Feng, 1952/3), or familiar messages about seeking an equilibrium at all times, the messages are all to the same effect: law is internally plural and subject to negotiation.[9]

Today, a Babylon of legal discourse exists, maybe one of the reasons for so much confusion and disagreement over the nature of law itself. As scholars of comparative law and legal theory, we simply do not speak with one voice and have not yet developed an agreed language for discussing law in a global perspective. For various reasons, it appears likely that we will never succeed in finding such agreement.[10] The 'intellectual labyrinth of jurisprudence' (Morrison, 1997: 3) remains deeply puzzling also if one takes a post-positivist perspective of plurality-consciousness. It may well be that no comprehensive legal analysis could ever capture this intrinsically dynamic process in a few words, but we can think about virtually unlimited plurality-consciousness in law in theoretical terms.

However, open recognition of the limitless nature of law as a plural global phenomenon leads allegedly towards an acceptance that 'anything goes'. Hence, radical relativism needs to be rescued from unjustified accusations of unprincipled liberality. But true liberalism in the form of a global 'rule of law' could never be a system of law based on one uniform set of norms.[11] A plurality-conscious analysis needs to be always highly sensitive to the dangers of imposing one's own presumptions and concepts of justice on others, who have equal claims

---

[8] On globalisation and Islam, Arkoun (2000: 180) notes that '[g]lobalization upsets all the known cultural, religious, philosophical and politico-juridical traditions; even modernity that issued from the reason of the Enlightenment does not escape from it', and that '[g]lobalization forces the Europeans themselves to speak of the limits and perverse effects of the reason of the Enlightenment'.

[9] Davis (2005) speaks now of 'intermediate realms of law' in relation to late medieval Indian laws, which indicates growing sophistication of recent comparative legal work.

[10] Morrison (1997: 14) notes that '[p]erhaps there is no limit to the stories we can tell . . . [B]eing human has to do with continual change, with events and projects, with dialogue and interpretation. And with the need to construct structures of orientation; hence the law.'

[11] Indeed, writing on the 'rule of law' indicates that it means vastly different things to different people (Peerenboom, 2003: 324).

to expressing their views and having them tested in the situation-specific cauldron of pluralist legal dynamism. A truly liberal legal order, whether at global or smaller level, right down to the family, must respect expectations that 'the others' are allowed to live their lives as they see fit, in their specific circumstances, and in light of their particular perceptions of what is good and bad, influenced by concerns for a larger common good or public interest. Who are we, at the end of the day, to totally prescribe to others, either as individuals or as groups, how to lead their lives? But who are we, too, as individuals striving for freedom, to insist on total autonomy? At all levels, therefore, the deeper challenge of realistic, plurality-conscious jurisprudence would seem to lie in working out myriad subtle balances between private and public interest.[12] I maintain that we can strive to achieve such balances in a spirit of plurality-consciousness, without having to give up on basic principles such as justice.[13] But we should also remain aware that justice remains normally just 'within reach' (Menski, 1996).[14]

The various historical roots of legal analysis, of course not only in Europe and ancient Greek history, were laid well before nation states took their recent prominent form, and long before international law became fashionable. Naming law primarily as 'rules', 'values', 'ethics', 'social norms' or 'customs', and insisting that some of these are 'legal' and others are not properly legal ('extra-legal') is simply unproductive. There are just too many types of law.[15] I was struck by the cryptic assertion of Dennis Lloyd in 1959,[16] noting that legal positivism 'is not enough' (Freeman, 2001: x) and his realisation that even Bentham and Austin, the fathers of English positivism, 'fully recognised the need to take account of human values and man's social and economic needs' (p. x). This came rather close to acknowledging the triangular structure of law as a global phenomenon as cultivated by the present study, taking account of positive law

---

[12] With reference to ancient Hindu law, Derrett (1968a: 99) highlighted that '[p]ublic opinion, the receptacle of transcendental and mundane ambitions, was the final arbiter: in this sense *dharma* was king even over kings. Public opinion has its own ways, alongside those of law.' Such comments match the Emperor Aśoka's general moral edicts, to the effect that all persons should simply be good (chapter 4, section 4.3) as well as the inherent expectations of central legal concepts like *dharma, shari'a, li,* various African equivalents and modern human rights claims, too.

[13] Twining (2000: 69) points to an overlapping consensus at world level about what constitutes intolerable situations *in other countries* (my emphasis).

[14] A realistic assessment of the lack of perfection shines through the comment of a wise old man of Indian origin with an ambivalent attitude to his own traditions. V. S. Naipaul (in *India Today* of 21 March 2005, p. 29) reminds us that '[w]e must strive to improve things. But we have to learn to live with the idea of imperfection. One kind of imperfection replacing another.'

[15] For a slightly deficient attempt to express this through the image of a 'bran-tub' of traditions see Glenn (2004). Glenn himself notes that traditions are of many different kinds, so the image chosen is not quite suitable.

[16] This is found in the Preface to the first edition of what is now Freeman (2001: vii–xi).

as well as values and social norms, but the argument was immediately fitted into the familiar binary debates about positivist law and moral values, hence dropping society. Maintaining, as a self-professed positivist, that 'there is nothing inconsistent or incompatible with a positivist outlook, in acknowledging the essential role of human values in law and human society (p. x), Lloyd suggested that positivists were merely uncomfortable about accepting 'the logical or practical possibility of establishing a scale of absolute values which govern mankind universally without distinction of time or place' (p. x). Going off into a universality debate relating to values, but ignoring society, this approach could not qualify as plurality-conscious. This example confirms that mainstream lawyers have been mesmerised by the positivism/natural law conundrum and forgot to include societies and cultures in relation to law.

However, the above statements by the forefathers of positivism also amount to a forceful rejection of uniformising claims to legal universality and a defence of the situation-specificity of all law. If that were agreed (which of course it is not), then positivism in itself could not be an enemy of the understanding of law. Rather it is the claim of its own superiority that is the problem of positivist methodology, its proud categorisation of everything that is not 'legal' as 'extra-legal', and its claim to be the only type of law that lawyers should properly be concerned with. It seems that such narrowing claims, enforcing positivist blinkers and shutting out the rest of all law, have indeed been significantly detrimental to the global understanding of the nature of law.

It is evident that politicking over legal terminology has confused legal analysts and encourages new writers to invent yet more terms or phrases. Despite claims to objectivity, legal scholarship has been intensely subjective and political, and polemically denigrating opponents is a much-used technique. In this context, the intriguing notion of 'dirty words' comes up. Law itself is not, in most contexts, a dirty word, though it stands sometimes for wanton abuse of powers as much as for the careful protection of basic rights. But doubts about the qualities of positivism are not infrequent. In 1959, Lloyd suggested in a footnote (Freeman, 2001: xi, n. 12) that '[i]t would almost seem that positivism is a "dirty" word in America, with overtones that it lacks in this country'. Indeed, various approaches in American realism opposed the idea that law can be just state-made rules and processes, isolated from social environments and constant value assessments (chapter 3, section 3.7.1). American protagonists of realist approaches went as far as claiming the invention of a fourth model of jurisprudence (Summers, 1982 and his pragmatic instrumentalism). However, that kind of approach seemed too parochial, asserting an American innovation and advance in this complex field which typically ignored the global dimension and has not been accepted, it appears. Maybe there is something 'dirty' about assertions of domination of any one particular national tradition of legal thought. General legal theory is, by definition, a globally focused enterprise and cannot be confined within national or jurisdictional boundaries. All legal

ven in its particularistic manifestations, is to some extent illustrative of
x global picture, which scholarship has been struggling to understand.
context, more 'dirty words' attract our attention. Discussing the rel-
f jurisprudence, Freeman (2001: 3) states that '[w]hen the first edition
ook appeared in 1959 jurisprudence was still something of a "dirty
nce then, it may be said to have come of age.' Being dirty is here asso-
th being young and unruly, perhaps not respecting established axioms.
e is more to this statement. Historically, it is easy to explain that, in
ial English legal education, with its focus on training lawyers on-the-
sprudence was seen as a superfluous discipline, somewhat a waste of
time. Roughly fifty years later, the intellectual value of studying jurisprudence
seems to have been accepted.[17] But today we are told that legal pluralism is a
dirty word, and that it irritates many lawyers. Is this more than just a familiar
reflection of conservatism in legal education? The currently ongoing slow process of accepting legal pluralism as a central aspect of legal theory is reflected
when Freeman (2001: 919–21) introduces a new, brief section on this topic,
observing (as do many others) that legal pluralism is an integral part of daily
life and that there is everywhere a plurality of legal orders in which state law is
only one player (p. 919). While there is continuing positivist agony over the loss
of pride of place, perhaps 'extra-legal' should now be seen as a dirty word, and
no longer pluralism, and certainly not jurisprudence, as may still have been the
case in the late 1950s. We have clearly moved on. Whether lawyers like this or
not, law itself is an internally pluralistic phenomenon. To fuss over boundaries
and to complain that the picture is getting too messy if we start talking about
pluralism (Tamanaha, 1993) is hardly a constructive academic response to pluralist reality. Paralysis of perspective (Mamdani, 1996: 3) is not only a problem
for analysing African developments.

Global legal realism demands, first of all, liberal inclusion of all potential
claimants under the wide umbrella of 'law' to allow us to test whether these
claimants actually make any contribution to the construction of what, at the
end of the day, we may perceive as 'living law' (Ehrlich, 1936), or, in Stammler's
neo-Kantian terminology of social idealism, as 'right law' (Stone, 1965: 171).
A globally inclusive, legal realist approach which dares to dream about justice
evidently requires much more than standard legal skills, it demands complex
interdisciplinary methodologies. It was no surprise to find that legal education
as currently conducted in most law schools does not prepare young people
adequately for becoming plurality-conscious skilled legal navigators (chapter 1,
sections 1.5 and 1.6).

The present study also found that, because of its multifarious nature, much
of law and particularly many elements of the continuous processes of dynamic

---

[17] Allott (1980: v) still indicates subtly that academics, rather than practising lawyers, are
interested to ask questions about the nature of law.

negotiation remain largely invisible because they take place in the human mind or in distant localities that the legal researcher does not reach. Too focused on positivist ideology and tangible manifestations of law, mainstream legal scholarship has so far failed to include and make visible those various legal elements and processes which have a huge impact on legal construction, but which do not appear as posited law or formal institutions. In particular, the vast field of values and ethics, primarily located in human minds, but also built – however invisibly – into all positive law and all social norms, remains evidently an area of darkness for positive lawyers. Tellingly, they have simply tried to define this particular problem away by claiming that law has little or even nothing to do with morality. We know, not only since Kelsen's intelligent efforts (and his ridiculously innocent protests about his theories being misused) how dangerous that approach has been and continues to be. Pure positivism on its own is simply not a sustainable legal science that could form the basis for a globally valid legal theory.

Comparatively few lawyers have been willing to argue coherently that socio-legal factors are critical to understanding all law, since law always plays itself out in social contexts. Historical school approaches remain tainted by powerful evolutionist paradigms that seem to exclude large regions of the world (chapter 2, section 2.2). Many shutters come down when one begins to talk about society and culture in relation to law, indicating a deliberate refusal to debate the innate plurality of law and to take account of different perspectives in a spirit of constructive engagement. The current unresolved (and probably never-to-be-concluded) debates about 'cultural defence' (Renteln, 2004) offer an indication that entrenched positions have been created from which cohorts of footsoldiers in jurisprudence and many other academic subjects shoot at each other instead of negotiating a plurality-conscious settlement.

However, the present study found significant evidence that even the stalwarts of legal positivism were not as single-mindedly positivist as their later acolytes presumed and wished. Austin would probably protest if he could speak to us today and realised what has been made of his simple axiom that 'law is the command of the sovereign'. Bentham, another giant of legal positivism, we are now told by those who closely study his work, left in his huge body of original writing many references to the recognition of social factors in relation to law. More recently, the so-called pope of legal transplant theorists protested in a telling 'Afterword' (Watson, 1993: 107–18) about his original work of 1974 being misread by those who argued that legal transplants were a magic remedy for legal development. Positivist axioms are not even built on strong steely foundations if the importance of social cement and the varnish of values is not recognised at the same time. But 'inclusive positivism', as we saw in chapter 3, section 3.6, becomes a contradiction in terms.

All of this confirms again that lawyers are often intensely politicised. Many legal scholars, not only various shades of international lawyers (chapter 1, section 1.2.1) and particularly comparative lawyers (chapter 1, section 1.2.2), have become all too willing handmaidens of particular politics, often of their own making. In this context, the prominent positivist and modernist orientation of legal instrumentalism and various schools of thought on social engineering through law have continued to privilege law over all other potential inputs in human development. Social theory has developed as a field of study apart from legal theory, as though the two could be kept separate, and it is often social theorists (e.g. Unger, 1976) who tell us more clearly about law and its predicaments in a plural environment than legal scholars. Some alert legal scholars argue that lawyers need to take more account of 'society' and 'community' (Cotterrell, 2003; Hinz 2003a), but how much impact do such clarion calls have? Becoming a socio-legal scholar is widely perceived as too much of a challenge for most academic lawyers (Cownie, 2004).

The politics of jurisprudence and interdisciplinarity take a yet different turn when lawyers begin to think about values and ethics. Here the same shutters as before come down when one speaks about society and community and their value systems and claims for legal recognition, especially now in ethnic minority contexts (chapter 1, section 1.3). Worse, as soon as one starts to speak of religion, many more blinkers appear. There is a kind of infectious phobia among Western lawyers, and their followers all over the world, of the historically powerful claims of religion as a superior force in human existence and global management. The history of Islamic jurisprudence (chapter 5) demonstrates that taking serious account of religion does not smother plurality-conscious jurisprudential debates. In metropolitan centres, though, ever since the Enlightenment, many lawyers have wanted to believe that law is higher than religion and argue that it can be fenced off by protective legal sheeting that prevents the perceived poison of religious authority from seeping from below into the legal domain. Dominant modernist perceptions of secularism have been entrenched to fight a war against religious terror. The politics of religion and law are worsened by continuing confusions over what we mean by 'secularism'. Perhaps the Indian way of looking at this problem offers some enlightenment to the world (Larson, 2001). It would not be the first time that non-Western wisdom has made a useful global contribution which we are reluctant to accept.

The matter of religion does not stop here, even if most states have become adept at preventing theocracies and theocratic interferences. Religion, like law, is everywhere a human construct. Whether God exists or not, and also which God or gods, is ultimately up to people as individuals and members of groups to decide for themselves, not for legal scholars to dictate to others in positivist fashion. Seen from this perspective, religion is intimately linked to values and ethics, which are in turn linked to specific cultures and social norm systems. Religious law, this study found throughout Asian and African legal systems, is thus a form of natural law in the widest sense. The various manifestations of natural law in Asia and Africa are all culture-specific variations of the systemic interlegality of specific communities, however defined.

Lawyers as educated human beings should know – and do normally know, because they will have their own personal views on such matters – that religion is not an aspect of human life that one can just define away. But, as scholars, people become purposely myopic in order to propound certain theories – Kelsen's 'pure' law theory is the most famous example. Instead of taking account of realism and plurality, modernist hubris has helped to divide the muddy field of law into private and public spheres, encouraging us to think and behave as though religion can be confined to a remote corner plot, an invisible mental space, or the semi-visible sphere of the home, while law claims to dominate the whole field of the public realm and the visible arenas of human activity and regulation. Chiba (1986: v) rightly highlighted that Western legal claims to universality and global validity unreasonably shut out non-Western perspectives. At a global level, this works neither in theory nor in practice. Where are the universally agreed boundaries between private and public, and between visible and invisible realms?

The answer that most lawyers have come up with is that law and religion are not the same thing, and that law has nothing to do with religion and *should* have nothing to do with religion. This is simply legocentrism in action, demanding recognition for law as the central element in the world. The fact that this is a ridiculously unrealistic approach does not appear to bother enough legal scholars, and it does not strike law students unless they are taught to think for themselves instead of being fed positivist axioms. When Twining (2000) diplomatically criticises the ongoing debates among lawyers as petty tribal squabbles with patricidal tendencies, he discloses deep dissatisfaction within legal positivist camps today about their own understanding of the global phenomenon of law. Even in the public sphere, culture-specific and individualised values and ethics are never absent. Atheism is still a religion, even if atheists protest that they wanted to get rid of God. Privileging secularism does not get rid of religion nor its influence, and to wipe out values and ethics seems entirely impossible. Positive law cannot simply eradicate another type of law by passing a statute – a grave statist fallacy critiqued in insightful writing about the limits of law (Allott, 1980).

A plurality-sensitive legal analysis clearly needs natural law input. We can argue about its form, but to deny a place in principle for this element of the conceptual triangle is entirely unrealistic and simply underpins demagogy, but not serious scholarship in any field. However, not all lawyers are positivists, and not all positivists deny a role for natural law – probably so long as it is not religious natural law, because that quickly becomes religious positivism, as our discussion on Islamic law (chapter 5) illustrated at length.

This is where a major impediment to applying a methodology of global legal realism was found in the present study. Western specialists of natural law and the many philosophies they produced over time should have come up with models of law that take account of all relevant aspects of human life and of the whole world. Instead, what has happened is that Western scholarship has rushed ahead to declare itself universal without checking, let alone asking, whether that would be universally acceptable. Above all, Western natural lawyers, almost by universal *ijma* of such scholars, have simply denied the rest of the world the right to have their own natural law theories and approaches. Any glimpses of evidence were measured against Western standards, and quickly dismissed as deficient (Weber, 1972). Current claims of globalising universality are simply one high point of such dictatorial systematic exclusions of the non-European 'other'. These can and must be challenged not only because they are unrealistic in view of glocalisation evidence everywhere, but also because they have been depriving the non-Western world of their own voices in the global chorus of legal theory. That in itself is probably the most important finding of the present study, with huge implications for how we need to research non-Western legal systems in the future.

Most natural lawyers have been and are academic philosophers, often with precious little interest in the realities of day-to-day legal battles. Probably they became philosophers because they did not want to be advocates or barristers, battling over positivist axioms every day, or solicitors, having to deal with people's (or large companies') woes. The resulting studies on natural law from the pens of such theorists are often vastly impressive efforts and flights of imagination, but fail to link sufficiently well with the other two major areas of legal analysis that the present study has identified out of a sea of legal theories, namely legal positivism and historical or socio-legal approaches.

The present study found that, with very few exceptions,[18] natural lawyers have not been able to break out of the magic boundaries erected around their field of expertise. They have remained deficient in reality-consciousness and seriously myopic in relation to plurality-sensitivity. As a result, they often philosophise about justice while forgetting real people and their concerns. Lack of respect for socio-legal analysis by natural law specialists is clearly one reason for the continuing dissatisfaction with so-called new natural law, which apparently needs to be defended (George, 1999) and requires new directions.

Apart from the failure to take society and its legal inputs seriously, something else has happened in the field of natural law which seems to have prevented its theoretical approaches from making the fullest possible contribution to global legal theorising. As noted, ever since the Enlightenment, it is documented that pursuing natural law does not necessarily mean that the scholar has to engage in a religious mission on behalf of one particular religion. Dropping the claim that religious law (and in reality, therefore, a particular religious law, namely

---

[18] I am thinking again particularly of Stammler (chapter 3, section 3.7.2) and his theory of 'right law', which indicates acute awareness of legal pluralism and situation-specificity.

Christian law) was conceptually superior, late medieval natural law theories freed themselves, so we thought, from the shackles of religious domination, as demanded by positivist axioms of modernity. However, as Western natural law scholarship gradually managed to free itself from such religious shackles, and could begin to challenge the claims of any particular religion to superiority over any form of law, eurocentric legal scholarship went to the other extreme. Religious orientation was deleted and virtually banned from the range of acceptable natural law philosophies. Now geophysics and other hidden forces are assumed to rule over all gods, hardly a new thought, but difficult for many people to accept. The result has been that so-called secular values now dominate the field of new natural law, so that we can today argue forever about universal concepts of human rights and international standards of 'justice', while it is evident that all of this might be wonderful to achieve, but is really rather idealistic. Secular dreams and idealising have replaced earlier visions of golden ages and bliss for all, which have been ridiculed unfairly by modernist scholarship (for Africa, see Chanock, 1978: 84).

Legal scholarship has not managed so far to explain convincingly why the values of one particular cultural group in the world should dominate the entire globe. Why is it that so-called Western values and ethics are pushed forward as universal values, when it is manifest that they are not universal values? To go into depth on these kinds of issues would require a different kind of book than the present study. What this study has achieved, though, is to demonstrate in depth that the values and ethics underlying Hindu, Muslim, African and Chinese legal systems are culture-specific and thus all slightly different, even if the same legal issues crop up everywhere and the same human predicaments are shared by all. The present study demonstrated that it is far too simplistic to classify all traditional non-Western legal systems more as cultural constructs than 'proper' legal systems. Further, the absence of positivist law in itself, while counted as a deficiency from eurocentric positivist perspectives, may be seen as a good sign from a non-Western standpoint. It certainly does not mean that there is no law in a particular social environment that the researcher encounters.[19] Global discussions about 'Asian values' illustrate that 'Asian legal systems have historically been given short thrift in studies of comparative law' (Peerenboom, 2003: xiv), while there are legitimate differences in values at stake (p. x). Evidently, the crucial legal input of non-positive laws everywhere in Asia and Africa is seriously undervalued.

Conversely, the positivist legal methodology of focusing on formal laws, such as modern legislation and case law, as it has emerged in ample diversity in non-Western jurisdictions, manages to catch only a glimpse of the respective official

---

[19] This confirms that journalists and our common use of language lack precision and due care in using the term 'lawless' to describe situations on the ground where a state does not appear to control the law.

law. Understanding the co-existing unofficial laws is a challenge that even socio-legal scholars find daunting, because it requires linguistic and cultural expertise and skills that many lawyers simply do not have. But the legal field, as Chiba (1986) so elaborately demonstrated, is not only composed of official and unofficial laws, there are also 'legal postulates' (Chiba, 1986: 6ff.). It seems that these have posed the greatest challenge to global legal scholarship. For eurocentric Western lawyers, such postulates are simply not legal elements and thus not worthy of attention. Whenever they emerge as cultural concepts from within local traditions, now all over the world and not just in the 'East' or 'South', legal scholars have developed skilful means of defining them away as 'extra-legal'.

Such secularity-based approaches achieve two important objectives at once. First, they manage to deny a legitimate place to any non-Western religion. This is not even perceived as discriminatory because we assume that in the West the majority Christian religion has been expelled from the realm of law by secularism. What we do not realise, or simply do not admit, is that by systematically accepting and thereby privileging the unspoken input and continuing infiltrations of Christian thought in Western laws and legal theories, we are closing all doors for a proper understanding of the legal expressions of values and ethics in other parts of the world. Having redefined European legal concepts simply as global legal values rather than culture-specific eurocentric norms, this approach is indeed not permitting others any voice at all in legal theory. The present study seeks to lift that ban and hopes to break the spell that seems cast on understanding the manifestations of legal pluralism in Asia and Africa.

Non-Western legal traditions have therefore faced a complex system of double exclusion from full participation in the arena of global legal theory. As so-called religious legal systems, Islamic and Hindu laws in particular are widely portrayed and dismissed as dangerous rogue elements that need to be reformed and prevented from having any impact on law-making. Manifestations of religion cause remarkable upsets, most visible now in the current Islamic headscarf controversies and their implications on other issues. Unsurprisingly linked to symbolic ethnicity, symbolic religion has become a political tool (Gans, 1994) and affects the identity constructions of whole communities (Modood, 1993). In Europe, we remain nervous about religion as a legal and political force, while in Asia and Africa (and now really all over the world) Muslims and Hindus are learning to make sense of their religious and legal traditions through plurality-sensitive postmodern reconstruction. That such processes do not occur without tensions and may occasionally break out into violence and terror does not justify the closing of minds about the continuing relevance of religious traditions all over the world. These are alternative natural law traditions, and, if we do not learn to accept them, we still have to live with the fact that they exist and deeply influence the lives, and laws, of the majority of humanity.

As the present study demonstrated in depth, so-called religious revivals, perceived as dangerous and negative, must be viewed from a comparative legal perspective as contemporary Asian and African renewals of natural law approaches. For our own good, we need to understand urgently that these are not necessarily just religious. From a non-Western perspective shared by all legal traditions studied in this book, they include every aspect of life, and thus also everything that we see as secular. Holistic approaches to religion effortlessly incorporate all secular aspects of life. Taking a macrocosmic perspective, as Hindu *rita*, Muslim *huqm*, Chinese *tao* and various African concepts all do, involves respecting the relationship between the individual and the global. While elaborately expressed by various cultural traditions, this is hardly ever explained to us by non-Western lawyers because such concepts are perceived as cultural and are so well known in their specific cultural contexts that no explanations are required. Hence, the presupposition of 'once religious, always religious' (Menski, 2002a: 108), which blindly taints all Hindu and Muslim manifestations of law, creates barriers of suspicion that comparative lawyers have been as much unwilling as unable to cross.

When dealing with African and Chinese legal traditions, the threat of religious domination seems far less tangible but is still there. Traditional African religions, barely perceived as properly religious, are presumed not to have the strength to dominate law. But African values remain powerful and make themselves felt everywhere, provided one opens one's eyes to culture-sensitive analysis. The intricate African models of legal balancing of competing sources contribute to legal theory in a significant way.[20] But, at the end of the day, they are not unique and reflect the shared experience of other chthonic peoples. The central challenge for African laws of the future, as the present analysis showed in detail (chapter 6), remains clearly how to make sense of elements of indigenous values and ethics for reconstructing postmodern African laws.

By the time we reached Chinese law (chapter 7), it became evident that there is no case at all for treating Chinese law as a unique example of a legal tradition that is more or less incomparable. Like all laws, it is simply a culture-specific manifestation of a universal phenomenon. Chinese legal scholarship, both Western and indigenous, has evidently become highly skilled in defining away the central role of various Chinese religions, celebrating instead the achievements of a formalised system of laws that did not properly survive into the twentieth century. Today's restructuring of Chinese laws, as secretive as Indian processes of postmodern reconstruction (chapter 4, section 4.10), but under far more intense scrutiny from a suspicious West, labours with the difficulty of how to legitimise culture-specific inputs into postmodern Chinese law without relying explicitly on vocabulary and discourses linked to religion and

---

[20] Forty years ago, Kuper and Kuper (1965: 17) perceptively identified three major potential contributors to legal negotiations in Africa: 'Probably there are many different theories of law in African societies, varying perhaps in their relative emphasis on imperium, tradition, and divine revelation. They have not been much studied in the past.'

Confucian tradition. The impossibility of shutting out culture-specific values and ethics, and the urgent need to inject natural law theorising into current Chinese debates became evident in the concluding sections of chapter 7 above.

What implications do such findings have for further analysis? The realisation and recognition that legal processes of testing plurality-sensitivity are often invisible mental processes rather than adversarial court battles with lawyers and judges involved in formal legal settings shifts the focus of some legal studies into the arenas of psychology and related fields of study.[21] Much law all over the world, as has been known for some time, never takes a formal shape, but legal theory has refused to fully accept this and fails to build such strategic absences properly into legal analyses. A globally valid, plurality-conscious analysis of law simply cannot overlook the predominant invisibility of legal phenomena, which mainly relates to Chiba's (1986) legal postulates. These, he stressed, were not themselves manifested in rules, but were embedded or implanted within the rules of official and unofficial laws. Since the present study includes values and social norms in the expanded definition of 'law', which is clearly more than state-made rules, it is evident that much law could never manifest itself in posited legislation or in courtroom activity. But the matter does not end there. Hidden beneath and embedded within legislation and case law are further layers of values and norms that only a plurality-conscious analysis, such as attempted here, can make visible.

At the same time, law everywhere, not only in Asia and Africa, appears in so many different forms that no study could ever describe it completely. And of course, over time, legal systems change, too. Those who argued that a complete analysis of law is futile therefore have a point, but the present efforts in thinking about law in a global perspective have yielded important results that might clarify why global jurisprudence is such a challenging field of study. Clearly, it remains a central dilemma of general legal theory that it cannot tackle all specificities. It is increasingly recognised today that the need for reflection and the acknowledgment of pluralism invites an endless process of questioning the nature of legal processes. Morrison (1997: 2) notes:

> Once this is apparent, it is obvious that no total or final account of these processes can be authoritatively offered – there could always be another twist to the tale, another item to be considered. All accounts emphasise certain features and neglect others.

The project of general theory can execute its plan of explaining a general phenomenon, in this case opening our eyes to the many levels of plurality that attach to law. However, no theory, as Unger (1976) evidently realised, and

---

[21] For example, a new doctoral study in progress, on why Indian men kill their wives for dowry, despite a legal system that has built up huge deterrent punishments, cannot rely merely on standard legal analysis. All we would find is that the existing law does not work – which we know anyway. But why do certain men kill in such situations?

Morrison (1997) confirms, can realistically claim to make visible all possible scenarios of these never-ending interaction processes. As we blink, there are multiple new scenarios, and, as we move across the world, legal tourism, of which comparative law has been maliciously accused,[22] becomes not a pleasurable timepass, but a painstaking lifelong search for the holy grail of plurality-conscious legal construction. The virtually unlimited options for the chemistry of rule-application, and the various possible processes that this may involve, preclude a finding that this sea of possibilities can ever be exhausted by academic analysis – we will always be surprised and confronted by yet more variants of informal and formal negotiation and application of these interlinking and competing networks of rules.

Such findings concur with Unger (1976), who argued that the ideal of a stable definition of law is impossible because the phenomenon we are trying to grasp is itself not stable. Law as an inherently voluble and fluid thing cannot be captured in words that describe adequately how this fluidity works in practice. Unger (1976: 49) suggests from a social theory perspective that 'law is simply any recurring mode of interaction among individuals and groups, together with the more or less explicit acknowledgment by these groups and individuals that such patterns of interaction produce reciprocal expectations of conduct that ought to be satisfied'. Any theoretical model is therefore limited by the realisation that the constant search for justice and for appropriate solutions in the specific contexts that arise precludes an analytical description that makes sense for all situations. This is, indeed, the dilemma of social science which 'must take a stand on issues of human nature and human knowledge for which no "scientific" elucidation is, or may ever be, available' (Unger, 1976: 267). Identifying that 'there is extraordinary promise as well as danger in the reunion of social study with metaphysics and politics', Unger (1976: 267) seems to say the same as Santos (1995) two decades later in his discussions of 'interlegality', exploring multiple pluralities within law and their constant interaction in often unexpected and unpredictable ways. This is precisely what the present study has also sought to explore, focusing all the time on the internally plural notion of 'law'.

If we cannot put this complexity in adequate words, can one represent law's intrinsic pluralism more elaborately in graphic form? The inevitably plural nature of law was earlier subtly indicated through Chiba's (1989: 180) concept of the 'identity postulate' of every law. This model culminates in a rather hidden global concept of 'legal culture' when Chiba (1989: 180) writes:

> In so far as a legal culture is preserved, a 'basic legal postulate for the people's cultural identity in law,' which I prefer to call the *identity postulate of a legal culture*, must be presupposed as functioning. It guides people in choosing how to reformulate the whole structure of their law, including,

---

[22] Twining (2000: 144) speaks of 'armchair legal tourism'.

among others, the combination of indigenous law and transplanted law, in order to maintain their accommodation to changing circumstances.

This identity postulate as a constantly negotiated central element of a legal culture is at all times closely and directly linked to ethical values, social norms and posited state-made legal rules as facts of human life in their various culture-specific manifestations. This means that law as a global phenomenon is only the same all over the world in that it is everywhere composed of the same basic constituents of ethical values, social norms and state-made rules, but appears in myriad culture-specific variations. This simply confirms the known basic premise that all laws are culture-specific and that legal matters like contract, marriage and murder are universal phenomena that seem to constantly change over time and space.

Beyond identifying three major types of laws created by society, by the state and through values and ethics, the present study, particularly in the applied sections of Part II of this book, demonstrated that all these three elements are in turn plural. In fact, it appears that each of them contains elements of the other two. We thus find a further level of intrinsic deep legal pluralism, which now yields nine visible elements or components of law rather than just three. After the preliminary efforts of chapter 3, section 3.8, it is now possible to illustrate this in a more elaborated graph of the internally plural nature of all three types of law that the present analyses of Asian and African legal systems so richly displayed.

The scheme used is actually quite easy to explain and understand. After all, legal realism is about common sense. To illustrate this model, we give the number 1 to the triangle of society, number 2 to the state, and number 3 to the realm of values and ethics. This sequence implies no intention of ranking or of relative superiority. A major point to make is indeed that it is the constant interaction of all three elements that counts, not primarily their relative power and status. This is why one type of legal theory on its own will not work to explain the intrinsically plural nature of law and only a pluralist analysis as presented here can achieve this.

To introduce the graphic representation of the second level of intrinsic legal plurality below, we start with the laws found in the social realm, because that is where laws are always located. As the present study confirms, there is no society without law, while there may well be less or almost no state law in a particular given local and cultural context. In this mainly social realm, we find rules, norms or inputs in legal negotiation that originate, more or less purely,[23] from within a particular society.[24] These we give the number 11, reflecting the

---

[23] In this intrinsically plural image of law, nothing is perhaps traceable purely to one origin.

[24] This society need of course not be a national society, but can be a small local community or group, perhaps even a clan or family. The precise definition of 'society' or 'community' (Cotterrell, 2004) would appear to depend on the respective identity postulate. If a

fact that all or most elements of this type of law originate from within this triangle. Rules in the realm of society that have been influenced by the presence of a co-existing state law are then given number 12, reflecting their more hybrid nature and the partial influence of state law. On the other side of the central axis in the triangle of society, we then give the number 13 to those social norms and processes that derive some of their validity and force from the sphere of values and ethics. That completes the image of the intrinsically plural nature of the triangle of society. It is evident that this is also the realm of 'culture', but culture is perhaps also intrinsically plural and extends into the realms of the state and of values, too. If that is so, cultural analysis would also benefit from applying plurality-conscious analytical methods.

Next, we move to the triangle of the state. While there may be no visible state in a given legal context, this study found that there would always be some kind of law. So the type of law directly originating from the state may be fairly small and even invisible, or it may be massive formal legislation. Whatever its shape and form, and whatever the precise nature of the state may be,[25] we give the central element of state law the number 22. This reflects the fact that such kinds of state law, which could again take the shape of rules, norms or inputs in negotiation, arise primarily from within this particular triangle. Next, we give number 21 to those kinds of state law that have been influenced by the social realm. We can immediately think of many examples of that kind of law, which in Chiba's (1986) terminology are known as the second type of official law, namely state law that was not really made by the state but accepted by it. The same reasoning can be applied, on the other side of the statist triangle, to those types of state-made law that are influenced by specific values and ethics. These we give number 23, reflecting the input of the third triangle.

We can then move to the triangle of natural law and its pluralistic elaboration. We give number 33 to those types of law originating from within this triangle which owe their origin mainly to inputs germane to this triangle. We then give number 32 to those values and ethical elements, Chiba's (1986) 'legal postulates', which owe most of their existence and form to the presence of the state, or to awareness of the presence of some rule-negotiating power originating from that triangle. We then complete this round by giving number 31 to those values and ethics that seem to owe their shape and form mostly to social inputs, and we are partly back in the wide realm of culture. The image as a whole would then look as shown in Figure 6.

We note that this representation of the intrinsically plural nature of all law can be still further refined. For, the various combinations of figures are still all

particular human group distinguishes itself from another group (or is itself distinguished from others, i.e. is 'ethnic'), we begin to see the emergence of a separate legal order.

[25] This is a problem left for political scientists, but the present study suggests that their field, too, would benefit from deeper plurality-conscious analysis.

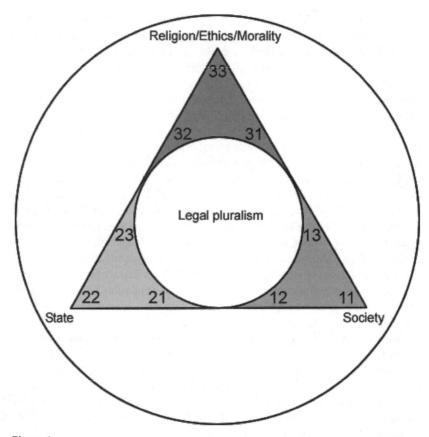

Figure 6

located outside the inner circle of legal pluralism. What happens if they were moved or extended inside the circle? In this case, quite clearly, the intensity of plurality increases, and at the final point of convergence, at the inner central point of the whole edifice, law becomes composed of all these diverse elements and approximates, indeed, an ideal conceptualisation of law. This is where the holy grail of all law appears to be hidden, right in the middle of the pluralist circle within the triangle.

One could use different images here, but they distract perhaps from the necessary realisation that all laws among all people are intrinsically plural as illustrated by the above figure. For example, it may be useful to imagine law as the wood in the tree. While we might not see this wood for the tree, the wood is not just the roots in the ground that provide the life blood for the entire tree (society and its rooted norms), nor just the impressive central pillar of the trunk that holds it all together (state positivism), nor the canopy of the branches as they stretch to the heavens to breathe and absorb the light (natural law and its ideas and ideals). All three together are a form of wood, and all three are required for the tree, as a complex structure of wood, to thrive and grow.

Like no tree is quite the same, so with law. We are therefore, as realist analysts, faced with the familiar dilemma that the universal phenomenon that we are seeking to analyse takes so many different forms that we will forever be busy identifying elements of the whole to make sense of an intrinsically plural totality. At the same time, we have to try and understand specific scenarios to work towards appropriate, justice-conscious solutions. At both levels, the global and the local, and everywhere in between, the challenge is one of constant negotiation, not myopic assertion of this or that perspective. For, the intrinsically plural nature of law always allows many perspectives. In a sense, therefore, all legal theory faces the predicament that emerged perhaps most pointedly from Islamic jurisprudence, where the key concept of *ikhtilaf,* tolerated diversity and recognition of the resulting margin of human error, privileged no single human conclusion on what the ultimate answer might be.

So that is what law is about. With eurocentric, positivistic and modernistic blinkers removed, we are free to explore the legal world in all its complexity and richness and we need not worry about politicking over the nature of law. The law of laws is that law is just law. The task remains to identify what, in any given context, we mean by it. In addition, the constant challenge remains to cultivate respect for the in-built need for negotiation of competing perspectives. Assertion of this or that perspective on its own is not a viable methodology in global legal realism. We can only handle such challenges constructively in a realistic spirit of negotiation with respect for plurality and diversity, rather than fighting over competing visions that seek to totally exclude other perspectives.

REFERENCES

Preface, Introduction, Chapters 1–3 and Conclusion

Alba, Richard and Victor Nee. 2003. *Remaking the American mainstream: Assimilation and contemporary immigration*. Cambridge, MA and London: Harvard University Press.

Allott, Antony N. 1968. 'African law'. In: Derrett, J. D. M. (ed.) *An introduction to legal systems*. London: Sweet & Maxwell, pp. 131–56.

1980. *The limits of law*. London: Butterworths.

Anleu, Sharyn L. Roach. 2000. *Law and social change*. London: Sage.

Arkoun, Mohammed. 2000. 'Present-day Islam between its tradition and globalization'. In: Daftary, Farhad (ed.) *Intellectual traditions in Islam*. London and New York: I. B. Tauris, pp. 179–221.

Ballard, Roger (ed.). 1994. *Desh pardesh: The South Asian presence in Britain*. London: Hurst & Co.

Ballard, Roger. 1996. 'Negotiating race and ethnicity: Exploring the implications of the 1991 census'. Vol. 30 No. 3. *Patterns of Prejudice*, pp. 3–33.

Banakar, Reza and Max Travers (eds.). 2002. *An introduction to law and social theory*. Oxford and Portland, OR: Hart.

Banakas, Efstathios. 2002. 'The contribution of comparative law to the harmonization of European private law'. In: Harding, Andrew and Esin Örücü (eds.) *Comparative law in the 21st century*. London, The Hague and New York: Kluwer, pp. 179–91.

Banks, N. K. Sam. 1999. 'Pedagogy and ideology: Teaching law as if it matters'. Vol. 19 No. 4. *Legal Studies*, pp. 445–67.

Bauman, Z.. 1992. *Intimations of postmodernity*. London: Routledge.

Baxi, Upendra. 1982. *The crisis of the Indian legal system*. Delhi: Vikas.

1986. *Towards a sociology of Indian law*. New Delhi: Satvahan.

2002. *The future of human rights*. New Delhi: Oxford University Press.

Beck, U. 2000. *What is globalization?*. Cambridge: Polity Press.

Bekker, J. C., J. M. T. Labuschagne and L. P. Vorster (eds.). 2002. *Introduction to legal pluralism in South Africa*, Part I, *Customary law*. Durban: Butterworths.

Bell, John. 2002. 'Comparing public law'. In: Harding, Andrew and Esin Örücü (eds.) *Comparative law in the 21st century*. London, The Hague and New York: Kluwer, pp. 235–47.

Bennett, T. W. 2002. 'The conflict of laws'. In: Bekker, J. C., J. M. T. Labuschagne and L. P. Vorster (eds.) *Introduction to legal pluralism in South Africa*, Part I, *Customary law*. Durban: Butterworths, pp. 19–33.

    2004. *Customary law in South Africa*. Lansdowne: Juta and Company.

Berman, Harold J. 1974. *The interaction of law and religion*. London: SCM Press.

Bhattacharjee, A. M. 2003. 'International law in ancient India'. Vol. 1. *Indian Journal of Juridical Sciences*, pp. 89–97.

Bistolfi, Robert and François Zabbal (eds.). 1995. *Islams d'Europe: Intégration ou insertion communautaire?*. Paris: Éditions de l'aube.

Bix, Brian. 1996. *Jurisprudence: Theory and context*. London: Sweet & Maxwell.

Bozeman, Adda B. 1971. *The future of law in a multicultural world*. Princeton: Princeton University Press.

Brundage, James A. 1969. *Medieval canon law and the crusader*. Madison: University of Wisconsin Press.

Butler, W. E. 2003. *Russian law*. 2nd edn. Oxford: Oxford University Press.

Caney, Simon and Peter Jones (eds.). 2001. *Human rights and global diversity*. London and Portland, OR: Frank Cass.

Cass, Deborah Z. 1996. 'Navigating the newstream: Recent critical scholarship in international law'. Vol. 65. *Nordic Journal of International Law*, pp. 341–83.

Chanock, Martin. 1978. 'Neo-traditionalism and the customary law in Malawi'. Vol. 16. *African Studies*, pp. 80–91.

Chatterjee, Hiralal. 1958. *International law and inter-state relations in ancient India*. Calcutta: Firma K. L. Mukhopadhyay.

Cheru, Fantu. 2002. *African renaissance: Roadmaps to the challenge of globalization*. London, New York and Cape Town: Zed Books and David Philip.

Chiba, Masaji. 1984. 'Cultural universality and particularity of jurisprudence'. In: Marasinghe, M. Lakshman and William E. Conklin (eds.) *Essays in third world perspectives in jurisprudence*. Singapore: Malayan Law Journal, pp. 302–26.

    (ed.). 1986. *Asian indigenous law in interaction with received law*. London and New York: KPI.

    1989. *Legal pluralism: Towards a general theory through Japanese legal culture*. Tokyo: Tokai University Press.

    2002. *Legal cultures in human society: A collection of articles and essays*. Tokyo: Shinzansha International.

Cochrane, Allan and John Clarke (eds.). 1993. *Comparing welfare states. Britain in international context*. Milton Keynes: Open University and Sage Publications.

Coleman, Jules L. 2001. *The practice of principle: In defence of a pragmatist approach to legal theory*. Oxford: Oxford University Press.

Collins, Hugh. 1999. *Regulating contracts*. Oxford: Oxford University Press.

Cotterrell, Roger. 1989. *The politics of jurisprudence: A critical introduction to legal philosophy*. London and Edinburgh: Butterworths.

2002. 'Seeking similiarity, appreciating difference: Comparative law and communities'. In: Harding, Andrew and Esin Örücü (eds.) *Comparative law in the 21st century*. London, The Hague and New York: Kluwer, pp. 35–54.

2003. *The politics of jurisprudence: A critical introduction to legal philosophy*. 2nd edn. London: LexisNexis.

2004. 'Law in culture'. Vol. 17 No. 1. *Ratio Juris*, pp. 1–14.

Coulson, Noel J. 1968. 'Islamic law'. In: Derrett, J. D. M. (ed.) *An introduction to legal systems*. London: Sweet & Maxwell, pp. 54–79.

Cowan, Jane K., Marie-Bénédicte Dembour and Richard A. Wilson (eds.). 2001. *Culture and rights. Anthropological perspectives*. Cambridge: Cambridge University Press.

Cownie, Fiona. 2004. *Legal academics: Culture and identities*. Oxford and Portland, OR: Hart.

David, René and John E. C. Brierley. 1978. *Major legal systems in the world today*. 2nd edn. London: Stevens & Sons.

Davies, Howard and David Holdcroft. 1991. *Jurisprudence: Texts and commentary*. London: Butterworths.

Davis, Donald R. Jr. 2005. 'Intermediate realms of law: Corporate groups and rulers in medieval India'. Vol. 48 No. 1. *Journal of the Economic and Social History of the Orient*, pp. 92–117.

De Cruz, Peter. 1999. *Comparative law in a changing world*. 2nd edn. London and Sydney: Cavendish.

2002. 'Legal transplants: Principles and pragmatism in comparative family law'. In: Harding, Andrew and Esin Örücü (eds.) *Comparative law in the 21st century*. London, The Hague and New York: Kluwer, pp. 101-19.

Dean, Meryll (ed.). 2002. *Japanese law: Text, cases and materials*. London: Cavendish.

Dembour, Marie-Bénédicte. 2001. 'Following the movement of a pendulum: Between universalism and relativism'. In: Cowan, Jane K. *et al.* (eds.) *Culture and rights. Anthropological perspectives*. Cambridge: Cambridge University Press, pp. 56–79.

Derrett, J. Duncan M. 1957. *Hindu law past and present*. Calcutta: A. Mukherjee & Co.

1963. *An introduction to modern Hindu law*. London: Oxford University Press.

1968a. 'Hindu law'. In: Derrett, J. D. M. (ed.) *An introduction to legal systems*. London: Sweet & Maxwell, pp. 80–104.

(ed.). 1968b. *An introduction to legal systems*. London: Sweet & Maxwell.

1968c. *Religion, law and the state in India*. London: Faber and Faber.

1970. *A critique of modern Hindu law*. Bombay: N. M. Tripathi.

1977. *Essays in classical and modern Hindu law*, Vol. III, *Anglo-Hindu legal problems*. Leiden: E.J. Brill.

1978. *The death of a marriage law*. New Delhi: Vikas.

1999. 'An Indian metaphor in St John's gospel'. (Third Series) Vol. 9 Part 2. *Journal of the Royal Asiatic Society*, pp. 271–86.

Derrett, J. Duncan M. *et al.* 1979. *Beiträge zu indischem Rechtsdenken.* Wiesbaden: Steiner.

Detmold, M. J. 1984. *The unity of law and morality: A refutation of legal positivism.* London: Routledge & Kegan Paul.

Dhagamwar, Vasudha. 2003. 'Invasion of criminal law by religion, custom and family law'. *Economic and Political Weekly,* 12 April 2003, pp. 1483–92.

Dias, R. W. M. and G. B. J. Hughes. 1957. *Jurisprudence.* London: Butterworths.

Diwan, Paras and Peeyushi Diwan. 1993. *Private international law: Indian and English.* New Delhi: Deep & Deep.

Doherty, J., E. Graham and M. Malek. 1992. *Postmodernism and the social sciences.* London: Macmillan.

Doshi, S. L. 2003. *Modernity, postmodernity and neo-sociological theories.* Jaipur and New Delhi: Rawat.

Drobnig, Ulrich and Sjef von Erp (eds.). 1999. *The use of comparative law by courts.* The Hague: Kluwer.

Dupré, Catherine. 2002. 'The importation of law: A new comparative perspective and the Hungarian Constitutional Court'. In: Harding, Andrew and Esin Örücü (eds.) *Comparative law in the 21st century.* London, The Hague and New York: Kluwer, pp. 267–79.

Dworkin, Ronald M. 1986. *Law's empire.* Cambridge, MA: Harvard University Press.

Edge, Ian (ed.). 2000. *Comparative law in global perspective.* Ardsley, NY: Transnational.

Ehrlich, Eugen. 1913. *Grundlegung der Soziologie des Rechts.* Munich and Leipzig: Duncker & Humblot.

1936. *Fundamental principles of the sociology of law.* Cambridge, MA: Harvard University Press.

Ellis, Stephen and Gerrie Ter Haar. 2004. *Worlds of power: Religious thought and political practice in Africa.* London: Hurst.

Eörsi, Gyula. 1973. 'On the problem of the division of legal systems'. In: Rotondi, M. (ed.) *Inchieste di diritto comparato.* Vol. II. Padua: CEDAM, pp. 179–209.

Farrar, John H. and Anthony M. Dugdale. 1990. *Introduction to legal method.* 3rd edn. London: Sweet & Maxwell.

Feng, Youlan. 1952–3. *A history of Chinese philosophy.* 2nd edn. Princeton: Princeton University Press.

Ferrari, Vincenzo (ed.). 1990. *Developing sociology of law: A world-wide documentary enquiry.* Milan: Dott. A. Giuffrè Editore.

Fikentscher, Wolfgang. 1993. 'Oikos und Polis und die Moral der Bienen: Eine Skizze zu Gemein-und Eigennutz'. In: *Festschrift für Arthur Kaufmann.* Heidelberg: C. F. Müller, pp. 71–80.

1995. *Modes of thought: A study in the anthropology of law and religion.* Tübingen: Mohr Siebeck.

Finnis, John. 1980. *Natural law and natural rights.* Oxford: Clarendon Press.

Fitzpatrick, Peter. 1984. 'Law and societies'. Vol. 22. *Osgoode Hall Law Journal*, pp. 115–38.

Flood, John. 2002. 'Globalisation and law'. In: Banakar, Reza and Max Travers (eds.) *An introduction to law and social theory*. Oxford and Portland, OR: Hart, pp. 311–28.

Foblets, Marie-Claire. 1994. *Les familles maghrébines et la justice en Belgique: Anthropologie juridique et immigration*. Paris: Éditions Karthala.

(ed.). 1998. *Femmes marocaines et conflits familiaux en immigration: Quelles solutions juridiques appropriées?*. Antwerpen-Appeldoorn: Maklu.

Foster, Nicholas. 2002. 'Transmigration and transferability of commercial law in a globalized world'. In: Harding, Andrew and Esin Örücü (eds.) *Comparative law in the 21st century*. London, The Hague and New York: Kluwer, pp. 55–73.

Francis, Andrew M. 2004. 'Out of touch and out of time: Lawyers, their leaders and collective mobility within the legal profession'. Vol. 24 No. 3. *Legal Studies*, pp. 322–48.

Fraser, Derek. 1984. *The evolution of the British welfare state*. 2nd edn. Basingstoke and London: Macmillan Press.

Freeman, M. D. A. 2001. *Lloyd's introduction to jurisprudence*. 7th edn. London: Sweet & Maxwell.

Friedmann, W. 1947. *Legal theory*. London: Steven & Sons.

1967. *Legal theory*. 5th edn. London: Steven & Sons.

Fukuyama, Francis. 1989. 'The end of history?'. Vol. 16. *National Interest*, pp. 3–18.

1992. *The end of history and the last man*. New York: Free Press.

Fuller, Lon Luvois. 1969. *The morality of law*. 2nd revised edn. New Haven and London: Yale University Press.

Funk, David A. 1987. 'Introducing world legal history: Why and how'. Vol. 18 No. 4. *University of Toledo Law Review*, pp. 723–803.

Galanter, Marc. 1981. 'Justice in many rooms: Courts, private ordering and indigenous law'. Vol. 19. *Journal of Legal Pluralism*, pp. 1–47.

1989. *Law and society in modern India*. Delhi: Oxford University Press.

Gans, Herbert J. 1994. 'Symbolic ethnicity and symbolic religiosity: Towards a comparison of ethnic and religious acculturation'. Vol. 17 No. 4. *Ethnic and Racial Studies*, pp. 577–92.

Geertz, Clifford. 1983. *Local knowledge: Further essays in interpretative anthropology*. New York: Basic Books.

George, Robert P. 1999. *In defense of natural law*. Oxford: Oxford University Press.

Giddens, Anthony. 1990. *The consequences of modernity*. Stanford, CA: Stanford University Press.

2000. *The third way and its critics*. Cambridge: Polity Press.

Gierke, Otto. 1950. *Natural law and the theory of society 1500–1800*. Trans. with an introduction by Ernest Barker. Cambridge: Cambridge University Press.

Gilissen, John (ed.). 1971. *Le pluralisme juridique*. Brussels: Editions de l'Université de Bruxelles.

Glendon, M. A. 1977. *State, law and family: Family law in transition in the United States and Western Europe*. New York: North-Holland.

Glenn, H. Patrick. 2000. *Legal traditions of the world: Sustainable diversity in law*. Oxford: Oxford University Press.

2004. *Legal traditions of the world: Sustainable diversity in law*. 2nd edn. Oxford: Oxford University Press.

Graveson, R. H. 1974. *Conflict of laws: Private international law*. 7th edn. London: Sweet & Maxwell.

Griffiths, Anne. 2001. 'Gendering culture: Towards a plural perspective on Kwena women's rights: In: Cowan, Jane K., Marie-Bénédicte Dembour and Richard A. Wilson (eds.) *Culture and rights. Anthropological perspectives*. Cambridge: Cambridge University Press, pp. 102–26.

2002. 'Legal pluralism'. In: Banakar, Reza and Max Travers (eds.) *An introduction to law and social theory*. Oxford and Portland, OR: Hart, pp. 289–310.

Griffiths, John. 1986. 'What is legal pluralism?'. No. 24. *Journal of Legal Pluralism and Unofficial Law*, pp. 1–56.

Guha, Ranajit (ed.). 1982. *Subaltern studies I: Writings on South Asian history and society*. Delhi: Oxford University Press.

Habermas, J. 1974. *Theory and practice*. London: Heinemann.

Hamilton, Carolyn. 1995. *Family, law and religion*. London: Sweet & Maxwell.

Hardiman, David. 2003. *Gandhi in his time and ours: The global legacy of his ideas*. London: Hurst & Co.

Harding, Andrew and Esin Örücü (eds.). 2002. *Comparative law in the 21st century*. London, The Hague and New York: Kluwer.

Harris, D. J. 1991. *Cases and materials on international law*. 4th edn. London: Sweet & Maxwell.

Harris, J. W. 1980. *Legal philosophies*. London: Butterworths.

Harris, Phil. 1988. *An introduction to law*. 3rd edn. London: Weidenfeld and Nicolson.

Hart, H. L. A. 1961. *The concept of law*. Oxford: Clarendon Press.

1994. *The concept of law*. 2nd edn. Oxford: Clarendon.

Hartland, S. 1924. *Primitive law*. London: Methuen.

Held, David, Anthony McGrew, David Goldblatt and Jonathan Perraton. 1999. *Global transformations: Politics, economics and culture*. Cambridge: Polity Press.

Helmholz, Richard H. 1996. *The spirit of classical canon law*. Athens, GA and London: University of Georgia Press.

Hepple, Bob and Erika M. Szyszczak (eds.). 1992. *Discrimination: The limits of law*. London: Cassell.

Hildebrandt, Hans-Juergen (ed.). 1989. *A. H. Post and the anthropology of law: A forgotten pioneeer*. Göttingen: Edition Re.

Hinz, Manfred O. 2003a. 'Jurisprudence and anthropology'. Vol. 26 Nos. 3–4. *Anthropology Southern Africa*, pp. 114–18.

2003b. *Without chiefs there would be no game: Customary law and nature conservation.* Windhoek: Out of Africa.

Hoebel, E. Adamson. 1954. *The law of primitive man: A study in comparative legal dynamics.* Cambridge, MA: Harvard University Press.

Holden, Livia Sorrentino. 2004. *Acting for equity: Women's legal awareness in Hindu customs of divorce and remarriage in central India.* London: SOAS (Unpublished PhD thesis).

Hooker, M. B. 1975. *Legal pluralism: An introduction to colonial and neo-colonial laws.* Oxford: Clarendon.

Hunt, Alan. 1986. 'Jurisprudence, philosophy and legal education – against foundationalism: A response to Neil MacCormick'. Vol. 6 No. 3. *Legal Studies,* pp. 292–302.

Huntington, Samuel P. 1998. *The clash of civilizations and the remaking of world order.* London: Touchstone Books.

Igarashi, Kiyoshi. 1990. *Einführung in das japanische Recht.* Darmstadt: Wissenschaftliche Buchgesellschaft.

Indian Law Institute. 1971. *An introduction to the study of comparative law.* Bombay: N. M. Tripathi.

Iyer, V. R. Krishna. 2004. *Leaves from my personal life.* New Delhi: Gyan.

Jones, J. Walter. 1956. *Historical introduction to the theory of law.* Reprint. Oxford: Clarendon.

Jones, Peter. 2001. 'Human rights and diverse cultures: Continuity or discontinuity?'. In: Caney, Simon and Peter Jones (eds.) *Human rights and global diversity.* London and Portland, OR: Frank Cass, pp. 27–50.

Jones, Richard and Gnanapala Welhengama. 2000. *Ethnic minorities in English law.* Stoke-on-Trent: Trentham Books.

Kagan, K. Kahana. 1955. *Three great systems of jurisprudence.* London: Stevens.

Kahn-Freund, Otto. 1974. 'On uses and misuses of comparative law'. Vol. 37 No. 1. *Modern Law Review,* pp. 1–20.

Kant, Immanuel. 1965. *The metaphysical elements of justice.* (trans. by John Ladd). New York and London: Macmillan and Collier Macmillan.

Kantowsky, Detlef (ed.). 1986. *Recent research on Max Weber's studies of Hinduism.* Munich, Cologne and London: Weltforum Verlag.

Kelly, J. M. 1992. *A short history of Western legal theory.* Oxford: Clarendon Press.

Kelsen, Hans. 1970. *Pure theory of law.* (trans. from the 2nd revised and enlarged German edn.). Berkeley: University of California Press.

Küng, Hans and Karl-Josef Kuschel (eds.). 1993. *A global ethic: The declaration of the parliament of the world's religions.* London: SCM Press.

Kuper, Hilda and Leo Kuper (eds.). 1965. *African law: Adaptation and development.* Berkeley and Los Angeles: University of California Press.

Lampe, Ernst-Joachim (ed.). 1995. *Rechtsgleichheit und Rechtspluralismus.* Baden-Baden: Nomos.

Larson, Gerald James (ed.). 2001. *Religion and personal law in secular India: A call to judgment.* Bloomington and Indianapolis: Indiana University Press.

Launay, Robert. 2001. 'Montesquieu: The specter of despotism and the origins of comparative law'. In: Riles, Annelise (ed.) *Rethinking the masters of comparative law.* Oxford and Portland, OR: Hart, pp. 22–38.

Legrand, Pierre. 1996. 'How to compare now'. Vol. 16 No. 2. *Legal Studies,* pp. 232–42.

1997a. 'Against a European Civil Code'. Vol. 60. *Modern Law Review,* pp. 44–63.

1997b. 'The impossibility of "legal transplants"'. Vol. 4. *Maastricht Journal of European and Comparative Law,* pp. 111–24.

Llewellyn, Karl N. and E. Adamson Hoebel. 1941. *The Cheyenne way. Conflict and case law in primitive jurisprudence.* Norman: University of Oklahoma Press.

Lloyd, Dennis. 1991. *The idea of law.* 8th edn. London: Penguin Books.

Lyotard, Jean-François. 1984. *The postmodern condition: A report on knowledge.* Manchester: Manchester University Press.

Macdonald, Ian A. and Frances Webber. 2001. *Macdonald's immigration law and practice.* 5th edn. London: Butterworths.

Mahajan, Gurpreet and Helmut Reifeld (eds.). 2003. *The public and the private: Issues of democratic citizenship.* New Delhi: Sage.

Maine, Henry Sumner. 1861. *Ancient law.* London: John Murray.

Malinowski, Bronislaw. 1926. *Crime and custom in savage society.* London: Kegan Paul.

Mamdani, Mahmood. 1996. *Citizen and subject: Contemporary Africa and the legacy of late colonialism.* Princeton: Princeton University Press.

2004. *Good Muslim, bad Muslim: America, the Cold War and the roots of terror.* New York: Pantheon.

Marcus, George E. M. and Michael M. J. Fisher. 1986. *Anthropology as cultural critique: An experimental moment in human sciences.* Chicago: University of Chicago Press.

Mattei, Ugo. 2001. 'The comparative jurisprudence of Schlesinger and Sacco: A study in legal influence'. In: Riles, Annelise (ed.) *Rethinking the masters of comparative law.* Oxford and Portland, OR: Hart, pp. 238–56.

May, Reinhard. 1985. *Law and society East and West: Dharma, li and nomos, their contribution to thought and to life.* Stuttgart: Franz Steiner Verlag.

McAleavy, Henry. 1968. 'Chinese law'. In: Derrett, J. D. M. (ed.) *An introduction to legal systems.* London: Sweet & Maxwell, pp. 105–30.

McDonald, Angus. 2002. 'Hundred headless Europe: Comparison, constitution and culture'. In: Harding, Andrew and Esin Örücü (eds.) *Comparative law in the 21st century.* London, The Hague and New York: Kluwer, pp. 193–209.

Melissaris, Emmanuel. 2004. 'The more the merrier? A new take on legal pluralism'. Vol. 13 No. 1. *Social and Legal Studies,* pp. 57–79.

Menon, N. R. Madhava (ed.). 1983. *Legal education in India*. New Delhi: Bar Council of India Trust.

Menski, Werner. 1987. 'Legal pluralism in the Hindu marriage'. In: Burghart, Richard (ed.) *Hinduism in Great Britain: The perpetuation of religion in an alien cultural milieu*. London and New York: Tavistock, pp. 180–200.

1988. 'English family law and ethnic laws in Britain'. 1988(1) *Kerala Law Times*, Journal section, pp. 56–66.

1993. 'Asians in Britain and the question of adaptation to a new legal order: Asian laws in Britain?'. In: Israel, Milton and Narendra K. Wagle (eds.) *Ethnicity, identity, migration: The South Asian context*. Toronto: University of Toronto Press, pp. 238–68.

1996. 'Introduction: The democratisation of justice in India'. In: Singh, Gurjeet, *Law of consumer protection in India: Justice within reach*. New Delhi: Deep & Deep, pp. xxv–liv.

2000. 'Introduction: Ethnic minority studies in English law'. In: Jones, Richard and Gnanapala Welhengama, *Ethnic minorities in English law*. Stoke-on-Trent: Trentham, pp. 1–7.

2001. *Modern Indian family law*. Richmond: Curzon Press.

2002a. 'Hindu law as a "religious" system'. In: Huxley, Andrew (ed.) *Religion, law and tradition: Comparative studies in religious law*. London: RoutledgeCurzon, pp. 108–26.

2002b. 'Immigration and multiculturalism in Britain: New issues in research and policy'. Vol. 12. *KIAPS: Bulletin of Asia-Pacific Studies* (Osaka), pp. 43–66.

2003. *Hindu law: Beyond tradition and modernity*. New Delhi: Oxford University Press.

Merry, Sally Engle. 1988. 'Legal pluralism'. Vol. 22 No. 5. *Law and Society Review*, pp. 869–96.

2001. 'Changing rights, changing culture'. In: Cowan, Jane K., Marie-Bénédicte Dembour and Richard A. Wilson (eds.) *Culture and rights: Anthropological perspectives*. Cambridge: Cambridge University Press, pp. 31–55.

Modood, Tariq. 1993. 'Muslim views on religious identity and racial equality'. Vol. 19 No. 3. *New Community*, pp. 513–19.

Moore, Joanne I. 1999. *Immigrants in courts*. Seattle and London: University of Washington Press.

Moore, Sally Falk. 1978. *Law as process: An anthropological approach*. London: Routledge & Kegan Paul.

1986. *Social facts and fabrications: 'Customary' law on Kilimanjaro, 1880–1980*. Cambridge: Cambridge University Press.

Moran, Mayo. 2003. *Rethinking the reasonable person: An egalitarian reconstruction of the objective standard*. Oxford: Oxford University Press.

Morrison, Wayne. 1997. *Jurisprudence: From the Greeks to post-modernism*. London: Cavendish.

Mungra, G. 1990. *Hindoestaanse gezinnen in Nederland*. Leiden: Faculteit der Sociale Wetenschappen.

Nader, Laura. 1992. 'The anthropological study of law'. In: Sack, Peter and Jonathan Aleck (eds.) *Law and anthropology*. Aldershot: Dartmouth, pp. 3–32.

Nandy, Ashish. 1983. *The intimate enemy: Loss and recovery and self under colonialism*. New Delhi: Oxford University Press.

Nelken, David (ed.). 1997. *Comparing legal cultures*. Aldershot: Dartmouth.

2002. 'Legal transplants and beyond: Of disciplines and metaphors'. In: Harding, Andrew and Esin Örücü (eds.) *Comparative law in the 21st century*. London, The Hague and New York: Kluwer, pp. 19–34.

Nelken, David and Johannes Feest (eds.). 2001. *Adapting legal cultures*. Oxford and Portland, OR: Hart.

Oda, Hiroshi. 1992. *Japanese law*. London: Butterworths.

O'Dair, Richard and Andrew Lewis (eds.). 2001. *Law and religion*. Oxford: Oxford University Press.

Okupa, Effa. 1998. *International bibliography of African customary law*. Hamburg: LIT and International African Institute.

Olivecrona, Karl. 1971. *Law as fact*. 2nd edn. London: Stevens & Co.

Örücü, Esin. 1999. *Critical comparative law: Considering paradoxes for legal systems in transition*. Deventer: Kluwer.

2002. 'Unde venit, quo tendit comparative law?'. In: Harding, Andrew and Esin Örücü (eds.) *Comparative law in the 21st century*. London, The Hague and New York: Kluwer, pp. 1–17.

Parekh, Bhikhu. 2000. *The future of multi-ethnic Britain*. London: Profile Books.

Pathak, R. S. and R. P. Dholakia (eds.). 1992. *International law in transition: Essays in memory of Judge Nagendra Singh*. Dordrecht: Martinus Nijhoff.

Pearl, David. 1981. *Interpersonal conflict of laws in India, Pakistan and Bangladesh*. London and Bombay: Stevens & Sons.

Pearl, David and Werner Menski. 1998. *Muslim family law*. 3rd edn. London: Sweet & Maxwell.

Peerenboom, Randall. 2003. 'The X-files: Past and present portrayals of China's alien legal system'. *Washington University Global Studies Law Review*, pp. 37–95.

(ed.). 2004. *Asian discourses of rule of law: Theories and implementation of rule of law in twelve Asian countries, France and the US*. London and New York: Routledge.

Peters, Anne and Heiner Schwenke. 2000. 'Comparative law beyond postmodernism'. Vol. 49. *International and Comparative Law Quarterly*, pp. 800–34.

Petersen, Hanne and H. Zahle (eds.). 1995. *Legal polycentricity: Consequences of pluralism in law*. Aldershot: Dartmouth.

Podgorecki, Adam and Christopher Whelan (eds.). 1981. *Sociological approaches to law*. London: Croom Helm.

Pospišil, Leopold. 1971. *Anthropology of law: A comparative theory*. New York: Harper & Row.

Poulter, Sebastian. 1986. *English law and ethnic minority customs*. London: Butterworths.

—— 1998. *Ethnicity, law and human rights: The English experience*. Oxford: Clarendon Press.

Rautenbach, Christa and N. M. I. Goolam (eds.). 2002. *Introduction to legal pluralism*, Part II, *Religious legal systems*. Durban: Butterworths.

Raz, Joseph. 1979. *The authority of law: Essays on law and morality*. Oxford: Clarendon Press.

Renteln, Alison Dundes. 1990. *International human rights: Universalism versus relativism*. Newbury Park: Sage.

—— 2004. *Cultural defense*. Delhi: Oxford University Press.

Riles, Annelise (ed.). 2001. *Rethinking the masters of comparative law*. Oxford and Portland, OR: Hart.

Roberts, Simon. 1979. *Order and dispute*. Harmondsworth: Penguin.

Robertson, Robbie T. 1986. *The making of the modern world*. London: Zed Books.

—— 1995. 'Glocalization: Time-space and homogeneity-heterogeneity'. In: Featherstone, M. *et al*. (eds.) *Global modernities*. London: Sage, pp. 25–44.

—— 2003. *The three waves of globalization: A history of a developing global consciousness*. Nova Scotia, London and New York: Fernwood Publishing and Zed Books.

Rohe, Mathias. 2001. *Der Islam – Alltagskonflikte und Lösungen. Rechtliche Perspektiven*. 2nd edn. Freiburg: Herder.

Rosenau, James N. and Hylke Tromp. 1989. *Interdependence and conflict in world politics*. Aldershot: Avebury.

Rouland, Norbert. 1994. *Legal anthropology*. London: Athlone Press.

Rutten, Susan. 1988. *Moslims in de Nederlandse Rechtspraak*. Kampen: Uitgeversmaatschappij J. H. Kok.

Sachdeva, Sanjiv. 1993. *The primary purpose rule in British immigration law*. Stoke-on-Trent: Trentham.

Sack, Peter and Jonathan Aleck (eds.). 1992. *Law and anthropology*. Aldershot: Dartmouth.

Sagade, Jaya. 2005. *Child marriage: Socio-legal and human rights dimensions*. New Delhi: Oxford University Press.

Said, Edward. 1979. *Orientalism*. New York: Vintage.

Sampford, Charles. 1989. *The disorder of law: A critique of legal theory*. New York: Basil Blackwell.

Santos, Boaventura de. 1995. *Toward a new common sense: Law, science and politics in the paradigmatic transition*. London: Routledge.

Sarkar, Benoy Kumar. 1975. *Chinese religion through Hindu eyes. A study in the tendencies of Asiatic mentality*. Delhi: Oriental.

Schnitzer, Adolf F. 1961. *Vergleichende Rechtslehre*. Band I–II. 2nd revised edn. Basel: Verlag für Recht und Gesellschaft AG.

Schoch, M. 1948. *The jurisprudence of interests*. Cambridge, MA: Harvard University Press.

Schott, Rüdiger. 1995. 'Rechtspluralismus und Rechtsgleichheit in den postkolonialen Staaten Afrikas'. In: Lampe, Ernst-Joachim (ed.) *Rechtsgleichheit und Rechtspluralismus*. Baden-Baden: Nomos, pp. 38–71.

Schuster, Liza and John Solomos. 2004. 'Race, immigration and asylum. New Labour's agenda and its consequences'. Vol. 4 No. 2. *Ethnicities*, pp. 267–87.

Schütt-Wetschky, Eberhard. 1997. *Interessenverbände und Staat*. Darmstadt: Wissenschaftliche Buchgesellschaft

Seidman, A. and R. B. Seidman. 1994. *State and law in the development process: Problem solving and institutional change in the third world*. Basingstoke: Macmillan.

1996. 'Drafting legislation for development: Lessons from a Chinese project'. Vol. 44. *American Journal of Comparative Law*, pp. 1–44.

Shah, Prakash. 1994. 'Legal pluralism – British law and possibilities with Muslim ethnic minorities'. Nos. 66/67. *Retfaerd*, pp. 18–33.

2003. 'Attitudes to polygamy in English law'. Vol. 52. *International and Comparative Law Quarterly*, pp. 369–400.

Shah-Kazemi, Sonia Nrîn. 2001. *Untying the knot: Muslim women, divorce and the Shariah*. London: Nuffield Foundation.

Shears, Peter and Graham Stephenson. 1996. *James' introduction to English law*. 13th edn. London: Butterworths.

Sheleff, Leon. 1999. *The future of tradition: Customary law, common law and legal pluralism*. London and Portland, OR: Frank Cass.

Singh, Mool. 1993. *Justice Iyer's jurisconscience*. Jaipur: RBSA.

Smart, Carol. 1989. *Feminism and the power of law*. London and New York: Routledge.

Smith, M. G. 1974. *Corporations and society*. London: Duckworth.

Steiner, H. J. and P. Alston. 2000. *International human rights in context: Law, politics, morals*. 2nd edn. Oxford: Clarendon Press.

Stone, Julius. 1965. *Human law and human justice*. Stanford, CA: Stanford University Press.

Summers, Robert S. (ed.). 1968. *Essays in legal philosophy*. Oxford: Basil Blackwell.

(ed.). 1971. *More essays in legal philosophy: General assessments of legal philosophies*. Oxford: Basil Blackwell.

1982. *Instrumentalism and American legal theory*. Ithaca and London: Cornell University Press,

2000. *Essays in legal theory*. Dordrecht: Kluwer.

Tamanaha, Brian Z. 1993. 'The folly of the "social scientific" concept of legal pluralism'. Vol. 20 No. 2. *Journal of Law and Society*, pp. 192–217.

2001. *A general jurisprudence of law and society*. Oxford: Oxford University Press.

Tan, Yock Lin. 1993. *Conflicts issues in family and succession law*. Singapore: Butterworths.

Teubner, G. 1998. 'Legal irritants: Good faith in British law, or how unifying law ends up in new divergences'. Vol. 61. *Modern Law Review*, pp. 11–32.

Tharoor, Shashi. 2000. *India: From midnight to the millennium*. New Delhi: Penguin.

Trubek, D. and Marc Galanter. 1974. 'Scholars in self-estrangement: Some reflections on the crisis in law and development studies in the United States'. Vol. 4. *Wisconsin Law Review*, pp. 1062–1102.

Twining, William. 2000. *Globalisation and legal theory*. London: Butterworths.

Unger, Roberto Mangabeira. 1976. *Law in modern society: Toward a criticism of social theory*. New York: Free Press.

Varga, Csaba (ed.). 1992. *Comparative legal cultures*. Aldershot: Dartmouth.

Vyas, Yash *et al.* (eds.). 1994. *Law and development in the third world*. Nairobi: Faculty of Law.

Waluchow, Wilfrid J. 1994. *Inclusive legal positivism*. Oxford: Clarendon Press.

2000. 'Authority and the practical difference thesis: A defense of inclusive legal positivism'. Vol. 6. *Legal Theory*, pp. 45–81.

Waters, Malcolm. 1995. *Globalization*. London: Routledge.

Watson, Alan. 1974. *Legal transplants: An approach to comparative law*. Edinburgh: Scottish Academic Press.

1993. *Legal transplants: An approach to comparative law*. 2nd edn. Athens, GA: University of Georgia Press.

Weber, Max. 1954. *Max Weber on law in economy and society* (ed. by Max Rheinstein). Cambridge, MA: Harvard University Press.

1968. *The religion of China: Confucianism and Taoism*. New York: Free Press and Collier-Macmillan.

1972. *Gesammelte Aufsätze zur Religionssoziologie II: Hinduismus und Buddhismus*. Tübingen: J. C. B. Mohr (Paul Siebeck).

Werbner, Pnina. 2004. 'The predicament of diaspora and millennial Islam: Reflections on September 11, 2001'. Vol. 4 No. 4. *Ethnicities*, pp. 451–76.

White, Ahmed A. 2001. 'Max Weber and the uncertainties of categorical comparative law'. In: Riles, Annelise (ed.) *Rethinking the masters of comparative law*. Oxford and Portland, OR: Hart, pp. 40–57.

Woodman, Gordon. 1988. 'Unification or continuing pluralism in family law in Anglophone Africa: Past experience, present realities, and future possibilities'. Vol. 4 No. 2. *Lesotho Law Journal*, pp. 33–79.

1998. 'Ideological combat and social observations: Recent debate about legal pluralism'. Vol. 42. *Journal of Legal Pluralism and Unofficial Law*, pp. 21–59.

Yilmaz, Ihsan. 1999. *Dynamic pluralism and the reconstruction of unofficial Muslim laws in England, Turkey and Pakistan*. London: SOAS. (PhD thesis).

2005. *Muslim laws, politics and society in modern nation states: Dynamic legal pluralisms in England, Turkey and Pakistan*. Aldershot: Ashgate.

Zweigert, Konrad and Hein Koetz. 1984. *Einführüng in die Rechtsvergleichung auf dem Gebiete des Privatrechts*, Band I, *Grundlagen*. 2nd edn. Tübingen: J. C. B. Mohr.

—— 1998. *An introduction to comparative law*. Trans. by Tony Weir. 3rd edn. Oxford: Clarendon Press.

Chapter 4, Hindu law

Agarwal, Bina. 1994. *A field of one's own: Gender and land rights in South Asia*. Cambridge: Cambridge University Press.

Agarwala, R. K. 2003. *Hindu law*. 21st edn. Allahabad: Central Law Agency.

Agnes, Flavia. 2000. *Law and gender inequality: The politics of women's rights in India*. New Delhi: Oxford University Press.

Ahuja, Sangeeta. 1997. *People, law and justice: Casebook on public interest litigation*, Vols. 1 and 2. London: Sangam Books.

Allott, Antony N. 1980. *The limits of law*. London: Butterworths.

Anagol-McGinn, Padma. 1992. 'The Age of Consent Act [1891] reconsidered: Women's perspectives and participation in the child marriage controversy in India'. Vol. 12 No. 2. *South Asia Research*, pp. 100–18.

Anand, A. S. 2002. *Justice for women: Concerns and expressions*. New Delhi: Universal.

Arthaśāstra, see Kangle.

Āśvalāyanagrihyasūtra, see Sharma.

Austin, Granville. 1966. *The Indian Constitution: Cornerstone of a nation*. Oxford: Oxford University Press.

Baird, Robert. D. (ed.). 1989. *Religion in modern India*. 2nd revised edn. New Delhi: Manohar.

—— (ed.). 1993. *Religion and law in independent India*. New Delhi: Manohar.

Bakshi, P. M. 1999. *Public interest litigations*. New Delhi: Ashoka Law House.

Banerjee, Tapas Kumar. 1962. *History of Indian criminal law*. Calcutta: Riddhi.

Banerjee, A. C. 1984. *English law in India*. New Delhi: Abhinav.

Basu, Srimathi. 2001. *She comes to take her rights: Indian women, property and propriety*. New Delhi: Kali for Women.

Baxi, Upendra. 1978. *K. K. Mathew on democracy, equality and freedom*. Lucknow: Eastern Book Company.

—— 1982. *The crisis of the Indian legal system*. New Delhi: Vikas.

—— 1985. *Courage, craft and contention: The Indian Supreme Court in the eighties*. Bombay: N. M. Tripathi.

—— 1986. *Towards a sociology of Indian law*. New Delhi: Satvahan.

—— 2002. *The future of human rights*. New Delhi: Oxford University Press.

—— 2004. 'Rule of law in India: Theory and practice'. In: Peerenboom, Randall (ed.) *Asian discourses of rule of law*. London and New York: Routledge, pp. 324–45.

Brihaspatismriti, see Jolly.

Bühler, Georg. 1975. *The laws of Manu*. Reprint. Delhi: Motilal Banarsidass.

Champappilly, Sebastian. 1988. *The Christian law.* Ernakulam: Continental.

Chaturvedi, Mahendra and Bhola Nath Tiwari. 1975. *A practical Hindi-English dictionary.* 2nd edn. Delhi: National.

Chiba, Masaji (ed.). 1986. *Asian indigenous law: In interaction with received law.* London and New York: KPI.

1989. *Legal pluralism: Towards a general theory through Japanese legal culture.* Tokyo: Tokai University Press.

Dahrendorf, Ralf. 1969. 'On the origin of inequality among men'. In: Beteille, André (ed.) *Social inequality.* Harmondsworth: Penguin, pp. 16–44.

Das, Veena. (ed.). 1990. *Mirrors of violence: Communities, riots and survivors in South Asia.* Delhi: Oxford University Press.

Dasgupta, Ramaprasad. 1973. *Crime and punishment in ancient India.* Varanasi: Bhartiya.

Datta, Bhakti. 1979. *Sexual ethics in the Mahabharata in the light of dharmashastra rulings.* London: Asia Publications.

David, René and John E. C. Brierley. 1978. *Major legal systems in the world today.* London: Stevens & Sons.

Davis, Donald R. Jr. 1999. 'Recovering the indigenous legal traditions of India: Classical Hindu law in practice in medieval Kerala'. Vol. 27. *Journal of Indian Philosophy,* pp. 159–213.

2005. 'Intermediate realms of law: Corporate groups and rulers in medieval India'. Vol. 48 No. 1. *Journal of the Economic and Social History of the Orient,* pp. 92–117.

Day, Terence P. 1982. *The conception of punishment in early Indian literature.* Waterloo, Ontario: Wilfred Laurier University Press.

De Cruz, Peter. 1999. *Comparative law in a changing world.* 2nd edn. London and Sydney: Cavendish.

Deolekar, Madhu. 1995. *India needs a common civil code.* Mumbai: Vivek Vyaspeeth.

Derrett, J. Duncan M. 1957. *Hindu law past and present.* Calcutta: A. Mukherjee.

1961. 'J. H. Nelson: A forgotten administrator-historian of India'. In: Philips, C. H. (ed.) *Historians of India, Pakistan and Ceylon.* London: Oxford University Press, pp. 354–72.

1962. 'Law and custom in ancient India: Sources and authority'. (3rd Series) Vol. 9. *Revue International de Droit de l'Antiquité,* pp. 11–32.

1966. 'The definition of a Hindu'. *Supreme Court Journal,* Journal section II, pp. 67–74.

1968a. 'Hindu law'. In: Derrett, J. D. M. (ed.) *An introduction to legal systems.* London: Sweet & Maxwell, pp. 80–104.

1968b. *Religion, law and the state in India.* London: Faber and Faber.

1970. *A critique of modern Hindu law.* Bombay: N. M. Tripathi.

1977. *Essays in classical and modern Hindu law,* Vol. 3. Leiden: Brill.

1978a. 'Justice, equity and good conscience in India'. In: Derrett, J. D. M. *Essays in classical and modern Hindu law,* Vol. 4. Leiden: Brill, pp. 8–27.

1978b. *The death of a marriage law.* New Delhi: Vikas.

1979. 'Unity in diversity: The Hindu experience'. Vol. 5. *Bharata Manisha*, pp. 21–36.

Derrett, J. Duncan M., G.-D. Sontheimer and Graham Smith. 1979. *Beiträge zu indischem Rechtsdenken.* Stuttgart: Franz Steiner Verlag.

Desai, Satyajeet A. 2004. *Mulla principles of Hindu law.* 18th edn. New Delhi: LexisNexis Butterworths.

Desai, Sunderlal T. (ed.). 1982. *Mulla principles of Hindu law.* 15th edn. Bombay: N. M. Tripathi.

Deshta, Kiran. 1995. *Uniform Civil Code: In retrospect and prospect.* New Delhi: Deep & Deep.

Dev, Bimal J. and D. K. Lahiri. 1983. *Lushai customs and ceremonies.* Delhi: Mittal.

Dhagamwar, Vasudha. 1989. *Towards the Uniform Civil Code.* Bombay: N. M. Tripathi.

1992. *Law, power and justice: The protection of personal rights in the Indian Penal Code.* 2nd edn. New Delhi: Sage.

2003. 'Invasion of criminal law by religion, custom and family law'. *Economic and Political Weekly*, 12 April 2003, pp. 1483–92.

Dhavan, Rajeev. 1992. 'Dharmashastra and modern Indian society: A preliminary exploration'. Vol. 34 No. 4. *Journal of the Indian Law Institute*, pp. 515–40.

Dirks, Nicholas B. 1987. *The hollow crown: Ethnohistory of an Indian kingdom.* Cambridge: Cambridge University Press.

Diwan, Paras. 1984. *Customary law (of Punjab and Haryana).* 2nd edn. Chandigarh: Panjab University.

1993. *Modern Hindu law.* 9th edn. Allahabad: Allahabad Law Agency.

Doniger, Wendy. 1991. *The laws of Manu.* London: Penguin.

Drobnig, Ulrich and Sjef von Erp (eds.). 1999. *The use of comparative law by courts.* The Hague: Kluwer Law International.

Ehrlich, Eugen. 1936. *Fundamental principles of the sociology of law.* Cambridge, MA: Harvard University Press.

Engineer, Asghar Ali. 1989. *Communalism and communal violence in India: An analytical approach to Hindu-Muslim conflict.* Delhi: Ajanta.

Falaturi, Abdoldjavad *et al.* 1986. *Beiträge zu islamischem Rechtsdenken.* Stuttgart: Franz Steiner Verlag.

Fawcett, Charles. 1979. *The first century of British justice in India.* Reprint. Aalen: Scientia.

Fisch, Jörg. 1983. *Cheap lives and dear limbs: The British transformation of the Bengal criminal law 1969–1817.* Wiesbaden: Franz Steiner Verlag.

Galanter, Marc. 1984. *Competing equalities: Law and the backward classes in India.* Berkeley: University of California Press.

1989. *Law and society in modern India.* Delhi: Oxford University Press.

Gledhill, Alan. 1956. *Whither Indian law? An inaugural lecture delivered on 7 December 1955.* London: SOAS.

Glenn, H. Patrick. 2000. *Legal traditions of the world.* Oxford: Oxford University Press.

2004. *Legal traditions of the world.* 2nd edn. Oxford: Oxford University Press.

Glucklich, Ariel. 1988. *Religious jurisprudence in the Dharmaśāstra.* New York and London: Macmillan and Collier Macmillan.

Griffiths, John. 1986. 'What is legal pluralism?'. No. 24. *Journal of Legal Pluralism and Unofficial Law,* pp. 1–56.

Hart, H. L. A. 1961. *The concept of law.* Oxford: Clarendon Press.

1994. *The concept of law.* 2nd edn. Oxford: Clarendon Press.

Heimsath, C. H. 1962. 'Origin and enactment of the Indian Age of Consent Bill, 1891'. Vol. 21 No. 4. *Journal of Asian Studies,* pp. 491–504.

Hoadley, M. C. and M. B. Hooker. 1981. *An introduction to Javanese law.* Tucson, AZ: University of Arizona Press.

Holden, Livia Sorrentino. 2004. *Acting for equity: Women's legal awareness in Hindu customs of divorce and remarriage in central India.* London: SOAS (Unpublished PhD thesis).

Hooker, M. B. 1975. *Legal pluralism: An introduction to colonial and neo-colonial laws.* Oxford: Clarendon.

Huntington, Samuel P. 1998. *The clash of civilizations and the remaking of world order.* London: Touchstone Books.

Indian Journal of Juridical Sciences. 2003. Vol. 1: Ancient Indian Legal Thought. Kolkata: NUJS.

Ingalls, D. H. H. 1954. 'Authority and law in ancient India'. Vol. 17 (Supplement). *Journal of the American Oriental Society,* pp. 34–45.

Iyer, Venkat. 2000. *States of emergency: The Indian experience.* New Delhi: Butterworths India.

Iyer, V. R. Krishna. 2004. *Leaves from my personal life.* New Delhi: Gyan.

Jacobsohn, Gary Jeffrey. 2003. *The wheel of law: India's secularism in comparative context.* Princeton and Oxford: Princeton University Press.

Jaffrelot, Christophe. 2003. *India's silent revolution: the rise of the lower castes in North India.* London: Hurst.

Jain, B. S. 1970. *Administration of justice in seventeenth century India.* Delhi: Metropolitan.

Jain, M. P. 1981. *Outlines of Indian legal history.* 4th edn. Bombay: N. M. Tripathi.

Jaswal, Paramjit S. 1996. *Directive Principles jurisprudence and socio-economic justice in India.* New Delhi: APH Publishing.

Jaswal, Paramjit S. and Nishtha Jaswal. 1999. *Environmental law: Environment protection, sustainable development and the law.* Delhi: Pioneer.

Jha, Ganganatha. 1942. *Purva-Mīmāmsā in its sources.* 2nd edn. Varanasi: Benares Hindu University.

Jois, Rama. 1990. *Seeds of modern public law in ancient Indian jurisprudence.* Lucknow: Eastern Book Company.

1997. *Dharma: The global ethic.* 2nd edn. Mumbai: Bharatiya Vidya Bhavan.

Jolly, Julius. 1977. *The minor law books.* Reprint. Delhi: Motilal Banarsidass.

Kane, P. V. 1968. *History of dharmaśāstra.* Vols. 1–5. Poona: Bhandarkar Oriental Research Institute.

Kangle, R. P. 1972. *The Kautiliya Arthashastra.* Bombay: University of Bombay.

Kantowsky, Detlef (ed.). 1986. *Recent research on Max Weber's studies of Hinduism.* Munich, Cologne and London: Weltforum Verlag.

Kautilīya Arthaśāstra, see Kangle.

Kelly, J. M. 1992. *A short history of Western legal theory.* Oxford: Clarendon Press.

Khan, Wahiduddin. 1996. *Uniform civil code: A critical study.* New Delhi: Islamic Centre.

Khodie, Narmada (ed.). 1975. *Readings in Uniform Civil Code.* Bombay: Thacker.

Kirpal, B. N. *et al.* (eds.). 2000. *Supreme but not infallible: Essays in honour of the Indian Supreme Court.* New Delhi: Oxford University Press.

Klaus, Konrad. 1992. 'On the meaning of the root *smri* in Vedic literature'. Vol. 36. *Wiener Zeitschrift für die Kunde Südasiens und Archiv für indische Philosophie,* pp. 77–86.

Kosambi, D. D. 1992. *The culture and civilisation of ancient India in historical outline.* Reprint. New Delhi: Vikas.

Kulke, Hermann (ed.). 1995. *The state in India 1000–1700.* Delhi: Oxford University Press.

Kumar, Virendra. 2003. 'Uniform Civil Code revisited: A juridical analysis of *John Vallamattom'.* Vol. 45 Nos. 3–4. *Journal of the Indian Law Institute,* pp. 315–34.

Kusum and P. M. Bakshi. 1982. *Customary law and justice in the tribal areas of Meghalaya.* Bombay: N. M. Tripathi and Indian Law Institute.

Larivière, Richard W. 1976. 'Dharmaśāstra, custom, "real law" and "apocryphal" smrtis'. In: Kölver, Bernhard (ed.) *Recht, Staat und Verwaltung im klassischen Indien.* Munich: R. Oldenbourg, pp. 97–110.

    1989. *The Naradasmriti: Text and translation.* Parts 1 & 2. Philadelphia: University of Pennsylvania Press.

    1991. 'Matrimonial remedies for women in classical Hindu law: Alternatives to divorce'. In: Leslie, Julia (ed.) *Rules and remedies in classical Indian law.* Leiden: Brill, pp. 37–45.

    1993. 'A persistent disjunction: Parallel realms of law in India'. In: Baird, Robert D. (ed.) *Religion and law in independent India*: New Delhi: Manohar, pp. 351 60.

Larson, Gerald James (ed.). 2001. *Religion and personal law in secular India: A call to judgment.* Bloomington and Indianapolis: Indiana University Press.

Legrand, Pierre. 1996. 'How to compare now'. Vol. 16 No. 2. *Legal Studies,* pp. 232–42.

Lingat, Robert. 1973. *The classical law of India.* Berkeley: University of California Press.

Lüders, Heinrich. 1959. *Varuna,* Vol. II, *Varuna und das Rta.* Göttingen: Vandenhoeck & Ruprecht.

Madan, T. N. 1987. 'Secularism in its place'. Vol. 46. *Journal of Asian Studies*, pp. 747–59.

(ed.). 1994. *Religion in India*. 2nd enlarged edn. Oxford: Oxford University Press.

Mahmood, Tahir. 1986. *Personal law in crisis*. New Delhi: Metropolitan.

Maine, Henry Sumner. 1861. *Ancient law*. London: John Murray.

Malik, Shahdeen. 1994. *The transformation of colonial perceptions into legal norms: Legislating for crime and punishment in Bengal 1790–1820*. London: SOAS. (Unpublished PhD thesis).

Mani, B. N. 1989. *Law of dharmasastras*. New Delhi: Navrang.

Manusmriti, see Bühler.

Mattei, Ugo. 2001. 'The comparative jurisprudence of Schlesinger and Sacco: A study in legal influence'. In: Riles, Annelise (ed.) *Rethinking the masters of comparative law*. Oxford and Portland, OR: Hart, pp. 238–56.

May, Reinhard. 1985. *Law and society East and West: Dharma, li and nomos, their contribution to thought and to life*. Stuttgart: Franz Steiner Verlag.

Menski, Werner. 1984. *Role and ritual in the Hindu marriage*. London: SOAS. (Unpublished PhD thesis).

1987. 'Legal pluralism in the Hindu marriage'. In: Burghart, Richard (ed.) *Hinduism in Great Britain*. London and New York: Tavistock, pp. 180–200.

1990. 'Uniform Civil Code in India: A false model for development?'. 1990(2) *Kerala Law Times*, Journal section, pp. 3–10.

1992a. 'Crime and punishment in Hindu law and under modern Indian law'. Vol. 57 No. 4. *Recueils de la Société Jean Bodin*. Bruxelles: De Boeck Université, pp. 295–334.

1992b. 'The role of custom in Hindu law'. Vol. 52 No. 3. *Recueils de la Société Jean Bodin*. Bruxelles: De Boeck Université, pp. 311–47.

1992c. 'The Indian experience and its lessons for Britain'. In: Hepple, Bob and Erika M. Szyszczak (eds.) *Discrimination: The limits of law*. London: Mansell, pp. 300–43.

1993a. 'Asians in Britain and the question of adaptation to a new legal order: Asian laws in Britain?'. In: Israel, Milton and N. K. Wagle (eds.) *Ethnicity, identity, migration: The South Asian context*. Toronto: University of Toronto Press, pp. 238–68.

1993b. 'Law and religion: The Hindu and Jain approach'. In: Bhattacharya, N. N. (ed.) *Jainism and Prakrit in ancient and medieval India: Essays for Professor Jagdish Chandra Jain*. New Delhi: Manohar, pp. 361–74.

2001. *Modern Indian family law*. Richmond: Curzon Press.

2002. 'Hindu law as a "religious" system'. In: Huxley, Andrew (ed.) *Religion, law and tradition: Comparative studies in religious law*. London: RoutledgeCurzon, pp. 108–26.

2003. *Hindu law: Beyond tradition and modernity*. New Delhi: Oxford University Press.

2004. 'Reluctant legislative activism'. 2004(1) *Kerala Law Times*, Journal section, pp. 35–41.

Menski, Werner, Ahmad R. Alam and Mehreen K. Raza. 2000. *Public interest litigation in Pakistan*. Karachi and London: Pakistan Law House and Platinium.

Menski, Werner and Tahmina Rahman. 1988. 'Hindus and the law in Bangladesh'. Vol. 8 No. 2. *South Asia Research*, pp. 111–31.

Miller, Jeanine. 1985. *The vision of cosmic order in the Vedas*. London: Routledge & Kegan Paul.

Mody, Perveez. 2002. 'Love and the law: Love-marriage in Delhi'. Vol. 36. *Modern Asian Studies*, pp. 223–56.

Mohanty, Saroj Kumar. 1992. *The concept of action: An analytical study*. New Delhi: Indus.

Monier-Williams, Monier. 1976. *Sanskrit-English dictionary*. 1st Indian edn. New Delhi: Munshiram Manoharlal.

Moore, Sally Falk. 1978. *Law as process: An anthropological approach*. London: Routledge & Kegan Paul.

Nanda, Ved P. and Surya Prakash Sinha (eds.). 1996. *Hindu law and legal theory*. New York: New York University Press.

Nāradasmriti, see Jolly.

Narang, Sudesh (ed.). 1988. *Dharmashastra in contemporary times*. Delhi: Nag.

New vision for legal education in the emerging global scenario. 2001. Bangalore: National Law School.

Nikam, N. A. and R. McKeon. 1962. *The edicts of Ashoka*. Bombay: Asia Publishing House.

Noorani, A. G. 2000. *Constitutional questions in India: The President, Parliament and the states*. New Delhi: Oxford University Press.

O'Flaherty, Wendy Doniger and J. Duncan M. Derrett (eds.). 1978. *The concept of duty in South Asia*. New Delhi and London: Vikas and SOAS.

Ojha, P. N. 1978. *Aspects of medieval Indian society and culture*. Delhi: B. R. Publishing.

Olivelle, Patrick. 2000. *Dharmasūtras: The law codes of pastamba, Gautama, Baudhāyana and Vasishtha: Annotated text and translation*. Delhi: Motilal Banarsidass.

Pandey, R. B. 1969. *Hindu samskaras*. Delhi: Motilal Banarsidass.

Parashar, Archana. 1992. *Women and family law reform in India*. New York: Sage.

Pearl, David. 1979. *A textbook on Muslim law*. London: Croom Helm.

Peerenboom, Randell (ed.). 2004. *Asian discourses of rule of law: Theories and implementation of rule of law in twelve Asian countries, France and the US*. London and New York: Routledge.

Price, Pamela. 1979. 'Rajadharma in Ramnad, land litigation and largess'. Vol. 13 No. 2 (New Series). *Contributions to Indian Sociology*, pp. 207–40.

Purohit, S. K. 1994. *Ancient Indian legal philosophy: Its relevance to contemporary jurisprudential thought.* New Delhi: Deep & Deep.

Raina, Dina Nath. 1996. *Uniform civil code and gender justice.* New Delhi: Reliance.

Rajan, Rajeswari Sunder. 2003. *The scandal of the state: Women, law and citizenship in postcolonial India.* Durham, NC and London: Duke University Press.

Ratnaparkhi, Madhukar Sadashiv. 1997. *Uniform civil code: An ignored constitutional imperative.* New Delhi: Atlantic.

Rocher, Ludo. 2002. *Jīmutavāhana's Dāyabhāga: The Hindu law of inheritance in Bengal: Edited and translated with an introduction and notes.* Oxford: Oxford University Press.

Rosen, Lawrence. 1995. 'Law and custom in the popular legal culture of North Africa'. Vol. 2 No. 2. *Islamic Law and Society,* pp. 194–208.

Sarkar, G. 1940. *Hindu law.* 8th edn. Calcutta: Sarkar & Sons.

Sathe, S. P. 2002. *Judicial activism in India: Transgressing borders and enforcing limits.* New Delhi: Oxford University Press.

Sathe, S. P. and Sathya Narayan (eds.). 2003. *Liberty, equality and justice: Struggles for a new social order.* Lucknow: EBC Publishing. (ILS Law College Platinum Jubilee Commemoration Volume).

Sharma, Narendra Nath. 1976. *Ashvalayana Grihyasutram.* Delhi: Eastern Book Linkers.

Shourie, Arun. 1993a. *Indian controversies: Essays on religion in politics.* New Delhi: ASA.

1993b. *A secular agenda.* New Delhi: ASA.

Shrivastava, Ashok Kumar. 1981. *Hindu society in the sixteenth century.* New Delhi: Milind.

Singh, Chhatrapati. 1990. 'Dharmasastras and contemporary jurisprudence'. Vol. 32 No. 2. *Journal of the Indian Law Institute,* pp. 179–88.

Singh, Gurjeet. 1996. *Law of consumer protection in India: Justice within reach.* New Delhi: Deep & Deep.

Singh, Mool. 1993. *Justice Iyer's jurisconscience.* Jaipur: RBSA.

Sivaramayya, B. 1988. 'Dharmashastra and contemporary Hindu law'. In: Narang, Sudesh (ed.) *Dharmashastra in contemporary times.* Delhi: Nag, pp. 67–76.

Smith, Graham and J. Duncan M. Derrett. 1975. 'Hindu judicial administration in pre-British times and its lesson for today'. Vol. 95 No. 3. *Journal of the American Oriental Society,* pp. 417–23.

Sontheimer, Günther-Dietz. 1977. *The joint Hindu family: Its evolution as a legal institution.* New Delhi: Munshiram Manoharlal.

Sontheimer, Günther-Dietz and Hermann Kulke (eds.). 1989. *Hinduism reconsidered.* New Delhi: Manohar.

Srinivas, M. N. 1973. *Social change in modern India.* Berkeley: University of California Press.

Subba Rao, G. C. V. 2003. *Hindu law.* 18th edn. Hyderabad: Gogia & Company.

Tarlo, Emma. 2002. *Unsettling memories: Narratives of the Emergency in Delhi*. Berkeley and Los Angeles: University of California Press.

Tharoor, Shashi. 2000. *India: From midnight to the millennium*. New Delhi: Penguin.

Tull, Herman W. 1990. *The Vedic origins of karma*. Delhi: Sai Satguru Publications.

Twining, William. 2000. *Globalisation and legal theory*. London: Butterworths.

Unger, Roberto Mangabeira. 1976. *Law in modern society: Toward a criticism of social theory*. New York: Free Press.

Venkataramiah, E. S. 1982. 'Certain aspects of adoption prevailing amongst the Hindus'. In: Sontheimer, G.-D. and P. K. Aithal (eds.) *Indology and law: Studies in honour of Professor J. Duncan M. Derrett*. Wiesbaden: Franz Steiner Verlag, pp. 225–47.

Verma, S. K. and Kusum (eds.). 2000. *Fifty years of the Supreme Court of India: Its grasp and reach*. New Delhi: Indian Law Institute and Oxford University Press.

Watson, Alan. 1993. *Legal transplants: An approach to comparative law*. 2nd edn. Athens, GA: University of Georgia Press.

Wezler, Albrecht. 1999. 'Über den sakramentalen Charakter des *dharma* nachsinnend'. In: Oberhammer, Gerhard und Marcus Schmücker (eds.) *Raumzeitliche Vermittlung der Transzendenz*. Vienna: Verlag der Österreichischen Akademie der Wissenschaften, pp. 63–113.

Wink, André. 1990. *Al Hind – The making of the Indo-Islamic world*, Vol. 1, *Early medieval India and the expansion of Islam, 7th-11th centuries*. Leiden: Brill.

Winternitz, M. 1968. *Geschichte der indischen Literatur*. Vols. 1–3. Reprint. Stuttgart: K. F. Koehler Verlag.

Chapter 5, Islamic law

Ahmad, Aqil. 1985. *Textbook of Mohammedan law*. Allahabad: Central Law Agency.

Ahmed, Ishtiaq. 1987. *The concept of an Islamic state: An analysis of the ideological controversy in Pakistan*. London: Frances Pinter.

Ajijola, A. D. 1989. *Introduction to Islamic law*. New Delhi: International Islamic Publishers.

Al-Azami, M. Mustafa. 1996. *On Schacht's origins of Muhammadan jurisprudence*. Oxford: Oxford Centre for Islamic Studies.

Allott, Antony N. 1980. *The limits of law*. London: Butterworths.

Amedroz, H. F. 1911. 'The mazalim jurisdiction in the Ahkam Sultaniyya of Mawardi'. Vol. 2. *Journal of the Royal Asiatic Society of Great Britain and Ireland*, pp. 635–74.

An-Na'im, Abdullahi Ahmed. 2002. *Islamic family law in a changing world: A global resource book*. London and New York: Zed Books.

Anderson, J. N. D. 1959. *Islamic law in the modern world*. London and New York: Stevens and New York University Press.

1960. 'The significance of Islamic law in the world today'. Vol. 9 No. 2. *American Journal of Comparative Law*, pp. 187–98.

1967. 'Pakistan: An Islamic state?'. In: Holland, R. H. C. and G. Schwarzenberger (eds.) *Law, justice and equity*. London: Sir Isaac Pitman and Sons, pp. 127–36.

1971. 'Modern trends in Islam: Legal reforms and modernisation in the Middle East'. Vol. 20 No. 1. *International and Comparative Law Quarterly*, pp. 1–21.

1976. *Law reform in the Muslim world*. London: Athlone Press.

1978. *Islamic law in Africa*. 2nd imprint London: Frank Cass.

Anderson, J. N. D. and Noel J. Coulson. 1967. 'Islamic law in contemporary cultural change'. Vol. 18 Nos. 1–2. *Saeculum*, pp. 13–92.

Ansari, Humayun. 2004. *'The infidel within': Muslims in Britain since 1800*. London: Hurst.

Arabi, Oussama. 2001. *Studies in modern Islamic law and jurisprudence*. The Hague, London and New York: Kluwer.

Asad, Muhammad. 1961. *The principles of state and government in Islam*. Berkeley: University of California Press.

Baillie, Neil B. E. 1865. *A digest of Moohammudan law*. Vol. I. London: Smith, Elder & Co.

Balchin, Cassandra (ed.). 1994. *A handbook on family law in Pakistan*. 2nd edn. Lahore: Shirkat Gah.

Ballard, Roger (ed.). 1994. *Desh pardesh: The South Asian presence in Britain*. London: Hurst.

Banerjee, A. C. 1984. *English law in India*. New Delhi: Abhinav.

Banerjee, Tapas Kumar. 1962. *History of Indian criminal law*. Calcutta: Riddhi.

Bharatiya, V. P. (ed.). 1996. *Syed Khalid Rashid's Muslim law*. 3rd revised edn. Lucknow: Eastern Book Company.

Bistolfi, Robert and François Zabbal (eds.). 1995. *Islams d'Europe: Intégration ou insertion communautaire?* Paris: Éditions de l'Aube.

Burton, John. 1994. *An introduction to the hadith*. Edinburgh: Edinburgh University Press.

Calder, Norman. 1993. *Studies in early Muslim jurisprudence*. Oxford: Oxford University Press.

Chaudhary, Muhammad Azam. 1999. *Justice in practice: Legal ethnography of a Pakistani Punjabi village*. Oxford: Oxford University Press.

Chiba, Masaji (ed.). 1986. *Asian indigenous law in interaction with received law*. London and New York: KPI.

1989. *Legal pluralism: Towards a general theory through Japanese legal culture*. Tokyo: Tokai University Press.

Cohn-Sherbok, Dan (ed.). 1997. *Islam in a world of diverse faiths*. Reprint. Basingstoke and London: Macmillan.

Cook, Michael Allan. 2000. *The Koran: A very short introduction.* Oxford: Oxford University Press.

Cotterrell, Roger. 2003. *The politics of jurisprudence: A critical introduction to legal philosophy.* 2nd edn. London: LexisNexis.

Coulson, Noel J. 1964. *A history of Islamic law.* Edinburgh: Edinburgh University Press.

1968. 'Islamic law'. In: Derrett, J. D. M. (ed.) *An introduction to legal systems.* London: Sweet & Maxwell, pp. 54–79.

1969. *Conflicts and tensions in Islamic jurisprudence.* Chicago and London: University of Chicago Press.

1971. *Succession in the Muslim family.* Cambridge: Cambridge University Press.

Daftary, Farhad. 1998. *A short history of the Ismailis: Traditions of a Muslim community.* Edinburgh: Edinburgh University Press.

Derrett, J. Duncan M. (ed.). 1968a. *An introduction to legal systems.* London: Sweet & Maxwell.

1968b. *Religion, law and the state in India.* London: Faber and Faber.

Diwan, Paras and Peeyushi Diwan. 1991. *Muslim law in modern India.* 5th edn. Allahabad: Allahabad Law Agency.

Doi, Abdur Rahman I. 1984. *Shari'ah: The Islamic law.* London: Ta-Ha Publishers.

Dupret, Baudouin, Maurits Berger and Laila al-Zwaini (eds.). 1999. *Legal pluralism in the Arab world.* The Hague: Kluwer Law International.

Dutton, Yasin. 1999. *The origins of Islamic law: The Qur'an, the Muwatta' and Madinan 'Amal.* Richmond: Curzon Press.

Edge, Ian (ed.). 1996. *Islamic law and legal theory.* Aldershot: Dartmouth.

(ed.). 2000. *Comparative law in global perspective.* Ardsley, NY: Transnational.

Ehrlich, Eugen. 1936. *Fundamental principles of the sociology of law.* Cambridge, MA: Harvard University Press.

El Alami, Dawoud Sudqi and Doreen Hinchcliffe. 1996. *Islamic marriage and divorce laws of the Arab world.* London: Kluwer.

El Fadl, Khaled Abou. 2001. *Speaking in God's name: Islamic law, authority and women.* Oxford: Oneworld.

Enayat, Hamid. 1982. *Modern Islamic political thought.* London: Macmillan.

Endress, Gerhard. 1988. *An introduction to Islam.* Edinburgh: Edinburgh University Press.

Esposito, John L. 1988. *Islam: The straight path.* New York and Oxford: Oxford University Press.

(ed.). 1995. *The Oxford encyclopedia of the modern Islamic world.* Vols. 1–4. New York and Oxford: Oxford University Press.

Esposito, John L. and Natana J. Delong-Bas. 2002. *Women in Muslim family law.* 2nd edn. New York: Syracuse University Press.

Falaturi, Abdoldjavad *et al.* 1986. *Beiträge zu islamischem Rechtsdenken.* Stuttgart: Franz Steiner Verlag.

Faruki, Kemal A. 1971. *The evolution of Islamic constitutional theory and practice.* Karachi: National Publishing House.

———. 1987. *Islamic jurisprudence.* Islamabad: National Book Foundation.

Ferdinand, Klaus and Mehdi Mozaffari. 1988. *Islam: State and society.* London: Curzon Press.

Fisch, Jörg. 1983. *Cheap lives and dear limbs: The British transformation of the Bengal criminal law 1969–1817.* Wiesbaden: Franz Steiner Verlag.

Fyzee, Asaf A. A. 1999. *Outline of Muhammadan law.* 4th edn. Reprint. New Delhi: Oxford University Press.

Fyzee, M. 1974. *A handbook of Muhammadan law.* 4th edn. Oxford: Oxford University Press.

Gerber, Haim. 1998. 'Rigidity versus openness in late classical Islamic law: The case of the seventeenth-century Palestinian Mufti Khayr al-Din al-Ramli'. Vol. 5 No. 2. *Islamic Law and Society,* pp. 165–95.

Gleave, Robert and E. Kermeli (eds.). 1997. *Islamic law: Theory and practice.* London: I. B. Tauris.

Glenn, H. Patrick. 2000. *Legal traditions of the world.* Oxford: Oxford University Press.

———. 2004. *Legal traditions of the world.* 2nd edn. Oxford: Oxford University Press.

Goldziher, I. 1981. *Introduction to Islamic theology and law.* Princeton: Princeton University Press.

Griffiths, John. 1986. 'What is legal pluralism?'. No. 24. *Journal of Legal Pluralism and Unofficial Law,* pp. 1–56.

———. 1999. 'Preface'. In: Dupret, Baudouin, Maurits Berger and Laila al-Zwaini (eds.) *Legal pluralism in the Arab world.* The Hague: Kluwer, pp. vii–ix.

Guraya, Muhammad Yusuf. 1985. *Origins of Islamic jurisprudence.* Lahore: Sh. Muhammad Ashraf.

Hai, Maulana Hakim Syed Abdul. 1977. *India during Muslim rule.* Lucknow: Academy of Islamic Research and Publications.

Hallaq, Wael B. 1984. 'Was the gate of ijtihad closed?'. Vol. 16 No. 1. *International Journal of Middle Eastern Studies,* pp. 3–41.

———. 1986. 'On the origins of the controversy about the existence of mujtahids and the gate of ijtihad'. Vol. 63. *Studia Islamica,* pp. 129–41.

———. 1992. 'Usūl al-fiqh: Beyond tradition'. Vol. 3 No. 2. *Journal of Islamic Studies,* pp. 172–202.

———. 1994. 'From fatwas to furu: Growth and change in Islamic substantive law'. Vol. 1 No. 1. *Islamic Law and Society,* pp. 29–65.

———. 1995. *Law and legal theory in classical and medieval Islam.* Brookfield, VT: Variorum.

———. 1997. *A history of Islamic legal theories: An introduction to Sunni usul al-fiqh.* Cambridge: Cambridge University Press.

———. 2001. *Authority, continuity and change in Islamic law.* Cambridge: Cambridge University Press.

Halliday, Fred and Hamza Alavi (eds.). 1988. *State and ideology in the Middle East and Pakistan*. London: Macmillan.

Hamidullah, Muhammad. 1987. *Muslim conduct of state*. Lahore: Sh. Muhammad Ashraf.

Hamilton, Charles. 1891. *The Hedaya, or guide: A commentary on the Mussulman laws*. London: T. Bensley.

Hasan, Ahmad. 1984. *The doctrine of ijma in Islam*. Reprint. Islamabad: Islamic Research Institute.

Hassan, S. Farooq. 1984. *The Islamic republic: Politics, law and economy*. Lahore: Aziz Publishers.

Hassan Syed Riazul. 1974. *The reconstruction of legal thought in Islam*. Lahore: Author.

Hidayatullah, M. (ed.). 1982. *Mulla's principles of Mahomedan law*. 18th edn. Bombay: N. M. Tripathi.

Hidayatullah, M and Arshad Hidayatullah (eds.). 1990. *Mulla's principles of Mahomedan law*. 19th edn. Bombay: N. M. Tripathi.

Hodkinson, Keith. 1984. *Muslim family law*. London: Croom Helm.

Hoebel, E. Adamson. 1954. *The law of primitive man: A study in comparative legal dynamics*. Cambridge, MA: Harvard University Press.

Hooker, M. B. 1975. *Legal pluralism: An introduction to colonial and neo-colonial laws*. Oxford: Clarendon Press.

Hosain, Saiyid Safdar. 1995. *The early history of Islam*, Vol. I, *Life of the Holy Prophet Mohammed*. Delhi: Low Price Publications.

Huntington, Samuel P. 1998. *The clash of civilizations and the remaking of world order*. London: Touchstone Books.

Hurvitz, Nimrod. 2000. 'Schools of law and historical context: Re-examining the formation of the Hanbali madhhab'. Vol. 7 No. 1. *Islamic Law and Society*, pp. 37–64.

Husain, Sheikh Abrar. 1976. *Marriage customs among Muslims in India. (A sociological study of the Shia marriage customs)*. New Delhi: Sterling.

Iqbal, Allama Muhammad. 1989. *The reconstruction of religious thought in Islam*. 2nd edn. Lahore: Iqbal Academy Pakistan.

Jan, Tarik *et al.* 1998. *Pakistan between secularism and Islam: Ideology, issues and conflict*. Islamabad: Institute of Policy Studies.

Johansen, Baber. 1997. 'Truth and validity of the qadi's judgment: A legal debate among Muslim Sunnite jurists from the 9th to the 13th centuries'. Vol. 14. *Recht van de Islam*, pp. 1–26.

    1999. *Contingency in a sacred law: Legal and ethical norms in the Muslim fiqh*. Leiden: Brill.

Kamali, Mohammad Hashim. 1991. *Principles of Islamic jurisprudence*. 2nd revised edn. Cambridge: Cambridge University Press.

Khadduri, Majeed. 1970. *Political trends in the Arab world: The role of ideas and ideals in politics*. Baltimore and London: Johns Hopkins Press.

Khan, Hamid. 1999. *Islamic law of inheritance*. 2nd edn. Karachi and London: Pakistan Law House and Platinium.

Khan, M. Mustafa Ali. 1989. 'Islamic polygamy – A blessing in disguise'. 1989(1) *Kerala Law Times*, Journal section, pp. 47–58.

Khan, Mansoor Hasan. 1993. *Public interest litigation: Growth of the concept and its meaning in Pakistan*. Karachi: Pakistan Law House.

Khan, Mohammad Ayub. 1990. *The Constitution of the Islamic Republic of Pakistan*. Karachi: Pakistan Law House.

Khare, R. S. (ed.). 1999. *Perspectives on Islamic law, justice and society*. Lanham, MD: Rowman & Littlefield.

Lau, Martin. 1995. 'Introduction to the Pakistani legal system, with special reference to the law of contract'. Vol. 1. *Yearbook of Islamic and Middle Eastern Law*, pp. 3–28.

1996. 'Pakistan'. Vol. 2. *Yearbook of Islamic and Middle Eastern Law*, pp. 375–86.

1997. 'Opening Pandora's box: The Saima Waheed case'. Vol. 3. *Yearbook of Islamic and Middle Eastern Law*, pp. 518–31.

2000. 'Pakistan'. Vol. 5. *Yearbook of Islamic and Middle Eastern Law*, pp. 439–52.

Legrand, Pierre. 1996. 'How to compare now'. Vol. 16 No. 2. *Legal Studies*, pp. 232–42.

Libson, Gideon. 1997. 'On the development of custom as a source of law in Islamic law'. Vol. 4 No. 2. *Islamic Law and Society*, pp. 131–55.

Liebesny, Herbert J. 1975. *The law of the Near and Middle East: Readings, cases and materials*. Albany, NY: State University of New York Press.

Loimeier, Roman (ed.). 2000. *Die islamische Welt als Netzwerk: Möglichkeiten und Grenzen des Netzwerkansatzes im islamischen Kontext*. Würzburg: Ergon.

Mahmood, Shaukat. 1973. *Constitution of Pakistan, 1973*. Lahore: Legal Research Centre.

Mahmood, Tahir. 1965. 'Custom as a source of law in Islam'. Vol. 7. *Journal of the Indian Law Institute*, pp. 102–6.

1977. *Muslim personal law*. New Delhi: Vikas.

1982. *The Muslim law of India*. 2nd edn. Allahabad: Law Book Company.

1986. *Personal laws in crisis*. New Delhi: Metropolitan.

Maine, Henry Sumner. 1861. *Ancient law*. London: John Murray.

Makdisi, John. 1985. 'Legal logic and equity in Islamic law'. Vol. 33. *American Journal of Comparative Law*, pp. 63–92.

Malik, Shahdeen. 1994. *The transformation of colonial perceptions into legal norms: Legislating for crime and punishment in Bengal 1790–1820*. London: SOAS. (Unpublished PhD thesis).

Mallat, Chibli. 1993. *The renewal of Islamic law*. Cambridge: Cambridge University Press.

Mallat, Chibli and Jane Connors (eds.). 1990. *Islamic family law*. London, Dordrecht and Boston: Graham & Trotman.

Mamdani, Mahmood. 2004. *Good Muslim, bad Muslim: America, the cold war, and the roots of terror.* New York: Pantheon.

May, Reinhard. 1985. *Law and society East and West: Dharma, li, and nomos, their contribution to thought and to life.* Stuttgart: Franz Steiner Verlag.

Mayer, Ann Elizabeth. 1984. 'Islamic law'. In: Kelly, Marjorie (ed.) *Islam – The religious and political life of a community.* New York: Praeger, pp. 226–42.

1990. 'The Shari'ah: A methodology or a body of substantive rules?'. In: Heer, Nicholas (ed.) *Islamic law and jurisprudence.* Seattle and London: University of Washington Press, pp. 177–98.

Mehdi, Rubya. 1994. *The Islamization of the law in Pakistan.* Richmond: Curzon Press.

Mehdi, Rubya and Farida Shaheed (eds.). 1997. *Women's law in legal education and practice in Pakistan.* Copenhagen: New Social Science Monographs.

Melchert, Christopher. 1997. *The formation of the Sunni schools of law, 9th to 10th centuries C. E.* Leiden: Brill.

2004. 'Review of Motzki, Harald, *The origins of Islamic jurisprudence: Meccan fiqh before the classical schools'.* Vol. 11 No. 3. *Islamic Law and Society,* pp. 404–8.

Menski, Werner. 1994. 'Maintenance for divorced Muslim wives'. 1994(1) *Kerala Law Times,* Journal section, pp. 45–52.

2001. *Modern Indian family law.* Richmond: Curzon.

Menski, Werner, Ahmad Rafay Alam and Mehreen Kasuri Raza. 2000. *Public interest litigation in Pakistan.* London and Karachi: Platinium and Pakistan Law House.

Mernissi, Fatima. 1975. *Beyond the veil: Male–female dynamics in a modern Muslim society.* New York: John Wiley.

Miller, Roland Eric. 1992. *Mapilla Muslims of Kerala: A study in Islamic trends.* 2nd revised edn. Madras: Orient Longman.

Modood, Tariq. 1993. 'Muslim views on religious identity and racial equality'. Vol. 19 No. 3. *New Community,* pp. 513–19.

Moore, Sally Falk. 1978. *Law as process: An anthropological approach.* London: Routledge & Kegan Paul.

Morgan, Peggy and Clive Lawton (eds.). 1996. *Ethical issues in six religious traditions.* Edinburgh: Edinburgh University Press.

Motzki, Harald. 1999. 'The role of non-Arab converts in the development of early Islamic law'. Vol. 6 No. 3. *Islamic Law and Society,* pp. 293–317.

2002. *The origins of Islamic jurisprudence: Meccan fiqh before the classical schools.* Trans. Marion H. Katz. Leiden: Brill.

Muslehuddin, Muhammad. 1980. *Philosophy of Islamic law and the Orientalists.* 2nd edn. Lahore: Islamic Publications.

Newberg, Paula R. 1995. *Judging the state: Courts and constitutional politics in Pakistan.* Cambridge: Cambridge University Press.

Nielsen, Jørgen S. 1995. *Muslims in Western Europe.* 2nd edn. Edinburgh: Edinburgh University Press.

Pearl, David. 1979. *A textbook on Muslim law.* London: Croom Helm.

Pearl, David and Werner Menski. 1998. *Muslim family law.* 3rd edn. London: Sweet & Maxwell.

Purohit, Nishi. 1998. *The principles of Mohammedan law.* 2nd edn. New Delhi and Allahabad: Orient Publishing Company.

Rahim, Abdur. 1994. *The principles of Islamic jurisprudence.* New Delhi: Kitab Bhavan.

Rahman, Fazlur. 1982. *Islam and modernity: Transformation of an intellectual tradition.* Chicago and London: University of Chicago Press.

Rosen, Lawrence. 1989. *The anthropology of justice: Law as culture in Islamic society.* Cambridge: Cambridge University Press.

Rosental, Erwin. 1958. *Political thought in medieval Islam.* Cambridge: Cambridge University Press.

1965. *Islam in the modern national state.* Cambridge: Cambridge University Press.

Said, Edward W. 1978. *Orientalism.* London: Penguin.

Sarup, M. 1993. *An introductory guide to post-structuralism and postmodernism.* 2nd edn. Hemel Hempstead: Harvester Wheatsheaf.

Schacht, Joseph. 1979. *The origins of Muhammadan jurisprudence.* Reprint. Oxford: Clarendon Press.

1984. *An introduction to Islamic law.* Reprint. Oxford: Oxford University Press.

Schneider, Irene. 1999. *Kinderverkauf und Schuldknechtschaft: Untersuchungen zur frühen Phase des islamischen Rechts.* Stuttgart: Franz Steiner

Shah, Nasim Hassan. 1999. *Constitution, law and Pakistan legal system.* Lahore: Print Yard.

Shaheed, Farida *et al.* (eds.). 1998. *Shaping women's lives: Laws, practices and strategies in Pakistan.* Lahore: Shirkat Gah.

Siddiqi, Aslam. 1981. *Modernization menaces Muslims.* 2nd edn. Lahore: Sh. Muhammad Ashraf.

Starr, June. 1992. *Law as metaphor: From Islamic courts to the palace of justice.* New York: State University of New York Press.

Stone, Richard. 2004. *Islamophobia: Issues, challenges and action. A report by the Commission on British Muslims and Islamophobia.* Stoke-on-Trent and Sterling: Trentham.

Tibi, Bassam. 1997. *Arab nationalism: Between Islam and the nation-state.* 3rd edn. Basingstoke and London: Macmillan.

Unger, Roberto Mangabeira. 1976. *Law in modern society: Toward a criticism of social theory.* New York: Free Press.

Watt, William Montgomery. 1999. *Islam: A short history.* Oxford: Oneworld.

Weiss, Bernard G. 1978. 'Interpretation in Islamic law: The theory of ijtihad'. Vol. 26. *American Journal of Comparative Law,* pp. 199–212.

1998. *The spirit of Islamic law*. Athens, GA and London: University of Georgia Press.

Wilson, R. K. 1921. *Digest of Anglo-Muhammedan law*. 5th edn by A. Yusuf Ali. Calcutta: Thacker.

Wink, André. 1990. *Al Hind – The making of the Indo-Islamic world*, Vol. 1, *Early medieval India and the expansion of Islam, 7th–11th centuries*. Leiden: Brill.

Yilmaz, Ihsan. 2005a. 'Inter-madhab surfing, neo-*ijtihad*, and faith-based movement leaders'. In: Vogel, Frank, Peri Bearman and Ruud Peters (eds.) *The Islamic school of law: Evolution, devolution and progress*. Cambridge, MA: Harvard University Press, pp. 191–206.

2005b. *Muslim laws, politics and society in modern nation states: Dynamic legal pluralisms in England, Turkey and Pakistan*. Aldershot: Ashgate.

Chapter 6, African laws

Achebe, Chinua. 1958. *Things fall apart*. London: Penguin.

Addai-Sebo, Akyaaba and Ansel Wong (eds.). 1988. *Our story: A handbook of African history and contemporary issues*. London: London Strategic Policy Unit.

Ajijola, A. D. 1989. *Introduction to Islamic law*. New Delhi: International Islamic Publishers.

Allott, Antony N. 1960. *Essays in African law: With special reference to the law of Ghana*. London: Butterworths.

1965. 'The future of African law'. In: Kuper, Hilda and Leo Kuper (eds.) *African law: Adaptation and development*. Berkeley and Los Angeles: University of California Press, pp. 216–40.

1968. 'African law'. In: Derrett, J. D. M. (ed.) *Introduction to legal systems*. London: Sweet & Maxwell, pp. 131–56.

1970. *New essays in African law*. London: Butterworths.

1977. 'The people as law-makers: Custom, practice and public opinion as sources of law in Africa and England'. Vol. 21 No. 1. *Journal of African Law*, pp. 1–23.

1980. *The limits of law*. London: Butterworths.

1984. 'On knowledge of customary laws in Africa'. In: *La connaissance du droit en Afrique*. Brussels: Académie Royale des Sciences d'Outre-Mer, pp. 122–36.

Altekar, A. S. 1958. *State and government in ancient India*. Delhi: Motilal Banarsidass.

Amadiume, Ifi. 1997. *Re-inventing Africa: Matriarchy, religion and culture*. London: Zed Books.

An-Na'im, Abdullahi A. 2002a. *Cultural transformation and human rights in Africa*. London and New York: Zed Books.

(ed.) 2002b. *Islamic family law in a changing world: A global resource book*. London and New York: Zed Books.

Anderson J. N. D. (ed.). 1968. *Family law in Asia and Africa*. London: George Allen and Unwin.

1978. *Islamic law in Africa*. 2nd imprint. London: Frank Cass.

Asante, Samuel K. B. 1975. *Property law and social goals in Ghana, 1844–1966.* Accra: Ghana Universities Press.

Ayittey, G. B. N. 1991. *Indigenous African institutions.* New York: Transnational.

Bastide, Roger. 1978. *The African religions of Brazil: Towards a sociology of the interpenetration of civilizations.* Baltimore: Johns Hopkins University Press.

Bekker, J. C., J. M. T. Labuschagne and L. P. Vorster (eds.). 2002. *Introduction to legal pluralism in South Africa,* Part I, *Customary law.* Durban: Butterworths.

Bennett, T. W. 1991. *A sourcebook of African customary law for Southern Africa.* Cape Town: Juta.

1995. *Human rights and African customary law under the South African Constitution.* Cape Town: Juta.

2004. *Customary law in South Africa.* Lansdowne: Juta.

Bohannan, Paul. 1957. *Justice and judgment among the Tiv.* Oxford: Oxford University Press.

(ed.). 1967. *Law and warfare: Studies in the anthropology of conflict.* Garden City, NY: Natural History Press.

Booth, A. 1992. '"European courts protect women and witches": Colonial courts as redistributors of power in Swaziland 1920–1950'. Vol. 18 No. 2. *Journal of Southern African Studies,* pp. 253–75.

Bozeman, Adda B. 1971. *The future of law in a multicultural world.* Princeton: Princeton University Press.

Canter, Richard S. 1978. 'Dispute settlement and dispute processing in Zambia: Individual choice versus societal constraints'. In: Nader, Laura and Harry F. Todd Jr (eds.) *The disputing process – Law in ten societies.* New York: Columbia University Press, pp. 247–80.

Chanock, Martin. 1978. 'Neo-traditionalism and the customary law in Malawi'. Vol. 16. *African Studies,* pp. 80–91.

1985. *Law, custom and social order: The colonial experience in Malawi and Zambia.* Cambridge: Cambridge University Press.

1995. 'Neither customary nor legal: African customary law in an era of family law reform'. In: Woodman, Gordon and A. O. Obilade (eds.) *African law and legal theory.* Aldershot: Dartmouth, pp. 171–87.

Cheru, Fantu. 2002. *African renaissance: Roadmaps to the challenge of globalization.* London, New York and Cape Town: Zed Books and David Philip.

Chiba, Masaji. 1984. 'Cultural universality and particularity of jurisprudence'. In: Marasinghe, M. Lakshman and William E. Conklin (eds.) *Essays in Third World perspectives in jurisprudence.* Singapore: Malayan Law Journal, pp. 302–26.

(ed.). 1986. *Asian indigenous law in interaction with received law.* London and New York: KPI

1989. *Legal pluralism: Towards a general theory through Japanese legal culture.* Tokyo: Tokai University Press.

CIMADE, INODEP and MINK. 1986. *Africa's refugee crisis: What's to be done?*. London: Zed Books.

Coker, G. B. A. 1966. *Family property among the Yorubas*. London: Sweet & Maxwell.

Comaroff J. L. and Simon Roberts. 1981. *Rules and processes: The cultural logic of dispute in an African context*. Chicago and London: University of Chicago Press.

Cotran, Eugene. 1963. 'The unification of laws in East Africa'. Vol. 1 No. 2. *Journal of Modern African Studies*, pp. 209–20.

1966. 'The place and future of customary law in East Africa'. *East African Law Today*, pp. 72–92.

Daniels, W. C. Ekow. 1964. *The common law in West Africa*. London: Butterworths.

David, René and John E. C. Brierley. 1978. *Major legal systems in the world today*. London: Stevens & Sons.

Davidson, Basil, 1970. *The African genius: An introduction to African cultural and social history*. Boston: Atlantic Monthly Press.

Davis, Darièn J. 1999. *Afro-Brazilians: Time for recognition*. London: Minority Rights Group.

Deng, Francis Mading. 1971. *Tradition and modernisation: A challenge for law among the Sudan*. New Haven: Yale University Press.

Derrett, J. Duncan M. (ed.). 1968a. *Introduction to legal systems*. London: Sweet & Maxwell.

Derrett, J. Duncan M. 1968b. *Religion, law and the state in India*. London: Faber and Faber.

Dhagamwar, Vasudha. 2003. 'Invasion of criminal law by religion, custom and family law'. *Economic and Political Weekly*, 12 April 2003, pp. 1483–92.

Dickson, Kwesi. 1974. *Theology in Africa*. London: Darton, Longman and Todd.

Ebo, Chukwuemeka. 1995. 'Indigenous law and justice: Some major concepts and practices'. In: Woodman, Gordon and A. O. Obilade (eds.) *African law and legal theory*. Aldershot: Dartmouth, pp. 33–42.

Elias, Taslim Olawale. 1954. *Groundwork of Nigerian law*. London: Routledge & Kegan Paul.

1956. *The nature of African customary law*. Manchester: Manchester University Press.

1962. *Ghana and Sierra Leone: The development of their laws and constitution*. London: Stevens & Sons.

1965. 'The evolution of law and government in modern Africa'. In: Kuper, Hilda and Leo Kuper (eds.) *African law: Adaptation and development*. Berkeley and Los Angeles: University of California Press, pp. 184–95.

1988. *Africa and the development of international law*. 2nd revised edn. London: Martinus Nijhoff.

Ellis, Stephen and Gerrie Ter Haar. 2004. *Worlds of power: Religious thought and political practice in Africa*. London: Hurst.

Farah, Nuruddin. 2000. *Yesterday, tomorrow: Voices from the Somali diaspora.* London and New York: Cassell.

Field, M. J. 1940. *Social organisation of the Ga people.* London: Crown Agents for the Colonies.

Fisch, Jörg. 1998. *Tödliche Rituale.* Frankfurt and New York: Campus Verlag.

Fortes, Meyer and G. Dieterlen (eds.). 1965. *African systems of thought.* London: Oxford University Press for the International African Institute.

Fortes, Meyer and E. E. Evans-Pritchard (eds.). 1940. *African political systems.* London: Oxford University Press.

Franklin, John Hope. 1947. *From slavery to freedom: A history of Negro Americans.* New York: Alfred A. Knopf.

   1983. *Negro. Die Geschichte der Schwarzen in den USA.* Frankfurt: Ullstein.

Freeman, M. D. A. 2001. *Lloyd's Introduction to jurisprudence.* 7th edn. London: Sweet & Maxwell.

Galanter, Marc. 1989. *Law and society in modern India.* Delhi: Oxford University Press.

Glenn, H. Patrick. 2000. *Legal traditions of the world.* Oxford: Oxford University Press.

   2004. *Legal traditions of the world.* 2nd edn. Oxford: Oxford University Press.

Gluckman, Max. 1955. *The judicial process among the Barotse of northern Rhodesia.* Manchester: Manchester University Press.

   (ed.). 1969. *Ideas and procedures in African customary law.* Oxford: Oxford University Press for the International African Institute.

Gorgendiere, L. de la *et al.* (eds.). 1997. *Ethnicity in Africa: Roots, meanings and implications.* Edinburgh: Centre of African Studies, University of Edinburgh.

Griffiths, Anne. 2001. 'Gendering culture: Towards a plural perspective on Kwena women's rights'. In: Cowan, Jane K., Marie-Bénédicte Dembour and Richard A. Wilson (eds.) *Culture and rights: Anthropological perspectives.* Cambridge: Cambridge University Press, pp. 102–26.

Griffiths, John. 1986. 'What is legal pluralism?'. No. 24. *Journal of Legal Pluralism and Unofficial Law*, pp. 1–56.

Grimes, Ronald L. 1982. *Beginnings in ritual studies.* Lanham, MD: University Press of America.

Gulliver, P. H. 1963. *Social control in an African society: A study of the Arusha, agricultural Masai of northern Tanganyika.* London and Boston: Routledge & Kegan Paul and Boston University Press.

Gupta, Dhruba. 1991. 'Indian perceptions of Africa'. Vol. 11 No. 2. *South Asia Research*, pp. 158–74.

Häckel, Erwin. 1974. *Afrikanischer Nationalismus.* Munich: Ernst Vögel.

Hameso, Seyoum Y. 1997. *Ethnicity in Africa: Towards a positive approach.* London: TSC.

Hampton, Janie (ed.). 1998. *Internally displaced people: A global survey.* London: Earth Scan.

Hart, H. L. A. 1961. *The concept of law.* Oxford: Clarendon Press.

Harvey, William B. 1966. *Law and social change in Ghana.* Princeton, NJ: Princeton University Press.

Hay, Margaret J. and Marcia Wright (eds.). 1982. *African women and the law: Historical perspectives.* Boston: Boston University.

Hinz, Manfred O. 1995. *Customary law in Namibia: Development and perspective.* Windhoek: University of Namibia.

  2003. *Without chiefs there would be no game: Customary law and nature conservation.* Windhoek: Out of Africa.

Hinz, Manfred O., Sam K. Amoo and Dawid van Wyk (eds.). 2000. *10 years of Namibian nationhood: The constitution at work.* Windhoek: University of Namibia.

Hoering, Uwe and Christa Wichterich. 1991. *Kein Zustand dauert ewig: Afrika in den neunziger Jahren.* Göttingen: Lamuv.

Holleman, J. F. 1974. *Issues in African law.* The Hague and Paris: Mouton.

Hood, Roger. 1992. *Race and sentencing.* Oxford: Clarendon Press.

Hooker, M. B. 1975. *Legal pluralism: An introduction to colonial and neo-colonial laws.* Oxford: Clarendon Press.

Howell, Paul. 1954. *A manual of Nuer law: Being an account of customary law, its evolution and development in the courts established by the Sudan Government.* London: Oxford University Press for the International African Institute.

Ihonvbere, Julius O. 1994. 'The "irrelevant" state, ethnicity and the quest for nationhood in Africa'. Vol. 17 No. 1. *Ethnic and Racial Studies,* pp. 42–60.

Jahn, Janheinz. 1961. *Muntu: An outline of neo-African culture.* London: Faber and Faber.

Jones, Richard and Gnanapala Welhengama. 2000. *Ethnic minorities in English law.* Stoke-on-Trent: Trentham.

Journal of African Law. 1984. (Special number: The construction and transformation of African customary law). Vol. 28 Nos. 1 and 2.

Kagan, K. Kahana 1955. *Three great systems of jurisprudence.* London: Stevens.

Keller, Edmond J. and Donald Rothchild (eds.). 1996. *Africa in the new international order: Rethinking state sovereignty and regional security.* London: Lynne Rienner.

Kenyatta, Jomo. 1938. *Facing Mount Kenya: The tribal life of the Gikuyu.* London: Secker & Warburg.

Kibreab, Gaim. 1985. *African refugees.* Trenton, NJ: Africa World Press.

  1987. *Refugees and development in Africa: The case of Eritrea.* Trenton, NJ: Red Sea Press.

Kuper, Hilda and Leo Kuper (eds.). 1965. *African law: Adaptation and development.* Berkeley and Los Angeles: University of California Press.

Ladley, Andrew. 1982. 'Changing the courts in Zimbabwe: The Customary Law and Primary Courts Act'. Vol. 26 No. 2. *Journal of African Law,* pp. 95–115.

Lapping, Brian. 1989. *End of empire.* London: Paladin Grafton.

Legrand, Pierre. 1996. 'How to compare now'. Vol. 16 No. 2. *Legal Studies*, pp. 232–42.

Levine, Robert M. and John J. Crocitti (eds.). 1999. *The Brazil reader: History, culture, politics*. London: Latin American Bureau.

Llewellyn, Karl N. and E. Adamson Hoebel. 1941. *The Cheyenne way: Conflict and case law in primitive jurisprudence*. Norman: University of Oklahoma Press.

Lloyd, P. C. 1962. *Yoruba land law*. London: Oxford University Press for the Nigerian Institute of Social and Economic Research.

Lowy, Michael J. 1978. 'A good name is worth more than money: Strategies of court use in urban Ghana'. In: Nader, Laura and Harry F. Todd Jr (eds.) *The disputing process – Law in ten societies*. New York: Columbia University Press, pp. 181–208.

Lugard, Frederick. 1922. *The dual mandate in British tropical Africa*. Edinburgh and London: William Blackwood and Sons.

Maathai, Wangari. 1995. 'Bottlenecks of development'. No. 169. *Resurgence*, pp. 4–10.

Maine, Henry Sumner. 1861. *Ancient law*. London: John Murray.

Malan, J. S. 1995. *People of Namibia*. Wingate Park: Rhino Publishers.

Malinowski, Bronislaw. 1926. *Crime and custom in savage society*. London: Kegan Paul.

Mamdani, Mahmood. 1996. *Citizen and subject. Contemporary Africa and the legacy of late colonialism*. Princeton: Princeton University Press.

Mann, K. and R. Roberts (eds.). 1991. *Law in colonial Africa*. Portsmouth, NH: Heinemann.

May, Reinhard. 1985. *Law and society East and West: Dharma, li and nomos, their contribution to thought and to life*. Stuttgart: Franz Steiner Verlag.

Mbiti, S. John. 1988. *African religions and philosophy*. London: Heinemann.

McAuslan, Patrick. 1996. 'Good governance and aid in Africa'. Vol. 40 No. 2. *Journal of African Law*, pp. 168–82.

Mensah-Brown, A. Kodwo. 1976. *Introduction to the law in contemporary Africa*. Owerri, New York and London: Conch Magazine.

Menski, Werner. 2001. *Modern Indian family law*. Richmond: Curzon Press.

Menski, Werner, Ahmad Rafay Alam and Mehreen Kasuri Raza. 2000. *Public interest litigation in Pakistan*. London and Karachi: Platinium and Pakistan Law House.

Middleton, John (ed.). 1997. *Encyclopedia of Africa south of the Sahara*. Vols I–IV. New York: Charles Scribner's Sons.

Middleton, John and David Tait (eds.). 1958. *Tribes without rulers: Studies in African segmentary systems*. London: Routledge & Kegan Paul.

Moore, Joanne I. 1999. *Immigrants in courts*. Seattle and London: University of Washington Press.

Moore, Sally Falk. 1978. *Law as process: An anthropological approach*. London: Routledge & Kegan Paul.

1986. *Social facts and fabrications: 'Customary' law on Kilimanjaro 1880–1980.* Cambridge: Cambridge University Press.

Morris, Henry F. and James S. Read. 1972. *Indirect rule and the search for justice: Essays in East African legal history.* Oxford: Clarendon Press.

Mothe, Gordon de la. 1993. *Reconstructing the black image.* Stoke-on-Trent: Trentham.

Mudimbe, V. Y. 1988. *The invention of Africa: Gnosis, philosophy, and the order of knowledge.* Bloomington: Indiana University Press.

Nader, Laura and Harry F. Todd Jr (eds.). 1978. *The disputing process – Law in ten societies.* New York: Columbia University Press.

Nandy, Ashis. 1983. *The intimate enemy: Loss and recovery of self under colonialism.* New Delhi: Oxford University Press.

Ojwang, J. B. 1995. 'Laying a basis for rights: Towards a jurisprudence of development'. In: Woodman, Gordon and A. O. Obilade (eds.) *African law and legal theory.* Aldershot: Dartmouth, pp. 351–97.

Okupa, Effa. 1996. *Ethno-jurisprudence of children's rights: A study of the Himba of Namibia.* London: SOAS. (Unpublished PhD thesis).

1998. *International bibliography of African customary law.* Hamburg: LIT and International African Institute.

Onyewuenyi, Innocent. 1991. 'Is there an African philosophy?'. In: Serequeberhan, Tsenay (ed.) *African philosophy: The essential readings.* New York: Paragon, pp. 29–46.

Parratt, John. 1987. *A reader in African Christian theology.* London: SPCK.

Pearl, David and Werner Menski. 1998. *Muslim family law.* 3rd edn. London: Sweet & Maxwell.

Peerenboom, Randall (ed.). 2004. *Asian discourses of rule of law: Theories and implementation of rule of law in twelve Asian countries, France and the US.* London and New York: Routledge.

Quaison-Sackey, Alex. 1963. *Africa unbound: Reflections of an African statesman.* New York: Frederick A. Praeger.

Radcliffe-Brown, A. R. and Daryll Forde (eds.). 1956. *African systems of kinship and marriage.* London: Oxford University Press.

Rautenbach, Christa and N. M. I. Goolam (eds.). 2002. *Introduction to legal pluralism* 'Part II' *Religious legal systems.* Durban: Butterworths.

Read, James S. 1997. 'Law'. In: Middleton, John (ed.) *Encyclopedia of Africa south of the Sahara.* New York: Charles Scribner's Sons, Vol. 2, pp. 526–59.

Reichmann, Rebecca (ed.). 1999. *Race in contemporary Brazil: From indifference to inequality.* University Park: Pennsylvania State University Press.

Reisman, Michael. 1982. 'The individual under African law in comprehensive context'. In: Takirambudde, Peter Nanyenya (ed.) *The individual under African law.* Gaborone: University of Botswana, pp. 9–27.

Roberts, Simon. 1979. *Order and dispute.* Harmondsworth: Penguin.

Rosen, Lawrence. 1989. *The anthropology of justice: Law as culture in Islamic society.* Cambridge: Cambridge University Press.

Rubin, Leslie and Eugene Cotran. 1960. *Readings in African law.* London: Cass.

Sachs, Albie and G. Honwana Welch. 1990. *Liberating the law: Creating popular justice in Mozambique.* London: Zed Books.

Sanders, A. J. G. M. 1987. 'Towards a people's philosophy of law'. Vol. 31 Nos. 1–2. *Journal of African Law*, pp. 37–43.

Santos, Boaventura de. 1995. *Toward a new common sense: Law, science and politics in the paradigmatic transition.* London: Routledge.

Sarbah, John Mensah. 1968. *Fanti customary laws: A brief introduction to the principles of the native laws and customs of the Gold Coast.* 3rd edn. London: Cass.

Sarup, Madan. 1991. *Education and the ideologies of racism.* Stoke-on-Trent: Trentham.

Schapera, Isaac. 1938. *A handbook of Tswana law and custom.* London: Oxford University Press.

    1955. *A handbook of Tswana law and custom.* 2nd edn. London: Oxford University Press.

Schott, Rüdiger. 1995. 'Rechtspluralismus und Rechtsgleichheit in den postkolonialen Staaten Afrikas'. In: Lampe, Ernst-Joachim (ed.) *Rechtsgleichheit und Rechtspluralismus.* Baden-Baden: Nomos, pp. 38–71.

Serequeberhan, Tsenay (ed.). 1991. *African philosophy: The essential readings.* New York: Paragon.

Shack, William A. and Elliott P. Skinner (eds.). 1979. *Strangers in African societies.* Berkeley: University of California Press.

Shah, Prakash. 2000. *Refugees, race and the legal concept of asylum in Britain.* London: Cavendish.

Shivji, Issa G. 1989. *The concept of human rights in Africa.* London: Codesria Book Series.

Shorter, Aylward. 1975. *African Christian theology.* London: Geoffrey Chapman.

    1991. 'African religions'. In: Hinnells, John R. (ed.) *A handbook of living religions.* Reprint. London: Penguin, pp. 425–38.

Takirambudde, Peter Nanyenya (ed.). 1982. *The individual under African law.* Gaborone: University of Botswana.

Tanner, Ralph E. S. 1966. 'Codification of customary law in Tanzania'. Vol. 2 No. 2. *East African Law Journal*, pp. 105–16.

Tempels, Placide. 1969. *Bantu philosophy.* Paris: Présence Africaine.

Tsanga, Amy Shupikai. 1997. 'Experiences from legal aid and legal literacy programmes in Zimbabwe'. In: Mehdi, Rubya and Farida Shaheed (eds.) *Women's law in legal education and practice in Pakistan. North South cooperation.* Copenhagen: New Social Science Monograph.

Turner, Victor. 1965. 'Ritual symbolism, morality and social structure among the Ndembu'. In: Fortes, M. and G. Dieterlen (eds.) *African systems of thought.* London: Oxford University Press, pp. 79–95.

1968. *The drums of affliction*. Oxford: Clarendon Press.

Twining, William. 1963. 'The restatement of African customary law: A comment'. Vol. 1 No. 2. *Journal of Modern African Studies*, pp. 221–8.

2000. *Globalisation and legal theory*. London: Butterworths.

Unger, Roberto Mangabeira. 1976. *Law in modern society: Toward a criticism of social theory*. New York: Free Press.

Vanderlinden, Jacques. 1972. *Bibliographie de droit africain 1947–1966*. Brussels: Presses Universitaires de Bruxelles.

Wanitzek, Ulrike. 1990–1. 'Legally unrepresented women petitioners in the lower courts of Tanzania: A case of justice denied?'. Nos. 30–1. *Journal of Legal Pluralism*, pp. 255–70.

Watson, Alan. 1993. *Legal transplants: An approach to comparative law*. 2nd edn. Athens, GA: University of Georgia Press.

Woodman, Gordon. 1988. 'How state courts create customary law in Ghana and Nigeria'. In: Morse, Bradford W. and Gordon R. Woodman (eds.) *Indigenous law and the state*. Dordrecht: Foris, pp. 181–220.

1995. 'Some realism about customary law – The West African experience'. In: Woodman, Gordon and A. O. Obilade (eds.) *African law and legal theory*. Aldershot: Dartmouth, pp. 145–69.

Woodman, Gordon and A. O. Obilade (eds.). 1995. *African law and legal theory*. Aldershot: Dartmouth.

Yelpaala, K. 1983. 'Circular arguments and self-fulfilling definitions: Statelessness and the Dagaaba'. No. 10. *History in Africa*, pp. 349–85.

Young, C. 1994. *The African colonial state in comparative perspective*. New Haven: Yale University Press.

Young, Josiah. 1986. *Black and African theologies*. New York: Orbis.

Zartman, I. 1985. *Ripe for resolution: Conflict and intervention in Africa*. Oxford: Oxford University Press.

Chapter 7, Chinese law

Ainsley, Clive. 1986. 'Chinese criminal law under Manchus and Marxists'. Vol. 20 No. 1. *University of British Columbia Law Review*, pp. 165–91.

Allott, Antony N. 1980. *The limits of law*. London: Butterworths.

Baker, Hugh D. R. 1979. *Chinese family and kinship*. London and Basingstoke: Macmillan.

Barrett, Jill. 1983. 'What's new in China's new constitution'. Vol. 9 No. 4. *Review of Socialist Law*, pp. 305–45.

Benecke, Gerhard. 1992. 'The comparative history of custom in Chinese law'. *Recueils de la Société Jean Bodin*, Vol. 53. La Coutume – Custom. Brussels: De Boeck Université, pp. 427–48.

Bianco, Lucien and Hua Chang-ming. 1988. 'Implementation and resistance: The single-child family policy'. In: Feuchtwang, Stephan, Athar Hussain and

Thierry Pairault (eds.) *Transforming China's economy in the eighties*. Vol. I, *The rural sector, welfare and employment*. Boulder, CO and London: Westview Press and Zed Books, pp. 147–68.

Bodde, Derek. 1954. 'Authority and law in ancient China'. Vol. 17. *Journal of the American Oriental Society*, pp. 46–55.

Bodde, Derek and Clarence Morris. 1967. *Law in imperial China*. Cambridge, MA: Harvard University Press.

Bonavia, David. 1982. *The Chinese*. Harmondsworth: Penguin.

Brady, James P. 1982. *Justice and politics in people's China: Legal order or continuing revolution?* London: Academic Press.

Butler, William E. (ed.). 1983. *The legal system of the Chinese Soviet Republic, 1931–1934*. Dobbs Ferry, NY: Transnational.

Buxbaum, David. 1971. 'Some aspects of civil procedure and practice at the trial level in Tanshui and Hsinchu from 1789 to 1895'. Vol. 30 No. 2. *Journal of Asian Studies*, pp. 255–79.

Callicott, J. Baird and Roger T. Ames. 1991. *Nature in Asian traditions of thought: Essays in environmental philosophy*. Delhi: Sri Satguru.

Chao, Chien-min and Bruce J. Dickson (eds.). 2001. *Remaking the Chinese state: Strategies, society and security*. London and New York: Routledge.

Chen, Albert. 1998. *An introduction to the legal system of the People's Republic of China*. Singapore: Butterworths Asia.

Chen, Fu-Mei Chang. 1970. 'On analogy in Ch'ing law'. Vol. 30. *Harvard Journal of Asiatic Studies*, pp. 212–24.

Cheng, Joseph Y. S. 1983–4. 'How to strengthen the National People's Congress and implement constitutionalism'. Vol. 16 Nos. 2–3. *Chinese Law and Government*, pp. 88–122.

1986. 'The present stage of state building in China and the 1979 electoral law'. Vol. 17 Nos. 1–2. *Internationales Asienforum*, pp. 99–130.

Chiba, Masaji (ed.). 1986. *Asian indigenous law in interaction with received law*. London and New York: KPI.

1989. *Legal pluralism: Towards a general theory through Japanese legal culture*. Tokyo: Tokai University Press.

Ching, Julia. 1993. *Chinese religions*. Basingstoke and London: Macmillan.

Clarke, Donald. 1995. 'The execution of civil judgments in China'. No. 141. *China Quarterly*, pp. 65–81.

Clarke, Donald C. and J. V. Feinerman. 1995. 'Antagonistic contradictions: Criminal law and human rights in China'. No. 141. *China Quarterly*, pp. 135–54.

Clayre, Alasdair. 1984. *The heart of the dragon*. London: Collins and Harvill.

Cohen, Jerome A. 1968. *The criminal process in the People's Republic of China, 1949–1963: An introduction*. Cambridge, MA: Harvard University Press.

Cohen, Jerome Alan, R. Randle Edwards and Fu-mei Chang Chen (eds.). 1980. *Essays on China's legal tradition*. Princeton: Princeton University Press.

Cottrell, Robert. 1993. *The end of Hong Kong: The secret diplomacy of imperial retreat.* London: John Murray

David, René and John E. C. Brierley. 1978. *Major legal systems in the world today.* London: Stevens & Sons.

De Bary, W. 1991. *The trouble with Confucianism.* Cambridge, MA and London: Harvard University Press.

De Cruz, Peter. 1999. *Comparative law in a changing world.* 2nd edn. London and Sydney: Cavendish.

Dicks, Anthony. 1989. 'The Chinese legal system: Reforms in the balance'. No. 119. *China Quarterly*, pp. 540–76.

  1990. 'New lamps for old: The evolving legal position of Islam in China, with special reference to family law'. In: Mallat, Chibli and Jane Connors (eds.) *Islamic family law.* London: Graham and Trotman, pp. 347–87.

  1995. 'Compartmentalized law and judicial restraint: An inductive view of some jurisdictional barriers to reform'. No. 141. *China Quarterly*, pp. 82–109.

Dikötter, Frank. 1990. 'Group definition and the idea of "race" in modern China (1793–1949)'. Vol. 13 No. 3. *Ethnic and Racial Studies*, pp. 420–31.

Dillon, Michael. 2001. *Religious minorities and China.* London: Minority Rights Group.

  2004. *Xinjiang – China's Muslim Far Northwest.* London and New York: RoutledgeCurzon.

Doo, Leigh-Wai. 1973. 'Dispute settlement in Chinese-American communities'. Vol. 21 No. 4. *The American Journal of Comparative Law*, pp. 627–63.

Elvin, Mark. 1970a. 'Early communist land reform and the Kiangsi rural economy'. Vol. 4 No. 2. *Modern Asian Studies*, pp. 165–9.

  1970b. 'The last thousand years of Chinese history'. Vol. 4 No. 2. *Modern Asian Studies*, pp. 97–114.

Evers, Georg. 1989. 'Geduldet oder akzeptiert? Die Religionen im nachrevolutionären China'. Vol. 25 No. 2. *Der überblick*, pp. 50–3.

Fairbank John K. and Kwang-Ching Liu. 1980. *The Cambridge history of China.* Vol. 11 Part 2. Cambridge: Cambridge University Press.

Fan, Jianhong. 1997. 'Die Rezeption der deutschen Strafrechtslehre und Strafvorschriften in der VR China'. Vol. 28 No. 4. *Internationales Asienforum*, pp. 361–74.

Feng, Youlan. 1952–3. *A history of Chinese philosophy.* 2nd edn. Princeton: Princeton University Press.

Fikentscher, Wolfgang. 1995. *Modes of thought: A study in the anthropology of law and religion.* Tübingen: Mohr Siebeck.

Folsom, R. H. and J. H. Minan. 1989. *Law in the People's Republic of China: Commentary, readings and materials.* Dordrecht: Kluwer.

Gasper, D. 1982. 'The Chinese National People's Congress'. In: Nelson, D. and G. White (eds.) *Communist legislatures in comparative perspective*. London: Macmillan, pp. 160–90.

Gellhorn, W. 1987. 'China's quest for legal modernity'. Vol. 1 No. 1. *Journal of Chinese Law*, pp. 1–22.

Glenn, H. Patrick. 2000. *Legal traditions of the world*. Oxford: Oxford University Press.

2004. *Legal traditions of the world*. 2nd edn. Oxford: Oxford University Press.

Gniffke, Frank L. 1969. 'German writings on Chinese law'. Vol. 15 No. 3. *Osteuropa Recht*, pp. 1–43.

Goodman, David S. G. and Gerald Segal (eds.). 1994. *China deconstructs. Politics, trade and regionalism*. London and New York: Routledge.

Hart, H. L. A. 1961. *The concept of law*. Oxford: Clarendon Press.

He, Ping. 1995. 'Perception of identity in modern China'. Vol. 1 No. 1. *Social Identities*, pp. 127–54.

Ho, Chin Ung. 2000. *The Chinese of South-East Asia*. London: Minority Rights Group.

Hsiao, Kung-Chuan. 1960. *Rural China: Imperial control in the nineteenth century*. Seattle: University of Washington Press.

Hsin-Chi, Kuan. 1984. 'New departures in China's constitution'. Vol. 17 No.1. *Studies in Comparative Communism*, pp. 53–68.

Hsu, F. L. K. 1944. 'Some problems of Chinese law in operation today'. Vol. 3 No. 3. *Far Eastern Quarterly*, pp. 211–21.

Huntington, Samuel P. 1998. *The clash of civilizations and the remaking of world order*. London: Touchstone Books.

Jones, W. C. 1989. *Basic principles of civil law in China*. Armonk, NY: M. E. Sharpe.

Kampen, Thomas. 1986. 'The Zunyi Conference and the rise of Mao Zedong'. Vol. 17 Nos. 3–4. *Internationales Asienforum*, pp. 347–60.

Keith, Ronald C. 1994. *China's struggle for the rule of law*. New York and London: St Martin's Press and Macmillan.

Keller , P. 1989. 'Legislation in the People's Republic of China'. Vol. 23 No. 3. *University of British Columbia Law Review*, pp. 653–88.

Kelsen, Hans. 1970. *Pure theory of law*. (trans. from the 2nd revised and enlarged German edn.). Berkeley: University of California Press.

Kolenda, Helena. 1990. 'One party, two systems: Corruption in the People's Republic of China and attempts to control it'. Vol. 4 No. 2. *Journal of Chinese Law*, pp. 187–232.

Ladany, Laszlo. 1992. *Law and legality in China: The testament of a China-watcher*. London: Hurst.

Lee, Hyeong-Kyu. 1987. 'Die Rezeption des europäischen Zivilrechts in Ostasien'. Vol. 86 No. 3. *Zeitschrift für Vergleichende Rechtswissenschaft*, pp. 158–70.

Leng, Shao-chuan. 1967. 'Pre-1949 development of the Communist Chinese system of justice'. No. 30. *China Quarterly*, pp. 93–114.

Leng, Shao-chuan and Hungdah Chiu. 1985. *Criminal justice in post-Mao China: Analysis and documents*. Albany, NY: State University of New York Press.

Li, H. Victor. 1970. 'The role of law in Communist China'. No. 44. *China Quarterly*, pp. 66–111.

Lin, Feng. 2000. *Constitutional law in China*. Hong Kong: Sweet & Maxwell Asia.

Ling, Trevor. 1988. *A history of religion East and West*. Reprint. Basingstoke and London: Macmillan.

Liu, Nanping. 1991. '"Legal precendents" with Chinese characteristics: Published cases in the Gazette of the Supreme People's Court'. Vol. 5 No. 1. *Journal of Chinese Law*, pp. 107–29.

Lloyd, Dennis. 1991. *The idea of law*. 8th edn. London: Penguin Books.

Lubman, Stanley. 1995. 'Introduction: The future of Chinese law'. No. 141. *China Quarterly*, pp. 1–21.

(ed.) 1996. *China's legal reforms*. Oxford and New York: Oxford University Press.

1999. *Bird in a cage: Legal reforms in China after Mao*. Stanford: Stanford University Press.

May, Reinhard, 1985. *Law and society East and West: Dharma, li and nomos, their contribution to law and to life*. Stuttgart: Franz Steiner.

McAleavy, Henry. 1968a. 'Chinese law'. In: Derrett, J. D. M. (ed.) *Introduction to legal systems*. London: Sweet & Maxwell, pp. 105–30.

1968b. 'Some aspects of marriage and divorce in communist China'. In: Anderson, J. N. D. (ed.) *Family law in Asia and Africa*. London: Allen & Unwin, pp. 73–89.

Meijer, M. J. 1971. *Marriage law and policy in the Chinese People's Republic*. Hong Kong: Hong Kong University Press.

Menski, Werner. (ed.). 1995. *Coping with 1997: The reaction of the Hong Kong people to the transfer of power*. Stoke-on-Trent: Trentham Books.

2001. *Modern Indian family law*. Richmond: Curzon Press.

Moore, Joanne I. 1999. *Immigrants in courts*. Seattle and London: University of Washington Press.

Morris, Clarence. 1967. 'Preface'. In: Bodde, Derek and Clarence Morris, *Law in imperial China*. Cambridge, MA: Harvard University Press, pp. v–ix.

Münzel, Frank. 1982. *Das Recht der Volksrepublik China*. Darmstadt: Wissenschaftliche Buchgesellschaft.

Murphey, Rhoads. 1967. 'Man and nature in China'. Vol. 1 No. 4. *Modern Asian Studies*, pp. 313–33.

Needham, J. 1956. *Science and civilization in China*. London: Cambridge University Press.

Oda, Hiroshi. 1992. *Japanese law*. London: Butterworths.

Orleans, Leo A. (ed.). 1979. *Chinese approaches to family planning*. New York: M. E. Sharpe.

Otto, Jan Michiel, Maurice V. Polak, Jianfu Chen and Yuwen Li (eds.). 2000. *Law making in the People's Republic of China*. The Hague: Kluwer.

Palmer, Michael. 1986. 'Adoption law in the People's Republic of China'. In: Butler, William E. (ed.) *Yearbook on socialist legal systems*. Dobbs Ferry, NY: Transnational, pp. 1–35.

1986–7. 'The People's Republic of China: Some general observations on family law'. Vol. 25 No. 1. *Journal of Family Law*, pp. 41–68.

1987a. 'The People's Republic of China: Problems of marriage and divorce'. Vol. 11. *Annual Survey of Family Law*, pp. 57–79.

1987b. 'The revival of mediation in the PRC: (1) Extra-judicial mediation'. In: Butler, W. E. (ed.) *Yearbook on socialist legal systems*. Dobbs Ferry, NY: Transnational, pp. 219–77.

1987c. 'The surface-subsoil form of divided ownership in late imperial China: Some examples from the New Territories of Hong Kong'. Vol. 21 No. 1. *Modern Asian Studies*, pp. 1–119.

1988. 'China's new inheritance law: Some preliminary observations'. In: Feuchtwang, S. D. R., Athar Hussain and Thierry Pairault (eds.) *Transforming China's economy in the eighties*. Vol. 1, *The rural sector, welfare and employment*. Boulder, CO and London: Westview Press and Zed Books, pp. 169–97.

1989a. 'Civil adoption in contemporary Chinese law: A contract to care'. Vol. 23 No. 2. *Modern Asian Studies*, pp. 373–410.

1989b. 'The revival of mediation in the PRC: (2) Judicial mediation'. In: Butler, W. E. (ed.) *Yearbook on socialist legal systems 1988*. Dobbs Ferry, NY: Transnational, pp. 143–69.

1991. 'Mediation in the People's Republic of China: Some general observations'. In: Mackie, Karl J. (ed.) *A handbook of dispute resolution: ADR in action*. London and New York: Routledge and Sweet & Maxwell, pp. 221–30.

1992a. 'Minors to the fore: Developments in the family law of the People's Republic of China 1990–91'. In: Freeman, M. D. A (ed.) *Annual Survey of Family Law, 1991*, pp. 299–308.

1992b. 'What makes socialist law socialist? – The Chinese case'. In: Feldbrugge. F. J. M. (ed.) *The emancipation of Soviet law*. Dordrecht: Martinus Nijhoff, pp. 51–72.

1995. 'The re-emergence of family law in post-Mao China: Marriage, divorce and reproduction'. Vol. 141. *China Quarterly*, pp. 110–34.

1996. 'Women to the fore: Developments in the family law of the People's Republic of China, 1992–4'. In: Bainham, Andrew (ed.) *The International Survey of Family Law 1994*. Leiden: Martinus Nijhoff, pp. 155–79.

1997. 'Protecting the health of mothers and their children? Developments in the family law of the People's Republic of China, 1995'. In: Bainham, Andrew (ed.) *The International Survey of Family Law 1995*. The Hague: Martinus Nijhoff, pp. 107–16.

1999. 'Environmental law in the People's Republic of China'. No. 156. *China Quarterly*, pp. 788–808.

Peerenboom, Randall. 2003. 'The X-files: Past and present portrayals of China's alien legal system'. *Washington University Global Studies Law Review*, pp. 37–95.

(ed.). 2004. *Asian discourses of rule of law: Theories and implementation of rule of law in twelve Asian countries, France and the US.* London and New York: Routledge.

Potter, Pitman (ed.). 1994. *Domestic law reforms in post-Mao China.* Armonk, NY and London: M. E. Sharpe.

Rausch, Karin. 1987. 'Immer einen Ausweg lassen. Soziale Kontrolle und Strafrecht in China'. Vol. 23 No. 3. *Der überblick*, pp. 40–3.

Rodzinski, Witold. 1983. 'A new survey of late Ch'ing history'. No. 1. *Journal of the Royal Asiatic Society*, pp. 74–82.

Saich, Tony. 1983. 'The Fourth Constitution of the PRC'. Vol. 9 No. 2. *Review of Socialist Law*, pp. 113–24.

Sarkar, Benoy Kumar. 1975. *Chinese religion through Hindu eyes: A study in the tendencies of Asiatic mentality.* Delhi: Oriental.

Saso, Michael. 1991. 'Chinese religions'. In: Hinnells, John R. (ed.) *A handbook of living religions.* Reprint. London: Penguin, pp. 344–64.

Schram, S. 1985. 'Decentralization in a unitary state: Theory and practice 1940–1984'. In: Schram, S. (ed.) *The scope of state power in China.* London: SOAS, pp. 81–125.

Schurmann, F. 1968. *Ideology and organization in communist China.* Berkeley: University of California Press.

Seidman, A. and R. B. Seidman. 1996. 'Drafting legislation for development: Lessons from a Chinese project'. Vol. 44. *American Journal of Comparative Law*, pp. 1–44.

Shapiro, Martin. 1981. *Courts: A comparative and political analysis.* Chicago and London: University of Chicago Press.

Shiga, Shuzo. 1992. 'Custom as source of law in traditional China'. *Recueils de la Société Jean Bodin*, Vol. 53. La Coutume – Custom. Brussels: De Boeck Université, pp. 413–25.

Stockman, Norman. 2000. *Understanding Chinese society.* Cambridge: Polity Press.

Tay, A. Erh-Soon. 1971. 'Law in Communist China – Part 2'. Vol. 6 No. 3. *Sydney Law Review*, pp. 335–70.

Townsend, D. E. 1989. 'The concept of law in post-Mao-China: A case study of economic crime'. Vol. 24 No. 1. *Stanford Journal of International Law*, pp. 227–58.

Tsien, Josiane. 1992. 'Rite et coutume en Chine'. *Recueils de la Société Jean Bodin*, Vol. 53. La Coutume – Custom. Brussels: De Boeck Université, pp. 391–411.

Unger, Roberto Mangabeira. 1976. *Law in modern society: Toward a criticism of social theory.* New York: Free Press.

van der Sprenkel, Sybille. 1977. *Legal institutions in Manchu China: A sociological analysis.* Reprint. London: Athlone Press.

von Senger, Harro. 1983. 'Rückbesinnung auf Konfuzius in der Volksrepublik China?'. Vol. 133 No. 2. *Zeitschrift der Deutschen Morgenländischen Gesellschaft*, pp. 377–92.

Wang, Chenguang and Xianchu Zhang (eds.). 1997. *Introduction to Chinese law*. Hong Kong: Sweet & Maxwell Asia.

Weng, B. 1982. 'Some key aspects of the 1982 Draft Constitution of the PRC'. Nos. 89–92. *China Quarterly*, pp. 492–506.

1984. 'The role of the state council'. Vol. 16 Nos. 2–3. *Chinese Law and Government*, pp. 153–92.

Zheng, Henry R. 1988. *China's civil and commercial law*. Singapore: Butterworths.

Zweigert, Konrad and Hein Kötz. 1998. *Introduction to comparative law*. Trans. from the German by Tony Weir, 3rd revised edn. Oxford: Clarendon.

absolutist rule 148, 337
academic lawyers 30, 32, 38, 49, 59,
    61, 65, 74, 83, 103, 108, 129, 157,
    162, 176, 195, 274, 367, 387, 444,
    466–7, 518, 600
accountability, *see* public interest
adat (local customary) law 336
Afghanistan 281
African law xii, 9, 21–2, 51, 82, 108,
    110, 111, 130, 133, 144, 193, 194,
    201, 242, 260, 281, 296, 331, 345,
    380–491, 508, 518, 593, 597, 600,
    605
  abuse of 405, 420, 427, 428, 440,
    460, 461–2, 472, 478–9, 480, 485,
    486, 487, 488, 587
  acephalous societies 435, 436, 440,
    461, 482
  alleged absence of law 77, 111, 194,
    281, 380–1, 382, 384–5, 387, 390,
    401, 466, 467, 499
  ancestors 108, 110, 411, 417, 420,
    421, 430, 454, 469, 472
  barbaric 405, 406, 465, 469, 472
  broken tradition 385
  chiefs, *see also* rulers 421, 436, 440,
    443, 461, 462, 482
  Christian influence 21, 385, 387,
    388, 413, 416, 417, 420, 454, 468
  chthonic character 381, 410, 453
  codification 449, 466, 478, 481, 484
  colonial influence on 21, 22, 382,
    385, 395, 398, 444–64, 472
  constructed nature of 463, 471,
    473–5, 487
  culture-specificity 381, 394, 409,
    414, 422, 492

customs 22, 43, 248, 382, 384–5,
    391, 394, 395, 398, 400, 402, 403,
    405, 412–13, 421–35, 451–2,
    453–9, 464, 470–8, 490, 491, 492
  definition of 380, 383–4
  dispute settlement 79, 382, 412–13,
    422, 435–44, 459–64, 477–80, 549
  duty focus 155, 409, 411, 466, 481
  dynamic interaction 400, 420
  environment 22, 381, 410, 412, 422
  equilibrium, *see* harmony
  equity 419
  globalising pressures on 22
  harmony 133, 412, 417, 420, 430,
    435, 437–8, 441, 443, 444, 453,
    459, 469, 473–4, 479, 482, 484,
    485, 489
  Himba 388, 411
  holistic 381, 387, 407, 439
  indigenous 394, 395, 464, 466, 471,
    472, 475, 487, 492
  'indirect rule' 390, 420, 424, 445,
    448, 450–1, 452, 454, 459, 461,
    462, 479, 480
  individual 404, 412, 421, 425,
    427–8, 429, 431, 443, 466
  interlinkedness 419
  internal perspectives of 22
  justice 389, 406, 426, 431, 438
  lawyers 433, 434–5
  legislation 434, 454
  litigiousness 460
  living law 383–4, 388, 396, 470
  Muslim influence on 21, 381, 382,
    383, 385, 387, 388, 413, 416, 417,
    430, 446, 451, 454, 465, 468
  native law 384–5, 394, 395

African law (*cont.*)
  natural law   22, 381, 468, 469, 476
  oral nature   9, 381, 382, 388, 394,
    396, 409, 422–3, 439, 457
  order focus   22, 411, 421, 607
  plurality of   21, 420
  positivism   425
  post-colonial   382, 464–84, 580
  pre-colonial   382
  public interest   426, 431, 443
  reconstruction of   383–5, 468
  reforms of   382, 457
  religious elements in   37, 381, 402,
    405, 407, 411, 413–21, 424, 607
  repugnancy   243, 390, 451, 455, 463,
    472
  ritual   414–16, 418
  rulers, *see also* chiefs   311, 330, 410,
    418, 447, 477, 480, 486, 538
  secularism   381
  self-controlled balancing   409, 411,
    421
  situation-specific   406, 411, 422,
    427, 442
  state   399, 402, 421, 427, 432, 435,
    437, 445, 461, 473, 481
  static nature of   408, 422, 453
  theory of   380, 391, 396–401, 492
  traditions of   382, 384–5, 390,
    404–21, 472
  ubuntu ('interlinkedness')   489
  unification   382, 458, 466, 473, 480,
    520
  witchcraft   416, 463
  women   460, 480, 491
African philosophy   21, 89, 131, 386,
  387, 388, 398, 408, 410, 428–9
African religions   387, 413
Africans in diaspora, *see* black people
Africanisation   486, 489, 491
Afropessimism   385
Allott, A. N.   xiii, 75, 76, 78, 102,
  108–13, 167, 178–9, 181, 202, 208,
  383–4, 389, 450, 456–7, 467, 489,
  527, 595
alternative dispute resolution   229, 534
American approaches, *see also* US law
  schools   150, 154, 164–6, 177,
  423, 599

American Indians   146
American realists   164, 166, 168, 599
analytical school, *see also* positivism
  155, 177
Anglo-Hindu law   19, 51, 116, 196, 197,
  200, 202, 234, 239–49, 254, 267
  bogusness of   246
Anglo-Indian law,   449, 455, 462
Anglo-Muhammadan law   281, 367,
  369
angrezi shariat (British Muslim law)
  61, 80, 97, 362, 470
anthropology   7, 16, 28, 29–41, 53, 62,
  83, 85, 86, 90, 104, 105, 108, 121,
  382, 388, 390, 392, 396, 424, 466,
  518
Aquinas, St Thomas   142–4, 145, 146,
  147, 148, 151, 204, 207, 285, 287,
  324
Aristotle   137, 139, 142, 162,
  222, 386
Asian despotism   87
Asian laws   120, 122, 127, 130, 144,
  155, 193, 250, 260, 331, 495, 496,
  512, 570, 583, 593, 605
Asian values   57, 122, 262, 264, 468,
  590, 605
Aśoka   218–19, 222, 269, 338, 425,
  539, 598
assimilationist pressures   64–5
Austin, John   18, 59, 86, 88, 98, 99,
  112, 130, 154, 155–7, 158, 176,
  181, 197, 199, 202, 226, 233, 285,
  326, 337, 440, 452, 535, 580, 598,
  601
Austro-Hungarian Empire   94
avoidance of disputes   34, 79, 238, 248,
  461, 476, 517, 533, 546

Bachofen, J. J.   88, 89
Ballard, Roger   62–3, 120, 121
Bangladesh   202, 261, 352, 368
Baxi, Upendra   12, 57, 119, 200, 203,
  230, 261
Bennett, T. W.   466, 470
Bentham, Jeremy   59, 87–8, 153,
  154–5, 164, 241, 598, 601
black box theories   8, 16, 18, 87, 129,
  173, 174, 409, 432, 496

black letter law 59, 69, 74, 78, 83, 129, 264, 470, 471, 474
black people, discrimination of 381, 382, 429, 467–8, 488
Blackstone, William 132, 154, 155
blasphemy 283, 324, 329
Boas, Franz 90
Bodin, Jean 86, 154, 519
Brazil 203, 383
Buddhist law 124, 145, 218, 287, 403

Canon Law 142, 151
Central Asia 23
Chagga law 57, 474
Chernobyl 12
Chiba, Masaji 36, 57, 64, 83, 96, 97, 104, 118, 119–28, 129, 153, 156, 179, 183, 184, 189, 197, 237, 363, 393, 399, 400, 402, 606
Chinese law xii, 9, 22–3, 51, 144, 153, 193, 194, 203, 222, 224, 345, 493, 597
  abuse of 529, 534, 586, 592
  ancestors 411, 430, 507, 514, 515, 517, 539, 560
  assisted self-control 525
  avoidance of law 547
  Board of Punishment 541, 564
  Buddhist influence on 498, 503, 504, 505, 562
  chthonic 498
  codes 493, 494, 495, 497, 499, 502, 521–5, 530, 535–8, 554, 564, 575, 592
  codification 579
  communist laws 495, 502, 561, 566–9, 576
  Communist Party 568, 569, 570, 585, 588, 592
  Confucian ethics 210, 493, 499, 500, 503, 504, 512, 514, 519, 522, 523, 524, 530, 532, 533, 540–1, 542, 545, 555, 563, 565, 567, 570, 571, 572, 575, 577, 581, 582, 585, 587, 588, 589, 593
  confucianisation of the law 210, 496, 521, 530, 531–4, 551, 585, 587, 590
  Confucius 516

Constitution 584
cruelty 493, 542, 544, 560, 564, 582
Cultural Revolution 260, 495, 570, 571, 576, 577, 578, 579, 580, 582, 583, 587, 590, 592
culture-specificity 494, 535, 547, 560, 575, 583, 593, 607
custom 22, 407, 493, 494, 507, 518–21, 530, 535, 550, 551, 554, 587
death penalty 505, 541, 559–60
democracy 579, 580, 587
dispute settlement 23, 517, 519, 546, 557, 590, 591
distrust of law 194, 497, 499, 516, 528
duty focus 556, 588
Emperor 330, 508, 518, 523, 526, 535, 538–41, 542, 563, 580
equity 551
fa (positive law, codes) 203, 223, 347, 502, 508, 510, 511, 521, 525–31, 533, 536
face, loss of 517, 552, 554, 557, 590
family 552, 553, 554, 555, 556, 557, 558, 591
feudal values 409, 566, 568, 571, 572, 573, 590
filial piety (*hsiao*) 514, 515–16, 517, 539, 555, 558
Golden Age 499
good governance 23, 144, 512, 524, 528, 532, 570
guilds 502, 553–4
harmony 494, 504, 505, 507, 513, 516, 518, 521, 523, 524, 529, 534, 538, 540, 546, 547, 548, 551
holistic 507
Hong Kong 519, 560, 568
hsing (punishment) 223, 347, 521, 527–8
human rights 23, 466, 480
Imperial system 23, 493, 495, 520, 541–7, 551, 553, 583
indigenous 499
individual 507–8, 512, 543
justice 542, 550, 560, 577, 585, 586
lawyers 433, 545–6, 574, 576, 588

Chinese law (*cont.*)
    legalism 210, 495, 503, 507, 523,
        524, 525–31, 540–1, 542, 577, 582,
        587, 591
    li (morality, duty, rites) 138, 224,
        294, 409, 501, 502, 505–12, 516,
        526, 530, 531, 544, 551, 570, 580
    li (sub-statutes) 536, 537
    litigiousness 546
    local norms, *see* custom
    lü (statutes) 536–7
    magistrates 543–5, 548, 549, 550,
        553, 556, 557
    Mandate of Heaven 206, 311, 440,
        504, 538–9, 540
    Mao Tse-tung 539, 567, 568, 569,
        570, 571, 573, 575, 576, 577, 578,
        586
    Maoist period 23, 570–8
    Mencius 508, 514, 515
    Miao people 527–8
    modern period 23, 494, 569
    Muslims 494, 563
    muyou ('friend behind the curtain')
        545
    natural law 22, 133, 493, 501, 504,
        510, 524, 581, 585, 593, 608
    orality 502, 520
    order focus 498, 499, 500, 503, 504,
        510–12, 523, 525, 536
    penal law focus 499
    philosophy 494, 496, 499, 500
    plural nature of 23, 493, 494, 538
    political nature of 501–2
    positivism 493, 516, 521, 528, 574,
        591, 592
    post-imperial system 23, 350, 495,
        520, 521, 560
    post-Maoist laws 529, 570, 579–84,
        585, 590
    postmodern 495, 569, 590, 592, 607
    PRC law 569–93
    public interest 570, 581, 585
    punishment, *see also hsing* 508, 518,
        523, 524, 529, 533, 549, 551, 555,
        557–9
    religion 495, 496–7, 498, 500–1,
        503, 504, 507, 514, 528, 530, 555,
        589, 607
    Republican period 260, 571
    secular 496, 500, 501, 507, 513, 514,
        525, 542
    self-controlled order 516, 522, 530,
        532, 547, 550, 555, 585, 591
    sinocentrism 561, 562, 563
    situation-specificity 530, 535, 557,
        560, 585
    socialist legality 23, 494, 495, 529,
        530, 566, 568, 569, 570, 571, 573,
        574, 579–80, 582, 583–4, 585, 586,
        589, 592
    state law 22, 494, 502, 512, 516,
        518, 523, 524, 548, 554, 555, 574,
        582, 583, 589, 592
    tao (cosmic Order) 80, 502, 503–5,
        526, 570, 607
    uniformity, impression of 22
    uniformisation 534
    village 552–3
    women 591
    wu lun (five relationships) 506,
        508, 516, 555
Christian law 103, 121, 130, 131,
    132, 141, 142, 143, 161, 220, 279,
    291
chthonic laws 85, 91, 103, 117, 130,
    131, 291, 296, 323, 380, 381, 387,
    393–4, 395, 402, 404, 488, 527
Church law, *see* Christian law
Cicero, Marcus Tullius 139, 140
civilising mission 11, 25, 37, 243, 424,
    444, 453, 465
clashes of culture, *see* conflict of
    civilisations
colonialism 37, 48, 89, 116, 386, 560
colonisation of the mind 37, 487
commercial law 35, 52, 53, 140, 147,
    263, 452, 536, 553
common law 45, 84, 154, 164, 171,
    172, 233, 246, 248, 332, 350, 475
Commonwealth 51, 158
community 53, 602, 610
comparative law xi, xii, 6, 21, 23, 30,
    40, 46–50, 66–9, 75, 79, 85, 104,
    161, 203, 225, 257, 263, 282, 287,
    337, 387, 394, 400, 490, 493, 508,
    582, 595, 597, 602, 607, 609
Comte, Auguste 162

conflict of civilisations 4, 161, 283, 379

conflict of laws, *see* private international law

consumer protection 127, 303

contract law 34, 140, 255, 272, 356, 452, 524, 536

convergence 41, 48, 195, 612

cosmic Order 135

Cotran, Eugene 458, 471, 480

Cotterrell, Roger 15, 53, 168, 169, 171, 172, 189, 602

Coulson, N. J. xiii, 288, 290–1, 308, 317, 352, 371–2, 373

Cownie, Fiona 168

Critical Legal Studies 168, 177

cultural defence 26, 601

cultural relativism of law 84, 90, 170

culture 30, 35, 51, 63, 67, 126, 127, 162, 173, 185, 189, 194, 590, 601

custom 33, 34, 37, 54, 59, 79, 83, 86, 87, 91, 96, 97, 107, 124, 125, 151, 152, 156, 172, 179, 184, 195, 336, 339, 476, 485, 519

custom in English law 87

Darwin, Charles 89

death penalty 230, 300

deep legal pluralism 29, 85, 118, 610

democracy 482, 486

Denmark 59

Derrett, J. D. M. xiii, 76, 77–8, 202, 231, 243–4, 247, 249, 264, 288–9

Dhagamwar, Vasudha 117, 260

difference 68, 160

divergence 53

Duguit, Jean 94, 97, 163

Durkheim, Emile 162, 164

Dworkin, Ronald 102, 159, 178

East Africa 383, 436, 446, 447, 448, 449, 462, 465, 467, 471, 478, 520

economic determinism 163

Egypt 123, 349, 350, 363, 386, 464

Ehrlich, Eugen 92–8, 106, 110, 114, 122, 165, 333, 363

Engels, Friedrich 163

English law 68, 76, 102, 150, 152, 172, 240, 242, 247, 263, 347, 369, 424, 448, 449, 456, 462, 600

Enlightenment 9, 11, 87, 149, 150, 498, 595, 597, 602, 604

environmental laws 127, 221, 504, 589

equality 13, 14, 31, 82, 138, 139, 142, 173, 190, 260, 266, 267, 273, 467

equality v. equity 15

equity 15, 17, 125, 419, 482, 596

essentialism 25, 32, 43, 204

ethnic implants 18, 26, 37, 58–65, 188, 456

ethnic minority laws 60, 97, 120, 124, 152, 382, 602

ethnic minority legal studies 34, 58, 61, 63

ethnicity 58, 62, 190, 284, 410, 467, 606, 611

Ethiopia 47, 448, 464, 483–4, 491

eurocentrism xi, xii, 6, 11, 23, 25, 32, 33, 46, 48, 49, 51, 56, 59, 77, 85, 99, 122, 128, 130, 131, 141, 146, 150, 161, 162, 175, 178, 186, 194, 195, 364, 389, 401, 605, 606, 613

European law 35, 40, 46, 156, 349, 384–5, 491, 564

evolutionism 28, 47, 85, 86, 89, 100, 162, 163, 392, 601

'exclusive legal positivism' 159

expert evidence 60

extra-legal 31, 32–3, 61, 64, 119, 158, 160, 173, 177, 217, 304, 497, 502, 517, 518, 519–20, 523, 534, 547, 551, 584, 598, 599, 600, 606

extra-territoriality 37, 58, 188, 348, 355, 562, 563

extremism 281, 283, 287

families of law, *see* legal families

Fatawa-I-Alamgiri 366

female circumcision 36

Finnis, John 169, 171, 173, 184

Fitzpatrick, Peter 127

folk law 85, 125, 394

Frank, Jerome 165

Freeman, Michael 158, 159, 162, 168, 174, 175

French law   70, 97, 242, 349, 355, 447,
    455
French Revolution   145, 149
Fuller, Lon   102, 160, 171–2
fundamentalism   16, 261, 273, 281,
    596

Galanter, Marc   37, 115, 119, 266
Gandhi, Indira   260, 262–3, 264, 265,
    266, 269, 273, 488, 489, 584
Gandhi, M. K.   37, 351, 488
Gandhi, Rajeev   276
general jurisprudence   129, 159, 160,
    161, 179, 195, 608
German law   60, 91, 562
Ghana   394, 395, 414, 442, 462, 464,
    465, 468, 478, 480
Giddens, Anthony   10
Gierke, Otto   91, 137
Gillissen, John   86, 114
Gledhill, Alan   264, 265
Glenn, Patrick   5, 8, 200, 252, 333,
    380, 496
global   9, 193
global village   9, 13, 49
globalisation   xi, xii, 3–17, 22, 23, 24,
    25–6, 37, 38, 41, 50, 53, 64, 76, 82,
    129, 131, 132, 139, 174, 195, 197,
    247, 282, 382, 399, 465, 467, 490,
    491, 495, 597
glocalisation   4, 12, 81, 195, 364, 491,
    596, 604
good governance   12, 38, 61, 144, 482,
    488, 597
Greek law   121, 132, 133, 134–9, 144,
    148, 153, 386, 512, 598
Griffiths, John   113–19, 237
Grotius, Hugo   132, 147, 148
grundnorm   113, 114, 116, 158, 201,
    204, 220, 251, 256, 259, 289, 324,
    379, 533

Hägerström, Axel   166
Hallaq, Wael   285, 337, 339, 343
harmonisation of laws   3, 16, 29, 38,
    39, 40, 42, 44, 46, 48, 195, 596
Hart, H. L. A.   34, 86, 98–103, 133,
    152, 156, 158–9, 160, 182, 218,
    225, 396, 436

Hart/Dworkin debates   159, 173
Hartland, S.   105
Hastings, Warren   116, 241, 243, 245,
    366
Hedaya   366, 377
Herder, Johann Gottfried von   90
Hindu   199, 201, 206, 207, 208, 282
Hindu fundamentalism   198, 199, 203,
    252
Hindu law   xii, 9, 19–20, 54, 94, 124,
    136, 137, 143, 144, 146, 147, 153,
    193, 194, 196, 279, 281, 285, 321,
    326, 345, 383, 384–5, 388, 402,
    451, 506
ahimsa (non-violence)   214
artha (possessions, wordly power)
    149, 214, 236
Arthaśāstra   226, 236, 245, 500, 526
assisted self-control   210, 224, 525
ātmanastushti (individual
    conscience)   78, 215, 216–17,
    257, 429
British intervention   236, 239–49,
    257, 350
caritra (good behaviour)   232–33
child marriage   220
chthonic law   197, 204, 205, 248
classical   196, 200, 209–34
codification of   196, 241–2, 245–6,
    251
colonial reconstruction   197, 246,
    250
continued relevance of   196, 197
cosmic nature   135
criminal law   225
culture-specific global vision   20,
    202
customs   201, 207, 208, 209, 218,
    219–20, 223, 226, 233, 236, 238,
    240, 241, 247, 248, 249, 254, 255,
    403, 457
danda (threat of punishment,
    retribution)   163, 200, 210, 223,
    262, 272, 347, 508, 527
Dāyabhāga   235, 246
deśāmāryāda (local law)   233
dharma (duty to do the right thing)
    137, 138, 148, 149, 198, 200, 201,
    204, 205, 208, 209–22, 223, 224,

225, 228, 230, 231, 236, 244, 248, 257, 270, 272, 287, 294, 368, 403, 409, 411, 413, 414, 506, 508, 509, 598

dharmaśāstra (Hindu cultural text) 209, 212, 214, 234, 244, 509

divorce 31, 249, 252, 253, 258

dispute settlement, *see vyavahāra*

duty focus 213, 215, 264, 267, 272, 276

equity 15, 202, 212, 219, 230

global claims 208

glorification of 197

'Golden Age' 209, 210, 222, 229

good governance 144, 149, 198, 259

holistic 201, 234, 270

individual 204, 205, 208, 209, 212, 221–3, 248

interlinkedness 9, 204, 205, 208, 237, 262, 265, 267, 273, 429

jurists 234, 244

justice focus 20, 200, 219, 230, 248, 257, 262, 264

kaliyuga (the 'bad' age) 204–34, 499

karma (action and its consequence) 145, 209, 211, 212, 225, 287, 403, 416, 504, 570

lawyers 228, 232

Manu 199, 213, 223, 509, 527

Manusmriti 198, 213, 214, 215–16, 217, 218, 223, 226, 230, 245, 255

marriage 31, 208, 209, 220, 253–5

mātsyanyāya (chaos, 'rule of the fish') 210, 224, 276

medieval 196, 237–9

mīmāmsā (technique of interpretation) 208, 220–1, 235

Mitāksharā 235, 246

modern 196, 249–58

Muslim rule 197, 200, 237–9, 240, 241, 348, 365–6

natural law 19, 131, 204, 205, 207, 257, 267

nibandha (digest) 238, 245, 246

oral basis 131, 204, 210, 212

order focus 19, 204, 205, 207, 226

pandit (learned man, priest, expert) 239, 241, 244–5, 246, 367

patriarchal basis 207

penances 225

personal law 237, 238, 240, 241, 243, 331

pluralism in 20, 31, 210, 213

polygamy 53–4, 234, 251, 252, 253

positive law 207, 222, 226, 231, 249

post-classical 196, 200, 234–7

post-colonial 20, 249, 263

postmodern 20, 203

public interest 205, 225, 264, 270, 272

rājadharma (duty of the ruler) 225, 233, 248, 262, 268, 436

rājaśāsana (ruler's verdict) 233

reforms of 250, 251, 252

religious nature of 20, 204, 214, 493, 496, 606

revelation 130, 143, 206, 207, 380

rita (cosmic Order) 136, 137, 147, 200, 204, 205, 206, 228, 234, 248, 255, 257, 387, 411, 504, 506, 607

rituals 204, 205, 206, 208, 211, 224–5

ruler (*rāja*) 149, 206, 207, 222, 223, 224, 225–6, 227–8, 229, 230, 231, 233, 234, 236, 248, 262, 311, 330, 346, 418, 538

sadācāra (correct, model behaviour) 217–18, 221, 232, 239, 257, 297, 299, 328, 425, 512

sadhu ('holy man') 198, 199, 202

saptapadī (seven steps, ritual of marriage) 253, 255, 256

satya (truth) 204, 205, 228

secular framework 20, 204, 205, 207, 234, 236, 500

secularisation 200, 209, 241, 249, 250, 252

self-controlled order 200, 203, 210, 219, 222–3, 227, 231, 236, 238, 246, 272

situation-specificity 202, 227, 230, 233, 246, 256

smriti ('remembered' text) 78, 204, 212, 216, 221, 233, 235, 238, 257, 297

śruti ('heard' text) 202, 204, 206, 216, 220, 221, 257, 321

Hindu law (*cont.*)
 state law   212, 218, 225, 228, 236,
  237, 246, 272
 texts   197, 198, 201, 212, 214–15,
  219–20, 221, 223, 231, 234, 235,
  236, 241, 243, 244, 245, 246, 554
 unity in diversity   202
 varnāśramadharma (duty in
  accordance with stage of life)
  214, 215, 221
 Vedas   143, 202, 204, 205, 206–7,
  216, 220–1
 vivāda (substantive 'law')   227, 230,
  231
 vyavahāra (dispute settlement)   200,
  210, 213, 227–30, 231, 232, 234,
  256, 272
Hindu law in Britain   60, 64, 197, 202
Hinduisation   209, 220
Hinduism   207, 209, 211
hindutva ('Hinduness')   130, 198, 208,
 259
Hinz, Manfred   13, 14, 16, 43, 84, 391,
 470, 482, 602
historical school   16, 47, 84, 85, 88–92,
 133, 149, 161, 162, 167, 170, 177,
 338, 394, 594, 601
Hobbes, Thomas   148, 154
Hoebel, E. Adamson   90, 369
holistic perspectives   86, 119, 175, 184,
 193, 195, 277, 607
Holmes, Oliver Wendell   165
Hooker, Barry   82, 86, 97, 103–4, 114,
 116, 118, 362, 363, 399, 453
human rights   3, 11, 12, 13–15, 25, 30,
 41–4, 61, 64, 122, 139, 145, 148,
 161, 261, 264, 268, 276, 360, 380,
 381, 399, 467, 576, 589, 595, 605
Hume, David   150, 153, 162, 386

identity postulate   64, 83, 128, 189,
 201, 237, 278, 284, 364, 381, 396,
 570, 606, 610
ideology   175, 176
immigration controls   45, 58
imperialism   12
'inclusive legal positivism'   159, 601
Indian law   76, 117, 123, 196, 249–78,
 363, 372, 373, 462, 487, 489

abolition of tradition   30, 117, 197,
 260
adoption   60
Buddhists   201, 250, 254
child marriage   43, 55
Christian law   200, 201, 250, 274
common law system   203, 263, 448
communal violence   199
composite legal culture   250, 260,
 269, 273, 277
Constitution of India   197, 201, 203,
 252, 258, 259–73, 581
consumer protection   197
crisis of   230, 260, 266
customary law   201, 253, 257
divorce law   274
Emergency   260, 262–3, 264, 266,
 267, 276, 489, 581, 582
environmental law   197, 269, 271,
 592
family law   197, 249–58, 273, 590,
 592
fundamental duties   269–70
fundamental rights   197, 267–8,
 269, 270
indigenous nature of   272
Jainas   201, 250
Jewish law   200, 250
judicial activism   269, 271
justice   263, 267, 268, 269, 272, 273
legal education   73
litigiousness   247, 256
maintenance   256, 275–7
Muslim law   54, 116, 200, 250, 252,
 274, 275–6, 277, 281, 342, 348, 366
Parsi law   200, 201, 250, 275
patriarchal context   252, 254, 256,
 276, 277
personal law system   117, 196, 200,
 250, 251, 274–5, 277
plurality of   249, 250, 273
postmodern   200, 203, 263, 273–8,
 590, 607
presumption of marriage   256
protective discrimination   266
public interest litigation   56, 149,
 205, 226, 264, 267–9, 431, 488
reconstruction   272–3
registration of marriage   254, 255

secular optional law 250

secularism 201, 251, 259, 260, 264, 265, 270, 370, 487, 602

Shah Bano case 275, 276, 305, 352

Sikhs 201, 250, 256

state 262, 270

Uniform Civil Code 118, 202, 250, 251, 252, 274, 275, 276

Indian legal positivism 253, 254–5, 258, 259, 270

Indian legal realism 273, 274

indigenous laws 97, 120, 122, 123, 125, 126–7, 128

individual agency 13, 31, 90, 94, 126, 132, 137, 146, 147, 148, 154, 157, 182, 183, 269, 272, 404, 598, 607

Indonesia 23, 203, 348

interdisciplinarity 18, 26, 68, 98, 164, 264, 393, 497, 502, 570, 596, 600

interlegality 8, 26, 29, 53, 81, 83, 160, 173, 392, 609

international law xii, 21, 37, 38–45, 83, 87, 156, 236, 394, 465, 468, 563, 589, 596, 598, 601, 605

interpersonal conflict of laws 44

Iran 123, 348

Islamic law xii, 20–1, 33, 59, 124, 130, 142, 143, 144, 146, 170, 193, 194, 201, 213, 215, 216, 221, 229, 237, 241, 275, 279–379, 383, 384–5, 402, 430, 602

Abbasids 303, 307, 309, 310–12, 348

ahl al-hadith (reliance on revelation) 283, 314, 345

ahl ar-ra'y (reliance on personal opinion) 283, 345

Caliphs 290, 298–302, 311, 320, 346

closing of the gates 280, 330, 339–44, 349, 352, 367, 402

codification 337–8, 356, 369

Companions 279, 284, 295, 296, 298–300, 304, 308, 320, 322

cruelty of 348

custom 21, 221, 283, 284, 292–3, 295, 296, 297, 299, 306, 316, 318, 321, 328, 331, 332, 334, 336–7, 344, 345, 356, 366, 368, 403

diversity of 20, 324, 328, 329, 330, 332, 336, 337, 339, 342, 353

divine judgment 145, 283, 345, 403, 429

divine legislation 21, 131, 151, 282, 285, 290–1, 380

divine revelation 280, 281, 282, 283, 284, 294, 302, 314, 315, 316, 319

divorce 45, 275, 305, 351, 376, 377

equality 283

equity 306, 311, 335, 347

fatwa (legal opinion) 239, 332, 339, 343, 366

fiqh (jurisprudence) 21, 78, 314, 339

fundamentalism 238, 309

global claims 20, 279, 353

good governance 144, 324

hadd (prohibitions and punishments for crimes against God) 223, 225, 347, 366, 374, 518

hadith (tradition, specifically of the Prophet) 298, 314, 316, 317, 319–23, 329

Hanafi school 313, 314, 315, 318, 325, 326, 328, 332, 333, 334, 350, 351, 356, 357, 360, 365, 366

Hanbali school 316, 325–6, 332, 333, 343

hisba (morality) 303

hiyal (device) 331

holistic 284

human interpretation 283, 284, 285, 286, 287, 295, 300, 306, 307, 308, 314–15, 316, 333, 343, 344, 352, 356, 374

huqm (global divine Order) 20, 286, 607

ibadat (obligations to God) 312, 346, 513

ijma (consensus, agreement) 215, 299, 300, 313, 316, 317–18, 327–8, 333, 340–1, 343, 350

ijtihad (individual effort) 21, 280, 283, 285, 286, 307, 312, 313, 314, 319, 326, 343, 351, 367, 371–2, 379

ikhtilaf (tolerated diversity, margin of error) 283, 285, 286–7, 308, 327, 328, 329, 330, 379, 548, 613

individual 215, 216, 283, 284, 285, 287, 293, 302, 305, 306, 312, 346, 350, 368

Islamic law (*cont.*)
  isnad (chain of transmission)   321,
    322
  istidlal (argumentation)   335
  istihsan (personal juristic preference,
    equity)   334–5
  istishab (presumption of continuity)
    335–6
  istislah (public interest)   334
  izzat (honour)   284
  jihad (endeavour towards a
    praiseworthy aim, struggle, holy
    war)   4
  jurists   142, 279, 282, 284, 285, 286,
    293, 294, 302, 304, 307–8, 309–10,
    311, 312–19, 322, 326, 327, 341,
    351
  justice   337, 344, 371–2, 378
  Kharijites   309, 314
  legislation   301, 311, 324, 336, 337,
    342, 345, 378
  living law   283, 287, 293, 333, 339
  local norms, *see* custom
  Majalla or Mejelle   350, 356–7
  Maliki school   306, 313, 314, 315,
    318, 325, 326, 332, 333, 334, 336,
    351
  margin of error, *see ikhtilaf*
  maslaha (public interest)   335
  Mazalim courts   288, 311, 331, 346,
    347
  methodology   280, 298, 305, 308,
    311, 313, 316, 319, 334, 342, 349,
    352
  minor sources   333
  minorities   281
  muamalat (obligations to
    individuals)   312, 346, 513
  mufti (jurist, authorised to give a
    fatwa)   332–3, 339, 341, 343, 344,
    350, 354, 367
  muhtasib (market inspector)   303
  mujtahid (scholar)   313, 317, 326,
    349
  natural law system   20, 21, 146, 281,
    284, 287, 294, 316, 324, 345, 375,
    379, 595
  neo-*ijtihad*   352, 372, 373
  Nizami courts   356

  nuclear family   295
  oral basis of   289, 320, 323
  personal law   283, 350, 357
  pluralism of   21, 65, 279, 280, 281,
    283, 285, 304, 326, 327, 337, 354
  polygamy   45, 282, 328, 352, 376
  positivism   151, 287, 300, 307, 308,
    309, 310, 311, 326, 330, 337, 346,
    356
  Prophet   20, 142, 221, 279, 280, 282,
    284–5, 286, 287, 289–98, 308, 313,
    315, 319, 320, 321, 324, 327, 328,
    337, 338, 343
  public interest, see also *maslaha*
    335, 346
  qadi (judge)   163, 279, 304–5,
    306–7, 310–11, 330–2, 343
  qanun (state-made law)   288, 354
  qiyas (analogical reasoning)   215,
    313, 316, 317, 319, 322, 326, 333
  Qur'an   21, 32, 143, 215, 221, 241,
    276, 279, 280, 281, 283, 284, 287,
    289–94, 295, 296, 298, 300, 302,
    305, 307, 308, 309, 314, 315, 316,
    371–2
  ra'y (human reasoning, personal
    opinion)   21, 280, 293, 295,
    307–8, 313, 315, 325, 327, 333–6
  reforms in   21, 344–58, 359
  religious nature of   20, 194, 279,
    316, 323, 332, 337, 338, 345, 349,
    352, 414, 493, 606
  riba (excessive interest)   331
  rulers   279, 284, 303, 330, 346–7,
    538
  Sa'd's case   296
  Schacht controversy   319, 321, 322,
    323
  schools of   310, 312–14, 317, 324–6,
    328–9, 334, 350
  secular approaches   238, 288, 299,
    303, 305, 309, 311, 337, 346, 349,
    355, 356, 357, 379
  shari'a (religious law, obligations
    system)   138, 287, 288, 290, 297,
    344, 346, 508
  Shafi'i   297–8, 312, 314, 315–19,
    320–1, 323, 324, 332, 333, 334, 339
  Shafi'i school   325, 333

Shi'a 285, 296, 300, 301, 302, 309, 322, 348, 350, 366

siyasa shar'iyya (governance in accordance with *shar'ia*) 144, 286, 288, 345, 346, 347, 350, 354, 370, 436

state 21, 279, 280, 284, 304, 316, 320, 337, 344, 346

succession 295, 296

sunna (custom, model action of the Prophet) 215, 235, 287, 291, 296, 297–8, 305, 307, 308, 309, 311, 312, 313, 315, 316, 317, 318, 319, 321, 322, 371–2, 470

sunna of the Orientalists 280, 323, 470

Sunni 301

takhayyur (selection) 350–2, 354, 357, 358, 368, 475

talaq (divorce) 358, 363

talfiq (patching) 351, 358, 475

Tanzimat reforms 355

taqlid (imitation) 280, 327, 329–30, 340, 341–2, 344, 351, 352, 367

ta'zir (deterrence, discretionary punishments) 347, 348

Umayyads 160, 303–7, 309, 311, 320, 324, 330, 331, 337

ummah (global Muslim community) 9, 281, 379

uniformity of 21, 279, 315–16, 324, 339

urf (custom) 334, 336

usul al-fiqh (sources of law) 316, 326

women 292, 293, 295, 297, 305–6, 312, 352, 358, 368

zann (conjecture) 307, 327

zina (extra-marital sex) 300, 347, 374

Islamisation 10, 21, 146, 280, 282, 295, 297, 302, 304, 308, 310, 315, 340, 348, 350, 365, 368

Islamophobia 282

ius gentium 140–1, 331, 449

Japanese law 9, 23, 37, 70, 94, 119, 120, 123, 128, 350, 493, 494, 500, 561, 562, 563, 564

giri (duty to do the right thing) 138, 409

Jhering, Rudolf von 67, 119, 162–3, 164

Jewish law 61, 124, 130, 220, 291, 300

judges 100, 165, 166, 168

Judicial Studies Board 60

judicial review 154

jurisprudence, teaching of 71, 73–4, 75, 600

justice 4, 5, 40, 81, 125, 132, 134, 136, 145, 146, 151, 152, 163, 164, 165, 169, 170, 171, 175, 177, 187, 212, 260, 261, 265, 267, 273, 360, 371–2, 373, 379, 477, 482, 489, 491, 595, 596, 597, 598, 600, 604, 605, 609

Justice, Equity and Good Conscience 56, 243, 247, 264, 334, 367, 451, 455

Kane, P. V. 197–8, 211

Kant, Immanuel 157, 386

Kelsen, Hans 82, 83, 85, 114, 131, 153, 157–9, 177, 204, 538, 601, 603

Kemal, Mustafa 359, 360, 361

Kenya 395, 411, 416, 457, 464, 468, 471, 472, 477, 479

Kerala 233, 238, 250, 271, 366

Kohler, Joseph 122

Krishna Iyer, V. R. 56, 264, 272

Kuper, Hilda 396–7, 403, 485, 607

Larivière, Richard 227, 228, 236

law xi, xii, 3, 5, 6, 7, 16–17, 18–19, 25, 33, 34, 35, 39, 66, 69, 72, 74, 80, 82, 83, 84, 85, 87, 94, 96, 98, 101, 104, 108–10, 113, 115, 119, 120–1, 123, 127, 128, 129, 130, 134, 136, 150, 151, 153, 156, 157, 159, 162, 163, 164, 166, 167, 168, 169, 170, 171, 172, 173, 176, 179, 180, 190, 193, 194, 195, 197, 198, 206, 227, 230, 233, 234, 235, 244–5, 246, 251, 261, 266, 282, 283, 286, 287, 288, 290, 291, 294, 324, 353, 375, 380, 382, 383–5, 388, 389, 391, 393, 419, 421, 453, 470, 473–4, 492, 493, 495–6, 497, 501, 523,

law (*cont.*) 529, 530–1, 540, 547, 569,
    572, 574, 578, 579, 580, 581–2,
    583, 584, 585, 586, 588, 591,
    594–611
  absence of agreement over 32, 33,
    34, 179, 397, 401, 496, 581, 595
  abuse of 25, 27, 79, 135, 137, 148,
    153, 160, 168, 171, 262, 511, 516,
    587, 592, 595, 599
  circular definition 113, 114, 153,
    154, 160, 179, 180, 186
  command of sovereign 156
  communication system 109–11
  culture-specific xi, xii, 16, 26–37,
    121, 128, 131, 132, 134, 144, 161,
    176, 179, 184, 194, 279, 353, 363,
    365, 379, 388, 404, 487, 495, 499,
    594, 603, 605, 609–10
  duty focus 148, 155
  dynamic interaction 119, 126, 127,
    167, 172, 174, 175, 184, 187, 594,
    595, 597
  eurocentric 5, 19
  expectations 172
  feminist analysis 6, 27, 41, 168
  global definition of 190
  'good law' 164
  interconnectedness 123, 124, 125,
    127, 129, 142, 159, 163, 187
  internalised 34
  limits of 108, 113, 167, 179, 261,
    362, 419, 476, 512, 603
  mentalité 68, 238
  negotiation of 5, 19, 79, 597, 601,
    613
  normative character of 111, 176
  piecemeal nature of 106, 112
  polycentricity of 40, 98, 104
  positivistic nature of 5, 82, 129
  plural nature of xii, 5, 26, 123, 127,
    136, 174, 180, 184, 186, 193, 595,
    597, 600, 612
  postmodern xi, 28, 277, 363
  religious foundations 131, 151
  rule focus 106, 155, 160, 162,
    166, 173, 174, 175, 176, 178,
    180, 595
  situation-specific 34, 171, 599
  social nature of 160, 161, 163, 333

  Southern perspectives 17, 26, 36,
    43, 55–8, 161, 468, 486, 492, 596,
    602, 604
  super-additivity of 17, 113, 581
  three dichotomies of 128, 189
  three-level structure of 123, 127,
    128, 432
  triangular model of 19, 130, 171,
    173, 186, 189, 203, 207, 210, 214,
    225, 234, 248, 253, 254, 261, 272,
    273, 279, 284, 285, 287, 316, 323,
    327, 333, 338, 344, 345, 353, 361,
    363, 364, 379, 381, 396, 400, 419,
    429, 430, 432, 445, 453, 485, 494,
    512, 583, 585, 589, 594, 598, 603,
    610–12
  uniformisation of 16, 117
  universality of xii, 3, 4, 9, 18, 112
  values in 35, 83, 119, 125, 128, 152,
    153, 156, 164, 170–1, 183, 193,
    581, 596, 598, 601, 602
  visions of 4, 13, 36, 38
law and development debates 11, 52,
    55, 399
law and language 77–8, 109, 168, 172,
    483
law and morality 131, 134, 152, 156,
    157, 159, 160, 169, 175, 179, 183,
    189, 214, 391, 418, 499, 599, 601
law and religion 31, 32, 33, 43, 144,
    161, 194, 214, 283, 287, 288, 387,
    418, 500, 603
law and society 29, 33, 57, 67, 105,
    107, 121, 164, 189, 537, 585
law of Nature 135, 137, 142,
    169, 170
legal centralism 55, 82, 113, 114–15,
    116, 117, 118, 119, 123, 160, 163,
    166, 185, 193, 194, 232, 257, 264,
    290, 319, 420, 479, 528, 594
legal education 17, 26, 30, 36, 45, 56,
    70, 71–81, 600
legal families 6, 19, 21, 40, 51, 72, 133,
    194, 281, 342, 380, 383, 493
legal instrumentalism 47, 252, 262,
    263, 345, 398, 580, 602
legal pluralism xi, xii, 6, 18, 26, 46, 66,
    81, 82–127, 129, 142, 159, 171,
    173, 177, 186, 187, 193, 203, 213,

226, 240, 280, 283, 328, 363, 369, 392, 401, 474, 491, 600, 604, 608

legal positivism   xii, 7, 27, 28, 143, 145, 150–60, 168, 252, 257, 262, 263, 284, 287, 336, 346, 452, 477, 529, 594, 598, 601

legal postulates   36, 119, 124, 125, 126, 127, 128, 153, 237, 294, 297, 445, 464, 471, 493, 560, 578, 583, 606, 608

legal realism   43, 164, 165–8, 177, 193, 226, 327, 579, 595, 600, 603, 610–12, 613

legal system   39, 109, 111, 112, 157, 158, 174, 178–9, 180, 181, 184

legal theory   xi, xii, 3, 5, 6, 7, 16, 18, 69, 83, 84, 85, 102, 129–89, 193, 257, 338, 398, 401, 485, 497, 594, 595, 596, 599, 608, 613

legal traditions   27, 84

legal transplants   26, 29, 37–8, 48, 49, 50–4, 59, 104, 128, 188, 242, 278, 303, 349, 350, 355, 484, 490, 561, 565, 601

legal unification   39

legislation   87, 89, 91, 96, 106–7, 143, 144, 152, 219, 336

legocentrism   6, 25, 33, 97, 121, 131, 163, 168, 179, 222, 250, 260, 266, 283, 291, 391, 400, 409, 420, 432, 444, 449, 452, 454, 457, 473–4, 476, 487, 497, 502, 509, 523, 529, 565, 572, 584, 588, 596, 603

Legrand, Pierre   3, 35, 36, 66–70, 74, 160, 179, 280

lex natura   114, 143

liberalism   5, 11, 13, 43, 118, 130, 164, 172, 402, 597–8

Lingat, Robert   208, 211, 214, 216–17

living law   92–3, 94, 95–6, 97, 110, 114, 125, 175, 184, 215, 217, 247, 257, 353, 361, 364, 378, 487, 600

Llewellyn, Karl   165, 166

Locke, John   148–9

Lugard, Frederick   450

Lundstedt, Vilhelm   167

Maathai, Wangari   399, 468–9, 472, 480, 486

Machiavelli, Niccolò   147

Maine, Henry   88, 89, 122, 208, 213, 216, 233, 338, 392, 393, 422, 439, 440, 474

Malawi   477

Malinowski, Bronislaw   83, 105, 106, 122, 390

Marx, Karl   89, 163

Marxism   13, 163, 425, 588

Mattei, Ugo   32–3

Mayer, Ann Elizabeth   337–8

'melting pot' image   165

migration   5, 18, 30, 55, 58

Mill, J. S.   241

millets (personal laws in Ottoman Empire)   359, 563

minority protection   41

mirror theory   52

model jurisprudence   121, 125, 127, 129

modernisation   8, 10, 491, 504, 529, 580

modernism   161, 250, 338, 342, 488, 491, 529

modernity   10, 29, 84, 353, 452, 595

monsters   12–13, 22

Montesquieu, Charles de   47, 51, 53, 86–7, 90, 149, 162

Moore, Sally Falk   57, 104–8, 113, 114, 118, 119, 176, 178, 184, 389–90, 393

Morgan, Lewis H.   89

Morocco   215, 281, 348, 383, 447, 464

Mozambique   383, 448, 464

Muhammadan law   281

Muslim, *see also* Islamic   281, 345, 353

Muslim legal pluralism   127

Muslims in Britain   60, 61, 64, 127

Namibia   4, 13, 33, 54, 73, 411, 413, 417, 421, 447, 464, 477, 485

Nandy, Ashis   37

Napoleon   47, 70, 91, 202, 223, 238, 284, 294, 360

nation state   3, 7, 8, 10, 11, 12, 83, 115, 117, 132, 146, 147, 152, 203, 259, 261, 270, 359, 465, 473, 479, 480, 596, 598

natural law   xii, 7, 13, 17, 41, 83, 84,
    85, 109, 114, 125, 129, 130,
    131–50, 154, 157, 161, 166,
    168–73, 177, 193, 248, 261, 269,
    279, 283, 286, 288, 289, 338, 370,
    386, 472, 487, 498, 504, 510, 584,
    589, 594, 595, 596, 599, 602, 603,
    604–5, 606, 611
  Christianisation of   130, 132, 141,
    145–6, 497, 606
  eurocentric nature of   146
  non-European theories of   133
natural rights   145
neocolonialism   11, 161, 263
Nepal   202
Nigeria   347, 348, 383, 394, 406, 432,
    450, 455, 461, 464, 479
nihilism   11
nomos   50, 138, 224
non-state law   119, 124, 130, 177, 185,
    218
'nonsense upon stilts'   154
normative pluralism   345, 407
norms   83, 93, 94, 95, 99, 110, 111–12,
    125, 157–8, 176, 178, 407
North Africa   383, 447

official law   7, 22, 36, 56, 57, 92, 93, 96,
    104, 116, 119, 124, 126, 127, 128,
    153, 183, 184, 189, 247, 258, 268,
    360, 364, 444, 453, 464, 475, 569,
    584, 605
Okupa, Effa   389, 395
Olivecrona, Karl   84, 144, 147, 153,
    154, 167, 168, 169, 173
Olivelle, Patrick   198, 211, 213
orality   85, 195, 320, 491
order   79, 174, 193, 194
Oriental despotism   144
Örücü, Esin   49–50, 53
Orwell, George   3
Ottoman Empire   348, 354, 359, 562,
    563
overlapping consensus   42, 57, 159,
    173, 267, 283, 324, 598

Pakistani law   21, 127, 153, 158, 251,
    261, 271, 300, 306, 353, 364–79,
    487

Ahmadis   280, 378
Anglo-Indian roots   365
divorce   275, 371–2, 375, 376–8
Hindu law in   202, 365, 369
Islamisation   21, 146, 279, 364–5,
    368, 369–70, 371–2, 373–5, 378,
    379, 487
legal education   72
polygamy   54, 371–2, 375–6, 378
public interest litigation   272, 335,
    371, 372, 431, 487
reforms in   251, 374, 376
women   373, 376
zina   371, 374, 377
Parsi law   291, 451
particular jurisprudence   159
patriarchy   31, 217, 289, 291, 352, 377,
    491, 568
Pearl, David   44
personal law systems   45, 60, 116
Plato   136, 137, 148, 164, 386
pluralism   3, 14, 32, 154, 160, 280
'positive law'   151, 152, 153, 248
positivism   32–3, 47, 84, 98, 127, 130,
    141, 142, 144, 154, 155, 157, 159,
    160, 161, 173, 176, 177, 182, 193,
    199, 248, 257, 261, 262, 266, 274,
    277, 279, 289, 338, 343, 371, 380,
    397, 399, 410, 423, 453, 479, 578,
    592, 599, 601
Pospišil, Leopold   114, 178
Post, Albert   89, 90, 122
post-colonial colonisation   18
post-colonial reconstruction   38, 56
post-colonialism   11, 89, 104
postmodernism   3, 8, 9, 10, 11, 35, 48,
    49, 82, 84–5, 103, 155, 168, 174,
    487, 570, 591, 596, 606
Poulter, Sebastian   59–60, 61–2, 63, 65,
    118
Pound, Roscoe   164–5
pragmatic instrumentalism   177
precedent   15, 434
primary rules   98, 99–101, 158,
    178, 225, 231, 237, 311, 376, 407,
    536
primitive law   99, 100–1, 105, 115,
    125, 135, 175, 291, 563
private international law   44–5, 60

private–public divide 119, 345, 346, 359, 392, 426, 431, 472, 491, 536, 598, 603
Privy Council 451, 465
property 144, 148, 149, 265, 272, 421, 426, 453
public interest 17, 173, 178, 486, 488, 583, 585, 598
public international law 38, 39, 48, 177
Pufendorf, Samuel von 132, 137, 148

qadi justice 163, 304

radical legal realism 193
Raz, Joseph 169, 173
received law 125, 126
reception of laws 5, 48, 51, 120, 123, 124, 126, 195, 348, 449, 452, 462, 495
Reformation 146–7
relativism 29, 41, 42, 119, 162, 597
religion 9, 44, 130, 143, 169, 183, 184, 189, 194, 254, 283, 284, 288–9, 290, 318, 338, 339, 402, 403, 409, 496, 584, 586, 589, 602–3, 604
religious centralism 194, 261, 283, 319
religious law 30, 124, 125, 127, 141, 220, 324, 606
religious positivism 141, 173, 220, 283, 287, 289, 344, 603
Renaissance 146–7
Restatement of African Laws 76, 457–9
right to culture 43, 477
Roberts, Simon 34, 174
Rocher, Ludo 227, 230
Roman law 50, 52, 89, 90, 91, 139–41, 151, 207, 213, 247, 303, 334, 392, 445
Roman-Dutch law 383, 446, 465
Ross, Alf 167
Rousseau, Jean Jacques 148, 149
rule of law 34, 38, 43, 47, 113, 130, 139, 169, 172, 177, 210, 259, 260, 261, 364, 444, 445, 463, 470, 473–4, 525, 575, 579, 583, 588, 597
Russian law 160, 566, 567, 568, 572, 574, 575, 590

Said, Edward 89
'salad bowl' model 58, 165
Sampford, Charles 174
Sanskrit 9, 89, 196, 198, 204, 246, 497
Santos, Boaventura de 7, 8, 14, 26, 43, 83, 609
Savigny, Carl von 89, 90–1, 122, 394
Scandinavian realists 166–8, 376
Schacht, Joseph 280, 295, 312, 316, 320, 341
Scottish law 52, 242
secondary rules 98, 99–101, 102, 158, 178, 218, 229, 236, 237, 299, 311, 337, 349, 376, 407, 536
secularisation 130, 140, 143, 147
secularism 31, 134, 144, 149, 151, 152, 161, 169, 251, 259, 283, 289, 304, 324, 500, 595, 602, 603, 605, 606
self-controlled order 79, 153, 203
semi-autonomous social field 104, 107, 114, 176, 184, 258
Shari'a Councils, see also Muslims in Britain 60
silence 55, 56, 57, 62, 118, 122, 133, 199, 201, 237, 248, 252, 261, 262, 274, 275, 277, 283, 321, 376, 425, 456, 468, 470, 500, 560, 581, 583, 590, 596, 608
situation-specificity 15, 172, 183, 195, 353, 413, 604
skilled cultural/legal navigation 63, 65
slavery 133, 138, 142, 145, 266, 385, 446
social contract 148, 149, 160
social engineering 358, 360, 365, 481, 584, 602
social justice 162
social theory 84, 171, 602, 609
socialist laws 127, 160, 494
socio-legal approaches xii, 7, 16, 85, 92, 96, 161–8, 171, 173, 177, 193, 261, 277, 279, 407, 594, 602, 604
sociological jurisprudence 92, 160, 161, 162, 164, 170
sociology of law 160, 162
Socrates 136, 137
SOAS xiii, 75–81, 264, 457
Somalia 382, 383, 408, 464, 465, 479
Somalis in Britain 64

Sophists 136
South Africa 4, 13, 14, 22, 45, 54, 73,
    107, 156, 203, 383, 417, 446, 447,
    464, 466, 470, 485, 489
South East Asian laws 23, 40, 318,
    494, 519
South–South borrowings 50
'sovereignty' 156
Spencer, Herbert 91, 162
Sri Lanka 123
Stammler, Rudolf 133–4, 170, 171,
    600, 604
state law 26, 79, 108, 124, 127, 128,
    136, 155, 156, 160, 168, 177, 183,
    185, 189, 193, 194, 195, 207, 266,
    269, 284, 361, 527, 529, 583, 591,
    611
state law pluralism 118
St Augustine 140, 141, 386, 402
St Thomas Aquinas, see Aquinas
Stoics 134, 135, 137, 138–9, 141, 503,
    570
Stone, Julius 92
strong legal pluralism 19, 103, 115,
    237, 420
subaltern perspectives 13
Sudan 382
Summers, Robert S. 88, 177, 179
symbolic legislation 277

Taiwan 494, 565
Tamanaha, Brian 82, 160, 179
Tanzania 440, 450, 464, 471, 480, 481,
    484
terrorism 283
Thailand 37, 123, 483
themis 135, 136
tolerance of diversity 5, 280
tort law 71, 263, 348, 356
tradition 30, 43, 127, 252, 254, 261,
    264, 273, 333, 382, 485, 499, 586,
    598
transnational communities 65, 383
transnational companies 12
transplants, see legal transplants
Tunisia 328, 352, 447
Turkish law 21, 49, 127, 279, 323, 349,
    353, 354, 355, 357, 359, 361, 365,
    370, 378, 379, 483, 561, 562, 579

amnesties 363
family law 360, 361, 362–3, 591
hybrid modernity 361, 363, 364
identity reconstruction 359
Islamic law 359, 360, 361, 363, 364
secularism 359, 361
transplants of European codes
    360–1
Twining, William xi, 5, 7, 16, 50, 84,
    87, 129, 155, 156, 159, 173, 174,
    603

Uganda 464, 471, 477
Unger, Roberto 130, 168, 170, 171,
    172–3, 174, 267, 501, 602,
    608, 609
uniformisation of laws 3, 40, 44, 139,
    161, 195, 197, 467, 529, 596
universalism 13–15, 30, 36, 41, 50, 52,
    138, 145, 161, 170, 171, 193, 282,
    604, 605
universality of law 11, 14, 109, 119,
    120, 121, 129, 132, 135, 146, 173,
    174, 178, 179, 180, 182, 184, 530,
    599
unjust laws 143, 144
unofficial law 36, 57, 60, 96, 119,
    124–5, 127, 128, 183, 249, 333,
    382, 445, 475, 554, 606
US law schools 71–2
utilitarianism 87, 144, 150, 154

Vanderlinden, Jacques 114, 391, 483
Volksgeist 91

War on Terror 4, 10, 602
Watson, Alan 29, 50–4, 601
weak legal pluralism 103, 115–16,
    117, 237, 453
Weber, Max 11, 122, 131, 133, 162,
    163–4, 204
Weiss, Bernard 286
welfare state 160, 166, 258, 274,
    276–7, 591
Woodman, Gordon 26, 66, 103, 118,
    187, 595
world legal history 26, 70–5

Yilmaz, Ihsan 65, 127, 324, 361